WORLD ARCHITECTURE

A Cross-Cultural History

Second Edition

RICHARD INGERSOLL

New York   Oxford

OXFORD UNIVERSITY PRESS

Oxford University Press is a department of the University of Oxford. It furthers
the University's objective of excellence in research, scholarship, and education by
publishing worldwide. Oxford is a registered trade mark of Oxford University
Press in the UK and certain other countries.

Published in the United States of America by Oxford University Press
198 Madison Avenue, New York, NY 10016, United States of America.

Library of Congress Cataloging-in-Publication Data
Names: Ingersoll, Richard, author.
Title: World architecture : a cross-cultural history / Richard Ingersoll.
Description: Second edition. | New York: Oxford University Press, 2019. |
   Includes index.
Identifiers: LCCN 2017059885 (print) | LCCN 2017060150 (ebook) |
   ISBN 9780190646479 (e-book) | ISBN 9780190646455 (pbk.)
Subjects: LCSH: Architecture—History.
Classification: LCC NA200 (ebook) | LCC NA200 .I54 2018 (print) |
   DDC 720.9—dc23
LC record available at https://lccn.loc.gov/2017059885

9 8 7 6 5 4

Printed by Marquis, Canada

Contents

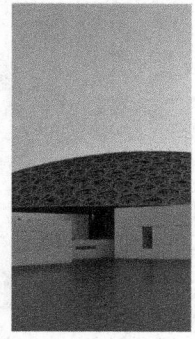

Preface

The Diversity of World Architecture

World Architecture: A Cross-Cultural History is a comprehensive survey of architectural activity from prehistoric times until today. While describing the beauty and ingenuity of a range of works, the text pursues the notion that buildings leave a meaningful trace, sometimes the only evidence, of past human existence. Much like the development of languages, distinct traditions of architecture emerged in specific geographic locations. Each culture exploited its technical and artistic skills to mediate particular conditions of landscape, climate, and materials. While the majority of buildings in any context appear ordinary, or vernacular, societies have always produced exceptional works that transcend the needs of dwelling and utility to express ambitions, hopes, and fears. This book addresses architecture both as a practical solution to the problems of everyday life and as a special, symbolic artifact resulting from the desire to either celebrate power or express poetics. It presents buildings from widely ranging regions of the planet and, although a few important cultures have been neglected, supplies a method for comprehending the diversity of architecture throughout the world.

Venice, Ca' da Mosto. Thirteenth-century palace with window details taken from Constantinople.

A User's Guide

*W*orld Architecture: A Cross-Cultural History offers the most accessible and comprehensive source-book for architectural history, with the following innovative features:

• Architecture presented as a phenomenon that occurs simultaneously in many different cultural and geographic contexts, thus having many histories rather than a single narrative
• Buildings considered as expressions of the diversity of cultures, situated within each culture's unique historical development
• Chapters strictly organized by chronology, using progressively shorter blocks of time, from thousand-year periods in antiquity to twenty-year intervals in the modern age
• Three sections in each chapter that address distinct locations, cultures, or themes during a given time period, showing simultaneous developments in architecture in different contexts—for instance, Chapter 5 (200 BCE–300 CE) has sections on imperial Rome, Han China, and early Mesoamerican civilization
• Sections that stand on their own as narratives, allowing the reader to select sections according to interests or requirements without having to read the entire book
• Pedagogical tools including time lines and maps at the beginning of each chapter and overviews of each chapter and section
• Text boxes pertaining to (1) religion, philosophy, and folklore; (2) culture, society, and gender; and (3) construction, technology, and theory
• Bibliographies of the latest scholarship, presented at the conclusion of each section
• Hundreds of graphics, drawings, and maps and over 800 color photographs

• A thorough glossary of terms, keyed to the section where the term is most relevant
• An open-access website with chapter summaries; cross-references to useful sites that pertain to specific buildings; links to UNESCO's list of world heritage sites, which appear in every chapter; review questions; downloadable image files by chapter; three-dimensional explorations of key buildings; and Google Earth maps

Lucca. Cathedral of St. Martin, medieval mason's labyrinth.

A Democratic Approach to Architectural History

The preparation of this book began like the renovation of a much-loved building, originally intended as a new edition of Spiro Kostof's groundbreaking text *A History of Architecture: Settings and Rituals* (1985). Over the years, teachers and students were inspired by Kostof's descriptions of different ethnicities and the great scope of his investigations. In the process of revision, however, I developed a new structure for this history, with a stricter sense of time periods and greater attention to distinct cultures, resulting in a completely different book. In this book, I have described and analyzed the works of over three dozen cultures, inserting extensive sections on Southeast Asia, Eastern Europe, sub-Saharan Africa, Central America, and pre-Contact Peru. I have treated each geographic context as a unique historical development rather than as a pendant to the Western tradition.

In writing this new text I have followed the spirit and method established by Kostof, who was my teacher. *World Architecture: A Cross-Cultural History* reflects a goal that was central to Kostof's work: to give a more balanced representation to world cultures and architectural traditions. In this book I pursue a wide range of social aspects, covering issues including the relation of architecture to culture, religion, gender, and class. For example, I follow the activities of women as patrons, users, and designers of buildings throughout the text. I have also addressed how new technologies and materials have influenced the development of architecture in different cultures.

Chronology and Architecture

The structure of this book divides history into twenty blocks of time, which become progressively briefer in numbers

Mali. Women villagers making annual restorations to mud buildings.

Cueta (Spanish Morocco). Civic library by Paredes Pedrosa conserving in the interior traces of a fifteenth-century traditional neighborhood, 2016.

the age of cathedrals in Western Europe. As the book progresses in time toward the nineteenth century, however, the sections become less geographically oriented because culture, through the expanse of world commerce and colonialism, became more globalized. Chapter 15 (1800–1850), for example, deals with three independent themes: the ideological use of neoclassicism, the revival of Gothic styles, and the spread of ferrovitreous technologies, all of which pertain to a variety of contexts.

By consulting the contents, the reader or the teacher can sort out the relevant sections according to interest or need. Not all courses in architectural history deal with Eastern Europe or Mesoamerica, and, if desired, these sections can be skipped without damaging the narrative flow. But likewise, one can skip the sections on ancient Rome or Renaissance Florence, which once represented the central focus of a Beaux-Arts education, and still receive a complete idea of the relevant themes in the field. Each section stands on its own and thus can be read in any sequence desired by the users. The book can just as easily serve a course devoted exclusively to the Western tradition as it can a survey of non-Western architecture.

The text is supported by several auxiliary tools. The frontispiece of each chapter displays a world map for geographic orientation and a summary of the entire chapter. Each section also begins with a brief summary and a time line of architectural and historic events. Throughout the text I have interjected a series of text boxes that provide case studies on thematic issues: (1) "Religion, Philosophy, Folklore," regarding the distinct cosmological beliefs of different cultures; (2) "Culture, Society, Gender," dealing with urban practices and social conditions in which a work was built; and (3) "Construction, Technology, Theory," addressing the structural, material, and conceptual issues of building. Each section concludes with a short bibliography of the most accessible current sources for further reading. The glossary at the end of the book covers terms used throughout the text, which have been cross-referenced to sections where they have the most relevance.

of years: the first chapter, for example, covers several millennia, the last just two decades. The book can easily be broken into two halves, Chapters 1–10, stretching from prehistory to 1500 CE; and Chapters 11–20, from 1500 to the twenty-first century.

Each chapter contains three independent sections, dedicated to different cultures, geographic areas, or themes. For instance, Chapter 8 (800–1200) presents the grand temple-building cultures of Southeast Asia, including Angkor Wat; the extravagant decorative traditions that evolved in Islamic Spain and Morocco; and the monastic culture that led to

Canonical Buildings and Stylistic Categories

It is inevitable that a comprehensive presentation of architectural history will deal with certain canonical, or rule-giving, works. In contrast to Nikolaus Pevsner's celebrated distinction between architecture and building—in which Lincoln Cathedral prevailed over a vernacular bicycle shed—I believe that both categories are of interest as acts of design and signs of life. The treatment of canonical buildings in this book has not inhibited the appreciation of common dwellings, nor has the interest in patronage excluded the role of ordinary people in the production of cities and monuments. While I have not ignored the Pantheon, Chartres Cathedral, and Fallingwater, I also highlight several non-Western monuments as part of the canon, such as the Great Stupa of Sanchi, the pyramids of Teotihuacán, and the Ise shrine. I also have attempted to pinpoint the simultaneity around the world of significant buildings, both vernacular and monumental. The Tuscan Renaissance town of Pienza appears in the same chapter as Machu Picchu in Inca Peru, and Borobudur in Southeast Asia shares a chapter with the cathedral of St. Denis, as does the Taj Mahal with New St. Peter's.

I have placed a great emphasis on chronology in order to downplay the use of style terms. Like Kostof, I am concerned that a work of architecture be considered as part of an ongoing process and not as an isolated or static expression of style. Instead of insisting on style categories, such as Romanesque, Baroque, or neoclassical, terms that were attributed to works retrospectively by art historians, I have tried to supply enough background to allow readers to comprehend why evident differences in style occurred. Architects, through their expertise, bring style to every project, but the social and political circumstances of a work deserve as much attention as the technical and formal solutions that produced them. As Kostof put it, "Every building represents a social artifact of specific impulse, energy, and commitment. That is its meaning, and this meaning resides in its physical form." His appeal to understanding the total context of architecture established a foundation for a more inclusive and sympathetic method of approaching this field.

Digital Support

Anyone working in the classroom today feels the exciting possibilities of the digital revolution. Students now appear more comfortable

Essen, Germany. Zollverein Coke Plant, Shaft 12, designed 1928 by Fritz Schupp and Martin Kremmer, UNESCO World Heritage Site, retrofit as Red Dot Design Museum by Foster + Partner, 1997.

London. St. Giles Central, mixed-use complex, Renzo Piano Building Workshop, 2012.

with laptops, tablets, or e-readers than with books. While one hopes that the book will not become obsolete, for a subject with such a great need of visual materials, digital technologies offer a marvelous resource. The open-access website that accompanies *World Architecture* was conceived as an organic pedagogical tool for parallel use by students and instructors. The reader can obtain instantaneous image support for the text that is layered and sophisticated, including:

• Chapter outlines to help prepare term papers and exams
• Links to pertinent websites dealing with specific architectural sites
• Links to UNESCO world heritage sites featured in the book and reports on their current condition (for instance, the recently destroyed works in Palmyra)
• Self-study questions to measure knowledge and comprehension of key information
• Downloadable versions of plans, drawings, and about 80% of the photographs in the text (available on the Instructor's Website)
• Google maps organized by chapter and section showing the location of all major monuments and buildings included in the text and links to major websites

New to This Edition

• Increased coverage of gender and architectural theory
• Updated and corrected coverage throughout with new information on historic sites
• Updated final chapter on architecture today
• Over 250 new images
• Web links to UNESCO heritage sites and other assets

Acknowledgments

Research assistants for the first edition: Sebastian Bentkowski, Claudia Ziegler, Sean Nelson, Matt Waxman, Joe Marci.

Graphics: Nicola Janucci (coordinator).

Colleagues who read and commented on certain sections in the second edition: Diane Favro, Zeynep Celik, Alick McLean, Jean-Francois Bedard, Lawrence Chua.

Special thanks for images: Don Choi, Stephen Harby, Alick McLean, Stefano Bertocci, Sebastiano Brandolini, Tim Hursley, Georg Gerster, Christophe Girot, Wojtek Palmowski, Hershel Parnes, Joe Staines.

At Oxford University Press, I am grateful to the original editor, Jan Beatty, and her successor, Richard Carlin; development editors for the first edition John Haber and Lauren Mine; assistant editors Jacqueline Levine and Grace Li; managing editor Lisa Grzan; production editor Janet Foxman; art director Michele Laseau; and original designer Bonni Leon-Berman.

The following outside readers offered invaluable comments and criticisms for the first and second editions of this book:

Jhennifer Amundson, Judson University
Eleni Bastéa, University of New Mexico
Vandana Baweja, University of Florida, Gainesville
Colin M. Cathcart, Fordham University
Zeynep Celik, New Jersey Institute of Technology
Carl Chapman, Catholic University of America
Meredith L. Clausen, University of Washington
Lyle Culver, Miami-Dade College
Jon Davey, Southern Illinois University
Suzanne Delahanty, College of the Desert
Pasquale De Paola, Louisiana Tech University
J. Michael Desmond, Louisiana State University School of Architecture
Roger Dunn, Bridgewater State College
Gabrielle Esperdy, New Jersey Institute of Technology
Ellen Glassman, Illinois Institute of Technology
Gayle L. Goudy, College of Charleston
J. Philip Gruen, Washington State University
Marta Gutman, City College of New York
Yvette Richardson Guy, College of Charleston
Kevin Harrington, Illinois Institute of Technology
Ira M. Hessmer, University of Hartford
Mark Hinchman, University of Nebraska–Lincoln
Kate Holliday, University of Texas at Arlington
Ann C. Huppert, University of Washington
Ralph B. Johnson, Florida Atlantic University
Douglas Klahr, University of Texas at Arlington
Nora Laos, University of Houston
Georgia Lindsay, University of Colorado Boulder
Christopher Long, University of Texas at Austin
Anne Marshall, University of Idaho
Brian McLaren, University of Washington
Terry Moor, Wentworth Institute of Technology
Hans Morgenthaler, University of Colorado Denver
Michael Rabens, Oklahoma State University
Mark Reinberger, University of Georgia
Michelle A. Rinehart, Catholic University of America
Elizabeth H. Riorden, University of Cincinnati
Shelley E. Roff, University of Texas at San Antonio
Jerzy Rozenberg, University of Kentucky
Steven Rugare, Kent State University
Sergio Sanabria, Miami University, Ohio
Anne-Catrin Schultz, Wentworth Institute of Technology
Melanie Shellenbarger, University of Colorado Denver
Elizabeth B. Smith, Pennsylvania State University
Julia Smyth-Pinney, University of Kentucky
Bruce Thomas, Lehigh University
Jeffrey T. Tilman, University of Cincinnati
Stefaan Van Liefferinge, University of Georgia
Susan Wadsworth, Fitchburg State University
Julia Walker, Binghamton University
Saundra Weddle, Drury University
Katherine Wheeler, Miami University
Janet White, University of Nevada Las Vegas
Margaret Woosnam, Blinn College
Christopher Yip, California Polytechnic State University
Craig Zabel, Pennsylvania State University
Brian Zugay, Texas Tech University
Kestutis Zygas, Arizona State University

Prehistory

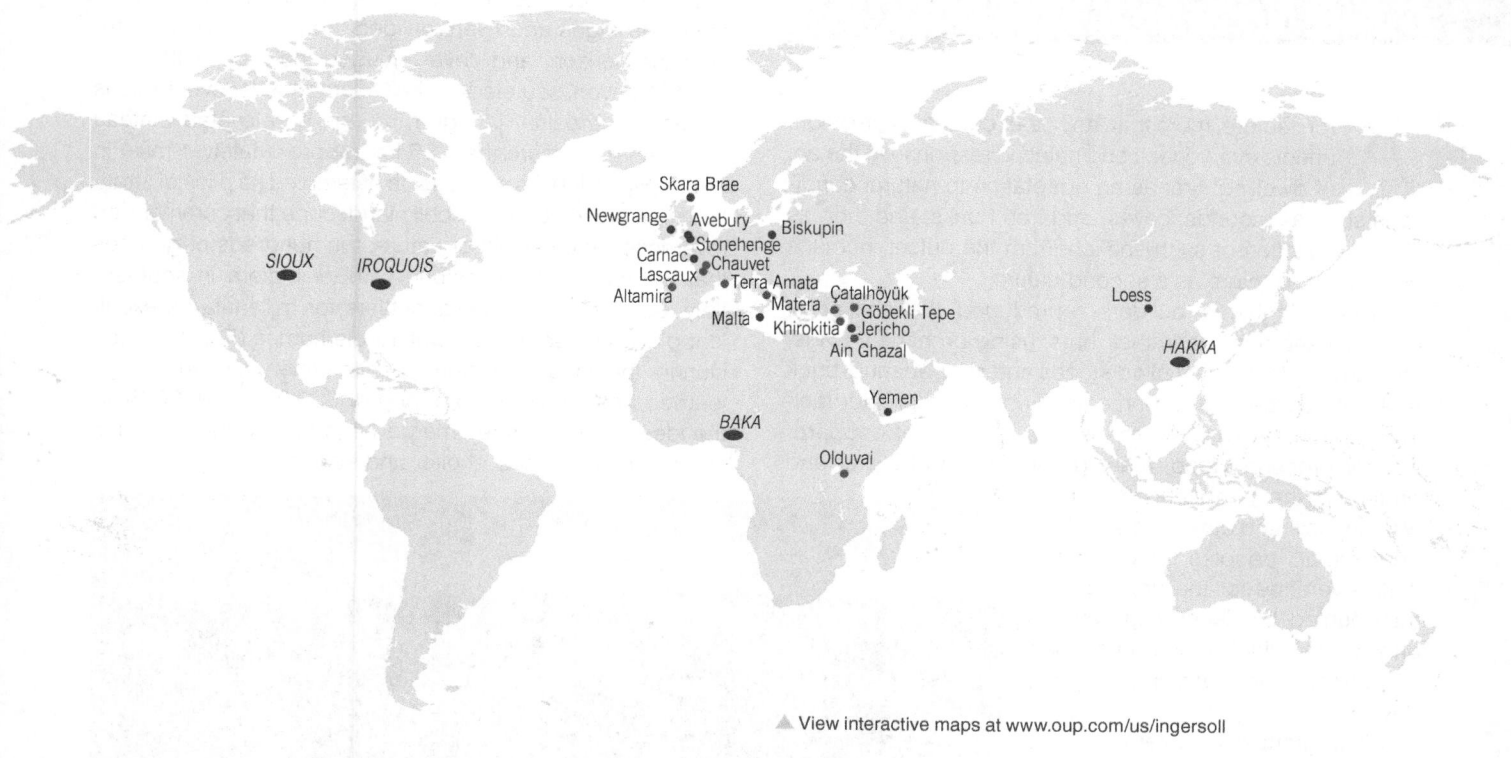

CHAPTER 1

Skara Brae
Newgrange Avebury Biskupin
Stonehenge
Carnac Chauvet
Lascaux Terra Amata
Altamira Matera Çatalhöyük
Malta Göbekli Tepe
Khirokitia Jericho
Ain Ghazal
Yemen
Loess
HAKKA
SIOUX IROQUOIS
BAKA
Olduvai

▲ View interactive maps at www.oup.com/us/ingersoll

1.1 ARCHITECTURE AS A SECOND NATURE: Sacred Caves and Primitive Huts

1.2 VERNACULAR ARCHITECTURE: A Language of Mud, Logs, Hides, and Stones

1.3 MEGALITHS AND STONE CIRCLES: Building as Memory

The first architects adapted the gifts of nature to their needs, improvising shelter in caves and trees. This led to construction techniques that imitated natural conditions. Logs were stacked, mud was mounded, hides were stretched over sticks, and stones were piled one over the next to create small dwellings. Each act of building became the tangible sign of a generation and led to the foundation of communities. In the effort to both preserve the memory of those who came before and assure the members of a community of their place in the world, monolithic stones that aligned with astral bodies in the heavens were raised as memorials to the dead. Architecture began as the creation of expedient enclosures to protect prehistoric dwellers but soon acquired a strong symbolic role of aiding human memory and registering the drama of life cycles.

1.1 ARCHITECTURE AS A SECOND NATURE
Sacred Caves and Primitive Huts

Architecture, more than any other cultural expression, affects everyone. It originated in response to the act of dwelling: first as an adaptation to natural conditions such as mounds, caves, and tree trunks, and then as the reproduction of such shelter. From the outset, humans created architecture as a second nature.

Prehistoric home builders reproduced the shelter of the cave and the tree in their huts, using branches, twigs, mud, and stones. They piled stones and shaped mud-brick walls into cave-like environments to achieve a greater feeling of security. To dwell required a process of cooperation for procuring food, making the warmth of a fire, and protecting the inhabitants from both wild animals and other humans. Pre-agricultural peoples documented their reverence for the great beasts they hunted by decorating caverns and caves, which they transformed into shrines for practicing religious devotions.

When groups of hunter-gatherers built structures for their cults, they imitated the great caverns of the past. As agricultural practices took hold, small villages of permanent dwellings cropped up near water sources. In the early agricultural settlements people drew little distinction between religious and nonreligious structures. The act of dwelling addressed at once the questions of creating shelter and making a symbolic environment to fulfill religious imperatives.

The Act of Dwelling: Shelter and Symbol

Before the appearance of architects, the world already possessed architecture. Natural processes had shaped the land: ridges and rivers divided the plains, hills punctuated the horizon, and caves gouged the rocky cliffs. The Grand Canyon, sculpted by the Colorado River over millions of years of erosion, plunged through an elevated plateau of tawny stone more than 1.5 km (approximately 1 mile) in depth (Fig. 1.1-1). Its succession of temple-like piles of stratified rock presented a symbolic landscape that commanded reverence. Another gift of nature, the hundreds of grottoes that perforated the limestone cliffs of Matera in southern Italy, appealed to primeval settlers for millennia as excellent places for safe and comfortable homes (Fig. 1.1-2a,b). During the long prehistoric period when human beings learned how to dwell, from roughly 500,000 to 3000 BCE, the idea of architecture emerged through the awareness of two recurring themes: shelter and symbol.

Figure 1.1-1 Grand Canyon, Arizona, formed through erosion by the Colorado River over several million years.

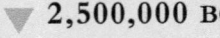

▼ **2,500,000 BCE**

Evidence of "Lucy," a hominid living in Ethiopia

Olduvai Gorge, Tanzania, earliest toolmakers

▲ **ca. 1,500,000 BCE**

▼ **ca. 500,000 BCE**

Neanderthal hunter-gatherers make fires in south of France and northern China

Terra Amata, France, earliest known huts

▲ **ca. 400,000 BCE**

Figure 1.1-2 Matera, southern Italy. (a) Grotto dwellings, lived in since the twelfth millennium BCE. (b) Section.

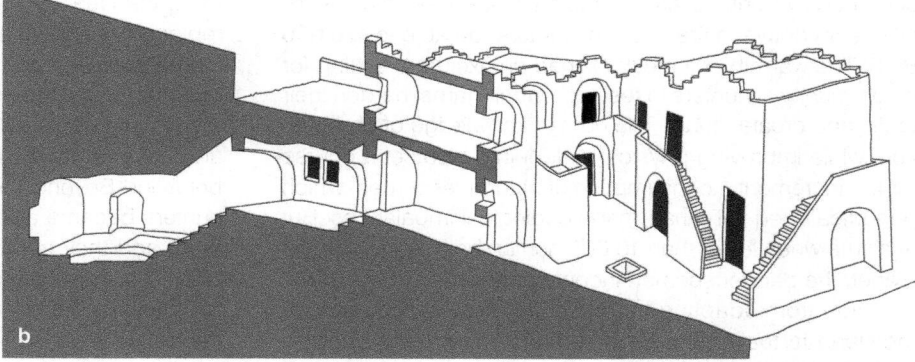

The art of building originated in many places and at different times. The so-called primitive hut, the mythical first dwelling, appeared all over the planet. Prehistoric structures and settlements offered fleeting interventions, at the outset conditioned by the nomadic way of life of hunter-gatherers. Early architects created similar building types—such as the rounded mud hut and the oblong, thatch-covered longhouse—on different continents at widely diverging moments, making it difficult to categorize them as part of a progressive sequence. The survival of architectural knowledge relied on the good fortune offered by geography and climate, as well as the tolerance of neighbors. Although dates can be attached to prehistoric artifacts through carbon-14 analysis, the interruptions in time and space of prehistoric works preclude an evolutionary or chronological understanding of them. Before the introduction of written language during the third millennium BCE, architecture must be allotted a certain timelessness.

Because the earliest designers constantly moved in search of a tolerable climate and food supply, their works remained tentative and unobtrusive. They made shelter in the pleats of the earth. Since the 1974 discovery at Hadar, Ethiopia, of so-called "Lucy" (*Australopithecus afarensis*), thought to be the first upright-walking humanlike species, further discoveries in Kenya have pushed the date of the emergence of our predecessors back from more than 3 million years ago to 6 or 7 million. Hominids forged ahead of other species through their domestication of fire. In the Olduvai Gorge in Tanzania, archaeologists have identified tools and circles of shelter dating back almost 2 million years. The Neanderthals (500,000–30,000 BCE) created hearths for heating, cooking, and toolmaking. They pursued the primal architectural act of building a fire as the key element of dwelling, driving the wild beasts from the caves to make the home of the moment safe.

The earliest known hearths, found at the great cave of Escale near Marseilles in southern France and the cave

▼ **ca. 40,000 BCE**

Cro-Magnons replace
Neanderthals; stone tools

Cave painters: Chauvet,
Lascaux, Altamira

▲ **ca. 30,000–15,000 BCE**

▼ **25,000–14,000 BCE**

Last Glacial Maximum
(Ice Age)

of "Peking Man" at Zhoukoudian, China, date from over 500,000 years ago. Deep within the Bruniquel cave in southwest France, archaeologists discovered two circular structures that Neanderthals built from pieces of stalagmites, scorched by bonfires, among the earliest evidence of the relationship between fire and architecture, datable to 176,000 BCE. The warmth of fire established an exclusive setting for a community of hunters to rest, cook their game, harden their tools, and create rituals. The human knowledge of combustion, while improving physical well-being, also set a course for the incremental consumption of natural resources, which periodically led to human-made ecological imbalances. But at a time when fewer than 10,000 human beings lived on the planet, the danger seemed inconsequential.

Aside from adapting to the shelter provided by nature, the Neanderthal hunter-gatherers built huts in the open as early as 400,000 BCE. The camp of Terra Amata, discovered near Nice in southern France in 1966, served many generations of hunters, who visited it briefly during the late spring. Archaeologists have identified traces of twenty oval huts, measuring as large as 6 × 15 m (18 × 47 ft), in a cove by the beach (Fig. 1.1-3). Bands of about fifteen persons built and occupied the huts for limited hunting forays, leaving them to collapse after their departure. The Neanderthal builders set rows of branches or saplings close together within a ring of stones. They pitched the boughs

from one side to the other, creating a vault-like covering over large posts that ran down the center to help support the roof. They dug out the site with fire-hardened wooden spears, pruning and trimming the branches with hand axes made of pieces of flint or limestone. Each year the seasonal builders set new huts over the site of the old ones or else nearby.

Anthropologists often refer to the long period of prehistory as the "Stone Age," named after the prevailing technology of stone tools. They further divide it into Paleolithic, Mesolithic, and Neolithic subperiods, the last beginning around 10,000 BCE and involving the earliest settlements and the transition to metal tools. Around 40,000 BCE, the Neanderthals coexisted with but were eventually replaced by the Cro-Magnon peoples, a distinct strain of *Homo sapiens sapiens*. The newcomers, smaller in stature but with larger brains than the Neanderthals, improved on the earlier people's stone tools, making cutting knives sharp and easy to grasp. They also began to formulate religious behavior. Beyond their day-to-day survival, the Stone-Age hunters became aware of their social destiny as a chain of lives, and they carefully buried or burned their dead relatives, leaving markers behind. Death remained a disturbing mystery, but through the performance of ritual acts and the creation of permanent shrines, primal hunters hoped to influence the cosmos to prolong their collective existence.

The cults that grew up to appease human anxiety prepared the foundations for architecture as the setting for ritual actions. The cave acquired a new status of **sanctuary**. At its mouth the hunter might still make a dwelling, while reserving the dark inner recesses for rituals addressing life, death, and the afterlife. Around 70,000 BCE, in one of the thirty caves of Monte Circeo, a limestone promontory south of Rome, the cave dwellers placed a single Neanderthal skull in a trench along the farthest wall, with stones arranged around it in an oval ring.

Göbekli Tepe (Turkey), round structures

▲ **11,000–8,000 BCE**

▼ **ca. 7500 BCE**

Jericho (Israel), Çatalhöyük (Turkey), Ain Ghazal (Jordan), earliest cities

Khirokitia (Cyprus), evidence of a street

▲ **ca. 6500 BCE**

The attempt to impose formal order expressed a symbolic need that went beyond the demands of shelter to define one's place in the cosmos.

During the slow development of primal cosmological beliefs, Stone-Age nomads began to use painting and sculpture to decorate special hillside caves. Explorers have discovered painted caves dating from the end of the last glacial period (between 30,000 and 12,000 years ago) in places as far from one another as Western Australia, Namibia, Patagonia, Yucatán, and southern India, as well as the better-known examples in southern Europe. This suggests the surprising possibility of a prehistoric global culture. The cave decorators used similar motifs, ranging from the stenciled outlines of hands, achieved by blowing pigments from one's mouth, to abstract patterns of grids, spirals, circles, dots, and zigzags. In some cases they depicted profiles of the majestic animals of the hunt. The evocative images of moving animals, which would have been animated by the flitting light of campfires, carried obvious symbolic intentions meant to accompany rituals. While the painted caves did not require acts of construction, the ceremonial organization of their spaces constituted the earliest form of religious architecture.

Nomadic hunters, chasing herds across the planet, brought with them the extraordinary gift of art to commemorate their cults based on animal vitality. The caves at Lascaux (Fig. 1.1-4), in southwestern France, and Altamira, in northwestern Spain, both occupied around 15,000 BCE, remain among the most magnificently decorated of the 200 painted caves discovered during the past two centuries in southern Europe. The followers of these cults crept into the caves from an upper entry, symbolically returning to a womb-like opening in the earth. They covered the walls and ceilings with realistic, polychrome images of the beasts of the hunt, sometimes up to 7 m (22 ft) in width. The artist-hunters depicted themselves as insignificant stick figures in the background, powerless in the face of the mystery-filled forces of nature. Using a mixture of ground minerals and charcoal applied either with hollow bone styluses or by being chewed up and spat, the cave painters narrated their relation to the flux and flow of life, moving with the herds, courting them, slaying the beasts reverently, and devising magic rituals to ensure their continued abundance.

The Chauvet Cave (Fig. 1.1-5), discovered in 1994 near Pont d'Arc in the Ardèche region of southern France, appears to be the oldest in Europe, tentatively dated to around 30,000 BCE. As at Lascaux and Altamira, one entered the cave from above, moving into a three-part sequence of descending spaces articulated by ritual markings. The cult members decorated the foyer, previously occupied by bears, with small pictures of mammoths. The central grotto

Figure 1.1-4 Dordogne, southwest France. Lascaux Caves, 17,000 BCE. The three chambers are covered with over 600 polychrome paintings and line drawings, executed by hunter-gatherers over many centuries during the last Ice Age.

The Great Goddess

The theory of the Great Goddess, a presumed archaic earth deity worshipped by the earliest cultures of Europe and Southwest Asia, was suggested by the discovery of numerous depictions of a corpulent female, such as this seated woman with royal felines found at Çatalhöyük. These commanding maternal figures appear to represent a matriarchal society and supply a necessary myth to counteract the prevalent patriarchal order found in most historical situations. Many archaeologists and anthropologists have put forward the notion of the Great Goddess as a means of interpreting the development of Neolithic cult sites constructed during the period of transition to agrarian society. While Çatalhöyük, Malta, and the later Minoan culture on the isle of Crete have been celebrated as peaceful, female-dominated societies, the evidence is in no way complete or conclusive. Phrenological studies indicate a surprising degree of equality in diet, work habits, and dwelling space between men and women in Neolithic communities, slightly contradicting the idea of matriarchy. The comforting figure of a primordial mother who ruled before the masculine militarization of society, when men armed themselves with metal weapons, nonetheless offers a story one would like to believe as an alternative to the tragic cycles of war and destruction that have littered the historical landscape.

Çatalhöyük, southern Turkey. Figurine thought by many to represent the Great Goddess, ca. 7000 BCE.

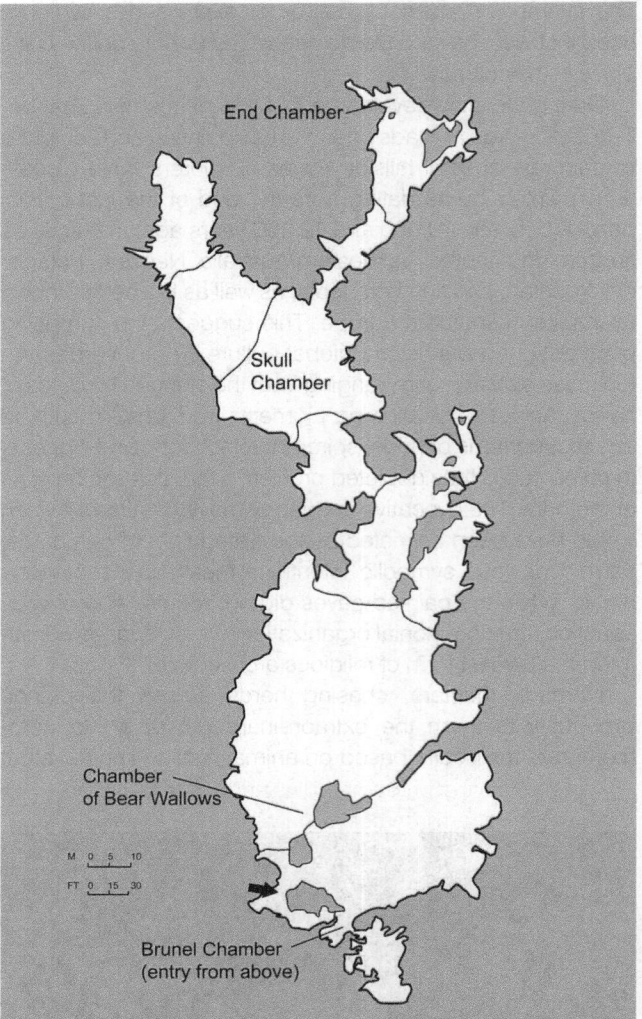

Figure 1.1-5 Ardèche region, southern France. Plan of Chauvet Cave, ca. 30,000 BCE, discovered in 1994. The central grotto extends as wide and as tall as a Gothic cathedral.

opens onto a space as large as a cathedral: 30 × 100 m (98 × 328 ft). The bears had dug out many of the nooks of the Chauvet Cave as hibernation spots, and the painters decorated them as if they were side chapels in a church. In one of the crannies the participants arranged an altar-like stone with the skull of a bear in its center as a sacrificial emblem. A collection of fifty-five bear skulls preserved the memory of the cave's previous occupants, presumably evicted after a struggle. Over 300 paintings and drawings of bears and spotted leopards, both fierce competitors for the hunt, cover the walls. The artists, working over the span of many millennia, depicted a collection of creatures including horses, woolly rhinoceroses, lions, bison, aurochs (wild oxen), panthers, mammoths, ibexes (wild mountain goats), and owls. Half of these species had become extinct by the time the decorators began working on Lascaux.

The "end chamber" of the Chauvet Cave has as its central icon a painting of a gigantic woman with bulging thighs, a prominent mound of Venus, and the horned head of a bison.

The image resembles sculpted figures found in later agricultural settlements, often associated with a presumed cult of the Great Goddess of the Earth. Leopards and horned bulls often accompany the image of the goddess, who sometimes holds a horn, the instrument for channeling animal force. In the depth of this metaphorical "womb" in the earth, the mother goddess of Chauvet may have received her due veneration.

The painted caves of primal hunters celebrated a timeless faith in the animal spirit. The wild beast represented both literal food and the life force. Stone-Age artists took little initiative to change the natural configurations of the caves but skillfully adjusted to their irregular spaces. Somewhat like the work of late-twentieth-century graffiti artists, their decorations presented ongoing projects to be added to by others. Numerous hands worked on the walls over the course of many centuries, if not millennia. The successive generations of hunters each added their own imprint to the existing shrines. Both in the making and in the presumed blessings of these magical environments, caves such as Chauvet, Altamira, and Lascaux became enduring community projects, which merged the present with hopes for the future and respect for the past.

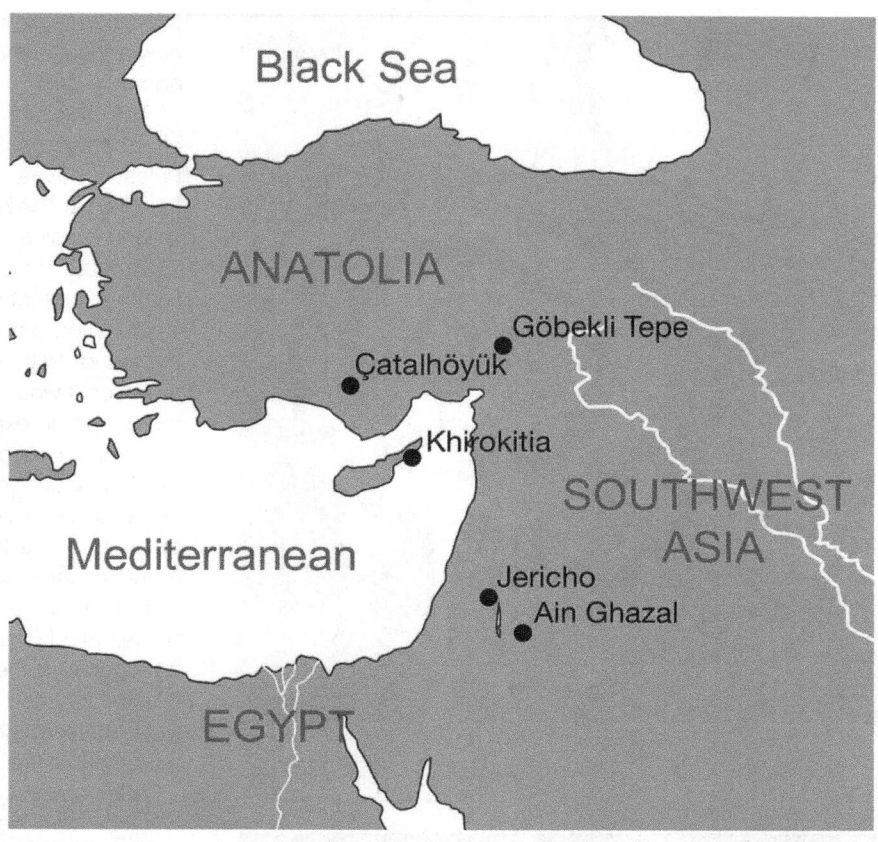

Figure 1.1-6 Neolithic Southwest Asia.

Living Together: Neolithic Settlements in Southwest Asia

Around 16,000 BCE the planet underwent a dramatic climate change, the last in the cycle of recurring ice ages that seriously threatened biological life with nine-month-long winters. A period of global warming followed, when a combination of water evaporation and greenhouse gases such as carbon dioxide formed a stratum in the atmosphere that retained solar energy. The milder weather and the gradual receding of the great ice sheets encouraged parts of the landscape to develop as forests and fertile plains. Between the twelfth and the fifth millennia BCE, the new stability of longer growing seasons permitted most of the nomadic hunter-gatherers in Europe, Southwest Asia, and East Asia to undertake farming and shepherding. They constructed dwellings near stable points of water supply where they found fertile soil.

With the cultivation of plant and animal resources and the introduction of improved tools, humans began to take more active control of the environment. Prehistoric agriculturalists created a second nature, reshaping the land by channeling water, terracing hillsides, and altering the fields through constant tilling. They fashioned shelters from the basic materials offered by the land—mud, wood, and stone—and covered them with woven grasses and animal hides. Over time they clustered their houses into villages both for sharing access

to prime resources such as water and for defense against raiders. The villages created religious ceremonies to bond their communities, reenacting stories of their origins and ideas about their place in the cosmos.

The earliest Stone-Age settlers migrated to Southwest Asia (Fig. 1.1-6), where wild grains grew in abundance, allowing the accumulation of a food surplus. The oldest structures in the region were unearthed in 1994 at Göbekli Tepe, a mound in southeastern Turkey that contains a cluster of two dozen cult buildings. The oval structures (Fig. 1.1-7a), only four of which have been excavated, range in diameter from 10 to 30 m (32 to 98 ft). Contrary to previous theories of human development that assumed agriculturalists to be the first architects, these early "temples" belonged to a community of hunter-gatherers. The buildings, in use from around 11,000 BCE until 8000 BCE, served the religious ceremonies of a highly organized nomadic society. The architects of the round structures at Göbekli Tepe set a series of T-shaped megaliths in radial positions to serve as ribs in the thick oval walls made of stone and rubble. About twice human height, the prized stones weighed up to 20 tons and required the effort of hundreds of people to drag them from the quarries. The builders carved the megaliths in relief with animal figures, reminiscent of the iconography of the painted caves. A pair of taller T-shaped pillars dominated the center of each temple. Carved with arms, they apparently represented humans (Fig. 1.1-7b).

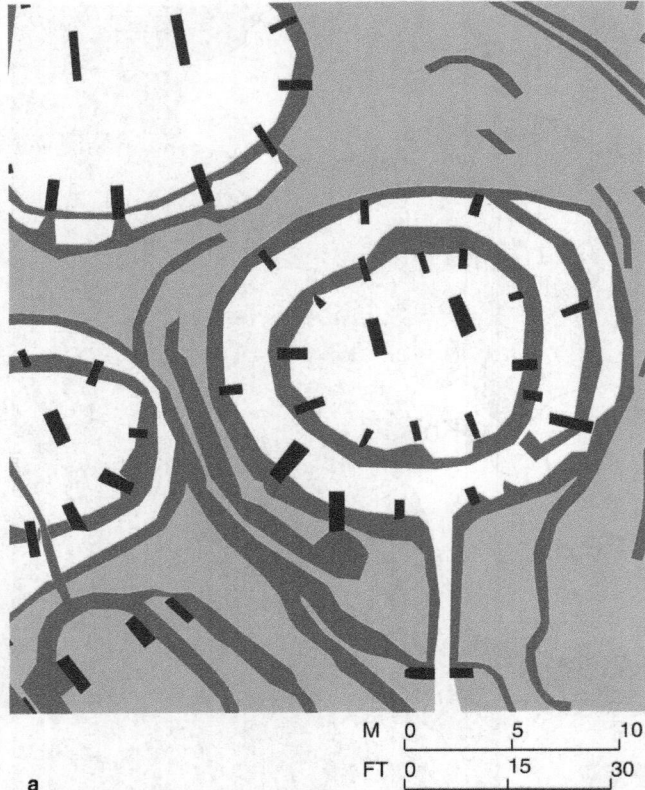

M 0   5   10
FT 0   15   30

a

b

Figure 1.1-7 Göbekli Tepe, southeastern Turkey. (a) Reconstruction of oval temples built by a preagricultural society, ca. twelfth millennium BCE. (b) Archaeological site showing an oval space with decorated pillars; roof was probably corbelled.

The roundness of the oval structures at Göbekli Tepe evokes the morphology of the painted caves, demonstrating an effort to reproduce the natural prototype. The hunter-gatherers would have assembled at the temples for ceremonies, similar to the religious use of the great painted caves. Sometime in the early eighth millennium the entire site was purposefully buried under a thick layer of soil. One can speculate that as the inhabitants of this region made the transition to the agrarian way of life, moving from the collection of wild grains to the cultivation of higher-yield grains,

the bizarre concealment of the oval temples signified the new agricultural regime's literal burial of old beliefs from the nomadic past.

The transition to agriculture inspired the earliest forms of urbanism in Southwest Asia. The region—comprising Palestine, Syria, southern Turkey, and Iraq—is often called the "Fertile Crescent" because of its abundance of spontaneous strains of wheat and barley. Jericho, settled around 7500 BCE, remains the best documented of thousands of settlements that sprouted up in the region during the Neolithic period, attracting the distinction as the oldest city in the world. With a population of fewer than 3,000 farmers, however, it would have appeared to today's eyes to be little more than an expanded village. The presence of imported obsidian, a hard, black volcanic glass indispensable for making sharp tools, demonstrates that these first towns in Palestine maintained distant trading relations, since the obsidian came from southern Turkey. The initial cluster of round houses at Jericho exploited the natural advantage of a reliable spring of freshwater that now gushes from a place called Elisha's Fountain. The life-giving value of such a resource in the arid region of the Dead Sea would have initially attracted the hunters, who likely followed their prey to the drinking hole and slowly converted to farming and a more settled life.

After several centuries of habitation, the occupants of Neolithic Jericho added an impressive fortification to protect their homes and silos. They built a wall 5 m (16.5 ft) high, with irregular, or cyclopean, masonry and set off by a deep ditch. Behind the wall they raised a conical tower, accessed by an interior stair made of single stone slabs (Fig. 1.1-8). They built small, round houses inside the walls, with mud walls set on stone foundations. Jericho's builders may have covered their houses with domes in imitation of the round tents of the nomadic hunters but more likely gave them flat roofs of reeds and clay. They periodically rebuilt houses on top of the originals. The floors of the houses lay below the ground level, requiring a wooden stairway to enter. Beneath the floors, each successive generation of deceased relatives lay buried, initiating a local tradition of stratification.

The site of ancient Jericho today presents a large mound near the oasis of the modern town, on the left bank of the Jordan River. Several layers of the city rose over the ruins of their predecessors. About 6500 BCE, the original town fell to outsiders. The newcomers built rectangular rather than round houses, with slightly rounded corners and open courtyards for cooking. Each house consisted of a few rooms, interconnected by wide, rounded doorways. The buildings set aside as shrines appear to have been similar to the houses, with identical rounded **doorjambs**.

Of the many towns and villages contemporary with Jericho, few have comparable archaeological traces. One of the better documented, Khirokitia, occupied a hillside on the southern coast of the island of Cyprus. Built around 6000 BCE, it shared a few architectural traits with ancient Jericho, including a ditch, a stone wall, and a series of small round houses (Fig. 1.1-9a,b). During its two-century existence Khirokitia doubled in size to perhaps 600 inhabitants. The inhabitants rebuilt the city walls with a formal gateway accessed by stone steps that rose in three flights set at right angles to each other in a *U* shape to negotiate the higher level of the ground inside the walls. The expansion of the town produced a unique urban feature, a paved street, probably by default. The trace of the earlier wall that now lay between the two halves of the town became an ad hoc thoroughfare, running uphill from the riverbank on the south side of the bend. It crossed the settlement and descended to the opposite side. Stone ramps led from this elevated path as tributary lanes to the houses. Halfway up the steepest part of the ascent from the south, the street widened into a platform about 4.5 m (13.5 ft) wide. This rounded plaza, with its splendid panorama of the Maroniou River valley and the sea beyond, doubtless served as a place of social exchange and assembly.

The public spaces at Khirokitia had no precedents, nor did they inspire contemporary imitators. Ancient Jericho grew without streets, the houses packed one alongside the next like a beehive. Likewise the inhabitants of Çatalhöyük—the largest and most complex Neolithic settlement of Southwest Asia, located on the Konya Plain of southern Turkey—left neither streets nor gaps between their buildings. Occupied between 7400 and 6000 BCE, the town spread as a dense fabric of rectangular cells (Fig. 1.1-10), accommodating perhaps 10,000 inhabitants. Çatalhöyük arose as a transitional settlement caught between nomadic and agricultural ways of life, developing into a society with diversified crafts and businesses.

Beyond any agricultural advantage it might have commanded, Çatalhöyük's success came from its control of the market for obsidian, the Neolithic period's most valued commodity. The city also hosted some of the first smiths working with metal. Lead and copper were mined and then shaped into ornaments and small tools such as awls and drills. In exchange for their crafts, the townspeople acquired luxury items—including marble, flint, sulfur, pumice, calcite, and alabaster—which they used to enhance the shrines for their daily rituals and to embellish their personal appearance. While temples have been found at Çatalhöyük, most of the houses also contained shrine spaces and chapel-like decorations. The recurring images of religious subjects in the domestic settings give the impression that the inhabitants specialized in religion and that the entire city may have functioned as a pilgrimage site. Similar to the structures at Göbekli Tepe built a few millennia earlier, the houses and decorations of Çatalhöyük seem to have been inspired by the painted caves of the hunter-gatherers.

One entered the typical house through a hole in the flat roof, served by a wooden ladder (Fig. 1.1-11). The aperture doubled as a smokestack for the hearth and oven located directly beneath the entry. The interior atmosphere would have remained dark and cavernous. Occasionally, the houses included an open courtyard, which doubled as

lavatory and rubbish dump. The house plans at Çatalhöyük were fairly uniform: each roughly 6 × 8 m (20 × 26 ft) with a single rectangular room, subdivided by a narrow, two-part storage space along one side and parallel, built-in platforms along two walls. One side served the men and the other the women of the household. They usually buried the dead (after their bones had been picked clean by buzzards) under the platforms.

The half-timber construction method used at Çatalhöyük remained a standard practice in this seismically challenged part of the world. A wooden frame of posts and beams divided the walls into a series of vertical slots filled with mud bricks and plastered over. The frame absorbed the **shear stresses** during a quake, while the mud was the most available material for thickening and patching up the walls. Rather than raise a defensive wall around the town, the inhabitants packed the houses tightly and protected themselves from the outside with continuous blank elevations penetrated by neither doors nor windows.

The social diversity of Çatalhöyük, a city that fostered merchants and artisans, encouraged the development of a complex religious life. Each house had its own shrine, and its walls were covered with religious imagery. The dead beneath the platforms remained like anchors holding the inhabitants to the place. The wall panels decorated with red plaster reliefs and paintings hearken back to the representations of wild animals found at Chauvet and Lascaux. The ritually active dwellers of Çatalhöyük incorporated the horns of wild oxen and the bones of other wild creatures into the benches and altars of their ceremonial platforms, infusing their dimly lit houses with the spiritual aura of the great caves. To dwell went beyond the need for shelter to become a sacred act.

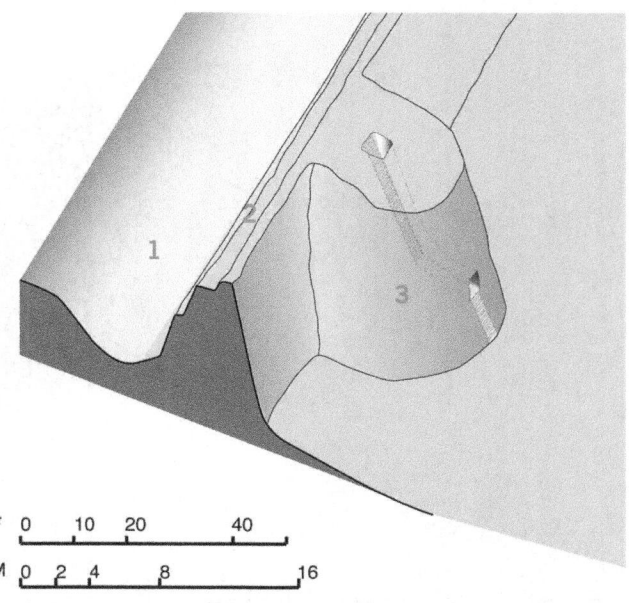

F 0   10   20   40

M 0   2   4   8   16

Figure 1.1-8 Jericho, ancient Palestine. (1) Ditch; (2) wall; (3) round tower with stair. Seventh millennium BCE.

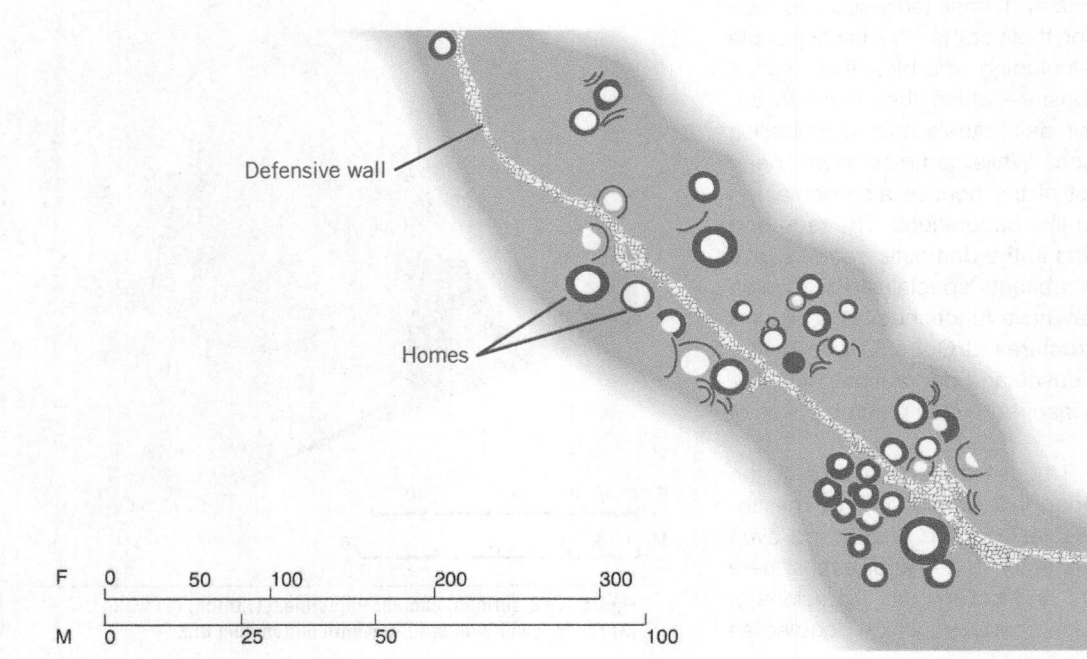

**Figure 1.1-9
Khirokitia, Cyprus.
(a) Street formed
on top of old
defensive wall,
sixth millennium
BCE. (b) Plan.**

Defensive wall

Homes

F   0   50   100   200   300

M   0   25   50   100

b

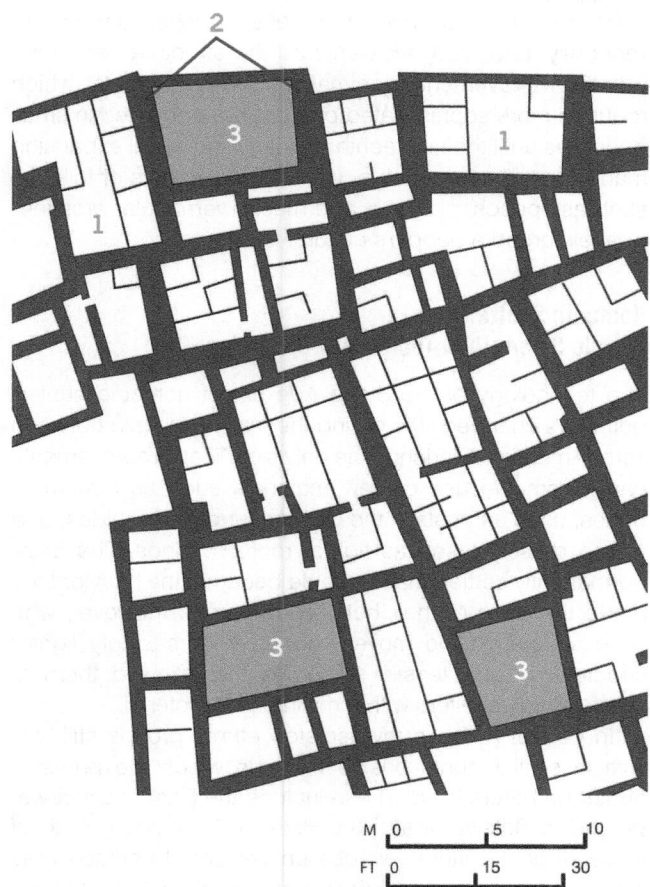

Further Reading

Bahn, Paul. *The Cambridge Illustrated History of Prehistoric Art.* New York: Cambridge University Press, 1998.

Cauvin, Jacques, ed. *The Birth of the Gods and the Origins of Agriculture.* Translated by T. Watkins. Cambridge: Cambridge University Press, 2000.

Clotte, Jean. *World Rock Art.* Santa Monica, CA: Getty, 2002.

Cunliffe, Barry, ed. *The Oxford Illustrated Prehistory of Europe.* New York: Oxford University Press, 1994.

Hodder, Ian. *The Leopard's Tale: Revealing the Mysteries of Catalhoyuk.* London: Thames & Hudson, 2006.

Gimbutas, Marija. *The Civilization of the Goddess.* San Francisco: Harper, 1991.

Mellaart, James. *Earliest Civilizations of the Near East.* London: Thames & Hudson, 1965.

Scarre, Chris, ed. *The Human Past: World Prehistory and the Development of Human Societies.* London: Thames & Hudson, 2005.

M 0 — 5 — 10
FT 0 — 15 — 30

Figure 1.1-10 Çatalhöyük, southern Turkey. Plan of a district of the city, seventh millennium BCE, showing (1) individual cellular units with platforms and internal parapets, (2) party walls connecting individual units (there were no doors in these walls; inhabitants entered through the roofs), and (3) courtyards between units.

Figure 1.1-11 Çatalhöyük, southern Turkey. Reconstruction of a dwelling, seventh millennium BCE. Ankara, Museum of Anatolian Civilizations.

1.2   VERNACULAR ARCHITECTURE
A Language of Mud, Logs, Hides, and Stones

Many animals—especially insects, birds, and fish—possess an uncanny instinct for building, rivaling that of humans. Animal architecture includes such structures as the common bee's hive, built as layers of hexagonal cells; the Australian compass termite's prodigious mud towers, more than head-height tall blades of mud oriented due north; the intricate canopies set between branches by weaverbirds; and the stone-lined pits of the jawfish. While humans doubtless share a similar genetic disposition to build, they differ from other animals in their capacity to go beyond instinct and learn how to build from others. Prehistoric designers at the outset imitated natural forms and, once they had established constructional processes, repeated and sometimes improved the solutions of previous generations. Builders borrowed tools and ideas from their neighbors.

While high-style architecture involves the patronage of elites and the skills of trained professionals and exhibits significant formal changes over time in response to religious and political pressures, the common buildings of vernacular architecture follow a plodding and constant evolution, like that of language. Vernacular architecture comprehends the traditions of building passed down from generation to generation. Unlike commissioned monuments, palaces, and religious structures, vernacular buildings respond to the local knowledge of materials, design, and construction. Thus, vernacular architects follow conservative building traditions but incorporate constant innovations meant to resolve the day-to-day problems of making shelter.

Vernacular builders invariably adapt to the constraints of regional materials and geological conditions. Both the nomad and the settled farmer, the two basic anthropological types of prehistoric humans, perfected their building methods through trial and error. Their creations ranged from the temporary shelter of tents and huts to more permanent structures in wood, mud, and stone. Notched timber, cut **masonry**, and fired brick entered the structural repertoire with the improvement of toolmaking. Glass and metal, which required more sophisticated processing, appeared in small quantities until the nineteenth century's industrial expansion made them more available. Like other elements of folk life, such as speech, cooking, and music, vernacular architecture reinforced a people's cultural identity.

Nomadic Shelter: Tensile Strength in Temporary Dwellings

The technology of the Stone-Age hut of nomadic hunter-gatherers changed little during the many millennia between Terra Amata and Jericho. The only significant improvements came from the use of new materials such as mammoth bones, used as posts in the Ukraine, and ropes, hides, and woven grasses used as tighter roof coverings. The more permanently settled that a people became, the heavier they made the walls of their huts. The nomads, however, who were always on the move, perfected increasingly lighter structures, using tensile strategies that allowed them to create sturdy shelters with a minimum of material.

In central Africa a few isolated ethnic groups still survive in similar conditions to those in which the primeval hunter-gatherers lived. These include the San, or Basarwa, people of Botswana and the Baka of Cameroon. Both of these distinct cultures, whose uninterrupted heritage may extend as far back as 20,000 years, continue to build temporary huts as they move through the wilderness. Although subject to vastly different climates, they both prefer half-dome structures made of intertwined branches, covered with woven grasses and leaves. The Baka live in *mongulu* huts (Fig. 1.2-1) built exclusively by the women, who weave slender branches into a thick arch stretching over a radius that comprehends the typical arm span of the famously short Baka. They insert parallel transverse poles into the gaps of the woven arch, bending them back as ribs to form the basket-like cup of a semidome. The Baka women then intertwine smaller branches laterally from rib to rib and attach the huge oval leaves of the mongongo tree to the exterior of the structure to create an impermeable covering. The same leaves, sometimes over 1 m (3.3 ft) in length, also serve as bedding. The Baka arrange their huts in a rough circle and live in them for up to three months before moving

▼ **ca. 7500 BCE**

Ain Ghazal settlement (Jordan)

Dugout village in Banpo (China)

▲ **ca. 5000 BCE**

▼ **ca. 3000 BCE**

Skara Brae settlement, Orkney Islands (Scotland)

Figure 1.2-1 Cameroon. Baka hut, or *mongulu*, a semidome of woven branches, covered in mongongo leaves.

on. The late-twentieth-century introduction of rectangular versions of the hut derives from neighboring peoples with whom the Baka trade and indicates a transition to more permanent shelters. Currently, both the Baka and the San peoples are being coerced toward permanent settlement because of political and environmental objections to their hunter-gatherer way of life.

Most hunter-gatherer nomads lived lightly on the land, more interested in conserving its natural resources and the habitat of their prey than altering them. One can still observe the inherent economy of the nomadic way of life in the Tuareg people, who have crossed the Sahara Desert for millennia as traders and shepherds, carrying the elements of their temporary shelters on their camels. They raise their tents by throwing a canopy of sewn hides and woven goat hair over a central pole, at the top of which is a supporting ring. From this central turban-like point they pull ropes in a radial pattern, fastening them to wooden stakes laid out on a square plan. They then insert lateral, curved branches between the ropes to coax the skin covering into a dome-like canopy and pull more ropes across the outside to secure it against the wind. The strength of Tuareg structures relies upon the tensile forces of the coverings and the ropes. When the nomads move on, they fold up the hides and bind them into a package with the sticks and poles to be carried on a camel's back to the next campsite.

The indigenous nomadic peoples of North America achieved a similar elegance in their dwelling places, using a minimum of materials and causing little disturbance to the land. The *tipi* (Fig. 1.2-2), named after a Sioux word meaning "to dwell," required only a few minutes for its assembly. Sioux builders in the Dakota territories sank four straight poles into the ground at the points of a square, 2–3 m (6.5–10 ft) per side. The poles converged into an interlocking crux made firm by binding the neck joint with strips of bark. With this basic structure in place, a dozen other poles were set in a polygonal or circular pattern and leaned toward the apex.

The tipi builders drew a conical covering of stitched buffalo hides over the frame, leaving an operable flap at the top to let the smoke out of the hearth and another flap to cover the entry at the base. Because of the prevailing western winds on the prairies, tipis frequently tilted to the west to brace against the elements. Like the Tuareg, the Native Americans of the Plains transported the basic ingredients of their dwellings with them as they moved across the continent.

Other nomadic peoples in North America, such as the Chippewa tribes, built domical **wigwams**, which served longer periods of settlement. Constructed of bent poles, the wigwam required more skill to prepare since the sapling branches had to be trained into shape. The arched ribs followed either a grid or a radial pattern, with a diameter of 3–4 m (10–13 ft). The structure looked like an overturned basket, with woven grasses, strips of bark, or sewn hides tucked into the ribs to keep out the elements. An **oculus**, a rounded hole at the top, served as a smokestack. The wigwam could be easily lifted intact and moved to another site. During seasonal migrations the occupants rolled up the coverings while leaving the skeletal frames in place for reuse when they returned to the site the following year.

The nomads of the steppes in Mongolia, Kyrgyzstan, Kazakhstan, and Turkmenistan build **yurts**, which are

Adobe arch in Ctesiphon (Iraq)

▲ **ca. 500** CE

▼ **ca. 1200** CE

Hakka people's tulous in Fujian Province (China)

Mud-brick tower houses (Yemen)

▲ **ca. 1200** CE

Bone Huts of the Ukraine: Building as Body

The hut type first documented at Terra Amata underwent subtle changes over the years according to site conditions and availability of materials. Among Stone-Age huts, some of the most spectacular were built with the bones of the great mammoths at Mezhyrich near Kiev in the Ukraine. Dating from 20,000 to 15,000 BCE, the bone huts show a pragmatic variation on the basic type: the oval shelters were raised on the skeletal remains of the hunters' prey. A single hut with a roughly 5 m (16.5 ft) radius consumed up to 150 bones, including three dozen sets of mammoth tusks that served to frame the doorway and hold the roof. The hut builders of Mezhyrich imitated the symmetry found in the skeletons of their prey and in their own bodies. This bilateral order derived from an analogy to the biological body, one frequently made in vernacular architecture. Buildings represented bodies, and at Mezhyrich, they were literally composed of body parts.

Ukrainian bone hut, ca. 15,000 BCE.

larger, more sophisticated versions of the wigwam. A yurt requires such a large quantity of wooden poles that it might be considered a timber building. Yurt builders create a cylindrical base from a grid of diagonally set wooden poles raised to head height. They then place dozens of slender poles in a radial pattern on top of the perimeter wall and fasten them to a central oculus, which acts as a compression ring. They cover this umbrella-like frame, held up in the

Figure 1.2-2 Pine Ridge reservation, Dakota territories. Sioux tipi photographed by John Grabill in 1891, showing canvas flaps for chimney and entry.

The Primitive Menstrual Hut

The so-called primitive hut frequently appears as the basis of Western architectural theory. If one considers that almost all preliterate cultures practiced some sort of segregation of women, sending them to a menstrual hut during their periods, a social theory about gender can be attached to the primordial structures. Among the Dogon people in Mali (see Section 9.3), women are required to retreat to a menstrual hut, or *penulu*, during their monthly cycle. In a polygamous society this serves to keep track of who is fertile. The Dogon situate the *penulu* hut on the outskirts of the village, thus segregating the women. The antiquity of such a practice is preserved in the orthodox Jewish *mikveh*, the obligatory

seven-day bathing requirement for women during menstruation, which goes back at least three millennia. While the ancient Greek physician Hippocrates considered menstruation to be a process of purification, the Roman historian Pliny the Elder, writing in the first century CE, expressed a more unsympathetic masculine bias, describing it as a form of impurity. Some argue that the segregation of women during menstruation became a source of empowerment for them in which they could celebrate their mystical connection with the lunar cycle, but the primitive menstrual hut generally enforced the subordination of women and remains an architectural legacy of the deep prejudices rooted in gender differentiation.

center by two slender columns, with substantial swathes of cloth, usually felt, and then lash ropes over it to bind the fabric to the roof.

Nomadic tents, quick to assemble and light, rely mostly on tensile strength. They achieve the goal of twentieth-century engineer Buckminster Fuller: to "make more with less" (see Section 20.2). Nomads travel with the ingredients of their dwellings the way others travel with clothing. Contrary to the significant alterations of the topography made by settled peoples, the flexibility of tents and huts allows the nomad to live lightly on the land, adjusting to its conditions without radically changing its ecology.

Building out of Earth

Unbaked mud provided the most common building material in the ancient world and remains very popular among traditional builders. Earth construction has both advantages and flaws. It is an incredibly flexible material, easily shaped and stiffened, but just as easily it loses its form when not protected from dampness or tremors. "Good boots and a nice hat," that is, stone footings and deep **eaves**, served as the traditional wisdom for protecting mud structures from moisture. To this one might add "a bit of makeup," such as bitumen-based or lime plaster, to help with impermeability. As to the vulnerability of mud structures to seismic tremors—they do not perform well unless reinforced with wood frames. The great tremor of 2003 in eastern Iran completely leveled the domes, towers, and houses of the ancient city of Bam, which was built exclusively of mud bricks. The magnificent **battered walls** of the fortress spread more than twice as thick as the upper wall at their base, anticipating the sliding forces of gravity, but unfortunately proved defenseless against lateral shear stresses.

One of the easiest ways to build with earth, and the safest protection from earthquakes, is to dig or cut into it. About 40 million Chinese people live in dugout houses in the northwestern Shaanxi Province just north of Xi'an, in an area as large as Spain known as the Loess Plateau. Winds and glaciers have packed the fine-grained silt and clay into solid, deep strata, so dense that trees do not easily grow on it. For three millennia builders have carved deep into the loess to make pit houses (Fig. 1.2-3) that yield an ideal thermal performance. They have cut some of the houses into the cliffs, which are accessed by ramps, while sinking others into the ground. They start the pit houses by carving out a courtyard 10 m (30 ft) deep and as many meters across. They then proceed to extract the rooms from the four faces of the court, as if they were cliffs. The entries into the loess dwellings are always through arches, and

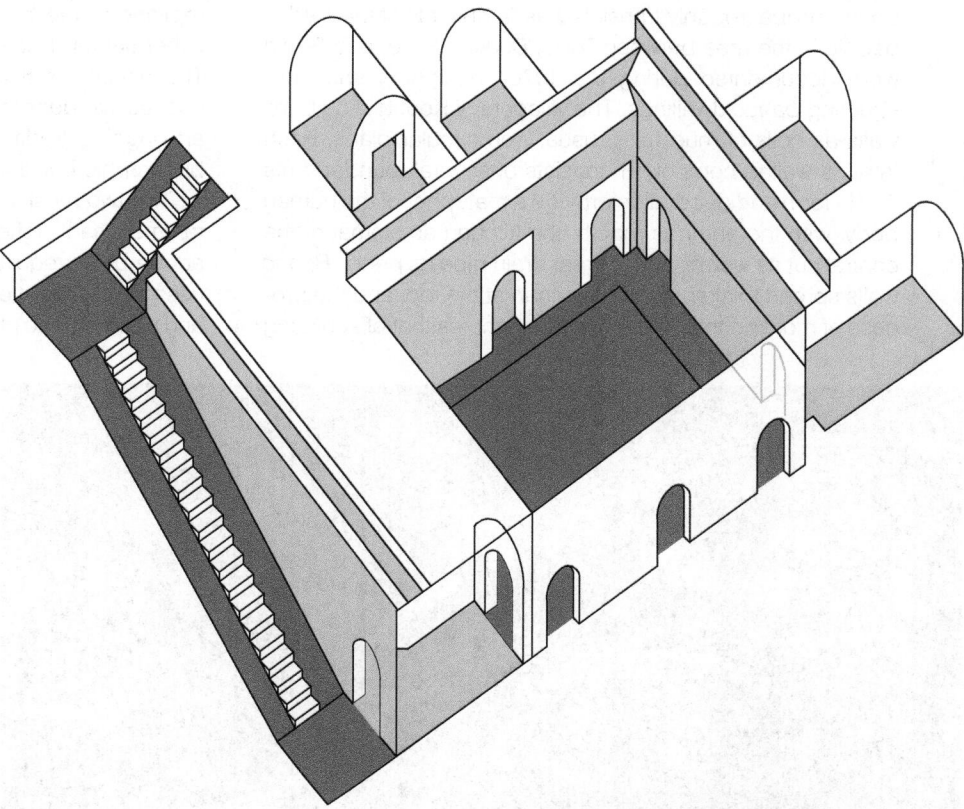

Figure 1.2-3 Loess Plateau, central China. Plan of cave house, or *yaodong*, dug into the dense soil. This typical earth dwelling has been used since the first millennium BCE.

the rooms are frequently carved with **vaults**, which have more compressive resistance than a flat beam or flat roofs. Rainfall in this region is scarce, making water retention the greatest problem. Pit-house courts do not have drains but attempt to collect the rainwater in cisterns.

Not far from the Loess Plateau, about 10 km (6 miles) east of Xi'an, lies one of the best-known prehistoric sites in China, the village of Banpo, with houses partially dug out of the earth. Dating from 5000 to 4000 BCE, the settlement supported about 500 inhabitants. Instead of building walls for their oval houses, the people of Banpo dug pits to a level of 1 m (3.3 ft) to serve as the walls. Pitched wooden beams were then set around each pit's perimeter to form conical roofs. Only the central building, which probably was used for assemblies, followed a different structural system. The builders of Banpo raised the rectangular hall 20 × 12.5 m (65.5 × 41 ft) off the ground on wooden posts. The fortifications of Banpo repeated the subtractive logic of the houses in the form of a deep ditch ringing the settlement.

While many Neolithic peoples dug pit houses out of the earth, geological conditions impeded others from doing so. Pit houses also have recurring problems with humidity. The next best method of building with earth involves mixing soil, water, straw, reeds, and leaves into balls that can be stacked. The piling up of mud balls is known as **cob technique** in English, and **banco** in West Africa, where until recently it was the most common form of construction. The

Batammaliba (roughly translated as "architects of the earth") people in the area between Togo, Burkina Faso, and Benin were documented during the 1970s designing and constructing *banco* dwellings. The villagers of Koufitoukou build walls as coils of mud balls, usually on circular plans. Each family's walled compound consists of several rounded huts that in form and decoration provide a metaphor of the human body, with the entry as mouth, the kitchen as stomach, the central hut as womb, and a great drain pipe as penis. *Banco* walls spread thicker at the base than at the top, and the process of molding their **elevations** resembles that of sculpting

replicas of the body. The Batammaliba roof the huts with either flat mud-paved surfaces or conical bundles of straw. The houses of Koufitoukou need yearly replastering, and successive generations completely rebuild them as part of an ongoing tradition of dweller-architects, who in making biomorphic buildings narrate stories about themselves.

The two most widespread varieties of earth construction, rammed earth (often called by the French word **pisé**) and adobe brick, require more skill and foresight. Rammed earth uses slightly moist earth poured into a rigid, wooden formwork and pounded into place, layer upon layer, with a heavy rammer.

The grand cylinders and cubes built as collective dwellings by the Hakka people in more than forty villages in Fujian Province, China, offer the largest and most beautiful examples. The village of Chuxi has five fortress-like compounds, known as *tulou* (Fig. 1.2-4a,b), built during the fifteenth century CE. As many as 200 rooms cling on wooden scaffolds to the solid mud perimeter walls. The occupants live in the concentric rows of structures built in the large open courts. The ingredients of *tulou* mud walls resemble a cake recipe, for in addition to clay-rich soil and straw, their builders included brown sugar, egg whites, and the juice of sticky rice to help bind the mixture. The outer wall, 3 m (10 ft) thick at its base and 1 m (3.3 ft) thick at the top, usually rose four stories high and was always set on a stone foundation to protect it from humidity. The absence of exterior windows on the first two levels indicates the defensive nature of the *tulou*. Their dwellers allowed only a single entry into these drum-shaped compounds, which could be carefully monitored.

Adobe, a Spanish word derived from the Arabic *al-tuba*, refers specifically to earthy substances shaped into unbaked bricks. Builders cast the earth mixture in rectangular bars, sometimes standardized through the use of wooden molds. After the bricks are sufficiently dried and hardened in the sun, they are laid in regular courses and bound together with mortar. The hand-molded mud bricks of Neolithic Jericho offer some of the first historical examples. The tradition of building with mud bricks continued in

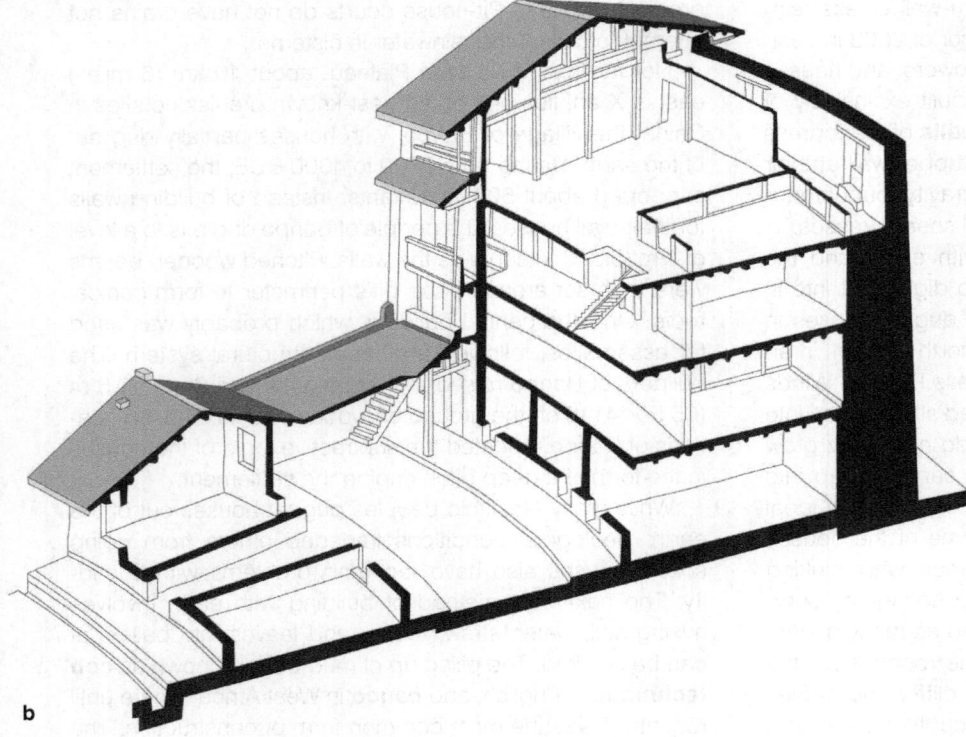

Figure 1.2-4 Chuxi, Fujian Province, China. (a) Hakka people's fortress houses, or *tulou*, made of rammed earth and dating as far back as the twelfth century. (b) Section.

Southwest Asia, culminating in the immense stepped towers, or ziggurats, built during the third millennium BCE (see Section 2.1).

The impressive mud-brick tower houses of Yemen (Fig. 1.2-5) derive from a centuries-old tradition. Their construction can be traced back to at least the twelfth century CE. In some cases the towers reach astounding heights of over 30 m (98 ft). The builders of Yemenite tower houses shape the frames of the windows and doors with mud thickened by white gypsum plaster, which can be carved into intricate geometric patterns like white lace after it sets.

In many semipermanent settlements in South America, Africa, and Asia, builders use wigwam-type frames to support a mud covering. The Fulani people, a minority group living in several different West African states, build their mud-walled huts on frames nearly identical to those of Chippewa wigwams. The sapling poles act as reinforcement for the thick mud walls, which are raised to head height. They then lay the domes over a skeleton made from lighter twined reeds that have been packed with mud and squared off, making them look like reinforced concrete beams. The Fulani's solidified wigwam huts suggest that the design of temporary nomadic structures served as the logical source for permanent architectural solutions such as the early round houses of Jericho and Khirokitia.

With skill and foresight builders can assemble mud bricks into sturdy vaulted coverings. Round houses built in Neolithic Southwest Asia probably had flat roofs made of reeds and plastered with mud, but in some cases they may have been covered with domes. Similar mud structures currently built in northern Syria often carry domes, whose mud bricks are placed in ascending spirals that gradually push in toward the center. During the 1960s the Egyptian architect Hassan Fathy (see Section 19.2) revived mud-brick vaults, known properly as "pitched" vaults, which can be built without expensive wooden scaffolds, or **falsework**, to hold them in place. The bricks are set in arching patterns on a 45° incline, which keeps them from slipping down. The great Arch of Ctesiphon, built by the Persian Sassanid regime in the early fifth century CE a few kilometers south of modern Baghdad, remains the most impressive adobe vault. Its shape is ovoid, similar to a modern **catenary arch**, like the inversion of a chain hung between two points. That the 25 m (75 ft) arch still stands speaks well of the spanning capacity and strength of mud bricks.

The Typical Structures of Spans

Baking mud bricks made buildings more durable. Fired bricks necessitated a greater quantity of materials, however, especially clay from quarries and firewood for the furnaces,

Figure 1.2-5 Sanaa, Yemen. Mud-brick high rises, sixteenth century CE.

which increased costs and required a more complex system of production. Standardized fired bricks were perfected by the third millennium BCE and used in both the Indus Valley and Mesopotamia. The orthogonal nature of bricks encouraged rectangular geometries that were more precise than the rounded forms created with mud. Building in the earth or out of earth has always been an organic process, and the forms became ready metaphors for bodies, but once designers started working with more specialized techniques such as fired bricks and drafted masonry, this meaning of architecture became less evident.

The Wooden Skeleton

The great forests of northern Europe initially provided a habitat and then the major building materials for the primeval settlers of the region, who usually lived in detached houses built of sticks and logs. Dozens of prehistoric sites show evidence of wooden **longhouses** (Fig. 1.2-6) built during the sixth and fifth millennia in a swathe of territory extending from the Black Sea to the British Isles. The longhouses of the village of Sittard in the Netherlands were structured on regularly spaced timber posts placed in parallel rows and braced at the top by roof beams. At Bylany, not far from modern Prague, there were over 100 houses, some up to 45 m (147 ft) in length, structured on five parallel rows of wooden posts. Boughs were woven around the exterior posts to create a basket-like wattle for the walls, which were then plastered with mud daub. The roofs of these **wattle-and-daub** structures were pitched to shed rain and snow and covered with either thatch or turf. The hearth was usually in the middle of the long central space, with a corresponding monitor cut in the roof overhead to admit light and vent the smoke. The designers divided the aisles into

Tension and Compression

All architecture struggles with gravity, using the forces of **compression** and **tension**. The first pushes down with its weight to stabilize the mass of a building, while the latter pulls in opposite directions. All structures need to control the downward pull of the forces of gravity and the lateral stress of wind and shear forces. Compression responds to the weight of mass pushing down and out. The walls of vernacular buildings are thus often twice as thick at the base as at the top. Tension exerts horizontal stresses like the elastic pull of a taut rope, allowing one to reduce mass. In the conventional **post-and-beam** (or **post-and-lintel**) structural system, the walls and columns support a horizontal member that spans between walls

or columns. The span favors the sort of tension found in fibrous materials like wooden beams. The tensile strength of spanning members can be assisted by a **cantilever**, an overhang beyond the supporting wall or column, which typically extends a third of the length of the member. Cantilevers can be used to stack stones or logs into corbelled arches or vaults, the components of which progressively step in toward the center as they rise until they reach a capstone that seals the system. The **true arch** developed from corbelled arches is among the strongest spanning methods. These arches are made of tapered masonry blocks, called **voussoirs**, which are arranged radially, each piece pushing against the next in total compression.

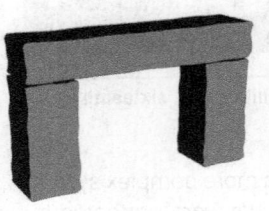
post & beam

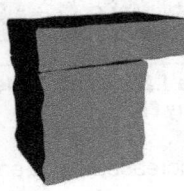
cantilever

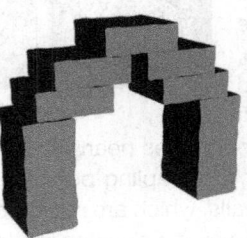
corbelled arch

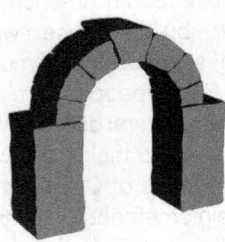
true arch

Structures of spans.

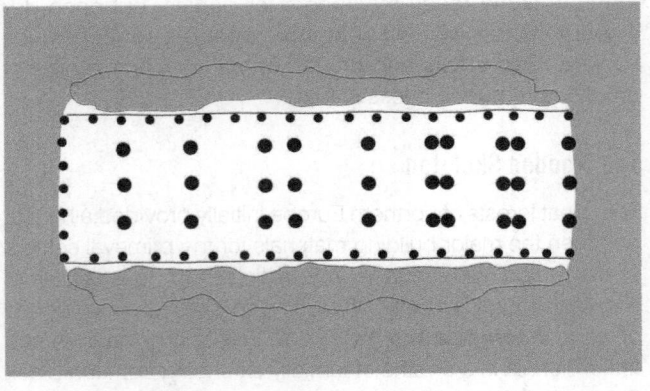

Figure 1.2-6 Cuiry-lès-Chaudardes, France. Plan of European longhouse, Neolithic period, ninth–fourth millennium BCE.

bays that served as stalls to shelter the livestock. Men and domesticated animals shared the dwelling. Like mud buildings, wooden buildings utilize organic materials, but the shape and stiffness of wood favors orthogonal geometry because of the natural right angles of intersecting timbers.

Variations of the Neolithic longhouse type have been found at European sites as widely spread as France, Norway, Romania, and Greece. Their configurations are not identical in terms of the positions of structural members. For instance, some have ridgepoles running down the center, while others have parallel

posts along the sides. The timber used in their construction, which has not survived, was probably joined by tying the members together. The top of the posts may have been forked to receive the crossbeams. Builders could not make accurate notches for diagonal **braces** and **mortise-and-tenon** joints until the introduction of metal tools. Mortise-and-tenon members fit a tapered ridge into a gouged-out groove. The longhouse builders invariably made rectangular structures, which were at least 10 m (33 ft) long, with spaces reserved for farm animals either at one end or along the sides.

In heavily timbered areas the Neolithic craftspeople made their longhouses with split logs or planks and occasionally added masonry walls when there was a ready supply of stone. They used thatch roofs made of branches and grasses almost universally, leading to highly flammable and insect-ridden environments. The houses were usually grouped in clusters of five or six, with each one thought to serve an extended family of twenty to thirty members. A Neolithic longhouse discovered in Mold, Austria, extended 80 m (262 ft) and would have accommodated an even greater number of residents under the same roof. The type endured for millennia among the peasant communities of Europe and was still being built in the thirteenth century CE.

The longhouse, as a single container for a large extended family and its animals, appeared in many other cultures outside Europe, including Southeast Asia and North America,

Figure 1.2-7 Reconstruction of an Iroquois longhouse, typical of the fifteenth century CE. Royal Ontario Museum, Toronto.

with similar social implications. The grass-covered, open-sided version in Borneo at Sarawak stretches nearly 60 m (197 ft) in length, with three rows of parallel posts. The Iroquois tribes built a 110 m (360 ft) long structure around 1400 CE at Howlett Hill near Syracuse, New York (Fig. 1.2-7). They made the walls of the structure from a palisade of slender posts between which they wove a bark covering and ran two parallel rows of thicker columns down the center to help support the vaulted roof. The structure may have housed up to 200 people.

The other major vernacular type of wooden building rises on stilts. Neolithic villagers along the Swiss lakes at Egolzwil built their modest wooden houses on raised piles to protect them from sudden floods. Measuring 3.7 × 9 m (12 × 29 ft), the stilt houses had timber floors, and their frames were among the first to be connected with mortised joints. Stilt houses continue to be a popular type in alluvial areas of Southeast Asia.

The timber-frame house possesses some of the expediency and tensile virtue of the temporary huts built with poles. Like the skeleton in the bodies of vertebrates, the timber frame absorbs most of the stresses that bear upon the structure. Not all regions possess abundant supplies of wood, but where there were great forests, such as in Eastern Europe and Scandinavia, it became the prime building material, leading to the construction of log cabins and plank houses. The Navajo in the American Southwest made their houses, or *hogans*, of unstripped logs without notches. For the oval version of this type the men tilted the logs toward the center in a manner close to the style of the huts of Terra Amata. The women built their version of the hogan as a spiraling hexagon. They corbelled the logs toward the center to create a dome with an oculus that let out the smoke. Lumber was used almost like piles of stone.

Wooden frames, while subject to fire and rot, proved particularly resilient in seismic locations and thus became the preferred construction method in places like Japan, California, and Turkey. Often, a combination of wooden frame with stone or mud infill, seen in the ancient houses of Anatolia at Çatalhöyük, transferred the flexibility of one material to the other in half-timber construction.

The **cruck frame**, found mostly in England, appears as one of the most primitive and spectacular versions of the wooden skeleton. The principal structural members of this type came from large trees that, instead of being milled into flat posts, were left in their natural state, split down the middle, and then pitched one half against the other into an arch shape. The effect recalls the mammoth tusks of the Ukrainian bone huts, resulting in a series of monumental pointed arches formed out of its rib-like structure.

While no examples of prehistoric wood joinery have survived, the various representations of wood sculpted in stone, seen at Stonehenge in Neolithic England, Saqqâra in ancient Egypt (see Section 2.2), and the Parthenon in classical Greece (see Section 4.2), give some indication of its ingenuity. Greek artists depicted wooden dowel pegs on their temples, while the builders of Stonehenge simulated the interlocking mortise-and-tenon method of joining timbers in which a projecting tongue (tenon) of one member fits into a hole (mortise) of corresponding shape in another member. The disposition of standing tree trunks, first seen in the Neolithic longhouses, established the basis for the systems of **columns** used in Chinese, Persian, and Western classical systems of architectural order.

Of Stones and Compression

While the majority of Neolithic builders used some combination of mud, sticks, timber, animal hides, and woven grasses, they chose stone, which was almost always available, for foundations, buttressing, and the hearth. Stone required the assistance of skilled masons to obtain and prepare, but it promised many advantages over the other materials, especially in its resistance to fire, the perennial destroyer. When Neolithic societies created religious structures, they usually chose stone as their medium for its permanence.

In some regions that have a ready supply of loose stone, such as the Orkney Island coast in northern Scotland, masonry construction became the easiest way to build.

The small village of Skara Brae, built around 3000 BCE, consisted of eight small stone houses linked by stone-lined alleys that formed a compact organism (Fig. 1.2-8a). The problem with building in stone comes from the degree to which it must be dressed, or sculpted, in order to fit one stone with the next. At Skara Brae the local supply came from a granite shelf that left loose stones in brick-like shapes, making it relatively easy to construct solid dry walls without mortar (Fig. 1.2-8b). Each of the small houses had a single

---

CONSTRUCTION, TECHNOLOGY, THEORY

The Ancient Wooden Town of Biskupin

Despite the perishable nature of wood, several well-preserved ruins of ancient timber architecture in Eastern Europe reveal the millennial practice of wood joinery. The foundations of a Neolithic wooden village at Lake Biskupin, Poland, built during the eighth and seventh centuries BCE, lay protected under the viscous mud of its island site until discovered in 1933. The prehistoric lumbermen assembled Biskupin's ramparts as **blockwork** boxes, 3 m (10 ft) on each side, filled with

mud and rubble. The oval wall enclosed 105 identical row houses arranged on twelve parallel streets paved with logs. Each of the log houses at Biskupin was built facing southeast, with an exterior porch and an internal hearth. Such urban regularity presages that of ancient Greek towns such as fifth-century-BCE Olynthus (see Section 4.2). The same construction technique of interlocking logs used in the Bronze Age endured well into the modern age throughout Eastern Europe (see Section 10.2).

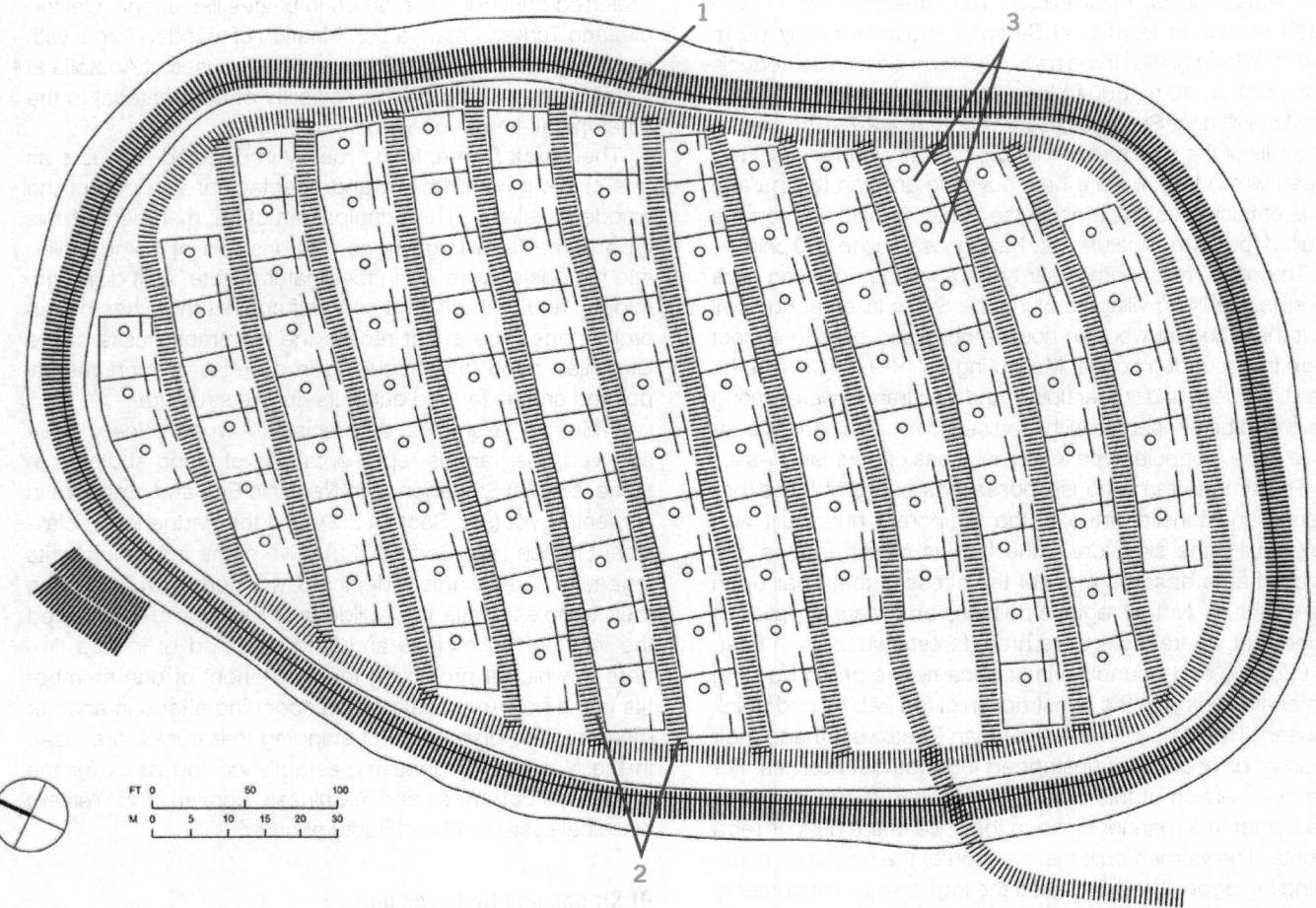

Biskupin, Poland. Reconstruction of Neolithic log houses and town plan, ca. 500 BCE, showing (1) ramparts made of blockwork boxes, (2) log-paved streets, and (3) row houses.

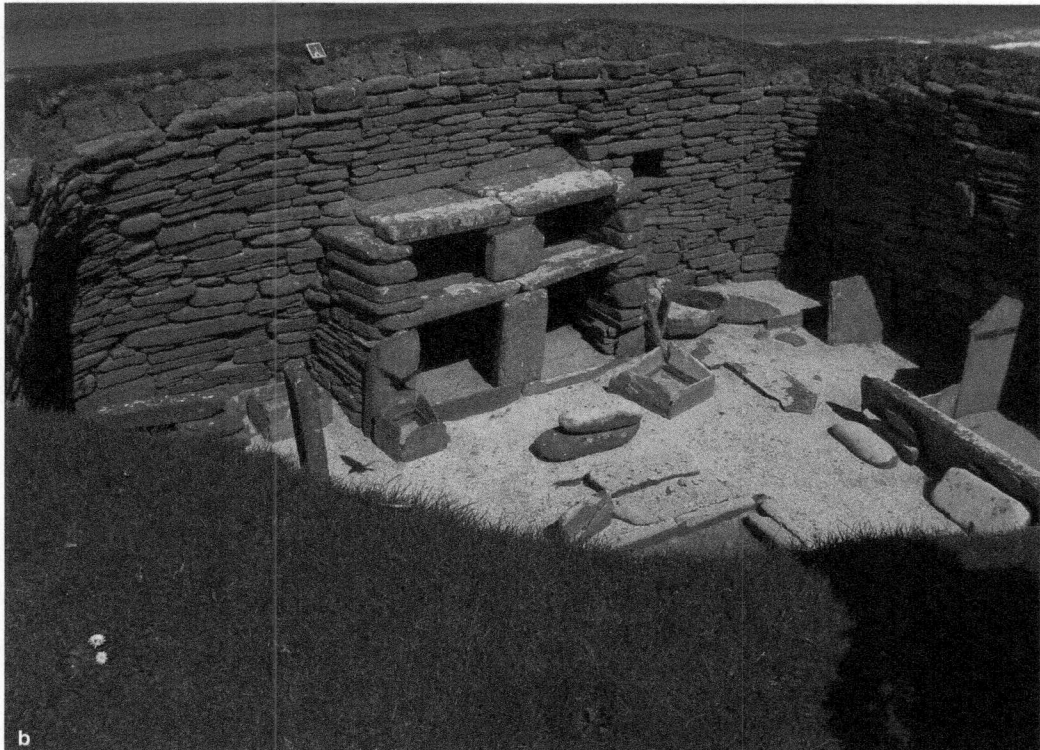

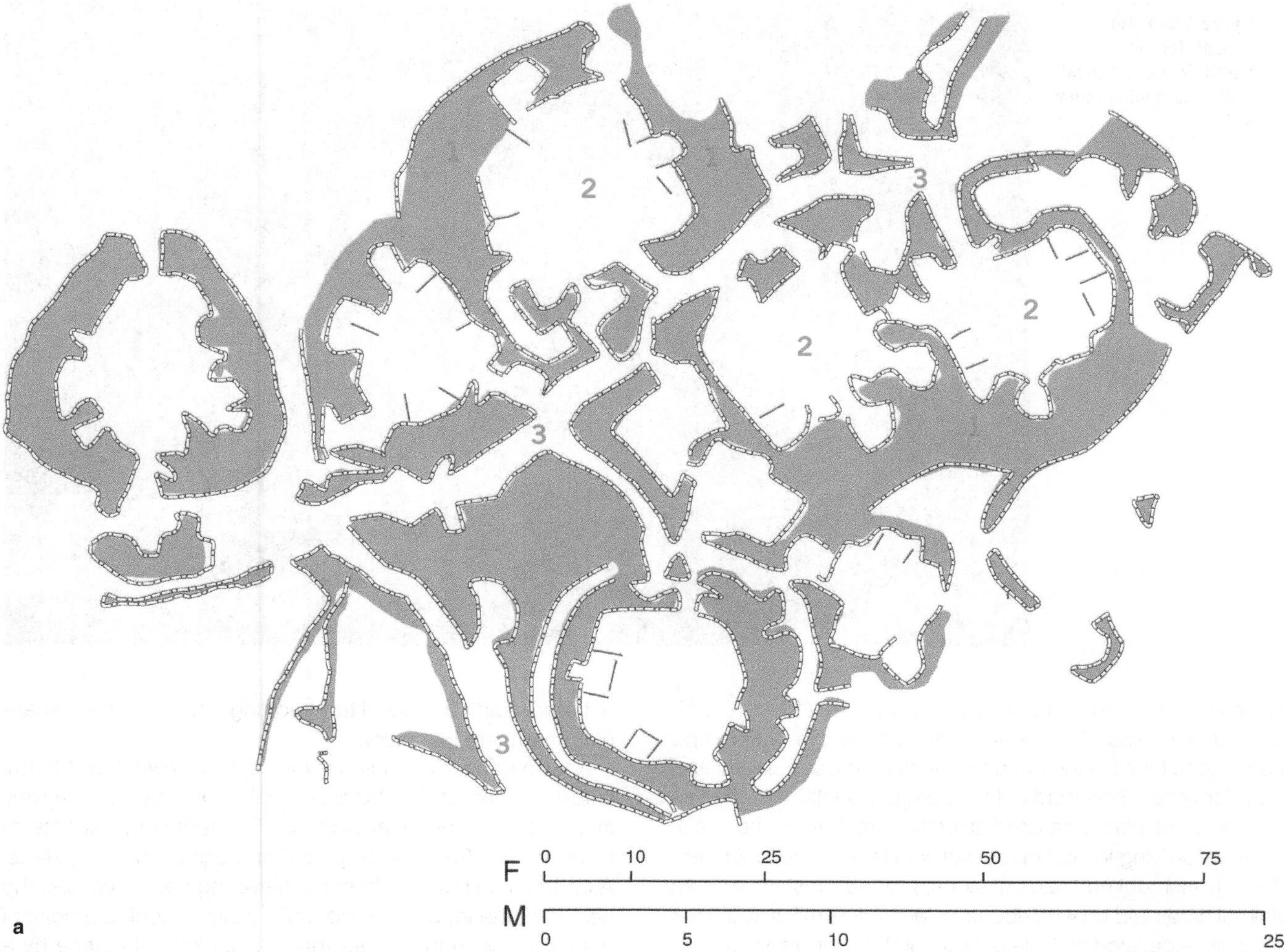
1
2
1
3
2
2
3
1
3
F
0 10 25 50 75
M
0 5 10 25

a

b

Figure 1.2-8 Orkney Islands, Scotland. Skara Brae, ca. 3000 BCE. (a) Plan, showing (1) thick walls built of dry-wall masonry, (2) individual lodgings featuring built-in furnishings made from stone slabs, and (3) narrow paths connecting the dwellings as a community. (b) Dry-wall masonry from brick-sized stones.

Figure 1.2-9 Ain Ghazal, Jordan. Neolithic stone "sack" walls, sixth millennium BCE.

room with rounded corners, typically 4 × 5 m (13 × 16.5 ft). The builders placed the hearth in the center of the room and used stone for all of their furniture, including beds, seats, and a system of shelves made of thin, broad panels. The shelves had pride of place, situated directly across from the entry, perhaps serving to hold objects of veneration. The roofs were the only element not made of stone, probably fashioned from animal hides laid on whalebone rafters. A few miles south the recently excavated cult site of Ness of Brodgar displays even more meticulous stone joinery of the same date, painted and decorated with reliefs and apparently topped with flagstone roofs. These temples were no doubt the progenitors of the great stone circle of Brodgar, built a few centuries later.

At Ain Ghazal, Jordan, a settlement built during the seventh millennium BCE and thus contemporary with Neolithic Jericho, the inhabitants constructed their houses of rectangular **sack walls** (Fig. 1.2-9). A sack wall is a sandwich of two outer layers of stone stuffed with mud and rubble infill. Such a system allowed builders to obtain a thick wall with much of the mass of mud construction while leaving a hard, impermeable exterior surface. Most of the structures at Ain Ghazal had squared-off corners, suggesting that cut stone often leads to orthogonal solutions.

The roof—usually built of organic materials (such as branches woven together), plastered with gypsum, and supported by wooden posts and beams—proved the weakest part of prehistoric houses. The caves of the nomads held solutions for a more solid way of spanning interior space. The easiest way to cover a room was to lay a solid slice of stone on top of two upright walls. The dolmen megalith tombs (see Section 1.3) built across Europe, Africa, and Asia during the third through the first millennia BCE offered ready examples, illustrating both the solidity and the limits of such a method, since slabs of stone rarely reach more than 3–4 m (10–13 ft) across. The megalith builders also had the extremely difficult task of transporting and lifting such spanning members into place.

One means of spanning involved the **corbel** (Fig. 1.2-10), introduced around 3000 BCE, which provided a relatively sturdy and fireproof alternative. The technique seems to have derived from the empirical process of stacking slabs. A corbel arch resulted from cantilevering one stone over the next from the tops of two opposite walls, reaching a point of convergence in the center that was locked into place by a **capstone**. A corbel vault could be formed by making a continuous series of corbel arches and a corbel dome by rotating a series of corbel arches around a central vertical axis. The various round stone houses with corbel roofs found around the Mediterranean, including the *trulli* of Puglia in southern Italy and the *borie* in southern France, hark back to the building techniques of Neolithic masons.

Neolithic masons shaped and dressed stones using stone axes and obsidian knives in a labor-intensive and imprecise process. They rendered the stones for the great megalithic works, such as the *T*-shaped monoliths at Göbekli Tepe, by adjusting to the forms offered by nature rather than completely controlling the form. They could sculpt limestone using tools made of harder stone, as some of the beautifully detailed temples on Malta indicate. In the Americas, where builders did not have metal tools until European contact during the sixteenth century CE, several cultures, such as the Mayans on the Yucatán Peninsula and the Inca of Peru, created impressive stone masonry joints with their limited stone tools.

In general, however, it was only with the introduction of metal tools that stonework became more precise and refined. As the masons perfected their craft, they used the clean lines of geometry to organize the laying of stones and draft perfectly rendered surfaces. The skill and theoretical knowledge needed to cut and design stone led to a class distinction among builders that elevated the chief masons

Figure 1.2-10 Alberobello, Puglia, Italy. Row of cone-shaped stone houses built with corbel dome roofs. Cone structures in the region date back to Neolithic times, but most *trulli* were constructed between 1500 and 1900.

with their "Masonic" secrets into the priestly caste. The high-style buildings commissioned for religious, princely, or community functions served an ulterior symbolic purpose that went beyond the expedient needs of shelter. In most parts of the world, such projects became the task of specialists working with stone masonry and the art of its assembly and decoration. Trained architects designed works intended to serve collective memory, which, unlike vernacular buildings, were built to endure beyond the span of a human life.

Further Reading

Blier, Suzanne P. *The Anatomy of Architecture: Ontology and Metaphor in Batammaliba Architectural Expression.* Chicago: University of Chicago Press, 1987.

Crouch, Dora, and June Johnson. *Traditions in Architecture: Africa, America, Asia, and Oceania.* New York: Oxford University Press, 2001.

Dethier, Jean. *Down to Earth: Adobe Architecture: An Old Idea, a New Future.* New York: Facts on File, 1982.

Guidoni, Enrico. *Primitive Architecture.* New York: Rizzoli, 1975.

Nabokov, Peter, and Robert Easton. *Native American Architecture.* New York: Oxford University Press, 1989.

Oliver, Paul. *Dwellings: The Vernacular House World Wide.* London: Phaedon, 2003.

Pallasmaa, Juhani. *Animal Architecture.* Helsinki: Museum of Finnish Architecture, 1995.

1.3 MEGALITHS AND STONE CIRCLES
Building as Memory

The formal distinction between high-style architecture and vernacular building comes from the difference in intention. The program for monumental architecture arose when communities desired to commemorate their forebears and was continued later when powerful patrons sought ways to mark their status. Rock formations and stone construction, because of their greater endurance, became forms of materialization of human memory. All cultures, once they became relatively settled, longed to remember their dead, and throughout the prehistoric world they raised stones and covered mounds as conventional markers of the deceased. The ***dolmen***, a chamber made from two **monolithic** side stones capped by a monolithic roof stone and then covered with earth, became a conventional tomb for important persons, found in places as distant from each other as England and Korea.

Prehistoric tomb sites inspired religious ceremonies, leading to the construction of stone and mud-brick temples and shaped landscapes. The earliest builders preferred to make rounded works reminiscent of the atmosphere of primordial painted caves. As they became aware of the sun's behavior and the movements of the celestial bodies, they began to design open landscapes to register the cycles of the heavens. By setting stone markers aligned to astronomical phenomena, they attempted to link human destiny to a greater cosmos in the sky. The prehistoric cults used megaliths and stone circles as a theater of memory for uniting themselves to the experience of all who had come before and all who would follow.

Menhirs, Dolmens, and Cairns: To Honor the Dead

Architecture became an act of communication when groups of prehistoric dwellers joined together to pile up stones for a collective purpose. Adolf Loos, a twentieth-century architectural thinker from Vienna, put it this way: "You find a rise in the ground, two meters long and one meter wide, heaped up in a rough pyramid shape, then you turn serious, and something inside you says: someone lies buried here. That is architecture." The need to commemorate the dead instigated the earliest design of monuments. **Megaliths**, large stones dragged across the land and erected as markers, acted as icons for remembering the lives of those who came before. The earliest megaliths almost always served to mark burial sites. The designers selected the stones for their impressive scale and usually left them in their raw state. While this was due partly to the megalith builders' poor tools for sculpting the rocks, it also was a form of reverence for the irregularly shaped stones as expressions of the sacred forces of nature.

Megalith markers have been found on all continents and were particularly common in the years 4000 to 1000 BCE. Their dating remains problematic, as there are no written traces and few remains of these structures that can be tested with radiocarbon methods. One of the greatest collections of megaliths appeared in northwestern France, in Brittany, where the stones set in the ground were known as *menhirs* (meaning "raised stones"). The towering Menhir Brisé ("Broken Menhir") at Locmariaquer once stood 21 m (69 ft) high but now lies in four pieces on the ground. The

technology for lifting this 350-ton mast served as the silent partner of design, a process that left few clues behind. One can only guess about the use of ropes, log levers, and earthen ramps to slip such a massive and bulky stone into its deep foundation hole. It surely required the group effort of hundreds of people, and as a landmark, once visible from great distances, the Menhir Brisé established the focus and identity for the regional community.

Not far away, in the farming town of Carnac (Fig. 1.3-1), lie four large fields of menhirs. The alignments of these funeral landscapes, dated between 4000 and 2500 BCE, suggest usage for mass ceremonies. One of the fields, Le Menec, possesses over 1,000 megaliths of local granite arranged in parallel lines that extend for 1.5 km (ca. 1 mile; Fig. 1.3-2). The dozen rows run east by northeast toward a rounded terminus. As they reach the circle, the megaliths grow in height from 1 to 4 m (3.3 to 13 ft) and shift their angle of alignment. Kerlescan, another field of megaliths at Carnac, has a few hundred menhirs arranged in a fanning series of lines. The stones get taller as the alignment widens, reaching a final height of 3 m (10 ft). They guide a procession toward a rectangular plaza 80 × 90 m (262 × 295 ft), shaped on three sides by megaliths and on the fourth by a burial mound. While the great stones initially served as burial markers, their function evolved into pieces of an astronomical observatory. The stone avenues at Carnac offered an intermediate architectural experience between openness and enclosure. The shadow-casting megaliths created a place for the community both to remember those who came before and to contemplate their connection to some greater collective destiny determined by the heavens.

During the same period between the fourth and third millennia BCE at Monte d'Accoddi near the northern coast of Sardinia a stepped pyramid accessed by a 40 meter long ramp lined with megaliths showed a similar interest in astronomical alignments. While the top platform was used as an altar for sacrifices, the structure's perfect northern orientation implies that it functioned as an observatory.

In contrast to the openness of the freestanding menhirs, Neolithic builders also created closed, cave-like spaces for their tombs. The basic tomb type, the dolmen, was a simple box-like chamber covered with earth. In its starkest form the dolmen comprised two lateral megalith slabs supporting a horizontal capstone. This **trilithon**, or three-stone assembly,

TIME LINE

▼ **ca. 4500 BCE**

Cairn at Barnenez (France)

Carnac (France) fields of upright megaliths

▲ **4000–2500 BCE**

▼ **ca. 3600–2500 BCE**

Hagar Qim, Malta, rounded stone temples

embodies the most rudimentary principle of architecture, the post and lintel, that is, two columns holding up a horizontal bar of **trabeation**. The mourners would have placed the remains of the dead under the dolmen's bench-like space, a chamber just large enough for two standing figures. Although dolmens appear today mostly as freestanding stone structures, they were intended to be covered with earthen mounds.

Many dolmens, such as the Chianca Dolmen (Fig. 1.3-3) near Bisceglie in southern Italy, were approached by an articulated pathway lined with a continuous series of **orthostats**, or broad, flat stones. This privileged axis became the **passage tomb**, common in the larger **tumulus** gravesites of Neolithic times. The designers of these great mounds of stone and earth, known as **cairns** in the British Isles and northern France, created tunnels made of linked dolmens leading to an interior vaulted chamber. One of the oldest cairns, the great oblong pyramid of Barnenez (Fig. 1.3-4), dating to around 4500 BCE, stands on a promontory overlooking the Bay of Morlaix in the Finistère area of Brittany. Eleven passage tombs line up parallel to each other inside the mound and terminate in corbel vaults nearly 5 m (16 ft) high. The burial chambers at the end of the passages served as multiple tombs. Similar mounded cairns accessed by orthostat-lined passages that terminated in a domical space appeared throughout Europe from Los Millares in southern Spain to Newgrange in Ireland, indicating that invasions by groups such as the Beaker people and trade led to a pan-European cultural synthesis.

The mounded tombs at Newgrange, 50 km (30 miles) north of Dublin, were built around 3000–2500 BCE (Fig. 1.3-5a). Even though the builders' Celtic successors of the first millennium no longer knew the figures to whom the mounds

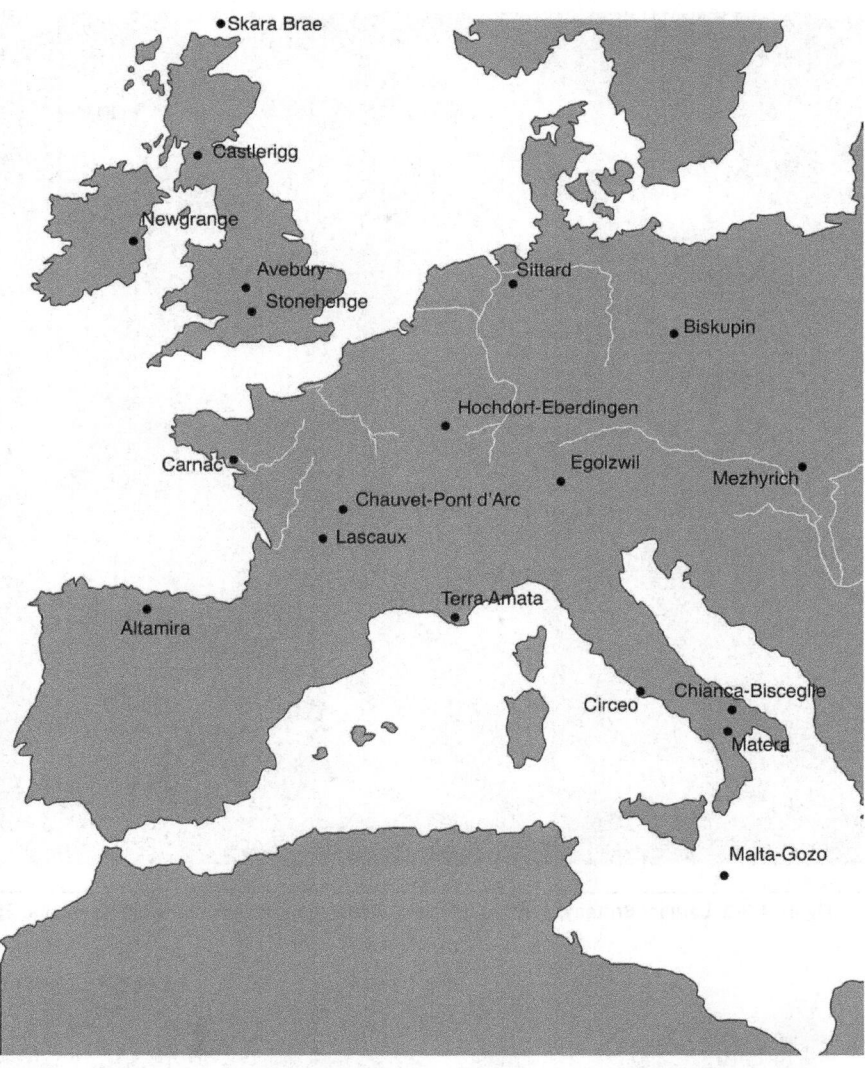

Figure 1.3-1 Monumental sites in Neolithic Europe.

were dedicated, they called the largest "Brú Oengusa," or house of the son of the Dagda, the king of the pre-Christian gods. This impressive pile, the grandest of over 150 cairns in Ireland, spreads over an 80 m (256 ft) diameter. It sits amid a diffused necropolis, within walking distance of two other similarly scaled cairns. Although more regular in shape than

Stone circles and megaliths (northern France, Ireland, and England)

▲ **ca. 3500–1000 BCE**

▼ **3000–2500 BCE**

Cairns of Newgrange, near Dublin

Avebury stone circle and Silbury Hill (England)

▲ **3000–2500 BCE**

▼ **3000–1600 BCE**

Stonehenge circle made with trilithons

Figure 1.3-2 Carnac, Brittany, northwest France. Aerial view of Le Menec alignments, ca. 2500 BCE.

Figure 1.3-3 Bisceglie, southern Italy. Chianca Dolmen, ca. 4000 BCE.

heart-shaped circle. They inserted a smooth **revetment** of gleaming white quartz masonry at the entry and inscribed most of the curbstones with spirals, **chevrons**, grids, and other abstract patterns commonly found in the painted caves.

At Brú Oengusa the artisans lined the interior passage with a series of dolmen-like megaliths. The path gently rises to a cruciform-shaped central chamber with three niches, 6 m (19.5 ft) across and 6 m high. The corbels of the vaulted ceiling form a conical shape. It took great foresight to leave a special window above the **transom** of the entry (Fig. 1.3-5b), which allows rays of sunlight to penetrate the passage to the center for twenty minutes each day during the winter solstice, a sure sign that the celebrants intended the monument as more than a tomb. They also raised a ring of thirty-eight standing megaliths, twelve of which are still upright, around the mound at regular 10 m (33 ft) intervals. These added features at Newgrange demonstrate that Neolithic communities moved from the cult of the dead toward a concern for sacred time, turning their

Barnenez, the Newgrange mound was by no means a product of calculated geometry. The designers defined its perimeter with a continuous series of ninety-seven megaliths set on their sides as a girdle of orthostats, yielding a rough,

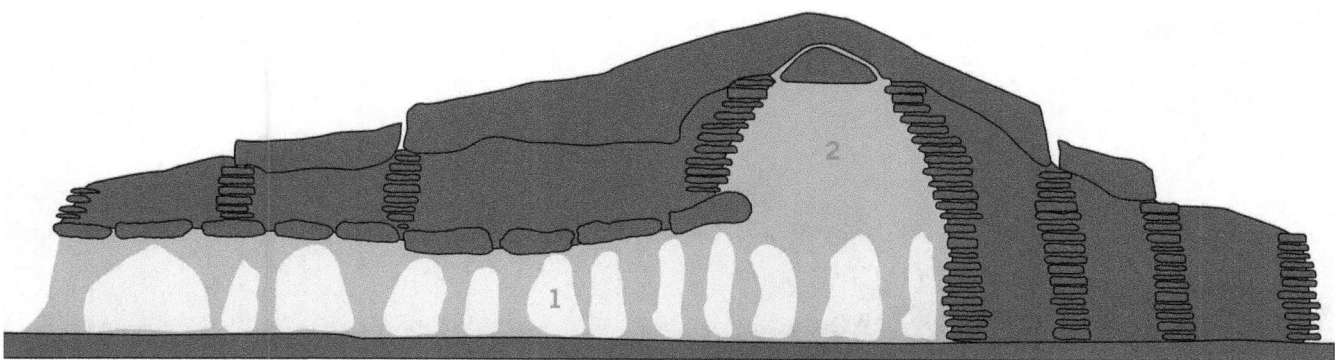

Figure 1.3-4 Barnenez, France. Section of a typical cairn tomb, ca. 4500 BCE, showing (1) main passage lined with raw megaliths, and (2) the central tomb space made with a corbel vault and closed with an immense capstone.

tomb structures into temples for observing the behavior of the celestial bodies.

Malta: The Roundness of Architecture

The prehistoric communities in the Maltese islands, located 90 km (56 miles) south of Sicily, produced an extraordinary collection of enclosed megalithic temples, built between 3600 and 2500 BCE. How these primordial places of worship came to be built in such a remote setting remains as mysterious as why their rounded forms had so little influence on the future of monumental architecture, which developed in almost all cases into a system of orthogonal geometry. The population on the two major islands of Malta and Gozo probably never exceeded 5,000. Their isolation from wild beasts and invaders, combined with a reasonable alimentary surplus from fishing and agriculture, allowed the Neolithic Maltese a certain advantage in the development of their cult sites.

All of the twenty-three temples on the Maltese islands correspond to a single design concept, seen in the complex of Hagar Qim (Fig. 1.3-6). Maltese designers began with a pair of rounded apses, which over time they multiplied, in a process similar to cell division. During a final phase they surrounded the curving cells by a layer of thick walls lined with megaliths. The outer walls of Hagar Qim rose independent of the interior, like a ring around the whole, leaving a sizable **poché** filled with rubble and smaller stones that in places stretched more than two body lengths across. They oriented the entry toward the rising sun and created an articulated threshold, capped on the exterior by a double row of horizontal spanning stones. This impressive concave facade, similar to facades at several other Maltese temples, provided stone benches at its base and opened to a paved plaza where people could gather. The designers seem to have conceived of the temple as a place of assembly for congregations in mourning, pilgrims seeking good fortune, supplicants with physical ailments hoping for relief, and prospective mothers longing for fertility. The votive offerings found at the site—ceramic statues of obese women, body parts, and horns—imply the undertaking of such quests.

On either side of the entry into Hagar Qim the architects made lobe-shaped rooms by propping up perimeter

orthostat walls of linked megaliths. Their craftspeople tooled the stones with great precision, leaving smooth joints between the stones and the recessed doorjambs. They plastered the walls in deep red tones to make them appear as continuous surfaces. Hagar Qim expanded during the course of the third millennium into a total of eight apses, interspersed with tiny side rooms thought to have been oracle chambers. The radius of each apse never exceeded 8 m (26 ft), a dimension probably determined by the limited spanning technology for the roofs. Although the roofs of these Maltese temples have completely disappeared, leaving the interiors exposed like courtyards, there is evidence of corbels at the top of the walls. Like the vaulted chambers inside passage tombs, the Maltese temples would have been roofed over with slabs of stone arranged into corbel vaults and then covered with turf. The interior atmosphere, without windows and with the walls plastered in red oxides, would have exuded mysterious, cave-like darkness.

The curving apses of Maltese temples seem to have been inspired by the great underground cemetery, or Hypogeum, at Hal Saflieni, where over thirty scooped-out chambers on three separate levels served about 7,000 graves. The niches in this multilevel grotto, many of them similar in shape and scale to the lobed spaces of the outdoor temples, served as sites for rituals honoring the dead. Some of the ceilings of the Hypogeum were carved like the negative of a stepped pyramid, hinting at the presence of corbel vaults that once covered the outdoor temples. The Maltese craftspeople subdivided the Hypogeum with walls and special doors placed in front of the niches. At some early point the celebrants used the cave to pursue two functions—the burial of ancestors and the propitiation of their spirits so that the dead could influence the good fortune of the living. In the apses of the outdoor temples, celebrants would have repeated the ceremonies begun in the underground niches of the Hypogeum.

The tiny "oracle chambers" nestled in the thick *poché* between the interior and exterior orthostats at Hagar Qim suggest the complex ritual use of the temples and the development of a hierarchical priesthood. Accessed by secret doors, these chambers would have allowed the oracle to speak through tiny square slots cut through the panels. Altars for votive offerings in some of the apses received the

Figure 1.3-5 Newgrange, Ireland. Mounded tombs, ca. 3000–2500 BCE. (a) Side view of the mound covering the passage tomb. (b) Entry.

most detailed sculptural treatment, raised on single pillars and carved with special images such as a palm-tree motif or delicate foliated spirals. The numerous representations of obese women, in one case a statue twice human height, suggests a cult of a mother goddess; but without written texts, one can only guess at the meaning and ritual life of the place. Certainly, the inhabitants made sacrifices of animals and perhaps humans there. Libations would have been poured into holes in the paving as gestures begging for divine intervention.

Within the dark sanctuaries of Malta, a devout Neolithic culture enacted its sacred rites of pacifying the dead, curing the sick, and ensuring fertility. The ancient Maltese made their sacrifices and listened to oracles uttered by mysterious voices through tiny slots from within concealed chambers. The sick and the crippled came to sleep in the wonder-working embrace of the temples in the hope of regaining their health. These shrines comforted and healed the islanders until sometime around 2500 BCE, when invaders overran Malta and left the rounded temples to fall into ruin. The sensuous curves of Maltese architecture almost completely disappeared from the religious architecture of successive cultures in the region, perhaps

CLOSE-UP

Figure 1.3-6 Malta. Hagar Qim, ca. 3600–2500 BCE.

(a) Concave orthostat façade.

a

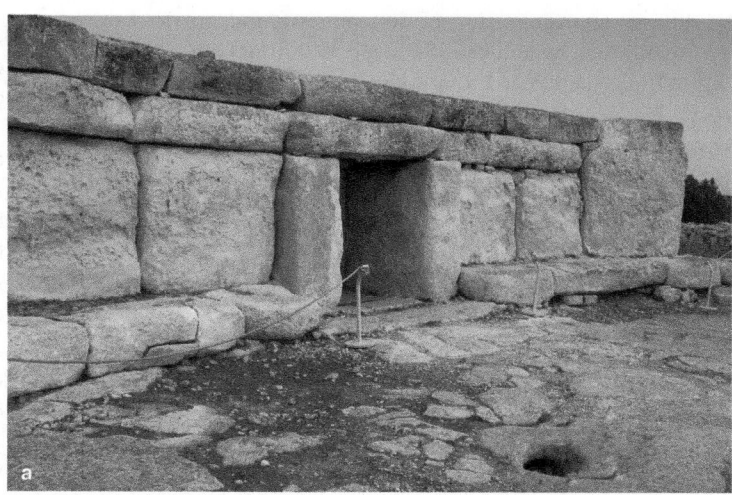

(b) Plan, aerial view.

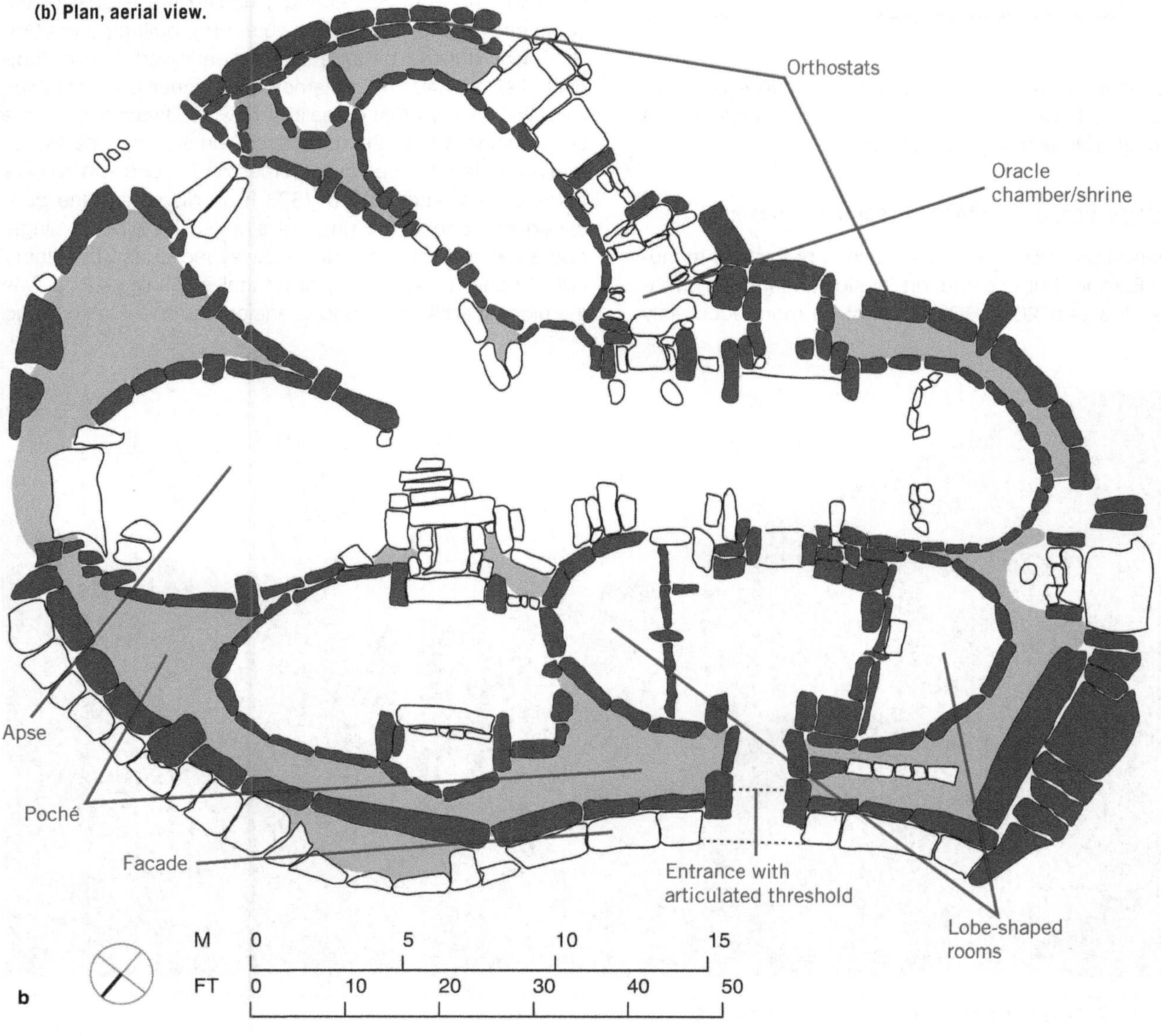
Orthostats
Oracle chamber/shrine
Apse
Poché
Facade
Entrance with articulated threshold
Lobe-shaped rooms
M 0 5 10 15
FT 0 10 20 30 40 50
b

Korean Dolmens

The greatest collection of dolmens is found on the Korean peninsula, where thus far over 30,000 have been studied. Often, the Korean tomb sites were built on slopes so as not to waste the arable land. The transport of the stones down the slopes was assisted by the force of gravity. In the village of Maesan there are 442 dolmens built between the seventh and third centuries BCE. Their shapes vary from straight-sided flanks carrying a flat slab to thicker blocks supported on four table-like legs. The largest capstone stretches 5.8 m (18 ft) in width, weighing 300 tons. The stability of the architecture results from the studied equilibrium between load and support. The heavier the ceiling is, the sturdier the walls must be. Although originally covered with soil and not intended to be seen, after several millennia the Neolithic dolmens in Korea and elsewhere have been left exposed as rather awkward freestanding archways. The accidental drama of these megalithic tombs as they stand denuded in the landscape evokes a sense of precarious stability, like a house of cards on the verge of collapse.

as a result of a greater concern with masculine divinities located in the heavens and a corresponding desire to plot out rational spaces using right angles.

Stonehenge: Responding to the Order of the Cosmos

Stonehenge prevails as the most famous prehistoric monument in Europe, but considering its significant transformation after the year 2000 BCE, it might be more accurately classified as a product of the Bronze Age. While neither the largest nor the oldest of the forty-six stone circles, or **henges**, in the British Isles, its final form reveals a superior refinement of craft, geometry, and astronomical knowledge. Just as Stonehenge has spawned the curiosity of millions of tourists today, it certainly attracted masses of pilgrims during its own time, people eager to participate in the rituals of a colossal timepiece.

An earlier stone ring, Castlerigg (Fig. 1.3-7) in Cumbria near the Scottish border, dates from 3200 BCE and provides a fine example of the precedents of Stonehenge. A bowl of hills surrounds the site on a treeless moor, and the circle looks from a distance like a group of people keeping silent vigil around a corpse about to be buried. Of the forty-two original megaliths, thirty-eight remain standing. The designers flattened the circle at the northern edge, perhaps to acknowledge the entry, and placed a rectangle of stones, known as "the cove," at the eastern end, probably for funerary rites. The megaliths ranged 1–2 m (3.3–7 ft) in height and were left in their raw shapes, each different from the other.

Avebury, an agricultural village in Wiltshire, 27 km (16 miles) north of Stonehenge, hosted the largest of the stone circles (Fig. 1.3-8). The outer ring, built around 2600 BCE, was defined by an enclosing earthwork and a deep ditch 427 m (1,401 ft) in diameter. The inner perimeter was lined with ninety-eight megaliths, of which twenty-seven are still standing. Within the great circle, an area now partly occupied by farmhouses and a crossroad, stood two smaller stone circles, each 100 m (328 ft) in diameter. One contained two concentric rings of stones, the other a single obelisk at its center. A ritual pathway led to nearby Silbury Hill, a conical stepped pyramid that at 39 m (128 ft) was the highest artificial mound in ancient Europe. These grand

Figure 1.3-7 England. Castlerigg stone circle, ca. 3000 BCE.

Figure 1.3-8 England. Reconstruction of Avebury, ca. 3000 BCE, showing (1) stone circles, (2) stone-lined ceremonial path, and (3) Silbury Hill.

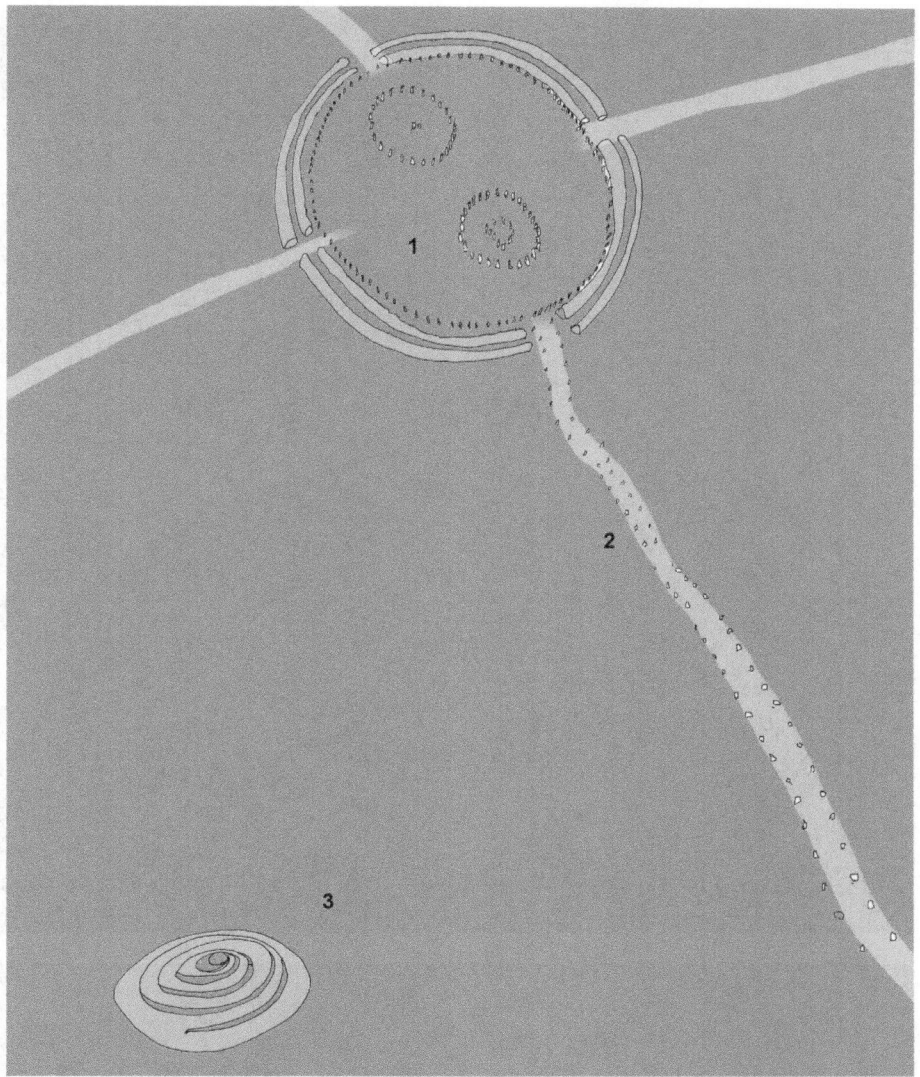

constructions, which had their origins in the desire to honor the dead, achieved a scale and order that surpassed the needs of burials and addressed transcendent cosmic themes. The Avebury circle and Silbury Hill clearly correspond to observations of the movements of the heavens. Their construction required the labor of masses of participants, and thus they can be interpreted as expressions of political will.

Stonehenge (Fig. 1.3-9a,b), set majestically on Salisbury Plain in southern England, belongs to the same heritage as these earlier stone circles but underwent at least five major phases of construction over the course of nearly two millennia. A first generation built the outer ring and ditch, probably around the time of Castlerigg in 3000 BCE, using an immense compass, probably a stretch of ox-hide rope attached to a wooden peg at the center. The builders dug the ditch through solid chalk, using tools such as picks made from antlers and shovels made from the shoulder bones of oxen. About 500 years later another team of builders added the so-called Aubrey holes, just within the earthwork, and a ring of timber poles, probably connected at the top with beams to increase their stability. The wooden circle, or *woodhenge,* resembled the scale of the inner circles of Avebury, which also date from this time. A rectangular wooden structure inside the ring probably served as a mortuary. The Heelstone, a bent marker placed outside the ditch, oriented the site to the moon. It was the only megalith erected during these early stages.

Around 2200 BCE new builders removed the timber columns at Stonehenge from the Aubrey holes, which they reused to bury the ashes of their cremated dead. The new design replaced the inner mortuary with a nearly perfect circle of rare bluestone megaliths, placed in radiating pairs with a marked entrance aligned to the Heelstone's avenue. The transport of these 4-ton chunks from the Preseli Mountains in Wales, 200 km (125 miles) to the west, remains a mystery, as an overland route would have been virtually impossible and a sea route almost as unlikely. Some have gone so far as to theorize that the stones were deposited in the Wiltshire area by a millennial glacial drift. The Heelstone was at this time incorporated into a 400 m (1,200 ft) long axis, now aimed at the rising sun during the summer solstice.

A fourth campaign came two centuries later, when the bluestones were replaced by thirty sandstone piers, known as "sarsens," taken from the quarry at Avebury. The new megaliths, over 4 m (13 ft) in height, stood several times the size of the earlier stones and weighed up to 45 tons. Unlike any of the earlier megaliths, the sarsens had been intentionally "dressed," shaped and smoothed into relatively standard tapering uprights, all with the same height. The stones were prepared as if they had been made of lumber: knobs were carved on the top of each pier to be caught in a corresponding groove scooped out of the **lintels**, like a carpenter's mortise-and-tenon joint. The horizontal members involved the most sophisticated execution of masonry, shaped according to the curve of the circle. They connected each pier to the next as a continuous ring. How Stonehenge's builders lifted these enormous crossbeams into place can only be conjectured. Perhaps they were handled like logs with ropes and levers or else dragged up temporary earthen mounds and slid into place. The interlocking pieces formed a single, compelling work of architecture.

Figure 1.3-9 England. Stonehenge, ca. 3000–1500 BCE. (a) Aerial view. (b) The Sarsens.

Five pairs of slightly taller trilithons, erected before the ring was completed, were set within the sarsen circle in a *U*-shaped configuration. The axis of the Heelstone focused on its entry. In a fifth campaign, sometime around 1600 BCE, a millennium after the first megaliths had been delivered, the bluestones were reintroduced into the design. The new builders set a ring of these smaller stones inside the trilithons and a circle of them outside the sarsens, considerably complicating the composition. They placed an altar in the center, leaving no doubt that Stonehenge now served as a temple. During these later phases, the original settlers of the area had been conquered by the so-called Beaker people, which may explain the radical changes in ceremonial usage. The cosmic understanding of Stonehenge, however, endured beyond its change in owners, even as the new authority desired to express its power through the process of rebuilding the monument.

The meaning of Stonehenge resided in the ritual life that humanized this calendar of stone and earth set in the open countryside. Its strong religious purpose explained the prodigies of engineering and labor that went into its making. The builders did not choose the bluestones or the gray sarsens for their practicality. To transport the great megaliths from such long distances would have become a form of sacrifice. The special materials and the colossal size of the project gave the majestic stone circle singular authority in the celebration of celestial events. Public architecture at its best aspires to be a setting for collective rituals that endow each participant with the pride of belonging to a reality that extends beyond the present. The construction of sacred space allows one to imagine daily life in relation to the greater cosmos.

Further Reading

Burl, Aubrey. *Prehistoric Stone Circles.* Aylesbury, UK: Shire, 2001.

Francis, Evelyn. *Avebury.* London: Wooden Books, 2001.

Hawkins, G. S. *Stonehenge Decoded.* Garden City, NY: Doubleday, 1965.

Joussaume, Roger. *Dolmens for the Dead: Megalith-Building throughout the World.* Ithaca, NY: Cornell University Press, 1988.

North, John. *Stonehenge: Ritual Origins and Astronomy.* New York: HarperCollins, 1997.

O'Kelly, Michael J. *Newgrange: Archaeology, Art and Legend.* London: Thames & Hudson, 1982.

Trump, David. *Malta: Prehistory and Temples.* Valetta, Malta: Midsea Books, 2002.

Visit the free website **www.oup.com/us/ingersoll** to view chapter outlines and study questions; Google Maps showing the location of key sites; links to UNESCO World Heritage Sites; and essays on topics that cross time and culture.

3000–1500 BCE

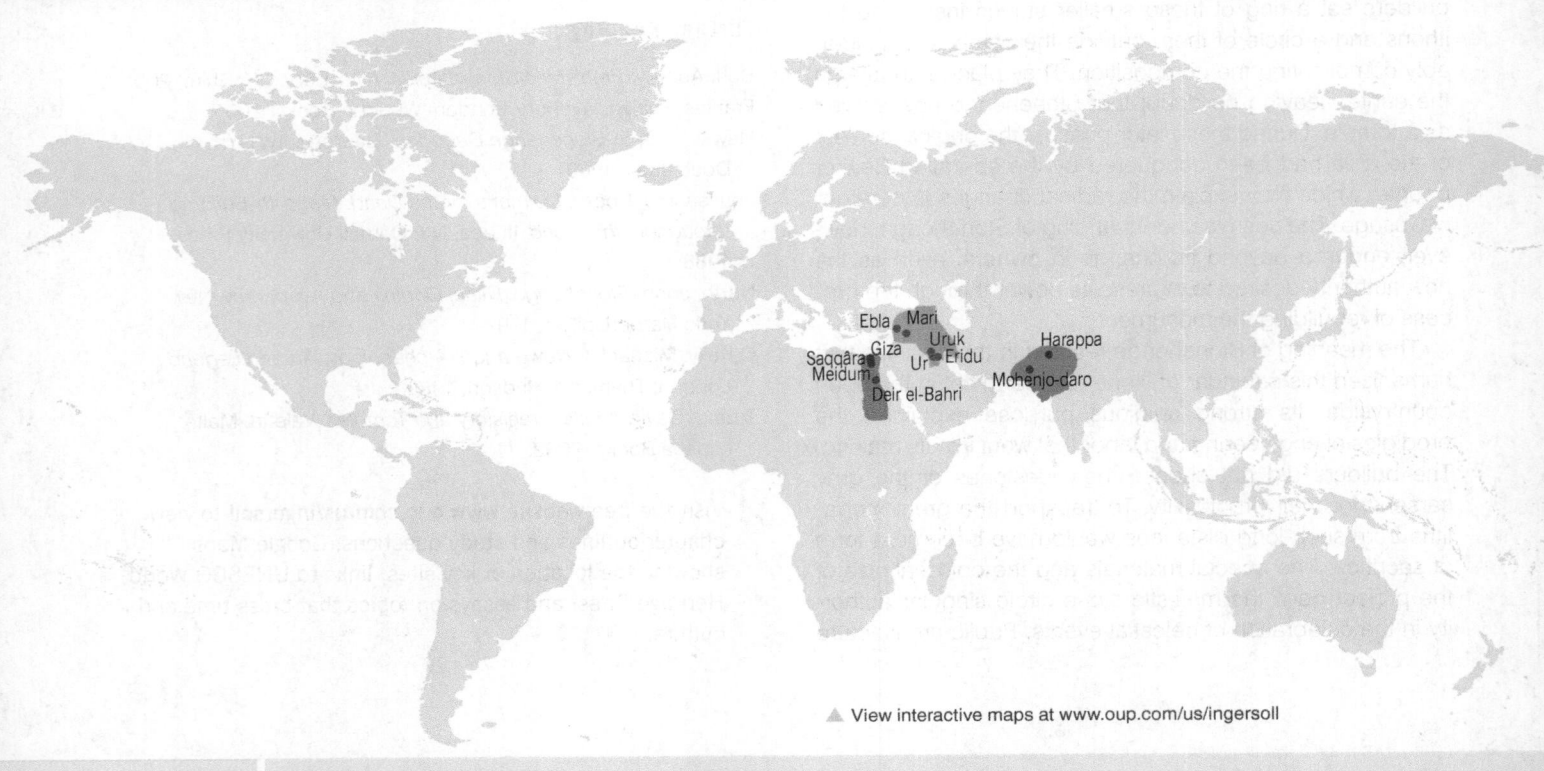

▲ View interactive maps at www.oup.com/us/ingersoll

The first truly urban cultures gathered around the great river systems in the sub-tropical regions stretching from Egypt to Southwest Asia to India. The specific conditions of each area led to the development of different political and religious orders. In Mesopotamia councils of elders and priests governed the city-states that grew up along the Tigris and Euphrates. They constructed massive mud-brick towers over their collective grain deposits. These stepped ziggurats represented the union of heavenly and human agency in the struggle to defend the area's precarious agricultural output. In Egypt the regular overflowing of the Nile yielded a much more stable agricultural supply, encouraging the formation of a strict hierarchy under a centralized monarchy. The grand stone monuments of the pyramids symbolized the continuity of daily life into the afterlife within the eternal cycle of the river's fertility. The Harappan culture in the Indus valley had greater difficulty controlling the floods of that region. Instead of grand tombs and religious structures, the inhabitants built massive walls around their cities to protect them from floods and created brick-lined sewers to control the course of effluents. They seemed to favor pragmatic over symbolic solutions to questions of survival.

2.1 CITIES OF MESOPOTAMIA
Mud, Gods, and Urbanism

In Southwest Asia architectural traditions developed in tandem with written language, responding to the religious and political needs of people sharing common goals. As communities in the first large cities amassed surpluses and developed specialized knowledge, they created texts and monuments to supplement human memory. Their architects designed monumental structures for storing surpluses, while their scribes composed indexes of wealth and codes of behavior. A religious hierarchy oversaw this cultural transition to the awareness of historical time. Design professionals helped to orchestrate a new type of urban order, distinct from the world of nature. As cities grew, they demanded the expertise of architects, even in the production of standard dwellings, to resolve matters regulated in written codes, such as street alignments, drainage, and roofing.

The Bronze-Age city-states of Mesopotamia, scattered in the delta region between the Tigris and Euphrates Rivers, began to take permanent form during the fifth millennium BCE, sprouting the first urban monuments. Their fabric of streets, canals, and dwellings comprised an immense collective work resembling cells seen through a microscope. These inhabitants considered their city a sacred place and gave it the name of a god as its founder, hoping to procure the protection of that deity. By piling up mud bricks into soaring stepped towers, or ziggurats, they created stairways to heaven as symbolic places of access to their gods. The ziggurat loomed as a tangible **axis mundi**, a sacred center of the world, where the privileged class of high priests and governors performed rituals to secure the city's destiny. Long after the decline of these first cities, successive cultures in the region continued to worship the gods of their temples, honoring them as the origin of both architectural and written knowledge.

The Urban Temple: Creating the Axis Mundi

The alluvial plains of the Tigris and Euphrates Rivers were known in antiquity by the Greek word *Mesopotamia*, "the land between two rivers" (Fig. 2.1-1). During the fifth through third millennia BCE this muddy expanse, which extends from the Persian Gulf in the southeast through modern Iraq to the foothills of Armenia in the northwest, spawned a great system of cities. By 3000 BCE over 80% of the inhabitants of the region qualified as urban dwellers, a proportion similar to that found among the industrialized societies of today. The climate ranged from fiercely hot summers to bitterly cold winters, and these early settlers lived with the constant threat of either flooding or droughts, which did not bode well for urban success.

The immense collective effort to harness the unwieldy rivers into canals and lay out irrigation systems for the agricultural fields helped to consolidate the Mesopotamian cities. Led by an urban elite that created a division of labor for complex tasks, managers and priests invented the first written language for keeping inventories of surplus

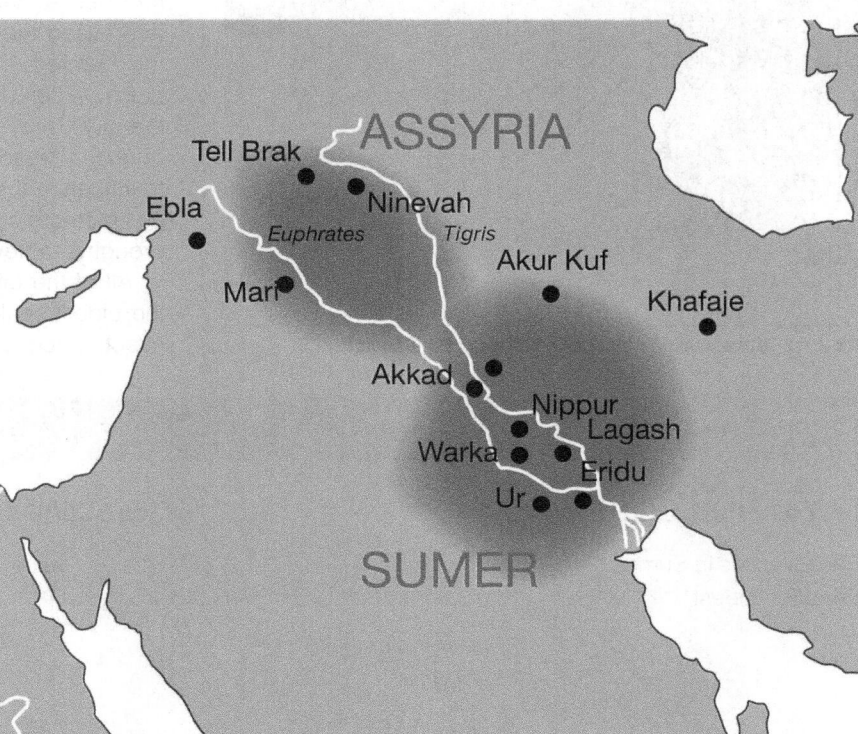

Figure 2.1-1 Mesopotamia, the land between the Tigris and Euphrates Rivers, showing the lower city-states in Sumer, 5000–1500 BCE.

agricultural products and tracking their distribution. Clay proved to be the most available medium of expression for both architecture and writing: in the cities of the plain, people built with mud bricks and wrote on mud tablets. As the ruling class perfected cuneiform characters (Fig. 2.1-2), the city itself became a type of language—a reproducible

Figure 2.1-2 Mesopotamia. Cuneiform cone, third millennium BCE.

architectural system that communicated religious hierarchy in its temples, military duty in its walls, water management in its canals, and the circulation of goods and people in its streets.

The earliest urban settlements in Mesopotamia date from 5000 BCE in Sumer, the southern delta area. Agricultural towns on the slower-moving Euphrates, such as Eridu, Uruk, Nippur, Lagash, Ur, and Kish, grew into sizable city-states with 10,000–20,000 inhabitants. Each city built a set of double walls and at least one towering temple as the center of its surrounding agricultural estates. The coordination of work teams to produce and maintain the **dikes** and canals for irrigation created the initial surpluses of these cities, leading to the stratification of their social systems. The elite class—which included an assembly of landowners, high priests, and usually an *ensi* (governor) or, in some cases, a *lugal* (king)—commanded the irrigation systems in the surrounding territory and controlled the wealth.

The Sumerian elites created architecturally distinct parts of the city for the storage of agricultural surplus and the orchestration of rituals meant to guarantee the land's continued fertility. Their architects designed sacred enclosures, what the Greeks later called **temenos**, using orthogonally aligned storehouses to frame elevated temples. The **ziggurat**, a temple that rose on one or more platforms to create a stepped profile, became the chief monumental expression of Sumerian cities, towering above the city's one-story fabric. Religious historians call such a vertical focus the axis mundi, a sacred marker indicating a local culture's center of the world. *Ziggurat* literally meant "house of the mountain, mountain of the storm, bond between heaven and earth," and its great height and palpable mass alluded to the origin of the hill peoples who had descended to the plains. Such a symbolic structure addressed the two prime themes of prehistoric religions, the comfort of the earth and heavenward aspirations. Earth deities dwelled inside the mountain, while those of the sky used its summit as their resting place. The ziggurats in Mesopotamia embodied the collective mandate to influence the sky gods in a region afflicted by precarious meteorological conditions, ranging from century-long droughts to devastating floods.

All of the city-states of Sumer acknowledged Eridu as the oldest settlement in the region, deserving of their respect. Once a seaport on the Persian Gulf, the site now

▼ **ca. 5000 BCE**

Earliest cities in Sumer; Eridu the oldest

White Temple at Uruk, first ziggurat

▲ **ca. 3400 BCE**

▼ **ca. 2600 BCE**

Gilgamesh epic written

Sargon the Great consolidates Syria, Armenia, and Sumer into the Akkadian Empire

▲ **ca. 2334–2279 BCE**

CULTURE, SOCIETY, GENDER

The Millennial Tell

Because of the perishable nature of mud buildings, the patterns of the earliest urban architecture underwent constant revision rather than assuming permanent form. Cities became part of an organic process that involved the habitual reproduction of types. Rather than clearing away the earlier buildings, new buildings rose on top of old ones, making use of the previous levels as foundations. The plans of the previous buildings persisted as the preconceived idea, or type, for the replacements; and the new buildings pushed up like fresh shoots from the older roots in the soil. After centuries of building in adobe on the same site, Mesopotamian cities generated prominent mounds, known in Arabic as *tells*. A site such as Tell Erbil (Arbil), on a northern branch of the Tigris near Mosul, Iraq, has been continuously occupied since at least 5000 BCE, resulting in a formidable plateau rising 40 m (131 ft) above the plain. Generation upon generation contributed to the stratification of this human-made topography.

Kurdistan, aerial view of Tell Erbil, also called Arbil (Iraq). The mound of the city arose as a result of successive generations building on top of one another since the fifth millennium BCE.

lies about 200 km (125 miles) inland due to silting. Over the course of three millennia Eridu's temple to Enki, god of deep water and wisdom, underwent eighteen rebuildings, each one raising the building higher into the air. The structure started around 5000 BCE as a tiny, thin-walled cubicle with sides only 3 m (10 ft) wide and two circular tables for burnt sacrifices (Fig. 2.1-3). Temple VII, a replacement structure built around 3800 BCE, used the area of the initial sanctuary as the foundation for one of four corner towers. The builders of the new version constructed thick walls studded with regularly spaced external **buttresses**, anticipating the pleated wall motif found on all later temples of the region. Inside, they placed **spur walls** to prop up the ceiling

beams and rafters over a narrow hall. The custom of rebuilding houses one on top of the other, seen in ancient Jericho (see Section 1.1), continued throughout Mesopotamia and extended quite naturally to the temples, leading to the succession of stages of the ziggurat. By the end of the third millennium BCE the Enki Temple had incorporated many previous versions into a colossal stepped mound that took the form of a proper ziggurat, covering a base ten times as large as that of Temple VII.

Shrines such as the Enki Temple at Eridu represented the theocratic political order of the early Sumerian cities, which were ruled by high priests. The fields and the produce of the city-state belonged to the temple of the city's

▼ **ca. 2300 BCE**

Palaces at Ebla and Mari, Syria, destroyed by Sargon the Great

Three-century period of drought weakens Sumerians, Egyptians, and Harappans

▲ **2200–1900 BCE**

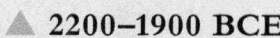

▼ **ca. 2140 BCE**

King Gudea rules parts of Sumer from Lagash

Khafaje, the Ritual Order of Mesopotamian Temples

The Oval Temple at Khafaje, begun around 2650 BCE, demonstrates the development of formal order in the creation of urban temples. Rather than adjusting to its surroundings, the new structure required the demolition of many nearby houses to accommodate the oval figure of its outer walls. The compound was entered through a formal gate flanked by thick guard towers. This threshold marked the transition from the profane world of the city streets into the *temenos*, the sacred world of the temple precinct. The entry court served as a public zone of offices for the temple administrators. A second portal on an axis with the first gate penetrated an inner, higher set of oval walls. The path ramped up a level to an inner court, a perfect rectangle set inside the rounded figure of the walls. In the center of the court, a well and circular basins for ablutions awaited the celebrants. Workshops, bakeries, and storage rooms fit into the court's perimeter. The upper sanctuary stood on a platform at the rear of the court, reached by a protruding stairway placed off axis at the southwest corner.

Mesopotamian temples contained two standard interior components: an altar table for sacrificial offerings; and a niche of epiphany, a place for the god to make an appearance. The niche usually framed a statue of the deity. Priests would have brought a sacrifice of food to the temple, rubbed it on the statue's mouth, and then distributed the rest to be eaten by the celebrants.

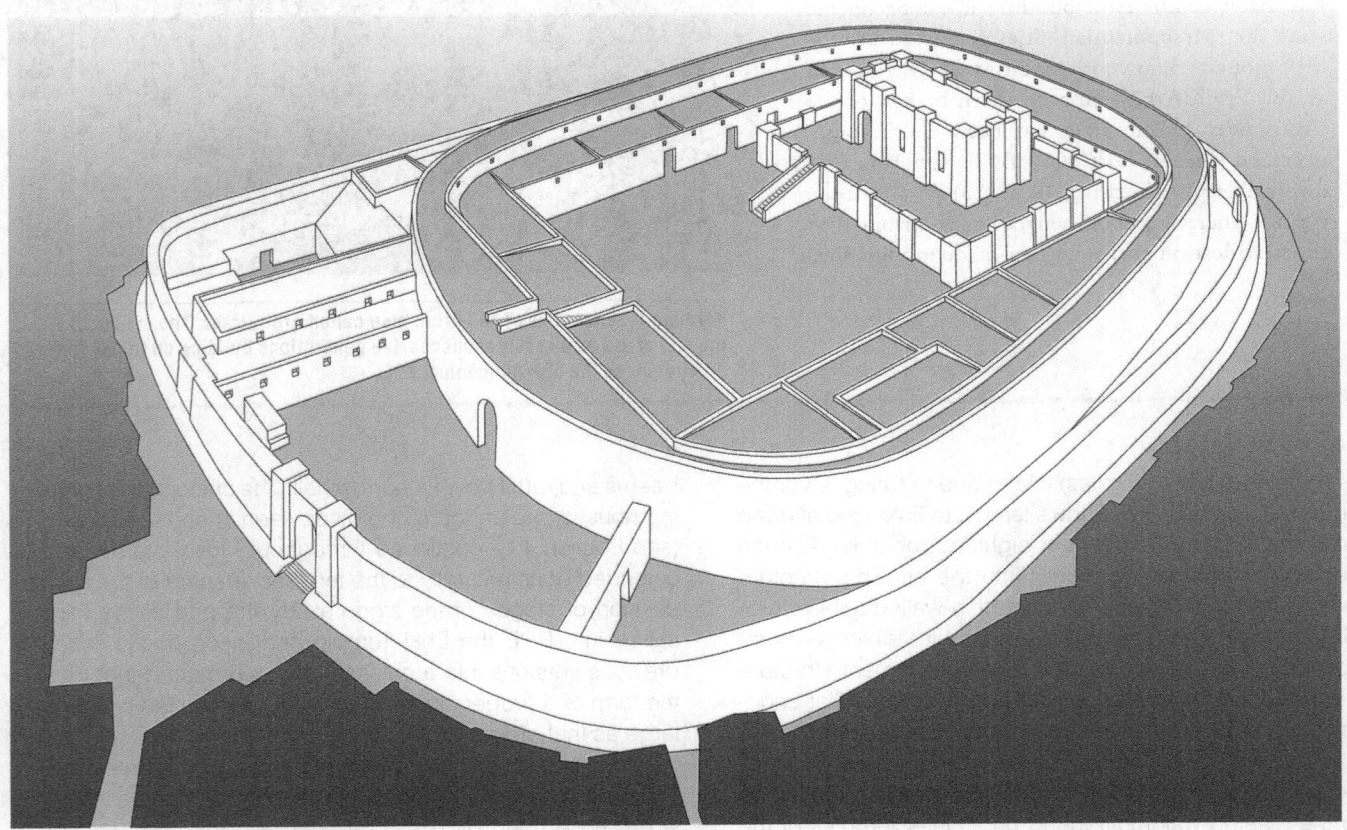

Khafaje, Mesopotamia (Iraq). Reconstruction of the Oval Temple, ca. 2650 BCE.

▼ **ca. 2040–2000 BCE**

Ziggurat of Ur built by Ur-Nammu and his son

Ur-Nammu publishes first code of written laws in Ur

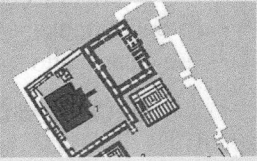

Palace at Mari destroyed by King Hammurabi and the Babylonians

▲ **ca. 2047–2030 BCE**

▲ **1759 BCE**

god. Cuneiform tablets discovered in Uruk, a close neighbor to Eridu, detail how the townspeople devoted their lives to the god Anu, the lord of the sky, while the ruling class of priests and elders exercised stewardship over the god's estates. The temple managed the canals, seeds, draught animals, and implements of tilling and stored the harvest on its grounds for distribution to the community, resulting in a system of "theocratic socialism." Craftspeople, organized into guilds, offered part of their output to the temple, as did builders who offered their labor and fishermen who shared their catch.

Uruk's White Temple (Fig. 2.1-4), dedicated to Anu, and the first true ziggurat, rose as the focus of the city's religion and government. It dates from the protoliterate period, between 3400 and 3000 BCE. Similar to the Enki Temple at Eridu, successive generations mounded this structure over earlier temples, buried underneath its platforms. The sloping base climbed 13 m (40 ft) above the skyline. Artisans embossed its battered walls with broad, regularly spaced grooves and cut a long access stair and ramp through its eastern mass. At the summit they placed a sanctuary, similar to Temple VII at Eridu, that took the form of a pure **parallelepiped**, a rectangular box, articulated with a uniform alternation of protruding buttresses and deep niches. While the priesthood entered the oblong interior hall on the broad southwestern facade, a special door on the short northwestern side was reserved for Anu to make appearances, probably in the form of a wooden statue. The interior of Sumerian temples sheltered a sacrificial **altar** for symbolically feeding the gods. Plastered and whitewashed in gypsum, the White Temple projected a gleaming stepped profile lording over the irrigated fields surrounding the city and visible from as far away as Eridu. The landmark testified to Uruk's divine patronage and oriented its residents to the axis mundi.

While the ziggurat offered a palpable symbol of Uruk and its founding deity, the city produced many other types of temples to important cults. About 100 m (300 ft) from the White Temple, the priesthoods of the moon god, Nanna, and the goddess of the morning star, Inanna, sponsored a collection of extraordinary monuments. Set within a bounded space, the designers encrusted several rectangular cult buildings with weatherproof, terra-cotta cone mosaics (Fig. 2.1-5). Thousands of baked cones, each about the size of a finger, were dipped in colored glaze and embedded into the mud walls and half-columns of the structures. The builders arranged

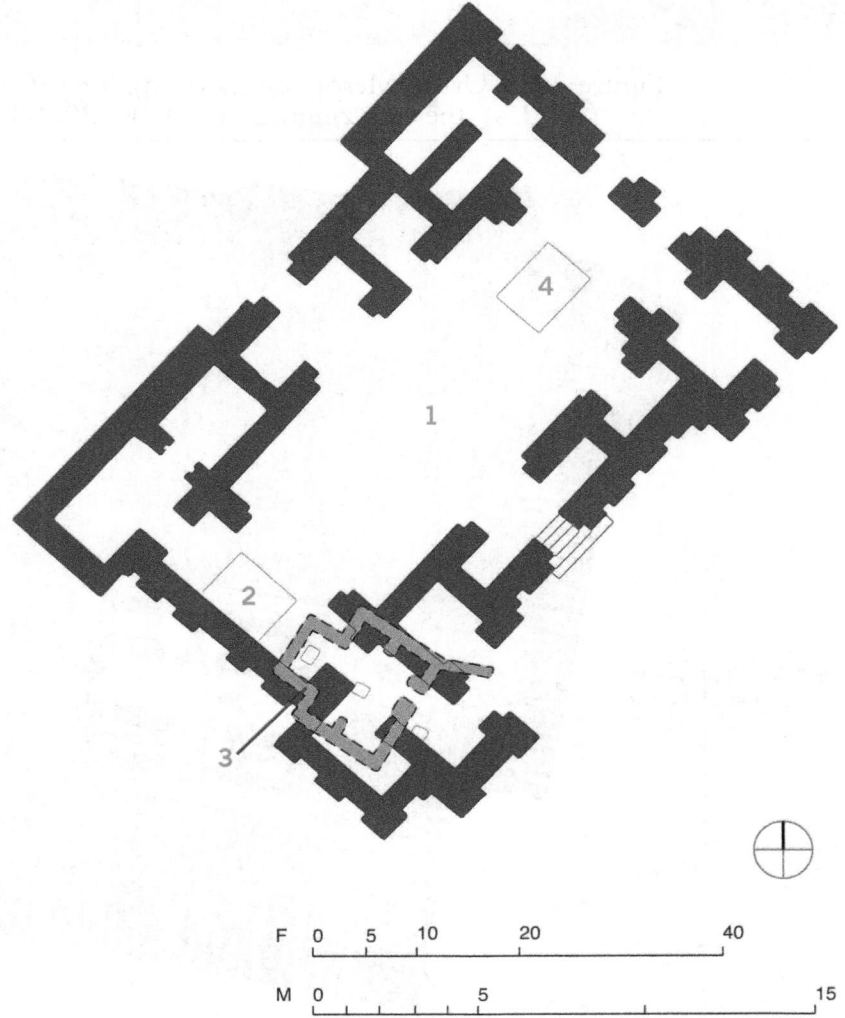

F 0   5   10   20   40

M 0   5   15

Figure 2.1-3 Eridu, Mesopotamia (Iraq). Development of the Temple of Enki from a single chamber built ca. 5000 BCE to the multichamber Temple VII of ca. 3500 BCE. Fifteen hundred years later this temple was covered over by a ziggurat. (1) Temple VII, ca. 3500 BCE (a rebuilding of the Enki Temple over nine previous versions); (2) niche for the wooden statue of the god; (3) trace of the earliest temple, built ca. 5000 BCE; (4) altar for sacrifices.

the red, white, and black dots of the **polychromatic** ceramic **cladding** into vibrant diamond and zigzag patterns like those of woven fabrics. A passage in the epic poem *Gilgamesh* (written around 2600 BCE) celebrates the temples of Uruk as marvels of baked bricks rather than mud.

The constant building and rebuilding of temples in Uruk came as a response to the fragility of existence in Sumer. Ever greater shrines served to beseech the mercy of the gods. After centuries of overworking the soil, the land underwent salinization, resulting in frequent crop failures and periodic famines. Droughts tormented the region from roughly 2200 to 1900 BCE, leaving a general feeling of anxiety in Sumerian cultures. The extravagant temple-building mission of Gudea, a high priest with kingly status

Figure 2.1-4 Uruk, Mesopotamia (Iraq). The White Temple of Anu,
the first ziggurat, ca. 3400–3000 BCE.

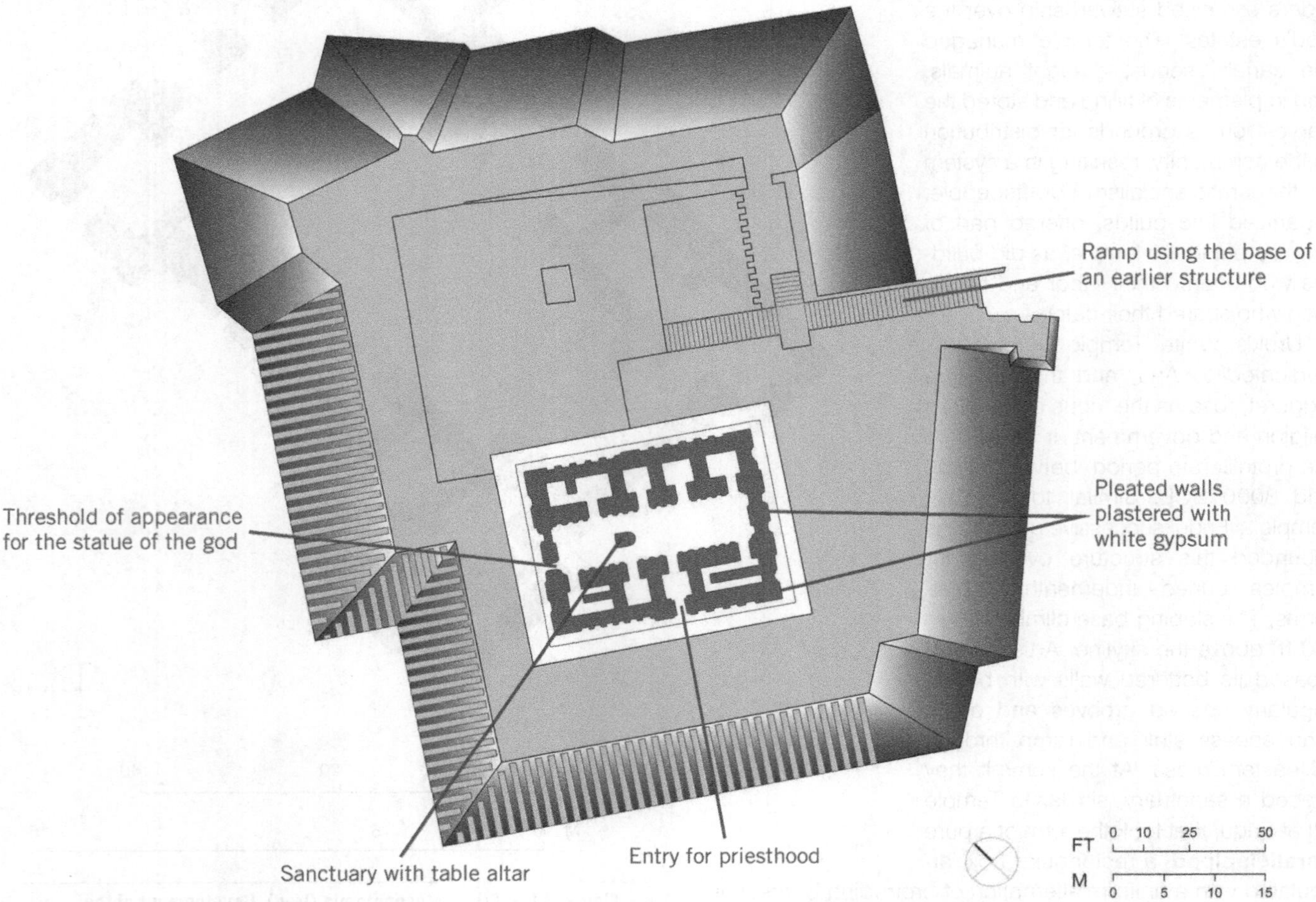

Ramp using the base of
an earlier structure

Pleated walls
plastered with
white gypsum

Threshold of appearance
for the statue of the god

Sanctuary with table altar

Entry for priesthood

FT   0 10 25   50

M   0   5   10   15

**Figure 2.1-5 Uruk, Mesopotamia
(Iraq). Cone mosaics covering
urban temples with more permanent
cladding, ca. 3400–3000 BCE.**

who commanded the city of Lagash east of Uruk, illustrates this desperate struggle for survival. Gudea reigned ca. 2140 BCE and left behind detailed written accounts of his rebuilding of the city's temples in which he invokes the environmental crisis of the Tigris River no longer rising to water the fields. He also claims that the city god Ningirsu has appeared to him in his dreams while sleeping in the old temple and promised, "When thou shalt set thy right hand to my temple, I will set my foot upon the mountain where the storm dwells . . . abundant rain shall pour for thee, it will give the heart's life to the land."

While undertaking the rebuilding of Ningirsu's temple, Gudea commissioned twenty stone statues of himself, intended as permanent witnesses to the glory of his god. In one version, Gudea is seated with his hands clasped in prayer above a drawing board with the plan of a temple on his lap (Fig. 2.1-6). The sculpture indicates that Sumerians invented not only written language but also architectural graphic conventions. In this rendering, parallel lines indicate the rippling outlines of an oblong temple's pleated walls, while five gaps represent the doorways. The proportions of Gudea's temple, his account reports, came to him in a dream, and he urged his people to gather materials for its construction. He and his family led rituals to purify the city and, on the site of the future temple, had the soil cut down to the bedrock for the foundations. After placing sacrifices there, his workers filled in the foundation trenches with purified sand before the piling of levels. Unlike the slave labor used by later imperial powers, Gudea's workers belonged to a theocratic regime that sought to redeem the city. They built the temples, but "the lash struck not, and none was oppressed with blows." Although early Sumerians worked hard for their gods, their piety was not always rewarded. By the end of the second millennium BCE the land could no longer support such large cities, and the population of the plains dwindled through starvation and warfare, leading to deportation of its inhabitants as slaves to neighboring kingdoms.

Kingship: The Emergence of the Palace

The Sumerian city-states periodically lost their autonomy to either local kings or foreign conquerors. The title "king of Kish" appeared around 2500 BCE, signifying that the *lugal*, or ruler, of one of the Sumerian cities claimed the right to command other cities in the region. Individual military leaders absorbed the governing authority of the earlier priesthoods. While the great cult sites in the original cities continued to be rebuilt into ever-higher piles, the region underwent a series of conquests. The power to rule in Sumer changed hands as frequently as the course of the twin rivers. The new status of kingship fostered the development of the palace complex as a new urban building type.

The most important political shift in Mesopotamia came around 2300 BCE, when a Semitic-speaking courtier, the charismatic Sargon the Great (r. ca. 2334–2279 BCE), seized power from the reigning king of Kish and proceeded to take control of as many as sixty-five cities. Sargon, whose name meant "legitimate king," ruled for half a century and

amassed the region's first empire, uniting the areas of Syria and Armenia with the old city-states of the Sumerian delta. He shifted the political organization to rule by hereditary dynasty, with imperial jurisdiction over a collection of cities. Sargon founded a new capital city at Akkad, on a site somewhere near modern Baghdad but not yet identified by archaeologists. By starting a new city instead of building on top of an existing one, he circumvented local power struggles inherent in existing cities with longstanding religious cults and political clans. Sargon's successors in the Akkadian dynasty took the grandiloquent title of "kings of the four quarters of the earth" and required the same forms of address allotted to the gods, establishing a tradition of deified rulers.

This transition from a system of loosely connected city-states to post-Sumerian empire building—with a more structured rule by a dynasty such as the Akkadians—led to the development of an enclave for the royal palace. Literary documents report that Sargon built a palace at Akkad capable of "feeding 5,400 courtiers." The design of such a compound no doubt relied on the precedents of bounded

Figure 2.1-6 Lagash, Mesopotamia (Iraq). Sculpture of King Gudea of Lagash with a plan of a temple in his lap, twenty-third century BCE.

Figure 2.1-7 Ebla, Syria. The _tell_ of the ancient city destroyed during the twenty-third century BCE by Sargon the Great.

cuneiform tablets of its archive into the more durable form of terra-cotta. Ebla's royal palace had orthogonally arranged interconnected rooms gathered around courtyards averaging 20 m (65 ft) in width. The devastated palace served as an excellent model for the conquering Akkadian culture.

At Mari, another ancient city in northern Syria that rivaled Ebla as the hinge for trade between the Mediterranean and Mesopotamia, the great palace was destroyed during the time of Sargon, rebuilt two centuries later, and destroyed definitively in 1759 BCE by King Hammurabi of Babylon. As in Ebla, the torching of the palace converted the mud-brick walls and the archive of cuneiform tablets into terra-cotta, inadvertently preserving the most complete set of documents of the period, including the "List of Kings." The palace at Mari served as both a royal residence and a religious center, consistent with the theophanic, or god-like, status of rulers during this period. It covered a site roughly 150 m (492 ft) per side and was divided into two halves, each structured around a great court (Fig. 2.1-8). The eastern side served the more public functions, the western the more domestic. While the architects plotted the layout of more than 260 rooms with orthogonal grids, they avoided placing the apertures and passageways in symmetry. They in fact went to great trouble to make the approach through the fortified entry gate at the northeast corner a twisting series of three antechambers to slow down entrants and allow the guards to better control their access.

religious enclosures. Sargon's palace at Akkad probably resembled those built in rival city-states, such as Ebla, near modern Aleppo, Syria, which then dominated the trade routes between the Mediterranean and Mesopotamia. At its core the ground of Ebla's compound rose 26 m (83 ft) above the rest of the city as a result of the work of many generations of builders. This human-made acropolis, or _tell_ (Fig. 2.1-7), served as the site for both the royal palace and the primary temple to the city goddess, Ishtar. As often happens with ancient monuments, the best preserved are the ones that were intentionally destroyed: Sargon's armies sacked Ebla and burned down the palace around 2300 BCE. The heat of the fires accidentally converted the clay of the walls and the

The eastern half of the palace served as the site for public encounters and ceremonies at the palace temple. The great court, measuring 50 × 30 m (164 × 98 ft), would have accommodated hundreds of functionaries and petitioners. A hall at the southern edge of the court may have served as the primary audience chamber. It was approached by a special set of semicircular steps, and its walls carried fresco paintings in deep red hues. The palace temple, the oldest part of the site, occupied the remote southeast corner, reached through a succession of four chambers. This secondary position indicated a less important role for the priesthood. The inclusion of temple-like spaces in the domestic areas of the palace suggests that the ruler carried out priestly functions and commanded quasi-divine status.

The second courtyard, in the western half of the Mari palace, served the ruler and his retinue. While parallel to the first court, there was no direct access between the two. The bureaucrats used a hollow chamber between the two courts as the palace archives, leaving behind a cache of 20,000 cuneiform tablets. Remarkable fresco paintings, representing scenes of sacrifice and the investiture of King Zimrilim by the goddess Ishtar, covered the southern walls of the second court. The paintings set up one's approach to the throne room, a space as large as the hall of a temple. A pair of massive, 2 m (6.5 ft) thick pillars placed on the central axis carried the loads of the ceiling. At the west end of the hall a raised platform served as the throne, while at the east end a special niche contained statues of two goddesses holding vases from which water flowed into a drain, representing the perennial concern for adequate water supply. The private living quarters of the royal family and a sizable harem were gathered around four smaller courts in the northwestern and western sections of the palace. The walls here were painted to imitate marble encrustation, and some areas were paved with alabaster slabs. The western flank housed a service wing with kitchens and baths, one of them with two terra-cotta tubs and a hole in the floor for a toilet. The labyrinthine plan of the palace at Mari allowed the paths of servants and troops to be segregated from that of the king. It ensured that the king's intimate life with his queen and forty concubines in the western half would remain independent from his duties and public display in the eastern half. This prototypical royal harem also guaranteed that the women would give birth only to the king's children.

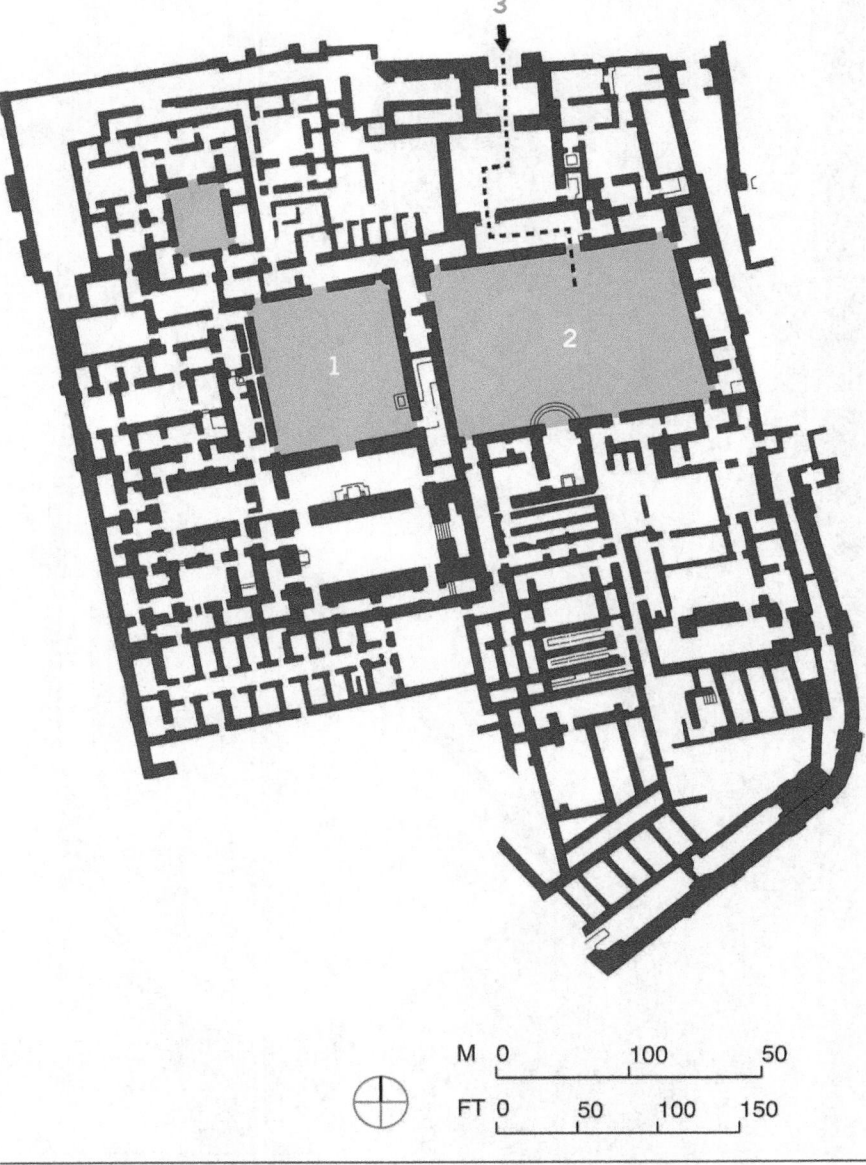

Figure 2.1-8 Mari, Syria. Reconstructed plan of the Palace of Zimrilim, ca. 2250 BCE, showing the private (1) and public (2) courts. The arrow path (3) traces the route through the three antechambers leading to the public court.

Ur: The City and the Ziggurat

The city of Ur emerged as the largest in Bronze-Age Mesopotamia following the demise of Sargon's Akkad. Like nearby Eridu, it began as a port city in Sumer, where the Euphrates meets the Persian Gulf, but now lies inland. The extensive archaeological excavations of Ur's temples, palaces, mausoleums, harbors, canals, streets, fortifications, shops, and common dwellings offer a unique vision of the urban fabric of this period. The city reached its maximum development during the period of the Third Dynasty, when King Ur-Nammu (r. 2047–2030 BCE) assumed the imperial ambitions of the Akkadians. Ur-Nammu improved the city's infrastructure of walls, canals, and public

spaces. He also published the first code of laws, revised three centuries later in Babylon as the celebrated Code of Hammurabi. Ur-Nammu's code protected the rights of the weak and restored "equity in the land." The code punished the crimes of murder and theft with death, established the proper treatment of slaves, sanctioned against sexual misconduct, levied heavy fines for violent crimes, and protected orphans and widows. Apart from his remarkable attention to the urban fabric and human rights, Ur-Nammu became famous for centuries to come as the patron of the Great Ziggurat of Ur, a monument completed by his son, Shulgi (r. 2029–1982 BCE).

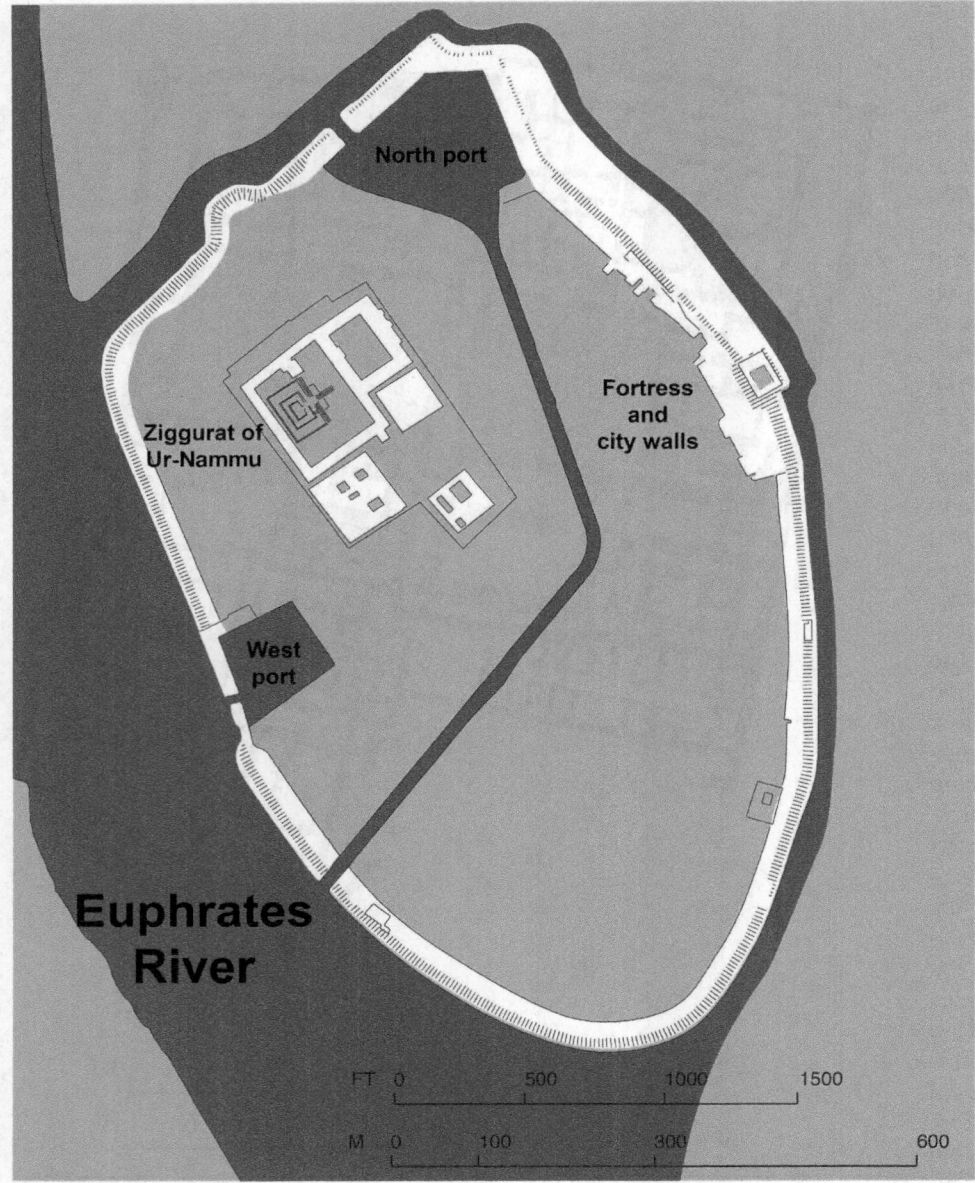

the wheel, it is hard to imagine much wheeled traffic in this congested maze.

The houses at Ur formed tightly packed blocks, built with party (shared) walls. Since the residents habitually dumped their refuse into the public space outside the front door, the level of the streets continually rose. Like the houses of ancient Jericho, the thresholds of Ur houses had to be constantly adjusted upward to keep pace with the rising street level. Inner steps descended to the house's original floor level. When in time the rising streets threatened to bury the ground story, the owners pulled the house down and laid a new floor on top of the old ceiling beams to match the current level of the street. This architectural metabolism constantly transformed the makeup of Ur's cityscape. Nothing about its streets or houses remained fixed or finished at any time, but like a living organism, the city continued the process of rebuilding itself.

A canal surrounded Ur-Nammu's city, and another bisected it. The oval shape of Ur's walls embraced a dense, twisted network of narrow, unpaved streets, relieved only by the port on the western edge, the harbor and a large palace in the north, and the great *temenos* for the ziggurat in the center (Fig. 2.1-9). The temple's orderly rectangular precinct of about 300 × 400 m (984 × 1,312 ft) covered an area as large as a city in itself. The street widths in Ur were never greater than 3 m (10 ft). An occasional open space, such as the so-called Baker's Square, resulted from the demolition of a few buildings according to a planned revision of the city fabric. Coordinated planning led to the rounding of corners at the street intersections. Perhaps initially the adobe edges were worn away by the frequent passage of pack donkeys, but in later times they were built expressly with nubbed bricks to accommodate the turning radius of carts. Although the Sumerians probably invented

Ur houses were mostly single-story structures of mud brick, with several rooms wrapped around an open court (Fig. 2.1-10). They usually contained no exterior **windows**, due to the repugnant nature of the street. The only connection to the outside, the constantly revised front door, opened to a small **vestibule** from which one moved cross-axially to enter the area of the courtyard.

A wealthier house in Ur, such as the two-story House III on Gay Street, would have been whitewashed inside and out. That house's footprint of 150 m² (1,623 ft²) proves larger than a typical middle-class apartment of today but would have housed three times as many occupants. The servants, or domestic slaves, used the ground floor for their chores, while the family lived upstairs. A typical plan included a wide and shallow reception room on the far side of the court for visitors and a main lavatory on the side facing the guest room, next to a staircase to the upper floor. In one corner was the kitchen. The courtyard generally had a strong formal order, usually a perfect square 4–5 m (13–16 ft) per side, defined by four wooden posts at the corners that held up a continuous wooden balcony for the upper rooms. The ***impluvium*** roof would have sloped gently inward, projecting beyond the balcony and carrying downspouts to the paved court below, where in some cases there was a drain.

The Mesopotamian courtyard house provided the primary cell of the city. This type of dwelling, which is still being built in the region, generated the courtyard houses in later cultures, such as the Greek *oikos* (see Section 4.2), the Roman *domus* (see Section 5.1), and the Moroccan *riad* (see Section 8.2).

Ur-Nammu strictly planned the temple district (Fig. 2.1-11) as a solemn void with orthogonal coordinates. The enclosing *temenos* established an obvious contrast between order and disorder—a perceptible distinction between the sacred and the profane. Thick double walls studded with buttresses surrounded the entire compound, and tall guard towers flanked the major gateway on the northeast leading to an oblong court as large as the base of the ziggurat. Here, the administrators of the cult of Nanna kept their offices. An oblique path led to a second court, twice as large as the first, which framed the ziggurat. While the platforms of the tower and its three-way stair rose in strict symmetry, the path to reach it remained intentionally non-axial. Other temples and sites for specialized functions, including a kitchen for preparing the sacrifices to Nanna, occupied the perimeter of the *temenos* of Ur-Nammu's ziggurat.

South of the tower, beyond its courtyard, stood the perfectly square palace of E-Gi-Par, with sides 100 m (328 ft) wide. It served the high priestesses, whose role in the cult of the moon god was considered essential to the survival of the community. One among them was selected each year to consummate a physical union with the god, a part probably acted by the king or a high priest, at the top of the ziggurat. The ritual copulation was believed to ensure the fertility of the land. Far more women than men were buried in the royal cemetery at the southeast corner of the precinct's walls, attesting to the important role of the high priestesses. Next to their palace the king used a similarly scaled square palace, the E-Hur-Sag, during religious occasions.

Ur-Nammu conceived his ziggurat as a calculated addition to a site that had been sacred for over a millennium. His heroic commitment to rebuilding the temple was partly

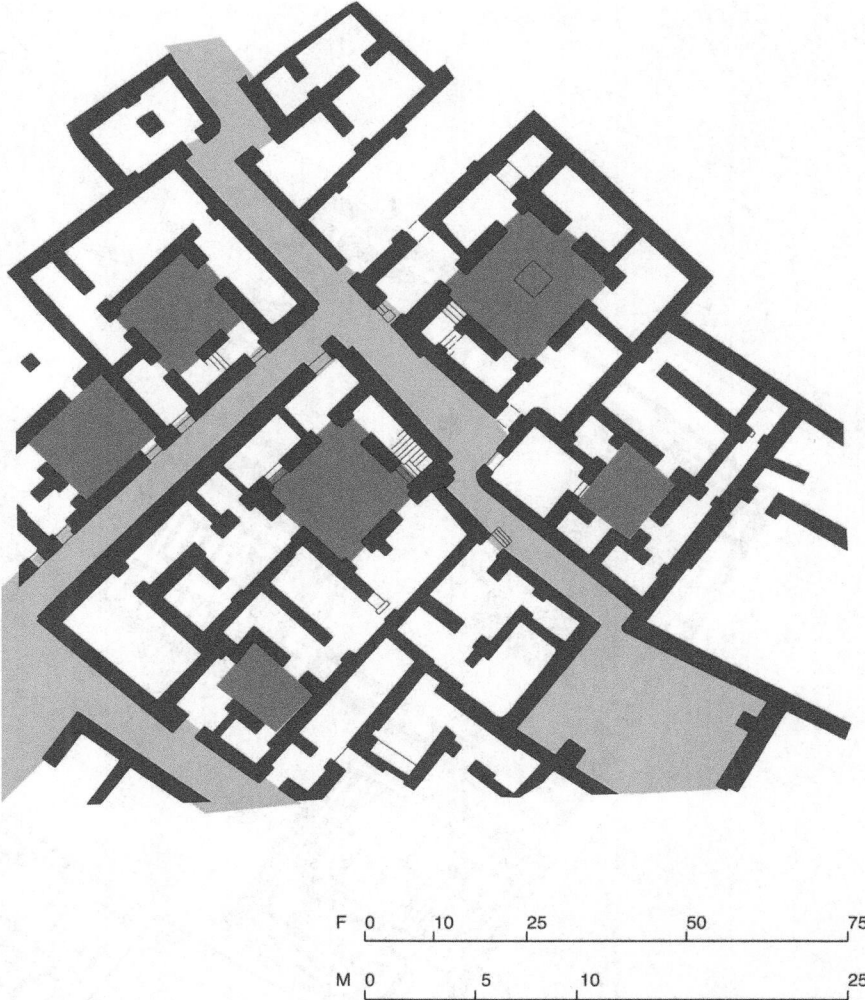

F 0   10   25   50   75

M 0   5   10   25

Figure 2.1-10 Ur, Mesopotamia (Iraq). Detail of neighborhood with courtyard houses, ca. 2000 BCE. Gray areas indicate streets; darker gray boxes show courtyards.

customary, as Sumerian rulers were expected to restore temples in the interests of the theocratic well-being of the city. It was also a strategy for advancing imperial claims over the surrounding city-states from which he exacted tribute. Records of the project give the impression that the king personally designed the staged tower and participated in its construction. A stele relief arranged in five narrative bands shows Ur-Nammu building the ziggurat (Fig. 2.1-12): on a lower level he carries the builder's tools and **mortar** basket for the approval of the god, and above this he pours libations for the god, who is holding a measuring rod. At the top, under the crescent moon, the king stands alone in reverence before the seated god.

The design of the ziggurat at Ur followed a preconceived geometric idea, and it was among the first to be built with materials meant to last. Unlike the majority of Mesopotamian temples, which have melted away as a result of their perishable adobe construction, much of the outer shell has remarkably survived, as it was encased in a 2.5 m (8 ft) skin of baked bricks, each stamped with the cuneiform slogan

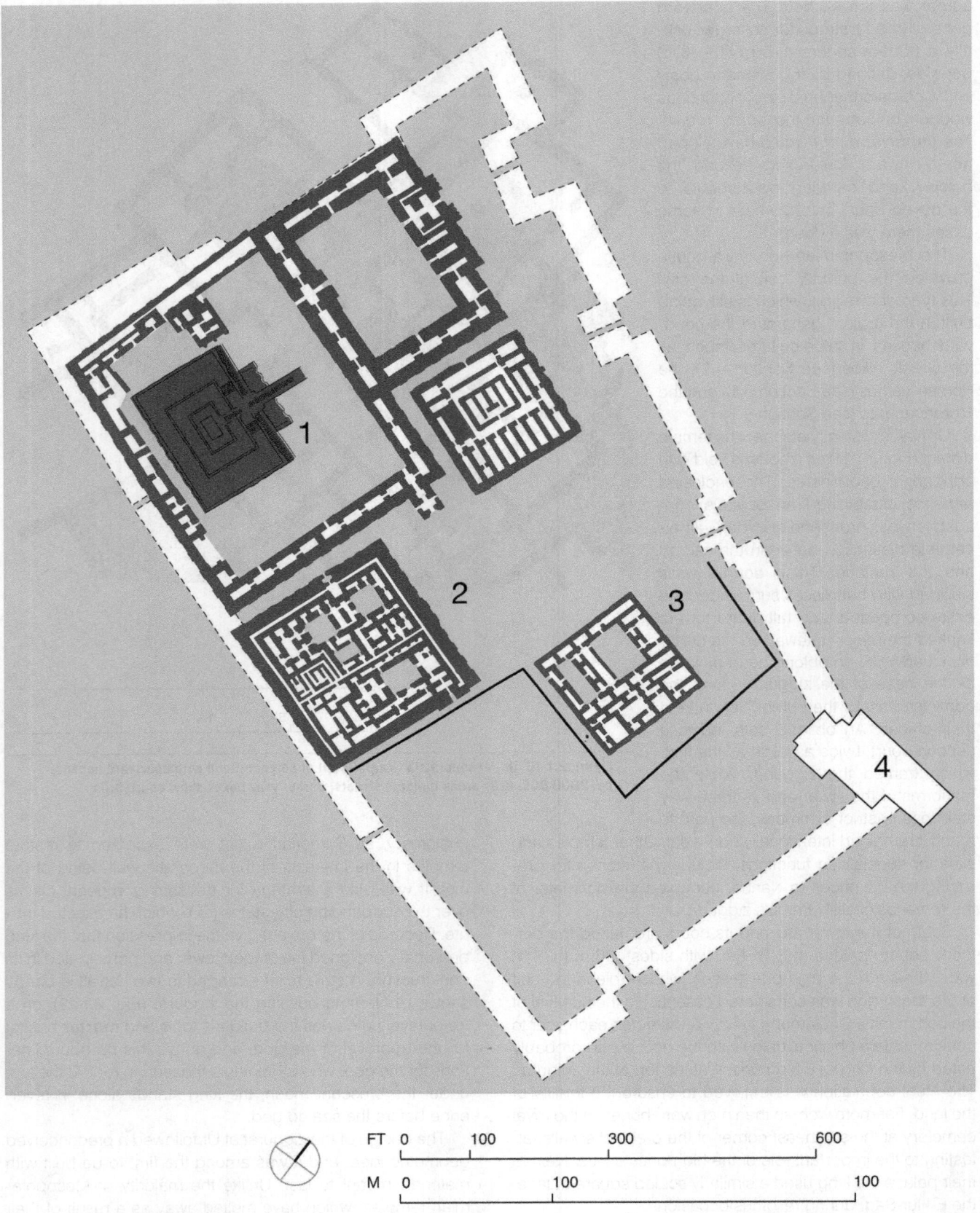

FT   0   100   300   600

M   0   100   100

Figure 2.1-11 Ur, Mesopotamia (Iraq). Plan of Ur-Nammu's temple compound, ca. 2100 BCE: (1) ziggurat; (2) palace of E-Gi-Par; (3) palace of E-Hur-Sag; (4) royal cemetery.

"Ur-Nammu, king of Ur, who built the temple of Nanna." Mud bricks filled the core of the tower, while masons set the baked bricks with straw bonds in bitumen mortar, utilizing the region's abundant supply of asphalt and petroleum byproducts. The builders cut narrow slits, or "weep-holes," at regular intervals through the baked-brick casing to drain the interior of residual moisture and prevent the walls from deforming.

As was customary, Ur-Nammu oriented the corners of his ziggurat to the cardinal axes. The triple staircase (Fig. 2.1-13), with its central branch pointing straight out and the other two ascending from the sides, emphasized the symmetry of the design. They converged at a pavilion gateway. From this point, a single flight of stairs ran straight up the next two platforms to the portal of the temple at the summit. The first stage of the tower rose 18 m (59 ft) and the next about half of that, following the same proportions in a plan of 2:3. The third level continued the pattern of diminishing in proportion by one-half. The Temple of Nanna, which served as the moon god's "bridal chamber," rested on top of the third **terrace**, about 6 × 10 m (20 × 33 ft) and plastered in blue. The ziggurat's cumulative height reached over 35 m (115 ft), more than ten times higher than any of the city's buildings.

The power embodied by Ur-Nammu's tower endured long after his dynasty's decline. The succeeding conquerors of the region dutifully maintained the Great Ziggurat of Ur and eagerly copied it elsewhere. After a three-century drought that devastated Southwest Asia, from roughly 2200 to 1900 BCE, new powers laid claim to the increasingly unfruitful plains between the Tigris and the Euphrates. After the new regime of Babylonians reunited the lands of Sumer and Akkad around 1800 BCE, they carefully restored and expanded the *temenos* of Ur as a sign of respect to the local gods. In the northern outpost of Tell al-Rimah near modern Mosul, the Babylonians constructed a new ziggurat attached to a vast temple. The next group to take power, the Assyrians, created the new capital city of Assur, on the upper Tigris, and crowned it with a series of three staged towers. The Kassites, during a short period of dominion in the fifteenth century BCE, built one of the tallest of the ziggurats, the 57 m (187 ft) Aqar Quf, near Baghdad. Much of its core still stands as a result of the layering of rope and reeds in bitumen mortar between the mud bricks. The Elamites in the thirteenth century BCE built a seven-level ziggurat at their capital

Figure 2.1-12 Ur, Mesopotamia (Iraq). Stele showing Ur-Nammu constructing the ziggurat and presenting himself to the god Nanna, ca. 2100 BCE.

Figure 2.1-13 Ur, Mesopotamia (Iraq). Axonometric drawing reconstructing the Great Ziggurat of Ur-Nammu, ca. 2100 BCE: (1) triple stair; (2) pavilion at the landing; (3) the "bridal" chamber at the summit.

CULTURE, SOCIETY, GENDER

A Map of Ancient Nippur's Territory

This clay tablet, created around 1500 BCE, describes land divisions belonging to the Sumerian city-state of Nippur. The cuneiform inscriptions refer to roads, canals, and sluices that were managed by the central temple of the city. Over the course of the second millennium, Nippur was incorporated into the neighboring city-states as a dependency but still maintained administrative autonomy. It became an important pilgrimage site during the period of the Third Dynasty of Ur-Nammu, often serving as the royal residence. The map shows evidence of sophisticated methods of two-dimensional spatial representation, using parallel lines to indicate a network of roads, canals, enclosures, and gateways. The temples maintained records not only of products and people, written in cuneiform letters, but of geographic and urban space, communicated with the sort of line drawings that became the convention for representing architecture. The cities of Mesopotamia during the Bronze Age invented written language and included as one of its subtexts communication about landscapes, space, and buildings.

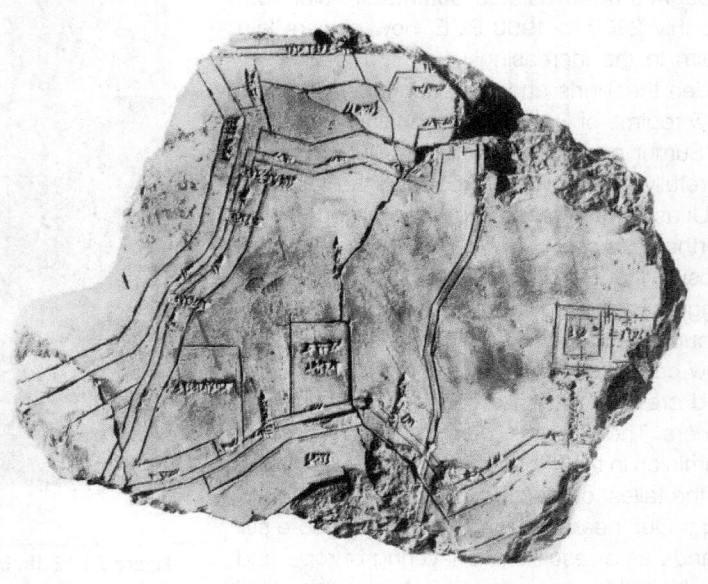

Nippur, Mesopotamia (Iraq). Clay map, ca. 1500 BCE.

in Choga in western Iran. Finally, more than fifteen centuries after Ur-Nammu's achievement, Nebuchadnezzar, king of the Neo-Babylonians, scrupulously restored the ziggurat at Ur and used it as the model for his own city's Entemenanki stepped tower, which at 90 m (295 ft) prevailed as the tallest ever built in the region (see Section 4.1).

The Mesopotamian ziggurat crowned the city, flaunting a tangible axis mundi, the vertical link to the supernatural. In a world full of dreadful uncertainties, including the threats of war, famine, and ecological catastrophe, the stairway to heaven transmitted the comforting illusion that humans could influence the gods for the good of their city. The factors of decline, however, such as the exhaustion of the soil, calamitous droughts, and the arrival of invaders, proved too great for religious faith to overcome.

Further Reading

Algaze, Guillermo. *Ancient Mesopotamia at the Dawn of Civilization: The Evolution of an Urban Landscape*. Chicago: University of Chicago Press, 2008.

Bottéro, Jean. *Everyday Life in Ancient Mesopotamia*. Translated by A. Nevill. Baltimore: Johns Hopkins University Press, 2001.

Fagan, Brian. *The Long Summer: How Climate Changed Civilization*. London: Granta Books, 2004.

Frankfort, Henri. *The Art and Architecture of the Ancient Orient*. Harmondsworth, UK: Penguin, 1970.

Hawkes, Jaquetta. *The First Great Civilizations: Life in Mesopotamia, the Indus Valley and Egypt*. New York: Alfred A. Knopf, 1973.

Lampl, Paul. *Cities and Planning in the Ancient Near East*. New York: Braziller, 1968.

Leick, Gwendolyn. *Mesopotamia: The Invention of the City*. London: Penguin Books, 2001.

Moscati, Sabatino. *The Face of the Ancient Orient*. New York: Anchor Books, 1962.

Postgate, Nicholas. *Early Mesopotamia: Society and Economy at the Dawn of History*. London: Routledge, 1992.

2.2 OLD KINGDOM EGYPT
Architecture for the Afterlife

The period of Old Kingdom Egypt, ca. 2700–2100 BCE, parallels that of the Sumerian city-states. While few traces remain of their cities, the ancient Egyptians left behind immense funerary monuments that constitute the most permanent **volumes** ever constructed. They created the **pyramids** as exquisite, abstract shelters for the spirits of the pharaohs, their queens, and their courtiers, who they believed would live in an eternal afterlife in the company of the lord of the sun. Specialist architects

emerged as key members of the royal court, calculating the precise geometry of the monuments and directing skilled masons in the assembly of the stones.

The great expense of the Egyptian pyramids suggests that in the society of the Old Kingdom the needs of the afterlife exceeded those of the here and now. The tombs served as investments to ensure good terms with the gods who regaled Egypt with the "gift of the Nile," the annual summer floods. The surplus of food produced by these floods and the lull in between growing seasons allowed the Egyptians extra time to pursue the complexities of their religion. Their construction of monuments and grand enclosures for the dead was believed to promote the well-being of their people, in this world and the next.

The Nile and Sacred Geometry

The geography of Egypt determined that it developed in relative autonomy. A thin, fertile strip along the Nile River, the kingdom's habitable land lay between parallel stone cliffs, beyond which stretched vast deserts. The river supplied the fundamental wealth of the land, while the cliffs offered a limitless quarry for stone monuments. The Nile's reliable annual floods encouraged the belief in an eternal order. The floodwaters left a deposit of rich black silt that could be sowed with little need for plowing. After each annual flood, farmers divided this "black land" into squared-off parcels using surveyor's cords. Although Egypt had a few heavily populated urban centers, the 5 km (3 mile) wide band of agricultural estates that straddled the river made the Nile valley more like a single, linear farming town, connected by the 1,000 km (620 mile) transportation artery from the first cataract at Aswan to the beginning of the river's delta at Memphis. The right angles used to plot the fields in relation to the river inspired the development of the Egyptians' precise knowledge of geometry, which they subsequently used to design the pyramids at the great funerary complexes.

Orthogonal planning came naturally to the ancient Egyptians. In their pictographic system of writing, they adopted a rectangle divided by a cross-axis as the hieroglyph for "province," or *nome*, and a circle similarly divided by intersecting axes as the sign for "town." The knowledge of right angles, combined with proportional systems obtained from triangles, enabled Egyptian engineers to plan immense works of astounding geometrical accuracy.

Unlike the solidity of their tombs, Egyptian houses were made with perishable materials. While scant evidence remains of urban dwellings, their forms appear in tomb decorations and in tomb architecture itself, which frequently imitated that of the houses. Aside from rectangular mud-walled structures covered with palm trunk roofs, the most frequent house type used vegetable matter: river reeds and papyrus stems, either bundled together for compressive strength or matted into **planar** surfaces stretched between wooden posts. In the south the desert climate favored tent structures, which were thought suitable even for the royal palace. Palace architecture in the north borrowed from Mesopotamian precedents,

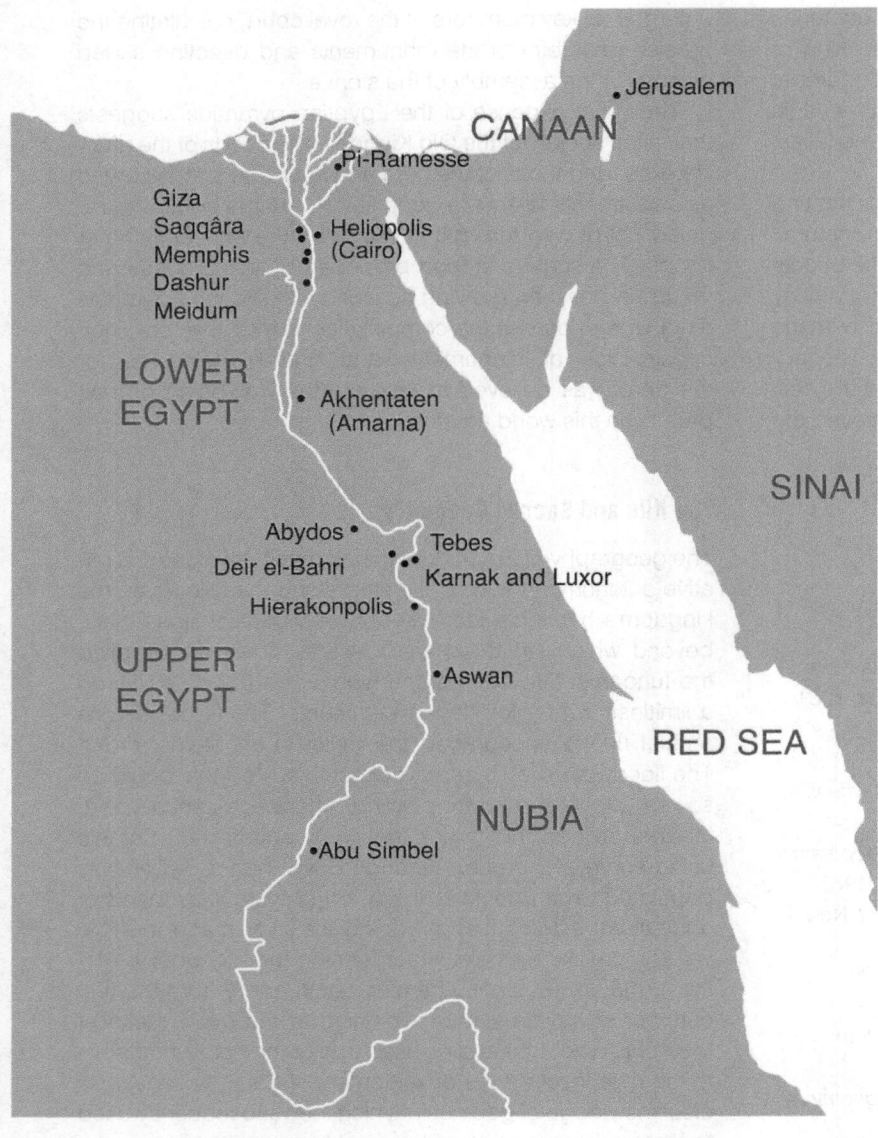

Figure 2.2-1 Ancient Egypt, 3000–1500 BCE.

Egypt, which extended 500 km (310 miles) south to Thebes (Fig. 2.2-1). The king, known later by the Greek name *pharaoh*, meaning "great house," wore a double crown as a symbol of the unified territories. Upon his death, he received a funeral in both lands: first in the south at Abydos, the ancestral home of the first kings, and then in the north, at a tomb site across the river from the capital city of Memphis.

Literary sources describe ancient Memphis as having magnificent white walls, which enclosed a grand palace for the pharaoh and the immense temple to Ptah. The temple compound covered 20 ha (50 acres), about twice the area of the *temenos* at Ur. The Babylonian name for the Egyptian temple, *Hikuptah*, led to the Greek pronunciation, *Aigiptos*, which became "Egypt" later on. The temple priesthoods of Egypt exerted great power within the kingdom, often influencing changes in dynasties, as they owned over 15% of the land and controlled about 2% of the population who worked the land. They promoted a major cult during the Old Kingdom period at the pilgrimage city of Heliopolis, 50 km (31 miles) north of Memphis, devoted to the sun god Ra. The temple focused on the *Ben-ben* monument, a tapered vertical **megalith** that symbolized the primeval mound on which the sun god had revealed himself at creation. This ancient stone, known only from representations, engendered both the prismatic shape of the pyramids and the pointed tip of **obelisks**.

As the ideology of a centralized Egyptian state took hold, the pharaoh became known as the son of Ra and was worshipped as a god. The belief that he joined the deities of the netherworld after his death encouraged a culture in which the buildings for the king's daily life appeared less substantial than those for his afterlife. During the third millennium BCE, the pharaohs and their courtiers erected hundreds of colossal

resulting in rectangular structures with large courts and pleated mud-brick walls with deep niches.

In the early third millennium BCE a centralized state emerged with a deified monarch, unifying the regions of Lower Egypt, the delta area north of Memphis, and Upper

---

TIME LINE

▼ **3000 BCE**

Two kingdoms of Egypt united under a single pharaoh

Royal Egyptian mastaba tombs at Saqqâra

▲ **2900 BCE**

▼ **2695–2625 BCE**

Imhotep builds staged pyramid for Pharaoh Djoser at Saqqâra

Pharaoh Sneferu adds Nubia and Libya to Egypt

▲ **2613–2589 BCE**

▼ **2600–2589 BCE**

Sneferu builds three pyramids at Meidum, perfecting smooth facades

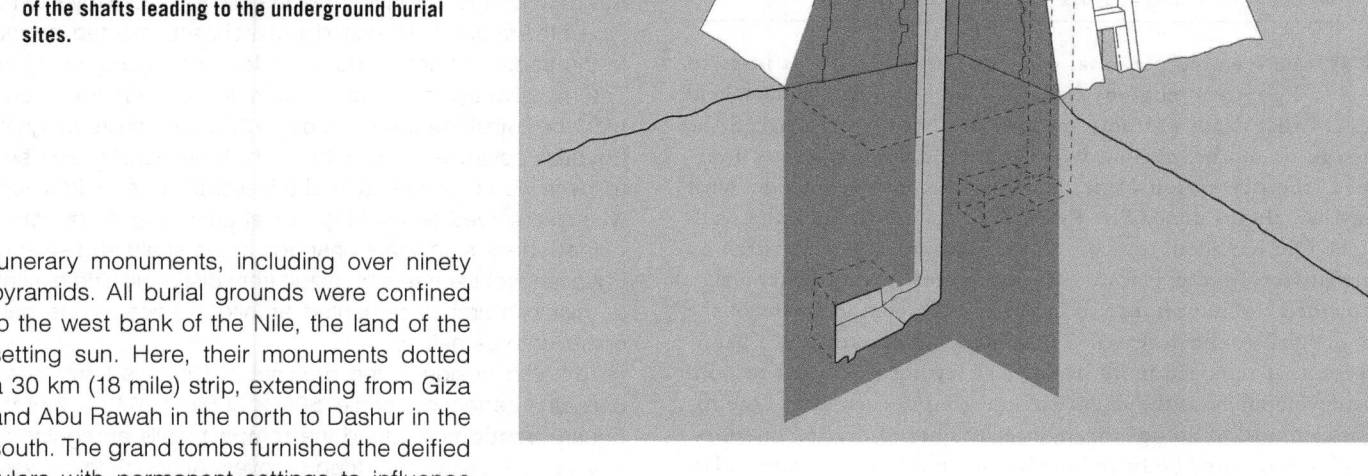

Figure 2.2-2 Ancient Egypt. Typical *mastaba*, section showing underground chamber, fourth millennium BCE. The cutaway section shows one of the shafts leading to the underground burial sites.

funerary monuments, including over ninety pyramids. All burial grounds were confined to the west bank of the Nile, the land of the setting sun. Here, their monuments dotted a 30 km (18 mile) strip, extending from Giza and Abu Rawah in the north to Dashur in the south. The grand tombs furnished the deified rulers with permanent settings to influence the gods for the country's well-being. Egypt's economic surplus went toward building the world's largest structures, solid environments for invisible spirits that could ensure the provision of the "gift of the Nile."

At first the Egyptians designed the royal tomb as a loaf-shaped rectangular tumulus, known in Arabic as a **mastaba**, the word for "bench." The memorials for the early pharaohs at Abydos had 5 m (16 ft) high brick perimeters filled with sand. A deep shaft extended under the sand to a secret burial vault (Fig. 2.2-2). As the royal tombs became cult sites for the worship of their deified occupants, the perimeter walls of the *mastabas* came to include altars for visitors that were framed with twin **stelae**. The patrons left endowments to maintain sacrifices in perpetuity. Many of the royal funereal landscapes seemed like the solidification of a royal palace. By filling in the voids of that palace they believed they could best house the *ka*, or spiritual double, of the deceased, who pursued the functions of life in the analogous mirror world of the afterlife. A special sealed chamber, known as the **serdab**, contained a statue of the pharaoh. A false door sculpted in relief stood opposite the image as the portal for the dead king's *ka* to enter and possess the statue.

Saqqâra came to prominence as a royal burial site around 2900 BCE. Here the exteriors of the tombs imitated the facades of the palaces of Memphis. A large rectangular casing, about 9 m (30 ft) high, enclosed the tomb of Queen Herneith. Its elevations carried intricate brick paneling, coated in white lime **stucco** painted with geometric designs. The palace-sized tomb of King Wadj also boasted colossal proportions, its perimeter about half the size of the *temenos* of Ur-Nammu. Fifty-six courtiers were buried alive with this pharaoh to care for him in perpetuity, but later, at the end of the First Dynasty, in the twenty-seventh century BCE, such human sacrifice was eliminated. The builders of the tomb of King Wadimu sealed the burial shaft with a stone **portcullis**, a mechanism that slipped into place to guard against tomb robbers. The last tomb of the First Dynasty, built for King Qaa, introduced the mortuary temple, a longitudinal hall lined with columns leading to an inner sanctum for visitors to celebrate the cult of the king. An endowment guaranteed that a priesthood would carry out rituals at the mortuary temples long after the death of the patron. Wooden boats buried in chambers alongside the royal tombs served the imaginary voyage of the pharaoh's spirit. In the afterlife he was believed to accompany the sun god Ra on his daily movement from east to west and at night his return by boat in the opposite direction through the underworld. Egyptian funerary architecture, in its incomparable solidity, made permanent records of one's role in the cosmos.

▼ **2550–2540**

Khafre builds second great pyramid at Giza, linked to the Sphinx

Pharaoh Khufu builds the largest pyramid at Giza

▲ **2589–2566 BCE**

Egyptian Middle Kingdom period established by Mentuhotep

▲ **2060–2010 BCE**

▼ **2000 BCE**

Construction of platform tomb at Deir el-Bahri for Mentuhotep

The Egyptian Cult of the Dead

The seemingly eternal cycle of the Nile's floods inspired Egyptian religious beliefs. The pyramid builders held that death did not conclude life but merely marked the passage to another region, where the Nile flooded, crops flourished, the dry season came, and people continued to do what they had always done. The *Pyramid Texts*, inscribed on the walls of the Old Kingdom tombs, and the *Book of the Dead*, written on papyrus scrolls and placed with mummies in their sarcophagi, explained the importance of death and the comportment of the *ka*, or spirit of the deceased. Through death one reached a parallel life that required more permanent settings. This led to both the development of the science of embalming corpses and the solidification of buildings through techniques of drafted masonry. One's mummified body and one's stone tomb were meant to last for eternity. The designers of tomb architecture believed that the *ka* moved through solidified spaces, and often they left a relief of a door within a door within a door as a ghostly point of impenetrable access.

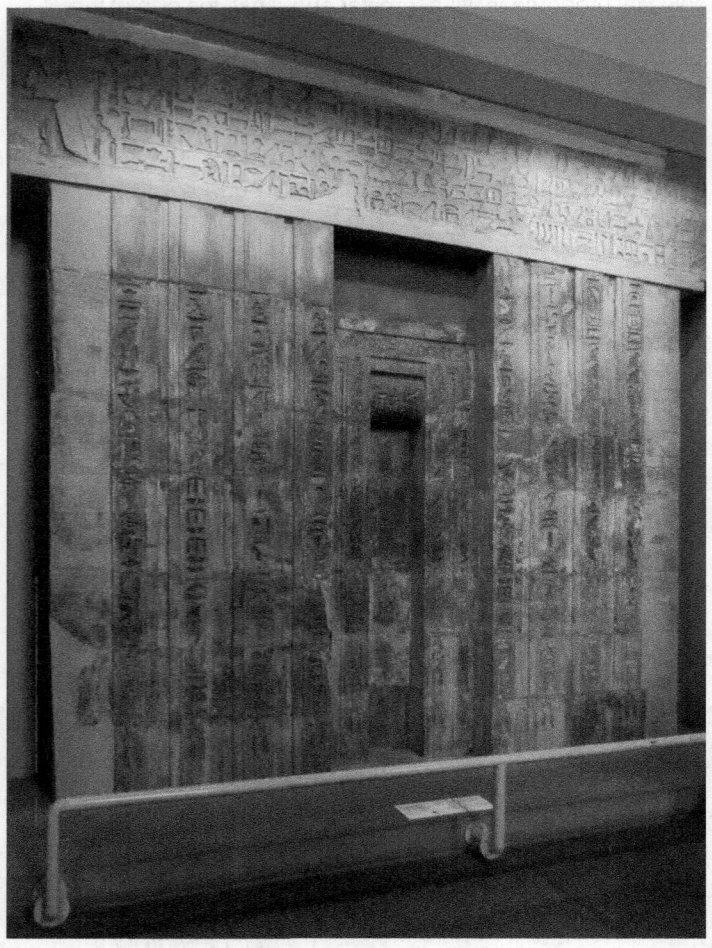

Saqqâra, Egypt. False door from the tomb of the courtier Ptahshepses, ca. 2400 BCE.

Saqqâra: The First Pyramid

King Djoser (r. 2691–2625 BCE), the probable founder of the Third Dynasty, transformed the Old Kingdom royal tomb type into Egypt's first pyramid. His architect, Imhotep, added to the traditional flat *mastaba* six levels of a staged tower. The massive enclosure of his complex at Saqqâra resembled the limestone walls of a city. Within, the entire range of Egyptian columnar architecture, which previously had been made in wood, appeared for the first time in stone. Imhotep, who also served as the king's chief advisor and physician, guided these significant changes in the scale and style of Egyptian architecture and, aside from distinguishing himself as history's first documented architect, became the only one ever to be deified.

Imhotep designed the precinct of Djoser's tomb complex as a perfect rectangle, 500 × 300 m (1,640 × 984 ft). Square **bastions** studded the **rampart** walls at regular intervals, articulated with deep grooves. Although there were fifteen gate towers, only one, at the southeast corner, could be entered. Here, a tall, narrow slot pierced through the thick mass of **ashlar masonry**. Once beyond this dark chasm one advanced to the Processional Hall (Fig. 2.2-3a,b) through a narrow corridor lined by rows of ribbed half-columns engaged to lateral spur walls. It was almost as if Imhotep doubted the bearing capacity of freestanding stone columns and felt obliged to anchor them to bearing walls. These flanges left a succession of side chapels, suitable for the placement of sculptures. The outer walls were lower than the central colonnade, allowing top light to filter in through **clerestory** gaps. The stone ceilings were carved with rounded beams resembling the palm trunks used to cover vernacular buildings. The corridor terminated in a wide chamber with four sets of twin half-columns placed in the center back to back. The drums of the columns, like most of the masonry in Djoser's complex, were made from small pieces of stone, comparable to the size of adobe bricks and never taller than 25 cm (10 inches).

After traversing the chasm-like Processional Hall, one emerged into the blinding light of the Grand Court, a space about twice the area of the stepped pyramid at its northern edge. Straight ahead stood a series of dummy granaries, completely solid volumes intended to store phantom provisions for the afterlife. A vaulted *mastaba* on the south covered an intricate tomb shaft as one of two burial chambers prepared for the pharaoh.

The spaces surrounding the pyramid served as the site of the Heb-Sed festival. This jubilee was a generational event, celebrated every thirty years during the reign of an incumbent pharaoh to test the monarch's capacity to rule. The five days of the festival involved the symbolic sacrifice and rebirth of the pharaoh, a double crowning, and a foot race to demonstrate his physical fitness. The two hoof-shaped markers in the Grand Court appear to have been goals for Djoser's ghostly reenactment of the race. Djoser evidently intended to repeat the festival regularly in the afterlife.

A secret passage in the first bay of the Processional Hall led circuitously along the ramparts to a narrow courtyard parallel to the Grand Court. Known as the "Heb-Sed Court," it was lined on the west with altars, behind which stood sham pavilions (Fig. 2.2-4). Each of the altars had a stone door set in a stone socket that was swung permanently into an open position. The facades of these ten stone pavilions resembled tent structures framed by **piers**, between which three slender engaged columns supported gently arched **transoms**. Twelve smaller altars lined the eastern side of the courtyard, and the ensemble apparently represented the *nome* gods of the twenty-two provinces of Upper and Lower Egypt. As in real life, so in the afterlife did Djoser need to obtain the consent of the provinces, one by one, to achieve his new term of office. His *ka* sat on a raised platform at the southern end of the court, where on back-to-back thrones he was awarded the cone-shaped white crown of Upper Egypt and the cap-like red crown of Lower Egypt.

A pair of smaller courts to the north of this court served as the king's "white" and "red" palaces. The first had half-columns with **lotus capitals**, the symbol of Upper Egypt, lining the walls. The second had flange-shaped half-columns crowned with flaring papyrus capitals, the emblematic plant of Lower Egypt. One of the traditions of Egyptian coronation ceremonies involved the lacing together of lotus and papyrus plants around a stake. Djoser's *ka* occupied a varied and magnificent ghost town set with storehouses, palaces, and temples that would help him carry on his kingly duties throughout eternity.

The stepped pyramid dominated Djoser's funeral complex, rising above the flat desert landscape like a vision of another world. Although it vaguely resembles the stepped ziggurat towers of Mesopotamia and was certainly inspired by them, Djoser's tower proved more abstract. Without stairs, doors, or windows, nothing about the structure relates to the scale of the human body. A prismatic stone occupied the summit, instead of a sanctuary for priests to mingle with gods. Egyptian pyramids rose as sublime forms for the exclusive use of the invisible protagonists of the supernatural.

The design of Djoser's tomb went through five phases. The initial *mastaba* was enlarged twice and then, during

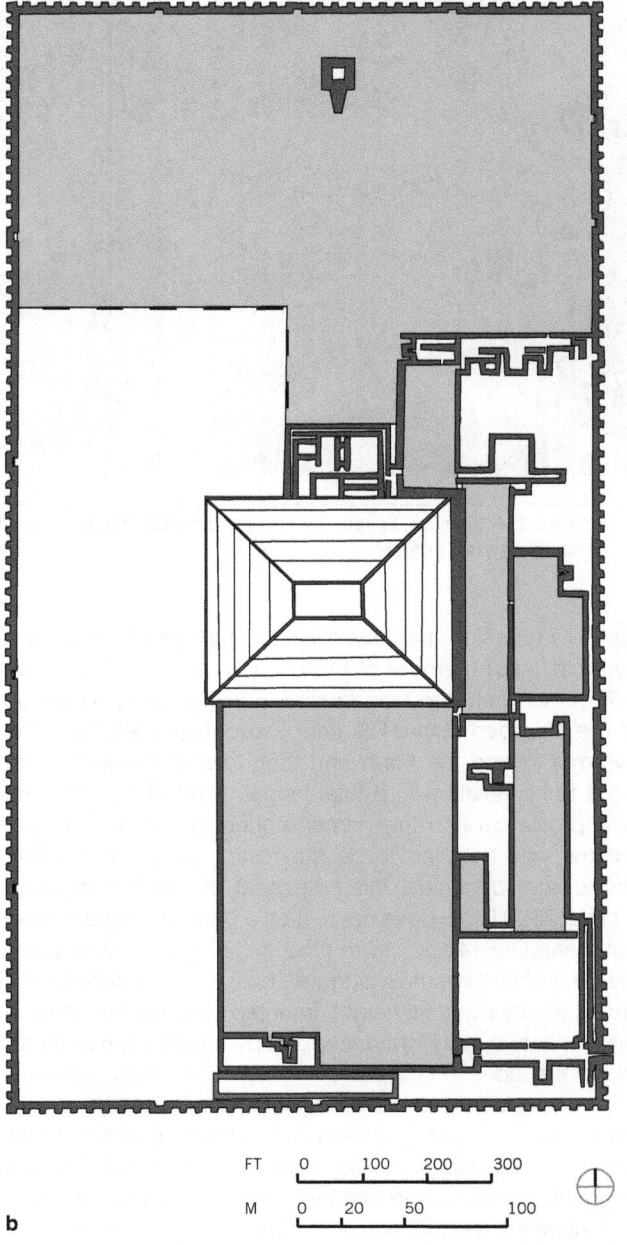

| FT | 0 | 100 | 200 | 300 |
| M | 0 | 20 | 50 | 100 |

Figure 2.2-3 Saqqâra, Egypt. (a) Djoser's tomb, Processional Hall with columns engaged to spur walls, ca. 2650 BCE. (b) Plan.

Figure 2.2-4 Saqqâra, Egypt. The stepped pyramid of Djoser, ca. 2650 BCE. Architect: Imhotep. View across Heb-Sed Courtyard, showing two of the twenty-two altars.

the third redesign, became the lowest stage of a four-level pyramid. As a member of the priesthood of the Heliopolis cult center, Imhotep was familiar with the tapering shape of the *Ben-ben* stone. His final two designs enlarged the pyramid toward the north and then toward the west, raising it to six levels with a total height of 62 m (203 ft). The new profile evoked the primal mound of creation, whose summit was believed to be the resting place of the sun. Unlike later pyramids, this first great pyramid, completed around 2600 BCE, does not rest on a perfectly square base but measures 140 × 118 m (459 × 387 ft). It covers twice the area of Ur-Nammu's ziggurat, built three centuries later, and is nearly twice its height. Imhotep improved his design with a second, unfinished stepped pyramid built nearby for Djoser's successor, the base of which is perfectly square.

The mortuary temple at Djoser's pyramid, where sacrifices were regularly conducted, stood adjacent to its north. The *serdab*, a sealed chamber built of solid blocks of granite, was inserted into the northern base of the tower. It sheltered a seated statue of Djoser and was perforated with two eye-level slots that would enable the *ka*-possessed

image to peer out from the darkness. In building the first pyramid, Djoser sought to improve his performance as pharaoh in the afterlife, assisting Ra on his daily journey and procuring good fortune for Egypt. As described in one of the *Pyramid Texts*, written two centuries later, the stepped tower allowed the king to "mount up to heaven thereby."

Giza: The Culminating Pyramids

While the true pyramid, a four-sided triangular prism, came to represent ancient Egyptian culture, it was the focus of a relatively brief season of tomb building during the twenty-seventh to twenty-fifth century BCE. The uncompromised geometry of the pyramid eluded any functional need, appearing as an extreme demonstration of the forces of gravity that push down from its pointed summit to the squared-off bottom corners. A pyramid's surging **mass** offered a fitting response to the flatness of the desert. Its cosmic significance as the stairway to unite the sun god Ra with his son the pharaoh inspired many costly and laborious efforts to improve on Djoser's staged scheme. During the century-long period of the Fourth Dynasty the type reached its smoothly pitched final configuration.

Djoser's immediate successors continued to build stepped pyramids. The last of these, built at Meidum, 50 km (31 miles) south of Saqqâra, was begun by a descendant of Djoser but completed by Sneferu (r. 2613–2589 BCE), founder of the Fourth Dynasty. The new king built two other pyramids and seems to have used architecture to bolster his legitimacy. Sneferu came from a nonroyal background and, in order to maintain the royal bloodline, married his half-sister. Then, to gain political favor, he carried out successful military campaigns in Nubia and Libya, bringing back thousands of captives, who were pressed into service for his progressively grandiose architectural projects.

At Meidum Sneferu attempted to smooth the stepped structure of the pyramid to obtain a solid prism. The 51° pitch rose too steeply to carry the loads, however, causing much of the tower to collapse. The exposed upper zones reveal that the inner structure of pyramids, including the initial one designed by Imhotep, rose in concentric vertical layers, like the skin of an onion. Sneferu's second effort, the Bent Pyramid at Dashur (Fig. 2.2-5a,b), proved even taller, with a greater slope. Halfway up, however, after cracking developed, he changed to a lower angle, giving the tower its name. Much of its smooth white casing, limestone from Tura across the river, still clings to its bulky mass, showing how luminous, if not blinding, the pyramids must have appeared at the moment of their completion. Sneferu began his third work, the Red Pyramid, a kilometer to the north. Over time its limestone veneer peeled off, revealing a core of red sandstone blocks, from which it gets its name. In his final effort, Sneferu adhered to the 43° slope used on the upper part of the Bent Pyramid, obtaining the first perfectly prismatic, if slightly squat, pyramid. A *pyramidion* capstone, a single pyramidal gilded limestone block, crowned the structure. Like Djoser's architect Imhotep, Sneferu was worshipped for over a millennium due to his architectural exploits.

Sneferu also created the first example of a valley temple. In this type, the colonnaded hall served as a reception area for the preliminary rituals honoring the deceased. A stone-lined **causeway** connected it to the mortuary temple next to the pyramid. For the interment ceremonies the king's corpse arrived by boat in the valley temple's dark, pillared hall. Here, the body was washed, purified, and embalmed—or, if already mummified, the embalming was reenacted. Once ready, the mummy underwent a magic rite known as the "Opening of the Mouth," which enabled the king to speak once more and partake in the offerings.

Sneferu's descendants continued to improve the pyramid type at Giza, on the southwest edge of modern Cairo (Fig. 2.2-6a,b). His successor, Khufu, more commonly known by the Greek name Cheops (r. 2589–2566 BCE), commissioned the first and largest of these structures. At 230 m (755 ft) per side, the pyramid rose 146 m (479 ft), as tall as a 60-story building. In terms of mass it still prevails as the largest building in the world. More than 2 million golden limestone blocks, each weighing over 2 tons, give it a total load of more than 6 million tons. The Great Pyramid of Khufu was accompanied by three or four small pyramids for the pharaoh's immediate family, a *mastaba* for his mother, and, to the east and west of the precinct wall, an orderly series of *mastabas* for his court. Khufu also provided five stone-lined troughs for docking the wooden solar boats, one of which was 43 m (141 ft) long.

Khufu's pyramid astounds not only for its bulk but also for its precision: it is perfectly aligned to the cardinal points with a tolerance of 0.015%. The maniacal accuracy of the structure, which was allegedly designed by the pharaoh's nephew Hem Iwno, left a difference of less than 20 cm (7 in) per side at its base. While most of the white Tura limestone blocks used for its smooth casing have been pillaged, they originally were set without mortar and had assembly joints of only half a millimeter. The structure's prismatic profile slopes 51.5°, like a perfect arrowhead.

It is difficult to fit a door on a pyramid, and it was intended to appear without visible points of access. Khufu put the secret entrance on the north face, a little east of center, about 20 m (66 ft) above grade (Fig. 2.2-7). The burial ceremony used temporary earthen ramps, such as those required for construction, to reach the entry. The initial entry shaft, about 1 m (3.3 ft) per side, descended more than 50 m (164 ft) below the base through the mass of the pyramid to the original burial chamber. Because of a shortage of oxygen, this room was abandoned for a second chamber centered on the vertical axis, at almost the same level as the entry, which in turn was scuttled for the third and final burial chamber, about 40 m (131 ft) above the base. The funeral party would have reached this chamber through an extension of the ascending ramp, where the tiny passage opened onto the Grand Gallery, an interior hall that continued the sloping ascent with ceilings 10 m (33 ft) high. Its polished, corbelled limestone blocks were arranged into seven steps like overlapping geological strata as they converged toward a central flat ceiling. A faint ray of natural light entered at the top of the passage through two minuscule air shafts.

The goal of the funeral route, the King's Chamber, contained a sarcophagus carved from a single piece of granite so large that it was put in place first and the chamber built around it. After the conclusion of the burial ceremony, three granite portcullis slabs were slipped into place between the antechamber and the King's Chamber, in an effort to block access forever. Above the burial room's flat ceiling, the engineers positioned five layers of monolithic stone, intended to relieve the compressive forces pushing down on the void. The top level had two slanting monoliths tilted up like a pitched roof within the solid core of the pyramid.

Khufu's successors sponsored the other two large pyramids at Giza. Khafre, known in Greek as Chephren, built his a few meters smaller than Khufu's, while Menkaure, or Mykerinos, made his half the size. Khafre's complex remains the best preserved, with some of the limestone casing at the pyramid's apex still in place. His valley temple led through indirect passages to a *T*-shaped **hypostyle hall**, a room

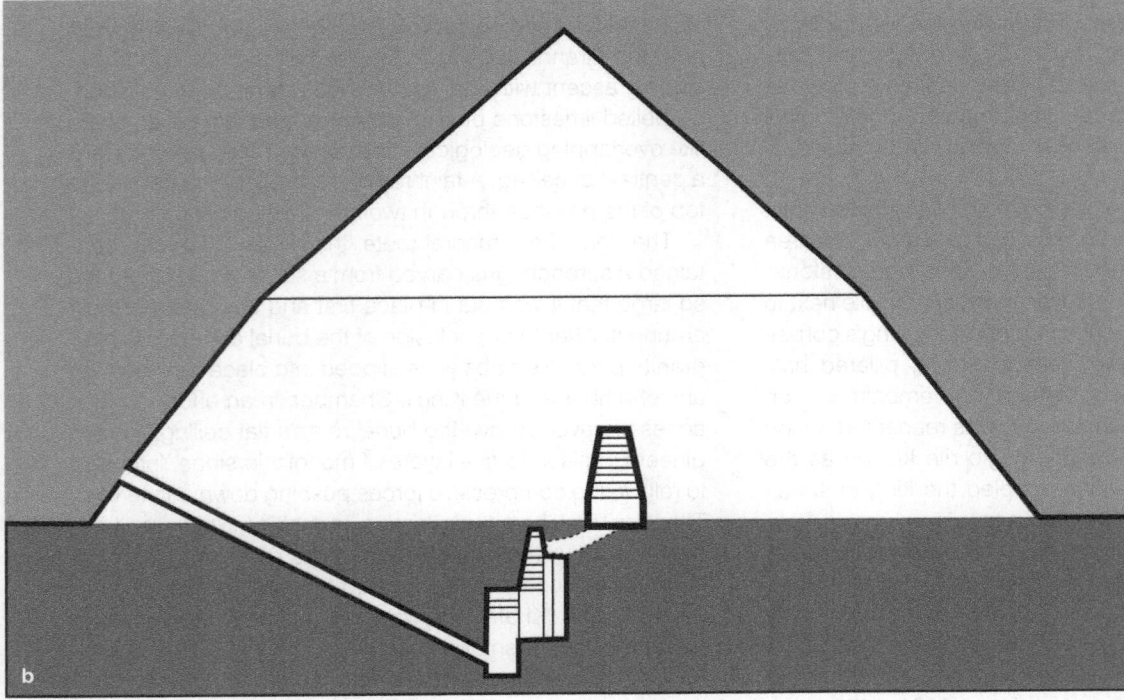

Figure 2.2-5 Meidum, Egypt. (a) Sneferu's Bent Pyramid, ca. 2550. (b) Section.

Figure 2.2-6 Giza, Egypt.
(a) Pyramids of Khufu on the left, Khafre in the center, and Menkaure on the right, twenty-sixth to twenty-fifth century BCE. Dozens of *mastabas* were built for the courtiers and set in a grid, and three small pyramids were built for Khufu's wives to the right of his tomb. (b) Plan of the pyramids: (1) pyramid of Khufu; (2) pyramid of Khafre; (3) the Sphinx; (4) pyramid of Menkaure.

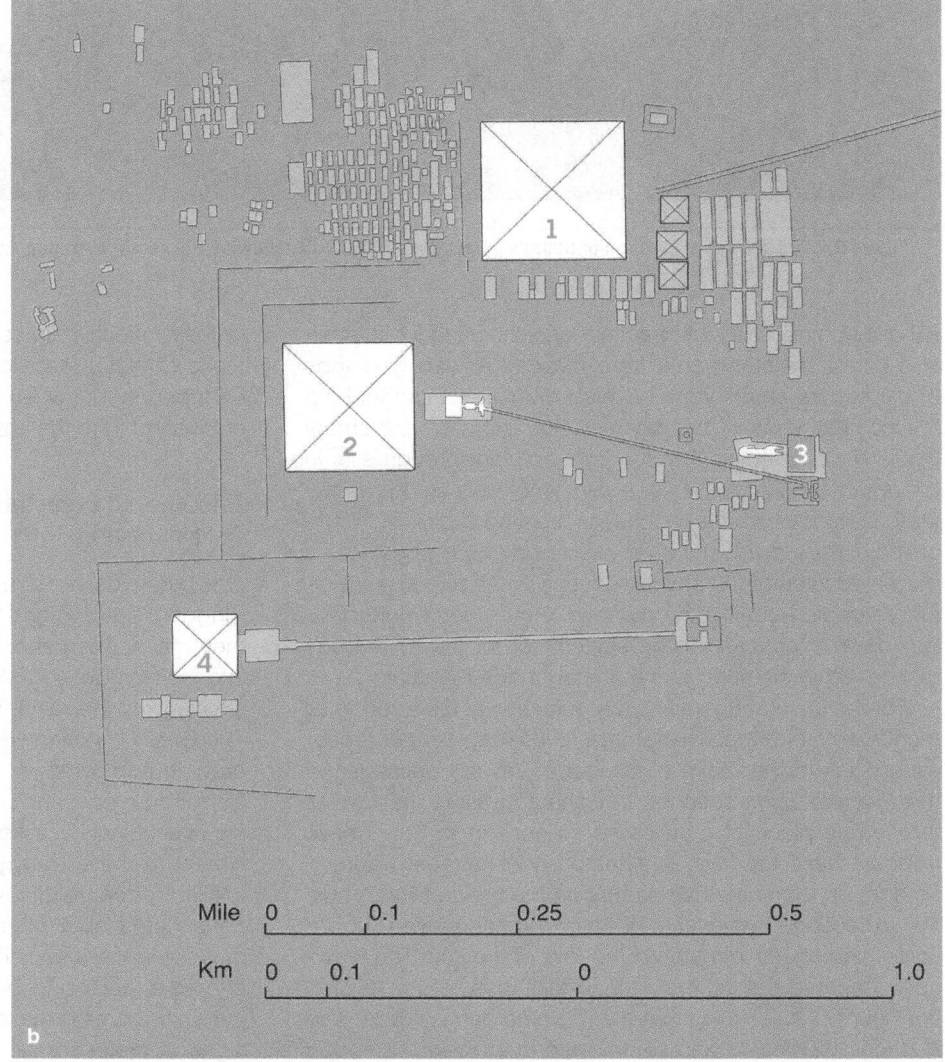

| Mile | 0 | 0.1 | 0.25 | 0.5 |
| Km | 0 | 0.1 | 0 | 1.0 |

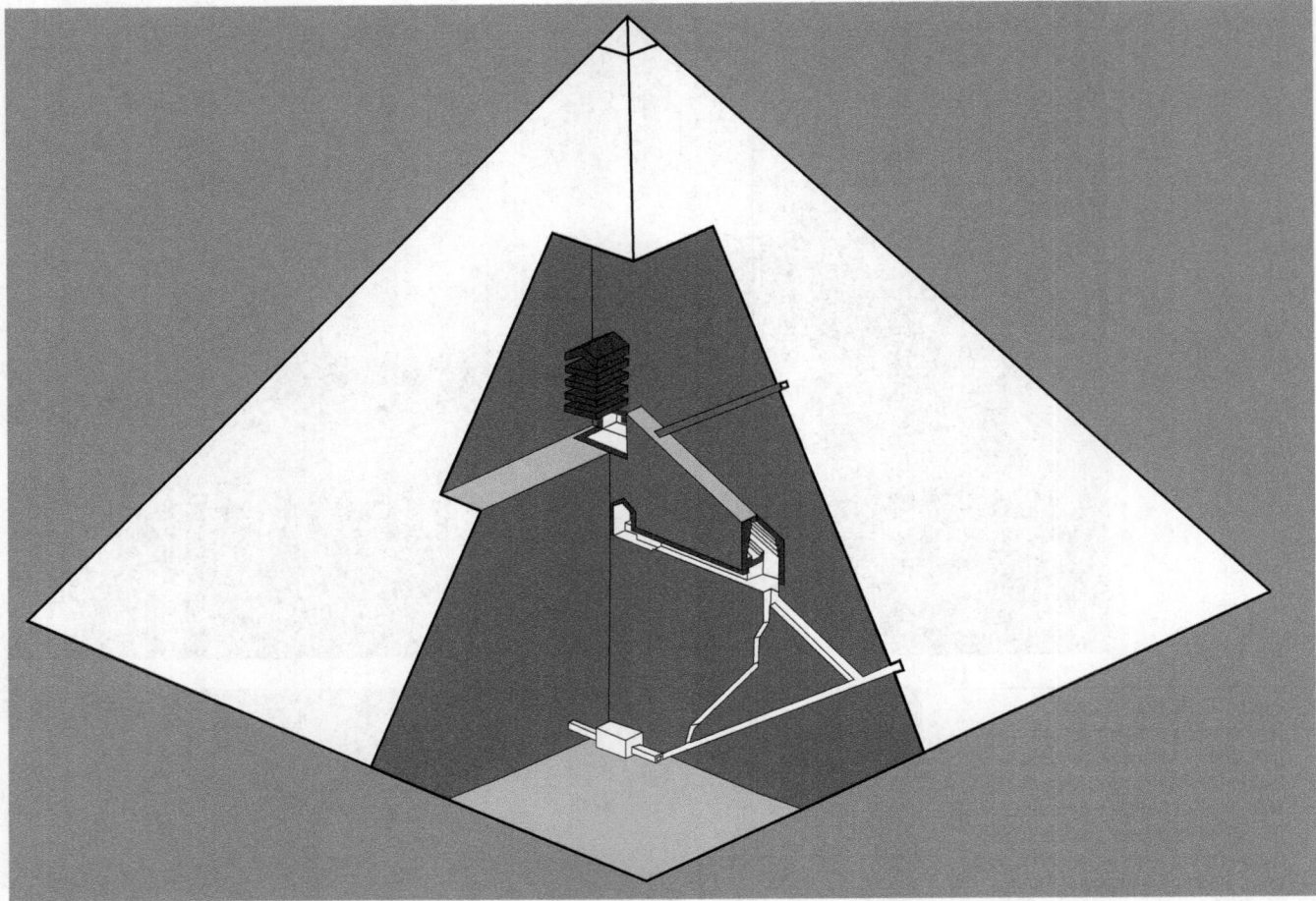

Figure 2.2-7 Giza, Egypt. Section of Khufu's pyramid, ca. 2570 BCE, showing the secret entrance and the three burial chambers.

full of columns. The pink granite monoliths used for its post-and-beam skeleton came from faraway Aswan. The tops of the square shafts were beveled to make joints that held the pointed ends of the beams. The alabaster pavement would have reflected the dim light coming through slits in the upper parts of the walls. Against the walls stood twenty-three statues of Khafre, each representing a different deification of the individual organs of his body. Only priests were permitted to enter the oblique causeway leading to the mortuary temple abutting the pyramid. Here, they would have laid down sacrifices for the sustenance of the royal body resting within the heart of the human-made mountain.

For the ancient Egyptians the pyramids at Giza shone as monuments of hope. These great piles represented a necessary link to the realm of the gods. Several passages of the *Pyramid Texts* describe the pharaoh using the rays of the sun, in place of a staircase, to ascend to Ra: "I have trodden these thy rays as a ramp under my feet whereon I mount up to my mother Uraeus on the brow of Ra." Thus, the exceptional materiality of the pyramids strived toward something utterly immaterial: the rays of the sun. The structures became palpable evidence for those who cultivated the bountiful Nile valley that the universe had an order and that their well-being and safety were guaranteed. Stripped

of their reflective limestone casing and the gold overlay of the pyramidion capstones, the pyramids now seem more earthbound, but when new they shone like luminous arrows emanating from the earth, leading the way to the sun.

The Lowered Expectations of Egypt's Middle Kingdom: The Limits of Eternity

The pyramids at Giza represented the climax of the Old Kingdom's artistic and theological ambitions. Confronted by their mass, one cannot help imagining the labor that went into their production. Were the millions of hours invested in such works the result of oppression or religious devotion? The Greek historian Herodotus (ca. 484–425 BCE) considered Khufu's pyramid the consummate act of tyranny. So did the modern poet and playwright Bertolt Brecht, who, speaking of such works, asked during the 1920s: "Was it the kings who hauled the craggy blocks of stone?" Yet the pyramids fulfilled a clear religious imperative and were built mostly by conscripted labor, often involving trained professionals. The mass of farmers, with little to do during the Nile's inundation, offered a ready pool of labor. The real burden of these final pyramids came in the form of bankrupting the economy. Few signs of protest or rebellion remain from the Old Kingdom

The Obelisk

Egyptians considered the obelisk, a tall needle with a pyramidal point, a materialized ray of sunlight, hearkening back to the primeval cult of the *Ben-ben* stone of Heliopolis. Obelisks frequently stood in relation to sacrificial altars, such as that of the Sun Sanctuary of Ne-User-Ra. Built of limestone blocks, the Ne-User-Ra obelisk rose 60 m (197 ft), almost as tall as Djoser's pyramid, and like the pyramids, it was capped with a shining pyramidion, a prism based on perfect isosceles triangles. Monolithic obelisks, such as the 21 m (69 ft) needle of Sesostris I, which was raised around 1950 BCE and remains the only significant monument still standing in Heliopolis, were typical of the solar sanctuaries of the Middle Kingdom. While obelisks today are usually seen as freestanding objects—such as the Lateran obelisk in Rome, planted at the end of the straight street leading to the Colosseum built for Sixtus V in 1587 CE (see Section 11.3)—the ancient Egyptians usually placed them next to a wall to cast a shadow.

Karnak, Egypt. Obelisk of Tutmosis IV at Temple of Amun, ca. 1400 BCE. Brought to Rome in the fourth century CE and placed at San Giovanni in Laterano in 1587.

period, but the overall well-being of the country and stability of the regime steadily declined during the next three centuries. In the twenty-second century BCE, the same period of Ur's decline, Egypt suffered comparable environmental disasters: the Nile refused to flood, and famine, disorder, and political shifts ensued.

After the monuments of the Fourth Dynasty, succeeding dynasties felt obliged to downplay the role of the royal tomb and give more attention to temples—in particular, solar sanctuaries dedicated to the sun god Ra. As the importance of the cult of the sun god increased, various powers outside the monarchy—including the provincial governors (or *nomarchs*), the priesthood of Heliopolis, and the landed aristocrats—began to assert their independence. In contrast to the masonry piles built in Lower Egypt, the tradition of rock-cut tombs in the south influenced the development of axial, columnar architecture toward the end of the third millennium.

The period known as the Middle Kingdom (ca. 2150–1750 BCE) took shape after more than a century of civil strife and anarchy. The founder of the Eleventh Dynasty, Mentuhotep I (r. 2161–2040 BCE), reunited the two lands of Egypt. Born in the south, he relocated the capital to Thebes, which became his base in the successful campaign to win

back the upper Nile. Mentuhotep sponsored a new type of platform funeral memorial, combining a solar sanctuary terrace temple to the sun god with a rock-cut tomb (Fig. 2.2-8). The king demonstrated a new theological modesty, placing himself in service to the deity. The principal shrine to Amon-Ra, the Theban sun god, stood at Karnak (see Section 3.2), directly aligned to Mentuhotep's funerary complex across the river beneath the spectacular cliffs of Deir el-Bahri. The funerary **program** began at the valley temple near the Nile and opened to a grand esplanade 35 m (115 ft) wide, more like a boulevard than the traditional submerged causeway. This road led to a sequence of three terraced enclosures, the lowest with a formal garden surrounded by a thick wall, in which regularly placed holes had been sunk in the arid terrain to be filled with topsoil for rows of tamarisks and sycamore trees. A broad ramp flanked with deep porticoes made of double rows of square columns bisected this planted court, and a false tomb with an empty sarcophagus stood inside the colonnade. The second level covered a square platform carved from the live rock. Here, another set of porticoes three rows deep surrounded the thick, battered walls of an interior temple, a flat-roofed shrine for the veneration of the local god Montu-Ra. The final level served as Mentuhotep's mortuary temple, carved directly into the base

How Were the Pyramids Constructed?

No ancient sources document the construction methods of the Giza pyramids, nor do scholars agree on the matter. The stone blocks weighed as much as 200 tons each and were dragged with sleds over a path paved with logs, as the wheel had not yet been introduced. The pyramid at Meidum shows that the cores were built first in vertical sections, but it is not certain whether the builders relied on a colossal earth ramp (examples a and b) or a system of spiral ramps that rose around the perimeter (example c) to drag the great stones to the upper areas. Other possibilities include a zigzagging ramp or a splayed or narrow axial ramp. None of these theories accounts for how a full pyramid was constructed, and it is likely that different combinations of techniques were used over the centuries and in different locations. The casing of Tura limestone could have been applied either after the understructure was complete, working from the top down, or at the same time as the understructure. The casing stones were beveled to fit the exact incline angle and set on a truly level plane.

Theories of how pyramids were built using ramps of sand:
(a) long wide ramp;
(b) long splayed ramp;
(c) spiral ramp;
(d) zigzag ramp;
(e) narrow axial ramp;
(f) splayed axial ramp.

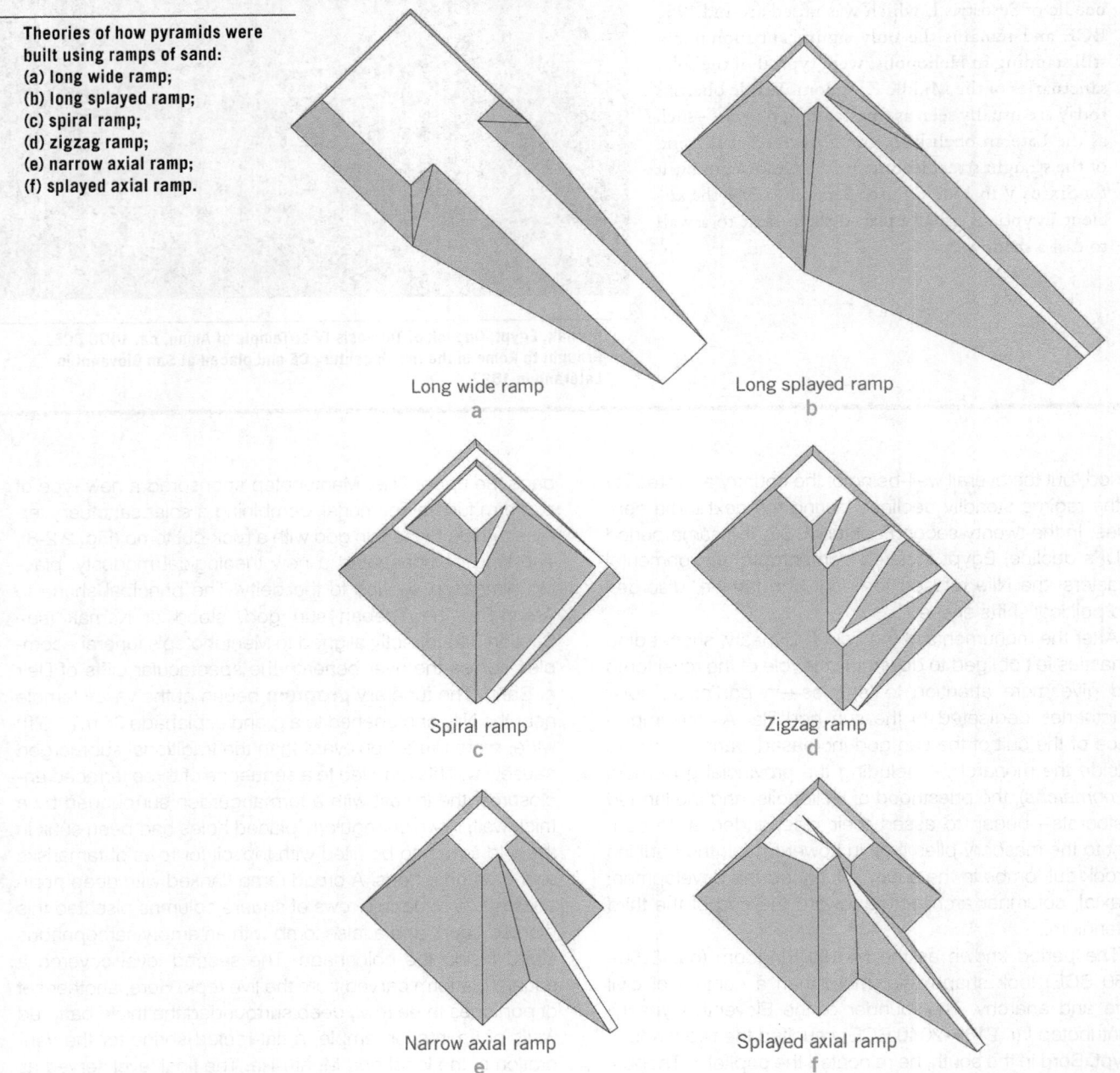

Long wide ramp
a

Long splayed ramp
b

Spiral ramp
c

Zigzag ramp
d

Narrow axial ramp
e

Splayed axial ramp
f

2.2 | OLD KINGDOM EGYPT   61

RELIGION, PHILOSOPHY, FOLKLORE

The Sphinx

Next to Khafre's valley temple rises the giant **apotropaic**, or guardian, figure of the Sphinx, a hybrid mythological creature with a lion's body and a king's head. The statue may have preceded the pyramids, attracting patrons to the site. The head of the Sphinx has lost its royal beard but still wears the royal headdress. Sculptors carved the recumbent leonine body from a 70 m (230 ft) outcropping of live rock and then encased it with the same Tura limestone used to wrap Khafre's pyramid. They made the diminutively proportioned head from a single block of limestone and set it over the base. The colossal scale of the statue, which acted as a solemn sentinel over the landscape, was without precedent.

Giza, Egypt. The Great Sphinx, ca. 2530 BCE. This colossal sculpture may have been created before or after Khafre built his pyramid. Its body was rock-cut on site, while the head was hewed from stones brought to the site.

of the cliffs. Mentuhotep's real tomb lay hidden deep in the cliff, approached by a long underground tunnel. The design of Deir el-Bahri achieved the antithesis of the pyramids of Giza. Rather than creating a gigantic, impenetrable mass that engaged most of the kingdom's capital for the benefit of a single user, Mentuhotep cut his temple out of the live rock and offered broad planted courts, colonnades, and interior halls as an accessible landscape geared to human scale.

The new attitude toward funerary architecture echoed the political transition to a more diffused system of authority. The eternal benefits of the Nile proved to have limits. Foreigners frequently invaded the region, and Egypt was drawn into conflicts beyond the isolated comforts of its river valley. The monarchy underwent cycles of restoration and decline, suggesting that the only place where the perfect order of society remained possible was in the realm of the dead. From Mentuhotep on, the pharaohs assumed a more human dimension in response to a theological shift in which the king became less important than the cult of the sun god.

Further Reading

David, Rosalie. *The Pyramid Builders of Ancient Egypt: A Modern Investigation of Pharaoh's Workforce*. London: Routledge, 1986.

Fassone, A., and E. Farraris. *Egypt: Pharaonic Period*. Berkeley: University of California Press, 2007.

Giedion, Sigfried. *The Beginnings of Architecture*. Princeton, NJ: Princeton University Press, 1964.

Michałowski, Kazimierz. *Art of Ancient Egypt*. Translated by N. Guterman. London: Thames & Hudson, 1969.

Silverman, David, ed. *Ancient Egypt*. New York: Oxford University Press, 1997.

Wilkinson, Toby, *The Rise and Fall of Ancient Egypt*. New York: Random House, 2011.

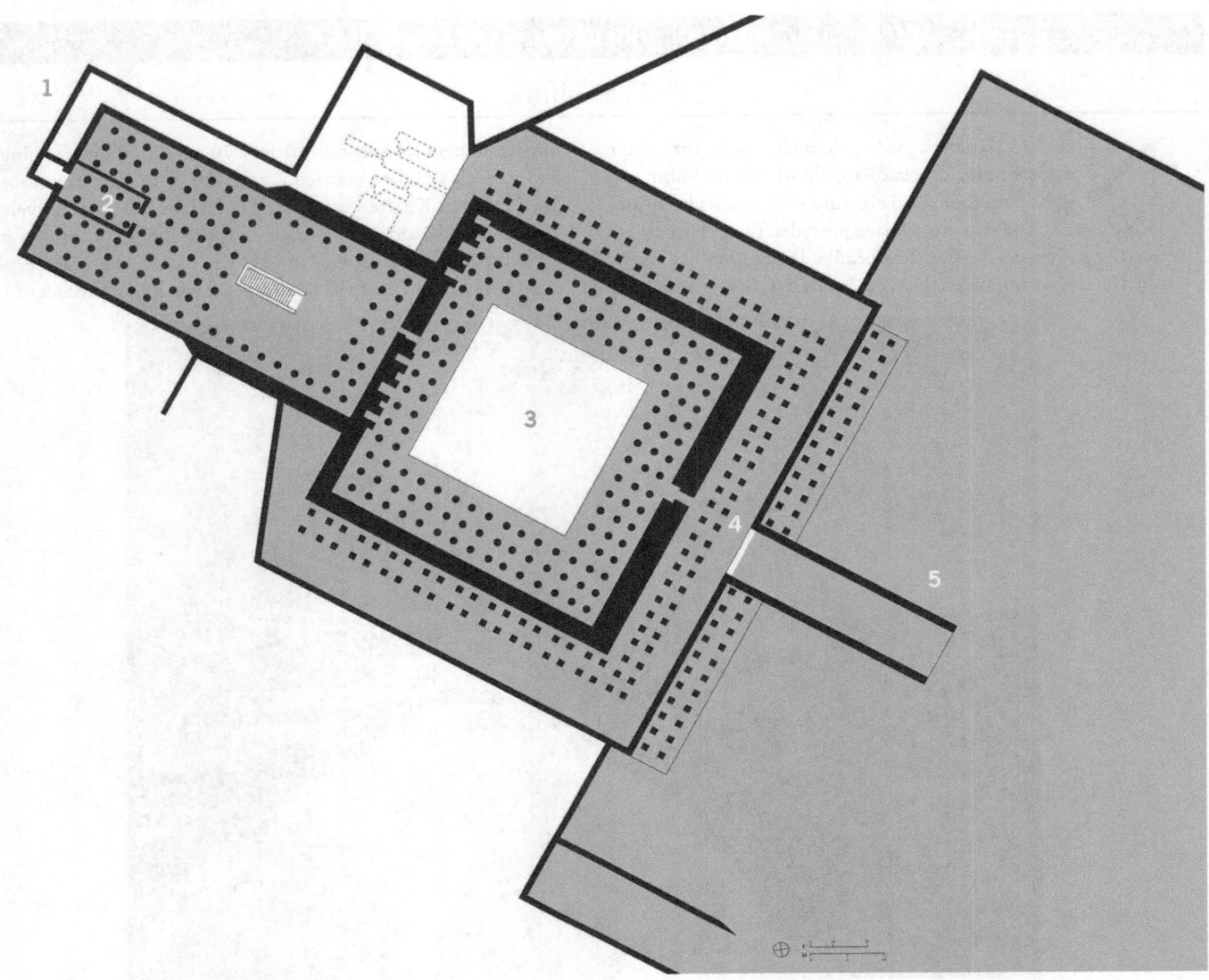

Figure 2.2-8 Deir el-Bahri, Egypt. Plan of the funeral complex of Mentuhotep I, ca. 2010 BCE. The progression moves west from planted forecourt to colonnaded terrace to rock-cut mortuary temple: (1) Mentuhotep I's tomb set in a tunnel within the cliff; (2) shrine to the god Montu-Ra; (3) square platform surrounded by colonnades; (4) porticoes with false tomb; (5) entry garden planted with tamarisk trees.

2.3   THE INDUS VALLEY
Cities without Monuments

The ancient Harappan culture of the Indus–Saraswati River system came to maturity during the third millennium BCE at the same time as the city-states of Sumeria and the pyramids of Old Kingdom Egypt. Unlike the other two cultures, however, the Harappans appear to have been the first urban society to intentionally avoid building monuments. The erratic behavior of monsoons, flooding rivers, and periodic droughts forced them to concentrate on hydrological projects rather than monuments. The archaeological evidence in hundreds of settlements shows extraordinary underground drains, lined with baked bricks, and formidable urban walls meant to resist floods. The only special buildings served as sites for ritual bathing and granaries. Harappan culture seems to have been governed by an austere moral agenda that would reappear among later peoples such as the ancient Spartans, seventeenth-century European Protestants, and twentieth-century socialists. These ancient cities without monuments offered the intriguing alternative that human resources might be better spent on utilitarian, rather than symbolic, projects.

The Indus–Saraswati River System: The Basis of a Hydraulic Civilization

The name of the Harappan culture comes from a town in northern Pakistan, literally translated "mound of the dead," where archaeologists explored the first ruins. While the Indus valley peoples surpassed Southwestern Asian cultures in terms of infrastructure, making towns with straight streets and supplying them with brick-lined drains, they were less attentive about keeping records. So few texts of the Harappan period survive that the language has yet to be decoded. One can only guess about the mentality of the people. As with many lost cultures, the Harappans are mostly understood through the traces of their architecture. The evidence suggests the existence of an urban culture that encouraged a fairly equitable distribution of wealth. Unlike the Mesopotamians and Egyptians, the Harappans left a complete absence of religious and dynastic monuments.

Mehrgarh, the earliest known settlement in the region, dates from as early as 6500 BCE. A system of linked agricultural towns between modern Lahore and Karachi took shape during the fourth millennium BCE. The Bronze-Age Harappans built settlements as far away as Oman and during the third millennium traded with Ur and other Mesopotamian cities. The ancient name of the Harappan territory may have been "Meluhha," since there is reference in Akkadian texts from the time of Sargon, during the twenty-third century BCE, to traders from an eastern place of this name who brought products typical of the Indus region. Harappan glass beads have been found in the Ur tombs. The most prized commodity from the Indus valley was cotton cloth, a fabric the Harappan people invented.

The two best-excavated sites, Harappa in the north and Mohenjo-daro 600 km (373 miles) to its south (Fig. 2.3-1a), are comparable in size to the Mesopotamian city-states. Population estimates range from 20,000 to 30,000. There were many other large cities between them as well, including Kalibangan, Dholavira, and Chanhudaro. Over 1,000 other settlements from this period have been identified. The port city of Lothal, destroyed by a flood ca. 1900 BCE and preserved under a layer of loam, offers some of the richest evidence of this civilization, while some of the largest Harappan cities, such as Gammeriwala and Lakhmirwala, have yet to be excavated. As an urban system, the Harappan culture covered more territory—most of modern Pakistan and the Indian state of Punjab—and was probably more populous than either Mesopotamia or Egypt.

The mystery of why the Harappans disappeared remains unsolved, but like other cultures that created a great civilization and then vanished, such as the Maya in Mexico (see Section 7.3), there was likely no single reason for their disappearance. Harappan cities probably underwent a combination of internal political dissension, environmental mismanagement, ecological disasters, famine, and plagues. The actual disappearance can in the long run be attributed to migration. The ruins show no signs of damage caused by invasion, nor is there forensic evidence of violence to the people. Environmental factors, then as now, were the bottom line of subsistence. The Harappans built their brick cities by clearing wetlands and deforesting the hills. The two rivers of the region, the Indus and the Saraswati (now called Ghaggar), underwent immense alterations. While the Indus seems to have subjected the area to intolerable floods, the Saraswati dried up as a result of the changing course of its Himalayan tributaries to become part of the Thar Desert east of the Indus. The same climate change toward the end of the third millennium BCE that influenced the decline of Ur and Old Kingdom Egypt, bringing colder weather and drought, affected the Indus valley as well. Extreme environmental calamities ultimately reduced the viability of a society based on agricultural surplus. Food shortages forced people to move away from the region.

Harappan culture built modest structures in baked bricks and mud (Fig. 2.3-1b). The Harappans' infrastructure appeared more interesting than their architecture. Instead of great stepped temples or massive pyramids, one finds unusually thick city walls, well-planned reservoirs, and sophisticated systems of brick-lined drains that kept the sewage away from the drinking water. They left no traces of grand palaces, temples, or mausoleums. Unlike the Mesopotamians, the Harappans used baked brick for the foundations of their buildings and for their elaborate drainage systems. Most of the houses in their cities were connected to the conduits, providing a level of sanitation unknown to other cultures until the time of the Romans, two millennia later (see Section 5.1).

The cities of the Indus valley followed a high degree of orthogonal order, indicating a sophisticated social organization and advanced engineering knowledge based on geometry and probably astronomy. Considering the greater sophistication of the geometric plans of the Harappans compared to the Mesopotamians, one can assume that the transmission to other cultures of design based on the right angle came from this eastern source.

▼ **ca. 2600 BCE**

Mohenjo-daro, largest of 1,000 cities in the Indus River valley

The Great Bath at Mohenjo-daro

▲ **ca. 2500 BCE**

▼ **ca. 1900 BCE**

Decline of Harappan culture

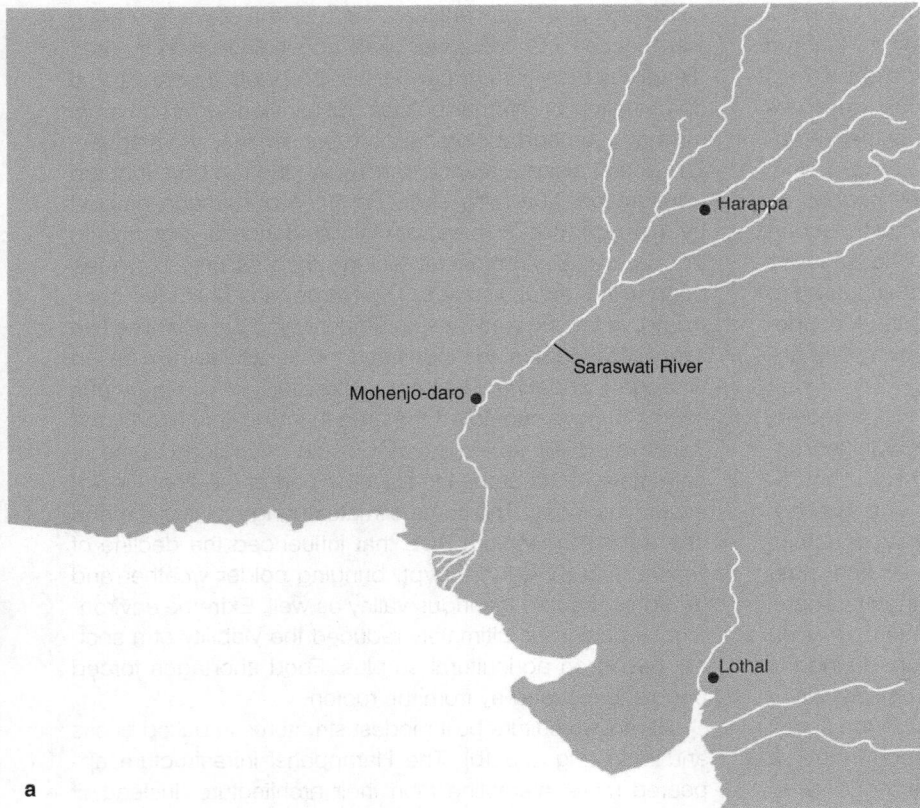

Figure 2.3-1 (a) The Indus valley region. The Saraswati (now Ghaggar) River changed course in the second millennium. Harappa can be seen in the north, Mohenjo-daro in the south, and Lothal on the southern coast at the Gulf of Cambay. (b) Mohenjo-daro. Detail of brickwork and drainage at the Great Bath, ca. 2500 BCE.

monarchs, or powerful rulers implies a relatively horizontal society run by assemblies. The similarity in the plans of Mohenjo-daro and Harappa, more distant from each other than Ur from Mari, suggests a unified regional government. A considerable amount of physical coordination went into the creation of Harappan street grids, walls, canals, and drains, requiring the services of specialized occupations, but the cities apparently prospered without a social or political hierarchy.

Water and Harappan Urbanism

While the Harappan cities appear to have been united into a federation, there is no sign that this was the result of empire building. Throughout the region one finds the same standard burnt-brick unit, with proportions of 4:2:1, and evidence of a universal decimal system for weights and measures that reinforces the suspicion that the cities were politically unified. Each town had impressive walls, but these seem to have been used to defend more against natural calamities than against human invasions. The walls, canals, and reservoirs became components of a system of water management that sought to control the periodic monsoon floods. Nowhere does Harappan culture express the celebration of military might and heroes, leading one to suspect these people of pacifism.

The cities of the Indus valley, such as Mohenjo-daro, usually included an elevated **citadel** area in the west and one or two lower districts, implying some sort of social hierarchy. As Mohenjo-daro was built mostly in fired brick, the large areas that have been excavated give a good idea of its urban fabric. The streets were wide and orderly compared to those of Ur, some of them 8 m (26 ft) across (Fig. 2.3-2). The ruins reveal vaulted drains and courtyard houses with shops in the front and stairways to upper floors. The only prominent monumental presence, a Buddhist stupa on the western mound, was built more than 2,000 years after the Harappan period. The small citadel of Mohenjo-daro followed a linear spine and possessed the most specialized buildings in the city. The Great Bath (Figs. 2.3-1b, 2.3-3) stood on a tapered platform adjacent to the largest building in the city, which was either a reception hall or a

The conspicuous lack of monuments in Harappan cities proves as interesting as the importance of monuments in others. The absence of large structures for high priests,

Figure 2.3-2 Mohenjo-daro, Indus valley. Typical street in lower city, which is unusually wide compared to those of the cities of Mesopotamia, ca. 2500 BCE. Note the covered drain on the right side of the street.

Figure 2.3-3 Mohenjo-daro, Indus valley. The Great Bath, ca. 2500 BCE.

granary, or perhaps both. Below it a hypostyle hall made with rectangular pillars may have served as a site for popular assemblies. The lower town stretched over an extensive set of rolling mounds to the east. The bulk of the population lived and worked in this 4 km^2 (2.6 mile^2) area. Two major cross streets on the cardinal coordinates, similar to the system used by the Romans two millennia later, divided this area into quarters. The houses adhered to a grid plan (Fig. 2.3-4), and the drainage system beneath connected them to a citywide system of public sanitation.

One of the greatest mysteries of Harappan cities remains their lack of religious buildings. Is it possible that an ancient culture devoted so little attention to the supernatural? This is especially hard to believe when one considers the high degree of religiosity in later Indian cultures. It is more likely that the Harappans pursued an experience-based religion without permanent shrines. Many primitive religions, including the Hebraic, specifically rejected architectural or iconographic solutions to the great questions of life, preferring the commitment of bodies in space as the principal form of devotion.

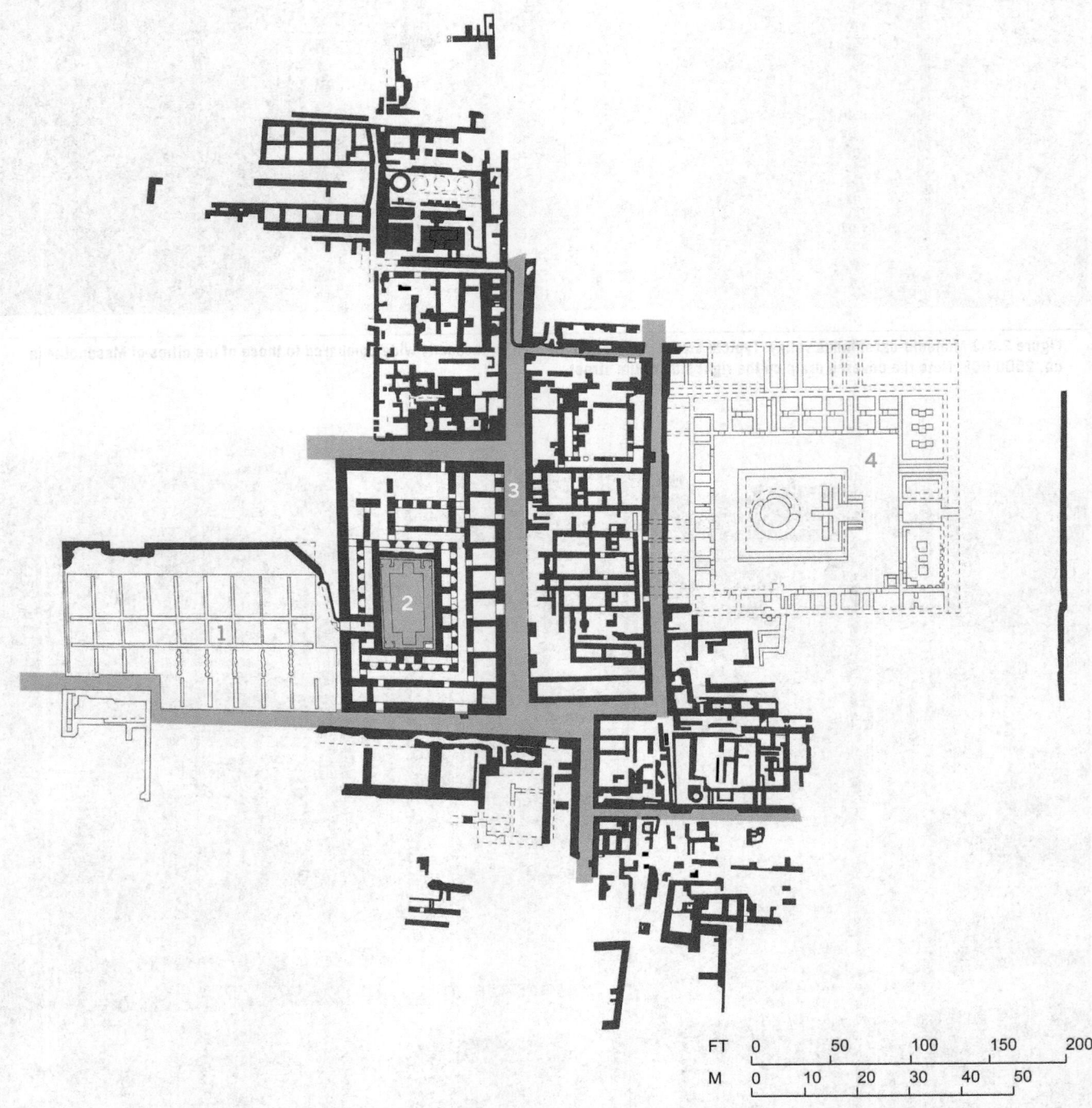

FT   0   50   100   150   200

M   0   10   20   30   40   50

Figure 2.3-4 Mohenjo-daro, Indus valley. Plan of lower town, showing regular orthogonal alignments and broad streets, ca. 2500 BCE: (1) granary; (2) baths; (3) central paved street with subterranean drain; (4) Buddhist stupa, added ca. 400 CE.

The most detailed building in Mohenjo-daro, the Great Bath, may have had religious functions as a structure for ritual bathing, a custom that has remained central to Indian religions. Small rooms and a portico made of brick piers surrounded the pool's courtyard. The pool measured 12 × 7 m (39 × 23 ft) and was 2.4 m (7.5 ft) deep. It was carefully constructed of sawn bricks set in bitumen mortar and sealed with gypsum-based plaster. Two stairways led down to a ledge around the pool for circumambulating the water's edge. In a society so concerned with managing hydraulics, this celebration of water suggests religious connections. The ablutions used in later Hindu and Muslim rituals continued as one type of religious use of water. Considering the region's cycles of droughts and floods, water was a volatile resource, yielding either too much or too little and thus requiring religious respect.

The question of both conserving water and protecting the city from floodwaters led to the construction of immense city walls, the most prominent examples of Harappan buildings. The walls of Dholavira, for instance, were 11 m (35 ft) thick, set in a parallelogram pattern around 1 km² (0.4 mile²) of city fabric. While such thick walls may have been useful for defense, they were much more helpful for flood control. Special elevated areas were put aside for the city's granaries. The walls doubled as reservoirs for water, since the city had no reliable freshwater supply and drought remained even more severe a problem than flooding. As at Mohenjo-daro, the citadel stood in the west, overlooking the rectangular district of the middle town, with its wide north–south axis, and below this the lower town, structured on a more informal grid.

The northern city of Harappa, which is partly occupied by a modern town, also had a citadel in the west, a grid of city streets, and the best-preserved drains of the region. Some of its sewers were covered with corbelled vaults, tall enough to walk through. There was also a large building apparently set aside as a formal granary. Judging from its foundations, it was quite large, reaching 45 × 45 m (148 × 148 ft). The granary was organized bilaterally into two rows of narrow rooms served by a broad corridor. In Mesopotamia and Egypt the priests and temples usually controlled the public granaries, but in Harappa neither iconography nor written traces suggest the presence of a supervising priesthood. Harappan houses had blank facades on the street side and were usually arranged around inner courtyards and built in two stories, with as many as a dozen rooms around the open space. Each house had its own well, a paved bathing place, and a drain leading to the civic sewers.

The Harappans appear to have been remarkably peaceful, equitable, and productive. But as there is no written evidence, one can only make conjectures about their political and religious life. What is obvious is that, unlike the Mesopotamians and Egyptians, they did not need to translate their surplus into great architectural statements. Instead, they seem to have invested in the greater civic concern for defense against the elements, grain storage, and public assemblies. Their cities grew to be large and remarkably well-organized, arranged in grids with wide streets, and their inhabitants enjoyed the sort of plumbing of which other cultures until recent times had never dreamed. The Harappan level of hygiene was much higher than that of many settlements in the same region today. The cities of the Indus valley offered the provocative possibility that humanity could live in relative harmony for over a millennium without recourse to religious or political monuments.

Further Reading

Kenoyer, Jonathon M. *Ancient Cities of the Indus Valley*. New York: Oxford University Press, 1998.

McIntosh, Jane. *A Peaceful Realm: The Rise and Fall of the Indus Civilization*. Boulder, CO: Westview Press, 2001.

Possehl, Gregory. *The Indus Civilization: A Contemporary Perspective*. Walnut Creek, CA: AltaMira Press, 2002.

Visit the free website **www.oup.com/us/ingersoll** to view chapter outlines and study questions; Google Maps showing the location of key sites; links to UNESCO World Heritage Sites; and essays on topics that cross time and culture.

1500–750 BCE

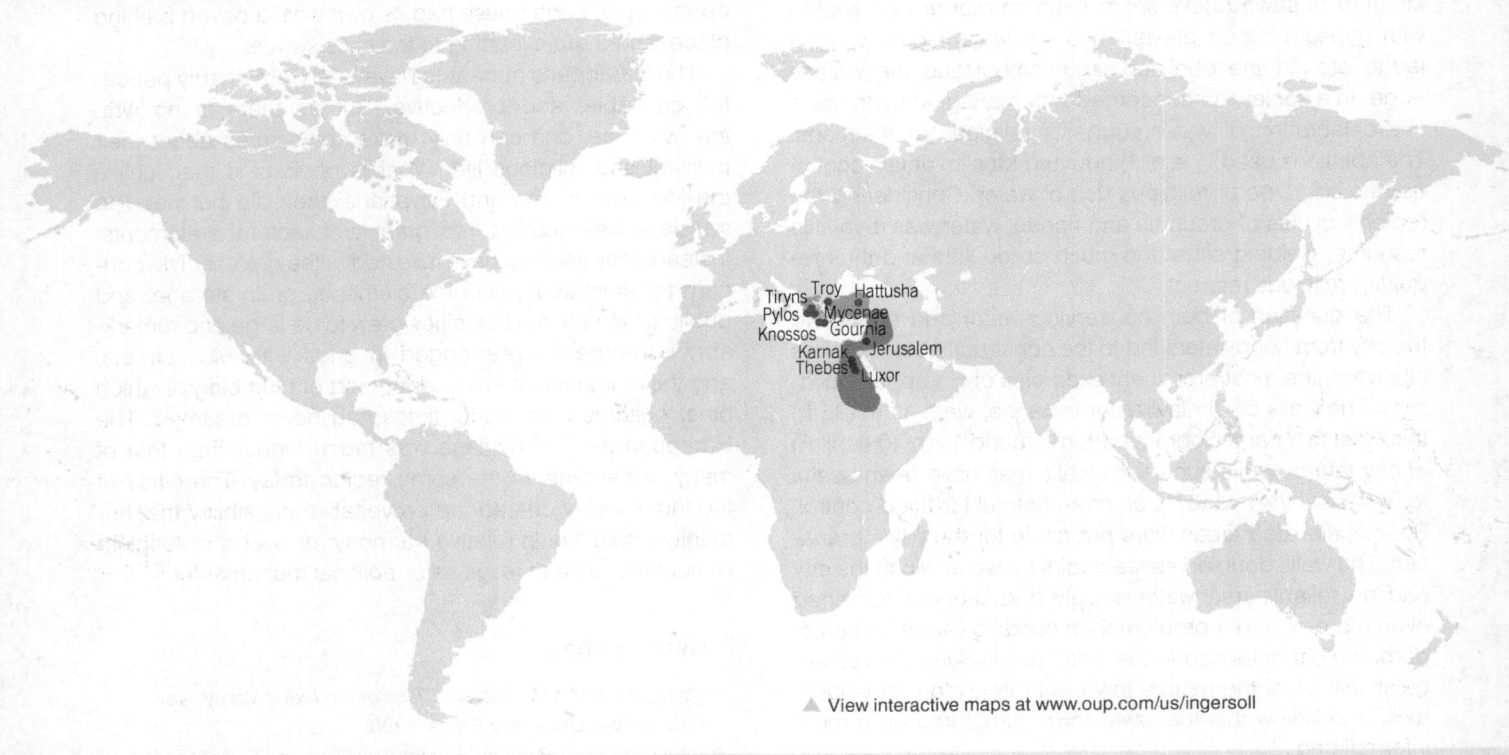

Troy
Hattusha
Tiryns
Pylos
Mycenae
Knossos
Gournia
Karnak
Jerusalem
Thebes
Luxor

▲ View interactive maps at www.oup.com/us/ingersoll

3.1   **THE AEGEAN IN THE BRONZE AGE:** Labyrinths and Cyclopean Walls

3.2   **NEW KINGDOM EGYPT:** Axial Temples and Colossal Statues

3.3   **BIBLICAL JERUSALEM:** Architecture and Memory

The Aegean and central Anatolia (Turkey) abound in rocky landscapes. On one of the region's islands, Crete, a singularly open, apparently peace-loving society emerged. Women played a central role in the religion and government. Lacking fortifications, Cretan architects designed their cities and temples with indirect circulation, giving rise to the legend of the Labyrinth. More war-like cultures, including the Mycenaeans on mainland Greece and the Hittites in Anatolia, built stone cities that appear to have had more fortifications than living space. Crete pursued trading relations with Egypt, while Egypt became the major military rival of the Hittites, culminating in the Battle of Qadesh, which both sides claimed to have won. The Egyptian monarchs, now in the third cycle of dynasties known as the New Kingdom, redirected their ceremonial life to Thebes, with its grand temples at Karnak and Luxor and the burial grounds at Deir el-Bahri. These vast longitudinal compositions were served by immense pylons, colossal statues, and hypostyle halls. During the twelfth century BCE a mass of outsiders, known in ancient texts as the "Sea Peoples," devastated the Aegean Islands and Anatolia and nearly conquered Egypt. In the aftermath of their attacks new powers took root, such as the Phoenicians and the Jews. During the reign of King Solomon, the Jewish dominions reached their largest extent. Relying on the expertise and labor of neighbors, Solomon sponsored the construction of a longitudinal temple on the rocky outcrop of Jerusalem to house the Ark of the Covenant, the token of a unique mandate to worship a single, invisible god.

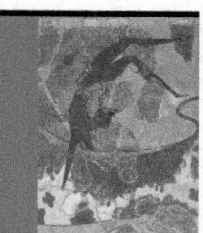

3.1 THE AEGEAN IN THE BRONZE AGE
Labyrinths and Cyclopean Walls

The cultures that developed around the Aegean Sea during the second millennium BCE sited their cities and temples with exceptional sympathy for the landscape. The settlements on Crete, in Greece, and in Turkey reflected a deep belief in the spiritual power of natural phenomena. Sacred hilltops, miracle-working trees, and mysterious grottoes served as the focus of their inhabitants' religious narratives and provided points of orientation for their architecture. These peoples chose hilly sites for their cities and integrated their architecture into the topography. Their architects used **cyclopean masonry,** or large, unrendered stones, to create structures that looked as if they had been formed by natural processes. The Greeks of the next millennium thought such works had been built by giants.

The inhabitants of ancient Crete designed elaborate, convoluted galleries for entering their principal shrines, reminiscent of the underground caves where they performed their primordial mysteries. Their largest compound at Knossos, later known as the Labyrinth, entered the realm of mythology as the path of mystery, where the monstrous Minotaur dwelled. While the symbolic world of Crete was charged with peaceful expressions, that of their contemporaries on mainland Greece and in Turkey privileged militarism. The Mycenaeans in Greece girded their cities with fearsome walls built of cyclopean masonry. They built subterranean galleries as defense strategies rather than for religious mysteries. Likewise, the Hittites in Anatolia, who controlled the Turkish coasts of the Aegean, where settlements traded with Crete and Mycenae, created even grander fortifications and tunnels. Their chief cult site at the capital of Hattusha integrated architectural structures with natural cliff formations. Among these early makers of metal tools, nature still prevailed as the source of divine manifestations, but it also offered itself as a landscape of pragmatic solutions for military agendas.

Minoan Crete: The Sacred Realm of the Labyrinth

One of the most extraordinary cultural awakenings of the Bronze Age occurred on Crete, a long, narrow island, 200 × 60 km (120 × 35 miles), on the southern rim of the Aegean Sea (Fig. 3.1-1). During the second millennium BCE, from roughly 1900 to 1600 BCE, the Cretans commanded large commercial fleets, trading with Egypt, ancient Turkey, and the cities of the eastern Mediterranean. They enjoyed a vibrant urban life that became legendary among the Greeks of the following millennium. Homer sang of Crete's "ninety cities," but in truth only a handful of its settlements reached a scale that could be called urban. The largest was Knossos, centrally located on the northern shore, which at its height may have had 50,000 inhabitants. The grand structure of the major religious complex at Knossos, later known as the Labyrinth, rose on the upper edge of the city. Once thought to be the palace of the legendary King Minos of Greek mythology, it more likely served as a convent-like temple compound run by powerful priestesses. There were no kings on Crete during the period of the great temple, and the existence of Minos remains in doubt, yet his name has endured to categorize the ancient culture of Crete.

Unlike most ancient peoples, the Minoans built their cities without defensive walls. The five major cities of ancient Crete rose on naturally protected hillsides but completely lacked fortifications, indicating an absence of internal conflicts. The various cities on the island belonged to a confederation with strong religious ties to the cult center at the Labyrinth of Knossos. Their maritime activities and colonial enterprise in the Greek islands and on the Ionian coast of Turkey ensured an awareness of the ways of warrior states. But in a society without pronounced hierarchies, rather than fortifying their cities, they built fortified communication towers along the coasts to link their various settlements and protect the entire island.

The Minoans enacted frequent processions to remote natural sites, performing sacrifices at sacred caves, sacred trees, and sacred mountaintops. At some sites they prepared paved platforms to accommodate crowds. The Skotino Cave rivaled Lascaux and other Neolithic precedents in grandeur. Its central cavern surpassed the dimensions of a Gothic cathedral. Other caves in Crete followed circuitous passages, suggesting a model for the indirect routes of the Labyrinth. The position of sacred landscapes influenced the orientation of Minoan urban temples. At the Labyrinth of Knossos the axis of the central Bull Court pointed to the sacred indented peak of Mount Juktas, where a walled *temenos* protected the entry to a sacred cave.

The ruins at Gournia, on the bay of Mirabello in the northeast, offer the best-preserved example of Minoan urban layouts (Fig. 3.1-2). With only about sixty houses, the city's population amounted to fewer than 1,000, yet the urban form of Gournia, which included a temple and a shaped public space, appears to have been more complex than a farming village. A tight mesh of narrow streets laced around the low hill. On the crest stood the temple compound, and the paved main street stretched from there across the hill. The intersecting alleys descended perpendicularly as flights of steps. A small assembly space opened at the western entry to the temple, while the southern edge of the compound overlooked a rectangular Bull Court, entered by an L-shaped arrangement of shallow steps.

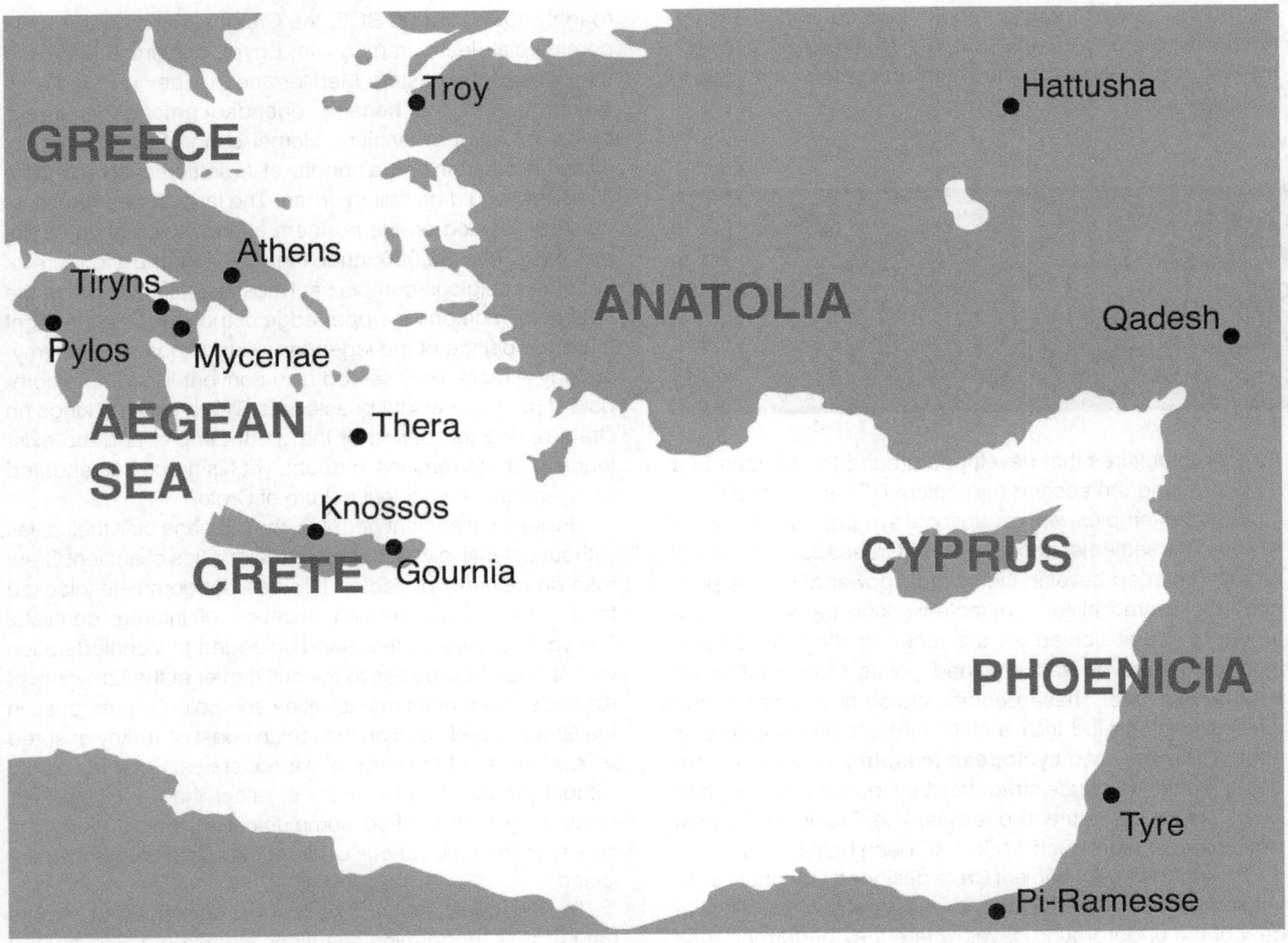

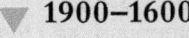

Figure 3.1-1 The Bronze-Age Aegean.

The houses at Gournia were small and densely packed. They showed remarkable equality in economic status and, while modest in size, boasted the luxury of indoor plumbing. The stone drains and flushable toilets of ancient Crete evoke the plumbing achievements of the Harappans during the previous millennium (see Section 2.3) and remain among the few ancient examples of sophisticated domestic hygiene. The Minoans built their houses with a lower story of small storerooms made of stone walls without doors or windows and an upper floor made of mud-brick walls with timber braces, which offered better seismic performance. Their artisans plastered the walls and decorated them with spirals and botanical motifs. The inhabitants entered the upper story by an external stair and used the lower level as a cellar. A remarkable series of ceramic tiles discovered at Knossos depicts the top stories of the houses with windows, an architectural element not found in other cultures of the time. These apertures, with four to six panes, required a transparent cover such as oiled parchment.

TIME LINE

1900–1600 BCE

Minoan culture flourishes on Crete

Eruption of Thera, Santorini (Greece)

▲ ca. 1600 BCE

1450 BCE

Temple of Knossos (Crete) rebuilt by Mycenaeans

Hittites expand Hattusha (Turkey)

▲ ca. 1400 BCE

Knossos, the center of the federation, had been settled since the sixth millennium BCE. Around 2000 BCE peoples migrating from Anatolia and the eastern shores of the Mediterranean supplanted an earlier village-based community. The economy of Knossos depended in large measure on overseas exchange for metalwork and textiles. The Minoan invention of clay turntables prefigured the potter's wheel and enhanced their much-admired ceramics industry. During the mid-second millennium BCE, trade with cities on the Ionian coast of Turkey and the Greek islands and mainland fostered the growth of a series of colonial depots in towns such as Miletus, Akrotiri on the island of Thera (now Santorini), and possibly Mycenae on the Greek mainland, the city that later conquered Crete.

The first Labyrinth of Knossos, the city's great temple complex, was constructed around 1900 BCE but collapsed in an earthquake two centuries later. After its reconstruction, it fell into ruin a second time during the volcanic eruption of Thera around 1600 BCE. The final version (Fig. 3.1-3), built under the new government of Mycenae around 1450 BCE, probably reproduced the design of the earlier temple. The bull imagery throughout the structure refers to the local prototype for Poseidon, honored by Greeks as the great earth-shaking god of the sea who had so seriously threatened the temple at the time of Thera's eruption. The structure, roughly 140 m (459 ft) per side, rose in isolation several kilometers inland from the port on a slope and was shielded from the sight of the sea by an intervening

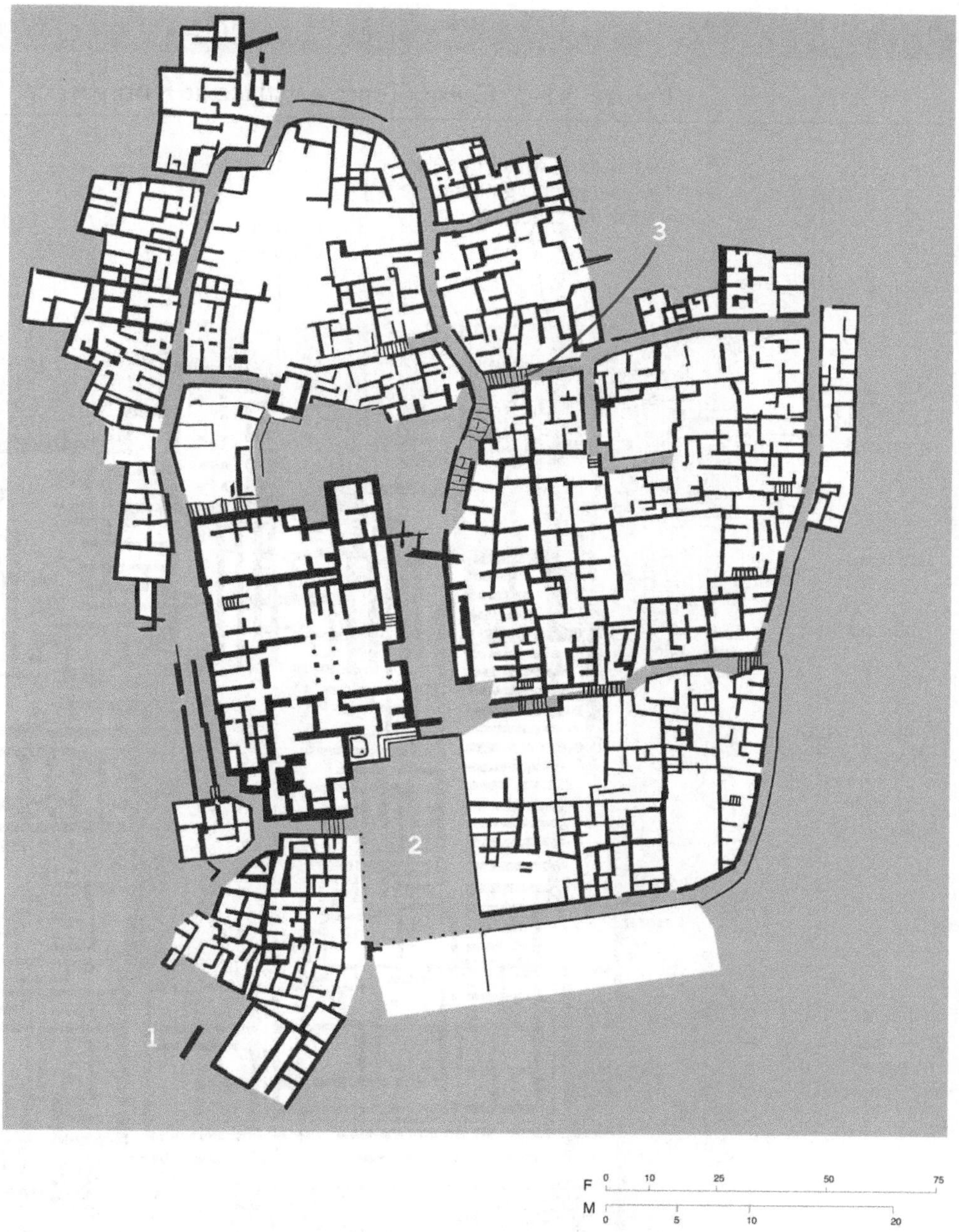

Figure 3.1-2 Crete. Plan of Gournia, ca. 1600 BCE: (1) palace-temple; (2) ceremonial court; (3) steep cross streets with stairs.

▼ ca. 1250 BCE

Rebuilding of Hittite sanctuary of Yazilikaya near Hattusha (Turkey)

Mycenae, Greece, rebuilds cyclopean walls, adds Lion Gate

▲ ca. 1250 BCE

▼ 1250 BCE

Beehive tomb, so-called Treasury of Atreus, built in Mycenae, Greece

Possible date of Trojan War

▲ ca. 1190s BCE

Figure 3.1-3 Crete. Temple/palace at Knossos, ca. 1450 BCE.

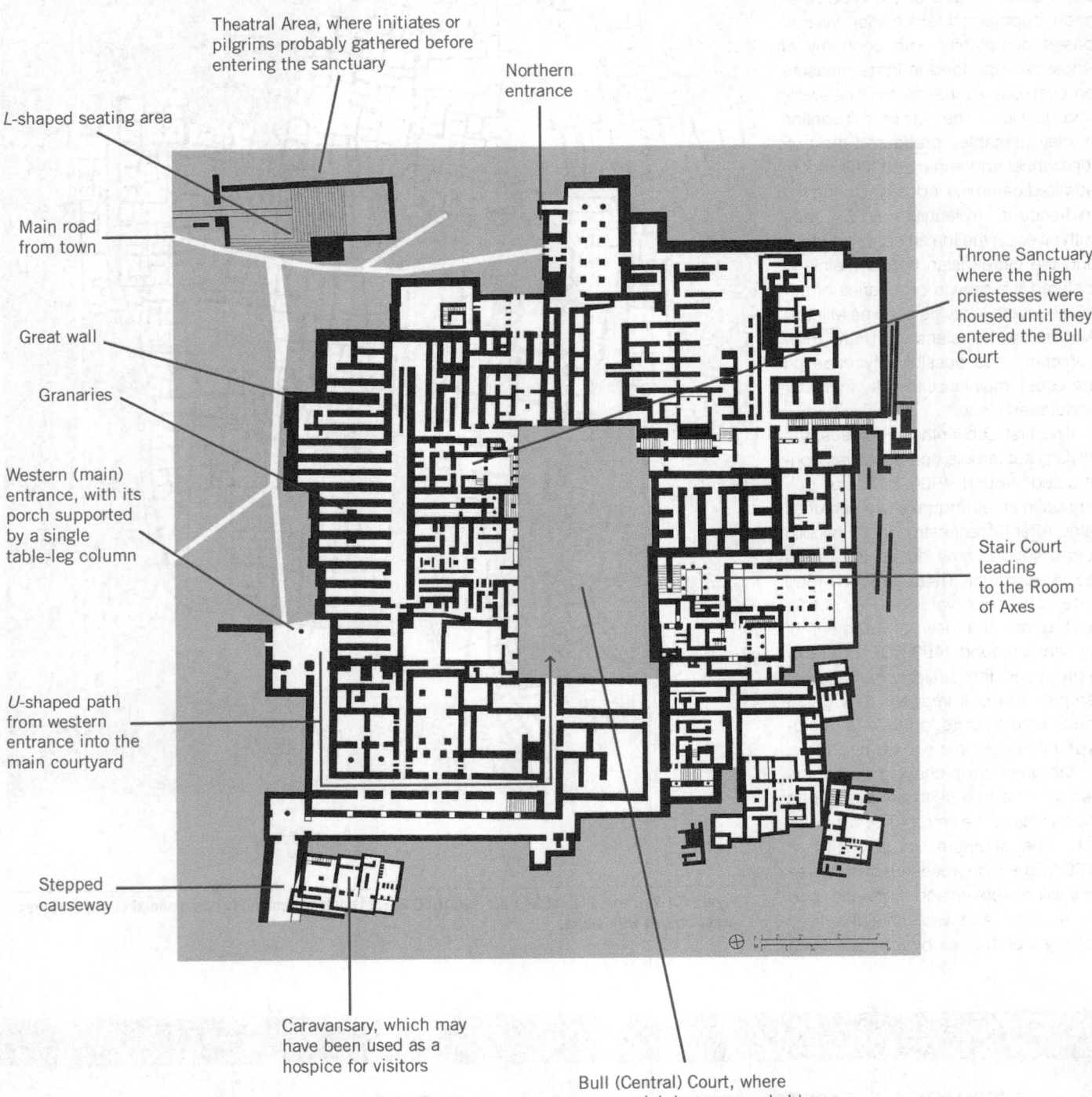

Theatral Area, where initiates or pilgrims probably gathered before entering the sanctuary

Northern entrance

L-shaped seating area

Main road from town

Throne Sanctuary, where the high priestesses were housed until they entered the Bull Court

Great wall

Granaries

Western (main) entrance, with its porch supported by a single table-leg column

Stair Court leading to the Room of Axes

U-shaped path from western entrance into the main courtyard

Stepped causeway

Caravansary, which may have been used as a hospice for visitors

Bull (Central) Court, where ceremonial dances were held

hill. A carefully paved road with a central rut for drainage extended in straight sections from the temple to the harbor city, passing by the so-called Little Palace, a secondary cult site for ceremonial functions. Aside from the improvised street at Khirokitia on Cyprus (see Section 1.1) and the well-drained streets of the Indus valley (see Section 2.3), there were no precedents for such a purposely constructed street. As the road approaches the temple it forks to the left, giving on to a paved enclosure, 15 × 10 m (48 × 32 ft), commonly called the Theatral Area (Fig. 3.1-4a). A thick retaining wall frames

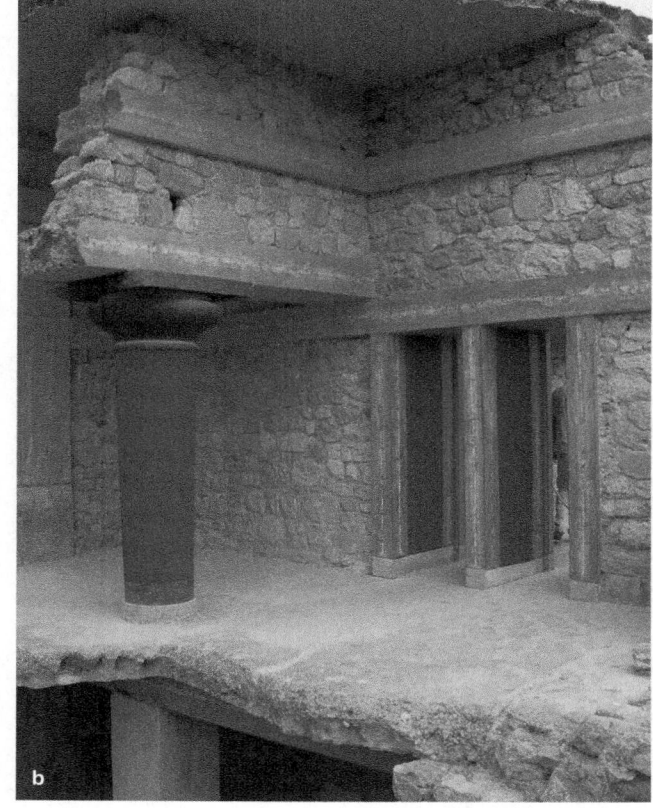

Figure 3.1-4 Knossos, Crete. (a) View of the Theatral Area.

the space on the north side, and two broad sets of stairs join to form an *L*-shaped seating area. It probably served as a gathering space for initiates or pilgrims before visiting the inner areas of the temple.

The western and northern **elevations** of the Labyrinth facing the city appear to have been fortified. Massive walls, 2.5 m (8 ft) thick, rose without windows, making them eminently defensible. The jogging contours of these walls resemble the buttressed corners of fortified palaces in ancient Southwest Asia. These thick stone walls protected a bank of long, narrow storerooms, similar to those built in Mesopotamian temple compounds (see Section 2.1). Like the palace-temples in other ancient cities, the Minoan Labyrinth served to amass agricultural tribute, monopolizing the grain supply. The giant *pithoi* storage jars for grain and olive oil seem to have been displayed for view from an interior gallery that ran along the western wing of the complex.

Another inherently defensive aspect of the Knossos temple was the disorientation caused by its maze-like circulation: none of the eight entry points led to a direct path to the central court. The principal entry at the West Porch rested on a single "table-leg" column—a red-tinted wooden post that tapered down in an oval section from a bulbous black capital (Fig. 3.1-4b). Such an eccentric

Figure 3.1-4 Knossos, Crete. (b) Table-leg column used throughout the temple/palace, ca. 1450 BCE.

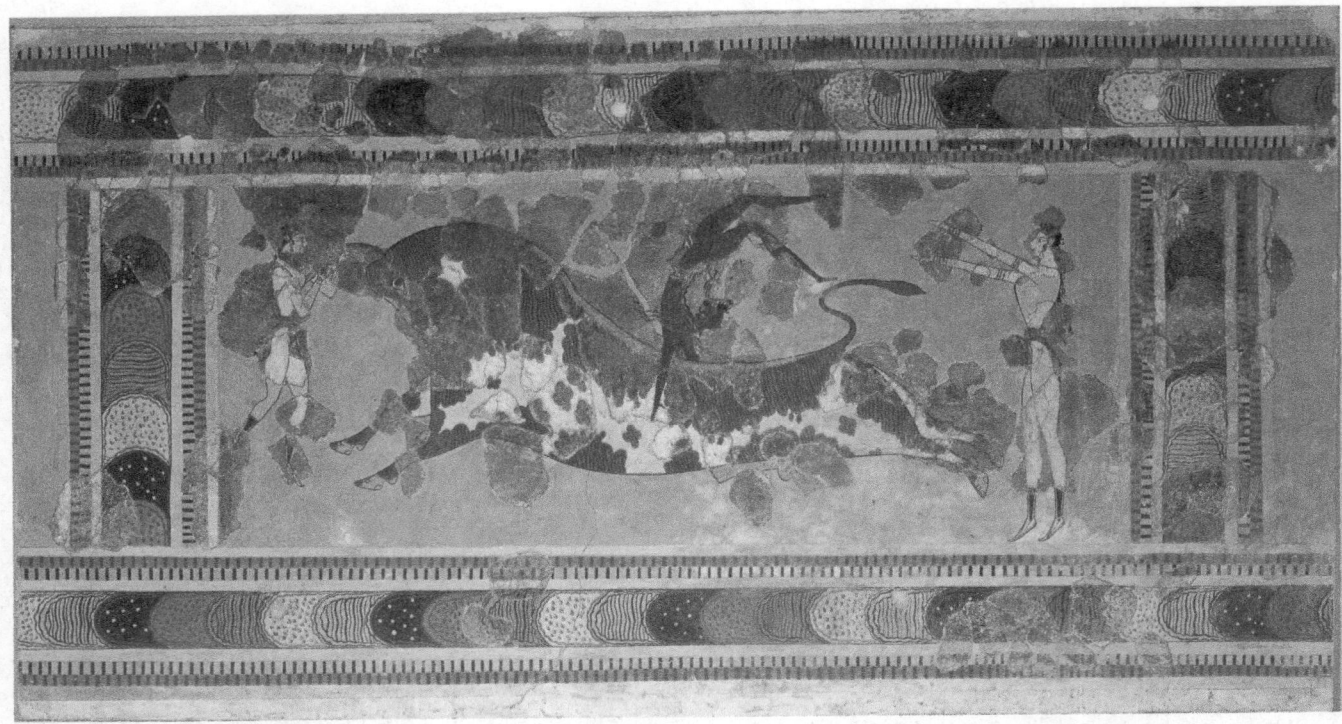

Figure 3.1-5 Knossos, Crete. "Toreador" fresco, ca. 1450 BCE.

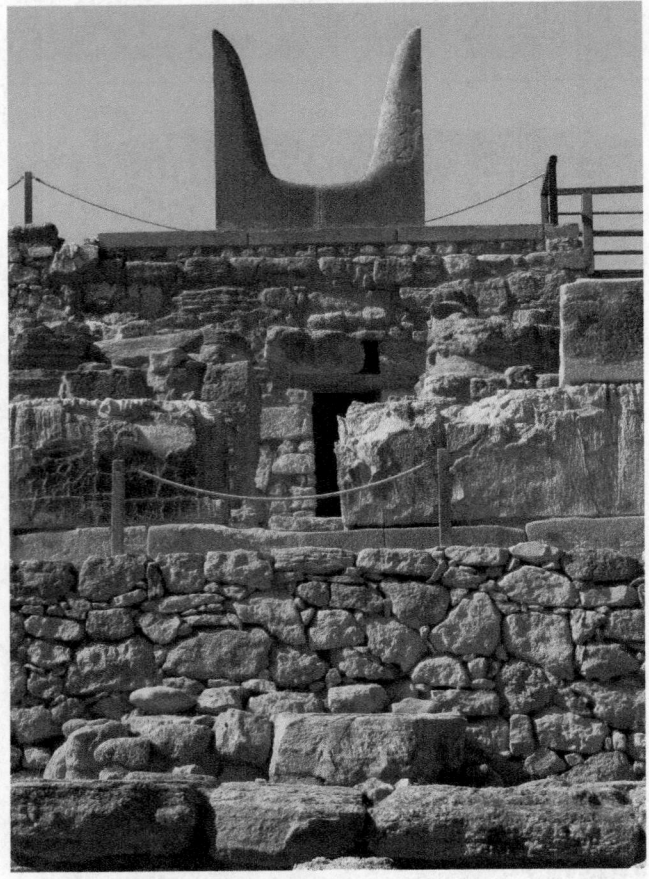

Figure 3.1-6 Knossos, Crete. Horns of Consecration overlooking the great court, ca. 1450 BCE.

column, antithetical to the compressive forces placed on it, acquired a deep symbolic significance as the manifestation of a god.

Whether the lower levels of the Labyrinth of Knossos were designed specifically as a maze or evolved as such, the winding paths inspired legends. Sources after the fall of the Minoans referred to the structure as the "Labyrinth." The entry sequence from the West Porch followed a 100 m (328 ft) long corridor that made two right-angle turns before reaching the Central Court. Hundreds of life-size painted images of young men and women bearing sacrificial offerings lined this Corridor of the Procession, leaving the first of many clues to the complex's religious function.

The Bull Court, a near-perfect rectangle at 53 × 27 m (174 × 89 ft), occupied the center of the Labyrinth. The similarity in size and proportions of the courts in the four other major Minoan temples of the time indicates a clear ritual standard. The bull dance, or *taurokatharpsia*, shown in the "Toreador" **fresco** (Fig. 3.1-5), was probably performed in these courts. In this painting a young boy is flipping over a bull, assisted by two female acrobats to either side. Throughout the temple stylized sculpted bulls' horns appeared as finials along the parapets, and the monumental Horns of Consecration (Fig. 3.1-6) on the southern terrace cast their shadow over the court while framing the perfect view of Mount Juktas.

The stairs and projecting balconies on the elevations facing the court purposely avoided symmetry. They led to rooms for hospitality, administration, production, religion, and dwelling. On the western side near the north corner, a ground-floor **loggia** opened to the so-called Throne

Figure 3.1-7 Knossos, Crete. Throne Sanctuary in the Labyrinth, ca. 1450 BCE.

Sanctuary (Fig. 3.1-7). This sequence of two rooms, with alabaster benches lining the walls and porphyry basins for lustrations in the center, probably served as a sanctuary for the high priestesses before their appearances to the crowds in the Bull Court. Ceramic statues depicting snake goddesses, their breasts freely exposed from the bodice of their gowns as they hold up snakes with hieratic authority, suggest how the priestesses might have performed their epiphanies when presenting themselves to mortals in the form of goddesses (Fig. 3.1-8). Evidence of the use of opium in trance-inducing rituals helps to explain some of the Minoans' euphoric decorations.

The Labyrinth of Knossos rose four stories high, with over 1,000 rooms. The western side served administrative functions and as granaries, the base of the northeastern quarter had workshops and bakeries, and the southeastern quarter housed the religious hierarchy. Winding corridors led to several sanctuary chambers in the latter area. The largest **chapel**, the Double Axe Sanctuary, carried numerous depictions of the *labrys*, the Minoan double-headed axe, from which the word *labyrinth* derives. The great stairway in the eastern wing rose as a switchback parallel to a colonnaded light well. This spacious light trap, which extended two floors below the level of the court and two above, would

have infused the dense collection of rooms with a bright feeling of openness.

The rear elevations of the Labyrinth were animated with numerous **colonnaded** loggias that opened to the landscape. A stepped bridge on the southern edge connected to a smaller structure on the other side of the stream known as the "Caravansary." This may have served as a hospice for visitors, or perhaps victims, who were received and ritually bathed there before being led through winding corridors into the temple's court.

The Minoans' attention to nature led them to build non-axial arrangements of space that were adapted to the topographic qualities of the land. They assembled their architecture piecemeal, adjusting it to the uneven terrain. They added windows, terraces, and loggias to keep these structures in contact with the landscape. While the devastating seismic catastrophes that struck them periodically should have led to a certain dread of nature, their buildings and decorations express a unique and joyful sense of oneness with it.

Mycenae: Cyclopean Walls and Megaron Palaces

Around 1450 BCE Minoan culture gave way to Mycenaean conquerors. Although the destruction of the cities and

Figure 3.1-8 Knossos, Crete. Ceramic figure depicting the Minoan priestess dressed as snake goddess, ca. 1600–1450 BCE.

temples of Crete has been linked to the great volcanic eruption that consumed the island of Thera around this time, it is now clear that the eruption occurred more than a century before the conquest of Crete by the Mycenaeans from the Greek mainland. The environmental damage this eruption caused undoubtedly weakened the Minoans' resistance. The Mycenaeans, proto-Greeks who ruled Crete until their downfall some time after 1200 BCE, demolished all of the Minoan temples except the Labyrinth of Knossos. Clay tablets found at Knossos, written in Mycenaean Linear B script, refer to the presence of Mycenaean kings, and the few vaulted beehive tombs for members of royalty built in the Mycenaean style substantiate this political transition. If King Minos ever existed, chances are he lived during this Mycenaean period, as there is little sign of kingship on Crete before this time.

Mycenae was a small hilltop city about 90 km (56 miles) south of Athens that gave its name to the war-like peoples who dominated the Aegean area between 1600 and 1200 BCE. During the expansion of Mycenaean power the Minoan artistic influence predominated. The Lion Gate in Mycenae (Fig. 3.1-9) shows two lions preening on either side of a Cretan table-leg column. The decoration of Mycenaean palaces and religious paraphernalia likewise exhibits strong borrowings from Crete. But in architecture, there could be no more different approach. Mycenaean designers created predominantly lithic, solid, and hierarchical structures based on military imperatives. Their cities clung to steep outcroppings like the Acropolis in Athens, which they girded with thick walls. The royal privilege of warrior kings seen in the **megaron** palaces and beehive tombs of the Mycenaeans differed immensely from the structures of the nonhierarchical Minoan society. Mycenaean houses were tiny and dark, without windows opening to nature. Their artistic intentions gravitated more toward dread than pleasure.

The great citadels of Mycenaean lords date from around 1400–1250 BCE, several centuries after the migratory wave that brought their forebears into Greece. These people positioned their cities strategically on defensible eminences with a good supply of water. The summit of Mycenae commanded the sea approach from Crete and the southern Aegean in general, as well as the land road to Corinth and central Greece beyond. It clung to a bold outcrop of hard limestone that they made impregnable by the addition of cyclopean walls—a descriptive term used by Pausanias in the second century CE that referred to the Cyclops, the one-eyed giant Polyphemus in Homer's *Odyssey* who tossed huge stones at the escaping

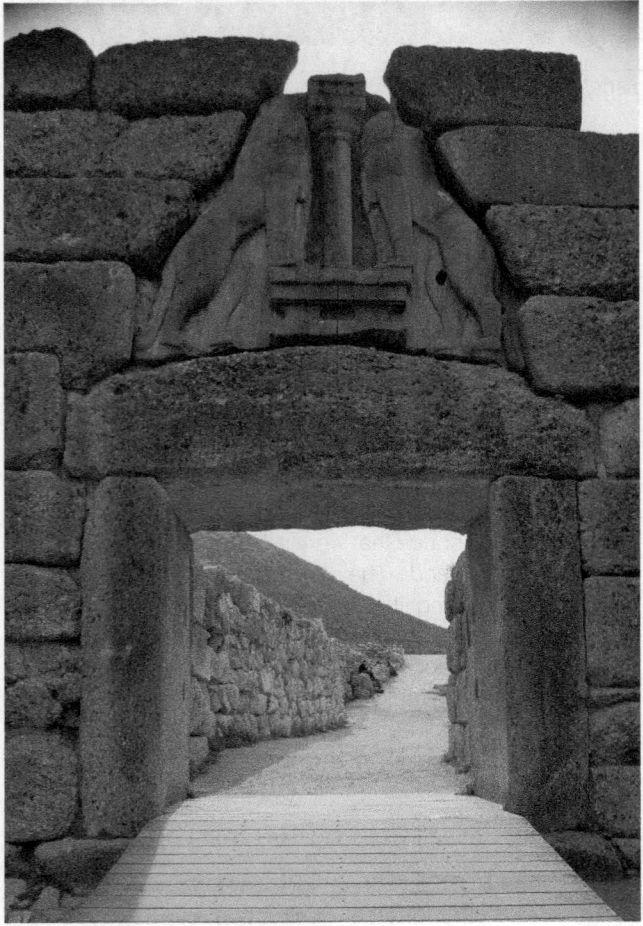

Figure 3.1-9 Mycenae, Greece. Lion Gate in the new set of walls, ca. 1250 BCE.

The Minotaur in the Labyrinth

The Labyrinth at Knossos acquired its name later in its history because of its resemblance to the legendary maze built to house the mythical Minotaur. The Temple of Knossos was built not as a maze but like earlier Assyrian palaces, such as the palace of Zimrilim in Mari (see Section 2.1), which had intentionally indirect passageways as a form of controlling access. A true maze for confounding intruders was built at Fayum, Egypt, as part of the funerary complex of Pharaoh Amenhemhat III during the eighteenth century BCE. The Labyrinth of Knossos was less maze-like than it might at first appear, with no passages more complex than the *U*-shaped processional entry with its frescoes of tribute bearers. The circuitous paths of the Labyrinth may have been inspired by the mysterious courses mapped through sacred caves and probably served as a stage for initiatory rites that culminated in the ceremonial courtyard. According to the founding legend of Athens, King Minos of Crete engaged the exiled Athenian architect Daedalus to build the Labyrinth. It was meant to conceal the shame of his family, the Minotaur, a monster with a bull's head and a man's body, born of the unhappy union between the king's wife and a bull. The Athenians were obliged by the Cretan king to send a yearly tribute of seven youths and seven maidens to be devoured by the Minotaur as compensation for the murder of Minos's son. One year the Athenian prince Theseus came to Crete as part of the tribute. There he befriended Minos's daughter Ariadne, who gave him a ball of twine to find his way out of the Labyrinth. Theseus killed the beast and escaped the Labyrinth but then abandoned the princess and, after unintentionally provoking his father Aegeus's suicide, rebuilt Athens as the city's hero-founder.

Pylos, Greece. Rendering of maze designed on a clay tablet, ca. 1300 BCE.

boats of Ulysses and his men after they tricked and blinded him. A second set of walls, added in 1250 BCE, has a thickness of 6–7 m (20–23 ft), employing rough-hewn boulders that weigh as much as 5 tons apiece. Mycenae's defenses protected the houses of the city's elite and served in times of danger as shelter for the population of the township, most of whom lived outside the walls on the adjacent slopes.

The Lion Gate, the main entry to the citadel of Mycenae, was added at the same time as the new walls. Made of monolithic pieces, its triangular lintel weighed close to 25 tons. The masons used metal tools to drill ruts into the threshold to secure the heavy wooden gates. A bastion enveloped the gate, providing a broad firing platform for the defenders to shoot at intruders using their unshielded right hands.

Mycenae controlled the coastal fortress of Tiryns (Fig. 3.1-10) a few kilometers to the east. The only access to its citadel burrowed through a thick, corbelled arch along the fortress's eastern flank. Bastions lined both sides of the ramp leading to the second gate, allowing the occupants to fire down on enemy invaders. A small plaza opened in front of the palace gate at the top of the ramp. **Casemates**, small chambers scooped out of the upper walls, were vaulted with formidable cyclopean corbels to serve as billeting stations during a siege. A long, secret tunnel passed under the walls and through a square bastion to the main water supply outside the citadel. Farther north, a second secret tunnel led to a subterranean spring that could be used during times of siege.

The Mycenaeans' heavily fortified hilltop towns resulted from local infighting among feudal lords. Each lord built a great hall, or megaron, that dominated the townscape. This oblong parallelepiped, entered by a colonnaded **porch**, rose taller than the other structures of the palace

CLOSE-UP

Figure 3.1-10 Tiryns, Greece. Plan of fortress, 1400–1200 BCE.

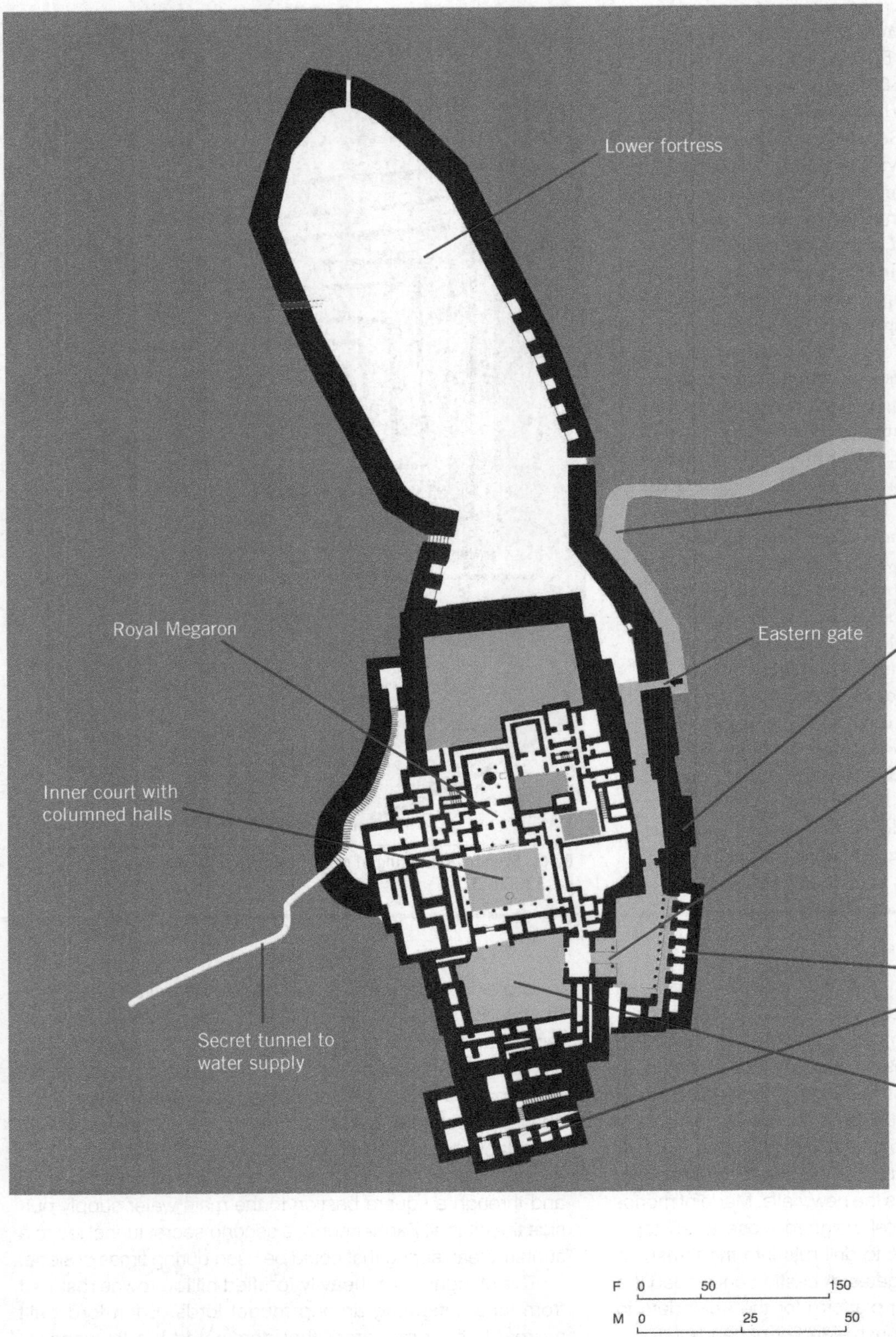

Lower fortress
Ramp
Bastions
Royal Megaron
Eastern gate
Great Propylon
(Portico)
Inner court with
columned halls
Casemates
Secret tunnel to
water supply
Plaza in front
of palace gate
F 0 50 150
M 0 25 50

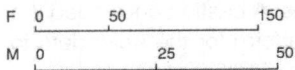

complex. The designers built the king's hall to be grand enough to offer hospitality to the gods, and during the next millennium the megaron type, with its *cella* and porch, inspired the layout of the classical Greek temple type. The royal megarons in Mycenae and Athens were in fact subsequently converted into temples. The megaron type probably migrated to Greece with settlers from Anatolia, although one related house type of the pre-Mycenaean period, the so-called hairpin megaron, appears to be a native Greek archetype, similar to the prehistoric long-house (see Section 1.2). Its *U*-shaped structure terminated in a curved apse, creating a semicircular back room. The primeval builders covered the early megarons with pitched roofs, but the Mycenaeans, influenced by Crete, left them flat.

The megaron of Pylos, a town 100 km (66 miles) southwest of Mycenae, offers the best-documented example of the type. The hall was roughly 10 × 20 m (33 × 66 ft), with an entry porch that established an axis through a pair of columns. The porch faced south, as did most Mycenaean royal halls. Guards would have stood duty in the vestibule between the porch and the inner hall. The great hall focused on a circular hearth about 5 m (16 ft) in diameter that was raised up a step and paved with stuccoed clay. Four posts formed a square around the hearth and held up a band of clerestory openings above the level of the rest of the roof, bringing top lighting into the hall and allowing the smoke to escape. The royal throne sat against the eastern wall flanked by painted griffins. The stuccoed floor was laid out in squares, each painted with a different abstract pattern in several colors. The walls carried frescoes of musicians, the hunt, soldiers' shields, and abstract patterns. While they clad the exterior of their megarons with finely cut limestone, the Mycenaeans built their walls of rubble, reinforced by a skeletal frame of horizontal and vertical timbers. The practice of using a thin **veneer** of stone to cover up inferior construction materials probably came from the Minoans, who lined the lower walls of their temples with alabaster **orthostats** to convey a sense of opulence.

Mycenaean architecture, made of rough cyclopean masonry and rubble walls, seems in keeping with a highly militarized society. The refined stonework of their funerary architecture, however, proves they could build with exacting smoothness and precision. Most of the gravesites of Mycenae lay along the first stretch of the road leading away from their citadel. They ranged from simple shaft tombs and a stone circle for collective graves (Fig. 3.1-11a,b) to the monumental **tholos**, or beehive, type (Fig. 3.1-12). Over 100 *tholoi* have been found at Mycenae, with the oldest dating to 1500 BCE. Just inside the Lion Gate, a circular stone wall 28 m (92 ft) in diameter enclosed the earliest royal tombs, which once stood outside the walls. Vertical panels, or *stelae*, marked the shaft graves as symbolic portals that let the wandering souls into and out of the tombs. The Mycenaean tombs contained gilded breast-plates and death masks of the buried princes.

The concept of shaft graves with false doors, the practice of swathing bodies in bandages and mummifying them, and the generous use of gold suggest direct familiarity with funeral practices in Egypt. Mycenaean mercenaries worked for the pharaohs during the sixteenth century BCE to help expel the foreign Hyksos rulers from the Nile delta area. Cretan ships transported this mainland army, reinforcing the links among the three cultures.

During the final century of Mycenaean power, the kings and queens commissioned mounded conical structures, the *tholos* tombs, built with corbelled domes of finely cut ashlar masonry. To build a *tholos*, they began by laying out a deep causeway, or **dromos**, for the stone-lined entry. After preparing a circular area, they raised a masonry corbelled dome and then covered it with earth to help stabilize the structure. An outer retaining wall that wrapped around the haunch of the dome added further support.

The finest *tholos*, the fancifully named Treasury of Atreus, had a *dromos* extending 36.5 m (120 ft). The side walls of this entry path rose in gradual steps as they reached the top of the two-story facade of the dome. The jambs of the doorway imitated the slant of Egyptian **pylons** and carried an immense lintel block that extended across the facade, locking into the blocks of the *dromos* walls. Half-columns of green limestone decorated with chevron bands framed the door. The downward tapering of these columns and their cushiony capitals clearly derived from Minoan precedents. Smaller half-columns stood above them at the second-story level, framing a relieving triangle that was originally screened over with a decorated slab. The triangle helped deflect the compressive forces pushing down on the lintel, not unlike the relieving slabs placed above Khufu's burial chamber inside the great pyramid at Giza (see Section 2.2). Bronze plaques fixed in place with bronze nails coated the double door of the tomb as well as the impeccably joined surfaces of the interior. The curve of the rotunda, which rose 13.5 m (44 ft), started at floor level, forming a sweeping arc over the buried prince. The designers attempted to make it more sky-like by adding bronze rosettes to the dome's surface.

The burial would have taken place in a small rectangular chamber to one side of the rotunda. The funeral procession would have marched down the *dromos* carrying the bodies of the king and his wife and an attendant or two, who may have been forced to kill themselves for the privilege of being buried with their lord. The celebrants would have lowered the king into his grave, commonly a pit beneath the floor, and arranged his treasures about him: bronze daggers inlaid with gold and electrum, cups of precious materials, ornaments, and seals. They would then have stacked logs over the opening of the pit and added valuable objects and clay pots with food and drink and then set the fire. The pyre would have collapsed into the grave pit as it burned. After filling the hole with earth to cover the king and the accompanying bodies, the celebrants placed large stone slabs over the grave and sealed the door to the *tholos*. They then

would have sacrificed horses in the *dromos* before filling it with earth. Such funeral rites descended from the traditions of the passage tombs in the Neolithic cairn mounds (see Section 1.3).

All of the Mycenaean cities and the settlements in the Aegean were destroyed during the late thirteenth century BCE, probably as a result of a combination of internal uprisings as well as invasions. As with the collapse of Mesopotamia and the Indus valley civilizations in the previous millennium, dramatic climate changes led to prolonged drought and famine. The mighty piles of stone fortifying the Mycenaean towns were ineffective at staving off hunger. Mycenae was sacked, and the Mycenaeans in turn may have gone off to sack other towns, desperate for sustenance. Their land, weakened by local infighting, devastated by invasions, and stricken with famine, prompted Homer to lament, "Among all creatures that breathe on earth and crawl on it, there is not anywhere a thing more dismal than man is."

Hattusha: The New Landscape of Militarism

The peoples of the Aegean during the Bronze Age could trace some of their culture to the earlier cultures of Southwest Asia. The Mycenaeans maintained strong connections to the more powerful Hittite Empire in Turkey, as remembered

Figure 3.1-11 Mycenae, Greece. (a) Aerial view. Bottom area includes new walls, Lion Gate, and circular grave, 1600–1200 BCE. (b) Circular grave.

Figure 3.1-12 Mycenae, Greece. *Dromos* (causeway) of beehive tomb, ca. 1250 BCE.

by Homer in the *Iliad*. He sang of how the proto-Greeks invaded the city of Troy at the northeast edge of the Anatolian peninsula to vindicate the abduction of Helen, the beautiful niece of Agamemnon of Mycenae. The story underlines the skill, valor, and invention of military strategies that now vied with the importance of ritual life in the design of cities.

The site of Troy was excavated at Hisarlick during the nineteenth century on the Ionian coast overlooking the southern tip of the Dardanelles. The various layers of this long-term settlement, dating from 1800 to 1100 BCE, reveal a town considerably smaller than Mycenae, which itself could contain only a few thousand people but would certainly have had many times that number living outside the walls in the surrounding territory. Like Mycenaean cities, Troy was crowned by an upper fortress set in a circuit of thick walls. A series of randomly oriented megarons flanked the royal megaron in the center. The ruins of Troy reveal the great similarity of typologies on either side of the Aegean.

Strong influences came from the Hittite Empire to the east, which at an earlier stage counted Troy, known also as "Iliam," among its colonial possessions. As a major imperial power in Southwest Asia during the late second millennium

BCE, the Hittites reached their apex during the same years as Mycenae's good fortunes, from roughly 1600 to 1200 BCE. They sited their towns defensively in the severe Anatolian hinterland, creating awesome fortifications, paved streets, monumental public buildings, and excellent drainage channels. Their great capital city of Hattusha, located in a hilly forest next to the modern town of Boğazkale (Turkey), about 200 km (125 miles) east of Ankara, grew to about 50,000 inhabitants. The city developed as a military base, relying on a network of supply and tribute that stretched to Mesopotamia and the coastal settlements of the eastern Mediterranean, such as Ugarit in Syria and Miletus on the Ionian shores.

Hattusha dominated a spur of rocky outcroppings at the end of a valley. Initially similar in size to Mycenae, its walled citadel clung to the north slope overlooking the valley. The Hittites adjusted their buildings, from their fortifications to their temples, to fit the irregular terrain of this craggy land. They exploited natural configurations for the purposes of defense, as well as wresting an inherent dignity from the rugged terrain. The gorges leading to Hattusha and the cliff against which it crouches offered the

Traces of an Aegean Diaspora

Knossos, Mycenae, and Hattusha all met a violent end sometime after 1200 BCE. The Egyptians referred to invaders known as the "peoples of the sea" as the common cause. The environmental crisis of prolonged droughts coupled with internal conflicts and violent over-throws forced the populations of the Aegean to move and may have induced them to become invaders themselves. The coincidental appearance of the Phoenicians and the Philistines on the Palestinian coast around 1200 BCE and the subsequent emergence of the Etruscans in Italy—combined with the enterprise of various Bronze-Age builders of conical towers in Puglia, Sicily, and Sardinia—all seem possible indications of a hypothetical Aegean *diaspora* (dispersion). The corbelled, domed *trulli* found in towns such as Alberobello, Puglia (see Section 1.2), follow an archaic vernacular tradition that shared a construction technique with that of the beehive tombs of the Mycenaeans. On the island of Sardinia more than 7,000 *nuraghi*, conical towers with corbelled domes, began to appear during this period of the late Bronze Age.

Sardinia, Santa Sabina, Bronze-Age *nuraghe*, reminiscent of Mycenaean beehive tombs, 1400–1000 BCE.

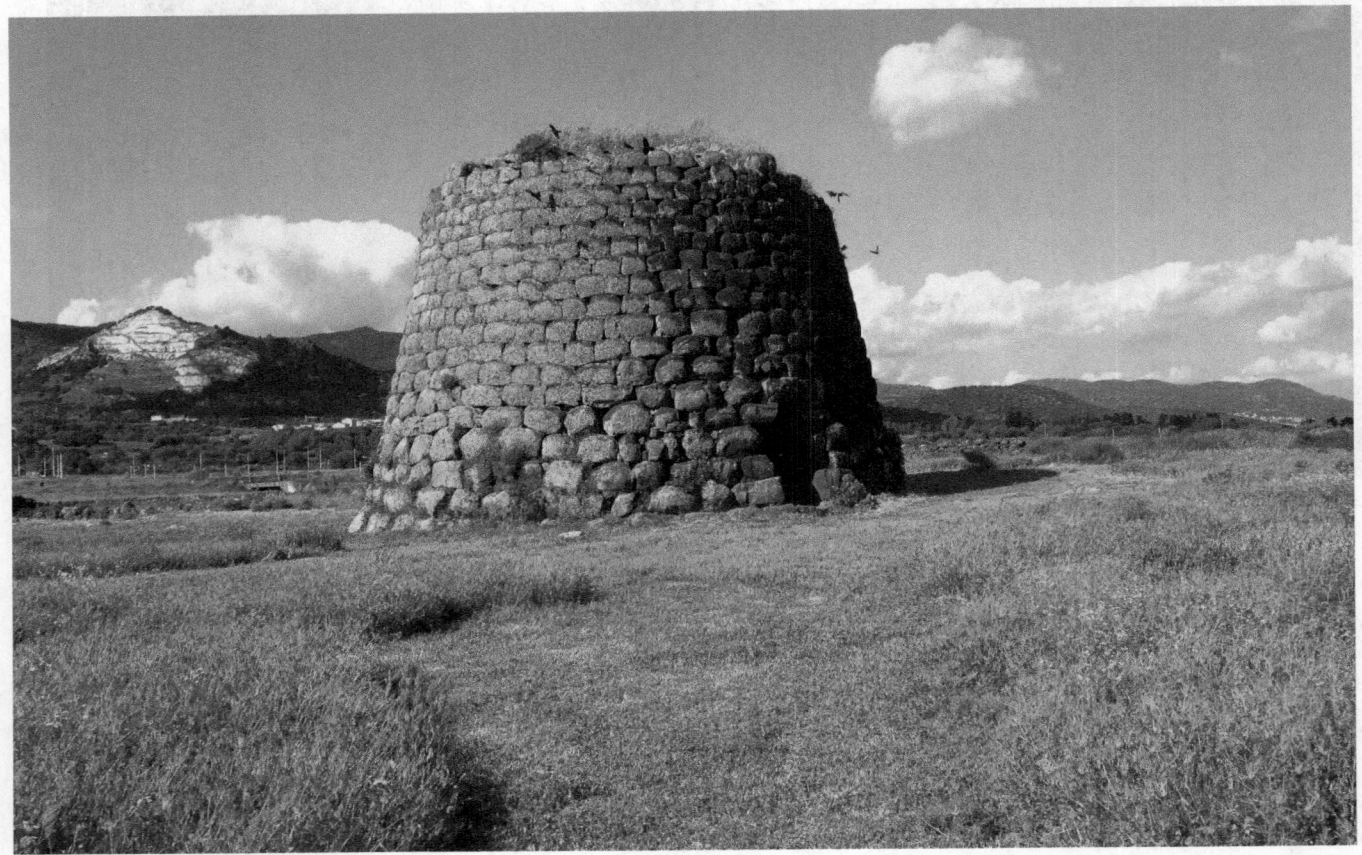

first elements of defense. The Hittites then piled up cyclopean boulders, left in an unfinished state, so that the city seemed rooted in a primordial landscape as an extension of the natural order.

Around 1400 BCE, the Hittites added a new crescent of fortifications around the exposed hillside to the south, tripling the area of Hattusha and raising it to the scale of Mesopotamian capitals such as Ur. The designers skillfully integrated the new walls with the land's contours, using a double shell of cyclopean masonry at points 10 m (33 ft) thick. The walls sheltered a series of bunker-like casemates, partitioned with internal **cross-vaults**. They placed guard towers every 30 m (98 ft) and between them a mud-brick superstructure along the parapets. Along the southern walls they dug an outer ditch and mounded up the stones to create a great, broad slope extending 100 m (328 ft). This slippery apron, which the Romans later called a ***glacis*** (derived from the Latin word for ice), served to break the momentum of a siege (Fig. 3.1-13a). Another thick wall capped the summit of the slope, followed by a second set of walls twice their height. The Hittites used corbel techniques that most likely influenced the masonry of the Mycenaeans,

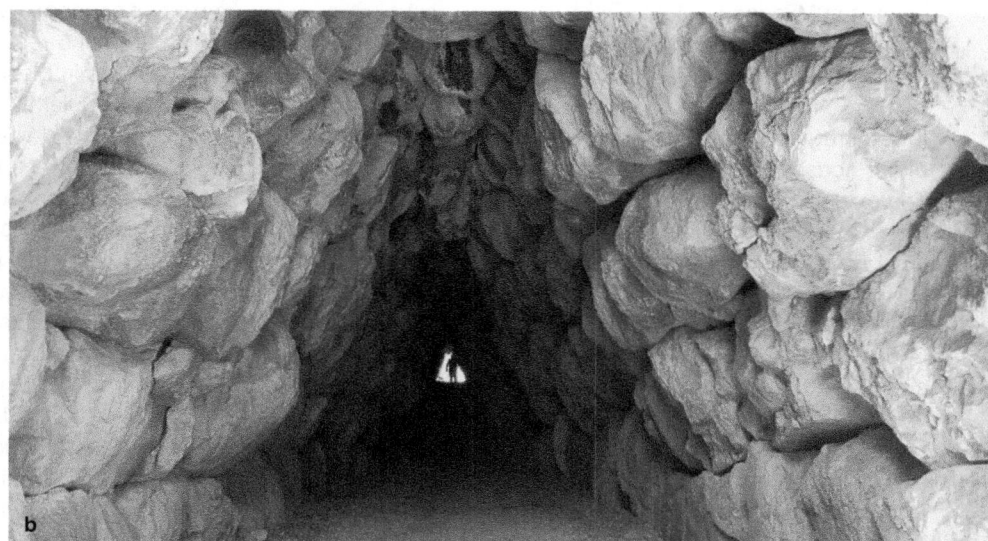

Figure 3.1-13 Hattusha (Turkey). (a) View of *glacis*. (b) Tunnel under the walls of the southern edge of the city, ca. 1350 BCE.

creating a secret tunnel (Fig. 3.1-13b) under the walls for the defenders to make surprise sorties.

The martial image of Hattusha mattered as much as the effectiveness of its defensive structures. Hittite engineers created sally port gates with two sets of portals made of monolithic jambs shaped as elliptical archways. They flanked the gates with fearsome towers built of huge cyclopean blocks. **Apotropaic** figures of lions and sphinxes

Figure 3.1-14 Hattusha (Turkey). Reconstruction of the Lion Gate, ca. 1350 BCE.

decorated the external jambs of the gates as magic guardians. The Lion Gate (Fig. 3.1-14) on the southwest served as the major entry, anticipating by a century the more refined version at Mycenae.

The residential arrangements in Hattusha conformed to the traditions of Southwest Asia: contiguous houses with five or six rooms gathered around small courts. The streets followed irregular patterns and boasted covered drains. Some of the houses had drains connecting to those in the street. The exterior walls of the houses were without windows, and the entry from the street led obliquely to the corner of an inner court.

The citadel of Hattusha (Fig. 3.1-15) covered an area slightly larger than the Labyrinth of Knossos, about 150 × 200 m (492 × 656 ft). A series of independent buildings surrounded two large courtyards. On the western side of the upper court rose a great audience hall, 30 × 30 m (98 × 98 ft). Its lower story was built of long, parallel walls and served as warehouses. The upper story carried the regularly spaced columns of a **hypostyle hall**, a type that may have been imported during the thirteenth century BCE from Egyptian precedents.

To the west of the citadel, Hattusha's principal urban temple (Fig. 3.1-16) became the focus of the "lower city." Dedicated to the weather god Hatti, it occupied a site as

large as the citadel. Warehouses and administrative structures wrapped around its *temenos*. Hittite temples, like those of Mesopotamia and New Kingdom Egypt, functioned as important economic entities, owning vast estates let to farmers for a ground rent in kind. Oriented to the northeast like most temples in Mesopotamia, the Hatti temple layout was much less regular than its precedents: the subsidiary buildings had crooked shapes that followed the lay of the land, while bent pathways led indirectly to the central cult building. The sanctuary was tucked into the back right corner without direct access. While not as convoluted a progression as the Labyrinth of Knossos, the Hatti temple shared a similar penchant for asymmetry.

The temples within the new walls of Hattusha after 1400 BCE did not conform to a standard orientation, but at least four of them linked perpendicularly to a sacred route, a paved street that led to the Hittites' chief cult site outside the walls, the sanctuary at Yazilikaya (Fig. 3.1-17a). Unlike the sealed chambers of both Egyptian and Mesopotamian temples, Hittite temples included ample fenestration in the sanctuary, which would have bathed the cult statue in natural light. Ample windows, framed by pilasters, pierced the perimeters of their temples.

The Hittites' desire for daylight in their temples may have been inspired by their outdoor sanctuary of Yazilikaya.

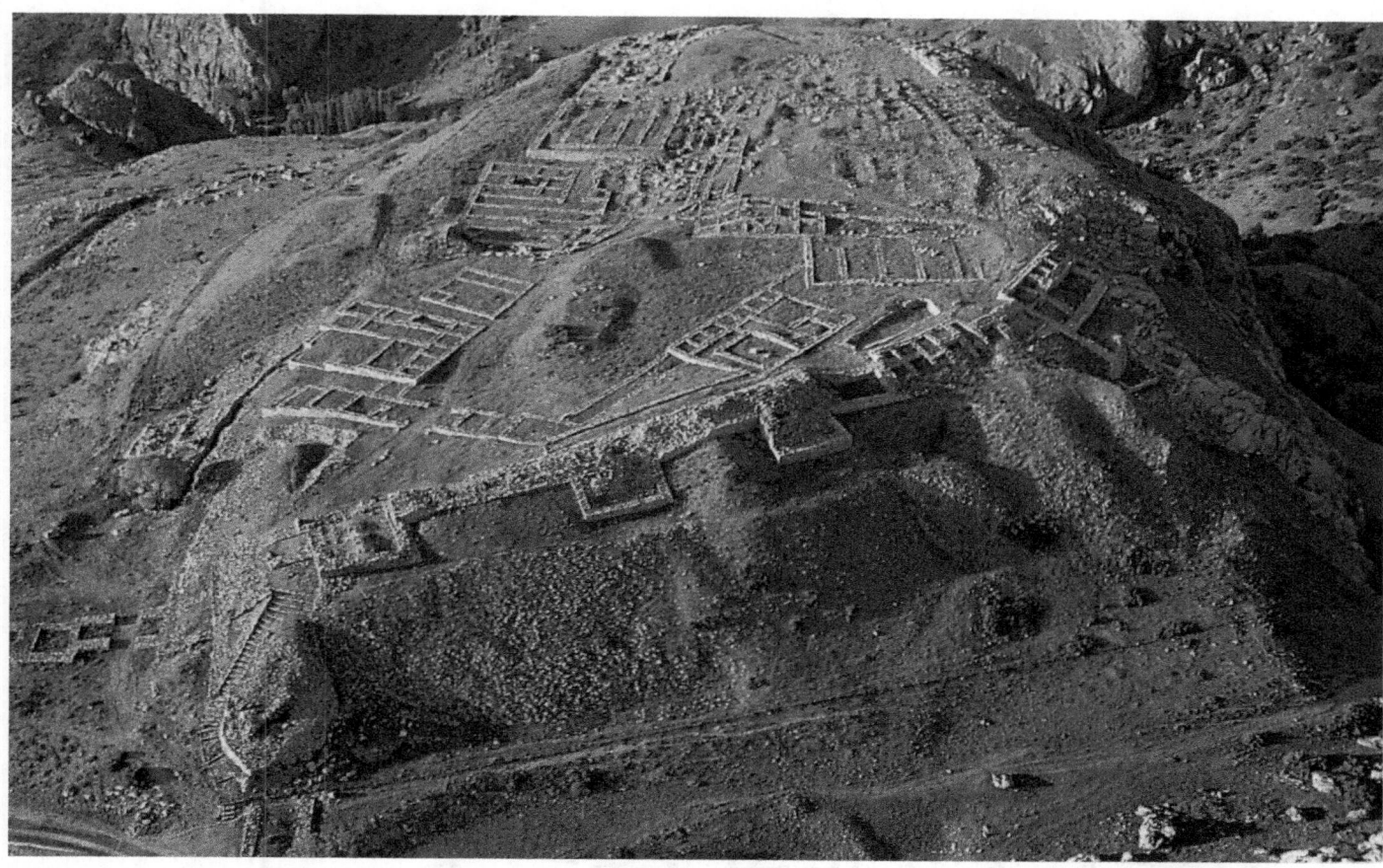

Figure 3.1-15 Hattusha (Turkey). Citadel, ca. 1350 BCE.

Set in a ravine 2 km (1.2 miles) northeast of Hattusha, the complex masterfully combined the natural order of grottoes with the architectural order of orthogonal halls (Fig. 3.1-17b). The shrine grew amid cliffs where a spring marked a sacred grove revered since prehistoric times. Stairs led to a gatehouse on the west, which continued the descent with two sets of interior stairs. These led down to a rectangular open-air court with a fountain pavilion that enclosed the southern end of the sacred grotto. From here one turned on a right angle to enter the two outdoor chapels. The major gallery, 5–10 m (16.5–33 ft) wide and 30 m (98 ft) deep, occupied a dramatic limestone ravine open to the sky and paved with turf and flowers. The Hittites carved sixty-six gods from their pantheon of 1,000 divinities into the rock elevations. Amid the reliefs appeared primitive versions of Ionic columns, which during the next millennium came to characterize the temples of the Ionian coast of Turkey. The solemn procession of the gods, males on one side and females on the other, converged toward a single isolated boulder. Worshippers would have come to witness the ritual coupling of Hatti, the male weather god, and Hepat, the female earth goddess: he stood on two mountains; she, reminiscent of the primeval earth goddess, stood on a panther.

The mid-thirteenth-century BCE decorations at Yazilikaya were commissioned by the wife of Hattusili III, Queen Puduhepa. Before her marriage she had served as a high priestess of the neighboring Hurrian culture and was known for her independence. The inscriptions on the figures were written in her language and not in Hittite. A narrow cleft to the right of this spectacular rock sanctuary led into a second gallery, hidden behind a crook, probably the holiest area of the site. Here, a strange dagger-god is depicted plunging into the rough base of the cliff, and next to him in the largest **frieze** appears the portrait of King Tudhaliya IV, son of Puduhepa, presented as a deified sovereign.

Around the time of Puduhepa's decorations at Yazilikaya, the Hittites went to war against Ramesses II of Egypt. Both sides claimed victory after the concluding Battle of Qadesh, fought in Syria. This left the Hittites with a short-lived international advantage. But despite their military prowess and the seemingly impenetrable fortifications of Hattusha, their culture, much like those of Mycenae and Knossos, collapsed around 1200 BCE. The same factors of internal dissension, famine, environmental crises, and the arrival of invaders undermined the survival of these three civilizations, all of which left precious lessons of how architecture can be integrated with the landscape.

CLOSE-UP

Figure 3.1-16 Hattusha (Turkey). Plan of the temple to Hatti, ca. 1350 BCE.

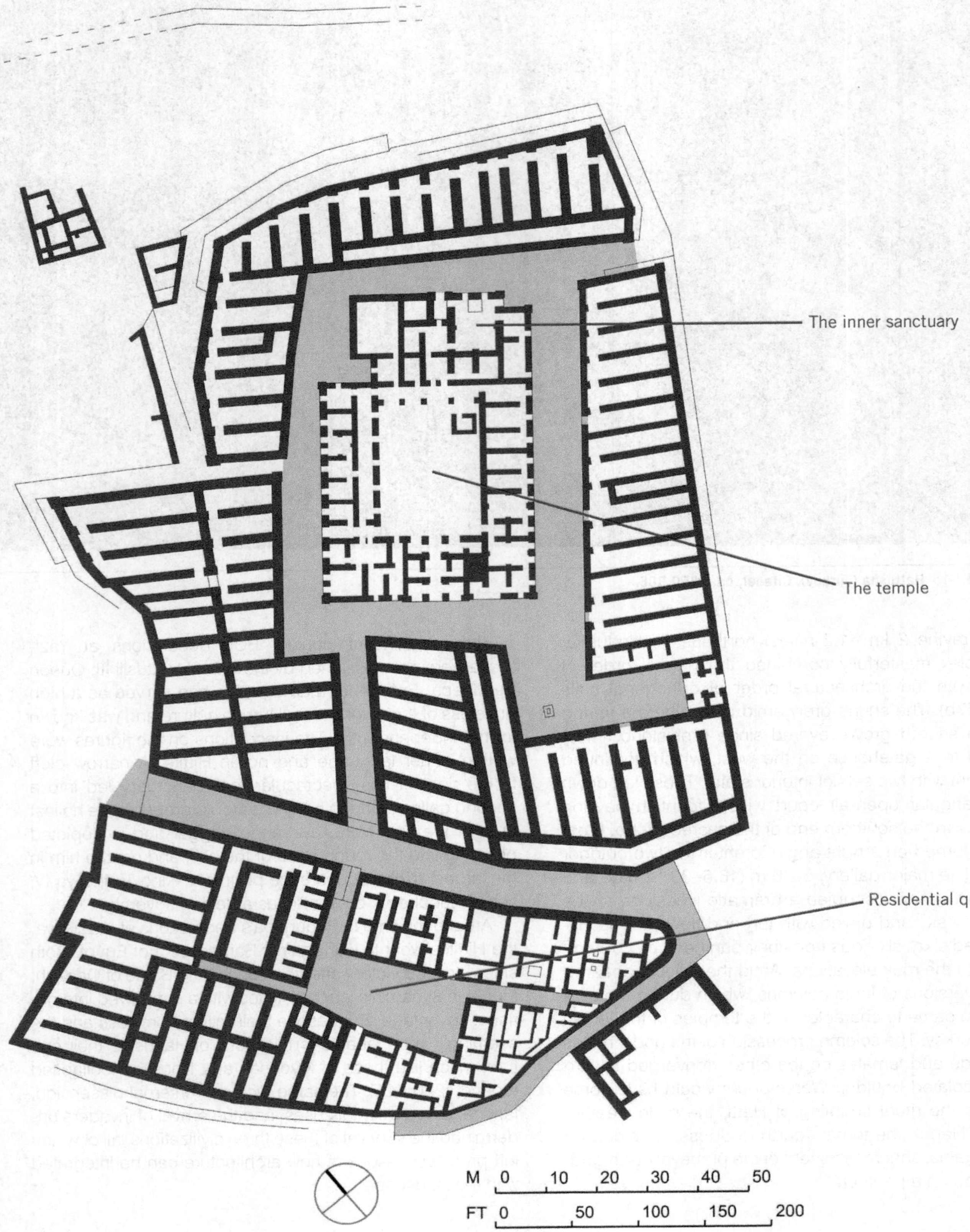
The inner sanctuary
The temple
Residential quarters
M 0 10 20 30 40 50
FT 0 50 100 150 200

Figure 3.1-17 Yazilikaya (Turkey). (a) The sanctuary's Major Gallery. (b) Plan of the sanctuary, ca. 1300–1250 BCE, showing (1) the western gate; (2) the altar; (3) the Major Gallery, set in a ravine and lined with friezes depicting the Hittite deities; and (4) the Second Gallery, lined with a procession of reliefs celebrating King Tudhaliya IV, ca. 1350 BCE.

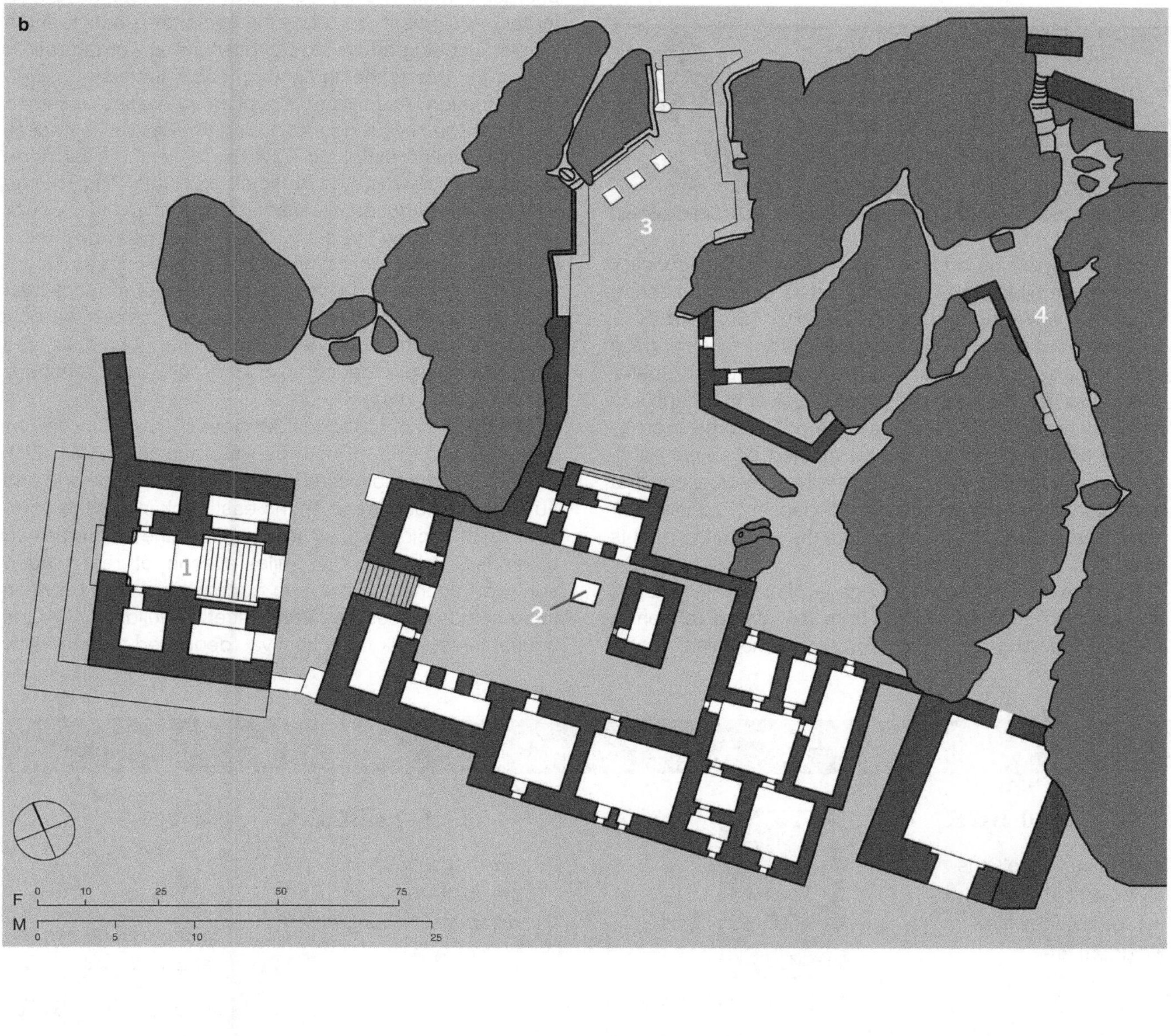

Further Reading

Bittel, Kurt. *Hattusha, Capital of the Hittites*. New York: Oxford University Press, 1970.

Castleden, Rodney. *Minoans: Life in Bronze Age Crete*. London: Routledge, 1993.

Hawkes, Jaquetta. *The Dawn of Civilization: Minoan and Mycenaean Origins of Greece*. New York: Random House, 1968.

Hooker, J. T. *Mycenaean Greece*. London: Routledge and Kegan Paul, 1977.

Lloyd, Seton, and Hans Wolfgang Muller. *Ancient Architecture*. Milan: Electa, 1980.

Sheeher, Jürgen. *Hattusha Guide: A Day in the Hittite Capital*. Istanbul: Ege Yayinlari, 2006.

Taylour, Lord William. *The Mycenaeans*. London: Thames & Hudson, 1983.

Willetts, R. F. *The Civilization of Ancient Crete*. Berkeley: University of California Press, 1978.

3.2 NEW KINGDOM EGYPT
Axial Temples and Colossal Statues

The pyramids of Old Kingdom Egypt left the concept of architectural space unexplored. During the period of New Kingdom Egypt, roughly 1560–1070 BCE, the southern capital of Thebes came to prominence and the great temples of Karnak and Luxor exhibited a new spatial awareness. Beginning with the patronage of Hatshepsut, a woman who bore the titles of a male ruler, Egyptian architecture acquired a sophisticated method of composition. Designers used the formal axis to explore sequences that alternated from open to closed experiences. Gigantic columns and colossal statues became the structuring agents of space.

About a century later a renegade pharaoh, Akhenaten, attempted to separate himself from the official religion in Thebes, founding the new capital of Akhentaten. In his buildings he introduced more light into the interiors, reflecting the emphasis of his new religion of light. He also set up the kinetic play of light amid the forests of columns in hypostyle halls as the new theme for Egyptian architecture. After the demise of Akhenaten and his religion, the pharaohs increasingly assumed the status of deified rulers. Ramesses II commissioned hundreds of colossal portraits of himself as physical reminders of his divine status. His statues reached such grand proportions that they seemed to take over the entire land, acting as ever-present sculpted surrogates of his person.

Thebes: The Great Temples of the New Kingdom

The continuous rule of Egyptian dynasties underwent a second crisis between the eighteenth and sixteenth centuries BCE with the intrusion of the Hyksos people. These "shepherd kings," tribal mercenaries from the Palestinian region, conquered Egypt and assimilated the trappings of pharaonic rule. The Hyksos introduced more advanced military equipment, including the horse, the chariot, and a regular standing army, into Egyptian military organization. During the late sixteenth century BCE Thutmose I ousted these foreign rulers and Egyptian dynasties resumed power as the New Kingdom. Using Thebes as its capital, the new regime extended Egypt's dominion as far north as the Euphrates and as far south as Nubia. The Theban cult of Amon acquired the associations with political power previously held by the cult of the northern sun god Ra of Heliopolis, leading to a synthesis of the two cults as Amon-Ra. The temples of Thebes, safely upstream, more than 700 km (434 miles) from the Nile delta, received the bulk of tribute coming from newly conquered territories and grew into ever-grander complexes structured on emphatic column-lined axes.

Thebes prospered as the "Mistress of Every City," growing as a long strip on both banks of the Nile (Fig. 3.2-1). The two major temple compounds, Karnak to the north and Luxor to the south, rose on the east bank inside their own mud-brick enclosures, while the rest of the city remained unfortified. A 4 km (2.5 mile) avenue of ram-headed sphinxes connected the two sanctuaries, and between them stood palaces and administrative buildings. For the annual three-week Opet Festival, dedicated to the fertility

Reign of Hatshepsut

▲ **1479–1458 BCE**

▼ **ca. 1500 BCE**

Thutmose I expels the Hyksos from Egypt and inaugurates the New Kingdom era

▼ **ca. 1479 BCE**

Hatshepsut expands the Temple of Amon-Ra at Karnak, building the Red Chapel

Hatshepsut begins the Temple of Luxor

 ▲ **ca. 1460 BCE**

of the gods, celebrants carried statues of Amon, his wife Mut, and their son Khonsu in boats on a circuitous path between one temple and the other to symbolically consummate the union of the gods and ensure the fertility of the Nile valley. The temple complexes sheltered a large priesthood, commanded thousands of workers, and owned hundreds of thousands of cattle, orchards, boats, and workshops. Facing this superb ceremonial setting across the Nile spread a ponderous series of mortuary temples for 10 km (6 miles) at the foot of the steep cliffs of Deir el-Bahri, behind which were the ravines and caves for royal tombs in the Valley of the Kings.

The bulk of the residential area of Thebes remained on the west bank of the Nile, between the river and the row of mortuary temples. Although Theban houses and palaces have mostly disappeared without a trace, their design can be reconstructed from representations and archaeological evidence at excavated sites (Fig. 3.2-2). Row houses lined the modest residential streets. Each had a small court and a shaded portico on the south side to take advantage of the northern breeze. A broad hall served as the main living space, and at the rear a kitchen with an independent staircase led to second-story bedrooms and a terrace above. The living room rose higher than the side rooms, allowing for clerestory lighting, a feature shared by both wealthy and humble dwellings.

Richer families had basements for their weaving looms and terraces to store grain in bins. Unlike the involuted and street-shy houses of Mesopotamian cities, Thebes enjoyed an extroverted street architecture. Facades were brightly painted and topped by balustrades of interwoven palm fronds. Perhaps earlier than the Minoans, the Thebans used windows with **mullions**, and tracery covered their lower halves for privacy,

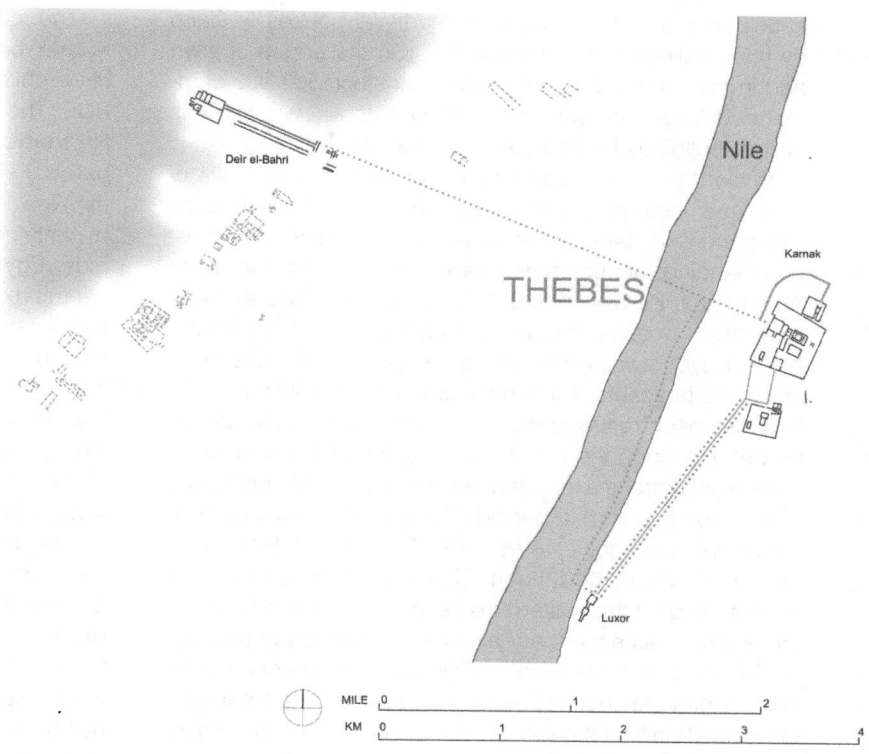

Figure 3.2-1 Thebes. Egypt's southern capital during the New Kingdom period, roughly 1560–1070 BCE. The mortuary temples at Deir el-Bahri sat across the river from the two major temple compounds, Karnak and Luxor.

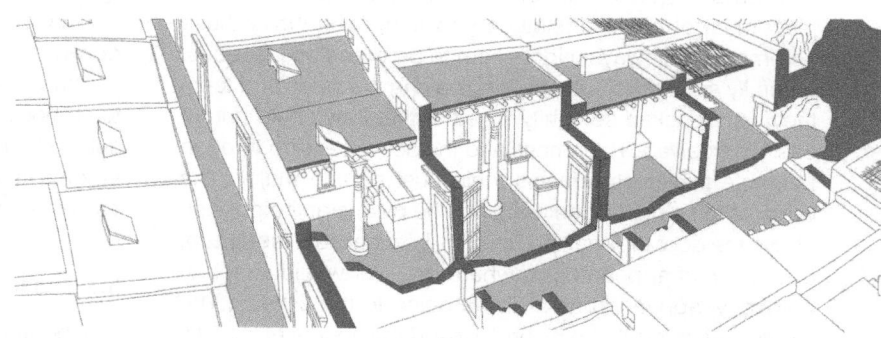

Figure 3.2-2 Ancient Egypt. Section of a typical New Kingdom house, reconstructed from the tomb-workers' village of Deir el-Medina, next to the Valley of the Kings, ca. 1500 BCE (after J. C. Golvin).

▼ **ca. 1460 BCE**

Mortuary Temple of Hatshepsut at Deir el-Bahri

Reign of Akhenaten (Amenhotep IV), who institutes monotheistic cult of Aten

▲ **1352–1336 BCE**

▼ **ca. 1340 BCE**

Foundation of Akhentaten (Amarna, Egypt) as new capital

Reign of Ramesses II

▲ **1279–1213 BCE**

▼ **1275 BCE**

Battle of Qadesh between Hittites and Egyptians in Syria

anticipating the *mashrabiyya* of medieval houses in Cairo by three millennia (see Section 9.1). On the edges of town and in the surrounding countryside, aristocratic villas commanded large independent plots with their own gardens and outbuildings for granaries and stables.

While the houses and palaces of Thebes were built of mud and expendable materials, the temples used solid limestone and have endured as splendid ruins. The most commanding monument in Thebes remains the Temple to Amon-Ra at Karnak (Fig. 3.2-3), occupying a site as large as a city. It boasted the greatest endowment of any institution in Egypt, owning 583,000 acres of farms and the labor of 83,000 peasants. The temple stood on an earlier cult site that had been resuscitated by the pharaohs of the Middle Kingdom. During the first three centuries of the New Kingdom, royal patrons expanded the temples to fill an enclosure of over 500 m (1,640 ft) per side. They added massive sloping pylons, ceremonial thresholds 10–25 m (33–82 ft) thick and up to 50 m (164 ft) high. Six pylon gates led from the river landing on the eastern axis and four from the southern cross-axis. This secondary axis proceeded to the precinct of Mut, the consort of Amon, following a sphinx-lined boulevard. A third precinct just beyond the northern gate honored the initial divinity of the site, Montu. Unlike the uncompromising coordinates of the pyramids, the axes of Karnak were skewed to follow the changing course of the Nile.

The monumental pylons at Karnak imitated those at the Old Kingdom temples in Memphis and Heliopolis, known only from graphic representations. Vertical slots were cut at regular intervals into their battered elevations for the placement of colossal statues and flagpoles. While these ceremonial gateways might seem to be grandiose facades, carefully articulated with moldings along the sides and tops, they were packed so tightly together that they could not be easily perceived. Their mass and the act of passing through palpable thickness remains their most salient quality. The builders left a cleft in the center of the pylons at the position above the door for what the Romans later called a **fastigium**, or window of appearances, where the ruler would enact an epiphany, appearing as a divine being to the crowds. The strong axis through the pylons evoked the course of the Nile pushing through its cliff-lined valley. Such a metaphor came from the major ritual of the temple, during which celebrants marched through the pylons carrying on their shoulders long boats in which stood wooden effigies of the gods.

The complex and imposing order of New Kingdom Karnak began under Thutmose I (r. 1505–1493 BCE) and his architect Ineny at the outset of the sixteenth century BCE. The program continued with the pharaoh's daughter, Hatshepsut, and her architect, Senenmut. As the premier national shrine, Karnak attracted the patronage of most of the New Kingdom pharaohs. The Greek-speaking Ptolemy dynasty continued to add to it in the third century BCE. Like most Egyptian temples, Karnak was organized around a central axis, approached by a colonnaded entry court that led to a more secluded hypostyle hall and a restricted inner sanctum. The pylons, colossal sculpted figures, and obelisks articulated hierarchical transitions for the ceremonies that would have been enacted there. The inclusion of obelisks, precious to the solar cult of Ra in Heliopolis, conveyed a precise political message of the fusion of the two cults into Amon-Ra.

The east–west extension of the Temple of Amon-Ra represented a cosmic timepiece. Each element of the sequence took the name of the hour that the sun passed directly above it. The easternmost gateway marked the station for the rising sun at the first hour. The inner sanctum, housing the sacred boat, indicated the ninth hour; the transverse hall between Pylons IV and V, the tenth hour; and the hypostyle hall, the eleventh. Beyond Pylon III signified the setting of the sun at the twelfth hour. To the southwest of the main temple stretched a sacred lake, referring to the primordial swamp out of which the sun emerged to create the world. A colossal granite scarab representing Khepri, god of the sun "growing toward noon," guarded the lake.

The precinct of the Temple of Amon-Ra contained a dozen smaller temples to other deities and pharaohs who together constituted an Egyptian pantheon. Karnak came to embody the nation's theological universe, serving as the setting for rituals such as coronations and the Heb-Sed ceremony. Its grandeur consumed a significant portion of the empire's new surplus.

King/Queen Hatshepsut: The Political Use of Patronage

Hatshepsut, a queen who was addressed with the masculine honorific of "king," ruled Egypt for twenty-one years, approximately 1479–1458 BCE. She emerged as the most intriguing and artistically influential royal patron of Karnak. In many ways the architectural style of the New Kingdom

Ramesses II completes temples at Karnak and Luxor

▲ **ca. 1250 BCE**

▼ **ca. 1250 BCE**

Ramesses II founds new capital of Pi-Ramesses in the Nile delta

Ramesses II sponsors gigantic rock-cut temples at Abu Simbel

▲ **ca. 1250 BCE**

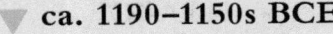

▼ **ca. 1190–1150s BCE**

Invasion of Sea Peoples throughout Aegean, Anatolia, Palestine, and Egypt

Figure 3.2-3 Karnak, Egypt. Temple of Amon-Ra, view through pylons, ca. 1400 BCE.

derived from her motivated patronage. She not only built a magnificent terraced mortuary complex at Deir el-Bahri (Fig. 3.2-4) but also sponsored numerous temples and monuments, including the central shrine of Amon-Ra at Karnak. Senenmut, her closest advisor, steward of the palace, and guardian of her daughter, served also as her chief architect, known by the portentous title "greatest of the great." As the administrator of the wealth of the temples of Luxor and Karnak, Senenmut executed most of the great works of his king/queen. That Hatshepsut's architecture represented power became clear in the aftermath of her projects: her successors pursued a campaign to destroy and erase signs of her patronage as king, which they perceived as threatening the primacy of masculine authority.

Although there are traces of powerful queens in other ancient cultures—in particular, the legendary founder of Babylon, Semiramis—and there had been two other Egyptian queens who had ruled as regents during interregnums, Hatshepsut became the first historically documented woman to rule with the complete authority of a man. Her father, Thutmose I, was the general who oversaw Egypt's first great imperial expansion into Southwest Asia during the late sixteenth century BCE. Due to the incestuous practices used to conserve the Egyptian royal bloodlines, Hatshepsut married her half-brother, Thutmose II, and after his death became regent for her infant nephew and stepson, Thutmose III, who had been born to a concubine.

A few years into her regency Hatshepsut orchestrated a bloodless coup d'état, crowning herself pharaoh and assuming all of the masculine attributes of power, including the fake beard worn by all pharaohs (Fig. 3.2-5). Her status changed from high priestess at the Temple of Amon-Ra at Karnak, where she was addressed as "god's wife of Amon," to "daughter of Amon." Inscriptions claiming Hatshepsut's divine origins covered her monuments and became the basis of her political power. She also introduced prophecy and propaganda as strategies for maintaining her authority. The queen's exceptional attention to architecture went beyond the conventional patronage expected of a pharaoh. She used architecture as a tool to bolster her rule. Aside from her funerary complex and the works at Karnak, she built five major temples, including the first temple at Luxor and the Medinet Habu, the holiest sanctuary of the region, honoring the alleged primordial site of creation.

Figure 3.2-4 Deir el-Bahri, Egypt. Hatshepsut's mortuary temple, 1480 BCE.

The Temple of Amon-Ra at Karnak has usually been attributed to Hatshepsut's father and stepson, yet she played the determining role in the development of the core of the temple. Her deep involvement with Karnak over a forty-year period, first as high priestess and then as pharaoh, accompanied her efforts to assert political control. When she promoted herself to the role of pharaoh, the support of this temple's powerful priesthood helped boost her status. Her father's architect, Ineny, began construction of the gateways of Pylons IV and V while Hatshepsut was high priestess, and they were completed under her tenure as pharaoh. Between them rose the first hypostyle hall, built of colossal cedar columns with papyrus bud capitals. Although from the central axis the hall would have appeared symmetrical, four pairs of columns were placed to the south, while only three stood to the north. Two granite obelisks 20 m (66 ft) high dedicated to her father flanked the entry to Pylon IV. Hatshepsut inscribed her own name on another more impressive pair of obelisks, one-third taller than her father's, within the hypostyle hall between Pylons IV and V. Her obelisks stood in light wells to gather light at the tenth hour and required the partial removal of the roof of her father's hypostyle hall. Their pyramidal tips, covered in gold foil, would have shone above the roofs.

During the initial building campaign at Karnak, colossal statues were introduced as architectural elements in the entry court in front of Pylon IV. The outer walls were lined with giant statues of Osiris, god of the underworld, and gigantic standing portraits of Thutmose I were placed between Pylons IV and V. Similar to the statues of Gudea in Sumeria (see Section 2.1), the stone portraits represented the patron as an eternal witness. Hatshepsut continued the tradition of colossal statues, placing another pair of obelisks and colossal seated figures of herself as pharaoh in front of Pylon VIII, the first gate on the perpendicular southern axis leading to the Temple of Mut. As with all such representations of the female king in male guise, the portraits were destroyed after her death.

Hatshepsut's greatest contribution to Karnak was the new inner sanctum housing the statue of the god and his processional boat. During the Middle Kingdom period the boat had been stored in a special elevated chamber known as the "White Chapel," constructed around 1920 BCE. This square pavilion, penetrated by ramps on two sides, was enclosed by a colonnade with three decorated square columns per side and capped with a coved entablature. Hatshepsut displaced it with the "Red Chapel," the terminating point of the Karnak axis behind Pylon V. This narrow hall, open at both ends, comprised two tall rectangular chambers, the first for the boat and the second for the wooden statue. Constructed of special interlocking red quartzite panels, the chapel was decorated with carved messages describing the queen's relationship to the god, first as his daughter and then as wife to his son. In the gloomy darkness of the final chamber a single beam of light would have fallen upon the statue from a slot in the ceiling. The priesthood fed, clothed, and ritually appeased the seated image on a daily basis. The contentment of Amon-Ra was believed to guarantee the benevolence of Egypt's rulers, the glory of its armies, and the continued abundance of the Nile. Hatshepsut's successor, Thutmose III (r. 1457–1425 BCE), dismantled the Red Chapel and replaced it with a similar chapel that ignored the existence of the king/queen. The masonry of both the White Chapel and the Red Chapel were recycled into the foundations of Pylon III, built about a century after Hatshepsut's reign.

While presiding over the works at Karnak, Hatshepsut also oversaw the burial arrangements for her father and her stepbrother/husband. During the preparation of their tombs in the Valley of the Kings, she decided to undertake her greatest architectural scheme: the terraced mortuary temple, initially intended for her father but named after her at Deir el-Bahri. The mortuary temple, a convention in use since the pyramids at Giza (see Section 2.2), received offerings to the *ka*, or spirit, of the deceased. The Temple of Hatshepsut, known in its day as *Djeser-Djeseru*, or "holiest of the holy," extended parallel to the ruins of the platform temple built by Mentuhotep I about five centuries earlier (see Section 2.2). Senenmut obviously borrowed ideas from the earlier work, but his temple for Hatshepsut covered three times the area and was more richly articulated. The choice of the site permitted terraces to be cut from the base of the rock, exploiting the 300 m (984 ft) height of the cliff as vertical mass greater than a pyramid for its backdrop. The real tomb sites were in fact on the other side of these cliffs, in the deep folds of the Valley of the Kings. The stone ranges of the terraces extended from the base of the cliffs as if nature had collaborated with Senenmut's design.

Hatshepsut's mortuary temple at Deir el-Bahri served not so much for burial rituals as for the annual Feast of the Valley, when the statue of Amon was transported in its boat from the temple at Karnak 9 km (6 miles) away to visit the mortuary temples of the earthly kings along the west bank of the Nile. The approach from the river followed a broad causeway, 31 m (102 ft) wide, lined with hundreds of sandstone sphinxes, the probable source for the sphinx-lined avenue built later as the connection between the temples of Luxor and Karnak. The long avenue terminated in a pylon gate that opened to the first of three terraced levels. Enormous, 7-ton red granite sphinxes with Hatshepsut's face lined the inner path of the first and second terraces, leading to gradual ramps from grade to grade. The abutment walls of each terrace were articulated with colonnaded porches two columns deep. Lining the wall of the third, upper terrace stood twenty-six colossal polychrome statues of Osiris engaged to the square piers. Once again the faces on these statues, despite their depiction of a male god, were portraits of the queen. Thutmose III ordered the defacement of all of these representations of Hatshepsut after her death.

On the upper terrace, after passing through a hypostyle court, the procession encountered the culmination of the axis, a narrow chapel cut into the base of the cliff and dedicated to Amon, and south of this, two narrow chapels, the larger for Hatshepsut and the other for her father and her husband. The proportions of these chapels resembled those of the Red Chapel at Karnak, and the celebrants left the statue of Amon in his boat here to visit with the *ka* of the defunct monarchs.

Hatshepsut designed her temple as an "earthly paradise" for Amon, reminiscent of the myrrh gardens of Punt, the mythical homeland of the gods. She sent an expedition to Somalia, which was thought to be the legendary Punt, to bring back myrrh trees for the terraced gardens. The atmosphere of Deir el-Bahri, which today appears stark, dry, and dusty, must have been cool and fragrant, with luscious gardens interspersed with small pools. The story of the expedition covers the walls of the colonnade on the second terrace, between the chapel on the north devoted to the jackal-headed Anubis, lord of cemeteries, and the chapel on the south dedicated to Hathor, the mother goddess, often depicted as a cow and associated with both love and death. The capitals of the columns in this hypostyle chapel

Figure 3.2-5 Ancient Egypt. Portrait of Hatshepsut with false beard, ca. 1480 BCE.

took the shape of Hathor's head. Inside Hathor's Chapel one finds the only representation of Hatshepsut to escape destruction, probably because it depicted the queen as a young girl and not in male guise as a pharaoh.

Aside from the anthropomorphic columns in Hathor's Chapel, the columns used in the porticoes on all three levels were designed in a particularly abstract manner. The square piers at the base of the two ramps seem sliced from the plane of the retaining wall. These shady porticoes would have contributed to the general sense of openness of the planted terraces. The interior columns of the porticoes were rounded off, their drums having a polygonal section of sixteen facets. In front of the unfinished Anubis Chapel at the northern edge of the second terrace, the same sixteen-sided columns, looking almost like the Greek Doric columns of a millennium later, stood fully exposed (Fig. 3.2-6). Their square capitals intersected with one of the facets to form a *T* on which hieroglyphs were inscribed.

The relation of the architect Senenmut to the queen seems to have been more than professional. He left his portrait behind every door in the complex and in many instances linked his name with that of Hatshepsut. Aside from his official tomb at another site, where he installed a sarcophagus identical to that of the queen, he also prepared a secret tomb next to the first terrace of Deir el-Bahri. Together, the king/queen and her architect managed a relatively peaceful and economically successful regime, creating impressive works of architecture that promoted the idea of their virtue. Hatshepsut's works had an immediate and lasting impact on the design of future monuments in their axiality, grand scale, and propagandistic iconography. While her successors pursued the revisionist program of defacement and substitution of her works, they also imitated her monumental flare. Despite the erasure of her name and face from the surfaces of her works, Hatshepsut's architecture, particularly her mortuary complex, remained without equal. No pharaoh before or after matched the peaceful serenity, openness, and harmonious play of her terraced temple.

CONSTRUCTION, TECHNOLOGY, THEORY

Egyptian Graphic Conventions

State architects like Imhotep and Senenmut worked from literary texts, such as *The Book of Foundations*, but then relied on the straight edge and triangle for drawing and modeling techniques to make their buildings. The ground plan of their works was based on an established module and two or more geometrical figures, to which was added a set of outline elevations for all sides of the building. Dimensions were based on the **cubit** (the length from the elbow to the tip of the middle finger) and the palm. Among the few architectural drawings that have remained from this period is a papyrus from Ghorab showing a portal drawn in black ink laid over a grid in red ink, demonstrating a rational system of proportional control.

Luxor and Amarna: Architecture after Hatshepsut

Hatshepsut's stepson, Thutmose III, became her co-ruler when he came of age. Although the younger pharaoh did not demonstrate hostility toward his stepmother during her lifetime and provided her a dignified burial, twenty years after her death he systematically destroyed her monuments, erasing her name and face wherever they were found in public. This case of what the Romans called *damnatio memoriae*, meaning the elimination from official memory, probably came as a political answer to her transgression of gender roles. While Hatshepsut's reign had been almost free of military engagement, Thutmose III pursued expansionism, resulting in the most successful Egyptian military campaigns in Mesopotamia and Syria. As a patron of architecture, he imitated his disgraced stepmother by continuing to add to the complex at Karnak using the spoils of his wars. Aside from remaking the Red Chapel, his greatest contribution to the shrine of Amon-Ra was the Festival Hall at the end of the eastern axis, which was used for the Heb-Sed Jubilee rituals. At Deir el-Bahri, between Hatshepsut's temple and that of Mentuhotep I, he inserted a smaller version of a terraced mortuary temple.

His successors, in particular Amenhotep III during the fourteenth century BCE, continued to build at an increasingly colossal scale, best seen in the additions to the Temple of Luxor. Hatshepsut initiated the Temple of Luxor in the mid-fifteenth century BCE as a small granite chapel consisting of three narrow docking chambers to receive the ritual boats of the deities. Its south-facing portico rested on four papyrus bundle columns. Amenhotep III's trusted architect and sculptor Amenhotep, son of Hapu, designed the significant additions, which, like the temple at Karnak, unfolded axially in three parts: an outer forecourt, a hypostyle hall, and an inner sanctuary for the cult statue. Devoted to the Theban triad—Amon, his wife Mut, and their son Khonsu—it became known as Amon's "southern harem," in honor of the god's fertility. The complex included a "birthing" room, alluding to the belief that the pharaoh had been sired by the god.

The rebuilt temple at Luxor extended a skewed axis from Hatshepsut's original porch through seven pairs of colossal 17 m (56 ft) high columns (Fig. 3.2-7). Capped with open papyrus blossom capitals, the columns carried crossbeams that held up a central roof that has since disappeared. At the terminus of the grand colonnade the designers placed a square peristyle court, 50 × 50 m (164 × 164 ft), ringed with a double row of papyrus bud columns. From here one proceeded to the hypostyle hall, where clusters of columns, four wide by four deep, stood to either side of the axis. The passage narrowed into progressively smaller rooms, with columns marking the axis. The inner sanctum behind the last room of the axial sequence could only be reached by a circuitous route, somewhat reminiscent of the indirect access seen at the major Temple of Hattusha.

The pharaohs were habitually worshipped as gods after their burial, but Amenhotep III became the first to assume god-like status during his own life. This identity shift accompanied his political strategy to wrest power from the temple bureaucracies that had grown stronger since the time of Hatshepsut. The walls of the ambitious additions to Karnak and Luxor were covered with narratives of Amenhotep's divine birth, and in the southernmost province of Nubia he was declared a living god. He commissioned his architect to produce suitable representations of this new divine status, resulting in the immense seated portraits at his mortuary temple near Deir el-Bahri, each over 20 m (66 ft) tall and known as the Colossi of Memnon.

The strange behavior of his successor, Amenhotep IV (r. 1352–1336 BCE), must thus be considered in this new context, wherein divine kingship served as a means for deterring the advance of the priestly class. Five years into his reign the new pharaoh espoused a new religion based on a single divinity, the solar disk Aten. He eliminated the other gods, including Amon-Ra at Karnak. He changed his official name to Akhenaten ("in the service of Aten") and founded a new capital at Akhentaten ("the horizon of Aten"), currently called Tell-el-Amarna, halfway between Thebes and Memphis, where he could reside at a safe distance from the conflicts with the established religious hierarchy in the old capital. In a state structured under the protection of Amon-Ra and the auxiliary deities, his turn to monotheism would have appeared an outrageous heresy.

Akhenaten's new city did not diverge completely from the architectural norms of Thebes, but it had some telling differences. The major buildings clustered around a single grand axis, 25 m (82 ft) wide, with the two major temples and a sprawling palace at the core. A bridge with a *fastigium* for official appearances connected the parts of the palace on opposite sides of the street (Fig. 3.2-8). Akhenaten programmed the Great Temple of Aten (Fig. 3.2-9) as a long, narrow structure, set in a walled compound, comparable in scale to the temple at Karnak. Once beyond the hypostyle entry hall of sixteen colossal columns, it offered an axial sequence of six planted, open-air courts. To either side of the axis stood 365 solar altars. The Temple of Aten had no hidden inner sanctum, only gardens and fountains. The solar disk, seen in full sunlight, became its sole object of veneration.

Akhenaten's new monotheistic religion inspired a completely different mode of representation. Artists portrayed the pharaoh and his wife, Nefertiti, naturalistically rather than as stiff, hieratic figures (Fig. 3.2-10). Some reliefs show them eating and others cuddling their children. They look distinctly human and not god-like. The pharaoh may have personally established these attitudes, as his chief architect, Bek, left an inscription referring to himself as "the assistant whom His majesty Himself taught."

After Akhenaten's demise, around 1333 BCE, the religious and political classes forced his successor, Tutankhamen, to move back to Thebes and restore the religious orthodoxy of

Figure 3.2-6 Deir el-Bahri, Egypt. Proto-Doric columns at Hatshepsut's temple, 1480 BCE.

the cult of Amon-Ra at Karnak. The royal widow, Nefertiti, continued to live in Akhentaten, but a dozen years later the city was completely destroyed, and fragments of its temples were dragged off to fill the walls of other temples in nearby Hermopolis. As with Hatshepsut, almost all references to Akhenaten were erased from public view in the effort to restore the power of the temples that had existed previous to his reign. This brief threat to the religious order that stood behind Egyptian political power stimulated the renewal of patronage for the conventional religious centers of Luxor and Karnak.

A generation later Ramesses II (r. 1279–1213 BCE) prevailed as the greatest contributor to these cult sites. At Karnak he added a temple to himself as deified ruler along the south wall and completed the great hypostyle hall between Pylons II and III. His architect, Penre, shaped the space into the most grandiose interior ever constructed in ancient Egypt or elsewhere, superhuman in its scale and dramatic in the thrust of its central axis. Ramesses loved to

Figure 3.2-7 Luxor, Egypt. Plan of the Temple of Amon-Ra, the southern harem, 1470–1250 BCE. Hatshepsut's initial temple can be seen at the upper left.

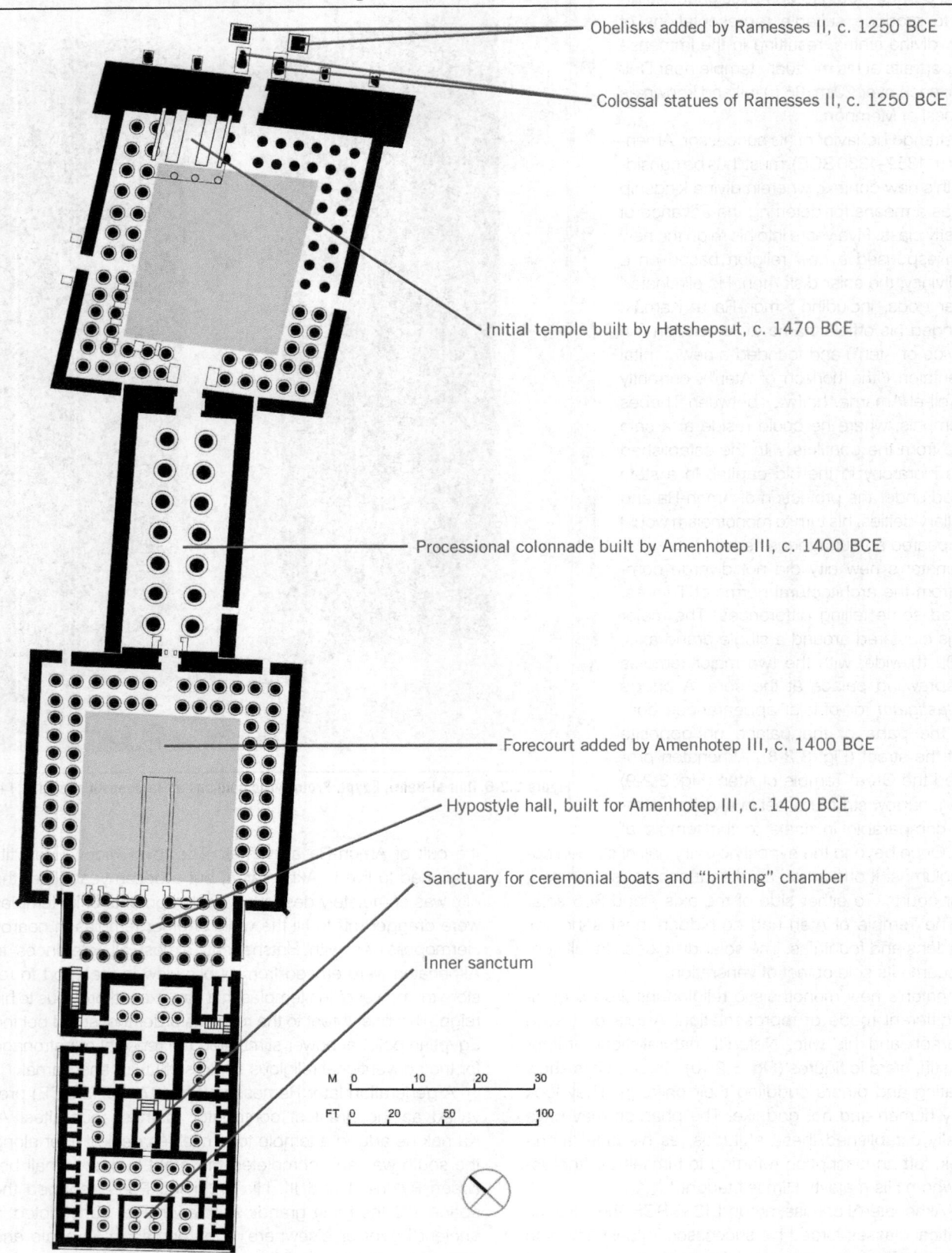

Obelisks added by Ramesses II, c. 1250 BCE

Colossal statues of Ramesses II, c. 1250 BCE

Initial temple built by Hatshepsut, c. 1470 BCE

Processional colonnade built by Amenhotep III, c. 1400 BCE

Forecourt added by Amenhotep III, c. 1400 BCE

Hypostyle hall, built for Amenhotep III, c. 1400 BCE

Sanctuary for ceremonial boats and "birthing" chamber

Inner sanctum

M   0   10   20   30

FT   0   20   50   100

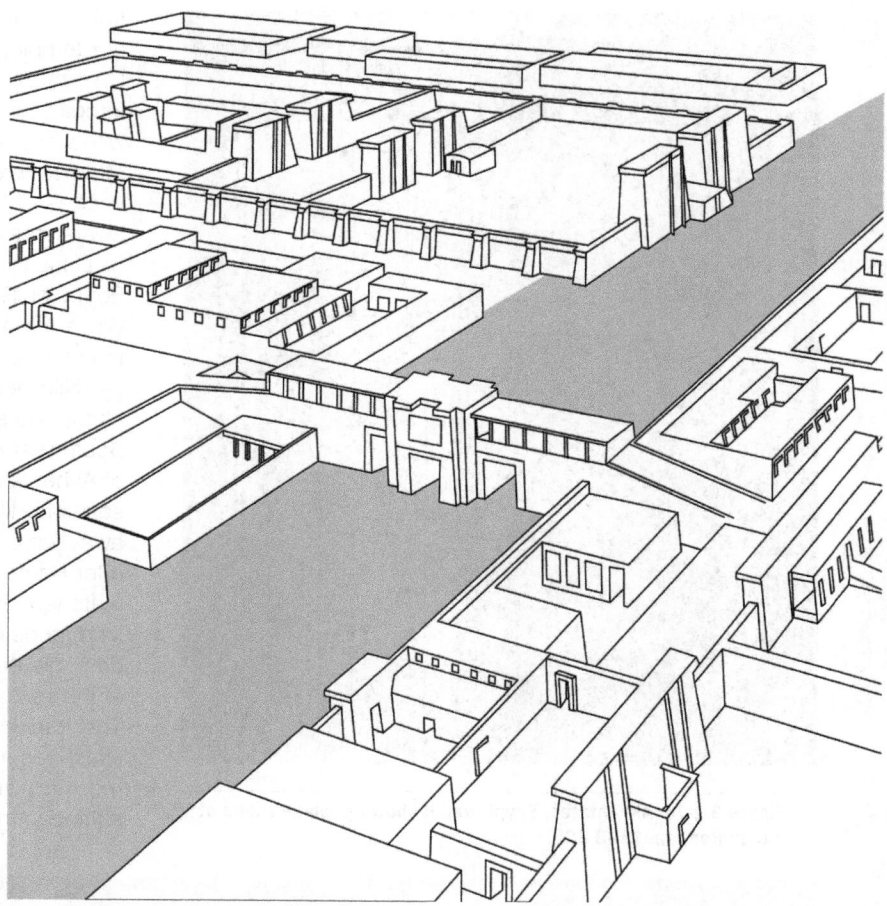

Figure 3.2-8 Akhentaten, Egypt. Hypothetical view of the *fastigium*, or window of appearances, bridging the main street and connecting parts of Akhenaten's palace, ca. 1340 BCE.

deploy a maximum of material to yield a minimum of space. The new hall, used for coronation ceremonies, overwhelms visitors with a field of 134 columns, each column over 4 m (13 ft) in diameter and ranging in height from 13 m (42 ft) on the sides to 23 m (74 ft) in the center. The five pairs of taller columns in the central row permit a grilled clerestory to bring light into the eerily dark interior. The papyriform columns on the sides were topped with closed bud capitals, while the capitals of the central aisles were designed as open papyrus flowers, offering a lyrical conceit of plants aspiring toward the light of the clerestories.

Ramesses II inserted the allée of ram-headed sphinxes, symbols of Amon, flanking the avenue between Karnak and Luxor as well as the colossal entry pylon (Fig. 3.2-11) at the latter monument. A century and a half after the completion of Amenhotep III's temple at Luxor, Ramesses added the great Northern Court, absorbing the original temple built by Hatshepsut into its double colonnades. The entry to the new court proceeded from the sphinx-lined avenue on the north through a massive pylon with two seated colossi of the pharaoh at the portal and several standing figures to the sides, as well as two obelisks. The plan of Ramesses's court followed a curiously skewed parallelogram as a result of the previous alignment of Hatshepsut's temple. The pylon carried friezes narrating the pharaoh's dubious victory over the Hittites at the Battle of Qadesh during the fifth year of his reign. Both sides claimed victory in this conflict and accepted a peaceful settlement, yet neither army actually prevailed. Ramesses, like his adversary Tudhaliya IV,

used the battle as propaganda, reporting it as a victory to increase his political clout at home.

During his nearly seventy-year reign Ramesses II left behind more colossal portraits of himself than any ruler in history. In the ancient capital of Memphis eleven colossal likenesses of him were found amid the ruins of the Temple of Ptau. For the new capital of Pi-Ramesse that he built in the Nile delta he commissioned no fewer than fifty statues of himself. His statues abounded at both Karnak and Luxor. An 18 m (59 ft) freestanding statue of the seated ruler, carved

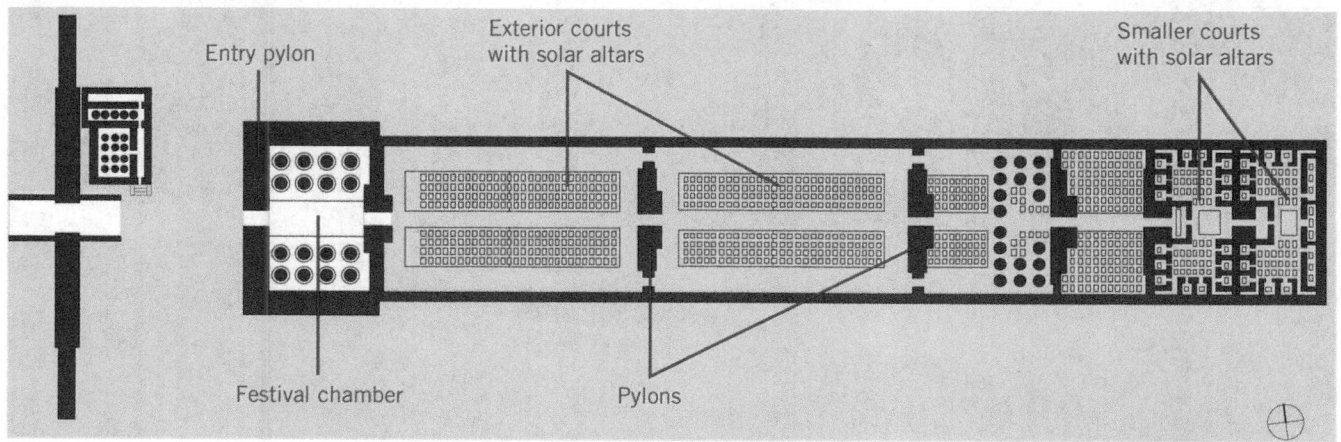

Figure 3.2-9 Akhentaten, Egypt. Plan of Temple of Aten, ca. 1440 BCE.

from a single block of sandstone, presided over his mortuary temple, known as the Ramesseum near Deir el-Bahri. Even taller portraits of him flanked the entries to the rock-cut temples of Abu Simbel. These statues served not just as witnesses for eternity but also as idols to be worshipped. Midway through his long career Ramesses even created images of the pharaoh worshipping himself, indicating his awareness of divine status.

Despite such ponderous expressions of power, the Egypt of Ramesses entered a phase of steady decline. While the national shrines remained in Thebes, Ramesses transferred the capital in the 1250s BCE to Pi-Ramesse in the Nile delta, a new city named after the divine king. He chose the site to be closer to the political trouble spots in Southwest Asia. Of the new capital, which was on the scale of Akhentaten and was used briefly by Ramesses's successors, only literary testimony remains, as the city was washed away with the changing course of the river. Nine pharaohs after Ramesses took his name, but none among them ever matched his power and divine status. Much like the urbanized lands of Southwest Asia, Egypt was weakened by the unstable environment, internal conflicts, and the invasions of the so-called Sea Peoples that began around 1200 BCE. The tradition of grand axes and colossal scale begun by Hatshepsut and brought to intimidating dimensions by Ramesses II subsided as the power of the pharaohs eventually shifted to the priestly class.

Figure 3.2-10 Akhentaten, Egypt. Relief showing family scene of Akhenaten, ca. 1340 BCE.

Figure 3.2-11 Luxor, Egypt. Pylon entry for Ramesses II, ca. 1250 BCE.

The Rock-Cut Temples at Abu Simbel

During the mid-thirteenth century BCE, Ramesses II built six temples in Nubia, Egypt's most unruly province. The temples confirmed the cult of the ruler and were the first indications of his deification during his lifetime, repeating a trend initiated by Amenhotep III a century earlier. The two temples at Abu Simbel, one dedicated to Ramesses and the other to his wife Nefertari, were cut from live rock. Four colossal seated portraits of the pharaoh guarded the entry to the king's temple. Smaller statues at his feet depicted important female members of the family and a young boy, the likely heir. The temple penetrated 60 m (192 ft) into the cliff, with hypostyle pillars in the entry hall. Six colossi guarded the queen's temple, including two portraits of Nefertari in the guise of Hathor, sandwiched between portraits of the pharaoh. From 1964 to 1968 CE, after the decision to flood the region with the construction of the Aswan Dam, the two temples were meticulously removed in 30-ton chunks and reassembled at a site 60 m (197 ft) above the original.

Abu Simbel, Egypt. Temple of Ramesses II, ca. 1250 BCE.

Further Reading

Michalowski, Kazimierz. *L'arte dell'antico Egitto*. Edited by Jean-Pierre Corteggiani. Milan: Garzanti, 2001.

Redford, Donald B. *Akhenaten: The Heretic King*. Princeton, NJ: Princeton University Press, 1984.

Reeves, Nicholas. *Akhenaten: Egypt's False Prophet*. London: Thames & Hudson, 2001.

Tyldesley, Joyce. *Hatchepsut: The Female Pharaoh*. London: Penguin, 1996.

———. *Ramesses: Egypt's Greatest Pharaoh*. London: Penguin, 2000.

3.3   BIBLICAL JERUSALEM
Architecture and Memory

Much of the history of ancient architecture relies on intelligent guesses about archaeological fragments, interpretations of literary and artistic documents, and the pursuit of legends. As urban artifacts disappeared through destruction, wear, natural calamities, and abandonment, so did the memory of them. Important cultures such as the Phoenicians—who from 1200 to 800 BCE dominated the trade of the Mediterranean and founded thriving colonies—have been poorly represented in general histories because of the lack of surviving built evidence. Despite their great importance during this period, Phoenician ports, such as Tyre, Sidon, and Byblos on the eastern Mediterranean coast, and the even more powerful colony of Carthage in Tunis, offer few traces of the significant culture that produced them.

In the case of Jerusalem, however, the memory of a city has endured despite the disappearance of its artifacts because the place came to represent an idea. Jerusalem has played a special role in world history because of the cosmological meanings attached to it by Jews, Christians, and Muslims. For Jews it is the place where the Messiah will come to unite all peoples in peace. For Christians it will be the scene of the Apocalypse, where heaven will descend to earth. For Muslims it signifies the site of the Last Judgment, where all souls will wait for deliverance. No other city in the world has been quite so burdened with religious expectation. During its 3,000-year history it has often been divided, sacked, and rebuilt. Even its name has been changed on a few occasions. But despite all attempts to erase or revise the "real" Jerusalem, over half of the world's population regards it, because of its supposedly sacred destiny, as an indelible *topos*, a place that represents a profound concept.

The City of the Jews and Many Others

Jerusalem would probably have remained in obscurity if it had not been claimed by the Jewish people and subsequently treated as their sacred center. Settled first by the Canaanites around 1800 BCE, it endures as one of the oldest continuously inhabited cities on earth and one of the least stable. Jerusalem has been destroyed through violent sieges seventeen times and ruled by twenty-five different peoples. Like Hattusha, it clings to a remote, defensible rocky site in the hills. To the east one can see where the desert begins to form, while the valleys sloping westward toward the Mediterranean appear verdant and the climate comfortable due to its high altitude. Although ancient Jerusalem had sufficient water from Gihon Spring to support a small city, it did not have access to a river and thus could never develop as a good site for trade or industry. Both its good fortune and its pitfalls have been mostly procured through religion, and like Eridu before it, Jerusalem for three millennia has been revered as the center of the sacred.

Seminomadic Jewish tribes claimed the city as their capital around the year 1000 BCE. The history of the Jewish people during the Bronze Age is seasoned by the legends assembled during the sixth century BCE into the five books of the Torah, the basis of the Bible. The twelve tribes of Israel shared a religious belief in a single, invisible God who occasionally communicated with the faithful through prophets. The compelling difference of ancient Judaism from other religions was its insistence that the divinity should not be represented, since that would create a substitute or false idol. Furthermore, even the name of God, "Yahweh," was prohibited from being uttered, leading to the deferential substitute "the Lord," used throughout the Bible. The Jewish people's mandate to worship a divine being that could not be seen appears as a constant struggle in the biblical stories. The first prophet, Abraham, convinced his people to leave Ur during the great drought at the end of the third millennium BCE and move west to the Mediterranean. Whether or not the Jews were among the Semitic Hyksos invaders of northern Egypt during the sixteenth century BCE, their subsequent servitude to the Egyptian state, particularly as construction workers for Ramesses II's new capital of Pi-Ramesse in the thirteenth century BCE, is well documented.

The Jewish liberation from Egypt and scattered resettlement in the coastal lands of Canaan between Egypt and Mesopotamia coincided with the overall strife that broke out in the eastern Mediterranean around the year 1200 BCE, when empires fell and invasions were common. The identity of the Jews as a people has endured as a result of their strict

▼ **ca. 1800 BCE**

Jerusalem settled by Canaanites

King David unifies Jewish peoples into the kingdom of Israel

▲ **1040–970 BCE**

▼ **ca. 950 BCE**

King Solomon commissions the First Temple in Jerusalem

adherence to sacred texts that document the nature of a single god. Attacks by the Philistines, who were probably settled descendants of the Sea Peoples, forced the Jews around the year 1000 BCE to consolidate militarily under the leadership of a warrior hero, the shepherd David. For strategic reasons David chose Jerusalem as the national capital, both to eliminate the competition of the resident Jesubites and to establish rule in a place that would not give unfair advantage to any of the previously settled villages of the Jewish tribes.

David's city (Fig. 3.3-1) clung to the top of a walled, oval-shaped hill, with steep fortifications built by the Jesubites, who after the conquest were peacefully absorbed into the city's population. Early Jerusalem appeared close in scale to Mycenae. Similar to the layout of Mycenaean citadels, the elite lived within the walls of the city, while the majority of the population resided in peripheral villages. A tunnel ran under the walls to an outside source of water, just as in Hittite and Mycenaean fortresses.

Being a seminomadic people, the Jews lacked traditions of masonry architecture, city building, and city administration. During the eighty years that David and his son Solomon reigned, Jerusalem followed the precedents of the nearby Phoenicians, with whom they had struck an alliance. Under King David, the status of the Jews changed from inconsequential outsiders to a dominant power, influencing a region that stretched from the Red Sea to the Euphrates River. The political mechanisms of alliances, intermarriages, and cultural exchanges guaranteed that wealth in the form of taxes and tribute flowed into the new capital. Like other regimes, David and Solomon realized that to maintain political control they needed a palace to represent the validity of their dynasty and, more importantly, a temple as the home of the deity that protected their rule. While the idea of a palace was perfectly acceptable, that of a temple created lasting antagonisms.

Against Architecture: The Rise and Fall of the Temple

For any other people the project of improving Jerusalem's architecture would have seemed quite normal, if not necessary, in order to continue the success of the unified state.

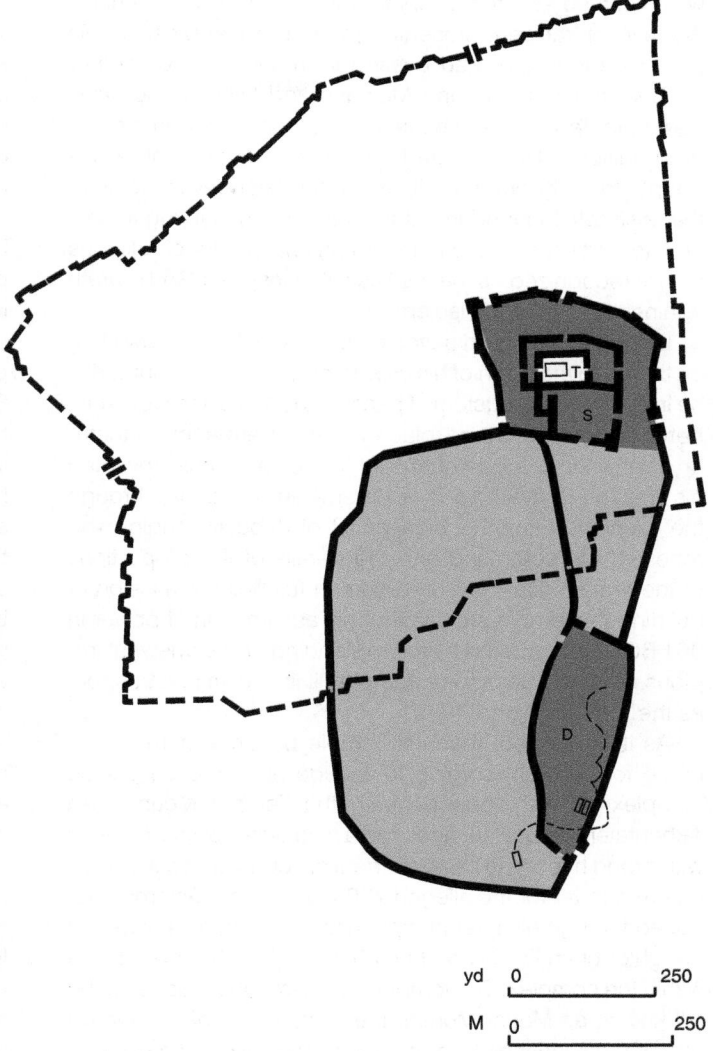

yd 0 _____ 250

M 0 _____ 250

Figure 3.3-1 Jerusalem. Plan of city, ca. 900 BCE: (D) David's city; (S) palace of Solomon; (T) First Temple. Dotted line indicates the existing sixteenth-century CE walls built by the Ottomans.

But for the Jewish tribes, which were saturated with nomadic habits, the creation of a temple next to a royal palace constituted a suspect act that might inspire divine retribution. Before settling in Jerusalem, the tribes had honored a mobile sanctuary, known as the Ark of the Covenant,

Jerusalem sacked and First Temple destroyed by Neo-Babylonians

586 BCE

▼ **535 BCE**

Construction begun on the Second Temple in Jerusalem

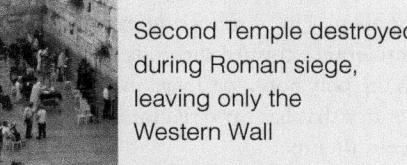

Second Temple destroyed during Roman siege, leaving only the Western Wall

▲ **70 CE**

which served as a repository for the Ten Commandments—the laws of Yahweh, presented to the prophet Moses. This portable tabernacle had passed from one tribe to another for brief tenures. Like the Minoans and Hittites, the Jews had gathered for ceremonies at outdoor sites, in groves or on hilltops. They needed only a congregation of twelve people to carry out their rituals. In the later Jewish texts of the *Mishnah*, the fundamental contradiction of trying to give architectural substance to the immaterial nature of religious faith is recognized as the fatal flaw that inspired God's wrath against the city of Jerusalem.

David programmed a stable ritual focus for the new state on the hill to the north of his city. To consolidate his authority, he interrupted the custom of passing the Ark of the Covenant between the tribes and placed it in a permanent sanctuary. Yahweh, as gods often did in Mesopotamia, revealed his desires to the king in a dream—in this case, through the prophet Nathan, a high priest of Jebusite origin, who received the command and the details of the proportions of the temple. David's son Solomon fulfilled the mission of building the temple shortly after his assumption of power in 961 BCE. Often called by the misleading and somewhat impious name of "Solomon's Temple," it is known in retrospect as the "First Temple."

As it developed, the First Temple became more than a home for Yahweh, coming to include an immense palace complex on the slope beneath the Temple Mount. Like Akhentaten, Jerusalem acquired a religious–political nucleus with grand hypostyle halls, residential courts, and a separate harem quarter for the alleged 700 wives whom Solomon acquired through his foreign diplomacy. One of these wives, a daughter of an Egyptian pharaoh, was given her own house within the complex. The temple rose above the palace on the hill known as Mount Moriah, the alleged site of Abraham's attempted sacrifice of his son Isaac. The hill may have previously served as an open-air cult site for the Jebusites. Like

Judaism and Monotheism

All cultures previous to the Jews believed in more than one god. Natural features were seen as expressions of divinity and cities as sacred, while even living people such as rulers and priests could achieve god-like status. The gods were perceived as being everywhere and very tangible. Through the guidance of the prophets of the Old Testament, beginning with Abraham, the Jews came to worship a single divinity. While this supreme being occasionally intervened on earth, speaking to select individuals such as Abraham and Moses, he remained invisible and his name could not be spoken. The abstract and exclusive nature of the Jewish god led to intolerance toward the gods of others. Monotheism, enforced through the holy book, or *Torah*, instilled in the Jews a powerful cultural identity that has survived innumerable displacements throughout three millennia.

Mesopotamian and Egyptian temples, the Jewish temple included a rectangular precinct, or *temenos*, enclosing the shrine formed by the walls of its storerooms. The people had access to its outer court, while only the priesthood could enter the inner court. The priests' court contained an outdoor altar for burnt sacrifices and a bronze basin for ablutions that rested on the backs of twelve sculpted oxen.

Literary sources of the sixth century BCE described the First Temple as a narrow, oblong volume raised on a tall platform reached by an axial stair (Fig. 3.3-2), similar to a Mycenaean megaron. While all could see it rising over the city, it could be accessed only by the religious elite. The porch facade had two columns, with the angelic names of Boaz and Jachin. They carried lily-shaped capitals. The main hall, approximately 30 m (96 ft) deep by 10 m (32 ft) wide, was lined with carved cedar panels. The rear sanctuary, or holy of holies, was a perfect cube 10 m (33 ft) per side, raised on a step above the level of the hall. Unlike all other temples of the time, the First Temple did not house a statue of the deity but only the effects of divinity, the Ark of the Covenant. Still, it was believed that God dwelled within the holy of holies. For the yearly feast of the Day of Atonement, the high priest risked entering the sanctuary alone to offer sacrifices for the sins of the people. The holy of holies seemed so dread-ridden to the ancient Jews that the priests would tie a rope around the high priest's waist so that if he died or fainted during the experience, they could pull him back into the hall without having to enter and profane the sanctuary.

Solomon enlisted the help of his ally Hiram I of the Phoenician port city of Tyre to build the First Temple. Hiram recently had undergone a similar experience of building a temple to the god Melqart for his own city. Thousands of Phoenicians came to carve the stones and teach the local masons. The Jews conscripted several thousand workers from their own people to finish the job. Solomon also built an aqueduct to bring water to the top of the hill from Bethlehem, 10 km (6 miles) to the south. During the twenty-year process, the king incurred an enormous debt to the neighboring Phoenicians, resulting in the siphoning off of some Jewish lands. The creation of the temple damaged the state's economy but established a seemingly unalterable urban fact, part natural, part human-made, that became the monumental pivot around which the city's history would revolve.

The temple and the palace in the upper city set the urban elite at a distance from the people through monumental architecture. Jerusalem now possessed a visible model of order that could be witnessed regularly through rituals. The problem arose from the fact that people could see through this sort of order, especially when it became a strain on their economy. The effect of Solomon's charisma began to dissipate soon after his passing, and he left an unclear line of succession. The state began to disintegrate and by 900 BCE had broken into two lands, with Jerusalem as the capital of Israel and Samaria as the capital of Judah. The latter kingdom fell to the Neo-Assyrians in the 720s BCE, and half the population was dragged off as slaves to build the new capital of Dur-Sharrukin for Sargon II (see Section 4.1). While

Figure 3.3-2 Jerusalem. (a) Plan of the First Temple, ca. 900 BCE.
(b) Model of the Second Temple at the time of King Herod, first century BCE.

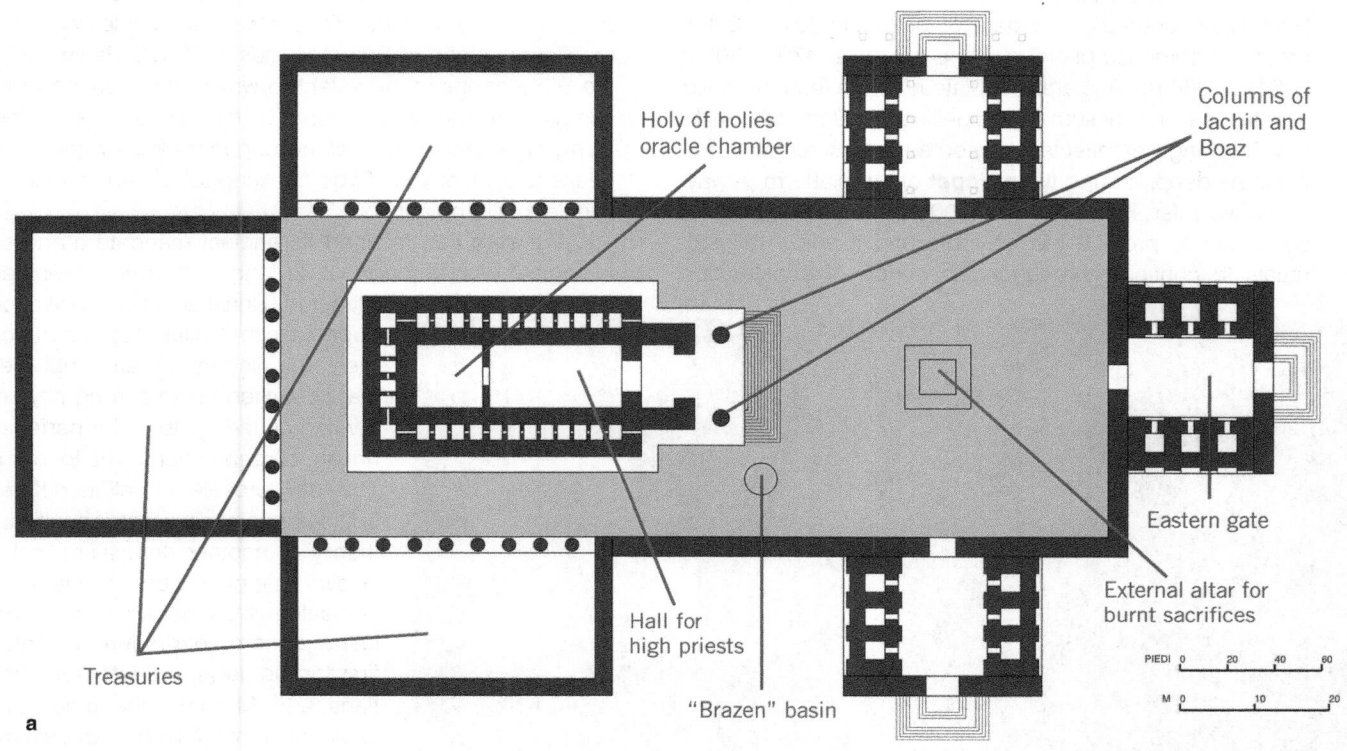

Holy of holies
oracle chamber

Columns of
Jachin and
Boaz

Eastern gate

External altar for
burnt sacrifices

Hall for
high priests

"Brazen" basin

Treasuries

a

b

Jerusalem escaped damage on that occasion, in 586 BCE it fell to the Neo-Babylonians. Nebuchadnezzar took 20,000 prisoners to Babylon and destroyed the First Temple completely. This event marked the beginning of what became known as "the diaspora," or scattering, of the Jewish people. When explaining retrospectively the troubles of the Jews, one of the prophets asked: "What is the sin of the house of Judah? Is it not Jerusalem?" The ambitiousness of the city and the vanity of its architecture seemed sins of hubris to those who regretted the loss of their nomadic virtue.

Despite the objections of the prophet Jeremiah, who felt that God could be honored without making great buildings, a Second Temple was hastily begun around 535 BCE after the Persians permitted the Jews to return to Jerusalem. During the late first century BCE the ambitious King Herod I completely rebuilt the Second Temple in grand style. Benefiting from the protection of the Romans, he transformed the hill into the largest temple mount of the Hellenistic period. His builders shored up the base of the mount 30 m (98 ft) to create an immense platform with a perimeter 470 × 300 m (1,541 × 984 ft). This artificial plateau, more than the buildings that sat on it, assumed compelling monumentality in the city. The king's architects wrapped a grand colonnade, four columns deep, around the **parapet** of the platform. Always a shrewd ruler, Herod trained 1,000 priests to be masons so as not to profane the holy site and to allow religious rituals to continue throughout its period of construction.

The grandeur of his project can still be observed in the huge ashlar blocks that sit at the base of the Temple Mount, some of them up to 4 m (13 ft) in length, rivaling the size of the blocks of the pyramids at Giza. Now known as the Western Wall (Fig. 3.3-3), the site draws Jews lamenting the loss of not only the First but also the Second Temple, which was destroyed a few generations after its completion during the Roman siege of Emperor Titus in 70 CE. Psalm 137 in the Bible captures the extent to which the absence of the Temple can taunt the memory: "If I forget you, O Jerusalem, let my right hand wither, let my tongue stick to my palate, if I cease to think of you, if I do not keep Jerusalem in memory even at my happiest hour."

Jerusalem has retained its ancient mandate as a cosmological pivot throughout its long history and eventually attracted Christian and Muslim occupants with similar religious attachments. It lingers in an ambivalent state between being a living city and serving as the symbol of a perfected notion of generations yet to come. The real Jerusalem in all its different editions has always carried with it a theory of another Jerusalem, not of its own time but of some timeless era. Jerusalem thus became more than just a place on earth: it represented, first for the Jews and later for Christians and Muslims, the theological explanation of a final human destiny.

Figure 3.3-3 Jerusalem. The Western Wall of the Temple Mount, ca. 20 BCE.

Further Reading

Armstrong, Karen. *History of God: The 4000-Year Quest of Judaism, Christianity, and Islam*. New York: Gramercy, 2004.

Moscati, Sabatino, ed. *I Fenici*. Milan: Bompiani, 1988.

Peters, F. E. *Jerusalem*. Princeton, NJ: Princeton University Press, 1985.

Rosenau, Helen. *Vision of the Temple: The Image of the Temple of Jerusalem in Judaism and Christianity*. London: Oresko Books, 1979.

Yadin, Yigael, ed. *Jerusalem Revealed: Archaeology in the Holy City, 1968–1974*. New Haven, CT: Yale University Press, 1976.

↗ Visit the free website **www.oup.com/us/ingersoll** to view chapter outlines and study questions; Google Maps showing the location of key sites; links to UNESCO World Heritage Sites; and essays on topics that cross time and culture.

700–200 BCE

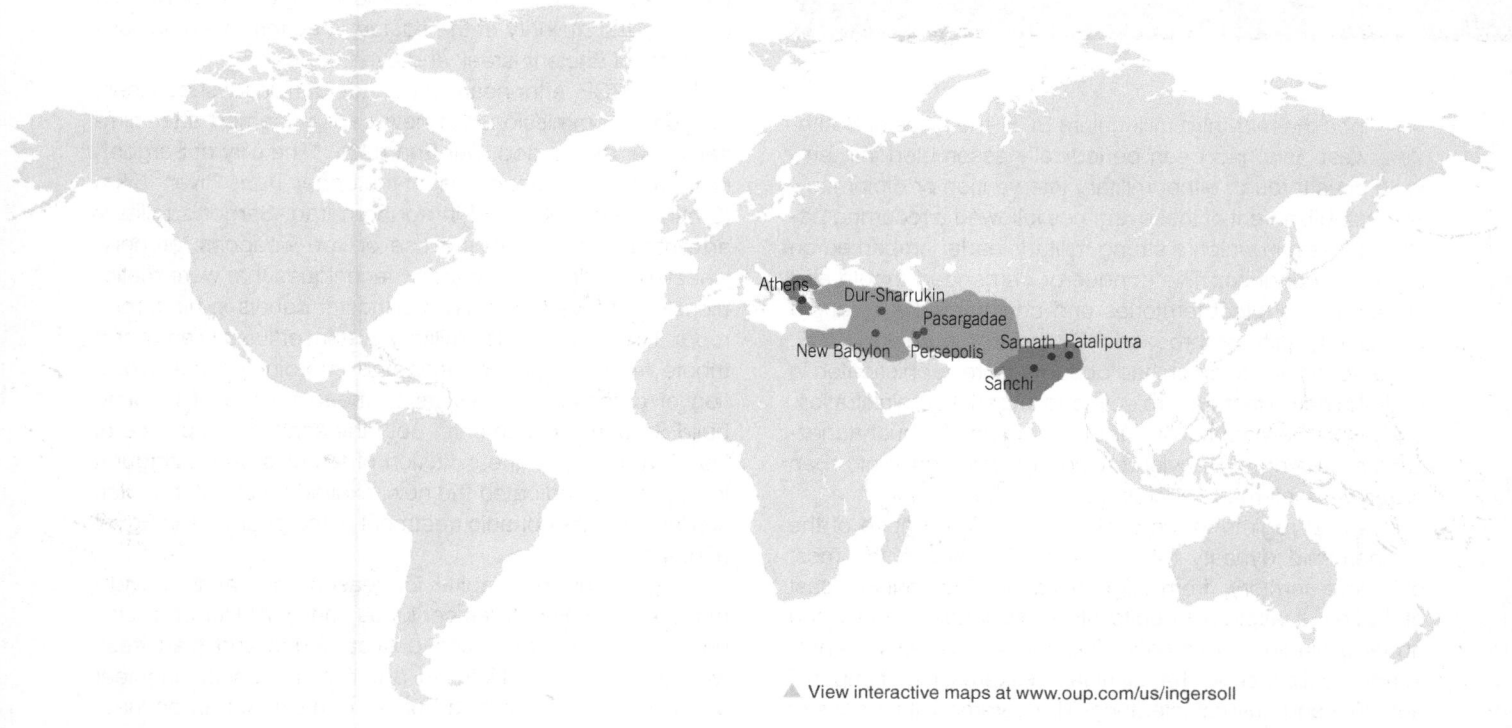

▲ View interactive maps at www.oup.com/us/ingersoll

4.1 SOUTHWEST ASIA AND ACHAEMENID PERSIA: A Cycle of Empires

4.2 THE GREEK CITY-STATE: Classical Architecture at the Acropolis and the Agora

4.3 MAURYAN INDIA: Emblems of Peace in Stone

During the first millennium, improved military techniques such as the wheeled chariot helped rulers amass ever-larger political empires. Command passed from the Neo-Assyrians in Nineveh to the Neo-Babylonians in Babylon to the Achaemenid Persians, who through a combination of military and diplomatic strategies incorporated all of Anatolia, Syria, Palestine, parts of Egypt, and Persia into a single empire. The Persian Achaemenid dynasty distributed its power to a series of regional *satraps*, who came yearly to Persepolis to pledge allegiance to the "king of kings." In the Aegean, Athens led the successful Greek resistance against the colonial efforts of the Persian Empire. This unique democratic society produced a splendid collection of monuments to celebrate its autonomy, including the great temple of the Parthenon. Alexander, the young king of the Macedonians, who had been educated in Greek ways by the great philosopher Aristotle, conquered the territories once ruled by the Achaemenids and attempted to spread Hellenistic culture throughout the world. His example of empire building was copied by the Mauryan dynasty in India, which unified diverse ethnicities and territories. The emperor Ashoka erected hundreds of memorial columns around India with pacific messages, as if to make amends for the violence of military expansion that accompanied the road to empire.

4.1 SOUTHWEST ASIA AND ACHAEMENID PERSIA
A Cycle of Empires

Since the mid-third millennium BCE, the cities of Southwest Asia had been periodically assembled into empires through either military intervention or diplomacy. The establishment of these regimes followed a recurring political pattern in which a strong military leader embarked on a path of conquest. The conqueror demanded tribute and slaves from subject territories and constructed a splendid capital city with the proceeds. By the eighth century BCE, the empires of the region had become more sophisticated in both their architectural projects and imperial administration. Sargon II's new capital of Dur-Sharrukin and Nebuchadnezzar's rebuilding of Babylon provided a new sense of urban order with well-made streets and city gates.

The last regime in the cycle, the Persian Empire of the Achaemenid dynasty (550–330 BCE), covered the most extensive territory, from Afghanistan to the Ionian coast of Turkey. It aspired to unite all of the lands of the world under a single government. The new Achaemenid capital at Persepolis rose as the culminating expression of imperial authority and cultural tolerance. The ceremonial terraces of the palace, with sculpted relief panels and vast hypostyle halls, attempted to demonstrate not just the power of the rulers but also their capacity to govern a grand multiethnic confederation.

Sargon II's Dur-Sharrukin: The Roots of the Charismatic Palace

Southwest Asia experienced a period of stagnation during the ninth and eighth centuries BCE. Invasions and famine kept the cities small until the Neo-Assyrians (not to be confused with the ancient Assyrians of more than 1,000 years earlier) amassed a huge army in northern Iraq and laid claim to the lands of the Fertile Crescent. Proud of their mastery of the most advanced military equipment of the day, they conquered a series of ethnically diverse states, attempting to restore the power of the original Sargon's Akkadian Empire. The new despot, Sargon II (r. 721–705 BCE), modeled himself on the Bronze-Age emperor, taking his name. He consolidated his holdings by annexing the northern territories of Armenia; the southern region of Babylonia (Sumer); the majority of the eastern Mediterranean, including most of ancient Israel; and even parts of Egypt.

In 713 BCE, after nearly a decade of military successes, Sargon II commissioned a new capital, named after himself rather than a god. Dur-Sharrukin, "The City of Sargon," now called Khorsabad, lies on the upper Tigris River 15 km (9 miles) north of Mosul in northern Iraq. Sargon's military advantage came from the use of iron weapons, archery, wheeled chariots, and cavalry, techniques that were meticulously portrayed on carved orthostat panels in his throne room. The Neo-Assyrian military system efficiently amassed tribute from conquered cities and coordinated the migration of defeated peoples as a cheap source of labor to build Sargon's monuments. Both the scale of his palace at Dur-Sharrukin and the inclusion of temples and a ziggurat in its precinct indicated the new, exalted nature of the ruler, similar to the theophanic treatment of the pharaohs in Egypt (Fig. 4.1-1).

Sargon built his capital for reasons similar to David's move to Jerusalem three centuries earlier. At Dur-Sharrukin he could avoid preexisting political feuds and start fresh without internal conflicts. In addition, he could engineer the new environment as a portrait of his rule. Sargon inaugurated his capital with a remarkable act of equity, compensating the landowners whose properties had been expropriated to create the site. He then lured thousands of construction workers to move there by absolving their debts. He increased their ranks with slaves gained through military conquests.

At Dur-Sharrukin one finds the first effort outside Egypt (and the vanished Harappan settlements) to design a city on an orthogonal plan (Fig. 4.1-2). But the scale and monumentality of Sargon's city surpassed all previous models. The outline of its walls followed a unique geometric figure, nearly square in shape: 1,760 × 1,630 m (5,774 × 5,347 ft). These walls enclosed four times the area of Ur and twice that of Hattusha (see Section 3.1). The walls rose 12 m (39 ft)

710 BCE

Sargon II builds Neo-Assyrian capital of Dur-Sharrukin (Syria)

Reign of Nebuchadnezzar and rebuilding of Babylon

▲ **604–562 BCE**

ca. 570 BCE

Neo-Babylonians build Entemenanki, last ziggurat

and were studded with slightly higher towers set at 10 m (33 ft) intervals, creating a serrated effect. Stepped merlons, known as **crowfoot parapets**, lined the battlements. The most prominent gate at the southern corner looked toward the earlier Assyrian capital at Nineveh. Most of the gates of Dur-Sharrukin corresponded to gates on the opposite side of the city, implying the existence of a grid of straight streets inside the walls.

Sargon set his palace, with its temples and ziggurat, astride the northern walls. His citadel rose on a grand terrace lined with pleated walls several stories above the level of the rest of the city. The two palace gates established the complex's colossal scale, with doorjambs framed by immense hybrid creatures made of a bull's body, an eagle's wings, and a bearded man's head. These **apotropaic**, or guardian, figures, known as *shedus* in the masculine and *lamassus* in the feminine, stood over 5 m (16 ft) high in carved granite (Fig. 4.1-3). While fearsome in scale, their bearded faces had serene, benevolent smiles.

Within the precinct of the Palace of Sargon stood a cluster of secondary palaces for the emperor's advisors and relatives and a temple to the Babylonian god of wisdom, Nabu. The temple's alignment diverged 10° east of that of the other buildings, perhaps for astronomical orientation. One entered the main palace by a broad ramp suitable for chariots. Triple portals at the top of the ramp were guarded by colossal pairs of *shedus*. Beyond these guardians lay an open square court, large enough to accommodate thousands of courtiers. While the designers used orthogonal coordinates throughout, they followed a longstanding tradition of setting the entries to the inner palace asymmetrically to discourage direct access. Bureaucratic offices lined the north flank of the first court, and in the north corner a passage led to the court of honor, about half the size of the first court. From here one turned left to enter through another pair of *shedus* into the suite of throne rooms. A relief beneath the throne showed Sargon in his chariot driving over the bodies of slain enemies while his men collected skulls, realistically depicting the violent methods of the Neo-Assyrian Empire. Stone orthostat friezes with larger-than-life portraits of the king and his courtiers on a hunt and at war clad the throne room's thick mud walls. Built primarily of unbaked mud bricks and without columns, the rooms of Sargon's palace were long and narrow. One technical innovation for the region

appeared under the royal quarters, where the designers inserted a vaulted drainage system. As in the Mesopotamian house type, the principal light source came from the courtyards distributed throughout the palace.

The western side of Sargon's palace contained six temples and a ziggurat. The combination of religious and secular spaces gave architectural expression to the attempt to deify the ruler. Sargon's ziggurat, the first to be constructed in the region for many centuries, presented both a revival and an improvement of the type. Square in plan, with 50 m (160 ft) per side and probably the same measure in height, it rose to seven levels on a continuous spiral path. This incorporation of the pathway into the geometric progression of levels provided an ingenious method for eliminating an extended stair. The walls along the ziggurat's path rippled with pleats and carried crowfoot parapets. The builders stained each level of the tower a different color, ascending from white to black, red, and blue.

Sargon died in battle a year after occupying his new palace at Dur-Sharrukin. His son, Sennacherib, immediately abandoned the city, preferring to rebuild the ancient city of Nineveh as his capital. The new king methodically eliminated references to his father in the many documents that have been preserved and refused to honor a cult site Sargon had dedicated to himself. Sennacherib's rejection of his father's cult and Dur-Sharrukin seems to have been as ideologically motivated as the Egyptian censure of Akhenaten and his new capital several centuries earlier. To witness Sargon's ziggurat and palaces standing empty must have seemed as uncanny as a visit to Djoser's mortuary complex in Saqqâra. The abandoned capital joined a long list of ideal cities in which a single patron attempted to produce an architectural materialization of uncompromised political order—in this case, a despotic one. Under the autocratic rule of Sargon II the palace type absorbed the religious functions to become a theater of absolute power and intimidation. Sargon's ambitious architectural adventure redefined the notion of the city as the stage for a god-like ruler in charge of a fierce war machine.

New Babylon: The Return to Ritual Order

Babylon stood on the Euphrates upstream from Uruk and Ur. Today it lies about 40 km (25 miles) west of Baghdad. Its name in the local Akkadian language, *Babilim*, or "Gate

King Cyrus of Achaemenid dynasty of Persia creates vast empire from the Aegean to Persia

▲ **539** BCE

▼ **ca. 530** BCE

Cyrus builds capital and tomb at Pasargadae

King Darius builds Persian capital at Persepolis

▲ **518** BCE

Figure 4.1-1 Dur-Sharrukin (Khorsabad, Iraq). Perspective view of Sargon II's palace (after Lloyd), 705 BCE.

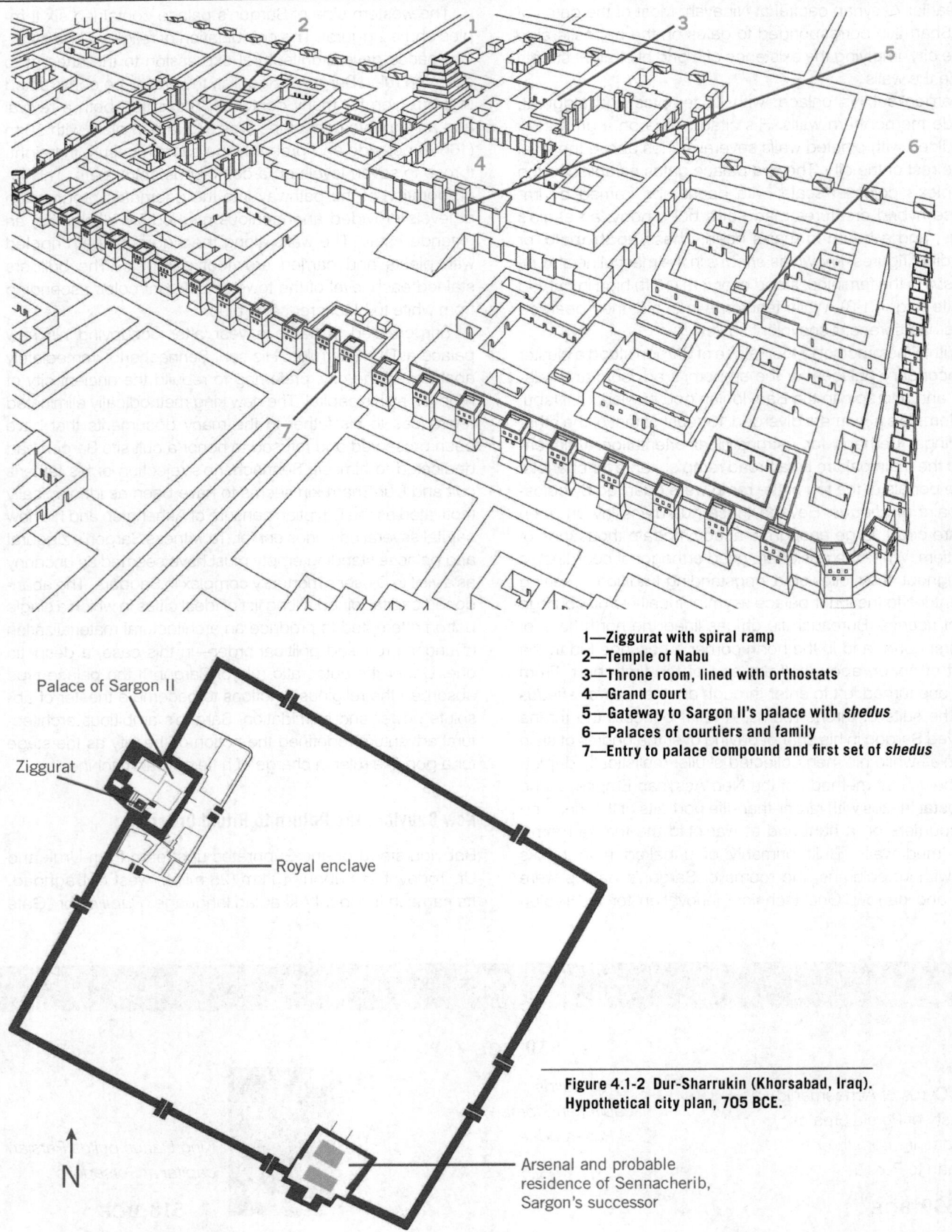

1—Ziggurat with spiral ramp
2—Temple of Nabu
3—Throne room, lined with orthostats
4—Grand court
5—Gateway to Sargon II's palace with *shedus*
6—Palaces of courtiers and family
7—Entry to palace compound and first set of *shedus*

Palace of Sargon II

Ziggurat

Royal enclave

Figure 4.1-2 Dur-Sharrukin (Khorsabad, Iraq). Hypothetical city plan, 705 BCE.

Arsenal and probable residence of Sennacherib, Sargon's successor

N

of God," indicates the city's religious caliber. Babylon came to political prominence under the rule of the Amorites, a proto-Arabic people, during the eighteenth century BCE. It lost political power around 1600 BCE but remained an important religious site. A millennium later, the Chaldean dynasty from southern Mesopotamia revived the city as the center of an empire. Under Nebuchadnezzar II (r. 604–562 BCE), New Babylon became an Iron-Age "melting pot," with as many as 500,000 inhabitants from twenty different language groups. It boasted forty-three temples to different national deities, including one for the Jews, who had been taken as captives after the destruction of the First Temple in Jerusalem. Babylon's new political fortune partly derived from its status as the region's primordial religious center and source of language. Unlike their Neo-Assyrian rivals, the rulers of New Babylon portrayed themselves as defenders of religion rather than champions of warfare. They planned major projects for Babylon's renewal, including great temples and the ceremonial procession route, to enhance the city's theological role. They discreetly set the royal palace, which covered more area than that of Sargon II, on the northern edge of the city, distinct from the religious center.

New Babylon repeated some of the same ideas as Dur-Sharrukin for its walls and elevated royal palace. The Greek historian Herodotus (ca. 484–425 BCE) admired the city for its architectural grandeur. The three sets of walls, the ziggurat of Entemenanki, the Esagila Temple dedicated to the god Marduk, and the vast imperial palace with its hanging gardens had no rivals. Like the Neo-Assyrians, the Neo-Babylonians brought hostages from conquered countries to build their projects, a process remembered by the Jews in the Bible as the "Babylonian captivity."

During the long reign of Nebuchadnezzar II, the walls of the inner city were twice rebuilt in a rectangular pattern. The new set of outer walls enclosed the Summer Palace in the north, increasing the city's area to twice the size of Sargon's capital. The Euphrates ran through the middle of the city, controlled by tall embankments. One reached the New Town on the western side of the river via an arched stone bridge. Nebuchadnezzar doubled the size of the royal palace, leapfrogging over the original walls to the north.

Figure 4.1-3 Dur-Sharrukin (Khorsabad, Iraq). A pair of *shedus*, apotropaic doorjambs, part bull, part eagle, and part nobleman, from the Palace of Sargon II, 705 BCE.

The designers of New Babylon repeated the orthogonal methods of Dur-Sharrukin, as seen in the squared-off walls (Fig. 4.1-4). A grand axis, 22 m (72 ft) wide, plowed straight through the heart of the city, bringing crowds to the major temples. Daily religious ceremonies took place on this Processional Way, called *Aj-ibut-shapu*, "the invisible enemy should not exist." This enigmatic name urged participants to make themselves visible, join the masses on procession, and partake in the greatness of Babylon. The first tract of the Processional Way ran alongside the new extension of the royal palace to meet the Ishtar Gate (Fig. 4.1-5). It then proceeded about a kilometer to the two major temple compounds in the center of the city. The new boulevard, intended to rid Babylon of "invisible enemies," constituted the first significant project for public space in this part of the world.

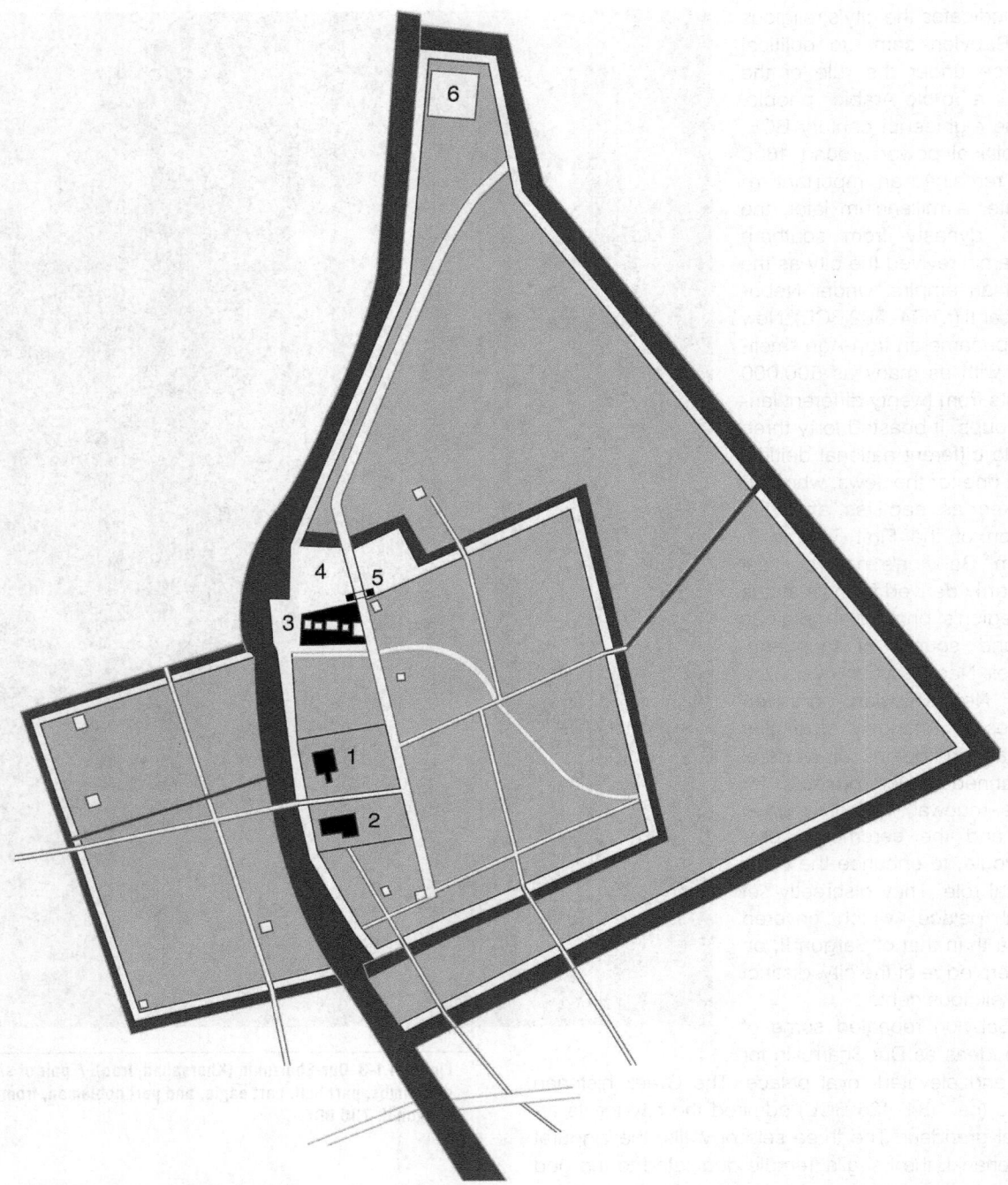

Figure 4.1-4 New Babylon (Iraq). Hypothetical plan of the city at the time of Nebuchadnezzar, ca. 570 BCE. The Ishtar Gate (5) on the north gave on to the broad Processional Way; the royal palace (3) and hanging gardens (4) were to its left. In the center, near the Euphrates, rose the great ziggurat of Entemenanki (1), and south of it the Esagila Temple (2), dedicated to Marduk. The Summer Palace (6) was built at the edge of the new northern walls.

Babylon's new ziggurat, known as Entemenanki (Fig. 4.1-6), "the house that is the foundation of heaven and earth," likely inspired the biblical story of the Tower of Babel. Nebuchad-nezzar at the same time restored Ur-Nammu's ziggurat at Ur, over 200 km (120 miles) to the south, as a gesture of theological continuity. The design of Babylon's stepped tower repeated that of the older one quite literally, with the same triad of stairs, one extended perpendicular and two lateral sets converging at the first landing. A grand *temenos*, 400 m (1,312 ft) per side, framed Entemenanki, with housing for priests and grain silos set in the thickness of its pleated perimeter walls. The ziggurat's footprint, which is all that remains of Entemenanki after centuries of looting of its bricks, was 91 m (299 ft) per side, nearly twice the width of Sargon's tower and 25% larger than that of Ur. Its broad stair-way protruded 50 m (164 ft) toward the south. Entemenanki rose in seven stages, each painted a different color, culminating in a blue pavilion temple at the top. The seven levels corresponded to the seven heavens, a notion quite important for a culture that had the most advanced knowledge of astronomy among the ancients. The height of Nebuchadnezzar's tower was double that of the ziggurat at Ur but one-third less than that of the pyramid of Khufu at Giza. Entemenanki, because of its urban situation, nonetheless appeared to be the tallest building in the world and, as such, attracted both awe and criticism. The Jewish interpretation of it in the Bible presented the tower as the materialization of the sin of hubris, the attempt of mortals to surpass the gods.

The entry to the other major cult site, the Esagila Temple, dedicated to the god Marduk, stood across the Processional Way to the south, directly on-axis with the stairs of Entemenanki. While set in a smaller enclosure, it had more ritual importance. Here, the religious hierarchy attempted to guarantee the city's power to control the fate of the world. The annual New Year's Festival, which included eleven days of ceremonies, began and ended in this court. The king took the leading role in these rites, requesting the intercession of Marduk, the king of the gods, to ensure the well-being of the city and its agricultural surplus. During the festival, the king would "take the hand" of Marduk and, from the Akitu Temple outside the city, conduct the wooden representation of the god and those of other gods, such as Nabu, Ishtar, and the mother goddess Ninmah, back into the city.

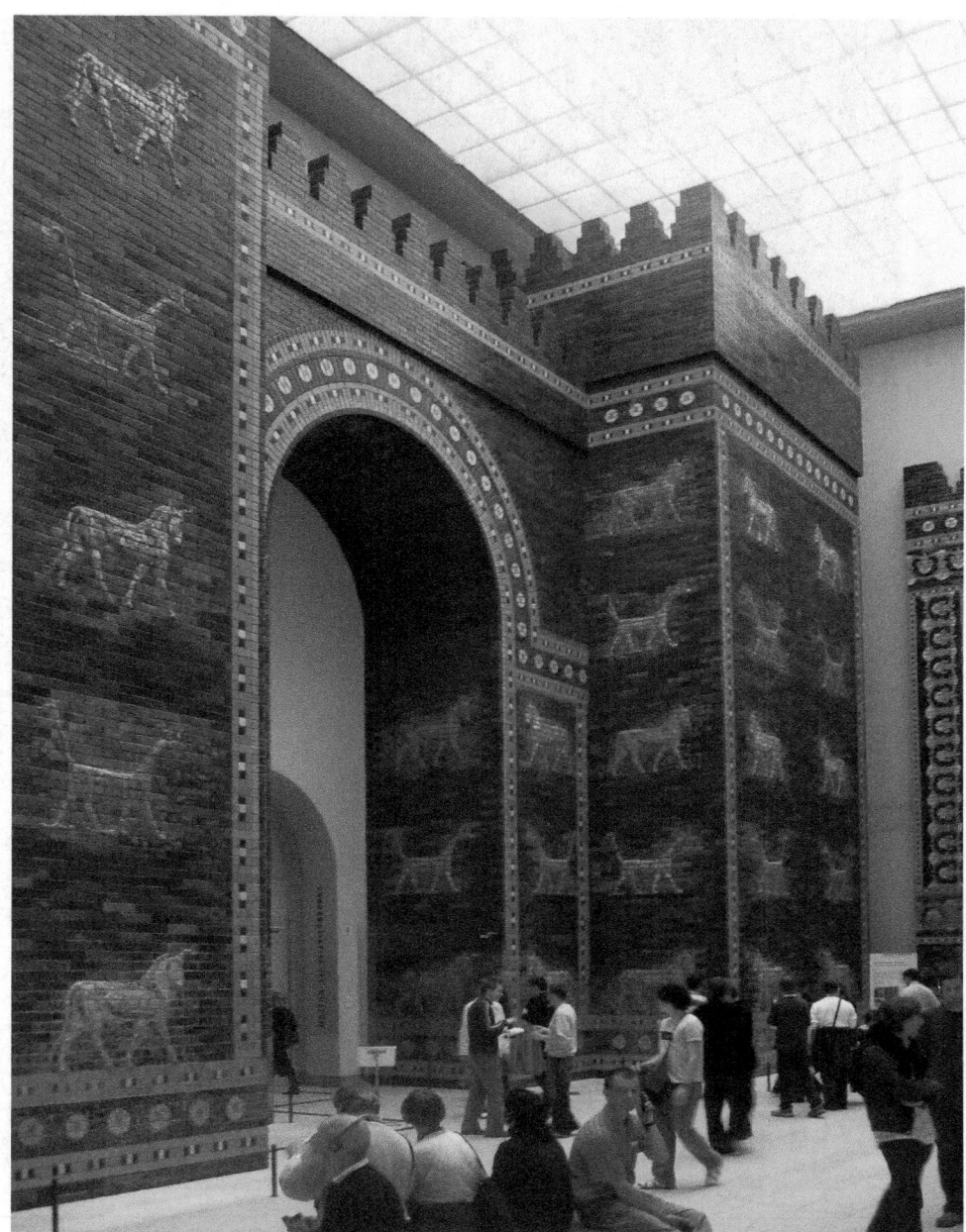

Figure 4.1-5 New Babylon (Iraq). Reconstruction of the Ishtar Gate, ca. 570 BCE. Pergamon Museum, Berlin.

The Palace of Nebuchadnezzar stood apart from these major cult sites, directly to their north. It grew as an agglomeration of existing palaces with many new additions, spilling over the earlier city walls. At 900 × 600 m (2,953 × 1,969 ft), it covered more than three times the area of Sargon's palace and was larger than most cities of the time. In opposition to the militaristic iconography of Sargon and the Neo-Assyrians, Nebuchadnezzar's throne room was lined with peaceful floral patterns in colorful glazed bricks. Winged *shedus* guarded the thresholds. The celebrated hanging gardens of Babylon, later included by the Greeks as one of the seven wonders of the ancient world, abutted the palace

on a series of fourteen vaulted chambers near the Ishtar Gate overlooking the Processional Way.

The expansion of the palace to the north included the rebuilding of the Ishtar Gate. Both sides of the northern approach to the gate were lined with uniform, symmetrically organized elevations, the walls of which were clad with colorful glazed bricks. Each bastion was decorated with two lions, symbols of Ishtar, goddess of love and war. The animals protruded in relief, made of special molded bricks (Fig. 4.1-7). The gate's towers were faced with blue-glazed bricks, decorated floral motifs, and molded figures of dragons and bulls. Its colorful threshold corresponded to a

Figure 4.1-6 New Babylon (Iraq). Model of the Entemenanki tower, 570 BCE, inspired by Ur-Nammu's ziggurat at Ur. Pergamon Museum, Berlin.

contemporary description of Babylon written on cuneiform tablets:

Babylon, the city of festivity, joy, and dance;
Babylon, the city whose inhabitants celebrate constantly;
Babylon, the privileged city that frees the captive;
Babylon, the pure city;
Babylon, the city of goods and chattels;
Babylon, the bond of nations.

Persepolis: A Terrace for the Unity of Nations

Despite Babylon's claim to be the "bond of nations," there was widespread discontent over its unfair tribute taxes. After the passing of Nebuchadnezzar II, the government succumbed to internal disputes. The last king neglected to perform the New Year's Festival rituals, causing widespread disaffection. As Babylon lost its grip on the region during the sixth century BCE, the Achaemenid dynasty of Persia took up the slack. Through their superior military organization and astute diplomacy the Persians amassed the largest empire yet, extending from the Indus valley in the east to the Nile valley in the west and including all of Turkey, the Greek-speaking Ionian coast, and even Macedonia, future birthplace of Alexander the Great. In 539 BCE, Cyrus the Great of Persia (r. 559–529 BCE) defeated the Babylonians. The Achaemenids neither sacked New Babylon nor interrupted its religious activities. The high priests at Entemenanki and Esagila continued to perform their sacrifices. The Persian ruler named his son *satrap*, or governor, of Babylon and

Figure 4.1-7 New Babylon (Iraq). Lion frieze on the Ishtar Gate, 570 BCE.

preserved the Babylonian state as a discrete province in the empire. In the land of their origins, east of Babylonia, the Achaemenids created new ceremonial landscapes meant to complement their ideology of rule. The Persians demonstrated superior military ability but also behaved as just rulers, praised for their clemency. They systematically apportioned the empire into twenty semiautonomous states ruled by satraps loyal to the king. Overseeing this federation, the king of Persia became the "king of kings."

Cyrus founded a new capital city at Pasargadae, near his birthplace in southwest Iran. The scattered layout of this first architectural initiative of the Persian Empire included a few randomly placed stone structures in a park surrounded by a defensive wall. The city included a gatehouse; a garden divided into four quadrants by water channels, or *Chahar Bagh* (see Section 12.1); a fire temple for the Mazda religious rituals; and the Tomb of Cyrus (Fig. 4.1-8).

Figure 4.1-8 Pasargadae (Iran). Tomb of Cyrus the Great, ca. 530 BCE.

Its informality reflected the nomadic origins of the dynasty. Like Sargon's palace, Cyrus's palace and audience hall stood on lofty platforms. One entered through broad colonnaded porches of the sort found among the Greeks. The main room of the palace was a hypostyle hall, six columns across and five deep, a type of interior space unknown to the preceding empires in the Mesopotamian region but common in Egypt. Just as the Persians amalgamated many nations into their empire, so they absorbed architectural knowledge from different cultures, sometimes as the consequence of using imported craftspeople.

When Darius I (r. 522–486 BCE) came to power after the seven-year reign of Cyrus's son, Cambyses II, he abandoned Pasargadae. Darius, who was not a direct descendant of Cyrus, chose to build a second Persian capital at nearby Persepolis to help consolidate his rule. The new city, begun in 518 BCE, included a grand palace complex set in the north against a backdrop of steep cliffs (Fig. 4.1-9). Mud-brick fortifications enclosed the palace, which loomed above the level of the city on a high stone terrace, accessed by a single extraordinary set of stairs (Fig. 4.1-10) arranged in the unprecedented pattern of bifurcated **switchbacks**. Laid out on broad, gradual treads, the stairs produced a theatrical effect as observers at the top landing viewed the visitors below. They also helped to guarantee the safety of the palace. Magnificent reliefs illustrating the ethnic variety

of the Persian Empire decorated the elevations of the stairs, with bearded courtiers and ambassadors shown carrying tribute for the king (Fig. 4.1-11).

Provincial representatives traveled across the empire to Persepolis to demonstrate their allegiance to the Achaemenids at the Nawruz Festival, a celebration of the vernal (spring) equinox. At the top of the entry stairs they passed through a freestanding pavilion known as the Gateway of All Nations. At the doorjambs of this threshold stood Assyrian-style *shedus*. From here the visitors turned right and proceeded across a court to a second ramp of bifurcated stairs flanked by painted reliefs of guards and imperial administrators carrying gifts to the king of kings. The stairs led to Darius's **Apadana** (Fig. 4.1-12), an immense, hypostyle audience hall with space for 10,000 visitors. A grid of thirty-six tall wooden columns filled the great square room, which measured 60 m (199 ft) per side. The columns, more than seven times human height, were plastered and painted with black and white geometric patterns. Like the hypostyle prayer halls built for Islamic worship many centuries later (see Section 7.1), the broad expanse of an indeterminate number of columns would have impressed visitors with a sense of nonhierarchical order. Colonnaded verandas, reminiscent of the facades of Hatshepsut's terraced mortuary temple (see Section 3.2), framed the exterior elevations of the Apadana on three sides.

Figure 4.1-9 Persepolis (Iran). Aerial view, ca. 500 BCE.

Figure 4.1-10 Persepolis (Iran). Southern entry stairway with carved reliefs moving up the bifurcated switchback stairs. Crowfoot parapets once lined the edges, ca. 500 BCE.

Darius's son Xerxes added a second hypostyle hall, the Hall of 100 Columns, behind the Apadana on a lower platform around 480 BCE. One entered this second throne room through a colonnaded veranda with a double row of eight columns. The square hall had the same dimensions as Darius's Apadana but contained 100 stone columns arranged in rows of ten. The columns amalgamated the style of Greek Ionic columns with that of Egyptian lotus columns. Floral motifs covered their bell-shaped bases, while the shafts had finer **fluting** than Greek columns. The capitals combined a cluster of Egyptian lotus buds with a set of double volutes curled up to connect to another set of double volutes curling down. Above these capitals, crowns of double-headed kneeling bulls formed notches to hold the ceiling rafters (Fig. 4.1-13). The density of the columns and the redundancy of the decorated capitals created a reverberating rhythm amid the solemn emptiness of the space.

Between the two hypostyle halls stood the monumental Tripylon Gate, leading into the private zones of the palace. The architects arranged the chambers for the king, his sons, the royal harem, and the treasury in parallel bands running toward the southern parapet. Unlike the dark, narrow interiors of Mesopotamian palaces, almost all of the rooms at Persepolis, no matter their dimensions, were square, exposed through exterior colonnades, and supported by interior columns.

Visitors reached Persepolis across stone highways constructed by the regime. These links between the twenty provinces began in Sardis, Turkey, and stretched all the way to the Silk Road at Taxila, Pakistan. The palace begun by Darius at Persepolis became a repository for tribute from across the empire. Built with design, labor, and materials drawn from a multiethnic pool of resources, it flaunted the empire's cultural differences. There were sculpted Assyrian monsters and crowfoot crenellations, Egyptian cavetto cornices, and Greek Ionic volutes. On the great Terrace for All

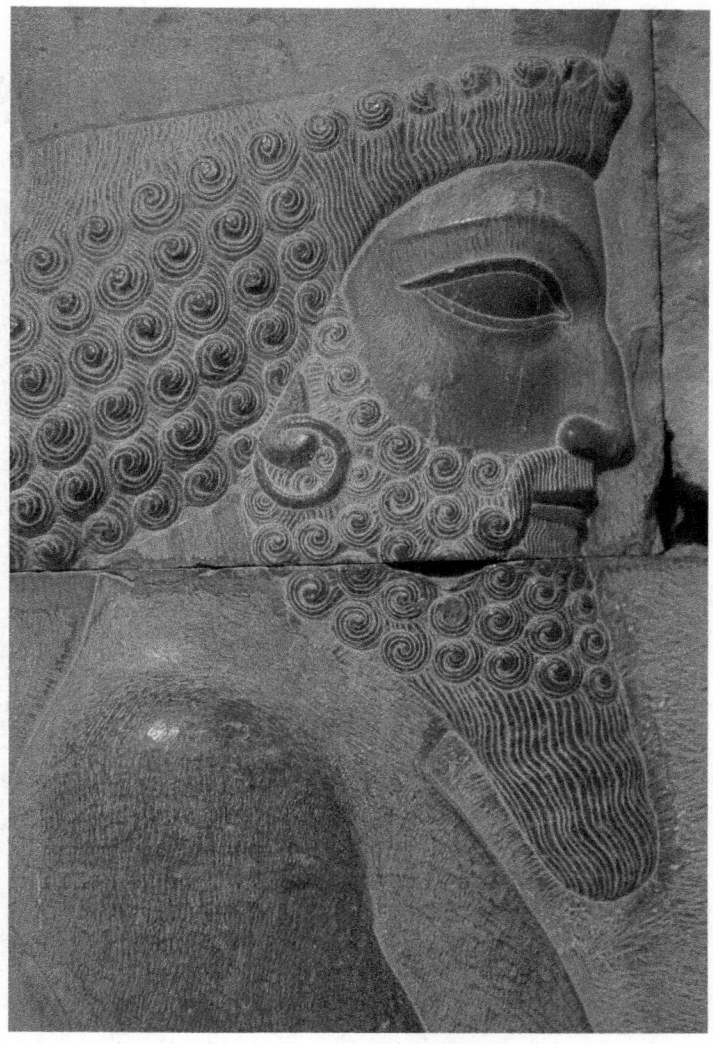

Figure 4.1-11 Persepolis (Iran). Relief on the Stairway of the Ambassadors, ca. 500 BCE.

RELIGION, PHILOSOPHY, FOLKLORE

Mazda Fire Temples

The Achaemenid ruling class adopted the monotheistic religion of Mazdaism, based on the teachings of the sixth-century-BCE prophet Zarathustra. Zarathustra promoted the belief in a single creator god, Ahura Mazda, and preached that justice should be the transcending objective of all humans, rejecting the fanaticism and superstitions of earlier cults. Mazdaism evolved into an ascetic faith, requiring only an outdoor altar for performance of its fire ceremony. Consequently, the Persians did not build significant temples. They celebrated their rituals on simple platforms known as "fire temples" that did not generate a strong formal presence. The winged disk became their sole form of religious iconography.

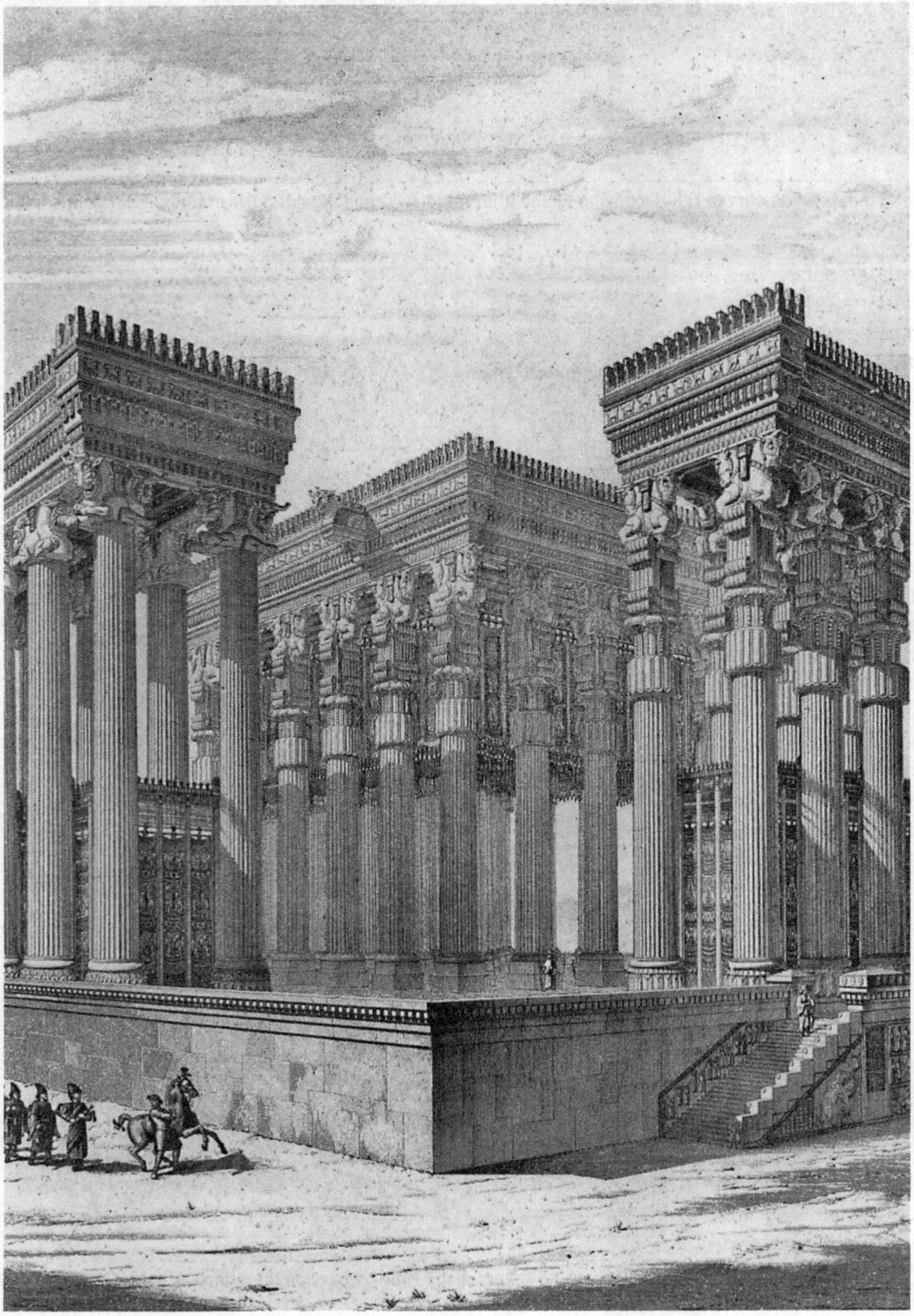

Figure 4.1-12 Persepolis (Iran). Reconstruction of the Apadana of Darius, ca. 500 BCE. Charles Chipiez (1890).

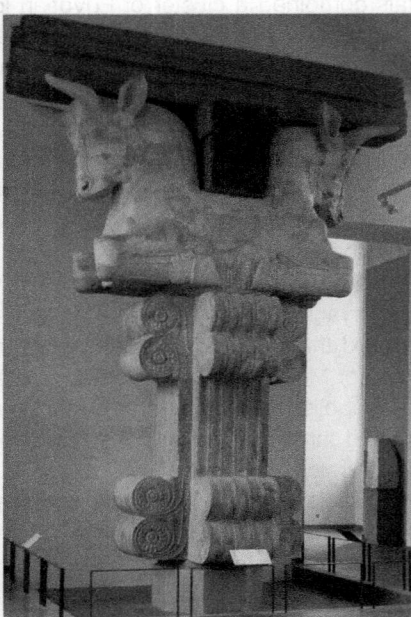

Figure 4.1-13 Persepolis (Iran). Detail of Achaemenid columns, ca. 480 BCE.

Rock-Cut Achaemenid Tombs and Monolithic Masonry

The Tomb of Cyrus evoked Babylonian types, with a stepped pyramid supporting a small chamber at the top. It reprised the seven-level theme of the ziggurats. The crowning chamber, built in solid stone, had a gabled roof. Cyrus's successors, less sympathetic to Babylon, abandoned this type of tomb for burial sites cut into cliffs, such as those overlooking the palace at Persepolis.

The cliff tombs at Persepolis displayed sculpted reliefs of columns and beams cut out of the cliffs. One recognizes the difficult transition from carving into stone to building out of stone by joining carved blocks in the remains of the Palace of Darius and Xerxes, where much of the masonry for elements such as doors, columns, and steps was carved from single pieces of stone. The frame of one doorway, for instance, instead of being made with two uprights supporting a lintel, was cut from a single block in a *U* shape. The columns in the hypostyle halls stood identical in height, but their shafts had differently sized **drums** of stone. The masons creating the great entry stair at Persepolis first pieced together interlocking monolithic blocks and then carved *in situ* the details for the steps and the crowfoot merlons. Most of the complex reveals a lack of knowledge of the concept of joinery, which derived from the traditions of timber construction.

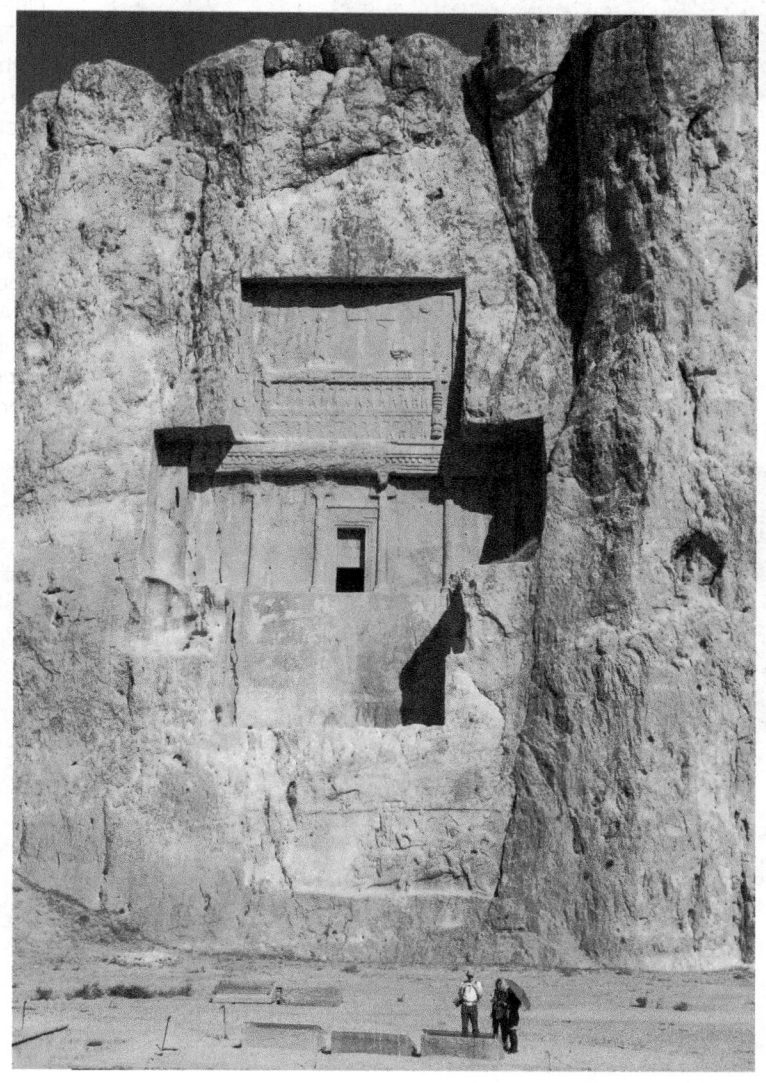

Persepolis (Iran). Rock-cut tombs of Achaemenid dynasty, overlooking the Palace of Darius and Xerxes, ca. 450 BCE.

Nations, the subjects of the Persian Empire would be flattered to find motifs of their people's own invention and materials from their own landscapes. The Mazda code of justice and the ethic of religious and cultural tolerance resonated in architectural expressions that mirrored the diplomatic spirit of the Achaemenids' all-embracing empire.

Further Reading

Frankfort, Henri. *The Art and Architecture of the Ancient Orient*. New York: Penguin Books, 1954.

Holland, Tom. *Persian Fire: The First World Empire and the Battle for the West*. London: Abacus, 2005.

Marzahn, Joachim. *The Ishtar Gate*. Mainz am Rhein, Germany: Philipp von Zaubern, 1995.

Oates, Joan. *Babylon*. London: Thames and Hudson, 1986.

Wiesenhofer, Josef. *Ancient Persia: From 550 BC to 650 AD*. Translated by A. Azodi. London: I. B. Taurus, 1996.

4.2   THE GREEK CITY-STATE
Classical Architecture at the Acropolis and the Agora

Ancient Greek architecture claims a special place in Western culture as the source of **classicism**. Classical architecture comprises both a system of proportional composition and a repertoire of decoration that includes sculpted **columns**, entablatures, and pediments. While all cultures produced styles that attained an optimal form and were copied by successive generations, the classical style of the Greeks has been revived by a variety of cultures, obtaining global universal acceptance. Classical architecture eventually came to represent two contradictory political ideas: the egalitarianism of Greek democracy achieved during the fifth century BCE and the authoritarian order of Hellenistic tyrannies and the Roman Empire that followed them.

The Greek city, or **polis**, gave birth to this new style of architecture. The *polis* also produced a democratic process of rule whereby political decisions and matters of justice became consensual, requiring public debate. The need for spaces for dialogue generated the buildings of classical Athens. The agora, the **stoa**, the council house, and the hillside theater all enabled exchanges of opinion. Even the Greek temple emerged as a product of dialogue, with its proportions, details, and cost subject to public debate.

After the decline of democratic Athens, Greek architects continued to improve on classical style for the various exponents of Hellenism. Alexander the Great enthusiastically promoted the Greek way in his campaign to unite the world into a single empire. As he attempted to convert the rest of humanity to Hellenism, he relied on the classical architecture of the *polis* as an agent of his civilizing mission.

The Greek *Polis:* The City of Public Space

The Greek city-states matured during the sixth century BCE at the western edge of the great empires of Southwest Asia (Fig. 4.2-1). From this peripheral position they developed a unique form of government quite different from that of the despots and autocrats to the east. Their rule by public assembly, which reached its most extreme form in the democracy of fifth-century BCE Athens, still seems exceptional for its degree of direct participation. Among other ancient civilizations, only the Phoenicians continued with the ancient Sumerian precedent of government by councils, but never on the scale of the Greeks. Instead of great palaces and tombs for tyrants and hierarchical temple compounds like those of Egypt, Assyria, and Persia, the Greeks designed open public spaces with a few colonnaded buildings for citizen meetings.

They called the city and its outlying territory the *polis*, the root for the word "politics."

Figure 4.2-1 The Aegean, ca. 400 BCE.

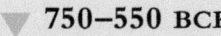

TIME LINE

▼ **750–550 BCE**

Foundation of Greek colonies around the Mediterranean

Cleisthenes creates democratic constitution for Athens (Greece)

▲ **508 BCE**

▼ **490 BCE**

Battle of Marathon, Delian League under leadership of Athens defeats the Persians

Persians invade Greece, sack Athens, destroy temples on the Acropolis

▲ **480 BCE**

▼ **479 BCE**

Greeks expel Persians

Their system of living under accountable institutions of self-government eliminated the perennial power struggles of dynasties, tribes, and clans. During the eighth century BCE, after several centuries of stagnation, the Greeks began to revive their cities through *synoikismos*, "or living together." The philosopher Aristotle (384–322 BCE) observed this process of confederation: "When several villages are united in a single complete community, large enough to be nearly or quite self-sufficing, the *polis* comes into existence." After the consolidating process of *synoikismos* occurred, a new civic consciousness required open public spaces and accessible public buildings.

The Greek mainland and surrounding islands evolved into an informal commonwealth that included about 700 city-states. While the different cities did not cohere into a single state, they shared the Greek language and religious beliefs with each other and honored national pan-Hellenic shrines such as Olympia, Delphi, and Epidaurus. Each city-state remained autonomous but when necessary, such as during the Persian invasions of the fifth century BCE, joined in league to expel an enemy. Their extraordinary invention of democracy derived partly from geographic peculiarities: a hilly interior, a jagged coastline, and hundreds of small islands. The fragmentation of this choppy landscape encouraged the growth and maintenance of independent, self-managed cities. Because a lack of arable land limited Greek agriculture, the main surplus came from more specialized occupations, such as maritime trade and shipbuilding.

As early as the eighth century BCE, cities on the Greek mainland began to establish colonies on the Ionian coast of Turkey. The wave of colonization continued during the seventh and sixth centuries BCE, spreading to the south of Italy and Sicily and resulting in the establishment of important urban centers, such as Neapolis (Naples) and Syracuse. These frequent acts of city building encouraged debates about the *polis* in terms of both urban form and institutions. Greek planners and political thinkers developed reproducible methods of orthogonal planning at the same time that they experimented with guaranteeing justice within a diversified class structure.

Athens, as the most powerful city in the Aegean, produced the most influential models of Greek architecture and urbanism. In the eighth century BCE, as the villages at the base of the **Acropolis** coalesced through *synoikismos*, the city spread informally along radial paths. The political focus of Athens shifted away from the Acropolis, which had served

as the fortress of Mycenaean princes, to the Agora in the flatland at its base. Aristotle explained that "an acropolis is suitable for oligarchy and monarchy, level ground for democracy." Democracy required that no citizen appear more privileged than any other. To Greek thinking, an acropolis, meaning "head of the city," seemed more appropriate as a home for the gods than as a place for citizens.

The **agora**, literally "gathering," served as the prime public space of the Greek *polis*. Other cultures had created large open spaces in front of temples and palaces, but the Greek agora sat as an indeterminate void in the middle of the city. The Athenian Agora occupied a space of roughly 200 × 250 m (656 × 820 ft), about half the area of the *temenos* of the Entemenanki in Babylon. It sloped up gently in the direction of the Acropolis and, while bounded by stone markers, or *horoi*, did not have a set shape. Groves of trees grew casually in its midst. This immense park-like setting served as the city's space of information, where every male, Athenian-born property owner could express his commitment as a citizen to fight for the city's interests and debate its affairs. The laws of the *polis* were built on two basic tenets: the right of private property and the goal of individual freedom. Both concepts weakened the hierarchical authority of a clan-based society. The *polis* proposed a community of equals, bound by their own decision making and administered by elected magistrates. Its citizens bore military and religious obligations. Each man carried his own weapons, just as each remained accountable for his relations with the divine protectors of the city.

The cultural difference between the Greeks and the Persians rings true in the sarcastic remark attributed to King Cyrus: "I never feared the kind of men who have a place set aside in the middle of the city where they get together to tell one another lies under oath." The emptiness of the Agora and its lack of architectural definition presented the opposite effect of the sense of fullness and order produced by the prescribed sequences of imperial palaces. From a social point of view the open space of the Greeks proved more interactive than the cult space of the Processional Way in Babylon. The Athenians left their Agora loosely defined to facilitate the dialogues of participatory democracy.

The major streets of Athens crossed the Agora, which accommodated a variety of activities, including market functions, religious ceremonies, athletic events, and theatrical performances (Fig. 4.2-2). Guardian *herms*, pillars with human heads and erect phalluses, marked the major entry points,

*Miletos
reconstructed
on grids*

▲ **470 BCE**

▼ **460 BCE**

*Pericles inspires Athens
to rebuild the Parthenon
and other monuments
on the Acropolis*

*Hephaisteion temple
built overlooking
Agora of Athens*

▲ **449 BCE**

▼ **447 BCE**

*Parthenon begun on the
Acropolis of Athens*

Figure 4.2-2 Athens. Plan of the Agora, ca. 450 BCE.

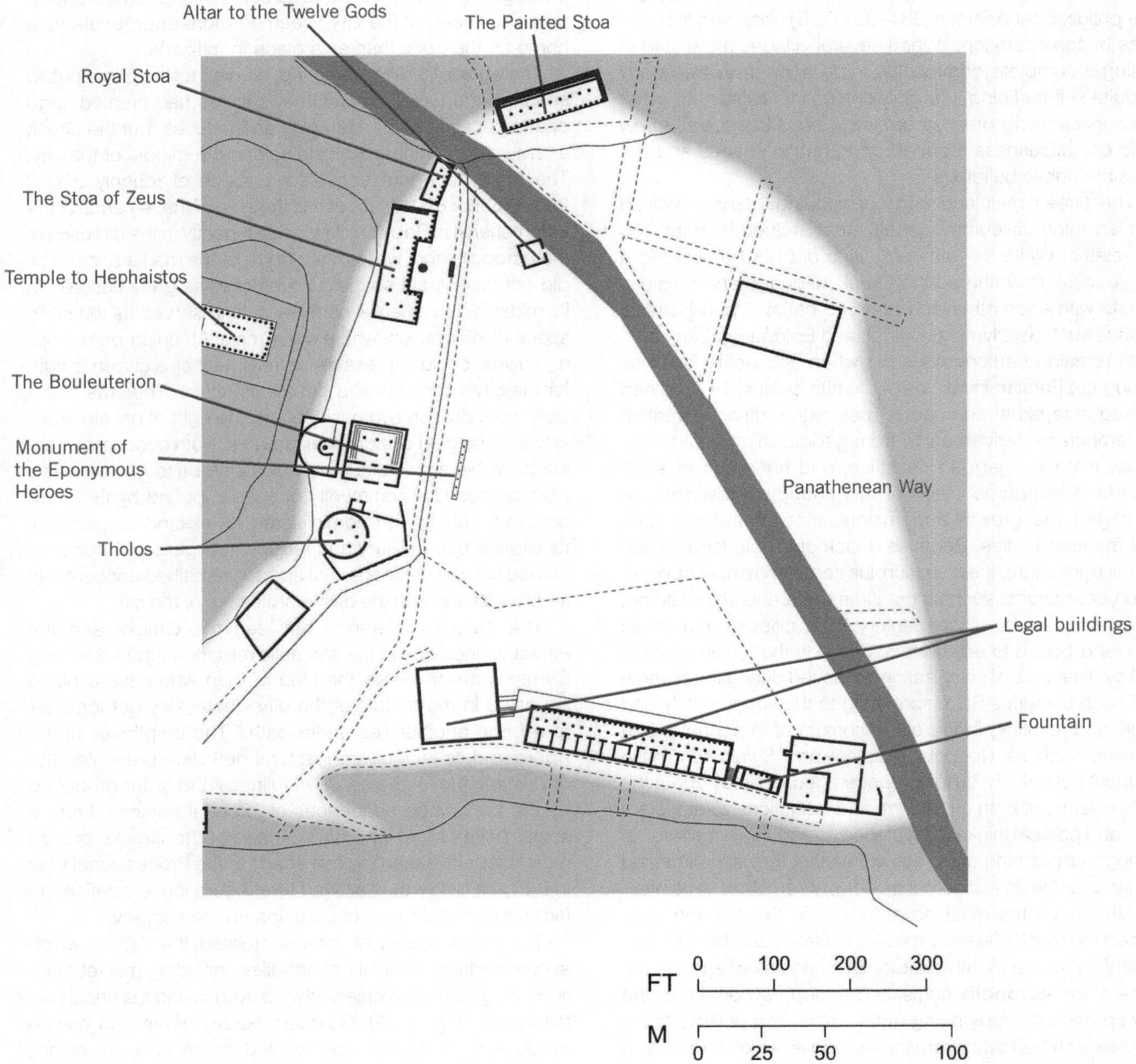

Altar to the Twelve Gods

The Painted Stoa

Royal Stoa

The Stoa of Zeus

Temple to Hephaistos

The Bouleuterion

Monument of
the Eponymous
Heroes

Tholos

Panathenean Way

Legal buildings

Fountain

FT   0   100   200   300

M   0   25   50   100

Peloponnesian Wars,
Sparta replaces Athens
as the leader of Greece

▲ 430–404 BCE

▼ 421 BCE

*Erechtheion
begun on the
Acropolis of
Athens*

*Mausoleum of
Halicarnassus*

▲ 353 BCE

▼ 336–323 BCE

King Alexander (the Great)
of Macedonia conquers
Egypt, Southwest Asia, and
Persia, spreading Hellenism
through the region

leaving little doubt of the male dominance of the prime public space. The processional route through Athens, the Panathenean Way, crossed the Agora diagonally from the northwest Dipylon Gate to the Acropolis. Paved with gravel, it served on occasion as a *dromos*, or track for foot races. At the northern edge of the Agora the open-air Altar to the Twelve Gods welcomed political refugees seeking sanctuary. Terra-cotta conduits and drains served a fountain house built on the southeast edge in the late sixth century BCE. Until the construction of a stone theater on the southern slope of the Acropolis in the fourth century BCE, the Athenians improvised theatricals in the Agora using temporary wooden bleachers.

The Greek Theater

Greek drama originated with festivals in honor of Dionysus, the god of wine, when groups of as many as fifty men chanted and danced. The **orchestra**, a circular play space, served as the site for their performances. To these revels the legendary Thespis introduced a single actor, who wore masks to portray different characters to a chorus. This evolved into dialogues between the actor and the chorus, and later, the number of actors increased to a maximum of three on stage at any time. In Athens the earliest dramas were performed in the Agora, with wooden bleachers improvised around the orchestra and an altar to Dionysus placed in the center. During the mid-fifth century BCE the Athenians built the first permanent *theatron*, a term derived from the verb "to see," on the south slope of the Acropolis. They exploited the hill to create a cup-shaped seating section above the orchestra, which they covered with wooden benches. The theater's rounded shape enhanced the space's acoustics. Behind the orchestra they later raised a platform as a stage for the actors, with three doors for entrances and exits.

The theater at the pan-Hellenic healing sanctuary of Epidauros, built in the mid-fourth century BCE, remains intact. The half-bowl shape of its seating area fits into the lay of the land and allows the audience to connect to the surrounding landscape. The thirty-four rows of seats for 6,000 spectators are accessed by regularly placed radial stairways.

Epidauros, Greece. Theater, mid-fourth century BCE.

ca. 330 BCE
Alexandria designed for Alexander on Nile delta in Egypt

▼ **ca. 250 BCE**
Attalid dynasty of Pergamon creates a monumental acropolis

Attalids commission the Pergamon Altar
▲ **ca. 180 BCE**

▼ **133 BCE**
Attalid dynasty of Pergamon wills itself to Rome

On the west side of the Agora the Monument of the Eponymous Heroes stood out as the most explicitly political marker. An oblong **podium**, it carried ten statues depicting the heroes of Athens who gave their names to the *polis*'s ten political groups, or *phylae*. In order to avoid the corruption of clan-based parties, the Athenian citizens apportioned themselves into arbitrarily assigned *phylae* that had proportional membership from throughout the city-state. The members of each *phyle* attached messages under the statue that represented their group, making the monument a political bulletin board for the *polis*.

As the complexity of Athenian government increased, each new function resulted in the development of a particular building type. The administrative buildings on the west side of the Agora included the Prytaneion, or city hall, which housed the city's metaphoric hearth. Next to it the Skias, a cylindrical **tholos** structure, served as the dining hall for the fifty members of the council, who served rotating two-month terms as the executive authority of the government. Close by stood the Strategeion, a chamber for debating military policies. Just north of the Skias was the square-shaped council house, or **Bouleuterion**, a theater-like structure lined on three sides with rows of perimeter seating. Four interior pillars held up its roof, similar to the square hypostyle rooms in the Persian palace at Persepolis.

Open porticoes, called *stoas*, loosely framed the edges of the Agora. These simple, box-like structures with colonnades were physically and visually accessible to all. They served as protected meeting spaces for lawsuits, official banquets, and occasional city council meetings. The Royal Stoa, built before the Persian Wars of 490–479 BCE, served as the office of a magistrate concerned with religious questions who was elected for a one-year term from the aristocracy and thus was considered "royal." It stood behind a row of eight columns and in its interior had four two-tiered columns to hold up the crest of the **gabled** roof. The city added the Painted Stoa, or Poikile, which was more than twice the Royal Stoa's size, in 479 BCE at the northern edge of the Agora. Here, painted wooden panels on the interior celebrated the recent victory over the Persians and depicted the mythological battle between the ancient Athenians and the female-warrior Amazons.

The early political congregations of Athens met in the Agora, but the increase of the assembly to 6,000 members during the early sixth century BCE required a larger, more undisturbed setting. For this, the Athenians cleared and leveled the great terrace of the Pnyx about 300 m (984 ft) to the south, overlooking the Agora (Fig. 4.2-3). They raked the terrace with a slight dip toward a cliff-like backdrop to obtain optimal acoustics. This acoustically calibrated shelf anticipated the auditorium seating of Greek theaters. The subsequent

Figure 4.2-3 Athens. The Pnyx, an open space for large assemblies located above the Agora and designed for good acoustics with a raked stone floor, early sixth century BCE.

invention of the theater emerged from the democratic need for dialogue. As a new architectural type, the rounded seating space for the audience and elevated stage for the actors distilled the relationships of the democratic process in the Agora.

Greek Colonies and Orthogonal Planning

The public spaces and colonnaded buildings of Athens served as models for other Greek cities in the Aegean region and beyond. The agora, the classical temple, and the Greek theater represented essential urban ingredients for colonists founding new cities. To these they added a normative grid. The Greek grid appeared in the seventh century BCE, organized in horizontal bands as an expedient way to divide the land, shape the structure of the city, and control its future growth.

While the tradition of orthogonal planning began with the Egyptians and the Harappans more than a millennium before, the earlier cultures made no effort to create a coherent system of public and residential zones. The Greeks used the *per strigas* (by bands) scheme to plan colonial cities such as Paestum, in southern Italy (Fig. 4.2-4). A small number of broad east–west avenues divided the site into long bands. North–south lanes were then struck to divide the rectangular urban blocks, each with six to ten building lots per block. The grid determined the size and shape of the public buildings, as can clearly be seen in the placement of Paestum's three prominent temples.

According to Aristotle, Hippodamus of Miletus (498–408 BCE) invented "the divisioning of cities." While the grid remained an indispensable tool for Hippodamian planning, Hippodamus's real contribution was a social theory of urbanism that took into consideration the differences among religious, public, and private zones. Hippodamus's ideal city had 10,000 citizens who were divided into three categories: artisans, farmers, and soldiers. His system structured the grid according to a rigorous geometric formula that divided the square into quarters and then further divided each quarter into six parts, leaving urban blocks measuring 30 × 46 m (98 × 151 ft) that were suitable for six courtyard houses. The agora, a square of 200 m (656 ft) per side, similar in scale to the Athenian Agora, provided the plan's largest dimension.

The Athenians rebuilt the colony of Miletus on the Ionian coast of Turkey in the 470s BCE after its destruction during

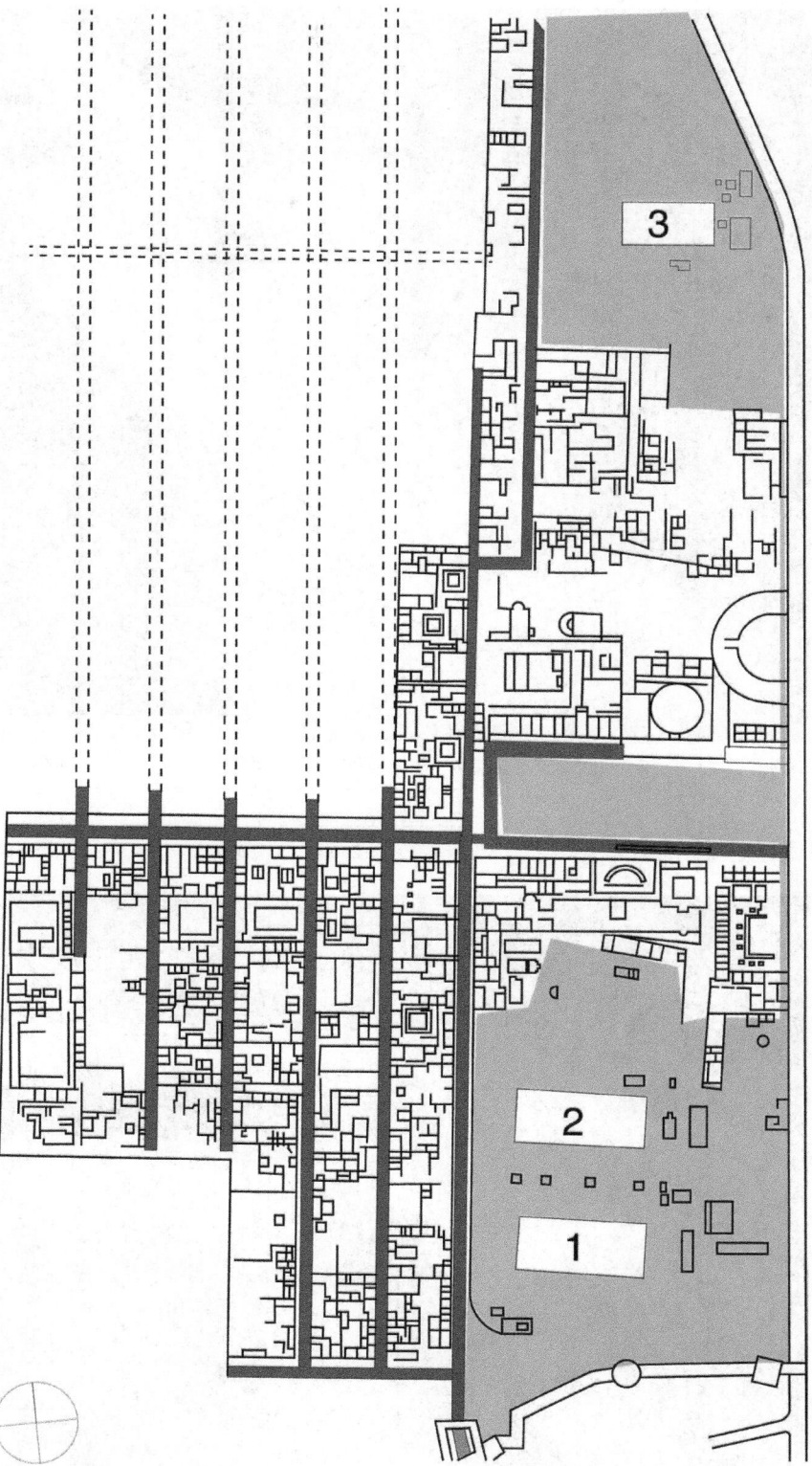

Figure 4.2-4 Paestum (Poseidonia), southern Italy. Greek colony laid out on *per strigas* grid of long blocks later rebuilt by Romans, eighth century BCE. (1) Heraion, or "basilica," devoted to Hera; (2) Temple of Poseidon; (3) Temple of Athena.

the Persian Wars. Whether Hippodamus designed it or not, the plan of his hometown closely corresponded to his theory. Even before the sack, Miletus was known among the Greeks as the birthplace of geometry, and its previous fabric surely

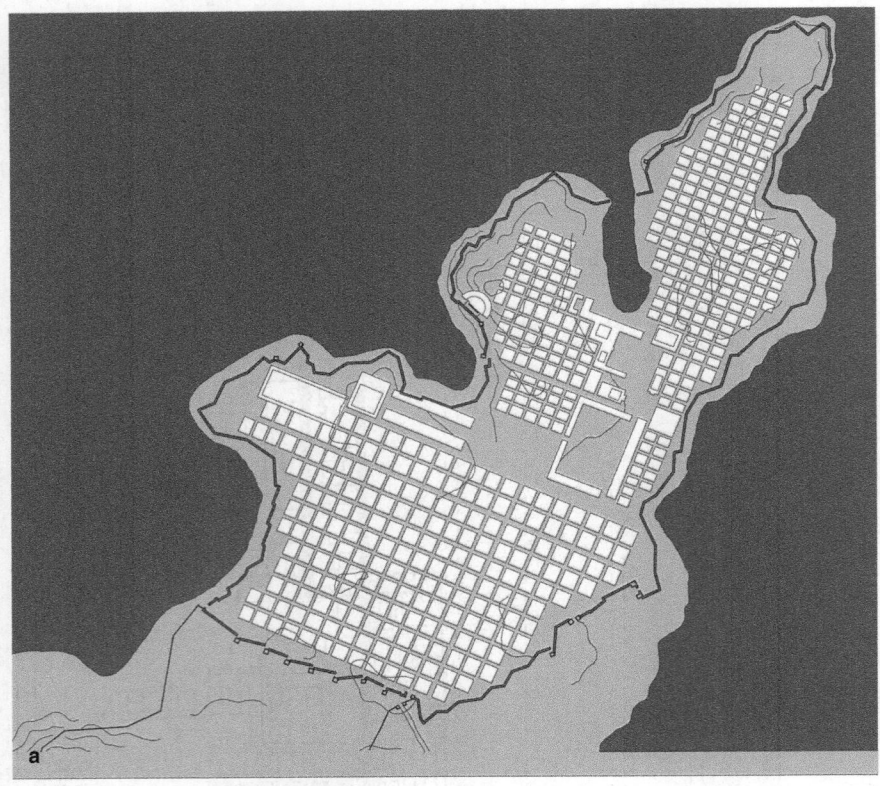

FT 0   750   1500   3000

M   0   250   500   1000

used a grid. The new plan for its expansion set three differently sized grids over the irregular terrain of three seaside promontories, to be built in phases (Fig. 4.2-5a). Between the grids, where there were natural changes in the topography, the planners left ample room to develop the complete repertoire of religious, political, and commercial spaces and buildings, using proportions generated by the grids. Starting with the *L*-shaped Harbor Stoa, the city built colonnaded courtyards, plazas, fountains, and temples at its monumental core, forming a special program of expanding and contracting public spaces. The sequence took several centuries to complete, concluding with the market gateway, rebuilt by the Romans as a monumental arched entry in the second century CE. Beyond this gate one found a perfectly rectangular agora (Fig. 4.2-5b),

**Figure 4.2-5 Miletus, Ionian coast of Turkey.
(a) Plan of Athenian colony as redesigned according to Hippodamian criteria, 470s BCE. The three promontories have different grid dimensions but correspond to the same axes. Gaps were left at the junctures to allow orderly spaces for public and religious functions. (b) Model of harbor agora after Roman interventions, second century CE. Pergamon Museum, Berlin.**

Figure 4.2-6 Priene, Ionian coast of Turkey. Reconstructed view of rebuilt town, ca. 350 BCE.

equivalent to thirty city blocks and a rational transposition of the Athenian Agora.

Priene, another colony on the Ionian coast, was rebuilt a century later with a more tightly integrated plan. Here, the public spaces were conceived from the start as colonnaded outdoor rooms, and the **prytaneion**, the bouleuterion, the theater, and the temple to Athena were fit carefully into a staggered pattern within the geometry of standard blocks (Fig. 4.2-6). Priene rose on a slope, which caused a series of dynamic oblique relationships between parts. The theater overlooked the temple, and the temple overlooked the agora. Broad avenues moved lengthwise across the hill, intersected by narrow stairways between the blocks. Only the walls and the stadium broke from the orthogonal patterns to fit the irregularities of the terrain. The planners of the grids of Miletus and Priene conceived of the entire urban territory as a rational form. This geometric organization of the *polis* established a controlled social experiment, meant to generate a community with an established growth target and a predetermined set of

institutions. While at first it may appear utilitarian, the grid facilitated the creation of the city as a work of art, a deliberate and artificial configuration that defined its own internal rules of architectural behavior.

The Greeks built the houses in their colonies comfortably but without distinction. The residential lots in the grids covered approximately 15 × 20 m (49 × 66 ft). The best-documented examples appeared in Olynthus, a northern Greek city rebuilt with an orthogonal *per strigas* plan around 470 BCE. The houses of Olynthus displayed remarkable uniformity, almost like modern row housing (Fig. 4.2-7). They suggest a society of equals. The house, or **oikos**, was usually one or two stories, built around a south-facing court that contained a cistern, or well, and an altar. The service functions generally occupied the short sides, while the living areas rose in a larger two-story volume at the rear. The *oikos* was constructed around a colonnaded veranda, known as the *pastas*, a semienclosed corridor somewhat like a *stoa*, set between the court and the rooms. It provided naturally cooled living spaces. The rooms were not strictly defined by

Figure 4.2-7 Olynthus, northern Greece. Plan of residential block of city rebuilt after the Persian invasion of 480 BCE. Every house, or *oikos*, is nearly identical, fitting into square plots on the *per strigas* blocks. (P) *Pastas*, veranda; (A) *andron*, men's dining hall.

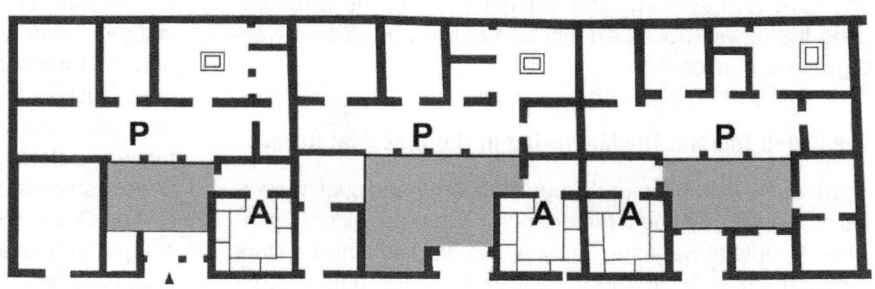

Women and the *Oikos*

Despite the new premise of equality introduced by the Greek *polis*, the majority of its residents, including slaves and women, did not enjoy any of the rights of the property-owning male citizens. While the Greek house, the *oikos*, represented the property of a free citizen, it also carried oppressive meanings as an instrument of confinement for wives and slaves. Women, often segregated within the house itself to quarters known as the *gynaikeion*, were not allowed to leave the *oikos*. Shopping and water retrieval were done mostly by the men and the house slaves. Once married, a woman was no longer called by her own name but was known to her husband simply as "*gyne*," or child-bearer, and to outsiders in terms of her relation to male members of the family. Wives were never expected to join in male conversation. Their exclusive duties were to cook, sew, and raise children in silent submission. During the later Hellenistic period, when governments became more tyrannical, Greek women paradoxically gained the freedom to go out in public space and, in some cases, own property.

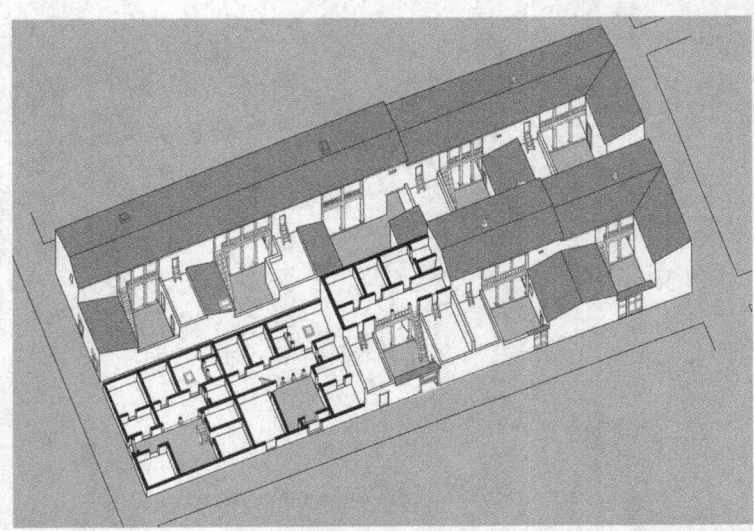

Olynthus, northern Greece. Reconstruction of the *oikos* (Greek house), 79 BCE.

function, excepting the **andron**, or men's dining room. Here, the men of the family and their guests reclined for meals and entertainment on a low platform that wrapped around the room's perimeter.

The typical *oikos* of Olynthus appears to have been a rationalization of traditional houses found in older Greek cities. The fabric of ancient Athens probably looked something like the winding streets on the island of Delos, which accommodated a variety of classes. In the wealthier Delian houses, which were usually about 300 m² (3,158 ft²) in area, the geometrically perfect court either led to a **pastas** set off by columns or was entirely surrounded by columns in a **peristyle**. The rest of the house followed a more casual order, adjusting to the irregularities of the neighboring houses and the uneven terrain.

The *oikos* served as the smallest common denominator of the geometrically ordered Greek *polis*. As the basic unit of a successful democratic society, it supplied the formal and etymological root for two important modern concepts, economy and ecology. The colonial plan for the *oikos* implied that a well-governed city was only as good as a well-organized household.

The Greek Temple: The Mastering of the Classical Orders

There are few architectural types that command such universal recognition as the Greek temple. The magnificent unfinished temple at Segesta, Sicily, which has remained a stark skeleton since its abandonment in the early fifth century

BCE, carries the imprint of the type: an oblong **peripteral** structure, girded on all sides by a screen of stone columns and crowned by a thick, horizontal **entablature** that sustains triangular **pediments** in the gables at each end. This formula reappeared with little variation wherever the Greeks settled from the seventh to the third century BCE. The Greek temple differed from the religious buildings of earlier cultures in two ways: its special relation to the landscape and its dazzling colonnaded exterior. The Greeks usually sited their temples in remote, nonurban settings as landmarks associated with the legends of their gods. Works such as the Parthenon in Athens looked over the city from afar. Their designers enhanced the view of the temple in the distance by wrapping its volume with beautifully crafted columns, creating a kinetic play of light and shade against the solid inner core.

The columns of Greek temples conformed to one of three styles: Doric, Ionic, or Corinthian. These became the basis of a language of architecture based on formulaic proportions. The diameter of the column established the module to measure all the other dimensions. The Doric **order**, for instance, was typically six modules high and left two modules of **intercolumnation** between one column and the next. Just as the orthogonal **per strigas** bands of Greek town planning could be easily communicated to builders in faraway colonies, so could the proportions and layouts of Greek temples be transmitted in simple numeric relations.

The Greek temples served either to mark sacred natural sites or to house treasuries of sacred images and the city's economic surplus. Early religious ceremonies used them as

Pan-Hellenic Cult Sites of Olympia and Delphi

The Greek city-states remained independent but shared common religious beliefs. The pilgrimage shrines of Olympia and Delphi unified pan-Hellenic culture. Olympia in southern Greece was honored as the primary sanctuary of Zeus and the eleven other major gods of Greek mythology. In a large grove at the base of a hill, the cities of the Greek commonwealth participated every four years in athletic games beginning in the seventh century BCE. Near the Olympic stadium they sponsored a grand collection of religious shrines during the next three centuries. These included two Doric temples dedicated to Hera and Zeus, a prytaneion (city hall), a row of eleven treasuries set up by individual city-states, and two *stoas*.

Another pan-Hellenic site evolved at Delphi, on the lower slopes of Mount Parnassus. Dedicated to Pythian Apollo, the prophet and musician, it became known as the mythological home of the Muses. The Doric Temple of Apollo, midway up the path, housed the Delphic oracle, whom rulers from across Greece and other parts of the Mediterranean consulted before making important decisions of state. During the oracular rite, the priestess of Apollo drank water from a sacred spring, chewed on leaves of laurel, and uttered statements only comprehensible to the priest of Apollo, who delivered them in often enigmatic and self-contradictory prophecies. One approached the temple on a winding path lined with a host of smaller temples, including a round *tholos* dedicated to Athena, treasuries, and above the temple a theater and a stadium. The buildings were sited carefully to be seen obliquely as one approached. At both Olympia and Delphi the visual connection of the temples to distant landscape features maintained a dialogue between architecture and nature.

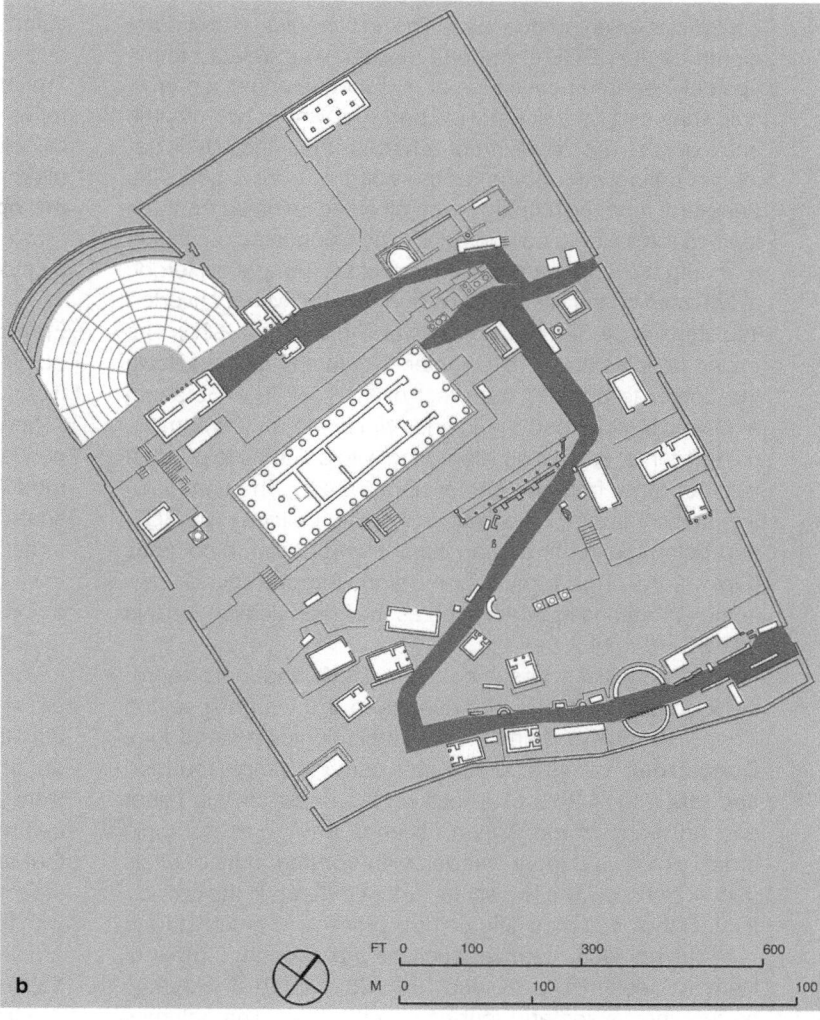

Delphi, Greece. (a) View of Temple of Apollo, fourth century BCE. (b) Plan of procession route through the Delphic shrines.

FT 0   100   300   600
M 0   100   100

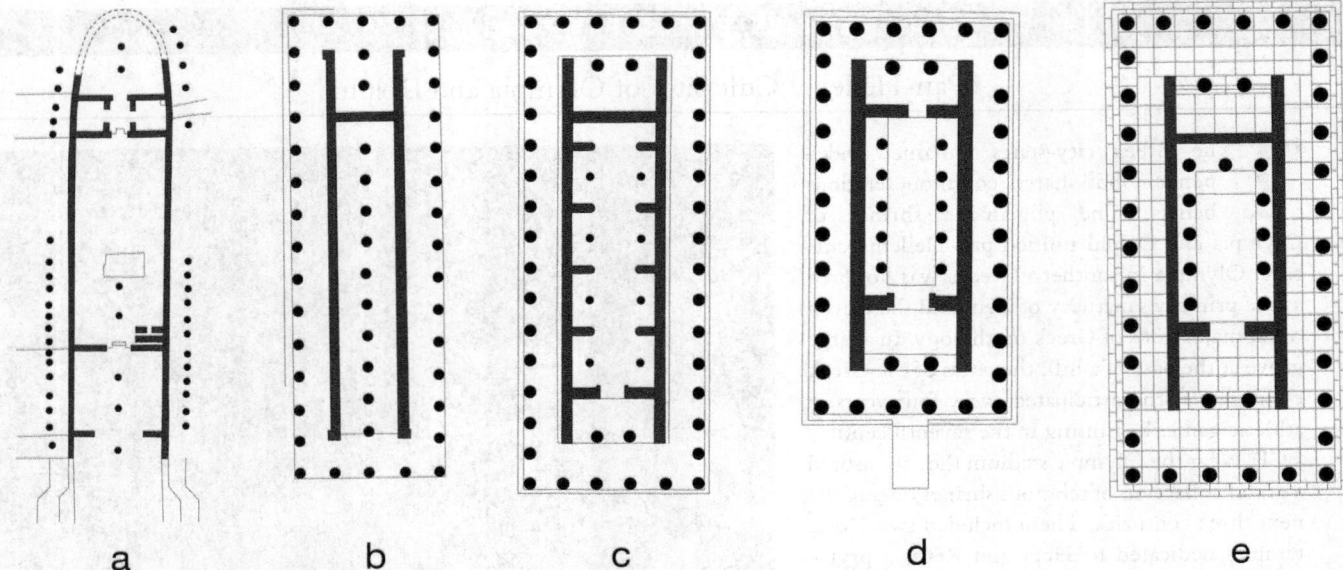

Figure 4.2-8 Ancient Greece. Plans of early Greek temples, which evolved from long buildings surrounded by timber poles to shorter forms with stone Doric columns. (a) Heroon at Lefkandi, Naxos, ca. 1100 BCE. (b) Temple of Apollo at Thera, ca. 1000 BCE. (c) Heraeum at Olympia, ca. 600 BCE. (d) Temple of Aphaea at Aegina, ca. 500 BCE. (e) Hephaisteion in Athens, ca. 449 BCE.

backdrops for an outdoor altar. The first temples, known from eighth-century BCE terra-cotta models, were related to the apsidal megaron house type of Mycenaean origin: a narrow hall, sheltered by a steeply pitched roof, and a two-column entry porch. The provision of a hearth underlined their domestic nature as a home for the cult statue of a god. The peripteral type, with columns on all sides, evolved from the tenth to the seventh century BCE. The wooden columns surrounding the long, narrow megaron of the Temple of Heroon at Lefkandi on the Isle of Naxos (Fig. 4.2-8a) were converted into stone at the Temple of Apollo at Thera (Fig. 4.2-8b). The earlier temples had a row of interior columns running down the center to support the crest of the roof. The Heraeum at Olympia increased the interior width into a central nave, using internal spur walls alternating with columns to support the roof away from the center (Fig. 4.2-8c). The final solution at the Temple of Aphaea on Aegina, built ca. 500 BCE, had both an exterior and an interior wrapped with columns (Fig. 4.2-8d). This formula for the Doric temple reached perfection in Athens in works such as the Hephaisteion, built in 449 BCE (Fig. 4.2-8e).

The two initial styles of columns, Doric and Ionic, represented specific zones of influence in the Greek-speaking world. The mainland and the western colonies preferred the **Doric order**, with its stout columns carrying simple rounded **capitals** (Fig. 4.2-9a,b). Those on the coast of Asia Minor and on many of the Aegean islands privileged the Ionic order, which was more slender, with **volutes** in its capitals (Fig. 4.2-10a,b). The two styles further differed in the proportions of their columns, intercolumnations, and entablatures.

A typical Doric temple, such as the second Temple of Hera at Paestum, built around 450 BCE, carried six columns on the short sides and fourteen on the long. The columns rose directly from the **stylobate** (the top step) on stout,

fluted **shafts** and were proportioned one **module** to five and a half. They concluded with broad, rounded capitals. The entablature, comprising an **architrave** beam, a decorative **frieze**, and a projecting cornice, spanned the rows of columns. The Doric frieze carried sculpted panels that alternated the three vertical grooves of the **triglyphs** with **metopes** depicting figures or symbols from a religious narrative. A triangular pediment above the entablature carried a sculptural composition.

For the **Ionic order**, as used in the Temple of Artemis at Ephesus (ca. 550 BCE), the columns rose from a slightly bulging **base** with slender shafts and a greater number of flutes. One of the largest temples of the age, the Temple of Artemis spread eight columns across and twenty deep. The conventional proportions of an Ionic column were set as one module to nine. Its capitals curled down on either side of the shaft as graceful volutes. The Ionic architrave often carried three undecorated, slightly corbelled bands finished with rows of egg-and-dart motifs, a continuous frieze above, and a cornice with tooth-like dentils.

The third Greek order, the **Corinthian**, initially appeared inside the Temple of Apollo Epicurius at Bassae, in the western Arcadian region of mainland Greece. Iktinos, one of the architects of the Parthenon, allegedly designed this temple during the late fifth century BCE. While its exterior columns were Doric, the interior chamber, or *cella*, was lined with eccentric versions of Ionic columns, engaged to short spurs that left niches along the walls. A lone Corinthian column stood like a statue at the end of the nave, its capital carved with rows of acanthus leaves. An aperture cut into the eastern flank of the *cella* would have brought a theatrical illumination to this exotic new order (Fig. 4.2-11a,b).

Greek temples were painted with colors as vivid as those on the ziggurats. Their designers left the columns unpainted

Figure 4.2-9   (a) Paestum. Doric second Temple of Neptune, mid-fifth century BCE. (b) Doric order.

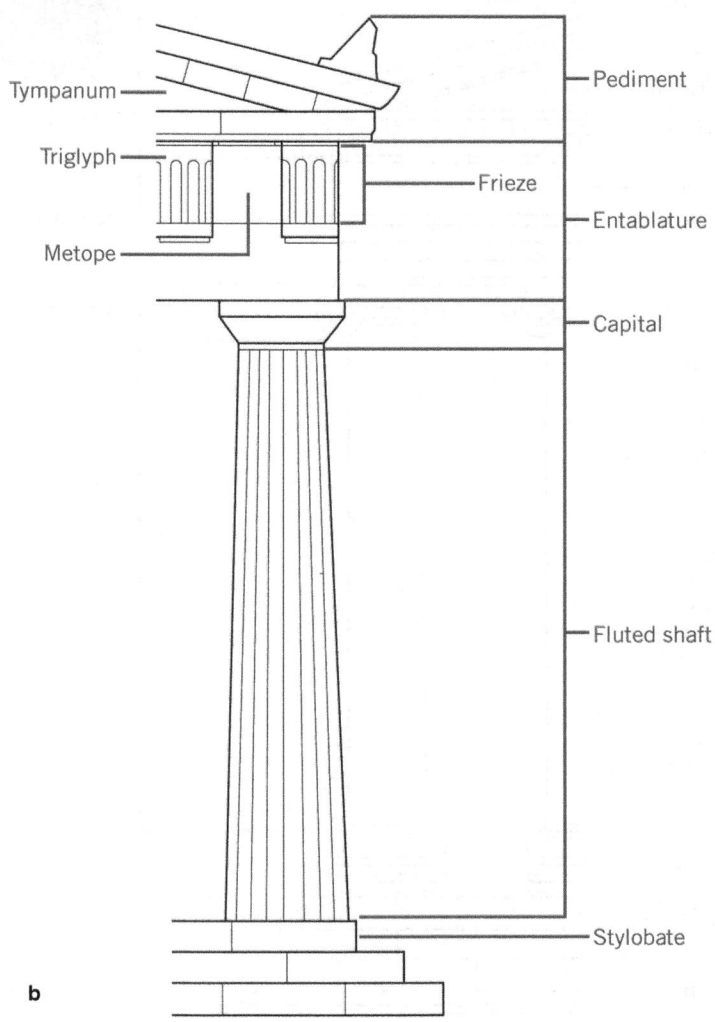

for the sake of structural clarity, **rendering** porous stone with a coat of **stucco** to cover up its rough texture and waxing the smooth marble columns so that they would shine in the strong Greek light, while painting the friezes above the architrave with blue triglyphs and red metopes. They also liberally tinted the sculptures in the pediments.

Greek temples attained a new degree of artistic sophistication during the fifth century BCE, when architects introduced visual correctives known as "refinements." They gently arced the ground plane of the temple platform toward the center to compensate for the way that straight lines seem to deflect when seen from a distance (Fig. 4.2-12a). At the Hephaisteion (built 449 BCE), the Doric temple overlooking the Agora in Athens, for instance, the rise of the base varies 6 cm (2.5 inches) from edge to middle on the fronts and twice that on the sides (Fig. 4.2-12b). Doric columns taper upward and swell with *entasis*, a slight convex bulging of the shaft that expresses their load-bearing function. The vertical fluting of the shafts also helps to convey the idea of compression, while distinguishing the column from the smooth background masonry of the walls. The designers tipped the four corner columns slightly inward 5 cm (2 inches), making them somewhat thicker than the others. Often, the intercolumnation at the corner columns on Doric temples was built narrower than elsewhere in the temple to give visual strength to the corners and compensate for the awkward alignment of the triglyphs in the frieze that were meant to fall directly

Figure 4.2-10 (a) Athens. Ionic North Porch of the Erechtheion, 420 BCE. (b) Ionic order.

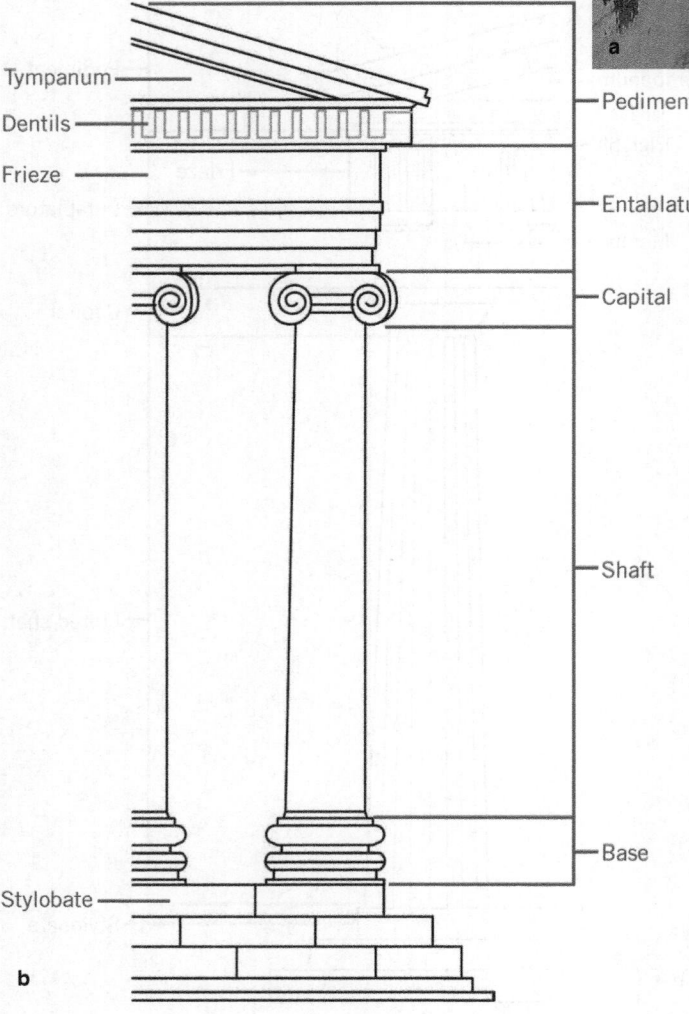

Tympanum — — Pediment

Dentils —

Frieze — — Entablature

— Capital

— Shaft

— Base

Stylobate —

b

on the center of each column. While some of the distortions, like the rise of the stylobate and the *entasis* of the columns, can be easily detected, most of the **refinements** remain barely perceptible, creating the illusion of the equality of the temple's members. A brilliant metaphor for a democratic society, Greek temples appeared to be made of identical parts, but no two were alike.

The Monuments of Democratic Athens

At the end of the sixth century BCE, Athens emerged as the leading city of Greece. The population of its *polis*, which included all of the peninsula of Attica, grew during this period to an estimated 320,000, with half of its residents living inside the walls of the city. The victories at Marathon in 490 BCE and ten years later at Salamis brought the city unexpected power and wealth. During the Persian Wars (490–479 BCE), Athens bonded with other Greek cities, an alliance that in the 470s BCE became the Delian League. As the commander of a union of nearly 300 Aegean city-states, Athens created a superior arsenal, a large navy, and an efficient administrative system. It became similar to an imperial capital, receiving annual tribute from all the other members of the league in support of the alliance. Some of this new wealth went toward building infrastructure and monuments for the city.

The Persians, before their final defeat, sacked Athens in 480 BCE, devastating the temples on the Acropolis. The Athenians at first elected to leave the ruins untouched, as a memorial to those who died at the hand of "the impious barbarians." The brilliant orator Pericles (495–429 BCE), however, convinced the assembly after two decades that both for the glory of the city and to honor the goddess Athena, who was believed to have secured the alliance's improbable victory, the Acropolis should be rebuilt. From 460 BCE until his death in 429 BCE, Pericles was the most influential citizen of Athenian democracy, regularly elected to the city's most important positions, including that of general. He advocated the construction of great buildings not just as aesthetic contributions but as public works to keep construction workers employed. He also convinced the Athenian assembly to liberalize its democracy, enfranchising more people to participate while further limiting the privileges of the elite. Through his influence, democratically selected juries received payment for jury duty so that not only the wealthy would have the time to sit on them.

The first reconstruction project undertaken after the sack of Athens began around 470 BCE at the Port of Piraeus. Hippodamus took charge of laying out the port's *per strigas* plan of orderly, rationally divided blocks, similar to those of Miletus (Fig. 4.2-13a). The assembly also approved the construction of a new set of stone walls, known as the "Long Walls," extending 6 km (3.5 miles) from Athens to the rebuilt port, which, with its three harbors, greatly contributed to the economic and military success of Athens (Fig. 4.2-13b).

For the reconstruction of the temples on the Acropolis, Pericles consulted a personal friend, the sculptor Phidias (ca. 490–430 BCE), who orchestrated the program on the temple mount into a coherent whole (Fig. 4.2-14a,b). The four major architectural projects of this program included the repositioning of the **Propylaia** gate; the construction of a new Ionic temple of victory, the Temple of Athena Nike, directly to the south; the rebuilding of the Parthenon to both house the colossal statue of Athena Parthenos and store the Delian treasury; and the replacement of the Doric Temple to Athena Polia with the Erechtheion, a hybrid building with porches on three levels.

Figure 4.2-11 (a) Bassae, Greece. Reconstruction of the interior of the Temple of Apollo Epicurius, mid-fifth century BCE. (b) Athens, Greece. Temple of Olympian Zeus, the largest temple completed in the Corinthian order, begun sixth century BCE, finished ca. 125 CE by Hadrian.

The temples of the Acropolis served as the terminus for the yearly festival of the Panathenea. Aside from religious ceremonies, the multiple-day event included democratically juried competitions for poetry, music, and athletics held in the Agora and other spaces beneath the hill. The festival culminated in a procession, which assembled at the Kerameikos cemetery just outside the northwest Dipylon gate and moved along the Panathenean Way through the Agora. It then took a detour to the Eleuseion, a hypostyle hall devoted to the Eleusinian mysteries, and

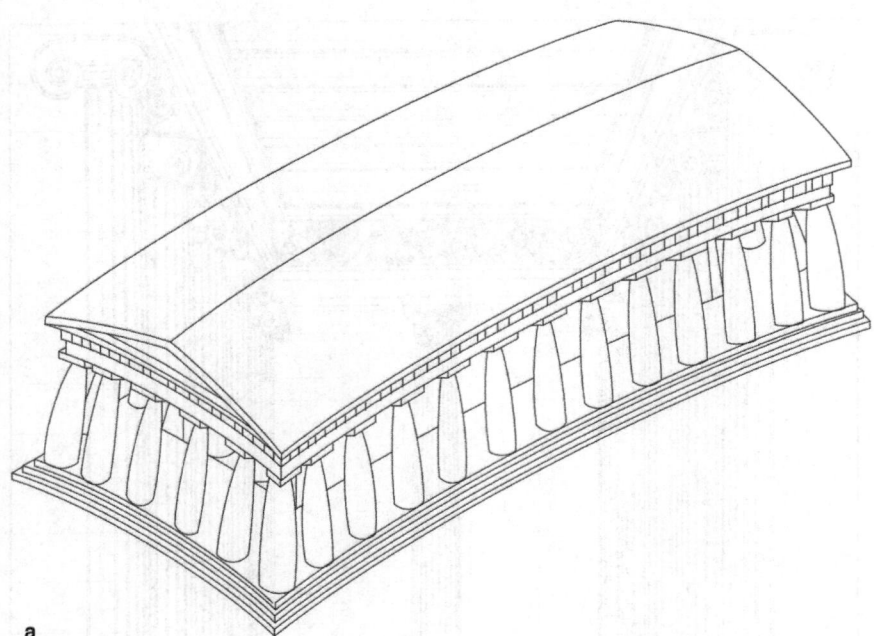

a

Figure 4.2-12 Greek "refinements." (a) Diagram of the distortions used to make Greek temples appear more harmonious (after Coulton). (b) Athens, Greece. Hephaisteion, constructed using the refinements, ca. 450 BCE.

b

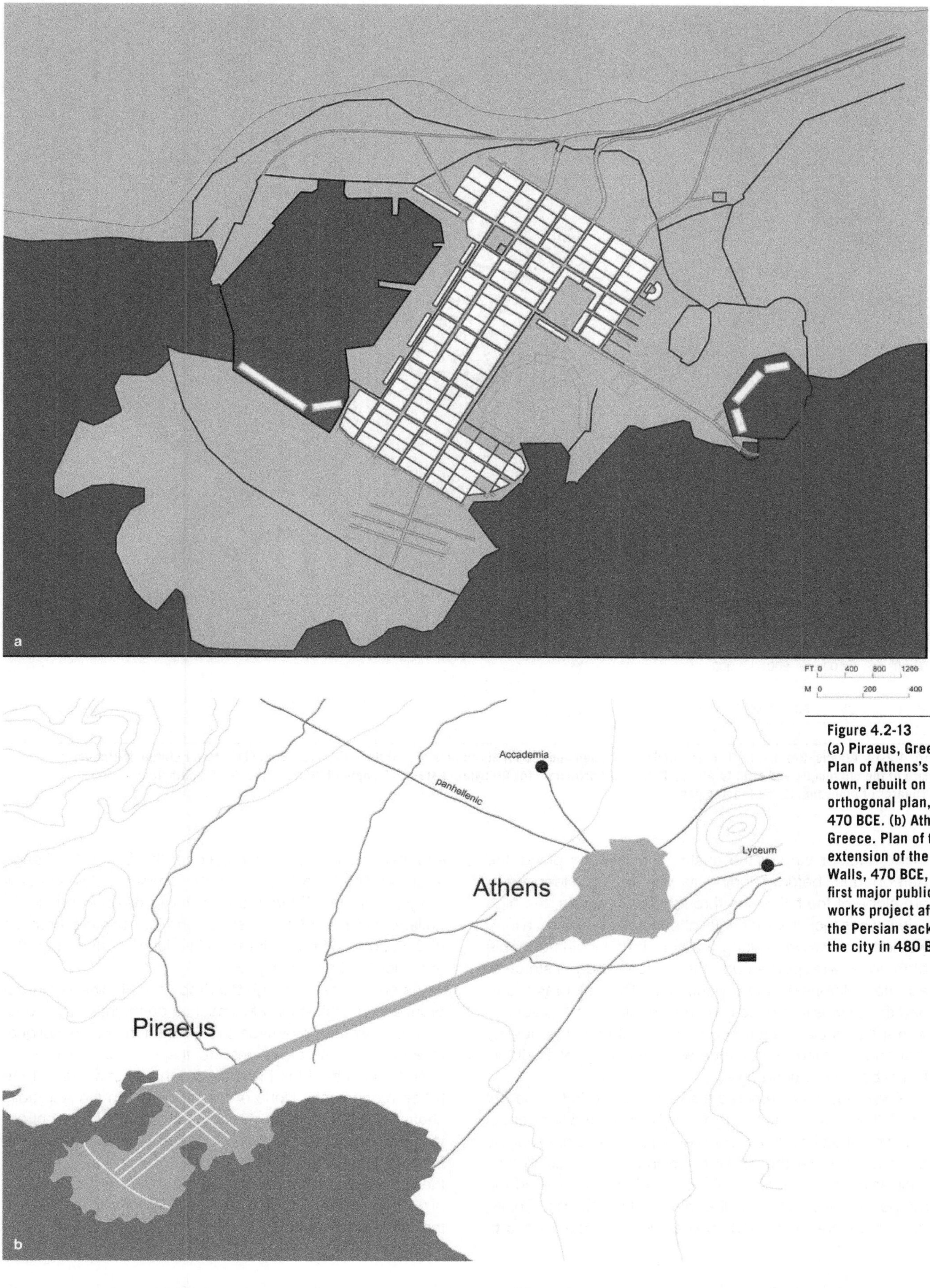

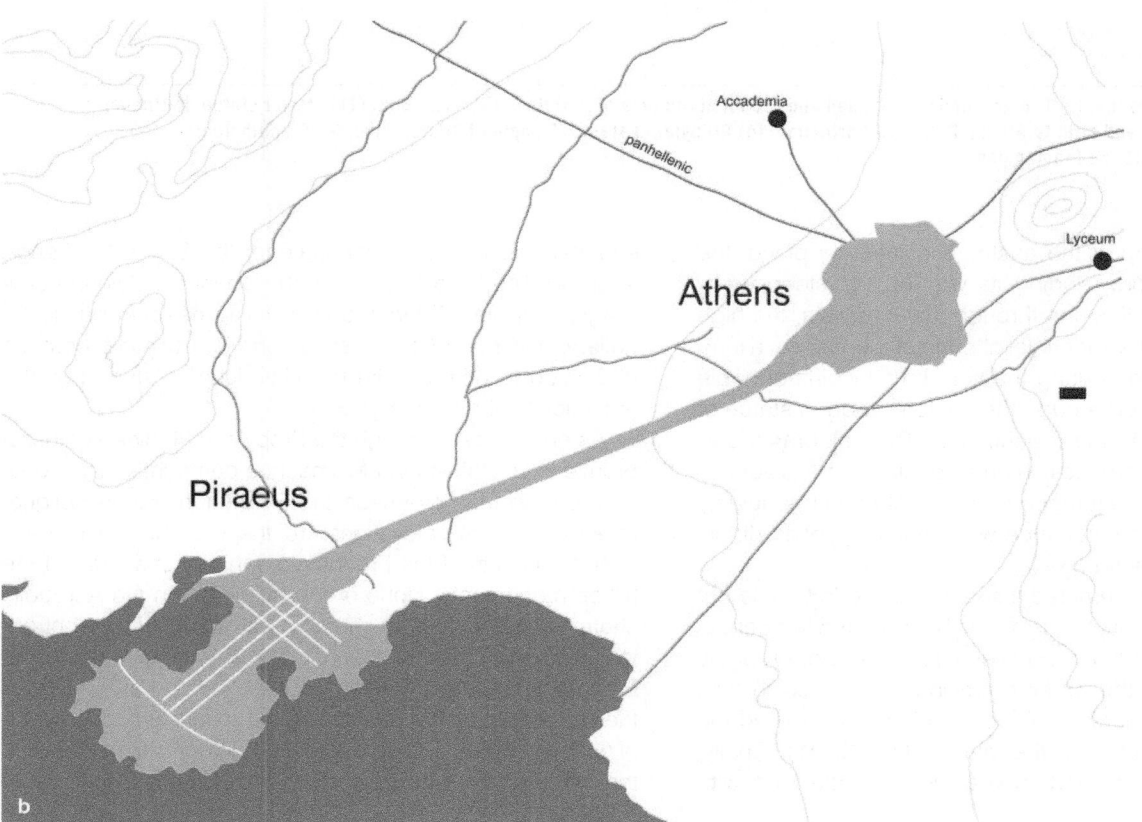

Figure 4.2-13
(a) Piraeus, Greece. Plan of Athens's port town, rebuilt on an orthogonal plan, ca. 470 BCE. (b) Athens, Greece. Plan of the extension of the Long Walls, 470 BCE, the first major public works project after the Persian sack of the city in 480 BCE.

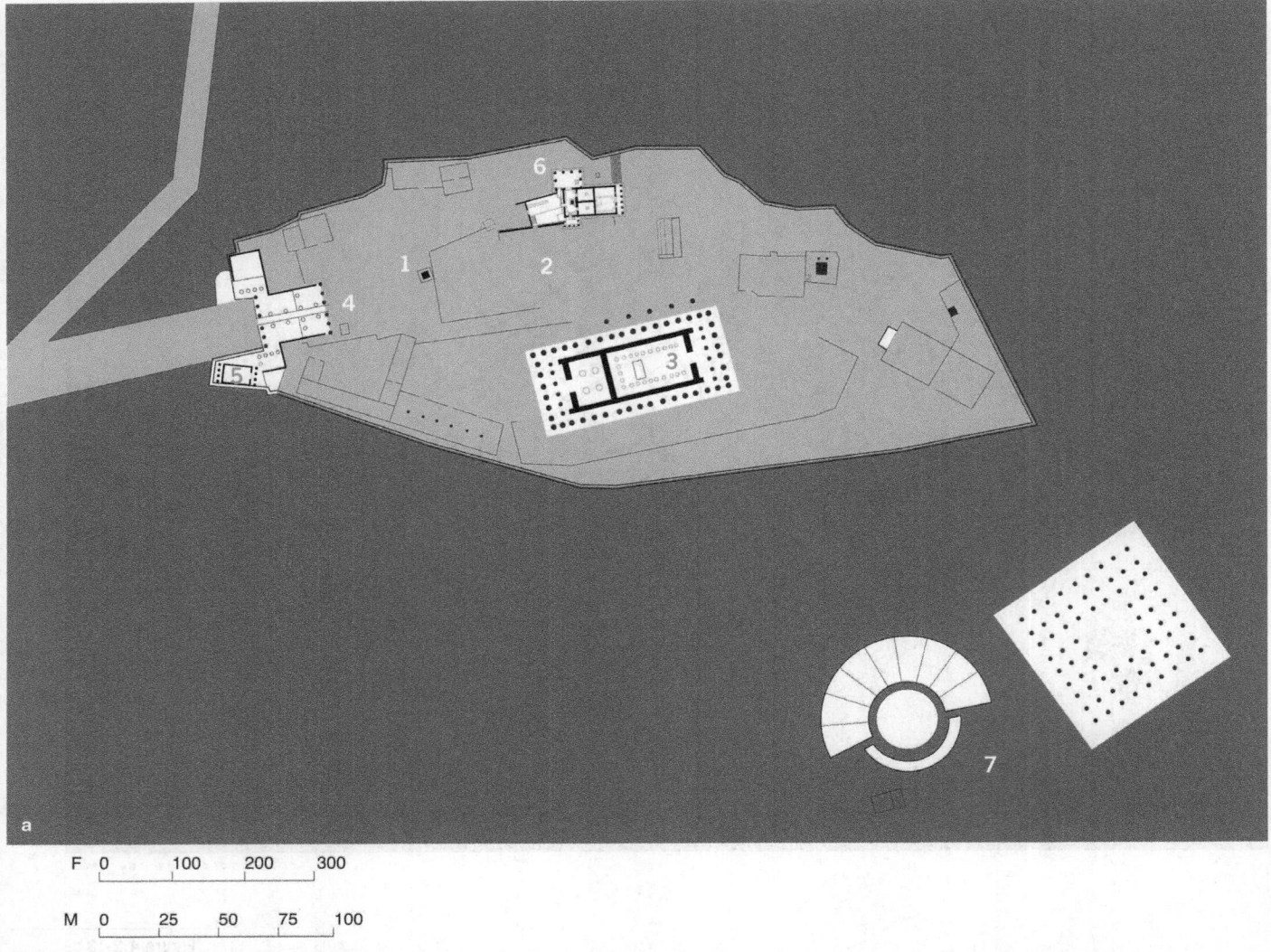

F 0   100   200   300

M 0   25   50   75   100

Figure 4.2-14 Athens, Greece. (a) The Acropolis, replanned and rebuilt at the time of Pericles, 459–420 BCE. (1) Exterior statue of Athena; (2) site of the old temple and altar to Athena Polia; (3) Parthenon; (4) Propylaia gate; (5) Temple of Athena Nike; (6) Erechtheion; (7) Theater of Dionysus. (b) See facing page.

made another stop at the aristocratic meeting place, the Aereopagus, before winding its way up the steep western slope of the hill. Once through the Propylaia, the high priestesses took the sacrificial offering of the *peplos*, a long woolen tunic woven during the year by four girls of noble birth, to be wrapped around the ancient wooden statue of Athena Polia inside the Erechtheion. The celebrants carried the *peplos* in procession on a special ship-like vehicle with a sail, a clear reference to the city's maritime destiny that had a strange resonance with earlier Egyptian rituals at Thebes (see Section 3.2).

The Propylaia resembled a six-column Doric temple but was full of eccentricities. The space between the two central columns stretched three modules instead of two, probably to accommodate the throngs arriving in procession with their animals for sacrifice. Slender Ionic columns lined the ramped pathway through the interior (Fig. 4.2-15). Finally, the rear facade presented another Doric temple front, with

squatter columns to compensate for the 2 m (6 ft) change in grade. The Propylaia's forecourt opened to two unequal wings, with the left leading to a dining hall and public art gallery, and the right to a small temple with Ionic porches dedicated to Athena Nike the Victorious, designed by the architect Kallikrates in 421 BCE.

As one passed through the Propylaia, Phidias's colossal bronze statue of Athena Promachos came into view. To its right one would have seen the Parthenon on the oblique, revealing two full elevations. To the left one would have seen fragments of the Erechtheion, the most sacred of the hilltop monuments. None of the buildings on the Acropolis shared alignments or symmetry with the others. Contrary to one's expectations, the primary entrances of both the Erechtheion and the Parthenon were located at the rear of the structures, as the east was the conventional orientation of Greek temples. This forced the participants to experience the full impact of the buildings by passing between them

(Fig. 4.2-16). In this zone between the two temples stood the prime ritual focus of the Acropolis: the great outdoor Altar to Athena Polia, built in 566 BCE, the year of the festival's origin.

The Parthenon was rebuilt from 447 to 432 BCE over the ruins of a temple that had been under construction at the time of the Persian sack. The architects Iktinos and Kallikrates designed the new temple on a grander scale, posing eight columns instead of six on its short sides and seventeen on the long sides (Fig. 4.2-17). The Pentelic marble of its columns glistened in the sun, projecting a luminous vision of order above the city, visible from far at sea. Due to its refinements, the Parthenon appeared harmoniously balanced and made of equal parts, but none of the Doric columns or the widths between them were the same. Part of the great cost of the temple accrued from this maniacal customization of its refinements, of which it remains the most sophisticated example.

The designers treated the Parthenon like an immense work of sculpture, laden with **relief** friezes and used primarily to contain a colossal statue of the goddess. The Greeks considered sculptors superior to architects at this time because they could reproduce the image of a god, which explains the prime role given to Phidias. His work on the east pediment depicted with fully rounded figures the birth of Athena, the virgin goddess who sprang fully grown from the brow of her father, Zeus. The west pediment narrated the dramatic struggle between Athena and Poseidon, god of the sea. The metopes of the frieze referred to the legendary battles dear to Athenian national honor: the Lapiths against the Centaurs, the Homeric Greeks against the Amazons and the Trojans, and the Olympian gods against the giants.

The artists at the Parthenon set the Panathenean frieze (Fig. 4.2-18) within the peristyle at the top of the exterior walls of the *cella*. This novel work, which ran 160 m (525 ft), had no precedent in terms of placement, subject matter, or technique. The upper areas protruded in higher relief to create a perspectival compensation for the angle of vision. The panels depicted Athenian society riding in tandem or solemnly marching: soldiers on rearing horses, musicians strumming their lyres, bearded elders in dialogue, boys leading reluctant sacrificial oxen and sheep, jug-bearing youths with their arms pulled around the back of their heads, maidens dressed in flowing gowns turning toward the viewer, and the *peplos* being passed on by a young boy to a character representing the *archon*, an authority figure from the age of kings. This human drama of different classes cooperating to ensure the well-being of the

Figure 4.2-14 Athens, Greece.
(b) Aerial view of Acropolis.

Figure 4.2-15 Athens, Greece. Section of Propylaia, showing the Doric order on the exterior and the taller Ionic order inside. Peter Connolly.

CLOSE-UP

Figure 4.2-16 Athens, Greece. Plans of the Parthenon and the Erechtheion.

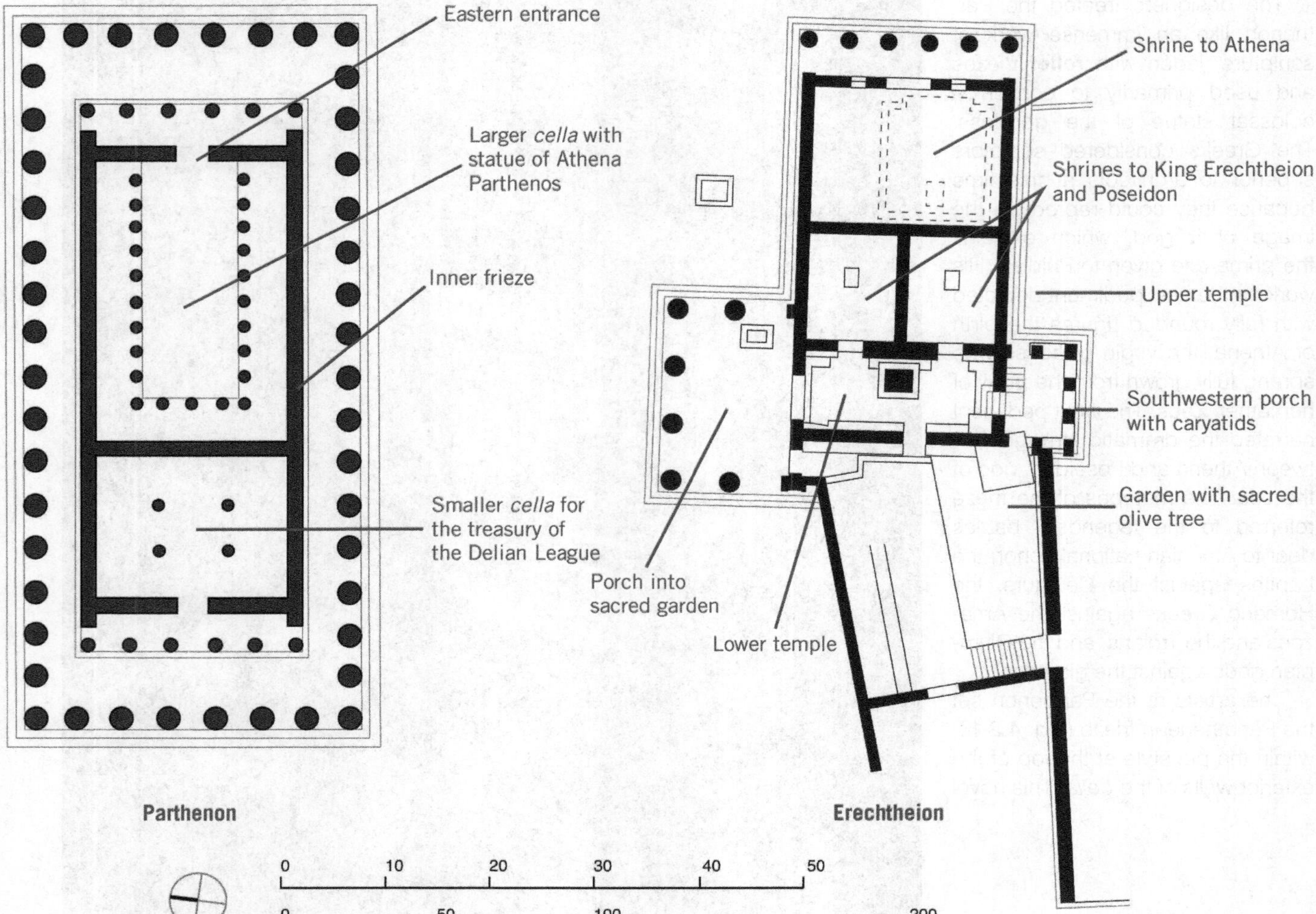

Eastern entrance

Larger *cella* with statue of Athena Parthenos

Inner frieze

Smaller *cella* for the treasury of the Delian League

Porch into sacred garden

Lower temple

Shrine to Athena

Shrines to King Erechtheion and Poseidon

Upper temple

Southwestern porch with caryatids

Garden with sacred olive tree

Parthenon

Erechtheion

| 0 | 10 | 20 | 30 | 40 | 50 |

| 0 | 50 | 100 | 200 |

The Parthenon, ca. 440 BCE, designed by Iktinos and Kallikrates, contained two *cellas*, the larger for Phidias's colossal statue of the virgin goddess, the smaller for the treasury of the Delian League. The Erechtheion, ca. 420 BCE, designed by Mnesicles, was more complex, with temples on two levels, the upper oriented east–west, the lower north–south, and the porch into the lower giving onto a sacred garden.

Figure 4.2-17 Athens, Greece. East facade of the Parthenon, 447–432 BCE.

polis begs to be compared with the analogous work of the rival culture at Persepolis, where a procession of stiff, hieratic Persians seemed perpetually halted on the stairs, unable to reach the Apadana.

On the day of the Panathenean festival the eastern bronze doors of the Parthenon would have been flung open to reveal the colossal 12 m (39 ft) figure of Athena Parthenos, also sculpted by Phidias. Poised over a reflecting pool, the statue of the goddess was dressed in full military attire encrusted with ivory and gold. She carried an effigy of victory in her right hand and with her left leaned on a great shield intertwined with a snake. In the space of the **cella** two tiers of Doric columns surrounded the statue on three sides, reiterating the kinetic qualities of the exterior peristyle. Like many Greek temples, the Parthenon had two back-to-back *cellas*. The minor

Figure 4.2-18 Athens, Greece. Frieze from the Parthenon, reconstruction of painted reliefs, ca. 420 BCE.

Greek Philosophy and the Peripatetic Use of Public Space

In the Agora the Poikile, or Painted Stoa, became the privileged site of philosophical dialogues during the fifth century. It offered a superb view of the Acropolis and became so closely associated with followers of the philosopher Zeno that they became known as "Stoics." The greatest teachers of Athens, such as Socrates (ca. 469–399 BCE), led their students on walks during which they would debate critical issues. The dialogues of the Socratic method as recorded by Plato employed a deductive mode of reasoning based on challenging foregone conclusions. The peripatetic system of learning while walking reached its mature form with Plato (ca. 428–348 BCE), who brought his students to the sacred grove of Athena, associated with the hero Akademos, about a mile north of the Dipylon Gate. Plato's Academy developed in 387 BCE into a conventional system for teaching with dialogical methods. The other great philosopher of the fourth century, Aristotle (384–322 BCE), also founded a school, the Lyceum, at a sacred grove dedicated to Apollo on the opposite side of Athens. Philosophical dialogue, a windfall of the democratic process, became the basic method for arriving at the notion of truth.

Athens, Greece. Rendering of Painted Stoa, site of Xeno's teachings, ca. 470 BCE.

cella contained the treasury of the Delian League and was articulated with four Ionic columns. Like the Propylaia, the Ionic columns on the interior willfully contradicted the Doric exterior. The use of the incongruous order distinguished the minor chamber from the shrine of the goddess and may have referred to the origin of the new wealth of Athens, which flowed from its Ionic dependencies.

The construction of the most unconventional of the new works on the Acropolis, the Erechtheion, began in 421 BCE, nearly a decade after the death of Pericles. Generally attributed to Mnesicles, it signaled a new taste for hybrid forms. From the east it appeared to be a conventional Ionic temple. This impression was contradicted, however, by a second, taller Ionic porch at the back edge of the north elevation. Here, one entered a lower sanctuary devoted to Athena's rival, Poseidon. The second porch also sheltered a gate leading into a walled garden that protected a sacred olive tree. On yet another level, the delightful Porch of the **Caryatids** protruded off of the rear southern corner, facing the Parthenon (Fig. 4.2-19). The six sculpted maidens supported an entablature on their heads. Like the girls of the festival, they wore flowing Ionic *chitons*. For some they were intended to represent the young women protected by the virgin goddess; for others, the sacrificial victims of King Erechtheos, who in the legends of Mycenaean times lived on the hill and was obliged to sacrifice his daughter. The sequencing of spaces, the great variety of styles, and the directed points of view of the Erechtheion demonstrated a new interest in **parallax**, a visual phenomenon that requires a viewer to move around a work to fully understand it. The multileveled, multichambered temple satisfied a rich program that celebrated the ground of a previous temple, the tomb of King Erechtheos, the sacred wooden cult statue of Athena, the salt spring where Poseidon's triton was said to have hit a stone, and Athena's sacred olive tree, which signaled her victory over the sea god in their rivalry to become the city's patron deity. The building's inscriptions reveal that the workers who constructed the Erechtheion were as varied as its facades: 54% foreign residents, 25% citizens, and 21% slaves.

Most of the works planned for the Acropolis were brought to term after the death of Pericles, during the thirty-year

Figure 4.2-19 Athens, Greece. Southwestern porch of the Erechtheion with caryatids, 430 BCE.

period of conflict with Sparta. The conclusion of the Peloponnesian Wars in favor of Sparta at the end of the fifth century BCE put an end to Athens's privilege as the dominant power of the Aegean. Yet the culture of Athens endured, and the gleaming figure of the Parthenon and the other works conceived during the time of Pericles exerted a determining influence on the Mediterranean and beyond for centuries to come.

Alexander the Great: The Diffusion of Hellenism

The Parthenon shone as the highest achievement of Athenian democracy, the most exquisite consequence of committees, councils, and competitions. Yet after the city's decline, it took on other meanings. For Alexander the Great (356–323 BCE), who a century after the temple's completion led Greek-speaking armies to conquer an even greater empire than that of the Persians, the Parthenon represented Greek cultural superiority. Despite his origin in backwater Macedonia, Alexander benefited from having as his tutor the great Athenian philosopher Aristotle, from whom he gained a broader understanding of the world. During his fifteen-year quest to unify the world under one rule, Alexander advanced from Egypt to Babylonia to absorb the Persian Empire but fell short of conquering India. He promoted Greek culture with missionary zeal, and his name became inseparable from **Hellenism**, or the transmission of Greek ideas. Alexander transformed the architecture and urbanism generated by democracy into set pieces for the autocratic rule of an empire. His charismatic presence, beyond the control of committees, raised him to a deified status common among eastern potentates.

The Hellenistic empire amassed by Alexander incorporated the hundreds of autonomous city-states of the Greek commonwealth into a vast international mosaic that also included the ruler-worshiping autocracies of Egypt and Southwest Asia. Greek rule no longer pertained to the Greek race alone, eradicating the civilization's age-old contrast with "barbarian" outsiders. Alexander, who considered himself a mixture of Achilles and Dionysus, was deified even before his death. The practice soon became commonplace among the rulers of successive regimes, who after his demise carved up the empire into three Hellenistic states, with the Ptolemy dynasty in Egypt and Palestine, the Seleucid dynasty in Mesopotamia, and the Antigonid dynasty in the Aegean region.

The new political atmosphere of deified rulers and powerful client states spawned a demand for formal urban spaces distinct from the casual layout of the original Athenian Agora. Authoritarian patrons sponsored grand settings for huge monuments to dynastic power. The **Mausoleum** at Halicarnassus (Fig. 4.2-20), built a generation before Alexander's rise, provided a prototype for these expressions. Although the form of this tomb cannot be reconstructed with complete accuracy, literary sources describe it as having a square base that supported a Greek peristyle of 10 m (33 ft) high columns, capped by a pyramidal tower of twenty-four levels. Pytheus of Priene designed the monument in 353 BCE for Mausolus, the satrap of the Persian region, which included the Greek-speaking Ionian coast. The immense pile, possibly 40 m (131 ft) high, loomed over Halicarnassus's bay and gave its name to the elevated tomb type.

Alexander's first experience with architecture came with the completion of the Philippeion, a *tholos* temple at Olympia dedicated to his father. Set in the precinct of the great pan-Hellenic shrine near two of Greece's oldest Doric temples, the round temple expressed both a sense of belonging and an impression of clear difference. Its correct proportional language proved the Macedonian usurpers worthy of the Greek geometric tradition, and the rounded *tholos* form, although unusual, had many precedents—such as the one at Delphi. The choice of an Ionic exterior in the midst of exclusively Doric temples, however, appeared incongruous, as did the unconventional use of the Corinthian order inside.

After founding the new city of Alexandria at the delta of the Nile in Egypt, the young leader established at least seventy other cities, many of them named in his honor. The plan of Alexandria followed the standard approach of

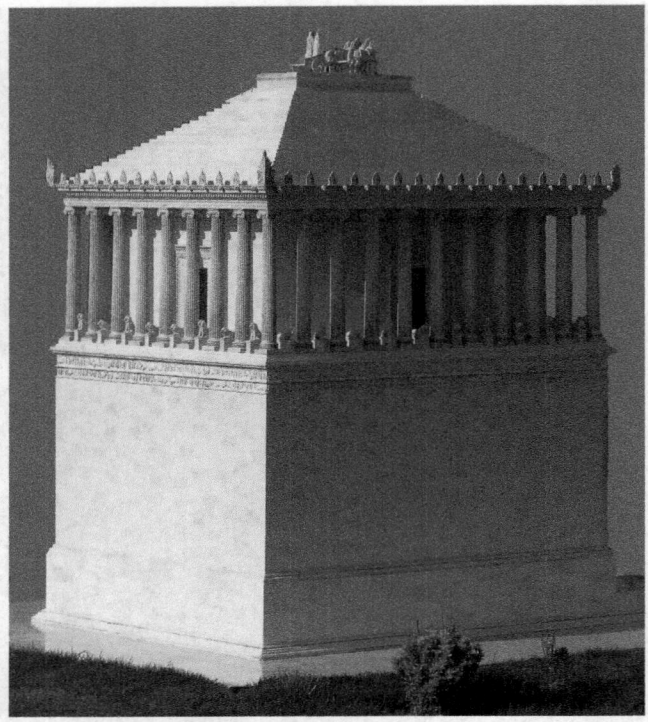

Figure 4.2-20 Halicarnassus (Turkey). Reconstruction of the Mausoleum, ca. 350 BCE. Miniaturk, Istanbul.

Hippodamian planning, with a rational grid of long blocks. A principal street, the Canopus, ran parallel to the coast, separating the public areas from the princely areas near the shore. In the center the Ptolemy dynasty placed an agora, a temple, a precinct for the mausoleum of Alexander, and to the side, looking toward the sea, a Greek theater.

The Roman architect Vitruvius, in his treatise on architecture (see Section 5.1), told the story of the architect Dinocrates, who in attempting to gain Alexander's patronage dressed up in a lion skin to resemble Hercules and offered the young emperor a model for a city to be carved out of a mountain as a portrait of the ruler. Although Alexander rejected Dinocrates's scheme as impractical, the theatrical and metaphoric approach came to characterize the design of subsequent Hellenistic public spaces. The famous **Colossus** of Rhodes, a bronze statue of the sun god Helios, offered a spectacular entry into that city's port. It stood 32 m (105 ft) tall, similar in scale to the Statue of Liberty in New York, with legs astride the mouth of the city's harbor. Rhodes, which retained its autonomy during the rise of Alexander, erected the monument in 280 BCE to commemorate the island's victory over the Macedonian general Demetrius I. The statue collapsed during an earthquake fifty years later.

At Lindos the Rhodians rebuilt the breathtaking sanctuary of Athena Lindia on the city's hilltop site, using the Acropolis in Athens as a model (Fig. 4.2-21a,b). Like the axial approach through the Propylaia, the entry was framed by colonnades. A sequence of three linked terraces stepped up the hill, each level enclosed with symmetrical sets of colonnades. After this grand sequence of symmetrical spaces, the

temple on the top platform broke the pattern, tucked off-axis into the northeast corner. This set up a surprise oblique view of its porch, reminiscent of the approach to the Parthenon.

Like Rhodes, the Attalid dynasty of Pergamon, a city-state on the Ionian coast of Turkey, also retained its autonomy. It entered the Hellenistic political checkerboard as a client state in the mid-third century BCE. The Attalids extended their authority over much of the Ionian coast, transforming Pergamon into a showcase of Hellenistic urbanism. With the wealth accrued from tribute and various industries, they shaped the rugged hillside stronghold into a spectacular series of monumental terraces. Their architects exploited the steep terrain with a flare unparalleled in the Greek world except perhaps in the Athens of Pericles, which served as their guide. The Attalids even chose the patron goddess of Athena Polia for the focus of their principal shrine. Athenian sculptors came to work on the Great Altar of Pergamon, as well as creating a replica of Phidias's statue of Athena.

Pergamon was divided into a lower city for commerce, education, and administration and an upper city for the royal palaces and major temples. The kings of Pergamon encouraged the development of a unique mixed government that allowed them absolute power over the state but permitted the city to be managed by democratic institutions. The upper city spread like a fan over a succession of terraces for shrines and public buildings, wrapping around a steep hillside theater. Starting from the arsenal and the **barracks** at the summit, the sequence of colonnaded terraces stepped down the hill. Successive kings constructed an archaic temple (replaced by a temple to the Roman emperor Trajan at the beginning of the second century CE; Fig. 4.2-22), a great library, the Temple of Athena Polia, a civic *stoa*, and finally the Great Altar, which occupied the most prominent terrace. Unlike the other monuments in the upper city, the Temple of Athena Polia did not obey the radial alignment to the theater. Instead, it pointed directly south to the Great Altar below, as if in dialogue with it. Built in the conservative Doric order, it appeared a conscious effort to quote the Parthenon.

So great was the Attalids' esteem for Athens that one of their last kings, Attalus II (r. 159–138 BCE), commissioned the eastern *stoa* of the Athenian Agora, a long colonnade with an internal row of columns and twenty shops along its back wall. The Stoa of Attalus reconfigured the Agora into an approximate rectangle with surrounding colonnades, making it somewhat like the terraces built at Pergamon.

The Great Altar at Pergamon became the hub of the royal city (Fig. 4.2-23). A broad flight of stairs led through an Ionic colonnade to an inner court for making burnt sacrifices. The exterior carried a colossal frieze of exceptional drama, with figures that seemed to burst out of the stone. The scene portrayed the battle of the Olympian gods against the giants, an allusion to the victory of Attalus I over the Gauls, the Celtic nomads from the north. Like the frieze of the Parthenon, it evoked the old duality of Greek versus barbarian that had been a constant theme in the classical *polis*. A frieze within the court offered a different mood, quieter and more delicate, celebrating the legitimacy of the Attalid

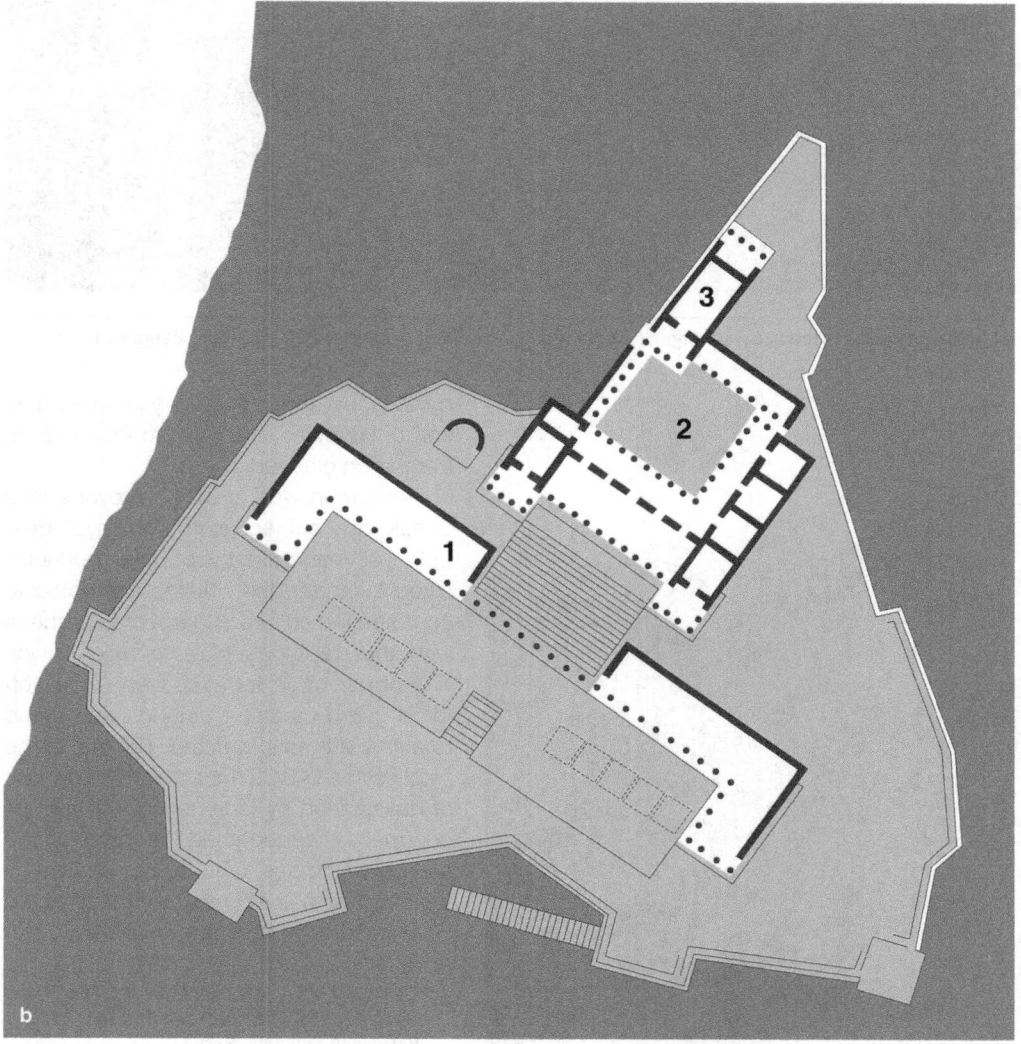

Figure 4.2-21 Rhodes, Greece.
(a) View of Sanctuary of Athena
at Lindos. (b) Plan of Sanctuary of
Athena at Lindos: (1) entry *stoa*;
(2) inner court; (3) Temple of
Athena Lindia, third century BCE.

Figure 4.2-22 Pergamon (Turkey). Model of the city's upper terraces, arranged in a fan around the hillside theater, 280–133 BCE. Pergamon Museum, Berlin.

dynasty by telling the story of Telephos, son of Hercules, from whom the kings of Pergamon claimed descent.

Pergamon was at once a royal and a Greek city, subject to the whim of despots yet managed by popular councils. Like Alexander, the Attalids attempted to combine the culture of democratic Athens with the trappings of autocratic power. The upper city's terraced sequences offered grand theatrical settings well suited to a final dramatic gesture. The last of the Attalids in 133 BCE, faced with the danger of devastation by local feuds and foreign occupation, bequeathed Pergamon to the powerful Romans, who in turn had much to learn from their new subjects about classical architecture and urbanism.

Figure 4.2-23 Pergamon (Turkey). The Great Altar, ca. 250 BCE, as reconstructed at the Pergamon Museum, Berlin.

Further Reading

Cahill, Nicholas. *Household and City Organization at Olynthus.* New Haven, CT: Yale University Press, 2002.

Camp, John M. *The Athenian Agora: Excavations in the Heart of Classical Athens.* London: Thames and Hudson, 1986.

Coulton, J. J. *Ancient Greek Architects at Work: Problems of Structure and Design.* Ithaca, NY: Cornell University Press, 1977.

Dinsmoor, William B. *The Architecture of Ancient Greece.* New York: Norton, 1975.

Keuls, Eva C. *The Reign of the Phallus: Sexual Politics in Ancient Athens.* New York: Harper, 1985.

Lyttelton, Margaret. *Baroque Architecture in Classical Antiquity.* London: Thames and Hudson, 1974.

Martin, Roland. *Greek Architecture.* Milan: Electa, 1975.

Pedley, John Griffen. *Greek Art and Archaeology.* New York: Pearson/Prentice Hall, 2007.

Woodford, Susan. *The Parthenon.* Cambridge: Cambridge University Press, 1981.

4.3 MAURYAN INDIA
Emblems of Peace in Stone

At the end of the third century BCE, Ashoka, grandson of the first great empire builder in India, sponsored a series of inscribed columns and ceremonial mounds to promote his political and religious convictions. As sovereign of the Mauryan dynasty he consolidated a realm that included most of what is now India, Pakistan, and Afghanistan. Ashoka's conversion to Buddhism led him to the exceptional contradiction of desiring to represent imperial dominion without celebrating its military basis. After a career of violent campaigns, he attempted to make amends by governing his kingdom according to a code of nonviolence. With the proceeds from his war chest Ashoka constructed multitudes of *stupas*, mounded shrines commemorating the life of Buddha. In key urban sites he erected hundreds of freestanding columns with inscriptions describing his peaceful ideology. Rather than financing grand buildings as testaments to his power, Ashoka preferred to sponsor humble, sacred landscapes of ritual contemplation, venerating the places associated with Buddha's life and preaching.

The First Indian Empire and Religions of Antimaterialism

In his campaign to conquer the entire world, Alexander the Great pushed as far as the Beas River in modern Punjab but failed to annex India. Before his retreat to Babylon in 326 BCE, however, he found enough time to establish new cities in the region: three with his name and one, Bucephalia, named after his recently deceased horse. Greek influence remained in the region for several centuries, particularly in the Bactria area of Afghanistan. The military leaders who created the first Indian empire, inspired by the example of the Greek invaders as well as the Persians before them, united the lands east of Taxila (near modern Islamabad) under the Mauryan dynasty soon after Alexander's demise. The new rulers emulated the political structure of the Persian and Hellenistic empires but did not build comparable architectural settings. Indian construction practices led to expendable buildings, few of which could resist time. The only lasting structures came from the new religions that took root during this period, especially Buddhism, which sponsored memorial mounds and monasteries.

The founding Mauryan emperor, Chandra Gupta, met Alexander some time before taking power in 320 BCE. The connection between the Mauryans and the Greeks was sustained through diplomatic relations with the Seleucids, the largest of the Greek successor states to Alexander's empire. The Indians exchanged their military equipment and elephants for parcels of Seleucid territory. The agreement between the two empires included the marriage of a Seleucid princess to a prince in the Indian royal family. In 305 BCE the Greek ambassador of King Seleuces I sent an account back to his ruler of the Indian emperor's capital city, Pataliputra (modern Patna), comparing its scale and grandeur to Persepolis, the only city that Alexander intentionally destroyed during his sweep east. The Indian capital occupied a key position in the Ganges valley. The Mauryan walls ran the length of the river, 15 km (9 miles) long and 2.5 km (1.5 miles) wide, resulting in a formidable linear city. However, the flimsy nature of Indian building materials, primarily mud and wood, and the waves of destruction by successive powers left almost nothing of the Mauryan capital that could be considered architecture. Among Pataliputra's scant archaeological remains are the stone bases of a hypostyle hall with over eighty wooden columns, reminiscent of the Persian emperor's Apadana (Fig. 4.3-1). Like the Persian emperors, Chandra Gupta consolidated his territorial power by installing regional governors and building a national road system. The Mauryans lined their roads with stone markers and supplied them with regularly placed hospices. The Great Royal Road stretched along the Himalayan border, connecting Taxila in the northwest to Pataliputra in the east.

Indian society, with perhaps as many as 50 million people at the time of the Mauryan unification, maintained rigidly structured social castes but was widely diversified into many feudal kingdoms with multifarious religious beliefs and expressions. The caste system of inherited social status began sometime after the Aryan transition in the twelfth century BCE, a period contemporary with the invasions of the Sea Peoples in the Mediterranean. The *Brahman*, or high priest caste, dominated the other three castes: *ksatriyas* (nobles and warriors), *vaisyas* (farmers and merchants), and *sudras* (workers). These four categories were in turn subdivided into many other hierarchies. At the very bottom, the

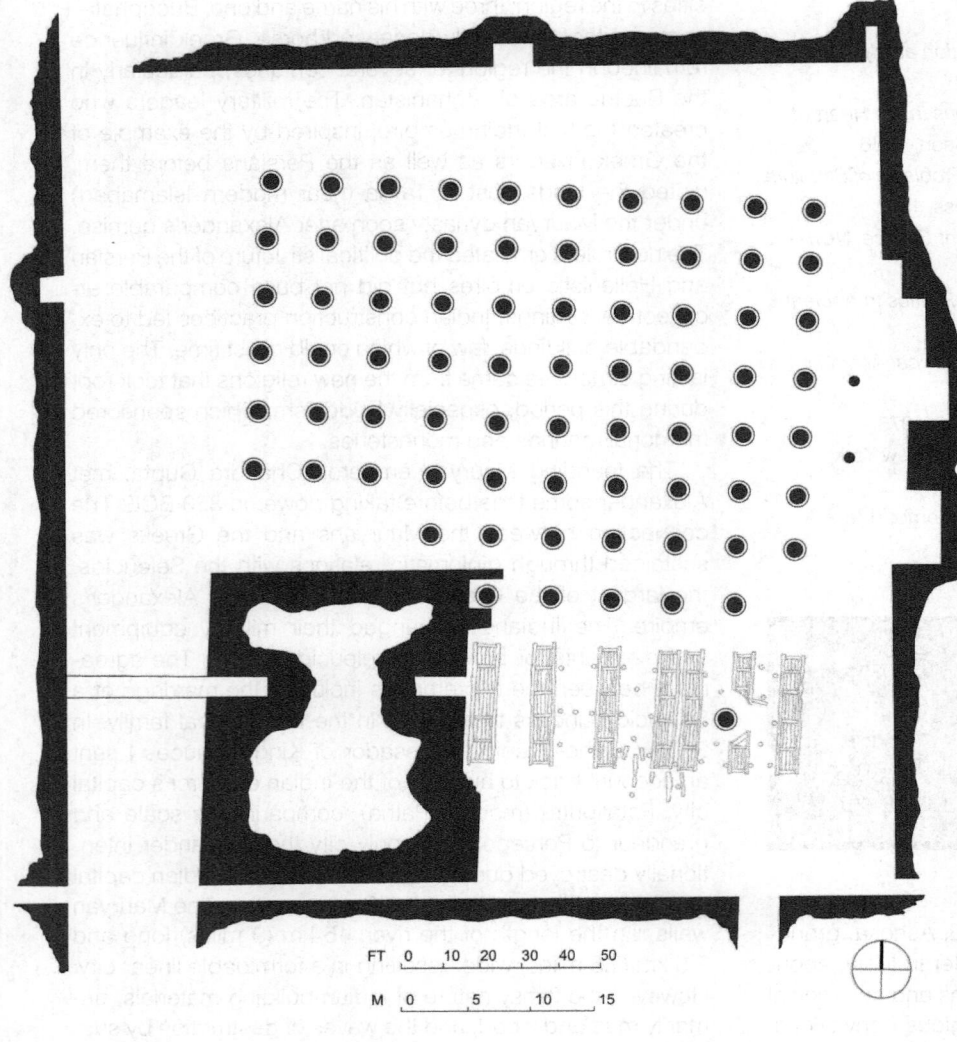

FT 0 10 20 30 40 50

M 0 5 10 15

with mythic stories and legends, date to the fifth century BCE.

Toward the end of his reign Chandra Gupta abdicated his throne and converted to the Jain religion. Jainism, which can be traced back to the sixth-century BCE teachings of the guru Mahavira, emphasized reincarnation while celebrating anti-materialism. Mahavira was the last of twenty-four wise men who predicated nonviolence as a means of attaining *moksha*, or enlightenment, a means of transcending *samsara*. As the religion developed, it branched into two strains, with the most ascetic known as the Dijambars, whose priests insisted on not wearing clothes to keep free of the corrupting influence of material things on the soul. Most Jains today adhere to the second strain, which is less radical. They nonetheless observe vegetarianism and object to the killing of all animals and even some plants. While in later centuries Jains sponsored glorious memorials with ornately sculpted columns, their anti-materialist philosophy in effect discouraged architectural display, and initially they did not build temples. The most enduring icon of Jainism, the *fylfot*, a flanged cross also known as the "swastika," represented the beneficial cycles of life and had nothing in common with the violent ideology that the German Nazis made of it in the twentieth century (see Section 18.3). Chandra Gupta was not known to have sponsored any enduring monuments to his faith. After he had accomplished his political and military goals, he retired to a life of asceticism in a monastery,

"untouchables" were destined to carry out the most onerous jobs. The culture's sacred texts, or *Vedas*, written in the Sanskrit language of the Aryan peoples, mapped out the underlying religious concept of *samsara*, or the inflexible cycle of birth, existence, death, and rebirth. While one could not change the destiny of one's birth, one was guaranteed that in a future life things would not be the same. The ancient literary epics the *Mahabharata* and the *Ramayana*, which blend the nascent theological concepts of the *Vedas*

TIME LINE

 ca. 500 BCE

The Buddha preaches throughout northern India

 320 BCE

Chandra Gupta leads Mauryan dynasty to control half of India

King Ashoka expands Mauryan power after Battle of Kalinga

Death of Buddha

▲ **ca. 480 BCE**

▲ **265 BCE**

devoting himself to the nonviolent precepts of his new religion. He left the rule of the new empire to his son in 297 BCE.

During the reign of Chandra Gupta's grandson, Ashoka, beginning around 270 BCE, the Mauryan dynasty produced its major cultural contributions. Ashoka ruled for thirty-seven years, expanding the regime's control over the subcontinent and, unlike his forebears, leaving an impressive monumental output. Due partly to political motivations and partly to his later conversion to Buddhism, Ashoka erected monumental columns known as *stambhas*, on which he inscribed his laws in several languages, including Greek. He also sponsored thousands of Buddhist memorial mounds in the form of domical **stupas**. Known as *Devanampiya*, "beloved of the gods," Ashoka spread his architectural patronage to all parts of the Mauryan realm. His chosen religion, Buddhism, developed into the most significant spiritual innovation within the Vedic traditions in India during the ancient period, offering an alternative to the established theological concepts obtained through divine revelation. Like Jainism, it posed a kind of resistance to the caste system in that its practice was not based on hierarchical rituals and thus seemed open to all.

Ashoka and Sanchi: Materializing the Immaterial

Like many successful rulers, Ashoka used architecture to demonstrate the extent of his power. Much like his grandfather, he underwent a religious catharsis after a career of violent conquest and battle. Ashoka turned to Buddhism after the horrendous Battle of Kalinga, in which 100,000 were reported slain and 150,000 deported. In an inscription on a *stambha* column, Ashoka describes the carnage of the battle scene as an unbearable vision of human suffering. It moved the emperor to promote the idea of consensus rather than warfare as a means of achieving political goals. To future generations he offered warnings against war and advocated "conquest by *dharma* to be a true conquest, and delight in *dharma* should be their whole delight." Ashoka felt that his great task as emperor was the maintenance and dissemination of Buddhist *dharma*, a code of nonviolence that promoted the tolerance of all religions and opinions, obedience and respect for elders and priests, generosity to others, and fair treatment of slaves. The emperor pursued the ethic of *dharma* by restoring the roads and hostels,

planting medicinal herbs, founding hospitals, and banning animal sacrifices and slaughter.

Ashoka's compassionate ideology, under which *dharma* replaced militarism, relied on Buddhism as a strategy for social harmony. In all, the emperor commissioned 256 *stambha* pillars to be erected throughout his empire, inscribing them with the benevolent message of *dharma*. The inscriptions on these columns were written either in the local languages or in Sanskrit. In the western province of Taxila he used Greek. Ashoka's *stambhas* were monolithic, polished sandstone, slightly tapered, and sometimes over 15 m (49 ft) high, approaching the scale of the obelisks of Hatshepsut. His engineers slipped the *stambhas* into stone foundations about 3.5 m (11 ft) into the ground, similar to their Egyptian precursors. The columns belonged to the ancient tradition of establishing a vertical axis as a cosmic sign of the union between heaven and earth. The most famous of Ashoka's pillars stood in Sarnath, on the Ganges River, the site of the Buddha's first sermon (Fig. 4.3-2a). Its capital resembled those in the Hall of 100 Columns at Persepolis (Fig. 4.3-2b). Above the sculpted petals of drooping lotus blossoms a ring of reliefs depicted sacred animals and *chakra* prayer wheels. At the top a composite of four lions pointed in the cardinal directions supported a bronze *chakra* wheel.

Not far from the *stambha* at Sarnath, Ashoka constructed a monumental *stupa*, a hemispherical mound to commemorate a holy site. Several centuries later this *stupa* was rebuilt into its current conical shape. According to some ancient accounts, Ashoka constructed 84,000 *stupas*, but among these only a few, such as those at Sravasti, Taxila, and Sanchi (Fig. 4.3-3), can be safely attributed to his patronage. The *stupa* descended from the Neolithic cairn, a tomb structure of piled stones laid over the ashes of the deceased (see Section 1.3). The perfectly rounded *stupa* type, a solid mass with no interior space, evolved as the typical Buddhist monument, containing relics and symbolizing religious beliefs. Pilgrims honored them as ceremonial settings and helped to enrich them with gates, fences, decorative finials, and symbolic sculptures.

After centuries of abandonment Ashoka's special site at Sanchi was rediscovered in the nineteenth century CE (Fig. 4.3-3). Set on a hill 7 km (4 miles) from the crossroads town of Vidisha in the third century BCE, the endowed monastery precinct remained active until the seventh century CE. The site lies at the exact geographical center of

▼ **260 BCE**

Ashoka as penitent erects columns

Ashoka sponsors the Great Stupa at Sanchi (India)

▲ **ca. 250 BCE**

Figure 4.3-2 Sarnath, India. (a) Ashoka's *stambha*, ca. 200 BCE. (b) Lion's capital.

the Mauryan Empire. Two of the major *stupas* stood within a walled *temenos* in an area a bit larger than the Agora in Athens. Most of the original monastic structures have disappeared, while all of the *stupas* were repeatedly modified.

Ashoka planned the largest of the three major *stupas* as a reliquary for some of the ashes of the Buddha. At its principal gateway on the south side he placed one of his *stambha* pillars. The Great Stupa was initially constructed of brick and rubble and smoothed over with plaster. From its earliest diameter of 20 m (66 ft), the *stupa* was nearly doubled in size during the next two centuries by later builders, who clad it with rough stones and skirted it with three levels of balustrades at the base, middle, and top (Fig. 4.3-4). Circular railings, made of log-shaped stones, enclosed a processional path at grade, used for the ritual *pradakshina*, the clockwise circumambulation of pilgrims (Fig. 4.3-5). The four gateways, or **toranas**, added in the second century CE were placed at each of the cardinal points. Rather than allowing direct access, the gates jog to the left, forcing the pilgrim to enter obliquely, turning his or her right shoulder toward the mound, the ritually prescribed position for acknowledging the presence of the Buddha.

The components of the fences surrounding the Great Stupa were clearly derived from timber joinery prototypes.

They screened off the processional path but allowed one to peek through the narrow gaps between the cross-stones. A bifurcated stair led to the middle level of the Great Stupa, reserved for priests and monks. The summit was capped by an inaccessible square balustrade surrounding a three-tiered sandstone parasol, or *harmika*, which indicated the presence of Buddhist relics inside the mound and represented the moment of enlightenment under the Bodhi tree.

A second *stupa*, about half the size of the Great Stupa, stood a few meters north of it. It reproduced many of the same features of the larger structure and was thought to contain the relics of Buddha's close disciples. A third large *stupa* built about 100 m (328 ft) below the main precinct contained two relic chambers with the ashes of ten enlightened monks from the time of Ashoka. Less ornate, it rose as a simple mound without the parasol or fence of an upper *harmika*. Dozens of smaller *stupas* filled the precinct area as reliquaries or funeral markers.

Like the Mesopotamian ziggurats and earlier tumuli, the *stupas* of Ashoka involved the piling of materials and then the refining of the mass with stairways and terraces. Architectural sophistication came later in the second century CE with the addition of carved railings and gateways. Ashoka eagerly commissioned architecture as propaganda to spread his

Buddhism and *Dharma*

Buddhism appeared around the same time as Jainism and was likewise a strong antimaterialist religion. Unlike the Jains, however, the Buddhists believed in conversion, and their religion had wide influence throughout Asia. The faith formed around the life and teachings of Siddhartha Gautama, the Buddha, or "perfectly enlightened one," whose long life of eighty years probably stretched from the mid-sixth century to the mid-fifth century BCE. The Indian sage lived at the same time as the Chinese lawgiver Confucius and the pre-Socratic philosophers in Greece. Born into a position of high status in a princely clan of Nepal, Buddha chose to live as a wandering ascetic. His ultimate moment of enlightenment came after a period of intense meditation under the Bodhi tree.

Buddha spent his life traveling throughout the Ganges valley region, spreading his teaching of liberation from *samsara*. The places he visited, such as Bodh Gaya, where he meditated under the Bodhi tree, and Sarnath, where he gave his first sermon, became pilgrimage shrines, monumentalized during Ashoka's reign. After his death Buddha's followers divided his ashes into ten parts to be enshrined in *stupas*. The ashes of his disciples received similar treatment. The Buddhist prayer wheel, or *chakra*, represents meditation on the cycle of life and became the most evident icon of the religion, emblazoned on Buddhist monuments.

Several centuries before the monastic movements of Mediterranean religions, many followers of Buddha chose to live in secluded monasteries, segregated from secular life. They lived in convents, or **viharas**, modest compounds with small individual cells surrounding a rectangular court. The Jaulian monastery near ancient Taxila is among the oldest of these institutions. Because so much of Buddhist thought emphasized transcendence, it inspired an architecture of restraint, initially avoiding monumental expression.

(a) Sanchi, India. *Torana* reliefs, ca. 200 CE. The footprints at the far right of the central transom indicated Buddha without showing his body. (b) Nalanda, near Pataliputra, India. Buddhist convent, or *vihara*, fifth century CE.

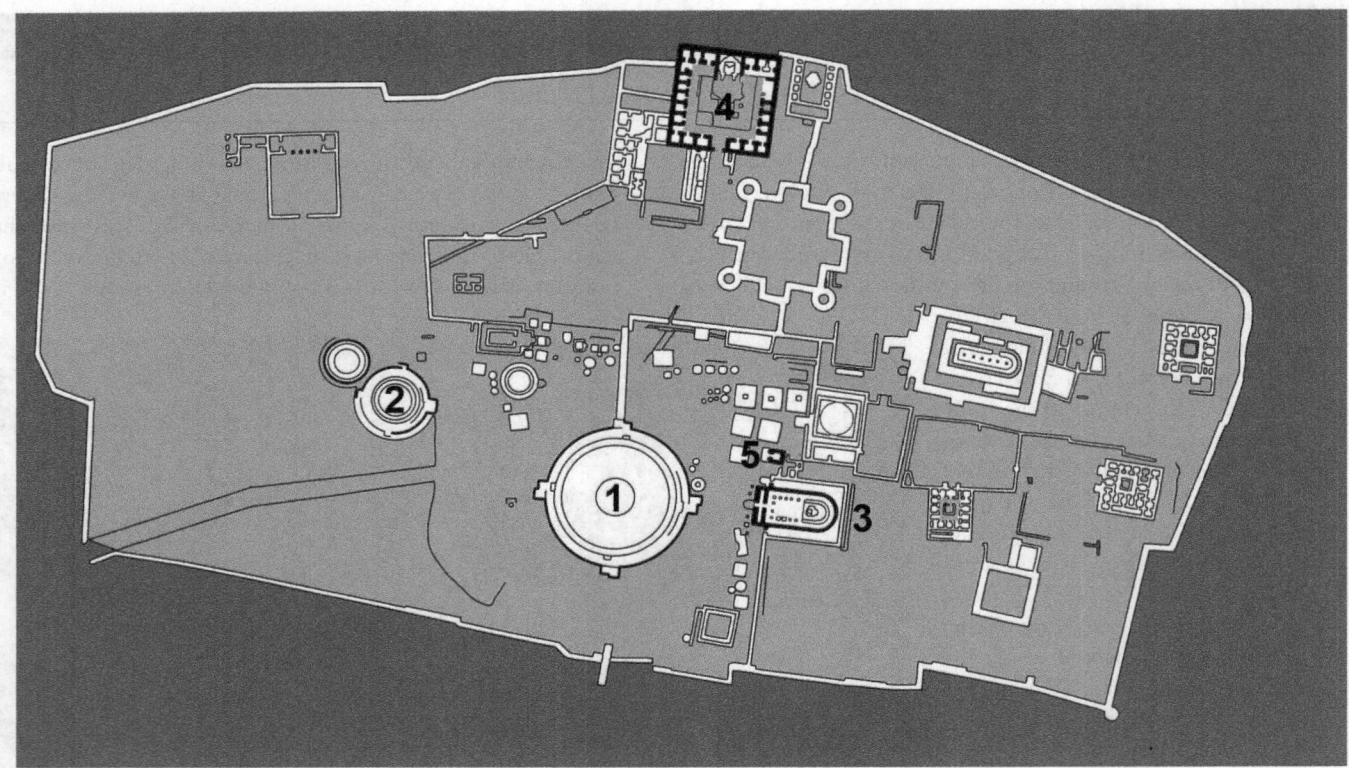

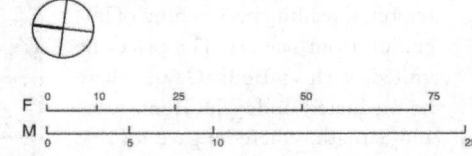

Figure 4.3-3 Sanchi, India. Ashoka's Buddhist enclave, begun in the second century BCE. (1) The Great Stupa; (2) the Second Stupa; (3) the *chaitya* hall, ca. 200 CE; (4) the *vihara* monasteries added ca. 200 CE; (5) Temple "17," ca. 400 CE.

Figure 4.3-4 Sanchi, India. The Great Stupa, memorial to Buddha, begun by Ashoka, mid-third century BCE. *Torana* gates added several centuries later.

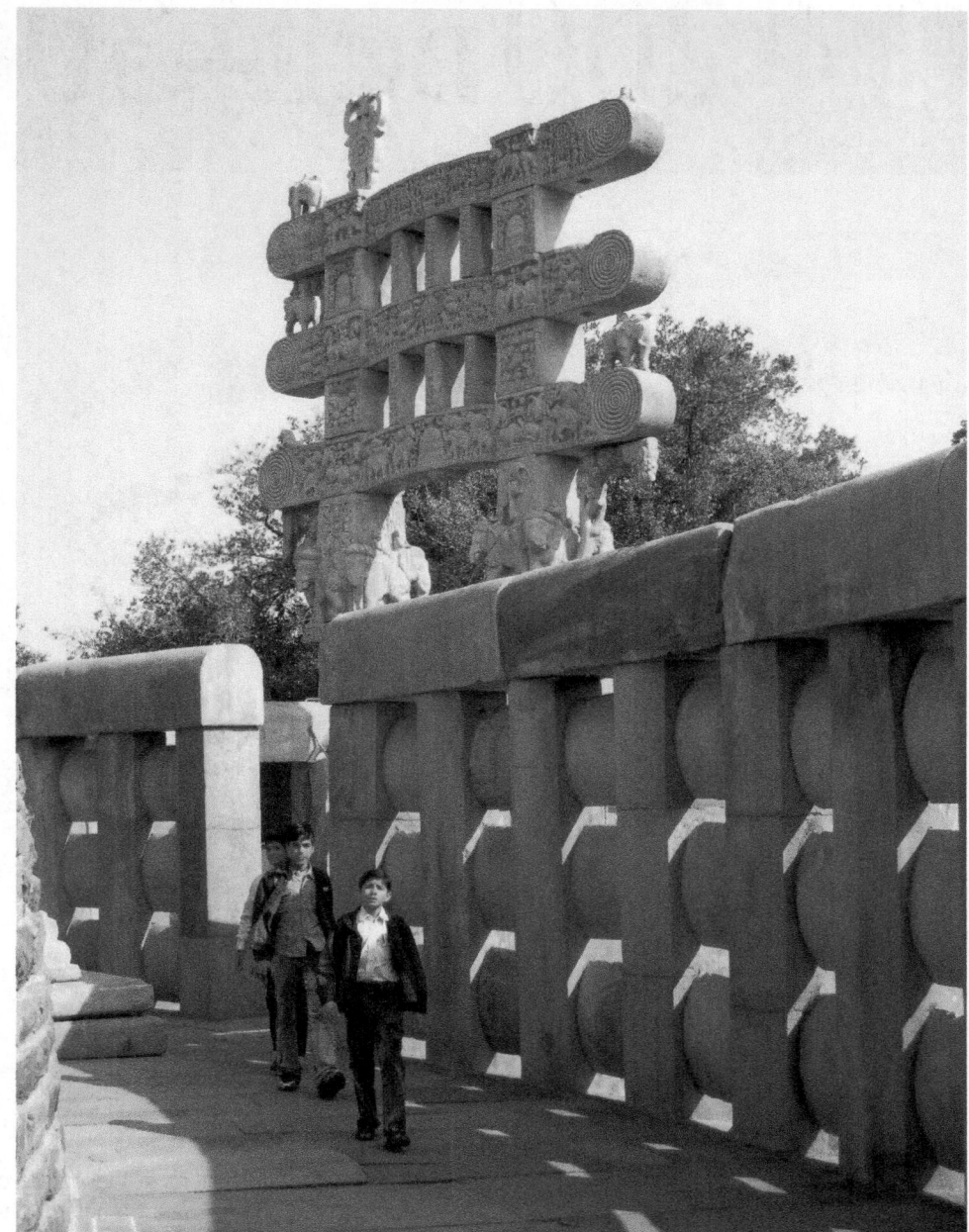

Figure 4.3-5 Sanchi, India. Pilgrim's path at base of the Great Stupa, mid-third century BCE.

ideology of *dharma*. The great scale and materiality of the *stupas* at Sanchi seem antithetical to the goal of transcending the material world, one of the tenets of Buddha's enlightenment. Nevertheless, similar to the tombs and temples of the pharaohs, the *stupas* helped Ashoka represent the most intangible spiritual ideas through the great masses of materials.

After Ashoka, the Mauryan dynasty began to lose its grip over the empire. Only the area around Pataliputra remained under its control, while the rest of India reverted to feudal divisions. By 185 BCE the capital city had been overrun, and new dynasties laid claim to it but did not last. The brief unity of India during the Mauryan period dissipated, and for several centuries the Indian subcontinent remained politically fragmented. Buddhism and Jainism, the religions of the emperors, however, continued to prosper.

Further Reading

Keay, John. *India: A History*. New York: Grove Press, 2000.

Rowland, Benjamin. *The Art and Architecture of India: Buddhist, Hindu, Jain*. London: Penguin, 1977.

Thapar, Romila. *Early India: From the Origins to AD 1300*. Berkeley: University of California Press, 2002.

Visit the free website **www.oup.com/us/ingersoll** to view chapter outlines and study questions; Google Maps showing the location of key sites; links to UNESCO World Heritage Sites; and essays on topics that cross time and culture.

200 BCE–300 CE

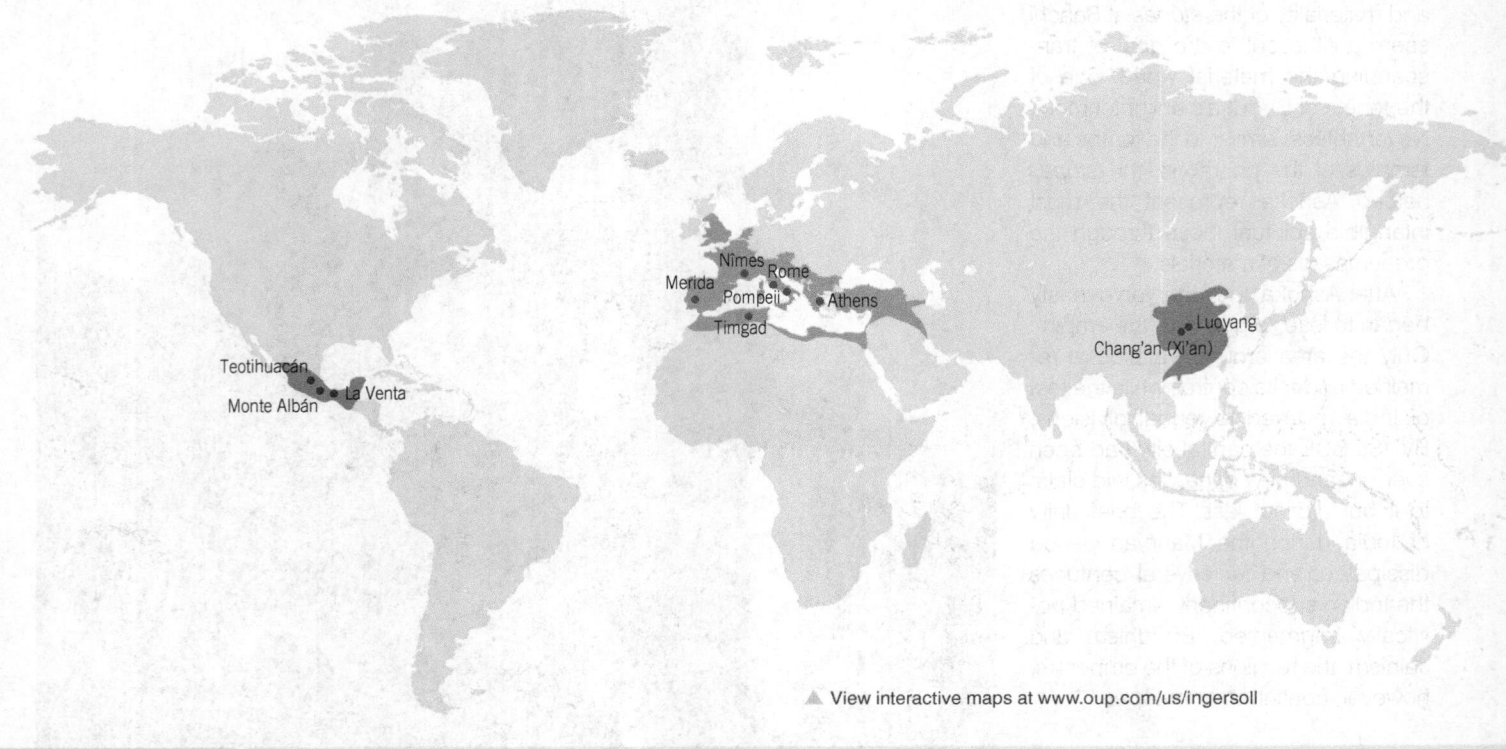

▲ View interactive maps at www.oup.com/us/ingersoll

Three large empires dominated world history at the outset of the first century BCE. In the East the Han dynasty ruled China from its capital of over a million inhabitants at Chang'an. Centered in the Mediterranean, the Romans absorbed much of the territory conquered by Alexander while adding the less settled areas to the west of Italy. The city of Rome likewise had more than a million residents. Across the Atlantic, far from the scrutiny of the Eurasian landmass, the Olmecs and Zapotecs in Mexico achieved great cultural feats, preparing the way for the religious metropolis of Teotihuacán. All three cultures perfected the grid in laying out buildings and cities. Chang'an and Teotihuacán both relied on an orthogonal structure with a broad central boulevard. Although Rome, owing to its hilly topography, never developed a rational urban layout, most of the numerous cities founded in the Roman Empire followed a strict grid. Religious activity guided the planning of Teotihuacán, with its two immense pyramids and hundreds of sacrificial altars spread throughout the city. In China the emperor was accorded semidivine status, and the palace compound was treated like a sacred precinct. For Rome the state became part of its theology, and the military triumph took on religious meanings. The Colosseum, the largest building in the Roman Empire, made tangible the policy of spectacle as a means of maintaining political stability, while the great Pantheon combined a temple front with the vaulted structure of bath buildings, obscuring the difference between sacred and secular.

5.1 ANCIENT ROME
Governing through Architecture

Most ancient cultures produced only a few buildings of high quality to represent religious or political ideals. The Hellenistic regimes in such cities as Pergamon and Alexandria, however, built entire cities as total works of architecture. The Roman Empire as it matured adopted this comprehensive approach to urban architecture with astounding results, building hundreds of cities throughout the Mediterranean that could boast of aqueducts, paved streets, and sewers, as well as ornate public buildings.

As the Romans conquered and absorbed different cultures of the Mediterranean, Southwest Asia, and Europe, their military leaders executed an integral program of urban set pieces, structured on **arches** and vaults and articulated with marble columns. The construction of magnificent temples, colonnaded streets and plazas, markets, theaters, aqueducts, baths, and triumphal arches assisted Rome in governing a wide range of peoples. The administrators of the Roman Empire delivered a complete architectural package that made the Roman way of life available to all. Architecture and urbanism served as instruments of governance, the tangible imposition of political will.

Roma Caput Mundi: A Regime of Architecture

Five centuries after its mythical founding on April 21, 753 BCE, the city of Rome considered itself *caput mundi*, the "head of the world." It commanded a vast international empire, secured through a system of rational military administration and civil law unknown to other ancient powers (Fig. 5.1-1). Roman generals settled conquered lands, using architectural projects to impose the power of the empire. Borrowing their models from Hellenistic cities, they created grand colonnaded enclosures, adding to them a new architectural repertoire of soaring vaulted interiors. The ethnic diversity of Rome's subjects ranged from the highly cultured city dwellers of the Aegean, Southwest Asia, and Egypt to the unlettered tribes of Western Europe. Throughout the empire Roman architects designed a new type of city, in which public space and public architecture provided a formal envelope for daily existence. The Romans offered conquered peoples an improved quality of life, an equitable legal system, a superb infrastructure of roads and aqueducts, efficient markets, public baths, and theaters as consolations for the loss of local autonomy. For many this was a desirable compensation.

Rome's ability to conquer other peoples matched its talent for mastering space. Using arches, vaults, and the new technology of concrete construction, Roman engineers devised unprecedented structures that defied gravity and overcame the irregularities of terrain. The architect-engineers of its army, such as Vitruvius, author of the single treatise on architecture (ca. 25 BCE) that has survived from this period, worked as agents of Rome's imperial expansion. The precise assembly of huge and complicated structures made from standard units extended the strict discipline of the Roman army to civil architecture. Multistoried arcuated structures, such as Trajan's Aqueduct in Segovia, Spain, still testify to Rome's pragmatic imposition of design over nature (Fig. 5.1-2).

At the time of its origin Rome seemed an unlikely spot to found a great empire. Set 30 km (18 miles) upstream from the mouth of the Tiber River, the city's fabled seven hills overlooked malarial marshlands. The site's only advantage lay in its broader geographical location, which was far enough away from the sea to escape coastal invasions yet close enough to reap the benefits of maritime trade (Fig. 5.1-3). Similar to Athens, Rome went through a process of *synoikismos*, in which villages joined together under a single legal code in an effort to reduce the influence of kinship groups. The legend of the city's founding demonstrates the Roman prioritization of law over blood relationships. Romulus, from whom Rome's name derived, ordered the execution of his brother Remus for trespassing the urban boundary line.

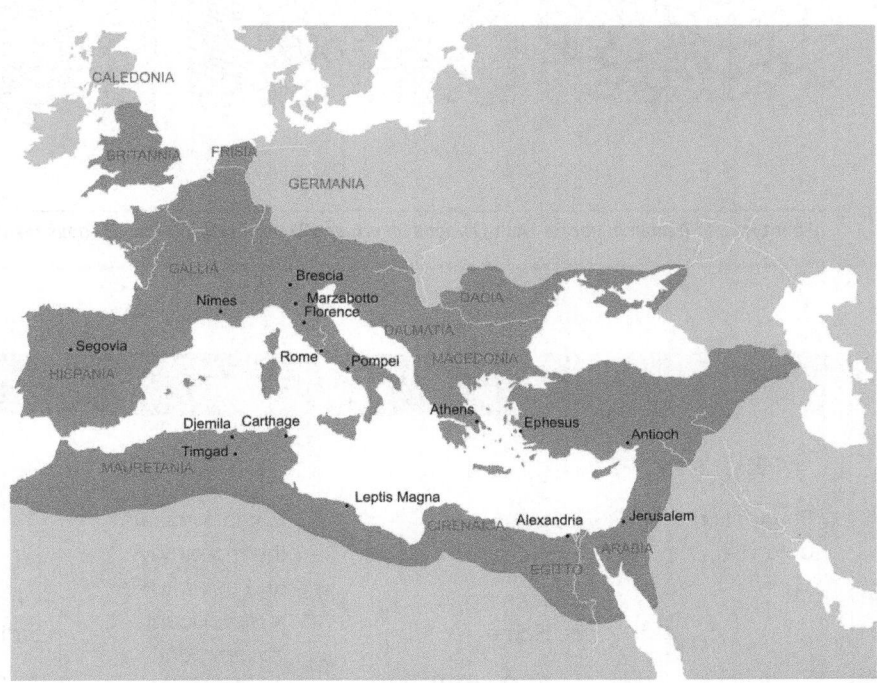

Figure 5.1-1 Roman Empire, ca. 125 CE.

The fratricide served to demonstrate that the sacred and legal bond to respect the *Pomerium*, a furrow plowed around the Palatine Hill with four gaps left for passage, superseded kinship ties.

During its first two centuries a monarchy governed Rome, borrowing legal codes, religious practices, and architecture from the more developed Etruscan culture. Etruscan architects brought with them the technology of arches and vaults, used for such works as the arched gateways of Perugia and Volterra. On the temple mount of the Capitoline Hill, the Romans installed their major cult building, an imitation of the Italo-Etruscan temple dedicated to Jupiter Optimus

CONSTRUCTION, TECHNOLOGY, THEORY

Roman Concrete Walls and the Vaulted Style

The Romans revolutionized construction and design during the second century BCE with their perfection of **concrete**, known as *caementitium*. They improved upon this versatile material by adding a natural bonding substance, *pozzolana*, a volcanic powder found in abundance between Rome and Naples. When mixed with water and aggregates and poured between two masonry or brick planes, it yielded durable "sack" walls as solid as stone. The masonry offered builders various solutions to architectural problems, such as the irregular *opus incertum*, the diagonally set bricks of *opus reticulatum*, the thinly stacked bricks of *opus testaceum*, and the alternating rows of stone and bricks of *opus mixtum*. Concrete could be shaped with the temporary support of wooden scaffolds, or formwork, into almost any geometric configuration. The complex carpentry of the formwork and the continuous pouring of the concrete to avoid

uneven drying required a huge workforce of militarily organized teams. The Romans initially used concrete on service buildings, such as the Emporium warehouses built along the lower banks of the Tiber in the second century BCE. By the early first century CE it had become the material of choice for most monumental structures, prized for its strength and fireproofing. It inspired the architecturally adventurous curving structures of the vaulted style of Roman theaters, baths, and **palaces**.

The superb hillside temple complex of Praeneste (now Palestrina, Italy), built around 120 BCE, provides one of the earliest examples of the Roman vaulted style. It stepped up the hill on a series of terraces accessed by bifurcated stairs. The colonnades supported concrete **barrel vaults** connected to concrete retaining walls. A hemicycle at the top of a curved set of stairs, shaped like the *cavea* of a theater, led to a U-shaped colonnade. Behind it rose a small *tholos* temple.

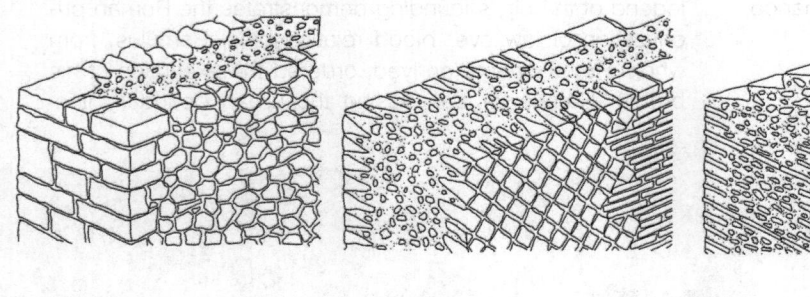 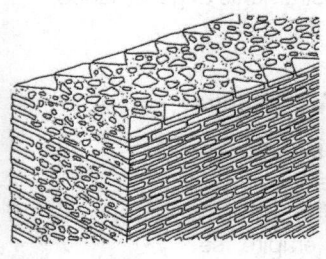 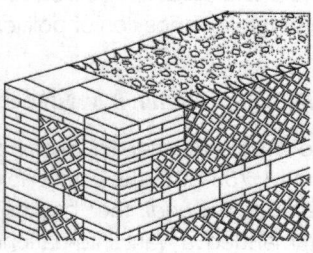

1   2   3   4

Four types of Roman concrete wall: (1) *opus incertum*; **(2)** *opus reticulatum*; **(3)** *opus testaceum*; **(4)** *opus mixtum*.

TIME LINE

▼ **753 BCE**
Foundation of Rome

Etruscan kings rule Rome
▲ **700–600 BCE**

▼ **509 BCE**
Rome eliminates the monarchy and establishes a republican government

Punic Wars with Carthage
▲ **264–146 BCE**

▼ **80 BCE**
Sulla builds Tabularium overlooking Roman Forum

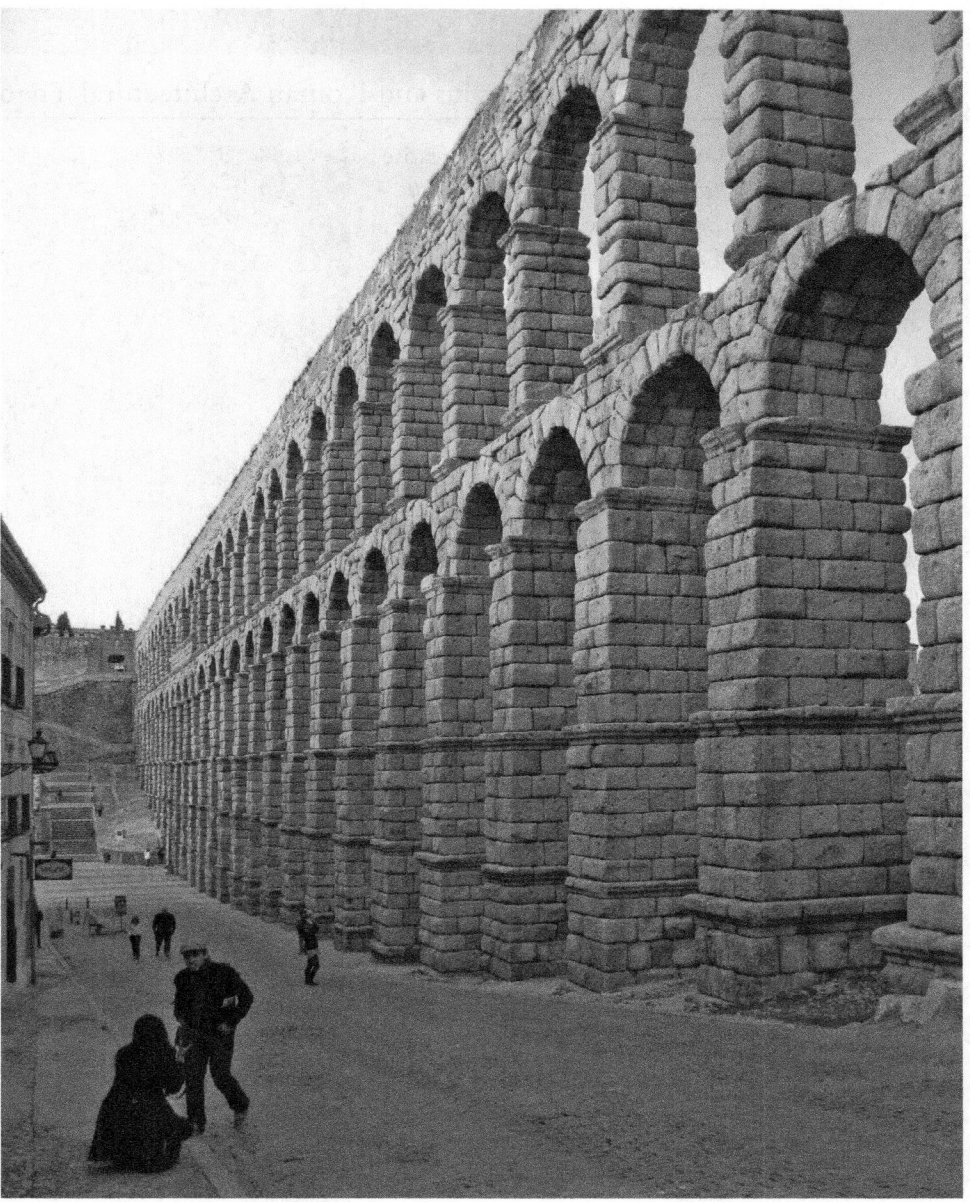

Figure 5.1-2 Segovia, Spain. Trajan's Aqueduct, ca. 100 CE.

Maximus. A reconstruction of the fifth-century BCE Belvedere Temple near Orvieto shows the typical Etruscan solution of a lateral tripartite *cella* under a low-pitched porch, accessed by axial stairs. The columns of the Tuscan order, the Etruscan version of the Doric, would have stood undecorated, stout, and wide apart. Most Roman temples repeated the Etruscan preference for frontal orientation, with a columnated porch rather than the Greek peripteral set of columns (Fig. 5.1-4).

In 509 BCE, the Roman republic replaced the monarchy with a representational form of government that lasted nearly five centuries. Under this system of rule the executive authority belonged to the Senate, a self-selected group of patrician landowners with hereditary power. The Senate in turn negotiated its policies with the plebeians, who elected representatives from the lower classes. The political space of the Roman Forum took shape in the valley bounded by four of the seven hills. Unlike the casual openness of the Agora in Athens, the Roman Forum evolved by the late republic into a tightly enclosed space about a third of its predecessor's area.

Roman expansionism began with its absorption of the neighboring Etruscans, other Italian tribes, and Greek settlements in Italy. During the third and second centuries BCE Rome emerged victorious from international conflicts with Carthage (modern-day Tunis) and Macedonia, allowing it to claim sovereignty over the Mediterranean. This increase in power and wealth put stress on the republican system, provoking long periods of internal strife, which concluded with the installation of a constitutional monarchy. The many

▼ **49 BCE**

Julius Caesar declared "dictator"

Spartacus leads slave rebellion against Rome

▲ **73 BCE**

Forum of Julius Caesar begun

▲ **44 BCE**

▼ **44 BCE**

Julius Caesar assassinated

Augustus (Octavian), the heir to Julius Caesar, proclaimed Rome's *princeps* (emperor)

▲ **27 BCE**

▼ **ca. 25 BCE**

Vitruvius publishes treatise on architecture

CONSTRUCTION, TECHNOLOGY, THEORY

Vitruvius and Roman Architectural Theory

Vitruvius wrote the architectural treatise *De Architectura libri decem* (*On Architecture, Ten Books*) between 33 and 14 BCE, during the reign of Augustus. It remains the most authoritative book on architecture known from antiquity. Vitruvius proposed the famous theoretical triad *firmitas, utilitas, venustas* (strength, utility, beauty) as the basic criteria of architecture and mapped out a series of rules for the construction and decoration of buildings. The buildings he described were conservative compared with the works the Romans constructed later in the vaulted style, and although he mentioned *pozzolana*, the basis of concrete, he lived too early to have foreseen its complex forms. His principles of beauty comprehended a system based on harmonic proportions, rational design layout, and the decorative use of the classical orders (the system of columns).

During the fifteenth century a Vitruvian revival explored his proposals of ideal proportions, as seen in Leonardo da Vinci's "Vitruvian man," a male figure whose body is inscribed in a circle and a square. Unable to fit the extended limbs of a man's body into the superimposition of the circle and the square, Leonardo staggered their positions.

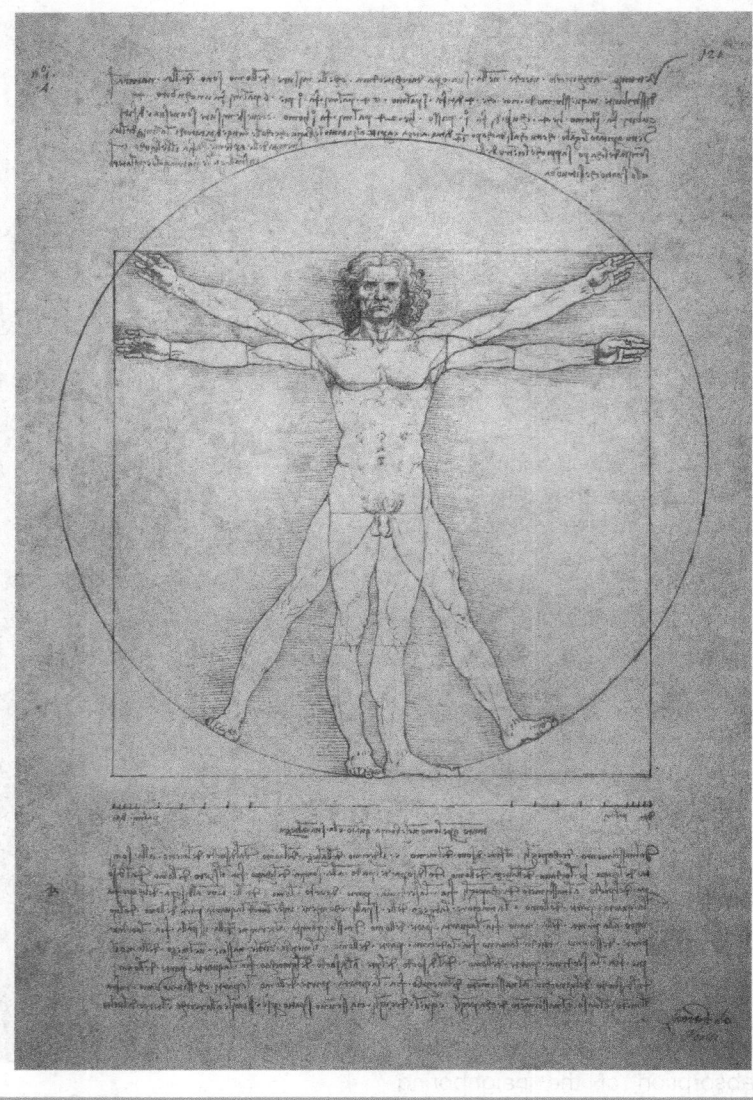

**Leonardo Da Vinci, "Vitruvian Man,"
ca. 1487. Galleria dell'Accademia,
Venice.**

decades of what was known as the Social War culminated with the assassination of Julius Caesar in 44 BCE by those who feared that his power as dictator, general, and high priest would endanger the autonomy of the republic.

Caesar's adopted heir, Augustus, completed the process of dismantling the republic and became the first Roman *princeps*. Augustus created a parallel government of appointed officials who could override the will of the Senate.

▼ **17 BCE**

*Theater of
Marcellus
completed*

▼ **ca. 30 CE**

Jesus of Nazareth
crucified in
Jerusalem

▼ **68 CE**

Nero forced to
commit suicide
by his troops

*Augustus adds
his new forum to
Julius's Forum*

*Nero begins
Domus Aurea
in Rome*

*Augustus dedicates
the Ara Pacis and
funeral monuments*

▲ **ca. 40–2 BCE**

▲ **65 CE**

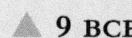

▲ **9 BCE**

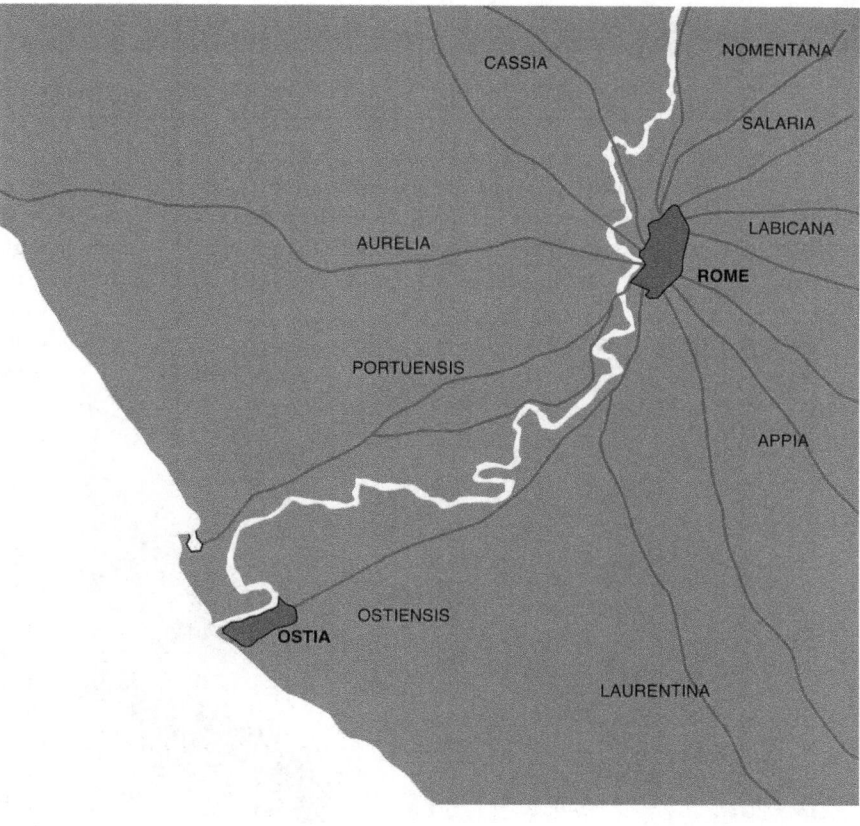

Figure 5.1-3 Rome. The city at its founding was located 30 km (18 miles) inland from the port city of Ostia, with the consular highways converging on the city—the source of the phrase "all roads lead to Rome."

He also organized the Praetorian Guard for his personal protection. With his family members, he used imperial patronage to transform the city, initiating a series of projects for shaped public spaces and grand monuments that boosted the authority of the state while initiating the cult of its rulers.

The Roman army founded hundreds of cities under both the republic and the emperors. They learned orthogonal urban design from Greek colonies such as Naples and Paestum in the south, and from the Etruscans, who built towns such as Marzabotto with the Greek right-angled surveying techniques. If topography permitted and there was no significant previous settlement, Roman planners usually founded their cities on a cross-axis of streets. Their religious beliefs, borrowed from the Etruscans, required them to adhere to the cardinal coordinates: the north–south **axis**, or *cardo*, crossed by the east–west *decumanus*. They equipped their towns with a standard set of monumental public buildings and spaces that became tangible propaganda for the *Pax Romana*, or "Roman peace." Most of the important cities across Europe and North Africa still show traces of this architectural investment. Timgad, Algeria, a **castrum** military camp founded around 100 CE, for example, was designed with typically colonnaded streets on a strict grid. Not all new Roman cities, however, followed a grid. The plan of Djémila, Algeria, built around the same time as Timgad, shows streets that followed the contours of a hilly site (Fig. 5.1-5).

The Roman Empire exerted political control over foreign cities through military force but held on to power through the provision of excellent infrastructure: paved roads, vaulted sewers, bridges, and aqueducts. In cities as distant as London, Segovia, and Antioch, occupying armies built grand public works and civic buildings. In the already mature cities of the eastern Mediterranean, such as Athens and Alexandria, Roman governors merely enriched the existing fabric with new building types such as basilicas, colonnaded streets, vaulted thermal bath structures, and freestanding theaters. In Athens, for example, the Romans by the second century CE had filled in more than half of the open space of the Agora with new public buildings. More than any previous culture, Romans relied on architecture and urbanism to control space and, by extension, determine people's behavior in it.

Pompeii: The Architecture of Public Space

The small city of Pompeii, which Rome acquired as a colony in 80 BCE, contains the best-preserved examples of Roman architecture. The eruption of Vesuvius in 79 CE completely destroyed the city but kept it intact. For nearly two millennia the

Romans destroy Second Temple in Jerusalem

△ 70 CE

▽ 79 CE

Pompeii destroyed by volcanic eruption

Flavian emperors build Colosseum over Nero's lake in Rome

△ 80 CE

▽ ca. 110 CE

Apollodorus of Damascus builds Trajan's Forum and markets

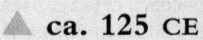

Hadrian builds Pantheon in Rome and Hadrian's Villa in Tivoli

△ ca. 125 CE

The Etruscans

Rome owed its greatness partly to its imitation and eventual conquest of the neighboring Etruscan peoples. From the eighth to the fifth century BCE the Etruscans dominated much of the Italian peninsula, settling and establishing autonomous city-states in Umbria, Tuscany, Emilia, and Lombardy. The Etruscans very likely originated from Asia Minor during the twelfth-century scattering of peoples around the Mediterranean, even though their language did not resemble other Indo-European tongues. Through trade with the Greek colonies in Italy they acquired many of the same gods and cultural habits. Although all of their initial towns were built on hilltops with irregular plans, when they founded the new town of Marzabotto in the fifth century BCE they used the long, rectangular *per strigas* blocks of the Greeks. The Etruscans built walls with rough cyclopean masses like the Bronze-Age defense works in Turkey and Greece but later refined the use of the **true arch** and the vault, seen in the gateways at Volterra and Perugia built in the fourth and third centuries BCE. These developments, along with frontally oriented temples and mounded tombs, remained their greatest architectural legacy to the Romans, while on the social level the Etruscans taught them about the organization of an oligarchic republic and the fair treatment of slaves and women. During the first century BCE Etruscan resistance to Roman dominion resulted in the destruction of most of their cities and the eradication of their language.

Cerveteri, Italy. Necropolis of Banditaccia, Etruscan mound tombs, ninth to third century BCE.

streets and buildings rested under a thick layer of volcanic ash. Unaltered by historical changes until excavations began in the mid-eighteenth century, Pompeii's complete urban system illustrates the importance of public space to Roman daily life.

The city pattern of Pompeii blended local Oscan, Etruscan, Greek, and Roman ideas. Extensions from the original nucleus included both the long orthogonal blocks preferred by the Greeks and typically Roman square blocks

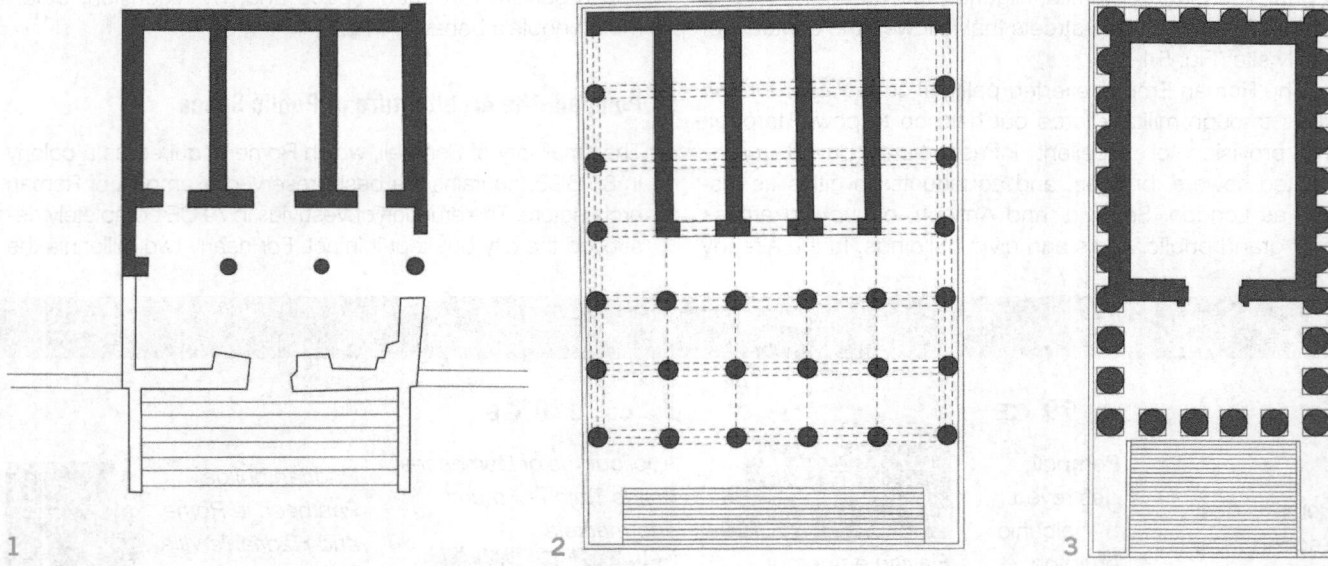

Figure 5.1-4 Evolution of the Etruscan temple type into the Roman temple: (1) sixth-century BCE Etruscan Belvedere Temple at Orvieto; (2) sixth-century Etruscan Temple of Jupiter Optimus Maximus on the Capitoline Hill in Rome; (3) Roman Maison Carrée in Nîmes, France, ca. 50 CE.

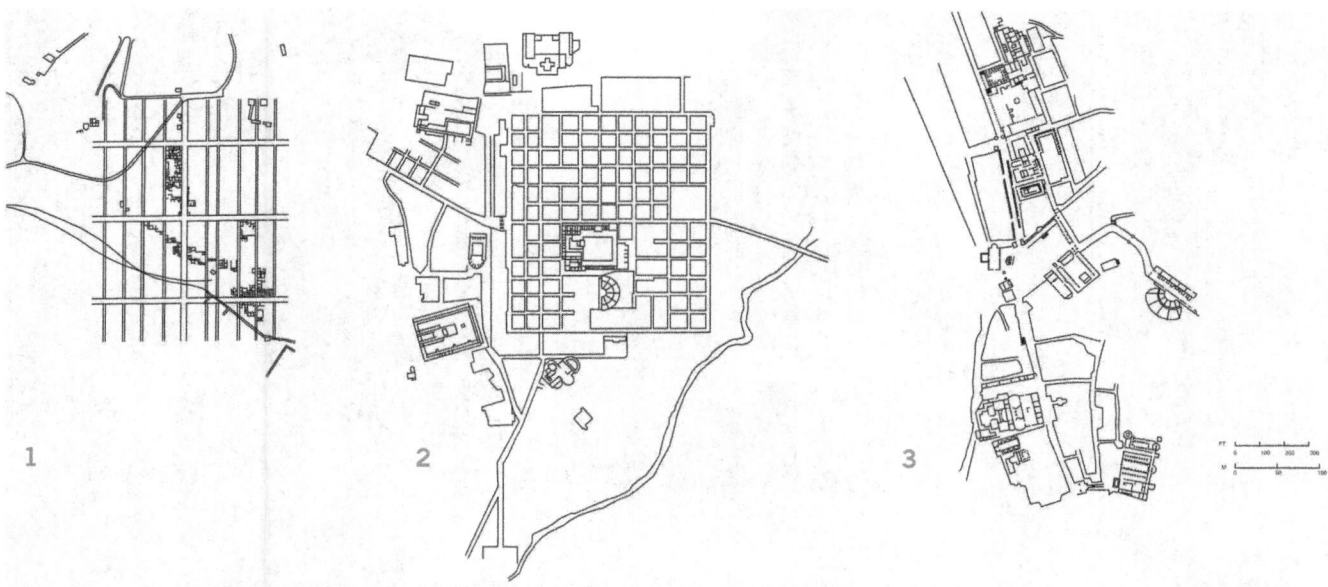

Figure 5.1-5 Roman Empire. Comparison of three town plans: (1) Etruscan city of Marzabotto, Italy, ca. 400 BCE, showing grid of long blocks; (2) Timgad, Algeria, ca. 100 CE, showing grid of short blocks with fora at crossroads and large public buildings on outskirts; (3) Djémila, Algeria, ca. 100 CE, which follows the natural topography while using typical Roman structures.

(Fig. 5.1-6). Pompeii's major north–south avenue obliquely intersected the main east–west avenue, Via dell'Abbondanza, which traversed the forum and led southwest beyond the walls to the Bay of Naples. All Pompeian streets were paved with the easily procurable dark lava stone. Deep ruts were carved in the pavement to guide wagons and carts. The streets were flanked by raised sidewalks and graced with a unique feature: stepping stones at their intersections allowing pedestrians to cross the streets without soiling their feet while water overflowing from the fountains flushed the streets clean (Fig. 5.1-7). The city's water came from a reservoir at the northern gate filled by an **aqueduct** and was distributed through lead pipes to public fountains, four public baths, and many private houses. Every other block had a neighborhood fountain.

The principal public space, the Forum of Pompeii (Fig. 5.1-8), showed the Roman preference for axial orientation. Restructured after an earthquake in 62 CE, the forum's new double-story colonnade wrapped around three of its sides, concealing the irregular positions of several of the surrounding

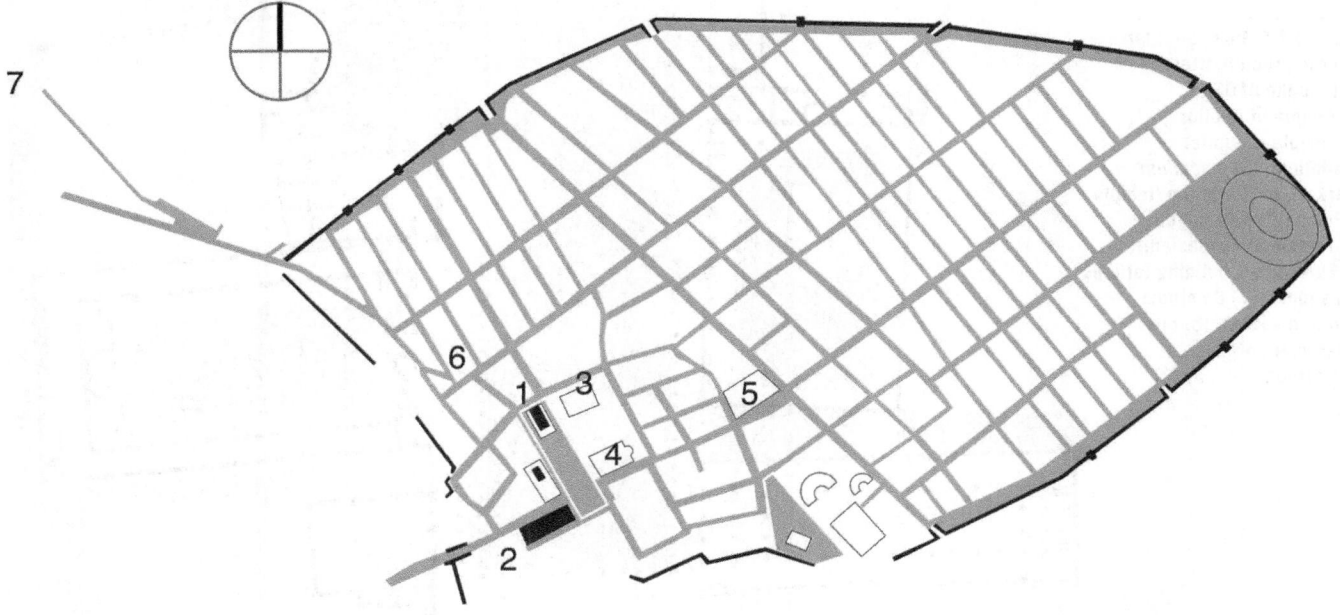

Figure 5.1-6 Pompeii. Plan of city, ca. 70 CE. (1) Temple to Jupiter in the rebuilt forum; (2) the basilica; (3) *macellum* (market); (4) Eumachia's building; (5) Stabian baths; (6) Domus of Pansa; (7) Villa of the Mysteries.

Figure 5.1-7 Pompeii. Typical street with raised sidewalk, fountain, and stones for crossing street with gaps left for the wheels of vehicles to pass, ca. 70 CE.

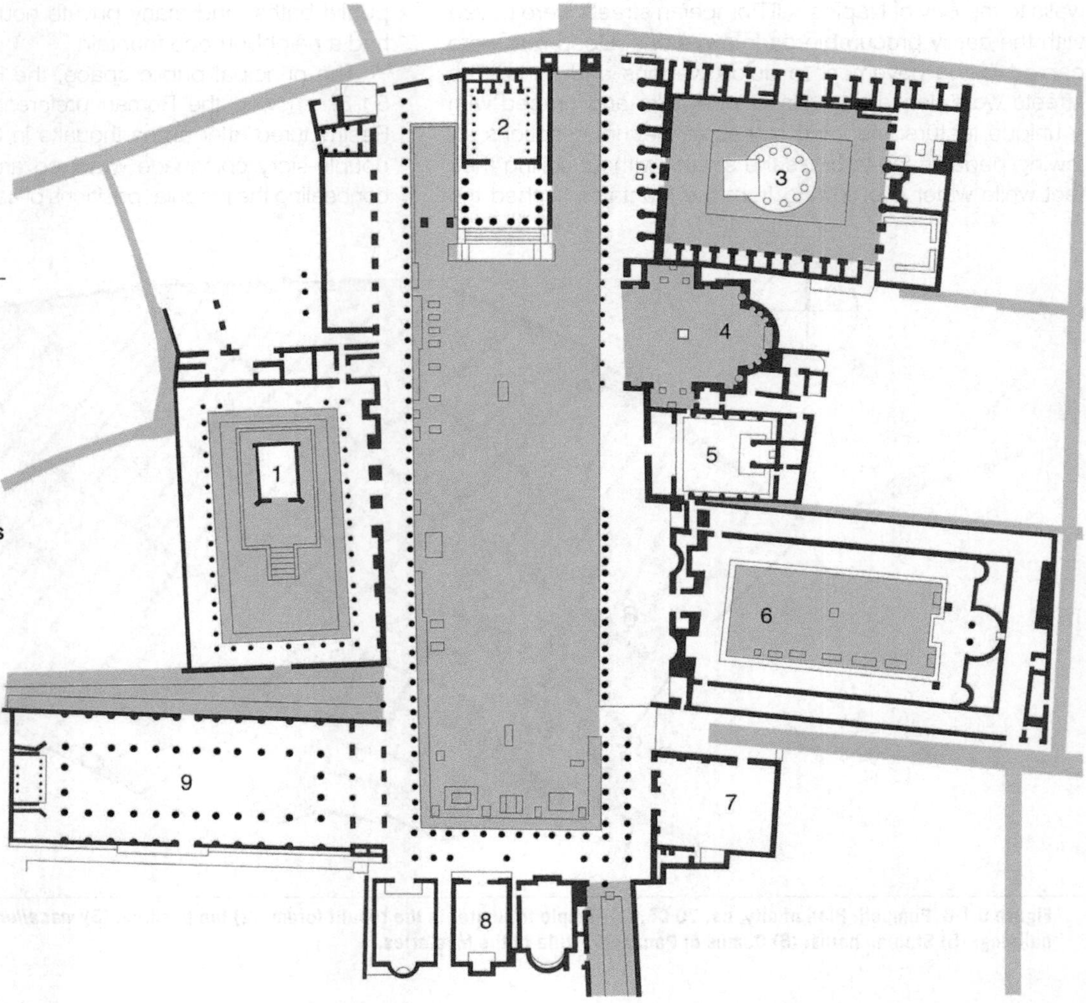

Figure 5.1-8 Pompeii. Plan of forum, rebuilt after the earthquake of 62 CE.
(1) Temple of Apollo;
(2) Temple of Jupiter Capitolium; (3) *macellum* (market); (4) Lararium (temple of Pompeii's patron gods);
(5) Temple of Vespasian;
(6) Eumachia's building (offices and shops); (7) Comitium (election space); (8) city government offices;
(9) basilica.

Figure 5.1-9 Nîmes, France. Maison Carrée, ca. 20 BCE.

buildings from earlier periods. Roman civic centers like Pompeii always included a **forum**, a temple, and a **basilica**. Typically, the temple stood at one end of the oblong space and a basilica, transversely laid out, closed off the other end.

The temple at the north end of the Forum of Pompeii was rededicated in the first century CE to the gods of the Roman Capitolium. As recommended by Vitruvius, the temple's depth was equal to twice its width. It stood on a high podium raised 1.5 m (5 ft), accessed by a single flight of stairs that enforced the axiality of the forum. The Corinthian porch of six columns across and four deep resembled the contemporary Maison Carrée in Nîmes, France, which has survived in nearly perfect condition (Fig. 5.1-9). The considerable geographic distance between these similar temples indicates that Roman architects followed easily reproduced standard models based on a modular proportional system.

The Basilica of Pompeii, a covered hall used for legal and administrative business, sat at the other end of the forum, in the southwest corner (Fig. 5.1-10). Most basilicas of the time were arranged transversely, with the entrances on the long side. Here, the principal entry stood on the short side, creating a strong axis from the forum colonnade to a pedimented tribunal at the other end of the basilica's interior. The central space rose double the height of the rest of the structure, lined with colossal columns and flanked on the sides by second-story galleries. Clerestory openings above the galleries brought natural lighting into the hall. The Roman basilica, with its grand clearspan hall, offered a comfortable improvement over the dark hypostyle halls used by earlier cultures for government tribunals and important business.

On the eastern flank of the Forum of Pompeii the colonnades concealed a walled-off market, the *macellum*. Its courtyard had shops under a perimeter awning, inspired by Hellenistic commercial spaces enclosed by *stoas* in cities like Miletus. The market featured a round columnar pavilion in its center for preparing fish before they were set out on stalls. Two smaller buildings that served as shrines to emperors and the offices and courtyard donated by the priestess Eumachia filled in the rest of this eastern flank. The northern entries into the forum were framed with special arches, showing the Roman skill in articulating grand public spaces.

Figure 5.1-10 Pompeii. Remains of the Basilica of Pompeii, ca. 70 CE.

Theaters and Baths: Roman Leisure Society

While the Romans resembled other ancient peoples in their need to build temples and tombs, they also produced a disproportionate number of secular monuments, such as theaters and baths. These halls of pleasure, socialization, and hygiene came to dominate Roman cityscapes during the first century BCE. Unlike the Greeks, who inserted their theaters into the contours of sloping sites, the Romans built freestanding monuments using arches and concrete vaults. Imperial administrators eventually exploited the political advantages of entertainment and sports as a means to appease the mob. Imperial Rome had a population of over a

Figure 5.1-11 Merida, Spain. Roman theater, first century CE. The double stories of columns represented the architecture of the Roman city.

million, the majority of whom, being poor and unemployed, could be quick to rebel. Following the strategy of *panem et circenses*, "bread and circuses," Julius Caesar instituted the *Annona*, a weekly grain allowance that served as a form of welfare, and his successors sponsored a constant array of spectacles and games during the year's 159 holidays.

The early Roman theaters usually included a temple to give religious sanction to the performances. The first permanent theater in Rome, built for the great general Pompey in 62 BCE, had a small temple perched atop its upper ranges overlooking the **cavea**, the sloped hemicycle for the seating. Unlike the Greeks, the Romans filled the orchestra with patrician seating. Opposite the temple stood the scene building, or **scenae frons**, with three levels of columns. Auditorium and stage created a prominent *D*-shaped volume, as exemplified by the Roman theater of Merida, Spain, which dominated the urban fabric as a cliff-like eminence (Fig. 5.1-11).

The largest site for spectacles in the empire, Rome's **Circus** Maximus (Fig. 5.1-12), accommodated 150,000

CULTURE, SOCIETY, GENDER

Eumachia and Female Patronage

Roman women, compared with those of ancient Greece and other parts of the ancient world, enjoyed exceptional freedom. They could own property, divorce their husbands, and circulate of their own free will, going to baths and theaters. They were nonetheless expected to remain obedient to the master of the house. A wealthy priestess of Pompeii, Eumachia, showed her power by donating the building in the southeast corner of the Forum of Pompeii. Within that structure she built a rectangular court as a commercial or administrative setting for

the cloth guilds. A bit larger than the *macellum*, its long axis terminated in a covered apse for a shrine. The entry foyer included a prominently set urinal to the right of the portal, which served as a place for collecting urine to be used for processing wool. An inscription attests to the unprecedented freedom of Roman women: "Eumachia, daughter of Lucius (Eumachius), public priestess, in her own name and that of her son, Marcus Numistrius Fronto, built with her own funds the porch, covered passage, and colonnade and dedicated them to Concordia."

Pompeii. Court of Eumachia, the largest court on the right side of the forum, ca. 70 CE. Model, Museo della Civiltà Romana, Rome.

Figure 5.1-12 Rome. Model of city, showing the Circus Maximus at left. Museo della Civiltà Romana, fourth century BCE to third century CE.

spectators around a 600 m (1,920 ft) track used for chariot races that in its origins had served as an arena to work out class differences through competitions. The bleachers were carved into the long, narrow valley between the Aventine and Palatine Hills as an extended *U* shape. Vaulted seating structures were added during the first century BCE at the southern end. Spoils acquired from foreign conquests, including an Egyptian obelisk, decorated the central spine as goal markers. The short ends acquired triumphal arches during the first century CE.

For the gladiatorial contests and other battles such as *venationes*, the pitting of wild animals against men, the Romans invented a new form of theater, the **amphitheater**, by joining two theaters end to end to form an ellipse. The immense stone and concrete shells of Roman amphitheaters held from 15,000 to 50,000 people. The crowds cheered on these spectacles of cruelty, which mirrored the violence of Rome's military campaigns. The arena, which got its name from the sand of its pavement, was rimmed by continuous stone bleachers that rose either on banked mounds of earth held behind retaining walls or on an elaborate system of radially composed, concrete vaulted substructures.

The Colosseum in Rome reigned as its greatest place of spectacle and, in terms of mass, the empire's largest building. Built mostly of concrete vaults, it covered an area of 156 × 188 m (512 × 617 ft). Its cliff-like exterior displayed tons

of **travertine** blocks fastened with iron clamps (Fig. 5.1-13). The facade rose on three levels of piers and arches, with half-columns engaged to the piers. A veritable dictionary of classical architecture, one found the Tuscan order at the base, with the Ionic followed by the Corinthian above, culminating in Composite pilasters on the **attic** story of solid walls.

The floor of the Colosseum and the metal barrier surrounding it have disappeared, exposing to view the intricate warren of hundreds of subterranean chambers on three levels that once housed beasts and gladiators, as well as staff, machinery, and services (Fig. 5.1-14). Thirty-two elevators hoisted the theatrical equipment and the participants in the gruesome spectacles to the combat space. The spectators entered through one of eighty arches, according to the number on their ticket, filtering past two annular corridors at ground level to ascend a series of stairs. The five different levels of the *cavea*, with stone seats, rose on a 37° incline, resting on a complex substructure of radially organized piers and vaults. The wooden bandstands in the top arcade were for women and slaves. Above the top level, a row of stone brackets anchored the poles that would have supported a canvas awning that shaded the *cavea*.

Roman baths, or **thermae**, were equally grand, covering even greater stretches of urban territory. Based loosely on Hellenistic prototypes, Roman baths were arranged in a sequence that began with a **palaestra**, a grassy arcaded court

Figure 5.1-13 Rome. Exterior of the Colosseum, the Roman Empire's largest theater, ca. 70 CE.

Figure 5.1-14 Rome. Colosseum interior, ca. 70 CE.

for outdoor exercise, and a *natatorium*, or swimming pool. One entered the Stabian Baths in Pompeii (Fig. 5.1-15), built in 80 BCE, through the *palaestra* and on the west side of the complex found the *natatorium*, flanked by rooms where one could oil oneself before exercise and scrape off the sweat and dirt afterward. The sequence of vaulted interiors proceeded from a lavishly decorated dressing room, with wall niches for storing clothes, to the **tepidarium**, where the body began to warm up, and then the much hotter **caldarium** steam bath. From there the visitor returned through the *tepidarium* and the vestibule to cool off in the **frigidarium**, a round room with four semicircular niches and an **oculus** in its **dome** for light. Here, steps led down to a cold pool, where freshwater gushed continually from a high spout.

Roman *thermae* were usually divided into men's and women's sections. The women's section at the Stabian Baths repeated on a smaller scale the sequence of vaulted rooms on the southeastern side of the court. Roman baths used **hypocaust**, or under-the-floor, heating, with hot air conducted from furnaces beneath the pavement (Fig. 5.1-16). This had

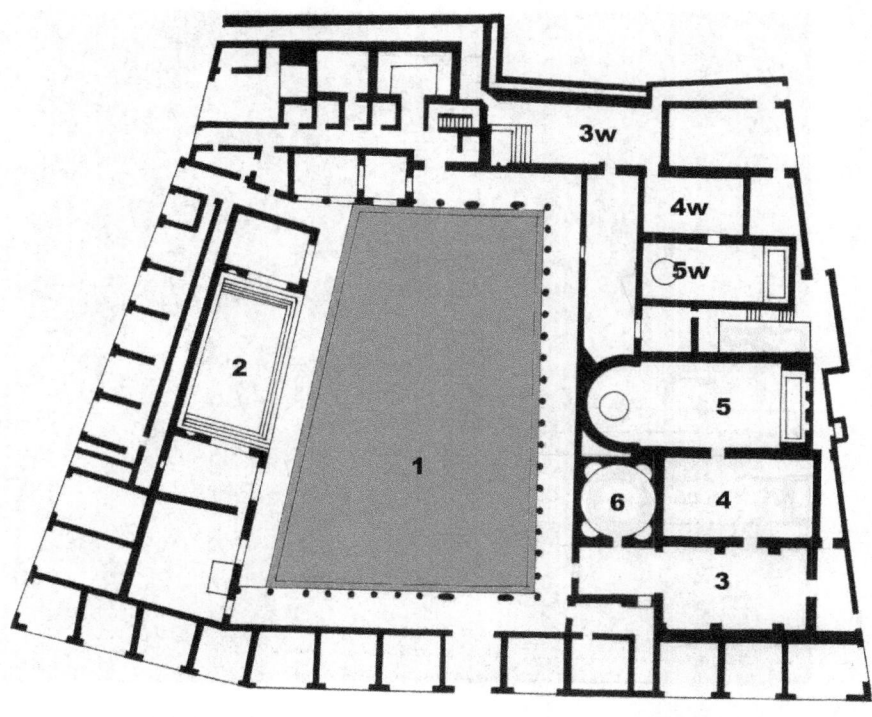

Figure 5.1-15 Pompeii. Plan of Stabian Baths, ca. 70 CE. (1) Open *palaestra* for games; (2) *natatorium*; (3) men's area with (4) *tepidarium*, (5) *caldarium*, and (6) *frigidarium*; (3w)–(5w) women's area with fewer rooms.

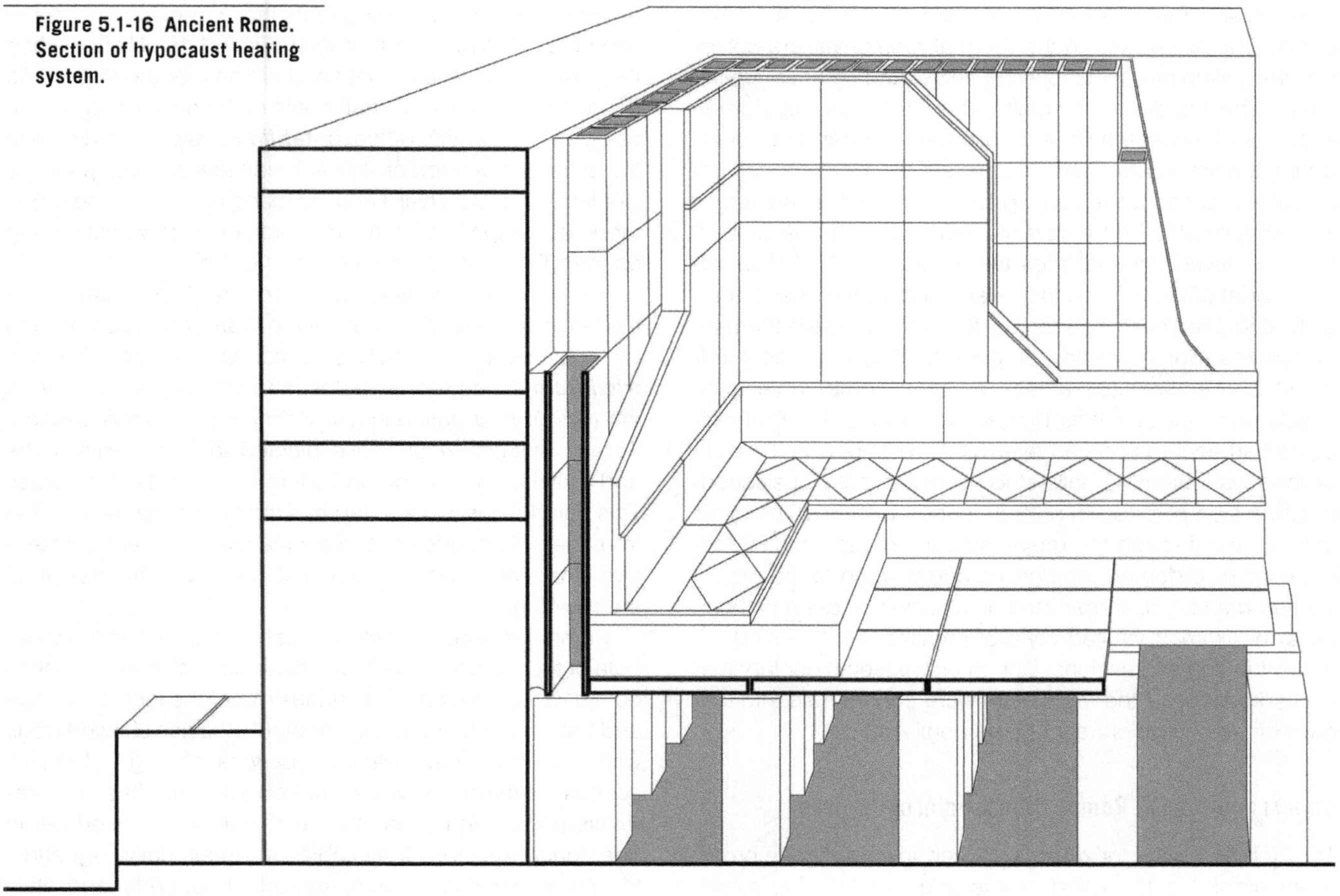

Figure 5.1-16 Ancient Rome. Section of hypocaust heating system.

Figure 5.1-17 Rome. Model of
the Baths of Diocletian, late third
century CE.

obvious advantages over the older system of heating by charcoal braziers, which smoked and smelled. A later technological improvement ran hollow **terra-cotta** pipes through the walls, carrying the hot air above floor level.

Typically, the inhabitants of Roman cities, rich or poor, would spend the morning working and the afternoon at the baths, where, aside from the thermal rooms, visitors could use the swimming pools, playing fields, and libraries. While there were hundreds of small baths in the city of Rome, known as *balnae*, the great public baths began to appear during the first years of the emperors. They were conceived as cultural centers, filled with prized works of art and libraries. Agrippa, the son-in-law of Augustus, built the first of Rome's eleven imperial *thermae* around 20 BCE. Toward the twilight of the empire, in the late third century CE, Caracalla and Diocletian sponsored the two grandest thermal complexes. Set in walled compounds, they each covered about 25 hectares (61 acres), an area comparable to a small Roman city, such as Timgad or Florence. The Baths of Diocletian accommodated over 3,000 visitors (Fig. 5.1-17). Inside, oval changing halls stood symmetrically positioned to either side of a 100 m (328 ft) long *natatorium*. The central axis led through the groin-vaulted *frigidarium*, past the more intimate domed *tepidarium*, and beyond to the groin-vaulted *caldarium*, surrounded on all sides by deep niches. Here the Roman vaulted style of architecture achieved its most stunning expressions. During the sixteenth century the vaulted spaces of the *frigidarium* were transformed into the nave of the church of Santa Maria degli Angeli.

Domus and *Insula*: Roman Domestic Architecture

The Roman house, or **domus**, looked inward, tightly organized around colonnaded courts (Fig. 5.1-18). The street facade often had shops to either side of the entry, with second-story dwellings for the shopkeepers. With the front doors open, one would have had a view into a luminous interior **atrium**, which served as a stage for the extended family and its clients. The atrium court, or **impluvium**, was rimmed with inward-sloping roofs that funneled rainwater to a marble catch basin at its center (Fig. 5.1-19). Niches along the walls of the atrium contained shrines for the household gods (*Lararium*) and portrait busts of the owner and his ancestors. The owner's office, or **tablinum**, stood on-axis with the entry and opened on its back side to a second, peristyle garden court. Courtyard houses made up most of the urban fabric of Pompeii. In Rome, however, only the wealthy living on the hilltops could afford the *domus* type.

The rear court in the typical *domus* at Pompeii served as the feminine zone of the household. Larger and surrounded by columns in a peristyle, it accommodated kitchens, **triclinium** dining rooms, baths, and privies. Benches lined the *triclinium* for eating in a reclining or semiprone position. Roman matrons would have planted the court with herbs and a kitchen garden around a formal fountain in the center. This colorful oasis in the depth of the house, partially visible from the atrium, offered a rare instance in ancient architecture of the integration of natural elements into the design of the dwelling.

Pompeian houses were profusely decorated. In the vestibule of the House of the Faun, the threshold mosaic spelled out *Have*, or "welcome," a curious mix of the local language and Latin. In other houses, threshold mosaics showed dogs with the words *cave canem*, "beware of dog." Narrative scenes covered the walls, framed with architectural elements painted in perspective. Within their simulated depth one found mythological subjects, small daily vignettes, friezes of miniature figures, sacred landscapes, and plain open sky. Ceiling beams were painted, gilded, or even inlaid with ivory. Small clerestory windows under the eaves were fitted with panes of a very thick glass or a translucent material known as *lapis specularis*, and wooden shutters kept out hot or cold air while preventing contact with the bustling streets.

The builders of Pompeii **stuccoed** and painted the exteriors of their brick and **half-timber** houses. The rental shops, or ***tabernae***, that lined the main streets usually took a *T* shape, formed by the placement of two display counters on either side of the threshold. Some shops had built-in food counters with braziers for keeping pots warm. *Tabernae* also lined the edges of public buildings like the forum baths. Commercial demand led to the stacking of single units with a first-story open front and a living space above. Second-story apartments became common in Pompeii. On the eve of the fatal eruption, crowding and increased ground rents had transformed the Pompeian *domus* into a multiple-family dwelling type.

During the Roman republic, wealthy Romans living in the capital dared not display their wealth in the architecture of their urban dwellings for fear of offending the ethic of moderation. They spent their fortunes on luxurious **villas** far from the scrutiny of the city, which they used to escape the heat and contagion of the city during the hot months of the summer. The villa type emerged in the second century BCE, mingling the courts of the *domus* type with gardens, orchards, and landscape vistas. Several "suburban villas" sat on the outskirts of Pompeii. The Villa of Mysteries, named after frescoes depicting female initiation rites on the walls of its *triclinium*, was less than 1 km (0.6 mile) from the city walls. It repeated the room types of the *domus*, but on a larger scale and with more openness to the landscape. Inverting the sequential order of the *domus*, one entered through a peristyle garden and followed an axis that terminated with an atrium court and *tablinum*. The patron's office overlooked a rounded terrace with a privileged view to the sea.

The demographic pressures visible in a country town like Pompeii during the first century CE had long before transformed Rome into a city of multilevel tenements. Most of the underclass remained renters in tall, poorly constructed blocks squeezed between the hills. The multilevel apartment block, or ***insula***, developed spontaneously from the simple shop with an attic room to a pile of several stories of apartments over ground-level *taberna*. Shoddily built of mud bricks or half-timber construction, with wooden floors, stairs, and ceilings, the tenement had no cooking facilities or privies and was highly flammable, subject to collapse, and frequently overcrowded. The state attempted to regulate heights and construction methods of these tenements, especially after

Figure 5.1-18 Pompeii. Detail of neighborhood showing the *domus*, with the house of Pansa occupying an entire block. Shops and rental units appear in the light gray areas on the perimeter, ca. 70 CE.

Figure 5.1-19 Pompeii. *Impluvium* court, Domus Vetii, ca. 70 CE.

Rome's Great Fire of 64 CE, which destroyed large sections of the city center. In the early second century CE, Rome's port city of Ostia sponsored exemplary *insulae*, entire blocks built of fireproof, brick-faced concrete set on wide streets. The four-story structures were rationally divided to accommodate multiple dwellings and ensure fire safety. This attention to housing indicated the degree to which the architecture of the city had become inseparable from the system of Roman governance.

While Roman colonial cities conformed to rigid order, the mother city remained chaotic. Rome developed without a plan, randomly following a pinwheel pattern set by its topographical irregularities. It lacked the major cross streets of *cardo* and *decumanus* and the gridded patterns of *castrum* towns. From the second century BCE onward, however, powerful Roman patrons contributed patches of order to the city as urban renewal projects. Using the spoils from military campaigns, they inserted colonnaded buildings and regular spaces, one adjacent to the next. Rome gradually acquired a piecemeal order.

Rome of the Emperors: From Brick to Marble

The urban renewal of Rome began as a means of spreading the wealth acquired through conquest. The city awarded a solemn procession, or triumph, to victorious generals, who in turn were expected to lavish the booty, or *manubiae*, of their campaigns on public works. Honorific columns and triumphal arches sprouted up along the triumphal route to the Capitoline Hill. A **triumphal arch**, such as the Arch of Septimius Severus, which stood in the Roman Forum at the foot of the Capitoline, served as a masonry billboard of imperial propaganda. The central arch was typically flanked by smaller arches half its size, while two pairs of engaged columns helped to sustain an attic panel, inscribed with the emperor's name and deeds.

The explicit political use of architectural patronage began with Lucius Cornelius Sulla (138–78 BCE), a successful general who from 82 to 79 BCE was named "dictator," a role of considerable power but without the negative connotations of modern dictatorships. His projects changed the monuments of the civic realm into statements of personal power. On the Capitoline Hill he rebuilt the Temple of Jupiter Optimus Maximus, the final destination of the ceremonies of the triumph, putting his own name in the entablature (Fig. 5.1-20). In the Forum he raised an equestrian statue of himself and doubled the size of the Curia Senate house. His most lasting contribution was the first major public building to be built in concrete, the Tabularium, completed around 70 BCE. Designed as a fireproof repository for public records and tax documents, the Tabularium's facade provided a grand backdrop to the northwest edge of the Forum, articulated with engaged half-columns and arches like the facades of theaters (Fig. 5.1-21).

Another general, Gnaeus Pompeius Magnus, or Pompey the Great (106–48 BCE), followed Sulla's example of self-aggrandizement, building Rome's first permanent theater—but also next to it a luxurious palace and a public garden in the style of Hellenistic tyrants. Pompey's chief rival, Julius Caesar (100–44 BCE), surpassed these architectural exploits, beginning an even larger theater, completed by Augustus in the name of Marcellus; rebuilding the basilicas on the long sides of the Roman Forum; and demolishing the Senate house, to be rebuilt in a completely new position (Fig. 5.1-22). The repositioned Curia prepared the way for the addition of a completely new forum. Measuring 160 × 75 m (525 × 246 ft) in area, the Forum of Julius Caesar matched the scale of its republican predecessor but was enclosed with perfectly orthogonal, continuous colonnades. It differed from Hellenistic precedents in its strict axial order. At

Figure 5.1-20 Rome. Reconstructed view of Capitoline Hill and Temple of Jupiter Optimus Maximus overlooking the republican Forum, ca. 100 BCE (before imperial transformations), with its temples, long basilicas, circular *comitium* outdoor assembly place, and at the right corner, the round Temple of Vesta.

Figure 5.1-21 Rome. View to Sulla's Tabularium, 70 BCE, revised during the thirteenth–sixteenth centuries.

the end of the longitudinal axis rose a Corinthian temple to Venus Genetrix.

Julius Caesar scripted a plan for Rome, the *Lex Julia Municipalis*, with which he intended to restructure the city's municipal districts and improve its roads and water supply. It included a law that prohibited wheeled traffic of large wagons through the city center during daylight. The most daring part of the plan proposed to reroute and straighten the Tiber River in an effort to avoid its regular flooding.

Octavian, Julius's adopted son and successor, became the first *princeps*, or emperor, after a decade of power struggles. The new ruler, who soon came to be known as Augustus (r. 27 BCE–14 CE), carefully plotted the transition from republic to monarchy. During his forty-year reign, he completed many of the unfinished projects of Julius, while adding others, including a temple to a deified Julius at the southern end of the Roman Forum. These renewal efforts prompted a court biographer to attribute to the first Roman emperor the saying that he "found the city in brick and left it in marble."

Augustus created a second imperial forum in his own name, placing a temple at the end of its axis dedicated to Mars Ultor. The Forum of Augustus, set perpendicular to that of Julius, contained approximately the same area but instead of the simple proportion of 1:2 followed that of 3:4. The temple had Greek-style Corinthian columns and seemed nearly square, with eight columns across and eight on the sides. In the center of the plaza an equestrian sculpture of Augustus carried the inscription *Pater Patriae*, the "father of the nation." An immense 33 m (108 ft) high fire wall wrapped the rear boundary of the new forum (Fig. 5.1-23). Its huge blocks of gray **tufa** stone protected the precinct from the visual and social chaos of the neighboring Subura district, the densest and poorest in the city. The project contained concealed **exedrae**, roofed-over semicircular halls decorated with sculptures celebrating the founders of Rome and the members of the new dynasty at the end of each of the flanking colonnades. With the addition of these imperial *fora*, Augustus converted the republican area of civic dialogue into a stage for celebrating the new imperial dynasty.

Augustus continued Julius's initiative to replan the capital, extending the *pomerium* boundary to more than twice the initial city's area and redistricting it from seven into fourteen regions. Rome now stretched beyond the Servian walls to include the Campus Martius, the area north of the Capitoline, where a new monumental district began taking shape. Rome's ancient defensive walls became superfluous. The new edges of the city acquired definition through clusters of monumental tombs, which by law stood outside of the city limits. On the western boundary, marking the road to Ostia, the magistrate Caius Cestius built in 12 BCE a 27 m (89 ft) high, marble-clad pyramid, inspired by the recently

Figure 5.1-22 Rome. Transformation of the republican Forum under Julius Caesar and Augustus, mid–first century BCE.

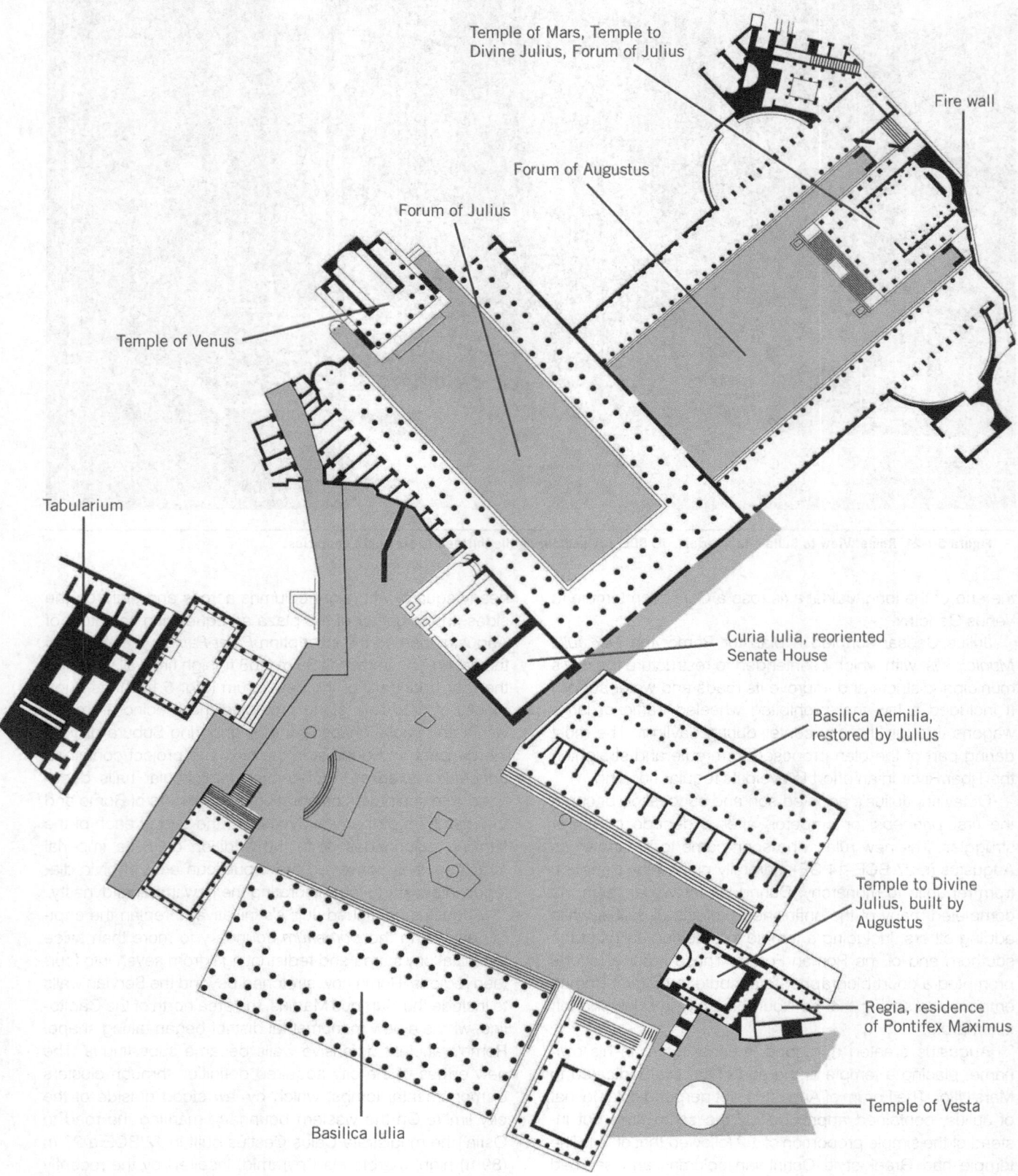

Temple of Mars, Temple to Divine Julius, Forum of Julius

Fire wall

Forum of Augustus

Forum of Julius

Temple of Venus

Tabularium

Curia Iulia, reoriented Senate House

Basilica Aemilia, restored by Julius

Temple to Divine Julius, built by Augustus

Regia, residence of Pontifex Maximus

Temple of Vesta

Basilica Iulia

Figure 5.1-23 Rome. Forum of Augustus, with fragments of the Temple of Mars and fire wall, 40–2 BCE.

Figure 5.1-24 Rome. The Ara Pacis, Emperor Augustus's legacy to the Roman Peace, 9 CE. Contemporary installation by Richard Meier, 2006.

conquered province of Egypt. The tomb of Eurysaces (30 BCE), an ex-slave who had made good as a baker, rose on silo-like cylinders and was punctured in its upper range with round slots, like a bread oven.

Inside the *pomerium*, the first emperor focused his personal patronage on the Forum and a temple on the Palatine Hill. Outside the urban boundary, at the northern approach to Rome, he indulged in a magnificent assembly of self-serving monuments that included a burial mound, a heroic altar, and an immense sundial. The massive pile of the Mausoleum of Augustus, 85 m (279 ft) in diameter, was begun in 28 BCE, the year of the emperor's investiture. Rising 45 m (148 ft), it was composed of a planted mound carrying a central square tower over a

travertine-clad cylindrical base. The memorial resembles Etruscan tumulus-type tombs, such as those at Cerveteri, about 40 km (25 miles) north of Rome, but may also have been inspired by the round mausoleum built three centuries earlier for Alexander the Great in Alexandria, a city that Augustus had recently conquered.

South of the mausoleum stretched a vast plaza for the Horologium. A 30 m (98 ft) high obelisk, taken as a spoil during the Egyptian campaign against Mark Antony and Cleopatra, stood as a cosmic needle, casting shadows on bronze meridian lines to mark the hours, months, and zodiac signs. To the east of the obelisk Augustus sited the Ara Pacis, the Altar of Peace (Fig. 5.1-24). The shrine came to symbolize the beginning of the long period of stability

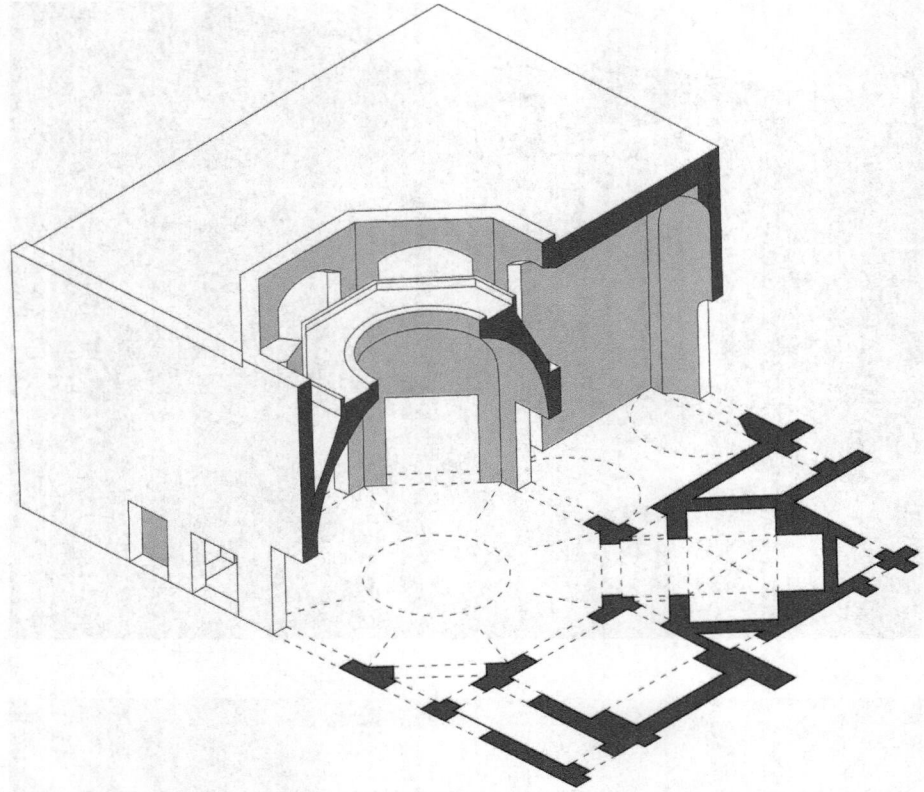

city's area. On the Esquiline Hill he installed a terrace lined with a linear succession of polygonal spaces with vaulted chambers. The colonnades of the terrace overlooked an artificial lake surrounded by miniature representations of the cities of the Mediterranean. Nero rebuilt the entry plaza of the Via Sacra with porticoes leading to the Roman Forum and here placed a 36 m (118 ft) high portrait of himself as Helios the sun god, a bronze colossus rivaling the erstwhile Colossus of Rhodes (see Section 4.2).

The *Domus Aurea* had more than 100 rooms. Nero's Greek-trained architects Severus and Celer prepared a succession of vaulted chambers whose mysterious atmosphere was enhanced by concealed clerestory lighting, cascading water elements, and shimmering marble and mosaic cladding. The Octagonal Hall in the east half of the *Domus Aurea* revealed the sophistication of this new spatial language (Fig. 5.1-25). Two concentric octagons formed a double shell for the central dome, which was lit by an oculus. Clerestories brought daylight from the crawl space between the domes, illuminating a series of radially arranged side chambers. While Nero's Golden House may seem like the eccentric fantasy of a spoiled tyrant, it nonetheless provided an appropriate setting for the new political ideology of a world empire governed by a single sovereign.

Although contemporary chroniclers blamed Nero's downfall on his squandering of money and his cruelty, his demise came from internal dissent among the military and his own Praetorian guards, who forced him to commit suicide on the eve of his thirtieth birthday. The Roman Senate, offended by his autocratic habits, ordered Nero erased from history, a victim of *damnatio memoriae*. His buildings, like those of Hatshepsut and Akhenaten, either underwent reinscription or were eliminated. The next dynasty, the Flavians, set out to make amends to the Roman people by burying the *Domus Aurea* under populist projects. The Baths of Titus were built atop some of the terraces of the villa, while Nero's lake was drained and replaced by the Colosseum. The face of the colossus received a new generic countenance representing Helios.

Thirty years after Nero's demise, Emperor Domitian (r. 81–96 CE) decided to improve the imperial residence on the Palatine Hill. The Romans had long conserved a thatched hut there to commemorate Romulus, thought to have founded

known as the *Pax Romana* (27 BCE–180 CE), the "Roman peace." A relatively small marble enclosure, 12 × 10 m (39 × 33 ft), open to the sky, it resembled Hellenistic hero shrines like the Altar of Pergamon. The reliefs decorating the Ara Pacis showed a procession of men and women of the Julio–Claudian dynasty and the chief magistrates of the time. Their solemn appearance evoked the Augustan ideal of maintaining stern republican values under the new monarchy. Augustus planned the entire monumental landscape to demonstrate the cosmic destiny of his imperial authority: the shadow of the obelisk penetrated the shrine's square aperture on his birthday, September 23, at noon.

Augustus and members of his family devoted their patronage principally to public works and temples. Their work on the imperial palace on the Palatine Hill was modest compared to later interventions. It took the flamboyant imagination of Nero (r. 54–68 CE) to begin the process of creating an imperial residence worthy of a Roman emperor. Nero, who came to power at age seventeen, prided himself on his talents as an actor, poet, painter, and musician and did not hesitate to add architecture to his cultural accomplishments.

Nero's first architectural project, the *Domus Transitoria*, connected the existing imperial residence on the Palatine Hill with the gardens of Maecenas on the Esquiline Hill. The barrel-vaulted structure was consumed, along with nearly half of the city, by the Great Fire of 64 CE. Faced with reconstruction, Nero behaved in the manner of eastern despots. The resulting estate, the *Domus Aurea*, or "Golden House," occupied three of Rome's hills, roughly 25% of the

the city on that site. Domitian's new palace covered most of the hilltop, presenting colonnaded facades toward the main approaches from the Forum and a great concave prospect toward the Circus Maximus. From this imperial loggia the emperor and his courtiers observed the games.

Domitian's architect, Rabirius, divided the palace into two parallel zones (Fig. 5.1-26). The *Domus Flavia* on the north was more public. Visitors entered through one of three halls. On the outer corner a barrel-vaulted basilica terminating in an apse served as the principal hall for imperial justice. Beside it, and nearly twice as large, lay a magnificent throne room, its side walls articulated by deep, rounded niches. The third hall served as a rectangular chapel. Visitors filtered through these reception spaces into a peristyle court where an octagonal maze surrounded a central fountain. The state dining hall, nearly as large as the throne room, overlooked the court from the opposite end. Its side walls

were screened with columns that opened to two intimate side courts with elongated oval fountains.

The other half of the palace, the *Domus Augustana*, contained more intimate suites for the imperial family. Rabirius arranged it on three levels around a square *impluvium* court with an elaborate fountain at its core (Fig. 5.1-27). He placed a sunken garden designed in the shape of a stadium along the southeast flank. Its shape recalled the stadium built by Domitian for the Agone Games in the Campus Martius, now known as Piazza Navona.

Both the *Domus Aurea* and the Flavian imperial palace complex show signs of a major architectural shift to the mature Roman vaulted style. Curves, countercurves, and ovals contribute to these structures' spatial complexity. The architects channeled water through the interior spaces, animating inert matter. They manipulated light for dramatic effect, letting its rays stream through *oculi* into closed

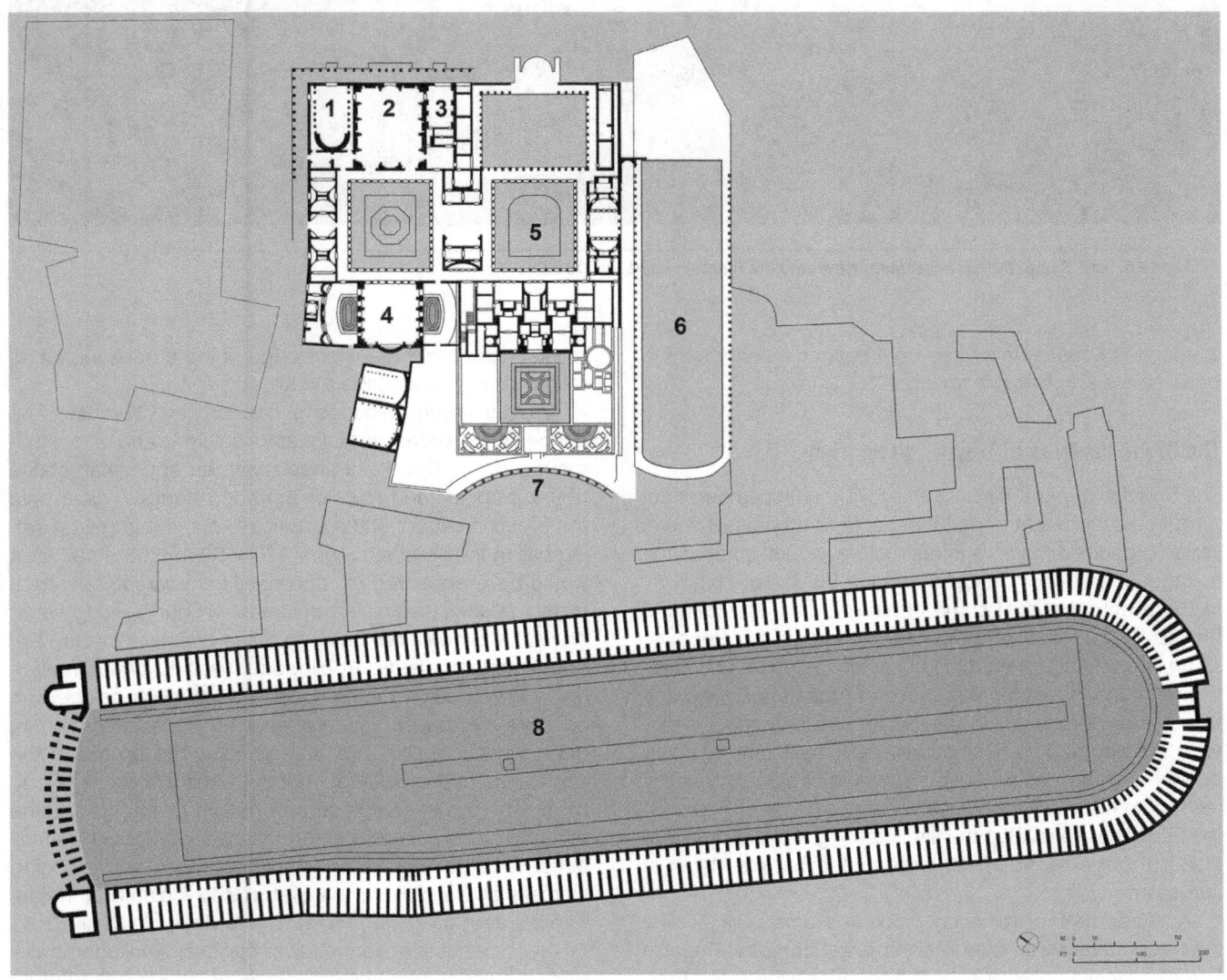

Figure 5.1-26 Rome. Plan of the Palatine Hill complex. The left side was known as *Domus Flavia* and used for political functions: (1) the basilica; (2) *Aula Regia* throne room; (3) *Lararium* with family shrines; (4) state *triclinium* dining hall. The right side (5) was known as *Domus Augustana*, the domestic half of the palace: (6) palace stadium; (7) concave terrace for viewing; (8) Circus Maximus.

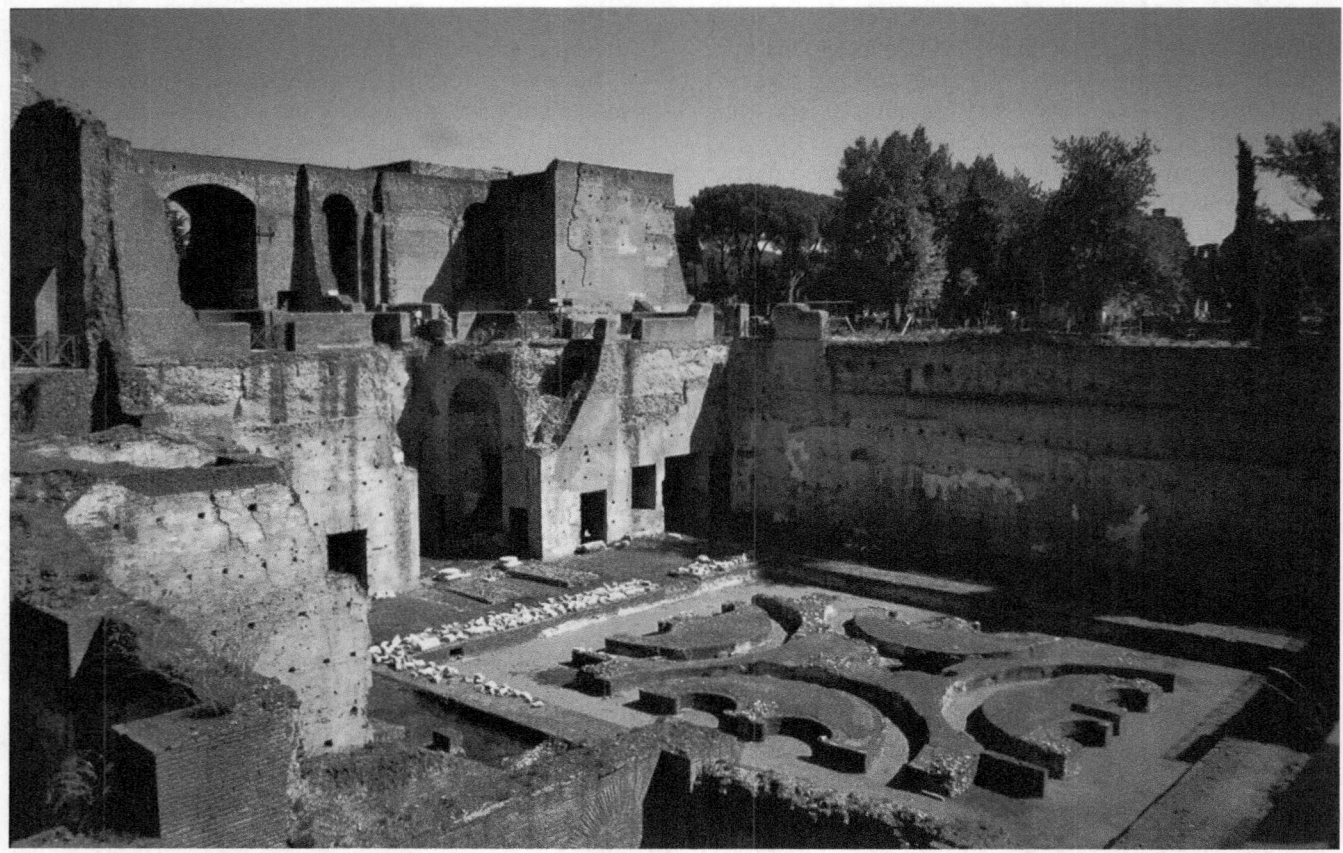

Figure 5.1-27 Rome. *Domus Augustana*, view onto the fountain court, ca. 100 CE.

interiors. Imperial architecture went beyond exterior form to become the art of interior space.

The Grand Projects of Trajan and Hadrian

The Spanish general Trajan (r. 98–117), the first emperor not born in Italy, brought imperial projects to a colossal scale. Trajan organized massive infrastructural works, such as the hexagonal port basin at Ostia and the Via Traiana highway to Benevento. He built some of his grandest structures in his native Spain, including the granite Aqueduct of Segovia, rising 30 m (98 ft) on double tiers of arches; the eighty-arch bridge of Merida; and the impressive Alcántara Bridge, the tallest ever attempted. In the capital the emperor's architect, Apollodorus of Damascus, assumed extraordinary power over the design of the public environment, literally reshaping the city's topography. For the Baths of Trajan on the Esquiline, he leveled the site, creating a platform 340 m (1,115 ft) per side, nearly as large as the Temple Mount in Jerusalem.

Apollodorus's culminating work in Rome was a new forum combined with a four-level market complex. Trajan's Forum covered an area almost three times the size of Julius's Forum (Fig. 5.1-28). To level the site required the demolition of the old Servian walls and the removal of a large chunk of the Quirinal Hill. The vaulted structures of the

markets flanking the eastern edge of the Forum served as retaining walls to stabilize the hill.

Trajan's Forum included a basilica, two libraries, four concealed exedras, a historiated column, and a posthumous temple. The plaza space, with an equestrian statue of the emperor and rows of boxwood hedges, gave onto the broad prospect of the Basilica Ulpia, the largest meeting hall in the empire, roughly 170 × 60 m (558 × 197 ft). It would have appeared exceptionally transparent, raised on evenly spaced Corinthian columns without bearing walls. As with a Greek *stoa*, one could see directly into the vast, double-height interior. Apollodorus used luxurious materials in this structure, composed in contrasting colors, with columns and pavers made of green pavonazzetto marble, golden *giallo antico*, and gray granite. The exedra at the short ends of the basilica were set behind screens of columns. The two vaulted libraries, one for Latin works and the other for Greek, stood behind the basilica, facing a small peristyle court. They framed the most original and imposing element of the project, the **historiated** Column of Trajan, with spiraling friezes that narrated his victory in Dacia.

As compensation to the lower classes, Apollodorus designed a series of commercial spaces abutting the Forum complex. The three lower ranges of the Markets of Trajan formed a hemicycle wrapping around the eastern exedra of the Forum, with 150 barrel-vaulted *tabernae*, each lit by

Figure 5.1-28 Rome. Forum and markets of Trajan, to the left of the four imperial fora, 110 CE. Model at Museo della Civiltà Romana, Rome.

Figure 5.1-28 Rome. Forum and markets of Trajan, to the left of the four imperial fora, 110 CE. Model at Museo della Civiltà Romana, Rome.

a clerestory over a transom (Fig. 5.1-29a,b). The shops on the ground level opened directly to the street, while those on the second level lined an **annular-vaulted** corridor, allowing views of the Forum through the arches on the facade. The third-story shops turned inward to a street halfway up the slope, the Via Biberatica, above which rose the irregular mass of the great market hall. Known as Aula Traiana, the hall's 9 m (29 ft) span combined a barrel vault with lateral groin vaults. The structural piers intersected arched buttresses that transferred with acrobatic skill the load of the vaults to six transverse barrel vaults on either side of the hall housing shops at the base.

Trajan's successor, Hadrian (r. 117–138), also raised in Spain, brought the Roman vaulted style to a new level of sophistication. During his reign the empire reached the apex of its material prosperity and the outermost limits of its growth, governing over 70 million people. Hadrian traveled over half of the years of his tenure, bringing with him a contingent of "geometers, architects, and every sort of expert in construction and decoration . . . whom he enrolled by cohorts and centuries, on the model of the legions." At the most unstable edge of the empire, the northern frontier between England and Scotland, he built a 130 km (78 mile) defensive boundary, the Vallum Hadriani (Hadrian's Wall). He ordered the construction of a wooden **palisade** to protect the strongholds along the Rhine and Danube, beyond which the mounted barbarians of Central and Eastern Europe— Sarmatians, Alamanni, and Visigoths—darted restlessly. The periodic movement for Jewish independence, first suppressed by Titus in 70 CE, flared up again briefly in

Figure 5.1-29 Rome. (a) Markets of Trajan, 110 CE, Apollodorus of Damascus. (b) Interior of the markets at Aula Traiana.

Figure 5.1-30 Rome. The Pantheon, 125–128 CE.

Hadrian's tomb projected a more commanding presence, looking over a new bridge back at the city across the river.

Hadrian achieved his greatest architectural legacy with the domed temple of the Pantheon, the most unorthodox religious building of ancient Rome. Completed between 125 and 128 CE, it represented a lifetime of research on the possibilities of curved space. As Hadrian's preferred site for holding court, the Pantheon embodied the ideal of sacred governance. Part temple and part throne room, its serene hemispherical space would have instilled a cosmic resonance in even the smallest of human gestures.

Palestine, to be definitively crushed in 135 CE. Hadrian renamed Jerusalem "Aelia Capitolina" after his family name. He razed the old city and rebuilt it with Roman colonnaded buildings, as if architecture could resolve its ethnic conflicts.

Hadrian aspired to the wisdom of Greek culture and donated several buildings to Athens. He enriched his architectural knowledge through contact with the sophisticated designers of Ephesus and Pergamon along the Ionian coast. The Market Gateway of Miletus, sponsored by Hadrian, showed in its broken central pediment and extruded corners the unconventional use of classical orders to obtain greater plasticity. Another contemporary work, the facade of the Library of Ephesus, had a similarly playful rhythmic alignment of aediculae that were staggered from the ground floor to the second story. Such theatrical facades derived from the stacks of columns used on the *scenae frons* of Roman theaters.

The architect-emperor indulged his architectural fantasies at his villa near Tivoli, with pumpkin-shaped vaults and reverse-curve plans. For his projects in Rome, however, he intended to reinforce the traditions of Augustus through the construction of almost exclusively religious buildings. Next to the Colosseum he built the largest temple in the city, a Greek-style peripteral volume dedicated to Venus and Rome. The interior had back-to-back *cellas*, also a Greek practice, and the combination of the goddess of the city with the goddess of love celebrated the well-known riddle that the city's name spelled backward yielded *amor*, or "love." In emulation of Augustus, Hadrian erected his family mausoleum as an Etruscan-inspired tumulus mound. The majestic cylinder, today known as Castel Sant'Angelo, rose over a cubic base and was clad in blocks of travertine. A helix ramp spiraled through its mass to the central burial shaft. Although not much larger than the mausoleum of Augustus,

The Pantheon combined Hadrian's desire to assimilate the values of the past while pushing the limits of concrete technology. The exterior seemed quite conventional: a temple front set within a colonnaded *temenos* (Fig. 5.1-30). Above the monolithic granite columns of the porch, the entablature carried an enigmatic dedicatory inscription to Agrippa, the patron of the original Pantheon, built in 27 BCE. The earlier rectangular building, oriented in the opposite direction, had been destroyed by fire. Hadrian thus paid his respects to the Augustan age by adopting a traditional temple front inscribed with the name of a well-loved patron from that period. The forecourt masked the bulging shape of the dome, greatly increasing the surprise of entering the Pantheon's rounded interior. Once past the colossal bronze doors, the hemispherical hall, 43 m (141 ft) in both height and diameter, comprised a world unto itself.

The apparent simplicity of the Pantheon was obtained through a marvelously complex structure, unparalleled in vaulted concrete technology. All structural considerations went toward the support of its 5,000-ton dome. The oculus at the top, 9 m (29 ft) in diameter, served both as the sole source of light and as a means of removing load at the most critical point (Fig. 5.1-31a,b). Like a **keystone** in an arch, the oculus works as a compression ring to lock the structure. The section of the dome thickens as it descends, shifting from light pumice aggregate in the upper concrete to heavier stones below. Although the Pantheon's formidable walls, more than 6 m (20 ft) thick, appear to be solid mass, they actually contain tiers of hollow chambers under relieving arches. It is as if a multilevel aqueduct with eight piers was wrapped around a cylinder. The barrel-vaulted entry and opposite it the semidome apse, along with the six niches with alternating **aedicules** that radiate around the central expanse, all belong to this system of hollows under relieving arches. The voids in the walls also helped to hasten the drying process of the concrete during construction.

Hadrian's Pantheon served as a temple to all the gods, whose statues, including those of the planetary deities, stood in the niches of the lower two stories of the interior. The beam of light from the oculus would have spotted some of the statues, at times bringing mysterious lighting into the niches, as it moved across the space during the course of the day. Here, religious meanings blended with political

CONSTRUCTION, TECHNOLOGY, THEORY

Hadrian's Villa

During his twenty-year reign, Emperor Hadrian expanded his villa near Tivoli into a vast estate as large and as complex as an entire city, with basilicas, theaters, baths, and terraced gardens. To the original nucleus built in the first century BCE he added accessory structures, including a ceremonial precinct lined with slender Doric pillars, vaulted libraries, and submerged *cryptoporticus* passages for services. Hadrian's additions were laid out in zones that obeyed internal symmetry but did not fit into a comprehensive geometric whole. Among the emperor's adventurous architectural solutions, the "scenic" *triclinium*, lit with a special light scoop and animated with running water, offered one of several examples at the villa of pumpkin-shaped vaults. The Water Court had a four-lobed, vaulted structure designed with reverse curves. The circular island enclosure, thought to be Hadrian's private domain, linked the early core to the lower platform. One reached the island palace from drawbridges over a wide moat. Its twenty-two interconnecting rooms were shaped with concave curves and included thermal baths, a *triclinium*, a library, and rooms for lounging.

Tivoli. Hadrian's Villa, 125 CE. (a) Model. (b) and (c) See next page.

CONSTRUCTION, TECHNOLOGY, THEORY

Hadrian's Villa (*continued*)

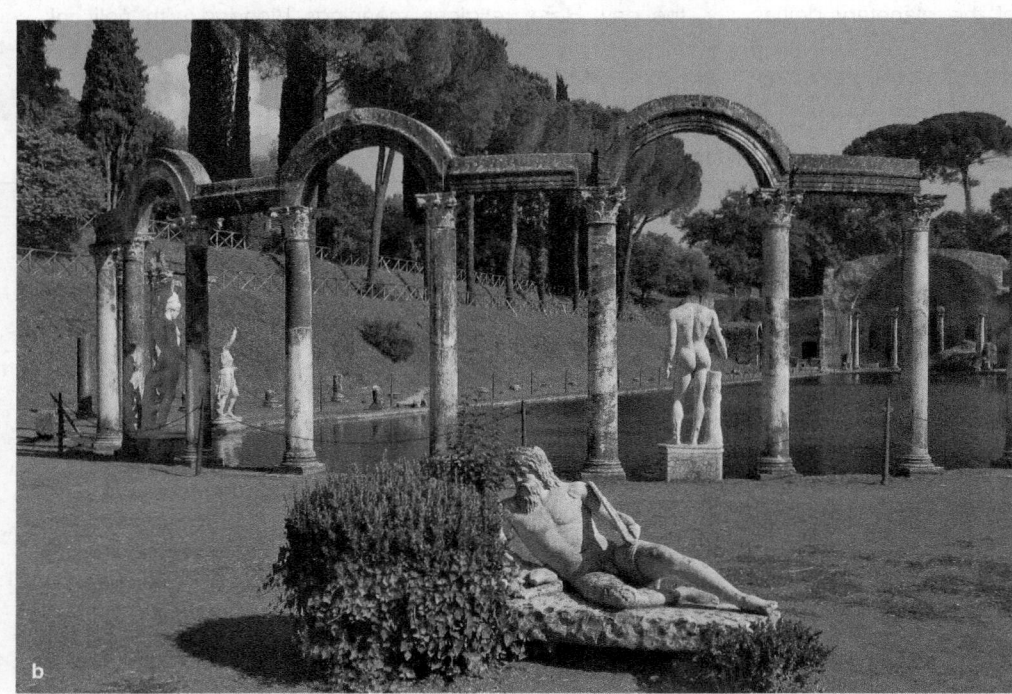

Tivoli. Hadrian's Villa, 125 CE. (b) View of the Water Court. (c) Plan.

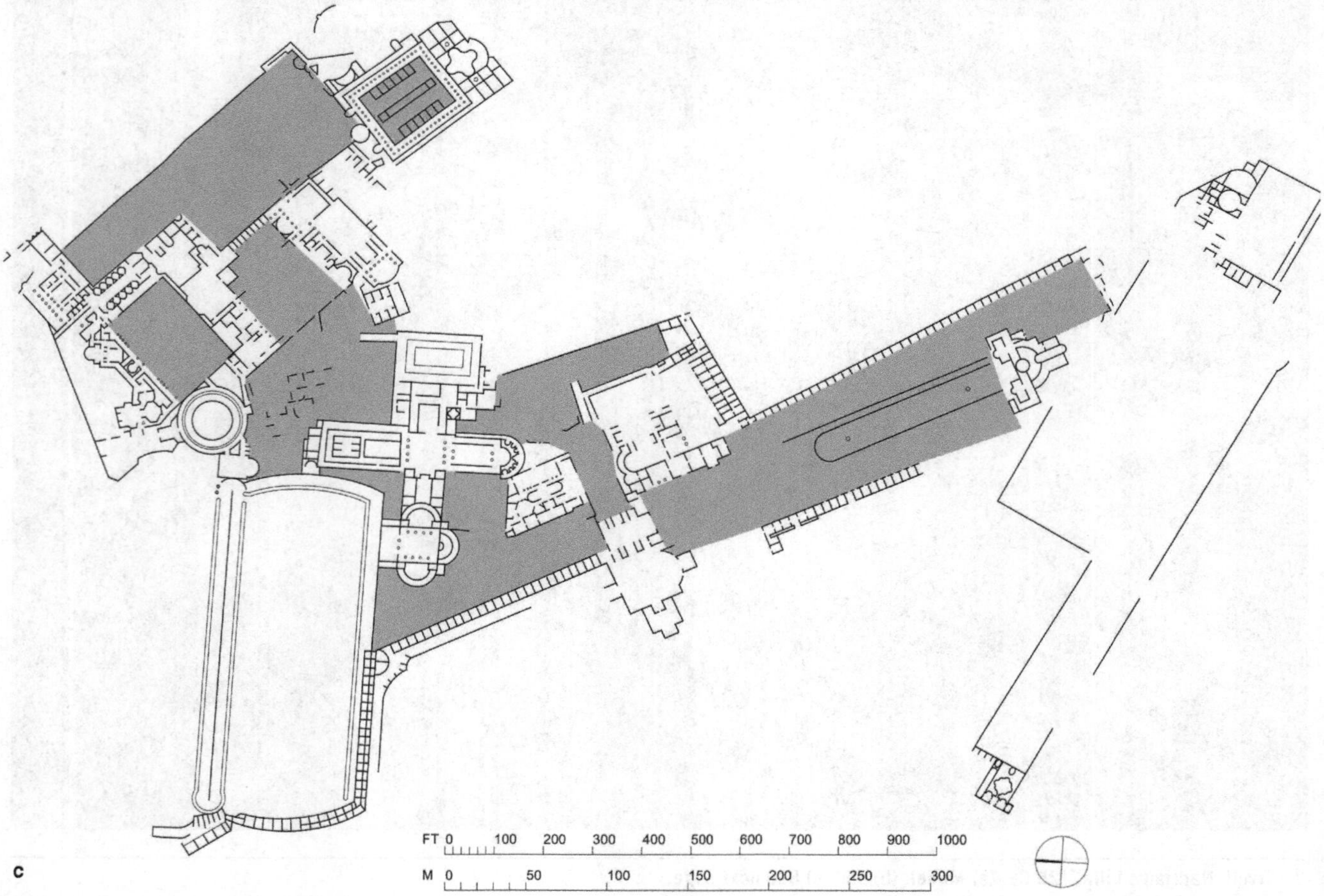
FT 0 100 200 300 400 500 600 700 800 900 1000
M 0 50 100 150 200 250 300

c

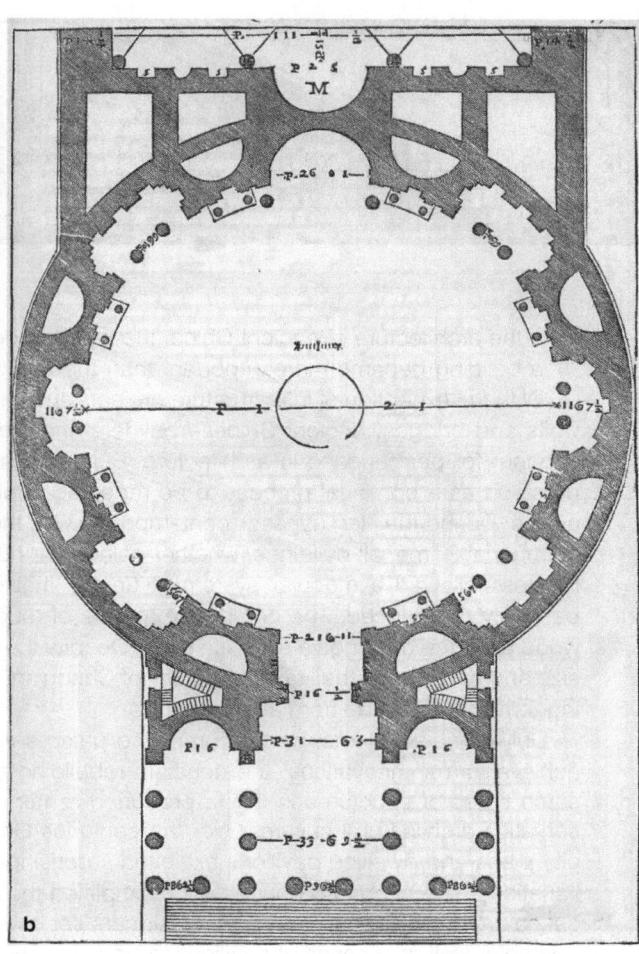

Figure 5.1-31 (a) Rome. Interior of the Pantheon, oculus, 125–128 CE. (b) Plan. Andrea Palladio, 1570.

signifiers, such as the statue of Augustus in the entrance vestibule and that of deified Caesar within. Hadrian's creation represented the dome of the heavens while promoting the notion of the empire's sacred mission to maintain the order of the world. Rome's true religion was Romanism, a force that, like the harmonious workings of the celestial spheres, bound the Mediterranean world together. Similar to the palace at Persepolis, the Pantheon became the repository of tribute from subject lands, with granite and **porphyry** for its columns and pavers from Egypt, colored marble for its paneling from North Africa, white marble for the capitals from the Aegean, and veined pavonazzetto from Asia Minor. Just as the Roman Empire absorbed other cultures and united them through a uniform legal system, so Hadrian assembled materials from throughout the realm in his Pantheon and held them together with the wondrous amalgamating capacity of concrete.

Further Reading

Adam, Jean-Pierre. *Roman Building Materials and Techniques.* London: Routledge, 1994.

Boatwright, Mary Tagliaferro. *Hadrian and the City of Rome.* Princeton, NJ: Princeton University Press, 1987.

Favro, Diane. *The Urban Image of Augustan Rome.* Cambridge: Cambridge University Press, 1996.

Hammond, Mason. *The City in the Ancient World.* Cambridge, MA: Harvard University Press, 1972.

Jones, Mark Wilson. *Principles of Roman Architecture.* New Haven, CT: Yale University Press, 2000.

MacDonald, William. *The Architecture of the Roman Empire,* 2 vols. New Haven, CT: Yale University Press, 1982, 1987.

MacDonald, William, and John Pinto. *Hadrian's Villa and Its Legacy.* New Haven, CT: Yale University Press, 1995.

McKay, A. G. *Houses, Villas, and Palaces in the Roman World.* Ithaca, NY: Cornell University Press, 1975.

Packer, James. *The Forum of Trajan in Rome: A Study of the Monuments.* Berkeley: University of California Press, 1997.

Richardson, L., Jr. *Pompeii: An Architectural History.* Baltimore, MD: Johns Hopkins University Press, 1986.

Taylor, Rabun. *Roman Builders: A Study in Architectural Process.* Cambridge: Cambridge University Press, 2003.

Yegul, Fikret. *Baths and Bathing in Classical Antiquity.* Cambridge, MA: MIT Press, 1992.

5.2   ANCIENT CHINA
The Pivot of the Cosmos in Mud and Wood

In the architecture of ancient China, the type, or idea, of a building became more important than the built work. With the exception of infrastructure projects such as city walls and bridges, ancient Chinese builders showed little concern for permanence in architecture. Building was understood as a continual process to be repeated in eternal cycles. During the Han dynasty, contemporary with the rise of imperial Rome, all buildings, whether palaces or humble houses, followed a modular system of design that could be easily reproduced. The common materials of mud and wood gave the buildings a short life span. Despite the great size and splendor of the Han capital city of Chang'an, nothing remains of it aside from a few mounds.

Unlike ancient Rome, where competing patrons vied to achieve formal innovations, the constant rebuilding of the same types of structures in China produced a more conservative architectural culture. Over the centuries Chinese city plans and dwelling pavilions exhibited surprisingly few variations. The courtyard house best exemplified the cyclical nature of Chinese buildings. Its designers set it within a perimeter wall as a series of pavilions to be added according to the family's need. Each successive generation would rebuild the individual pavilions in identical form. Chinese builders followed simple modules and prescribed plans, and through constant repetition the type of their buildings proved more lasting than any specific work.

The Unification of China behind the Great Wall

Chinese architectural traditions and written language extend back seven millennia. While the Romans were consolidating their empire around the Mediterranean, Chinese emperors amassed an even larger territory in Asia. They relied much less than their western contemporaries on architecture and urbanism in the governing of their empire. Their use of nondurable materials such as mud bricks and wood meant that few ancient Chinese buildings survived beyond a few generations outside of literary and archaeological traces. The only durable structure, the Great Wall along the northern and western frontiers, was an amalgam of several walls (Fig. 5-2.1). Begun in the second century BCE as a series of defensive structures, it offered a formidable symbol of Chinese identity. Most of its earliest parts crumbled with time and were rebuilt by later dynasties.

The first records of China as a unified political dominion come from the Xia dynasty, around the time of Ur, 2200 BCE. More accurate written records came with the next rulers, the Shang dynasty, who held power from 1750 to 1100 BCE. Their core territory spread around the Yellow River (Huang Ho), to which the territory surrounding the other great Chinese river system to the south, the Yangtze, equally rich in cultural development, was later annexed (Fig. 5.2-2).

The Zhou dynasty replaced the Shang in 1100 BCE and ruled sporadically until 256 BCE. The Zhou originated in the western provinces and around the year 1000 BCE created the capital city of Chang'an, near the modern city of Xi'an. The name meant "city of everlasting peace." Peace, however, did not endure, and the city underwent devastation and abandonment, to be revived as the capital on several occasions.

During the first millennium the Chinese emperor acquired the semidivine status of "son of heaven," a role adopted by all successive dynasties. The title signified military and political sovereignty as well as sacramental authority. The combination of political and religious roles assumed by the emperor projected a compelling sense of centrality and hierarchy on the organization of the state, capital cities, and palace compounds. The early Chinese state created a confederation of feudal warriors and governed through the participation of a sizable class of civil servants. After the fall of the Zhou capital at Chang'an in 771 BCE, the government moved to a new capital in a safer position at Luoyang, 200 km (120 miles) to the east. This alternation between Chang'an and Luoyang was repeated on two other occasions during Chinese history.

When the Chinese founded a capital city, they relied on a set of general rules. The model came from the ideal Zhou capital, known as the *wangcheng*, or "ruler's city." It proposed a quadrangle, with three gates on each side, three sets of triple avenues running straight from the gates, and the palace occupying a large enclave in the center

TIME LINE

▼ ca. 550 BCE
Confucius

Great Wall of China

▲ **221 BCE–1368** CE

▼ 221 BCE
Shi Huangdi founds Qin dynasty

Figure 5.2-1 China. View of the Great Wall, 221 BCE–1368 CE.

(Fig. 5.2-3). Chinese geography likewise followed orthogonal diagrams: a territory was defined as a series of linked squares, at the center of which lay the square capital of the empire. The regime and its architecture were structured according to a cosmic diagram centered on the figure of the emperor, who was invested with the "Mandate of Heaven," the power to rule bestowed by the grace of heaven.

Like the Romans, the Chinese attributed profound religious significance to the cardinal directions. The imperial palace in the center of their capital cities commanded the main north–south axis, facing south in the direction of the Red Phoenix region of summer and fire. To the east lay the symbolic region of the Blue Dragon, representing spring, growth, and the upright tree and corresponding to the eastern position of the Temple of the Ancestors. The symbol of the White Tiger in the west meant autumn and its harvest, as well as war and the harvest of men, leading planners to place the Altar of the Earth in this direction. From the north came cold winter and marauding hordes bent on destruction, leading to the choice of the symbolic color black and the tortoise. The emperor's dwelling faced away from the north, and the dubious activities of commerce and markets were allocated to this sector of the city behind the palace.

In the emperor's palace compound the principal buildings followed a tripartite diagram: a foundation platform, a rectangular timber frame made of interlocking parts, and a decorative roof. Architects by the first millennium BCE had designed official buildings using a modular system that comprised eight different ranks of buildings, defined by the number of **bays** and the scale of the module. They made structures with simple post-and-beam techniques, based on the *jian*, or the repetition of framed bays. They added multilevel brackets, or **dougong**, to embellish the structure holding up the roof. These interlocking, branch-like supports diffused the loads of the roof and in some cases thrust up the corner **eaves**.

Terra-cotta warriors at tomb of Shi Huangdi

▲ **210 BCE**

▼ **206 BCE**

Gaozu founds Han dynasty

Chang'an (Xi'an) built as Han capital

▲ **204 BCE**

▼ **25 CE**

Han dynasty relocates capital to Luoyang

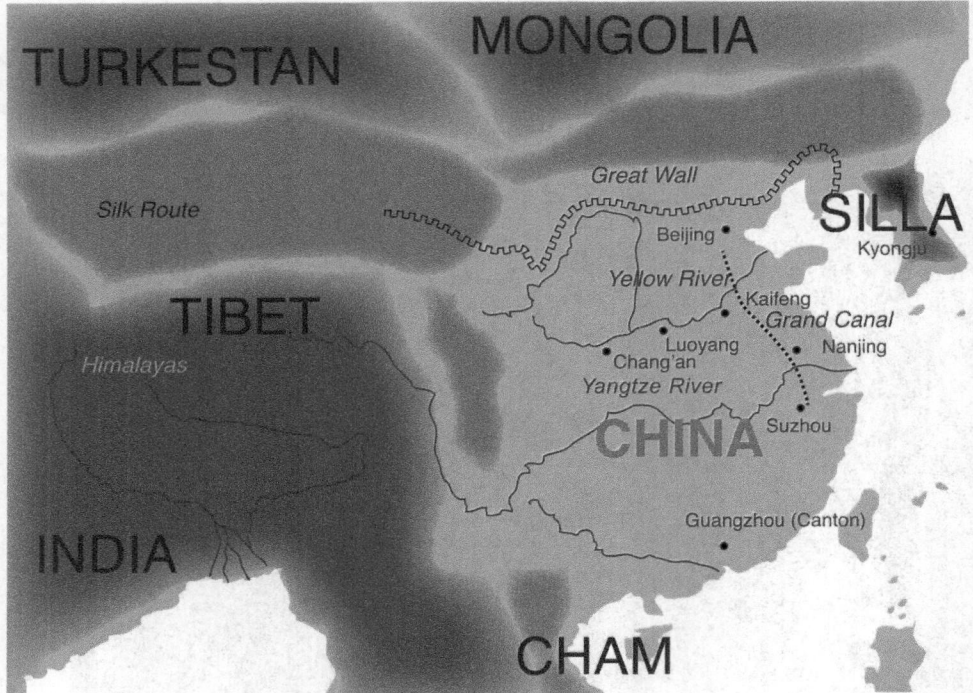

Figure 5.2-2 Ancient China. Growth of the empire, 200 BCE–600 CE.

China underwent significant cultural development after iron replaced bronze as the principal metal in the seventh century BCE, increasing the efficiency of both agriculture and weaponry. New prosperity led to the decentralization of power and a wider diffusion of literacy. During the so-called Spring and Autumn Period (722–481 BCE), the two great schools of Chinese philosophy emerged around the figures of Confucius (ca. 551–479 BCE), an administrator from Lu Province, and the legendary Laozi, who may have lived at the same time but whose existence remains undocumented.

Although the Zhou dynasty continued to claim sovereignty from the eighth to the third century BCE, China perennially disbanded into a number of competing kingdoms. Emperor Shi Huangdi (r. 221–210 BCE), founder of the Qin dynasty, united the seven warring kingdoms into the first true empire of China in 221 BCE. A ruthless military leader with superlative organizational skills, Shi Huangdi reapportioned the states of the empire into a system of thirty-six provinces administered through a centralized bureaucracy with military governors. The population of the empire grew to over 50 million inhabitants. To further consolidate the authority of his rule, the first emperor enforced the use of a universal written language and a universal currency. He promoted Chinese unity through a network of straight highways that connected the provinces. He then literally outlined the state with the world's greatest public work: the first version of the Great Wall, integrating several partial barriers begun by earlier regimes.

The Qin Great Wall, known as the "wall of 10,000 *li*" (the *li*, or Chinese mile, equaled 415 m [1,361.5 ft] in antiquity and today is approximately half a kilometer), was a series of walls that stretched over 3,500 km (2,100 miles). The state conscripted 400,000

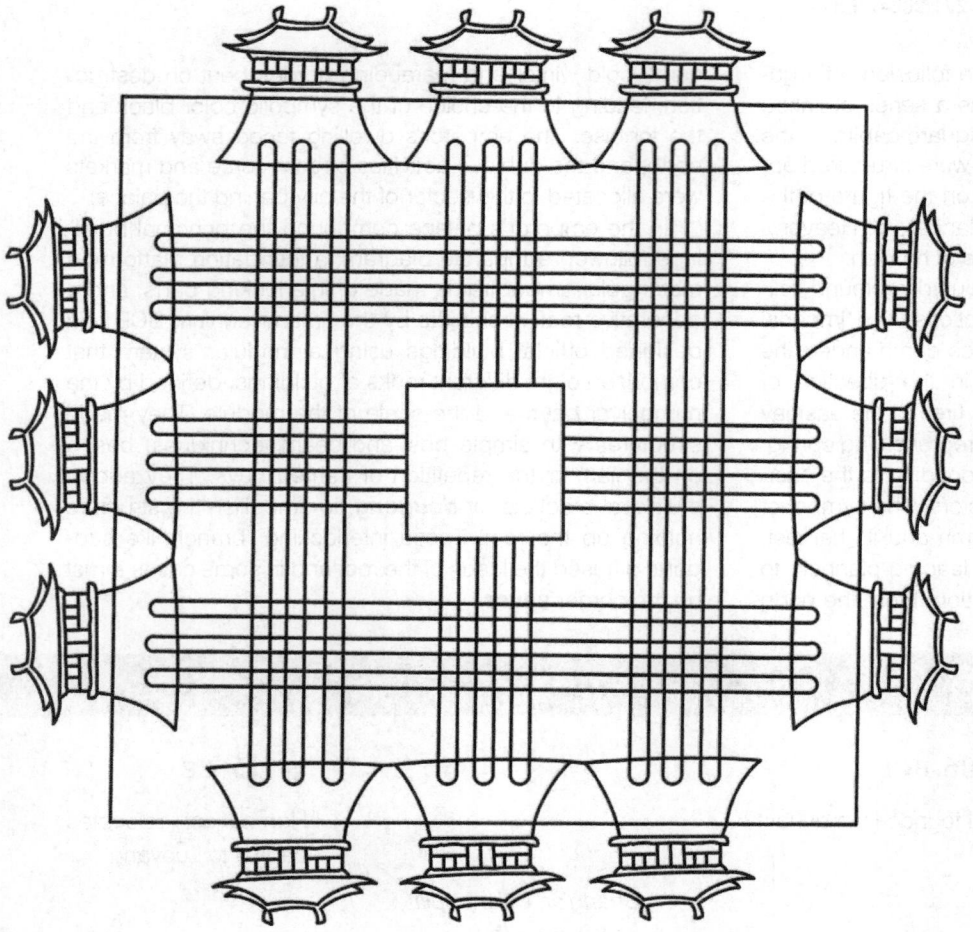

Figure 5.2-3 Ancient China. *Wangcheng* diagram for the "ruler's city," ca. 700 BCE.

laborers to work on the project over the course of ten years. The materials used in its construction changed according to the region, ranging from pounded earth (*pisé*) over wooden palisades to fired bricks to stones. Parts of the Qin Great Wall rose as high as 6 m (20 ft), stretching 4 m (13 ft) across. The planners placed guard towers at intervals of roughly 130 m (427 ft) for communication relays. The Han emperors, who succeeded the Qin, improved the wall during the next century, planting permanent veterans' colonies along its length to both control the passage of nomads and prevent the exit of settled populations.

The Great Wall that one visits today was rebuilt sixteen centuries later during the Ming dynasty. It is doubtful that any of the original Qin and Han dynasty wall has survived. The current wall, which is made of many walls, comprises the single largest structure in the world, stretching thousands of kilometers. The eastern sections of the current wall, which in some places have parallel sets of walls, extend for over 500 km (300 miles) without interruption at an average height of 11 m (36 ft), with towers every 700 m (2,296 ft). Despite its forbidding appearance, the Great Wall did not always deter raiders from attacking China; as late as 1550 CE, Mongol invaders besieged Beijing. Two of China's major dynasties in fact came from among those who breached the Great Wall.

Shi Huangdi initiated many other ambitious projects, including the Qin dynasty's capital of Xianyang, located 25 km (15 miles) northwest of Chang'an and enclosing an area 6 × 7.5 km (3.5 × 4 miles). The Qin capital covered a greater area than Rome and may have had a larger population. As part of his effort to break down feudal authority, the emperor forced 120,000 nobles to relocate to his new city. He used more than half of the gridded urban area for royal palace enclaves, leaving behind the foundation mounds of eight palatial compounds. A bridge across the Wei River connected the emperor's urban palace to the suburban Ebang Palace, a walled compound 1,400 × 450 m (4,500 × 1,400 ft), and the Shanglin Park. According to legend, Shi Huangdi built hundreds of palaces throughout the empire, each connected to the next by a covered gallery. He could thus move surreptitiously from one to the other without his enemies guessing his whereabouts.

While little remains of Shi Huangdi's grand palaces, his vast funeral complex at Lintong, discovered in 1974, eliminated any doubts about his penchant for grand scale. Located 40 km (25 miles) east of Xi'an, it includes a huge pyramid mound built of rubble and earth. Shi Huangdi's pile, the first and largest Chinese tumulus, measured 350 m (1,148 ft) per side and rose 75 m (246 ft), one-third larger than the Great Pyramid of Khufu in Egypt but only half its height. Shi Huangdi's architects set the precinct behind massive walls, measuring roughly 1 × 2 km (0.5 × 1 miles). Colossal stone animals, apotropaic figures, guarded the base of the pyramid. A few kilometers east of his funerary park Shi Huangdi built a vast underground sepulcher for a terra-cotta army of 8,000 life-size foot soldiers, archers, and charioteers (Fig. 5.2-4a,b). Most of the figures were organized into nine orderly linear cohorts, four across. Each

The *Jian* Module

Beginning in the first millennium, the *jian*, or bay, served as the basic unit of architectural order in China. Structural timber posts defined the *jian*, which had an average size of 3 × 6 m (10 × 20 ft), setting the size of a room. Chinese designers made their spaces through a process of addition, and a hall usually expanded to an odd number of *jians*.

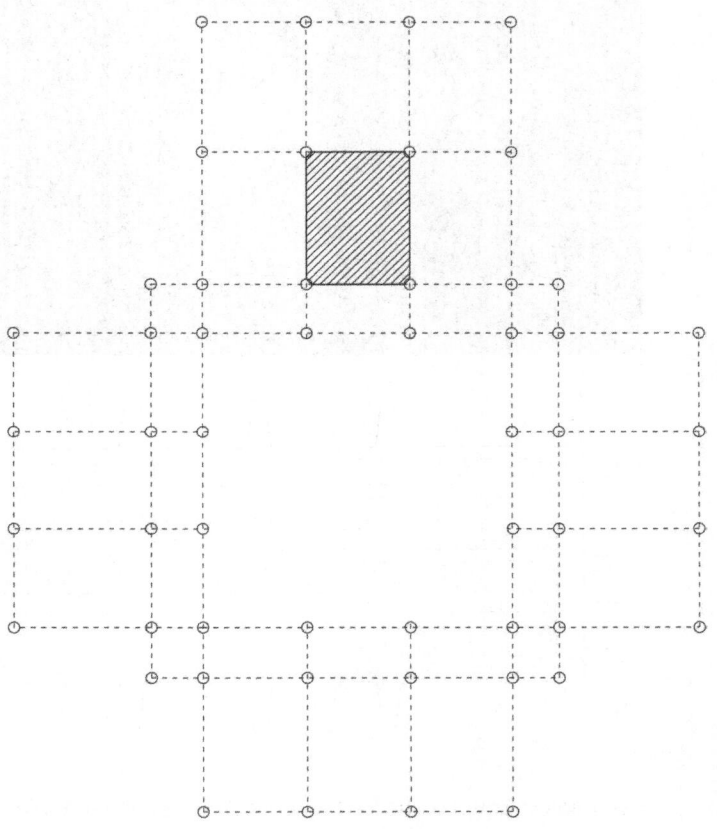

Ancient China. *Jian* proportional bays used in Chinese buildings.

terra-cotta soldier was given a different face and personalized headgear. These portraits of the emperor's honor guard were intended to protect him in eternity while advancing his power during his life.

Many later historians trained in Confucian doctrines condemned Shi Huangdi for his acts of repression. There are mixed opinions, however, about his regime. While the Confucian chroniclers maintained that his legal apparatus was cruel and arbitrary, the laws and punishments of his successors appear to have been no different yet went without criticism. Shi Huangdi also received blame for compelling a large portion of the population to construct his monuments and the Great Wall. His architectural projects, however, may have been part of a public works strategy to keep people working, a practice used in the construction of the great

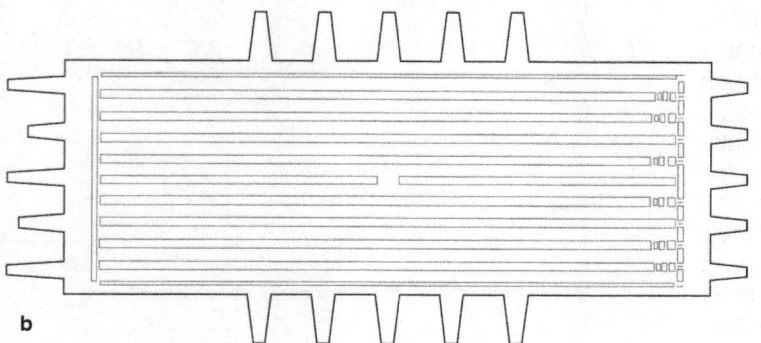

Figure 5.2-4 Xi'an, China. (a) View of sepulcher for Shi Huangdi's terra-cotta army, 210 BCE. (b) Plan.

pyramids in Egypt or the Parthenon in Athens and far nobler than Romans' use of slave labor for their monuments. The strongest accusations against the first emperor concerned his attempt to burn all of the texts that preceded his regime, eliminating historical and philosophical challenges to his policies, and his alleged execution of Confucian scholars, a claim for which there is no tangible evidence. The stories condemning the first emperor may have been a form of scholarly revenge, since Shi Huangdi's laws did not always adhere to Confucian doctrine. A few years following his death the Qin dynasty was overthrown, and the capital was destroyed by fire during subsequent rebellions.

Han Chang'an: Enclosed Urban Types

The ruling dynasties of China did not conceive of architecture as a form of public service. Their concern for the people might instead be shown through gifts to the poor, the granting of amnesties, or the remission of taxes. The central task of government in the cities remained social control. Walls enclosed each residential sector to monitor the population, helping impose curfews at night and facilitating census taking and recruitment for military service and forced labor. While the streets seem to have been abnormally wide, nothing in Chinese urban theory provided for the sort of shaped public space found around the ancient Mediterranean. The main avenue of the city led directly to the emperor's enclave, not to a civic or religious space for public life.

After the fall of the Qin dynasty, Gaozu, "the great progenitor" (r. 206–195 BCE), restored order to China, founding the Han dynasty. The new emperor came from modest agricultural origins, and his dynasty took its name from the word for "farmer." The Han dynasty, with a brief interruption at the beginning of the first century CE, ruled for over four centuries. Gaozu's clemency after the alleged cruelty of Shi Huangdi encouraged national solidarity. He refounded Chang'an on the *wangcheng* principles. His city was constructed as a variation of the grid plan of the old capital city of the Zhou dynasty. Chang'an flourished as the eastern terminus of the Silk Road, the main conduit for trade and ideas with India, Persia, and the West. Syrian and Persian middlemen exchanged silk from China with gold from the West. Thus, the Romans in the first century BCE referred to China as *Seres*, the "land of silk," while the Chinese called Rome the "Great *Qin*," or empire.

The Han dynasty retained many of the policies of Shi Huangdi, enforcing provincial allegiances through a system of tributes. The state obliged the feudal lords of distant provinces to pay homage to the emperor in Chang'an and leave behind a prime hostage, such as a crown prince, with the court. In return, the lords received imperial honors and gifts. At the same time the Han dynasty attempted to reduce the influence of the feudal nobility by increasing their number and thus diminishing their individual status. At the outset in 206 BCE there existed fifteen commanderies, ruled by government-appointed grand administrators, and ten feudal kingdoms. At the close of the first phase of the dynasty in 9 CE, China had eighty-three commanderies and twenty kingdoms. While some of this expansion came from the accretion of more territories, most was the result of a political strategy of reapportionment. The Han state was subdivided into 1,587 prefectures administered by specially trained scholar-officials. This new class of bureaucrats, which contributed immensely to the stability of the Chinese state, came to power through a system of meritocracy, which was formalized in the seventh century CE under the short-lived Sui dynasty. After sufficient years of studying Confucian texts and legal precedents, anyone in China, even the sons of the poor, could apply to take the qualifying examinations and, if they passed, enter the administrative corps of scholar-officials.

During the Han dynasty, Chang'an's population grew to 250,000. Its 22.7 km (13 miles) of walls enclosed about twice the area of Rome. As specified by the *wangcheng* diagram, three gates punctuated the walls in each of the four directions. The main thoroughfare, which extended from the central southern gate, had the dimensions of a modern six-lane highway, stretching 50 m (164 ft) across. It ran straight north for 5.5 km (3 miles) but diverged to the east before reaching the exit gate on the north. Contrary to the *wangcheng* model, the imperial palace did not occupy the precise center of the city but stood to the north. As in Shi Huangdi's capital, much of the space inside the walls of Chang'an was occupied by walled palace compounds, with the Changle and Weiyang Palaces in the southeast and southwest quadrants constructed before the walls of the city. The expansionist Emperor Wudi (r. 140–87 BCE) added two later palaces in the northeast and northwest, plus the Jianzhang Palace directly outside the western wall. Chang'an's two markets, following tradition, stood near the northwest gates (Fig. 5.2-5).

The Weiyang Palace enclave, in the southwest quadrant of Han Chang'an, stretched about 2 km (1.2 miles) per side, considerably larger than Nero's estate in Rome. It contained over forty halls, six hills, thirteen ponds, and a hundred residential pavilions. The traditional method of establishing distinction for a great palace was not to increase its size but to elevate its base. The principal hall at Weiyang Palace stood on a rammed-earth platform that rose 15 m (49 ft) above the plain.

RELIGION, PHILOSOPHY, FOLKLORE

Confucianism and Daoism: Order and Indirect Access

During the fifth century BCE, contemporary with the great cultural awakening in Greece, China produced two major philosophical schools: Confucianism and Daoism. The Chinese philosopher Confucius (ca. 551–479 BCE) exerted a profound impact on the order of the Chinese state, community, and family. Confucian texts advocated the creation of an orthodox ritual order for the world, emphasizing the importance of social hierarchy, respect for elders, and subordination of women. The fixed order of urban space in the *wangcheng* diagram corresponded to the Confucian notion of rigid hierarchies. Confucius often phrased his moral precepts in an indirect manner, such as his Chinese version of what Christians call the Golden Rule: "Do not do to others what you would not like to have happen to yourself."

The other great Chinese system of philosophy, Daoism, grew into a cult-like movement based on the study of Laozi. The aphorisms associated with Laozi, known as *Dao*, or "the Way," were even more indirect than those of Confucius and often quite challenging, such as "being originates in non-being." The basic theory that everything exists in relation to its necessary opposite was captured in the *taijitu*, the traditional yin-yang emblem, a reversed *S* shape in a circle in which a black *yin* zone sat in opposition to a white *yang* zone, with dots of the opposing color in each. While scholar-officials frequently cited Confucius to justify their strategies of intervention in maintaining order, Laozi's maxims corresponded to a more passive, indirect practice. Daoism had a strong impact on Chinese geomancy, known as *feng shui* ("wind and water"), which recommended avoiding an axis and seeking an oppositional relationship between water elements and mountains.

CULTURE, SOCIETY, GENDER

Chinese Pyramids

The burial of Han emperors followed the example set by Shi Huangdi. Emperor Gaozu and his wife Empress Lu were buried in a pair of tumulus pyramids, his 32.5 m (107 ft) high, hers slightly lower. Thick walls and sets of triple gates like those to the city enclosed their funerary park. The axial approach, lined with apotropaic sculptures, served as the prototype for the "spirit path" conventionally used for the tombs of emperors and important officials during the Han dynasty. Each of the seven successors of Gaozu constructed a similar funerary park and tumulus, which like the Egyptian pyramids usually included a town for the tomb workers organized on an orthogonal plan. The state forced members of rich and powerful families to move to these Chinese funerary towns as a form of political control. The funeral towns eventually grew into complete urban systems with shops, offices, and artisans, housing as many as 50,000 inhabitants.

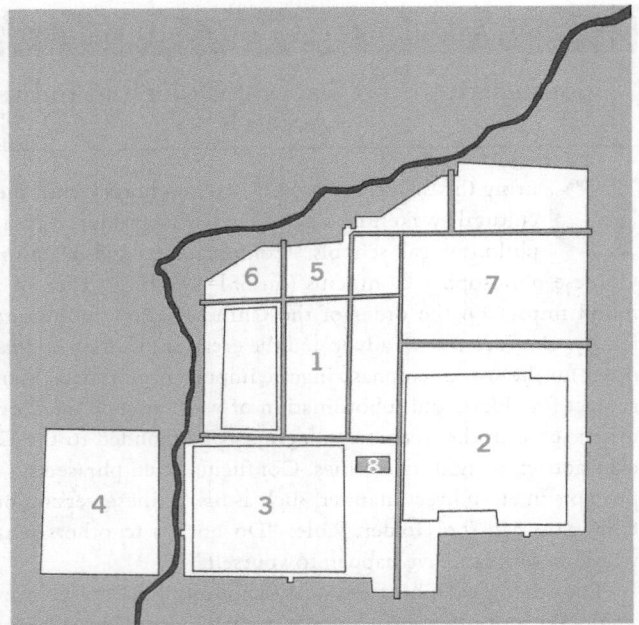

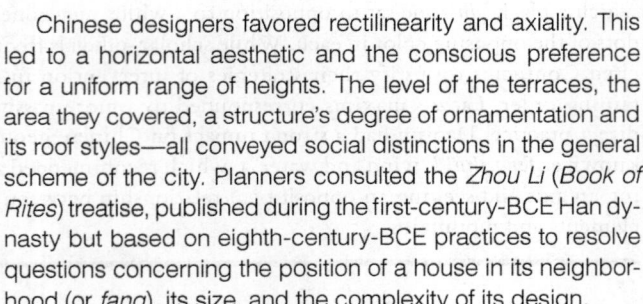

Figure 5.2-5 Chang'an, China. Hypothetical diagram of the Han capital, 200 BCE: (1) North Palace; (2) Changle Palace; (3) Weiyang Palace; (4) Jianzhang Palace (outside walls); (5) eastern market; (6) western market; (7) Mingguang Palace; (8) arsenal.

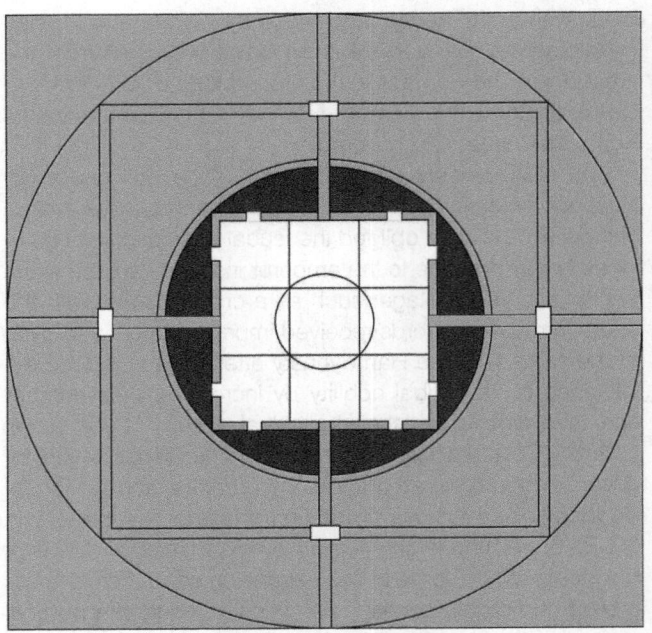

Figure 5.2-6 Chang'an, China. Plan of the Mingtang Temple, 100 BCE.

Chinese designers favored rectilinearity and axiality. This led to a horizontal aesthetic and the conscious preference for a uniform range of heights. The level of the terraces, the area they covered, a structure's degree of ornamentation and its roof styles—all conveyed social distinctions in the general scheme of the city. Planners consulted the *Zhou Li* (*Book of Rites*) treatise, published during the first-century-BCE Han dynasty but based on eighth-century-BCE practices to resolve questions concerning the position of a house in its neighborhood (or *fang*), its size, and the complexity of its design.

The principal religious focus of Chang'an, the Mingtang Temple, stood in the southern suburbs. Chinese religion did not ascribe to a creation myth but considered the world as an organic whole that interacted with such gods as the Queen Mother of the West and the King Father of the East. It also emphasized homage to family ancestors and natural phenomena such as the equinoxes. The emperor played a unique role in this system as the instrument of the Mandate of Heaven, obliged to perform rituals to secure the well-being of the state. At crucial moments during the year he alone came to the Mingtang Temple to make sacrifices connected to fertility and harvests. The layout of the temple focused on the cosmological role of the emperor as the conduit of divine grace. The square temple rose on a circular terrace of pounded earth 60 m (197 ft) wide, surrounded by a square colonnade that in turn was enclosed by an outer circular platform and a square moat (Fig. 5.2-6). The repetition of circles and squares came from the basic symbols of the earth as a square and the heavens as a circle. The three-level structure in the center had protruding porches on all four sides. The emperor moved from hall to hall according to the ritual calendar, his itinerary geared to nature's seasonal

changes. As the "son of heaven" he represented the pivot of the universe for millions of subjects in an expanding empire.

After the twelve-year interval of Wang Mang's Xin dynasty concluded with the reassertion of the Han dynasty in 25 CE, the capital was relocated to Luoyang, following the precedent of the Zhou dynasty. Han Chang'an faded into oblivion through sacking and neglect. Luoyang became the center of the empire for the next two centuries. It covered about half the area of Chang'an. An elevated walkway, like the legendary secret passages of Shi Huangdi, connected the two imperial palaces, Beigong in the north and Nangong in the south. While the site of the imperial capital changed, the cycle of rebuilding remained constant.

Chinese Domestic Architecture: Growth by Addition

The Chinese character for "house" (*jia*) shows a pig under a roof, an allusion to agricultural well-being. The house, whether humble or princely, had as its focus an inner courtyard isolated by a walled envelope that surrounded the compound (Fig. 5.2-7). In some cases freestanding pavilions stood within the courtyard, arranged according to the status of the occupants, with the elders situated in the most prominent central hall.

One entered the Chinese courtyard house, or **siheyuan**, through a front gate that set the domestic boundary for peddlers or strangers. An independent roof framed the entry, and a wall behind it blocked the direct view into the interior. The approach from the side conformed to the *feng shui* preference for indirect access (Fig. 5.2-8). The Chinese believed that this layout helped to retain the positive energy within the *siheyuan* while keeping negative energy at bay. The

Figure 5.2-7 Ancient China. View of a typical *siheyuan* courtyard house.

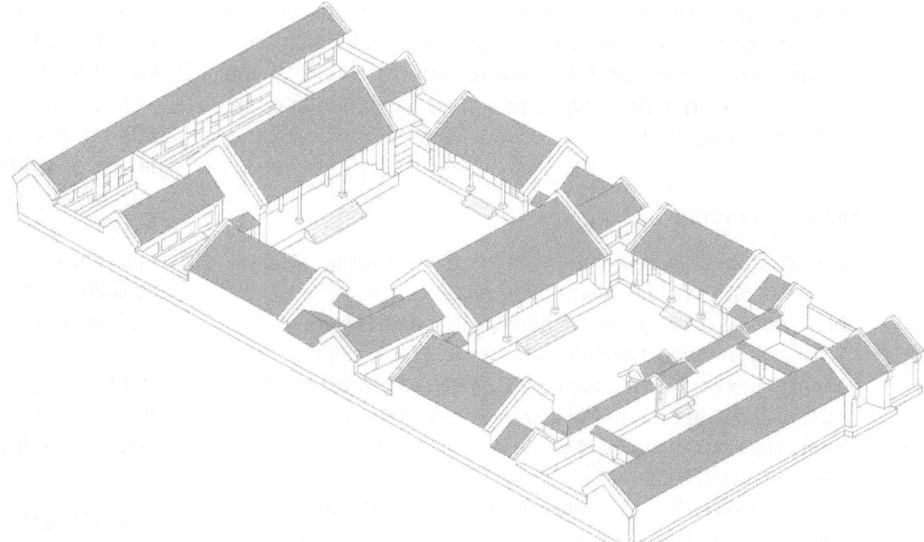

siheyuan resembled the Roman *domus* in its succession of courts but differed greatly from its counterpart in conception: the Chinese assembled many units around a void through a process of addition, while the Romans conceived of the house as a whole from which they subtracted the voids.

Movement through the *siheyuan* followed an oblique path. This screened the intimate world of the house from the bustle of the streets to protect the internal rules of behavior and allow the spatial sequences to unfold according to a protocol of "graduated privacy." Friends and relatives were received in the porches of the central room (the *ming*), which sat on its own platform a little higher than the rest of the house. Beyond this area, the family reserved rooms for the women and the daily routines of family life. The etiquette of the royal palace, with its many courtyards and pavilions, differed only by degree and scale.

A Han dynasty treatise describes in great detail the protocol of a visit to a courtyard house. The overriding duty of the participants was "to humble oneself in order to honor others."

> At each gateway the host must respectfully urge his guest in until they arrive at the door of the inner courtyard. The host excuses himself to enter first so that he may place the mats personally. . . . The host enters the doorway and . . . proceeds to the eastern stairway, while the guest proceeds to the west. . . . As the host lifts his left foot to ascend the eastern stairs, the guest lifts his left foot to ascend the western stairs.

Figure 5.2-8 Pingyao, China. The courtyard in a *siheyuan* house.

The life expectancy of Chinese buildings, public or private, rarely exceeded a generation. Their materials of rammed earth, mud brick, and timber decayed quickly. Successive generations salvaged and reused materials from the obsolete buildings as they rebuilt. The architectural plans rarely varied: a long and shallow rectangle divided into *jian* bays, with pillars to support a superstructure of ceiling beams and a truss roof. The skeletal armature between ceiling and roof consisted of progressively shorter lateral beams and a vertical spine at the top that held up the ridge. The walls served merely as spatial dividers between **point-loaded** frames.

All basic Chinese roof types were already present in the Han period: the gable roof with or without overhangs, the hipped roof of four slopes, and the roof known as "nine spines." The upturned-eaves style, which became so characteristically Chinese, postdates Han practice, but already roofs were being built with a change of pitch halfway up, as if they had given way under their own weight. Chinese builders covered their roofs with cupped terra-cotta tiles, not so different from those used in the Mediterranean, except that they terminated at the eaves with inscribed cylinders. The roof dominated Chinese buildings, giving them style.

The Chinese built in earth and wood out of choice, not necessity. Their skill at masonry is apparent in their stone bridges, defensive works, and tombs. Eastern Han tombs, for example, exploited a full array of vaulting techniques from slabs to corbels to true arches. But the majority of Chinese buildings avoided masonry. Building and rebuilding, while always repeating the same type of structure, served as an allegory of the life cycle of each generation. Chinese architecture represented an eternal return, in which the faithful repetition of archetypes prevailed over changing historical circumstances.

Further Reading

Boyd, Andrew. *Chinese Architecture and Town Planning, 1500 BC–AD 1911*. London: Alec Tiranti, 1962.

Ebrey, Patricia Buckley. *The Cambridge Illustrated History of China*. Cambridge: Cambridge University Press, 1996.

Jullien, François. *Detour and Access: Strategies of Meaning in China and Greece*. New York: Zone Books, 2000.

Knapp, Ronald. *China's Old Dwellings*. Honolulu: University of Hawai'i Press, 2000.

Liu, Laurence G. *Chinese Architecture*. New York: Rizzoli, 1989.

Loewe, Michael. *Everyday Life in Early Imperial China during the Han Period, 202 BC–AD 220*. London: Batsford, 1968.

Steinhardt, Nancy S. *Chinese Imperial City Planning*. Honolulu: University of Hawai'i Press, 1990.

———, ed. *Chinese Architecture*. New Haven, CT: Yale University Press, 2002.

Wood, Frances. *China's First Emperor and His Terracotta Warriors*. New York: St. Martin's Press, 2008.

5.3 ANCIENT MEXICO
Pyramids and Sacrifice

Most cultures designed structures using the grid, an idea that seems rooted in human consciousness. Ancient societies in the Western Hemisphere produced grid patterns, as well as pyramids and axial streets, in apparent isolation from the influence of Asia and Europe. During the same period of urban expansion in Han China and the Roman Empire, several cities in ancient Mexico came to rival their complexity and formal order. At Teotihuacán, the

Pyramid of the Sun rose as majestically as the great ziggurats of Southwest Asia, while the boulevard at its base revealed a geometric plan as orderly as that of Chang'an.

The ancient cultures in the Americas were markedly different from those of Europe and Asia. They left little evidence of written language until the second century BCE and lacked primary technological devices such as the wheel and metal tools. Their great urban centers served as stages for the continual performance of religious rituals, including human sacrifice. While the Romans contrived a total architectural setting for the control of a secular society, the ancient Mexicans produced a theocratic environment, commanding the behavior and respect of neighbors and pilgrims. Later cultures remembered the compelling ritual order of Teotihuacán as "the home of the gods."

Early Mesoamerican Cultures: The Space of Ceremonies

The cultures of ancient Mexico (part of what is usually called "Mesoamerica"), though less technologically equipped than the Romans or the Chinese, tended to build more imposing monumental spaces. Cities such as Monte Albán and Teotihuacán produced towering pyramids and carefully composed platform enclosures, demonstrating that intelligence in design usually transcends the means of its production.

Three cultures of ancient Mexico attained high architectural expression during the period from 200 BCE to 300 CE: the Teotihuacános in the Valley of Mexico, the Zapotecs centered at Monte Albán in the Valley of Oaxaca, and the early Mayans (see Section 7.3) in the Guatemalan rain forests (Fig. 5.3-1). All of these cultures, despite their differing languages, honored their ritual and artistic origins in the earlier culture of the Olmec ("the rubber people"), a society centered on the swampy Gulf Coast region near Vera Cruz. Their religion honored various male, female, and animal gods, revered as the bringers of maize, and included among its rituals a ball game after which the losers on occasion were sacrificed and eaten.

The first surviving monumental Olmec center, now called San Lorenzo, dates to around 1500 BCE and reveals a gigantic earthwork, an artificial 1 km (0.6 miles) long plateau built of clay and rubble. This platform served as a ceremonial center for the dozens of neighboring towns and villages subject to the Olmec kings. Carved thrones and ten colossal heads (Fig. 5.3-2), the largest nearly 3 m (10 ft) high, lined the pathway leading to the seat of dynastic authority.

TIME LINE

 ca. 1500–1200 BCE

Olmec civilization at San Lorenzo

 ca. 500–200 BCE

Zapotec peoples build monuments of Monte Albán

Olmec civilization at La Venta
ca. 900 BCE–400 BCE

Figure 5.3-1 Ancient Mexico, 1200 BCE–200 CE.

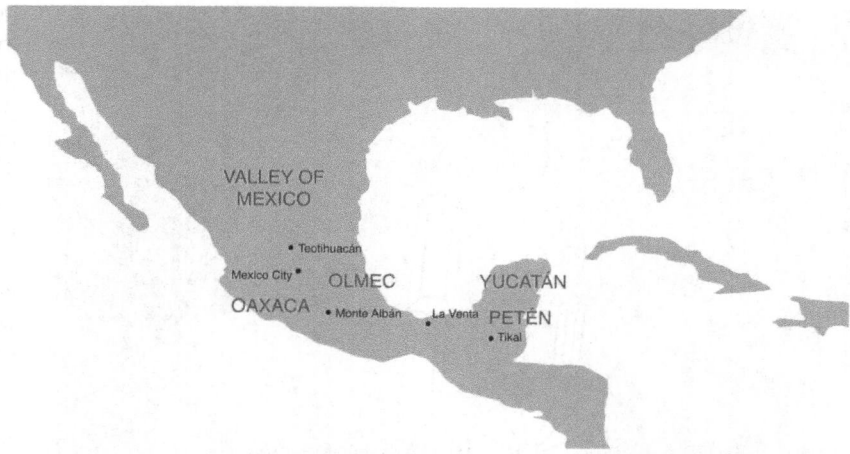

Artisans used obsidian blades to chisel these colossal portraits of Olmec rulers from solid blocks of basalt and then transported them more than 80 km (50 miles) on rafts, from which they were rolled up to the platform. At the same time that violent changes occurred in the Mediterranean around 1200 BCE, San Lorenzo underwent violent destruction. Subsequent erosion of this wetland area removed most of the traces of the city's design.

La Venta, 90 km (55 miles) east of San Lorenzo, grew to prominence around 900 BCE as a second ritual city ruled by Olmec kings. Like the earlier site, its designers decorated the ceremonial precinct with giant stone heads and thrones. The major artifacts fit a clear geometric pattern (Fig. 5.3-3) dominated by a radially composed pyramid, which sat on a square base, 128 × 114 m (420 × 374 ft), and rose to 30 m (98 ft). Made of mud bricks that have dissolved into a mound, the exact shape of the great pile can only be guessed. A set of parallel mounds beyond this area seems to have served as the arena for the ritual ball game, a sport played throughout Mesoamerica. The axis at La Venta extended with supplementary altars to a total length of 1.5 km (1 mile).

La Venta also fell to invaders some time around 400 BCE. The Olmec culture transmitted to neighboring cultures the crafts of carving basalt and jade with obsidian tools, the art of fresco painting, methods of paving with mosaics, and the design of underground tombs. Above all, the designers of La Venta introduced the compositional practice of creating spaces from raised terraces while imposing axial alignment on orthogonal elements.

The Zapotecs, about 300 km (180 miles) to the south at Monte Albán, elaborated the Olmec system of order, framing a grand elevated plaza with stepped platforms (Fig. 5.3-4a,b). In this drier climate they had the advantage of working with more permanent materials. Perched on a 400 m (1,312 ft) acropolis that dominated the Oaxaca Valley, the Zapotec designers created monumental terraces and elaborate tombs beginning in the fifth century BCE. Their culture continued for

Figure 5.3-2 San Lorenzo, Mexico. Olmec head, 1200 BCE.

Pyramid of the Sun built in Teotihuacán

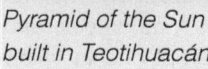
▲ **ca. 150** BCE

▼ **100** CE

Temple of the Feathered Serpent built at Teotihuacán

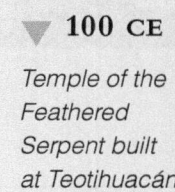

Pyramid of the Moon rebuilt in Teotihuacán

▲ **ca. 200** CE

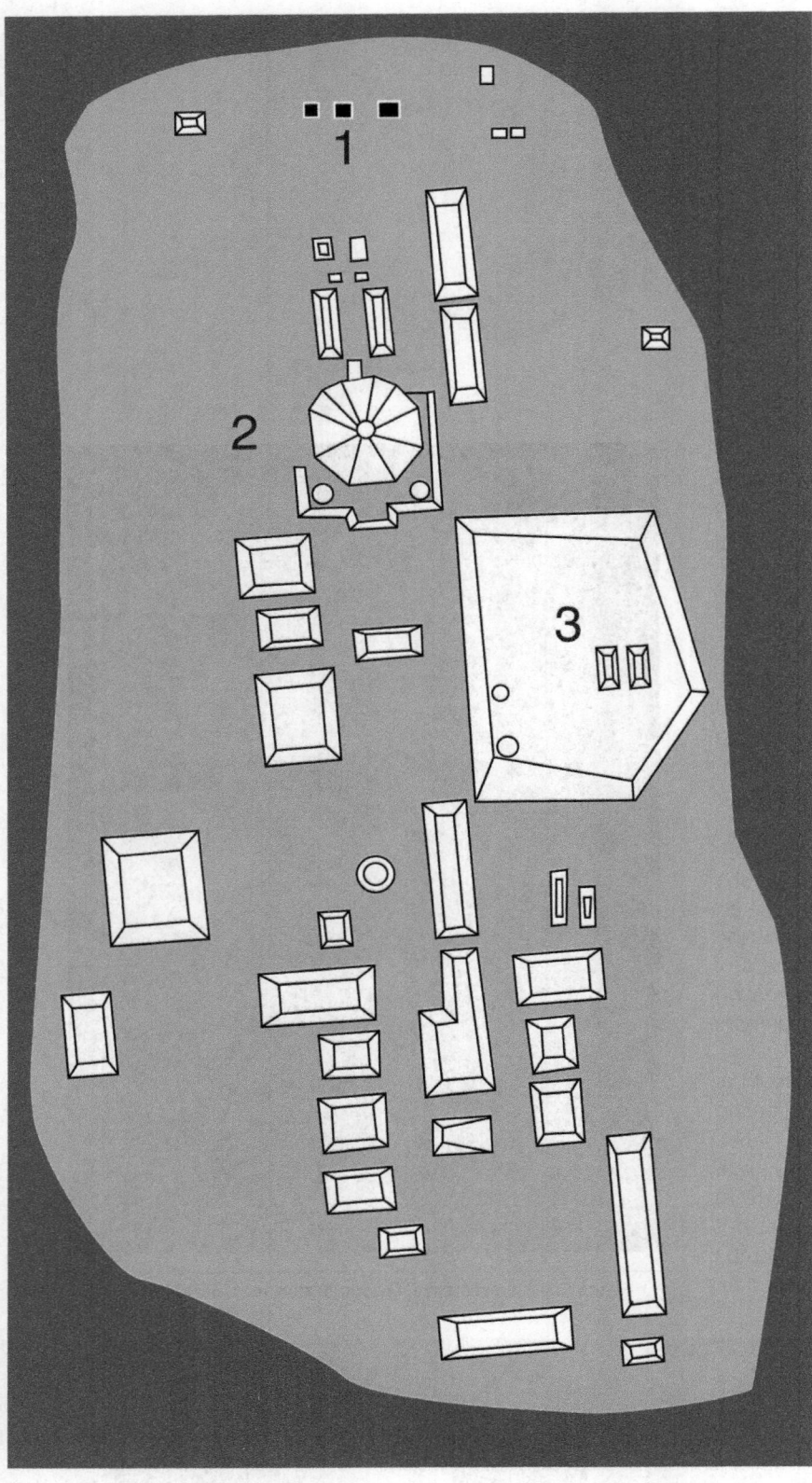

Figure 5.3-3 La Venta (Mexico). Plan of city, 400 BCE. (1) Placement of colossal heads; (2) radial pyramid; (3) terrace with ball court.

nearly a millennium. For their principal ritual site they leveled the top of the hill at Monte Albán and ringed it with a series of stepped platforms. All of their temples focused on an immense internal plaza in the shape of a near perfect rectangle, 100 × 250 m (328 × 820 ft), about the same size as the open space of Trajan's Forum in Rome. In the center stood an oblong, three-part sanctuary with steps on all sides. To its south lay the only building in the complex that broke with strict orthogonal alignment, an arrowhead-shaped bastion rotated 45° to the central axis. Its shape and alignment suggest use as an astronomical observatory. An *I*-shaped ball court for the ritual game fit into the series of platforms on the western flank of the plaza. Steep slopes rose on both sides of the play space to deflect the rubber ball. Like the amphitheaters in Roman cities, the ball courts gave shape to the Mesoamerican city and performed a similar function of ritualizing violent conflict.

The monumental buildings of ancient Mexico embodied the cyclical nature of political power. Rather than constantly rebuilding their structures as the Chinese did, however, they added successive layers over them. At Monte Albán the platform temples and pyramids are layered like the skin of an onion. Each ruler or priesthood fulfilled the community's religious duty by building a fresh layer over the cult structures as a symbol of renewal.

The acropolis of Monte Albán consisted almost entirely of stairways and altars, closer in spirit to Sumerian environments than to those of Rome or China. The ancient cities of Mesoamerica used the altars and the ball courts as places of tribute to display a hierarchical system of authority based on military and cultural primacy. Their military battles were probably less violent than those fought elsewhere in the world since the chief objective of warfare was to take hostages, who were then publicly sacrificed to be eaten. The theatrical arrangement of altars served as gruesome stages for butchering the captives. The hearts that were cut out of the living victims were meant to satisfy the gods and strengthen the victors. As in Rome, where city dwellers gathered to watch the violent spectacles in the Colosseum, the ritual bloodshed in Mesoamerica served as an instrument of social control.

Teotihuacán: City of the Gods

Architecture alone cannot determine human behavior, but in some cases, grand scale and articulated directionality prompt one to follow

Figure 5.3-4 Monte Albán (Mexico). (a) Aerial view. (b) The *I*-shaped ball court at center left side.

the dictates of buildings. Teotihuacán, the largest ancient city in Mexico and its prime ritual center, had such an effect. Confronted with its grand axis, one had little choice but to pursue the pyramids at its end. The pyramids marked the axis mundi, the cosmic center of a community's known world. They also invariably signified domination: the thousands of tons of material that comprised them required the labor of hordes of construction workers. Their human-made mass seemed greater than nature and thus the work of the gods.

The urbanism of Teotihuacán rivaled the grandest ensembles of the ancient Mediterranean. Located in the high, semiarid Valley of Mexico, the city became the region's

pilgrimage center and premier market town. That it survived for nearly a millennium without need of defensive structures indicates the respect it commanded as a sacred place. From about 100 BCE to 200 CE Teotihuacán produced its two great pyramids, hundreds of platform temples, and 2,000 palaces. The city's grid spread about 30 km^2 (11.5 miles^2), exceeding both Rome and Chang'an in area.

The central axis of Teotihuacán was a sunken, 50 m (164 ft) wide avenue, now called *Miccaotli*, or "Avenue of the Dead" (Fig. 5.3-5a). Over 6 km (3.5 miles) in length, it surpassed the axial thoroughfares of all other preindustrial cultures. The avenue runs about 15° east of true north,

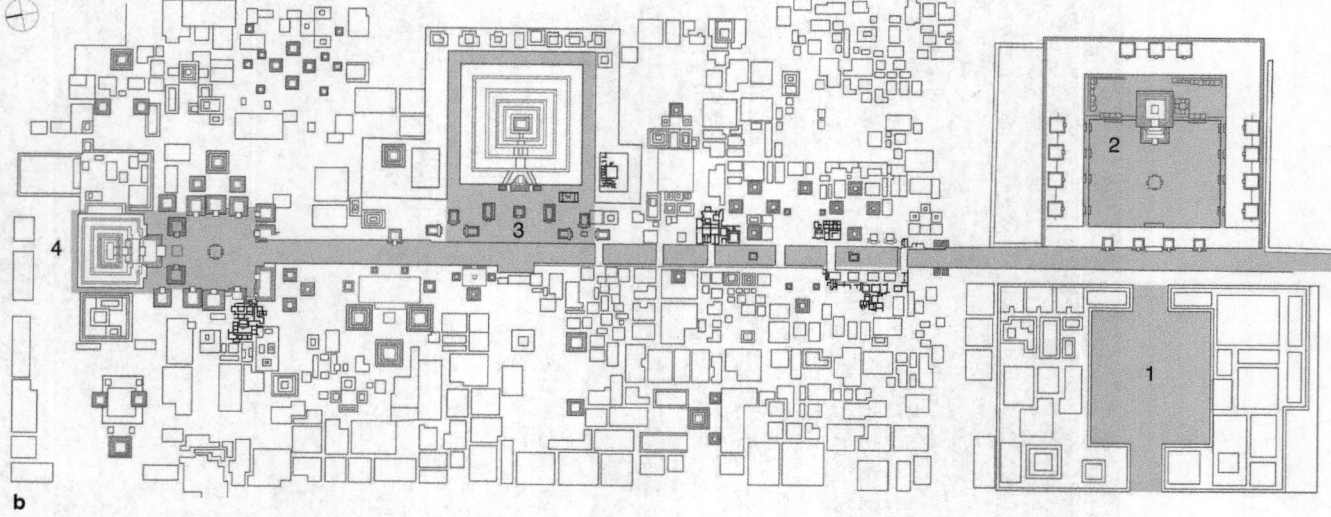

Figure 5.3-5 Teotihuacán (Mexico). (a) Avenue of the Dead, ca. 100 BCE–200 CE. (b) Plan: (1) market; (2) Temple of the Feathered Serpent compound; (3) Pyramid of the Sun; (4) Pyramid of the Moon (after René Millon).

intended to align with the extinct volcano of Cerro Gordo, whose springs provided a major source of water to the region's inhabitants. The Teotihuacános planned the great axis to connect the temple district of the two pyramids, which dates from the first century BCE, to the crossroad, where two monumental enclosures were constructed on either side of the axis about a century later (Fig 5.3-5b). The avenue had no southern terminus, as if it could extend infinitely toward the southern highlands of Guerrero.

The great compound at the crossroad served as a marketplace and administrative center where pilgrims from areas such as Monte Albán and the Mayan country came to trade. Across from it rose a more imposing compound, 400 m (1,280 ft) per side. This so-called *ciudadela* (citadel) probably functioned as a royal palace during the brief period of monarchical rule in the first century CE. A high terrace rings the citadel site, with four temples lining the top of each side like guard towers. A broad set of stairs served as the sole entry from the Avenue of the Dead. The citadel court, about three times the area of Trajan's Forum, could contain an assembly of the entire population, which at its height probably numbered 100,000.

The Temple of the Feathered Serpent, a small pyramid built around 100 CE, dominated the central axis of the *ciudadela*. *Talud-tableros*, horizontal panels cantilevered over a battered base, articulated its terraces. Inside the frame of the **tablero** were exquisite reliefs of toothy feathered serpents and scaly, goggle-eyed creatures (Fig. 5.3-6). The pyramid probably served as a dynastic mausoleum. It covered the remains of more than eighty soldiers who were ritually sacrificed for a king's funeral.

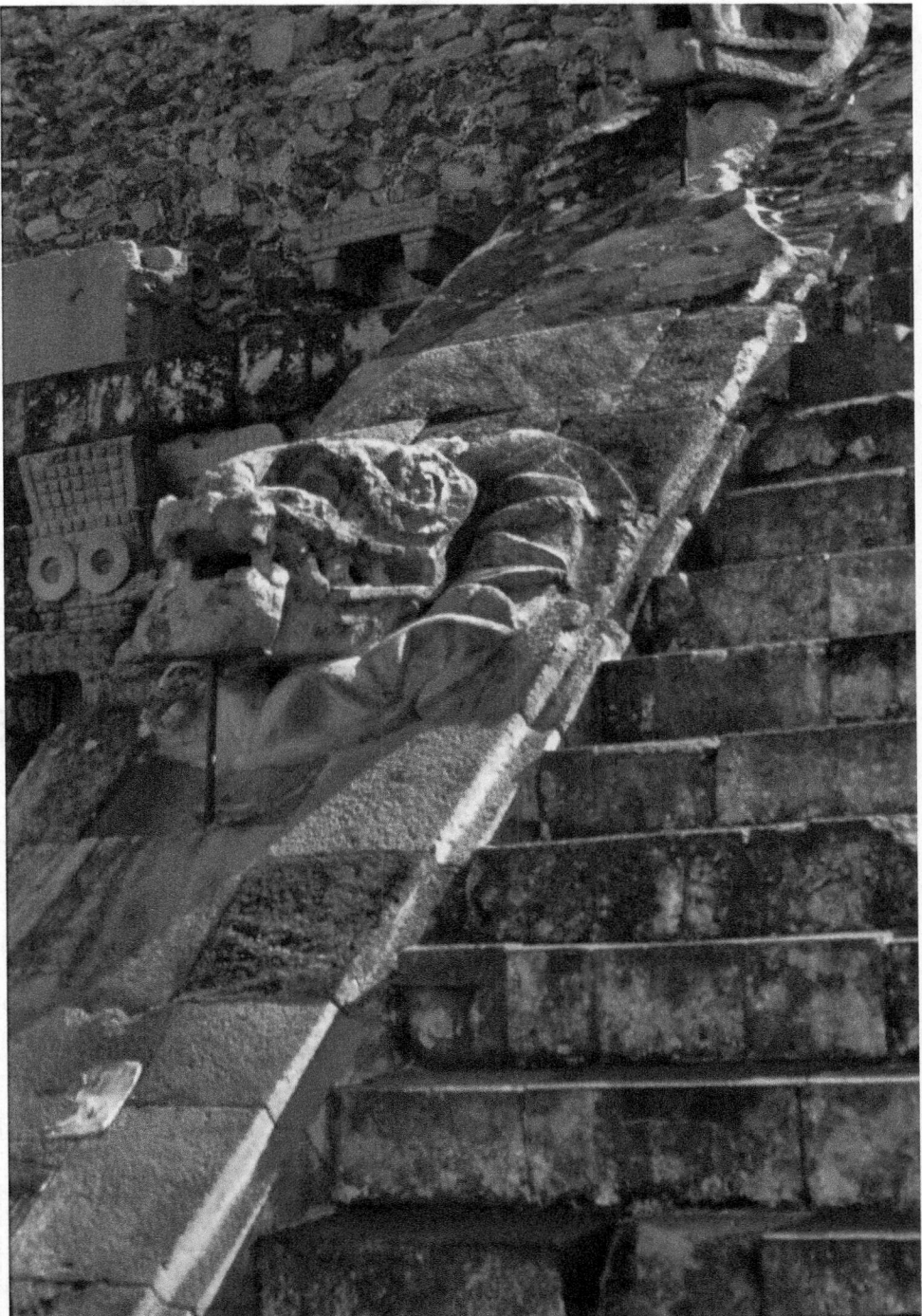

Figure 5.3-6 Teotihuacán (Mexico). Temple of the Feathered Serpent, detail, 100 CE.

While Teotihuacán had no walls, the Temple of the Feathered Serpent confirms the presence of military conflicts.

The central crossroad divided Teotihuacán into four distinct quarters. These were then broken into what the Spanish later called **barrios**, or neighborhoods, each specializing in a dominant craft or activity. Shops for obsidian, essential to the other crafts in the absence of metal tools, were quite common. Aside from potters, painters, masons, and merchants, the city maintained a sizable priesthood, which occupied gracious courtyard buildings in the vicinity of the temple precincts. While all of the blocks of the city were arranged orthogonally, they did not fit perfectly onto a grid. The blocks fit instead together like a mosaic made of differently sized pieces. Thus, only the *Miccaotli* and the cross-axis at the citadel were straight, while the side streets were narrow and crooked lines.

The blocks of Teotihuacán were organized as self-contained enclosures. They resembled palaces but contained apartments for as many as 100 inhabitants per block. Both the commoners and the wealthy classes lived in these apartment blocks, single-story structures built with stone posts, wooden beams, and mud-brick walls. As in Mesopotamia, the rooms lacked windows, taking light from inner courts. On the east side of the central **patio** of most blocks stood a small stepped altar. The more than 2,000 apartment blocks in Teotihuacán ranged in size from 400 to 7,000 m² (1,312 to 22,966 ft²). This exceptional collective dwelling type had no precedent outside of Mesoamerica. Many scholars assume it served a communitarian social order run by a theocratic priesthood. The hundreds of altars and temples scattered throughout the city indicate the religious importance of Teotihuacán as one of the greatest pilgrimage destinations on earth.

The scale and position of the two great pyramids also convey the religious primacy of Teotihuacán. One occupied the end of the axis, and the other sat to its side midway from the crossing. Platform temples covered both sides of the procession route and spread throughout the city. More than twenty of the urban altars appeared in triadic clusters. Pilgrims walking along the gently rising processional avenue would have encountered a series of six mysterious "locks," stepped barriers 5 m (16 ft) high, which would have greatly impeded their progress. The five resulting depressions served as protective filters to slow down the crowds before they reached the sacred precinct. Their dimensions, roughly the same size as the ball court at Monte Albán, suggest that these hollow spaces may have served that quasi-religious sport. All Mesoamerican cities except Teotihuacán had at least one *I*-shaped ball court, and the stepped flanks of the "locks" would have served the game well.

The final "lock" corresponded to the city's oldest and largest monument, the Pyramid of the Sun (Fig. 5.3-7). This great pile rose perpendicular to the grand axis, approached through a forecourt with a triad of altars. Like Shi Huangdi's pyramid in China, it was larger in area than the Pyramid of Khufu at Giza but less than half the height. Begun in the second century BCE, it covered a cave that extends 100 m (320 ft) under its mass, a natural phenomenon revered as the origin of the world. The pyramid faced 15° north of west, coinciding with the setting sun on June 21, the solstice day of its zenith passage. A monument both to the origins of the earth and to the cosmic movements of the sky, its coordinates informed the orientation of the rest of the city's orthogonal blocks.

CONSTRUCTION, TECHNOLOGY, THEORY

The *Talud-Tablero*

The **talud-tablero** was a horizontal motif that became as pervasive in ancient Mexican architecture as the classical column in the Greco-Roman world. It consisted of a *tablero*, a framed horizontal casement, which cantilevered over a battered *talud* base. Artists filled in the frame of the *tablero* with either painted panels on plaster or relief sculptures.

The use of burnt lime as a bonding agent in many of Teotihuacán's structures accounts for the survival of some of the magnificent jutting terraces made of *talud-tableros*. While the type may have originated elsewhere, it came to indicate the supremacy of Teotihuacán's religious influence when reproduced in places such as Monte Albán and Tikal.

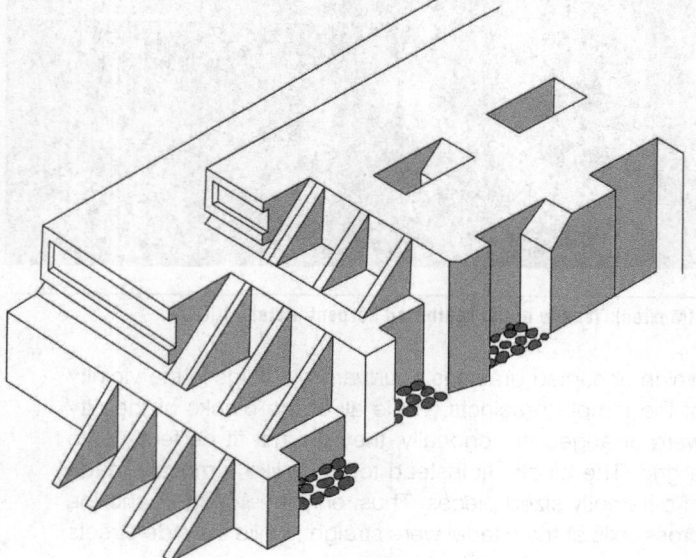

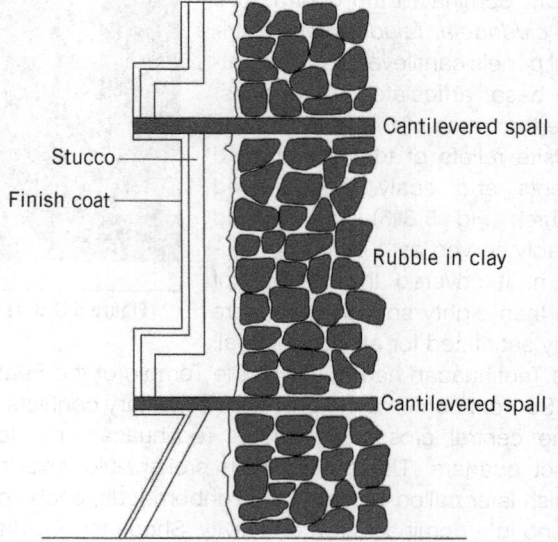

Stucco

Finish coat

Cantilevered spall

Rubble in clay

Cantilevered spall

Talud-tablero, cutaway section (after Kubler), found at Teotihuacán, ca. 100 BCE–200 CE.

Figure 5.3-7 Teotihuacán (Mexico). View to the Sun Pyramid, ca. 100 CE.

Figure 5.3-8 Teotihuacán (Mexico). Moon Pyramid, 200–400 CE.

The builders of the Pyramid of the Sun used construction techniques similar to those used to build the ziggurats in Mesopotamia (see Section 2.1), stacking it in four stages with horizontal layers of clay. They clad it with rough-hewn stones. For the second great pile, the Moon Pyramid at the end of the axis, they employed a new technique of construction, building a core of vertical tufa piers with the shafts between them filled with rubble. They buttressed this core with fin walls, which determined the slope of the main terraces. At the pyramid's base a later generation built an access platform on five terraces articulated with *talud-tableros*. The broad axial staircase of the pyramid continued up three more stages to the summit, aligned with the axis of the Avenue of the Dead.

The ceremonial landscape of Teotihuacán climaxed at the base of the Moon Pyramid (Fig. 5.3-8). The powerful members of the priesthood made their sacrifices here in a linked series of platform temples enclosing a square plaza with the same dimensions as the base of the Moon Pyramid. Next to the bottom of the stair stood a special temple surrounded by a low parapet and entered from a single breach on the west. The nine altars around its perimeter focused radially on a central altar. Considering the numerous representations of hearts skewered by daggers found in the paintings and pottery of Teotihuacán, it seems likely that this open-air sanctuary served as a superb operating theater to carve up the victims of the "heart" ceremony.

Teotihuacán's succession of raised platforms along the Avenue of the Dead would have provided a dizzying rhythm for processions toward this plaza. The strenuous hike to the ritual center in unrelieved sunlight would have required a strong physical commitment. The alignment of the axis and the looming masses of the pyramids put the pilgrim in the midst of an immense cosmic model, where mortals came to sacrifice, or perhaps to be sacrificed, in the quest to find their place in the universe.

Further Reading

Berlo, Janet Catherine, ed. *Art, Ideology, and the City of Teotihuacan.* Washington, D.C.: Dumbarton Oaks, 1992.

Berrin, Kathleen, and Esther Pasztory, eds. *Teotihuacan: Art from the City of the Gods.* London: Thames & Hudson, 1993.

Coe, Michael D., and Rex Koontz. *Mexico: From the Olmecs to the Aztecs.* London: Thames & Hudson, 2002.

Diehl, Richard A. *The Olmecs: America's First Civilization.* London: Thames & Hudson, 2004.

Heyden, Doris, and Paul Gendrop. *Pre-Columbian Architecture of Mesoamerica.* New York: Electa/Rizzoli, 1988.

Knight, Alan. *Mexico: From the Beginning to the Spanish Conquest.* Cambridge: Cambridge University Press, 2002.

Kubler, George. *The Art and Architecture of Ancient America.* New Haven, CT: Yale University Press, 1990.

Millon, Rene. *The Teotihuacan Map.* Austin: University of Texas Press, 1973.

Pasztory, Esther. *Teotihuacan: An Experiment in Living.* Norman: University of Oklahoma Press, 1997.

↗ Visit the free website **www.oup.com/us/ingersoll** to view chapter outlines and study questions; Google Maps showing the location of key sites; links to UNESCO World Heritage Sites; and essays on topics that cross time and culture.

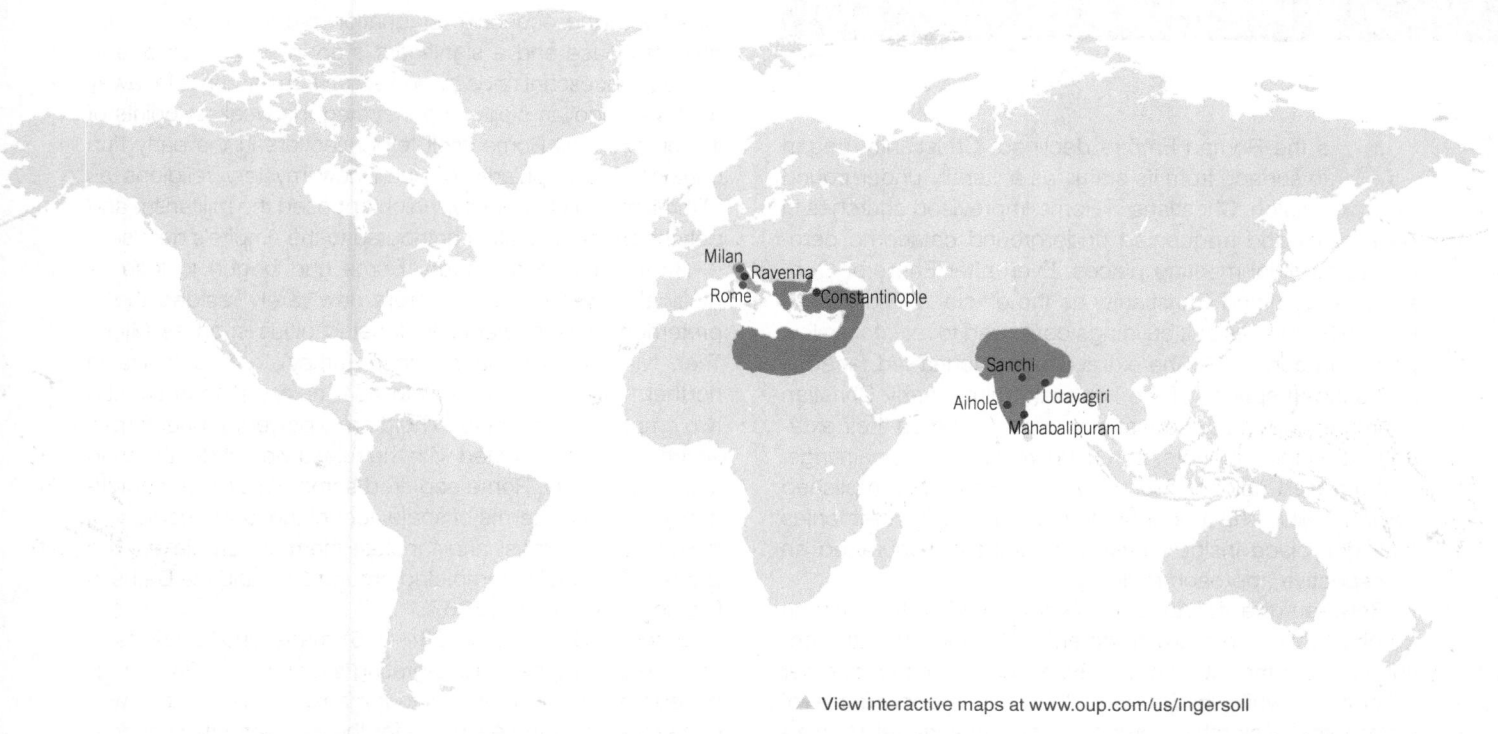

▲ View interactive maps at www.oup.com/us/ingersoll

During the fourth century CE, the Roman Empire broke into two and began a long process of disintegration. The state adopted the Christian religion, once confined to the poor, and the church took up the slack as the political and military structures of Roman society began to disappear. Constantine, the first Christian emperor, built churches and baptisteries wherever he held court. Sensing the weakened social fabric in the west, he moved the political center from Rome to Constantinople, which became the fulcrum of the Byzantine Empire. The great church of Hagia Sophia, rebuilt in the sixth century, crowned the tip of the city's peninsula with a new type of monument that focused attention on the interior. The infiltration of outsiders into the empire's western territories resulted in tentative barbarian kingdoms, all of which corrupted the language and practices of the Romans while embracing the Christian faith. In India during the same period, the Gupta dynasty attempted to revive the imperial reach of the Mauryans. These rulers encouraged the construction of rock-cut cave structures for Buddhist and Hindu halls and monasteries, leading to a building technique of carving out space from piles of stone. A generation after the Huns invaded Western Europe, they swept across Gupta India, destabilizing political control and outlawing the Buddhist religion.

6.1 EARLY CHRISTIAN ITALY
The Inward Orientation of the Church

As the Roman Empire declined, Christianity began to surface from its status as a literally underground religion. Christians in Rome improvised churches in basements and frequented underground catacomb cemeteries as ritual meeting places. Even after Emperor Constantine promoted Christianity as the official religion of the Roman Empire, its cult buildings continued to maintain a low profile. In contrast to the extravagant colonnaded facades and shaped spaces of the imperial regime, early Christian churches appeared modest and unassuming on their exteriors. Only their interiors, brimming with mosaics, paintings, and marbled colonnades, showed signs of accomplished design skills. The frequent processions and ceremonies that took place inside Christian churches encouraged an introspective approach to design.

Between the fourth and sixth centuries the Roman Empire broke into many fragments. The eastern half continued under the rubric of the Byzantine Empire for another millennium, while in the west "barbarian" contingents of Ostrogoths, Visigoths, Lombards, and Franks set up warlord kingdoms. After driving out the Roman administrators from the European provinces of the empire, the invaders eventually adopted both Roman law and the Christian religion. Rome and Milan underwent alternating periods of brilliance and decline during the twilight of the Roman Empire. The papacy emerged as the most powerful institution in Rome and sponsored the last expressions of classical architecture in the great churches of the fifth century. In Milan the struggle between different interpretations of Christianity led to markedly different solutions for **church** architecture, always expressed most powerfully in the interior, where the congregations convened to demonstrate their faith.

The Advent of Constantine: The First Christian Emperor

The rise of Christianity coincided with the gradual dismantling of the Roman Empire. By the late second century the *Pax Romana* had begun to falter as a result of internal and external conflicts. The stability of the empire suffered from a weakened army, staffed mostly by foreign mercenaries, combined with the economic stagnation produced by a dwindling tax base and a significant drop in population due to plagues. Incessant raids by horsemen from lands as far away as the Mongolian steppes penetrated the weakest points of the empire until Rome itself fell to sackers in the early fifth century. The popularity of such new mystery religions as Mithraism and Christianity, which opposed the militarism and polytheism of the state, contributed to the empire's demise.

By the mid-third century Rome had begun to lose its political primacy. The emperors now rarely resided there, preferring more strategically located cities such as Milan, Trier, Nicomedia (modern Izmit, Turkey), and Salonika in northern Greece. From 235 to 284, no fewer than twenty-two emperors attempted to hold on to power for brief terms, which usually terminated with the ruler's violent death. Amid such uncertainty, Rome acquired some of its most magnificent buildings in terms of scale, technique, and decoration, including the largest and fanciest thermal complexes, the Baths of Caracalla, completed around 210, and the Baths of Diocletian, finished in 306.

Emperor Diocletian (r. 284–305) made drastic efforts to salvage the empire's disintegrating structure. In 294 he proposed the establishment of a four-man executive system, with one emperor for the east, one for the west, and two younger emperors for the Danube territories and the empire's Southwest Asian holdings. In theory, the two older tetrarchs would retire after ten-year terms to allow their younger alternates to take power. Diocletian dutifully retired in 305 to Spalato, or the "little palace," on the Dalmatian coast near his birthplace, modern Split, Croatia. Organized like a military *castrum* on a cross-axis inside a nearly perfect square set of walls, his palace had three entry gates on the west, north, and east sides flanked by octagonal guard towers. The southern elevation, accessed from a lower dock, overlooked the Adriatic Sea. Two intersecting streets divided the palace into quarters. They were lined with colonnades that carried a series of

▼ 294
Diocletian establishes the tetrarch system of four emperors, with two in the east and two in the west

Diocletian builds his retirement palace at Spalato

▲ 290s

▼ 300
Constantine rebuilds his father's capital of Trier, adding basilica

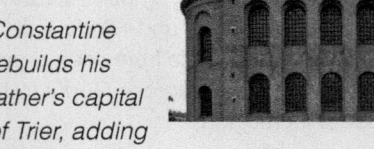

Constantine defeats Maxentius while carrying the Christian cross on his banners, takes Rome
▲ 312

arches instead of an entablature—one of Diocletian's many breaks from classical tradition. The north–south axis passed through an outdoor hall that terminated in a monumental gabled porch supported by four colossal columns. Diocletian's architects inserted an arch into the pediment between the two central columns, creating a **fastigium**, a stage-like space, for imperial appearances. This broken-pediment motif derived from the sophisticated Hellenistic styles of Southwest Asia, such as the third-century CE **propylon** at the Temple of Zeus at Baalbek in Lebanon. A small rectangular temple and an octagonal mausoleum stood to either side of the palace's entry court. Spalato's major domestic and official functions were carried out in the two-story wing in the southwestern quadrant. From the sea the facade appeared as a continuous, arcaded gallery between the corner towers. The predominantly defensive appearance of Diocletian's palace set the precedent for the fortified castles of medieval Europe.

Diocletian's abdication ushered in a decade of dynastic infighting, punctuated with violent succession disputes. Constantine, son of one of the tetrarchs, began his campaign for power from the northern capital of Trier on the Moselle River in southwestern Germany. Here, during the first decade of the fourth century, he continued the policies of his father, erecting new city walls; one of the largest bath complexes outside of Rome; and, adjacent to the stadium, an imperial palace with a formidable basilica (Fig. 6.1-1). Built entirely in brick and roofed with wooden trusses, it took the shape of an axial, rectangular hall, roughly 30 × 60 m (98 × 197 ft). The side walls rose on tall arches similar to those of an aqueduct. The two tiers of arched windows between the piers of each bay gave the interior exceptional luminosity. The building served as an audience hall, with Constantine's throne placed under the large **semidome** at the end of the axis. Hypocausts under the pavement heated the basilica like a thermal bath. The starkness of the side elevations of Constantine's basilica, once covered in plaster but now left as exposed brick, produced a stern

architectural character that influenced the later churches sponsored by the same patron.

Constantine's chief rival, Maxentius (r. 306–312), son of another tetrarch, introduced a quite different style of basilica in Rome, one of the grandest vaulted concrete structures in the world. The central groin-vaulted nave of the Basilica of Maxentius (Fig. 6.1-2), 80 × 25 m (262 × 82 ft), rested on massive piers that supported three **coffered** transversal barrel vaults per side. The central hall imitated the scale and fluid form of the *frigidarium* in the recently completed Baths of Diocletian. Maxentius promoted his claim to power through the lavish patronage of public projects. He restored the Senate house and the Temple of Venus and Rome that stood next to his new basilica; built a new **hippodrome** attached to his palace on the Via Appia; and next to it erected an impressive rotunda, the Mausoleum of Maxentius, a copy of the Pantheon at half scale.

The rivalry between the two sons of tetrarchs climaxed in 312 at the Battle of the Milvian Bridge on the outskirts of Rome. Constantine prevailed and attributed his victory to his sympathy for the Christian religion. Only a decade earlier, under

Figure 6.1-1 Trier, Germany. Constantine's Basilica, ca. 300.

▼ 313

Edict of Milan approves Christianity as the official religion of Rome

Constantine sponsors first official church of St. John's in the Lateran, finishes the Basilica of Maxentius

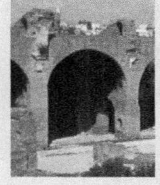

▲ 315

▼ 315

Arch of Constantine made with spolia *from earlier monuments, Rome*

Council of Nicaea (Iznik) takes a position against Arian theory of Jesus

▲ 325

Figure 6.1-2   Rome. Basilica of Maxentius, begun in 306 by Maxentius and finished by Constantine.

Diocletian's "great persecution," thousands of Christians had been martyred and imprisoned, churches destroyed, and scriptures burned. Diocletian's policy inspired broad contempt, and both Constantine and Maxentius sought to demonstrate tolerance of Christians, hoping to win back popular support. Constantine, whose mother, Helen, had already become a convert to Christianity, went one step further by openly favoring the religion. According to legend, he dreamed that an angel appeared and promised him victory in the sign of the cross. By painting crosses on his soldiers' shields and uniforms, Constantine gained the sympathy of Rome's Christians, who by this time constituted about one-third of the population, and entered the city as their champion.

As a pro-Christian interloper, Constantine alienated the Roman senatorial class, which nonetheless rewarded him with the Arch of Constantine (Fig. 6.1-3) in 315, next to the Colosseum. The Senate reconfigured a triumphal arch originally dedicated to Hadrian and Marcus Aurelius, changing the portraits on the reliefs to depict Constantine, and adorned it with recycled fragments, or **spolia**, from other monuments, including eight of the Dacian slave figures from Trajan's Forum. The inscription on the attic, while not specifically naming Christianity, discreetly alludes to the divine favor bestowed on Constantine. While the use of *spolia* might seem

a matter of thrift or expediency, it also conveyed an organic continuity with the greatness of Rome.

To prove his gratitude to the Christians, Constantine built Rome's first imperially sponsored church, St. John's in the Lateran (Fig. 6.1-4). Located just inside the Aurelian Walls, about a kilometer southeast of the Colosseum, the city's new **cathedral** turned its back on the imperial core to avoid conflicts with Roman shrines in the Forum district. The Lateran's remote site previously contained the barracks for Maxentius's imperial cavalry. The emperor also donated the palace next to it, which came from his wife's dowry, to the bishop of Rome. Known as the "pope," or "father" of the faithful, Christianity's chief cleric began to accumulate political status from this base. Instead of an impressive colonnaded facade, Constantine's new church carried a nondescript exterior. Christians kept their rituals mostly indoors, where the faithful gathered in prayer and moved in procession. The layout of the Lateran followed a five-**aisle** longitudinal plan. The architects avoided typological associations with pagan temples, using the **basilica** meeting hall type, familiar to Constantine as part of his works in Trier. While some concrete went into the walls of the Lateran's **apse**, the roofs were timber beams rather than vaults. The columns in the nave supported conventional flat trabeation, while those of the side aisles held up round arches, similar to the colonnades at Spalato. Such arcades with rounded arches soon became a standard element of church interiors. The central aisle, or **nave**, pushed above the pairs of side aisles to allow clerestory windows to illuminate the space. At its terminus a freestanding archway rose on four bronze columns as the "triumphal arch of Christ." Behind this screen a semidome covered a rounded apse for the altar. The placement of the apse at the west end of the church instead of the conventional eastern orientation seen in almost all later churches was a peculiarity shared by other Constantinian churches in Rome.

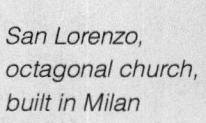

Figure 6.1-3 Rome. Arch of Constantine, made with *spolia* from earlier monuments, 315.

Soon after beginning the Lateran Basilica, Constantine commissioned a separate **baptistery** behind the apse. Much altered on its interior during the following centuries, the Lateran Baptistery (Fig. 6.1-5), an octagonal, central domed space wrapped by a colonnaded **ambulatory**, provided the model for the type throughout Italy. The original ceremony of baptism, the Christian initiation rite, required full immersion in a tub of water. Thus, the polygonal, vaulted baptisteries of the early Christian era borrowed from thermal bath structures and usually stood independent of the main churches.

Constantine distrusted Rome and resided there only for brief periods. During his final visit in 326, he sponsored the most important church in Christendom, Old St. Peter's (Fig. 6.1-6). Located near the Vatican Hill across the river from the Campus Martius, it served as a funeral basilica around the tomb of Peter, the first pope. Old St. Peter's, like all of the early churches, had an unassuming facade. One entered a grand colonnaded atrium that focused on a monumental bronze pinecone-shaped fountain of the second century CE, placed under a canopy in the center. At the end of this court a transversal **narthex** served as a vestibule between the atrium and the church interior. Slightly larger than the Lateran, the basilica of St. Peter's had a similarly tall nave flanked by pairs of side aisles. Its 100 columns, *spolia* from other monuments, ranged from green cipollino and yellow breccia to gray and red granite. A **crossing**, or **transept**, created a *T* shape at the western end of the church, which allowed more space for visiting the tomb of St. Peter in the **crypt** beneath the central altar. The apse and crossing eventually

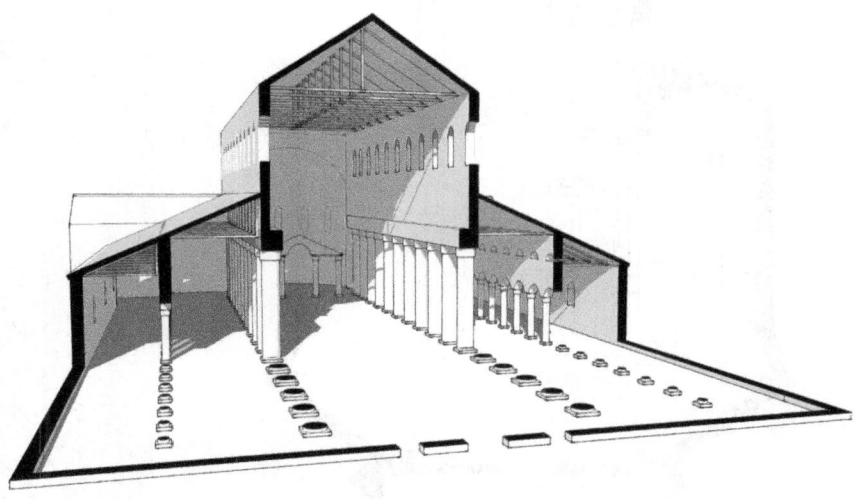

Figure 6.1-4 Rome. St. John's in the Lateran, 315 (after Donati).

Jesus of Nazareth

The Christian religion hinges on the figure of Jesus of Nazareth, born in Palestine during the reign of Augustus before the death of King Herod in 4 BCE. He was brought to trial and died a martyr's death in Jerusalem, crucified by Roman officials as a subversive on a date sometime before 36 CE, when the Roman governor Pontius Pilate left the region. Christians consider Jesus to have been the messiah, or Christ, the spiritual leader foretold in Jewish prophecies who would lead humankind to redemption. Among the mysteries of the religion are the Savior's being born to the Virgin Mary, his nature as both human and divine, and his resurrection from the Holy Sepulcher, followed by his bodily ascension into heaven.

Jesus probably received religious training from the Essenes, an order of apocalyptic monks who lived as strict vegetarians, took vows of chastity, and prepared their souls for the ultimate struggle between darkness and light. Following the example of his cousin, the prophet John the Baptist, Jesus spent most of his adult life as an itinerant preacher, offering moral lessons to the poor. Many of his teachings made both the Jewish hierarchy and the Roman governors uncomfortable, in particular statements such as "Render unto Caesar what is Caesar's and to God what is God's." Thought to be seditious, Jesus was arrested, tried, and condemned. After his death by crucifixion, his followers, the twelve apostles, elaborated on his life story of miracles and martyrdom, teaching his message of brotherly love, humility, and charity. The "Four Evangelists"—Matthew, Mark, Luke, and John—scripted the core texts, or gospels, of the New Testament, which became the basis of Christianity's theology of spiritual redemption. Early Christians emphasized the importance of the afterlife and prepared for the end of time. They believed Christ would return for the Last Judgment to condemn unrepentant sinners to the eternal punishment of hell, while permitting the saved to sit with God, the saints, and the angels in heaven.

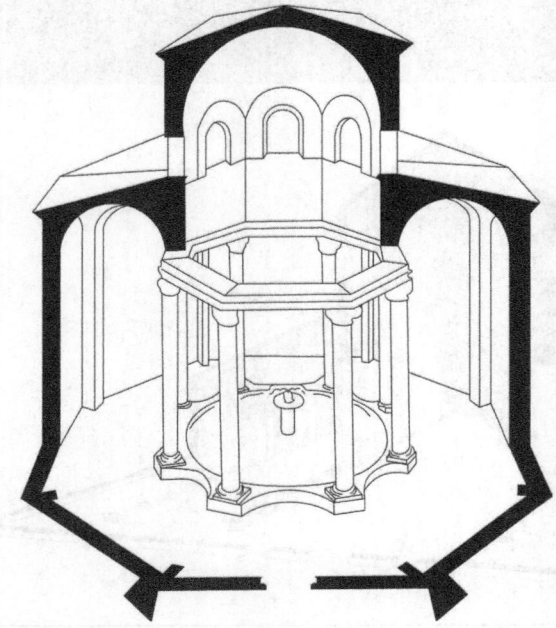

Figure 6.1-5 Rome. Reconstruction of the octagonal Lateran Baptistery, 315 (after Donati).

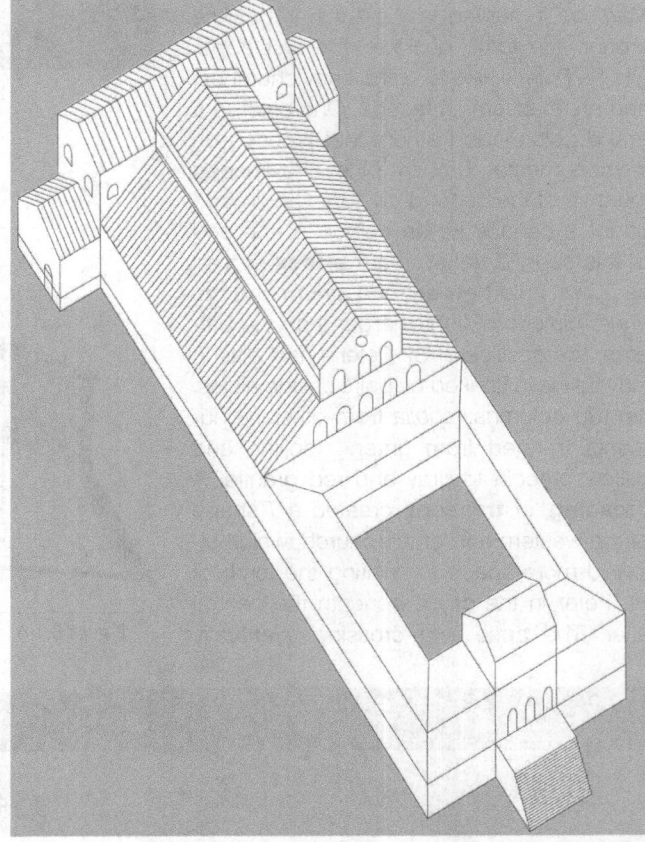

Figure 6.1-6 Rome. Reconstructed axonometric view of Old St. Peter's, begun in 326.

accommodated the growing ranks of the clergy. A sparkling mosaic of Christ the Redeemer, flanked by Peter and Paul and the palms of paradise, covered the semidome of the apse, and on the diaphragm arch in front of the apse another mosaic showed Constantine donating the building to Jesus. Here, an inscription made the emperor's intentions clear: "Because under Your guidance the world rose triumphant to the skies, Constantine, himself a victor, built You this hall."

Before definitively leaving Rome, Constantine completed the basilica begun by Maxentius, adding to it a second apse on the long axis and a porch fronting on the Via Sacra. In the new apse he placed a colossal seated portrait of himself, fragments of which are now in the courtyard of the

The Clandestine Church

Like the Jews, the early Christians had good reason to maintain a low profile. The Romans periodically persecuted them for their refusal to conform to the state religion and worship its deified rulers. At times this friction led to mass arrests, exile, extermination, and occasionally the use of Christians as bait for the gruesome games presented in Roman amphitheaters. The new religion did not follow any set **typology** for making churches, often improvising a sanctuary in the home of a wealthy member as a "community house," or *domus ecclesia*. The New Testament describes Jesus as treating women with exceptional fairness, and many women became the most influential converts to the new religion. Wealthy female patrons donated meetinghouses and properties for cemeteries. Beneath the medieval church of Santi Giovanni e Paolo lies a fine example of such a meetinghouse: a double-height hall fashioned out of the lower floor of an apartment block, or *insula*. This meetinghouse has two aisles, with an altar table placed toward the center. Aisled pathways eventually became the standard solution for ritual processions to receive the sacrament of the Eucharist, the symbolic transformation of bread and wine into the body and blood of Jesus. Competing cults also used underground sites, in particular the followers of Mithraism, a Persian religion that revered a redeemer figure, Mithra, in secret sanctuaries called "**mithraeums**."

Because of the Christian theological emphasis on the afterlife and bodily resurrection at the end of time, cemeteries played an important role as cult sites. Roman underground burial sites, such as the Catacombs of Callixtus, begun around 200 CE, became an elaborate maze of tomb-lined corridors carved out of the soft tufa stone on four intertwining levels.

Detail from an early Christian marble relief showing the cross surmounted by the Christ, or Constantinian, monogram (*chi rho*) within a wreath with doves picking its fruits, ca. 340.

The **catacombs** proved too cramped for church services, but Christians gathered there on the anniversaries of the deaths of famous martyrs. Such observances, known as the *refrigerium*, involved the pouring of libations and partaking of meals.

Capitoline Museum. The emperor thus put his stamp on the city before abandoning it for a new capital at Byzantium, leaving behind a simulacrum with eyes looking heavenward and one hand holding the Christian standard with the Greek letters *chi-rho* (X, P), the first two letters of Christ's name. Constantine thus projected both the scale of his power and the nature of his religious commitment.

Rome after Constantine: The Last Classical Buildings

After Constantine's departure from Rome in 326, the city slowly yielded power to the Christian Church. As the senatorial class lost its political authority and the population dwindled, the church survived as the only viable institution. During the fifth century, despite Rome's shrinking fabric and reduced fortunes, the city saw the foundation of a series of large churches. These early Christian basilicas constituted the final works achieved within the classical tradition of ancient Roman architecture (Fig. 6.1-7).

The Visigoths entered Italy at the outset of the fifth century to find the Roman troops unable to resist. After nearly two years of negotiations, Alaric I ordered the Sack of Rome in 410, an assault that damaged the city's pride more than its buildings. While looting and torching occurred, the barbarian leader forbade mass slaughter, ordered that the churches be left unharmed, and ushered refugees safely to the major churches. At midcentury, successive invasions by the Vandals and the Ostrogoths brought the city to its knees. The Roman Empire officially expired in the west in 476 with the deposing of the last western emperor, a teenager with the pretentious name of Romulus Augustulus.

Between the two sacks, Rome experienced a brief recovery under papal leadership. By now the popes had taken the place of the emperors as the prime source of patronage. They sponsored several new churches, including Santa Sabina, Santa Maria Maggiore, and Santo Stefano Rotondo, using a particularly refined classical style as a statement of Rome's ability to survive with dignity. They

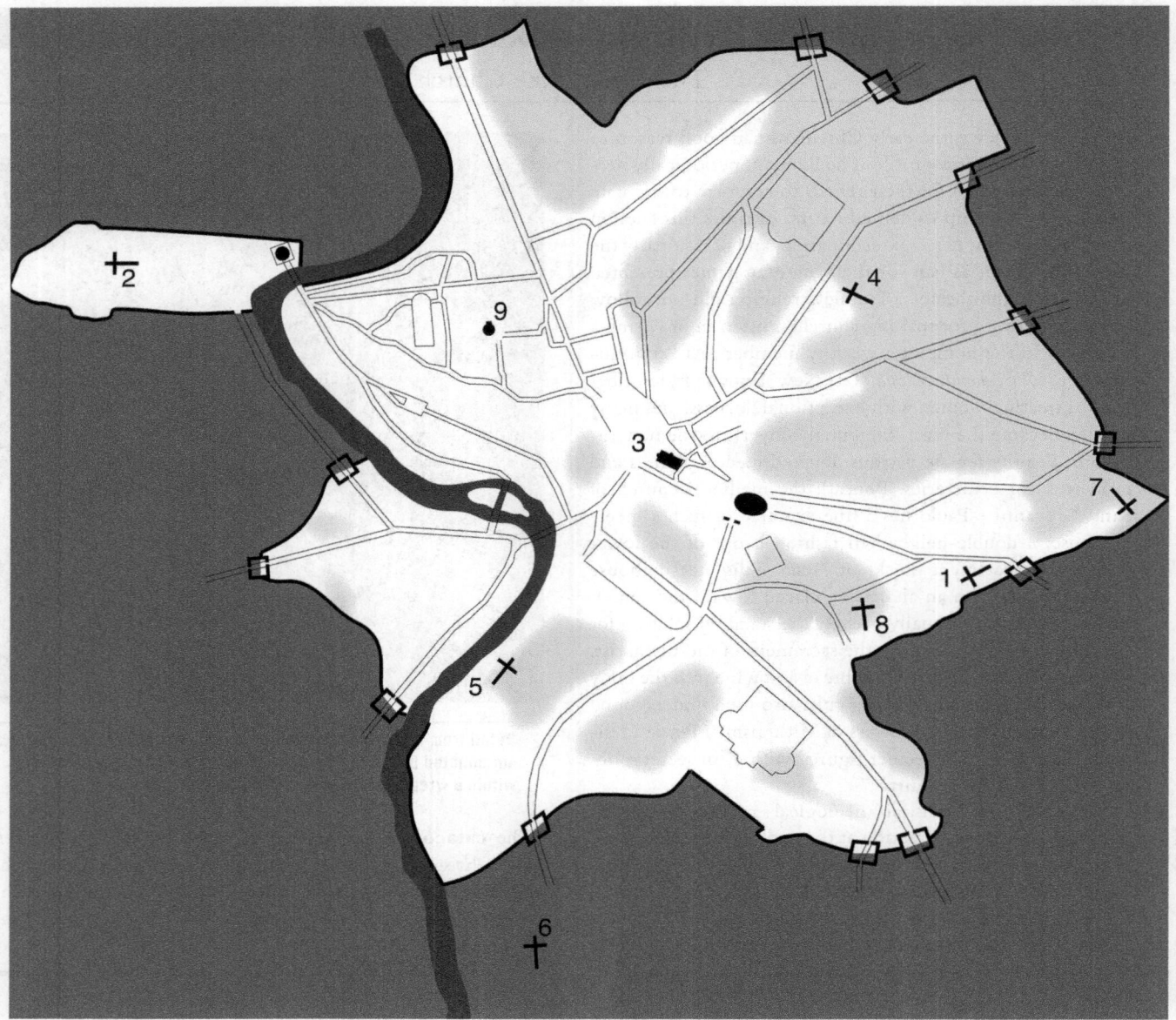

Figure 6.1-7   Rome, ca. 500. (1) St. John's in the Lateran; (2) St. Peter's; (3) Basilica of Maxentius; (4) Sta. Maria Maggiore; (5) Sta. Sabina; (6) St. Paul's Outside the Walls; (7) Sta. Croce in Gerusalemme; (8) Sto. Stefano Rotondo; (9) Pantheon.

sited the three-aisle basilica Santa Sabina (Fig. 6.1-8) in 430 on the Aventine Hill, a sparsely populated area greatly damaged during the sack of Alaric. Its austere brick exterior recalled Constantine's basilica at Trier. The interior looked as well coordinated as the great reception halls of the empire. The only stylistic license taken in its use of classical precedents was the use of arches rather than flat trabeation over its recycled Corinthian columns.

Santa Maria Maggiore (Fig. 6.1-9), completed around 440, in contrast, used columns with flawless Ionic capitals supporting well-proportioned flat entablatures. As Rome's first church to the cult of the Virgin Mary, the mother of Jesus, the choice of the Ionic order corresponded to Vitruvius's proposal that it be used to honor female deities.

The architects rigorously coordinated the church's proportions, leaving the attic story above the entablature the same height as the lower order and articulating it with perfectly scaled Corinthian pilasters. The flat coffered ceilings and the geometric patterns of the pavement gave Santa Maria Maggiore the feel of interiors such as the Basilica Ulpia in Trajan's Forum (see Section 5.1).

The third and most original of these Roman churches, Santo Stefano Rotondo (Fig. 6.1-10a), built between 468 and 483, remained unfinished. The patrons intended it to appear like an imperial mausoleum, with a central domed space wrapped by an annular vaulted ambulatory. On the edge of this ring, four rectangular **chapels** extended radially in the four cardinal directions, connecting to a second,

The Barbarian "Integration"

The ancient Greeks introduced the term *barbaros* ("foreign") in their complaints about outsiders whose languages they could not understand. From the third to the seventh century, the empires of Europe and Asia—including China, India, and Persia, as well as Rome—succumbed to waves of barbarian marauders. These horseback-riding, nomadic warriors originated in places as remote as Scandinavia, Mongolia, and the Arabian Desert. Various Germanic and Eastern European Gothic peoples had also settled on the Roman Empire's borders since the second century CE. Through trade and offering themselves as mercenaries, they assimilated into Roman society and religion.

Other more unpredictable and violent invaders arrived from the north and the east, uprooting both the Romans and the newly settled Gothic tribes. The military organization of these mounted nomads from the Asian steppes usually relied on the emergence of a charismatic leader, such as Attila the Hun, who during the period 435–453 invaded Gaul and then settled in Hungary, where he received tribute from the Byzantine emperor. In Europe the pressures exerted by the arrival of the Alans and the Huns from the east forced the more domesticated Germanic tribes to migrate to Gaul, Spain, Italy, and North Africa. After the initial turmoil of these barbarian intrusions, the invaders adopted Roman urban culture and the Christian religion. In hindsight the barbarian invasions destroyed the cultural unity of the Romans but generated a significant "integration" of peoples, leading to the development of the Romance languages, including Portuguese, Spanish, French, Romanian, and Italian.

Barbarian kingdoms, fifth to tenth century.

Figure 6.1-8 Rome. Sta. Sabina on the Aventine Hill, mid-fifth century.

fortunes of Rome, however, they never completed the central dome of Santo Stefano. To help support the pitched roof over the cylindrical core, they improvised an incongruous arcaded plane that sliced the central space in half (Fig. 6.1-10b).

The devastation of Italy continued throughout the sixth century as a result of the struggles between the Gothic contingents from Eastern Europe and the Germanic Lombards. After floods, famines, plagues, and invasions, Rome dwindled to as few as 30,000 inhabitants. During the chaos, when the funding for churches subsided, the popes transformed some of the great imperial monuments of the city, including the Senate house and the Pantheon, into shelters for the church and its institutions. While legislation to convert pagan temples into churches had existed since 407, Romans remained reluctant to mix pagan and Christian cult sites. One major exception was the Pantheon, originally dedicated to all of the gods and used as Hadrian's throne room, which underwent an elegant transition, rededicated in 609 to all the Christian martyrs.

Milan on the Eve of the Gothic Advance

Milan was known in antiquity as *Mediolanum*, or "the land in the middle." The most important crossroads city in the middle of the plains of northern Italy's Po valley, it replaced Rome for most of the fourth century as the capital of the western empire. Its new political prominence led to numerous imperial and ecclesiastic projects. The authority of the city's bishop often conflicted with imperial will, lead-

Figure 6.1-9 Rome. Sta. Maria Maggiore, fifth century.

external ambulatory that encircled the whole. The designers had hoped to install four planted courts in the residual spaces between the chapels. The Valerio family, who paid for the church, had traveled to Jerusalem several times and sought to approximate the Anastasis, the Church of the Holy Sepulchre, built by Constantine. Due to the sinking ing to competitive patronage for the city's churches. Waves of invaders devastated Milan in the early fifth century, erasing most of its Roman fabric.

Although Constantine declared Christianity the official religion of the state, deeply rooted pagan beliefs persisted. Only in 356 did an imperial decree call for the

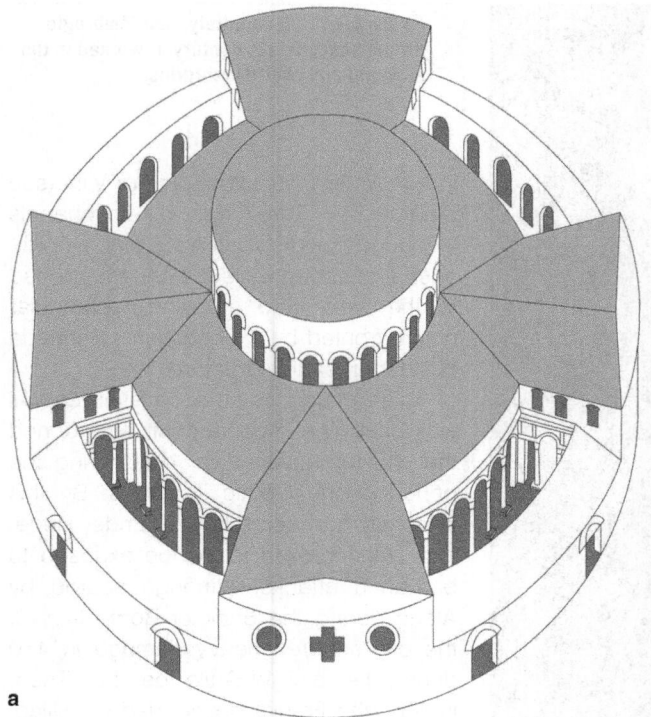
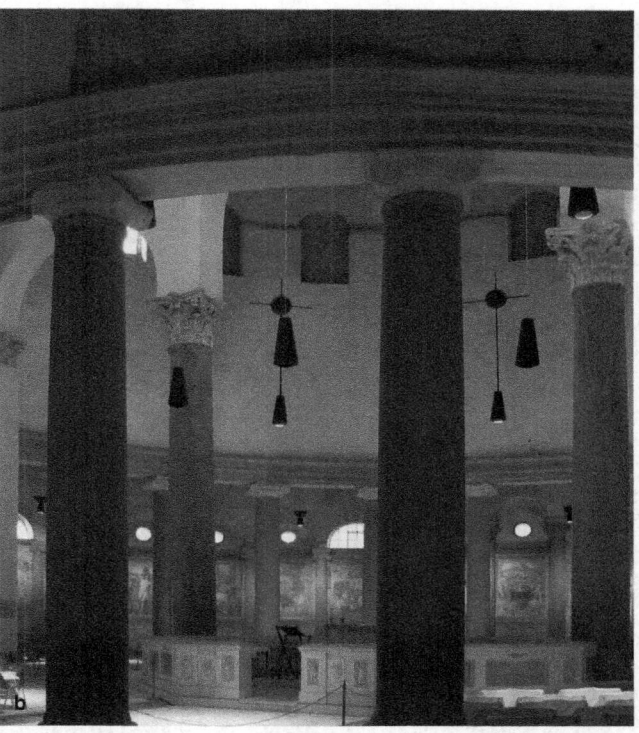

Figure 6.1-10 Rome. Sto. Stefano Rotondo, 470s. (a) Reconstruction of church (after Spencer Corbett). (b) View of the interior.

closure of pagan temples throughout the empire. With the exception of Emperor Julian "the Apostate," who briefly ruled from 361 to 363 and embraced a new solar cult, Constantine's successors eagerly espoused Christianity. Religious conflicts, however, arose from different interpretations of Christian doctrines. One such division occurred over the thesis of Arius, a priest from Alexandria who proposed that Jesus should not be worshipped as God but instead venerated as a prophet. Constantine was baptized by a key exponent of Arianism, and his son, Constantius II, also showed sympathy for this faction. During the fourth century, imperial policy vacillated on the issue, sometimes siding with the dogma of the Council of Nicaea, which insisted on the simultaneous divinity and humanity of Jesus, and sometimes siding with the Arians. The barbarians who had converted to Christianity tended to support the Arian thesis.

When the barbarians began to infiltrate Italy as settlers, mercenaries, and eventually rulers, Christian bishops emerged as the rulers of Italian cities. Milan's bishop at this time, St. Ambrose (ca. 338–397), wielded a mixture of secular and religious authority during the late fourth century. He arrived in Milan as the Roman governor of the province in 370, and four years later the citizens chose him to be their bishop, even though he had not yet been baptized. He made his base in the recently built cathedral of Santa Tecla. The five-aisle basilica, constructed around 350, appeared almost as large as the Lateran. Its skewed, rhomboid contours adjusted to the boundaries of its densely packed site

in the center of town. The octagonal baptistery recalled the Lateran Baptistery in its form and placement.

Ambrose sponsored the construction of three large churches on the outskirts of Milan: Sant'Ambrogio (Fig. 6.1-11), which was named after him later; the Basilica Apostolorum (now San Nazaro); and San Simpliciano, named after Ambrose's successor. He programmed these churches as martyrs' cemetery churches, similar to the covered cemeteries founded by Constantine outside Rome. Sant'Ambrogio, heavily rebuilt in various campaigns from the eighth to the eleventh century, now stands as a three-aisle basilica with a colonnaded atrium. Ambrose placed his own sarcophagus under the main altar of the apse next to two legitimate martyrs. The only one of Ambrose's churches still partly intact, San Simpliciano, had tall blind arches built in brick and was a modest construction resembling Constantine's basilica in Trier, but with the addition of a broad transept.

Ambrose's imperial rivals created the most impressive early Christian church in Milan. Now called San Lorenzo, the church has a luxurious double-shell structure that supports a dome (Fig. 6.1-12). The peculiar form of its **central plan** was an outgrowth of the ideological struggle between the bishop and the pro-Arian emperor. Built in the 380s, San Lorenzo's octagonal dome soared over four two-story piers alternating with four conches that formed colossal exedra. On the exterior, four square stair towers abutted the four exedra at the corners. In plan San Lorenzo resembled a quatrefoil, reminiscent of the reversed curves of the pavilion

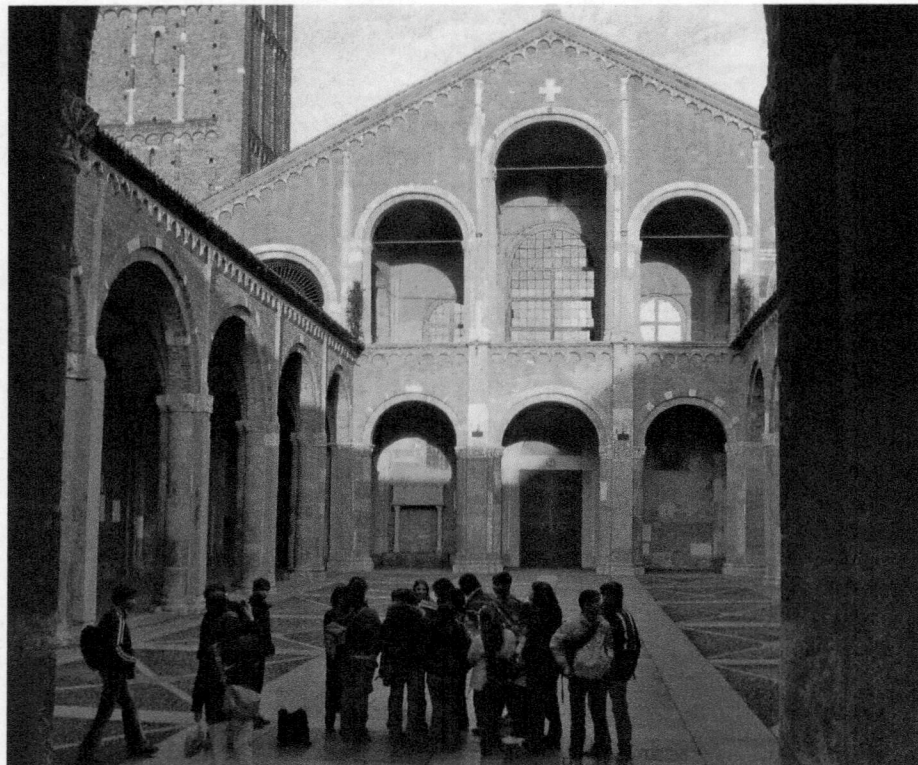

Figure 6.1-11 Milan, Italy. Sant'Ambrogio, atrium court, fourth century, reworked in the eleventh and twelfth centuries.

in the Water Court at Hadrian's Villa (see Section 5.1). Three mausoleum chapels extended from its outer walls on the north, east, and south, while the church opened to the west onto a grand rectangular atrium fronted by a Corinthian colonnade built for an earlier structure.

Milan's success as a Christian capital was brief. The imperial court abandoned the city for Ravenna in 402, during the period of the Gothic invasions. By this time Italy had come heavily under siege, and Milan proved to be too exposed to barbarian attacks. Although spared by Alaric during the Sack of Rome in 410, the city suffered heavy damage in 450 during the raids of Attila the Hun. Then, in 539, the Franks descended on Milan, exterminating the population and reducing most of the city to rubble. When the Lombard warlords sought an Italian base in 568, they rejected Milan, which was too devastated, preferring Pavia. The early Christian churches of Milan, however, survived relatively unharmed due to the respect that barbarians retained for Christian monuments.

Further Reading

Brown, Peter. "Late Antiquity." In *A History of Private Life*. Edited by P. Veyne. Cambridge, MA: Harvard University Press, 1987.

Jones, Mark Wilson. *Principles of Roman Architecture*. New Haven, CT: Yale University Press, 2000.

Krautheimer, Richard. *Rome: Profile of a City, 312–1308*. Princeton, NJ: Princeton University Press, 1980.

Krautheimer, Richard, and Slobodan Curcic. *Early Christian and Byzantine Architecture*. New Haven, CT: Yale University Press, 1986.

Figure 6.1-12 Milan, Italy. San Lorenzo Maggiore, double-height conch, 380s.

6.2 BYZANTIUM
The Dome as an Act of Faith

After Constantine began his great churches in Rome, he transferred his political capital east to Byzantium. Here, at a safe distance from the old center of power, he produced the first Roman city plan to include Christian churches as primary urban components. The emperor also sponsored projects in Jerusalem, including a dome to cover the tomb of Christ. Its central-plan form, the common type for imperial mausoleums, became an alternative to the longitudinal basilica for church design. The domes of subsequent Byzantine churches rose as prominent symbols of Christianity, culminating in Emperor Justinian's rebuilding of Hagia Sophia during the early sixth century. This extraordinary vaulted space advanced the design of churches to become full-fledged monumental figures in the city.

During the fifth century Constantine's successors in Constantinople favored Ravenna on the Adriatic coast as their base for governing Italy. One of their trusted mercenaries, Theodoric, an Ostrogoth prince, usurped Byzantine control of the city and established the first important barbarian kingdom in Italy. After his death, the Byzantines regained Ravenna, which they held for the rest of the sixth century, and completed several exceptional churches there, including the dome of San Vitale. For a brief moment this Byzantine outpost shone as brilliantly as Constantinople, shimmering in the glow of its mosaics.

Constantinople: The First Christian Capital

Few patrons have so single-handedly changed the course of architecture as Constantine. He both installed Christianity as the principal religion of the Roman Empire and imposed the major types for its principal cult buildings. During his long reign he moved frequently, setting up capitals and palaces and sponsoring new churches wherever he settled. His patronage in Trier, Rome, Jerusalem, Antioch, and, above all, his new capital of Constantinople established models for three major church types still in use: the aisled basilica, the central-plan memorial church, and the pavilion-like baptistery.

Constantine's greatest work, the foundation of *Nova Roma*, "New Rome," soon took on his name as Constantinople. He ordered the construction of the new capital after stabilizing his power in the eastern half of the empire in 324. It emerged as the last city founded according to imperial Roman criteria and the first to have an expressly Christian identity. The emperor dedicated his new Rome in 330 "to the God of the martyrs," putting his imprimatur on the city through his palace, hippodrome, **palatine chapel**, triumphal plazas, and imperial mausoleum.

Constantine settled Constantinople as an extension to the ancient Greco-Roman city of Byzantium, which had a population of about 20,000. It straddled a hilly, triangular peninsula bounded by the Bosporus strait to the north, a narrow inlet known as the Golden Horn to its northwest, and the Marmara Sea to the south. The Mese, a grand, colonnaded central boulevard, dominated the urban structure of the peninsula. At its widest point the street stretched 25 m (82 ft), and the major juncture boasted a tetrapylon like the one in Palmyra. Every half-kilometer or so, the thoroughfare opened onto a shaped public plaza. In the midst of the Mese's final stretch, the curved Forum of Constantine focused on a colossal column carrying contradictory messages: a Christian chapel as its base and a statue of the emperor as the sun god on top. The urban sequence culminated at the Milion, the original milestone marker, and the Augusteon Forum, lined with colonnades on all sides. This space approximated the scale and function of the Forum of Julius Caesar in Rome.

On the east side of the Augusteon Forum stood the Senate house and the Chalke, a bronze arch for entering the Great Palace. The imperial enclave had formal dining halls, basilica meeting chambers, and a series of domestic courtyards that stepped down the promontory. Like the *Domus Flavia* in Rome, Constantine's palace overlooked a stadium, the Hippodrome. A special box, known as the "Kathisma," set on its western elevation, served as a place for the emperor and his court to watch the races. The long, *U*-shaped Hippodrome covered an area about three-quarters the size of the Circus Maximus.

To the conventional collection of Roman building types Constantine added churches. But unlike those in Rome, his churches occupied nodal points of the new city. The palace church of Hagia Sophia, or the Holy Wisdom of Christ, took the northern flank of the Augusteon Forum, directly adjacent to the palace complex. On several occasions the first Christian emperor conflated the cult of the imperial ruler with that of Christ, most pointedly at the Apostoleion, a church he built beyond the walls as his own mausoleum. The designers of the basilica of St. Mark's (San Marco) in Venice (see Section 9.1) copied the Apostoleion as it appeared in the eleventh century before its destruction, a **Greek-cross** plan, with arms of equal length in all directions (Fig. 6.2-1). Its five domes formed a *quincunx* scheme. The Apostoleion abutted an imperial residence with baths, guardhouses, dining halls, and fountains. At the center of the church lay the sarcophagus of Constantine, meant to support the main altar. Surrounding the crossing the emperor installed twelve empty sarcophagi representing the twelve apostles of Christ, demonstrating his desire to be remembered as the thirteenth apostle. Constantine may have had many virtues, but his well-known sins, including the execution of his eldest son, the murder of his wife, and the betrayal of his allies, made it difficult to accept him as a saint. To position the emperor's tomb as the sacred center of the church seemed so inappropriate from a theological point of view that his heirs later moved the sarcophagus to a round mausoleum attached to the apse.

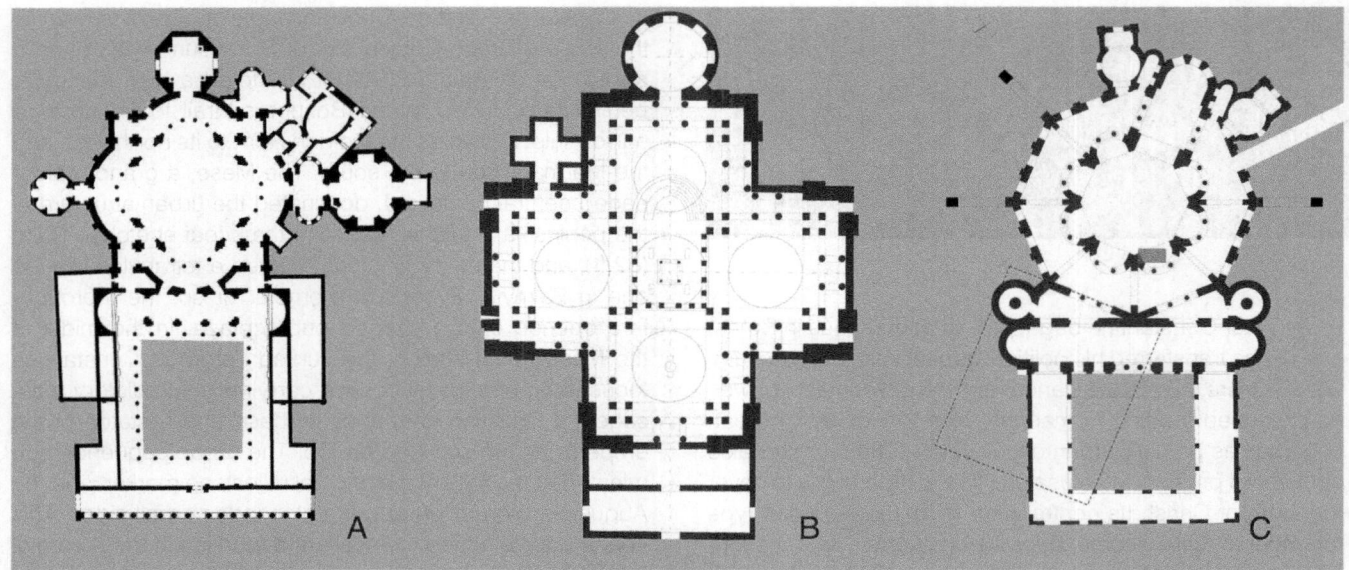

Figure 6.2-1   Byzantine Empire. Central-plan churches, equidistant on all axes from the crossing: (A) San Lorenzo Maggiore, Milan, 380s; (B) Apostoleion, Constantinople, 330s; (C) San Vitale, Ravenna, 526.

Constantine's city succeeded beyond all expectations as the new Rome. Within a single generation, the population grew to 100,000. The emperor offered incentives to senatorial families to move there from "old" Rome, and by the mid-fifth century an inventory listed 4,388 domuses, eight baths, twenty state bakeries, four harbors, four forums, and twelve churches in the city. The zoning laws of the next century prohibited the construction of buildings more than 30 m (96 ft) high, indicating that multistoried *insulae* continued to be built in the new Rome, with all the attendant problems of fire safety, sanitation, and crowding. Because the city's fabric included primarily timber buildings, it suffered constant conflagrations, leaving few buildings from this period. And what fires did not destroy, earthquakes finished off. The clarity of the Roman armature was blurred by frequent rebuilding to the point that Constantinople developed into a city of densely interwoven fragments dotted with a few distinct monuments.

The change in architectural attitudes from the extroverted colonnaded spaces of imperial Rome to the mysterious, inwardly oriented church halls of the early Christians took root during Constantine's reign. Among the most visible projects stood the original church of Hagia Sophia, begun by Constantine in 326 as an adjunct to his palatine complex. Construction continued until 360 during the reign of his son, Constantius II (r. 337–361). Although Constantine's church can only be partly reconstructed from archaeological remains and literary descriptions, the plan clearly followed the examples of the Lateran and Old St. Peter's: a five-aisled basilica entered through a short atrium. Its rounded apse pointed east, setting the standard for later churches. Another difference from the Roman churches was the use of upper galleries in the nave for the *matroneum*, an area reserved for women, in the tradition of Jewish **synagogues**.

Constantine's Hagia Sophia shared much with the Basilica of the Holy Sepulchre in Jerusalem, designed during the same years by the same team of designers. The emperor's mother, Helen, one of the most enthusiastic promoters of early Christianity, traveled at age seventy-five to Palestine to venerate and protect the sites associated with the life of Jesus. Using faith-based archaeological methods, she identified his birthplace, the cross on which he died, the place of his

TIME LINE

▼ **330**

Official inauguration of "New Rome" (Constantinople) by Constantine

▼ **424**

Galla Placidia sponsors cathedral and baptistery in Ravenna

Theodoric, king of the Ostrogoths, conquers northern Italy, takes Ravenna as capital

▼ **ca. 520**

Mausoleum of Theodoric in Ravenna

Constantine builds the first Hagia Sophia and the Apostoleion

▲ **330s**

▲ **488**

Figure 6.2-2 Jerusalem. Church of the Holy Sepulchre, begun 326; crypt with *U*-shaped monument capped with a wooden lantern added in later centuries. Constantine's Hagia Sophia was designed by the same designers.

ascension, and his tomb. Constantine commissioned special monuments for all of these sites. The most important, the Church of the Holy Sepulchre, begun in 326, has been destroyed and rebuilt twice. The original church repeated the five-aisle basilica plan, adding second-story galleries over the central nave. The rounded apse contained an underground crypt (Fig. 6.2-2) for the relic of the "True Cross" that Helen allegedly found on the site. Behind the apse, a peristyle court framed an outcropping believed to be the rock of Golgotha, the site of Jesus's crucifixion. This court served as a transitional space between the basilica and a domed **martyrium**. Known as the Anastasis, the Greek word for "resurrection," it sheltered Christ's tomb. Its double-shell, wood-frame dome, 20 m (64 ft) in diameter, covered the shrine with a glistening gilded skin. The dome rose on a ring of a dozen columns regularly interspersed with eight square piers. The lower ambulatory and upper gallery served as spaces for pilgrimage processions around the sacred site of Jesus's miraculous return to life.

The central plan and vaults of the Anastasis derived from the architecture of royal tombs. Constantine began a similar tomb for himself on the outskirts of Rome during the 320s before moving to Byzantium. Likewise, his daughter sponsored a burial rotunda in Rome in 340, which became the church of Santa Costanza (Fig. 6.2-3). Its **mosaic**-clad rotunda remains one of the best-preserved works of the period. Twelve sets of twin columns positioned radially supported a central domed space wrapped by an annular vault. Although it lacked upper galleries, Santa Costanza's curved space covered about the same diameter as the martyrium in Jerusalem and reproduced the shimmering atmosphere of the original Anastasis.

Saints Sergius and Bacchus begun in Constantinople

▲ 525

▼ 526

San Vitale, pro-Byzantine monument, built in Ravenna

Justinian becomes Byzantine emperor

▲ 527

▼ 532

Justinian rebuilds Hagia Sophia after Nika riots

Byzantines briefly regain control of Italy

▲ 540

Figure 6.2-3 Rome. Sta. Costanza, tomb for Constantine's daughter Costanza, 340.

Hagia Sophia after Constantine

Constantine's successors continued his policies, and Constantinople grew into the largest city of the Mediterranean during its first century. Imperial power proved shaky, however, and rioters devastated Constantine's Hagia Sophia in 404. After reconstruction, a second wave of rioters destroyed it again during the Nika riot of 532. On this occasion, the Blues and the Greens, two of the rival sports factions at the races in the Hippodrome, joined forces to protest against Emperor Justinian's punishment of some of their members. They stormed the imperial palace shouting "*Nika!*," the stadium cheer meaning "Victory!" The mob ran wild for three days, sacking the palace and destroying the buildings near the Hippodrome, including the churches of Hagia Sophia and Hagia Eirene. The emperor sent his trusted general Belisarius to suppress the conflict with the help of barbarian mercenaries. The Hippodrome subsequently acquired a new function as the execution site for as many as 30,000 rioters.

Justinian's reconstruction of Hagia Sophia responded to a tense political situation. He had come to power under dubious circumstances in 525. Members of the old imperial family rejected his claim to the throne because his uncle, who preceded him as emperor, had seized power through a coup, sidestepping hereditary succession. Justinian further alienated the local aristocracy by marrying a known courtesan, Theodora. Together the imperial couple forged a path to legitimacy that included reforming the Roman legal code and constructing forty-eight churches. Justinian founded the first public hospital for the sick and destitute, the Hospice of Sampson, and built the city's largest reservoir, the Basilica Cistern, an underground hypostyle expanse. Theodora sponsored a hospice for ex-prostitutes, known as the Metanoia, or "redemption."

Two influential works preceded the reconstruction of the Hagia Sophia, with the first being the church of Saints Sergius and Bacchus (Fig. 6.2-4), attached to a convent sponsored by Theodora at the southeastern tip of the city. Construction on the church began before the Nika riots and ended around 535. The designers proposed a double-shell structure, with the square outer walls enclosing an inner octagonal figure that supported a shallow dome. Narrow conches alternated between the wedge-shaped piers of the tall octagonal central space. The sixteen segments of the dome recalled Hadrian's "pumpkin" domes at his villa in Tivoli. While quite different in scale and design from Hagia Sophia, Saints Sergius and Bacchus established the concept of a domed central space nested inside a larger orthogonal figure. That the inner shape of the double shell was built slightly askew did not help the stability of the structure. The church's sagging and deflected surfaces required constant repair, problems that probably alerted the emperor to consult specialists for the reconstruction of Hagia Sophia.

Justinian was also inspired by the church of Hagia Polyeuktos, which no longer exists. A powerful female patron, Anicia Juliana, daughter of an emperor of the previous imperial dynasty, commissioned this large domed church between 524 and 527 as part of her campaign to promote her son's claim to the throne. Hagia Polyeuktos apparently resembled the reconstructed church of Hagia Eirene ("church of peace"), which Justinian sponsored during the same years as Hagia Sophia. The latter church was a longitudinal basilica with massive square piers in the center, supporting thick barrel-vault arches 8 m (26 ft) deep. A dome rose over the center on **pendentives**, triangular concave **spandrels**, and rested on a short drum with a ring of clerestories. Screens of columns and upper galleries ran along the sides, emphasizing the long dimension of the church. A deep, rounded apse covered by a semidome at the east end terminated the sequence. At the base of the apse lay a *synthronon*, a concentrically arranged series of curved benches for the clergy that stepped up seven levels like the *cavea* of a theater.

Justinian desired to surpass Anicia Juliana's dome at Hagia Polyeuktos. The reconstruction of Hagia Sophia (Fig. 6.2-5) served as both a token of expiation for the riot and an expression of personal ambition. While the ingenuity of its design might seem inspired by a great formal vision, some of it came from the ordinary need for fire safety. The rebuilt church contained a minimum of flammable materials in its construction, with arches, vaults, and a dome made of stone, bricks, and lime. Iron and timber served only as ties between arches and clamps for bonding pieces of masonry. Construction began forty days after the end of the

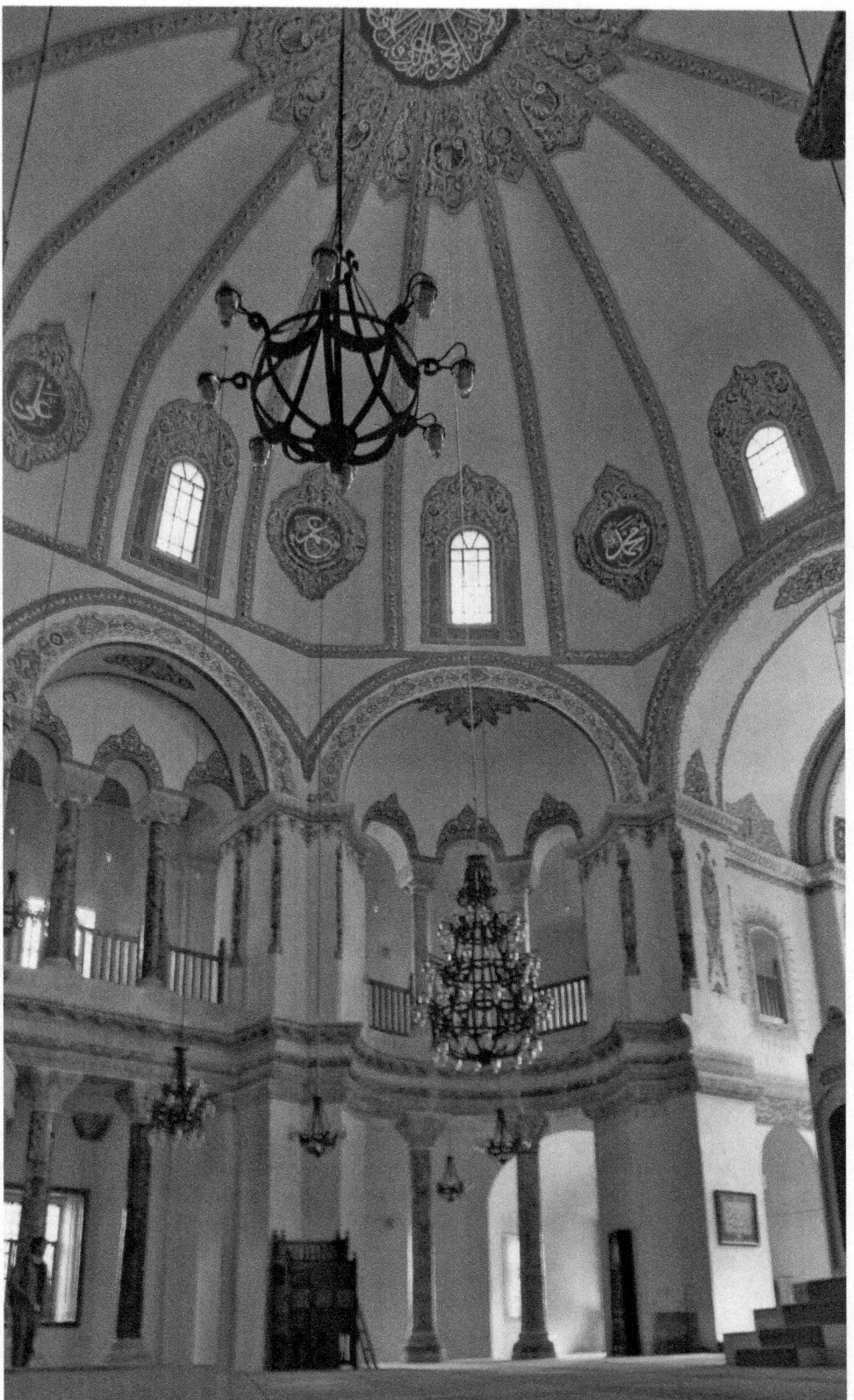

Figure 6.2-4 Constantinople. Saints Sergius and Bacchus, begun 526.

Nika riot with a plan by two designers better known as scientists than architects: Anthemius of Thralles, an expert in projective geometry and an inventor of mechanical devices, and his colleague Isidorus of Miletus, a teacher of stereometry and physics who at one time had served as the director of the Platonic Academy in Athens. Their highly theoretical approach to structure fostered a colossal experiment, one of the greatest challenges ever lodged against the common sense of architectural conventions.

Anthemius and Isidorus planned the central dome, 32.6 m (107 ft) in diameter, to rise more than 50 m (164 ft) above the nave (Fig. 6.2-6a,b). A shallow drum pierced with forty clerestory windows supported it so that it seemed to float. These windows were placed at the points where cracking had been witnessed in solid domes such as that of the Pantheon in Rome. Delicate concave pendentives lifted the drum and dome from four broad arches, but much of the **thrust** was absorbed by massive buttresses, which were enlarged during later restorations. Two semidomes flowed down from the eastern and western arches, while the northern and southern sides stood as if sliced by planes of windows. Each of the two semidomes stepped down to three smaller arches sheltering scooped-out conches at the diagonals and a barrel vault at the center. The eastern end of the axis terminated in a deep, rounded apse, like that of Hagia Eirene. It once contained a *synthronon*. The western end led to the imperial portal of the narthex. Hagia Sophia's complex succession of concave hollows, suspended above the nave with no apparent mass for their support, created an atmosphere of unparalleled drama: the space swelled magnificently as an organic system of billowing vaults pushed to perilous heights.

Hagia Sophia covered almost as much area as the Basilica of Maxentius in Rome. Its dome, when combined with the radii of the two semidomes, reached a greater continuous span than the diameter of the Pantheon. But unlike Roman engineering, in which the relation of vault thrust to wall mass was clearly visible, the structure of Hagia Sophia seemed less clear, its vaults appearing to levitate. The colored marbles used for the columns and wall revetments, the shimmering gold mosaics, and the airiness of the galleries and multiple clerestories added to its feeling of evanescence.

a

Figure 6.2-5 Constantinople. Hagia Sophia, built by Justinian in the 530s.

While the space of the nave of Hagia Sophia appeared unitary, its details showed great discrepancies. The number and scale of the columns from one level to the next did not correspond. The conches, for instance, had two monolithic red porphyry columns on the ground level and six green *verde antico* columns above—*spolia* taken from Baalbek and Ephesus, respectively. In contrast to the classical sense of order, the spacing of the upper columns did not correspond to that of those below. The central colonnades of the nave below the dome had four tall green columns below and six shorter ones above (Fig. 6.2-7). The mismatched proportions continued into the aisles, where the columns holding up the groin vaults under the galleries assumed yet another size. While many of the original golden mosaics of the dome and vaults have been lost through collapse or covered over, many fine examples still shine on the walls in the upper galleries. The wainscoting of the aisles and galleries carries yellow, green, gray, and purple slabs of marble, arranged in symmetrical book-matched sets like pairs of butterflies, enhancing the interior's overall glowing effect and giving it a sense of incomprehensible unity.

Like most early churches, Hagia Sophia had no real facade. At first impression it appeared a great bulging mass. The four slender minarets added by the Ottomans to its corners during the fifteenth and sixteenth centuries introduced an orderly frame for its complex shape (see Section 11.2). Unlike a Mesopotamian ziggurat or a Greek temple, for which the combination of architectural parts led to a coherent whole, Hagia Sophia's profile cannot be reduced to a simple figure made of proportional elements. The dome, cupped shapes, and buttresses create a complex form, like a mountain range. One perceived each part, indispensable to the structural whole, on its own.

Built in just five years, Hagia Sophia's central dome collapsed only twenty years after completion as a result of an earthquake. Rather than abandoning the design, Justinian had it rebuilt, raising the dome higher on ribs and thickening the buttresses. Despite all of its successive collapses and its transformation into a mosque, Hagia Sophia survived as the quintessential expression of the new Rome's **genius loci**, the spirit of the place. It seemed to take its shape from the city's hilly topography and in turn crowned Constantinople with mounded forms. Justinian's court historian, Procopius, aside from noting the emperor's boast of having surpassed Solomon in Hagia Sophia's construction, explained the power of the new church's space thus: "Whenever one enters this church to pray, he understands at once that it is not by

Figure 6.2-6 Constantinople. Hagia Sophia, 530s. (a) Under the central dome. (b) See facing page.

Figure 6.2-6b Constantinople. Hagia Sophia, 530s. Plan.

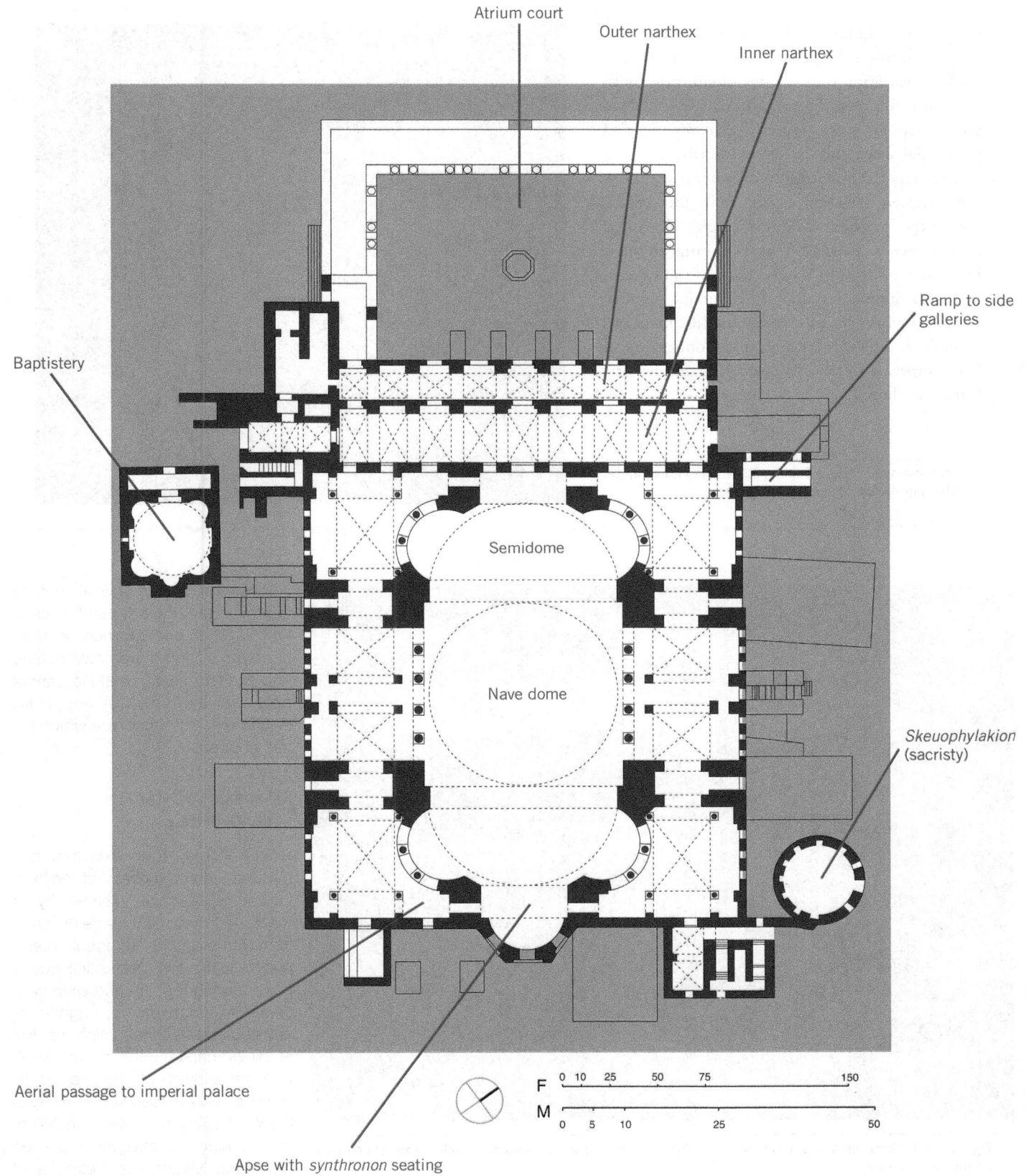

Atrium court

Outer narthex

Inner narthex

Ramp to side galleries

Baptistery

Semidome

Nave dome

Skeuophylakion (sacristy)

Aerial passage to imperial palace

Apse with *synthronon* seating

F

M

0 10 25   50   75   150

0   5   10   25   50

Byzantine Capitals

The capitals of the heterogeneous columns at Hagia Sophia were carved as a variation on the Corinthian order with very fine filigree. The acanthus leaves in Byzantine capitals were flattened into an inverted pyramidal shape and delicately inscribed, almost like jewelry, terminating in tiny spiral scrolls. A sophisticated variation occurred in the gallery above the narthex, where a single, elongated capital covered pairs of columns, similar to those in Santa Costanza in Rome. Each of the capitals in Hagia Sophia was slightly different, some of them carrying the monogram of Justinian and Theodora, others carrying the monograms of later emperors involved in repairing and beautifying the church.

Constantinople. Hagia Sophia, 530s. Byzantine capital with filigree and imperial monogram.

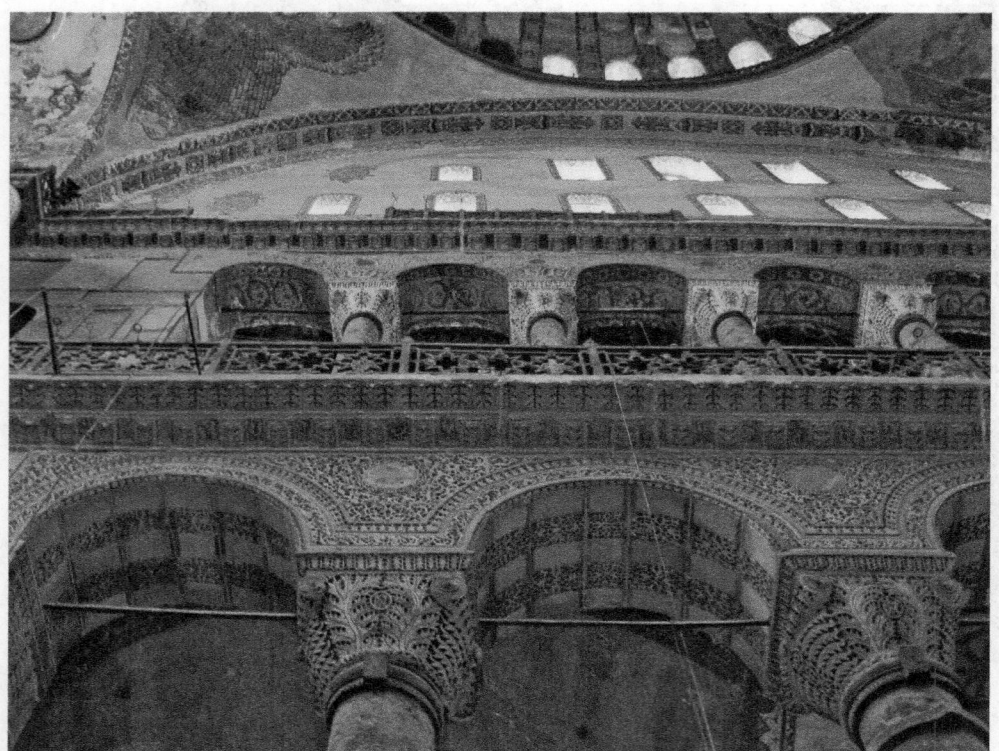

Figure 6.2-7 Constantinople. Hagia Sophia, 530s. Interior elevation, showing misalignment of columns on the second level.

any human power or skill, but by the influence of God, that this work has been so finely turned. And so his mind is lifted up toward God and exalted, feeling that He cannot be far away, but must especially love to dwell in this place which He has chosen."

Ravenna: The Byzantine Satellite in Italy

As the Roman Empire in Italy disbanded into a mosaic of political fragments, Ravenna, a small city on the Adriatic coast set a safe distance from Rome and Milan, acquired surprising luster as a Byzantine power base. During the fifth and sixth centuries it underwent a magnificent architectural reconstruction as the empire's capital city in the west, with the addition of churches, baptisteries, and mausoleums. As with the ecclesiastical projects in Milan, the theological struggle between Arian and Nicene interpretations of

Figure 6.2-8 Ravenna, Italy. Byzantine capital of Italy, fifth to sixth century. (1) Cathedral and Orthodox baptistery; (2) Sta. Croce and Mausoleum of Galla Placidia; (3) St. John the Evangelist; (4) Arian Baptistery; (5) Theodoric's palace and Sant'Apollinare Nuovo; (6) Mausoleum of Theodoric; (7) San Vitale; (8) road to Sant'Apollinare in Classe.

Christianity often motivated these commissions. The integration of barbarian regimes with the surviving Roman culture further sharpened the conflict.

Ravenna began as a Roman *castrum* town in the first century BCE, plotted on a grid about 400 m (1,312 ft) per side. The surrounding marshes of the Po River delta provided excellent defense against both land and sea attacks. Canals set the city's boundaries to the north and east. The Byzantines developed the small town of Classe about 5 km (3 miles) to the south as a suburban port for maritime exchanges with Constantinople. After the relocation of the imperial court from Milan at the beginning of the fifth century, Ravenna expanded beyond its canals, tripling in size to accommodate palaces, a circus, and numerous churches (Fig. 6.2-8).

A female patron, Galla Placidia, was responsible for the first important structures of imperial Ravenna. Daughter of an emperor, sister of another, wife of a third, and mother to yet another, her life touched the apex of Byzantine power. During the Sack of Rome in 410 she was abducted and

brought to Gaul, where she was wed to the Visigoth king. After his assassination, she returned to Italy and, through a new marriage, became the Byzantine empress. Her direct influence over politics in Ravenna spanned the years 424–438, when she served as regent for her son. Throughout her career in the new capital she maintained a palace on the Mese in Constantinople, where she had been born. She also traveled frequently to Rome, where she commissioned mosaics for St. Paul's Outside the Walls and oversaw the design of her family's tomb in Old St. Peter's, where she is thought to have been buried.

Some time after her arrival from Constantinople in 424, Galla Placidia built the large three-aisle Basilica of St. John the Evangelist in the new eastern district of Ravenna. She commissioned it as an *ex-voto* in thanks for being spared from a violent storm at sea. At the same time, she also built the church of Santa Croce, in the new northern district of the city next to a new palace. Its cruciform shape provided one of the first explicit instances of a church plan referring to the

Figure 6.2-9 Ravenna, Italy. Mausoleum of Galla Placidia, 430.

Figure 6.2-10 Ravenna, Italy. Orthodox Baptistery, begun during the regency of Galla Placidia, 430s.

Christian emblem. While neither church nor palace has survived, a small cruciform chapel dedicated to St. Lawrence, the so-called Mausoleum of Galla Placidia (Fig. 6.2-9), once attached to the narthex of Santa Croce, remains intact. Mosaics with intense indigo backgrounds and striking contrasts of red, yellow, and gold decorative bands cover the short barrel vaults of its four wings and the central pendentive dome. The little chapel, now freestanding in the yard near the church of San Vitale, has a stark brick exterior, articulated with regularly spaced blind arches, and seems particularly modest compared to its lavish interior.

Galla Placidia also sponsored Ravenna's new cathedral and baptistery, built in the first half of the fifth century. They are now called "orthodox" to distinguish them from the Arian versions built at the end of the fifth century. The basilica, replaced in the eighteenth century, had five aisles like the Lateran and a baptistery to one side. The octagonal structure of the Orthodox Baptistery (Fig. 6.2-10) remains beautifully preserved, even if the level of its pavement, like all ancient structures in Ravenna, lies more than 1 m (3.3 ft) below grade as a result of subsidence. Its modest brick shell conceals an interior space of superb decorative complexity. The mosaics, painted stucco, colored marbles, and inscriptions impose a sacred hierarchy over its frame. As with most of the vaulted structures of Ravenna, the designers built the dome using interlocking terra-cotta tubes to lighten the compressive loads. The mosaics in the dome descend in concentric circles. The twelve apostles, dressed in white and gold robes and holding crowns, look to the central scene of the baptism of Christ, set on a background of pure gold. The curious figure of Jordan, a pagan river god, emerges from the waters, demonstrating a holdover from pre-Christian iconography.

At the end of the fifth century the Byzantine emperor in Constantinople entrusted a faithful barbarian general, Theodoric (r. 493–526), the king of the Ostrogoths, with ousting a barbarian pretender who had attempted to take control of Italy. Theodoric not only succeeded in eliminating this rival but seized power for himself in Ravenna. As the new conqueror of Italy, he replaced the collapsed authority of the Roman emperors while attempting to establish rule "in the name of Rome." Despite his origins, he carefully imitated the style of Roman religious and funerary architecture. For his barbarian followers and others of the Arian religious persuasion he duplicated the cathedral and baptistery in the eastern half of the city. The Arian Cathedral, just like the Orthodox Cathedral, was dedicated to the Anastasis, or Christ's resurrection. The Arian Baptistery, though smaller than its Orthodox counterpart, appeared identical to it, with an octagonal mosaic-encrusted dome. Theodoric sought to imitate without offending tradition, letting the Arian faction coexist with the Orthodox as separate but equal.

Like Constantine and other rulers, he planned a monumental tomb for himself in 526. The Mausoleum of Theodoric (Fig. 6.2-11), located about 1 km (0.6 miles) beyond the northeast gate of the city, stood as the only great work in Ravenna built in stone. It originally flanked the Basilica of San Giorgio, which has since disappeared. The lower story rises on massive half-piers and arches as a ten-sided polygon. The voussoirs have jogged interlocking joints to resist slipping, a detail often found in Syrian masonry. The interior on the lower level does not correspond to the exterior, as it is cruciform rather than polygonal, with a groin vault over the center. The three niches accommodated sarcophagi. The upper story stepped back to accommodate the columns of an exterior arcade that have since disappeared, leaving uncanny traces of their outline on the masonry. The most extraordinary feature of Theodoric's mausoleum was its monolithic dome, a single, cup-shaped, 300-ton block of Istrian marble 11 m (36 ft) in diameter. While the mausoleum adhered to an overall classical idea, its roof evoked the dolmens and megalithic tombs still used by Gothic royalty. Twelve pierced spurs crowned the perimeter of the dome, serving as hooks for the hoist ropes. While not aligned with the facets of the polygonal plan, each spur carried the name of an apostle, perhaps making reference to Constantine's mausoleum at the Apostoleion in Constantinople.

During the year of Theodoric's death in 526, work began on two great churches in Ravenna: Sant'Apollinare in Classe and San Vitale. Pro-Byzantine propagandists promoted their construction as a symbolic rejection of Ostrogoth rule. Theodoric's remarkable success and good government in Ravenna became a threat to Byzantine power. The new government of Justinian in Constantinople, which took power in the same year as Theodoric's death, sought to reassert control over Italy and the lost provinces of the empire. The new churches stood far from Theodoric's palace and the Arian district in the center of Ravenna, literally keeping their distance from the barbarian king. The Orthodox bishop sponsored the works, while the wealthy banker Julianus Argentarius financed them. As a supporter of the imperial Byzantine faction, Julianus served as more than a casual donor: he owned the brickyards that produced the thin Byzantine-style bricks used to build both churches. His frequent visits to Constantinople might also explain the close stylistic connections between these structures in Ravenna and works in the capital.

Sant'Apollinare in Classe (Fig. 6.2-12), located near Ravenna's port, was a three-aisle basilica with a design

Figure 6.2-11   Ravenna, Italy. Mausoleum of Theodoric, 520s.

close to that of Santa Sabina in Rome. One entered the church through a courtyard atrium, which has since disappeared, to find the nave lined with arcades resting on well-proportioned columns, a dozen on each side. The Corinthian capitals carried swirling patterns of acanthus leaves, and as in the other Ravenna churches and many examples in Constantinople, the **imposts** above the capitals rose as inverted pyramids. The tall clerestory windows in the nave and the golden mosaics in the apse contributed to a glowing interior.

San Vitale (Fig. 6.2-13) proved unlike any church in Italy except San Lorenzo in Milan. It followed a central plan as a martyrium dedicated to Ravenna's first bishop, St. Vitalis, whose tomb now appears as a rectangular pool, since the water table has risen over it. One originally entered the church through a square atrium next to a palace. The court was

Figure 6.2-12   Ravenna, Italy. Sant'Apollinare in Classe, begun 526.

reconfigured as a cloister for a monastery, which may explain the uncanny oblique rotation of the narthex 22° from the octagonal plan, forcing entry at an angle through one of two facets. San Vitale's octagonal, double-shell structure shares many typological traits with Saints Sergio and Bacchus in Constantinople, built during the same years. The style of Constantinople supplied the church's details, with column shafts and capitals imported from the imperial workshop of Proconnesus. The capitals on the ground-floor arcades imitated the flattened version of the Corinthian order used in Hagia Sophia, while those on the upper story imitated those used in Sant'Apollinare in Classe. The great panels of butterfly marble repeated those used to decorate the wainscots of Hagia Sophia. A drum of eight wedge-shaped piers connected by arches supported

CULTURE, SOCIETY, GENDER

Byzantine Revisionism

In the most famous of Theodoric's churches, originally dedicated to the resurrection but today called Sant'Apollinare Nuovo, one sees a curious instance of Byzantine revisionism perpetrated by the subsequent rulers of Ravenna in their efforts to erase signs of the Ostrogoths. One of the mosaics in the nave labeled "Palatium" shows a prominent three-arch porch. On some of its columns one still sees the detached hands that once belonged to the figures of Theodoric and his courtiers standing between the columns, now replaced by curtains. The Palatium mosaic

probably represented the Chalke, or entry gate to Theodoric's palace, located to the south of the church in imitation of Constantine's palace in Constantinople. During his youth, Theodoric resided for ten years as a hostage in the Great Palace, and this experience formed his taste and style of rule in Ravenna. He dressed like a Byzantine emperor and reproduced variations of the Great Palace's reception halls, throne room, peristyle courts, and triclinium with apses in his rambling palace in Ravenna.

Ravenna, Italy. Sant'Apollinare Nuovo, "Palatium" mosaic, ca. 530.

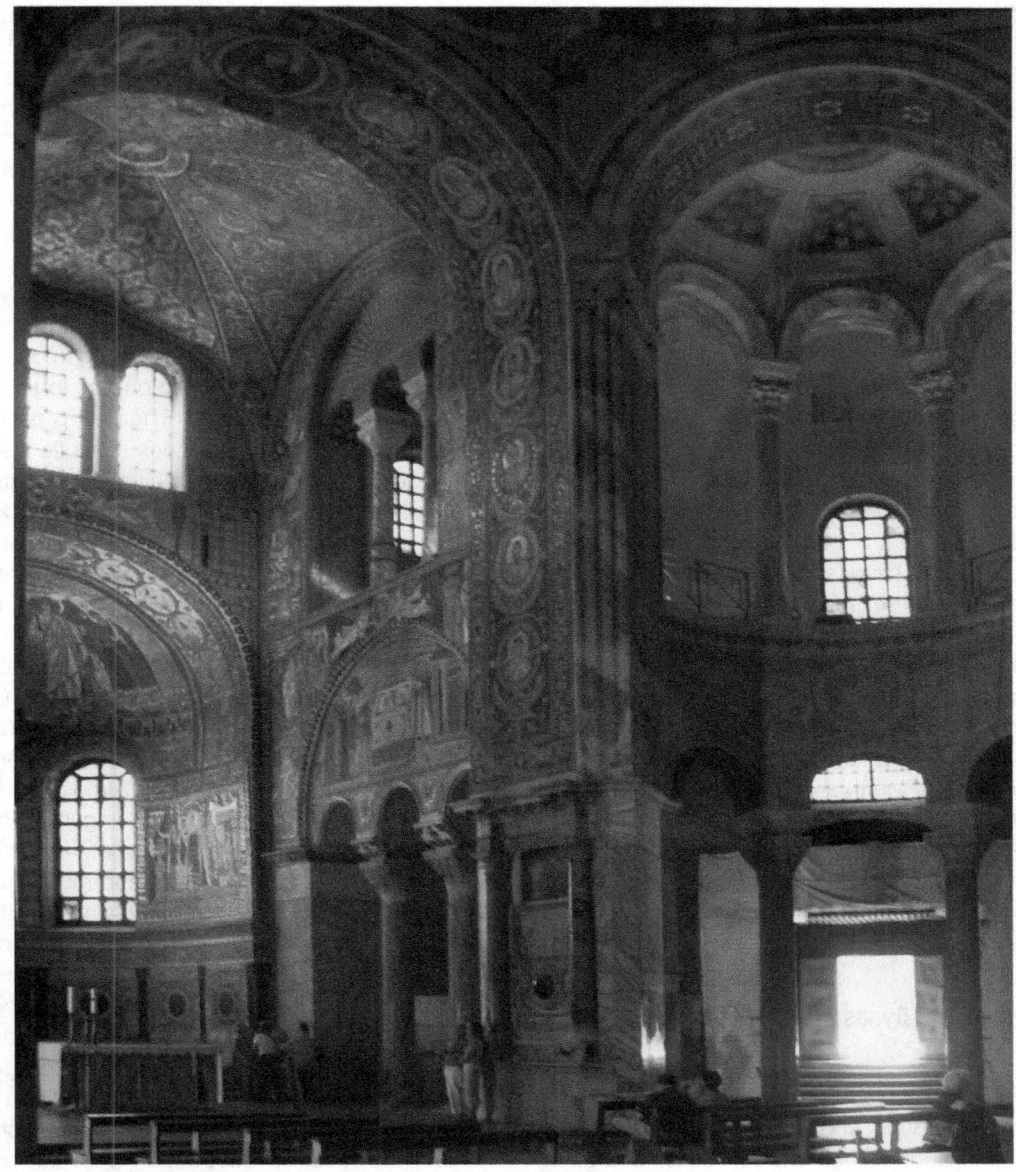

Figure 6.2-13   Ravenna, Italy. San Vitale, 526–540.

the **cupola** of San Vitale, which seems to soar above the structure, its height three times its diameter. Two-story conches cut into seven sides of the octagon. A rectangular sanctuary interrupts the eighth side of this annular sequence, opening to a protruding apse. The sanctuary walls carry golden mosaics illustrating the emperor and empress, Justinian and Theodora, and their retinues, who bear the "gifts" of bread and wine for the sacrament of the Eucharist.

The armies of Justinian repossessed Ravenna from the followers of Theodoric in 540, a few years before the completion of the two churches. While the propagandistic value of the works cannot be judged, they heralded the political transition. The Byzantines precariously ruled central and southern Italy for another 200 years through appointed governors. Despite the fine portraits of Justinian and Theodora in San Vitale, neither of them ever set foot in the church or the city. San Vitale represented the summit of Byzantine expression in

Italy, a work that, like Hagia Sophia, transcended its circumstances. Even after numerous changes to the atrium and the narthex, the addition of flying buttresses on the exterior, and the layering of incongruous Baroque frescoes in the upper vaults, it still rouses feelings of spatial rapture.

Further Reading

Herrin, Judith. *Byzantium: The Surprising Life of a Medieval Empire.* London: Penguin Books, 2007.

MacDonald, William L. *Early Christian and Byzantine Architecture.* New York: George Braziller, 1963.

Mainstone, Rowland J. *Hagia Sophia: Architecture, Structure, and Liturgy of Justinian's Great Church.* New York: Thames & Hudson, 1988.

Mauskopf, Deborah. *Ravenna in Late Antiquity.* New York: Cambridge University Press, 2010.

6.3   GUPTA INDIA
Rock-Cut Architecture and the Art of Subtraction

Since the age of the megalith builders many cultures have found intrinsic spiritual value in pure stone. Indian temple builders from the first to the eighth century carved into stone cliffs or out of piled rocks, making an art of subtraction. Subtraction as a design method allowed one to forgo such functional criteria as foundations, support systems, and roofs but required ingenious strategic organization for the displacement of material. Once material has been removed, it cannot be easily replaced. The structure of rock-cut temples thus relied on what nature provided. The inclusion of columns and vaults served as reminders of other, less permanent structures.

The tradition of rock-cut works reached its zenith during the Gupta period in the fourth and fifth centuries. The dynasty attempted to revive the extent of Ashoka's empire, returning to many of the Mauryan projects. The age of the Gupta inspired the great cave monasteries, the sublime rock-cut temples carved from single masses of stone, and the first important masonry temples built like pyramids over small sanctuaries. Rock-cut works embodied the highest Indian method of praising the divine.

The Stones of the Gupta Dynasty: From Caves to Piles

The ancient empire of the Mauryan dynasty fell apart in the early second century BCE, and India reverted to feudal fragmentation. A multitude of local dynasties took charge of many small states. In the fourth century the Gupta princes succeeded in reconstituting the empire. Multiple sources of religious and secular authority, however, continued to discourage national unity. In contrast to the relatively uniform monotheism of Christianity after the fall of Rome, religious beliefs in India during the same period seem to have

multiplied. Hinduism, Buddhism, and Jainism remained nonhierarchical, permitting a multiplicity of divinities and varied strains of dogma. A great exchange of theological ideas circulated among these cults. Pilgrimage shrines and sacred relics acquired greater ritual importance than the centers of political power. The principal temples and monasteries appeared in remote areas away from the major cities and attracted a continuous flow of pilgrims.

Buddhism, which tended to appeal to wealthier patrons, produced the earliest architectural prototypes, later reworked for Hindu and Jain buildings. Buddhists sponsored projects for **chaitya** halls and *viharas* (monasteries) across the northern and central regions of India, but few were built in permanent materials. The best-preserved examples remain those carved in the cliffs. Despite the shifting political order, local rulers and wealthy merchants continued to build *stupas*, temples, monasteries, and rock-cut sanctuaries in relative isolation. The Ghats, hills formed from horizontal shelves of stone in the central western regions of India near Mumbai, served as the site for many of the great rock-cut works.

The caves at Bhaja, about 100 km (60 miles) southeast of Mumbai, were among the earliest Indian rock-cut temples, carved during the mid-first century BCE. They made quite explicit the crossover of the traditions of wooden architecture into the stone hall. Almost like a mold or impression taken from a freestanding building, the hollow temples in fact give an idea of what the vanished wooden structures, finished with reeds and mud, probably looked like. One entered the great *chaitya* hall at Bhaja through a horseshoe-shaped arch with **struts** carved under its recessed gable in imitation of wooden purlins. The original wooden vestibule door and clerestory window that protected the entry have long since disappeared, exposing its longitudinal cavern. Twenty-seven octagonal columns, simple posts without bases or capitals, lined the U-shaped nave. While the columns seemed constructed, they were in fact the result of subtraction from the monolithic cliff. The builders carved a barrel vault over the flat architraves and willfully perverted the structural nature of their materials, inserting curved teak ribs to the self-supporting stone ceiling so that it appeared as if the timber carried the load. Between the ribs the carvers simulated horizontal crossfrets in stone.

TIME LINE

 321

Chandra Gupta I conquers most of northern India

Samudragupta adds twenty kingdoms as "king of kings"

 335

 380

Chandra Gupta II encourages pan-Indian culture

Gupta dynasty of northern India sponsors cave monasteries at Udayagiri

▲ **ca. 400**

At the end of the axis of the *chaitya* hall at Bhaja a *stupa* rests on a cylindrical **pedestal**, capped with a square *harmika*. The plan bears some resemblance to that of early Christian basilicas, with a wide nave flanked by side ambulatories. The apse of a church, however, was reserved for an altar and did not accommodate circulation, while in an Indian hall pilgrims circulated around the perimeter of the colonnade as a form of devotion to the object or concept marked by the *stupa*. The central nave served as a site for congregational activities. Pilgrims traveled great distances to reach the remote sanctuary at Bhaja, following the river gorge and climbing the steps to the mouth of the cave. They entered from the left, obeying the convention of clockwise movement around the *stupa*, going slowly between the octagonal columns and the rock wall of the cave. The walls were polished smooth and gentle to the touch. Approaching the *stupa* in the dark, its smooth surfaces would have glowed with reflected light like a cosmic egg, a mysterious origin of the universe, in the dark heart of the sanctuary.

The largest and most ornate of the early rock-cut *chaitya* halls was built around 120 CE at Karli, not far from Bhaja (Fig. 6.3-1a,b). It covered a little less than half the area of the Lateran Basilica in Rome. The designers of the screen door and clerestory windows of the vestibule combined stone with wooden details. Sculpted friezes of elephants and lusty couples served as the guardians of the vestibule. Fifteen columns stood on each side of the nave, poised on pot-shaped bases and crowned with complex Persian-style capitals. Each capital stacked an inverted lotus flower above pairs of elephants carrying pairs of *mithuna*, lovers representing the union of male and female energies. In contrast to these exuberant capitals, the seven columns of the apse remained unadorned octagonal posts without bases or capitals. The *harmika* on top of the *stupa* rose as an inverted stepped pyramid capped by a wooden umbrella. The Buddhist builders at Karli used pointed and flat chisels and iron mallets to carve and finish the stone. They scooped out the barrel vault first, removing the rubble through the clerestory window. Then they hewed the lower section, probably beginning at the entrance. As at Bhaja, they hoisted in superfluous teak ribs, weighing as much as 3.5 tons each, and secured them to the polished surface of the vault with dowel pegs.

During the Gupta period of the fourth and fifth centuries the same carving techniques used at Karli appeared in the production of freestanding temples. Contemporary with Constantine's taking of Rome, the Gupta dynasty in India attempted to restore the empire of the Mauryans of several centuries earlier. Although these rulers did not descend from the earlier dynasty, they borrowed Mauryan names and retraced their geographical steps with acts of patronage. Chandra Gupta I used the same name as the founder of the Mauryan dynasty and reestablished the Mauryan capital of Pataliputra. Seeking to surpass the titles of Persian rulers, he chose the honorific title *Maharajadhiraja*, "supreme king of great kings." Despite such grandiose claims, the Gupta kings did not attain absolute rule but remained more like brokers within a federation of kingdoms. Through diplomacy and coordinated administration they guided most of India through a relatively stable, peaceful, and culturally prolific moment from 300 to 500.

The Gupta dynasty left most architectural patronage to the high-ranking members of the court, reserving as royal projects several of the sites preferred by Ashoka's dynasty, in some cases adding new inscriptions to his *stambha* columns (see Section 4.3). To his sacred Buddhist shrine at Sanchi, just a few meters south of the Great Stupa, Gupta designers around the year 400 added a small square temple with a colonnaded porch, now known as Temple 17 (Fig. 6.3-2). Built of mortarless ashlar blocks, it is almost as if a rock-cut temple had been extracted from the cliff and transported to the site. The porch carries two pairs of monolithic columns that, like the columns in the *chaitya* at Karli, appear quite complex, rising from a tall, square base to a short octagonal shaft that becomes an even shorter sixteen-sided shaft before reaching an inverted lotus capital. Above each capital the builders placed a squared-off impost with two crouching lions on each facet. A single slab of stone covered the porch, ennobled with rounded moldings. Two spouts, looking almost like cross-timber beams, stuck out on the sides. The perfectly square, windowless *cella* of Temple 17 remained as dark as the rock-cut caverns and served as a site for the devotional contemplation of an image.

The Gupta court also sponsored caves, quite similar in format to Temple 17, on a cliff only 5 km (3 miles) from Sanchi, known as Udayagiri. Carved during the same years, Caves 6 and 7 share a similar treatment of *T*-shaped doorjambs and pilasters in the same style as the porch columns at Sanchi. One suspects the same artists designed them.

▼ ca. 400

Gupta designers add Temple 17 to Ashoka's Buddhist shrine at Sanchi

Huns led by King Toromana invade India, breaking Gupta power

▲ ca. 500

▼ 530

Huns outlaw Buddhism in India

Last Gupta ruler, Vishnugupta

▲ 550

In this case, however, the builders dedicated the caves to Hindu deities, demonstrating the dynasty's fluid exchange with Buddhist precedents. The caves of Udayagiri included the colossal relief of the god Vishnu as Varaha, the cosmic boar, depicted with the body of a man and the head of a boar, striding heroically as he saves the earth goddess.

A rival clan to the Gupta dynasty sponsored many of the twenty-nine caverns built for Buddhist monasteries at the cliffs of Ajanta, Maharashastra, in the fifth century (Fig. 6.3-3). Among their splendid decorations, which included copious statues of Buddha, were a series of frescoes that depicted typical buildings of the period. The frescoes showed wood-framed, pitched-roof structures covered with thatch as the mainstay of Gupta cities and palaces with open verandahs held up by decorated wooden columns in pot-shaped bases. In the scenes, horizontally placed

Figure 6.3-1 Karli, India. (a) *Chaitya* hall, ca. second century CE. (b) See facing page.

▼ **550s**

Chalukya dynasty (southern India) sponsors seventy-nine temples at Aihole

Elephanta rock-cut temple carved on an island near Mumbai

▲ **ca. 590**

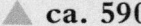

▼ **ca. 600s**

Pallava dynasty (southern India) sponsors temples at Mahabalipuram

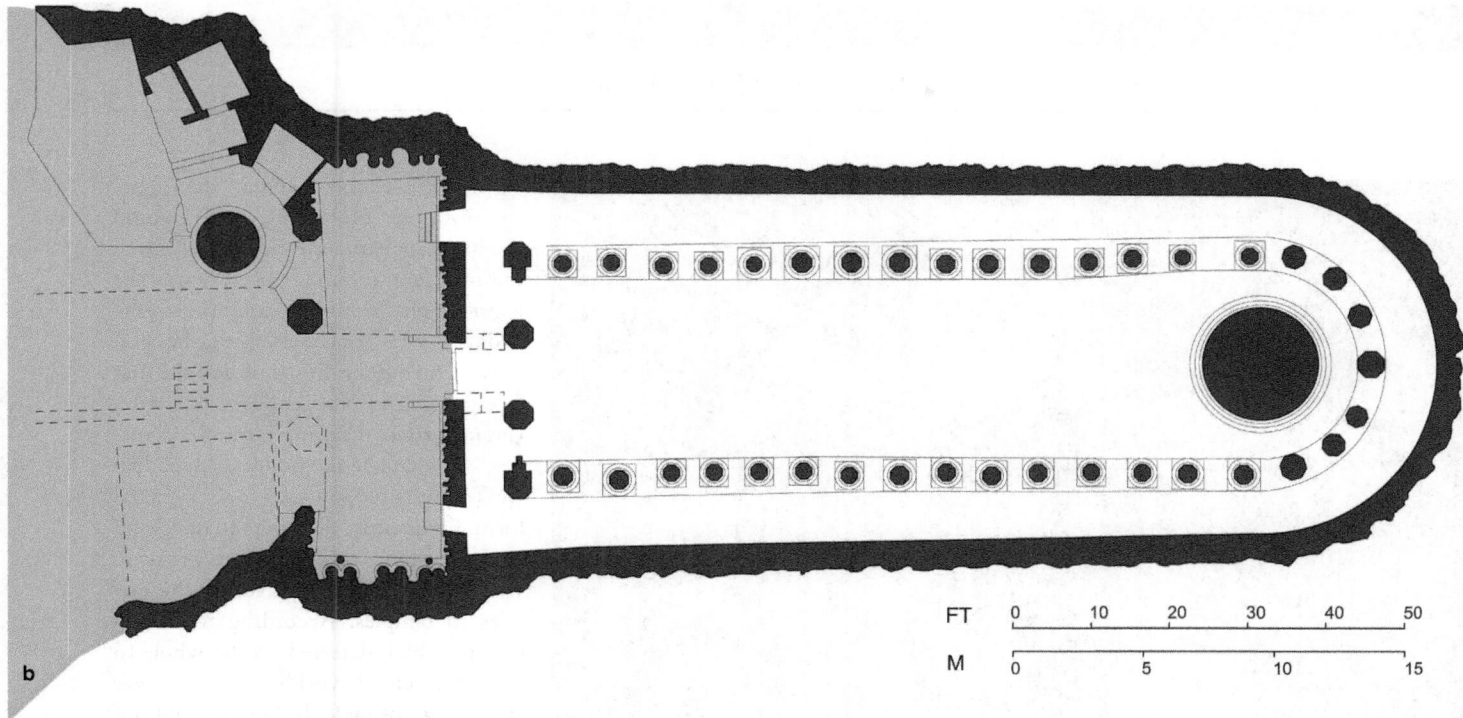

Figure 6.3-1 Karli, India. (b) Plan of *Chaitya* hall.

barrel vaults, or *shalas*, capped the city gates. Their gables had pointed horseshoe arches known as *gavak-shas*, which apparently predated the use of pointed arches in Islamic and Christian buildings.

Some of the *vihara* monasteries at Ajanta included a hypostyle assembly space known as a *mandapa*. The most spectacular of this type of hypostyle cave was cut toward the end of the sixth century into the cliffs in the harbor of Mumbai on the island of Elephanta, a name given to it by the Portuguese in the sixteenth century after the statue of an elephant guarding its northern entry. The patrons of this Hindu shrine were southern rivals of the Guptas. The great *mandapa* hall, which reaches a depth of 40 m (131 ft), was carved in a cruciform configuration, penetrable from three sides. The columns were set in progressively widening rows of two, four, and six, creating a diamond pattern in plan. They rose on tall, square bases; made the transition to round, fluted shafts; and were capped by bulging, rounded cushions. One of the columns has eroded over time, leaving only the cushiony capital dangling from the ceiling and thus revealing the subtractive process of its making. In the southern niche, the darkest wing,

Figure 6.3-2 Sanchi, India. Temple 17, ca. 400 CE.

awaited the proud cult image of the god Shiva, a 5 m (16 ft) high bust with three heads, signifying the creator, the conserver, and the destroyer. An elevated, freestanding cubical *cella*, with doors and steps on each side guarded by giants, occupied the western arm of the hall.

The Sex of the Hindu Temple

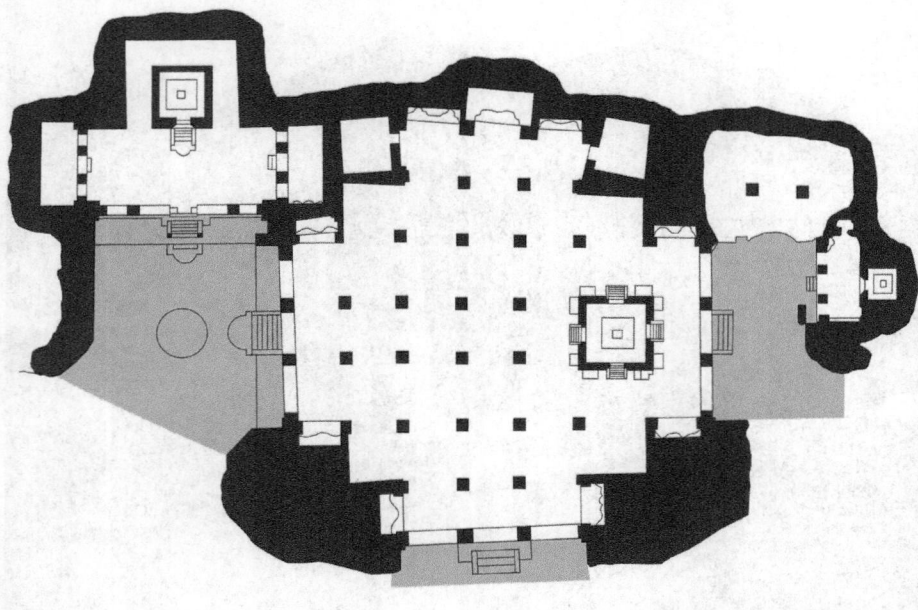

In sixth-century India, the sexualization of architecture would have appeared clear to all. Among the most common cult objects was the *lingam*, a phallus object, sometimes embedded with the likeness of the god Shiva. During the Gupta period the first freestanding Hindu temples sheltered a **garbha griha**, meaning "womb chamber." The cult of the goddess Mahadevi was represented by the *yoni*, a vulval form. Frequently, the sculpted images of bare-breasted women, known as *shakti*, were prominently displayed at the entries to temples. According to Hindu beliefs, which deferred on the whole to a male-oriented worldview, the power and energy of male divinities could not be achieved without union with the female. Consequently, the dialogue of genders occupied the core of the Hindu cosmic vision.

During the Gupta period a Hindu priest, Mallanaga Vatsyayana, compiled the *Kama Sutra*, a synthesis of various treatises on the art of living. Conceived as a religious tract, this celebrated manual of eros described love and courtship and offered detailed advice on a wide variety of methods for lovemaking. Unlike the taboos associated with sexuality found in Christianity, Indian theology promoted the art of love as necessary for achieving an equilibrium between religious propriety and professional virtue. The *Kama Sutra* investigated one's relation to desire in order to gain control of the senses rather than being dominated by them.

Elephanta, India, 590. (a) The *garbha griha* chamber, containing a *lingam*. **(b)** Plan of hypostyle *mandapa* with *garbha griha* on the right.

Figure 6.3-3 Ajanta, India. View of twenty-nine caves with *vihara* (Buddhist monasteries) and *chaitya* halls, fifth century.

Post-Gupta Dravidian Temples

The authority of the Gupta dynasty began to falter in 467 after the invasion of the Huns. These warriors from the Central Asian steppes shared the same origins as the followers of Attila, who terrorized Europe during the same period. A second invasion in 510 demoted the Guptas to minor political players, while rival dynasties emerged in the south of India, generically known as "Dravida." The Huns and their allies actively discouraged Buddhism, allowing other cults to absorb the style of Buddhist temples.

The Chalukya dynasty intermittently commanded the Deccan Plateau from the mid-sixth century, after the demise of the Gupta, as they were relatively safe from the invaders in the north. At their first capital city in Aihole they built over seventy temples using a wide range of styles. Their works show the evolution of rock-cut temples to constructed ones. The Durga Temple (Fig. 6.3-4), built in the mid-seventh century, remains the most sophisticated. Oblong, with a rounded apse, it derived from the *chaitya* type and was skirted by a colonnaded ambulatory. Over the *garbha griha* chamber of the temple the designers raised a pyramidal *shikhara* tower, using thin, horizontal layers decorated with architectural reliefs.

The Dravidian temple architecture of southern India, much like its northern counterpart, appeared inherently sculptural, developed from rock-cut caverns into mounded piles. The seventeen temples at Mahabalipuram, begun in the seventh century by the Pallava dynasty in the region of Tamil Nadu, at India's southeastern tip, illustrates the transition from monolithic works carved out of single boulders found *in situ* to masonry structures built of joined stones. The temple district of Mahabalipuram included many rock-cut caves and the extraordinary precinct known by the somewhat misleading name of Pandava *ratha*, the term for the festival carts used all over India for religious processions. The *rathas* corresponded to the belief that each of the Hindu gods had a particular means of transportation: the faithful ox Nandi, for instance, always accompanied Shiva.

The Pandava *ratha* at Mahabalipuram (Fig. 6.3-5), a series of cart-like monuments each carved from a single stone, lacked wheels but included five monolithic buildings and a few outsized animals. One elephant was carved from a massive loaf of gneiss stone 60 m (197 ft) long and 12 m (39 ft) high. A rectangular walled precinct surrounded the whole complex in the Indian version of a *temenos* known as a **prakaram**. Four of the temples followed a linear

Figure 6.3-4 Aihole, India. Durga temple, seventh century.

cupola with typical *shala* vaulted roofs and horseshoe gables. The series of aedicules, later known as *chhatri* (see Section 12.1), probably alluded to the mythical palaces allotted to the thirty-three gods of the Hindu pantheon. Among the statues in the niches at the pyramid's base stood a portrait of the patron, King Narasimhavarman I (r. 630–668). Most of the Mahabalipuram temples were carved from single stones but looked like they had been built from pieces, imitating the structure of wooden precedents.

The so-called shore temples at Mahabalipuram were built around 720 (Fig. 6.3-6). Situated a twenty-minute walk from the Pandava *ratha*, they were among the first structural temples built in durable materials in this region. As with most medieval monuments in India, their engineering was limited to spanning with corbels. The two adjacent pyramids, one 30 m (98 ft) tall and the other 15 m (49 ft) in height, sat on the beach like eroded lighthouses. They shared a common ambulatory terrace, repeating the vocabulary of decoration used in the aforementioned *ratha* pyramid, with ascending rows of *chhatri* capped by an octagonal cupola. The *garbha griha* chamber of the large pyramid faced east and contained a basalt **lingam**, while that of the smaller pyramid held a representation of the god Shiva with his wife Parvati and their child Skanda. The two pyramids stood in a bounded *prakaram*, subdivided into terraces with sculpted bulls lining the parapets.

Figure 6.3-5 Mahabalipuram, India. Pandava *ratha*, a series of cart-like monuments each carved from a single stone, seventh century.

sequence like a procession, depicting stone simulacra of conventional buildings of the time. The first offered a cube articulated with pilasters and capped by a swollen pitched roof like a thatched hut. The penultimate took the form of a two-story palace that was carved from a single block of stone but looked as if it were built of wooden joinery. Its barrel-vault roof carried horseshoe arch dormers and tiny balconies. The last of the *ratha*, a pyramid, represented the mythical Mount Meru, the origin of the Hindu universe. Three rows of **aedicules** descended beneath its octagonal

The Chalukya commissioned the largest of all the rock-cut temples during the 760s at Ellora, an area of cliffs in the same region as Ajanta. One of dozens of shrines, the Kailasanatha temple (Fig. 6.3-7a,b) demonstrates the evolution from cave to freestanding masonry architecture. The designers sliced a rectangular *prakaram* out of the hillside, 90 × 40 m (295 × 131 ft), and then whittled down the remaining stone into four monumental volumes and a few subsidiary chapels and freestanding columns. One entered the complex through a **gopura**, a propylon capped by a second-story attic. A bridge from the second story of the *gopura* led on the axis to a square pavilion for Nandi, Shiva's ox, and continued on this level to the hypostyle *mandapa* hall with sixteen columns. At the end of the axis awaited a three-story pyramid crowned by an octagonal cupola, close in style to those at Mahabalipuram. The sculptors meticulously scooped out the complex from the top down, but the individual structures appear to have been built from the ground up, with columns, walls, and roofing.

The Gupta dynasty attempted to consolidate the cultural unity of India but exercised limited political control. In the end they allowed their rivals to show themselves as more accomplished patrons. An overall attitude of religious tolerance prevailed, with Buddhist, Jain, and Hindu sects practicing simultaneously. After the invasions of the Huns, however, the Guptas' pretense of empire lost credibility. The Huns enforced discrimination against Buddhism. Various forms of Hinduism came to predominate the religious landscape, and the Buddhist *chaitya* hall type and many decorative solutions were incorporated into the ensuing religious expressions. Likewise, the rock-cut architecture of the Gupta period influenced most of India's subsequent religious buildings, which were conceived as if lovingly extracted from solid stone.

CONSTRUCTION, TECHNOLOGY, THEORY

Elements of the Hindu Temple

At Bhitargaon, in Uttar Pradesh, Gupta patrons sponsored a small, brick temple to Vishnu during the early fifth century, one of the earliest masonry versions of rock-cut precedents. Set on a raised platform, the square womb chamber supported a tower, now mostly in shambles, which rose to about three times its width in a gently tapering section. The tower element, known as a **shikhara**, distinguished the Hindu temples from their Buddhist precursors. The *shikhara* had ascending rows of horseshoe-shaped *gavaksha* gables, used as frames for sculptures. The progressive intensity of the sculpted decoration of the *shikhara* towers during the next few centuries eventually gave them a sponge-like quality. The architecture of Hindu temples evolved into northern and southern tendencies— respectively, the Nagara and the Dravida. The differences between these strains appeared in their treatment of the *shikhara*: the convex curves, or beehive shape, of the Nagara type, such as the seventh-century Parashurameshvara Temple in Bhubaneshwar, Orissa, versus the tiered, pyramidal approach of the Dravida style, seen in the shore temples at Mahabalipuram.

Figure 6.3-6   Mahabalipuram, India. Shore temples, seventh century.

a

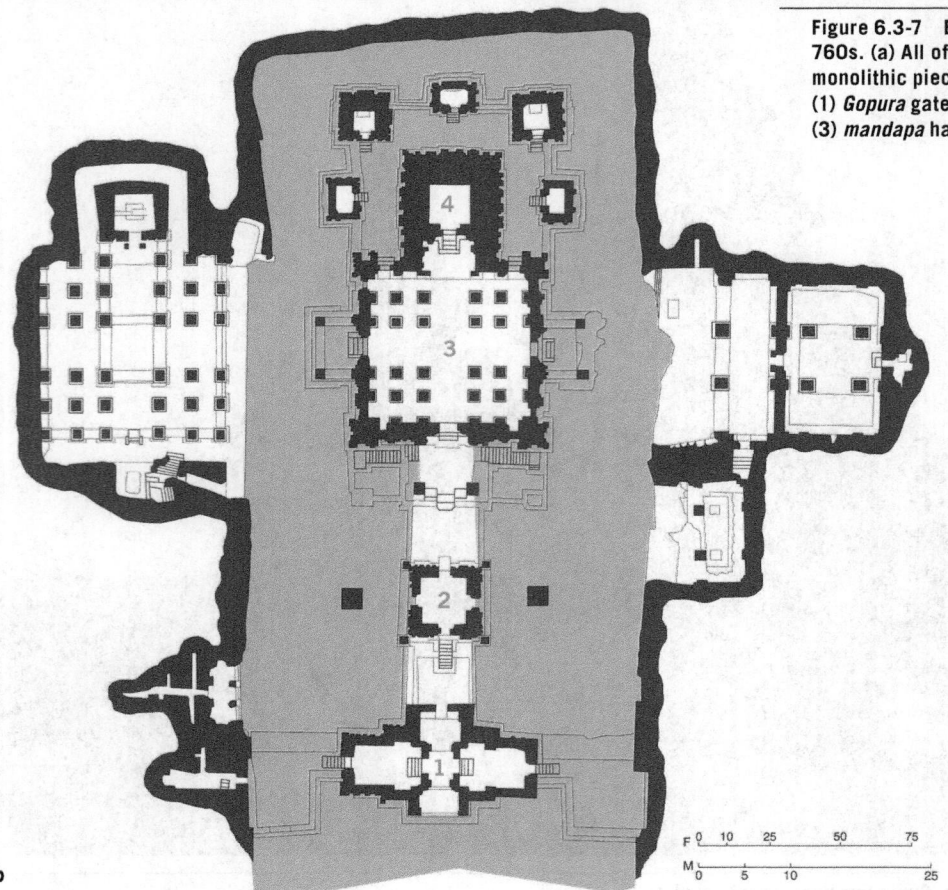

b

Figure 6.3-7   Ellora, India. Kailasanatha temple, 760s. (a) All of the buildings were carved from monolithic pieces, including the bridges. (b) Plan. (1) *Gopura* gateway; (2) pavilion devoted to Nandi; (3) *mandapa* hall; (4) *garbha griha* for *lingam*.

RELIGION, PHILOSOPHY, FOLKLORE

Buddha Leaves India

The post-Gupta rulers of India actively discouraged Buddhism, forcing the practitioners of the religion to migrate. The faith soon flourished outside of India in Nepal, China, and Southeast Asia, and the image of the Buddha became an item of export. In its origins Buddhism opposed idolatry and deification, and images of the Buddha were absent from sites such as Sanchi. His presence was signified by such enigmatic signs as footprints. But with the increasing importance of venerable images in the Hindu cults during the Gupta period, pictures and statues of the Buddha as objects of worship became more frequent. In one of the *chaitya* halls at Ajanta, the end of the axis terminated not in a simple *stupa*, but in a figure of the Buddha set in a colonnaded niche over which rose a rounded *stupa*, capped by umbrellas. In another *chaitya* hall at Ajanta, the perimeter walls of the ambulatory hosted the first colossal statue of the Buddha, a reclining figure 4 m (13 ft) long. What had once seemed conspicuous by its absence now loomed bold like the giant statues of Hindu gods.

Long after the areas controlled by the Gupta stopped building rounded Buddhist *stupas*, the form survived both in the south on the island of Sri Lanka and in the north in Nepal at the base of the Himalaya Mountains. In Kathmandu, Nepal, the Swayambunath Stupa, a smooth mound with perimeter chapels puncturing its base, was originally built in the fifth century CE and has been periodically renovated. As at other *stupas* in this region, the artisans painted a pair of squinting eyes on each side of the cubical *harmika* at the summit of the mound. In effect, this personification of the monument acknowledged the *stupa* as the embodiment of the presence of the Buddha.

The two great colossi of Bamiyan, carved into cliffs at a point of convergence with the ancient Silk Road between Persia and China, were among the earliest and largest images of the Buddha. Designed between the third and fifth centuries, the largest at 70 m (230 ft) surpassed the rock-cut portraits of Ramesses at Abu Simbel (see Section 3.2). They derived from the Indian rock-cut temple traditions and indeed served to frame a series of monasteries that honeycombed the cliffs. The hollows of the rock out of which the

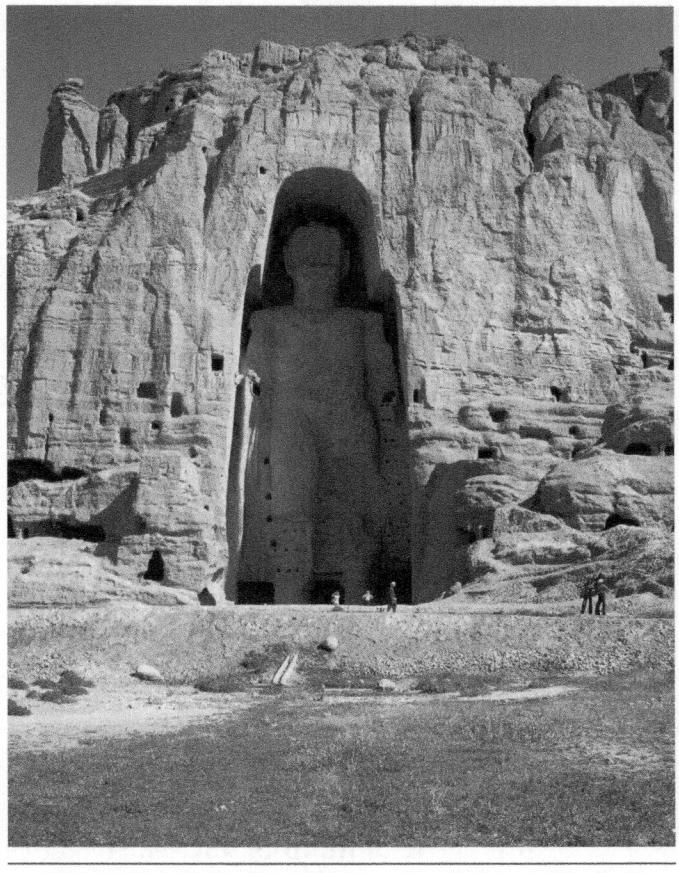

Bamiyan, Afghanistan. One of the two colossal statues of the Buddha (third to fifth century CE) prior to its devastation in 2001.

statues had been cut provided deep hoods to protect the figures, which were originally plastered and gilded. While intended as peaceful apotropaic guardians between borders and as welcome signs for pilgrims, the immense scale of the Buddhist colossi became an iconographic threat to the Islamic fundamentalists of the Taliban government of Afghanistan, who destroyed them in 2001.

Further Reading

Bussagli, Mario. *Oriental Architecture,* vol. 1. Translated by J. Shepley. Milan: Electa, 1981.

Kramrisch, Stella. *The Hindu Temple.* Delhi: Motilal Banarsidass, 1980.

Michell, George. *Hindu Art and Architecture.* London: Thames & Hudson, 2000.

———. *The Hindu Temple: An Introduction to Its Meaning and Form.* Chicago: University of Chicago Press, 1988.

Rowland, Benjamin. *The Art and Architecture of India: Buddhist–Hindu–Jain.* London: Penguin, 1977.

Spink, Walter. *Ajanta: History and Development.* Boston and Leiden: Brill, 2006.

Thapar, Romila. *Early India: From the Origins to AD 1300.* Berkeley: University of California Press, 2002.

Williams, Joanna G. *The Art of Gupta India: Empire and Province.* Princeton, NJ: Princeton University Press, 1982.

Zimmer, Heinrich R. *The Art of Indian Asia: Its Mythology and Transformations,* 2 vols. Edited by J. Campbell. New York: Pantheon Books, 2001.

↗ Visit the free website **www.oup.com/us/ingersoll** to view chapter outlines and study questions; Google Maps showing the location of key sites; links to UNESCO World Heritage Sites; and essays on topics that cross time and culture.

CHAPTER

7

600–800

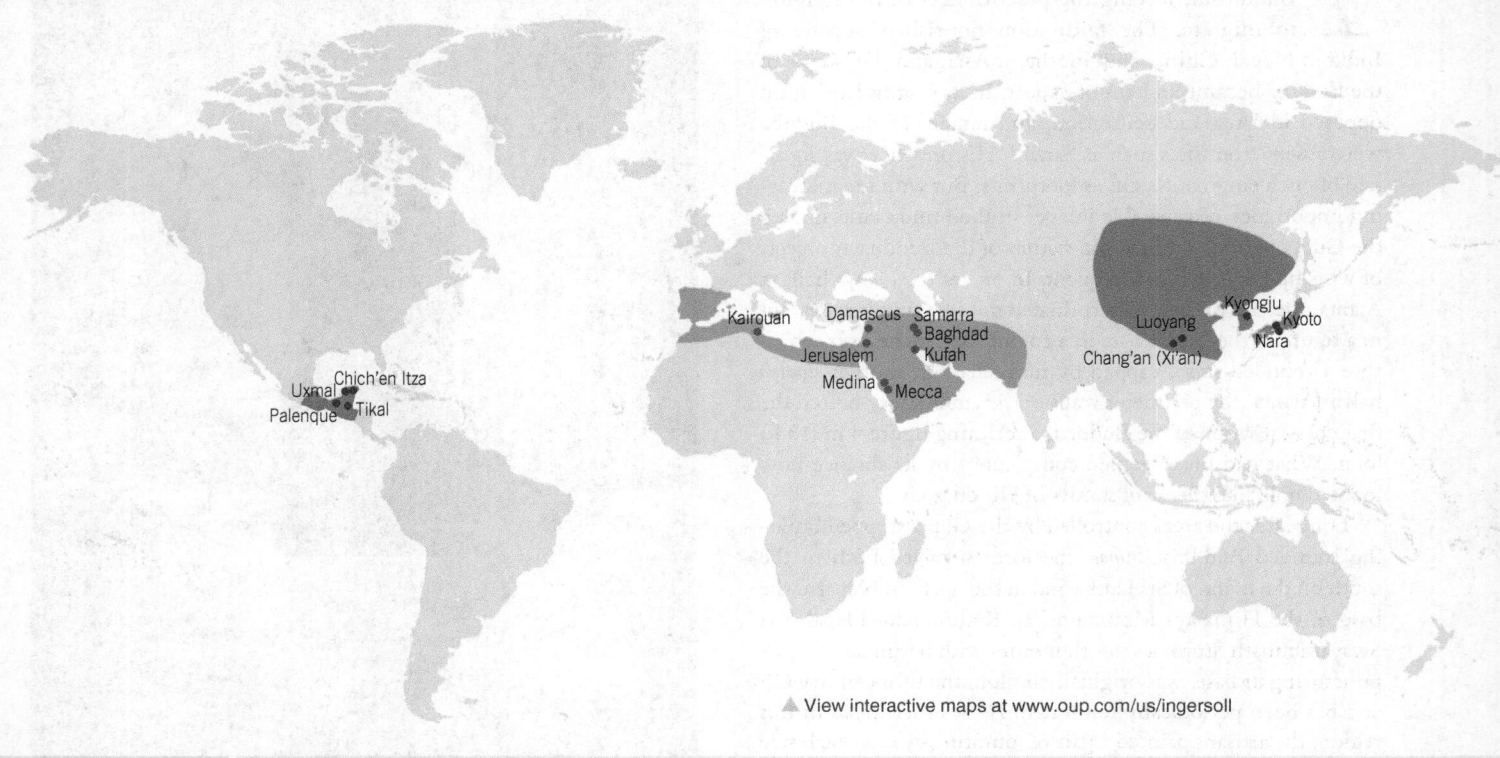

Kairouan
Damascus Samarra
Baghdad
Jerusalem Kufah
Medina Mecca

Luoyang
Kyongju
Kyoto
Nara
Chang'an (Xi'an)

Uxmal Chich'en Itza
Palenque Tikal

▲ View interactive maps at www.oup.com/us/ingersoll

7.1   **THE SPREAD OF ISLAM:** Hypostyle Mosques and Soaring Minarets

7.2   **TANG CHINA AND EAST ASIA:** Gridded Capitals and Lofty Pagodas

7.3   **THE MAYA OF CENTRAL AMERICA:** Reproducing the Mountain of Creation

Islam, the new monotheistic religion of the Prophet Muhammad, spread from Arabia to Southwest Asia, Persia, and North Africa. Within a century this new empire covered as much territory as that of Alexander. The Umayyad leadership constructed the exceptional central-plan structure of the Dome of the Rock on the Temple Mount in Jerusalem to attract attention from other faiths. Throughout Islamic territories patrons sponsored conventional hypostyle prayer halls as the Friday mosques of their cities, accompanied by tall minarets for the *muezzins* to call the people to prayer. As Islam spread into Central Asia, the Buddhist religion spread rapidly through the Chinese empire and eastern Asia. The powerful empress Wu Zetian sponsored numerous monasteries and pagodas, using religious sympathy to gain political support. The Silk Road through the territory of the steppes to the west enjoyed new stability because of the increased protection offered by the empires at either end of the route. During the same period in the Western Hemisphere the Maya culture reached its apex. The struggle to control the scarce resources of the region led to numerous military conflicts and inspired competitive patronage for ever-greater monuments, which eventually exhausted the carrying capacity of the land.

7.1 THE SPREAD OF ISLAM
Hypostyle Mosques and Soaring Minarets

Islam, the religion that developed around the teachings of the Prophet Muhammad (570–632), began in the seminomadic setting of the southern edge of the great Arabian Desert. The new monotheistic religion gained wide approval because it appeared to be nonhierarchical, easy to grasp, and tolerant of differences. Like Christianity at the time of Constantine, Islam spread as an urban phenomenon tied to military and political power. Within a century of the Prophet's death, Islamic rulers amassed an empire through military conquest and conversion that included most of the southern half of the Roman Empire plus all of the Persian Empire (Fig. 7.1-1).

The **mosque**, usually built as a multicolumned prayer hall, provided the new religious focus of the cities under Islamic rule. The minaret, a slender tower for the *muezzin*, or crier, to call the faithful to prayer, added a new vertical axis to urban skylines. The earliest cities built by Muslims appeared as orderly as Roman military camps, but gradually urban development in places such as Damascus and Baghdad yielded patchworks of neighborhoods, or *herats*, without through streets or open public spaces. Despite this apparent disorder, all of the Islamic world shared an underlying sense of order in the radial orientation of mosques, tombs, and prayers toward the theological fulcrum of Mecca.

Mecca and Medina: The Cities of Muhammad and His Followers

The Arabian Desert touches both Mesopotamia to the north and Egypt to the south. Although the inhabitants of this sparsely settled region had witnessed urban civilizations since the seventh millennium BCE and had traded with the major cities of the Roman, Byzantine, and Persian Empires, theirs remained for the most part a nomadic culture. The cooler climate of the hills of the Hejaz region on the southeastern flank of the Red Sea stimulated the growth of the oasis settlements of Mecca (sometimes spelled Makkah) and Medina (formerly Yathrib), where the new religion of Muhammad took root. During the seventh century Islam spread rapidly, uprooting various pagan cults while seeking to convert Jews and Christians through intellectual persuasion, economic incentives, and military force.

Mecca had long been a major cult site for the nomadic tribes of Arabia, attracting religious pilgrims to the Kaaba (Fig. 7.1-2), a cubical granite house containing many idols, including a mysterious black meteorite. Muhammad belonged to the Quraysh tribe of Mecca, which claimed responsibility for maintaining the Kaaba. The earliest conflict of Islam involved the local rejection of the Prophet's espousal of monotheism. Forced to leave Mecca in 622, Muhammad spent ten years in exile in Medina, where he refined his new religion. After many battles, Muhammad conquered Mecca and stripped the Kaaba of its pagan iconography. He taught that the angel Gabriel had given

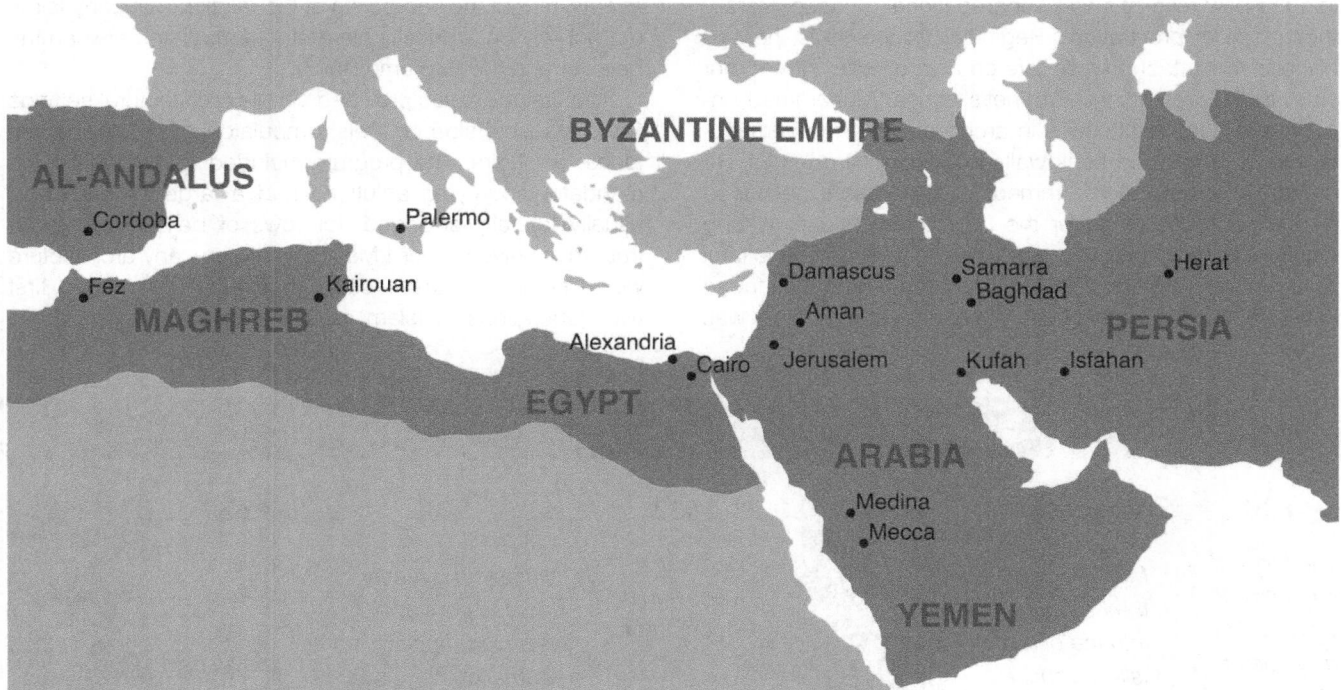

Figure 7.1-1 The spread of Islam, 630 to 750.

Figure 7.1-2 Mecca. The Kaaba, a pre-Islamic cult site that became the focus of Muslim pilgrims. The box-like structure was rebuilt during the life of Muhammad; the black silk veil was placed over it toward the end of the seventh century.

the sacred black stone to Abraham and that both Abraham and Ishmael participated in building the original structure. Muslim pilgrims still circumambulate the Kaaba seven times as an act of supreme devotion to God. During the latter half of the seventh century a black silk drape was introduced to shield the Kaaba, transforming the shrine into a veiled abstraction. The surrounding court, or *haram*, was rebuilt over the centuries. As the focus of Muslim prayers, the Kaaba represents the unity of the faithful.

Aside from the Kaaba in Mecca, Muhammad directly influenced the transformation of his own house in Medina into the new religion's first congregational mosque, literally the "place of prostration." Beginning in the 620s, he and his followers attached a square courtyard, 56 m (184 ft) per side, to the west of the Prophet's house. Muhammad encouraged ascetic attitudes in architecture, using vernacular methods for mud-brick walls and a palm-trunk roof. He insisted that he and his immediate successors be buried without monuments under the floor of the house. A long covered portico, two columns deep, protected the faithful on the north side from the sun. His initial prayer hall faced Jerusalem, which, previous to the conquest of Mecca, was

favored by the Prophet as the **qibla**, or direction of prayers. Muhammad had made his legendary "night flight" to Jerusalem, thus involving his followers with the city revered by both Jews and Christians. After his conquest of Mecca, however, he redirected the *qibla* to the Kaaba. In Medina his followers added a second portico to the south side of the Prophet's mosque to shelter those facing Mecca.

The Mosque of the Prophet in Medina probably resembled a small traders' **caravansary**. Muhammad's modest approach to architecture echoed his nomadic origins. Like the early Christians, the first Muslims rejected the form of pagan temples, preferring to base their cult buildings on secular structures. The earliest mosques took the place of the forum–basilica core of Roman cities. The ruler, or his official representative, led prayers inside. The sermon that followed usually had political content, ending invariably with a declaration of allegiance by the community. In contrast to Christian liturgy, Muslim services had no dramatic action or ceremonies like processions, communion, or baptism. Holy men, known as *imams*, taught the fine points of the religion, but early Islam did not rely on a priestly hierarchy to mediate between the believer and the Supreme Being.

The first mosques provided simple architectural settings without apses, side chapels, ambulatories, crypts, baptisteries, or choirs. The program included a fountain for the mandatory purifying ablutions and a large covered hall, usually laterally arranged, for rows of believers to prostrate themselves toward Mecca. In theory, any architecture would suffice for these basic requirements, and the first two generations of Islam requisitioned diverse structures

TIME LINE

▼ **620**

The Prophet Muhammad creates first mosque in Medina

Muhammad and his followers take Mecca, convert the Kaaba into the prime Islamic shrine

▲ **630**

▼ **632**

Death of the Prophet Muhammad

Umayyad dynasty locates capital of Islamic empire in Damascus

▲ **661**

▼ **687**

Dome of the Rock built by Umayyads in Jerusalem

Muhammad and Islam

Muhammad ibn 'Abdullah (570–632), known as the Prophet, abandoned a career as a merchant in Mecca to preach monotheism to the desert tribes of Arabia. Although his new creed, Islam, had common origins with Judaism and Christianity, with followers of all three faiths viewing themselves as "people of the Book," he claimed that Arabs descended from Abraham's son Ishmael, rather than Isaac. The Prophet's teachings were initially transmitted orally and later written down in the *Quran* ("word of God"). Concerned mostly with moral lessons, the holy book of Islam has less historical narrative than the Torah or the New Testament. The new religion required five simple tasks: the first, to honor a single God, a rule familiar to both Christians and Jews, with a new clause that "Muhammad is His messenger"; the second, to worship God five times daily—the *muezzin* sings from a lofty place to call the faithful to prayer at the appointed times (on Fridays, all male believers are expected to attend a midday service to listen to a sermon); the third, to set aside Ramadan, the ninth month of the Muslim calendar, as a period of abstinence, requiring fasting and sexual restraint during the hours of daylight; the fourth, to give alms to the poor; and the fifth, to make the *hajj*, or pilgrimage, to Mecca at least once.

While Islam's rapid diffusion during the seventh century came partly through military conquest and partly through the political economy of levying lower taxes on Muslims, the religion undoubtedly had broad theological appeal. The militant aspect of Islam related to Muhammad's own background as a warrior. From his exile in Medina he personally conducted his followers in battle against the Quraysh clan to take Mecca in 630. "Islam" literally means "submission," inferring that one should turn one's face humbly to God. To underline this sense of humility, all mosques and tombs are oriented to Mecca as the spiritual pivot of Islam, creating a subliminal order known as the *qibla* that often contradicts the geometry of street patterns.

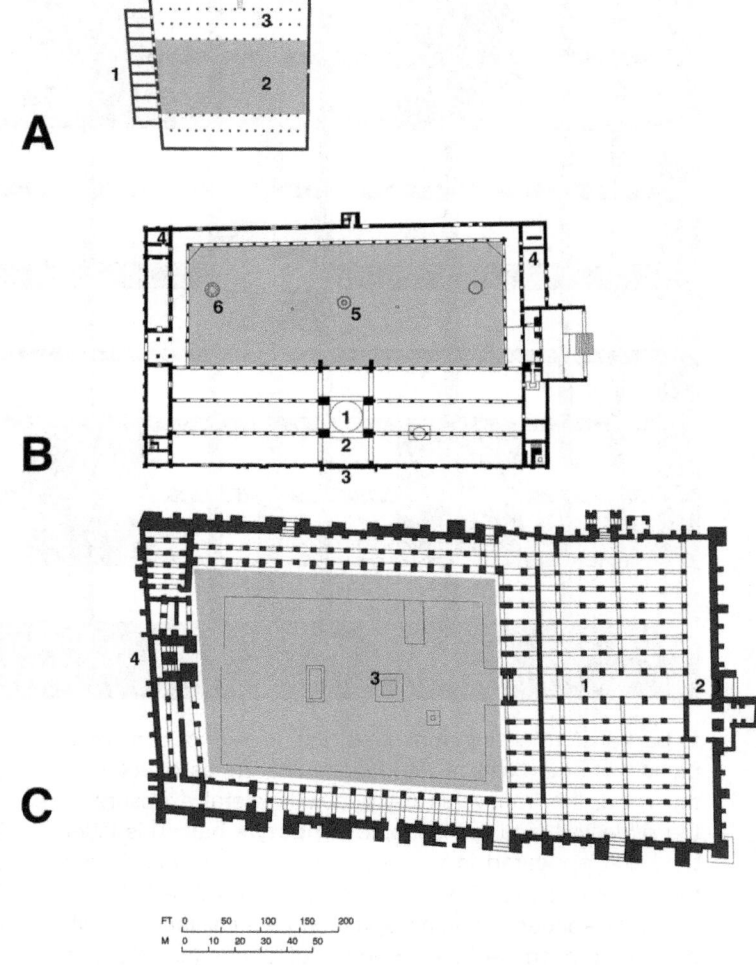

Islamic world. Comparison of hypostyle plans. **(A)** Mosque of the Prophet in Medina, ca. 634: (1) house and burial site of the Prophet; (2) *sahn*, or court; (3) first pergolas oriented to Jerusalem. **(B)** The Great Mosque of Damascus, eighth century: (1) dome over *qibla* direction; (2) *maksura area* for royal family; (3) *mihrab* niche; (4) corner towers used as minarets; (5) fountain; (6) treasury. **(C)** The Great Mosque in Kairouan, 836: (1) nave on *qibla*; (2) *mihrab* niche; (3) fountain house; (4) tower minaret.

Umayyad dynasty begins construction of the Great Mosque of Damascus

▲ **707**

▼ **750**

Abbasid dynasty exterminates the Umayyad dynasty

Al-Mansur founds the round city of Baghdad (Iraq) as Abbasid capital

▲ **762**

▼ **820**

Al-Mutasim founds Samarra (Iraq)

Aghlabid dynasty commands Tunisia and Sicily

▲ **830**

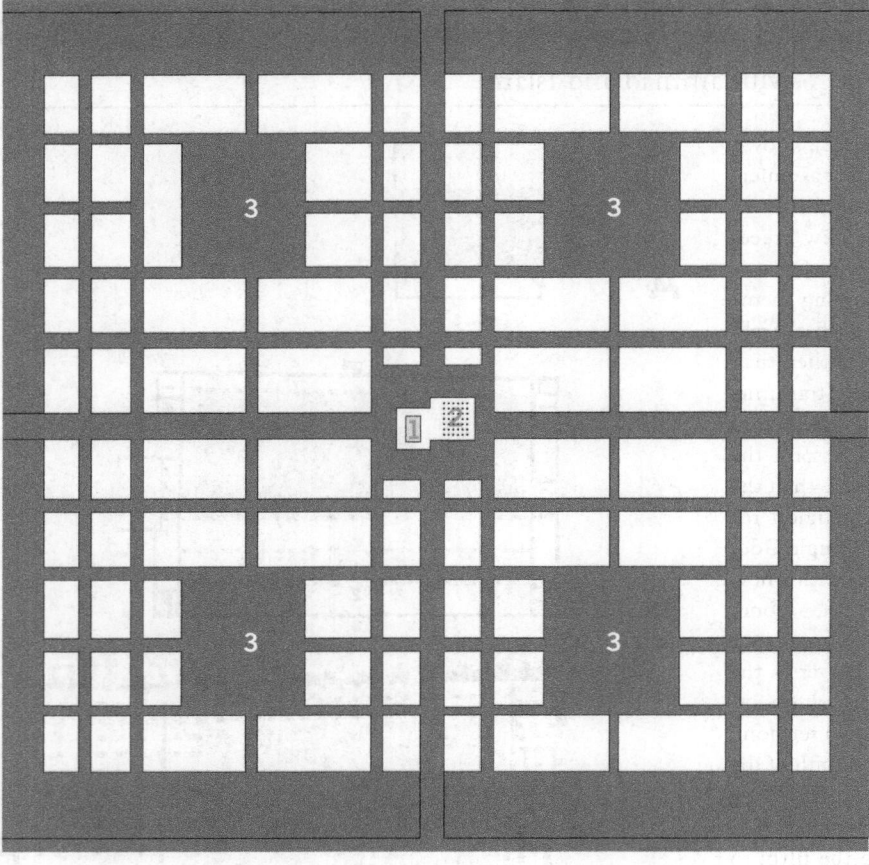

Figure 7.1-3 Kufah, Iraq. Reconstructed plan of new capital city built in **638** on a strict orthogonal plan, with the hypostyle mosque (1) and palace (2) in the center, surrounded by four quadrants, each with an open plaza, or *maydan* (3), in the center (after Nezar Alsayyad).

Persians, the Arabs founded Kufah in 638 on a site not far from ancient Babylon. The city's architect, Abu al-Haiyaj, followed the Greco-Roman precedents of Byzantine towns in the region. He structured the new city on a grid with two broad cross streets (Fig. 7.1-3). At the principal intersection he placed the governor's palace and the Friday mosque back to back. Each of the four quadrants of Kufah contained an open plaza, or ***maydan***, surrounded by orthogonally arranged streets 9 m (29 ft) wide. Narrow lanes, one-third the width of the main streets, subdivided the blocks. Although the cities of this region later took on gnarled, informal patterns, the initial Arab foundations proved almost as methodically geometric as those of the ancient Romans.

to be transformed into mosques. The three most common plans were the basilica with longitudinal aisles directed to the *qibla*, the transverse basilica with lateral exposure to the *qibla* wall, and the isotropic **hypostyle hall**. This latter type first appeared in the new city of Kufah, Iraq, in the mid-seventh century, where a square hall with a forest of regularly spaced columns spreading equidistant in both directions resembled the Apadana of Darius (see Section 4.1). It was served by a large open court, or *sahn*.

The Arab domination of Sassanian Persia and the southern Mediterranean relied upon the ideology of *jihad* (the religious duty of conquest). Muhammad's army founded garrison towns in the eastern part of the empire in order to segregate the Arab troops from tribal representatives of the conquered populations. After the victory against the

The Umayyad Period: Jerusalem and Damascus

The original promoters of Islam assumed that religious and political authority descended from Muhammad. The Prophet's followers chose his close friend Abu Bakr (r. 632–634) as the first caliph, or successor. The troops elected the next successor, Umar (r. 634–644). After the third elected caliph, Uthman (r. 644–656), was assassinated, Muhammad's cousin and son-in-law Ali (r. 656–661) took power, claiming his right to authority through the bloodline. To avoid disputes, he moved the political capital of Islam from Mecca to Kufah, the geographic center of the territory taken by conquest. Following the assassination of Ali, the rival Umayyad clan established a

▼ **836**

Great Mosque of Kairouan built for Aghlabids of Tunisia

Great Mosque of Samarra built with spiral minaret

▲ **ca. 850**

▼ **870**

Ibn Tulun takes control of Egypt

Ibn Tulun's mosque in Cairo modeled on Great Mosque of Samarra

▲ **880**

hereditary dynasty, attempting to bring stability to the new empire. Husayn, one of the sons of Ali, however, continued to demand his family's right until his assassination at Karbala, Iraq, in 680, an event that spawned the Shiite faction of Islam. Shiites maintain that only the blood relatives of the Prophet should serve as caliph. The Umayyads settled in the Greco-Roman city of Damascus, Syria, where they sponsored a brilliant urban culture partly based on the example of the Byzantines in Constantinople. Through the production of fine architecture and grand ceremonies, they attempted to create a charismatic setting to smooth over the succession disputes.

Like other nomadic peoples, the Arabs had scarce knowledge of masonry architecture. They borrowed forms and techniques from Persian, Roman, and Byzantine precedents. Abd al-Malik (r. 685–705), the patron of the first great Umayyad monument, the Dome of the Rock in Jerusalem, most likely hired a Byzantine architect and mosaic artists from Constantinople. Constructed on an elevated terrace toward the center of the Temple Mount between 687 and 692 (Fig. 7.1-4a), the central-plan structure resembled a Christian martyrium. Its dome followed the example of the nearby Anastasis built over the tomb of Christ and had the same 20 m (64 ft) diameter (see Section 6.2). Inside the Dome of the Rock a frieze of interlacing **kufic script** encircled the base, distinguishing it as Islamic. The new religion rejected the representation of people and things as idolatry, favoring decorative inscriptions, or *alfiz*, instead of narrative scenes with human figures. The arcade surrounding the central rock that gave the site its name had two other characteristics that became common in Islamic architecture: pointed arches and **ablaq**, alternating bands of different-colored masonry (Fig. 7.1-4b). An octagonal ring of double ambulatories served as paths for pilgrim circulation around the sacred site. The dome rose as a double-shell structure over a cylindrical drum. The outer shell was covered in gilded copper and appeared to slightly bulge at its base. The Iznik tile decoration on the lower elevations is a sixteenth-century embellishment.

The Umayyad project for the Dome of the Rock had clear political motivations. Since a rival clan controlled Mecca at that time, the Umayyads sought to propose Jerusalem as an alternative pilgrimage site. By creating the most visible monument in the city, they transmitted a major propaganda statement to attract non-Muslims. The site could not have been more significant: here, Solomon built the initial Jewish Temple with its holy of holies, allegedly over the rock of Abraham's sacrifice at Mount Moriah (see Section 3.3). The rock was also believed to have served as the base for the ladder to heaven for Muhammad's legendary "night flight" to visit God. The Temple Mount, known in Arabic as *Haram ash-Sharif*, "the noble sanctuary," prevailed as the largest of all Greco-Roman platforms, 470 × 300 m (1,541 × 984 ft). The new shrine occupied about 10% of this *temenos*, bound by eight sets of broad stairs, each framed at the top by a freestanding row of arches, added in the eleventh century.

The Dome of the Rock differed from most central-plan Christian churches in its use of two concentric ambulatories (Fig. 7.1-5), which accommodated the pilgrims' ritual of circling the rock under the dome. The major structural elements of the interior piers and arcades followed the intersection of two superimposed nine-square grids, one rotated 45° over the other to create an eight-pointed star. The discrepancy of the alignment between the columns and piers of the two ambulatories unchained a superb kinetic effect as one moved in a circular path toward the rock.

Mecca fell to the Umayyads a year after the completion of the Dome of the Rock, and the realm of Islam regained a sense of unity. Abd al-Malik's son, al-Walid I (r. 705–715), built three impressive mosques to celebrate the consolidation of the empire. The first entailed the enlargement of the Mosque of the Prophet in Medina, to which he added mosaics and the earliest **mihrab**, a decorated niche indicating the *qibla* to Mecca. The second, the al-Aqsa Mosque, begun in 705, took the form of a congregational hypostyle hall on the Temple Mount in Jerusalem. Raised over Herod's South Stoa, it lined up with the southern portal of the Dome of the Rock. Destroyed and rebuilt several times over the years, the mosque in its origins had a basilica plan, with a central nave and seven aisles to either side.

Al-Walid I's third project, the Great Mosque of Damascus (Fig. 7.1-6), took form between 707 and 714. It abutted the al-Khadra, the Green Palace, a dynastic residence begun by his grandfather and known for its green tiled dome, which has long since vanished. This fusing of the mosque with the palace compound drew upon the Byzantine precedent of combining temporal and religious authority, notably in Constantinople, where the imperial palace connected to Hagia Sophia. Similar to the Dome of the Rock, the new mosque in Damascus reutilized the principal Greco-Roman *temenos* of the ancient city. The Byzantines had destroyed the original temple at the end of the fourth century and inserted inside the compound a five-aisled basilica church dedicated to St. John the Baptist. During the seventh century Christians and Muslims shared the precinct. After the demolition of the church to make way for the mosque, the Umayyads conserved the prized relic of St. John's head in a side chamber as a benevolent gesture to the city's Christians, who still outnumbered its Muslims.

The new structure for the prayer hall of the Great Mosque of Damascus rose against the southern wall of the ancient *temenos*. This left a generous lateral courtyard, slightly larger in area than the prayer hall, articulated with arcades on two levels. The great **sahn** enclosed an ablution fountain, a kiosk for a clock, and an arcane octagonal pavilion known as the "treasury," which was used for symbolically storing the wealth of the empire under divine surveillance in full view of the community. This windowless structure, encrusted with glittering mosaics, rose on eight Corinthian columns, capped with a small cupola. The columns there and throughout the complex originated as spoils from the earlier Roman temple that had sat on the site. On the corners of

Figure 7.1-4 Jerusalem. Dome of the Rock, 690. (a) Aerial view of setting on ancient Temple Mount. (b) See facing page.

the southern wall of the *temenos*, the existing guard towers served as platforms for the *muezzin*'s call to prayer. These towers served as the first minarets, which evolved into the most monumental element of later mosques.

The entry portal to the Great Mosque of Damascus rose three stories above the court between two square buttresses. The triad of ground-floor arches, as well as the arched windows above them, was recessed inside a single grand arch. Above this rested a triangular pediment. The Byzantine-style mosaics depicted a verdant vision of paradise with fruit trees and fine buildings instead of saints and angels.

Past this portal a central nave led to the *mihrab*, which was further accentuated by a dome above its central section. The Umayyads introduced the *mihrab* niche as the termination of a princely axis. The door next to it on the left led directly into the caliph's palace, while a screened area to the right, known as the ***maksura*** (Fig. 7.1-7), served to protect the caliph and his court. The *maksura* imitated the screened areas in palatine churches that separated Byzantine emperors from the congregation. Next to the *mihrab* rose an elevated sitting platform, or ***minbar***, a podium that referred back to the Prophet's two-stepped wooden seat in

Figure 7.1-4 Jerusalem. Dome of the Rock, 690. (b) Detail view through freestanding gates; tile cladding from sixteenth century.

Medina. The pulpit served as the *imam*'s primary position during Friday prayer meetings. To either side of the central nave stretched long, three-aisled wings similar to those of basilica churches. The colossal Corinthian columns had Byzantine inverted pyramidal imposts supporting stilted horseshoe-shaped arches. A second level of smaller columns and arches was stacked above the arcade, supporting the open web of wooden crossbeams. The kinetic effect of the double-story arcades and their evanescent lighting gave the interior a magnificent sense of transparency.

Although nothing remains of the Umayyad palaces in Damascus, the ruins of the so-called desert palaces provide evidence of great splendor. These remote residences served as trading caravansaries, administrative centers of agricultural estates, hunting lodges, and pleasure grounds. Their rural locations conformed to the Arab ruling class's tendency to remain aloof from the masses in the cities. While the palaces had high solid walls and seemed fortified, these protections proved more symbolic than functional. Among the finest examples of such structures one finds the Qasr Mshatta, near Amman, Jordan, built in the 740s. Its square set of walls stretched 144 m (472 ft) per side, nearly as large as Diocletian's palace at Spalato (see Section 6.1). Octagonal towers flanked the gate. The outer walls were encrusted with delicately carved limestone rosettes framed in chevron patterns. The plan was rigorously symmetrical: the central entry hall led to a formal court with a mosque on one side and baths on the other (Fig. 7.1-8a,b). Beyond the reception court lay a larger court, 50 m (164 ft) per side. The axis terminated in a long vault, or **iwan**, with a triconch room, similar to a Byzantine triclinium. Such a luxurious atmosphere, though contrary to the humble tenets espoused by the Prophet, corresponded perfectly to the imperial scale of Umayyad power, soon to be eclipsed by the Abbasids.

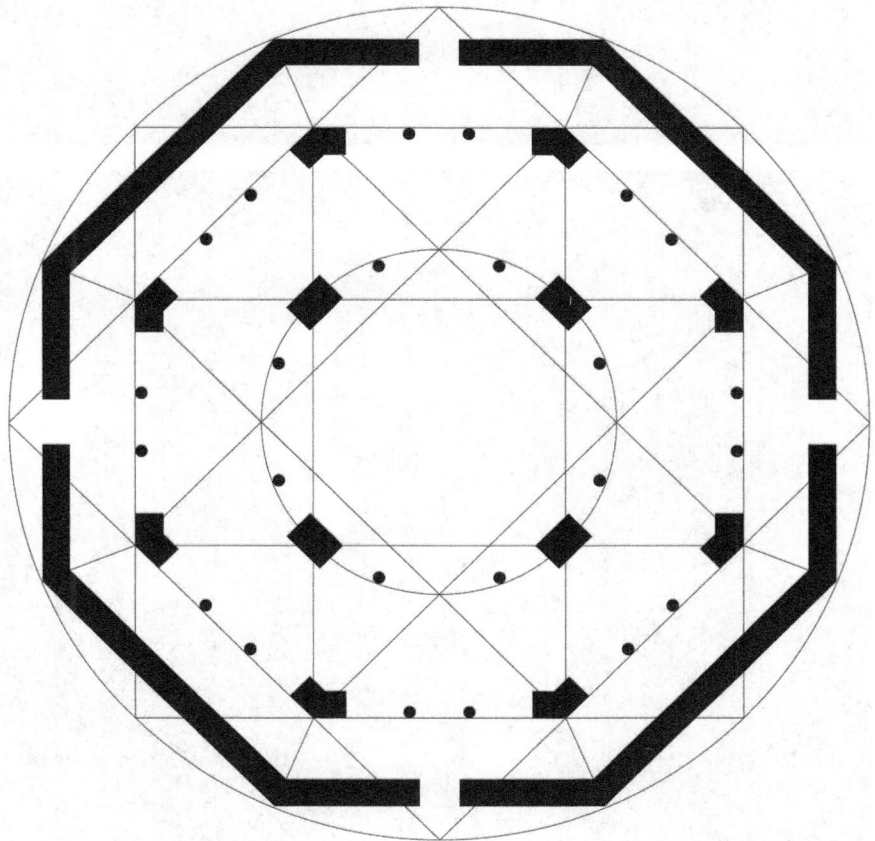

Figure 7.1-5 Jerusalem. Dome of the Rock, plan, 690.

Figure 7.1-6
Damascus. The Great
Mosque, eighth century
(dome rebuilt in the
twelfth century).

Figure 7.1-7 Damascus.
The Great Mosque,
eighth century. Interior,
looking onto the
maksura area.

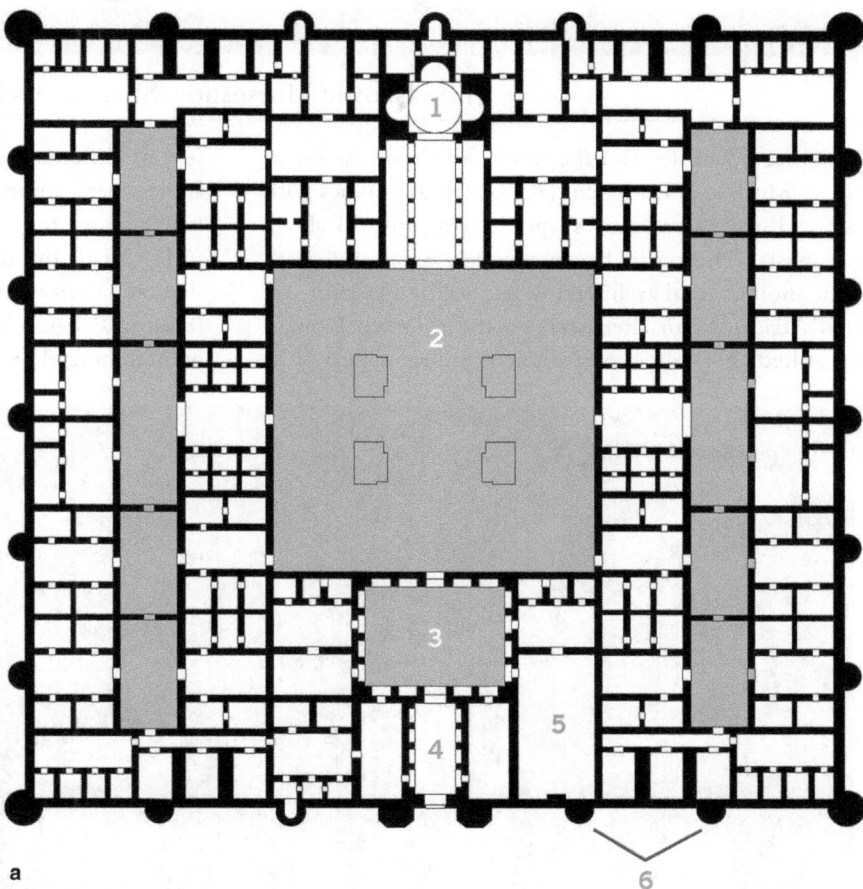

Figure 7.1-8 Jordan. Qasr Mshatta, 740s. (a) Plan, showing (1) Royal Hall of three apses; (2) Grand Court; (3) reception court; (4) entrance hall; (5) palace mosque; (6) pseudo-bastions. (b) Walls with luxurious reliefs using natural motifs, partially conserved in the Pergamon Museum, Berlin.

The Abbasid Succession: New Capitals in Baghdad and Samarra

The Umayyad dynasty brought the empire of Islam to its farthest extent, from the Indus valley in the east to Spain and Morocco in the west. Rebellions led by the Shiites and others disaffected with Umayyad rule came to a climax under the leadership of Abu'l-Abbas, a descendent of the Prophet's youngest uncle. The Battle of Zab near Kufah transferred power in 750 to the Abbasid dynasty. The new rulers systematically murdered all of the members of the Umayyad clan, excepting one. The lone survivor fled to Morocco and a few years later restored the Umayyad line on the Iberian Peninsula, a rule that lasted for another three centuries (see Section 8.2).

Shortly before their demise, the Umayyads relocated their capital to the new circular town of Harran on the upper Euphrates to be closer to the areas of revolt. The second Abbasid caliph, al-Mansur (r. 754–775), likewise created a perfectly round city in 762 on the Tigris River, which he called Madinah al-Salam, or "city of peace," but which the locals called Baghdad. Several generations later a second Abbasid capital emerged a day's journey upstream at Samarra. Here, the caliphs constructed several grand imperial palaces on a scale that surpassed all precedents, including Roman, Byzantine, and Persian.

No trace of the round city of al-Mansur remains because, like its ancient precursors in the region, it was built entirely of adobe. Baghdad's initial plan can be reconstructed from literary sources: a perfect circle 2.6 km (1.5 miles) in diameter (Fig. 7.1-9). The designers rotated its four symmetrically placed gates 45° from the cardinal points so that the southwest gate pointed toward Mecca. Each entry had a deep vault arch, known as an *iwan*, and over it a hall with a golden dome for diplomatic ceremonies.

Like Kufah, early Baghdad had two major cross-axial streets, but instead of being lined with arcades, they were covered by vaults, creating a cool climate for the shops that lined them. The forty secondary streets led radially from the center.

The outer ring of Baghdad's blocks contained houses for the caliph's family members and the nobility, while the

The Islamic Horseshoe-Shaped Arch

The side aisles and the north arcade of the Great Mosque of Damascus (707–714) carry arches with distinct horseshoe shapes, flaring inward above the imposts. The motif became widely associated with Islamic monumental architecture, especially in Spain and North Africa. As an alternative to the rounded Roman arch, stilted, horseshoe, and pointed arches appeared in several different places after the fall of Rome. Pointed arches were common in India during the Gupta period (see Section 6.3), and the motif passed through Persia to Baghdad. In Spain, the Visigoths already used horseshoe arches in many churches, such as San Juan de Baños (built in Palencia in 660), before the arrival of Islam. The pointed horseshoe arch thus eluded ethnic association.

Damascus. Horseshoe arches in the court of the Great Mosque, eighth century.

inner ring hosted military barracks and administrative buildings. A vast central void, over 1 km (0.6 miles) in diameter, framed the caliph's palace and the adjacent Great Mosque in the center. The palaces of his sons and chief administrators stood as freestanding blocks at the perimeter of the void. A green dome capped with an equestrian figure rose 45 m (147 ft) above the palatine complex. The only other structure allowed in the inner circle served as police headquarters. The city's radial plan placed all of the occupants under close scrutiny, and eventually the chief members of

the royal family and high officials moved to less controlled palaces on the city's outskirts.

A decade later al-Mansur himself abandoned the claustrophobic center of the round city for the less confined al-Khuld Palace 1 km (0.6 miles) to the north. His grandson, Harun al-Rashid (r. 785–805), transferred the capital to Ar-Raqqah (Syria) in the 780s, laying out the town on an octagonal plan. Baghdad remained the administrative center until the 830s, when the caliph al-Mutasim (r. 833–842) took his 70,000 Turkish mercenaries 80 km (48 miles) north of

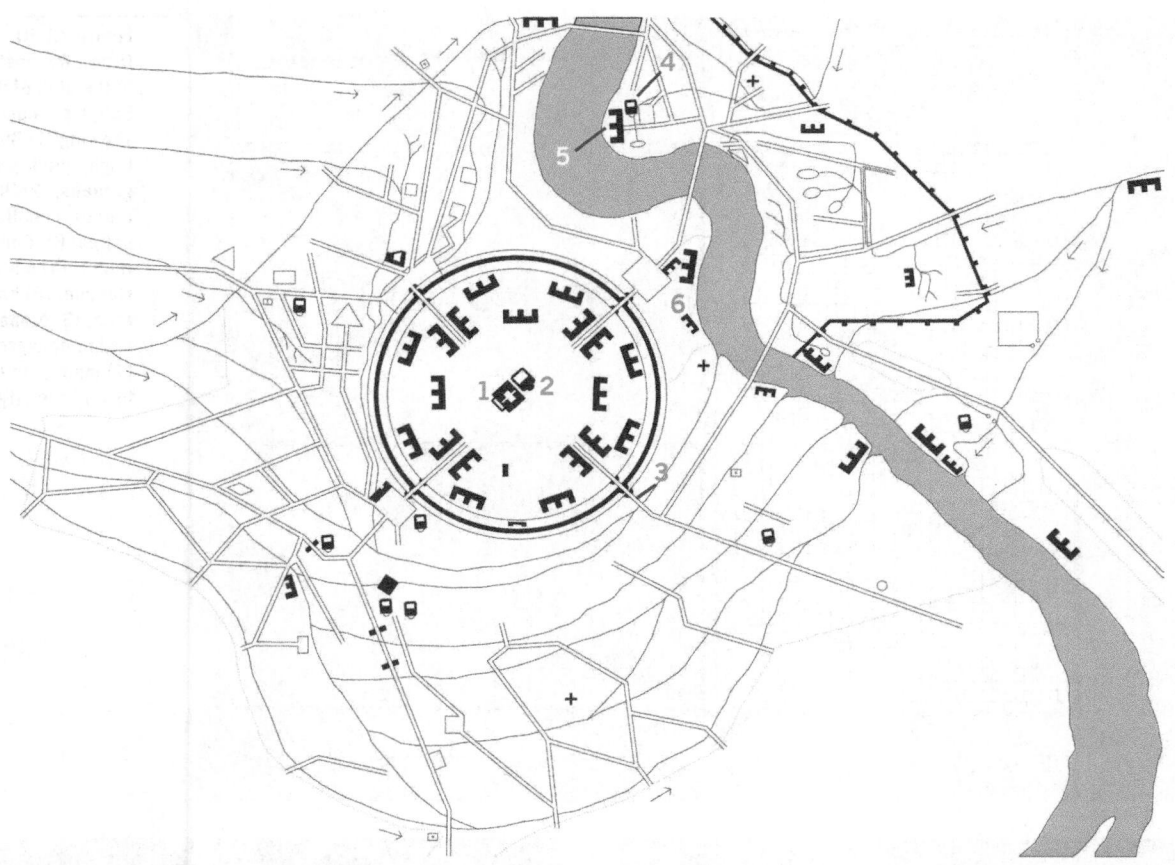

Figure 7.1-9 Baghdad. The round city, under the second Abbasid caliph, al-Mansur, eighth century. (1) Caliph's palace; (2) the Great Mosque; (3) market streets leading to the four major gates; (4) New Friday Mosque; (5) Rusafah Palace; (6) al-Khuld Palace.

Baghdad to the new capital at Samarra. The large geometric enclaves of Abbasid palaces and mosques built in Samarra formed a strip of orderly patches that spread for 25 km (15 miles) along the Tigris River. The first of its grand residences, Jausaq al-Khaqani, known as the Caliph's Palace, was built in 836. The palace occupied nearly the same area as al-Mansur's Baghdad. Broad stairs led to it from the river, rising 17 m (56 ft) to meet the gateway of the Bab al-'Amma (the Gate of the People), formed by three vaulted *iwans* (Fig. 7.1-10). The palace gate marked the point of contact between the people and their ruler, a place where petitions might be presented, justice administered, and admittance to higher authority requested. The grounds included a central esplanade 180 × 350 m (590 × 1,148 ft), a circular amphitheater, 170 acres of flower gardens and orchards, and a 0.5 km (0.3 miles) long polo field with grandstands. The northern barracks for 3,000 troops had its own mosque and guarded the enclosures for the treasury and the arsenal. To the south, a maze-like building served as quarters for the harem. The Caliph's Palace surpassed the scale of the imperial complex in Constantinople and was matched only by the imperial palaces of Tang dynasty China.

Samarra came to full maturity under al-Mutawakkil (r. 847–861), who installed one of his three sons in the

Caliph's Palace and built two more palaces almost as large for the other two sons. Such a colossal scale of architecture imposed a solemn distance between the people and their rulers. To complete the city, he commissioned the largest mosque in the world, the Great Mosque of Samarra (Fig. 7.1-11a), which covered roughly the same area as the Temple Mount in Jerusalem. An outer set of walls created a perimeter court for service functions. The inner *sahn* of the mosque had arcades four columns deep. The hypostyle prayer hall stretched nine columns deep and twenty-four across, with a slightly taller central nave. A spiral **minaret** (Fig. 7.1-11b), evoking the ancient ziggurats of the region, dominated the whole on the north. Standing 52 m (170 ft) high, it served more as an icon than as an acoustic device.

The grandson of al-Mutawakkil brought the Abbasids back to Baghdad, leaving the sprawling mud-and-brick enclosures of Samarra to slowly disintegrate. After a century of rule and constant threats of revolt, the Abbasid caliphs began to lose their authority over the provincial governors, or *viziers*. In Tunisia the Aghlabid dynasty took root around 800. These rulers rebuilt the Great Mosque of Kairouan in 836 (Fig. 7.1-12) in imitation of the Great Mosque of Baghdad, using tiles and wooden panels imported from that city. The mosque's layout followed a slightly skewed

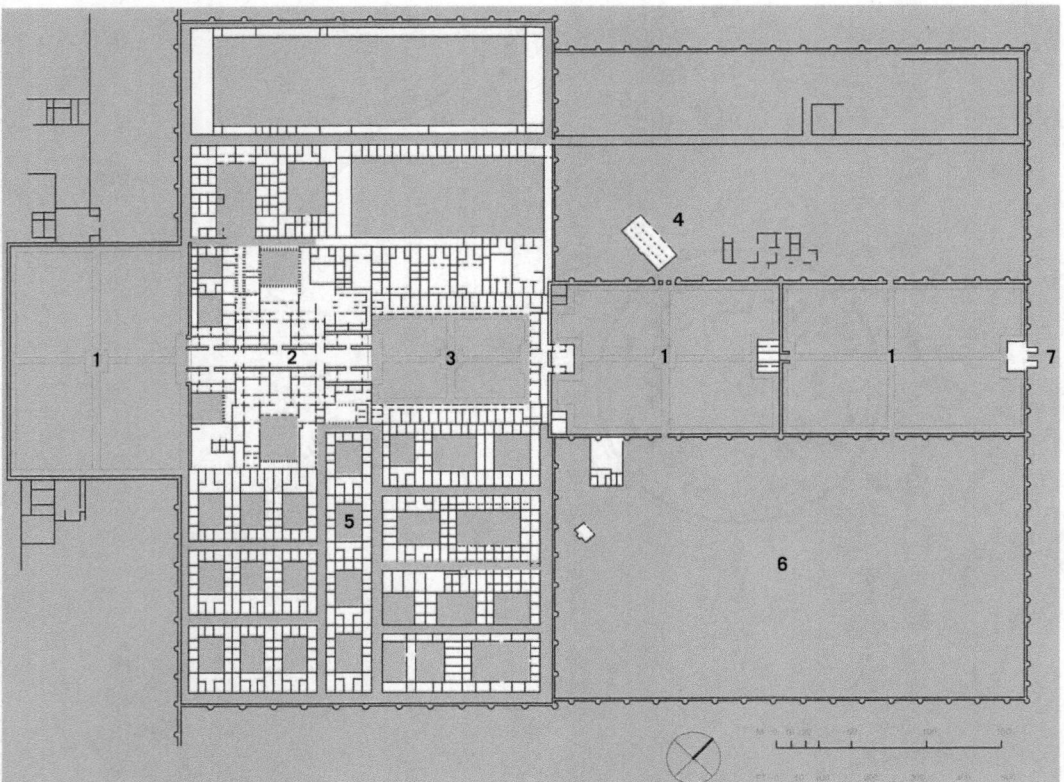

Figure 7.1-10 Samarra (Iraq). Reconstruction of the plan of the Caliph's Palace, 836, showing (1) Chahar Bagh, quadripartite gardens; (2) the great cruciform hall of the caliph; (3) Court of Honor; (4) palace mosque; (5) harem area; (6) probable site of polo grounds; (7) main gate looking toward the city.

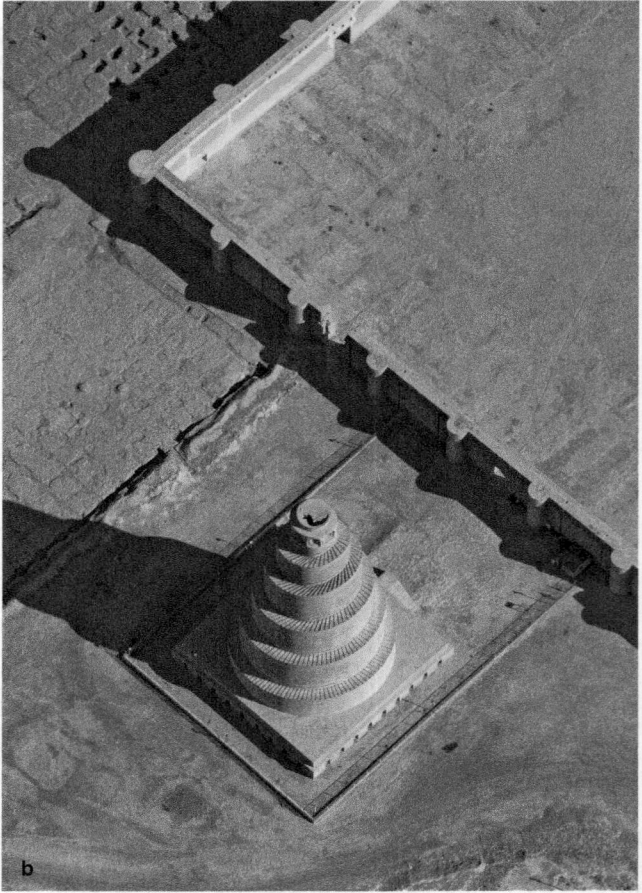

Figure 7.1-11 Samarra (Iraq). The Great Mosque, ca. 850. (a) Aerial view. (b) Spiral minaret.

parallelogram, adjusting to the position of the previously built structures surrounding it. The arcades of its *sahn* were two columns deep, and the hypostyle prayer hall spread across sixteen aisles, using over 400 columns taken from ancient Roman sites. A central nave, crossed at the *qibla* wall by a transept, formed a *T*. A scalloped cupola over the entry and another over the *mihrab* signaled a princely axis. The most innovative element of the Great Mosque of Kairouan remained its 35 m (115 ft) high minaret, a three-tiered tower apparently inspired by the Lighthouse of Alexandria, which was still visible as a ruin at this time. The alignment of the minaret stood in symmetry with the outer wall but fell to one side of the prayer hall's axis. For over a century the Aghlabids thrived as a semiautonomous dynasty, paying annual tribute to the Abbasids in Baghdad and gaining extra power and influence through their conquest of Sicily and southern Italy. In 846 they led yet another sack of Rome.

In Egypt Ahmed Ibn Tulun (r. 868–884), the son of a Turkish slave from Bukhara, became the Abbasid vizier. Soon he established an autonomous dynasty, the Tulunids, and proceeded to eliminate vestiges of Abbasid power. Remembering the new works in Samarra, which he had witnessed before leaving Iraq, Ibn Tulun created a new palace district at al-Qatai and furnished it with courtyard gardens, an aqueduct, a hippodrome, and barracks for his 10,000 loyal troops. Although the succeeding regime destroyed his palace after his dynasty fell from power in 905, the Mosque of Ibn Tulun remained intact (Fig. 7.1-13). It greatly resembles the mosques of Samarra, standing in a square double enclosure 162 m (531 ft) per side, about half the size of the mosque at Samarra. Its perimeter court served market functions. Despite the availability of limestone from the nearby Muqattam cliffs, the Tulunids built the entire structure of baked brick and plaster, suggesting the presence of Mesopotamian builders unfamiliar with stone construction. The pointed arches of its hypostyle hall and those of the arcades surrounding the *sahn* were raised on broad piers, each articulated with engaged columns at the four corners. Perforated spandrels relieved the mass of the construction, while the perimeter walls carried lace-like perforated merlons. The original minaret of the Mosque of Ibn Tulun had a spiral shape, emulating those at Samarra. The current tower, built in stone during the thirteenth century, preserves the spiral but rises to the side of the main axis. The round, domed fountain house in the center of the *sahn* was added at the same time.

While the first two centuries of Islamic design pursued strict geometric order for cities, palaces, and mosques, the texture of Arab Islamic cities evolved into a dense snarl of covered markets and tightly packed courtyard houses occasionally interrupted by orderly religious complexes. Where there had once been straight streets, such as the central colonnaded avenue of Damascus, the long process of merchants impinging on public space resulted in a winding

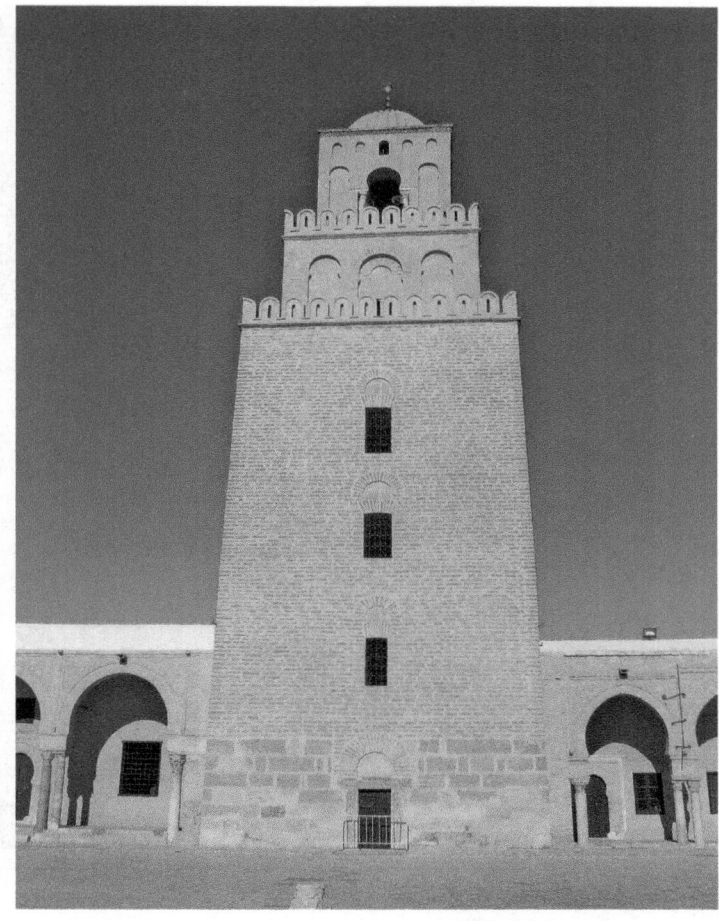

Figure 7.1-12 Kairouan, Tunisia. Mosque built for Aghlabid dynasty, 836.

fabric of narrow alleys. The typical urban neighborhood, or **herat**, gathered around a blind alley, its entry controlled by a trusted member of the community. The popular realm of the *herats*, attached one to another in clusters, gave Islamic cities their unfathomable complexity.

Further Reading

AlSayyad, Nezar. *Cities and Caliphs: On the Genesis of Arab Muslim Urbanism*. New York: Greenwood Press, 1991.

Ettinghausen, R., and O. Grabar. *The Art and Architecture of Islam, 650–1250*. New York: Viking Penguin, 1987.

Grabar, Oleg. *The Formation of Islamic Art and Architecture*. New Haven, CT: Yale University Press, 1987.

Hattstein, M., and P. Delius. *Islam: Arte e Architettura*. Cologne, Germany: Konneman, 2000.

Hillenbrand, Robert. *Islamic Architecture: Form, Function and Meaning*. New York: Columbia University Press, 1994.

Hoag, John D. *Islamic Architecture*. Milan: Electa, 1975.

Stierlin, Henri. *Islam from Baghdad to Cordova*. Cologne, Germany: Taschen, 1997.

Figure 7.1-13 Cairo. Mosque of Ibn Tulun, ca. 880.

7.2 TANG CHINA AND EAST ASIA
Gridded Capitals and Lofty Pagodas

The political unity of China periodically broke down under the pressure of feuding kingdoms until a new dynasty emerged to impose a strong central government. The Tang dynasty came to power at the beginning of the seventh century and for nearly three centuries led China to a high level of cultural and political order. Following the brief Sui dynasty, Tang emperors rebuilt the gridded capital of Chang'an, the world's largest city; perfected China's national civil service examinations; and exercised military and cultural influence over Vietnam, Korea, and Japan. They initially encouraged Buddhism as a common religion, and Buddhist monasteries, pagodas, and colossal rock-cut statues appeared as new architectural programs in China. The Silk Road led to Chang'an as its final destination and put the West in regular contact with Tibet, India, and the Islamic regimes. To the east, both Korea and Japan looked to Chinese urbanism when designing their

TIME LINE

 580

Sui dynasty rebuilds Chang'an and starts Grand Canal

Great Wild Goose Pagoda, louge type, built in Chang'an

▲ **652**

 660

Gaozong and Wu Zetian begin new Daminggong Palace in Chang'an

Silla dynasty unifies Korea, builds capital at Kyongju using Chinese conventions

▲ **676**

Dougong: Tang Brackets

Only four examples of Buddhist temples from the Tang period survived the purge of the mid-ninth century. The East Hall of the Foguang Monastery at Mount Wutai, built in 857, remains the finest example, displaying intricate roof brackets, or **dougong**, made of interlocking wooden joinery. Precedents for this type of construction in stone can be seen in the Han dynasty tombs. The temple rose on a stone terrace reached by balustered side stairs. The plan followed the typical modular column system. While the rows of evenly spaced columns might at first seem to be a grid in plan, they in fact followed a concentric series of rectangular figures, with the central space defined by two rows of five columns surrounded by an outer ambulatory of four by seven columns.

The complex system of *dougong*, which crisscrossed at the top of the columns, connected the columns to the beams and rafters. The five tiers of brackets equaled half the height of the columns. The cantilevering of the arms of the *dougong* diffused the load of the roof, each bracket extending slightly farther out than the one below it. The addition of midspan brackets and brackets above the beams to support a higher set of rafters created burgeoning clusters of branch-like forms. The *dougong*'s even distribution of stresses from the roof performed well in earthquakes.

Duocun, Shanxi Province. Tang brackets in Foguang Monastery, eighth century.

▼ **682**

Empress Wu Zetian begins Tang dynasty funeral park at Qianling

Empress Wu Zetian moves Chinese capital to Luoyang

▲ **685**

▼ **707**

Small Wild Goose Pagoda, miyuan type, built in Chang'an

Japanese build capital at Nara on plan of Chang'an

▲ **710**

capital cities, and the multilayered pagodas that originated in Tang China became prominent vertical accents in cities throughout Asia.

Tang Chang'an: The End of the Silk Road

After several centuries of feudal division in China, the Sui dynasty (580–618) reunited the north and south of the empire. Although the regime lasted less than four decades, its renewal of imperial structure prepared the way for the success of the Tang dynasty. The most radical innovation of these rulers involved the redistribution of agricultural land, guaranteeing that every Chinese farmer possessed the same-sized plot, approximately 13 acres, and paid a tax partly in grain and partly in silk to the central government. The Sui instituted a national civil service examination, which reduced the privileges of the rich, who previously had gained appointments through recommendations. Now, chief scholar-officials were selected according to their proficiency with the Confucian texts that were the basis of law. The Sui initiated China's second grandest work of infrastructure by piecing together various canals into the Grand Canal, which at 1,770 km (1,100 miles) remains the world's longest artificial waterway. The canal served to transport the imperial grain tribute from the south to the north. The short-lived Sui dynasty also began to rebuild the capital city of Chang'an (which they called Daxing) on a site 10 km (6 miles) southeast of the abandoned Han capital (see Section 5.2). The Tang emperors filled out the grand plan, creating the largest city in the world, with over 1 million inhabitants.

Costly wars with Korea to the east and the Turkish tribes in the western steppes led to the downfall of the Sui. After the Tang dynasty made peace with the Turks, a move that allowed them to later rely on the Uighurs for military support, they pursued a more open policy regarding foreign trade and foreign religions, such as Buddhism. The legendary Silk Road to the west acquired new importance, and China extended its control through the steppes to protect trade with lands as far as the Transoxiana areas of modern Uzbekistan and Tajikistan.

The Silk Road offered no singular, or easy, itinerary. The physical danger of traversing the vast deserts and treacherous mountains vied with the threat of pirate raids from nomadic hordes. With most of Southwest Asia and Persia dominated by the new Islamic empire, first under the Umayyads and then under the Abbasids, traders received the most protection at either end of their journey. The combined strength of these two imperial spheres guaranteed safe passage through the perilous territories that separated them.

Chang'an (modern Xi'an) lay at the eastern terminus of the Silk Road, welcoming traders who came via the Himalayas from India, those who meandered across the steppes from Afghanistan and Persia, and those who came from farther north by passing through Kazakh lands from the Black Sea and the Mediterranean. Chang'an's two markets covered more area than most cities of the time. The process of traveling from a western point, such as Damascus, to Chang'an could take anywhere from nine months to two years and was usually handled as a sequence of relays, with middlemen carrying the goods back and forth along various stretches of the road. In Chang'an the trading communities built Buddhist temples, mosques, Nestorian Christian churches, and Zoroastrian fire temples. The strong influence of Islam became apparent with the construction of Chang'an's Great Mosque in 742, designed with Chinese-style roofs.

The Sui dynasty relied on the extraordinary talent of the architect Yuwen Kai (555–612), who produced the new plan of Chang'an, conceived the Grand Canal, and was probably involved in the making of the **segmental arch** Anji bridge of Zhaozhou, with its 37 m (121 ft) span across the Nanjiao River (Fig. 7.2-1). As imperial image maker and problem solver, Yuwen Kai seems to have gained a status similar to that enjoyed by Apollodorus of Damascus in Trajan's Rome. The architect's scheme for Chang'an followed the longstanding grid traditions of the *wangcheng* diagram, with three axial streets intersected by three cross-axial streets and the palace placed in the center (see Section 5.2) (Fig. 7.2-2). The scale of the new capital proved many times larger than that of any city ever conceived in China or elsewhere, covering 84 km^2 (32 miles^2), more than three times the area of ancient Rome. Chang'an had three gates, on the east, south, and west, each with three arches, and the major streets were divided into three paved lanes, with the central lane reserved for the emperor and his court.

▼ **743**

Todaiji Temple, Nara, becomes national center of Buddhism

Bulguk-sa Temple (South Korea)

▲ **751**

▼ **784**

Kyoto founded as new imperial capital of Japan

Buddhism outlawed in China

▲ **842**

Figure 7.2-1 Nanjiao River, Hebei Province. Zhaozhou Bridge (Anji Bridge), 605–616.

The breadth of Chang'an's streets has never been matched: the central avenue, at 155 m (508 ft) across, stretched considerably wider than the widest of Hauss-mann's nineteenth-century boulevards in Paris (see Section 16.1). The other streets in the main grid measured 100 m (328 ft) across, about three times the typical size of nineteenth-century American streets designed for the passage of fire trucks. To soften the starkness of the broad roadways, the designers planted elms and junipers along their sides. Deep drainage ditches also lined the sides, requiring the construction of multiple bridges at the intersections. The dimensions of Chang'an's boulevards proved intimidating in their regimentation and exposure, not to say daunting to those who had to cross them. Rather than serving to connect parts of the city, like the armature of Roman colonnaded streets (see Section 5.1), they served to keep them segregated.

Chang'an's grid of nine south–north streets and twelve east–west streets aligned to the cardinal points and contained a total of 108 blocks, known as *fangs*, or "wards," larger in area than a city block. These village-sized wards, normally about 0.5 km (0.3 miles) per side, sat within their own walls. A large police force, with as many as thirty guards at the intersections, enforced a strict curfew that prohibited residents from leaving the wards after dark. Internal streets

40 m (131 ft) wide subdivided each ward. The larger wards contained as many as sixteen sub-blocks inside their walls, between which ran the only intimately scaled streets in the city. The Taijigong district for the imperial palace and the administrative city occupied the equivalent of twelve wards, or about one-tenth of the whole.

Buddhism, which arrived in China with Indian merchants and monks during the first century BCE, became the most important foreign influence during the Sui and Tang periods. The path of Buddhist influence led from the colossal statues of Buddha at Bamiyan in Afghanistan (see Section 6.3) to the various caves of "a thousand Buddhas" found along the Silk Road in way stations between Kashgar, the westernmost Chinese outpost, and Chang'an. The Buddhist influx also came from the mountain kingdom of Tibet to the south. During the same years as the Tang dynasty's ascendancy, the kingdom of Tibet emerged as a serious regional power. The matrimonial exchange of princesses between Chinese and Tibetan dynasties indicates the Tang's recognition of the smaller state's importance.

Contact with Buddhist kingdoms on the Chinese periphery may explain the appearance of the most distinctive building type of Chinese Buddhism: the **pagoda**. This layered wooden structure that protected a *stupa* memorial for a relic or act of the Buddha, came to maturity in the

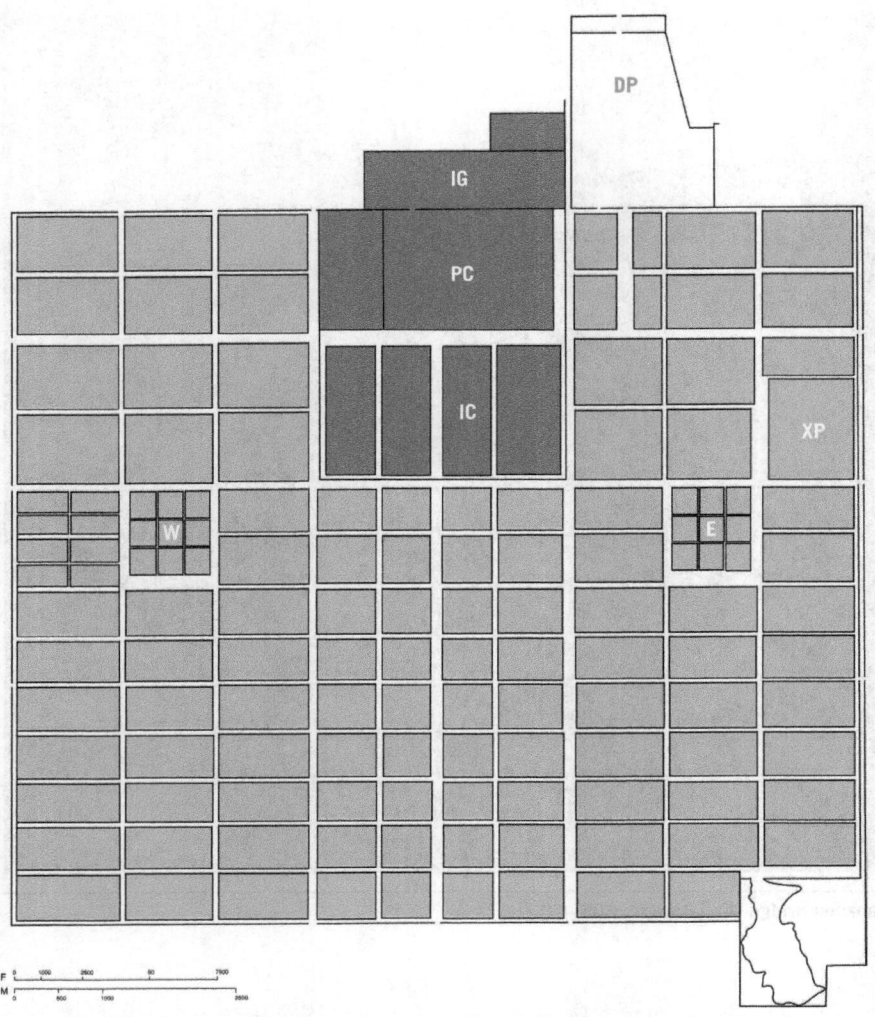

Figure 7.2-2 Chang'an. Rebuilt during Sui dynasty, ca. 580, and developed by the Tang dynasty during the seventh century. (W) West market; (E) east market; (IC) Imperial City for administrators; (PC) Palace City for court; (IG) imperial gardens; (XP) Xingqing Palace; (DP) Daminggong Palace.

The spread of Buddhism, which frequently benefited from imperial and aristocratic patronage, spawned a building boom for religious complexes in Tang dynasty China. By the eighth century the state census listed over 40,000 monasteries. They ranged from modest structures for a small brotherhood of three or four monks to very expensive buildings on vast sites on a par with the palace designs of the period. The monastery of Shaolin, 50 km (30 miles) south of Luoyang, allegedly hosted 10,000 monks, its "forest of pagodas" suggesting the presence of great numbers.

Chang'an itself boasted several large monasteries ranging from 300 to 400 members and occupying entire wards. The wealthy Buddhist monasteries followed the planning logic of palace compounds: they were entered through a gateway with a series of halls and pavilions surrounding a courtyard, usually ordered with axial symmetry and sometimes connected by linked verandahs. The front gate, or *shanmen*, usually had more than one story and blocked direct entry into the court. The major hall, or *dadian*, sat on the central axis from the gate and housed the most important images of Buddha. The Dabei pavilion at Longxing monastery (Zhengding county, Hebei), a five-story hall housing a 21 m (69 ft) Buddha, resembled the prayer halls built in Chang'an during the eighth century. Other important halls for meditation, library pavilions, and in some cases the abbot's quarters lined the major axis of the complex, while the sleeping halls for the monks and storage areas sat along the sides of the courts.

Buddhist monasteries became the wealthiest institutions of the city, receiving substantial endowments of land and funds from the emperors and wealthy patrons. They operated shops and services such as public baths, and often their substantial treasuries served as pools of funds for usury, the practice of lending money at high rates of interest, on which they did not pay taxes. By the ninth century the economic power of the monasteries had contributed to the impoverishment of the agricultural peasants, and they had come to be perceived as a threat to imperial authority. An official interdict outlawed Buddhism, leading to the destruction of 46,000 monasteries between 842 and 845. The Buddhist movement in China never recovered from this blow.

Himalayan regions of Nepal and Tibet during the sixth and seventh centuries. Two of the only buildings in Chang'an that remain intact from the Tang period represent the two categories of Chinese pagodas. The Great Wild Goose Pagoda (Dayan Ta) (Fig. 7.2-3), built in 652 in the Ci'en monastery, offers a fine example of the multistoried *louge* type. The first two levels were built to house the 1,300 volumes of sutras imported from India by the pilgrim Xuanzang. The pagoda steps up, with each story of its brick structure slightly smaller in area than the one below, reaching a height of 60 m (197 ft). The Small Wild Goose Pagoda (Xiaoyan Ta) (Fig. 7.2-4), with many rows of projecting eaves, corresponds to the *miyuan* type. The pilgrim Yi Jing sponsored this tower in 707 for a monastery. Above the ground-floor space of the shrine, fifteen densely set layers of eaves rise around a hollow to 45 m (148 ft). With over ninety Buddhist monasteries, the two-story skyline of Tang Chang'an bristled with these many-eaved towers.

The Shrines of Japanese Shintoism: Ise and Izumo

Buddhism spread from China to Japan, where it became the state religion in the seventh century, yet the Japanese continued to honor the indigenous beliefs of Shintoism, "the way of the *kami* ('spirits')." Shintoists revered natural phenomena and elements, such as trees and mountains, and did not in essence require cult buildings. The two principal Shinto monuments, the Ise and Izumo shrines, were dedicated, respectively, to the sun goddess Amaterasu and to Okuninushi, the spirit of fish, silk, and good fortune.

Shinto temples evoked the forms of primordial wooden buildings on stilts with thatched roofs. The periodic rebuilding of both of these shrines came to represent the supreme ritual gesture of imperial authority. Somewhat like the privileged Mingtang temple reserved for the Chinese court, the sacred precincts at Ise and Izumo could only be entered by the emperor and his entourage. The formal obligation to rebuild the imperial Ise shrine at twenty-year intervals was established in 792, not long after the abandonment of Nara and the reduction of the role of Buddhism in the state. The act of reproducing the exact same buildings without changing their form represented the power of imperial authority over the uncertainty of the material things of the world. In a certain sense the ritual rebuilding of Ise replaced the previous tradition of building a new imperial palace with each change of regime.

The *shoden*, a modest wooden structure at its core, 15 × 10 m (49 × 33 ft), rises on stout poles, sheltered by a pitched thatch roof. Except for its gilded roof details, it resembles an agricultural storehouse. The ten ridgepoles supporting the spine of the roof intersect the forking rafters, or *chigi*, that stick out at the gables. These extravagant roof elements are sheathed in gilded bronze and historically were the only part of the shrine visible to the people. The two massive columns at either end of the gables lean slightly inward to support the ridge beam. Behind the *shoden* stand two treasuries, smaller versions of the same building but without porches. The *temenos* at Ise is divided into halves: on one half stands the current version of the *shoden* surrounded by a succession of three fences, and on the other, where the temple will be rebuilt, stands a simple wooden shed covering the "heart pillar" on an otherwise vacant lot covered with white pebbles. The outer fence is made of horizontal slats, while the inner three fences progress from open railings to pickets to solid boards. The *torii* gateways mark the ritual progress of the emperor toward the *shoden*. The reconstruction of the Ise shrine requires the felling of 13,600 cypress trees and takes eight years and a succession of thirty-two ceremonies. The final rite involves the transference of the sacred mirror from the old *shoden* to the new. The ritual rebuilding of the Ise shrine provides a compelling analogue for the precarious state of most preindustrial architecture in East Asia, where each generation established itself by remaking its environment. Though always new, the buildings always appeared the same as the ones they replaced.

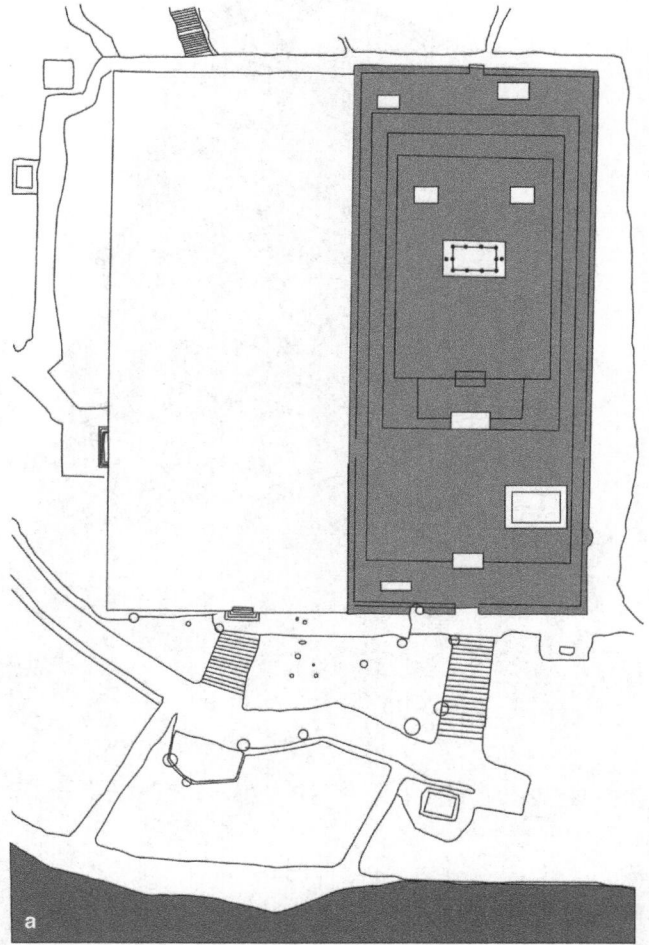

Ise, Japan. (a) Plan of the imperial Shinto Great Shrine, rebuilt every twenty years since 792 on the adjacent site. (b) Aerial view of the shrine with its concentric fences, *torii* gates, *shoden* temple, and treasuries under construction in the left enclosure.

Figure 7.2-3 Chang'an. Great Wild Goose Pagoda, 652. *Louge*-type pagoda.

The Patronage of Empress Wu

Many of the works and policies attributed to the third Tang emperor, Gaozong (r. 649–683), were either inspired or directed by his ambitious wife, the much-maligned Wu Zetian (the "supreme empress"). Empress Wu (623–705) became the only woman to rule China using the masculine title of "emperor" and established her own dynasty, the

Zhou (690–705). Like Hatshepsut in Bronze-Age Egypt (see Section 3.2), she proved to be an able ruler and one of the greatest patrons of architecture. Through her patronage of buildings and religious institutions the empress attempted to gain legitimacy.

Wu Zetian remains one of the most controversial figures in Chinese history. While blamed for conducting a reign of terror and mismanaging the military defense of the borders, China indeed expanded during her reign and prospered through agricultural reforms and improved foreign commercial relations. Because Confucianism strongly discouraged women from assuming roles of power, historians steeped in this philosophy have not been kind to her. They report that Wu Zetian strangled her infant daughter to pin the blame for her death on her rivals. She has also been accused of forcing one of her sons to commit suicide so that her claim to the throne would go unopposed, poisoning relatives to avoid dynastic struggles, and using a succession of lovers, including a professional wrestler and twin brothers, to carry out her dirty work. The need to discredit a female protagonist in order to conserve the Confucian respect for male power proved as strong in Tang China as it was for those who erased Hatshepsut's name and image from her monuments in Luxor.

Wu Zetian came from a merchant's family, was educated in a Buddhist convent, and entered the imperial palace at age fourteen as a fifth-level concubine to Gaozong's father. Following court protocol, the concubines were dismissed to a convent upon the death of the emperor. Wu Zetian succeeded in returning to the palace, however, as a second-level concubine to Gaozong. She assumed the role of imperial consort in 655 after the suspicious disappearance of both the new emperor's first wife and the chief concubine. Five years later her husband suffered a series of strokes that left him incapacitated, and Wu Zetian took control. For the next two decades she literally became the power behind the throne, usually speaking for the ailing emperor from behind a screen.

Wu Zetian's first act of patronage involved building a second imperial palace in Chang'an, the Daminggong Palace, just outside the northeast edge of the walls. The unforgiving Confucian historians suggest that she desired to leave the Taijigong Palace because it was haunted by the ghosts of her victims. Begun in 662, the Daminggong Palace duplicated most of the functions of its precursor in a 3 km^2 (1.16 miles^2) area, with a grand reception hall overlooking a vast court that had two separate audience halls on either side of a *U*-shaped configuration. The Hanyuandian, or Hall of Enfolding Vitality, stretched fifteen columns across and rose on a pyramidal mound 10 m (33 ft) above grade, approached by a gradual brick ramp with stone stairs and balustrades on the sides. Its 200 m (656 ft) wide courtyard space could accommodate thousands of courtiers on major public occasions.

After Gaozong's death, the empress dedicated the large monastery that housed the Small Wild Goose Pagoda to her husband's memory and initiated the immense **necropolis** at Qianling that would serve as her final resting place as well. With her youngest son installed as emperor she acted as regent until he was eventually forced to step aside. In 690, after nearly thirty years of *de facto* rule, Wu Zetian officially reigned as "emperor." Her government continued successfully for fifteen years. Much like Constantine moving from Rome to Byzantium, she transferred her capital 300 km (186 miles) east to Luoyang, a city that had been rebuilt by the Sui emperors in 605 on the scale of Chang'an. The second capital's perimeter walls ran 27 km (17 miles) in circumference, containing 104 walled *fangs*, just slightly smaller than the other capital. While farther removed from the hub of the Silk Road markets, Luoyang sat strategically at the terminus of the Grand Canal. By changing cities Wu Zetian left behind factional disputes that made it difficult to control Chang'an and brought with her the 100,000 courtiers and retainers willing to comply with her rule.

Figure 7.2-4 Chang'an. Small Wild Goose Pagoda, 707. *Miyuan*-type pagoda.

Like Hatshepsut, Wu Zetian exploited religion to reinforce her power, building numerous Buddhist temples, gaining the support of powerful monasteries, and instituting a tradition of prophecy to prop up the propriety of her rule. Upon ascending the throne she declared the superiority of Buddhism to Taoism and promoted the translation of the *Flower Garland Sutra*, which she copied with her own hand. This sutra voiced tolerance for female authority and alluded to the notion of a centralizing deity that accompanied centralized political power. Under Wu Zetian's rule every prefecture of China sponsored a monastery bearing the name *Dayun si*, meaning "Great Cloud Temple." This official recognition along with her generous patronage ensured the loyalty of

Figure 7.2-5 Qian, China. Qianling imperial necropolis, begun 680s under the patronage of Empress Wu.

the Buddhist movement. The empress donated hundreds of statues of Buddha to the caves at Longmen, a few kilometers south of Luoyang, including a colossal 13 m (43 ft) high statue of the cosmic Vairocana Buddha that was placed in the largest of the caves, Fengxian Si.

In Luoyang Wu Zetian relied on the resourcefulness of a man who Confucian historians proposed was one of her lovers, a merchant turned Buddhist abbot named Xue Huaiyi. He oversaw the construction of the towering five-story Heavenly Palace temple (Tiantang), which housed a colossal 30 m (96 ft) bronze statue of Vairocana Buddha. In the same area he also erected the new capital's Mingtang, or Hall of Light, the primary temple of monarchical authority used for imperial New Year's ceremonies. Neither of these wooden buildings survived later conflagrations. The towering structures had the distinction of being several stories taller than any other Chinese building. The Mingtang climbed from a square base to a twelve-sided second level, followed by a nearly cylindrical twenty-four-sided upper level. It was capped with a conical roof and a 3 m (10 ft) iron phoenix.

Like other powerful rulers, Wu Zetian exploited the magnificence of architecture to transmit the impression of her power's inevitability. The Qianling tombs remain the most impressive and enduring of her many works. Located 80 km (48 miles) northwest of Chang'an, the mausoleum district occupied a park with dimensions similar to that of the city, making the necropolis an analogue of

the capital. Construction began in 682 after the death of Emperor Gaozong. The empress dictated the program for a grand landscape that combined the natural position of three hills with the constructed tomb. More than 100 colossal sculptures, including a group of sixty-one "ambassadors," and pylon-like gate structures lined the central spirit path (Fig. 7.2-5). Like the principal avenue of Chang'an, the path was flanked by paved drainage ditches, with regular side bridges placed every 20 m (66 ft). The axis passed between two natural mounds, on which sat small pavilions. A pyramid-shaped hill concluded the axis, and at its base the ramp plunged to an underground palace, a site that has yet to be excavated by archaeologists. The imperial tomb was surrounded by seventeen satellite tombs for family members, several of whom were the empress's alleged victims. The tombs that have been opened reveal frescoed walls depicting courtly life in the buried person's palace settings. The monumental slab dedicated to Wu Zetian at the entry to her tomb remained uninscribed, while that of her husband Gaozong was brimming with hagiographic details. Either her surviving son was too ashamed of her acts to have them recorded, or, like Hatshepsut, the direct mention of her accomplishments in a masculine role proved untenable to, and thus unmentionable by, her survivors because of the Confucian distrust of women in power.

Under Wu Zetian women achieved more economic independence and could seek education in philosophy and the arts. Like women during the Roman Empire, they also achieved the right to divorce. Women continued to influence the Tang court for a decade after Wu Zetian's death, until the execution in 713 of Empress Wei and her daughter Taiping, both of whom were accused of conspiracy. The official suppression of Buddhism during the next century was partly motivated by its connection to feminine power at court, and Confucian officials created new barriers to keep women from becoming political protagonists in government.

Variations on Tang Urban Types: Korea and Japan

When a culture has limited architectural experience, it borrows indiscriminately from its neighbors. Even when there has been hostility with a neighbor, as in the cases of Korea and Japan with Tang dynasty China, the lesser states have willingly copied the dominant powers' models of architecture and city planning as valid settings. Korean and Japanese architects developed Chinese models into new forms that represented their respective national identities.

During the late seventh century, the Silla dynasty in Korea relied on Chinese artistic ideas from Chang'an to produce its own capital cities. The southern city of Kyongju (sometimes spelled Gyeongju) and the northern capital of Pyongyang near the border with China both adopted a strict grid with great, broad avenues, setting a walled palace and administrative sector in the northern part of the city. Kyongju probably had a population of 1 million at its height and appeared like a smaller version of Chang'an. The 8 × 10 km (5 × 6 miles) outline of the old city still shows up in aerial photographs. Contrary to the Chinese model, the *fangs*, or blocks, of Kyongju were small—one-tenth the size of those in China but 100 times as numerous, resulting in over 1,300 blocks. A Japanese invasion during the late sixteenth century (see Section 12.3) left the old Silla capital in ruins.

Buddhism entered Korea officially in the fourth century and during the seventh century became the state religion for the Silla aristocracy, who sponsored variations on Chinese temple courtyards, often using more permanent materials than their neighbors. The use of twin pagodas to the southeast and southwest of a central prayer hall, as seen at the Wolssong-kun Temple, derived from the type built in wood at the monasteries of Chang'an and Luoyang. Among the remaining structures of the Silla period, the Bulguk-sa Temple closely resembles a Tang prayer hall (Fig. 7.2-6). The masonry structure included an exceptionally well-crafted series of stone stairways supported on structural vaults, a method of construction rarely seen in Chinese precedents.

Local Korean traditions appear to have been less dependent on China when it came to tomb architecture. The Silla tombs rose as great stone cylinders capped with cup-shaped grassy knolls, more like Etruscan or Mycenaean burial mounds than Chinese pyramids. The Daereungwon Tumuli Park near Kyongju possessed twenty-three large mounded tombs that formed an enchanted undulating landscape of hillocks (Fig. 7.2-7).

In Japan, the *kofun*, keyhole-shaped burial mounds built during the third through sixth centuries, likewise presented a completely different local design approach as the first monumental expressions of a unified state. While more isolated than Korea, the nascent Japanese state likewise looked to the architecture and urbanism of the Chinese for inspiration. Before the foundation of Nara in 710 (originally called *Heijo-kyo*, "capital of the peaceful citadel"), the imperial government changed capitals at the death of each ruler. They considered the rebuilding of the royal palace to be an act of purification that renewed each generation. During the seventh century they built no fewer than seventeen different capitals. In the efforts to reform the Japanese state along the lines of the Tang government, the imperial rulers planned the new capital at Nara to be permanent, directly inspired by Chang'an. As part of Empress Wu Zetian's diplomatic strategy of expansion through culture, numerous Tang officials and Chinese religious advisors came to Japan at this time.

During the height of its power, Nara may have housed a population of 1 million. It covered one-third of the area of Chang'an, and the royal palace was one-third as large as the Daminggong Palace in the Chinese capital. While the central north–south avenue covered half the width of its Chinese precedent, at 74 m (243 ft) it stretched wider than any thoroughfare west of Chang'an. Similar to the wards in Chinese cities, Nara's wards extended a half-kilometer per side, divided into sixteen internal blocks (Fig. 7.2-8). The palace complex at the north end of the axis focused on the Daigokuden Audience Hall, a near replica of the Hanyuandian Hall at Daminggong Palace that was served by the same sort of *U*-shaped courtyard. The palace complex at Nara sat behind a thick wall, but the city itself remained unwalled. Japanese cities, perhaps not as susceptible as their Chinese neighbors to international invasions, were regularly built without fortifications.

During the sixth century the Buddhist religion increased in influence in Japan, paralleling the rise of Chinese political influence on central administration. Buddhism became the state religion in 604, and in the first half of the eighth century, the Todaiji Temple complex in Nara became the religion's national focus. The temple covered almost as much area as the royal palace. It was foregrounded by twin *louge*-type pagodas in the southeast and southwest, following Chinese precedents. The pagodas framed the Great Temple, the Daibutsuden (Fig. 7.2-9), which housed a colossal bronze statue of the seated Vairocana Buddha, 11 m (36 ft) high. The statue represented the same cult of the Flower Garland Sutra promoted by Empress Wu in China. The great hall rose nearly 50 m (164 ft), the largest timber-frame building in the world. Although the treatment of the roofs changed with the eighteenth-century remodeling, the original two-level structure had rafters supported by Tang-style *dougong*.

Feminine influence entered Japanese political life during the period of Empress Wu's rule of Tang China, and on four occasions during the Nara period, female sovereigns ruled the country. In 766, after Empress Shotoku named a Buddhist monk as prime minister, the aristocratic faction demanded a ban on women taking the throne. In 784 the conflict of the

Figure 7.2-6 Bulguk-sa, Korea. Buddhist temple, seventh century.

Figure 7.2-7 Kyongju, Korea. Daereungwon Tumuli Park of twenty-three Silla tombs, seventh to eighth century.

state with religious institutions provoked the transfer to a new capital 35 km (28 miles) north at Kyoto, where the imperial family remained for the next ten centuries. Female rulers became anathema to the Japanese political system, while Buddhist temples and monasteries were pushed outside the city limits. Kyoto's plan repeated that of Nara but eliminated prominent sites for temples. The two state-run temples were placed at the southern edge of the city, far from the imperial palace in the north, creating a clear separation of religious institutions from politics.

Further Reading

Benn, Charles. *China's Golden Age: Everyday Life in the Tang Dynasty*. New York: Oxford University Press, 2002.

Boyd, Andrew. *Chinese Architecture and Town Planning*. London: Alec Tiranti, 1962.

Coaldrake, William H. *Architecture and Authority in Japan*. London: Routledge, 1996.

Cotterell, Arthur. *The Imperial Capitals of China: An Inside View of the Celestial Empire*. Bournemouth, UK: Pimlico, 2007.

Heng Chye Kiang. *Cities of Aristocrats and Bureaucrats: The Development of Medieval Chinese Cityscapes*. Honolulu: University of Hawai'i Press, 1999.

Kazuo Nishi and Kazuo Hozumi. *What Is Japanese Architecture?* Translated by H. Mack Horton. Tokyo: Kodansha International, 1985.

Steinhardt, Nancy S. *Chinese Architecture in an Age of Turmoil, 200–600*. Honolulu: University of Hawai'i Press, 2014.

———, ed. *Chinese Architecture*. New Haven, CT: Yale University Press, 2002.

Wood, Frances. *The Silk Road: Two Thousand Years in the Heart of Asia*. Berkeley: University of California Press, 2002.

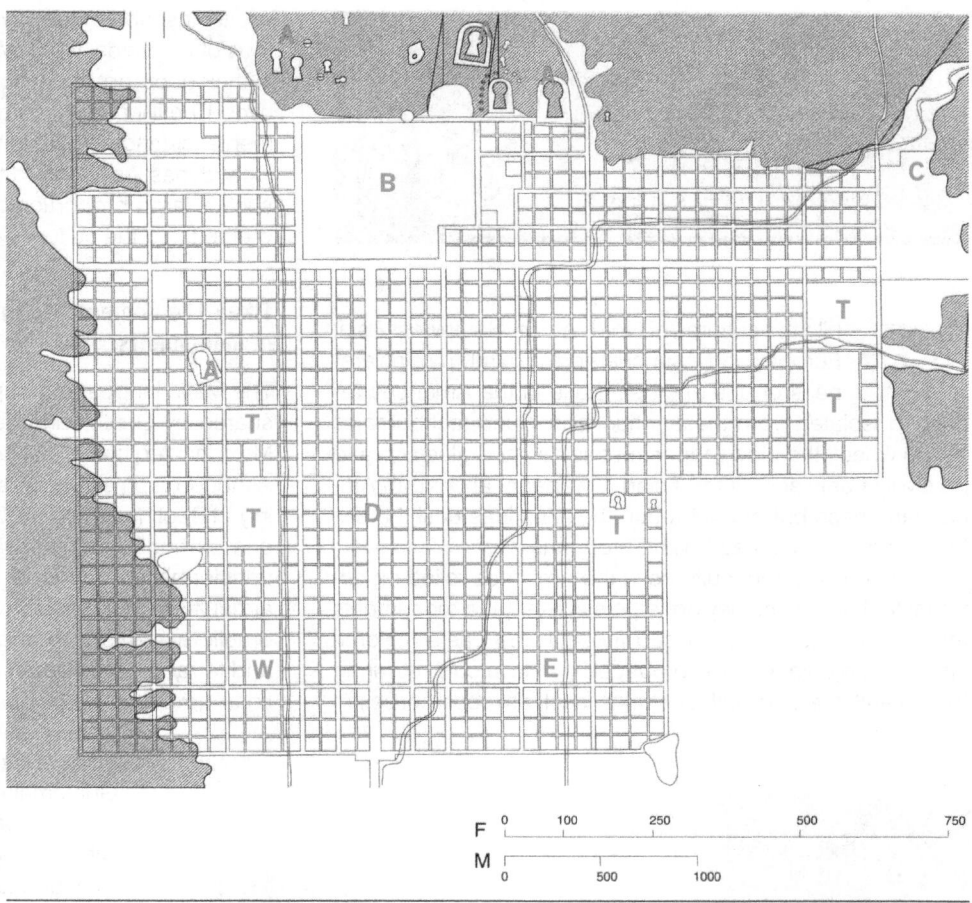

Figure 7.2-8 Nara (Heijo-kyo). Japan's first permanent capital, 710. (A) "Keyhole"-shaped tombs of Heijo dynasty; (B) royal Heijo palace; (C) Todaiji Temple, the major Buddhist shrine in Japan; (D) Scarlet Phoenix Avenue, 74 m (236 ft) wide; (T) temple compounds; (W) West Market; (E) East Market.

Figure 7.2-9 Nara, Japan. Todaiji Temple, Daibutsuden Hall, 743.

7.3 THE MAYA OF CENTRAL AMERICA
Reproducing the Mountain of Creation

vaults, inscribed stairways, and fanciful **roofcombs** on the tops of pyramids, were symbolic expressions deeply rooted in their geographic context. The Maya population swelled to over 10 million at its height, producing spectacular monumental settings. In the long run, however, the buildings that local dynasties intended to perpetuate their power required such a large proportion of the region's resources that they precipitated the culture's collapse.

W hile the cultures of North Africa, Southwest Asia, Europe, and Asia shared a minimum of awareness of one another, those in the Americas remained isolated from these influences. Such technologies as the wheel, the plow, paper, metallurgy, and glass spread relatively freely across the Asian, European, and North African landmass but did not reach the Americas until the sixteenth century "Contact" with Europeans.

While pre-Contact cultures in the Americas relied on different technologies, they nonetheless executed monuments that in some cases surpassed those in the Eastern Hemisphere. The unique forms produced by Maya culture during the seventh through ninth centuries, such as cross-corbelled

Tikal: The Competitive Production of Monuments

The Maya language group evolved in the semitropical zone shared by Guatemala, Belize, northern Honduras, and the Mexican regions of Chiapas and the Yucatán Peninsula. Although some Maya settlements predated the founding of Teotihuacán (see Section 5.3), the culture remained one of modest agricultural villages until a sudden political transformation occurred around the first century BCE. As agricultural techniques evolved from slash-and-burn to hydraulic systems with irrigation ditches, canals, reservoirs, and terraces, the villages grew into cities with large populations governed by kings (*ajaws*). The first important Maya cities grew up along the Usumacinta River in the Petén region straddling the Mexico-Guatemala border (Fig. 7.3-1). The fierce competition among these cities, combined with the region's limited agricultural productivity and difficult transportation connections, discouraged any single city from prevailing as the imperial ruler over the others. While Tikal, Guatemala, with its grand monumental core, appears in retrospect to have been the dominant city in the region, it remained in cyclical competition with Calakmul, Mexico, 40 km (60 miles) to the north. Both Tikal and Calakmul had populations of about 50,000 at their cores and perhaps 350,000 in their overall territories.

The urban pattern of Maya cities differed radically from those of other preindustrial cultures, closer in its low density to the scattered expanse of twentieth-century sprawl. Tikal's urban territory covered 200 km^2 (77 miles^2).

Figure 7.3-1 Map of Mayan lands between Mexico and Guatemala, seventh to ninth century.

▼ **570**
King of Tikal (Guatemala) takes refuge in Palenque (Mexico)

Monuments of Palenque
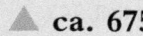
▲ **ca. 675**

▼ **685**
Tikal conquers Calakmul and begins new phase of pyramid building

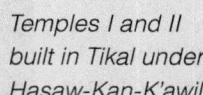
Temples I and II built in Tikal under Hasaw-Kan-K'awil
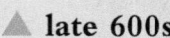
▲ **late 600s**

Maya cities housed as few as 1,200 people per square kilometer, in correspondence to the low agricultural yield of the land. At their core rose a monumental cluster of palaces, assembly halls (*popol nahs*), sweat baths, ball courts, and funerary temples for the kings and the court. A precinct wall bounded the urban core, which included great public plazas and elevated avenues paved with plaster, known as "white ways," or *sak behs*. A large plaza on the edge of the monumental district served as a market area. The rest of the residences cropped up randomly without connecting streets. Extended families built thatched-roof longhouses on raised platforms that typically formed groupings of three or four around a farmyard court. Craftspeople belonged to hereditary guilds, living in multiple-household compounds with as many as fifty to sixty-five residents. The aristocracy and professionals, who made up about 10% of the urban population, lived in the city center, where the pyramids, palaces, stelae, and ball courts reinforced the divine sanction of the kings. Here, they narrated their primacy in war and created the ritual setting for blood sacrifices.

The hilly terrain of most Maya sites discouraged the use of the grid, leading to the apparently informal placement of buildings. The individual compounds, however, were strictly orthogonal and usually composed according to a proportional grid. While each individual monumental complex conformed to internal orthogonal coherence, often established by symmetrically placed pairs of pyramids, it did not appear to relate to the geometry of the whole. A hidden structuring principle based on triangles, however, seems to have governed the organization of Tikal (Fig. 7.3-2), where several monumental courtyard compounds fit on a triangle of *sak behs*. If one draws straight lines between the major temples and palaces, it yields a remarkable series of right-angled triangles, suggesting planned alignments.

Maya cities constantly went to war with one another in the struggle to control trade and tribute and to take hostages for sacrifice. The dynasties ruling Maya cities carefully documented their power in stone inscriptions, and their lineages often endured for centuries. The *ajaws* of Tikal traced their origins to a third-century king named Yax-Moch-Xok. During the seventh and eighth centuries they continued to revere Toh-Chok-Ich'ak (True-Great-Jaguar-Claw), the longest-living *ajaw*, who ruled the city from about

RELIGION, PHILOSOPHY, FOLKLORE

The *Popol Vuh* and the Corn People

Shortly after the Spanish conquest of Maya territories in the sixteenth century, Spanish friars transcribed the sacred stories of local religious beliefs in the *Popol Vuh* (*The Community Book*). The book presents a worldview in which humans lived suspended in the Middle World between the overworld of the gods and the underworld of hell. The ruler served as the pivotal mediator with nature, and his blood represented the life force, or *k'ul*. This required frequent blood sacrifices, performed in the ritual bloodletting of the sovereign, the capture and sacrifice of the king or a noble of a rival city, or the sacrifice of the losers in a ball game tournament. On ritual occasions the Maya kings went into trance states to communicate with their ancestors and their gods. Music, dance, psychoactive herbs, sleep deprivation, and bloodletting induced altered states of consciousness.

Much of the *Popol Vuh* concerns the creation myths of the Maya. The gods had failed to create humans from mud and wood and eventually succeeded with maize, or corn. Hero twins through their guile defeated the lords of the underworld, vindicating their father and uncle, who had been executed for rowdy ball playing. These lost relatives returned to life as celestial bodies. The ball game ritualized the regenerative process, which allowed humans to be successfully created out of corn dough. The Maya called the ball courts, which are found in the most prominent places in their cities, the "crack in the top of the mountain of creation" from which the maize god could be reborn.

317 to 378. His descendants carefully preserved his palace as a sacred monument on the western edge of the Central Acropolis. Steep corbelled vaults (Fig. 7.3-3), unknown to other Mesoamerican cultures, covered each of the palace's narrow rooms and established a spatial module that endured throughout Maya history. The section of a typical room evoked that of a Maya hut, with its pitched thatch roof. Even the wooden beams spanning the spaces at the base of the vaults imitated the stabilizing timber joists used in huts. Toh-Chok-Ich'ak's tomb took pride of place in the middle of the central axis of the North Acropolis amid a cluster of sixteen pyramidal temples built for the royalty of Tikal over

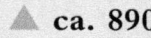

730

New Maya regime begins at Uxmal in Yucatán

Chichén Itzá (Mexico) comes to prominence as ally of Uxmal

800

869

Last Maya inscription at Tikal

El Caracol observatory and El Castillo radial pyramid built at Chichén Itzá

ca. 890

the course of four centuries. As an old man Toh-Chok-Ich'ak had led his people to victory against their closest neighbor, Uaxactun, but died from the wounds of battle. His victory secured Tikal's momentary control of the region, commanding cities as far away as Palenque and Copán.

The bank of kitchens on the southern edge of Toh-Chok-Ich'ak's palace complex overlooked one of six reservoirs. These key hydraulic tanks filled in the hollows left by the quarries used for the monuments of Tikal. The paved areas of the central city channeled the water runoff into catchment areas, the largest being 60 hectares and holding 900,000 cubic meters of water. During the four months of annual drought, the water was distributed through sluice gates. Thus, the monumental core of Tikal served as both a ritual center for dynastic propaganda and the nodal point of hydraulic infrastructure.

During the sixth century Calakmul sacked Tikal. The city began to reassert itself a century later, when the king of Tikal was forced to take his court into exile to Palenque. From there he organized successful military campaigns

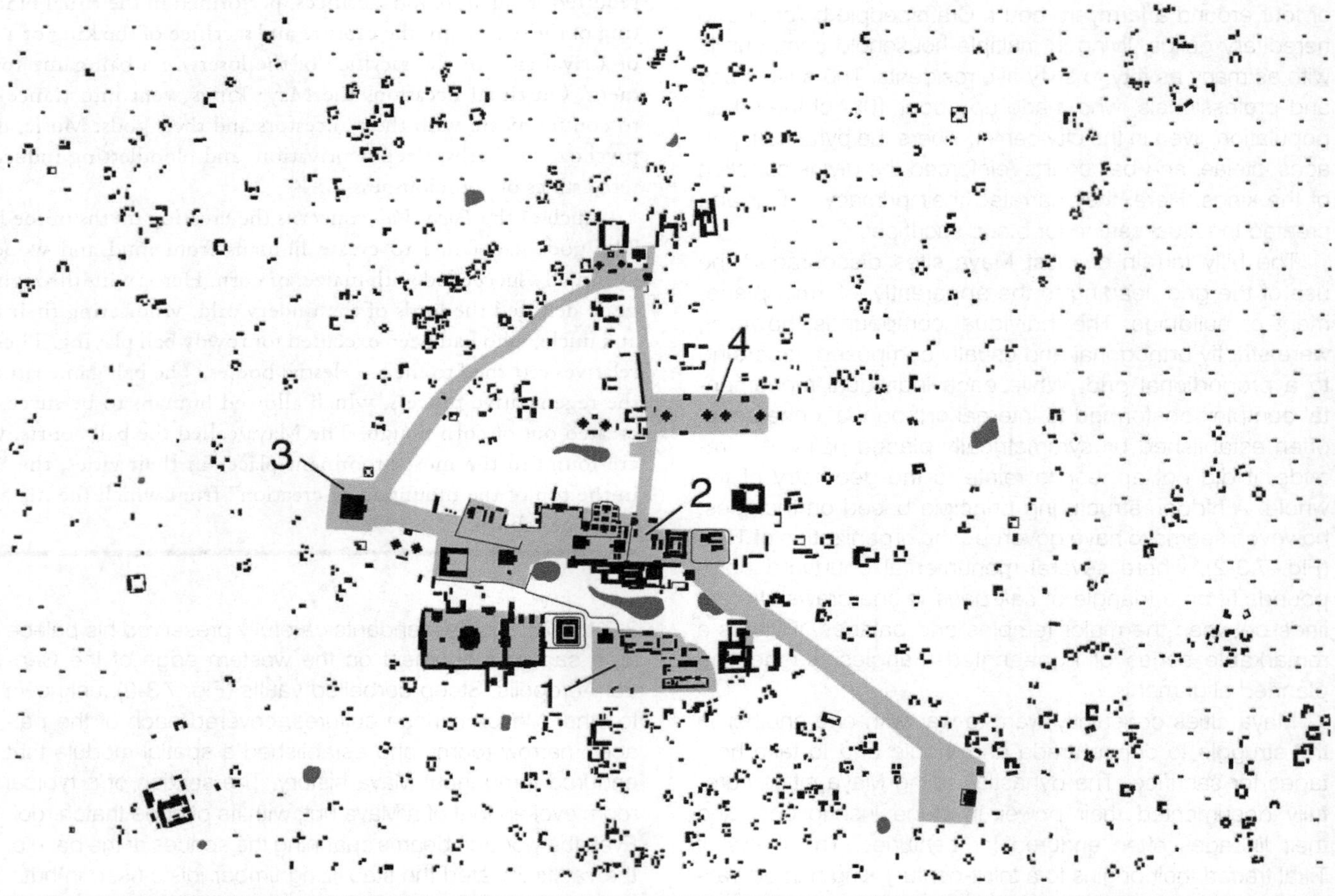

Figure 7.3-2 Tikal, Guatemala. Plan showing the diffused layout of the city around the triangle of the ceremonial center, which guarded the reservoirs, ca. 600–800. (1) Palace-shrine of Toh-Chok-Ich'ak; (2) Hasaw-Kan-K'awil's Great Plaza with Temple I and Temple II; (3) Temple 4; (4) *Katun*, calendar shrines.

▼ **ca. 900**

Pyramid of the Magician and the Nunnery built at Uxmal

Temple of the Warriors and Group of a Thousand Columns built at Chichén Itzá

▲ **ca. 900**

Figure 7.3-3 Tikal, Guatemala. Mayan stone corbelled vaults as an inverted V with wooden stabilizing poles, ninth century.

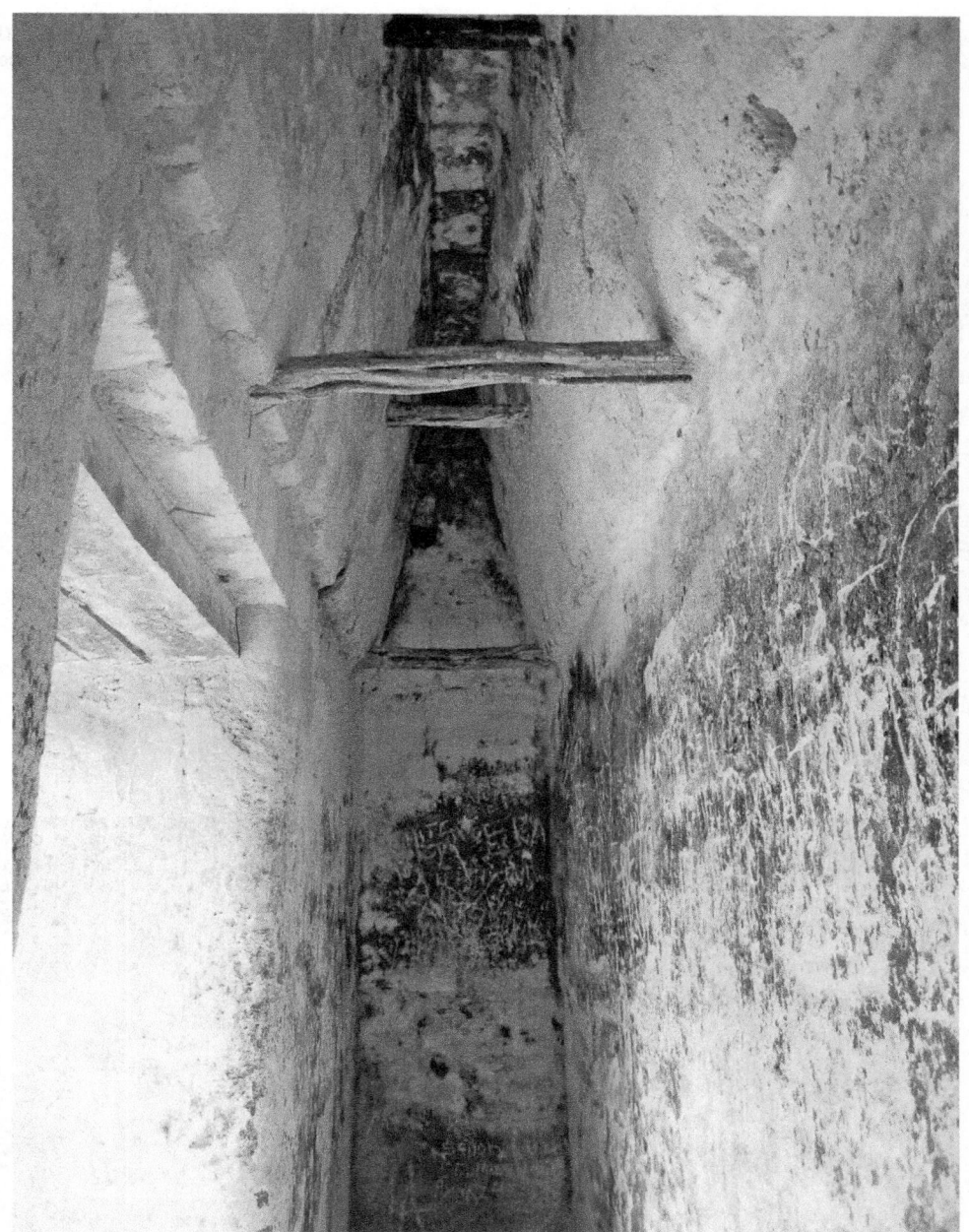

against Calakmul's ally, the city of Dos Pilas, in the 670s. Twenty years later, Hasaw-Kan-K'awil (r. 682–734) captured the king of Calakmul, reversing Tikal's bad fortune. The date of this victory fell at precisely thirteen *katuns* (the twenty-year cycles of the Maya calendar) since the fourth-century victory of Toh-Chok-Ich'ak over Uaxactun. After holding the captured king for thirteen days, Hasaw-Kan-K'awil sacrificed him and proceeded to sack the rival city.

Hasaw-Kan-K'awil celebrated his victory by rebuilding Tikal with new monuments. He first commissioned a new ball court and a radial temple adjacent to it in 695, aligning them to Toh-Chok-Ich'ak's palace and using styles taken from other cities. Above the sloping sides of the ball court, the upper galleries had six rounded columns, a novelty for Tikal but a motif frequently used in the recently conquered Calakmul. The radial temple recalled the style of Teotihuacán, using the *talud-tablero* motif, which alluded to the legendary place of origins.

The victorious *ajaw* also built Tikal's first tall pyramid, Temple 33, as his father's tomb, initiating the formation of the Great Plaza. To either side of this massive pile, Hasaw-Kan-K'awil added even taller structures as tombs for himself and his wife, closing off the eastern and western ends of the plaza. Known as Temple I and Temple II, these staged towers rose steeply to 48 and 41 m (157 and 134 feet), respectively, and faced each other across the space. Temple I, to the east, had nine levels, accessed by a single vertiginous flight of stairs on a 70° pitch (Fig. 7.3-4). The tomb of the king lay beneath the foundations of the structure, while at the summit a single-chambered sanctuary served as a space for priests and royal relatives to make sacrifices to his memory. The flamboyant roofcomb sprouted a full 10 m (33 feet) above the upper chamber. Temple II rose on three levels with a similarly steep flight of stairs leading to a tall roofcomb (Fig. 7.3-5). The crests of the pyramids resembled the ornate headdresses worn by the kings and appeared

as flat billboards decorated with anthropomorphic and zoomorphic motifs. The plaster ornaments, which have since worn away, represented huge masks of seated figures. The Maya called their pyramids "mountains" and in their myths considered mountains as living beings. Thus, they decorated them with animate creatures. Hasaw-Kan-K'awil's son and grandson continued to add staged pyramids to the core of Tikal.

During the seventh and eighth centuries the victorious kings of Tikal built six sets of twin radial pyramids as shrines to the *katun*. Set on raised terraces, the complex incorporated a long palace on the south, two radial platform temples on the east and west, and a walled, open-air altar on the northern edge. The altar contained a stela commemorating each monarch's celebration of the end of

Figure 7.3-4 Tikal, Guatemala. Temple I, late seventh century.

Figure 7.3-5 Tikal, Guatemala. Model of ceremonial center with Temples I and II, mid-eighth century.

Maya Time

The Maya used a written language in the form of bulging glyphs, which were both phonetic and pictographic. The earliest datable inscription, on a stela at Tikal traceable to 292 CE, indicates the local concern for historical time. The Maya calendar was based on a year with 365 days, twenty-year groupings, and 400-year cycles. The majority of inscriptions detail the time and names of dynastic rulers and their military accomplishments. The Maya relied on a cyclical, rather than a progressive, concept of time. Similar to the Sumerians, their yearly calendar followed precise astronomical observations and, with 365 days divided into eighteen months of twenty-one days with five extra days, was the most accurately calculated calendar of all preindustrial civilizations. The *katun*, or twenty-year period, represented the opening and closing of repeated events. The great twin pyramid terraces of Tikal rose as monuments to cyclical time, celebrating the *katun* of a ruler, an event similar to the Heb-Sed festival of the pharaohs of ancient Egypt (see Section 2.2).

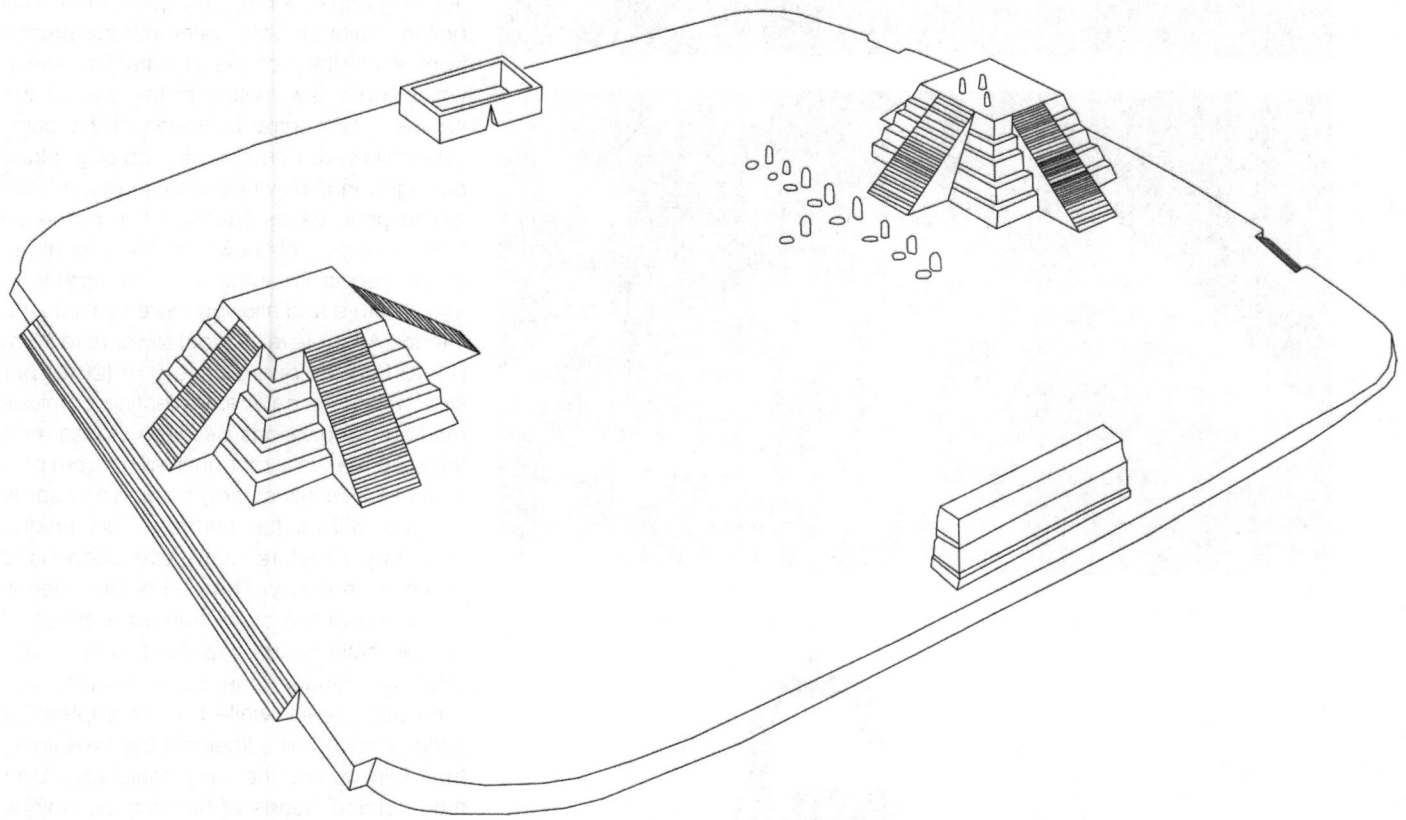

Tikal, Guatemala. Rendering of radial platforms commemorating twenty-year katun, late seventh century.

a *katun*. The gateway to the altar chamber took the form of a Maya arch, a steeply pitched triangular corbelled arch. The long palace in the south of the precinct had nine doors, signifying the realm of the underworld. Identical four-level radial pyramids, with stairs set in the cardinal directions, represented chronological markers on top of which priests performed ceremonial dances. The *ajaws* of Tikal left more than 3,000 inscribed monuments as testament to their cycles of power, the last dating from 869. After this date, civil wars and famines led to the city's abandonment. To build the monuments of Tikal required enormous quantities of wood and much time taken away from agriculture. Inadvertently, the pyramids helped to exhaust the area's resources and livelihood.

The Royal Pyramids of Palenque

Palenque, a city on the western outskirts of the Maya region, never grew to a population of more than 10,000. It related to Tikal as an ambitious provincial town to a brilliant capital city. Located about 250 km (155 miles) from Tikal, it served as the refuge for that city's exiled king in the mid-seventh century.

a

b

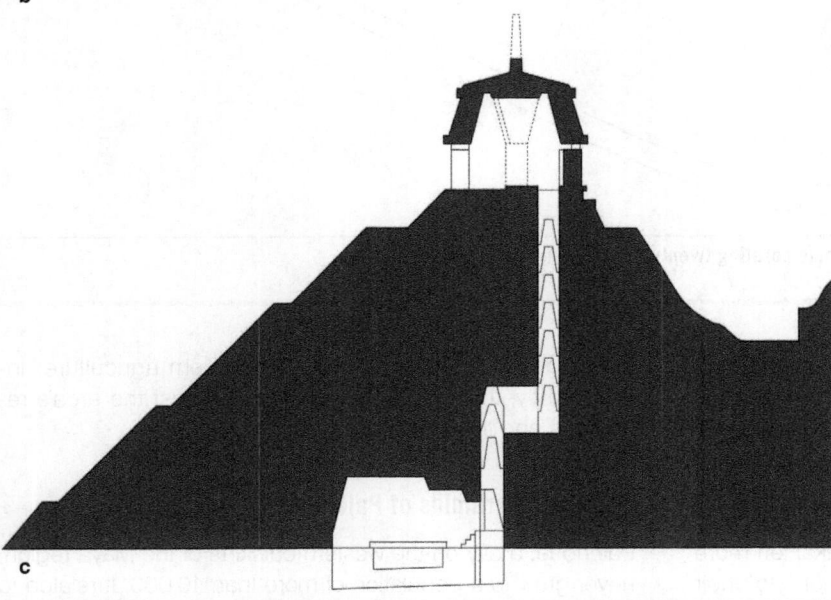

c

Figure 7.3-6 Palenque, Mexico. (a) Palace of Hanab Pakal, ca. 680. (b) Temple of the Inscriptions, built as the tomb of Hanab Pakal, 680. (c) Section showing secret stairway in the Temple of the Inscriptions.

During this period the *ajaw* of Palenque, Hanab Pakal (r. 615–683), reigned as the city's greatest ruler, leaving several inscriptions that noted the hospitality given to his superior from Tikal as one of the city's finest achievements. The distinguished exile seems in fact to have cross-fertilized the architectural imagination of the smaller city, which in turn inspired the increased scale of Tikal.

Hanab Pakal built a palace complex and a pyramid for his own tomb, now called the Temple of the Inscriptions, forming the eastern and southern edges of the city's great plaza. He set the palace on berms raised over previous structures and skirted the perimeter with stairs, protecting it from flooding (Fig. 7.3-6a). An aqueduct on corbelled vaults brought water into the palace from a tributary of the Usumacinta River, which ran a few meters to the east of the palace. The central buildings of the complex followed conventional oblong plans arranged in a pinwheel configuration. Corbelled groin vaults spanned two of the interior spaces. This new masonry technique introduced at Palenque both strengthened the structure and allowed more light into the interior. A four-level lookout tower rose 22 m (72 ft) from a square base 8 m (26 ft) per side within the palace. Projecting cornices marked the divisions between stories, and the solid masonry roof pushed up from projecting eaves into steeply sloping mansards capped with a flat surface. This unique multistory structure may have been used as an observatory. The perimeter galleries at the top of the stairs framed a series of sunken patio courts decorated with carved orthostat panels. One panel documented a military defeat, while a more impressive series showed nine kneeling captives lining the stairs where the king could step over the sculpted heads of his victims. Unique *T*-shaped windows appeared in several of the rooms of the palace and in the Temple of the Cross at Palenque. The vaulted rooms of the palace were decorated with paintings of life-size figures representing the city's dynastic legends.

In 675 Hanab Pakal initiated work on the Temple of the Inscriptions, a massive stepped pyramid adjacent to the palace, piled 36 m (118 ft) over his tomb (Fig. 7.3-6b). Originally designed to have eight stages, its principal northern side had to be buttressed to keep it from collapsing during construction, resulting in a new configuration of three levels. Today, it has been restored to the original eight levels. The structure may have been weakened by the inclusion of an internal stair to the king's burial chamber at the pyramid's core (Fig. 7.3-6c). This secret access descended through the sanctuary from the summit of the temple on a series of switchbacks. After the king's burial, his successor filled the stairs with rubble, leaving a conduit, now known as the "psychoduct," to allow the spirit of the defunct king to ascend to the upper temple to communicate with his heirs during their ceremonial trances. Three cross-vaults intersected the corbelled vault of the burial chamber, repeating a sophisticated structural solution invented by the architects of the palace. Hanab Pakal's gigantic sarcophagus, cut from a single 15-ton piece of limestone and capped with an exquisitely carved slab, occupied most of the tomb. The relief carvings depicted the king in a falling position as he entered the underworld, next to a cruciform "world tree," while the edges of the lid documented six generations of his ancestral heritage. The walls carried painted stucco portraits of nine previous rulers, including his mother, who, as regent, had preceded him for several years. At the door lay the corpses of five attendants, sacrificed with the king.

Ironically, the success of Palenque and many other small Maya cities, including Bonampak, Piedras Negras, and Seibal, during the seventh and eighth centuries may have contributed to the overall decline of the region around 900. The transformation of the ceremonial center of Dos Pilas into a fortress, for which stones for a new set of walls were scavenged from its temples, indicates a destructuring process caused by political competition. The fragmentation of the political centers of Tikal and Calakmul and the general overpopulation of the region led to constant strife in the struggle for resources.

Spaces of Assembly in the Yucatán: Uxmal and Chichén Itzá

The cities in the Petén area declined during the ninth century, exhausted by warfare and no longer able to agriculturally sustain large populations. The elite apparently migrated north to the lowlands of the Yucatán Peninsula. Here, they founded the last great Maya cities of Uxmal and Chichén Itzá. In this heavily forested hill country over a dozen cities reached their prime between the eighth and tenth centuries, contemporaneous with the decline of areas once controlled by Tikal and Calakmul to the southwest. The lack of rivers or springs in the region made water management the key to power.

The monumental core of Uxmal sat inside an oval mound of walls, roughly 1 km × 600 m (3,280 × 1,968 ft). The contiguous structures of three large courtyards surrounded the Great Pyramid in the south. Its north-facing stairs looked over a vast esplanade to a second complex of courtyards next to a second pyramid. The tallest structure in Uxmal, retroactively called the Pyramid of the Magician (Fig. 7.3-7), equaled Temple I at Tikal in height. Begun by an earlier culture in the sixth century, the final two layers were added in the late eighth and ninth centuries after the arrival in 731 of new rulers. The elites accessed the temple on the west by an extremely steep stairway with a 70° pitch leading to an ornately carved portal in the form of an inverted *T* surrounded by interwoven stone mosaics. Like the roofcombs of Tikal, the portal presented in more durable materials a colossal mask, with spiral-shaped eyes, a protruding curled nose (which has broken off), and a wide mouth. The eastern stairway, built a generation later, stepped more gradually to a temple poised one level above it on the western side.

The Pyramid of the Magician overlooked one of the best-preserved and most fancifully decorated Maya courtyard complexes, now called the "Nunnery" (Fig. 7.3-8). King Chan-Chak-K'ak'nal-Ahaw dedicated this complex in 907. The disposition of over sixty cell-like rooms in the four 80 m (262 ft) long volumes suggested the analogy of this ceremonial center to a convent. The king's designers set the entire trapezoidal court on an elevated platform reached by broad stairs on the south. A two-story, arrowhead-shaped arch led into the southern entry. The four doors on either side of the arch were placed at progressively shorter intervals as they moved away from the center, indicating the use of a proportional grid. Masons adorned the mansards with friezes depicting *itz* flowers, which were associated with magic. Above each door they placed a realistic representation of a thatch-roofed house with monsters and maize above it, probably referring to the creation myths about beings formed from cornmeal dough. The stone mosaics on the interior of the court included diagonal grilles resembling canes used on hut construction, *V*-shaped corn cribs, spiral cloud motifs that refer to the *popol nah* community house,

Figure 7.3-7 Uxmal, Mexico. Pyramid of the Magician, ca. 740.

Figure 7.3-8 Uxmal, Mexico. The Nunnery, ca. 750.

and long-snouted creatures representing the *Izamna*, the great bird poised on top of the world tree.

Chan-Chak-K'ak'nal-Ahaw also commissioned the ball court of Uxmal and the Governor's Palace, a narrow building almost 100 m (328 ft) long with decorations using the same intricate stone mosaic technique and motifs found in the Nunnery. For this structure the builders again used corbelled arches to separate the central block from two side wings and constructed the mass of the walls and vaults with a local cement infill, which required the extravagant burning of wood to obtain lime. Maya concrete was not as strong as the pozzolana-based concrete of Rome but was nonetheless a sign of highly advanced construction methods. The masons at Uxmal worked the limestone with such accuracy of detail and plasticity that it is hard to believe they used only obsidian blades.

The great profusion of monuments at Uxmal at the end of the ninth century coincided with the alliance made with Chichén Itzá in 883, resulting in a larger regional state. The 18 km (11 mile) interurban road constructed between Uxmal and Kabah indicates the strong union of the territory. Chichén Itzá, about 150 km (93 miles) east of Uxmal, became the dominant power in the region and produced a brilliant collection of monuments, signs of great wealth from both tribute and trade. The inland city controlled the coastal port at Isla Cerritos, where it imported obsidian from central Mexico and enforced a monopoly on salt, the region's most sought-after commodity.

Until recently archaeologists attributed Chichén Itzá's surprising production of new building types, such as hypostyle halls, to the migration of Toltecs from Tula in central Mexico, where several similar structures had been found. New evidence from a thorough interpretation of the inscriptions, however, indicates that the structures at Chichén Itzá predated those of Tula and the new settlers came from the Petén region. The Itzá probably fled from the conflicts between Tikal and Calakmul. The great mixture of styles found in their capital might also indicate the presence of refugees from Teotihuacán, which was abandoned in the late seventh century. The *Chilám Balám* book of prophecies, transcribed in the late sixteenth century, referred to the Itzá as heathens, heretics, stupid foreigners, and, worst of all, "people without fathers and mothers." Instead of the typical Maya dynasty, the rulers of Chichén Itzá seem to have established a more diffused system of power, relying on warriors' councils to form policy. Their atypical colonnaded structures probably served the new function of tribal council halls.

Chichén Itzá was located near two sinkhole reservoirs, or *cenote* (Fig. 7.3-9). The local populace revered the Sacred Cenote as a pilgrimage site before, during, and after the reign of the Itzá. One approached this site from the edge of the northern precinct on a long paved *sak beh* avenue. Visitors threw sacrificial offerings into its deep waters 20 m (64 ft) below grade. One reached the second *cenote* at the juncture of the northern and southern precincts on a similarly raised avenue.

The central core of Chichén Itzá had two walled precincts. The style of several of the buildings in the southern precinct resembles the stone mosaic motifs found at Uxmal. The most intriguing complex, however, is a unique round structure known as the *Caracol*, or "snail," its cylindrical tower rising three stories (Fig 7.3-10a). The concentric corbelled vaults supporting its spiral stair were pierced with narrow slots at four positions to reveal the alignment to Venus at different times of the year (Fig. 7.3-10b). While the lowest platform of this observatory conformed to the geometrical coordinates of the surrounding monuments, its second terrace was rotated 10° and the doors of the cylinder were rotated another 5° to give it a perfect cardinal alignment.

The radial pyramid known as the *Castillo*, or "castle," dominates the northern precinct of Chichén Itzá (Fig. 7.3-11). Pitched on nine levels, the ninety-one steps of each of its four elevations add up to 364, making a clear reference to the yearly calendar. The railings of the stair depict the feathered serpent known as Kulkukan, the Maya version of Quetzalcoatl. During the equinoxes, the stepped corner of the pyramid projects an undulating shadow on the northern stairs that resembles the sinuous snake. A square pavilion caps the summit of the Castillo.

The large compound to the east of the Castillo contained the most extensive use of colonnaded architecture in all of Mesoamerica, known as the Group of a Thousand Columns (Fig. 7.3-12). North of this hypostyle, the Temple of the Warriors rose 20 m (66 ft) on a four-staged mound. Rendered in the *talud-tablero* style of Teotihuacán, its friezes depicted jaguars and eagles dining on human hearts, a probable reference to the valor of the city's military hierarchy. The temple's entry hall spread twenty-eight columns wide and four deep, like the colonnaded prayer halls of Islam. Corbelled masonry vaults supported the roof. At the threshold of the Upper Temple sat a *chacmol*, a sacrificial altar more commonly found in central Mexico, designed in the form of a man lying on his back, knees bent, and propped up on his elbows with a plate on his belly for depositing the hearts of sacrificial victims. The sacrificial furniture stood between two colossal serpent columns, mouths open at the base and tails bent up to form brackets for the lintel. The impressive collection of colonnaded structures around the Group of a Thousand Columns seems to have accommodated an alternative political order based on assemblies.

The Great Ball Court of Chichén Itzá (Fig. 7.3-13), the largest and most ornate in Mesoamerica, was dedicated between 849 and 869. Located west of the Castillo, the *I*-shaped arena was placed next to a *T*-shaped altar for the skull racks, or *tzompantli*, where those who lost in the tournaments were sacrificed. The playing field measured 146 × 36 m (479 × 118 ft), larger than a football field. Sculptural friezes and interior paintings explained its meaning as the "crack in the mountain of creation." The walls stood 10 m (33 ft) thick, and their outer profiles were slanted like

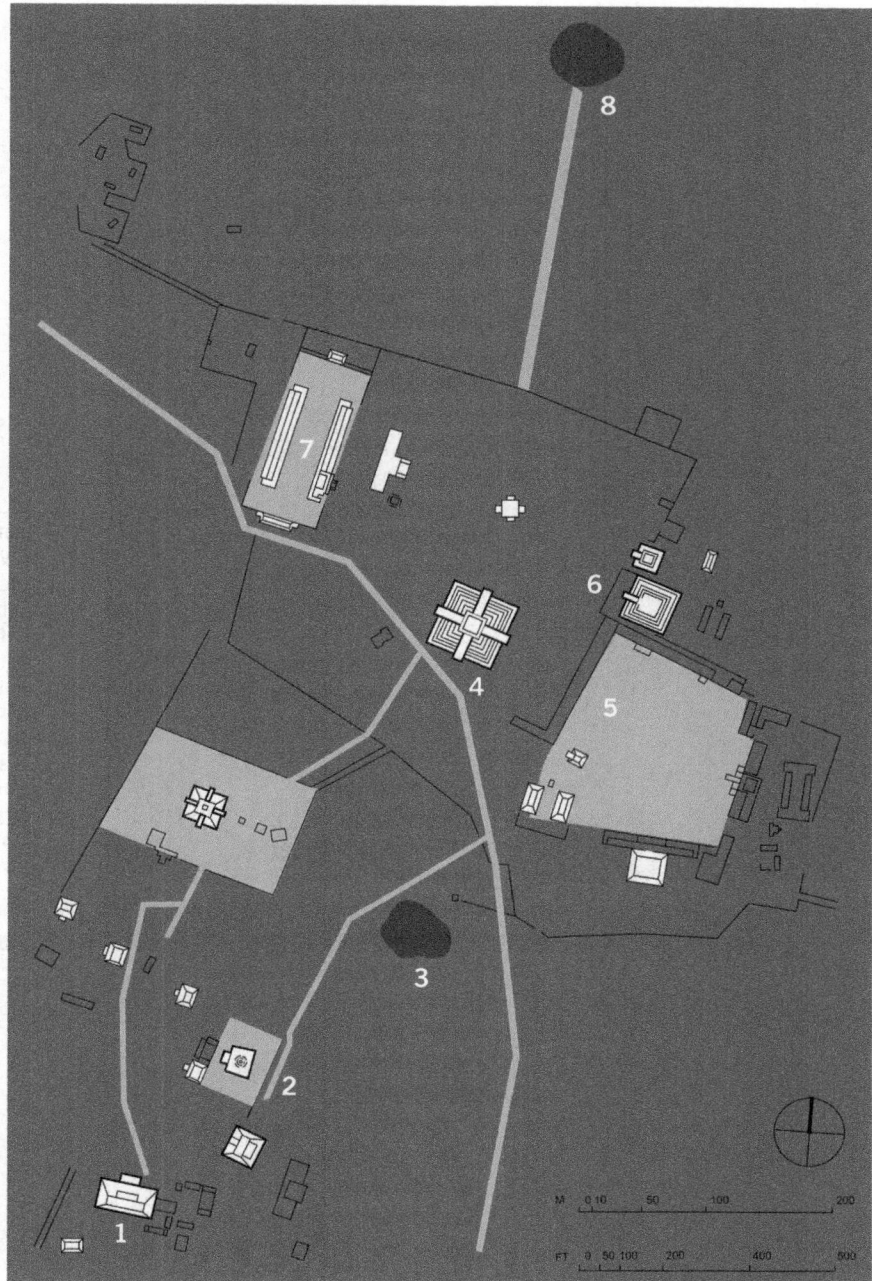

Figure 7.3-9 Chichén Itzá, Mexico. Plan, ninth century: (1) the Nunnery; (2) El Caracol observatory; (3) small *cenote* watering hole; (4) El Castillo radial pyramid; (5) Group of a Thousand Columns; (6) Temple of the Warriors; (7) ball court; (8) large *cenote* watering hole.

a stepped pyramid. They rose straight up above the field 8 m (26 ft), leaving the typical slope at their base, lined with a 1.5 m (5 ft) high bench on which friezes described the game. The impractical height of the goal rings 7 m (23 ft) above grade has led some scholars to suspect that the court merely represented a symbolic space for imaginary giants to play. The iconography, however, featuring scenes of seven-man teams and the sacrifice by decapitation of the losers, indicates that it served its designated purpose. At the north end of the court stood a small elevated pyramidal

pavilion, perhaps a tribunal for the elite. On the south a long pavilion with a six-column portico housed a *chacmol* dressed as a player in the game. The Jaguar Temple was perched on top of the southeast corner of the ball court, and one entered it through colossal serpent columns like those of the Temple of the Warriors. The upper hall contained an extraordinary table supported by fifteen sculpted warrior figures in ceremonial costumes. These ornate **atlantids** have been likened to the ruling hierarchy of Chichén Itzá, with the table a symbol of their federated unity in rule.

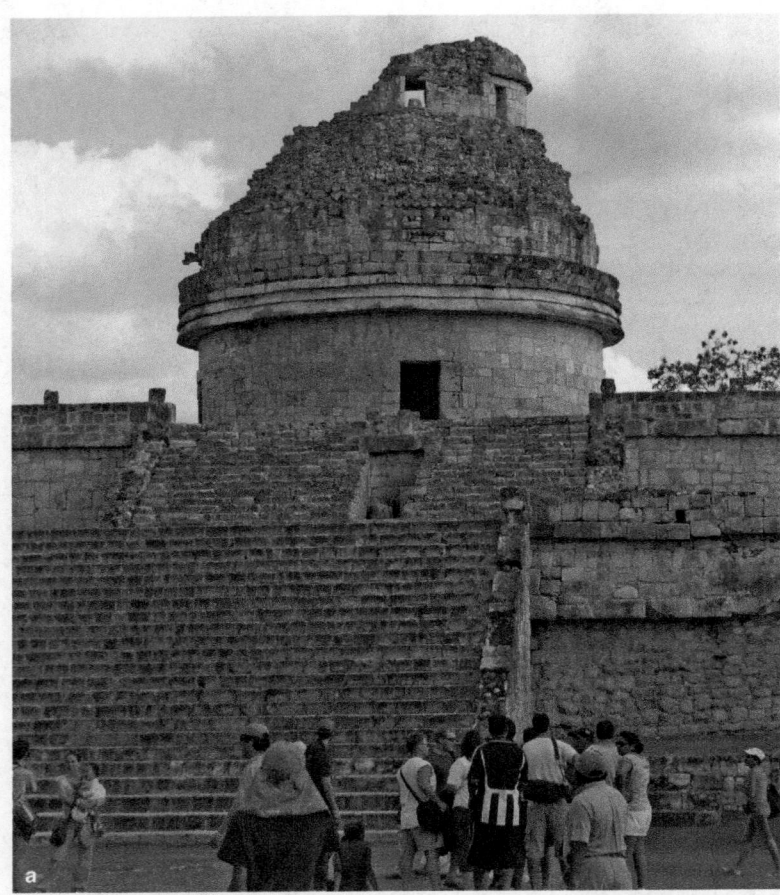

Figure 7.3-10 Chichén Itzá, Mexico. (a) View of El Caracol, the "snail," observatory, ca. 890. (b) Plan of observatory: (A) Square outer platform aligned to other monuments of Chichén Itzá; (B) inner platform rotated to align with cardinal points; (C) spiral staircase in round tower with windows aligned to Venus and the setting sun at the summer and winter equinoxes; (D) niche in the entry stair aligned to Venus at the May 30 solstice; (E) small sanctuary or prayer hall.

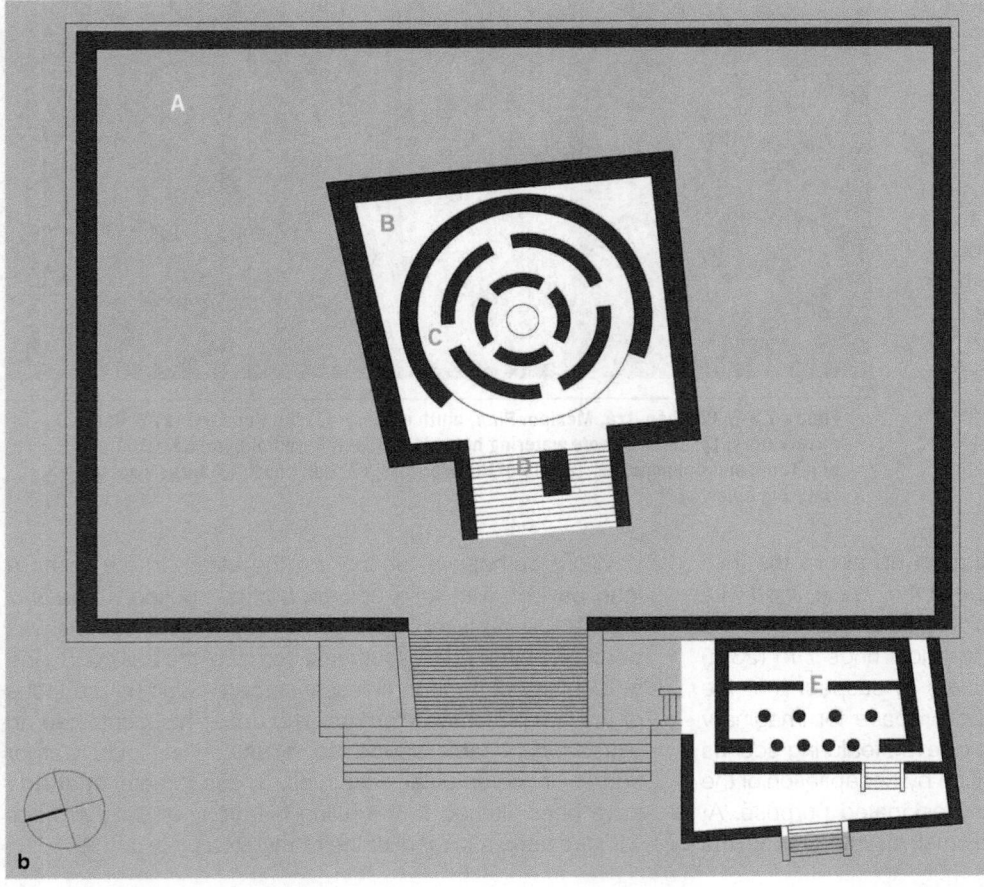

Figure 7.3-11 Chichén Itzá, Mexico. El Castillo radial pyramid, ca. 890.

Figure 7.3-12 Chichén Itzá, Mexico. Temple of the Warriors and Group of a Thousand Columns, ca. 900.

Despite its apparent power, Chichén Itzá was abandoned in the middle of the tenth century. Its decline may be explained in part by its alternative political structure, which instead of a dynasty relied on a consortium of rulers, which in time may have become difficult to coordinate. Certainly, environmental factors of drought and famine also influenced the economic difficulties. The region quickly reached a population greater than the land could sustain. As the iconography of the ball court and the Temple of the Warriors attests, the capital city itself became a significant drain on the local population in terms of tribute, forced labor, and human sacrifice, and according to the *Chilám Balám*, this led the subject cities to rebel against their overlords.

Figure 7.3-13 Chichén Itzá, Mexico. Great Ball Court, ninth century. The court symbolized the crack in the mountain of creation.

Further Reading

Abrams, Elliot M. *How the Maya Built Their World: Energetics and Ancient Architecture.* Austin: University of Texas Press, 1994.

Harrison, Peter D. *The Lords of Tikal: Rulers of an Ancient Maya City.* London: Thames & Hudson, 1999.

Miller, Mary Ellen. *Maya Art and Architecture.* London: Thames & Hudson, 1999.

Schele, Linda, and Peter Mathews. *The Code of Kings: The Language of Seven Sacred Maya Temples and Tombs.* New York: Scribner, 1998.

Schele, Linda, and Mary Ellen Miller. *The Blood of Kings: Dynasty and Ritual in Maya Art.* Fort Worth, TX: Kimbell Museum, 1986.

Whittington, E. Michael. *The Sport of Life and Death: The Mesoamerican Ballgame.* Charlotte, NC: Mint Museum, 2001.

Visit the free website **www.oup.com/us/ingersoll** to view chapter outlines and study questions; Google Maps showing the location of key sites; links to UNESCO World Heritage Sites; and essays on topics that cross time and culture.

800–1200

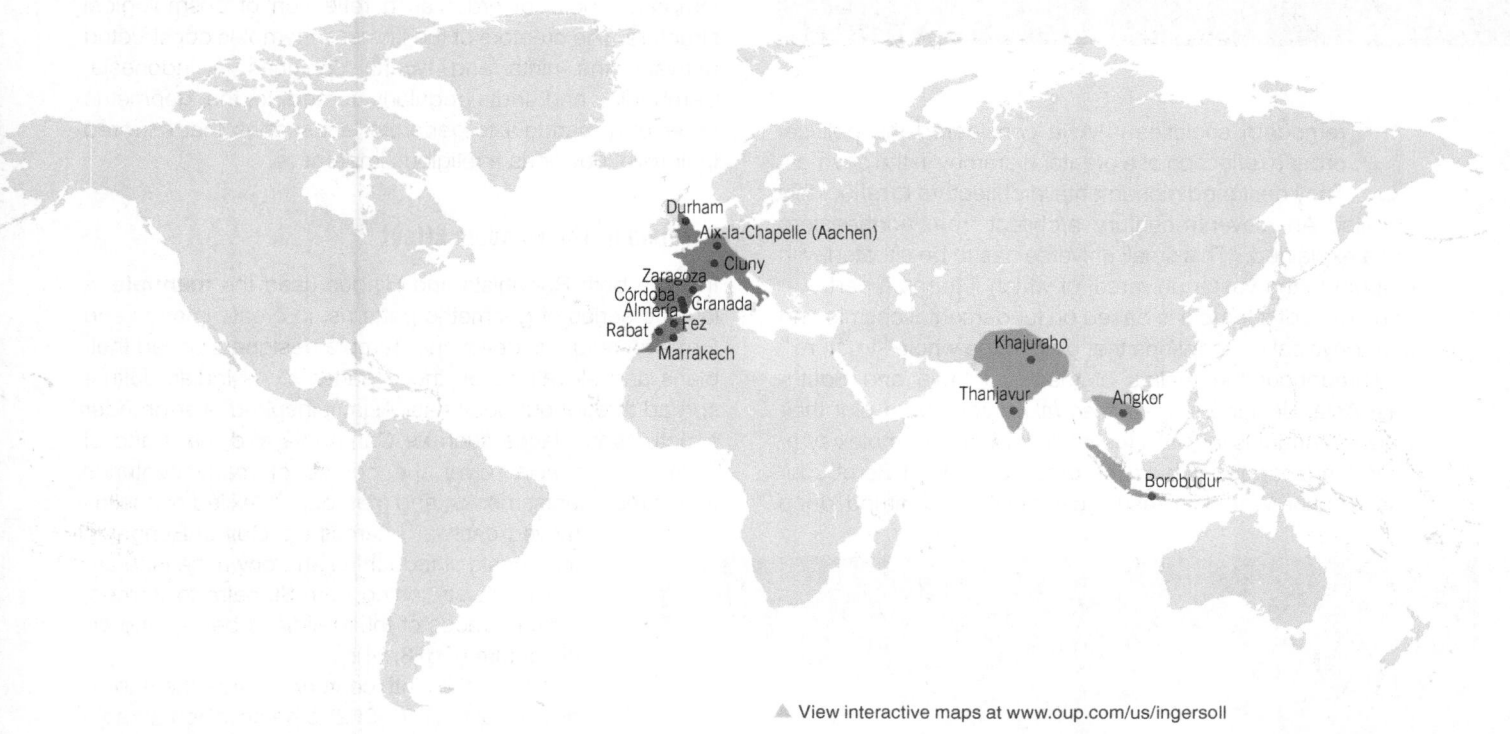

Durham
Aix-la-Chapelle (Aachen)
Cluny
Zaragoza
Córdoba
Almería Granada
Rabat Fez
Marrakech
Khajuraho
Thanjavur
Angkor
Borobudur

▲ View interactive maps at www.oup.com/us/ingersoll

8.1	**SOUTHEAST ASIA AND SOUTHERN INDIA:** Lived-In Models of Cosmic Order
8.2	**ISLAMIC SPAIN AND MOROCCO:** Interlacing Forms in al-Andalus and the Maghreb
8.3	**WESTERN EUROPE AFTER THE ROMAN EMPIRE:** Monks, Knights, and Pilgrims

Indian merchants and exiles crossing the Gulf of Bengal helped spread their religions and architectural methods throughout Southeast Asia. Some of the grandest interpretations of the Indian *mandala* rose at the maritime hinge between Indian and Chinese cultures, in places such as Borobudur on the island of Java and Angkor in Cambodia. By the eleventh century the dynasties in the south of India had kept pace with the gigantic structures of the Khmer. Islamic Spain underwent a similar process of cultural stimulation from abroad as a result of the enlightened exile Abd al-Rahman I, the sole survivor of the Umayyad dynasty, who brought his memories of the glories of Damascus to Córdoba. The Umayyad monuments, starting with the Great Mosque of Córdoba, inspired the architectural programs of a series of rulers in the *taifa* states of Spain and the Berber regimes of Morocco and Spain, culminating in the spectacular fortress palace of the Alhambra in Granada. Such grandeur sparked the envy of Christian rulers to the north. Charlemagne, who around 800 united parts of Europe into the tenuous confederation of the Holy Roman Empire, attempted to evoke the monuments of Byzantine Ravenna while aspiring to the grandeur of Abd al-Rahman's achievements in Spain. Ecclesiastic institutions, especially the great monasteries such as Cluny, determined much of the political climate in Europe during the eleventh and twelfth centuries, sponsoring pilgrimages and launching the Crusades to Palestine, both of which inspired the ambitious architectural programs of the great vaulted cathedrals.

8.1 SOUTHEAST ASIA AND SOUTHERN INDIA
Lived-In Models of Cosmic Order

Premodern societies in Asia considered the political order a reflection of a greater hierarchy in the cosmos. They designed monumental architecture to reflect this parallel. An eleventh-century architect from northeastern India explained, "This small universe has to be situated with respect to the vaster universe, of which it forms a part. . . . The layout of a temple is based on fundamental cosmic and metaphysical conceptions that govern the whole structure."

Throughout the realms of medieval India and Southeast Asia, designers used *mandala* diagrams to plot their works. Mandalas inspired the composition of complex symbolic landscapes such as the great temples of Borobudur and Angkor Wat. The resulting architecture carried deep

religious significance while providing a demonstration of authority. Harnessing the labor needed to build such monumental structures was among the greatest political acts of the region. When a society constructed a grand pyramidal composition that focused on the axis mundi, the sacred center of the world, it signaled the desire to treat the contemporary political order as a reflection of cosmological structure. The creators of the immense temples constructed between the ninth and twelfth centuries in Indonesia, Cambodia, and India regularly turned to the geometric order of a mandala to generate landscapes that mirrored their royal power as a religious imperative.

Borobudur: The Mandala Effect

In India both Buddhists and Hindus used the **mandala**, a layered series of geometric patterns, to create images and forms for religious devotions. Temple designers based their plans and elevations on these patterns. As Indian culture spread throughout Southeast Asia, it inspired ever-grander structures in places such as Cambodia and the island of Java in Indonesia. Over the course of many centuries Indian merchants, monks, and members of exiled dynasties moved eastward across the Gulf of Bengal to the coasts of Indochina and down the long arc of islands stretching from Sumatra to Borneo, leaving traces of their religious beliefs and architecture (Fig. 8.1-1).

During the ninth century on Java, the Sailendra dynasty (770–862) created a remarkable series of monuments, including one of the largest temples of all time, the Buddhist shrine of Borobudur (Fig. 8.1-2). Rival dynasties built Hindu temples, locally known as *candi*, on a similar scale. The *candi* of Java provide the only architectural evidence of the urban civilization that crafted them. The craftspeople of Borobudur completed this great pile of lava stone sometime around the year 800 on a knoll in open country near the Sailendra capital of Yogyakarta. A consummate realization of a mandala in three dimensions, it presented

Figure 8.1-1 Southeast Asia and India, 800–1200.

TIME LINE

▼ **800**

Sailendra dynasty builds Buddhist monument of Borobudur on Java

Khmer dynasty consolidated by Jayavarman II in Cambodia

▲ **ca. 800**

▼ **ca. 800–900**

Khmer dynasty creates several capitals in the district of Angkor

Sanjaya dynasty builds Hindu temples of Prambanan (Java)

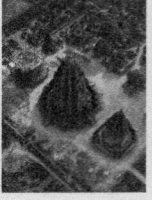

▲ **910**

Figure 8.1-2 Borobudur, central Java (Indonesia). Buddhist shrine built by the Sailendra dynasty, ca. 800.

a concentric succession of geometric figures leading from the **redented** squares of the five outer platforms to the three oval rings of *stupas* on the upper terraces, terminating in a giant *stupa* at the summit. The base covered about the same area as the small pyramid at Giza. Its mountain-like profile symbolized the legendary Mount Meru, center of the Vedic and Buddhist cosmos and home of the gods in Indian mythology.

The Sailendra masons carved the temple of Borobudur from a pile of stones: more than 2 million blocks of volcanic rock, set without mortar. The designers showed little concern for structural invention other than finding a way to brace the mass of the outer terraces from sliding outward. During a

second building campaign they covered the lowest terrace with stone buttressing. They used conservative stepped corbel techniques for the rounded arches placed over the stairways, which had no function other than supporting their own weight and indicating independent thresholds.

Borobudur's designers composed with a mandala plan based on *padas* (squares in a grid) organized in rows of either 8 × 8 or 9 × 9 and then further subdivided by a radial pattern of eight segments with twenty-four subdivisions. The number eight, which in Buddhist doctrine refers to the eightfold path for reaching enlightenment, recurs throughout the Borobudur complex, from the number of its levels to the multiples of its details. The pilgrim would

▼ **ca. 1000**

Rajarajesvaram built by Chola dynasty in southern India

Chandela dynasty in northeast India builds Khajuraho temples

▲ **1020**

▼ **1130**

Angkor Wat begun for Suryavarman II

Angkor destroyed by Chams of Vietnam

▲ **1177**

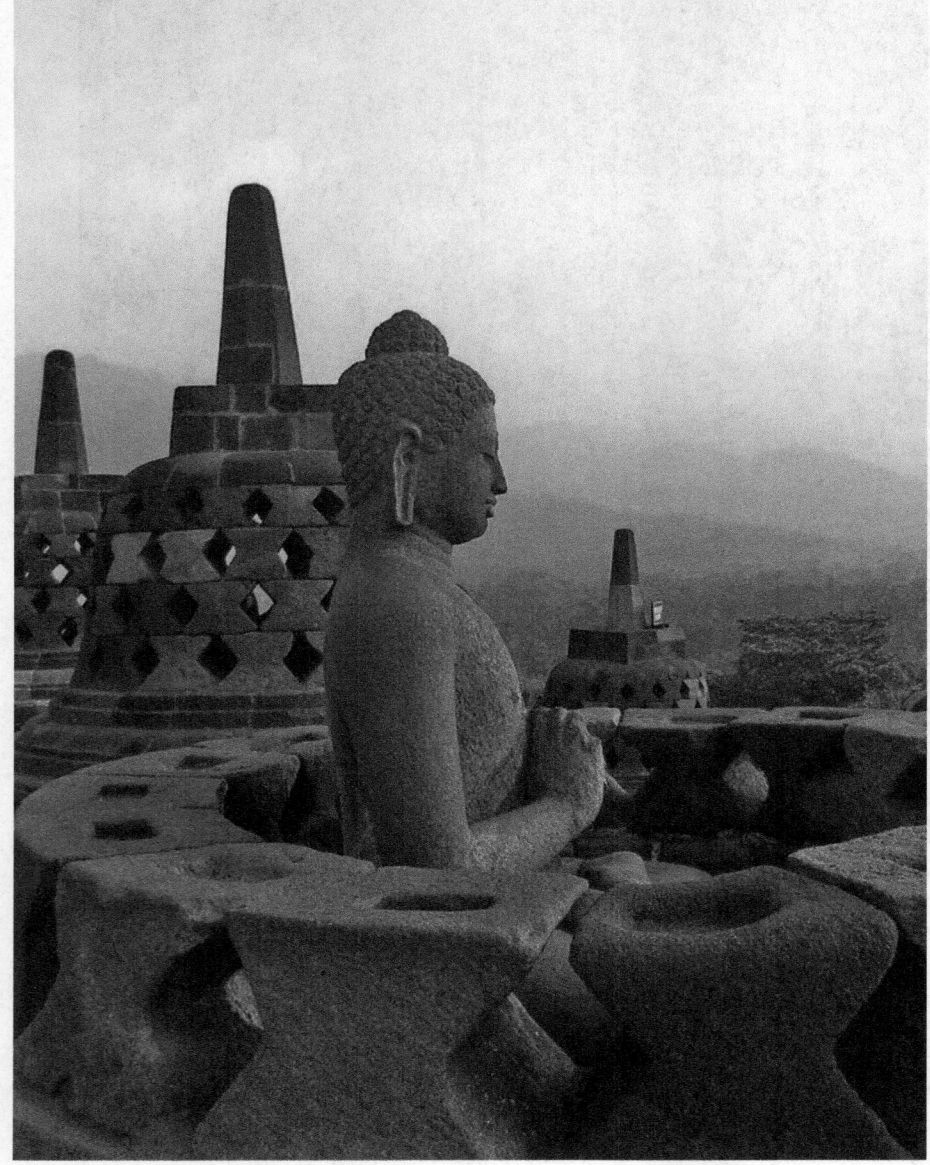

Figure 8.1-3 Borobudur, central Java (Indonesia). Upper terraces of the Buddhist monument with perforated *stupas*, each containing a statue of a cross-legged Buddha, ca. 800.

one that was later covered up, carried 160 relief panels describing the causes of human suffering. The intermediate levels described the realm of form in partially sunken galleries traversed by a path lined with more than 1,000 sculpted panels and hundreds of niches containing life-size statues of Dhyani, the transcendental Buddha (Fig. 8.1-3). A head-height parapet lined the outer edge of these galleries so that even though the terrace remained open to the sky, it felt enclosed. To walk the entire 3 km (2 mile) itinerary, encircling the monument on its lower levels, required at least an hour.

The pilgrim, upon reaching the top three terraces of Borobudur, would have found a stark contrast, representing the realm of enlightenment. The oval terraces were set in concentric rings of seventy-two bell-shaped *stupas*. Diamond-shaped grilles perforated the carefully carved *stupas*, allowing one to peer inside at life-size statues of the Buddha sitting in a cross-legged lotus position. The central *stupa* at the summit, five times larger than the others, once contained a giant bronze Buddha that has since disappeared. In the temple's completed state the statue occupied an inaccessible hollow that no one could see, an architectural allegory of the Buddha's transcendence of the material world.

have circumambulated each level on a clockwise path, contemplating the multitude of images of the Buddha and the scenes of his life. The route followed a narrative based on three states of being: the realm of desire, the realm of form, and the realm of formlessness. The lowest level, the

Few records remain of the Sailendra patrons who produced this colossal vision. Their control over central Java lasted less than a century. By the end of the ninth century, the rival Sanjaya dynasty, based on the eastern tip of the island, had intermarried with them and eventually supplanted

▼ **1181**

Jayavarman VII builds Angkor Thom to restore Khmer center

Pandya dynasty in southern India builds Madurai to rival Cholas

▲ **ca. 1250**

RELIGION, PHILOSOPHY, FOLKLORE

The Mandala and Magic Numbers

An Indian building manual of the seventh century, the *Manasara-silpasastra*, explained the theory of organizing buildings and cities on the diagrams of the mandala, a layered series of concentric geometric figures that was used by both Buddhists and Hindus for meditation. The mandala represented cosmic order and in its simplest form followed a square grid. Its mythological connection to architecture came from the story of Vastu Purusha, a cosmic being positioned facedown in the square of the grid as divine punishment for evil deeds. This scapegoat character provided the metaphoric sacrifice upon which to assemble the rest of the structure. The plans ordered by the grids usually contained sixty-four or eighty-one subdivisions, known as *padas*. The squares radiated from a central figure representing Mount Meru, the origin of the Hindu cosmos, to peripheral *padas* representing the gods. The mandala generated the complex order of Buddhist and Hindu temples, which followed symmetrically deployed subdivisions around a central vertical axis.

Buddhist and Hindu architects who started their designs from the mandala followed magic numerical sequences. The number 15 held a particular fascination when used in the nine-square diagram. A variety of integers placed in sequences adding up to 15 could be counted across, down, and diagonally:

6 + 7 + 2

1 + 5 + 9

8 + 3 + 4

(a) Mandala of Kalacakra (the wheel of time). Tibetan *tangka*, eighteenth century. (b) Vastu Purusha in the mandala grid.

them, imposing Hinduism as the island's principal religion. The Sanjaya constructed their major temple of Prambanan in 910 (Fig. 8.1-4), achieving nearly as grand a setting as Borobudur. Four concentric rings of 224 small *candis* surrounded a central precinct with three soaring pyramids dedicated to Brahma, Shiva, and Vishnu and five smaller altars. The tallest *candi* in the temple's center was also dedicated to Shiva, the Destroyer, perhaps invoking the volatile seismic situation of the island. Although there is evidence of exchanges between the Cholas of southern India and the kings of Java and Sumatra into the eleventh century, it appears that the effects of volcanic eruptions curtailed Sanjaya power in central Java by the mid-tenth century. The splendid redundancy of the *stupas* of Borobudur

Figure 8.1-4 Prambanan, Java (Indonesia). Major shrine, built by the rival dynasty to the Sailendra, dedicated to the Hindu trinity of Brahma, Shiva, and Vishnu, ca. 900.

and the *candis* of Prambanan present stunning visions of a hieratic society that sacrificed an enormous quantity of hours in labor to produce a habitable image of the perfect order of a mandala.

Angkor: Living in a Microcosm

The Khmer dynasty in Cambodia went even further toward designing representations of the cosmos of such magnitude they could almost replace the real world. Angkor, with its dozens of temple complexes, oblong reservoirs, canals, and sculpture-lined causeways, comprised the largest monumental setting in the world, covering an area of over 350 km^2 (135 miles^2) (Fig. 8.1-5). The Khmer owed obvious debts to the monumental and religious traditions of both India and China, borrowing from Hindu and Buddhist beliefs while imitating the Chinese system of divinely sanctioned monarchy. Local geographic peculiarities contributed significantly to the culture's unique formal development. During the rainy season, Tonle Sap (the "Great Lake") in the interior of Cambodia swelled to four times its normal size and then receded, leaving fertilized land and fish behind. Somewhat like the regular flooding of the Nile, the Great Lake ensured a ready surplus of foodstuffs while imposing a lag time during the flood season that could be devoted to ambitious

architectural pursuits. Most of the monumental complexes of the Khmer involved impressive hydraulic manipulations related to the annual floods.

The Khmer dynasty began its monuments about the same time that Borobudur was nearing completion. The dynasty's founder, Jayavarman II (r. ca. 770–835), was a military adventurer who may have been aware of the *candis* of Java. The projects of the Khmer showed certain affinities with the island's structures, such as pyramidal massing and mandala-based plans. As *chakravartin*, or "universal monarch," Jayavarman created a new capital at Hariharalaya between the Great Lake and the sacred mountain of Phnom Kulen. The initial coronation ceremonies established a theocratic mold: Jayavarman II became the universal king, while a simultaneous rite declared the kingship of a supernatural being. The Khmer rulers were thus believed to share their power with the king of the gods. As a consequence they lived highly ritualized parallel existences in temple cities designed for the gods. The first few generations of Khmer rulers at Hariharalaya sponsored three basic architectural programs: (1) a grand waterwork, (2) an ancestor temple, and (3) a pyramidal state temple that functioned as a mausoleum.

The scale and complexity of Khmer hydrological engineering, which included great basins, canals, and formidable dams and bridges, reveals the advanced organizational capacity of this highly centralized and hierarchical society. The construction of enormous temples in the political center and at pilgrimage sites throughout the region necessitated the imperial subjugation of masses of laborers. The Khmer's constant military expansion allowed its rulers to distribute generous land grants and endowments to the temples of monastic communities, which guaranteed a network of religious support. While the temples of Angkor seemed serene visions of harmony, the state that paid for them pursued an aggressive military policy. The commoners of Cambodia suffered heavy taxation and were overworked. The Khmer hierarchy expressed their contempt for their slaves, calling them "dogs."

During the first century of Khmer rule, the work that literally set the dynasty apart in the region involved the preparation at Hariharalaya of the huge rectangular Indratataka reservoir, known locally as a *baray*. The Khmer's efforts resulted in a perfectly geometrical stone-lined basin, 3,800 × 800 m (12,467 × 2,625 ft). The function of the *baray* is still debated. It may have been more symbolic than practical. Much like the ancient Egyptians, who built a stone-lined basin at Karnak to represent the primordial source of life, the Khmer described their origins in a cosmic sea, where they were whipped into life by the tail of the Nagy, the snake with seven heads. The *baray* might also have represented the Great Lake of Cambodia, the natural source of the country's well-being. On a practical level it could have served fishing and transportation needs as part of the canal network of the area, while acting as a catchment area for floodwaters.

South of the basin, the vast enclosures for the ninth-century temples of Preah Ko and Bakong covered sites as large as Borobudur with great cross-axial compositions, wide **moats**, and tufted roofscapes. During the next century the successors of Jayavarman II surpassed the scale of Hariharalaya at nearby Angkor. Originally known as Yashodharapura ("glory-bearing city"), Angkor stood 15 km (9 miles) to the northwest in a similar relation to the Great Lake and Phnom Kulen Mountain. The first pyramidal temples overlooked the East Baray of Angkor, a vast rectangular reservoir eight times larger than its precursor at the old capital of Hariharalaya. Although the stone-lined perimeter of the lake is still well preserved, it partially dried up forty years after its construction. The Khmer regime built the even larger West Baray, 2 × 8 km (1.2 × 5 miles), a century later and added a final reservoir, about half the size of the earlier two, around 1200 to the northwest of the East Baray. These oblong bodies of water established a staggered geometric frame around the central monumental core of Angkor, an area roughly 6 km (3.5 miles) per side, reinforcing the reverential distinction of the sacred and political core. During the course of three centuries the Khmer built over thirty temple compounds in central Angkor, using vast planes of water as stunning voids.

The Khmer sponsored two basic temple types, the terrace temple and the pyramid temple, which varied greatly in section but in plan had only slight differences. The diagram of the terrace temple of Banteay Srei, commissioned by a Brahmin guru in 968, appeared quite similar to that of the pyramidal temple of Angkor Wat built two centuries later. Both followed a mandala pattern of concentric geometric enclosures, framing a core of symmetrically organized galleries, junctures, and pavilions that were mostly cruciform in plan.

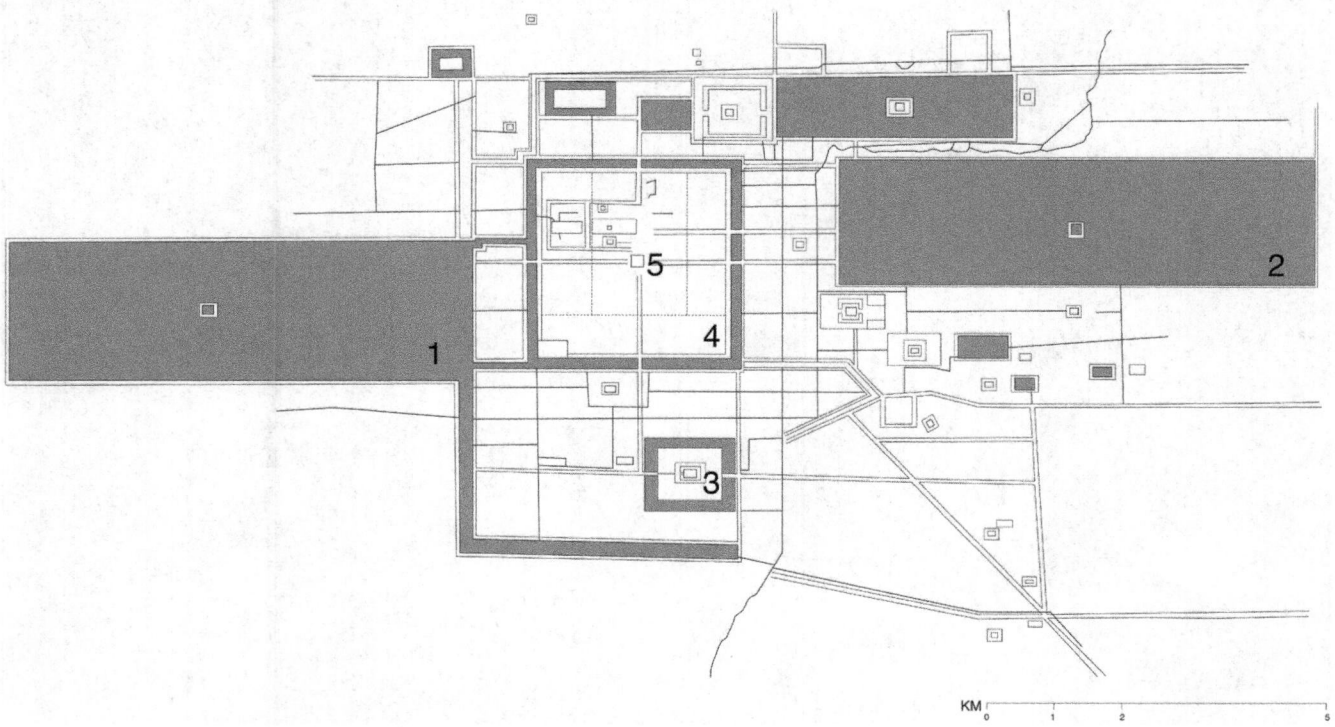

Figure 8.1-5 Angkor, Cambodia. Plan, ninth to thirteenth century. (1) West Baray; (2) East Baray; (3) Angkor Wat; (4) Angkor Thom; (5) the Bayon.

The Banteay Srei (Fig. 8.1-6a,b), also known as the "citadel of the women" because of its many depictions of female divinities, stood at the periphery of the capital, 20 km (12 miles) to the northeast of Angkor Wat. The temple consisted of a succession of four **prakarams**, or perimeter spaces, often enclosed with walls. One approached from the east through a cruciform *gopura*, an elevated gate with stepped upper stories, and a long causeway lined by sixteen pairs of sandstone pillars. Covered galleries with colonnaded porches opened toward the path like Greek *stoas*. A second *gopura* at the end of the causeway controlled entry to the next *prakaram*, where the temple spread on an island in the midst of a wide moat. The island contained two more *prakarams*, protected by gates, that stood between the moat and the inner sanctum, where two small "libraries" sat to either side of a central *T*-shaped set of chambers raised on a platform. The central vestibule opened to a tall *garbha griha*, housing a *lingam*, flanked on either side by pavilion shrines. The roofscape mounted in a succession of flamboyant gables, like a cluster of pinecones. The **blind windows** at Banteay Srei carried ornately turned balusters, while the red sandstone masonry of the inner sanctum displayed intricately inscribed floral patterns like a woven tapestry.

Angkor Wat (a modern name, meaning "temple city") had a completely different section but used a similar sequence of *prakarams* (Fig. 8.1-7a,b). The patron, Suryavarman II

(r. ca. 1113–1150), began this largest of Angkor's temples around 1130. His grand gesture came partly as a strategy for legitimating his rule after usurping the throne. He further boosted his power through diplomacy and military exploits, reestablishing mercantile treaties with China while invading the Cham people in Vietnam. The remarkable dimensions of Angkor Wat reflected the magnitude of his imperial ambitions.

Angkor Wat is the only temple in Angkor oriented to the west, in honor of the god Vishnu. In its design, the representations of the god and the king became interchangeable. The area of the temple precinct, 1,470 × 1,650 m (4,823 × 5,413 ft), covered a site many times larger than the enclosures at Karnak, the Temple Mount in Jerusalem, and the Great Mosque of Samarra. The moat stretched 150 m (492 ft) across, emphatically setting off the complex as an island removed from the rest of the world. The causeway across the moat led to the first set of walls and a *gopura* entry. Beyond this point it continued at an elevation on-axis and passed a pair of basins to either side, terminating at a raised cruciform terrace used for dancing ceremonies. The composition then thickened into a succession of three formal enclosures, culminating in a central pyramid. The first *prakaram* presented colonnaded galleries facing outward for use as a didactic ambulatory, analogous to the semisubmerged paths on the lower levels of Borobudur. Although no

a

Figure 8.1-6 (a) Angkor, Cambodia. Banteay Srei, 968. Inner shrine **(b)** See facing page.

Figure 8.1-6b Angkor, Cambodia. Banteay Srei, 968. Plan.

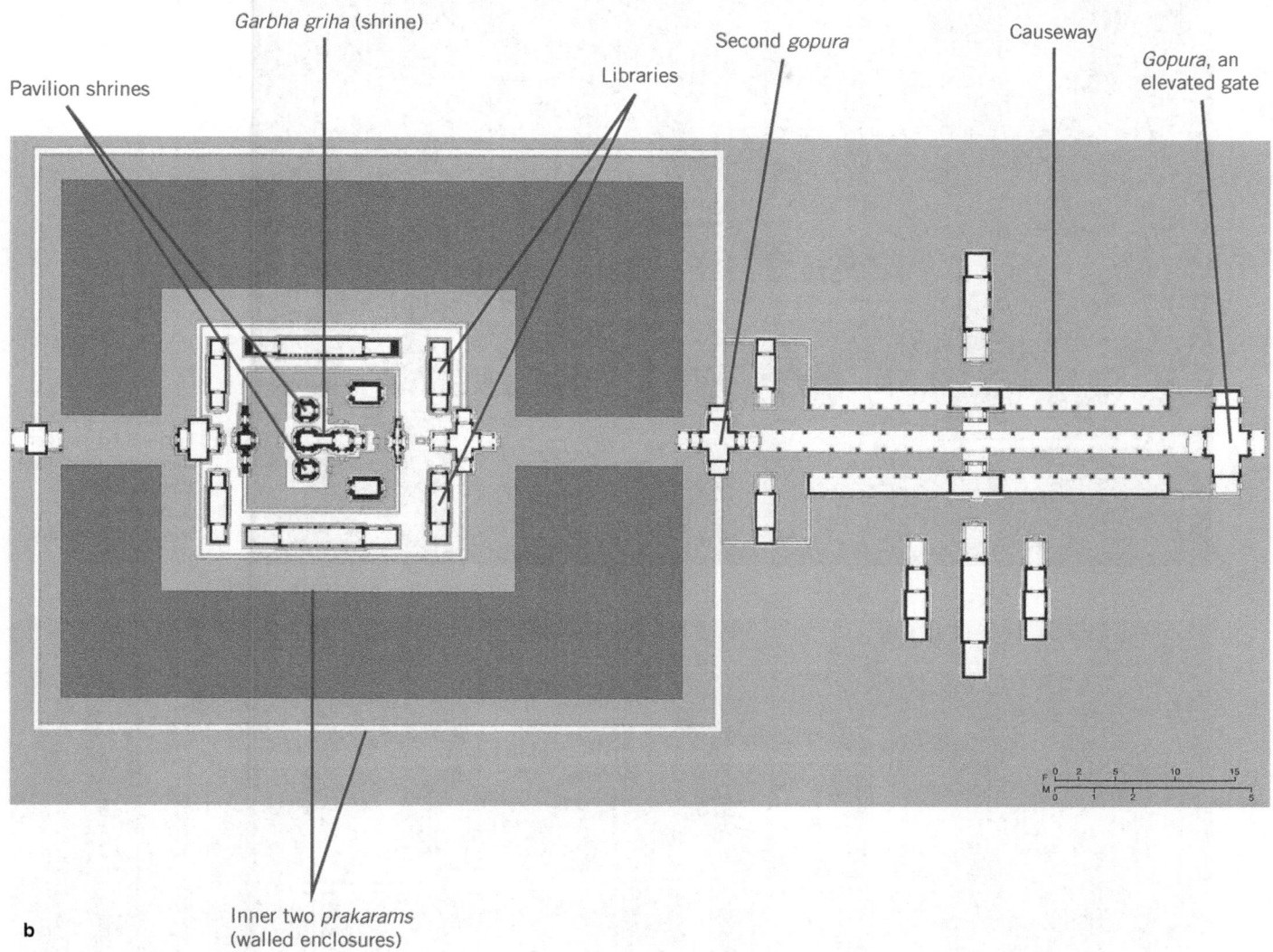

Pavilion shrines

Garbha griha (shrine)

Libraries

Second *gopura*

Causeway

Gopura, an elevated gate

b

Inner two *prakarams* (walled enclosures)

Maya influence was possible, the corbelled ceilings of the Khmer vaults appear structurally similar to those at Tikal and Palenque (see Section 7.3).

The inner *prakaram* of Angkor Wat stepped up 15 m (49 ft) above the rest of the complex, with a pinecone-shaped tower at each corner. The rippling contours of its staged towers rose dramatically above the moat. Galleries extended around the inner enclosure, reflected by ponds in each of the four quadrants. The central pyramid spread on a cruciform base, rising 35 m (115 ft). Beneath its tower a concealed shaft plunged 23 m (75 ft) below grade to provide a hiding place for royal treasure and the ashes of the king. This secret cavity contributed to a supreme axis mundi.

The grand spaces, perfect geometry, and infinitesimal sculptural detail of Angkor Wat's monuments overshadowed the dwelling spaces of the common people of Angkor. While Buddhist monks have continued to inhabit the temples since the fall of the Khmer dynasty in the fifteenth century, with the galleries and "libraries" perhaps serving as living spaces, no evidence indicates their use for the daily life of the city. Both the rich and the poor built domestic structures of expendable materials that have left no trace. The typical dwellings would have resembled the vernacular houses one still finds in the region, raised on wooden stilts with an elevated living level enclosed by woven reed walls and covered with thatch or banana leaves. The living space usually lacked internal divisions or furniture. The kitchen and toilet functions remained outside the house at a safe distance from the structure. The houses looked to the east and were spaced at substantial distances from each other, usually in hamlets of five to ten. Narrow paths meandered between the clustered dwellings. Like Maya cities, the Khmer capital spread at very low density over a vast territory.

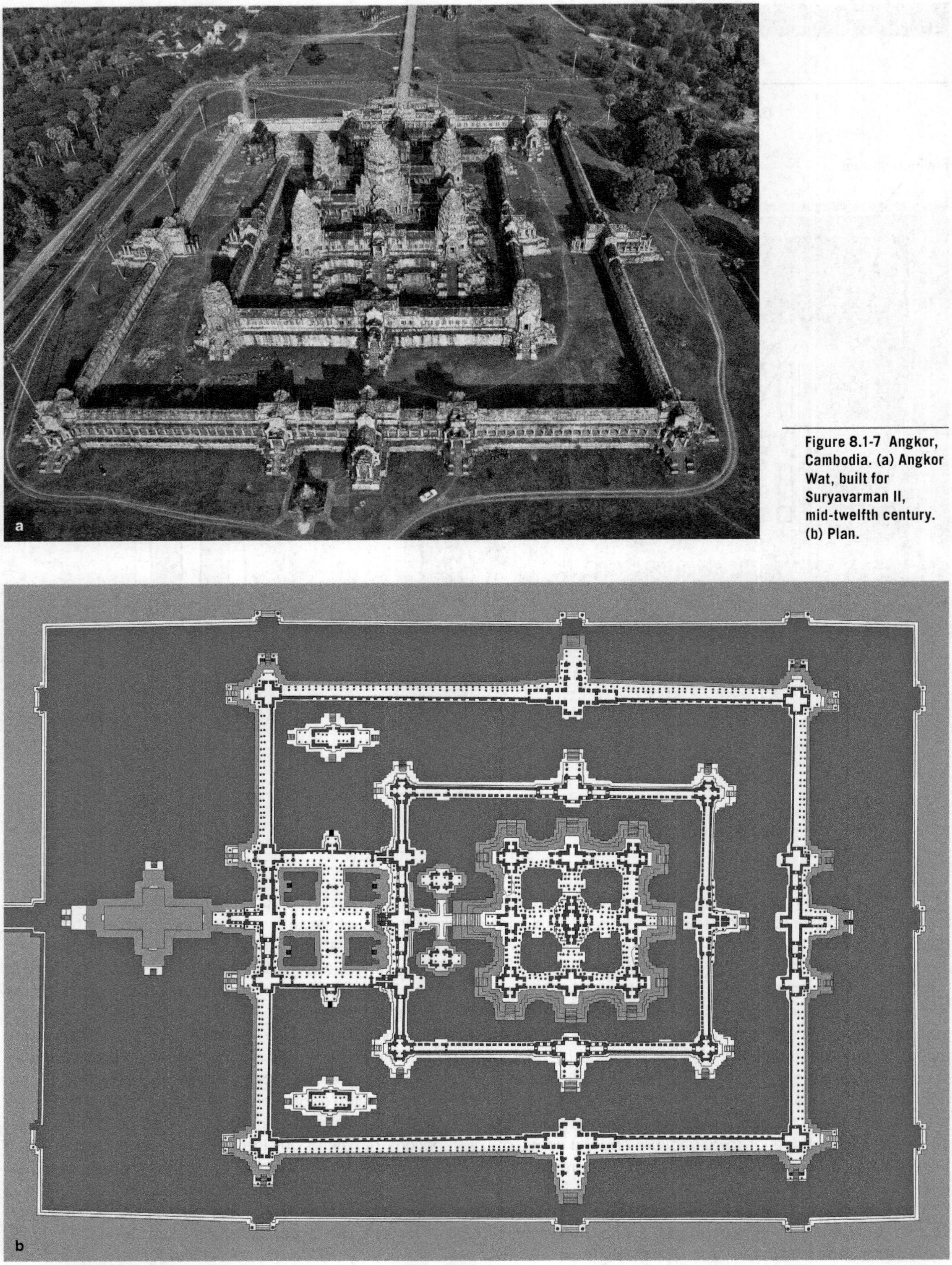

Figure 8.1-7 Angkor, Cambodia. (a) Angkor Wat, built for Suryavarman II, mid-twelfth century. (b) Plan.

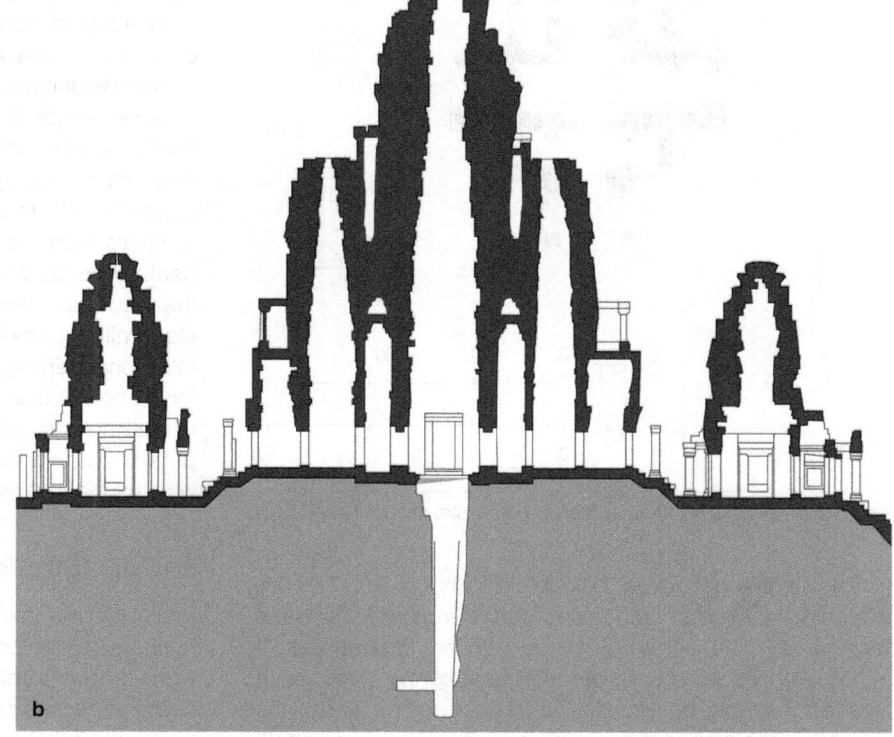

Figure 8.1-8 Angkor, Cambodia.
(a) The Bayon, central temple of
Angkor Thom, built for Jayavarman VII,
ca. 1200. (b) Section of the Bayon,
showing a deep shaft. (c) See next page.

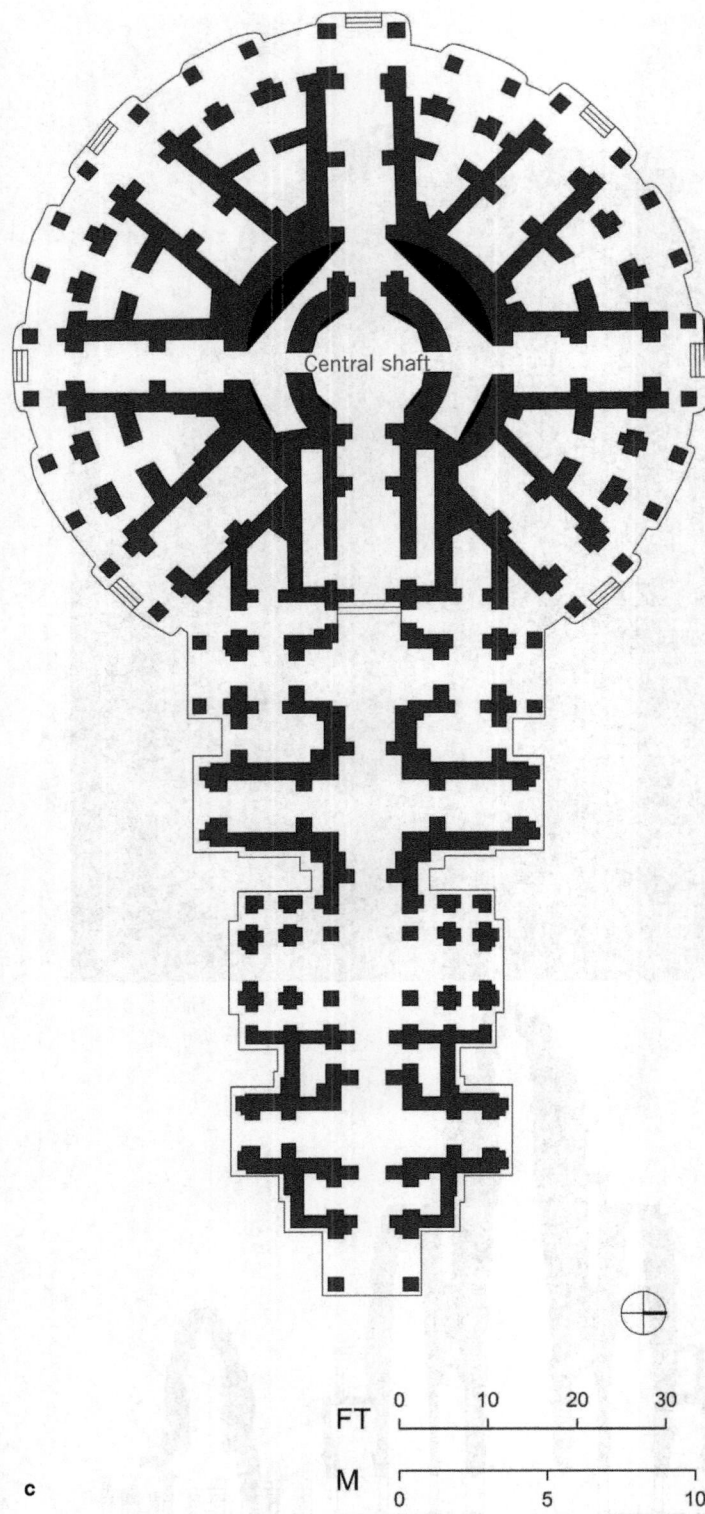

Central shaft

FT 0 10 20 30

M 0 5 10

c

Figure 8.1-8 Angkor, Cambodia. (c) Plan of the Bayon, showing central shaft.

The Chams destroyed the center of Angkor in 1177. Until this point the Khmer had used palisades and bodies of water for defense. The last great Khmer builder, Jayavarman VII (r. 1181–1219), came to power after ousting the Vietnamese invaders in a naval battle on the Great Lake and expanded the borders of the empire to their farthest extent. Jayavarman VII

refurbished the country's infrastructure while building a multitude of hospitals. On top of the ruined city he established the new city of Angkor Thom (the "Great City"), surrounded by 8 m (26 ft) thick walls that stretched 3 km (1.8 miles) per side and a moat nearly as broad as that at Angkor Wat. The royal family and a court of nearly 100,000 resided inside the walls, between the East and West Barays, the new Jayatataka Baray to the northeast, and Angkor Wat 1 km (0.6 mile) to the south. Five monumental *gopuras* marked the entries into the new city, each with a tower made of four colossal Buddha faces looking in the cardinal directions.

The eccentricity of the Bayon (Fig. 8.1-8a,b,c), the principal temple in the center of Angkor Thom, may derive from Jayavarman VII's commitment to Buddhism. Although he specifically dedicated the temple to Mahayana Buddhism, he was careful to include the other gods worshipped by the Khmer, in particular Shiva and Vishnu, in its iconographic program. Constructed around 1200, Angkor Thom's plan repeated the formula of three successive enclosures but appeared much more tightly packed than Angkor Wat. The inner cruciform-shaped enclosure surrounded a cylindrical tower, the only round temple in Angkor. Jayavarman VII placed a 3 m (9.8 ft) high portrait of himself as a cross-legged Buddha protected by the *naga* snake inside the central cell. The designers of the Bayon placed towers made of four colossal faces at every juncture, similar to those on the city gates. Because of generally poor construction, only thirty-seven of the fifty-four towers have remained upright. In places one finds masonry courses with stones placed one directly over the other, instead of being staggered. In its original state, a total of 216 colossal heads smiled down serenely from the monument. These bizarre facades literally made of faces may have represented Avalokitesvara, the Compassionate Buddha; the king himself; or perhaps a community of gods. While similar to the colossal Buddhas carved in China and Sri Lanka, the heads at the Bayon served as unique, habitable works of architecture.

Jayavarman VII built six other grand temple complexes, the last and costliest monuments of the Khmer, works that may have bankrupted the state. The *chakravartin*'s devotion to Buddhism and his overzealous urge to build inspired reprisals from the Hindu religious hierarchy, which after his death organized the destruction of thousands of statues of the Buddha. Although Buddhism later reemerged as the state religion, the Khmer dynasty lost its power in the mid-fourteenth century, and the new regime abandoned Angkor for a capital closer to the sea. The great hydrological works of the Khmer silted up, the agricultural fields no longer prospered, and the monuments quickly became enshrouded with luxuriant vegetation.

Southern India: The Exalted Scale of Pyramid Temples

While the models for Indonesian and Cambodian temple builders originated in India, Indian patrons did not achieve works of comparable scale and refinement until the eleventh century. Despite periodic territorial disputes, the eastern and southern regions remained less affected by invasions than the northern and central areas. The towering temples built there after the year 1000 served as both a vision of cosmic order and a demonstration of resistance to outsiders.

The Chola dynasty in southern India (the region of Tamil Nadu) sponsored huge religious enclosures outside their capital of Thanjavur (Tanjore). The Chola's architectural exploits followed ambitious military campaigns, including raids on the north and the devastation of Sri Lanka's millennial capital at Anuradhapura to the south. During the first part of the eleventh century, after conquering lands in the northeast near the Ganges River, they set out to plunder the islands of Indochina, reaching Sumatra. After conquering their neighbors, they redistributed the booty as endowments to monasteries. Like the Khmer in Cambodia, the Chola boosted their political authority through the distribution of land grants to hundreds of monastic communities, engendering bonds similar to those seen in European feudalism during the same period.

The principal Chola monument, the Temple of Brihadeesvara, dedicated in 1010, was also known as the Peruvudayar Koyil (Fig. 8.1-9a) but was commonly called the Rajarajesvaram after its patron, Rajaraja I (r. 985–1014). The largest temple in India for many centuries, it housed hundreds of monks, musicians, and dancing maidens to provide a complete religious spectacle. Like the temples of Angkor, Rajarajesvaram included a succession of grand *prakaram* enclosures isolated by a moat. One entered the central *prakaram* through a sequence of two *gopura* pyramidal gateways (Fig. 8.1-9b). The double colonnade framing the inner *prakaram* rivaled the great Hellenistic *temenos* of Herod's Temple Mount in Jerusalem. The sequence passed axially from a pavilion for Shiva's ox, Nandi, through two hypostyle *mandapa* halls, to terminate in the great pyramid.

The builders of the Rajarajesvaram pyramid transported large granite blocks by boat from a distant quarry. They piled the stones over a square base, 30 m (98 ft) per side, which was articulated with regularly spaced half-columns alternated with recessed niches, similar to the rhythms of Hellenistic facades. At the top of dozens of progressively smaller terraced levels—a summit that surpassed the pyramids at Tikal by 20 m—they placed a gilded monolith weighing several tons. How they lifted it into place remains a mystery. Another large stone, a 4 m (13 ft) *lingam*, the largest in India, awaited in the womb chamber at the base of the great pyramid.

The Pandya kings, located about 200 km (124 miles) to the west, competed with the Chola dynasty and by 1200 had gained control of the south of India. To celebrate their success, they built the Meenakshi Amann Temple in the center of Madurai, imitating the architectural types and scale of the Rajarajesvaram. They arranged their brightly colored, towering shrines much more casually, however, in relation to a sacred pool, the **kunda**. The dense collection of twelve staged towers gave the impression of a modern high-rise city (Fig. 8.1-10). Each level of the towers was stepped slightly back to provide a podium for a riotous lineup of columns, statues, and gables. Over the centuries, the temple's keepers regularly repainted the intricate decorations in vibrant reds and blues, not unlike ancient Greek temples.

At the turn of the millennium, temple building resumed in the north of India as well. Various local dynasties attempted to keep up with the Chola in the south. The Solanka kings in the northwestern region of Gujarat sponsored the temple to Surya, the sun god, at Modhera in 1025 to celebrate the momentary expulsion of their Muslim overlords. Its magnificent water tank, or *kunda*, sank like an inverted pyramid, ringed by a rippling succession of five levels with multiple sets of bifurcated stairs. The *kunda*, used for ritual cleansing, became an increasingly important ingredient in Hindu temple complexes.

From the ninth to the twelfth century, the Chandela dynasty in the northeast created India's most extensive collection of temples at Khajuraho. Of the original eighty-five temples, only twenty-five remain standing after centuries of neglect. Rather than creating *kundas*, the Chandela exploited the natural pools of the area. The random position of these sacred ponds determined the irregular siting of the temples. The shrines in the eastern cluster belonged predominantly to the Jain faith, while those in the western group were Hindu. A sizable residential area stretched between the two cult areas.

Among the earliest permanent temples at Khajuraho stood the Lakshmana (Fig. 8.1-11), dedicated to the goddess Lakshmi (wife of Vishnu) in 954. It established a type that was repeated in many variations in the complex, organized in an axial sequence intersected by a double transept. The profile of the roofs stepped up from a piled crown above the porch to a banded cupola above the *mandapa* assembly space to a thirteen-level, square-based pyramid above the first transept crossing. The sequence culminated in a 20 m (66 ft) beehive-shaped **shikhara**. Instead of enclosing the temple with a *prakaram*, the designers achieved a feeling of enclosure by raising the complex on a 2 m (6.5 ft) high rectangular podium. They articulated the corners of this platform with miniature replicas of the central *shikhara*, creating a vision of the five peaks of Mount Meru.

The Kandariya Mahadeva (Fig. 8.1-12a), the largest and most artfully coordinated of the western cluster of temples at Khajuraho, was constructed around 1020. It repeated the double-transept type of the Lakshmana Temple but handled the transitions in the roof with greater dynamism. The rippling forms led to the towering *shikhara*, padded on all sides with progressively smaller versions of its beehive shape. Dedicated to Shiva, it housed a marble *lingam* at its core. The north and south flanks carried the most explicitly erotic sculptures ever conceived for a religious building (Fig. 8.1-12b). While it was conventional to find *mithuni* (amorous couples) and bare-breasted *shakti* figures languidly posing at the entries to Hindu temples, the friezes of the Kandariya Mahadeva regaled visitors with an array of sexual acrobatics that surpassed the art of love described in the *Kama Sutra* (see Section 6.3). This uninhibited panoply of scenes of copulation elaborated the theological narrative of the marriage of the gods Shiva and Parvati.

The Muslim conquest of northern India at the end of the twelfth century put an end to the construction of grand temple complexes such as Khajuraho, which probably

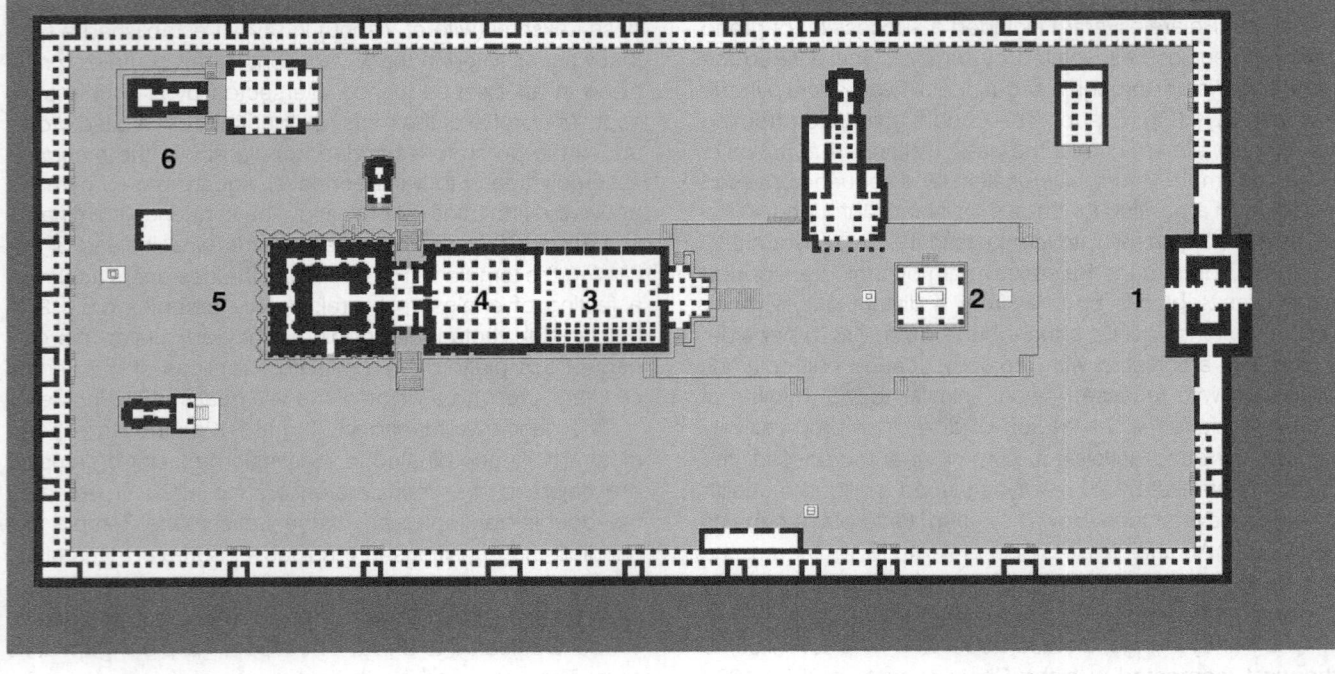

Figure 8.1-9 Thanjavur (Tanjore), southern India. (a) The Temple of Brihadeesvara, or Rajarajesvaram, central tower, ca. 1000. (b) Plan of *prakaram*: (1) *gopura* gateway; (2) pavilion devoted to Nandi; (3) first *mandapa*; (4) second *mandapa*; (5) pyramid over *garbha griha* for *lingam*; (6) Subrahmanya Temple.

survived vindictive demolitions because of its remote jungle location. The patronage for Hindu temple building moved south to places such as Konarak, where the thirteenth-century Surya Temple took the form of a massive *ratha* with great stone wheels. Despite the progressive refinement of sculptural detail and formal articulation at such temples in Khajuraho and Konarak, Indian religious architecture remained essentially an exterior phenomenon at the service of cave-like interiors. The patterns generated from the mandala nurtured an art of mass rather than one of space.

Figure 8.1-10 Madurai, southern India. Meenakshi Amann Temple, built by the Pandya dynasty around a sacred *kunda* pool, thirteenth to seventeenth century.

Further Reading

Bernet Kempers, A. J. *Ageless Borobudur*. Wassenaar, the Netherlands: Servire, 1972.

Bunce, Fredrick W. *The Iconography of Architectural Plans: A Study of the Influence of Buddhism and Hinduism on Plans of South and Southeast Asia.* New Delhi: D. K. Printworld, 2002.

Bussagli, Mario. *Oriental Architecture.* Vol. 1, *India, Indonesia, Indochina.* Translated by John Shepley. Milan: Electa, 1981.

Coe, Michael D. *Angkor and the Khmer Civilization*. London: Thames & Hudson, 2003.

Laur, Jean. *Angkor: An Illustrated Guide to the Monuments.* Paris: Flammarion, 2002.

Mannika, Eleanor. *Angkor Wat: Time, Space, and Kingship.* Honolulu: University of Hawai'i Press, 1996.

Figure 8.1-11 Khajuraho, north central India. Lakshmana Temple, 945.

Figure 8.1-12 Khajuraho, north central India.
(a) Kandariya Mahadeva.
(b) Panels depicting the loves of the gods, 1020.

8.2 ISLAMIC SPAIN AND MOROCCO

Interlacing Forms in al-Andalus and the Maghreb

During the seventh century, Islamic rule spread across the southern coasts of the Mediterranean and into Spain, or al-Andalus. Here, the exiled branch of the Umayyad dynasty consolidated its rule over the Iberian Peninsula and Morocco and sponsored an exuberant style of architecture, beginning with the Great Mosque and royal palaces of Córdoba. The dynasty's architects stacked arches over arches and eventually intertwined them into lace-like patterns. They perfected the kinetic effects of **interlacing arches** and vaults with star-shaped ribs.

After the demise of the Umayyad dynasty in the early eleventh century, al-Andalus splintered into smaller states, or *taifas*, which for brief periods produced brilliant urban set pieces modeled on Córdoba. In Morocco, the Berber dynasties, which frequently destabilized power in Spain, borrowed the Umayyad style to shape their royal cities of Fez, Rabat, and Marrakech. The last Islamic dynasty to rule part of Spain, the Nasrids of Granada, maintained their autonomy through alliances with Christians. Aware of their tenuous situation, the Nasrids withdrew into the luxurious trappings of ornate palaces and lush gardens on the hilltop site of the Alhambra, cultivating in isolation the finest testament to the architectural skill and sensitivity of a culture destined for extinction.

Córdoba: The Sea of Arches in the Great Mosque

At its height the Umayyad capital of Córdoba in southern Spain (Fig. 8.2-1) may have had a population of 500,000, rivaling Constantinople as the greatest city of medieval Europe. A census taken in the tenth century claimed the city had 200,000 houses, 60,000 palaces, 80,000 shops, and 600 public baths—a

scale of building that verged on that of ancient Rome. While the Christian-ruled countries of Europe suffered from near-universal illiteracy, with only a few small libraries in remote monasteries, Córdoba boasted seventy libraries and a population enamored with poetry competitions. The caliph's collection alone counted 400,000 volumes. Patronage for architecture proved no less impressive, resulting in a brilliant style that wove arches into interlacing forms.

Between the collapse of Roman power in the fifth century and the Islamic conquest in 711, Spain came under the loose grip of Christianized Visigoth warlords. The rule of Islam gained force when the only surviving member of the Umayyad dynasty, the nineteen-year-old Abd al-Rahman I (r. 756–788), moved to Spain in the 750s. Reigning as the western emir, he gained control of the Iberian Peninsula, known as "al-Andalus," and much of Morocco, known as "the Maghreb," the "western lands" of Islam. He set up an autocratic but tolerant regime, which for three centuries fostered a brilliant cultural synthesis, combining ancient Greco-Roman knowledge, Byzantine style, and Islamic religious tenets amid a multiethnic population. Córdoba, a prominent city of Roman foundation, sited 150 km (90 miles) inland on the Guadalquivir River, remained a safe distance from coastal raids but was still easy to access by boat. Its multilingual population included Christians, known as *Mozarabs*; Jews, known as *Sephards*; and North African

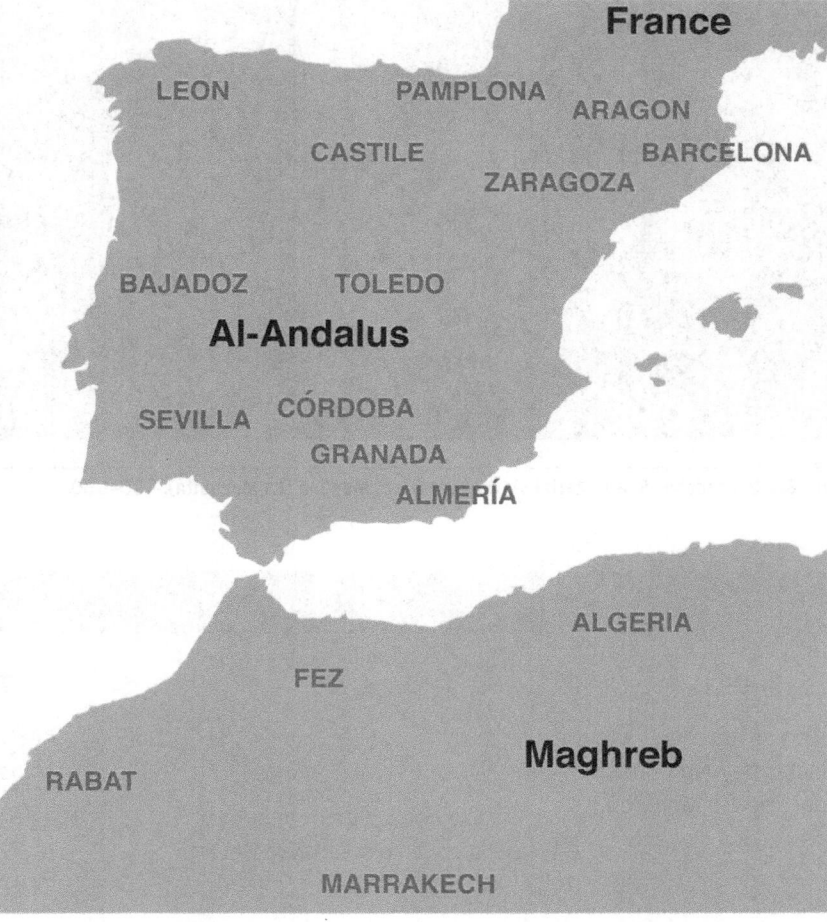

Figure 8.2-1 Map of al-Andalus and the Maghreb region, ca. 800–1200. The cities defined most of the territories of Islamic Spain and, from the tenth century until the fall of Granada in the fifteenth century, were often ruled as independent *taifa* kingdoms.

Berbers, Muslim converts descended from the nomadic tribes of North Africa. The Umayyads governed through the *dhimma*, a pact that guaranteed non-Muslim "people of the book" the right to live in semiautonomous internal enclaves with their own places of worship.

Few traces of Roman Córdoba survived aside from the city's magnificent sixteen-arched bridge and the ruins of an amphitheater. A dense urban fabric with narrow, winding streets and closed *herats* structured on blind alleys, much like those in Damascus and Cairo, enveloped the Umayyad capital. The city abounded with mosques, **suqs** (covered markets), *funduks* (hostels for foreign traders), hospitals, schools, and *hammams* (thermal baths). The caliphs also permitted churches and synagogues. The principal monument of the city, the Great Mosque (Fig. 8.2-2), later known in Spanish as the *Mezquita*, rose next to the *alcázar*, the prince's urban palace, offering a unique patch of orthogonal order. Set in the center of the city near the river, the Great Mosque of Córdoba advertised Umayyad political independence, identity, and well-being. Begun in 785 during Abd al-Rahman I's final years, it sent a message that the western emir had made

his break from the caliphate of the Abbasid Empire. His successors expanded the mosque in four campaigns over the course of two centuries as an ongoing architectural project. Its wondrous multitude of columns, capitals, arches, and ceiling decorations folded into an endless repetition of more than 500 arcuated bays, infusing the whole with a compelling sense of unity like the waves of the sea.

In many ways Abd al-Rahman I attempted to reprise the Umayyad mosque in Damascus, a project that had been central to the imperial ambitions of his forebears. Like the earlier mosque, the Mezquita occupied a site that had been shared by both Christians and Muslims. The position of the previous building, a church built more than a century earlier by the Visigoths, seems to have conditioned the Mezquita's structure and orientation, since the *qibla* wall remained significantly misaligned, situated 50° south of Mecca. The initial eleven aisles of columns repeated in twelve bays gave the founder's mosque the sort of spatial redundancy typical of early hypostyle mosques, such as the al-Aqsa Mosque in Jerusalem (see Section 7.1). Unlike the mosque in Damascus, the arches in Córdoba ran perpendicular to the *qibla* wall.

The hypostyle hall of the Great Mosque of Córdoba produced incomparable kinetic effects as a result of hundreds of double arches poised gracefully on rows of recycled Roman columns (Fig. 8.2-3). The voussoirs of the stacked arches were rendered in *ablaq*, alternating red brick and white limestone, which intensified the sense of scintillation. While the horseshoe-shaped arches in Córdoba had a local precedent, the Visigoth church at San Juan de Baños in Palencia, it is more likely the motif was transmitted from Damascus (see Section 7.1). The second level of arches rose on thick masonry piers that protruded slightly from the imposts over the columns. The upper arches were semicircular and twice as thick as the lower ones, and thus the structure broadened upward, to catch the crossbeams of the roof.

Figure 8.2-2 Córdoba, Spain. Aerial view of the Great Mosque (La Mezquita), 785–990.

TIME LINE

 750

Abd al-Rahman I, the last Umayyad prince, escapes to Morocco

Córdoba, Spain, becomes the western Umayyad capital

▲ **756**

 786

Abd al-Rahman I begins construction of the Great Mosque of Córdoba

Figure 8.2-3 Córdoba, Spain. The Great Mosque, interior, 785–990.

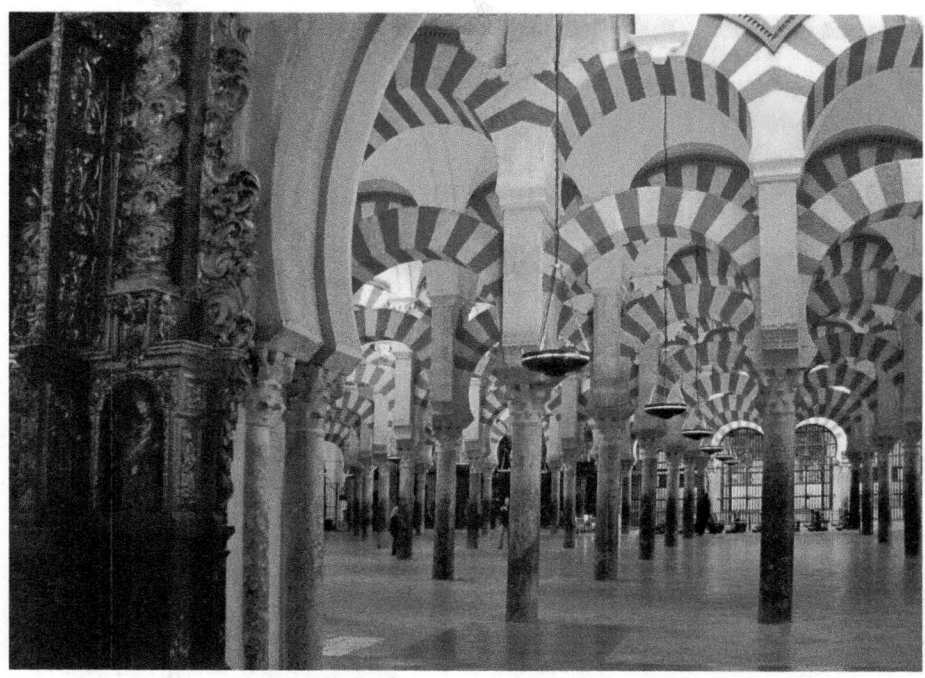

During the ninth century the Great Mosque was extended eight bays toward the bridge (Fig. 8.2-4), and during the tenth century it was extended again under Abd al-Rahman III (r. 912–961) and his son al-Hakam II (r. 961–976). The father, secure in his rule of Spain and Morocco, directly challenged the Abbasids by claiming the title of caliph. At the same time he promoted culture, increasing the city's libraries, starting free schools, commissioning translations of ancient texts, and sponsoring works of poetry and philosophy. To the mosque he added the formidable minaret, a 34 m (112 ft) square-based tower, which, like the one at Kairouan, rose straight up and stood slightly off-axis. He doubled the *sahn* with new arcades that imitated those of the court in Damascus. Although now famous for its fragrant orange trees fed by water channels, the court originally enclosed a paved void with a fountain for ablutions.

Abd al-Rahman III's most radical changes came in the form of a new ritual. Perhaps borrowing from the ceremonies of the Byzantines, with whom the Umayyads had always maintained friendly relations, the caliph introduced an imperial procession through the mosque, a ceremony without precedent in Islam. Arranged according to hierarchy, the court followed two porters carrying a revered copy of the Quran, thought to have been transcribed by Uthman, the third caliph after Mohammed and progenitor of the Umayyad dynasty. The ceremony involved depositing the book in the richly decorated *mihrab* niche. Al-Hakam II increased the interior of the mosque by one-third, adding its most ornate features: the exquisite domes over the *maksura* and the new *mihrab*, which evolved from a niche into a hexagonal domed chamber, similar to a Christian chapel. The three lateral bays in front of the *mihrab* chamber carried luxuriant intertwining arches that set off the *maksura* as the restricted area for the caliph and his court. The arches had cusped lobes and sprouted intermediary arches from their keystones that extended into the upper arches (Fig. 8.2-5). The complexity of these crisscrossing arches evoked the intertwining floral patterns of damask embroidery. Each of the three lateral bays of the *maksura* supported a small dome that through the windows of its drum allowed diffused light into the space. The ingenious system of arched ribs, deployed in different star-shaped patterns in each of the cupolas, helped reduce the weight of the structure while increasing the area for clerestories. At the threshold to the *mihrab*, the caliph's designers created a grand horseshoe arch with exceptionally long, gilded voussoirs.

After the death of al-Hakam II, the ambitious vizier al-Mansur ("the Victorious") commandeered the government as regent for the underage Umayyad heir. He reigned for the last quarter of the tenth century, pursuing aggressive military policies against the northern Christian states that ultimately

▼ **930**
Abd al-Rahman III builds Madinat al-Zahra Palace

Alfonso II of Castile begins the *Reconquista*

▲ **900**

Al-Hakam II adds maksura to the Great Mosque of Córdoba

▲ **963**

▼ **1013**
Córdoba taken by Moroccan Berbers

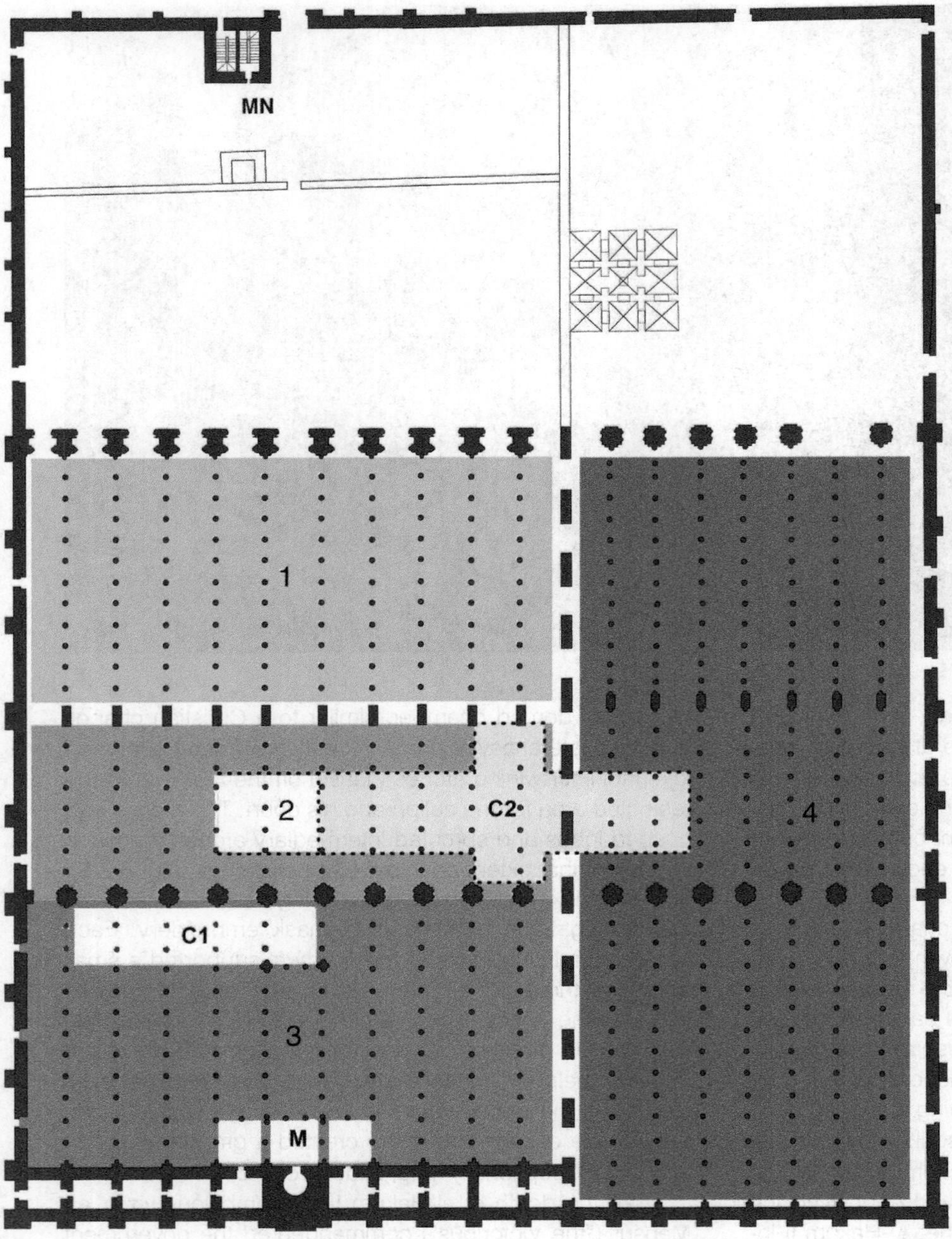

MN

1

2   C2   4

C1

3

M

Figure 8.2-4 Córdoba, Spain. Plan of the Great Mosque, showing phases of construction: (1) Abd al-Rahman I's original area, 785; (2) ninth-century addition; (3) addition of *maksura* by Abd al-Rahman III and his son al-Hakam II, 950–980; (4) completion of plan by al-Mansur, ca. 1000; (M) *maksura* area; (C1) late-fifteenth-century Christian church; (C2) cathedral begun in 1523; (MN) transformation of the minaret into the belfry, sixteenth century.

ushered in the ruin of Córdoba. As regent, al-Mansur added eight new aisles to the eastern side of the Great Mosque, nearly doubling its area to a total of 544 bays.

Al-Mansur committed two egregious strategic errors that seemed beneficial in the short term but had disastrous consequences for the continuity of the Umayyad state: first, he welcomed Berber mercenaries into the caliph's armies, and second, in 997 he ordered the sack of the Christian pilgrimage city of Santiago de Compostela. Upon his death in 1002, Córdoba was consumed by civil war between the supporters of the Umayyads and those of the vizier's heirs. The Berbers turned on their ex-employers in 1013, completely destroying the city and the suburban palaces of al-Mansur and the caliph. Meanwhile, the Christians in the north organized the *Reconquista*, a crusade against Islamic Spain, which endured for four centuries until the final purging of Islam from the Iberian Peninsula.

The Great Mosque survived the transition to Christian rule, reconsecrated as the city's cathedral in 1236. At first the Christians introduced discreet changes to the perimeter of the mosque: a small chapel carved out of the western wall and a polygonal chapel to the east of the *mihrab* chamber intended as the mausoleum for the kings of Castile. In the late fifteenth century they became more courageous, inserting an east–west nave counteraxial to the hypostyle space, an addition that necessitated the removal of eight columns. In the sixteenth century the minaret received new facades during its conversion into a bell tower. Finally, in 1523, royal

Aljafería Castle built in Zaragoza (Spain)

▲ **1049**

▼ **1062**

Marrakech founded by Almoravid dynasty

Toledo taken by Christians

▲ **1085**

▼ **1180s**

Koutoubia minaret, Marrakech

The *Munya* Palace

Abd al-Rahman I built the first of many *munyas*, or country palaces, 3 km (1.8 miles) north of Córdoba, calling it "al-Rusafa" after one of the Umayyad palaces outside of Damascus. Nothing remains of this first royal palace, for which the exiled monarch allegedly imported palms from his native Syria. The impressive ruins of the most ambitious Córdoban *munya*, the Madinat al-Zahra, built ca. 950 by Abd al-Rahman III, offer an intimation of Umayyad grandeur.

The Madinat al-Zahra spread over a hill 13 km (8 miles) to the northwest of the city on a scale similar to that of the Abbasid palaces in Samarra. Its fortified walls enclosed an area comparable to a small city, extending over a grand series of terraces from which one could survey the outlying productive landscape. Famous for specialized luxury foods and scents, its royal workshops produced costly ivories and textiles that defined the high standards of courtly life in al-Andalus. Abd al-Rahman III's *munya* combined landscaped platforms, shaded courts with fountains and reflecting pools, vaulted throne rooms framed with interlacing archways, pleasure pavilions, both male and female harems, and a palace mosque. The rotation of the latter provided the correct *qibla* alignment to Mecca, which was famously not observed at the Great Mosque in Córdoba. Umayyad country palaces functioned like ancient Roman imperial villas, part plantation and part setting for the government's court, far from the din of urban complications. Both Abd al-Rahman III and his son al-Hakam II kept a male harem at the Madinat al-Zahra palace. This same-sex preference, while perfectly acceptable at court, posed a problem for the political continuity of the dynasty, as the son neglected to produce an heir until late in life.

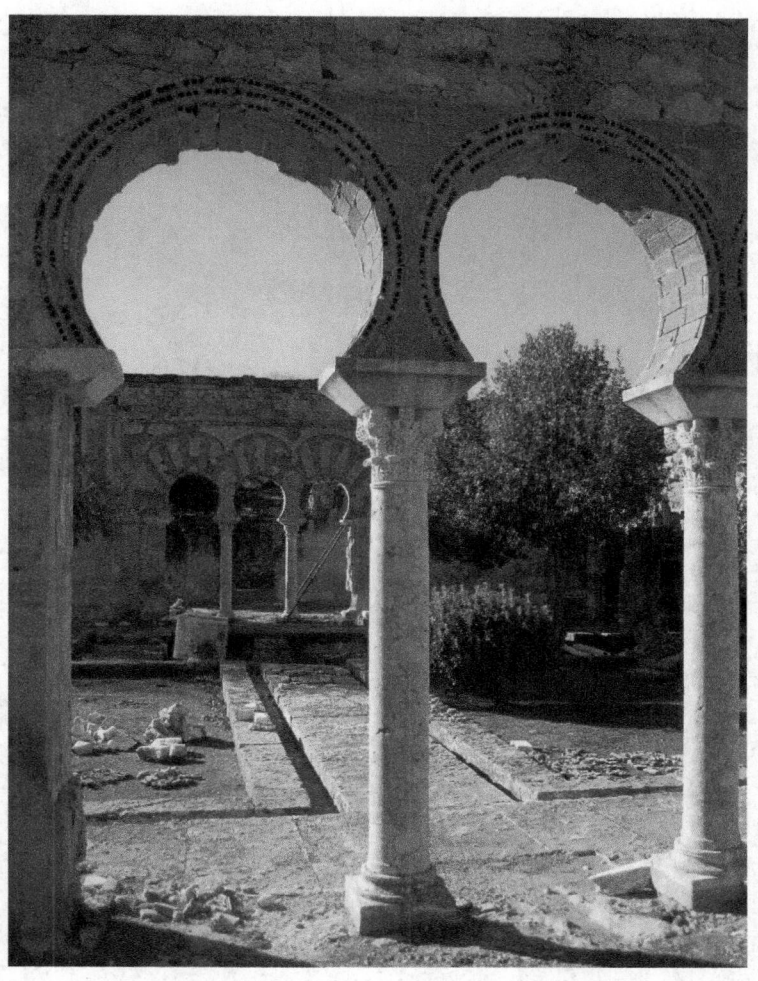

Córdoba, Spain. Caliph's Palace of Madinat al-Zahra, built 13 km (8 miles) outside the city for Abd al-Rahman III, ca. 930.

architects began a substantial cruciform basilica set in the midst of the mosque, counteraxial to the *qibla*. This required the subtraction of more than fifty columns. Despite these intrusions, the Great Mosque's lacy hypostyle expanse survived as the majority of the structure, offering a seemingly limitless view of undulating arches.

Hassan Mosque begun in Rabat (Moroco)

▲ 1190

▼ **1236**
Córdoba falls to Christians

Height of the Alhambra's construction by the Nasrid dynasty in Granada (Spain)

▲ 1350

▼ **1492**
Last Islamic dynasty, the Nasrids of Granada, forced to leave Spain

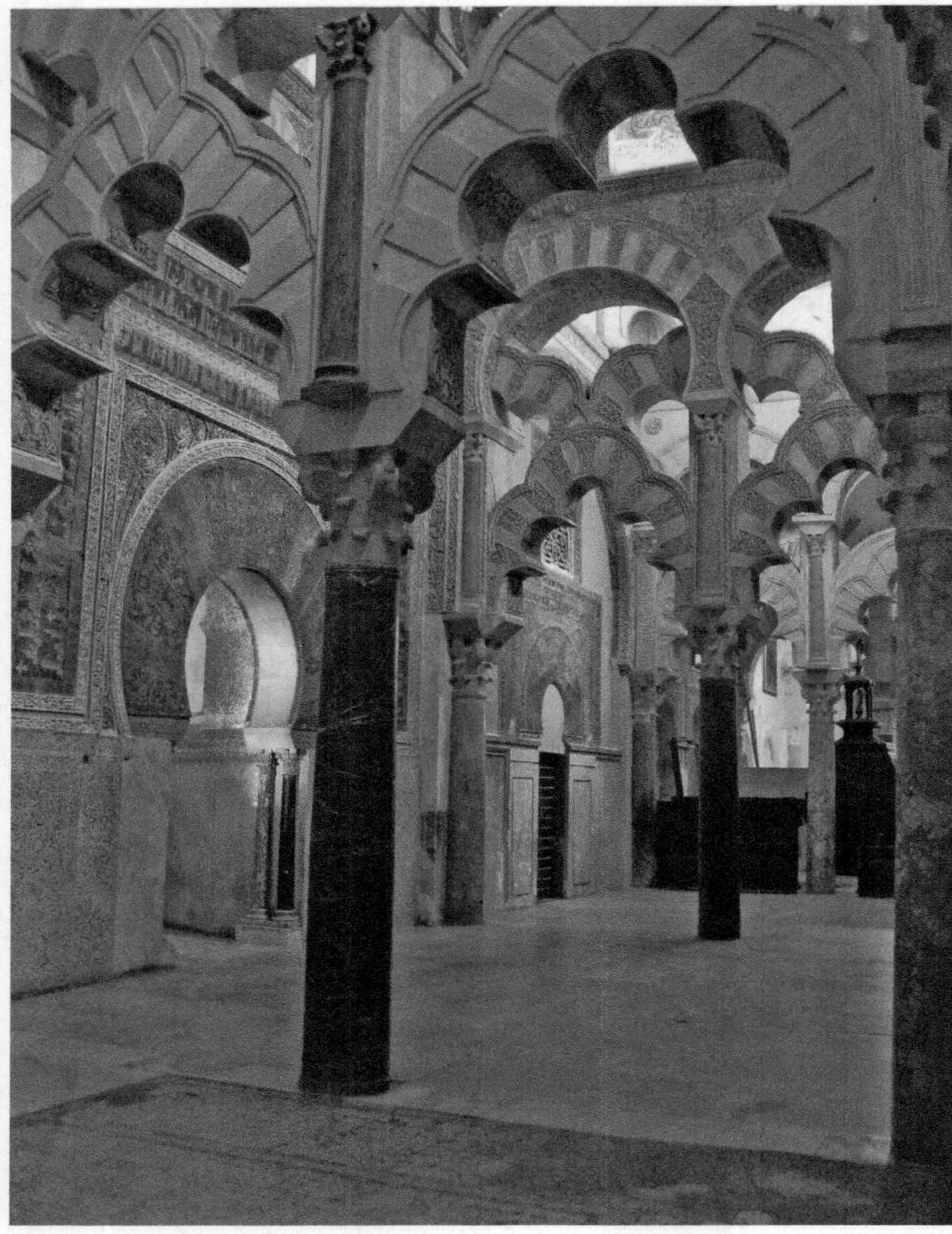

Figure 8.2-5 Córdoba, Spain. Great Mosque, *maksura* space in front of *mihrab* niche decorated with interlacing cusped arches, 963.

Fez, Rabat, and Marrakech. Despite their distaste for the Umayyads, the new rulers adopted and elaborated on most of the architectural elements of their precursors.

During the Almoravid ascendancy Fez emerged as the major crossroads city of the Maghreb, midway between Marrakech and the tip of Spain. By the thirteenth century it boasted 120,000 houses, 700 mosques, a university, and numerous **madrasas**, or religious colleges. During the ninth century a female patron belonging to an exiled community from Kairouan (see Section 7.1) founded the Qarawiyin Mosque, the city's principal mosque (Fig. 8.2-6). In 1144, a decade before the Almoravids lost power to the Almohads, the mosque received significant additions, including the pleated, green-tiled roof; domes with star-shaped ribs; and a polygonal chapel-like *mihrab* chamber inspired by the one in the Great Mosque of Córdoba. The designers included the novel decorative device of **muqarnas**, a complex pattern that subdivided the curvature of a pendentive into a multitude of rows of **squinches** carved in plaster in one of the domes on the *qibla* axis. The Umayyads in Spain did not use *muqarnas*, and thus, the motif must have come from Baghdad or some eastern source.

The Maghreb: The Courtyards of the Royal Cities

The Umayyad regime in Córdoba intermittently administered the territories of the Maghreb until the mid-eleventh century. The Almoravid dynasty then took control of Morocco, adhering to a fundamentalist religious program. Rather than sponsoring translations of Greco-Roman texts, the Almoravids preferred burning books thought to be dangerous and returning to the sole text they could trust, the Quran. After founding their capital in the southern city of Marrakech in 1062, this Berber movement of nomadic desert peoples swept north to take Fez and Algiers by the end of the century. Following the fall of Toledo to the Christians in 1086, the Almoravids made their move on Spain. They plowed the proceeds from their victories into the construction of mosques in

The Marinid dynasty, which controlled Morocco from the thirteenth to the fifteenth century, was in power during the building of most of the neighborhoods surrounding the Qarawiyin Mosque in Fez. Blind alleys led to the entries of the most important houses. The intersections of the main streets contained the neighborhoods' prime services: a fountain, a small mosque, a public bakery, shops, and a *hammam*. The Moroccan courtyard house, or **riad**, took form from the inside out, arranged around one or more geometrically perfect courts. The Sqali House, for example, a wealthy family's residence of the Marinid period, focused on a 6 × 8 m (20 × 26 ft) court. Brilliantly colored tiles and the deep reveals of double-height *iwan* arches helped to moderate the desert temperatures, assisted by an octagonal fountain in the court's center. A pergola-like cupola, with clerestories for

CONSTRUCTION, TECHNOLOGY, THEORY

The Ribbed Dome

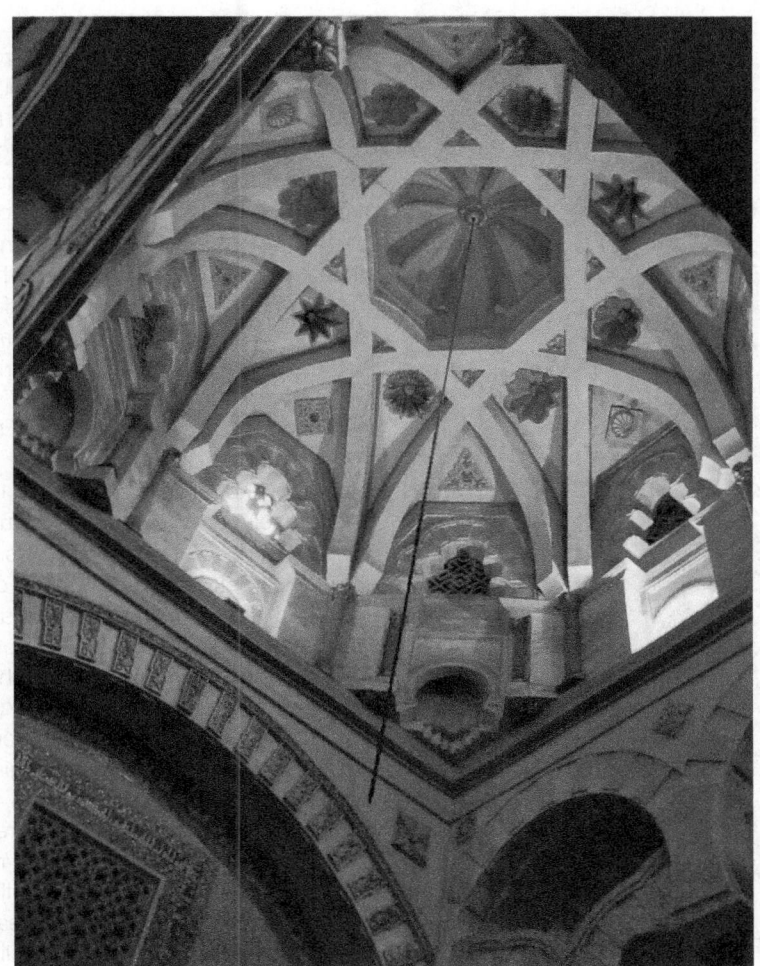

Three domes made with ribbed arches covered the *maksura* area of the Great Mosque of Córdoba. The most ornate stood over the bay in front of the *mihrab* chamber. Its eight ribbed arches sprang obliquely from the corners of an octagonal drum, extending over two sides. A scalloped dome covered with mosaics imported from Constantinople occupied the central octagonal void. In the domes to either side, the ribs reached perpendicularly over three sides of the octagon to form a star shape, repeating a geometrical pattern similar to that of the square rotated diagonally on another square seen in the plan of the Dome of the Rock in Jerusalem. These sophisticated ribbed structures lightened the load of the domes. Their intertwined assembly may have been inspired by basket-weaving techniques or perhaps Berber tents.

Córdoba, Spain. One of the side domes covering the *maksura* in the Great Mosque, ca. 970.

Figure 8.2-6 Fez, Morocco. Qarawiyin Mosque, begun ninth century, expanded by Abd al-Rahman III of Córdoba, ca. 930, and given definitive form by the Almoravids in 1144.

Figure 8.2-7 Marrakech, Morocco.
Koutoubia minaret, 1180s.

light and air, protected the court from direct sunlight. Sections of the house belonged to different branches of the family. Each *bait*, or semiautonomous dwelling unit, extended centrifugally around the court. The rooms of one part of the family did not communicate with those of another. While the courts of a *riad* observed perfect symmetry, they always had indirect entries from a side corridor, requiring two or more changes of direction.

During the mid-twelfth century the Almohad dynasty seized power in Morocco and ruled for the next 100 years, seeking to correct the attitude toward Islam of their predecessors through greater austerity. They demolished the Almoravid palace and mosque in Marrakech as symbols of luxury and corruption and in their place built the Koutoubia Mosque in 1147. Ten years later they rebuilt the same mosque using the original plan but correcting its *qibla* axis 5°. Despite the Almohads' austere rendering of arches, their style did not prove noticeably different from that of the Almoravids. The nave leading to the *mihrab* of the Koutoubia Mosque included domes with fanciful *muqarnas*, which by this time had become conventional decorations. At the northwest corner of the mosque, Ya'qub al-Mansur (r. 1184–1199), the most successful of the Almohad caliphs, commissioned the formidable Koutoubia minaret (Fig. 8.2-7), which rose 69 m (226 ft). Built in the rose-colored sandstone of the region, its decorations of interlacing lobed arches derived from Córdoba.

The same prince transferred the capital to Rabat, where he hoped to build the largest mosque in the world. His Hassan Mosque (Fig. 8.2-8) stood more than 1 km (0.6 miles) from the fortified seaport town, overlooking an inlet that divided Rabat from the twin city of Salé. The death of the patron in 1199 halted construction, leaving the minaret as a prominent

Figure 8.2-8 Rabat, Morocco. Columns of incomplete Hassan Mosque, 1190.

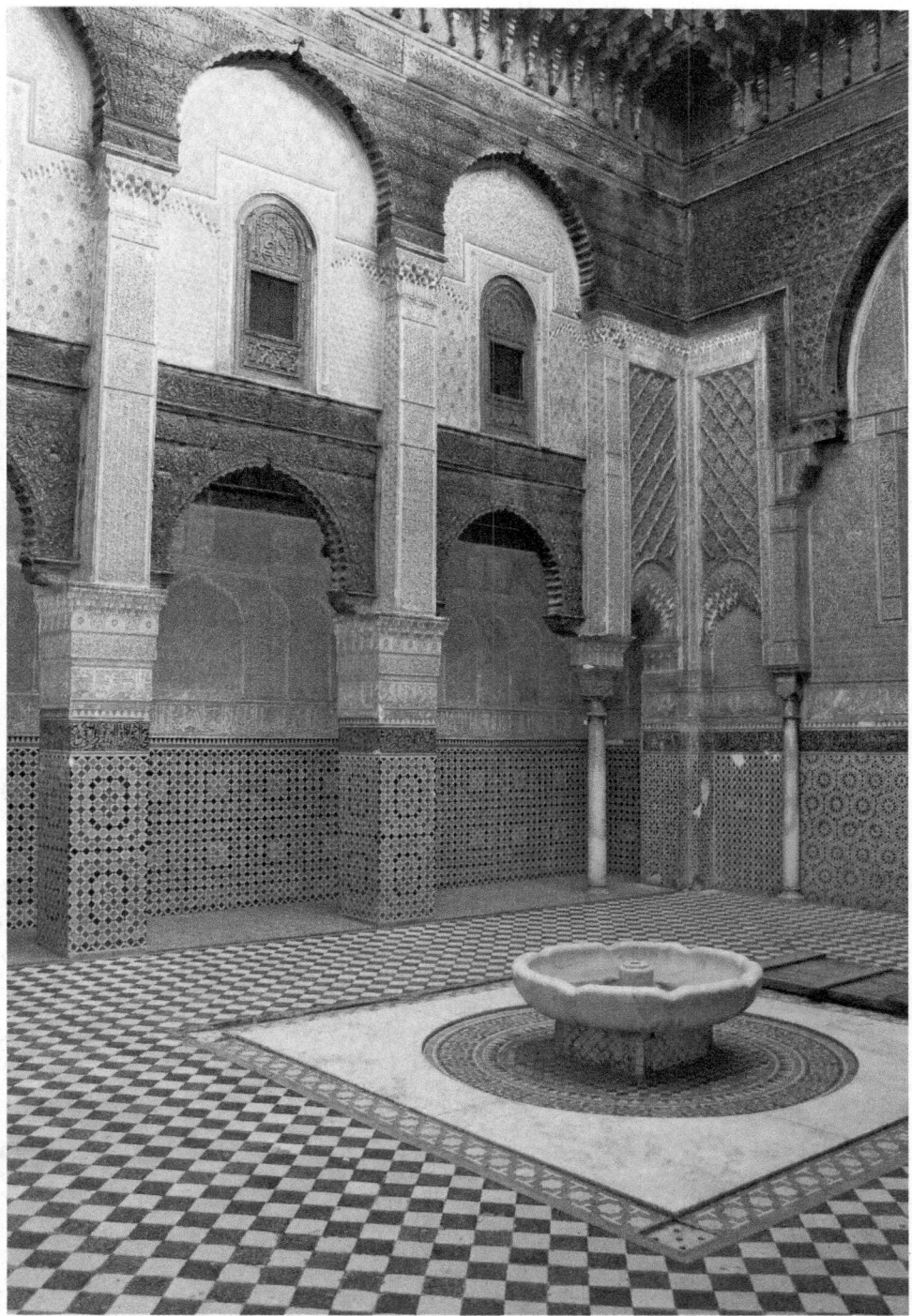

Figure 8.2-9 Fez, Morocco. Bou Inania Madrasa, ca. 1350.

stub, only half of its intended 80 m (262 ft) height. The vast platform, 446 × 449 m (1,463 × 1,473 ft), bristled with the partially erected stone columns of the unrealized hypostyle prayer hall. Aside from the laterally arranged entry *sahn*, the Hassan Mosque would have had two longitudinal interior courts to help illuminate the hall. The Almohads held power for another half-century, but their architectural patronage slowed down as they struggled to hold on to conquered territories. Their Marinid successors picked up the slack and during the next two centuries created dozens of religious institutions in Morocco's royal cities. At the Bou Inania Madrasa, founded in the 1350s, as well as at *madrasas* in Fez (Fig. 8.2-9) and Meknes, they continued to elaborate on the lacy motifs of the two earlier regimes.

From the *Taifa* States to the Gilded Confinement of the Nasrids at the Alhambra

The demise of the Umayyad regime ended the political and cultural pre-eminence of Córdoba in al-Andalus. Amid efforts at invasion by the Almoravids and Almohads from Morocco, Spain broke into various *taifas*, or petty principates. Each regime built a new capital city, aspiring to the splendor of Córdoba. The autonomy of these city-states usually endured for one or two generations. More than forty were founded, but most fell to outsiders by the end of the eleventh century. For brief moments Almería, Zaragoza, Toledo, and Seville shone as promising new centers of power. The onslaught of the Moroccan competitors from the south and the pressure of the Christian *Reconquista* from the north, however, regularly destabilized these tiny kingdoms. Only the Nasrid dynasty in Granada, which appeared toward the end of the *taifa* period, succeeded in maintaining an independent Islamic principate until the late fifteenth century.

The southern city of Almería was the first to break from Córdoba in 1011. The Alcazaba castle (Fig. 8.2-10), begun for Umayyad caliph Abd al-Rahman III in 955, became the setting for the independent emir's court. The largest of the Islamic fortresses in Spain, it had a ship-shaped outline and culminated in a square castle **keep** that gave clear views over the port and to the northern valleys. Al-Mutasim (r. 1037–1091) transformed it into a site for luxurious palaces with hanging gardens and fountains. Inside the walls a large collection of dwellings below the royal palace accommodated up to 20,000 people in times of siege. The Alcazaba's battered walls, rounded towers at the gates, and switchback entry made it the most sophisticated fortress in eleventh-century Europe. After the death of al-Mutasim in 1091, the city fell to the

Figure 8.2-10 Almería, Spain. Alcazaba, the largest fortress in Islamic Spain, ca. 1060.

Almoravids, then to the Christians, and for most of the fourteenth and fifteenth centuries remained under the Nasrids of Granada.

Zaragoza withstood as the northernmost Islamic stronghold for most of the eleventh century. The Aljafería Castle, built in 1049 for the *taifa* dynasty on the western outskirts of the city, faintly recalled the Umayyad desert palaces of the early eighth century in Jordan and Syria (see Section 7.1). The outer walls carried evenly spaced, rounded towers, while the central residential block stood symmetrically between two garden courts (Fig. 8.2-11). The inner arcades of the Aljafería Castle overlooked a reflecting pool and displayed a dazzling pattern of interlacing lobed arches, closer in spirit to embroidery than masonry. The octagonal

Figure 8.2-11 Zaragoza, Spain. Courtyard of *taifa* palace of Aljafería, ca. 1050.

palace mosque repeated the crossed-rib cupola first seen in the Great Mosque of Córdoba. Despite the help of the Castile-exiled Christian knight Rodrigo Díaz de Vivar, better known as El Cid, who defended the independence of Zaragoza during the 1080s, the city-state fell at the end of the eleventh century, first to a succession of Islamic Moroccan dynasties and a century later to the Christian kings of northern Spain.

Toledo, the most centrally located city in Spain, resisted incursions for seventy years as a *taifa*. Its rulers sponsored remarkable walls and gates, including the Puerta del Sol, decorated with interlacing arches. A small mosque, the Bab al-Mardum, rose next to the southern gate, with three cupolas structured on star-shaped ribs like those in Córdoba. After surrendering to the Christian king of Castile in 1085, Toledo became a multiethnic capital in which Christians initially showed the same tolerance for other religions as the Umayyads of Córdoba had. Muslims continued to worship in their mosques and speak their own language, and the Jews built synagogues. A fusion of motifs from Córdoba found its way into the religious buildings of Toledo's three faiths, resulting in the **mudéjar** style of lace-like, cusped arches. An impressive synagogue begun in 1180, now known as Santa Maria

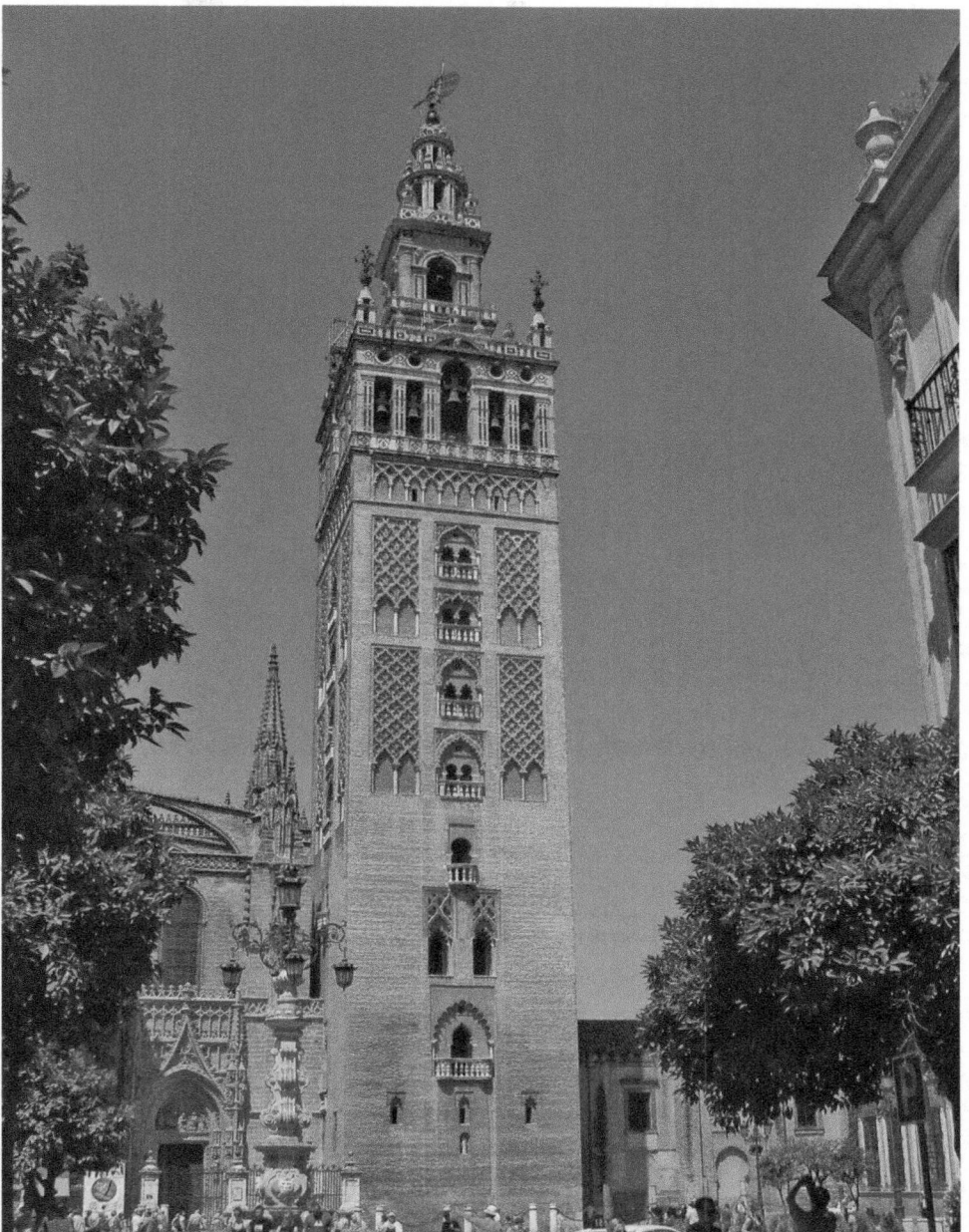

Figure 8.2-12 Seville, Spain. Giralda Tower, minaret of the Great Mosque designed in 1184 and transformed into cathedral's bell tower in thirteenth century.

la Blanca, offered a superb example of this combination of styles. Muslim masons built its five aisles of horseshoe arches, which resembled those of a hypostyle mosque. Capitals with extraordinary intertwining fern motifs capped the building's thick octagonal columns. The success of the Christian *Reconquista* at the end of the fifteenth century, however, led to the definitive expulsion of both Muslims and Jews from Spain in 1492 and the conversion of their buildings into churches. Those who converted were known as *moriscos*. The *mudéjares*, "those who remained," paid a special tax to live in autonomous communities and gave their name to the style of interlacing arcuate forms that emerged.

Seville flourished during the ascendancy of the Almoravids and became the capital of the Almohads in

Spain during the late twelfth century. In the mid-thirteenth century it fell to the Christians, who transformed the city's Great Mosque into the base of a new Gothic cathedral. The Giralda Tower (Fig. 8.2-12), which features a parapet with interlacing lobed arches similar to those on the Koutoubia minaret in Marrakech, was initially designed as a minaret in 1184 by the Almohad architect Ahmad ibn Baso.

Granada, the last independent Muslim state in Spain, survived until the fifteenth century by negotiating alliances with Christians against other Islamic principates. The Nasrid dynasty developed the Alhambra (Fig. 8.2-13a,b), a fortress on a steep promontory, into a pleasure palace that remains the crowning achievement of Islamic architecture in al-Andalus. Begun in 1039 as a dwelling for the Jewish

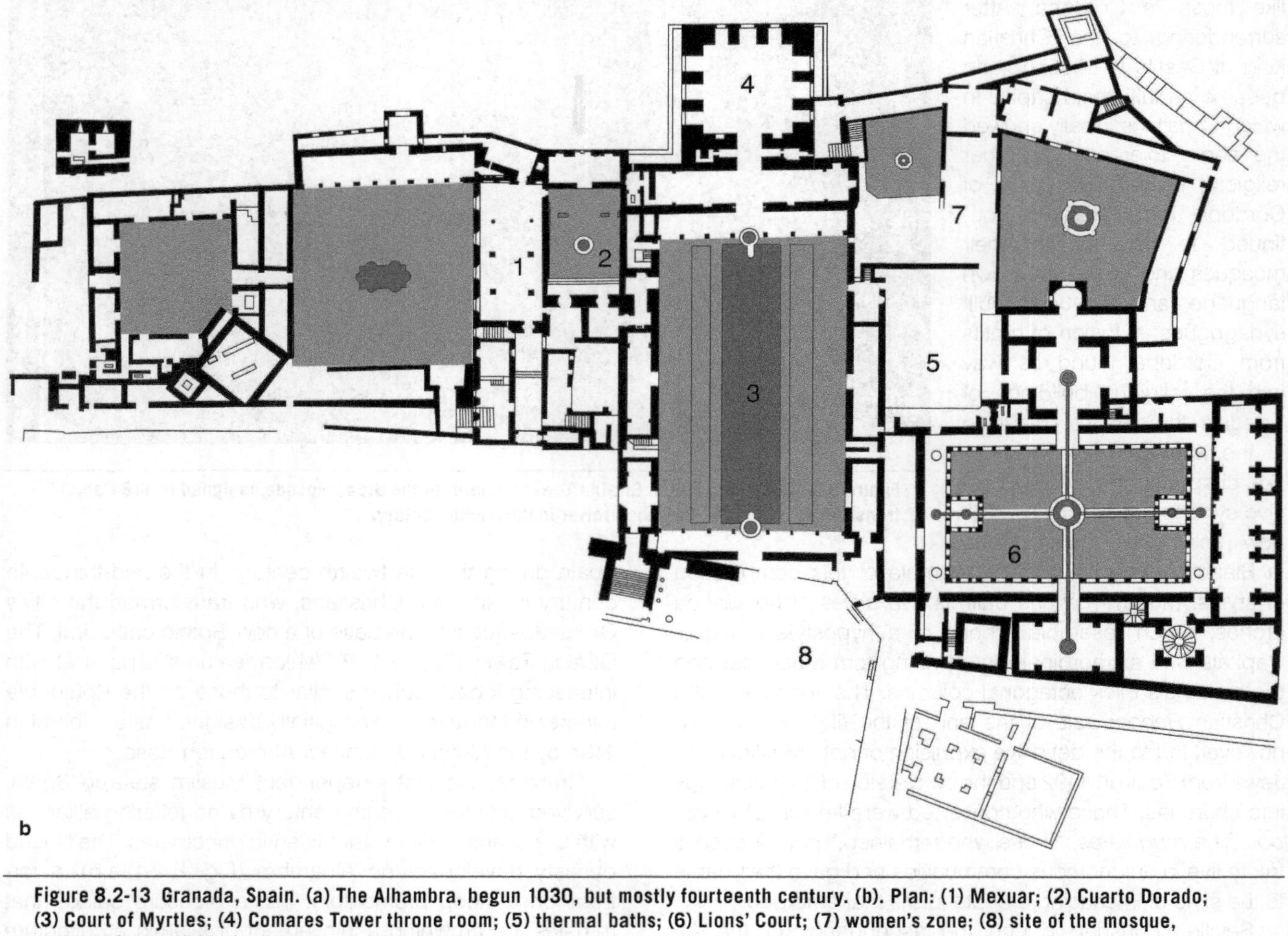

Figure 8.2-13 Granada, Spain. (a) The Alhambra, begun 1030, but mostly fourteenth century. (b). Plan: (1) Mexuar; (2) Cuarto Dorado;
(3) Court of Myrtles; (4) Comares Tower throne room; (5) thermal baths; (6) Lions' Court; (7) women's zone; (8) site of the mosque,
replaced in the 1520s by the palace of Charles V.

Figure 8.2-14 Granada, Spain. The Alhambra, Court of Myrtles, 1350s.

poet Ishmael ibn Nagrila, chief vizier to the first generation of the *taifa*, the site took its name from the red clay that tinted the hilltop. From 1236 until the definitive Christian takeover in 1492, the Nasrids governed the region while pledging feudal allegiance to the Christian kings of Castile, assisting in their *Reconquista* of Seville. The increasing magnificence of the Alhambra during the fourteenth century accompanied the dynasty's progressive isolation and entrapment in Christianized Spain.

The Alhambra grew into a dense palace-city of courts and gardens, about twice the area of the Acropolis in Athens. The sole public entry passed through the southern Gate of Justice. Most of the court resided in the lower "Medina" levels beneath the palace and reached the palace by skirting the military compound of the Alcazaba. The complex actually comprised a series of five different palaces built adjacent to each other, each with its own magnificent courtyard. This growth by addition explains the convoluted circulation from one courtyard to the next.

The first palace, the Mexuar, served as a site for public interactions with the caliph's representatives, the viziers. At its entry one found a mosque in the southern corner, demolished in the sixteenth century to make way for a palace with a circular courtyard, built for Emperor Charles V. Beyond this point access was restricted to intimates of the caliph, who entered through the Cuarto Dorado (the Golden Chamber) into the second palace of the Comares. The ornate eaves of this courtyard extended over the patio as a royal canopy under which the prince would greet official visitors at the threshold before accompanying them further. The circulation followed an *S*-shaped corridor like the entry foyers in Moroccan *riads*. It led to the Court of Myrtles (Fig. 8.2-14), where cropped myrtle hedges lined a long reflecting pool fed by circular fountains at each end. Alcoves with exuberant clusters of *muqarnas* in their ceilings stood under the arcades at opposite ends of the pool. The north axis opened to the massive Tower of Comares, which housed the throne room. Three deeply recessed windows on each side of this hall revealed the extraordinary thickness of the walls, more than 2 m (7 ft). The window niches offered stunning views of the populous Albaizín quarter across the valley.

The Lions' Court (Fig. 8.2-15) ran perpendicular to the Court of Myrtles on a slightly

Figure 8.2-15 Granada, Spain. The Alhambra, Lions' Court, 1350s.

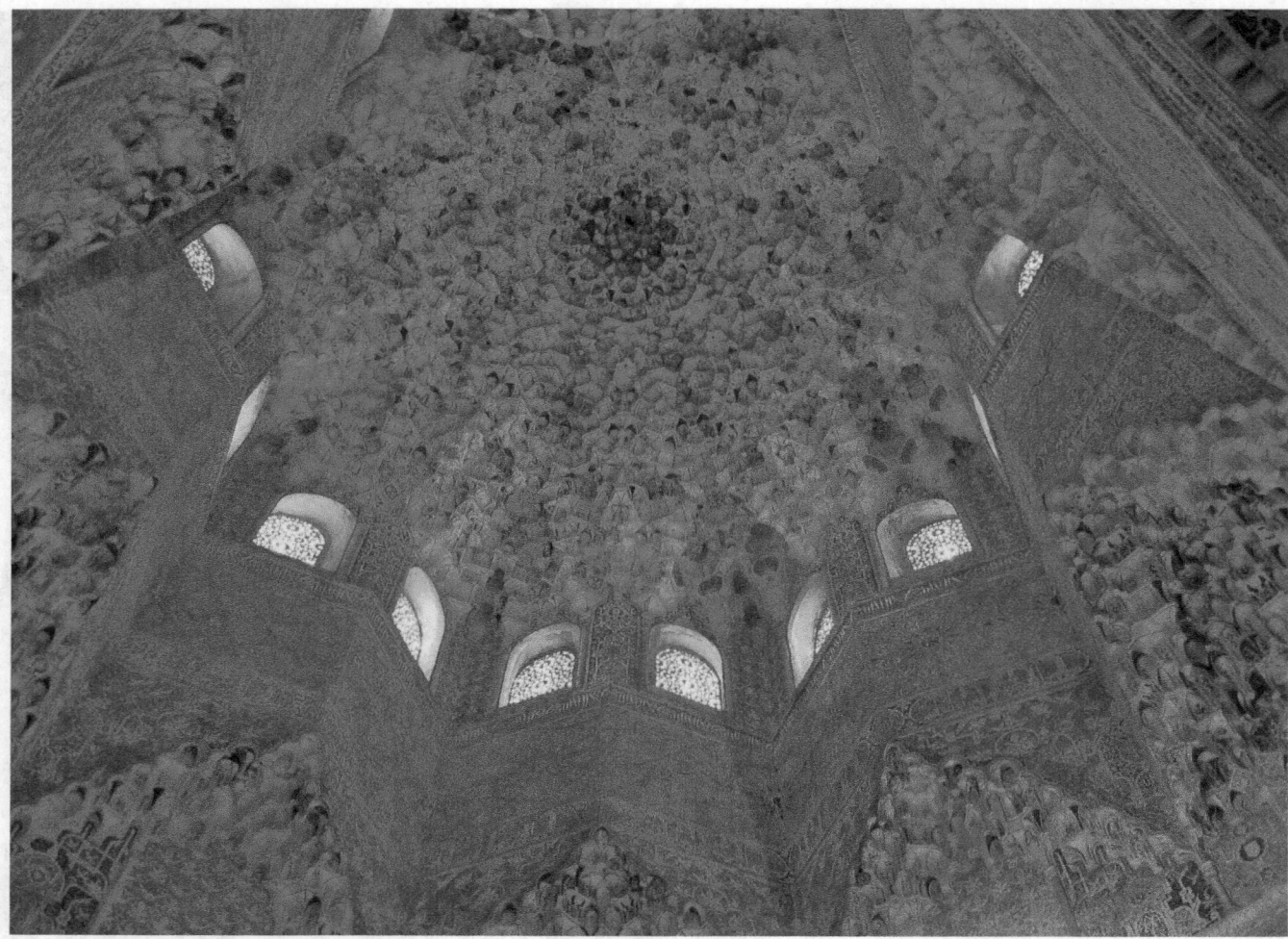

Figure 8.2-16 Granada, Spain. The Alhambra, *muqarnas* in the dome of the Hall of Two Sisters, ca. 1350.

lower level and served the domestic needs of the caliphs. The columns of its arcades followed an uncanny syncopated rhythm that was different on each elevation of the court, with various combinations of single and double columns. The Alhambra's unique cubic capitals and tall, stilted arches proved a sophisticated local invention. The design of the Lions' Court literally radiated from the central fountain, a ten-sided basin held up by ten lions squirting water from their mouths. Four narrow cross-axial troughs collected the run-off and continued the flow of water along a thin trough into the rooms. The interior halls of the Lions' Palace possessed the most intense display of *muqarnas* ever conceived. The cupolas in the Hall of the Two Sisters on the north and the Hall of the Abencerrajes opposite it achieved a paroxysm of refracted decoration, with thousands of scalloped, gilded pieces as precisely ordered as beehives (Fig. 8.2-16).

The fourth palace, the Lindaraja, was added in the six-teenth century by the Spanish kings, probably replacing the zone previously occupied by the harem. The final palace, the Partal, stood east of the others, with a large pool framed by arcades that looked out over the landscape. Here, by the still water of the pool, the court pursued its preferred pastimes of poetry and music while observing the horizon

for signs of impending doom. The walls of the Alhambra carried inscriptions with comforting imagery like "mouths of boon, bliss, felicity" and "celestial spheres over the glowing pool of dawn," alluding to the promise of paradise in the Quran. While awaiting their inevitable demise, the Nasrids devoted their dwindling resources and substantial creativity to refining the luxurious palaces and gardens of the Alham-bra and the neighboring Generalife Palace, pursuing the rich style of life initiated by the Umayyads. As their chances for survival declined, their taste for decorative *muqarnas* in-tensified, almost as if some sort of salvation lurked within the infinitesimal folding of their fluttering coves.

Further Reading

Barrucand, Marianne, and Achim Bednorz. *Moorish Architecture in Andalusia*. Cologne, Germany: Taschen, 2002.

Bianca, Stefano. *Urban Form in the Arab World: Past and Present*. London: Thames & Hudson, 2000.

Dodds, Jerrilynn D. *Architecture and Ideology in Early Medieval Spain*. University Park: Pennsylvania State University Press, 1990.

Hoag, John D. *Islamic Architecture*. Milan: Electa, 1975.

8.3 WESTERN EUROPE AFTER THE ROMAN EMPIRE

Monks, Knights, and Pilgrims

From the fifth century until the year 1000, the cities of the western half of the Roman Empire underwent invasions, famines, plagues, and economic hardship. Political power diffused to barbarian warlords and to smaller feudal states led by military strongmen huddled in hilltop castles. As the population dwindled, so did international trade. Church bishops remained the only figures with legal authority in the cities. The feudal system divided society into those who fought, those who prayed, and the great mass who toiled. Most of Europe became a mosaic of feudal duchies, locked into a self-sufficient but chronically impoverished existence. This relatively static order, while laced with ignorance, hardship, and taboos, produced a model of ecological restraint.

Christian monasteries remain the most inspired expressions of European feudal society. They became important stabilizing elements, sustaining a community that produced what it consumed, wasted nothing, and limited its size by selecting new members rather than breeding them. Organized like little cities, productive in both agriculture and crafts, and stocked with libraries, they attracted the patronage of ambitious leaders.

After the year 1000, a new sense of cultural and economic openness encouraged the journeys of Christian pilgrims. They traveled from England, Germany, and France to either Jerusalem, Rome, or Santiago de Compostela, Spain. The protection of pilgrims became a pretext for the military exploits of the crusaders, who reclaimed Jerusalem as their "Holy Land." The subsequent contact with Muslim societies, in both war and trade, stimulated European cities. The grand churches, hospitals, monasteries, and castles built all over Europe after the millennium represented an optimistic architectural expression of a progressive social order.

Charlemagne: The Revival of the Roman Empire and the Role of Monasteries

During the long reign of Charlemagne (r. 768–814), the Franks patched together the territories of France, Germany, Switzerland, Czechoslovakia, and Austria. At the request of Pope Leo III, they entered Italy in 774 to oust the Lombards from their capital in Pavia, while pushing the Byzantines to the south. The pope crowned Charlemagne in 800 as the first Holy Roman emperor, a title as pretentious as "Raja-raja" ("king of kings"), since the unity of this empire was as tenuous as its claims to being "Roman" or "holy." After the reign of Charlemagne's son, Louis the Pious, the empire dissolved into three kingdoms. Frequent Viking incursions from the north and Magyar and Saracen raids from the south had left Charlemagne's legacy in tatters by the end of the ninth century. The formerly centralized political power dissipated to the scattered feudal system of a myriad of duchies and monasteries.

Charlemagne's fleeting vision of *Renovatio Romanae Imperii*, the revival of the unity and greatness of the Roman Empire of Constantine, inspired a feverish few decades of architectural patronage. Aside from numerous imperial palaces built for his itinerant court, he sponsored the construction of sixteen cathedrals and over 200 monasteries, financed through the spoils of his conquests. Like the Khmer rulers of Southeast Asia, Charlemagne relied on the support of monastic settlements to bolster his regime. This in turn empowered the religious orders, and by the eleventh century the network of Benedictine monasteries, increasingly under the authority of the **Abbey** of Cluny, had assumed a determining role in European politics.

Charlemagne's palace (Fig. 8.3-1) and chapel at Aix-la-Chapelle, now called Aachen, was a key project in his far-flung efforts to revive the Roman Empire. The court architect, Odo of Metz, borrowed liberally from the Byzantine works in Ravenna to construct this complex. The palace

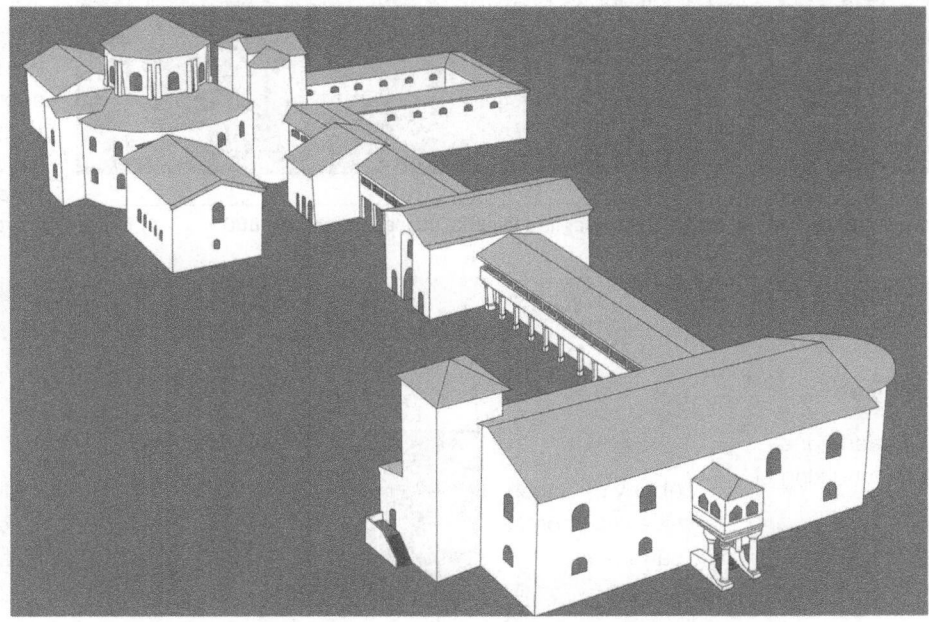

Figure 8.3-1 Aachen (Germany). Reconstruction of Charlemagne's palace, ca. 800.

derived its organization from Theodoric's palace in Ravenna, which had been inspired by the imperial palace in Constantinople. A long upper gallery passed from a basilica meeting hall through the major gateway and into the palatine chapel, similar to the **viaduct** that passed through the Chalke Gate, connecting Hagia Sophia to the palace in Constantinople. In the center of Charlemagne's courtyard stood an equestrian statue of Theodoric taken from Ravenna, a perfect precedent for a barbarian king of the Romans.

In 791 Charlemagne commissioned the Palatine Chapel (Fig. 8.3-2), which, despite significant additions, is the only piece of the imperial complex in Aachen that remains intact. His architect attempted to copy San Vitale in Ravenna for the emperor's mausoleum, producing a stiff approximation of the two-storied octagon supporting a dome on a drum. Built entirely in stone instead of brick, its structural components were thicker than those of its precedent, leaving the interior spaces darker than those in Ravenna. Instead of the soaring scooped-out conches and complex annular vaults, the piers rose in flat facets, and behind them were ordinary groin vaults. One flaw in the interior details betrayed the imperial chapel's distance in time and space from Roman and Byzantine sources: the marble columns in the upper galleries, *spolia* dragged across Europe from Roman sites, reached up directly into the **intrados** of the arches without a mediating entablature. This contradicted both the structural and grammatical logic of columns and arches. Another peculiarity, seen for the first time in Christian architecture, was the alternation of black and white voussoirs in the arches, similar to *ablaq* patterns in the Great Mosque of Córdoba. The craftspeople covered the

Figure 8.3-2 Aachen (Germany). Charlemagne's imperial chapel interior, ca. 800.

TIME LINE

 768

Charlemagne crowned king of the Franks

Abbey of Lorsch receives imperial patronage

▲ **774**

 792

Charlemagne crowned Holy Roman emperor in Rome

Vikings destroy Lindisfarne Abbey (England)

▲ **793**

 800

Charlemagne's palace and church constructed at Aachen

Figure 8.3-3 Westphalia (Germany). Abbey of Corvey, westwork facade, with imperial chamber, 873.

lower ranges of the chapel with Byzantine-style marble slabs of butterfly revetment.

Above the main entry to the Aachen chapel rose the two towers of the *castellum*, or fortress. A special chamber on the second level served as the emperor's official loggia, offering a view of the main altar. During the next century the twin-towered facade became known as a **westwork** and lost its direct military associations. These monumental thresholds initially served as throne rooms for the itinerant emperor's visits but in later churches housed chapels for the relics sought by pilgrims. The westwork at the Abbey of Corvey in 873 in Westphalia, the only Carolingian example intact, anticipated the twin towers on the facades of most of the great cathedrals of northern Europe built during the eleventh through fourteenth centuries (Fig. 8.3-3). Some of the members of Charlemagne's court produced another distinct type, the **double-ender** church, with full apses in both the east and the west ends, such as the abbeys of Fulda and Centula (now called St. Riquier). Most of the churches with imperial patronage during the Ottonian revival of Charlemagne's empire in the eleventh century, such as St. Michael at Hildesheim (1010), adhered to this type.

One of the Carolingian westworks that may have influenced the chapel at Aachen, the Abbey of Lorsch, received imperial patronage in 774. Although the church succumbed to a fire in the eleventh century, the surviving gatehouse to its convent, built after 800, offers a rich example of the Carolingian reinterpretation of ancient types (Fig. 8.3-4). The gate suggested a triumphal arch to celebrate Charlemagne's return from his imperial coronation in Rome. The designers presented a local interpretation of a well-known Roman precedent, using three arches flanked with classical half-columns

capped by an attic story with pilasters. There the resemblance blurs, as the emperor's designers clad the facade in alternating red and white sandstone panels, square at the base, rotated into diamond patterns in the fascia at the level of the capitals, and star-shaped in the attic. The fluted Ionic pilasters of the upper bays carried an entablature fused with a continuous series of pediments, creating a novel sawtooth pattern. The rounded staircase turrets on either side and the spacious hall on the

Figure 8.3-4 Lorsch (Germany). Gatehouse to imperially sponsored convent, ca. 800.

The *opus dei*, or "God's work," consisted of prayer, participation in collective services seven times daily, and a life of poverty and chastity.

The double-ender, three-aisle church, with two freestanding towers for its west-work, dominated the monastery's plan. It was sited on the north so as not to block the sunlight to the major structures. The brothers would have built the majority of the buildings, except the church, in wood, which explains why so little remains of these early structures. The animal pens, barns, workers' lodgings, and other ancillary functions occupied the southern edge of the complex. The eastern wing for the novitiates had its own little church and **cloister**. The infirmary and cemetery flanked this mini-nucleus. The visitors' spaces north of the church included a compound for vassals and knights serving the emperor, a house for distinguished guests, a **hospice** for pilgrims and paupers, a school, rooms for visiting clerics, and kitchens for the different categories of visitors. While the monks could not leave the convent, the plan anticipated a constant flux of pilgrims, visitors, and patrons, including the emperor.

upper floor have no parallel in Roman triumphal arches but relate to ancient city gates, such as the Porta Nigra in nearby Trier. The pitched roof, which originally had a lower pitch, made a practical concession to the colder climate. The mix of Italian and barbarian motifs both enriched and contradicted the classical Roman type, leading nineteenth-century historians to label the works of this period "Romanesque."

Although none of the convents from the age of Charlemagne have survived fully intact, the extraordinary graphic document of the ideal plan of St. Gall reveals the form and social order of a Benedictine **monastery**. The drawing accompanied a letter of ca. 816 intended to guide the building of a convent. The designer plotted the plan on a grid using a 12.5 m (41 ft) module subdivided into sixteen units, each obtained through continuous halving. The convent's organization illustrates the theoretical balance of the devotional life of prayer and study and the productive life to sustain the community. One-third of St. Gall's spaces concerned monastic duties, one-third agriculture and crafts performed by the serfs, and one-third hospitality. The monks lived in strict observance of the *Rule of St. Benedict*, which they read aloud daily in the warming room, or chapter house.

The arcaded cloister at the core of the plan of St. Gall represented the heart of the religious community. The principal ingredients of the monks' segregated existence gathered around this void: the church on the north, the warming hall with a dormitory on the second level to the east, the **refectory** and kitchen to the south, and the larder and cellar to the west. The cloister at the twelfth-century Abbey of St. Pierre at Moissac gives an idea of the typical structure's form and peaceful mood (Fig. 8.3-5). The beautifully carved columns of the arcade, alternating single with paired, rose from a hip-height parapet to frame a planted void. While in plan the cloister vaguely resembled a forum, the raised arcades discouraged one from entering the open space, which served as a vision of paradise that monks and visitors could use in meditation.

From the tenth to the twelfth century, monastic institutions acquired exceptional power and authority in Western Europe. The two major centers emerged at Gorze, located

▼ **1061**

Normans take southern Italy and later Sicily

Normans invade England

▲ **1066**

▼ **1088**

Cluny III church (France) rebuilt

Cathedral built at Durham as part of monastery complex next to the royal palace of the Normans

▲ **1093**

▼ **1098**

Cistercian order begins at Citeaux, France

Crusaders take Jerusalem, establish four crusader kingdoms

▲ **1099**

Figure 8.3-5 Moissac (France). Cloister of St. Pierre, ca. 1100.

in northern France near Metz, and Cluny, in central France. The former was associated with the imperial court, while the latter catered to the interests of the papacy in Rome. Cluny began with papal patronage in 909 as a reformed Benedictine community and enjoyed singular independence, electing its own abbots. The layout of its initial scheme repeated much of the program of St. Gall, including an infirmary, a refectory, and a kitchen to the south of the cloister; a storeroom to the west of it; and a cemetery, a hospice for pilgrims, and a separate house for the abbot. Instead of a complex series of workshops and agricultural buildings, Cluny retained only a modest stable and a row of tiny workshops because the monks deferred the physical labor to their tenants and serfs. This left them more time to pursue a

life of purely liturgical purpose. By praying, saying the mass, and singing vespers, they fulfilled their founder's invocation to "stand in choral prayers that our soul may be in harmony with our voices."

By the end of the eleventh century, Cluny commanded a monastic empire with jurisdiction over nearly 1,500 monasteries, half of them in France and the rest in Spain, Italy, England, and Germany. The alterations that had been made to the abbey's plan, making it more like an imperial palace, set inside substantial walls, reveal its political importance. The abbot St. Hugh of Semur began the third version of the church in 1088, transforming fragments of the apses of the second church into an expanded cloister. The old church's atrium became the courtyard of a new palace for the abbot,

▼ **1142**

Impenetrable fortress of Krak des Chevaliers built by Hospitallers in Syria

Norman Cathedral of Monreale, Palermo

▲ **1150**

▼ **1187**

Saladin defeats crusaders at Jerusalem

Frederick II begins Castel del Monte

▲ **1240**

a dwelling suitable to receive heads of state. The warming room became the **chapter house**, the monastery's council chamber, where the priors managed their international affairs. Attached to this vaulted hall stood the **Lady Chapel** devoted to the Virgin, reserved for the private use of the monastery's hierarchy. By this time the Cluny community included over 1,200 monks and *conversi*, the lay initiates who carried out the monastery's more menial tasks. Twin palaces for up to forty noblemen and thirty noblewomen hosted the likes of kings, queens, popes, and emperors. Running water from concealed conduits fed twelve bathhouses and a number of fountains. The inspiration for such luxurious settings probably came from the grand palaces of Islamic Spain.

The construction of Cluny III (Fig. 8.3-6) coincided with the election of a Cluniac as pope. The order consciously planned to build the largest church in the world, and St. Hugh defended the expense of his mission to produce splendid music and great architecture by portraying them as suitable offerings to God. The expansion of the church attracted the patronage of Alfonso VI of Castile, fresh from his victory over the Muslims in Toledo in 1085. The new church's architect, Gunzo of Baume, was a retired abbot renowned as a musician and thus a master of proportions. Chanting ceremonies remained one of the key elements of Cluny III's program. With the addition of a second transept, the choir could accommodate 450 monks. The apse terminated with an ambulatory, off of which radiated five rounded chapels.

This apron of chapels, known as the **chevet**, improved the circulation for pilgrims, who could visit the reliquaries without disturbing the choir. The final dimensions of Cluny III covered nearly twice the area of St. Peter's in Rome. At a height of 30 m (98 ft), the pointed barrel-vault nave seemed dizzying, initiating a competition to build ever-higher vaulted roofs. A square steeple rose over the crossing, and octagonal towers studded the crossing of the second transept and the ends of the transept, creating a spiky, crown-like profile, not dissimilar to its contemporary at Angkor Wat.

The extravagance of Cluny, with its gilded pilasters and painted chapels, attracted the disdain of the Cistercian order, which advocated a return to the austerity of the initial Benedictine rules of poverty, chastity, and obedience. One of its leaders, St. Bernard of Clairvaux (1090–1153), lashed out against Cluny: "The church is resplendent in its walls, but its poor go in want; she clothes her stones in gold, and leaves her sons naked; the rich man's eye is fed at the expense of the indigent." From the Cistercian motherhouse in the marshes of Cîteaux near Dijon, teams of twelve monks set out to establish other monasteries in out-of-the-way wilderness sites during the early twelfth century. They founded more than 700 Cistercian settlements during the next two centuries, from Ireland to Greece to Palestine. Their architecture appeared severe and disciplined, governed by a rigorous building ordinance. The order spawned an international style that varied little in form, decoration, or content, no matter how different the site.

CONSTRUCTION, TECHNOLOGY, THEORY

The Chevet in Pilgrimage Churches

The chevet, an apse with an ambulatory and radiating chapels, became a chief characteristic of pilgrimage churches in the eleventh century. It was inspired by a tragic event in Reims in 1046, when a crowd pushing into a *T*-shaped transept to witness the relics of St. Remi trampled many people to death. St. Hugh, the patron of Cluny III, was present at the disaster and became one of the chief proponents of the chevet as an elegant solution for more fluid circulation. The chevet at the Abbey of Fontevrault resembled that of Cluny, with cascading conches around the apse, a type that was repeated at most churches along the pilgrimage trails.

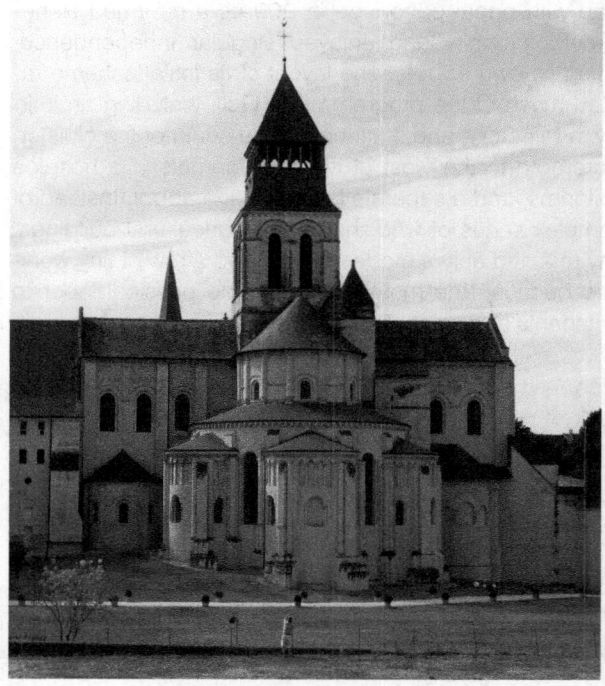

Anjou (France). Abbey of Fontevrault, chevet apse with radiating chapels, 1100.

The austere program of the Cistercians shaped Le Thoronet Abbey (Fig. 8.3-7a,b), built in the south of France from 1157 to 1175. The abbey's builders rejected decoration, relying on bare structure for their aesthetic pleasure. St. Augustine's "perfect" ratio of 1:2 controlled the elevations and ground plan: the width of the nave was double that of the side aisles. Cistercians eschewed monumental facades, and only a simple bell tower rose over the roof of the apse. They eliminated intermediary galleries above the side aisles and gave the windows clear panes instead of stained glass. St. Bernard explained Cistercian iconoclasm: "We forbid

there to be any statues or pictures in our churches or in any other rooms of a monastery of ours, because, when attention is paid to such things, the advantages of sound meditation and training in religious gravity are often neglected."

The cloister of Le Thoronet followed an irregular layout owing to its sloping terrain, but the same rigor applied to the design of the church affected the construction of its vaulted arcades and the thick piers surrounding the cloister. A single eccentric element, a hexagonal pavilion for the water supply, had a pointed roof that stuck out like a pencil point above the cloister roofs. The monks at Le Thoronet

---

CULTURE, SOCIETY, GENDER

Convents for Women

Monasticism represented a primarily masculine worldview, and monks, perhaps because of their vows of chastity, had a vocational aversion to women. During the eleventh and twelfth centuries, however, a number of abbeys were founded for women and attracted the patronage and participation of the well-born. St. Hugh, the builder of Cluny III, founded a convent for his mother and sister in 1055 at Marcigny, not far from his own abbey. The great abbess Hildegard of Bingen (1098–1179) organized two women's abbeys, neither of which have survived, at Rupertsberg and Eibingen on opposite sides of the Rhine, 50 km (31 miles) west of Frankfurt. Here, she produced her celebrated musical compositions and illuminated manuscripts, the *Scivias*, describing her mystical visions.

The Abbey of Fontevrault was built in 1100 as a double monastery, one side for monks and the other for nuns. It attracted royal patronage and became the pet project of Eleanor of Aquitaine (1122–1204), who spent her final years there, turning the church into her family's mausoleum. A forceful patron who divorced her first husband, Louis VII of France, and attempted to depose her second husband, Henry II, king of England, Eleanor saw to it that monks served the nuns of the convent.

Aside from the distinctive nave of the church of Fontevrault, which instead of having barrel vaults was spanned by a succession of four domes, the twelfth-century abbey was endowed with an extraordinary building for the kitchens. It stood at the edge of the cloister, an octagon 15 m (49 ft) in diameter, with a central chimney forming a colossal prismatic spire surrounded by seven apse-like chambers, each with smaller conical chimneys. Separating the kitchen from the body of the monastery became common

practice for fire safety, one recommended earlier in the plan of St. Gall. In this case the kitchen acquired monumental status as a culinary temple, indicating the importance of setting a good table for the abbey's aristocratic clientele.

Anjou (France). Abbey of Fontevrault, kitchen, 1100.

Figure 8.3-6 Cluny (France). Model of Cluny III church and convent (based on J. K. Conant, 1960), ca. 1100.

achieved a tighter version of the plan of St. Gall, excluding ingredients such as bathhouses and a separate abbot's residence. They constructed everything, even the latrines and corridors, with smooth stones and vaulted ceilings. Cistercians always chose sites where a stream could be diverted into the grounds of the monastery for sanitary and industrial purposes. Their attention to labor led to numerous technological advances in milling and metalworking, forms of proto-industrial production. Cistercians formulated an alternative aesthetic to that of Cluny, conceiving of beauty as the direct consequence of expedient structure without decoration.

The Norman Invasions: An Architectural Cross-Fertilization

Throughout the ninth century, Viking raiders from Scandinavia menaced the stability of much of Europe. To appease them, the king of France granted the Vikings the duchy of Normandy in 911, leading to their new identity as Normans. From their earlier role as destroyers of monasteries, they became the most enthusiastic sponsors of their reconstruction. Following the example of Charlemagne, members of the Norman hierarchy founded monasteries to reinforce their network of territorial control. Around the year 1000 they began rebuilding the spectacular island sanctuary of Mont-Saint-Michel (Fig. 8.3-8), which had been destroyed in a Viking raid. An Italian monk from Cluny, William de Volpiano (962–1031), expanded the site into a monastery, and during the next two centuries the various functions—including cloister, refectory, chapter house, and dormitory—were stacked vertically on three levels.

William the Conqueror (1028–1087), before launching the Norman invasion of England, established his capital at the coastal town of Caen in 1060, building a castle and the monastery of St. Etienne. The church's sheer facade, articulated with four thick buttresses, demonstrated the conversion of the Frankish westwork into a flat plane with twin towers. The nave and side aisles of the church displayed one of the first uses of ribbed groin vaults. The twin-tower facade and the ribbed vaults became conventional elements for most of the subsequent cathedrals built in France and England.

Figure 8.3-7 Provence, southern France. (a) Le Thoronet Abbey, church crossing, ca.1100. (b) See facing page.

Figure 8.3-7b Provence, southern France. Plan of Cistercian convent of Le Thoronet, mid-twelfth century; the dashed line shows the course of water from a natural source.

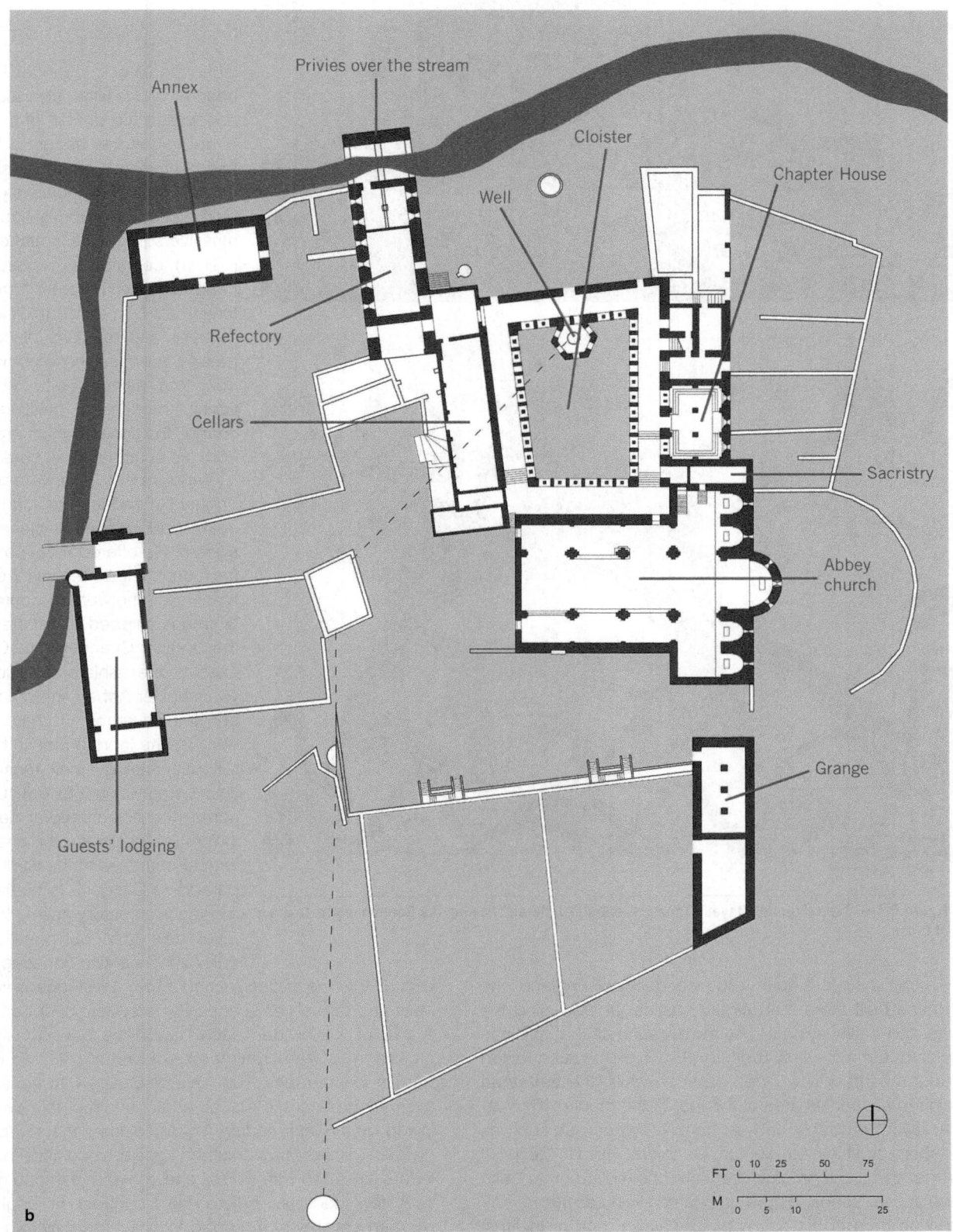

Figure 8.3-8 Normandy (France). Mont-Saint-Michel, destroyed by Vikings in the tenth century and rebuilt as a Benedictine convent by Normans (ex-Vikings) during the eleventh century.

Figure 8.3-9 Caen (France). Bayeux Tapestry, ca. 1070. Detail showing the Norman motte castle of Dinan.

stone donjons in France; its solid square volume with buttressed walls anticipated the design of the White Tower in London, begun in 1078 as the new king's official residence. One of the largest secular structures built in Europe since antiquity, this massive square pile stretched 40 m (131 ft) per side. A severe block capped with four corner turrets, the tower had 5 m (16 ft) thick walls at its base and regularly placed buttresses between the windows. The boxy form gained a bit of eccentric variety through the position of the chapel, the apse of which protruded from the southeastern corner.

William's new government in England introduced a highly centralized administration to the feudal system. He offered royal patronage for monasteries as a means of extending his network of control. The Normans shipped limestone across the English Channel from Caen to execute the ashlar construction of Westminster Abbey and many other convent churches. Durham Cathedral, in the northernmost Norman outpost, rose as their most ambitious commission (Fig. 8.3-10). At its completion, the cathedral measured 140 m (459 ft) in length, one of the largest churches in the world, comparable to Cluny III. It loomed over a steep promontory above the Wear River next to a polygonal donjon built for William two decades earlier.

Among their first acts in the conquest of England, the Normans built more than eighty castles, at first using the motte-and-bailey system. The **motte**, such as that at Dinan depicted in the Bayeux Tapestry (Fig. 8.3-9), was a raised lookout mound with wooden palisade walls, the **bailey** an enclosed residential area at the foot of the mound. This circular layout probably derived from Viking camps such as Trelleborg, built in ninth-century Denmark. From these initial earth-and-wood fortresses the Normans moved on to build stone castle "keeps," known in Normandy as **donjons**. William was born in the castle of La Falaise, one of the first

Like St. Etienne at Caen, it had a twin-tower facade, with the nave and side aisles spanned by a system of ribbed vaults. A pair of X's divided each bay of the ceiling with crisscrossing ribs. The craftspeople of Durham steered clear of Roman iconography. The nave resonates with the effect of alternating piers, the first as a tall bundle of thin poles, followed by the intermediary squat columns that support the galleries. These latter columns appear as colossal pure cylinders inscribed with vibrant chevron and diamond motifs.

A few decades before the conquest of England, a Norman contingent departed for southern Italy to serve as

Figure 8.3-10 Durham, England. Cathedral built as part of the monastery complex next to the royal palace of the Normans, 1093.

mercenaries and protectors of pilgrims. In 1059 Pope Nicholas II granted these Normans feudal rights in the region, and two years later their rule was extended from Aversa to all of southern Italy and Sicily, establishing a kingdom with its capital in the Muslim-dominated city of Palermo. As a minority in these lands, the Norman rulers avoided imposing cultural or religious preferences, while nonetheless exercising a highly centralized government. Their strategy of rule resembled that of the Umayyads in Córdoba: staying aloof from the base; making expedient use of local talent; and allowing Muslims, Jews, and Christians to follow their own beliefs. The impressive architectural output of the kingdom under the Norman rulers relied on local Muslim craftspeople and Byzantine artists for its vigor.

North African Muslim dynasties had ruled Sicily during the previous two centuries. The Normans transformed their *alcázar* at the southern edge of Palermo into the "Norman" Palace in 1131, using a mixture of Arab and Byzantine styles. On its rear exteriors one finds *mudéjar* interlacing arches. In its Palatine Chapel, the craftspeople combined Byzantine mosaics with inscriptions in Greek and cupolas with Arab-inspired *muqarnas*, a unique use of this element in a Christian church.

The most compelling example of Norman stylistic fusion appeared at the Abbey of Monreale (Fig. 8.3-11), located in the hills 7 km (4.3 miles) south of Palermo. Here, William

II envisioned a monastery that would also serve as the mausoleum of the Norman kings of Sicily. Contrary to Italian practice, the entry facade had twin towers like churches in Normandy. The interior resembled a timber-ceilinged basilica of the early Christians, its narrow aisles set off by classically proportioned Corinthian columns that carried Islamic-inspired pointed arches. The space literally glowed from the intensity of the golden mosaics executed by Byzantine masters. Interlacing arches articulated the exterior elevations of the three apses.

The Sicilian Normans showed their desire to emulate the models of luxury at North African courts in the design of La Ziza (Fig. 8.3-12). William I began the villa in the 1160s on the outskirts of Palermo, but it could easily be mistaken for a work commissioned by the previous Muslim rulers. Three *iwan*-like arches, stilted and pointed like those in Abbasid Baghdad, led from the principal facade to lush gardens and geometrical fountains. The central arch rose two stories. Recessed arches framed the smaller **biforium** windows of the upper two stories, creating a rhythmic pattern with the ground-floor arches. On the rear wall of the interior hall *muqarnas* covered a niche decorated with mosaics. The water from a fountain in the niche spilled down a small stair to form a thin channel that passed through a succession of basins into a reflecting pool in front of the central arch, providing one of La Ziza's several passive cooling features. The

Figure 8.3-11 Monreale, Palermo (Italy). Norman Cathedral, with interlacing arches typical of Arab decoration, 1150.

their palaces and villas they created a precocious expression of secular magnificence for Christian Europe.

The Pilgrim's Progress: Rome and Compostela

The fragmentation of medieval Europe into semiautonomous demesnes controlled by feudal castles and monasteries led to both social experiments and widespread immobility. The religious pilgrimage became popular as the single legitimate pretext for travel. During the eleventh and twelfth centuries, the attempt to serve and attract pilgrims stimulated the exchange of design ideas, particularly between central France, northern Spain, and Italy.

Christian pilgrimages to sacred relics in faraway sites began with St. Helen's trips to Palestine in the early fourth century. Three tombs became the principal goals for medieval pilgrims: Christ's Holy Sepulcher in Jerusalem, St. Peter's crypt in Rome, and the tomb designed for the recently discovered body of St. James in Compostela, Spain. The new enthusiasm for pilgrimages paralleled Islam's emphasis on the *hajj* to Mecca. The church promised Christians "indulgences" upon reaching their goals, such as the absolution of sins, favor for their vows, or benefits in the hereafter. Pilgrims undertook their journeys as penitential acts in "the economy of salvation." The tympanum at the entry of Ste. Foy at Conques (Fig. 8.3-13), one of the major churches on the pilgrims' path through France to Compostela, depicted the familiar scene of the Last Judgment awaiting humankind at the end of time. It reminded the pilgrim

builders integrated wind-catcher flues (*malqaf*; see Section 9.1) at each end of the building and placed vents in the central chamber to draw off the hot air. This integration of architecture and passive cooling recalled the fountain courts in al-Andalus. The Normans in no way let their religious commitments inhibit their efforts to equal the grandeur and comfort of the palaces of their North African contemporaries. In

that through the pardon obtained by visiting the holy shrines one could gain redemption from eternal punishment in hell.

Bethlehem and Jerusalem, the sites of Christ's birth and death, respectively, remained the most prized but difficult to reach destinations. Rome—a city of saints, martyrs, and popes—offered itself as the more common goal for international journeys. Large crowds descended from the north

Figure 8.3-12 Palermo (Italy). Norman La Ziza Palace, showing mosaics and niche decorated with *muqarnas*, built with Muslim designers as a Norman pleasure palace, 1160s.

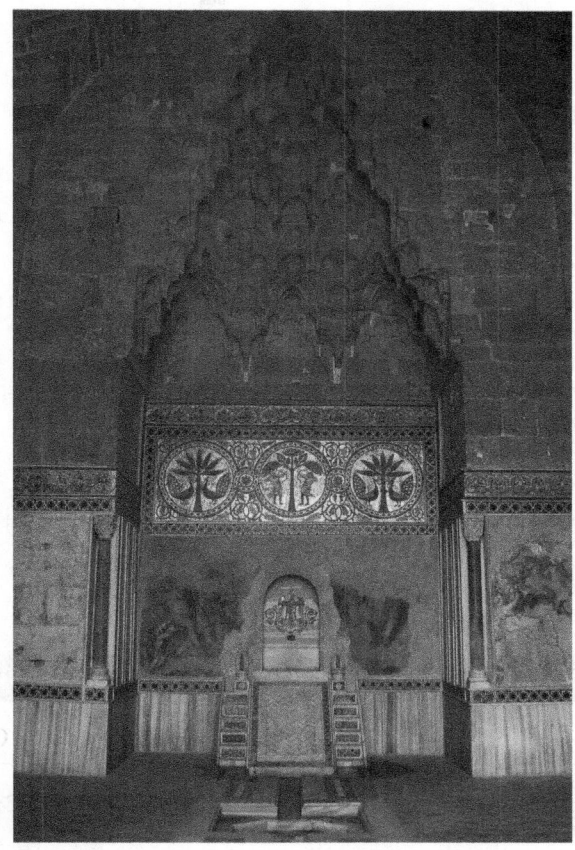

every year to pay homage to Peter and Paul, both of whom had been martyred in Rome, and made the rounds to the other major stations within the city and the nearby countryside. For some the route began in Canterbury, England, crossed France, and proceeded over the Alps into Italy at the Pass of St. Bernard. The Via Francigena passed through Pavia and the church of San Michele, used for the coronations of kings and emperors. Then it crossed the Apennines to Sarzana, proceeding via Lucca, Siena, and Viterbo to Rome.

Once in Rome pilgrims had no shortage of churches and relics to visit, but the city at the end of the twelfth century stood in a shambles. The Normans had led the last sack of the metropolis in 1084, resulting in a truce and the remodeling of major Roman churches and convents, such as Santa Maria in Trastevere, San Clemente, and Santi Quattro Incoronati. These works followed the style of early Christian basilicas with few significant changes, excepting the decorative porches and the addition of the new vertical element of the **campanile**. St. Peter's and most of the major pilgrimage churches acquired slender towers by the year 1200 to help orient pilgrims searching the horizon for the next holy shrine. Some campaniles, such as the one added to Santa

Figure 8.3-13 Conques, France. Tympanum of Ste. Foy showing the Last Judgment, 1060–1140.

Maria in Cosmedin, seemed incongruous because of their disproportionate height and the contrasting color of their brick construction.

During the height of the influence of Cluny in the eleventh and twelfth centuries, Compostela became a serious alternative to Rome. The cult began shortly after the body of the apostle St. James miraculously appeared in 813 on the nearby shores of this remote northwestern tip of Spain. The draw of Compostela intensified after al-Mansur of Córdoba sacked the shrine in 997. While the act of pilgrimage was by definition pacific, armed knights usually accompanied the pilgrims for their protection, and their passage through the predominately Muslim territories of al-Andalus became an inherently political act. The decision by Alfonso VI (r. 1065–1109), ruler of the northern Spanish states of Léon and Castile and one of the major protagonists of the *Reconquista*, to sponsor the rebuilding of Cluny III in 1088 deepened the political connection, which is revealed in the stylistic similarities of the church of Santiago at Compostela with Cluny III.

The four official routes to Compostela (Fig. 8.3-14) encouraged the development of abbeys, inns, and hospices along their way. The *Via Turonensis* began at the Tour St. Jacques in Paris and proceeded to the Cluniac abbey of St. Martin in Tours, one of four major convent churches in France that specialized in the pilgrims' progress (Fig. 8.3-15). Although St. Martin was demolished, it resembled two other key pilgrimage churches: Ste. Foy at Conques (1050–1120) and St. Sernin at Toulouse (1060–1119). These were aisled basilicas, the nave roofed with tall barrel vaults and the side aisles with groin vaults. The aisles continued around the transepts. Second-story galleries, known as **tribunes**, wrapped around the nave and transept and served as places of rest for pilgrims. The designers of Conques attempted to free the nave from the heaviness of earlier barrel-vaulted churches by making the bays narrow with tall, rounded arches between the slender piers; extending ribbed arches from each pier across the nave; and punching external windows into the tribune galleries to bring daylight to the upper ranges.

RELIGION, PHILOSOPHY, FOLKLORE

The Italian Campanile

A tall bell tower, or campanile, provided the Italian answer to the minaret. Rather than using the *westwerk* (westwork) or the symmetrical twin towers of French cathedral facades, most Italian church builders placed a tall, detached campanile to one side of the church, adding a solitary figure to the skyline. During the twelfth and thirteenth centuries, these towers competed symbolically with the secular towers built by both the baronial feudal families and the new citizen republics.

The master mason Deusdedit built one of the oldest surviving campaniles at the Abbey of Pomposa in 1063. The monastery sat on an island in the Po delta, 30 km (18 miles) north of Ravenna. The builders demonstrated an empirical understanding of statics: as the tower rose 50 m (164 ft) they progressively lightened the load of its nine levels, from a single loophole arch at the bottom to four open ones at the top, before terminating in a cone.

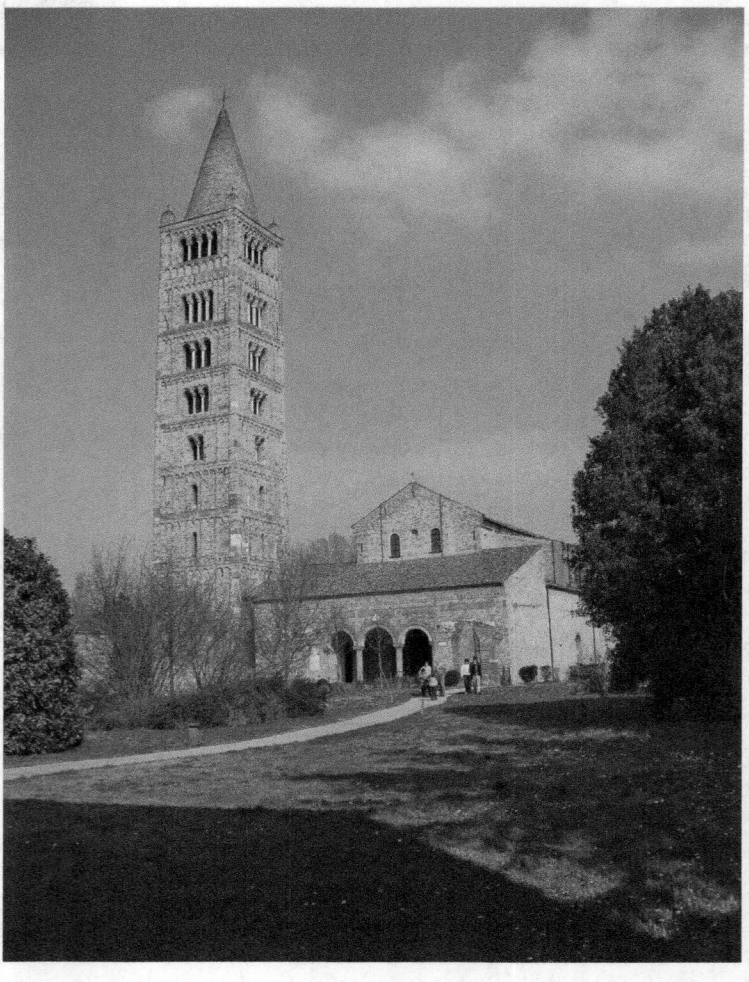

Pomposa (Italy). Abbey of Pomposa, campanile, 1063.

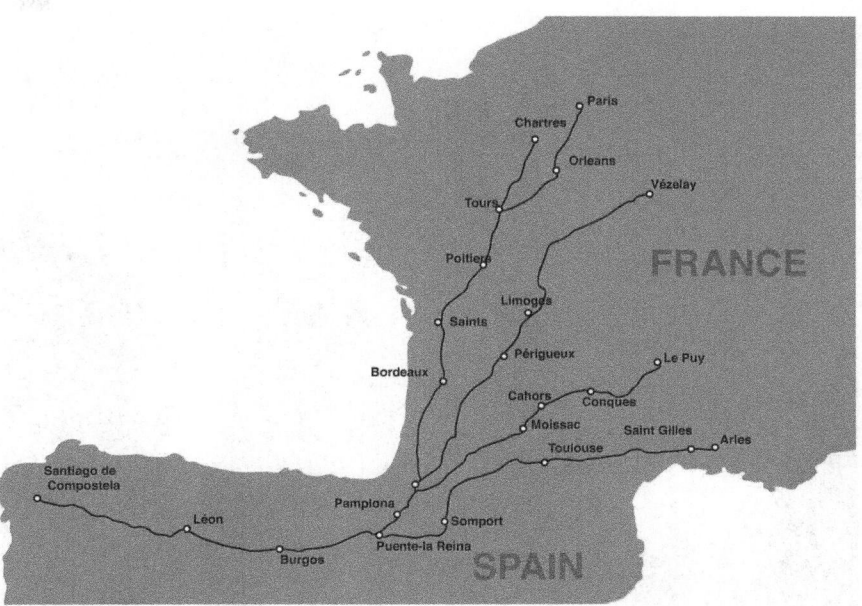

Figure 8.3-14 Western Europe. Four principal pilgrimage routes from France to Compostela, beginning in Paris, Vézelay, Le Puy, and Arles, and converging at Puente la Reina near Pamplona.

The stilted arches surrounding the choir also brought in more light and recalled Andalusian sources.

The second route, *Via Lemovicensis*, began in Burgundy, at the Cluniac abbey of Ste. Madeleine in Vézelay (1120), which housed a relic of Mary Magdalene. The alternating colors in the voussoirs of the nave recalled the *ablaq* motif of *mudéjar* builders in Spain. The name of the route came from the city of Limoges, the site of the pilgrimage church of St. Martial, now destroyed.

The third route, *Via Podiensis*, took its name from its starting point at the hill town of Le Puy, south of Lyon, where the sanctuary of St. Michel d'Aiguilhe (Fig. 8.3-16) perched miraculously atop a conical lava outcrop overlooking the city. It rose 85 m (279 ft) on a natural pedestal, slightly higher than its contemporary, the pyramid of Rajarajesvaram in southern India. The major church on this route was Ste. Foy at Conques.

The final, southern route, *Via Tolosana*, departed from Arles at the church of St. Trophime (ca. 1170) (Fig. 8.3-17) and nearby St.-Gilles-du-Gard (ca. 1170). Both of these abbey churches had partially finished facades that seemed cribbed from Roman triumphal arches. The route passed through Toulouse to the church of St. Sernin, where a soaring octagonal spire over the crossing beckoned the pilgrims. The three northern routes converged at a point in

the Pyrenees known as St.-Jean-Pied-de-Port, just before entering into Spanish territory. Here, the weary pilgrims planted the wooden crosses they had been carrying on the Calvary-like hill.

Once in Spain, the pilgrims enjoyed the luxury of the Camino Francés (the "French highway"), a new roadway sponsored by Alfonso VI at the end of the eleventh century. Just beyond Pamplona, at the new town known as Puente la Reina, the fourth itinerary joined the other pilgrim trails at a bridge built in the early twelfth century by Queen Urraca (r. 1109–1126), daughter and successor of Alfonso VI. This magnificent five-arched stone structure over the Arga River came to a gentle apex at its center and had hollow relieving arches over its piers (Fig. 8.3-18). From this point the route continued another 300 km (186 miles) to Compostela.

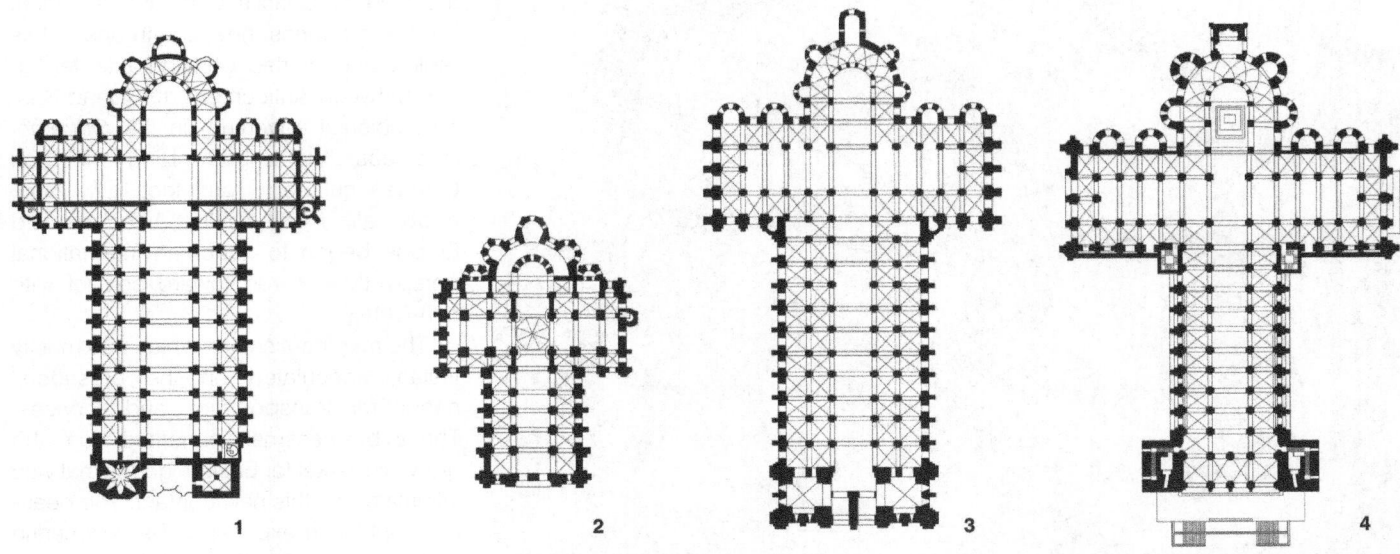

Figure 8.3-15 Western Europe. Principal pilgrimage churches, eleventh to twelfth century: (1) Tours, St. Martin; (2) Conques, Ste. Foye; (3) Toulouse, St. Sernin; (4) Compostela, Santiago. All four churches repeated Cluny's barrel-vault nave and chevet with radiating chapels.

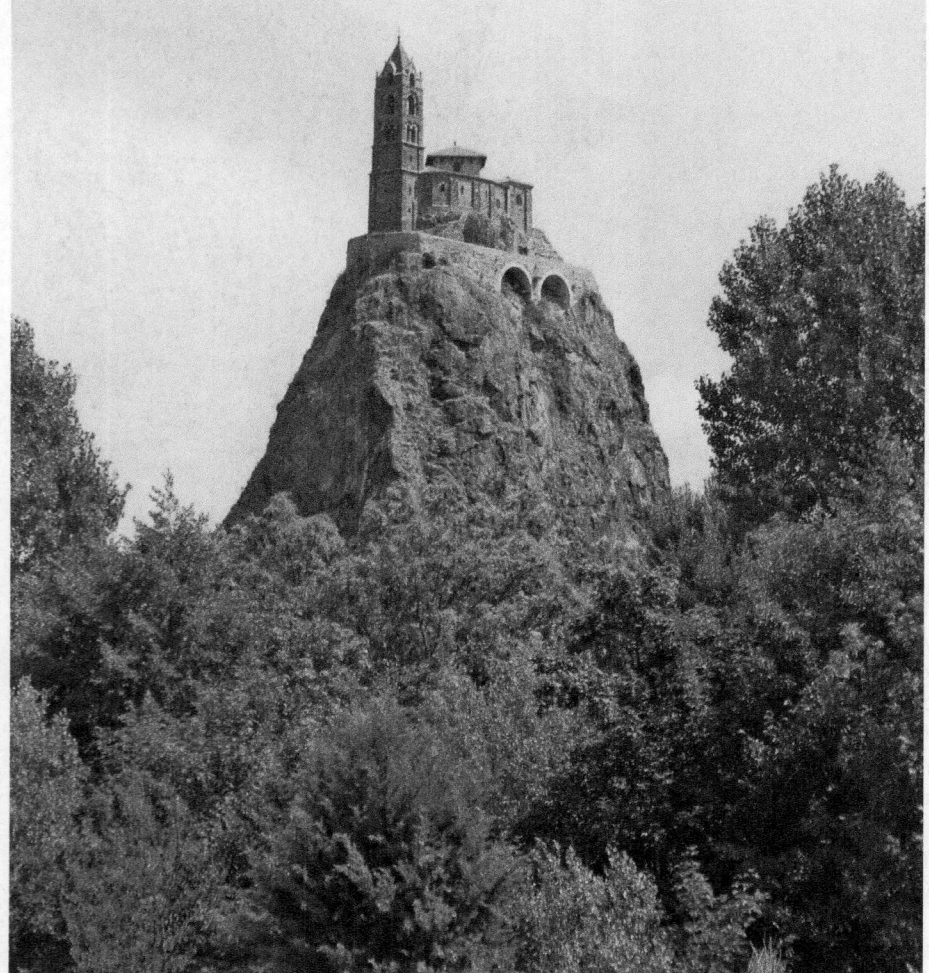

Figure 8.3-16 Le Puy, France. St. Michel Aiguilhe, tenth century.

In Compostela pilgrims were welcomed at the Portico de la Gloria, the major western entrance, finished in 1180, which repeated the familiar icon that had motivated their journey, Christ at the Last Judgment, accompanied by the twenty-four elders of the Apocalypse arranged radially on the tympanum's edge like voussoirs. An octagonal tower above the crossing brought diffused light to the center of the church, illuminating a gilt and jeweled statue of St. James and the high altar over the reliquary in the crypt. Having reached the goal of their months-long journey, pilgrims approached the statue from the rear of the altar, to embrace it and place on the saint's head their own hats decorated with a scallop shell, the symbol of St. James, found on the Atlantic beaches.

The Crusades: The Architectural Consequences of Christianity's Holy War

The protection of Christian pilgrims traveling to Jerusalem became one of the motives for launching the Crusades at the end of the eleventh century. Under papal and royal supervision, bands of feudal lords, mostly of French or Norman origin, invaded Syria and Palestine to reclaim the land of Christ's birth and sacrifice. For two centuries they sent troops to this region and settled considerable territories between Antioch and the Dead Sea. This colonial adventure in the *Outremer* (overseas) had a galvanizing effect on Europe—culturally, architecturally, and, above all, ideologically. A fragmented Europe began to adopt an international perspective geared toward conflict with non-Christians.

The merchant sector, which was mostly Italian, speculated on the crusaders' needs for transportation and services. These businessmen benefited from the growing market for Eastern goods that was stimulated by this new contact. The peasant population experienced a new sense of freedom as participants in the colonizing process. The technology of castle building improved through the encounter

Figure 8.3-17 Arles, France. St. Trophime, 1100.

Figure 8.3-18 **Puente la Reina, Spain. Bridge built by Queen Urraca over Arga River, 1120.**

between East and West, and the design of European castles changed radically from the tall, rectangular keeps seen in places such as Loches (1040s) to the concentric layout with rounded **battlements** seen in such structures as the thirteenth-century walls of Carcassonne (see Section 9.2).

The ideology of the Crusades originated with Pope Gregory VII (r. 1073–1085) and Pope Urban II (r. 1088–1099), both of whom had strong connections to the Abbey of Cluny. They promoted a unitary vision of "Christendom," proposing that Christian warriors stop killing each other and turn their strength toward the enemies of the church. Muslims had controlled Jerusalem for over four centuries but permitted a steady flow of pilgrims to travel to Palestine relatively undisturbed throughout the eleventh century. There was nonetheless always the threat of Arab, or even Byzantine, hostilities. In 1009 al-Hakim, known as the "mad sultan" of Cairo, vindictively destroyed the Church of the Holy Sepulchre.

Urban II brought European leaders to Clermont in 1095 to discuss the "liberation" of Jerusalem. The leaders proposed an invasion as a form of pilgrimage, promising its participants that "sins will be forgiven for those who fight." Many of these Christian soldiers believed that if they died

in the process, they would be considered martyrs, the one certain method to get to heaven. Like the first Christian army of Constantine, the crusaders sewed the emblem of the cross onto their clothes and shields. In 1097 a force numbering perhaps 100,000 mustered in Constantinople to move toward Palestine.

When the crusaders finally took Jerusalem in 1099, they massacred the entire population of Jews and Arabs. Contrary to the pope's plan of installing a bishop to rule the city, they set up a secular kingdom, which soon broke into four feudal states. The new European overlords constructed over fifty castles to control the region. They hoisted a golden cross over the Dome of the Rock, now called the Temple of the Lord. A new monastic order, the Templars, who combined monastic oaths with service as fighting knights, occupied the al-Aqsa Mosque in 1118. They took their name from the site's association with the Temple of Solomon.

While the earliest castles built by the crusaders resembled the tall, stone keeps of Normandy and England, later designs showed signs of ballistic innovation. The crusaders built the castles of Saone, Margat, and Krak des Chevaliers (Fig. 8.3-19) near Aleppo in Syria with prominent round

Figure 8.3-19 Syria. Krak des Chevaliers, built for the monk-knights of the Hospitallers order, ca. 1140.

bastions, sloped *glacis* embankments, and concentric successions of battlements. While round bastions had appeared on ancient Roman walls and were visible in the ninth-century desert palaces built by the Umayyads, they remained quite rare in Europe. They had the advantage of eliminating the dead zones that hid attackers from the view of the defense.

The Hospitallers order, competitors of the Templars, founded Krak des Chevaliers in 1142 and improved it in the early thirteenth century. The stonework of its bastions, perhaps the work of Armenian masons, seemed to be assembled without mortar. The entry recalled Mycenaean fortifications: one had to climb a 200 m (656 ft) dog-leg ramp controlled by "murder holes" to reach it. The builders set off the inner fortress with a slippery stone *glacis* on the south and the west. The great vaulted substructures of Krak des Chevaliers served as enormous storehouses, capacious enough that 2,000 occupants could withstand a siege for over a year. The monks rebuilt the formal hall and its portico around 1200 with Norman-style ribbed groin vaults and delicate biforium windows—in strong contrast to the otherwise stark volumes of the fortress. It proved so effective that Saladin, the warrior from Cairo who regained Jerusalem for Islam in 1189, refused to attack it. Despite the declining fortunes of the crusader states during the thirteenth century, the Hospitaller brotherhood held on to it until 1271.

Norman Sicily subsequently passed into the hands of the Holy Roman emperor Henry VI through his marriage

to the Norman queen, and then to their son Frederick II (r. 1220–1250), who maintained the title of Holy Roman emperor and through his second marriage also became king of Jerusalem. By all accounts he was an extraordinary ruler, fluent in Arabic as well as Latin and Greek and educated enough to write a treatise on falconry. Like Charlemagne, he understood that the patronage of architecture was essential to maintaining an empire. Frederick II had a geographic vision behind his version of *renovatio*, one that aimed to reconstitute the Roman Empire in the Mediterranean.

The geometric rigor of Frederick II's fortresses in Sicily and Puglia was without equal. His architects built his principal residence at Lucera with a perfect square keep in an octagonal courtyard, set off by a steeply battered, two-story **glacis**. In Prato in 1238 he commissioned the Imperial Palace (Fig. 8.3-20) at the base of the mountain pass where imperial goods and soldiers arrived from the north. His architects made the castle perfectly square, with four corner towers and a tower at the midpoint of each wall, and lined the walls with Ghibelline **merlons**, **crenellations** with a cleft, which became an emblem of imperial allegiance. The design served more as a statement of imperial power to frighten the nearby Florentines than as a working fortress.

In Puglia, at the southeastern tip of Italy, Frederick II left the enigmatic Castel del Monte (Fig. 8.3-21a), set on a knoll overlooking the plains between Lucera and Bari. It appeared like a gigantic crown, an octagonal prism

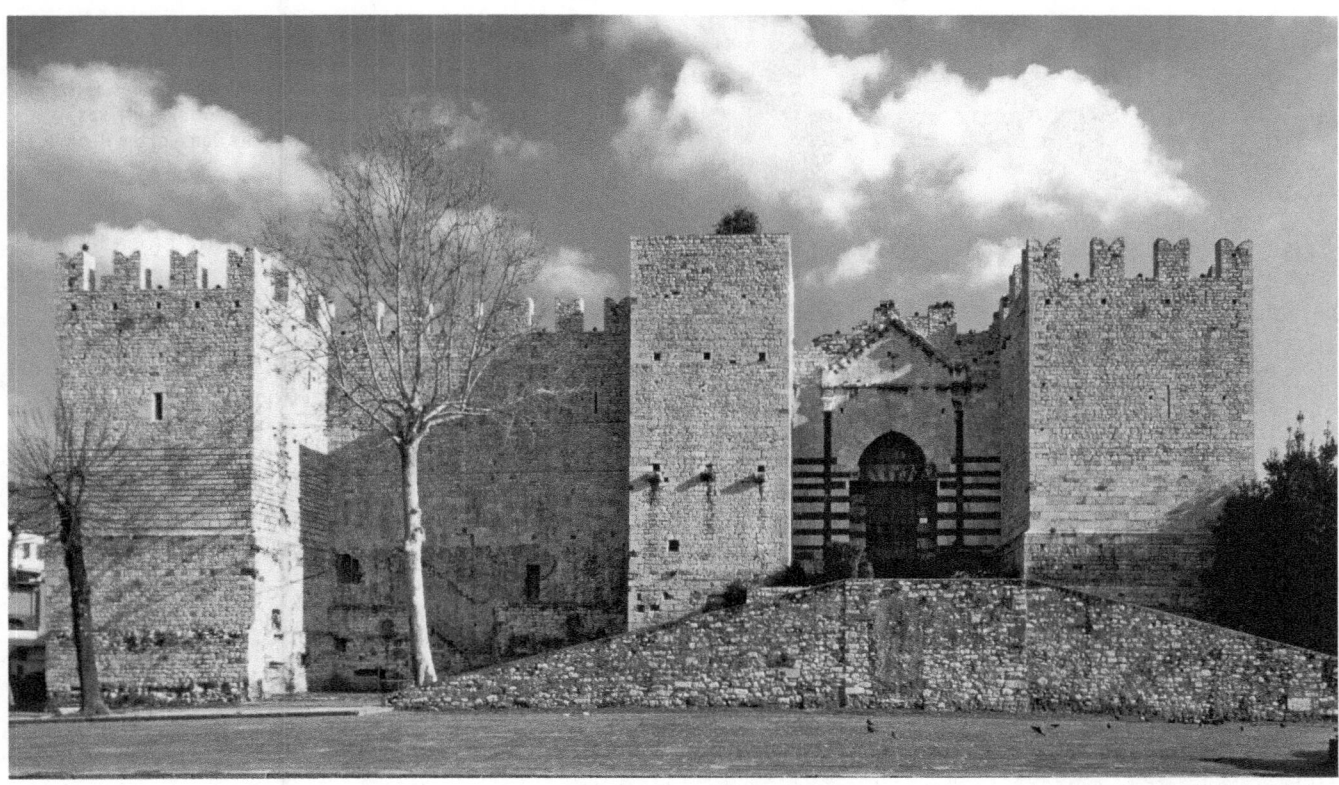

Figure 8.3-20 Prato, Italy. View of castle built for Frederick II, showing Ghibelline merlons, crenellations with a cleft, 1238.

Figure 8.3-21 Puglia, Italy. (a) Castel del Monte, 1240–1250. (b) See next page.

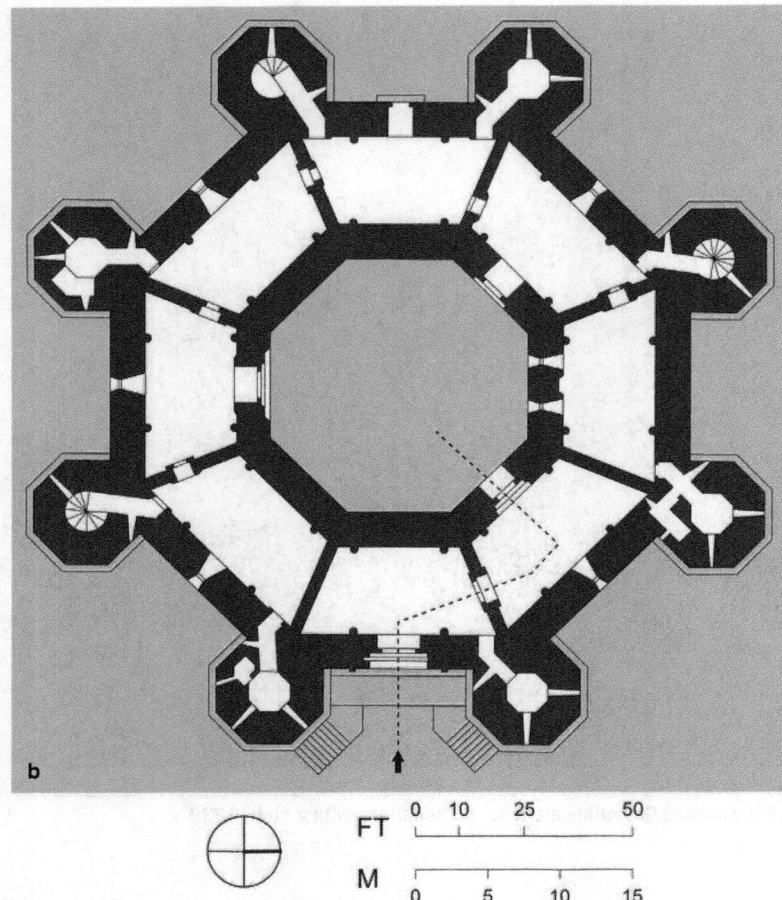

b

FT 0   10   25   50

M   0   5   10   15

Figure 8.3-21 Puglia, Italy. (b) Plan of Castel del Monte. More of a pleasure palace than a fortress, the entry recalled the indirect approaches of Islamic palaces. The octagon of the central court was nearly identical in size to the Dome of the Rock in Jerusalem.

central-plan churches built by crusader organizations. Frederick II's synthesis of religious and secular forms at Castel del Monte resulted in the highest expression of the idealism that began with Charlemagne for the revival of the grandeur of imperial Rome.

Further Reading

Barber, Malcolm. *The Two Cities: Medieval Europe, 1050–1320*. London: Routledge, 1992.

Braunfels, Wolfgang. *Monasteries of Western Europe: The Architecture of the Orders*. London: Thames & Hudson, 1972.

Calkins, Robert. *Medieval Architecture in Western Europe*. New York: Oxford University Press, 1998.

Clapman, A. W. *Romanesque Architecture in Western Europe*. Oxford: Clarendon Press, 1936.

Conant, Kenneth John. *Carolingian and Romanesque Architecture, 800–1200*. London: Penguin, 1959.

Duby, Georges. *The Age of the Cathedrals: Art and Society, 980–1420*. Translated by E. Levieux and B. Thompson. Chicago: University of Chicago Press, 1981.

———, ed. *A History of Private Life: Revelations of the Medieval World*, vol. 2. Cambridge, MA: Harvard University Press, 1988.

Kennedy, Hugh. *Crusader Castles*. Cambridge, UK: Cambridge University Press, 1994.

McLean, Alick. "Romanesque Architecture in Italy." In *Romanesque Architecture, Sculpture, Painting*, edited by R. Tolman. Cologne, Germany: Konemann, 1997.

Stalley, Roger. *Early Medieval Architecture*. New York: Oxford University Press, 1999.

↗ Visit the free website **www.oup.com/us/ingersoll** to view chapter outlines and study questions; Google Maps showing the location of key sites; links to UNESCO World Heritage Sites; and essays on topics that cross time and culture.

with octagonal towers at each corner. Like Hadrian's island retreat at Tivoli or the Lions' Court in the Alhambra, Frederick's castle transcended all functional programs to project the patron's worldview. No one had attempted a secular building in Europe on this scale and with this sophistication of geometry since the time of Hadrian. The castle's footprint covered about the same area as the Pantheon, although the more direct influence on its design surely came from the octagonal form of the Dome of the Rock in Jerusalem. The diameter of the courtyard of Castel del Monte was nearly identical to that of the dome. Like an Arabic house, the architects designed the entry with an indirect approach: from the **portal** one turned to the right and passed through another room before gaining the court (Fig. 8.3-21b). The octagon recalled religious typologies, such as baptisteries, Charlemagne's chapel, or the

1200–1350

CHAPTER 9

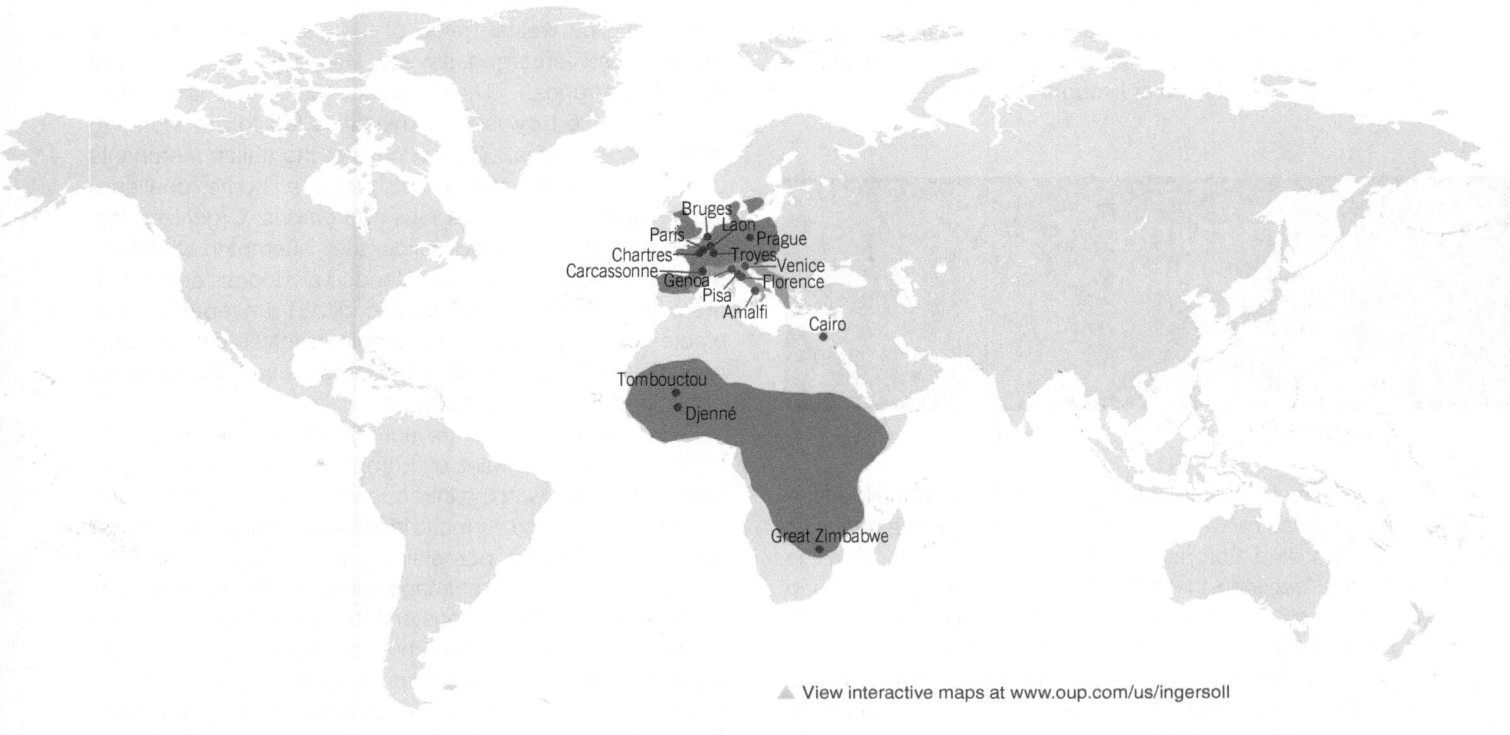

▲ View interactive maps at www.oup.com/us/ingersoll

9.1 THE MERCANTILE MEDITERRANEAN: New Facades for Old Cities

9.2 GOTHIC EUROPE: The Fabric of the Great Cathedrals

9.3 SUB-SAHARAN AFRICA: Living Architecture

After the year 1000, European cities began to show new cultural vigor and rapid population growth. The maritime republics in Italy initiated fluid trade relations across the Mediterranean with Byzantine and Islamic ports. The Champagne fairs centered around Troyes (France) in the twelfth and thirteenth centuries opened exchanges between northern and southern cities. While Italy hosted the largest number of merchant republics, cities such as Valencia and Barcelona (Spain), Bruges and Ghent (Belgium), Hamburg and Lübeck (Germany), and Novgorod and Pskov (Russia) also claimed autonomy from monarchical authority. Fanciful domes and slender towers began to sprout up in the cities around the Mediterranean, in both Islamic and Christian contexts, as did luxurious marble cladding in alternating bands of color. Every European city-state invested in a grand religious structure, such as the cathedral of Pisa, and sponsored prominent municipal buildings, such as the Belfry at Bruges, to represent civic well-being. As the French state consolidated in the Île-de-France region surrounding Paris, its king encouraged the Gothic style pioneered at the royal abbey of St. Denis. This style spread to the cities surrounding Paris, such as Chartres. Using pointed arches, ribbed vaults, and flying buttresses, the builders of Gothic cathedrals achieved scaffold-like masonry structures that allowed modulated light to become the protagonist of vast interiors. As designers and masons migrated to building sites around

Europe, they brought with them the new Gothic style, which lost its nationalistic connotations and blended into the local styles. Only traders in North African cities were aware of the rich architectural culture south of the Sahel (the Sahara Desert) in such cities as Axum, Tombouctou, and Djenné. Africans built exclusively with mud, which meant that their architecture required restoration every year after the rains. By the late fifteenth century the European interest in Africa, however, had found a new focus: the traffic of human slaves exported to the colonies or brought to Europe.

9.1 THE MERCANTILE MEDITERRANEAN
New Facades for Old Cities

The revival of international shipping around the Mediterranean between the eleventh and thirteenth centuries boosted European well-being. The profits from the exchange between the large eastern markets of Cairo and Constantinople and traders from the Italian maritime republics of Amalfi, Pisa, Genoa, and Venice helped finance new monumental expressions on both sides of the sea. While scores of stilted domes rose above the skyline of Cairo, Italian cities added magnificent marble facades to their cathedrals.

By the end of the eleventh century the new power of the Italian merchant class in Venice and other cities north of Rome had generated citizen-led governments. The nascent republics established complex bureaucracies and juridical institutions, improving the quality of both public space and citizens' rights. During the mid-thirteenth century they introduced an unprecedented building type, the public **palace**, to represent the collective interests of the republic. The autonomous city-states invested in infrastructure, churches, and civic buildings, resulting in such purposefully shaped public spaces as Piazza San Marco in Venice and Piazza del Campo in Siena. The merchant ruling class promoted the ideal of civic beauty as part of its program to maintain the freedom of the citizens against the oppression of tyranny.

Italian Maritime Republics: The Taste for Marble Facades

Around the year 1000 four Italian ports—Amalfi, Pisa, and Genoa on the western side of the peninsula and Venice on the east—emerged as key shipping powers around the Mediterranean. Their contact with Byzantine cities and ports ruled by Islamic dynasties led to the founding of trading "colonies." The success of the Italian merchants abroad greatly enhanced their status at home, challenging the feudal order of bishops and barons. Organized into democratically managed guilds, they attempted to defend themselves against the rule of landed aristocrats and the hierarchy of the church by founding citizen-run republics with elected officials. The merchant regimes fostered a new civic consciousness, which led to the construction of impressive public and religious monuments.

This contact with lands across the Mediterranean affected the development of European taste. That of food literally changed with the introduction of spices such as cinnamon, ginger, and turmeric from Asia, while the decoration of imported silks, porcelains, and jewelry stimulated the artistic and architectural imaginations. At the beginning of the second millennium Constantinople, Córdoba, and Cairo prevailed as the largest and most culturally advanced cities in the Mediterranean, providing formal models for the Italian maritime republics. The stilted arch windows of Byzantine Constantinople reappeared on the facades along the Grand Canal in Venice. Fatimid Cairo's enthusiasm for **ablaq**, the alternating bands of contrasting colored masonry used on mosques and *madrasas*, found its way into important Italian religious works such as the twelfth-century cathedral of San Lorenzo in Genoa (Fig. 9.1-1). The North African and Andalusian cultivation of the pointed arch, interlacing arches, and ribbed vaults accompanied the transmission of other foreign tastes to Italy.

Amalfi, south of Naples, was the first Italian city to operate an important medieval port, winning trading privileges with Islamic ports of call in Sicily and along the North African coast. The tenth-century logbooks of Amalfi merchants reported activities in Marseilles, Barcelona, Kairouan, and

▼ **1050**
Florence begins Roman-style Baptistery

Normans defeat Aghlabid dynasty in Sicily and southern Italy

▲ **1060s**

▼ **1063**
Pisa begins building its cathedral

Venetians begin palatine church of San Marco

▲ **1063**

Alexandria. The Normans curtailed Amalfi's independence in the late eleventh century in order to dominate the south of Italy.

Amalfi's decline accompanied the rise of Pisa (Fig. 9.1-2), which had allied itself with the Normans, participating in the sack of Muslim-ruled Palermo in 1063. Pisa remained distant enough from the Norman strongholds in southern Italy to elude their sphere of political control. In 1085, the city established a republican government, or *commune*, administered by an oligarchy of thirty wealthy families. Emperor Henry IV officially sanctioned Pisan autonomy, making Pisa one of the earliest independent city-states in Italy. A decade later the city's fortunes soared when it played a key role in the transport and supply of the First Crusade in 1096–1100. The new wealth from this colonial endeavor financed the construction of Pisa's new cathedral, baptistery, and campanile.

The Italian name for a cathedral, *duomo*, derives from the Latin *Domus Domini*, the "house of the Lord." The open, grassy setting for Pisa's duomo complex proved unusual (Fig. 9.1-3). This verdant **piazza** remained outside of the old city limits, away from political spaces, until it was enclosed within the northern perimeter of the new city walls in the 1150s. By the mid-thirteenth century the Pisans had added the marble-clad Campo Santo cemetery on the north side of the piazza and the long elevation of the pilgrims' hospice to the south, further defining the area as an enclosed *temenos*. Roughly 100 × 350 m (328 × 1,148 ft), it covered one-third the area of the Temple Mount in Jerusalem. The Pisans intended just such an association, having aided the establishment of the crusader kingdom of Jerusalem and having sent the Pisan archbishop to serve as the patriarch of Jerusalem during the first decade of the twelfth century. The conscious correspondence of the city to Jerusalem continued throughout the twelfth and thirteenth centuries as Pisan mariners transported soil from Palestine as ballast in their ships to be spread in their new cemetery.

Figure 9.1-1 Genoa, Italy. Cathedral of San Lorenzo, with banded masonry, twelfth century.

The Pisans gladly mixed ingredients from abroad into their duomo. An inscription on the facade from 1063 boasted of the spoils taken during the siege of Palermo, including the granite columns from the mosque of Palermo used in the new church's nave. A Byzantine master mason, Buschetto, oversaw the first decades of the building's construction. By the 1150s the dome was complete, rising from an oval plan to a section that followed the profile of a pointed arch, similar to contemporary domes in the eastern Mediterranean area. A small, bulb-like **finial** served as a cap and made the eastern inspiration explicit.

Pisa's proximity to one of the world's greatest marble quarries at Carrara benefited the exterior of the Duomo. The builders encased the elevations in marble, slipping narrow bands of dark gray stone in between the thick panels of creamy white like the *ablaq* pattern fashionable in Cairo and Damascus. They completed the facade in 1165, giving the ground level a blind arcade of uniform columns carrying arches of differing widths and curvatures. The four upper-level **galleries** stood detached from the wall, creating a kinetic play of light and shade (Fig. 9.1-4). Sculpted waves lined the profile of the roof, hinting at the maritime source of the city's wealth. The multitude of columns recalled the *scenae frons* of ancient Roman theaters (see Section 5.1).

▼ **1085**

Pisa establishes republican commune for oligarchical rule

Doge Sebastiano Ziani expands Piazza San Marco and starts the Arsenal in Venice

▲ **1170s**

▼ **1172–1440**

Palazzo della Ragione built in Padua, Italy

Saladin builds Citadel of Cairo

▲ **1176**

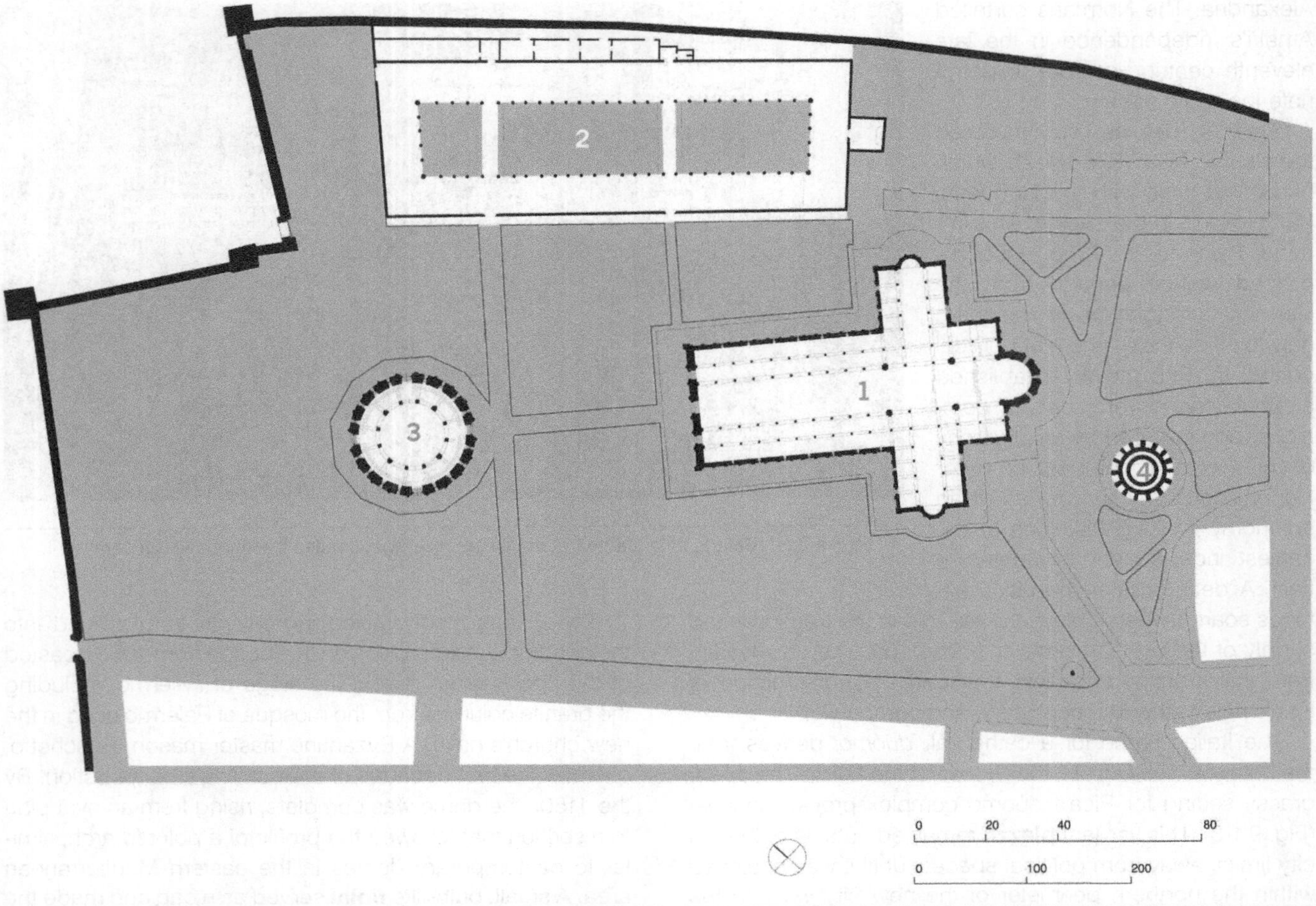

Figure 9.1-2 Pisa, Italy. Plan of Piazza del Duomo, eleventh to thirteen century: (1) cathedral; (2) Campo Santo; (3) baptistery; (4) campanile.

Cathedral facades indeed served as the theatrical backdrop for Passion plays, ceremonies of justice, and pilgrims' rituals.

The Pisan baptistery, begun in 1182 by the master builder Diotisalvi, stood in axial alignment with the central portal of the Duomo. It made clear reference to the Anastasis in Jerusalem (see Section 6.2), and Diotisalvi's successors even copied the strange conical dome that had been added to the Holy Sepulchre during the mid-twelfth century. The outer rounded dome added a few generations later partially concealed this uncommon profile. Like the cathedral's facade, the baptistery carried a girdle of marble arcades. The sculptor Nicola Pisano (ca. 1220–1285) and

his son Giovanni (ca. 1250–1315) completed the two upper registers, working from 1265 well into the next century, alternating slender floriated pinnacles with steeply pitched pediments to frame busts of the saints (Fig. 9.1-5). This brittle tracery resembled finely worked embroidery.

Behind the Duomo, the campanile, or Leaning Tower of Pisa, revealed the structural problems of the city's marshy soil. The tower's unitary mass led to subsidence. This problem seems to have prefigured Pisa's decline as a major naval power toward the end of the thirteenth century. The fall of the crusaders' kingdoms blocked access to the markets of the East, while closer to home Genoa prevailed over

▼ **1187**

Saladin regains most of the crusader kingdom of Jerusalem

Fourth Crusade, on the advice of Venetians, takes Constantinople

▲ **1204**

▼ **1215**

Palazzo del Broletto, public palace, built in Como, Italy

Death of St. Francis of Assisi

▲ **1226**

CONSTRUCTION, TECHNOLOGY, THEORY

Amalfi and the Diffusion of the Pointed Arch

Amalfi's contacts with North African cities inspired the use of *ablaq* and pointed arches on the eleventh-century facade of the city's cathedral (replaced in the nineteenth century, leaving only the belfry from the original structure). Amalfi's pointed arches were

contemporary with the rebuilding of the nearby convent of St. Benedict at Monte Cassino (rebuilt in 1066, but destroyed in World War II), which in turn informed the designers of Cluny III (begun in 1088) (see Section 8.3). The cathedral's stunning cloister of San Andrea, rebuilt in the 1260s, displays one of the most complex uses of interlacing arches in Christian architecture: they crisscross, each arch stretching over three sets of columns to be intersected in six places. The residual gaps between each pair of slender, bone-like columns leave lancet-like pointed apertures.

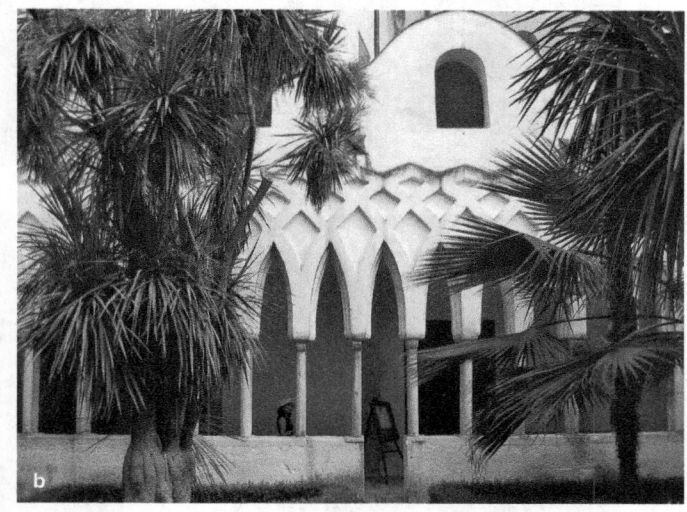

Amalfi, Italy. (a) View of cathedral, eleventh century, with facade rebuilt during nineteenth century. (b) Detail of cloister with interlacing arches, twelfth century.

Pisa in the naval skirmishes of the 1280s. The last significant expression of Pisan patronage came with the tiny chapel of Sta. Maria della Spina (Fig. 9.1-6), located on the banks of the Arno River. Constructed in 1323 as a votive shrine for a thorn from Christ's crown, it reprised many of the details of

the baptistery, introducing even steeper pitches to the pediments and pinnacles in a design appropriate to the spiky relic it housed.

Pisa's greatest threat came not from the sea but from Florence, 70 km (44 miles) upstream. The Florentines competed

1250 Shagar al-Durr, widow of al-Salih Ayyub, rules Egypt for ten months

Genghis Khan destroys Baghdad **1258**

1280s Genoa defeats Pisa at sea

Mamluk sultan Qalawun builds madrasa and tomb with dome in Cairo **1284**

1297–1330 *Noveschi Council of Siena sponsors new public palace and Piazza del Campo*

Figure 9.1-3 Pisa, Italy. View of Piazza del Duomo from the south, with baptistery on the far left, eleventh to thirteenth century.

Figure 9.1-4 Pisa, Italy. Facade of Duomo with four levels of galleries, 1064–1150.

with the Pisans militarily and culturally and eventually acquired Pisa in the early fifteenth century. Florence pursued a different style for its churches, more planar and more chromatic. At San Miniato al Monte, a Benedictine abbey begun in 1018 on a hill overlooking the city, the facade followed a flattened, geometrical scheme (Fig. 9.1-7). The designers alternated green and white marble panels in the compartments of a lower blind arcade and an upper temple front. The elevation seemed almost as well proportioned as a classical temple, but on closer inspection it harbored eccentric flaws that contradicted the rules of classicism. The corners of the entablature of the top story bent down at right

Florentine republic builds public palace (now Palazzo Vecchio)

▲ **1299–1330**

▼ **1347–1348**

Black Death spreads from China to the Mediterranean

Al-Nasi Hasan builds last, and grandest, Mamluk madrasa–tomb complex in Cairo

▲ **1356**

▼ **1430**

Ca' d'Oro built by Contarini family on Grand Canal in Venice

Figure 9.1-5 Pisa, Italy. Baptistery, detail of upper decorations by Nicola and Giovanni Pisano, mid-thirteenth century.

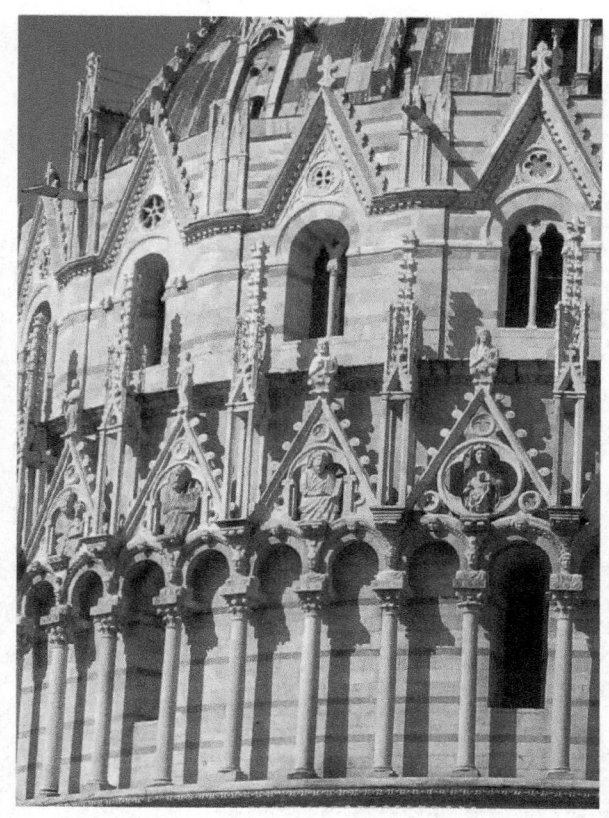

angles and extended a few centimeters to meet the capitals of the Roman-inspired fluted pilasters, while grotesque human figures supported the pediment at either end.

Florence began its major church, the Baptistery of San Giovanni, during the same years that Pisa began its duomo. Pope Nicholas II consecrated the domed structure in 1059, the rectangular apse and lantern were added during the next century, and Arnolfo di Cambio contributed the banded piers in the late thirteenth century. Taking inspiration from the Pantheon in Rome, the Baptistery's walls rose as a thick, hollowed-out base to support a double-shelled dome (Fig. 9.1-8a). Each facet of the octagon concealed four internal buttresses, 3.5 m (11 ft) deep. The leaves of its prismatic roof, clad with flat white marble panels, sloped straight instead of following the curve of the interior dome. The dome had a pointed profile, made from intersecting segments of rounded arches. It was capped with a temple-like lantern. Byzantine craftspeople taught the Florentines the art of mosaic, and local artists covered the interior of the dome with golden mosaics during the thirteenth and fourteenth centuries (Fig. 9.1-8b). Much of the exterior panel

CONSTRUCTION, TECHNOLOGY, THEORY

The Leaning Tower of Pisa

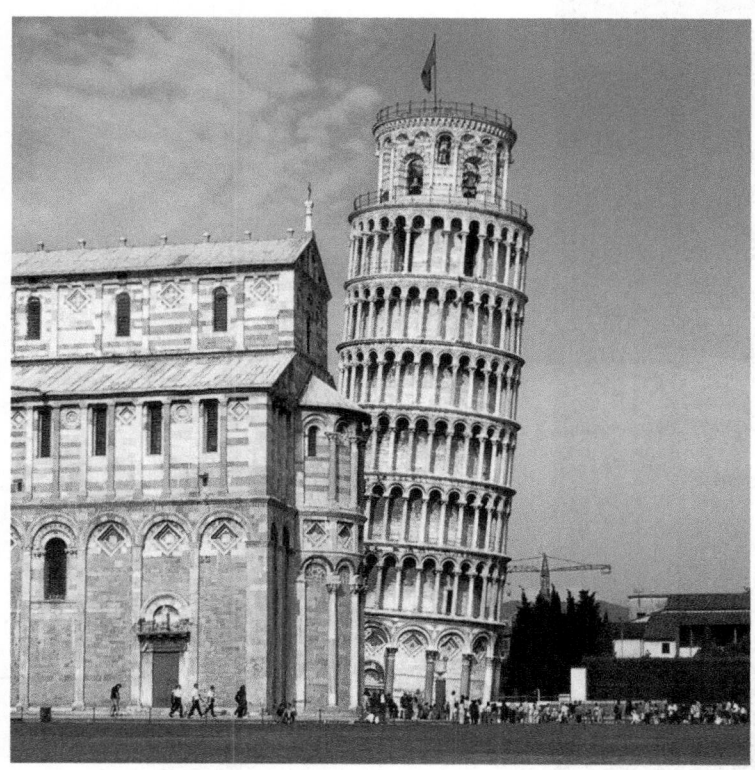

Pisa, Italy. Campanile (Leaning Tower), 1173–1350.

Berta de Bernardo, the widow of a wealthy Pisan merchant, financed the campanile of Pisa in 1173. The initial designer, Bonanno Pisano, designed its uncommon cylindrical shape as a colossal shaft. During the construction of the first three levels, the tower began to sink to the south. Work on the upper five levels resumed in 1275 under Giovanni di Simone, who attempted to compensate for the structure's tilting by giving it a slight curvature. It remained miraculously oblique, more than 4 m (13 ft) out of plumb. Although intended to extend two levels higher, the tower's construction was halted around 1350 at 55 m (180 ft).

Over the centuries the Leaning Tower continued to subside, reaching a critical point in the 1980s. From 1990 to 2001 a team led by the Polish-born Italian engineer Michele Jamiolkowski stopped the sinking by using 1,000 tons of lead counterweights as a crutch and a temporary steel-cable corset wrapped around the tower for stability. The soil conditions were too unstable to insert the planned deep anchors, and in the end the engineers consolidated a wider base, like bigger shoes, to prevent the structure from further displacement.

Figure 9.1-6 Pisa, Italy. Sta. Maria della Spina, with votive chapel set on the river, 1323. The facade borrows many of the motifs used on the dome of the baptistery.

Figure 9.1-7 Florence. San Miniato al Monte, eleventh century.

Figure 9.1-8 Florence. (a) Baptistery of San Giovanni, 1060–1170. (b) Interior of dome covered with Byzantine-style mosaics showing Christ at the Last Judgment.

work, including the classical aedicular windows, was completed in the same years. The merchant guilds oversaw the commission of the Baptistery, indicating its civic importance as a triumphal statement of Florence's power in the region.

Mamluk Cairo: A Thousand and One Domes

Cairo commanded the largest trading economy of the Mediterranean in the thirteenth century, providing the hinge between Asia and the Italian merchants. Its wealth and religious monuments became a standard against which to measure the contemporary achievement of Italian cities. The Egyptian city's fortunes advanced through three geopolitical events. First, the Christians of the Fourth Crusade in 1204, following the advice of the Venetians, invaded Constantinople instead of Palestine, further weakening the power of the Byzantine Empire. Second, the Mongolian hordes of Genghis Khan destroyed Baghdad in 1258, bringing the Abbasid caliphate to an end. And finally, during the late twelfth century the Ayyubid leader Saladin successfully regained parts of the crusader kingdoms in Palestine and Syria.

By 1300 Cairo had emerged as the greatest concentration of political and commercial power in the Mediterranean, and its population may have swelled to half a million. While hostile to Christian crusaders, the Egyptians welcomed European merchants, in particular the Venetians, whom they met at the port of Alexandria to exchange spices for slaves. The only Europeans allowed to enter Cairo were privileged traders, ambassadors, and political prisoners. Here such individuals witnessed multitudes of stilted domes and bulbous finials poking above the city's dense, sand-swept fabric. The itinerant Moroccan scholar Ibn Battuta (1304–1369) remembered such a grand vision as the "mother of cities."

Three centuries earlier the Fatimid Dynasty from Tunisia had conquered Egypt and changed the capital's name from al-Fustat to al-Qahira (the forerunner of the modern "Cairo," meaning "the Victorious"). As was common among Islamic rulers, the new regime lived in an isolated compound away from the local inhabitants. The Fatimids built their enclave 5 km (3 miles) north of the old city, in a rectangular walled area large enough for 30,000 residents (Fig. 9.1-9). The major street, the Qasba (now "Casbah"), ran straight through the middle, and two royal palaces rose in the center on either side of it. While the Fatimids permitted merchants to open shops inside the walled city, only the ruling class and its dependents could reside there. Foreign military elites lived in compounds within the walls known as *herats*, a term that eventually came to signify "neighborhood."

The Fatimids built their first great mosque, the al-Azhar, toward the end of the tenth century inside the walls near the eastern palace. It became the principal Islamic study center

Figure 9.1-9 Cairo. Map of the city, ca. 1300, showing the extension north from al–Fustat to the Fatimid compound of al–Qahira and to the east the Citadel begun by Saladin and used by the Mamluks.

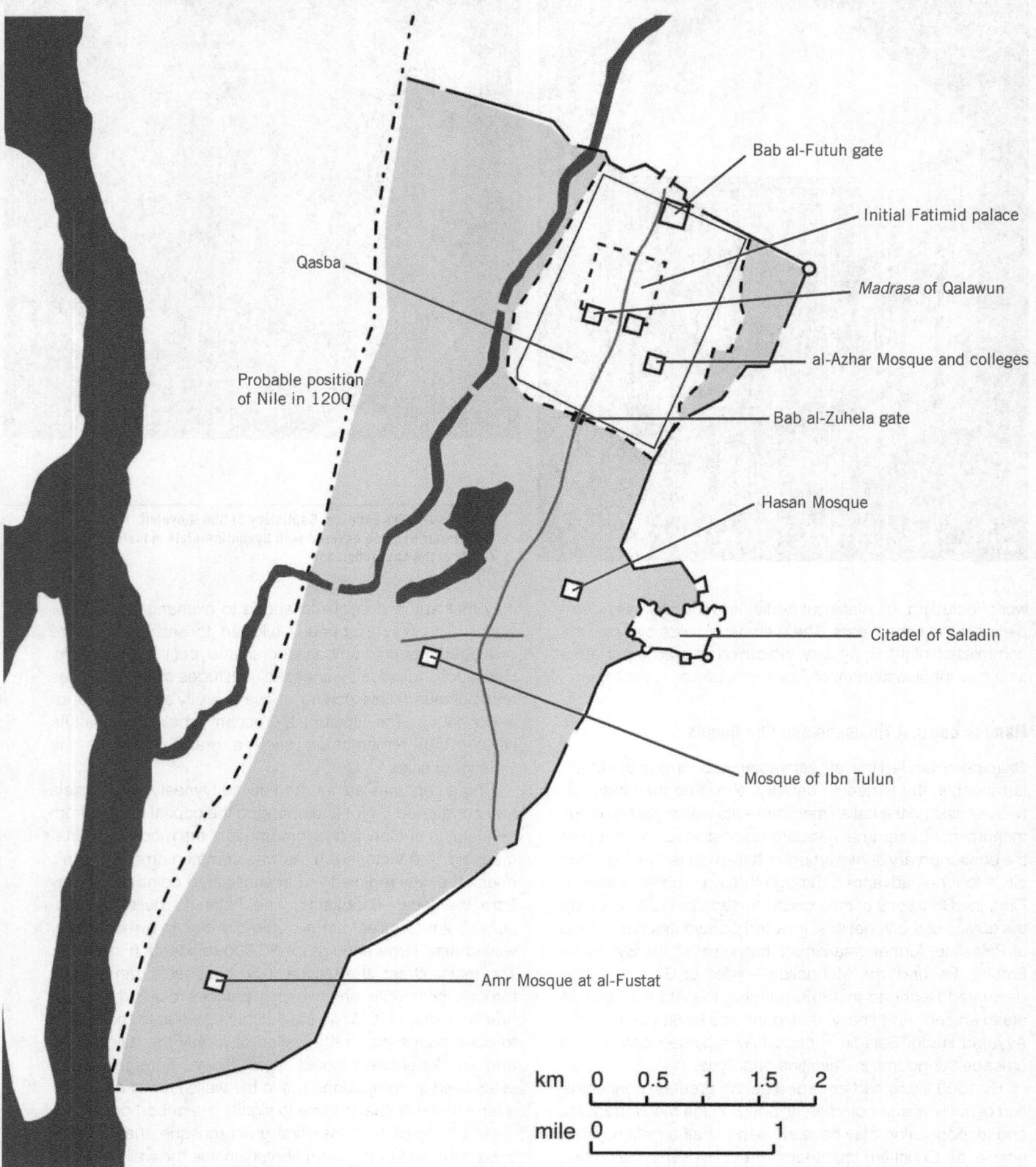

Bab al-Futuh gate

Initial Fatimid palace

Madrasa of Qalawun

Qasba

al-Azhar Mosque and colleges

Bab al-Zuhela gate

Probable position of Nile in 1200

Hasan Mosque

Citadel of Saladin

Mosque of Ibn Tulun

Amr Mosque at al-Fustat

km 0   0.5   1   1.5   2

mile 0   1

and basis of the city's university, a function it still retains. The original hypostyle interior had five rows of arches running parallel to the *qibla* wall, with three cupolas set perpendicular to them to mark a central aisle to the *mihrab*, similar to the mosque in Kairouan. Three centuries later four new rows were added behind the original *qibla* wall at a slight skew, as if seeking a more precise orientation to Mecca. Fatimid arches and niches acquired a distinct style, rising from rounded edges into a triangular apex. The builders of the al-Azhar scavenged most of the columns from ancient Roman ruins in Alexandria, capping each with a different style of Corinthian capital.

The other important Fatimid mosque begun at the end of the tenth century, the Friday Mosque of al-Hakim (r. 996–1021), sat just outside the walls of the princely city, its two minarets set atop sloping bastions. A century later, when the new walls were expanded to include the mosque, the north minaret was incorporated into them as a bastion. Adjacent to it, the graceful rounded towers of the northern gate of Bab al-Futuh displayed broad recessed arches, the "eyebrow" motif, imported by Armenian masons (Fig. 9.1-10).

Figure 9.1-10 Cairo. Bab al-Futuh, the northern gate, with eyebrow arches, ca. 1100.

During the thirteenth century Cairo became a city of domes. The trend began with a female patron, Shagar al-Durr (r. 1250–1257), wife of the last of Saladin's heirs, al-Salih Ayyub. After her husband's sudden death in 1250 during preparations to thwart the invasion of crusaders at Damietta, she secretly assumed power to avert a crisis of confidence, becoming the first woman to command a premodern Islamic state. After eighty days of rule, however, Shagar al-Durr tactfully married the chief Mamluk guard, who soon took on the role of sultan.

Mamluk literally meant "the owned." The Mamluks descended from a warrior caste of slaves originating in the Turkish steppes. The practice of enslaving non-Muslim children, converting them to Islam, and training them as an elite military guard began in Baghdad during the ninth century to eliminate conflicts of interest in the military. The Mamluks gained high esteem and reaped significant rewards for their services but were forbidden to leave their property or titles to their families. During their first century of rule in Cairo they elected each new sultan from their highest-ranking emirs to avoid succession disputes.

Cairo's first dome, built for Shagar al-Durr in the 1250s, crowned the funerary monument to her first husband, al-Salih Ayyub, set as an appendage to a *madrasa* he had commissioned. The monument inspired a series of domed mausoleums, including the sultana's own tomb. Across from al-Salih Ayyub's tomb the sultan Qalawun (r. 1279–1290) began his own tomb in 1284 as the culminating element of a *madrasa* complex (Fig. 9.1-11). Its octagonal plan may

have derived from the Dome of the Rock in Jerusalem. The section of the dome resembled the pointed-arch profile of the dome in Pisa. While formal ideas at this time usually moved from the East to the West, here the direction was reversed: the pointed arches of the biforium windows of Qalawun's mausoleum appeared remarkably like those of European cathedrals. The similarity to the windows in the crusader churches indicated the craftsmanship of conscripted Christian prisoners taken during the siege of Acre and engaged by Qalawun for his mausoleum.

Qalawun established the first hereditary succession among the Mamluks, leaving his sons, al-Ashraf Khalil (r. 1290–1293) and al-Malik an-Nasir (r. 1293–1340), to rule Cairo during its most prosperous period. Nasir built a *madrasa* next to that of his father, into which he incorporated a significant spoil from Acre: one of the doors from the Christian cathedral there (Fig. 9.1-12). His designers framed it with interlocking *ablaq* masonry to enshrine this obviously alien presence within familiar patterns. His *madrasa* borrowed its typology from Abbasid Baghdad, with four pointed-arch *iwans* placed cross-axially around an open court. Like the Normans, the Mamluks initially had no particular style of their own and thus synthesized local craft traditions with ideas taken from conquered or admired peoples. They also benefited from the expertise of those who fled the Mongolian occupation of Baghdad.

The Mamluk emirs of Cairo, unable to will their property to their families, spent their fortunes on great tombs and religious structures as memorials. Much of their wealth diffused to charitable foundations, the *waqfs*, which constructed and maintained mosques, *madrasas*, *khanqahs* (monasteries), and hospitals. Their tombs became increasingly showy, as seen in the tall, fluted cupolas of the mausoleum of the

Figure 9.1-11 Cairo. *Madrasa* and tomb of Qalawun, with windows inspired by Christian churches at St. Jean d'Acre, 1285.

emirs Salar and Sangar al-Gawli (1303) and that of Barkuk (1400), with its deep-grooved, horizontal chevrons.

The Mamluk emirs also placed domes over the great houses of Cairo. The entry to the house of Emir Taz (1352) presented a tall, recessed niche decorated with sculpted *muqarnas*. Once past the bends of the entry corridor, one came upon a longitudinal hall, known as a *qa'a*. At the Bashtak House (1336) the center section of the three-part *qa'a* space rose triple-height, capped by a clerestory-lit dome and flanked by second-level galleries screened with wooden lattices. Pointed diaphragm arches framed the two side areas. Mamluk palaces, such as that of Uthman Kathuda (1350), incorporated passive cooling devices called wind-catchers (**malqaf**), which rose like chimneys to face the prevailing northeast winds. Cool air wafted through a downward shaft in the evenings, while hot air vented out the dome's clerestories. The emirs often placed a niche, similar to a *mihrab*, on the southeast wall of the *qa'a* space, facing Mecca. Ornate wooden screens, **mashrabiyyas**,

Figure 9.1-12 Cairo. Portal into Nasir's *madrasa* taken from a crusader church in Acre, 1310.

covered exterior windows to help keep the interiors cool and served as architectural veils to shield the women of the house from public view.

Foreign traders lived in **fonduks**, in Cairo usually called *wekelas*, hotel-like compounds (Fig. 9.1-13). Unlike the houses, the entries to these hotel-like structures usually allowed a direct view into the court because of their commercial function. In the al-Ghuri *fonduk*, a six-story block built during the late fifteenth century, the first two levels under the arcades were used for business and storage, while the upper ranges contained stacks of three-story apartments with *mashrabiyyas* covering the top windows. Few European traders were allowed to visit Cairo, confined to doing business in *fonduks* in Alexandria.

Construction of the grandest Mamluk monument, the Madrasa of al-Nasir Hasan, commenced in 1356, eight years after the devastating Black Death wiped out more than one-third of the population. The young sultan came to power in 1347 at age thirteen, was shortly after deposed, and reassumed rule in 1354. By this time a council of emirs administered the government, leaving Sultan Hasan free to pursue his passion for architecture. His architect, Muhammed Balah al-Muhsini, supplemented the ruler's mosque and

mausoleum with an immense *madrasa* for over 500 students (Fig. 9.1-14a). The niche of its principal entry, a six-story hollow, stood as an independent volume rotated 15°, which accentuated the complex's exceptional height of 40 m (131 ft) (Fig. 9.1-14b). Like most of Cairo's religious monuments, the *madrasa* was designed with *ablaq* patterns, alternating courses of red and white masonry. The inner court derived from Persian models seen in thirteenth-century Baghdad before the Mongolian sack. Four colossal *iwan* vaults framed a domed fountain house in the center of the court. The *iwans* provided generous semienclosed spaces without columns or hypostyles. The four different schools of the *madrasa* and requisite housing for their students and teachers filled the four multistory corners between each of the spans of the *iwans*. Hasan's mausoleum rose behind the southeastern *iwan*, reserved for the mosque's *qibla*. The diameter of its dome equaled the diameter of the Baptistery in Florence. *Muqarnas* helped negotiate the transition from the corners of the square room to the octagonal **drum**. The parapets were lined with a perforated lily motif, also used in the interlocking voussoirs of the *mihrab*. The dome of the Hasan complex rose as the most prominent of the age and with the sheer elevations of the *madrasa* gave form to Mamluk

Figure 9.1-13 Cairo. The al-Bazar Wekela (or *fonduk*), hospice for foreign traders, ca. 1600.

The *Mashrabiyya* and the Women of the Cairene House

The Abbasids in Baghdad were the first Muslims to require the systematic seclusion of women, a rule imposed toward the end of the eighth century. Men and women were separated in mosques, as in Jewish synagogues and Byzantine churches. During the ninth century the Abbasid regime encouraged the separation of male and female areas of the house and obliged women to cover their faces with a veil.

The strictly gendered zones of the Cairene house repeated the ancient Greek tradition of the *gynaikeion* (see Section 4.2). Windows to the public street carried elaborate screened wooden boxes, or *mashrabiyya*, that jutted out to allow the sequestered women to look out onto the activity without being seen. *Mashrabiyya* also helped to cool the house and create an atmosphere of sparkling, diffused light.

Cairo. (a) View of *herat* neighborhood, with the windows of the house on the right fitted with wooden *mashrabiyya*, in the Qasbah of central Cairo.
(b) Detail of a *mashrabiyya* inside a Mamluk house, fourteenth century.

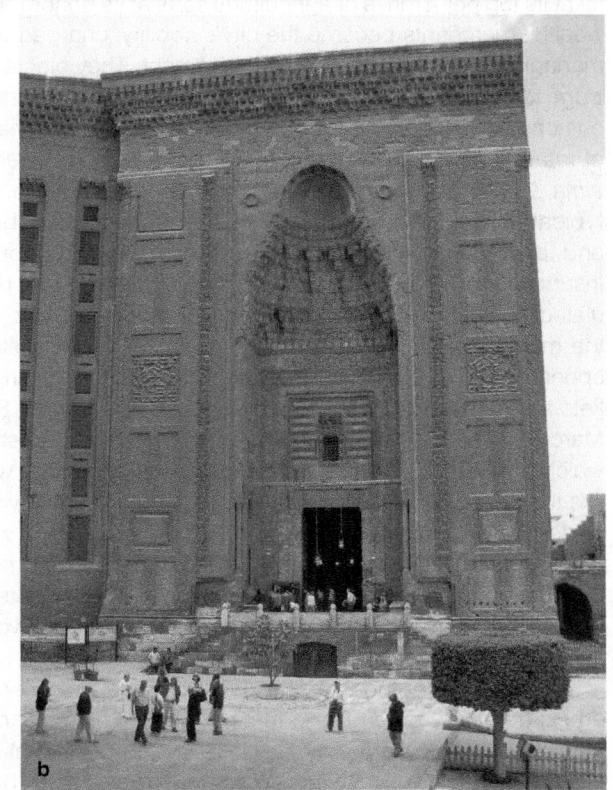

Figure 9.1-14 Cairo. (a) Hasan Mosque, with tomb and *madrasas*, 1350s. (b) Hasan Mosque, the great five-story scoop of main entry.

Cairo's major space of representation, the Rumayla. Here, the elite of the Citadel, built by Saladin, performed in festivals and polo matches against an orderly backdrop.

Venice: City without Land

Venice, a city that grew from a cluster of sixty islands in a marshy lagoon at the northern tip of the Adriatic Sea (Fig. 9.1-15), kept pace with Cairo as the greatest of the Italian maritime republics from the eleventh to the fifteenth century. Since its legendary foundation in 421 CE, the city's fortunes came from the water, first through fishing, then through piracy, and finally through trade. The Venetians created a maritime empire through special treaties with the eastern Mediterranean ports. By the fourteenth century they controlled most of the Dalmatian coast and many Aegean islands. Venice initially gained its political autonomy through its connections with the Byzantines and remained the only Italian city not aligned with the Holy Roman Empire. These connections with eastern powers explain the appearance of strong traces of Byzantine and Arabic styles in Venetian

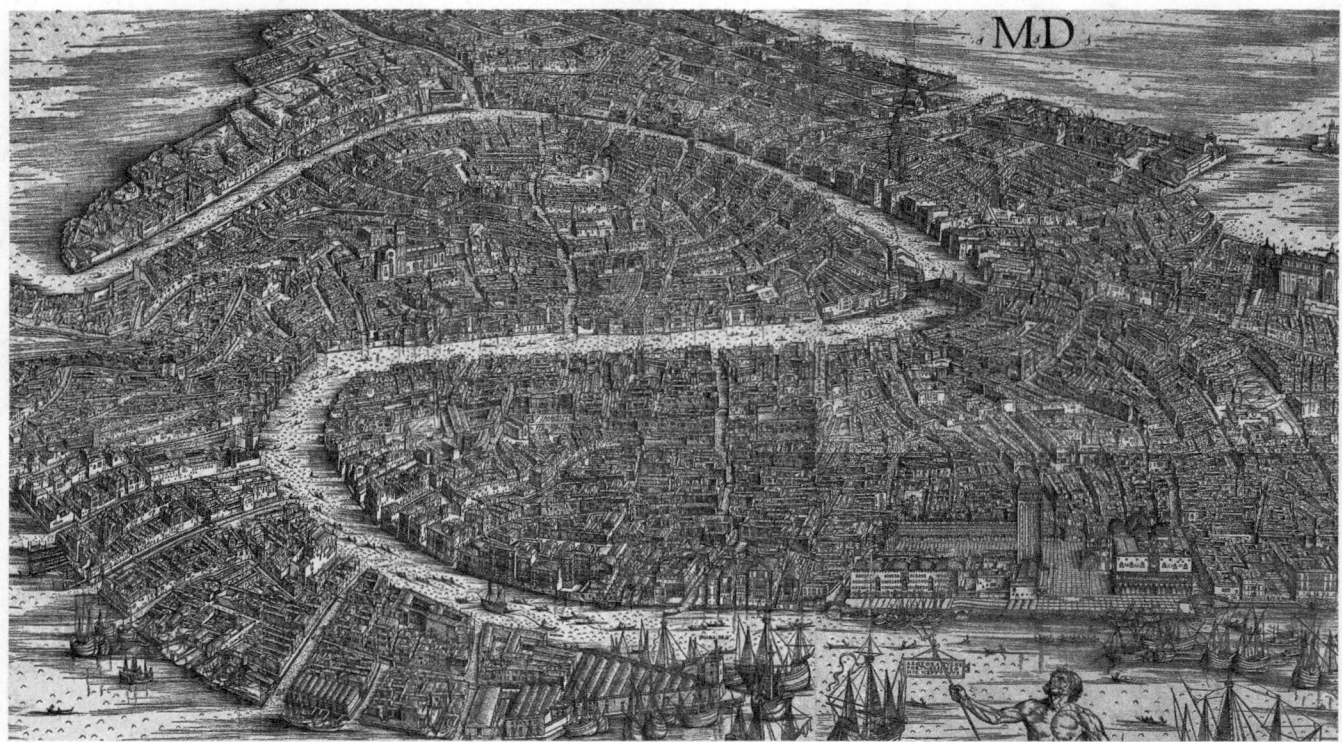

Figure 9.1-15 Venice. Jacopo Barberi's aerial view of Venice, 1500, showing the Grand Canal, the Rialto Bridge, and the Piazza San Marco.

architecture, including stilted arch windows, floriated merlons, and the *fonduk* type.

The lack of land in Venice encouraged the development of its unique class structure, which had neither a landed nobility at its top nor a mass of agricultural serfs at its bottom. The wealthy merchants became the city's nobility, charged with managing a highly democratic government. They elected a *doge* to a lifetime monarchical position but imposed numerous checks to his power through elected committees made of rotating members. Venice became known as *la Serenissima*, "the most serene," because it did not undergo the typical struggles between citizens and a land-based nobility and, after the mid-twelfth century, never witnessed popular insurrections. The state monopolies on grain and salt regulated supplies during shortages to avoid bread riots. As the most stable and long-lasting republic in Italy, the state sponsored a wide array of projects, including the Rialto markets and bridge and the civic spaces and buildings of San Marco. It also created the industrial district of the Arsenal, which employed 16,000 people. The nine procurators, who like the doge were elected to lifetime positions, oversaw the budget and programs for the *proto*, or state architect, who managed the construction of not only churches, government buildings, piazzas, and bridges, but also such elements of welfare as a state granary and housing for the retired workers of the state-managed naval operations.

Venice's small islands and network of canals resulted in an extraordinary urban fabric that had almost as many discontinuous streets as the *herats* of Cairo. The city's dual circulation on canals and streets favored those traveling by boat as the more expedient mode of transportation for goods and people. The great serpentine Grand Canal flowed through the center of the city as an exceptional public thoroughfare. At 30 m (98 ft) across, it proved wider than any street in Europe prior to the emergence of nineteenth-century boulevards, but of course it served boats only. The banks of the Grand Canal attracted the patronage of noble Venetians, who built more than 100 magnificent palaces on either side. This private investment in magnificent architecture advanced the status of the merchant families while creating a rich backdrop for the city. Ca' Loredan and Ca' Farsetti (Fig. 9.1-16), begun in the early thirteenth century, lacked any of the defensive battlements and towers found in the great houses of the rest of Italy at this time. They included more fenestration than wall, with windows raised on the stilted Byzantine arches used in Constantinople. Many of their neighbors preferred the **ogive** arch with pointed cusps common to both North African mosques and Gothic cathedrals.

Venetian merchants, many of whom learned Arabic during their travels, called their great palaces *fontego*, after the Arabic *fonduk*. While the layouts differed from the generous courts of the *fonduks* of Egypt and Syria, Venetian palaces combined commercial functions and warehouses on the ground floor and living functions above. The Venetian state sponsored a few compounds that truly imitated the Arabic type, such as the Fondaco dei Tedeschi (Fig. 9.1-17), built in 1225 as a rental property for German merchants. The state rebuilt it on the same plan in the 1520s after a fire. The structure wrapped around a large open courtyard with semi-independent apartments above.

Figure 9.1-16 Venice. Ca' Loredan and Ca' Farsetti, thirteenth-century palaces with stilted "Byzantine" arches based on palaces in Constantinople.

Many of the *fontego* palaces along the Grand Canal quoted the decorative fenestration of the Doge's Palace. These buildings belonged to noble families that either produced a doge, such as the Foscari of Ca' Foscari (1430s), or aspired to the office, such as the Contarini, who built Ca' d'Oro (1425). The palaces were accessed by boat on the canal facade and by land on the minor side elevations. Venetians loved a variety of window styles and asymmetrical placements. The palaces' exceptional quantity of windows, verging on the openness of a modern curtain wall, responded to the need to keep structures light. It also reflected the city's singular lack of concern for fortifications.

The shapers of the political center of Venice aspired to the power of Constantinople. The Doge's Palace, the palatine church of San Marco, and the elongated piazza repeated the relationship of the Byzantine imperial palace, Hagia Sophia, and the hippodrome. Doge Sebastiano Ziani (r. 1172–1178), who had spent many years as a diplomat in the Byzantine capital, replanned Piazza San Marco, doubling its length to rework it into the shape of a stadium (Fig. 9.1-18). The elevations surrounding the piazza were filled with three stories of unified, arcaded facades, similar to the exterior of Roman theatrical structures. The long buildings belonged to the procurators, who used them for their own dwellings and offices, or were rented as shops, offices, and housing. Ziani also transferred the Arsenal from the palace district to a site he owned and filled in the old shipyards to create the Piazzetta, a space analogous to the Augusteon Forum in Constantinople. The two Columns of Justice, placed where the Piazzetta opened a vista to the canal, imitated the position of the Byzantines' Milion milestone. The *L*-shaped configuration of the two piazzas provided the largest and most magnificent public space of medieval Europe, serving as a theater for civic rituals. At the juncture the builders inserted the towering campanile, as tall as the Lighthouse of Alexandria.

Figure 9.1-17 Venice. Fondaco dei Tedeschi, rebuilt by the Venetians for the German trading delegations, attributed to Girolamo Tedesco, 1508.

The Venetians undertook the rebuilding of the church of San Marco in 1063, the same year that the Pisans began their cathedral. The plan came directly from Constantine's Apostoleion in Constantinople, a quincunx composition of five domes on a central-plan Greek cross. While common in Byzantine-controlled territories, the type appeared the antithesis of Italian basilical churches. Many of the facade decorations were added in the thirteenth century after Venice emerged victorious over the Byzantines. In 1204, the Venetians convinced the leaders of the Fourth Crusade to invade Constantinople instead of Palestine, leaving Venice in control of three-eighths of Byzantine territories. Over the next eighty years Venetians brought back spoils to display on San Marco, including hundreds of ancient columns, the four bronze horses from the Hippodrome, and the porphyry statues of the Tetrarchs. Eschewing classical order they stacked the columns tightly at the five entry porches on two levels, like a merchant's stockpile. During the same years they tripled the exterior height of the domes of San Marco, adding wood-framed superstructures over the original hemispherical vaults for tall, stilted cupolas covered with sheets of lead (Fig. 9.1-19). These double-shell domes evoked both

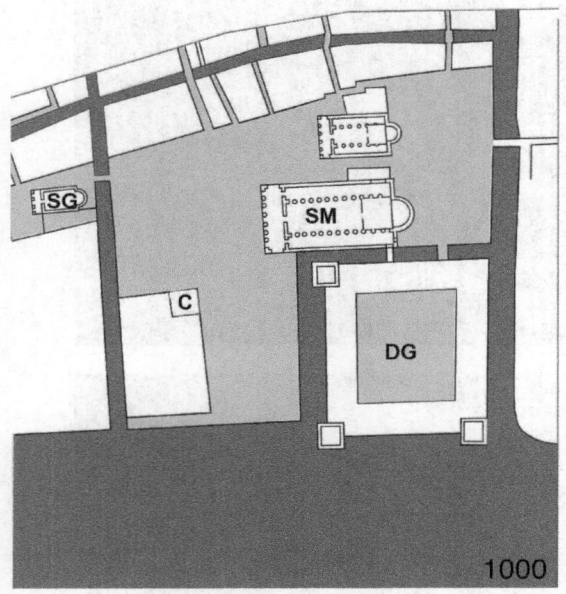

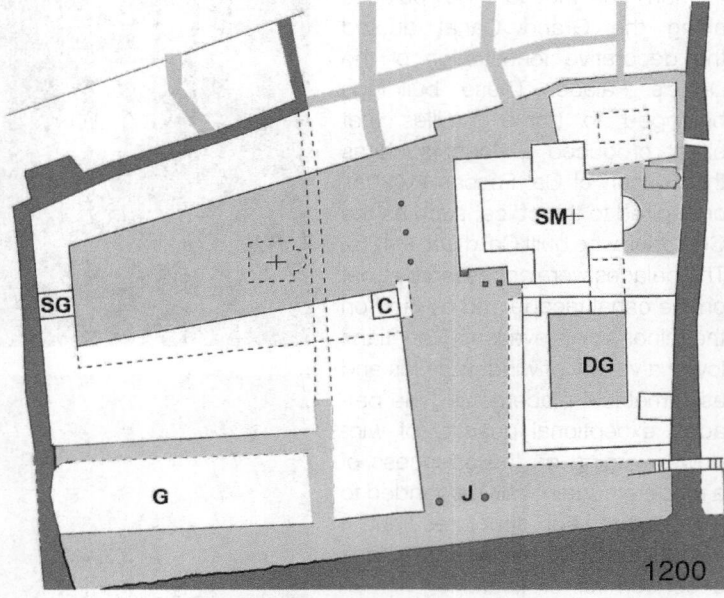

Figure 9.1-18 Venice. Transformation of the Piazza San Marco, before (left) and after (right) the late twelfth century: (SG) S. Gemignano; (SM) S. Marco; (DG) Doge's Palace; (C) campanile; (J) Columns of Justice; (G) granary.

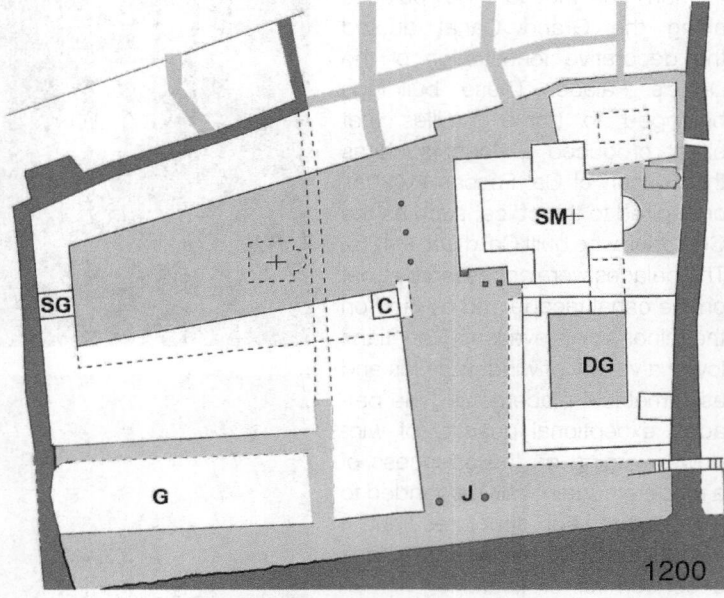

Figure 9.1-19 Venice. S. Marco, cupolas, eleventh century.

the structure of the Dome of the Rock in Jerusalem and the shapes of domes in Cairo, a source that was underlined by the use of crowning bulbous lanterns and starburst metal ornaments.

Doge Ziani also took the initiative to rebuild the Doge's Palace in the 1170s, giving it an overall cubic shape, with three wings surrounding a large open court, closed on the fourth side by the apse of San Marco (Fig. 9.1-20a). The three wings of the palace corresponded to the offices of justice on the Piazzetta side, the hall of the Great Council overlooking the water, and on the east the doge's apartments and spaces where the inner councils met. The renovation of the palace during the 1340s on the eve of the Black Death accommodated the expansion of the Great Council to 1,200 nobles. The procurators commissioned facades that conveyed the sense of grandeur, transparency, and accountability associated with republican ideology. The two public sides of the palace dissolved at their base into

two-story arcades. On the ground level the broad pointed arches rested on stout columns of different thicknesses, each with a different narrative in the capital. The second level opened to a deep loggia with twice the number of columns, now more slender and uniformly matched. From their capitals sprouted the tracery of sinuous trilobe arches and **quatrefoil roundels**, similar to the motifs used on Gothic cathedrals in northern Europe (Fig. 9.1-20b). The porous and lacy merlons lining the parapets resembled the hem of an expensive gown, closer to the floriated finials of Hasan's *madrasa* in Cairo than to the design of the fortified public palaces found on the Italian mainland. The upper two stories carried cladding of alternating white and pink blocks of marble, arranged in bold diamond patterns, almost like wallpaper. The builders punched large pointed-arch windows through these planes and, in the center of both facades, placed a grand balcony framed by slender turrets and capped with an ornate canopy sheltering the image of the

---

CONSTRUCTION, TECHNOLOGY, THEORY

The Foundations of Venice

Venetian buildings required a unique and costly foundation technology because of the lack of solid land on the marshy islands. Builders drove 3 m (10 ft) long wooden piles into the soft clay, as many as nine timbers per square meter. They covered these piles with wooden rafts and then a layer of limestone, almost like ballast at the bottom of a ship. They then laid brick curtain walls with ample fenestration on top of this to reduce the bearing loads of the exterior walls. Great palaces like Ca' d'Oro have more window than wall to maintain lightness.

Venice. (a) Venice wall. (b) Section of the foundations of a Venetian palace.

Figure 9.1-20 Venice.
(a) Doge's Palace seen
from the Piazzetta, 1170s.
(b) Detail of quatrefoil
tracery.

winged lion, symbol of St. Mark. The cathedral-like tracery of the second-level arcades suggested the sacred role of the state. It also signified a change in the direction of architectural sources as Venice began to look to the Gothic West.

The Italian Commune: Public Palaces versus Private Towers

During the Middle Ages, the cities of Italy shrank but never truly disappeared, and after the year 1000, they began a quick recovery. Over 100 cities in the northern and central regions of Italy established independent **communes**, citizen-led governments with a general council and elected officials. Although these republics often started off with the participation of the bishop and included members of the feudal nobility, the emerging merchant class eventually excluded both sectors from the government. The conflicts they encountered appeared in the skyline of a small city like San Gimignano, 30 km (18 miles) southwest of Florence, where a cluster of fourteen slender military towers represented feudal families and their fortified urban compounds (Fig. 9.1-21). The commune sponsored a city hall with a grand staircase and a bell tower taller than the other towers. This hall overlooked a paved civic piazza that it shared with the cathedral, which likewise built a tower for its **belfry**. As the Italian city-states became more prosperous, the merchant regimes forced members of the nobility to cut down

their towers to the four-story scale of the rest of the city. Talented designers focused on a new building type, the public palace, which during the twelfth to fourteenth century offered a novel secular program for architectural expression parallel to the creation of the great cathedrals.

The Palazzo del Broletto in Como, built in 1215, remains among the oldest surviving examples (Fig. 9.1-22). A two-story structure attached to the cathedral, it stood out from the rest of the city's fabric with its chromatic walls made from contrasting bands of pink, black, and white limestone. Octagonal columns and pointed arches held up the open ground-floor level, used for a market. An external stair led to the upper hall, used for council meetings. The large **triforium** windows framed in recessed arches looked as important as those of the cathedral. The loggia sheltered urban officials, who regulated weights and measures, and accommodated stalls for the sale of privileged goods such as iron, wine, herbs, and the city's prime monopoly, salt. The Broletto's upper story served as offices for jurists, notaries, scribes, and official estimators. From the austere campanile, built in rusticated stone on the short side away from the cathedral, the bells rang either to convene the council members or to alert the citizens to muster for battle.

While the early republican assemblies often used churches, the frequent disputes between the bishop and the citizen governments led to the construction of independent council halls as large as the nave of a church. Padua

Figure 9.1-21 San Gimignano, Italy. City studded with twelfth-century tower houses.

Figure 9.1-22 Como, Italy. Palazzo del Broletto, loggia for city hall and market, 1215.

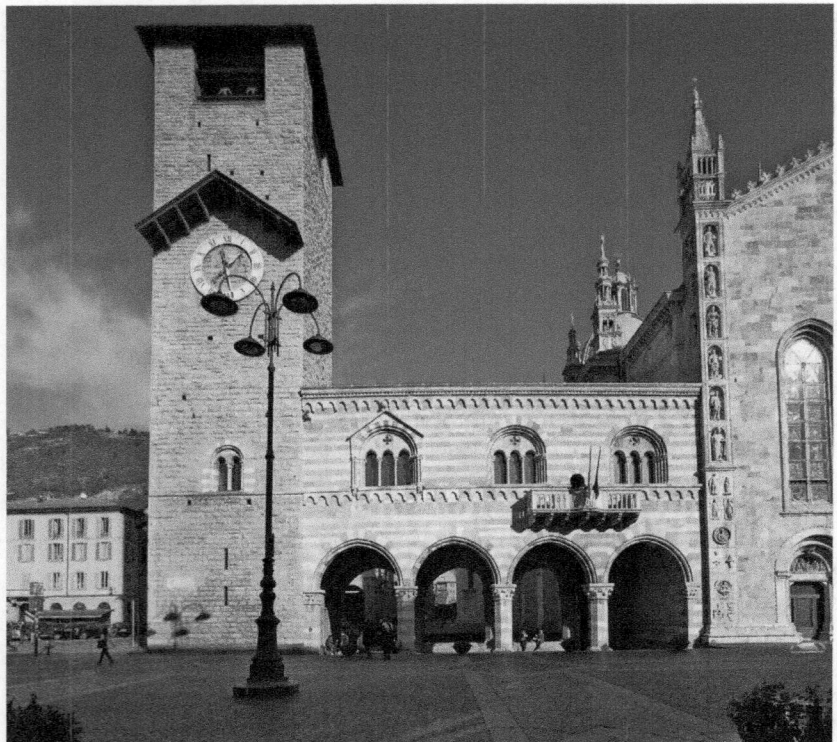

built the largest and most impressive, the Palazzo della Ragione, begun in 1172, to which the celebrated engineer-monk Fra Giovanni degli Eremitani added the extraordinary roof in 1305 (Fig. 9.1-23). The ground-floor plan looked like a broken fish spine with a long row of back-to-back shops. The skewed orientation of the structure between two market piazzas resulted in an uncanny parallelogram. The two-story side arcades contained gracious stairways to the upper hall. The interior, which was given its definitive shape in 1420, recalled the scale of ancient Roman basilicas, measuring about half the area of Trajan's Basilica Ulpia. The walls curved up to meet a soaring, hull-shaped wooden vault, clearly influenced by shipbuilding techniques from nearby Venice.

Public stairs and spacious loggias created the image of accountability at the public

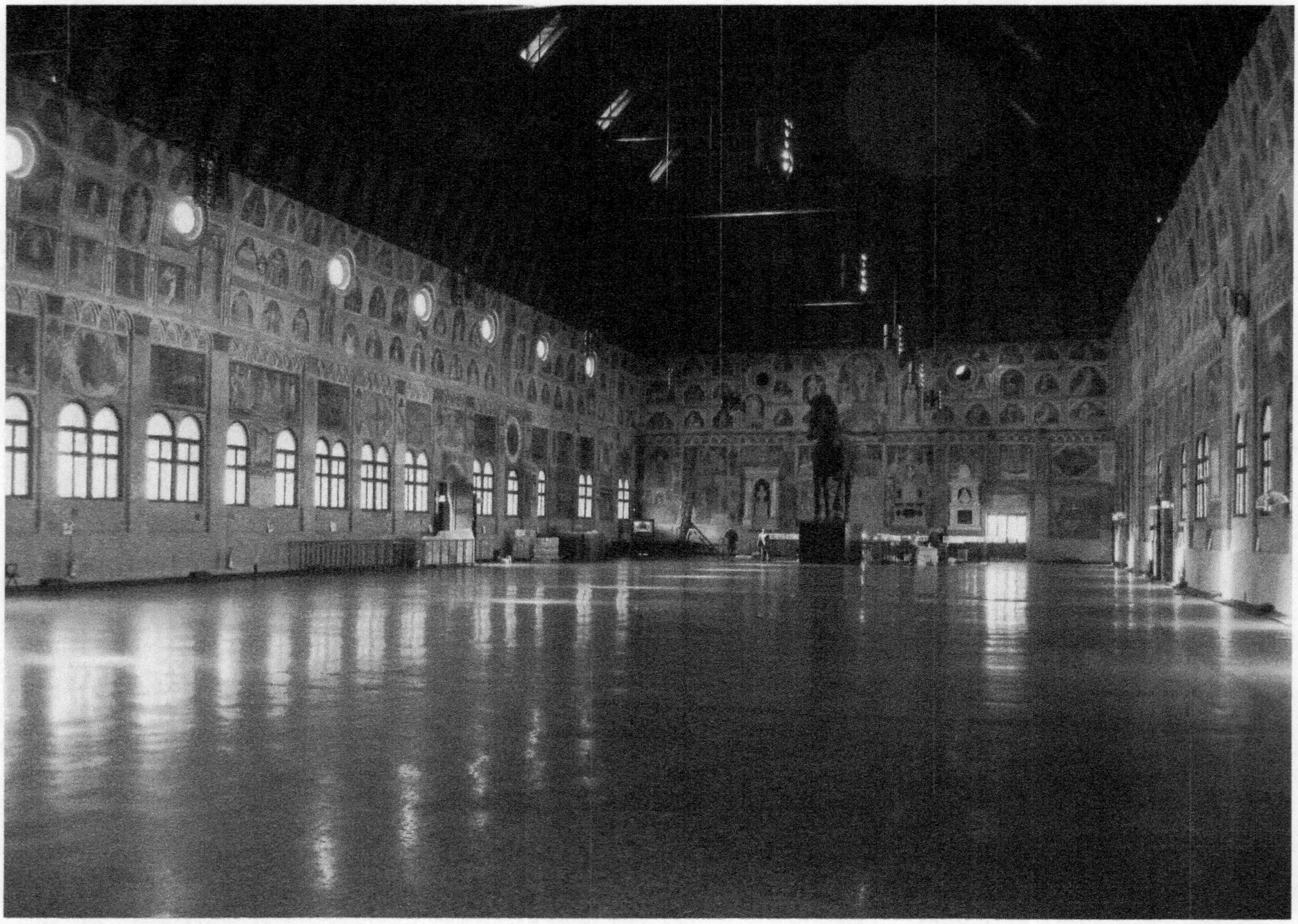

Figure 9.1-23 Padua, Italy. Palazzo della Ragione, 1172–1440.

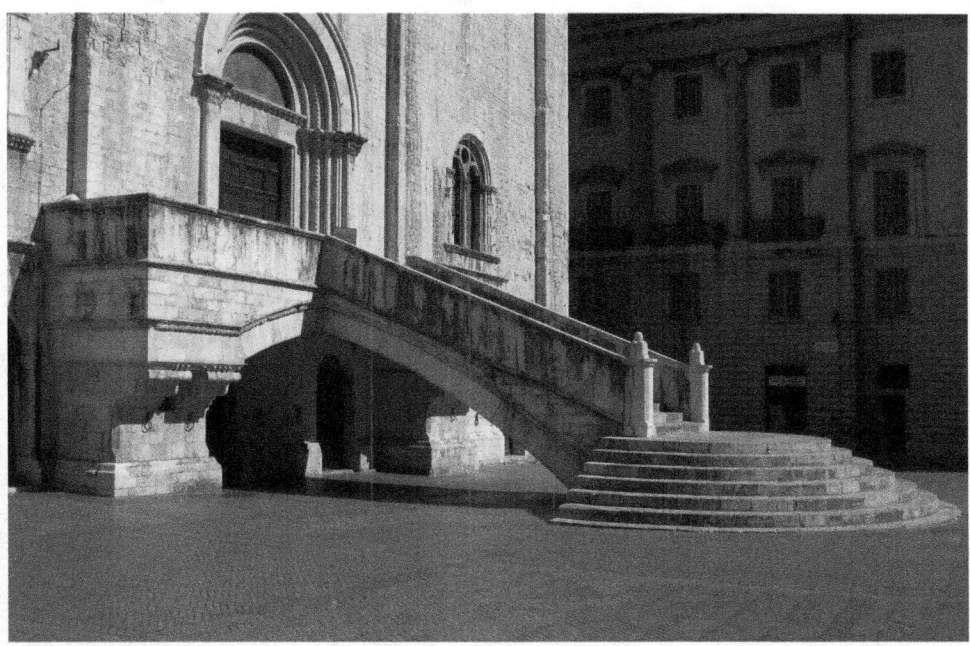

palaces in central Italy, often serving as sites for civic spectacles. Palazzo dei Consoli, in Gubbio, designed in 1332 by Angelo da Orvieto, captured the full scenographic value of formal stairs (Fig. 9.1-24). Situated at the top of a steep hillside, the civic piazza occupied a broad terrace set over a retaining wall supported on colossal barrel vaults. This urban veranda, framed by the two principal civic buildings, offered a breathtaking vista to the valley. An ingenious bridge-like staircase accessed the tall facade of the palace. The upper landing in front of the portal rested on a deep arch cantilevered over thick piers, and the steps mounted over a segmental vault. At the base the stairs spilled out on semicircular treads.

Florence constructed its second public palace, now called Palazzo Vecchio (Fig. 9.1-25), at the end of the thirteenth century, taking advantage of the city's class disputes. The communal authorities expropriated the houses of the Uberti clan as a political reprisal and, by demolishing the family's tower house, made room for a new civic piazza. The public palace, attributed to the sculptor Arnolfo di Cambio (ca. 1240–1310), appeared like a fortress, with heavy, rusticated masonry and high windows. At the top a *ballatoio* jutted out on arched **machicolations** that supported square crenellations. The belfry added a generation later rose taller than any of the buildings in the city, at 94 m (308 ft). Arnolfo's design showed a new degree of proportional rigor, placing the five bays of the original facade in strict symmetry, with biforium windows uniformly detailed in delicately carved white marble colonnettes and **trefoils**. The public palace loomed above Florence as an incontrovertible statement of the power of its citizen-run government.

Figure 9.1-25 Florence. Palazzo dei Priori (now called Palazzo Vecchio), Arnolfo di Cambio, 1299.

During the years 1287–1355, Siena's ruling party of the Noveschi, the council of nine priors, oversaw a period of great prosperity, stability, and demographic expansion. The Noveschi commissioned the greatest expression of the city's collective imagination, the Palazzo Pubblico (Fig. 9.1-26), and its *cavea*-shaped Piazza del Campo. Construction began in 1297 and continued for the next four decades. The architecture reflected multiples of three: the building was divided into three wings, articulated with triforium windows. The open arches of the ground-floor arcades, later transformed into windows and doors, used a typical Sienese motif of a segmental arch set inside a pointed arch. Unlike the fortifications atop Florence's Palazzo Vecchio, the crenellations on Siena's public palace seemed more symbolic than functional. The bell tower, known as the Torre del Mangia, rose to the left side like an obelisk, at 102 m (334 ft) the tallest building in the city.

The three wings of the Palazzo Pubblico consolidated several governmental functions: on the left, the dwelling and judiciary chambers of the *podestá* (an outside arbiter with judicial authority); in the center, the council hall for 300 citizens; and on the right, the offices and lodgings of the Noveschi, who were obliged to live in the

Figure 9.1-26 Siena, Italy. Palazzo Pubblico, 1320s. The ground-floor arches were originally open.

During the late thirteenth century, Florence's perennial rival to the south, Siena, pursued a comprehensive program of public works as an investment in overall well-being. The city promoted its own style, offering incentives for the alignment of brick-and-stone facades along the curved streets and the use of pointed arches and ornate windows with colonnettes. The government financed the major monuments and institutions, including the brilliantly decorated duomo, the additions to the hospital of Santa Maria della Scala in front of it, the public palace, and its piazza. The Sienese state also subsidized five convent churches at the city's edges, reasoning that the popularity of the new mendicant orders of St. Francis and others contributed to its political interests while helping to develop the sparsely inhabited parts of the city.

palace during their two-month terms. The lower levels contained prisons and the salt monopoly warehouses. One incongruous feature, the small marble canopy for an altar attached to the left corner of the palace, marked the influence of the Black Death, which in 1348 wiped out over half of Siena's 55,000 inhabitants. While the city never made a full recovery, the Cappella di Piazza, begun in 1352 and finished during the next century, attempted to appease the supernatural as an **ex-voto**.

The shell-shaped Piazza del Campo sloped down to the Palazzo Pubblico like a grand outdoor theater (Fig. 9.1-27). At its edges, the palace waited with its two outer wings bent 10° to embrace the space. The piazza's nine wedges of brick paving left a subtle reference to the Noveschi

Figure 9.1-27 Siena, Italy. Piazza del Campo, 1330s.

patronage. The council sent its urban magistrates, later known in Siena as officers of *ornatum*, or beauty, to encourage the new facades on the piazza to use biforium windows with stone colonnettes and to refrain from adding balconies or outcrops. The coordination of dozens of properties surrounding the Piazza del Campo encouraged architectural variety within a prescribed figure, demonstrating that the republican ideals of accountability and dialogue could generate a masterpiece of public space.

Further Reading

Abu-Lughod, Janet. *Before European Hegemony: The World System, AD 1250–1350*. New York: Oxford University Press, 1989.

Benton, Tim, and Diana Norman, eds. *Siena, Florence, and Padua: Art, Society and Religion, 1280–1400*. New Haven, CT: Yale University Press, 1995.

Bowsky, William M. *A Medieval Italian Commune: Siena under the Nine, 1287–1355*. Berkeley: University of California Press, 1981.

Brucker, Gene. *Florence: The Golden Age, 1138–1737*. Berkeley: University of California Press, 1998.

Goy, Richard. *Venetian Vernacular Architecture: Traditional Housing in the Venetian Lagoon*. Cambridge, UK: Cambridge University Press, 1989.

Howard, Deborah. *Venice and the East: The Impact of the Islamic World on Venetian Architecture, 1100–1500*. New Haven, CT: Yale University Press, 2000.

Lane, Frederic C. *Venice: A Maritime Republic*. Baltimore, MD: Johns Hopkins University Press, 1973.

McLean, Alick. "Italian Architecture of the Late Middle Ages." In *The Art of the Italian Renaissance: Architecture–Sculpture–Painting–Drawing*. Edited by R. Toman. Cologne: Könemann, 1995.

Nevola, Fabrizio. *Siena: Constructing the Renaissance City*. New Haven, CT: Yale University Press, 2007.

Ragette, Friedrich. *Traditional Domestic Architecture of the Arab Region*. Beirut: Editions Axel Menges, 2003.

Raymond, André. *Cairo*. Cambridge, MA: Harvard University Press, 2000.

Schulz, Juergen. *The New Palaces of Medieval Venice*. University Park: Pennsylvania State University Press, 2004.

Trachtenberg, Marvin. *The Dominion of the Eye: Urbanism, Art and Power in Early Modern Florence*. Cambridge, UK: Cambridge University Press, 1997.

9.2 GOTHIC EUROPE
The Fabric of the Great Cathedrals

The success of the Italian merchants in the Mediterranean stimulated the rest of Europe with new possibilities for commercial and cultural exchange. During the twelfth century the Champagne fairs in central France offered a neutral ground for trade between northern and southern merchants. Markets began to thrive in the cities, and the demand for public space and new **cathedrals** followed. The municipalities of hundreds of cities and new towns placed themselves in opposition to the feudal lords by encouraging the serfs to abandon their feudal bonds to become taxpaying city dwellers. Great market cities such as Bruges, Paris, Lübeck, and Cologne more than doubled in size by 1300.

In France the shared interests of the monarchy and the clergy promoted the new style retroactively known by the derogatory name of "Gothic." At the time the style was most commonly called *Opus Francigenum*. In contrast to the heavy barrel vaults of Romanesque churches, the designers of Gothic cathedrals explored a structural system that combined pointed arches, ribbed vaults, and flying buttresses to achieve dazzling heights and mysterious luminosity. Traveling masons helped spread the style from France throughout Europe, leading to local interpretations wherever it appeared, to the point that the English, Germans, Spanish, Polish, and Czechs each considered Gothic their own.

The City Returns: Market Towns and New Towns

The groundswell of medieval European urbanism coincided with the birth of the Gothic architectural style. From 1150 to 1350, after centuries of decline, the population of Europe expanded from approximately 40 million to 70 million. A relatively stable political structure worked in the region's favor. So did a new military pride stemming from the Spanish *Reconquista* and the First Crusade. The monasteries improved farm tools and practiced crop rotation, leading the rest of Europe to agricultural surplus and greater life expectancy. The new prosperity of the cities encouraged the expansion of city walls and the construction of gigantic cathedrals and impressive civic buildings, such as town halls, covered markets, and hospitals. The quest for emancipation from feudal bonds inspired the foundation of hundreds of new towns across Europe, most built on orthogonal plans that revived the idea of public space.

In northern Europe the counts of Champagne and Flanders discovered that the tariffs on fairs and foreign merchants that they could collect yielded more than their estates. Their sponsorship of the Champagne fairs held in Troyes and three nearby towns during the twelfth and thirteenth centuries stimulated the axis of medieval European commerce extending from London to the Low Countries, through the Rhineland, and down the Rhone valley to Milan in northern Italy. The seasonal markets rotated among the four Champagne towns in two-month durations throughout the year. The local feudal lords raked in duties from sales, rents, stables, and the administration of justice in exchange for policing the city and the region and guaranteeing the safe conduct of the merchants on the roads and in the towns.

The Champagne fairs took place initially outside the city gates, where they generated permanent settlement areas known in French as *faubourgs*. The walls surrounding the city of Troyes doubled in circumference in 1250, enclosing the western *faubourg* of the market district. In this western half of the city the streets took the names of the goods sold and the money changed. The new district included a synagogue, a large building for the crusaders' Templar order, and two hospitals. The counts of Champagne and the bishop of Troyes maintained their palaces in the old town, away from direct contact with the bartering. They encouraged commerce by sponsoring barn-like wood-beamed halls in the market district, similar to the market still standing in Montpazier (Fig. 9.2-1).

The growing economy of Troyes led to the rebuilding of the cathedral, the founding of the new church of St. Urbain, and the foundation of a new hospital in the mid-thirteenth century. St. Urbain (Fig. 9.2-2), begun in 1262 when a cleric from Troyes was elected to the papacy as Urban IV, took only thirty years to finish and exemplified the new French manner of increasing heights and reducing walls to skeletal frames. The hospital of Troyes looked something like

TIME LINE

 1119

Zähringer counts build new towns in Switzerland and southern Germany

Abbot Suger completes the choir of St. Denis, France, initiating Gothic style

▲ **1145**

▼ **1190s**

Construction begun on Lincoln Cathedral, England

Chartres Cathedral rebuilt, France

▲ **1194–1250**

Figure 9.2-1 Montpazier, France. Semi-enclosed market hall, fifteenth century.

the Hospital of Notre-Dame de Fontenilles at Tonnerre, built in the same period (1250–1293) in Burgundy, a long 100 m (328 ft) hall covered with a wooden barrel vault and terminating with a small chapel. The type and technique came from monastic designs for refectories and dormitories.

The transformation of Troyes prefigured that of numerous mercantile cities throughout Europe: urban perimeters fattened with concentric layers linked by radial streets that converged on an administrative and economic hub. The merchants of Bruges, one of the major distribution points, gained the right to own their houses and land as freeholders in 1127 from the counts of Flanders. This led to the formation of guilds and citizen councils similar to those in the Italian republics. By the end of the thirteenth century Bruges had rebuilt its walls as a gigantic oval enclosing the two earlier rings (Fig. 9.2-3). The city also improved its canal system and constructed several significant civic monuments, including the Belfry, the Cloth Hall, and the Waterhalle. The Belfry, begun in 1280, stood nearly as tall as Venice's campanile. It was incorporated into the Cloth Hall, built for the guilds and used for municipal meetings. Its courtyard structure resembled the *fonduk* type in Cairo—but without the traders' apartments above—and became the model for European stock exchanges built

Figure 9.2-2 Troyes, Champagne (France). St. Urbain, built ca. 1240 in flamboyant Gothic style to honor Pope Urban IV, born in Troyes.

▼ **1215**

Cathedral of Laon, northern France, completed in Gothic style

Ste.-Chapelle, Paris, exemplifies the web-like rayonnant style of Gothic

▲ **1240**

▼ **1240s**

Carcassonne, southern France, fortified as stronghold against Cathars

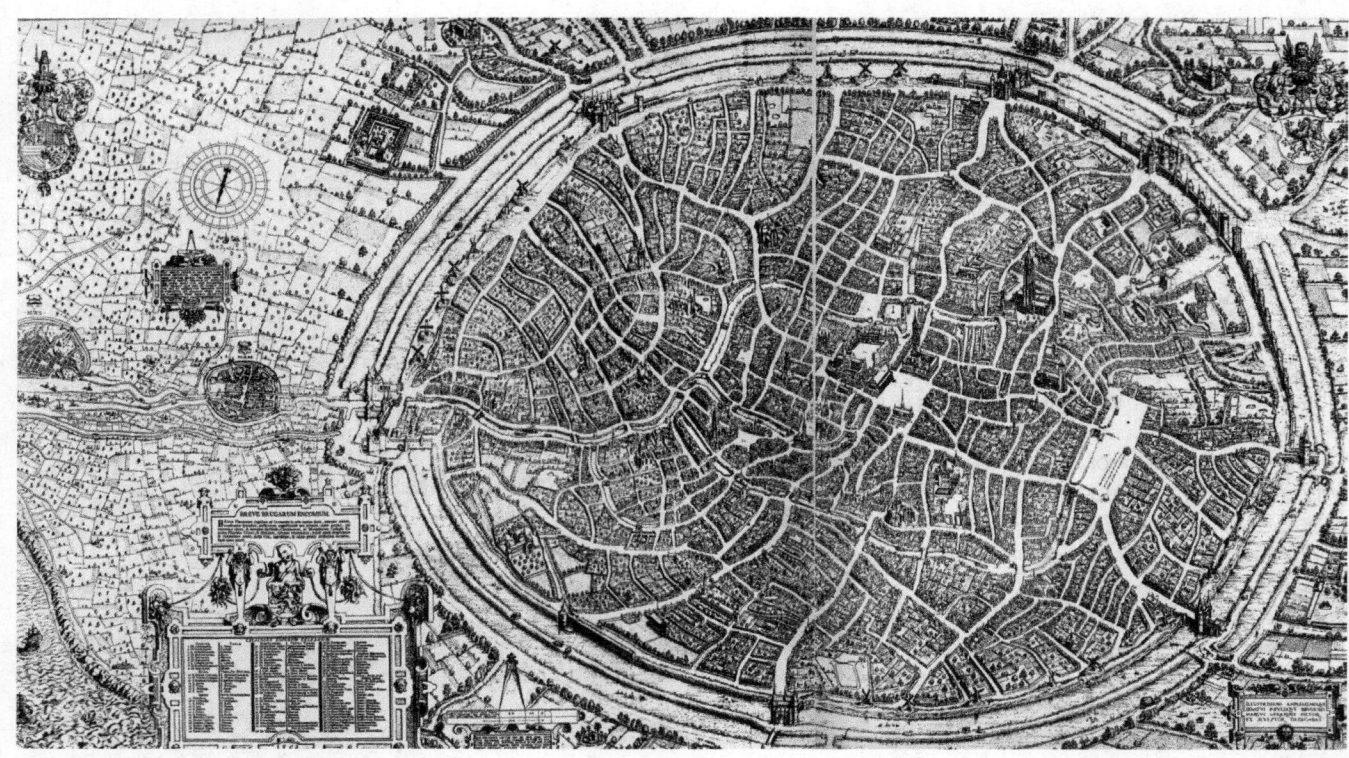

Figure 9.2-3 Bruges, Belgium. Map of expanded city, fattened into an oval, in late thirteenth century.

during the next four centuries. During the same year the merchant regime of Bruges financed an innovative commercial structure, the Waterhalle, an immense covered hall, fifteen bays long, that straddled the canal (Fig. 9.2-4). Traders unloaded their goods directly from the barges to the merchandisers' stalls in a protected environment without the need for extra hauling. The designers articulated the pitch of the roof at each end with stepped gables.

As the citizens of older towns struggled to gain new liberties, new towns were founded throughout Europe promising similar rights to those who would settle them. The aristocratic patrons of these planned settlements used them as either a financial investment or a colonial ploy, or both. The Zähringer counts, lords of parts of southern Germany and Switzerland, initiated the concept of the town as an enterprise. Between 1119 and 1228 they sponsored a dozen market towns, each structured on a broad central street. The most successful of these, Freiburg im Breisgau and Berne,

developed into important trade centers. Toward the end of the twelfth century, as Freiburg prospered, its planners created a second street, set cross-axial to the first. The central market street of Berne stretched nearly 25 m (82 ft) across, about five times the width of typical medieval streets. Confined to a narrow promontory overlooking the river, Berne grew in a linear progression, doubling the length of its three parallel streets. During the fourteenth and fifteenth centuries the town council permitted property owners to add deep arcades to the front of their buildings in the form of single arches propped up on thick piers. The Zähringer planners did not designate specific sites for cathedrals and town halls, but once a city had proven itself as a successful market, the citizens found sites in secondary positions on the side streets for the religious and institutional buildings.

The French king Louis IX (r. 1226–1270), later canonized as St. Louis, led the Seventh Crusade in the mid-thirteenth century to Palestine and Alexandria against Islam. He also

Second, rayonnant, phase of Notre-Dame of Paris

▲ **1250s**

▼ **1280**

Bruges, Belgium, builds Belfry and Waterhalle for its merchant republic

Montpazier, France, founded by English

Florence builds new town of San Giovanni Valdarno on geometric grid

▲ **1300**

▼ **1350**

Peter Parler designs St. Vitus Cathedral in Prague

Figure 9.2-4 Bruges, Belgium. Waterhalle, 1280, detail from painting of the *Wonders of Bruges*, by Pieter Claessins, mid-seventeenth century.

CULTURE, SOCIETY, GENDER

The Beguinage

The merchant society of Bruges fostered the foundation of the Beguinage in 1230, a unique social institution that served as a shelter for unwed women. Behind an enclosing wall, this all-female community lived in dozens of small white houses gathered informally around a large park and served by a small church. The Beguinage of De Wijngaard was something like a convent, except that the women did not take religious vows, nor did they relinquish their property rights. Residence there became a dignified alternative to married life, religious cloistering, or prostitution, since each woman resided in her own house within the compound, living a sheltered but independent existence.

Bruges, Belgium. Beguinage, 1230.

conducted a campaign in the south of France against renegade Christians of the Cathar sect. His armies destroyed
countless mountain communities between Toulouse and
Bayonne. In 1240 the king took one of the prime rebel forts,
Carcassonne, and rebuilt it as the French crown's bastion
against the Cathars, whose houses were demolished. The
pretext of the struggle against heretics served the expansionist policies of the French state, which doubled its territories in the process. On a flat site adjacent to the fortress
of Carcassonne, the king commissioned a new polygonal
town with an approximate grid of square blocks for the resettlement and control of the Cathar population. One square
in the center of the new town was left vacant for the city's
market. The hilltop fortress walls of Carcassonne, heavily
restored in the late nineteenth century (see Section 15.2), included round turrets and a semicircular barbican entrance
with a drawbridge to the castle keep, or donjon, on the highest peak of the hill (Fig. 9.2-5a, b).

**Figure 9.2-5
Carcassonne,
southern France.
(a) Fortified city
built to dominate
the Cathars and
settle the south of
France for Louis IX,
1240s. (b) Fortress
with double wall.**

During the late thirteenth century the French and the English both claimed Gascony and built hundreds of **bastides**, the French name for new towns, to consolidate their respective power over southwest France. The English controlled the port of Bordeaux as a crucial player in their trading triangle with Bruges, sending English wool for the textiles of Flanders to be exchanged for the wines of Gascony. The dozens of new towns built by the English in the wine country of southwestern France served this colonial effort. The French supporters of Louis IX countered with just as many new towns of their own in their effort to take control of the region. There were no formal differences between Montpazier, founded by the English in 1284, and Villefranche de Perigord, founded by the French in 1261. Each followed a simple grid plan with streets about 7 m (22 ft) wide (Fig. 9.2-6). Surveyors laid them out by string alignments. They subdivided the blocks into oblong "gothic lots," usually 5 × 10 m (16 × 32 ft), which the local peasants obtained by drawing lots. Each settler was obliged to build a house within a year and participate in the expenses of preparing the town's streets, walls, and marketplace. The dimensions of the "gothic lot" related to the standard lengths of timber and allowed for two bays of windows per facade. A town charter determined the selection and procurement of the site, the recruitment of settlers, and the establishment of their legal privileges. The founding lord, or representative of the king, would dig a hole at the center of the site and raise the *bastidor*'s arms on a stake called the *palum*, declaring the town open. He would also pledge his recognition of the liberties to be enjoyed in the name of God, the Virgin Mary, and all the saints: "A man whatever his status may be, who dwells there for a year and a day without being challenged shall be free." The new towns initially competed for regional agricultural products but eventually entered into the international conflict of the Hundred Years' War, begun in the 1330s.

Other medieval new towns served specifically as military bases, such as in Caernarvon, Wales, a northern complement to the English *bastides* in France, and Santa Fe, Spain, where the *Reconquista* stationed troops to unseat the last *taifa* in Granada. Florence sponsored the most systematically designed towns to hold down its borders in Tuscany. The designers calculated their spaces using proportional divisions of the sort reserved for cathedrals. San Giovanni Valdarno (Fig. 9.2-7) had five parallel streets that diminished progressively in width, from 11 to 7 m (35 to 22 ft). They allotted much more attention to public space, creating an oblong central piazza intersected directly by each of the streets. The new towns and the expanded merchant cities increased people's accessibility and freedom of movement, reducing the intimidating presence of feudal control. This ushered in a greater sense of social order and a new way of seeing the world.

The Gothic Cathedral: The Crown of the City

The building boom in European cities during the thirteenth and fourteenth centuries nurtured the new Gothic style in church building, an architecture as distinct in its details as the classical style of the Romans. The designers experimented with slender structural members to accentuate

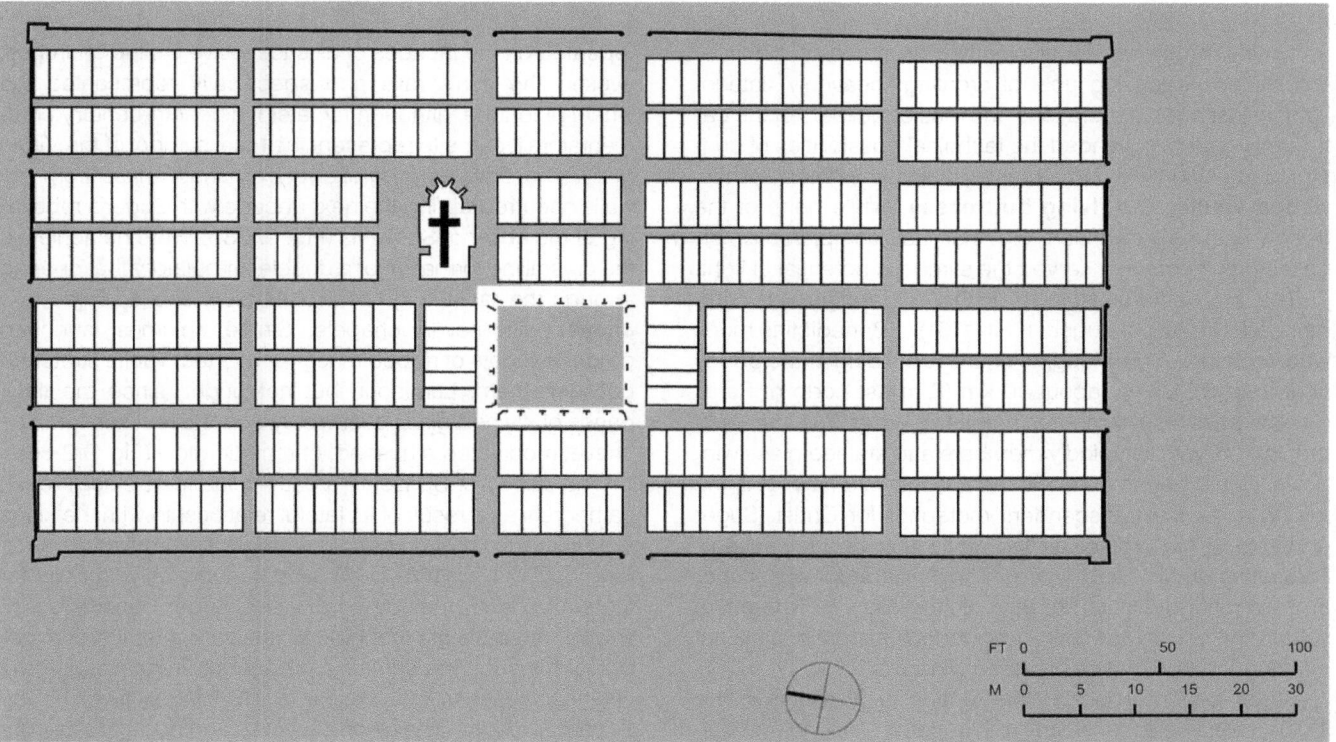

Figure 9.2-6 Montpazier, France. Plan of new town, 1284.

Figure 9.2-7 San Giovanni Valdarno, Tuscany, Italy. Reconstructed axonometric view of town ca. 1300 by Massimo Tosi.

verticality, progressively eliminating the mass of the walls to fulfill an underlying goal of creating "heavenly" interior light. In just a few generations, the master builders of the cathedrals greatly advanced the technical possibilities of construction using three structural expedients: pointed arches, **ribbed vaults**, and **flying buttresses**. While none of the three was a new invention, together they comprised an architectural theory that served the symbolic potential of light.

The architectural attitude of *Opus Francigenum* commenced with Abbot Suger (1081–1151), a Benedictine monk who wrote down his thoughts on the rebuilding of the abbey church of St. Denis, about 10 km (6 miles) north of Paris, with the passion of a modern manifesto writer. The interior of the church, with its spindly members and stained glass windows, would become the means to achieve a new light, the *lux nova*, as the transcendent metaphor for Christ. Suger understood his project as the realization of the heavenly Jerusalem of the Apocalypse: "The wall thereof was jasper and the city pure gold like unto clear glass. . . . The entire sanctuary . . . pervaded by a wonderful and continuous light entering through the most sacred windows."

Suger began rebuilding the facade of St. Denis in the 1130s, retaining associations with imperial Carolingian westworks while inserting between the two towers an *oculus*, a wheel-like round window (Fig. 9.2-8a). This novel motif,

repeated on the facades of all successive Gothic churches, evoked the sun's rays and specifically represented the wheel of fortune, although for later nineteenth-century commentators it came to represent the rose, symbol of the Virgin Mary. The drive to progressively eliminate mass from the walls occurred during the next decade with Suger's rebuilding of the **choir** of St. Denis (Fig. 9.2-8b). Here he achieved the crystalline formation of a double ambulatory that opened through the radial alignment of its piers and columns to a **chevet** with seven chapels. Single columns launched graceful shoots of ribbed masonry with taut vaults stretched between them. Luminous but not bright, since the thick panes of stained glass shone only under direct sunlight, the chevet modulated a hushed, chromatic glow (Fig. 9.2-8c).

The abbey of St. Denis greatly influenced other French cathedrals as a result of its fateful relationship with the kings of France. In 1124 Abbot Suger's good friend and patron King Louis VI (r. 1108–1137) used it as the rallying point for the supporters of his growing realm. Suger became so involved with the state that in 1145, the year after the completion of his choir, he served as regent of France during the two-year absence of Louis VII (r. 1137–1180), away on the Second Crusade. The union of sacred and political was consecrated in Suger's choir, which became the site of the state burial of all the subsequent kings and queens of France.

Figure 9.2-8 Saint-Denis, France. Cathedral of St. Denis. (a) Facade, with wheel-like rose window, 1130. The church originally had a second tower. (b) Plan of the choir, apse, and chevet. (c) See next page.

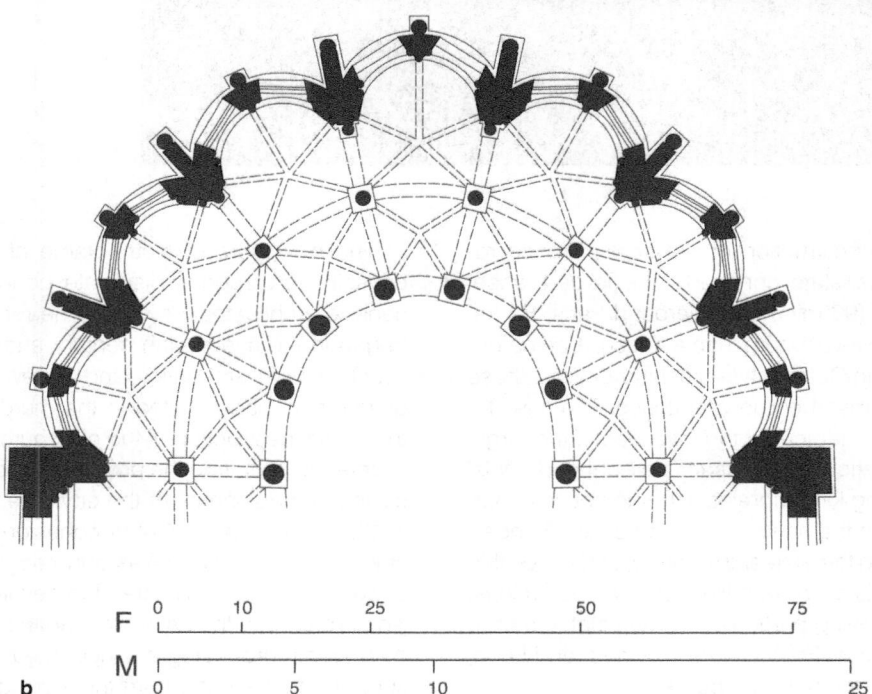

F | 0   10   25   50   75

M | 0   5   10   25

b

Figure 9.2-8 Saint-Denis, France. Cathedral of St. Denis. (c) View into the chevet.

During Suger's reconstruction of St. Denis, France remained a relatively small state, confined to the Île-de-France, which fit in a 160 km (96 mile) radius around Paris. By the end of the century, however, more than a dozen large cathedrals were underway in Gothic style, pushing beyond these borders as the state absorbed new territories. The new cathedrals, most of them dedicated to *Notre Dame*, the Virgin Mary, provided dramatic backdrops for political and social conflicts waged among kings, prelates, noble houses, merchants, and artisans in the newly awakened cities. France's territories tripled during the thirteenth century, and the Gothic style accompanied this expansion to cities such as Amiens, Troyes, and Rouen, leaving particularly strong statements in Reims, where the kings of France were crowned, and Laon, a strategic location on the northern borders.

The designers of Notre-Dame at Laon (Fig. 9.2-9a,b) consolidated Suger's disparate concepts into a comprehensive architectonic system. The rebuilding of the church began in the mid-twelfth century after a major conflict between church authorities and a newly established citizen government had resulted in the murder of the bishop and the partial destruction of the old church. The king of France intervened, restoring the power of the bishop while acknowledging the autonomy of the city. The cathedral, finished in 1215, provided a symbol of cohesion for the once-divided city. In plan, the apse was squared off without the typical chevet, while the choir extended beyond the transept almost isomorphic with the nave. Sexpartite ribbed vaults spanned both areas, producing a syncopated rhythm in the slender supports that sprang from the stout ground-floor columns.

Pointed Arches, Ribbed Vaults, and Flying Buttresses

Gothic architects created structures that combined pointed arches, ribbed **groin vaults**, and flying buttresses. Pointed arches are made by intersecting two half-circles drawn from different centering points. They have a double advantage over round-headed arches, as they disperse loads more effectively and have greater flexibility for the width of span. One can easily vary the width of a pointed arch while still touching the same crown line. Groin vaults, compared to barrel vaults, also have more flexibility. While the barrel vault exerts uniform pressure on the walls, **cross-vaults** shift the loads to the groins and then down to the four corners of the bay. These points of maximum thrust can then be buttressed individually with the half-arches of an external flying buttress—a technique clearly more economical than having to counter the outward push of a barrel vault with thicker walls.

The erosion of mass into thin lines of support followed an empirical process of trial and error. Medieval masons converted the solid walls of a building into a skeletal frame on which to hang thin membranes, mostly of stained glass. Of the numerous structural failures among the Gothic cathedrals, that of St. Pierre at Beauvais, begun in 1230, proved the most spectacular. The tallest nave ever attempted, it rose 52 m (171 ft) but collapsed in 1284, never to be completed.

Villard de Honnecourt, sample page of master builder's notes, twelfth century.

These piers alternated bundles of five shafts corresponding to the **ribs** at the primary arches, with three shafts at the minor arches between each bay. The ribbed vaults, supported by external flying buttresses, rose between large voided areas for the tall clerestory windows that brought abundant daylight into the **tribunes** and the nave. The four levels of the interior elevations included an intermediary triforium level with blind arches just beneath the top windows. Laon's spindly towers flanking the south, west, and north entries exhibited the same degree of harmony, with novel aedicules set obliquely on the corners to shelter a menagerie of full-scale sculpted animals, including many horned oxen.

The cathedral at Chartres (Fig. 9.2-10a,b), a small city on the western edge of the Île-de-France region, began as a smaller church that was rebuilt and expanded after a devastating fire in 1194 that consumed half of the city. The city's prized relic, the tunic of the Virgin Mary, miraculously withstood the flames in the church's crypt, increasing the cathedral's strong attraction for pilgrims. Crowning the top of the hill, the new church seemed outsized for a city of fewer than 10,000 residents. The strong vertical lines of its spires and buttresses beckoned pilgrims from 30 km (18 miles) away as a new Christian axis mundi in the heart of France.

Verticality became a theological imperative for Gothic cathedral builders. The ribbed vaults in the nave of Chartres reached an astounding 38 m (125 ft), considerably higher than Cluny III. The piers of the nave alternated round and octagonal columns supporting the pointed arches of the lower

Figure 9.2-9 Laon, France. (a) Cathedral facade, 1215. (b) Interior nave.

arcades. This subtle rhythm interrupted the continuous line of shafts holding the quadripartite ribbed vaults. From the crossing to the apse the shafts rose without interruption to the spring of the vaults, greatly enhancing the verticality in the progress toward the sacred crypt. The flying buttresses on the exterior of Chartres exhibited a similar progress from heavier to lighter as they proceeded toward the choir. Exterior flying buttresses received the thrusts of the vaults as **exoskeletal** "flyers," arches extended to tower-like exterior piers placed in correspondence to the interior columns of each bay (Fig. 9.2-11). The lower fliers sprouted rows of stout columns like the spokes of a wheel. Where the choir joined the transept, the fliers intersected in a grid of skeletal supports that suggested their similarity to, and probable origins from, wooden scaffolding.

The windows of Chartres conveyed a broad spectrum of patronage. King Philippe Auguste appeared, along with the count of Dreux and his family, in the southern **wheel window**. Later in 1228 the count's enemy, Queen Blanche of Castile, financed the entire north transept window. Many of the noble families of Île-de-France had their coats of arms included, as did the local guilds. The king used his

patronage to discourage the power of the local feudal nobility, while the bishop encouraged the participation of the merchant class, appointing individuals from its ranks as honorary members of the chapter. The local funding for Chartres came from the city's lucrative grain trade, the silver mines owned by the bishop, and taxes on the textile and munitions industries. The cathedral grew as a symbol of the city's prosperity and indeed served as much as a community center as it did a hall of faith, used for town meetings, law courts, and theatrical events. This community at Chartres did not include everyone, however, and in 1256 Louis IX ordered the top of the hill walled off to protect the cathedral, the bishop's palace, the hospital, and the merchants' hall from civil uprisings, such as the one that occurred at Laon. Such unrest led the bishops of the cathedral towns to fortify their residences with ample space for an army and a prison.

During the mid-thirteenth century Louis IX reopened work at St. Denis under the direction of his favored architects, Jean de Chelles and Pierre de Montreuil. The resulting structures, which reduced the walls to shockingly thin skeletons of stone, acquired the style name **rayonnant** ("radiating") during the nineteenth century. Under Chelles

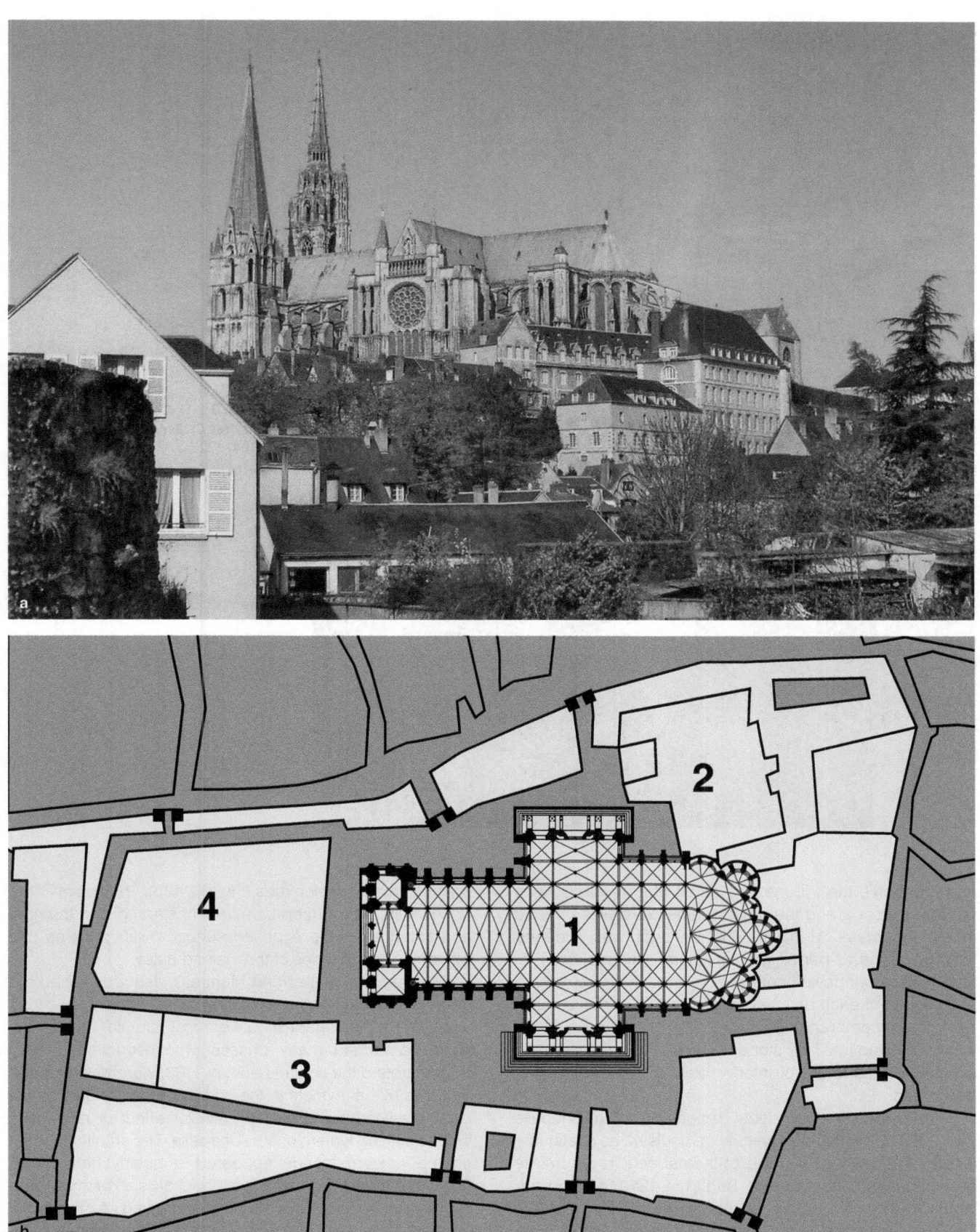

Figure 9.2-10 Chartres, France. (a) Cathedral, 1194–1225. (b) Fortified enclave surrounding the cathedral, showing (1) the cathedral; (2) bishop's palace and gardens; (3) old hospital; (4) canon's houses.

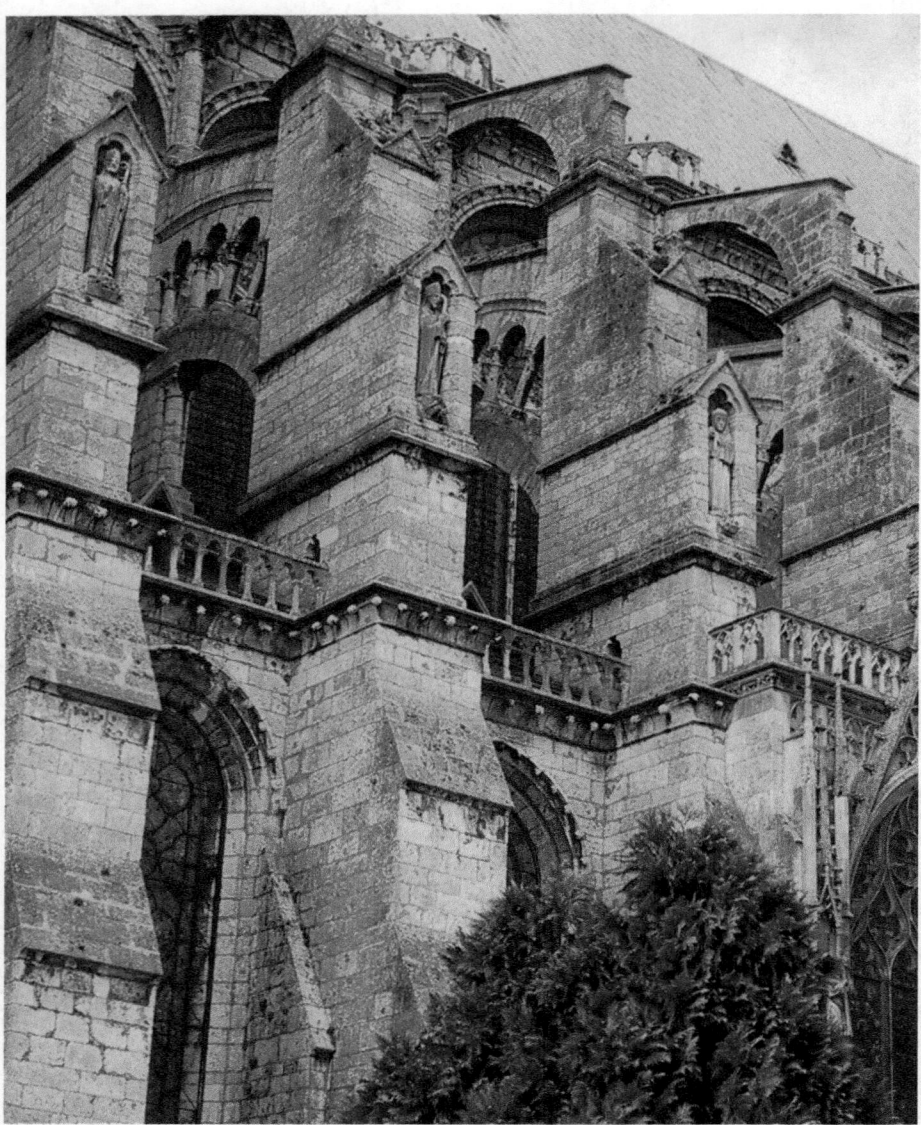

Figure 9.2-11 Chartres, France. Chartres Cathedral, flying buttresses, 1194–1225.

and Montreuil, the tribune, the squat attic level between the lower arcade and the upper clerestories, was opened to stained glass windows. The transept was widened into five aisles to permit greater lateral fenestration, with upper wheel windows courageously stretching across the entire width of each bay, held together with intricate, lead-reinforced membranes (Fig. 9.2-12). The exterior walls were dissolved into lacy stone **tracery** strung between the scaffold-like structure of interior piers and exterior flying buttresses.

In Paris the same architects designed the Ste.-Chapelle (Fig. 9.2-13a) for France's saint/king, Louis IX, as a reliquary (container) for Christ's crown of thorns, acquired from the deposed Byzantine emperor. Begun in 1240, it stood adjacent to the royal palace on Île de la Cité, the island in the Seine that served as the heart of medieval Paris. In the upper chapel the designers attempted to reduce the mass of the walls to leave an ethereal curtain of stained glass. They enhanced the structure of the thin piers with cleverly

concealed iron tension rods (Fig. 9.2-13b). They painted the groin vaults with a deep blue field of stars, gilded the ribs, and tinted all of the exposed surfaces with patterns that blended with the tones of the stained glass.

The team of Chelles and Montreuil also redesigned the transept of Notre-Dame of Paris (Fig. 9.2-14a), a few steps away from Ste.-Chapelle. Like most Gothic cathedrals, Notre-Dame had many phases of construction. Initially begun around the time of Laon, in 1163, work was resumed by Louis IX's architects in the mid-thirteenth century to enlarge the windows, creating a similar effect of *rayonnant*, like the shining lantern of Ste.-Chapelle. The architects' work on the western facade appeared singularly harmonious (Fig. 9.2-14b,c). They created a triadic division of three vertical bays intersected by three horizontal levels. A mezzanine entablature spread above the entry porches with twenty-eight niches for sculpted portraits of the French kings, creating an ideological synthesis of church and state. On the next level, to either side of the wheel window, biforium

Figure 9.2-12 St.-Denis, France. Cathedral of St. Denis, north transept and wheel window, Jean de Chelles and Pierre de Montreuil, 1240s.

windows set in large pointed arches maintained the equilibrium of the level below. Above this a continuous screen of interlacing pointed arches concealed the pitched roof of the nave. Finally, twin towers rose in squared-off form, carved with deep lancet arches for the carillon bells.

Like the temples of the Khmer, the great Gothic cathedrals doubled as marvels of engineering and immense piles of sculpture. Statues were tucked into the niches, cut into the columns, and pitched on the roofs. The pyramidal pinnacles piled on the tops of the buttresses of Notre-Dame sprouted **crockets** above the level of the flyers like vegetal outgrowths. The pinnacles, once thought to be pure decoration, served as counterweights to the thrust of the flyers. **Gargoyles**, grotesque creatures sculpted on the downspouts, stuck out as fetish elements animating the upper

ranges of the cathedrals (Fig. 9.2-15). As diabolical figures they haunted the house of God the way sins disturb human consciousness.

The Spread of Gothic: International yet Local

The first few bays of the pavement in the nave of Chartres Cathedral contained a labyrinth. In its center were portraits of the master builders who designed the structure. The Christian faithful entering the cathedral followed its twisted path on their knees, awestruck by the majesty of the soaring vaulted interiors. They revered the stones of the cathedral as sacred and paid homage to the masons who brought order to their complex assembly as heroes of a great mystery. These well-paid problem solvers, constantly migrating as the funding for

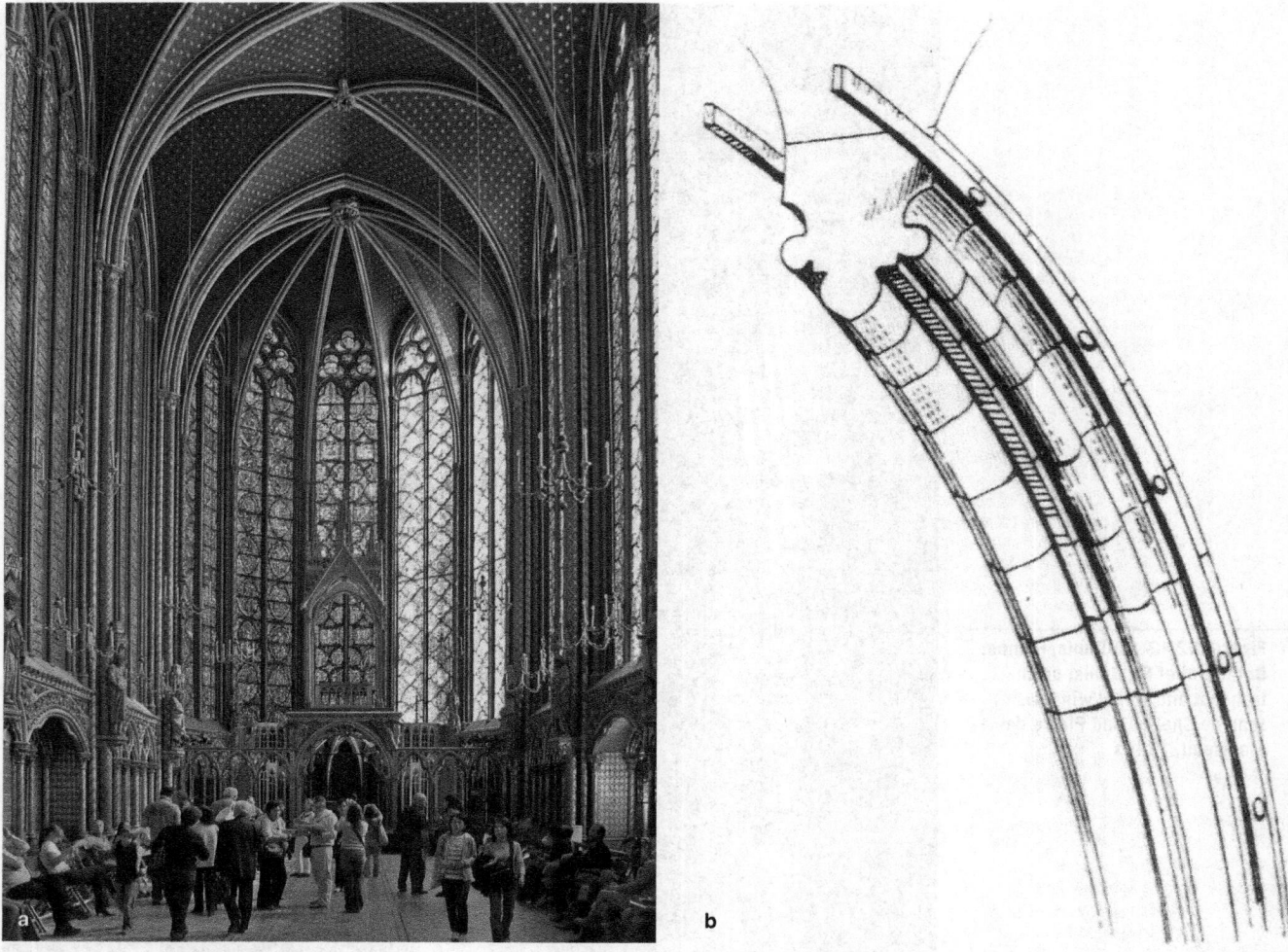

Figure 9.2-13 Paris. (a) Ste.-Chapelle, view of upper chapel with almost completely glazed enclosure, Jean de Chelles and Pierre de Montreuil, 1240s. (b) Drawing of Ste.-Chapelle by E. Viollet-le-Duc, showing metal reinforcing rods for the vertical piers, 1850.

one project subsided and that for another appeared, created the most meaningful artifacts of the booming cities.

William of Sens, one of the earliest documented master masons, was lured to England in 1175 to rebuild Canterbury Cathedral, which had partly burned down. His work on the Gothic cathedral of Sens, under construction for two decades, gave him excellent qualifications, and the chevet he added to the new choir of the English church showed his preference for French precedents. William died of complications after a fall from a scaffold at Canterbury, evidence that he was deeply involved in the building process as master mason, structural engineer, and building contractor.

Outside of France, Gothic style, or *Opus Francigenum*, carried associations with French nation building. After its assimilation into a foreign context, however, Gothic soon shook off its associations with the French to become English, German, Dutch, Spanish, Czech, Portuguese, and even reluctantly Italian. The English, because of their Norman heritage, were as much responsible for the development of the style as the French. Ribbed vaults had appeared very early at Durham and were arranged in astounding

combinations at Lincoln Cathedral during the 1190s, contemporary with the construction of Chartres. The vaults over St. Hugh's choir looked in plan like adjacent *Y* figures, with one inverted, leaving a rhomboid gap between them (Fig. 9.2-16). Perhaps the designers intended to redistribute the loads of one vault from pushing against the other. In any event, these eccentric structures have neither collapsed nor attracted imitators. A generation later, in the nave of Lincoln Cathedral, the masons raised vaults with a profusion of radiating ribs that made each bay look like a starfish, anticipating the fan vaults of later centuries.

Several features at Wells Cathedral (Fig. 9.2-17) demonstrate that empirical engineering methods existed outside of France and that the English masons could arrive at quite innovative solutions on their own. One of the most common structural failures in English cathedrals involved the collapse of the central tower over the crossing. This occurred at both Lincoln and Ely Cathedrals. The designers at Wells, anticipating the stresses at the intersection of the crossing, inserted huge "scissor" arches in the 1330s. These curving *X*-shaped forms dramatically interrupted the flow of the nave, adding tangible support to the base of the spire.

Figure 9.2-14 Paris. Notre-Dame, 1250s. (a) View from the southeast, showing the flying buttresses. (b) Transept wheel window. (c) Western facade, with niches for the kings of France on the mezzanine level.

Figure 9.2-15 Paris. Notre-Dame, gargoyle, 1250s.

Figure 9.2-16 Lincoln, England. Lincoln Cathedral, St. Hugh's choir with *Y*-shaped rib vaults, 1220s.

The notebooks of Villard de Honnecourt, compiled during the first half of the thirteenth century, catalogued the type of knowledge an itinerant master mason could contribute to a foreign context. Gothic style appeared in Germany through both the arrival of French masons and the taste preferences of elite patronage. At Trier, near the border with France, the choir windows of the Liebenfraukirche of the 1220s imitated those of Reims Cathedral, revealing the presence of French masons. Villard drew the exact same windows in his notebooks. In 1248 the archbishop of Cologne desired to reproduce the plan and tracery of Notre-Dame at Amiens for his new cathedral. From this project there was further diffusion of the style to Burgos, Spain. Although the towers of Cologne remained incomplete until the nineteenth century, their design of open-web steeples directly inspired copies at the Spanish church (Fig. 9.2-18), executed in 1442 by the master mason Juan de Colonia, or Johan of Cologne.

Even Italy, which resisted Gothic style in favor of its strong Roman heritage, produced new versions of ribbed vaults and pointed arches. Gothic became the preferred style of the Dominican order, which built grand churches such as SS. Giovanni e Paolo in Venice. The Franciscan order likewise opted for Gothic in the design of its mother church in Assisi. The decision would no doubt have perturbed the order's founder, St. Francis (1181–1226), who even more than St. Bernard preferred modest, unpretentious buildings. The great cathedrals planned in fourteenth-century

Figure 9.2-17 Wells, England. Wells Cathedral, scissor piers at the crossing to support tower, 1330s.

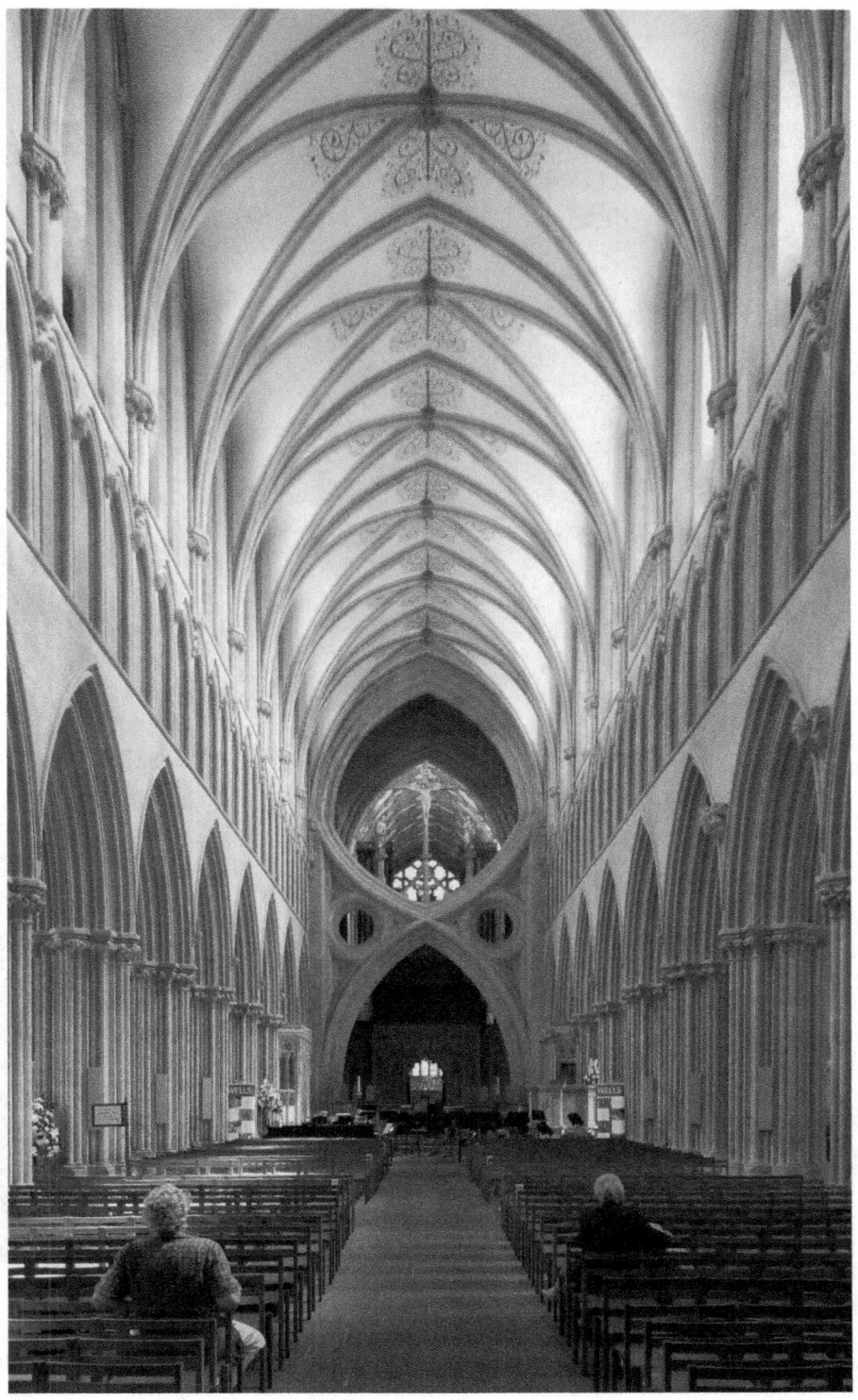

Florence and Bologna opted for a purified Gothic, without flying buttresses or complex tracery. In Milan, however, the Visconti tyrants in 1386 promoted the full-fledged flamboyant Gothic, which required the advice of French and German experts because of its adventurous structural demands (Fig. 9.2-19).

One of the French Gothic masters, Eudes de Montreuil, had worked for Louis IX during the Crusades and migrated on commission to remote Sweden to design the Uppsala Cathedral from 1248 to 1254. Villard in his notebooks wrote with great pride of being invited to Hungary for his services. While his drawings would not suffice to carry out a building, they provided a great wealth of details, proportional methods, and techniques to assist potential clients and helpers.

The masons' lodges at the cathedrals, where the designers and workers resided during a building campaign, became the architecture schools of the age. They involved a dozen or so specialists who lived together like a family and, in some cases, belonged to the same family. The best-documented dynasty of master masons descended from Heinrich Parler of Cologne in the fourteenth century. To what degree Parler worked on Cologne Cathedral cannot be determined. His name apparently derived from the French term for a contractor's foreman, *parlier*. He and his descendants pursued a clear style and signed their works with a family emblem, a stylized hook.

His son Peter worked with him on the cathedral of the Holy Cross at Schwäbisch Gmünd, Germany, after which they gained the commission for the Frauenkirche at the marketplace of Nuremburg in the 1350s. Like the other great church in Nuremburg, St. Sebald, the side aisles of the Frauenkirche rose as tall as the nave. The uniform height of this **Hallenkirche** type allowed more light into the interior. Peter caught the attention of Emperor Charles IV, who brought him to work on the new cathedral of St. Vitus in Prague. As in the churches designed with his father, he treated the ribs of the vaults like a radiating series of nets rather than lines converging on a central spine (Fig. 9.2-20). Prized as both a sculptor and an engineer, Peter also designed Prague's Charles Bridge in

Figure 9.2-18 Burgos, Spain. Cathedral steeples, inspired by Cologne Cathedral, 1442.

1357. The ornate, three-story gateway tower at the first pier signaled the connection of the "old town" on the river with its new cathedral and the castle town across the river on the hill.

Another member of the Parler clan, Michael, and perhaps his son Heinrich, worked on Strasbourg Cathedral in the 1360s. The initial design for the structure by Erwin von Steinbach, constructed in 1236–1276, borrowed from Parisian models. Although only one of the two western towers reached completion, its spindly structure, the tallest in

Europe, vied with the west tower of Ulm Cathedral, where Michael Parler was known to have worked. Another family member, Johan Parler, designed the late-fourteenth-century choir and tower of the Freiburg Cathedral, in the successful Zähringer new town. The project showed a working knowledge of Strasbourg. The chain of commissions then passed to Johan's son Wenzel, who took charge of the design of St. Stephen's in Vienna, begun in 1399.

Teams and families of master masons, such as the Parlers, disseminated the Gothic approach to architecture so

Figure 9.2-19 Milan, Italy. Duomo, begun 1386, with Mannerist front portals and windows added in the 1560s. Facade completed ca. 1900.

thoughtfully explored in the notebooks of Villard. Cohorts of experienced builders, under the patronage of knowledge-able clients, added their interpretations. Gothic became an agreed-upon language of design that through a variety of regional situations developed into numerous local dialects.

Figure 9.2-20 Prague. St. Vitus Cathedral, Peter Parler, 1350s.

Further Reading

Bowie, Theodore. *The Sketchbook of Villard de Honnecourt.* Bloomington: Indiana University Press, 1959.

Bruzelius, Caroline Astrid. *The Thirteenth-Century Church at St-Denis.* New Haven, CT: Yale University Press, 1985.

Coldstream, Nicola. *Medieval Architecture.* New York: Oxford University Press, 2002.

Erlande-Brandenburg, Alain. *The Cathedral: The Social and Architectural Dynamics of Construction.* Translated by Martin Thom. New York: Cambridge University Press, 1994.

Friedman, David. *Florentine New Towns: Urban Design in the Late Middle Ages.* Cambridge, MA: MIT Press, 1988.

Gies, Frances, and Joseph Gies. *Cathedral, Forge and Waterwheel: Technology and Invention in the Middle Ages.* New York: Harper, 1994.

Gimpel, Jean. *The Medieval Machine: The Industrial Revolution of the Middle Ages.* London: Penguin, 1976.

Grodecki, Lawrence. *Gothic Architecture.* Translated by I. M. Paris. New York: Abrams, 1977.

Harvey, John. *The Master Builders: Architecture in the Middle Ages.* New York: McGraw-Hill, 1971.

James, John. *Chartres: The Masons Who Built a Legend.* London: Routledge & Kegan Paul, 1982.

Mark, Robert. *Experiments in Gothic Structure.* Cambridge, MA: MIT Press, 1982.

9.3 SUB-SAHARAN AFRICA
Living Architecture

Sub-Saharan Africa possesses the most ancient traces of human existence yet remains among the least documented areas of the world. The impermanence of African architecture and urbanism likewise complicates a historical understanding of the region. For millennia most Africans built clusters of cell-like structures, but to determine when variations occurred in their designs proves as difficult as establishing a precise chronology for the evolution of biological species. The perennial "primitive hut" evolved but did not leave traces of its development. Buildings made of mud and straw offered shelter for a wide variety of societies in Africa and survived in relative autonomy as the primary type of shelter for subsistence farmers and simple shepherds.

As designers and builders of their own homes and villages, Africans created a truly living architecture, involving most of the members of their communities in the process. The constant reproduction of dwellings yielded a traditional African architecture that always seemed the same but in fact continually changed according to circumstances, such as the life situation of the occupants, the political choices of the community, and the resource potential of the territory. While shapes and layouts in African architecture remained constant, technical, material, and social influences led to subtle refinements.

Eastern Africa: Ethiopia, the Swahili Coast, and Zimbabwe

Excepting the ancient states of Nubia south of the first cataract of the Nile and the realm of Axum in the Ethiopian highlands overlooking the Red Sea, one finds scarce evidence of urbanization and permanent architecture on the African continent south of the Sahara before 1000 CE. Intense heat, low-yielding agriculture, and tropical diseases prevented most African regions from easy urban development. These contexts favored small-scale vernacular structures in villages rather than monumental expressions.

Since the third millennium BCE the Nubians had posed serious competition to the Egyptians. Their rulers built pyramids, temples, and monuments in the effort to rival their neighbors. Ramesses II created his most ambitious works in Nubia to demonstrate his hegemony over the region. During the New Kingdom period the land of Axum, led by the *negusa negast* ("king of kings"), created hundreds of funeral stelae, some taller than the obelisks in Luxor. These flat needles, the last dating from the third century BCE, carried inscriptions with architectural details and terminated in head-shaped rounded tops.

During the transition to Byzantine power both Nubia and Axum converted to the Coptic version of Christianity in the fourth century CE and continued exchanges with the Byzantines for many centuries. The churches of Christian Nubia, known only from ruins at Faras and Old Dongola, generally followed central plans like Byzantine churches. The most important Ethiopian churches were initially built in the old capital of Axum. During the thirteenth century, however, the Zagwe dynasty attempted to revive the declining status of Ethiopia, building a series of extraordinary rock-cut churches in the southern city of Lalibela, named after

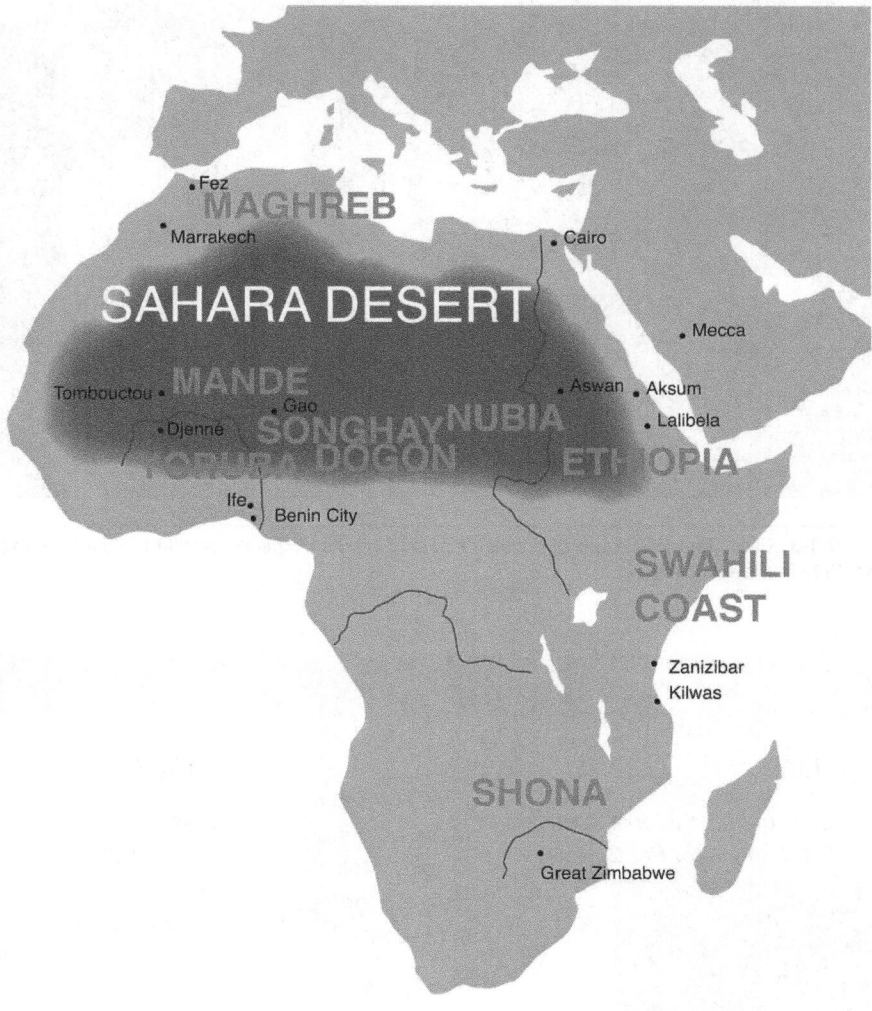

Figure 9.3-1 Map of Africa, 1000–1350.

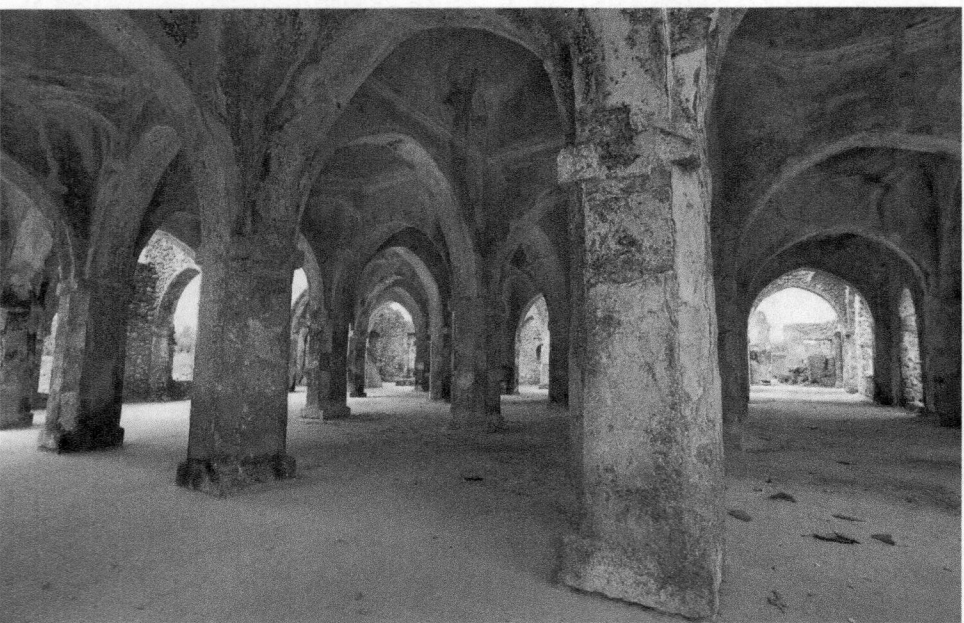

the first of their priest-kings, Lalibela (r. ca. 1181–1221). The twelve new churches cut from the local volcanic tufa stone represented a new Jerusalem. They cut the Bet Giorgis as a cruciform prism within a 13 m (43 ft) deep quadrangular chasm (Fig 9.3-2). One approached the church from above and first encountered its flat roof, decorated with three superimposed Greek crosses. A hidden tunnel far off to one side served as a passageway to reach the entry. The ground level had blind windows that featured monkey-head nubs at the corners, a motif found on ancient Axumite walls with timber frame reinforcement. As with Indian rock-cut temples, the builders at Lalibela carved the stone to simulate the less permanent building systems of wood.

Nubia maintained its independence from Islamic rule until the fourteenth century as the major supplier of black slaves to Cairo. The slave markets were found on the eastern, or Swahili, coast of Africa (modern Tanzania) and saw significant urbanization after the year 1000. The emir of Kilwa, Husuni Kubwa, supplied the mass of *zanj*, black slaves, for sale to Baghdad and other Southwest Asian markets in exchange for salt and spices. There he built a palace in adobe with vaulted chambers and lumber reinforcements, successfully imitating the luxury and details of the structures belonging to his Muslim trading partners (Fig. 9.3-3). The palace contained a thermal bath and focused

Figure 9.3-3 Kilwa, Tanzania. Ruins of the emir's palace overlooking slave market of Husuni Kubwa, eleventh to fourteenth century.

1167
King Lalibela of Ethiopia sponsors rock-cut church of Bet Giorgis

King Mansa Musa of Mande Empire, Mali, makes pilgrimage to Mecca
1324

1327
Mansa Musa sponsors Djinguereé Mosque in Tombouctou, Mali

Sankoré Mosque begun in Tombouctou, Mali

1340

on an octagonal court with a tiled pool, decorated with Kufic inscriptions. It occupied a defensible position on a bluff overlooking the city and its slave market. Kilwa went into irreversible decline during the Black Death of 1348.

While climate generally discouraged urbanization in other parts of East Africa, a few highland areas attracted denser settlements, such as Engaruka near Lake Manyara in modern Tanzania and, south of this, Great Zimbabwe, in modern Zimbabwe. The elevated position of the latter on the high plateau of the Zambizi savannah, over 1,000 m (3,280 ft) above sea level, lowered the average temperatures and reduced the threat of *tsetse* flies and other bearers of tropical diseases. Zimbabwe came to prominence through trade with the Swahili coast in the thirteenth century, marketing ivory, gold, and leather. Here the elites of the region created an extraordinary monumental setting, leaving the only large stone structures in Africa south of the Nile. Other parts of Africa occasionally used stone in the footings of huts or at thresholds, but rarely for an entire structure.

The Shona people built the magnificent granite drywalls of the Great Zimbabwe enclosure between the twelfth and fifteenth centuries (Fig. 9.3-4a,b). It was the largest and most carefully crafted of at least seven major *zimbabwes* (literally "stone structures") constructed at distances of 150 km (90 miles) from one another by the competing cattle-raising elites of the region. The formidable walls of the stone enclosures, in places 10 m (33 ft) high and 5 m (16 ft) thick, had no apparent practical function. They rose too high and remained too open for use as fortifications or shelters. They most likely served as fetish objects, derived from the nearly universal custom of piling up rocks as religious or funerary markers. The rulers built massive stone walls to convey distinction, commanding thousands of hours of labor, coming from either slaves or those owing tribute. The *zimbabwe* builders claimed the greater part of the cattle reserves for themselves, and the stone walls stood as a tangible symbol of their superior status.

The stones of Great Zimbabwe came as a gift of nature: as at Skara Brae (see Section 1.2), the strips of granite in this region crumbled

into brick-size pieces, which facilitated their assembly into smooth walls. The builders did not need metal tools to quarry or work the masonry but simply gathered the stones, preselecting them by size to keep the courses of the walls regular. They set each course slightly inward from the one below, giving the walls on both sides a gentle rake. Near the top the builders laid the stones in decorative patterns—zigzags, chevrons, and checkerboards—which lightened the load and gave a sense of termination to the parapets. At their base the walls included drains to keep the interior of the compound dry. Great Zimbabwe stretched 110 m (361 ft) across its elliptical length, similar

Figure 9.3-4 Zambezi savannah, Zimbabwe. Great Zimbabwe, twelfth to fifteenth century. (a) View of the Hill Ruin and elliptical enclosure. (b) See next page.

in area to the Gothic cathedrals. In some respects the enclosure evoked an outsized version of the typical African dwelling compound, with cells placed inside a perimeter fence. A conical tower, located just inside the curve of the southern walls, peeked out a meter or so above the perimeter wall like a grain silo. Solid to the core, without internal space or stairs to reach its summit, the tower remained a purely symbolic artifact. One approached it through a long, narrow passage that set it off in a restricted sanctuary of profound ceremonial significance, Zimbabwe's holy of holies.

Like many of the peoples of Africa, the Shona adhered to animistic beliefs, according to which all of the elements of nature possessed a spirit. The great rocks of the original settlement at the Hill Ruin would have seemed like gigantic beings, which most likely offered themselves to an evolving tradition of stone worship. As the power of the kings increased, they attached the huge walls to the large monoliths to provide even more impressive objects for cult veneration.

Conical finials capped the top of the walls, similar to the mounds for ancestor worship built in other parts of Africa.

The demise of the *zimbabwe* builders during the fifteenth century came as the result of the ecological exhaustion of the region. The overworked land could not support such large numbers of cattle and people living near the great stone enclosures. The builders' disappearance also coincided with the arrival of the Portuguese fleet, which favored the coastal regions, along the Swahili coast. With time the mud dwellings disappeared, leaving only the venerable stone walls.

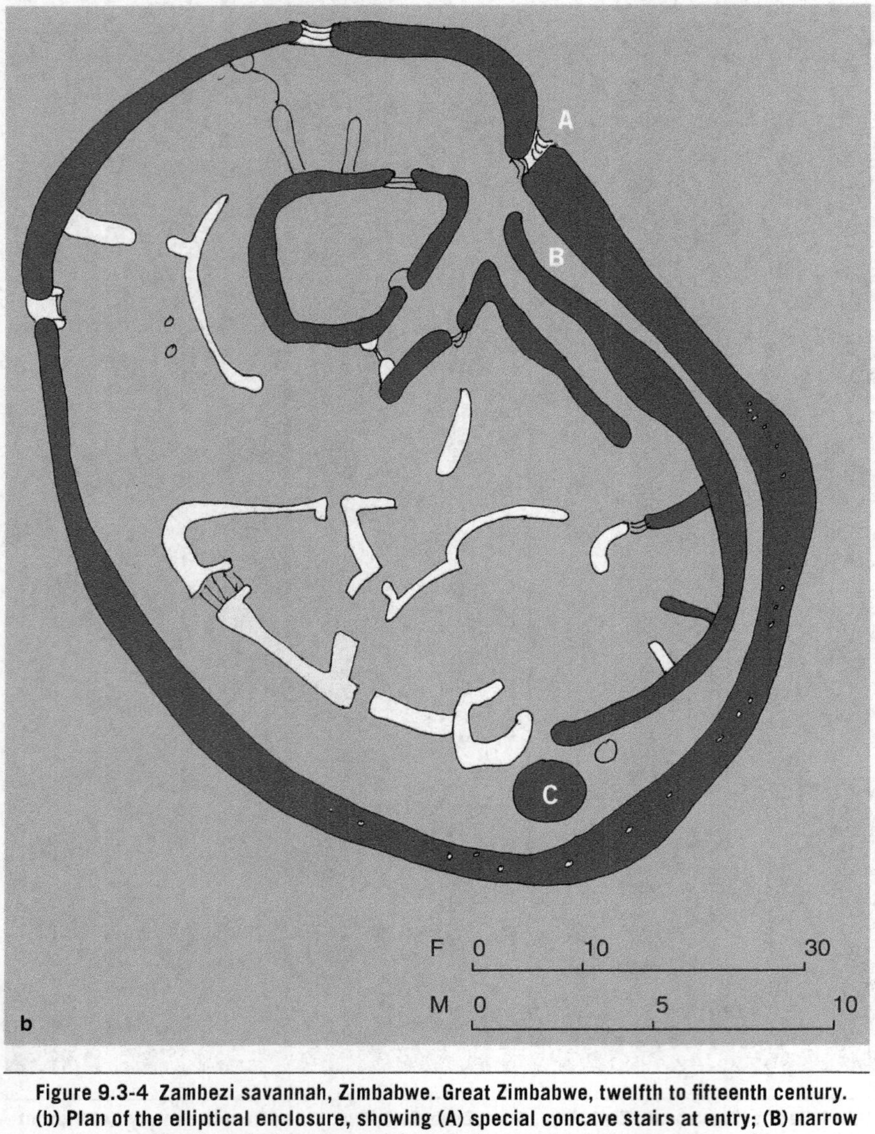

West Africa: From Dogon Villages to the Yoruba Metropolis

Geography determined the slower urban development of the majority of sub-Saharan Africa: the tropical climate in some regions reached 50°C for long stretches of the year, preventing agriculture from flourishing. Limited foodstuffs, combined with the waterborne tropical diseases and parasites, kept the population at a relatively low density. Most Africans, from the Transvaal plains in South Africa to the rain forest in central Africa to the West African savannah, lived in rounded cell structures in small villages. Each year they fixed, added to, or totally rebuilt their shelters. Building became inseparable from living. These vernacular builders honored the spirits of their ancestors with conical votive mounds while expressing the spirit of daily life in the constant renewal of their dwellings.

West African villagers usually organized their huts in clusters, often arranging them into oval or circular enclosures. Depending on the agricultural yield of the land, the proximity of the individual cells of a village would vary from extremely close to widely scattered, and from as few as a half-dozen to over 100. At the village of Kasuliyili in central Ghana, the Dagamba tribe lived in over three dozen clusters of six to ten cells, which were scattered 5 to 50 m (16 to 164 ft) from each other. In Tongo, a Tallensi village located 100 km (62 miles) farther north, clusters of similar dimensions spread, with cells separated more than 1 km (0.6 miles) from each other. The land in the south could feed a higher number of inhabitants per hectare. The village of Tongo presented a social diagram based on the hierarchy of wives' courtyards, organizing the wives in chronological order and containing their cooking areas, an area for married sons, another for unmarried sons, a livestock pen, and granaries. The granary stood out as the most articulated element of African villages, raised off the ground on a base of logs or stilts to avoid dampness. The **silos** stood taller than the regular huts and were often crowned with

Figure 9.3-4 Zambezi savannah, Zimbabwe. Great Zimbabwe, twelfth to fifteenth century. (b) Plan of the elliptical enclosure, showing (A) special concave stairs at entry; (B) narrow sanctuary path; (C) conical tower, reminiscent of grain silos but completely solid.

Figure 9.3-5 Mali. Dogon village.

a parapet and sculptural decoration. An entry hole large enough for a man to slip in was placed halfway up the elevation, accessed by a ladder that could be removed when not in use to discourage rats. As the treasury of the community's alimentary surplus, the granary assumed a monumental function, comparable to the role of domes in the Mediterranean.

While indigenous buildings tended to be round, derived from either the basket-like structures of woven twigs or the coiled adobe construction made of **banco** (wads of mud), orthogonal geometry occasionally appeared in exceptional contexts. The Dogon culture in the modern state of Mali, for instance, tended to build its villages with square stone cells. Since at least the fourteenth century they settled along the great Bandiagara escarpment, a 200 km (124 mile) length of cliff that in places rises 600 m (1,968 ft). Here, the geometry was conditioned by the formidable stone cliffs, which established a geological precedent for right angles. The availability of brick-shaped stones taken from the cliffs likewise encouraged orthogonal plans. The square huts of the Dogon repeated the order of villages made with round structures, forming clusters focused on the granaries (Fig. 9.3-5).

The language used to name buildings and their parts in a Dogon village reveals a traditional anthropomorphic theory of design. Every element corresponded to the parts of the human body, a conceit that appears in many other West African societies. According to this anthropomorphic view, the council building (*toguna*), its plaza, and the blacksmith's forge represented the head; the family huts stood for the torso; the menstrual hut signified the hands; the granary and crushing platform represented the female genitals; the conical shrines represented the male genitals; and the altars at the outskirts of the village were the feet. Dogon builders also conceived the house in anthropomorphic terms: the kitchen cell as the head, the open court as the torso, the storage rooms as the arms, and the whole complex symbolizing the sexual union of man and woman.

The Tamberma people of Togo shared this carnal interpretation of architecture, making beehive-shaped, mud-walled dwellings representing a body (Fig. 9.3-6): windows like eyes, doorway frames like lips, interior granaries like

Figure 9.3-6 Togo. Tamberma dwellings.

stomachs, grinding stones like teeth, and the roof drainpipe like a penis. In this metaphorical system, the dwelling became a mirror of one's being and an index of one's life. The changes enacted on these regularly rebuilt structures served as the history of a people.

The Niger River system of West Africa passes through a mosaic of savannah and rain forest areas. Its natural abundance encouraged the growth of several large city-states that created significant artistic and architectural works from the twelfth through fifteenth centuries. The Yoruba-speaking tribes emerged as the most urbanized of the West African peoples, now mostly found in modern Nigeria. Like the

Dogon, they built with orthogonals, but on a much grander scale. The great fertility of the Niger River led to a larger concentration of surplus and population, which allegedly reached 25 million by the fourteenth century. The Yoruba traditions related to a sophisticated political structure based on interregional cults, centralized power, capital cities, slave labor, and a pretense of empire.

The earliest Yoruba capital at Ile-Ife dates to the ninth century. Set in a hilly forest, a concentric series of five oval walls surrounded its central palace complex, 4 km (2.4 miles) across. The royal architects arranged the single-story rectangular structures into clusters gathered around small *impluvium* courts, with the roofs sloping toward the center. They lined the courts with stone pavers. Though smaller and lower than the Roman *domus* type and lacking classical symmetry, the tightly packed Yoruban courtyards recalled the fabric of ancient Pompeii. According to legend, the Yoruba creator god, Oduduwa, sent his children from Ile-Ife to be the rulers of the twelve major cities of the region and thus transferred divine status to the kings and queens. The stunning bronze heads sculpted in Ile-Ife served as surrogates for the immortal rulers, who continued to live in sculptural form after their deaths.

Although Ile-Ife degenerated during the fourteenth century and was periodically abandoned, all the peoples of the Niger River valley revered it as a sacred city, the source of the Yoruban pantheon of over 600 gods. After its decline political power first passed northwest to the king of Oyo, 170 km (106 miles) northwest of Ile-Ife, before moving downstream to Benin. Benin City (not to be confused with the modern state of Benin) emerged as the new dominant city, controlled by non-Yoruba, Edo speakers. A deified king, known as the *oba*, ruled Benin. He lived in the center of the city in a large palace with many *impluvium* courtyards surrounded by fortified walls. The city spread over an immense terrain covering approximately 20 × 40 km (12 × 24 miles), a scale similar to

---

The *Toguna*: A Male Meeting Hall

Each Dogon village had a special open loggia structure, the *toguna*, or "house of words," where the men congregated to discuss political and social problems, similar in function to an ancient Greek *stoa*. The columns of the loggia were carved in either stone or wood and often represented female bodies, an African version of the caryatids (see Section 4.2). The *toguna*, which is still used today, is only high enough for men to sit in it, but not stand, since they are less likely to squabble from a sitting position.

Mali. Dogon village, *toguna*, loggia for male assemblies.

the sprawl of a modern metropolis, such as modern Lagos, or about twice the area of Angkor. Each of Benin City's dozens of adjacent enclaves had its own enclosure, adding up to 16,000 km (9,940 miles) of rammed-earth walls. The city spread as large as a state, and the impressive landworks spoke of its imperial capacity to press others into service.

After the arrival of Portuguese traders in the 1490s, Benin City became even more prosperous, expanding the already thriving local slave trade into an international export market. The majority of the 12 million slaves shipped from this region to the Americas between the sixteenth and nineteenth centuries spoke Yoruban dialects. The complicity of the Benin ruling class with the Portuguese taskmasters allowed them several centuries of prosperity. The slaves who were sent abroad, cut off from the spirit of their native villages, attempted to conserve some of their cosmic traditions in the meeting spaces, lean-to shelters, impromptu shrines, and, above all, music that traveled with them across the Atlantic.

The Sahel: An Islamic–African Synthesis

The West African edge of the Sahara Desert, known as the Sahel, or the "coast," began to attract urban development from the tenth century onward. Regular caravan trade became a constant, and the use of camels as "ships of the desert" added another maritime metaphor for the world's greatest uninterrupted expanse of arid land. Islam filtered into the cities of this region to mix with strong local belief systems. While mosques and minarets became dominant features of the skylines, indigenous technologies and religious functions, such as fetish veneration, blended into the new urban architecture. Ibn Batutta, while visiting the empire of Mali in 1353, noted what he perceived as the local inhabitants' alarming mixture of Islamic ritual with native animistic practices.

The houses in the cities of the Sahel conformed to the orthogonal models imported from Islamic North Africa, densely packed around courtyards. The dwellings nonetheless maintained the anatomical metaphors of West African mud structures. The entry stood for the head; the court for the belly; and the side rooms, one for males and another for females, for the two arms. Despite the strict Islamic dogma adopted by the rulers of these cities, the spirit of earlier beliefs survived in the language and iconography of the dwellings.

Songhay emerged in the ninth century as the first of the indigenous states in the Sahel. Its capital of Gao, on the eastern bend of the Niger River, dominated the region until the rise of the Mande Empire in the thirteenth century. Two centuries later Songhay returned to prominence, a rise marked by the construction of the mausoleum of Askia Muhammed, begun in 1495. Although its shape has greatly changed over the centuries, the mausoleum's impressive pyramidal form represents the culmination of the fusion of Arab and local sources. The great adobe pile, studded with gnarled *toron* sticks, rose like a prickly ziggurat. The sloping walls were smoothly mounded into three stages, with an external stairway that snaked its way to the summit, leaving a dynamic oblique pattern on the southern elevation. Originally, Askia Muhammed's tomb rose 20 m (66 ft) in seven stages, which corresponded to the local belief that the sky consisted of seven superimposed beds. Today, after considerable melting, it stands 11 m (36 ft) high. As with all mud buildings, if not resurfaced on a yearly basis, the mass dissolves through contact with the elements. The elevations of the tomb were articulated with crooked *toron* sticks, placed at regular half-meter intervals, a practice derived from local icons of regeneration. The *torons* added lateral reinforcement to the walls and served as scaffolding for the yearly plastering, while keeping alive contact with the fetishes of pre-Islamic faith.

The legendary magician-king Sundiata Keita brought together the Mande-speaking region north of the Niger Valley during the mid-thirteenth century. The Mande Empire reached its apex under his grandnephew, Mansa Musa (r. 1312–1337), who, after his famous pilgrimage to Mecca in 1324, began an ambitious building campaign. The king hoped to equal the marvels he had visited in Mecca, Cairo, and North Africa. As described by the Tunisian writer Ibn Khaldun (1332–1406), Mansa Musa traveled with an entourage of 40,000, including twenty pack camels loaded with gold bullion. While most of Mansa Musa's palaces and religious structures have not survived, two works in Tombouctou belong to this flourishing period of the mid-fourteenth century. The Andalusian poet-architect Abu Ishap Es Saheli Altuwaidjin, who accompanied the king on his return to Mali, designed the Great Mosque, or Djinguéré, at the southwest edge of the city in 1327 (Fig. 9.3-7). In the 1580s Imam

Figure 9.3-7 Tombouctou, Mali. Djinguéré (Great Mosque), begun 1327.

al-Akib rebuilt and enlarged the structure, which was almost entirely made of *banco*, dried adobe balls combined with organic materials such as fiber, straw, feathers, and wood chips. The builders created a broad structure of twenty-seven rows of rounded arches facing the *qibla* wall, some made of limestone and burnt-brick blocks, a rare application of masonry in this region. The thickness of the piers and lack of windows rendered the interior exceptionally dark. The somber light filtered through two inner courts. One of the two original minarets has survived, rising on a square base with sloping walls and *torons*. It was capped with a conical turret that closely resembled the traditional pre-Muslim ancestor shrines. Another conical turret rose above the *mihrab* on the *qibla* wall, further conserving the memory of folk religion.

The other important mosque in Tombouctou, the Sankoré Mosque (Fig. 9.3-8), was begun by a female patron of Tuareg origin in 1340. It also was rebuilt by Imam al-Akib in the 1580s. Its perfectly square court, 14 m (45 ft) per side, emulated the dimensions of the Kaaba in Mecca in negative. The center of the southern elevation hosted a massive ziggurat-shaped minaret rising about 15 m (49 ft), with similar geometry and style to the Askia Muhammed

mausoleum in Gao. The northern part of the shrine, known as the "university-mosque," served as classrooms for the celebrated University of Sankoré. During the fifteenth century there may have been as many as 25,000 students in Tombouctou. Since 1952 the sands of the advancing desert have nearly engulfed its volume.

The city of Djenné, 400 km (248 miles) west of Tombouctou, like Gao emerged in the ninth century as a commercial hub and during the mid-thirteenth century, through the aegis of the local king, Koi Konboro, converted to Islam. When asked what a virtuous follower of the religion should do, the king replied, "Plant a tree, dig a well, and build a mosque." The Great Mosque of Djenné, built in the fourteenth century, melted into ruin and was later abandoned for several centuries. In 1907, during the period of French dominance of Mali, the colonial government sponsored the rebuilding of the Djenné Mosque (Fig. 9.3-9). The architect, Ismaila Traore, chief of the local building guild, worked within the centuries-old traditions of earth construction, maintaining the synthesis of Islamic and local homage to the spirit cults. He designed the new structure directly on the site of the old mosque without using modern graphic tools, resulting in a curious parallelogram layout. The turreted buttresses

Figure 9.3-8 Tombouctou, Mali. Sankoré Mosque with ziggurat-shaped minaret, begun 1340.

Figure 9.3-9 Djenné, Mali. Great Mosque, built by traditional designers in 1907 over the remains of an earlier, fourteenth-century mosque.

and mask-like portals closely resembled traditional Sahel mosques of the fourteenth century. The conical tips of the vertical pylons evoked the spirit mounds of ancestor worship in pre-Islamic Africa. They are also strangely reminiscent of the pinnacles of Gothic churches, while the *torons* jut out suggestively like gargoyles. These fetish icons added a sense of primordial religion to the structure.

The Great Mosque of Djenné requires replastering every year and relies on community volunteers to do the work as part of the Ramadan festival. With each application of mud, the building's contours take on a slightly altered shape. Like the mud huts of West African villages, the mosque belongs to a living process. It can only survive through a continual commitment to restoration. The *torons*, now placed with strict regularity, poke out of the elevations and, in the flickering of their shadows, gesture that the spirit world continues into the present.

Further Reading

Blier, Suzanne P. *The Anatomy of Architecture: Ontology and Metaphor in Batammaliba Architectural Expression*. Chicago: University of Chicago Press, 1987.

Bourdier, Jean-Paul, and Trinh T. Minh-ha. *African Spaces: Designs for Living in Upper Volta*. London: Africana, 1985.

Connah, Graham. *African Civilizations: An Archaeological Perspective*. Cambridge, UK: Cambridge University Press, 2001.

Garlake, Peter. *Early Art and Architecture of Africa*. New York: Oxford University Press, 2002.

Iliffe, John. *Africans: The History of a Continent*. Cambridge, UK: Cambridge University Press, 1995.

Morris, James, and Suzanne Preston Blier. *Butabu: Adobe Architecture of West Africa*. New York: Princeton Architectural Press, 2004.

Pikirayi, Innocent. *The Zimbabwe Culture: Origins and Decline of Southern Zambezian States*. Walnut Creek, CA: Altamira Press, 2001.

Prussin, Labelle. *Architecture in Northern Ghana: A Study of Forms and Functions*. Berkeley: University of California Press, 1969.

———. *Hatumere: Islamic Design in West Africa*. Berkeley: University of California Press, 1986.

↗ Visit the free website **www.oup.com/us/ingersoll** to view chapter outlines and study questions; Google Maps showing the location of key sites; links to UNESCO World Heritage Sites; and essays on topics that cross time and culture.

CHAPTER 10

1350–1500

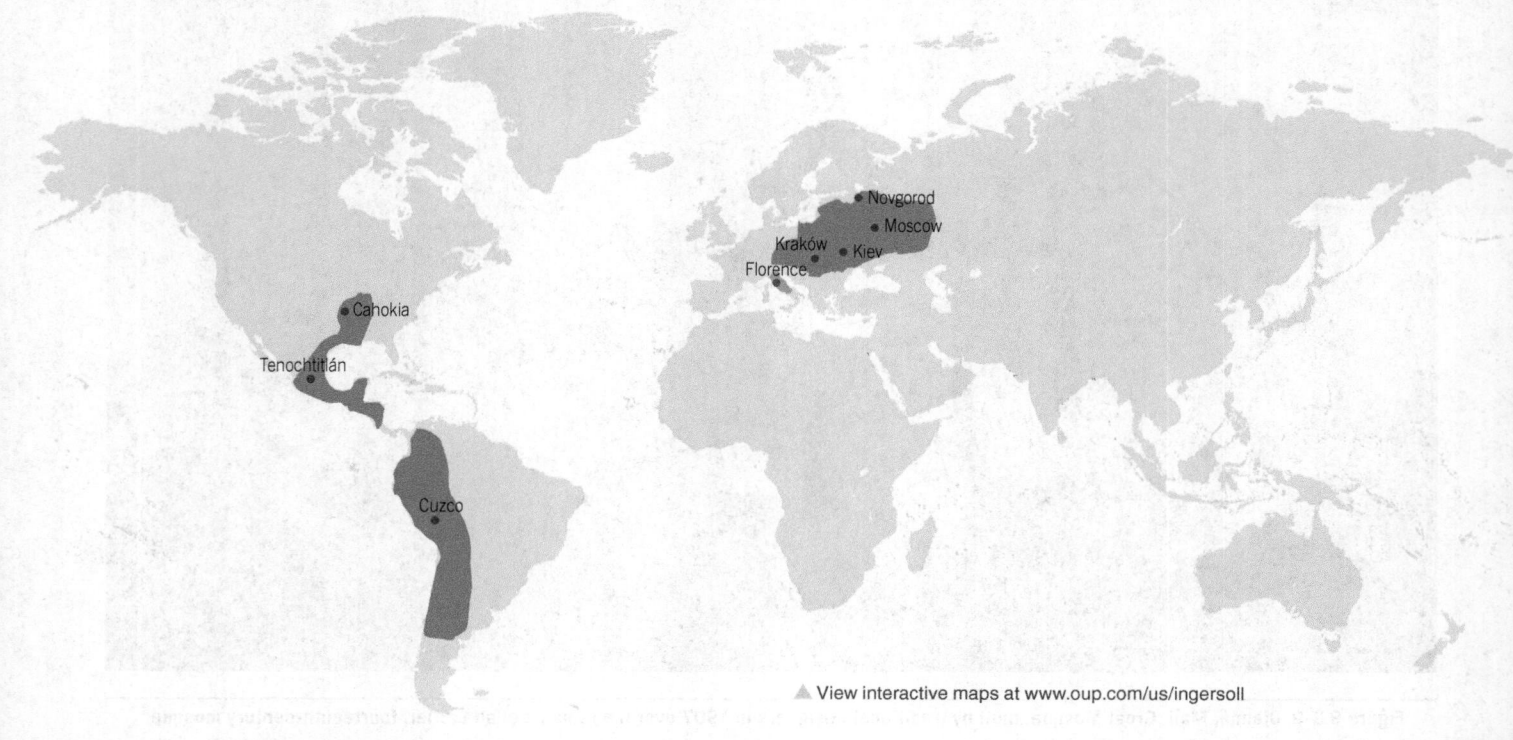

▲ View interactive maps at www.oup.com/us/ingersoll

10.1 HUMANIST ITALY: Public Spaces and Private Palaces of the Renaissance
10.2 EASTERN EUROPE: From the Spirit of Wood to the Conventions of Masonry
10.3 PRE-CONTACT AMERICA: Empires of the Sun

The idea of a *renaissance*, the rebirth of ancient Greco-Roman culture, grew naturally on Italian soil, where the ruins of ancient Rome were much in evidence. The well-educated humanist scholars in the merchant republic of Florence stimulated the desire for *all'antica* palaces, emulating the ancients. Among the Florentines the Medici family demonstrated how patronage for religious and secular buildings could perpetuate a clan's fame while adding to the magnificence of the city. This magnificence inspired the popes in Rome, such as Pius II, and the tyrants of Italy's many autonomous city-states, such as the duke of Montefeltro, to pursue a new style based on symmetry, harmonious proportions, and classical columns. Returning to the wisdom of ancient philosophers such as Plato, the humanists reconsidered the role of the city in human culture, leading to proposals for an ideal city. The balanced classical vision of Leon Battista Alberti and others appealed to rising powers abroad. During the late fifteenth and early sixteenth centuries, the monarchs of both Russia and Poland imported Italian designers to work on their key symbolic projects. Soon after the Atlantic crossings of Columbus, the humanists were able to match their own theories of a return to the grand unified state of ancient Rome with the immense empires discovered in the Americas: the Aztecs in Mexico and the Inca in Peru. The Aztec capital of Tenochtitlán appeared larger and more orderly than any city in Europe, while the Inca produced an efficient bureaucracy to manage the lands and labor of an empire more populous than the combined states of Europe.

10.1 HUMANIST ITALY
Public Spaces and Private Palaces of the Renaissance

The movement to revive ancient Greco-Roman culture, known in hindsight as the "Renaissance," had its epicenter in fourteenth- and fifteenth-century Florence. It began with the leaders of the Italian merchant republics, who educated their young as humanists, exposing them to ancient Greek and Latin sources of history, science, philosophy, art, and poetry. Humanism spread to the arts from the great Tuscan poets Dante, Petrarch, and Boccaccio. Architects attempted to create a correspondence through **all'antica** details from Greco-Roman culture. Artists and architects in Florence went beyond copying antiquity, however, eager to discover the underlying principles of design in order to surpass their models. Painters led the way by perfecting perspective vision, a scientific mode of seeing that put all the parts in relation to the whole. Architects followed, discovering harmonious proportions linked to the classical orders.

The new palaces and churches influenced by humanism changed the character of Italian cities, giving them a more uniform scale and geometric basis. The rebirth of ancient art and architecture not only carried an aesthetic agenda but also implied the restoration of a lost ideal of social and political order.

The Dome of Florence and Its Architect, Filippo Brunelleschi

The Florentine commune, a republic with elected officials, reached relative stability by 1300, having subdued the quarrelsome feudal nobility, which during the twelfth and thirteenth centuries had overwhelmed the center city with more than 100 tower houses. The wealthiest families from the merchant guilds dominated the artistic output of Florence. At first their republican creed discouraged them from demonstrating their individual fortunes for fear of attracting envy or heavier tax burdens. They channeled their collective resources into great civic projects, including the public palace (now called Palazzo Vecchio), the new cathedral of Santa Maria del Fiore, the public grain market of Orsanmichele (later turned into a church), the city walls, and a series of bridges. They managed the city's public works through the guilds, seeking to improve their corporate status through the grandeur of civic architecture.

Most public works in late-fourteenth-century Florence used rounded arches, symmetrically placed bays, and harmonious proportions based on whole numbers, such as 1:1, 1:2, and 2:3. To this the Florentines added a new way of seeing, treating buildings as freestanding objects in proportional space. The emergence of perspective vision accompanied the development of the principal public space of the city, the L-shaped Piazza della Signoria that surrounded Palazzo Vecchio (Fig. 10.1-1). In 1356 the urban magistrates cleared a final patch of houses to connect the

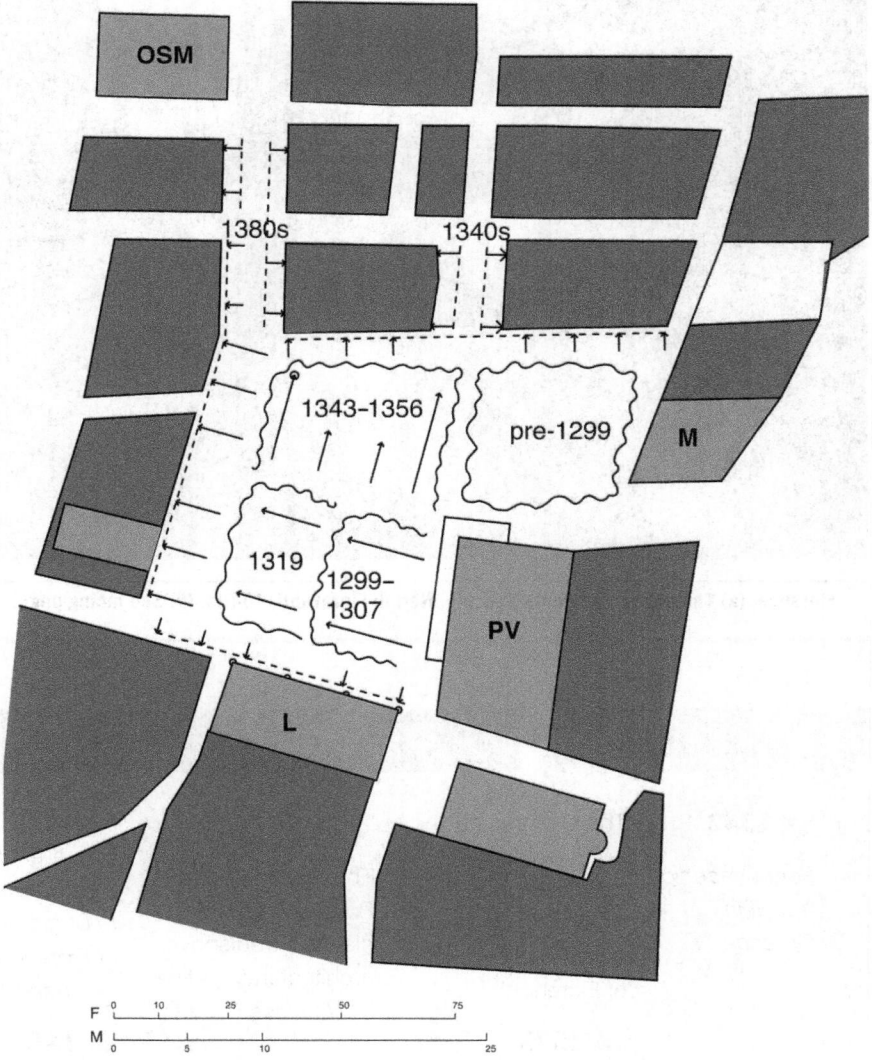

Figure 10.1-1 Florence. Expansion of the Piazza della Signoria, 1299–1380s. (PV) Prior's Palace, also called Palazzo Vecchio; (L) Loggia dei Priori, later Lanzi; (M) Mercanzia, the commerce office; (OSM) Orsanmichele church and grain market.

CONSTRUCTION, TECHNOLOGY, THEORY

Ponte Vecchio and the Segmental Arch

After the flood of 1333, the Florentines rebuilt their "old" bridge, Ponte Vecchio. The reconstructed bridge scale and symmetry set a new standard for the city. The designer, Neri di Fioravanti, began the reconstruction in the 1340s with financing from the Arte della Lana, the powerful wool guild. He spanned the river with three arches rather than the original five, introducing the new spanning technique of placing **segmental**

Florence. (a) The shop-lined Ponte Vecchio, Neri di Fioravanti, 1340s. (b) See facing page.

TIME LINE

▼ **1342**

Ponte Vecchio rebuilt in Florence

The *Ciompi* (the lower class of wool carders) rebel against the republican oligarchy of Florence

▲ **1378**

▼ **1414**

The Florentine Poggio Bracciolini claims to rediscover architectural treatise by Vitruvius

▲ **1418**

Filippo Brunelleschi wins competition to begin dome of Florence's cathedral

▼ **1420**

Pope Martin V ends schism in church and returns papacy to Rome

arches between the piers, which until then had only been seen at the scale of windows and doors. As a segment of a circle, this type of arch appeared flatter than a rounded arch but had the same compressive strength. Fioravanti doubled the width of the bridge to 18 m (59 ft) and lined it with regularly placed, single-bay shops that were clad in brownstone and crowned with a uniform parapet. He left a gap at mid-span for a perfectly square piazza overlooking the river. Ponte Vecchio became a model for a new type of urbanism based on symmetry and geometric order. It also proved a sound economic venture, as the rent from its forty-three shops offset the expense of construction. A few generations later the shopkeepers disrupted the unity of the facades by improvising dwellings propped up on brackets above the shop level, giving the bridge its current picturesque charm.

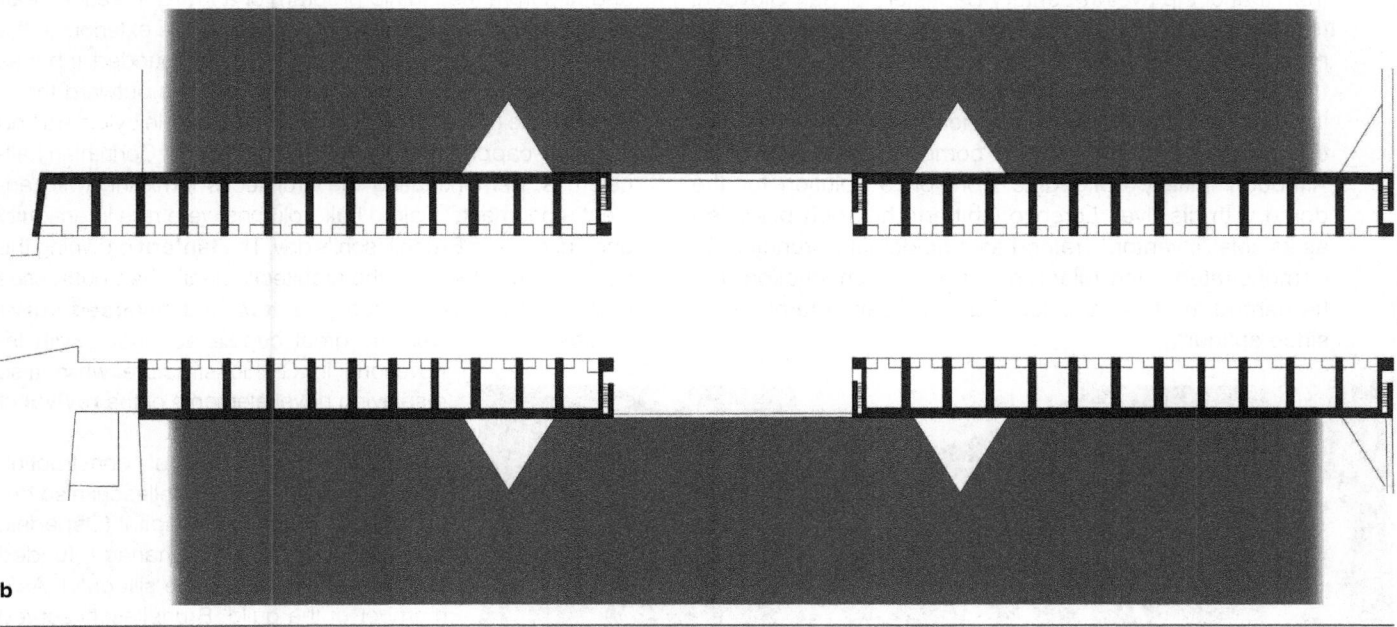

b

Florence. (b) Ponte Vecchio, plan, 1342.

initial rectangular piazza on the north to a second piazza that served the new southwest entry. The enlarged space, brought together on a grid of flagstones and brick pavers, allowed one to view the formidable volume of the city's public palace and bell tower in relation to its surroundings.

Construction began on Florence's greatest civic project, the cathedral of Santa Maria del Fiore, in 1296. Like all civic projects of this period, the design was entrusted to Arnolfo di Cambio, who proposed a simplified Gothic style, with quadripartite ribbed vaults spanning the nave and two side aisles. The Black Death of 1348 halted construction, and when it resumed a few years later Francesco Talenti extended the length of the nave an extra bay and outlined the area for a huge octagonal dome over the crossing, intended

Brunelleschi and Michelozzo begin work rebuilding church of San Lorenzo, Florence

▲ **1420s**

▼ **1434**

Cosimo de' Medici (the Elder) returns to Florence from exile

Roman Catholic Church holds Council of Florence in Santa Maria Novella

▲ **1439**

▼ **1444**

Palazzo Medici begun by Michelozzo in Florence

to surpass the domes of the rival cities of Pisa and Siena. In 1367 the commune charged a committee with setting the dimensions of the cupola as wide as the Pantheon in Rome and nearly twice its height. Neri di Fioravanti produced a scale model showing the dome's central octagon, which stepped down to three partial octagons, each of which contained five radiating chapels. In the 1380s the urban magistrates used **eminent domain** to clear the surrounding buildings and legislated that the houses be rebuilt with stone cladding and round-arched doors to echo the unusual outline of the dome (Fig. 10.1-2).

The structural concept for Fioravanti's dome derived from that of the twelfth-century Baptistery of San Giovanni (see Fig. 9.1-8a for comparison). Its unprecedented size, more than one-third wider and over twice the height of the Baptistery, posed tremendous logistical problems for its construction. Filippo Brunelleschi (1377–1446) took charge of the project after a competition held in 1418. Although initially obliged to work on a solution for the dome with his rival, Lorenzo Ghiberti, he soon prevailed as its sole "inventor." Trained as a goldsmith, Brunelleschi demonstrated such talent in the art of construction that he earned the title "architect," a qualification rarely used since antiquity.

The architect astounded the city by proposing to build the new dome without **falsework**, contriving a structure that supported itself during the process of construction. His scheme substantially reduced the costs of lumber and carpentry for temporary wooden supports. The secret of Brunelleschi's double-shelled structure lay in a combination of clever masonry techniques and a ribbed skeleton girded by nine horizontal supports concealed between the two layers (Fig. 10.1-3). He also invented such laborsaving machines as an ox-driven hoist, a turnstile with gears, and sprockets used for lifting materials onsite.

While Brunelleschi borrowed the dome's pointed arches and ribs from the Gothic program of a few generations earlier, he added several all'antica details to the exterior. At the base of the octagonal drum he inserted rounded tribunes between the three apses to help absorb the outward thrust of the dome (Fig. 10.1-4). Each of these marble cylinders had five shell-capped **niches**, flanked by pairs of Corinthian half-columns, demonstrating the architect's familiarity with ancient monuments. Paired half-columns were rare in antiquity and unknown in Brunelleschi's day. The **lantern** crowning the dome, completed after the architect's death, had buttresses made with classical fluted **pilasters** and **reversed-curve** volutes (Fig. 10.1-5). The great cupola abounded with innovations in Gothic structure while also displaying novel elements of the **revival** of ancient Roman style.

In 1419, the year that construction began on the dome, Brunelleschi also designed the Foundling Hospital (Ospedale degli Innocenti), an orphanage funded by the Arte della Seta, the silk guild. As a member of the guild, Brunelleschi served on its building committee. While his design, completed by others during the next three decades, respected the conventions of earlier hospitals in Florence, using long

Figure 10.1-2 Florence. Buildings surrounding the cathedral of Santa Maria del Fiore, 1296–1380s. Their stone cladding and round-arched doors echo the unusual outline of the dome, as dictated by urban magistrates in the 1380s.

Leon Battista Alberti begins redesign of San Francesco as a mausoleum for Malatesta of Rimini ▲ 1450

▼ 1452 Leon Battista Alberti publishes treatise on architecture titled *De re aedificatoria*

Mehmed II (Fatih, "the Conqueror") takes Constantinople for the Ottoman Turks ▲ 1453

▼ 1460 Pope Pius II Piccolomini transforms village of Corsignano into ideal city of Pienza Filarete (Antonio Averlino) proposes ideal city of Sforzinda to duke of Milan

Alberti completes facade of Santa Maria Novella, Florence ▲ 1470

Figure 10.1-3 Florence. Cathedral dome, Filippo Brunelleschi, 1419–1446, on top of the church designed by Cambio and Talenti.

halls and courtyards set behind a public **loggia**, the facade had a distinct classical appearance, with ancient-style Corinthian columns and pilasters (Fig. 10.1-6). He set the level of the loggia above head height on a nine-step base. This stage-like relation to the piazza added an even greater sense of drama to the anonymous act of leaving an orphan at a window on the far left of the loggia. A century later a nearly identical loggia was built directly opposite the hospital, completing the symmetry of the piazza. The site, which was named Piazza Santissima Annunziata, Florence's most

elegant and formally controlled public space and site of the annual Passion play reenacting the Annunciation, reached completion in 1601 with the addition of the equestrian statue in mid-space and a loggia on the church.

Another project begun in 1419 by Brunelleschi, the Old **Sacristy** of San Lorenzo (Fig. 10.1-7), was commissioned by the Medici family. Giovanni di Bicci de' Medici invested in his family's status by financing this chamber to the side of the main altar where the clergy stored vestments and sacred paraphernalia. The program included a tomb for the patron

▼ **1470**

Leon Battista Alberti designs the pilgrimage church of Sant'Andrea in Mantua

Federico da Montefeltro sponsors ducal palace of Urbino

▲ **1460–1470**

▼ **1486**

Giuliano da Sangallo begins Villa of Poggio a Caiano for Lorenzo de' Medici

Sangallo designs the largest palace in Florence for banker Filippo Strozzi

▲ **1489**

▼ **1494**

Florentines, following Fra Savonarola, expel Medici family

Savonarola put to death as a heretic

▲ **1498**

Figure 10.1-4 Florence. Duomo, with rounded tribunes placed between the octagonal apses, Brunelleschi, 1419–1446.

Figure 10.1-5 Florence. Buttress of the Duomo's lantern with reversed curves, begun by Brunelleschi, finished by Michelozzo, 1460.

Figure 10.1-6 Florence. Foundling Hospital (Ospedale degli Innocenti) portico, Brunelleschi, 1419.

and his wife beneath the table in the center of the room. The dome rose from the cubic volume on pendentives, assuming the shape of a hemispherical umbrella divided by twelve round-arch ribs. A smaller hemispherical dome covered the altar. Corinthian pilasters and a classically proportioned entablature framed the altar niche, and an arch rose over the middle bay, forming a stylized version of a triumphal arch.

A decade or so later Brunelleschi probably designed the Pazzi Chapel (Fig. 10.1-8a), completed in the 1460s by his colleague Michelozzo di Bartolomeo (1396–1472). Built for a family that initially supported the Medici but in the 1470s became their most hostile enemy, the chapel served as the chapter house in one of the cloisters of the Franciscan convent of Santa Croce, with a porch resembling a triumphal arch. Like the Old Sacristy, the Pazzi Chapel had a curious flaw where the pilasters met the corners. In the former, a single pilaster folded into a right angle, half on one wall and half on the adjacent wall. In the Pazzi Chapel, the corner pilasters were bent, leaving a thin strip on the side wall

corresponding to a single flute of the shaft and the outer volute of the capital (Fig. 10.1-8b). These eccentric details demonstrated the struggle to reconcile mathematical correctness in proportions of the volume with the iconographic conventions derived from ancient classical elements.

Brunelleschi also initiated the plan in the 1420s to rebuild the church of San Lorenzo, a project completed during the following four decades by Michelozzo, the Medici family architect, for the budding dynasty. The architects' solution for the reconstruction of the oldest church in the city, founded in the fourth century, resembled the early Christian basilicas of Rome, such as Santa Maria Maggiore (see Section 6.1). Over the nave they placed a flat coffered ceiling, while setting the side aisles behind arcades raised on slender Corinthian columns. The arcades show stylistic improvements over the **portico** at the Foundling Hospital: the width of the bays extended only half of their height, which complemented the slender scale of the Corinthian columns, and the rounded arches sprang from isolated chunks of

CONSTRUCTION, TECHNOLOGY, THEORY

The Structure of the Dome of Florence

Brunelleschi's dome rose on a double-shell structure. Parallel sets of walls with a 1 m (3.3 ft) wide hollow between them concealed a grid of horizontal and vertical ribs that helped to absorb the lateral thrusts. In plan, a circle could be comfortably inscribed between the concentric octagons of the two shells, suitable for inserting tension rings made of oak chains. The interlocking masonry also kept the dome from buckling. Brunelleschi placed a succession of nine rings at roughly 3 m (10 ft) intervals to brace the dome as the construction progressed. Between each of the eight major vertical ribs he inserted two internal vertical ribs that added extra stiffness to the frame. The cupola performed as a continuous shell, like an egg, which allowed the architect to assemble the walls on a herringbone pattern of bricks that ascended in spiral courses, leaving the dome to support itself as it was being built.

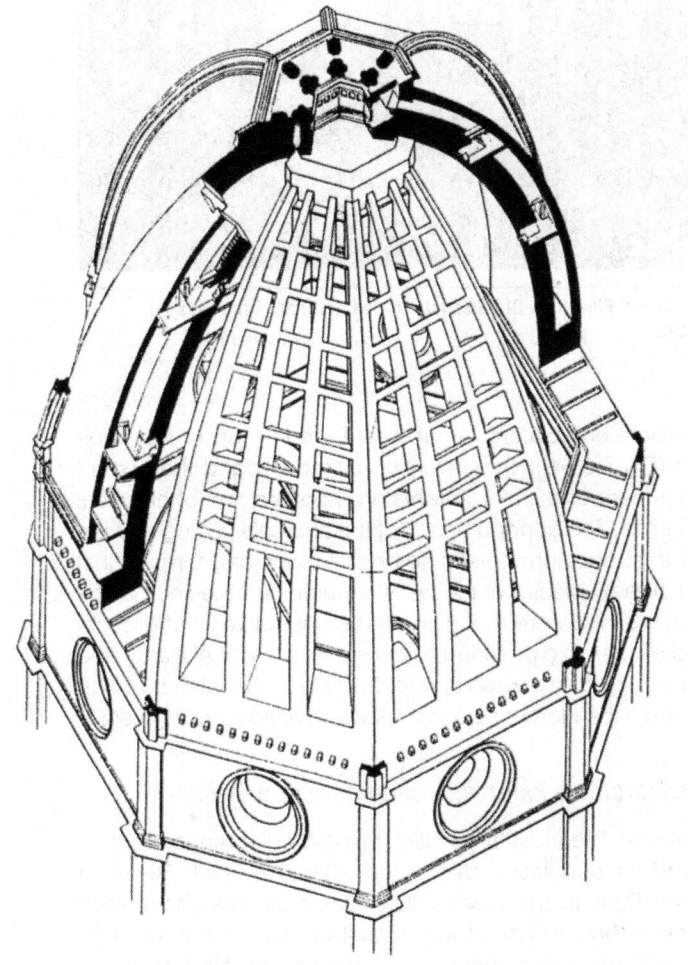

Florence. Section of Brunelleschi's dome, 1419–1446.

Figure 10.1-7 Florence. Old Sacristy in San Lorenzo, Brunelleschi, ca. 1420.

classical entablature rather than from the top of the capitals (Fig. 10.1-9). This invention acknowledged the correct placement of a linear entablature above a row of classical columns. The gridded bands of the church's paving and the contrast of its gray *pietra serena* columns and trim against the creamy plaster of the walls accentuated the lines of the space as if it were a constructed perspective. Brunelleschi and Michelozzo provided a new sense of rational clarity and luminosity for a sacred space, fulfilling in the interior of San Lorenzo the Florentine quest for an *all'antica* environment.

The Florentine Palazzo: Architecture as a Civic Duty

Florence, like most large cities in the Mediterranean region, found its population decimated after the Black Death of 1348. Prior to the plague the city's cloth merchants and bankers had amassed the largest concentrations of capital in Europe, and those who survived received an unexpected economic windfall as considerable inherited wealth

Figure 10.1-8 Florence. (a) Facade of Pazzi Chapel at Sta. Croce, attributed to Brunelleschi but finished by Michelozzo in the 1460s. (b) Interior showing corner pilaster.

Figure 10.1-9 Florence. S. Lorenzo, Brunelleschi and Michelozzo, 1420–1460.

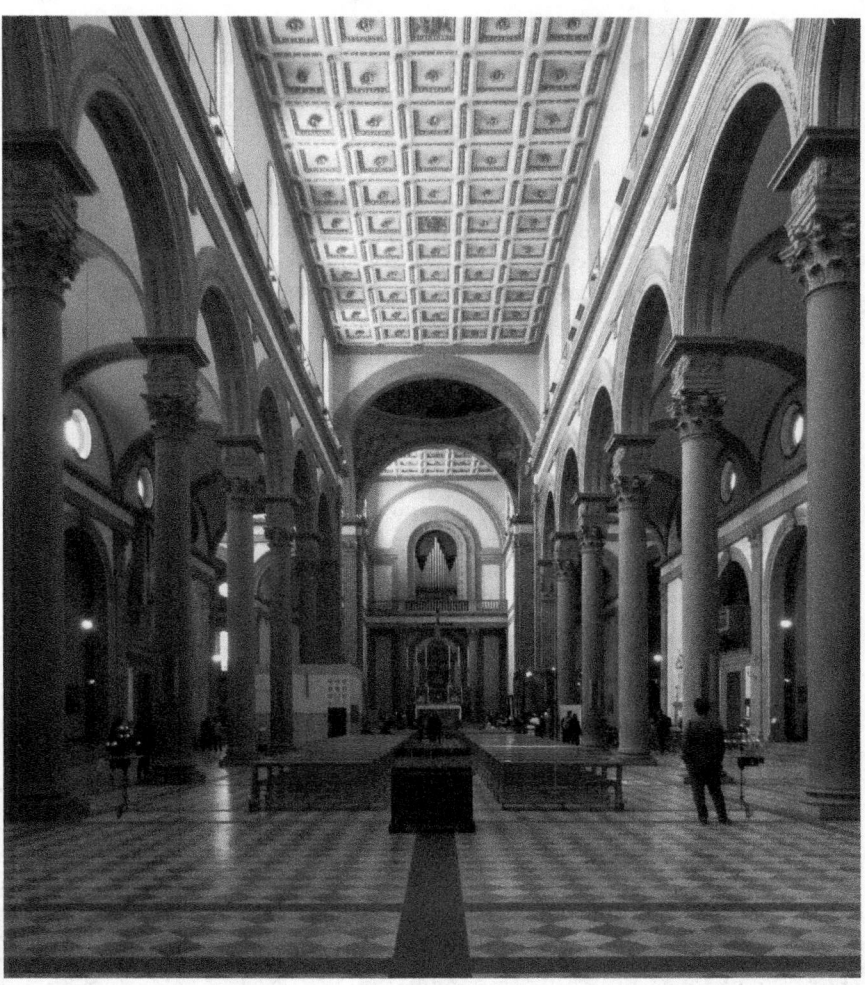

remained in fewer hands. This solid economic base stimulated patronage for exceptional works of public and private art. In addition to the ambitious civic projects begun before the plague, including the public palace and the Duomo, wealthy Florentines commissioned magnificent stone-clad private palaces that infused the city with a new sense of material cohesion and scale. By 1500 Florence appeared the most orderly city in Europe, with well-paved and drained streets, monumental civic buildings, and a fabric of stately cubic palaces.

The fortress-like Palazzo Vecchio, with its **rustication** of rough blocks and regularly spaced biforium windows, exerted a prime influence on the development of the Florentine merchant's palace. During their two-month terms as priors on the six-member executive council, these representatives of the wealthy merchant class were obliged to live in the public palace and thus knew it intimately. While the city magistrates had outlawed the tall, anarchic tower houses of the feudal nobility, they encouraged the production of the palaces of Florence's urban elite. A new ethic for architectural patronage took root, best expressed by the banker Giovanni Rucellai in the 1470s, who stated that his patronage "serves the glory

RELIGION, PHILOSOPHY, FOLKLORE

Italian Humanism

Humanism, the secular study of science, history, and language, provided the intellectual background of the ruling classes of the Italian Renaissance. The interest in recuperating Latin and Greek texts began in the thirteenth and fourteenth centuries with the leaders of the republics of central Italy. To guarantee justice against tyranny, the communal councils drew upon examples from the history of the ancient Roman republic. This inspired a new curriculum of study, taught by classically trained scholars. Poggio Bracciolini (1380–1459), a notary from Florence, became a leading humanist scholar, translating ancient texts and writing a history of Florence on the model of the ancient Roman historian Livy. He traveled all over Europe in the hunt for ancient texts. In 1414 he brought back to Florence precious manuscripts from medieval monasteries in Switzerland and Germany, including works by the Epicurean philosopher Lucretius and the architectural treatise of Vitruvius.

Cosimo de' Medici, influenced by the arrival in Florence of Greek scholars from Constantinople during an ecumenical council, sponsored the founding of an academy, modeled on Plato's school in ancient Athens, in the 1440s. He commissioned Michelozzo to add a library to the convent of San Marco, arranging the Latin books on one side of a central vaulted passage and the Greek books on the other. The donor of the books, Niccolò Niccoli, stipulated that they be accessible to all the citizens of Florence. The Florentine Academy promoted some of the greatest scholars of the Renaissance, including Marsilio Ficino (1433–1499), who translated all of Plato's works from Greek to Latin. Ficino also researched geometry and astronomy and was known for his mystical interests. Within this atmosphere of scholarship Pico della Mirandola (1463–1494) published his treatise "Oration on the Dignity of Man" advocating the ancient Greek wisdom of using the human being as the measure of all things. The premise that humans are the only creatures of God with the ability to change their situations inspired both patrons and artists to produce ever more original works.

Women in the Renaissance Palazzo

The great size of Florentine palaces left an immense amount of interior space for relatively small families of four to six members, plus a commensurate number of servants. Because of the active political and commercial life of their merchant patrons, the palaces often became the exclusive domain of young wives and children. The women left the house only for ceremonies and formal occasions. They used the spaces of the palace for their own education and that of their children and usually undertook its administration. The letters written in the late fourteenth century between Francesco Datini, who spent most of his time in Florence tending to business, and his wife, Margherita, who managed Palazzo Datini in Prato, 15 km (9 miles) to the west, offer a detailed view of Florentine gender politics.

Margherita's letters document her regret at being "treated like an inn-keeper" in her own house, while also revealing her superior command of language.

The Florentine palace became a display space for patrons to show their taste in art, luxury furnishings, and fancy clothing. Women's gowns were worn only at home because of the republic's sumptuary laws forbidding ostentation in public. While Florentine women were often considered more as ornaments than as equals, they nonetheless had the most to gain from living in the great palaces, where they were empowered by their continued education and their management of the household economy. The palazzo presented a masculine statement of family power on the facade, while inside it nurtured a space of culture dominated by feminine values.

Florence. Fresco by Domenico Ghirlandaio in the Tornabuoni Chapel in the church of Sta. Maria Novella (1485–1490) illustrating the "Birth of the Virgin Mary" in a setting that depicts the luxury of Florentine palace interiors and the brocaded gowns that Florentine women could only wear in private.

of God, the honor of the city, and the commemoration of myself."

The rebuilding of the Medici family palace in the 1440s by Cosimo de' Medici ("the Elder," 1389–1464), the patron of San Lorenzo and other religious institutions, redefined the Florentine **palazzo** type for many generations. The Medici architect, Michelozzo, made clear references to Palazzo Vecchio in the palace's overall cubic shape (doubled in the seventeenth century by the Riccardi family) and the rugged *bugnato* rustication on its ground floor, the chunks of which were at least three times the size of medieval precedents. He clad the upper two stories in progressively smoother, drafted masonry, creating the illusion of greater height (Fig. 10.1-10a). Michelozzo orchestrated another perceptual refinement by pulling the southeast corner of the palace a few degrees forward, making the outer walls of its square plan slightly oblique (Fig. 10.1-10c). This gave the corner more prominence when seen from the steps of the Duomo.

Cosimo was the prototypical humanist patron, amassing a famous collection of ancient texts and statues. He desired to build a residence more like an ancient Roman *domus* than an urban fortress. Classical details, such as the Corinthian colonnettes of the biforium windows, replaced military imagery. The grand classical **cornice**, with its **brackets**, dentils, and egg-and-dart motif, resembled fragments that one could find in the Roman Forum. It cantilevered more than 1 m (3.3 ft) over the street, hiding the pitched roofs and contributing to the illusion of the volumetric purity of the whole. The perfectly square arcaded courtyard aspired to the *impluvium* court found in the atrium of a *domus* (Fig. 10.1-10b). Its area occupied more than half of the ground floor and served as a museum for the Medici collection of ancient and modern statues. This courtyard presented a dilemma similar to that faced by Brunelleschi in the Old Sacristy, with the convergence of two planes resting on a single column. Later designers, seeing this design as cramped and overloaded, placed a square pier or doubled the columns in the corners. Most palaces for the next two centuries followed the plan organization of Palazzo Medici: a series of interconnecting, or **enfilade**, rooms set around

a square arcaded court. The only break in the sequence of rooms came with the insertion of a private chapel in the northwest corner, a rare privilege granted to Florence's wealthiest family.

The Medici Palace embodied the attitude of *magnificenza*, whereby Florentine patrons contributed to the improvement of the public realm through the propriety of their private palaces. Cosimo's example inspired the construction of more than sixty palaces in Florence during the second half of the fifteenth century, as well as countless imitations in other cities. The construction of such large structures improved the local economy, boosting employment. It also could have damaging consequences to individual fortunes, as in the case of the Boni, who built a palace (Fig. 10.1-11), now named after the Antinori family, that led the family to bankruptcy. The Florentine palace type—with a stone bench, a rusticated base, regularly placed biforium windows, a classical cornice, and an arcaded courtyard—bred imitations in Bologna and Milan and even appeared

Figure 10.1-10 Florence. (a) Palazzo Medici-Riccardi, designed by Michelozzo in the 1440s. (b) and (c) See next page.

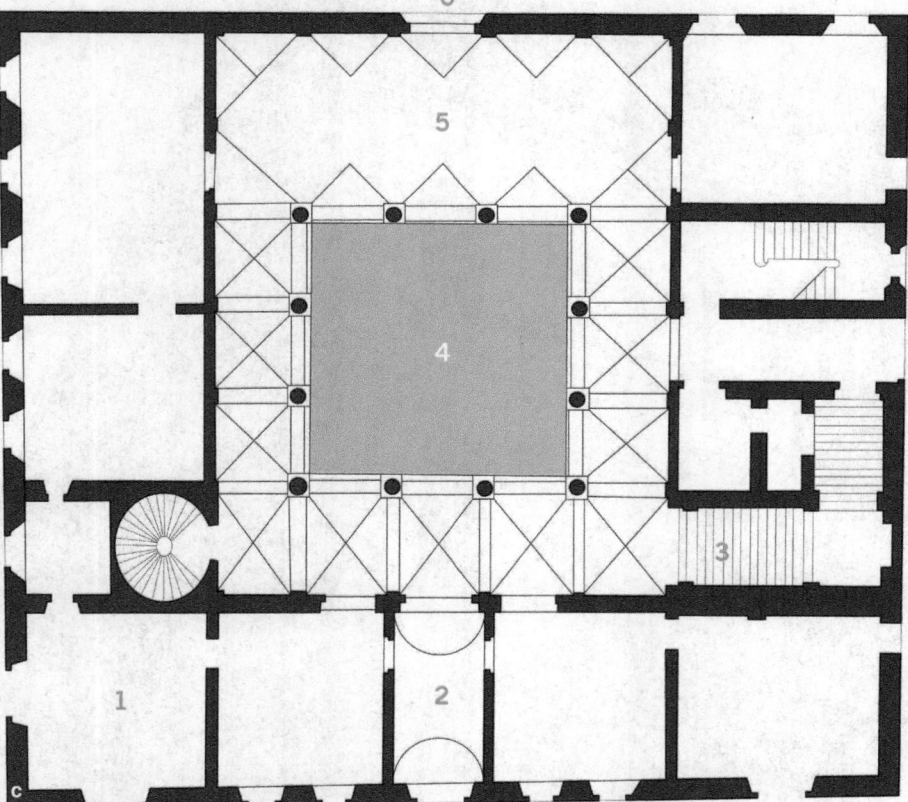

Figure 10.1-10 Florence, Palazzo Medici-Riccardi. (b) Courtyard. (c) Plan of palazzo as it was in the 1440s, showing (1) banking hall, originally open to the street; (2) vaulted entry to the palace; (3) grand stairway to *piano nobile* with four landings; (4) central square courtyard for displays of sculpture; (5) back colonnade of the courtyard, built twice as wide as the other three colonnades to accommodate meetings and lectures; (6) rear garden, enclosed by its own wall.

da Sangallo (1445–1516), the personal architect of Lorenzo de' Medici (the "Magnificent"), to prepare the initial model, with a classical cornice and rustication similar to those of Palazzo Medici. As completed by Benedetto da Maiano (1442–1497) and Simone del Pollaiolo (1457–1508), the palace became considerably taller, its three stories as high as six, with the cornice doubled, like a grand visor for the facade. The rounded cushions of its *bugnato* rustication diminished almost imperceptibly in depth from the bottom story to the top. This grander scheme resulted from Lorenzo's insistence on *magnificenza* as a civic duty, which proved a clever political strategy to tie up the capital of competing families. Although Filippo Strozzi died two years after construction began, he dedicated his fortune to the building's completion as a permanent testament to his status and the future greatness of his clan. His son, also named Filippo, born two years before the original patron's death, resumed construction in the 1530s but, due to his role in the resistance to Medici rule, was incarcerated and died in prison in 1538, the year of the palace's completion.

Giovanni Rucellai (1403–1481), the third wealthiest man in the city and one of the most documented patrons of the Florentine palace boom, began construction on his family palace in 1453. Built with the advice of his friend, the humanist scholar Leon Battista Alberti, and supervised by the sculptor-architect Bernardo Rossellino (1409–1464), the facade of Palazzo Rucellai included pilasters to create a more classical look (Fig. 10.1-13). The designers partitioned the facade into eight bays across three levels, using the pilasters to mark the coordinates of a proportional grid. The two bays of the doorways stood half a module (the width of a pilaster) wider than the others to subtly emphasize the entries, while the pilasters on each successive story were proportionally shorter

in the rival city of Siena, where the Florentine architect Giuliano da Maiano built Palazzo Spannocchi for an expatriate Florentine banker.

Filippo Strozzi, the second richest man in Florence and with a family history of bitter rivalry with the Medici, reconciled the two families' differences and began the city's largest palace in 1489 (Fig. 10.1-12). He commissioned Giuliano

by half a module. Alberti and Rossellino improved on the medieval biforium window by placing small entablatures above the well-proportioned Corinthian colonnettes. At the base level above the stone benches they inserted an imitation of ancient *opus reticulatum* in a diagonal grid as an erudite *all'antica* reference. They etched the harlequin pattern, like the outlines of the pilasters, into the blocks of the stone cladding solely for iconographic effect. The eighth bay of Palazzo Rucellai remained unfinished because of an uncooperative relative who refused to yield that part of the site.

The patron compensated for the modest dimensions of Palazzo Rucellai's courtyard by the creation of a triangular piazza in front of the palace, cleared at the intersection of converging streets. Opening toward the palace like a funnel, it allowed one to view the facade in perspective. Rucellai built an independent loggia at a right angle to the palace facade, to be used for ceremonies by all of the members of the clan. Outer Corinthian piers held up a frieze carrying the patron's emblems, while elegant Corinthian columns stood at widths half the height of the apex of the arches to frame the open, theatrical space of the loggia. With such a scheme, Rucellai challenged the moral constraints of the early republic concerning conspicuous spending for private projects. In his diary he noted, "I have given myself more

honor and my soul more satisfaction by having spent money than by having earned it, above all with regard to the building I have done."

Leon Battista Alberti: Humanist and Architect

Behind the harmonious proportions and classical details of Palazzo Rucellai was one of the greatest humanists of the fifteenth century, Leon Battista Alberti (1404–1472). Born into an important merchant clan of Florence as an illegitimate child, he received an elite education but was deprived of an inheritance. Alberti found support for his humanist research in the papal bureaucracy and eventually entered the priesthood. His motto, *Quid Tum* (Latin for "what next"), and his emblem of an eye with wings captured his restless efforts to achieve fame through knowledge. Alberti's need to be accepted as worthy of his class motivated a prolific output of treatises on such diverse topics as the Tuscan language, sociology, code encryption, horseback riding, painting, and sculpture. His most enduring work remains his treatise on architecture, *De re aedificatoria*, written mid-century in Latin, the language of patrons, not craftspeople.

Alberti's treatise encouraged patrons to demonstrate their virtue and achieve fame by sponsoring appropriate buildings.

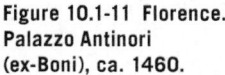

Figure 10.1-11 Florence. Palazzo Antinori (ex-Boni), ca. 1460.

Figure 10.1-12 Florence. Detail of the cornice of the Palazzo Strozzi, begun by Giuliano da Sangallo and completed by Benedetto da Maiano and Simone del Pollaiolo, 1490–1500.

Despite the author's collaboration with popes and tyrants, his sympathies lay clearly with the republican ideal of moderation. "We should not so much praise sobriety," he commented, "as condemn an unruly passion for building: each part should be appropriate . . . born of necessity, nourished by convenience, dignified by use; and only in the end is pleasure provided for, while pleasure itself never fails to shun every excess." He put such values to the test with Rucellai, a lifetime friend, for whom he designed two other works, a mausoleum inspired by the Holy Sepulchre in Jerusalem (see Section 6.2) and the facade of the Dominican church of Santa Maria Novella, both a short walk from Rucellai's palace. Alberti's version of the Holy Sepulchre, a freestanding marble-paneled memorial, oblong with a solid round apse at one end, was better proportioned than the original.

For the completion of the facade of Santa Maria Novella (10.1-14), the lower parts of which date from the mid-fourteenth century, Alberti framed the existing base of *avelli* niches for the tombs with monolithic green Corinthian columns and added an attic level punctuated with intarsia squares and an upper story in the form of a flattened temple front. To connect the two levels he extended scrolls with reversed curves. In the entablature of the triangular pediment he inscribed in large Roman-style letters Rucellai's name and the date 1470, a bold display of individualism by a private citizen in public space.

Alberti's fame as a humanist and his elite acquaintances brought him to the most powerful courts of Italy. The ambitious tyrant of Rimini, Sigismondo Malatesta (1417–1468), engaged him to restructure the thirteenth-century church

Figure 10.1-13 Florence. Palazzo Rucellai, L. B. Alberti and B. Rossellino, 1450–1470.

of San Francesco as a mausoleum (Fig. 10.1-15). His crew began in 1450 to encase the old church in a thick marble envelope of classical architecture, lining the side elevations with deep arches like an aqueduct for the tombs of Malatesta's courtiers. Alberti dressed the facade of Malatesta's "temple" with fluted half-columns, imitating some of the details on the nearby Arch of Augustus of the first century BCE. On the entablature of the church he emblazoned the tyrant's name with the date 1450. The upper story of the church facade and a planned dome remained unbuilt as a result of the patron's fall from power in 1461.

Alberti's friendship with Ludovico Gonzaga (1412–1478), marquis of Mantua, led to two final ecclesiastical projects. In 1459 he designed the central-plan church of San Sebastiano on the outskirts of the city (Fig. 10.1-16a,b). He positioned it over a hypostyle vaulted substructure to avoid the humidity of the site, while leaving space below for a mausoleum. His antiquarian interest in ancient Etruscan temples led to the church's unconventional central plan. Over the central space he placed a groin vault that extended in each direction as barrel vaults over the entry and three side chapels. The layout appeared so strange to Cardinal Gonzaga, son of the patron, that he wondered whether it was a church, a mosque, or a synagogue.

San Sebastiano was only partly finished at the death of the architect in 1472 and, like Alberti's other project in Mantua, the pilgrimage church of Sant'Andrea in the center of the city, was continued under the guidance of the Florentine architect Luca Fancelli (ca. 1430–1494). Construction on the latter church began in 1472 and

Figure 10.1-14 Florence. Facade of Sta. Maria Novella, Alberti, 1470.

Figure 10.1-15 Rimini, Italy. Church of S. Francesco, Alberti, 1450s.

proceeded in stages, culminating with the addition of the dome by Filippo Juvarra in the eighteenth century. The facade of Sant'Andrea fulfilled the Albertian concept of "invention," combining two conventional elements, a triumphal arch and a temple front, to obtain something new (Fig. 10.1-17). The pilasters of the central arch rose at one scale from the top of the steps, while those supporting the pediment took a slightly larger scale, pushed up from tall **pedestals**. The elements of the facade, such as the coffered barrel vault over the entry porch, were repeated on the interior elevations of the nave. The repetition of the rhythmic system of the facade on the interior offered a rare instance in fifteenth-century architecture of an organic correspondence between inside and outside. Emulating ancient works such as the Basilica of Maxentius in Rome (see Section 6.1), Alberti designed Sant'Andrea with a barrel-vaulted longitudinal nave without side aisles. He argued in favor of this more open solution for economic reasons and because it could better accommodate large crowds coming to view the church's reliquary containing the blood of Christ.

Unlike other designers of the time, Alberti came from the upper class and had a university background, remaining closer to the patrons of architecture than to the craftspeople. When he wrote that an architect should use craftspeople as his tools, he was referring to his own experience as an intellectual supervising design. Many of his contemporaries, including his friend Federico da Montefeltro, duke of Urbino, took active roles in the design and details of their building projects. Alberti visited Urbino frequently during the 1460s,

Figure 10.1-16 Mantua, Italy. (a) Church of S. Sebastiano, Alberti, ca. 1470. (b) Interior.

Figure 10.1-17 Mantua, Italy. Pilgrimage church of Sant'Andrea, Alberti, begun 1470s.

Figure 10.1-18 Urbino, Italy. Courtyard of Palazzo Ducale, L. Laurana, late 1460s.

the most active period of construction of the duke's grand palace. The courtyard of Palazzo Ducale (Fig. 10.1-18), designed by Luciano Laurana (ca. 1420–1479) in the late 1460s, reflected Alberti's sensibilities. The corners consisted of square piers framing sets of arcades. This early solution to the corner problem strengthened the points where the planes intersected. It also allowed the capitals of the flat piers to carry an entablature, which otherwise would have rested awkwardly on the crests of the arches. The Latin inscriptions on the entablature celebrated Federico's virtues and were even more grandiloquent than the inscriptions on Alberti's churches.

Lorenzo de' Medici (1449–1492), grandson of Cosimo the Elder, figured among the readers of Alberti's treatise on architecture. In 1472, after his sister married Rucellai's son, he and his new brother-in-law went with Alberti to Rome to visit the ruins in the Forum. A few years earlier the Medici family had commissioned Giuliano da Sangallo to prepare measured drawings of the great works of antiquity in Rome. The resulting notebooks served many generations of architects as a source for *all'antica* types and details. Sangallo's drawings of the Arch of Constantine, the Colosseum, the Pantheon, and the Basilica of Maxentius codified the graphic conventions of plans, elevations, sections, and axonometrics still used today. His graphic familiarity with ancient Roman buildings paralleled the humanist scholars' knowledge of ancient texts. Lorenzo used the architect for cultural politics, sending Sangallo to design a villa as a favor to the king of Naples in 1488.

After Lorenzo obtained the estate at Poggio a Caiano in an exchange with Giovanni Rucellai, Sangallo began construction on an innovative villa there in 1486. Lorenzo's death halted progress on the building, which was completed two decades later for Lorenzo's son, Giovanni, who had become Pope Leo X. Alberti had praised the villa type as the conscious revival of an ancient form that made an economic contribution as a farm while offering its patron a place of *otium*, or relaxation, away from the business and distractions of the city. Despite its value as a dairy farm, Lorenzo and his architect treated Poggio a Caiano as an ideal work of architecture, without the usual compromises imposed by preexisting buildings or specialized functions. The *H*-shaped plan fit on a perfectly square podium. The rooms in each of the four wings were arranged in discrete clusters rather than the typical *enfilade*, and between them a double-height transversal hall stretched, capped with a coffered barrel vault worthy of the ancient villas of Nero or Hadrian. The facade boasted the first appearance of a temple front on a secular building, a Doric porch encrusted with Medici emblems.

Alberti established a standard for Renaissance patrons and architects. Rather than copy the past, he recommended that the revival of ancient architecture follow a coherent set of rules with which one could approximate the grandeur of the ancients yet create something new. His theory of *concinnitas* held that beauty resulted from the harmonious use of symmetry and proportionality, reasoning that the design of buildings would thus be as sensible as the organisms produced by nature. He derived principles both from observing ancient architecture and considering relationships in nature.

Ideal Cities: Between the Real and the Ideal

Alberti's treatise on architecture lacked illustrations, making it even less accessible to unlettered practitioners. His friend Federico da Montefeltro attempted to visualize the new architecture and urbanism of the Renaissance by commissioning a series of perspective city views. Among them, the so-called Ideal City panel (Fig. 10.1-19) depicts a harmonious collection of palaces set on a gridded piazza, overlooking a round church in the center (the *opus reticulatum* on the church's base has led some scholars to attribute the painting to Alberti). For this vision of classical order, the artist made all the buildings similar in scale but slightly different in detail, using a common vocabulary of colonnades and pilasters. This ideal city had neither a castle nor a poor person's dwelling, implying an ideal republican social context in which everyone was equally well-off.

As a member of the papal bureaucracy from the 1420s until his death, Alberti worked for a succession of popes, including two with excellent humanist credentials, Nicholas V (Parentucelli, r. 1447–1455) and Pius II (Piccolomini, r. 1458–1464). He likely provided advice, if not a helping hand, in their architectural endeavors, but such activities are undocumented. Nicholas imagined an ideal revision of the Vatican Borgo, the area surrounding St. Peter's in Rome, but his plan remained literary, offering a description of three parallel streets lined with porticoes that would connect two geometric piazzas at either end. Pius, frustrated with the turmoil of Rome, took his patronage to the Tuscan countryside south of Siena, where he rebuilt his birthplace, the small farm town of Corsignano, into the dignified city of Pienza.

Pius completed the transformation of Pienza in the brief period from 1459 to 1464 (Fig. 10.1-20). Its design adhered to many of the ideas in Alberti's treatise, such as using a slightly curved main street to make a small town appear larger. Pius widened and leveled the main street and placed a gridded piazza at its summit. He then instigated the construction of nearly forty buildings for himself and his supporters, with the assistance of Rossellino. In the center the travertine-clad facade of the cathedral pushed slightly above the uniform fabric of the town, decorated with a sculpted pediment and classical columns. Despite this classical exterior, the interior reproduced the Gothic *Hallenkirche* that the pope had admired during his years as a diplomat in Germany. To the east stood the largest secular building, the brownstone, Florentine-style Palazzo Piccolomini, intended as the dynastic seat of Pius's family. To the other side of the church, the papal secretary of state, Rodrigo Borgia, rebuilt the bishop's palace, with Roman-style cruciform windows. Opposite the church, the pope commissioned a new city hall with a spacious Ionic loggia on the ground floor and a brick campanile. All of the entries of the principal building aligned to the grid of the piazza, an approximate trapezoid 25 m (82 ft) wide and 20 m (65 ft) deep. Like the "Ideal City" painting, each building relied on the same palette of materials, brownstone and travertine, but with different combinations of details, resulting in harmonious variety.

Palazzo Piccolomini closely resembled Palazzo Medici in plan, with a nearly identical courtyard, while the pilasters of its elevations recalled Palazzo Rucellai. There was one subtle difference between them: the pilasters of Palazzo Piccolomini were shortened progressively by one module from floor to floor. The rear, or southern, elevation remained Pius's greatest architectural contribution, built with continuous colonnaded

Figure 10.1-19 "The Ideal City" *cassone* **panel, attributed to Giuliano da Sangallo, painted ca. 1460.**

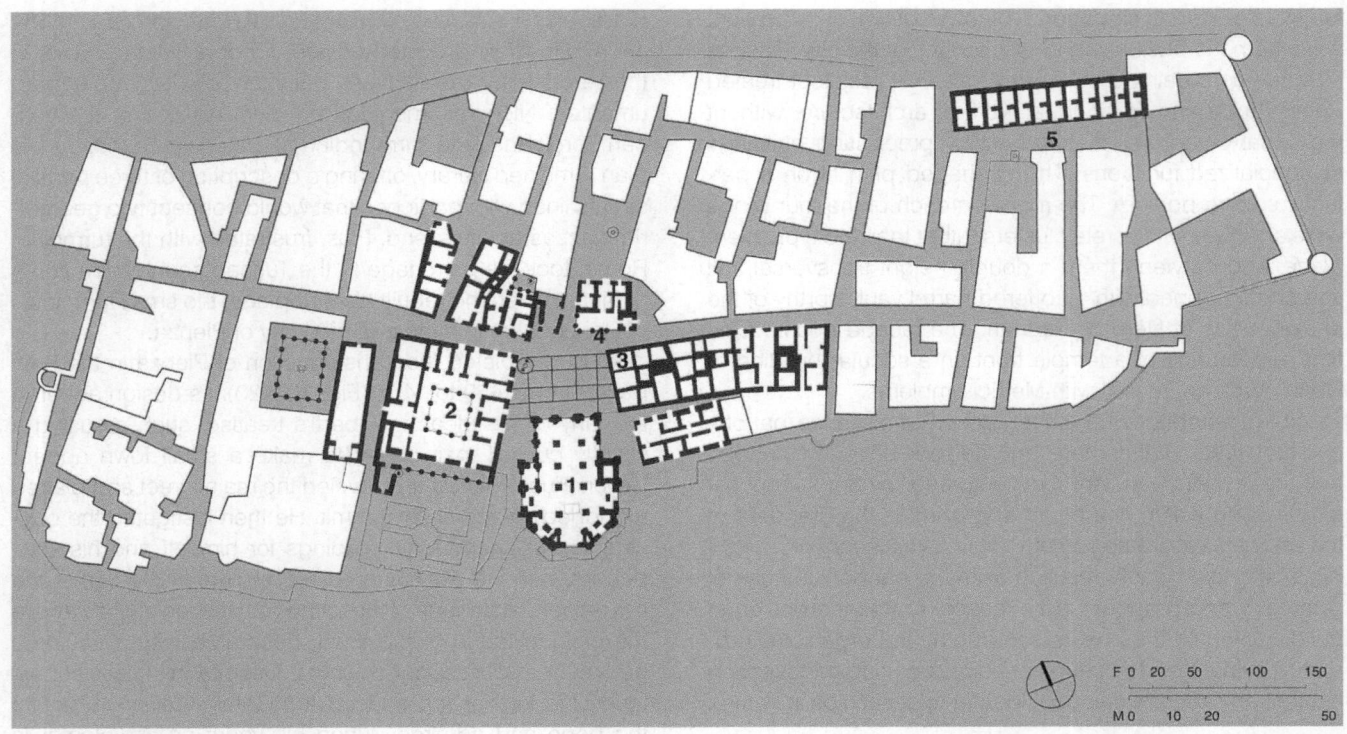

Figure 10.1-20 Pienza, Italy. Plan of city, built for Pius II (Piccolomini) in the 1460s: (1) *hallenkirche*-**style cathedral; (2) Palazzo Piccolomini; (3) bishop's palace; (4) public palace; (5) row houses for those displaced by new construction.**

Figure 10.1-21 Pienza, Italy. Palazzo Piccolomini, rear loggia, B. Rossellino, 1460.

openness of the city hall denoting the desire to allow all classes a good life. The pope further demonstrated his liberal concept by commissioning nine units of subsidized row housing for the families displaced by the construction in the city center (Fig. 10.1-22).

The humanist interest in urbanism led Antonio Averlino, better known by his pseudonym Filarete (ca. 1400–1469), to create the fictional city of Sforzinda. Trained as a sculptor in Florence, he worked in Rome designing the bronze doors of St. Peter's during the 1430s and 1440s. Filarete came to Milan in 1451 to work for Duke Francesco Sforza (r. 1450–1466), for whom he designed

loggias on all three levels to offer privileged vistas to a geometric hanging garden at grade level and beyond this to the valley of Mount Amiata (Fig. 10.1-21).

Despite his status as a monarch and his family's feudal control over the town, Pius intended to create an environment that appeared a model of social equilibrium and justice. Pienza resembled a balanced republic, with the

parts of the ducal fortress, the Castello Sforzesco, and made plans for the city's new hospital. During his last years he composed an illustrated treatise in the form of a novel that described a star-shaped city, which, like Pienza, derived its name from its patron. He gave Sforzinda an ideal diagram, inscribing it in a circle framing an eight-point star obtained by rotating a square diagonally on its axis (Fig. 10.1-23).

Figure 10.1-22 Pienza, Italy. Row houses built for those displaced by Pius II's urban renewal, 1460s.

Figure 10.1-23 Filarete's star-shaped plan for the fictional city of Sforzinda, ca. 1460.

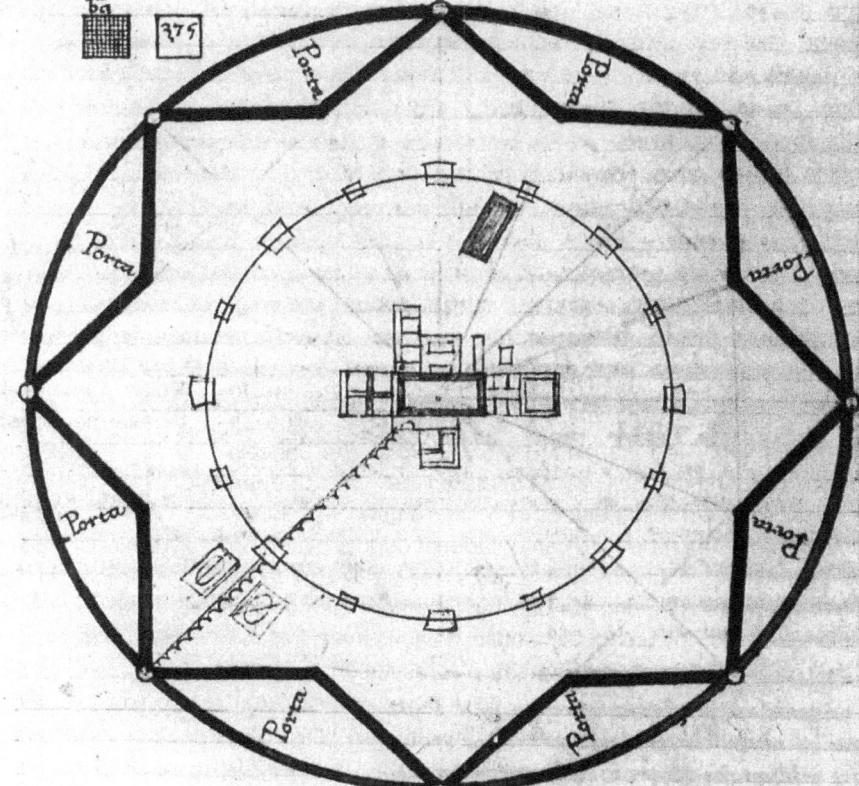

Figure 10.1-24 Filarete's House of Vice and Virtue for the fictional city of Sforzinda, ca. 1460.

young men. Inspired by ancient arenas and perhaps an attempt to visualize Dante's progress through the rings of hell, purgatory, and heaven in the *Divine Comedy*, he planned it as a tall, cylindrical structure with a central court at the edge of town. Part bordello and part convent, the structure would have served as a place to initiate youths into the extremes of both lust and piety. As they moved up the sequence of nine levels, advancing to the top, the graduates would take their place beneath a verdant pergola to look back at the star-shaped city with a privileged perspective. Like Pius II, Filarete dreamed of a city that would combine the best practices of the medieval republics with the new authority of an enlightened monarchy to approximate the grandeur of the past while dealing with the problems of the present.

The humanist revival of classical culture in fifteenth-century Italy, following the examples built in Florence and the theoretical positions of Alberti, led to diverse attempts to perfect the visual order of the city. The full-scale experiment in Pienza was designed like a game board for a well-balanced social hierarchy. In the fictional Sforzinda, Filarete anticipated a complete social system and unwittingly introduced a recurring theme in architectural utopias: the belief that form can influence behavior for the betterment of society.

Filarete proposed radiating streets and canals that led to the center. Here, around a rectangular piazza, twice as long as it was wide, he placed the cathedral, the prince's palace, and the city hall. He gave the prince's palace open loggias like the public palaces of northern Italy. Sforzinda's cathedral was crowned with an octagonal cupola based on that of Florence but at the four corners had bizarre, minaret-like bell towers. Two smaller piazzas to either side catered to popular life, including the public palace, the mint, the taverns, the butchers, the houses of prostitution, and the *bargello* for the police. Among his innovative programs, Filarete proposed to abolish the death penalty, which necessitated the construction of a large prison. He included his design for Milan's new hospital as part of the plan, conflating real and ideal.

Filarete's most exotic invention for his ideal city was a multistory tower known as the "House of Vice and Virtue" (Fig. 10.1-24), proposed for use in the moral education of

Further Reading

Clarke, Georgia. *Roman House–Renaissance Palaces: Inventing Antiquity in Fifteenth-Century Italy.* Cambridge, UK: Cambridge University Press, 2003.

Fiore, Francesco Paolo, ed. *Storia dell'architettura italiana, il quattrocento.* Milan: Electa, 1998.

Goldthwaite, Richard A. *The Building of Renaissance Florence: An Economic and Social History.* Baltimore, MD: Johns Hopkins University Press, 1980.

Grafton, Anthony. *Leon Battista Alberti: Master Builder of the Italian Renaissance.* New York: Hill and Wang, 2000.

Hollingsworth, Mary. *Patronage in Renaissance Italy: From 1400 to the Early Sixteenth Century.* Baltimore, MD: Johns Hopkins University Press, 1994.

Origo, Iris. *The Merchant of Prato: Francesco di Marco Datini, 1335–1410.* Boston: David Godine, 1986.

Smith, Christine. *Architecture in the Culture of Early Humanism: Ethics, Aesthetics, and Eloquence, 1400–1470.* New York: Oxford University Press, 1992.

Tavernor, Robert. *On Alberti and the Art of Building.* New Haven, CT: Yale University Press, 1998.

Trachtenberg, Marvin. *Dominion of the Eye: Urbanism, Art, and Power in Early Modern Florence.* Cambridge, UK: Cambridge University Press, 1997.

10.2 EASTERN EUROPE
From the Spirit of Wood to the Conventions of Masonry

While the architects of Italy and the Mediterranean relied primarily on masonry techniques, Eastern Europeans built exclusively with wooden planks and logs. From the Baltic Sea in the north to the Black Sea in the south, they used timber for their fortresses, churches, and houses and in some places even paved the streets with tree trunks. The abundant supply of timber from vast conifer forests offered a seemingly inexhaustible supply of building materials, while the dry assembly of wooden structures better suited the region's extremely cold winters. Wood provided both shelter and fuel in lands that during the winter were covered with a blanket of snow. The early settlements in this region considered the dark forests both a resource and a mysterious place of dread. Pre-Christian cults revered sacred groves and wood spirits. Many builders in this part of the world still place a live tree at the top of a building during construction, even when erecting a steel and concrete structure, to attract the sacred blessing of the forests.

The introduction of masonry into Eastern Europe followed religious and political changes. The Byzantine influence coming from the south brought imperial ideology, while the Benedictine monks coming from the west transmitted religious stability. By the end of the fifteenth century, the leading courts of Eastern Europe had imported Italian architects and engineers to supply authoritative models of both stone construction and Renaissance style. While fetish-like elements referring to ancient timber traditions survived in the new architecture and country people continued to build wooden structures, the durability of masonry construction, especially for monumental works, supplanted the ancient spirit of wood.

The Formation of Russia: From Log Houses to Onion Domes

The vast, timber-using areas of Eastern Europe were sparsely settled, treacherous, and among the coldest climate zones on earth (Fig. 10.2-1). Here, great rivers moved sluggishly through the broad, permeable plains, leaving desolate marshes in their wake. *Grody*, wooden fortresses made of sharpened log palisades, dotted the countryside. Viking bands from Scandinavia, whose compatriots had so convulsed Western Europe during the eighth and ninth centuries, referred to the region as the "land of forts." These same Vikings, after raiding the Slavic-speaking territories along the trade routes between Scandinavia and Constantinople, in the ninth century participated in the rebuilding of both Kiev and Novgorod, consolidating trade with these cities. The ethnic name "Slav," which literally meant "noble,"

Figure 10.2-1 Eastern Europe, ca. 1500.

came to signify "servitude" in other European languages because of the active slave trade that had operated in the region since the time of the Romans. Venetian merchants in the thirteenth and fourteenth centuries still loaded their ships with Slavic captives auctioned at Kaffa on the Black Sea to supply Mamluk clients in Cairo.

The Byzantine Empire exerted the primary cultural influence north of the Black Sea, and the Greek Orthodox faith spread through Kiev to greater Russia after the conversion of Vladimir the Great (r. 980–1015), who ordered mass baptisms, married the Byzantine emperor's sister, and built Russia's first cathedral. Vladimir's church of the Tithe in Kiev, finished around the year 1000 by masons from Constantinople, became the region's first monument in stone. Although

rebuilt in later centuries, its original plan resembled that of typical Byzantine churches, with three aisles leading to three rounded apses in the east and a central crossing for a dome, intersected by a transept. This central-plan model of a cross within a square served as the pattern for most Ukrainian and Russian churches for the next five centuries.

In Novgorod, Vladimir commissioned a cathedral in timber, crowned with thirteen domes, one for Christ and the others for the twelve apostles. The abundance of timber made it more practical to build with logs. Local craftspeople assembled the majority of the early Russian Orthodox churches using the traditional **blockwork** construction method. They notched the logs on their ends and stacked them at right angles into interlocking, box-like forms. This dry assembly, free of mortar or adobe, allowed them to build even in subzero temperatures.

The oldest wooden church in Russia, the fourteenth-century Church of St. Lazarus on Kizhi Island at Lake Onega (Fig. 10.2-2), survived because it was encased inside of a larger seventeenth-century church. Its plan related to the standard blockwork type with dimensions corresponding to the 3 m (9.6 ft) optimal length of the timbers. The first cubic volume, made of linked staves, served the western porch and narthex, followed by a slightly wider and taller cube for the nave, made of logs, and a smaller, lower cube for the sanctuary, also made of logs. Over the ridge beam of the nave's plank roof rose the sole symbolic element, a bulbous **lukovitsa** dome. The onion-shaped dome, which has come to characterize Russian style, arrived with the thirteenth-century Mongolian invasions. Domes before this time were saucer- or helmet-shaped. The use of *lukovitsas* increased in the mid-sixteenth century as a patriotic gesture after Ivan IV's

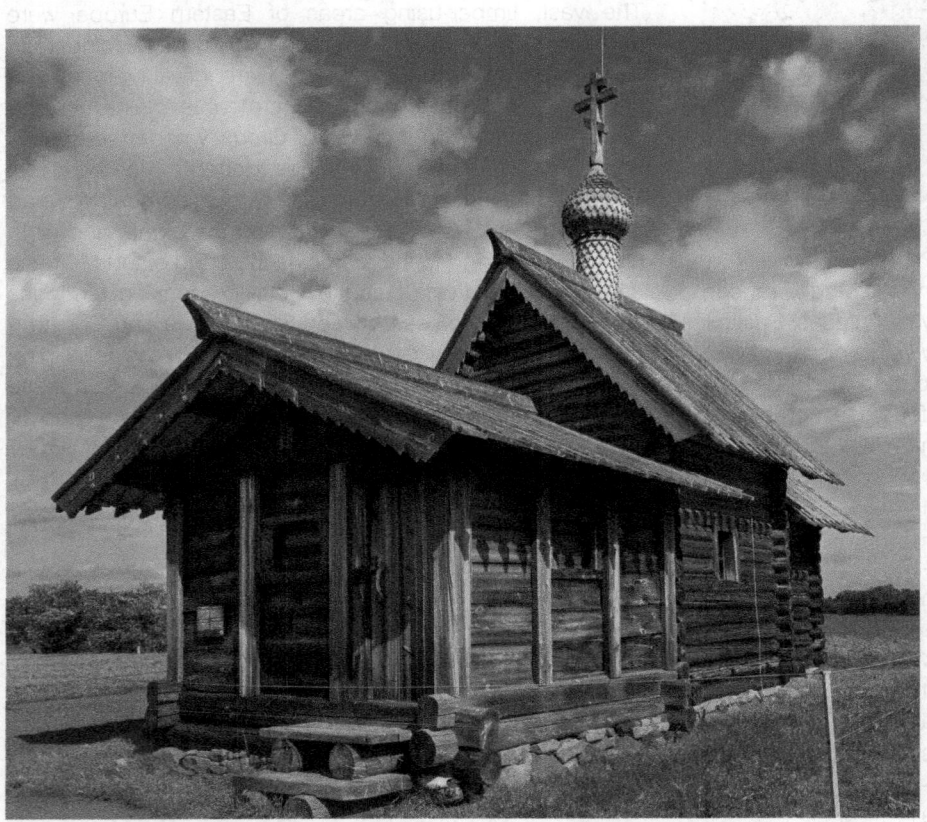

Figure 10.2-2 Kizhi Island, Russia. Church of St. Lazarus, fourteenth century, typical of the early wooden churches of Russia, structured on three blockwork bays, covered with a stave roof, and capped by a bulbous *lukovitsa* dome.

TIME LINE

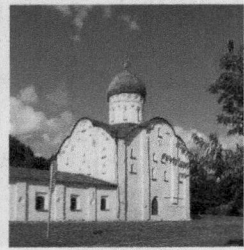

▼ **1360**

St. Theodore Stratelates, Novgorod

Kasimir III commissions Sukiennice (Cloth Hall) for market of Kraków

▲ **1360s**

▼ **1364**

Kasimir III rebuilds Wawel castle and finishes Gothic cathedral in Kraków (rebuilt in 1550s)

Figure 10.2-3 Kizhi Island, Russia. Cathedral of the Transfiguration, with its flamboyant use of *lukovitsas* and *kokoshniks*, eighteenth century.

definitive victory over the Tatar capital of Kazan. The dome on St. Lazarus did not open to the interior but served only to give the exterior a vertical focus. The more ornamental wooden churches, such as the eighteenth-century Cathedral of the Transfiguration (Fig. 10.2-3), also on Kizhi Island, had roofs that ascended into a crescendo of multiple *lukovitsas* and pointed barrel vaults, or **bochkas**, and **kokoshnik** gables, a term that derived from the bulbous headdresses worn by Russian women at festivals.

The use of masonry in Slavic lands was usually associated with royal clients and imperial intentions. The Church of St. Sophia in Kiev, built in 1025 and later expanded, remains the oldest example. Its name came from the palatine church

of Hagia Sophia in Constantinople. Its Byzantine masons used *opus mixtum* construction, alternating bands of brick and stone. The plan originally had a central domed bay and side aisles, with a series of thick piers lining the central nave (Fig. 10.2-4b). As the church expanded, the side aisles multiplied, extending laterally like a hypostyle mosque. St. Sophia in Kiev initially carried thirteen domes but over time acquired ten more. The thick dimensions of the walls and piers came from both the builders' lack of engineering experience with stone structures and the traditions of blockwork construction based on 3 m (10 ft) bays.

During the thirteenth century the Mongolian cavalries of the Golden Horde devastated Russia. Known locally as

▼ 1471

Ivan III subdues
Novgorod

*Aristotile Fioravanti builds
Cathedral of the Dormition
in Moscow's Kremlin*

*Church of St. Lazarus, oldest
wooden church in Russia*

▲ ca. 1400

▲ 1475

Figure 10.2-4 (a) Novgorod, Russia.
St. Sophia, 1045–sixteenth century.
(b) See facing page.

both sides of the Volkhov River. Like Kiev and other Russian cities, it encompassed a scattered series of walled enclaves. Its Kremlin fortress, an elongated oval, 200 × 500 m (656 × 1,640 ft), stood on the highest outlook, with smooth walls rebuilt in brick during the fourteenth century.

Near the center of Novgorod's Kremlin the merchant regime sponsored the rebuilding in stone of Vladimir's wooden cathedral of St. Sophia in 1045 (Fig. 10.2-4a). The builders borrowed motifs from the church's namesake in Kiev and imported Byzantine architects for assistance. They divided the square plan into nine squares, forming a quincunx roofscape with a central dome and a series of four smaller domes at the corners, like many churches in Greece. The domes had tall shafts, but the distinctive ogive caps were most likely added three or four centuries later. At the southern edge of Novgorod's Kremlin members of the oligarchy built themselves sturdy wooden houses, and the *posadnik* sponsored the construction of St. Theodore Stratelates (Fig. 10.2-5). Built in 1360 on a square plan and crowned by a single dome, later transformed into an onion-shaped *lukovitsa*, it was graced by an undulating roofline formed by trefoil vaults set at cross-axes, a motif that was copied in many later churches.

The Tatar invaders brought little cultural stimulation to the region but unwittingly inspired Russian national unity through their tax policies. By relying on the nobility of Moscow to administer their tax collection, they consolidated the loyalty of a future ruling class. By 1480 Ivan III (the Great, r. 1462–1505) had succeeded in both expelling the Tatars and subduing the independent city-state of Novgorod. Concentrating on Moscow as the fulcrum of a centralized state, he planned stone monuments to reinforce the dynasty's religious and political independence.

Ivan III replanned Moscow to be a "third Rome," successor to both Rome and Constantinople, and assumed the

Tatars, they began their incursions in the 1220s and, under the leadership of Batu, a grandson of Ghengis Khan, concluded their sweep of the territory with the siege of Kiev in 1240. Kiev had been in economic decline since the beginning of the thirteenth century, and the Tatars delivered the finishing blow, from which the city never recovered. The Tatars established their capital in Kazan and continued to threaten Russian autonomy until the mid-sixteenth century.

The northwestern city-state of Novgorod went unharmed during the period of Tatar dominion, protected by its remote position amid forests and swamps. The city maintained its independence by paying tribute to the new Mongolian overlords. Novgorod emerged in the twelfth century as a key trading market in the network of the Hanseatic League. The state's wealthy merchants, influenced by the autonomy of burghers in northern Germany and the Low Countries, declared a republican form of government, eschewing the control of a prince or royal dynasty. Novgorod's sovereignty for the next three centuries remained in the hands of an assembly, or *veche*, made of powerful citizens who, like the Great Council in Venice, elected a duke and appointed a *posadnik*, a magistrate like an Italian *podestà* who could override the duke's orders. The *veche* refused to acknowledge the power of a single ruler or a hereditary authority. Novgorod spread out on a butterfly pattern to

▼ **1487**

Faceted Palace begun inside the Kremlin of Moscow by Venetian architects

Florentine Bartolommeo Berrecci begins Sigismund Chapel in Kraków for tomb of Sigismund I of Poland

▼ **1552**

Ivan IV (the Terrible) commissions church of St. Basil on Red Square

▲ **1516**

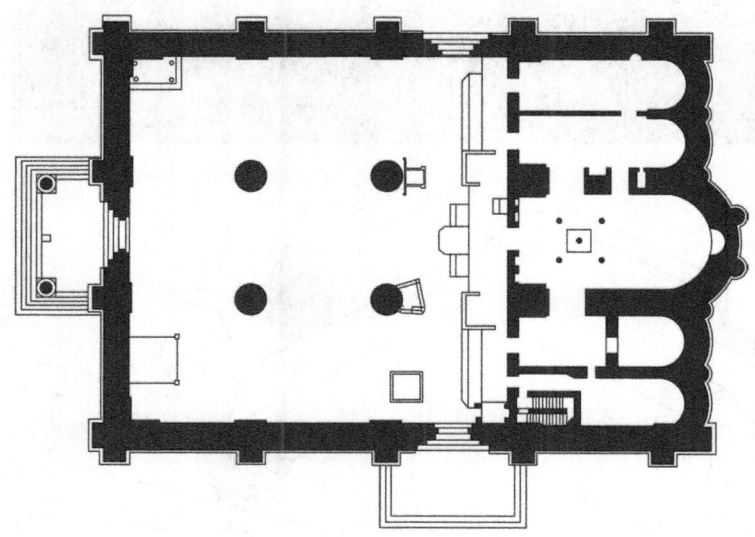

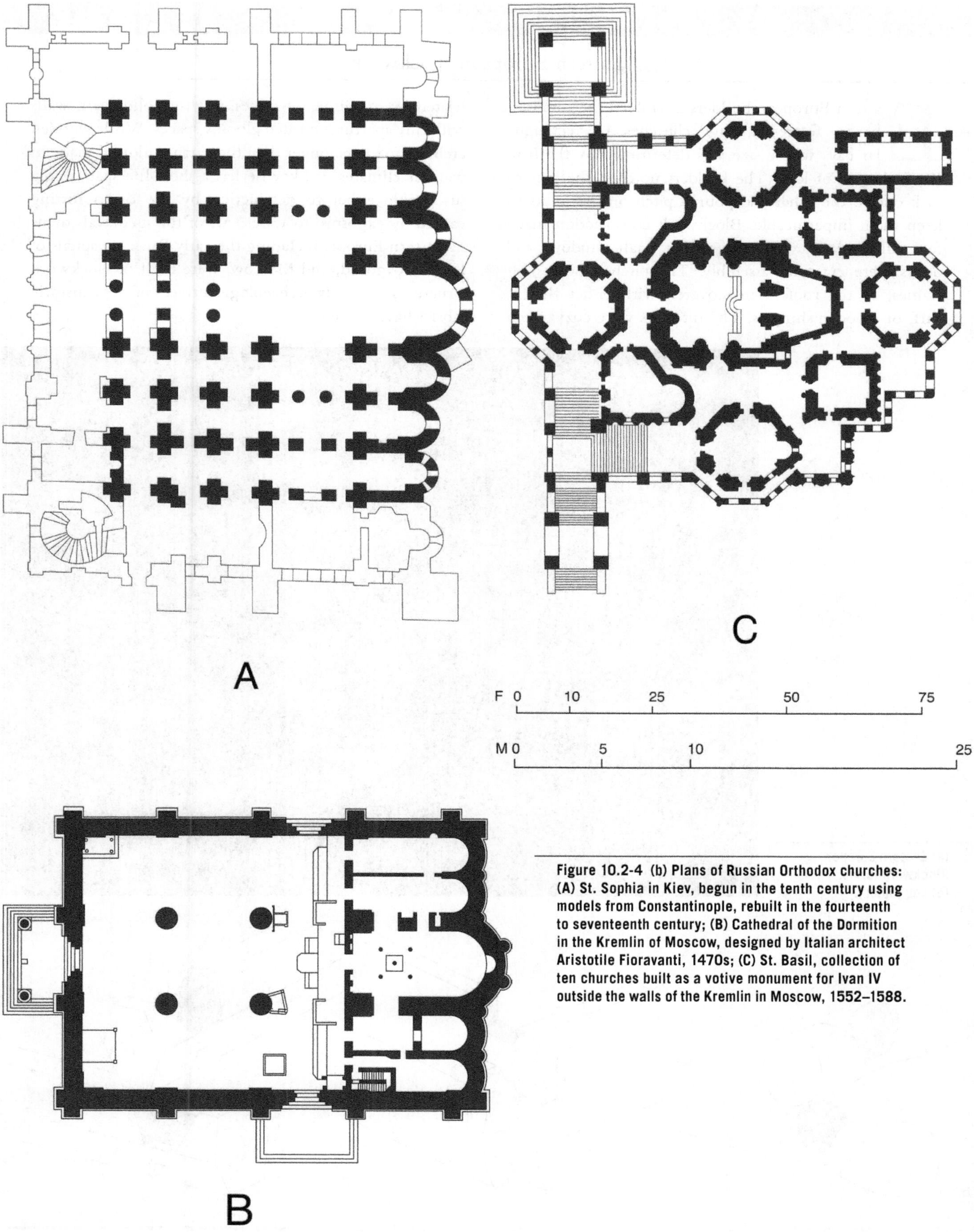

A

B

C

F 0   10   25   50   75

M 0   5   10   25

Figure 10.2-4 (b) Plans of Russian Orthodox churches: (A) St. Sophia in Kiev, begun in the tenth century using models from Constantinople, rebuilt in the fourteenth to seventeenth century; (B) Cathedral of the Dormition in the Kremlin of Moscow, designed by Italian architect Aristotile Fioravanti, 1470s; (C) St. Basil, collection of ten churches built as a votive monument for Ivan IV outside the walls of the Kremlin in Moscow, 1552–1588.

Eastern European Blockwork

Eastern European builders assembled their houses, barns, fortresses, and churches in rectangular bays whose size was determined by the 3 m (10 ft) length of logs. The builders notched the logs to lock one to the other and poured pitch on the joints to keep them impermeable. Blockwork construction made for well-insulated walls into which small windows and doors were cut after assembly. The pitched beams, or frames, of the roofs were covered with either thatch, turf, or wooden shingles. The interiors were cozy, often heated by monumental stoves, but the solid, dark walls with tiny apertures created gloomy spaces. While wooden architecture lasts longer than the earth buildings made in warmer climates, it likewise has a short life span, being susceptible either to destruction by fire or to rotting caused by exposure to water. All of the medieval towns in Eastern Europe, including the early Russian capitals of Kiev, Novgorod, and Moscow, were built of blockwork structures, but only archaeological traces of their historic fabrics have survived.

(a) Eastern Europe. Blockwork forms.
(b) Log joinery.

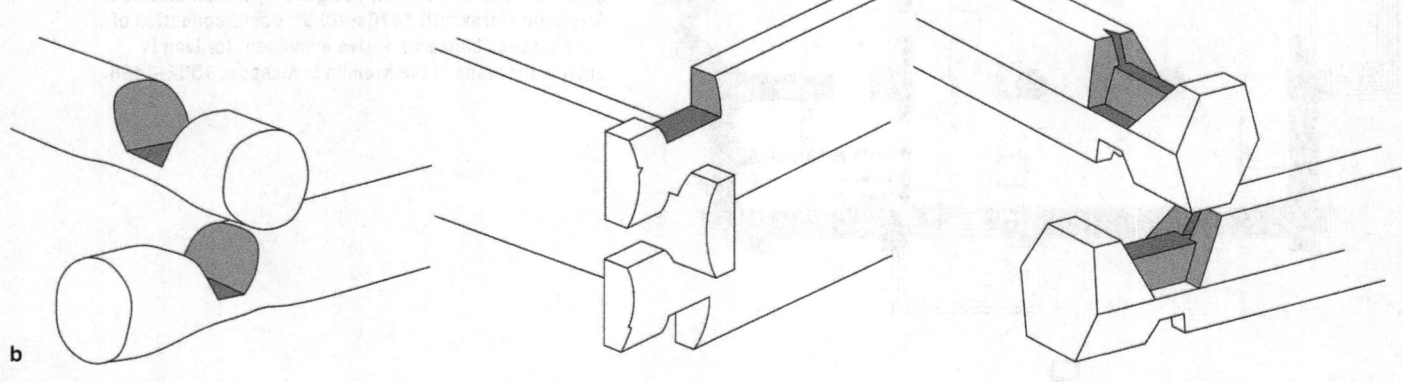

Figure 10.2-5 Novgorod, Russia. St. Theodore Stratelates, 1360.

title of *tsar*, Russian for "caesar." While most of his capital was built in wood, he commissioned the new buildings for the Kremlin exclusively in stone and brick (Fig 10.2-6a,b). For his campaign he drew upon the more developed masonry skills of Novgorod and Pskov. He also sent an envoy to Venice to hire Italian professionals. Aristotile Fioravanti (ca. 1415–1486), an engineer from Bologna who a decade earlier had ventured to Hungary to work for the court of King Matthias Corvinus, served as the first of a succession of northern Italian designers in Moscow. Fioravanti rebuilt Moscow's Cathedral of the Dormition (Uspensky Sobor) (Fig. 10.2-7), the church used for royal investitures, from 1475 to 1479. He based the design on the church of the same name in Vladimir, built during the latter half of the twelfth century with the probable participation of Lombard masons. Fioravanti respected the traditional Byzantine cross-domed plan while introducing new masonry techniques, including the reinforcement of deep foundations with oak beams, the strengthening of thin walls and piers with iron tie-rods, the addition of light brick vaults, and the use of stronger mortar for the masonry. The result corresponded stylistically to Russian Orthodox churches but appeared extraordinarily open and light compared to earlier structures. Only a few details, such as the colonnettes in the blind arcade above the entry, the groin vaults, and the slender and round-arched windows in the domes, betrayed the architect's northern Italian style.

Opposite Fioravanti's church, Ivan ordered the rebuilding of the palatine chapel, the Cathedral of the Annunciation (Blagoveshchensky) (Fig. 10.2-8), in the 1480s. Although the external classical pilasters and rounded arches might at first appear to be the work of Italians, the architects came from Pskov and were obviously attempting to learn from and keep up with the Italian competition. They added a cluster of seven gilded *lukovitsa* domes to the church as a distinctly Russian crown.

Between these two churches Ivan III stationed an extraordinary secular building, purposefully alien in style, known as the Faceted Palace (Granovitaya Palata) (Fig. 10.2-9). Built in 1487 for diplomatic occasions, the tsar intended it as a familiar atmosphere for European guests. The Lombard architects Marco Ruffo and Pietro Antonio Solari encrusted it with northern Italian motifs, such as foliated columns and diamond-shaped revetment. The staggered placement of the upper windows, however, betrayed a curious lack of compositional rigor, somewhat like the arbitrary cutting of windows into log buildings. These features acted as clerestories for the great hall's groin vaults, which radiated from a massive central pier. Italian masons further shaped the look of the Kremlin in Moscow in the design of the majestic red walls and bastions, planned by the Milanese architect Alvisio da Carcano in 1493.

Ivan's final church, the Cathedral of the Archangel Michael (Fig. 10.2-10), served as his dynasty's mausoleum. Begun in 1505, the year of his death, by the Italian Alvisio Lamberti da Montagnana (also known as Novy), it was the most Italian-looking church in the Kremlin, positioned as a freestanding object in space with two levels of classical pilasters that framed bays capped with shell-shaped conches, reminiscent of those seen on Venetian churches of the period.

After the death of Ivan III, his successor commissioned another Italian designer, Marco Bon, to build an octagonal belfry directly in front of the palace. The tower, which today is named after Ivan, rose in three stages, with the third completed at 81 m (266 ft) in 1600. Another Italian builder, Petrok Maly, who came from Rome in 1528 and Russified his name, produced the accompanying Belfry of the Assumption, which housed the great bell and, with the Tower of Ivan, contributed to a total of twenty-four bells, providing the visual and aural focus of the royal enclave.

Figure 10.2-6a Moscow. Plan of the Kremlin walled city, site of the royal palace and six churches, 1490.

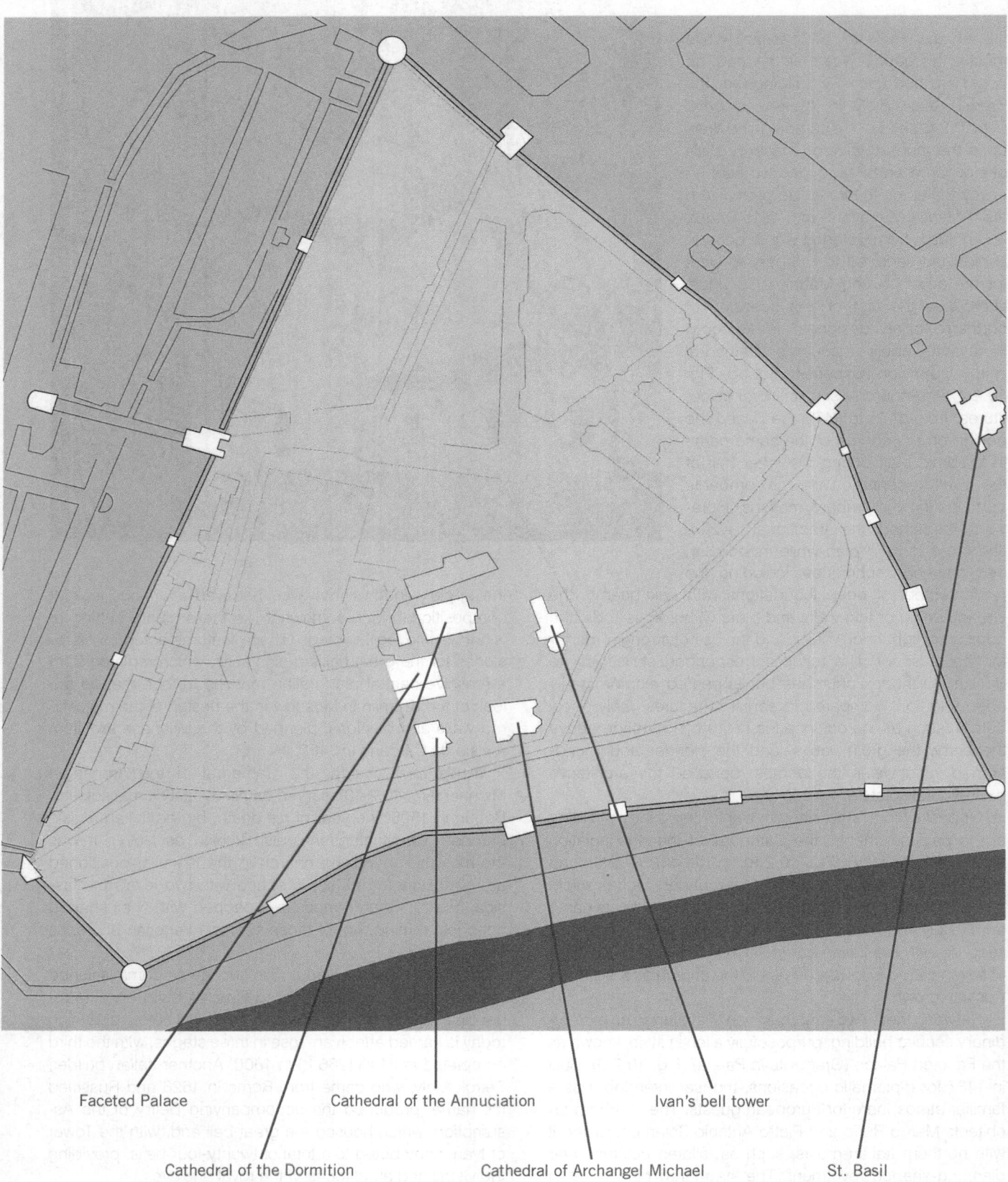

Faceted Palace

Cathedral of the Annuciation

Ivan's bell tower

Cathedral of the Dormition

Cathedral of Archangel Michael

St. Basil

Figure 10.2-6b Moscow. Walls and towers built for Ivan III by Italian engineers in the 1490s.

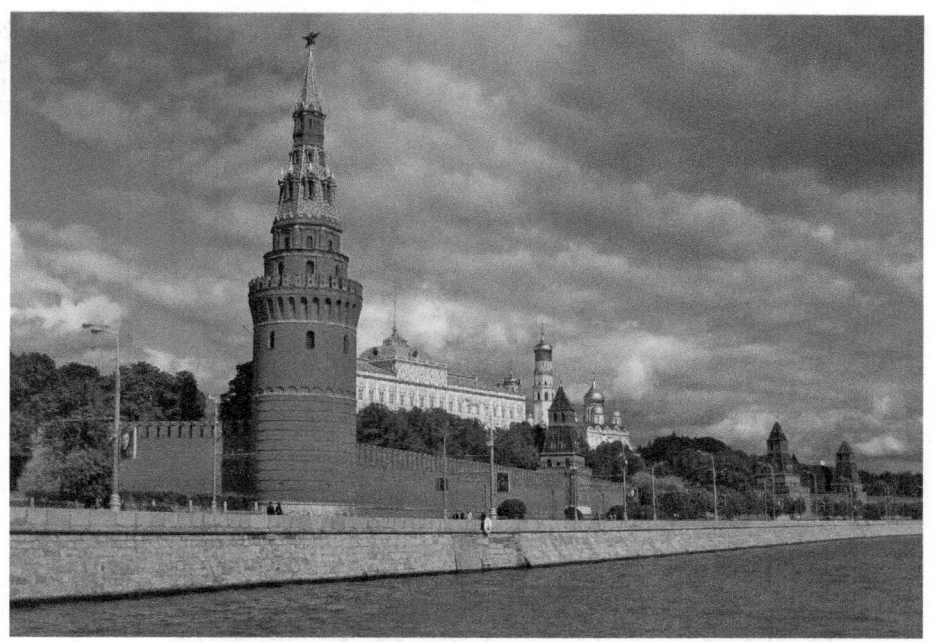

The Russian enthusiasm for Italian Renaissance design was interrupted by the construction of Moscow's most ostentatious church, popularly known as St. Basil the Blessed, but formally called the Church of the Intercession on the Moat (Fig. 10.2-11). After each victory against the Tatars, Ivan IV ("the Terrible," r. 1547–1584) placed a domed wooden chapel adjacent to the fourteenth-century Church of the Trinity. With the final conquest of Kazan in 1552 he commissioned a new church on the site, which became St. Basil. Its unprecedented roofscape of variegated cupolas apparently replicated the earlier jumble of ex-votos, since each chapel belonged to a different saint on whose feast day a major battle had been won. The wild assembly of bulbous *lukovitsas* with stacked gables girding their extended drums represented a conscious rejection of Italian classical style. The central church was flanked by eight smaller churches, much like the Persian **hasht bihisht** scheme for a nine-square grid (see Section 12.1). The tenth church was appended to the northwest corner of the symmetrical composition in 1588 over the tomb of the saintly fool Vasily, or Basil, an ascetic who lived a life of deprivation as a critique of the vanity and materialism of his times. While much of the brightly colored ceramic decoration of the domes was added in later centuries, the central tent-roof tower and the cascade of pointed and arched gables appeared in the original building campaign as a revival of the elements of Russia's wooden churches. The victory monument provided a riotous counterpoint to the severity of Krasny Ploshchad ("Red Square"), the broad 200 m (656 ft) wide paved space built by Ivan the Great as a firebreak and public display grounds in 1493. Seen against the stark red walls of the Kremlin, St. Basil proffered a fanciful forest of surging cupolas

Figure 10.2-7 Moscow. Kremlin, Cathedral of the Dormition, Aristotile Fioravanti, 1470.

Figure 10.2-8 Moscow. Kremlin, Cathedral of the Annunciation, built by Russian architects from Pskov, influenced by early-fifteenth-century painter Andreij Rublev, 1484.

Figure 10.2-9 Moscow. Kremlin, Faceted Palace, Marco Ruffo and Pietro Solari, 1485–1491.

Figure 10.2-10 Moscow. Kremlin, Cathedral of Archangel Michael, Alvisio Lamberti da Montagnana (Novy), 1505.

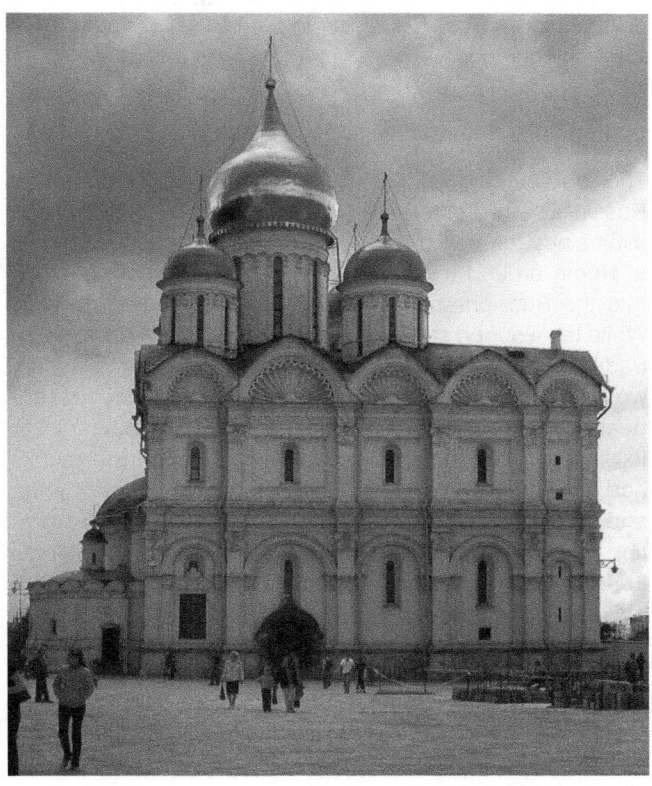

Figure 10.2-11 Moscow. Red Square, Cathedral of St. Basil, built for Ivan IV (the Terrible) in honor of Russia's victory over the Tatar territory of Kazan, 1552–1561.

and pointed *kokoshniks*, asserting the Russian traditions of wooden churches.

Unified Poland: Catholicism and Masonry

The political consolidation of Poland paralleled that of Russia. The two emerging states diverged in religion, however, since the Polish monarchs chose the Western Church of Rome around the same time, in the late tenth century, that the Russians opted for the Eastern Greek Orthodox. While the wooden structures of Poland adhered to the same traditions of blockwork found in Russia, the new masonry works in the first Polish monasteries and churches appeared markedly different from those in Moscow, closer to the models coming from the West. Benedictine monks had built over 200 new monasteries in the region by the end of the thirteenth century, greatly furthering the rejection of wood construction in favor of the more conventional European architecture of masonry. On rare occasions Polish builders included vertical battens on flat elevations to recall the articulation of earlier wooden structures.

The southern city of Kraków, strategically positioned at the foothills of the Carpathian Mountains, became the base for the unification of Poland in the mid-eleventh century. It also led the movement toward stone architecture. Kraków had to be rebuilt after the Tatar incursions of the 1240s, the same that ruined Kiev. The Wawel Hill compound (Figs. 10.2-12 and 10.2-13), which was a bit smaller than the Kremlin of Novgorod, served as Kraków's original castle and cathedral, overlooking the Vistula River. North of the Wawel Hill, the Polish crown sponsored the construction of a rationally designed new town, now known as Stare Miasto, or "Old Town," toward the end of the thirteenth century. Here, the Franciscans and Dominicans built their convents and churches, using masonry to create permanent structures. The plan of Stare Miasto resembled those of other medieval new towns in Europe, particularly those in neighboring Bohemia like České Budějovice. The new town boasted an abnormally large market square, the Rynek Główny, over 200 m (656 ft) per side, more than twice the size of Florence's main public space. Around this central plaza the planners set a checkerboard grid of forty blocks.

Kasimir III ("the Great," r. 1333–1370) led Poland to a new position of well-being, strengthening ties to the West while expanding eastward into Russian territory. He commissioned over fifty castles and fortified towns and many churches as a means of consolidating his own power and establishing a national system of defense. His insistence on building in masonry rather than the more expedient timber significantly altered the building traditions of the region. Parallel to the famous encomium of Augustus, who "found Rome in brick and left it in marble," Kasimir's promoters claimed he "found Poland in wood and left it in stone."

Aside from his ambitious military efforts, which brought tribute from the Ukraine, Kasimir also optimized the exploitation of the Wieliczka Salt Mine as a major income-producing resource. The expanded structure of the mine's subterranean levels could be thought of as the largest building in medieval Poland. The state monopoly on Wieliczka salt yielded 30% of the royal budget, allowing Kasimir to rebuild the principal structures of the Wawel Hill, connecting the castle wings and completing the Gothic cathedral. The Wawel Cathedral, finished in 1364, became an important symbol of the union of the monarchy with the church, used for coronations and the royal mausoleum. Its Gothic vaults, in particular the star-shaped vaults over the narthex and over the altar, resembled the style used by Cistercian

Figure 10.2-12 Kraków. Wawel Hill compound, view to the cathedral, ca. 1350.

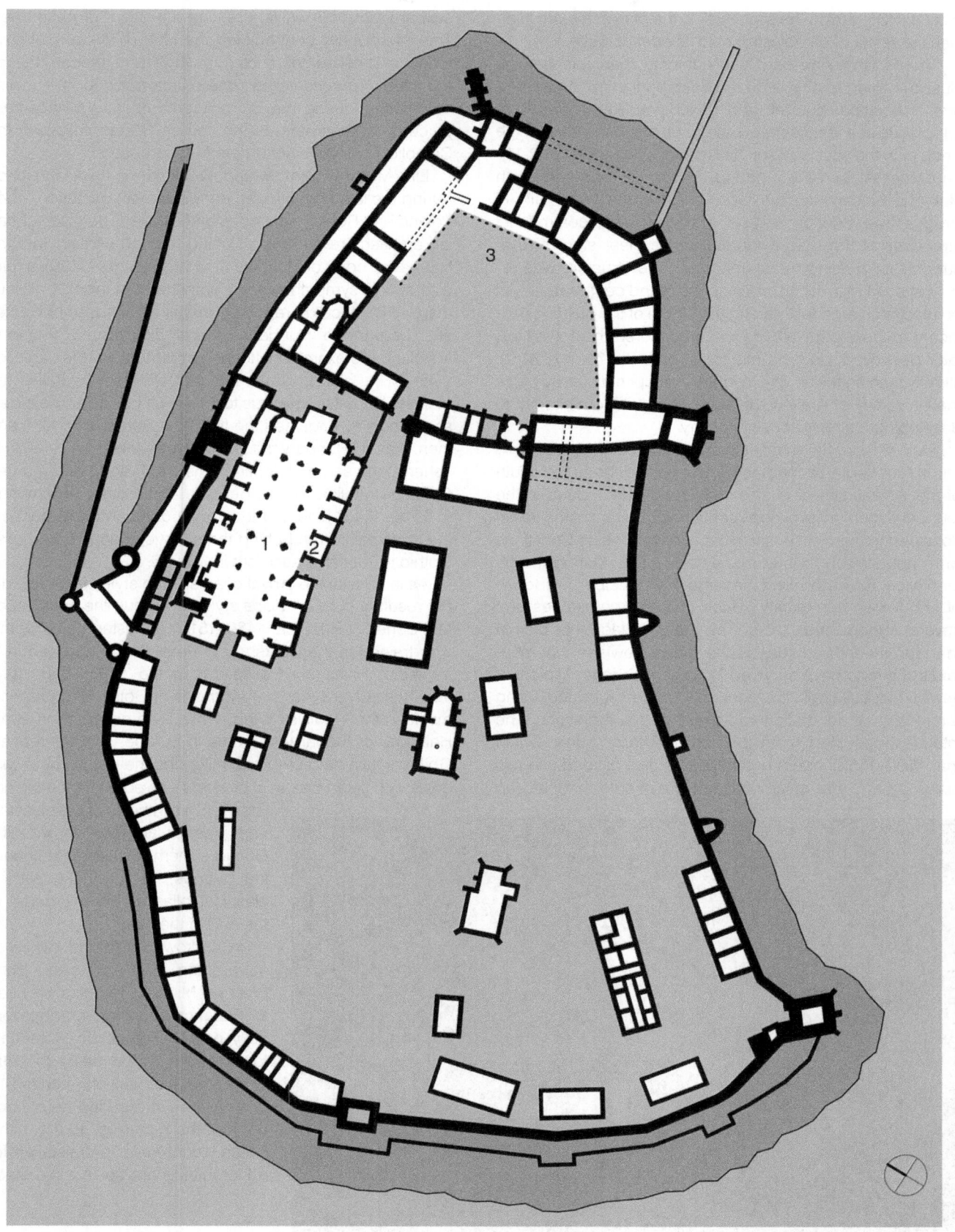

Figure 10.2-13 Kraków. Plan of the Wawel Hill town, ca. 1350–sixteenth century, showing (1) Gothic cathedral finished for Kazimir III, ca. 1350; (2) Sigismund Chapel, added ca. 1520; (3) addition of Renaissance portico to the old castle, ca. 1515.

monks in Bohemia. The slight kink in the plan at the crossing was the result of an adjustment to its confined site.

The Polish kings had less authority than the tsars in Russia, having to answer to the Sejm parliament on all matters of taxation, budget, and diplomacy. Kasimir thus attempted to use architectural patronage to win the favor of the people. In the vast plaza of the Rynek Główny (Fig. 10.2-14), he commissioned the arcaded, 108 m (354 ft) long Cloth Hall (the Sukiennice), similar in scale to the Waterhalle in Bruges (see Section 9.2). One of the finest commercial structures of the age, it represented a clear sign of royal support for a rising merchant class. The structure was rebuilt after a fire in 1555, retaining the grand central vault and pointed-arch arcades running the length of the building. Adjacent to the Cloth Hall, the king sponsored the Town Hall, later destroyed, and the municipal belfry, a 70 m (229 ft), slightly leaning tower. The king also set up in a nearby block the University of Kraków, demonstrating his commitment to developing a strong secular society.

As in Russia, Polish cities grew in discrete patches. Kasimir III founded a second new town, Kazimierz, to the south of the Wawel, similar in size to Stare Miasto. Poland in the fourteenth century proved exceptionally tolerant of the Jews, considering them essential to the economy, since Christians were not allowed to lend money at interest. During the fifteenth century Kazimierz became the principal residence of the Jewish community, which built two cemeteries and several **synagogues** there. The Stara Synagogue, built in the late fifteenth century, is the oldest Jewish monumental structure to have survived in Eastern Europe. Typical of Jewish cult buildings, the exterior appeared subdued, using a minimum of decoration so as not to attract attention. The interior, redesigned in the 1550s by the Italian Mateo Gucci (ca. 1500–1555), had a nearly square hall, divided into two aisles by a row of columns down the middle that held up

sexpartite ribbed vaults, creating the effect of palm trees. This intentionally contradicted the idea of the central nave found in Christian churches (Fig. 10.2-15). Although Kazimierz initially represented a zone of autonomy for the Jewish community, during the late sixteenth century it became a place of confinement as the Jewish Ghetto, following the Catholic Church's strict orders for segregation.

Like Moscow, Kraków underwent strong Italian influence during the late fifteenth and early sixteenth centuries, when Poland and Russia were constantly at war. The taste for Italian architecture arrived in Poland through contact with the Hungarian court of Matthias Corvinus (r. 1458–1490), a ruler with strong sympathies for Florentine humanism. Corvinus married Beatrice d'Aragona from the royal house of Naples and brought to Hungary several Florentine artists and scholars. His example influenced members of the Jagiellon dynasty in Poland, who in the 1460s invited the Italian humanist Filippo Callimachus to tutor their children. The eldest son, Vladislav II, gained the throne of Bohemia in 1470 and then that of Hungary after Corvinus's death in 1490. He ushered the same Florentine artists to Prague and married Corvinus's Italian widow, Beatrice. His brother Sigismund I (r. 1506–1548) inherited the crown of Poland and became the principal patron behind the stylistic change from Polish Gothic to Tuscan classicism in Kraków.

As in Russia, the arrival of artists and styles from Italy did not result in pure *all'antica* style. In Prague the court architect Benedict Reid (ca. 1430–1516), a master of late Gothic who trained in the workshop of Peter Parler, had begun to transform Hradčany Castle during the 1490s (Fig. 10.2-16). This led to a startling synthesis of Gothic and classical motifs in the Vladislav Wing. While Reid covered the Great Hall, one of the largest rooms in Europe, with flamboyant Gothic vaults held by branch-like ribs, he detailed the windows with fluted classical pilasters carved by Florentine artists. Reid's synthesis of the classical language of architecture with the Gothic system resulted in astounding hybrids, such as the twisted classical pilasters on the portal at the end of the hall.

In Kraków, Sigismund I likewise married an Italian princess, Bona Sforza of Milan and Naples. He hired a Florentine designer, appropriately named Francesco Florentino, to revise the Wawel castle in 1516. While the intervention resulted in one of the first arcaded courtyards north of the Alps (Fig. 10.2-17), this castle would never be mistaken for a Florentine palazzo. A triple stack

Figure 10.2-14 Kraków. Rynek Główny plaza, view to the belfry and market hall of Sukiennice, after 1350.

Figure 10.2-15 Kazimierz district, Kraków. Stara Synagogue, Matteo Gucci, rebuilt mid-sixteenth century.

Figure 10.2-16 Prague. Great Hall of the Hradčany Castle, Benedict Reid, 1490s.

Figure 10.2-17 Kraków. Wawel castle courtyard, Francesco Florentino, ca. 1516.

of arcades surrounded the trapezoidal court on three sides. The lower two levels had stout classical columns, supporting round-headed arches, while the upper loggia soared double height, with the awkward stacking of a row of classical columns upon another without intervening trabeation. Such eccentricity demonstrated that ingredients of *all'antica* language were freely borrowed without regard for syntax.

A bit later, however, at the Sigismund Chapel, one of the many chapels that padded the perimeter of the Wawel Cathedral (Fig. 10.2-18), Florentine style arrived intact. The designer, Bartolommeo Berrecci (1480–1537), had trained under Giuliano da Sangallo and practiced a more rigorous style of classicism. He set the hemispherical cupola over an octagonal drum, with indented oculi windows reminiscent of those of the Duomo of Florence. With Albertian clarity he articulated the cubic base with drafted rustication, fluted Corinthian pilasters, and an inscribed frieze. Berrecci's decorations included numerous references to pagan mythology, typical of humanist programs, and in the lantern of the cupola of the Sigismund Chapel he proudly inscribed: "Bartholo. Florentino. Opifice."

After the transfer of the capital of Poland to Warsaw in 1596, the patronage of important buildings migrated north. Kraków provided Poland with its finest models of stone-clad architecture, in which the traditions of log construction had been completely displaced by a new classical language of architecture. Sigismund I set a pattern of patronage for other European regimes that imported the Renaissance style of Italy to evoke the power of ancient Rome and partake in the sophisticated culture of pan-European humanism.

Figure 10.2-18 Kraków. Sigismund Chapel of Wawel Cathedral, Bartolommeo Berrecci, 1520s.

Further Reading

Berten, Kathleen. *Moscow: An Architectural History*. New York: St. Martin's Press, 1990.

Brumfield, William Craft. *A History of Russian Architecture*. Cambridge, UK: Cambridge University Press, 1993.

Buxton, David. *The Wooden Churches of Eastern Europe: An Introductory Survey*. Cambridge, UK: Cambridge University Press, 1981.

Crossley, P. *Gothic Architecture in the Reign of Kasimir the Great: Church Architecture in Lesser Poland, 1320–1380*. Kraków: Ministerstwo Kultury i Sztuki, Zarza̧d Muzeów i Ochrony Zabytków, 1985.

Kaufmann, J. E., and H. W. Kaufmann. *The Medieval Fortress: Castles, Forts, and Walled Cities of the Middle Ages*. Cambridge, MA: Da Capo Press, 2001.

Kaufmann, Thomas da Costa. *Court, Cloister, and City: The Art and Culture of Central Europe, 1450–1800*. Chicago: University of Chicago Press, 1995.

Opolovnikov, A., and Y. Opolovnikova. *The Wooden Architecture of Russia: Houses, Fortifications, Churches*. New York: Harry N. Abrams, 1989.

Shvidkovsky, Dmitry. *Russian Architecture and the West*. Translated by A. Wood. New Haven, CT: Yale University Press, 2007.

10.3 PRE-CONTACT AMERICA
Empires of the Sun

The European maritime exploits of the late fifteenth century changed the notion of "center" for most people in the world. Until then, each society, both in Europe and on other continents, related to itself as the center of the world. Once the colonization process began, however, those who lived outside Europe found themselves in a peripheral relationship. Arguably the largest and most elegant buildings of the fifteenth century were built on this margin in the Americas. In both North and South America, several indigenous cultures created bold monuments. Many of these civilizations disappeared shortly before the arrival of the Europeans, while others terminated as a consequence of that fateful contact.

The empires of both the Aztecs in Mexico and the Inca in Peru took root during the late fourteenth century and reached the height of their development on the eve of the Spanish arrival in the early sixteenth century. The Aztec capital of Tenochtitlán (now Mexico City) developed into the largest and most diversified city in the world, its skyline studded with pyramidal temples. The Inca regime in South America during the fifteenth century unified all of the territories touching the western slopes of the Andes into the

largest empire of the age, excepting that seen in China. The Incas' capital city, Cuzco, represented the sacred center of the world. The cut stones of their monuments commanded religious obedience. The arrival of the Spanish threw into crisis the cosmic certainties of Native Americans, undoing their sense of centrality in the world.

North America before the Contact with Europeans

What Europeans called the "New World"—the Caribbean Islands, Central America, South America, and North America—proved to be very old (Fig. 10.3-1). Prehistoric wanderers and settlers had lived there for more than 15,000 years, repeating many of the phases of culture experienced in the "Old World." Ancient American cave artists and megalith builders created works at the same time that their counterparts were producing Lascaux and Stonehenge. The pyramids of Caral in Peru (2600–2000 BCE), although of much cruder construction, were contemporary with those at Giza and almost as large. Mound builders raised enigmatic hillocks of earth throughout the central region of North America, similar to those in Europe and Asia. While the inhabitants of the Western Hemisphere did not have the wheel, the horse, or metal tools and created only limited forms of written language, they designed monuments and spaces of superb craft and beauty.

Before the arrival of Europeans the architectural development of America north of Teotihuacán remained discontinuous and heterogeneous. The hunter-gatherers in the northeast constructed nomadic structures such as wigwams and **tipis**, while those living in the warmer climate zones built more permanent pit houses. Log structures, comparable to the blockwork of Eastern Europe, appeared in some parts of North America, but pole and thatch houses were more common. The longhouse, a type built throughout Europe since Neolithic times, had a corresponding type among the Iroquois and other peoples of the American Northeast. The Iroquois, whose name literally means "longhouse people," built oblong structures with poles sunk into the soil at the base, tied together at the apex with leather strips, and covered with hides and bark.

Earthworks, mounded figures made from piles of dirt, provided the most durable Native American monuments in the midwestern areas of what is now the United States. A set of six concentric circles at Poverty Point, Louisiana, date to around 1000 BCE, and more recently discovered mounds at nearby Watson Brake may date to 3500 BCE. The Adena culture of Ohio left more than 300 mounds around 500 BCE, which served mostly as tombs. The same culture probably produced the magnificent Serpent Mound (Fig. 10.3-2), a sinuous shape extending over 400 m (1,370 ft), some time around 300 BCE. The snake figure, which may have been related to astronomical alignments, appeared at one end to have an open mouth devouring an egg.

Urban development had sporadic beginnings in pre-Contact North America. Cahokia, located at the exact geographic center of the continent, on the east side of the

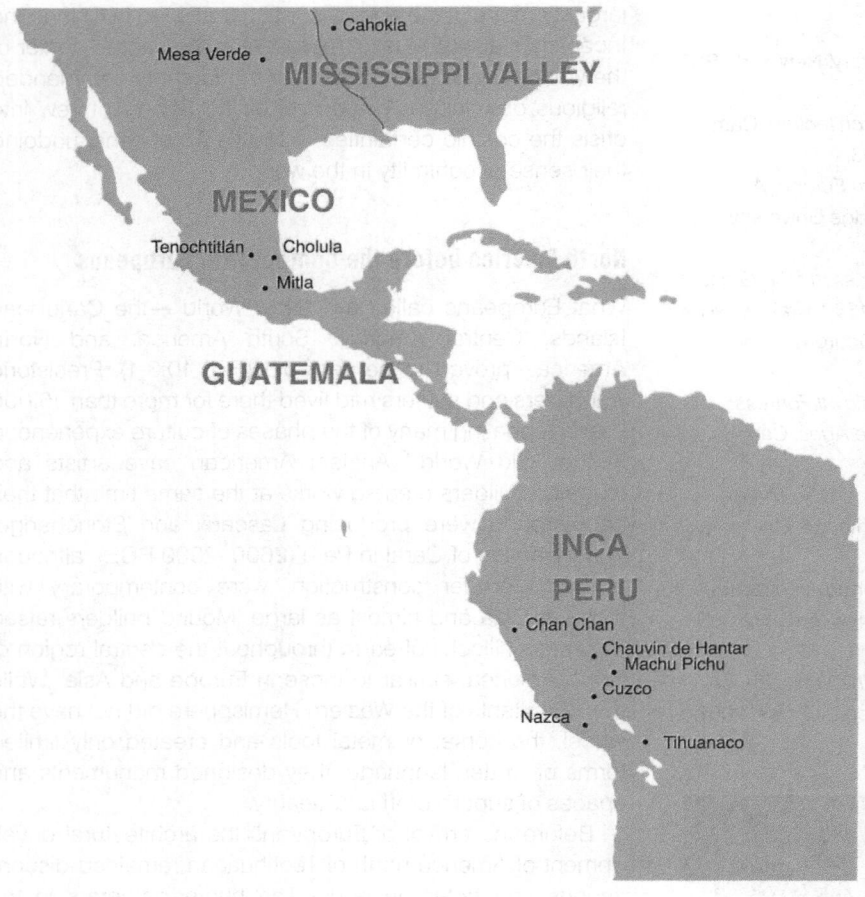

Figure 10.3-1 Pre-Contact Americas.

from the south. Depletion of resources, droughts, and increased warfare in the thirteenth century led to the decline of Cahokia. Most of the mound-building cultures of the Mississippi, excepting those in the Southeast, disappeared around 1400.

The other significant urban culture in pre-Columbian North America settled in the Southwest at the "four corners" between present-day Colorado, Utah, Arizona, and New Mexico. The Hohokam, Mogollon, Anasazi, and other peoples of this region acquired the name "Pueblos," from the Spanish word for their towns. Their settlements, subsequently known as "Great Houses," were usually multistoried, collective structures made of either adobe walls or joined masonry, housing several hundred inhabitants. The Great House builders exploited natural topography for shelter and defense at Anasazi sites such as Mesa Verde (Fig. 10.3-4), tucked under the protective cliffs of Colorado, or Pueblo Bonito, set in the shadow of a cliff in the Chaco Canyon of New Mexico. The Pueblos were strongly influenced by the more settled cultures to the south. The Hohokam in Arizona, for instance, until their disappearance in the fourteenth century, built ball courts for the ceremonial game imported from Mesoamerica. Many of the Pueblo sites honored the Mexican sky god known as Quetzalcoatl, the Plumed Serpent.

The architecture of the Anasazi remained relatively autonomous from that of Mexico and, unlike that of the Mississippi cultures, lacked temple mounds or pyramids. The Anasazi planned their sacred spaces in underground circular chambers, known as **kivas**. The Cliff Palace at Mesa Verde formed part of a cluster of three Great Houses under the protective canopy of a monolithic rock shelf. The complex included twenty-three circular kivas amid more than

Mississippi River facing what eventually became St. Louis, attained a uniquely high level of development (Fig. 10.3-3). Around 1050–1200 CE a population of 15,000 participated in the creation of this vast ceremonial landscape, set on 13 km² (5 miles²). Monks Mound, the great pyramid of Cahokia in the north, dominated an oval-shaped *temenos* enclosed by a log stockade. The Cahokians built a type of blockwork structure for this barrier, similar to the *grods* of Eastern Europe. A vast plaza to the south and two minor plazas to the east and west provided ceremonial settings for seventeen other mounds built with layers of clay. While the compositional similarity of Cahokia to Mesoamerican ceremonial spaces such as Monte Albán and Teotihuacán (see Section 5.3) might suggest the cultural, or perhaps colonial, presence of Mexicans, there is no solid evidence of migrations

TIME LINE

 1325
Aztecs settle in the Valley of Mexico at island city of Tenochtitlán

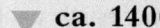 Mound-building cultures of Mississippi disappear

▲ **ca. 1400**

 ▼ **ca. 1400**
Palace at Mitla, Oaxaca, Mexico, built by Mixtecs

Figure 10.3-2 Adena, Ohio. Serpent Mound, ca. 300 BCE.

200 orthogonal dwelling chambers. The cliff offered a natural defense advantage, and the builders stacked the rooms as high as four stories, buttressing their walls with round and square towers. They used wooden ladders to enter their dwellings, while lower-level tunnels offered internal circulation. The roofs made of corbelled logs could support considerable live loads, including terraces and rooftop gardens.

About 200 km (124 miles) south of Mesa Verde, another branch of the Anasazi built a grander power base at Chaco Canyon. By the thirteenth century the clans living here had assumed imperial control over the region, and their clustered Great Houses served as a capital city. Pueblo Bonito commanded a 10 km (6.2 miles) stretch of a dozen communities.

Its elite created the largest and most refined of the Great Houses in five phases over the span of four centuries, evident in the differing styles of masonry bonds. They shaped the southern-oriented crescent with a low outer wall that gave it a perfect *D* shape. Over two dozen *kivas*, including the central Great Kiva, 20 m (66 ft) in diameter, dotted its inner court. The holes at the top of the walls of the Great Kiva indicate that large timbers once supported its roof. The crescent rose in five receding levels against the protective backdrop of a prominent cliff to the north. The palatial *enfilade* sequences and the lack of domestic facilities, such as kitchens, suggest that the orthogonal rooms of Pueblo Bonito housed a priestly elite. The hemicycle's alignment to

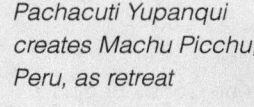

Pachacuti Yupanqui rebuilds Cuzco, Peru, including Sacsahuamán site

▲ **1440s**

▼ **1460s**

Pachacuti Yupanqui creates Machu Picchu, Peru, as retreat

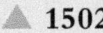

Moctezuma II begins reign

▲ **1502**

The *Kiva*: A Sacred Space for the Male Retreat

The womb-like form of the *kiva* derived from primordial pit houses dug into the ground by Pueblo ancestors. It was conceived as an exclusively male space for congregational councils and religious rituals. Some *kivas* had a flange to the west for ventilation, which gave the plan a keyhole pattern. One entered a *kiva* through an oculus in the roof, and the protruding poles of the entry ladder acquired symbolic meaning, something like the steeple of a church. Built-in adobe or stone benches lined the interior walls. A shrine dug into the floor represented the navel of the world from which life emerged, while the paved floor stood for the second world of human life. The area above the benches signified the third world of animals, and the space of the roof, the current world.

Chaco Canyon, New Mexico. Great Kiva of Pueblo Bonito, twelfth century.

 1510

Moctezuma II rebuilds the Great Temple pyramid and creates immense palace at Tenochtitlán

 Hernán Cortés begins conquest of Mexico

1519

 1524

Francisco Pizarro begins conquest of Peru

Figure 10.3-3 Collinsville, Illinois. Monks Mound, the centerpiece of Cahokia Mounds State Historic Site, ca. 1050–1200 CE.

the cardinal directions made it perform well for passive solar energy but also signaled a cosmological orientation with the solar equinox. Pueblo Bonito was abandoned in the mid-twelfth century, and after recurrent droughts the Anasazi culture disappeared around 1300, its population dispersing to the south and east.

Tenochtitlán: The Aztec Metropolis

The Aztecs, known in their own time as *Mexicas*, settled in the Valley of Mexico in 1325. Following the augury of an eagle devouring a serpent atop a cactus, they founded their capital, Tenochtitlán (Fig. 10.3-5), on an island near the western shores of the valley's network of five lakes. From here they dominated fifty warring city-states. With the snow-clad volcanoes Popocatépetl and Iztaccíhuatl as a back-drop, the Aztecs developed their city into a spectacular setting, rich with temples and palaces. The island metropolis proved larger, cleaner, and closer to the ideal city of the Renaissance than any city in Europe of the same period, including Florence.

Aztec policy set a religious mandate for constant warfare to gain tribute and to stock the altars with sacrificial victims. Through the triple alliance of Tenochtitlán, Texcoco on the eastern shore of the lakes, and Tlacopán on the western shores, the Aztec Empire acquired all of the territories around the highland lakes. About one-third the size

of Spain, it comprised 10 million inhabitants. Local agriculture could not sustain this growing population, which provided the underlying motive for constant colonial warfare. The protection of Tenochtitlán's important merchant population also often served as the pretext for initiating military campaigns.

Similar to Venice (see Section 9.1), Tenochtitlán grew on land recuperated from marshes. The Aztecs created a grid of shallow canals for both drainage and circulation, providing transportation by canoes and flatboats for the merchant and military sectors. Aztec hydraulic engineers rivaled the ancient Romans, bringing freshwater to the center of their capital via a 6 km (3.7 mile), stone-lined aqueduct from Chapultepec Hill. From the mainland they built three paved causeways, which functioned as both highways and dikes to keep the saltier water of the eastern Lake Texcoco from polluting the western freshwater lakes. By the late fifteenth century Tenochtitlán had absorbed the neighboring town of Tlatelolco to the north, extending its area to 14 km² (5.4 miles) and its population to almost half a million.

The Aztec capital remained unique among Mesoamerican cities because of its density. While not as crowded as European cities, its island blocks were tightly packed. Government magistrates enforced orthogonal street and canal alignments and strict sanitary measures to avoid polluting the lakes. In the center stood a walled ceremonial precinct, 500 m (1,640 ft) per side, stocked with a collection of over

Figure 10.3-4 Mesa Verde, Colorado. Anasazi cliff palace, twelfth century.

forty brightly colored monuments. From here four cross-roads divided the city into quarters, each further subdivided into *calpulli*, or wards. The commoners lived as clans or artisan groups in these neighborhoods of about 200 households and collectively farmed the lake garden *chinampas*, maintained a temple, and sponsored a military school for their young. Each island possessed a warriors' house for the men to congregate, the equivalent of the Pueblo *kiva*. The members of a *calpulli* went to war as a combat unit. Like the island parishes in Venice, each ward cherished its

autonomy, and the wooden bridges that connected the islands during the day were drawn up at night.

The common Aztec dwelling type gathered two or more one-room structures around a patio, similar to the *siheyuan* house type in China. Because of the region's seismic volatility and frequent earthquakes, the residents of Tenochtitlán built their houses low, with wattle-and-daub walls and thatch roofs. The women dominated the management of the household and attended to their work of food preparation and weaving in a segregated zone of the house known

Figure 10.3-5 Tenochtitlán, Mexico. Plan, 1525.

as the *cihuacalli*. Each house had a flushing toilet, and the night soil was carefully collected on flatboats to be used as fertilizer. The citizens of Tenochtitlán bathed once or twice a day, and the elite enjoyed steam baths.

The Aztec councils initially elected a "speaker," or *tlatoani*, to rule, but during the fifteenth century this role evolved into a hereditary monarchy. Moctezuma II (r. 1502–1520), king at the time of the arrival of the Spanish captain Hernán Cortés (1485–1547), created an immense palace in stone, 180 m (590 ft) per side, with over 100 rooms. Each suite had

its own bath and several courtyards. The palace included enclosed gardens for such curiosities as an aviary, a zoo, and an apartment for deformed humans. Moctezuma's palace may have resembled a well-preserved structure at Mitla near Oaxaca (Fig. 10.3-6), built a century or so earlier by the Mixtecs. The Aztecs conquered this area during the fifteenth century and conscripted builders from the conquered lands to work on their capital. The builders at Mitla used stone panels to form the flat-roofed volumes. A broad stairway with three wide entry portals led to windowless

Figure 10.3-6 Mitla, Mexico. Palace that anticipated Aztec palaces, fourteenth century.

rooms. The deep transom beams carried geometric fret-work in stone mosaics. Depictions of Moctezuma's palace show similar portals and friezes with the geometric step motif and linked circles. This latter symbol, which appeared frequently on the friezes of the monuments in Tenochtitlán, represented water.

The Aztec city differed from most urban cultures in two chilling details: the constant recourse to human sacrifice and the normalization of cannibalism. Human sacrifice occurred throughout the Americas, but never with the intensity and pace of the Aztecs. The king enacted a daily sacrifice, and each of the many temples scattered throughout the city slaughtered at least fifty victims per year. The Aztec ruling class thrived on cannibalism, which provided the ritual fuel to appease the patron god Huitzilopochtli and secure the fortunes of the city. The Eagle Warriors' compound to the north of the Great Temple served as a council chamber and banquet hall for feasting on the victims. The Aztec sacrifices corresponded to acts of war in other societies. Rather than killing their enemies in the field, they brought them back alive to be offered to the city. They fed the hearts of rival warriors to the deity while cooking up the rest of the body for the victors.

As the city's high priest, Moctezuma II declared himself a god and commanded that no one look at him directly. Like his forebears, he rebuilt Coatepetl, the Great Temple of Tenochtitlán (Fig. 10.3-7a,b), named after the legendary "mountain of the serpents." This final version of the steep pyramidal sanctuary rose 60 m (196 ft), rivaling the dome of Florence in monumentality. The pyramid had been rebuilt at least six times, and, similar to ancient Sumerian ziggurats, each new version enveloped the earlier ones, conserving the inner layers. On the broad platform at the summit stood two shrines: one, painted blue, to the rain god Tlaloc on the left; and the other, painted red, to Huitzilopochtli, the chief Aztec deity of the sun and war. A *chacmol* figure waited splayed with a dish on his belly to welcome the sacrificial victims in front of the shrine of Tlaloc, while inside the shrine of Huitzilopochtli stood an effigy of the god. The still-palpitating hearts cut from the live victims were stuffed into the statue's mouth. At Santa Cecilia Acatitlan there is a restoration of the typical Aztec pyramid temple (Fig. 10.3-7c).

Behind this lust for blood resided an apocalyptic vision of human life, according to which the Aztecs had already suffered four annihilations. The sacrifices served as a compensation to the earth for what people had taken in terms

Figure 10.3-7 Tenochtitlán, Mexico. (a) Model of Coatepetl, the Great Temple. (b) Detail. (c) Santa Cecilia Acatitlan, an intact Aztec temple similar to those in Tenochtitlán.

Figure 10.3-8 Peru. Nazca lines, second to seventh century.

which aside from religious monuments included extensive systems of agricultural terracing, tunnels for mining precious metals, rope suspension bridges, and a network of 30,000 km (18,640 miles) of paved roads connecting the four quarters of the empire.

Inca architectural know-how began with the agricultural infrastructure of irrigation canals and stone terraces in a land characterized by high mountains and coastal deserts. The pyramids at Sipan, built in adobe bricks by the Moche culture from the first to the sixth century, were still used for ceremonies in the fifteenth century by the Chimu, the Inca's chief rivals. The Inca were probably familiar with the mysterious geoglyphs cut into the desert by the Nazca culture perhaps 1,000 years earlier, 200 km (124 miles) west of Cuzco. These colossal incisions, some over 300 m (984 ft) in breadth, depicted such figures as a condor, a whale (Fig. 10.3-8), an alligator, a monkey, and the so-called astronaut, a humanoid figure that appears to be wearing a pilot's helmet. The Nazca lines were cut into the stony desert floor with 30–40 cm (11–13 inch) deep grooves between the second and seventh centuries. They probably served as a way to chart the positions of the stars, leaving the icons as metaphors for the constellations on a vast, treeless shelf that provided an ideal astronomical observatory.

Members of the Inca ruling class made regular pilgrimages to three ancient sites that informed their monumental endeavors. They paid homage to the seventh-century BCE sanctuary of Chavín de Huántar, a temple with a function similar to that of Delphi for the ancient Greeks. Inside its massive stone walls one passed through a circular court to underground labyrinths to seek the advice of the oracle. They also prized the oracle at the coastal site of Pachacamac, 30 km (19 miles) south of Lima, where they restored the pyramidal mud-brick structure of the Temple of the Sun, begun between the fourth and seventh centuries. The final site revered by the Inca, Tiahuanaco, a temple that represented the origins of human culture, was relatively close to their capital at Cuzco, on the Bolivian side of Lake Titicaca. The cut-stone masonry of its perfectly square Sunken Court (Fig. 10.3-9) and the monolithic Gate of the Sun, carved from a single 10-ton block of red andesite granite, inspired the formidable masonry achievements of Inca engineers, who used even larger stones in their structures.

The Inca practiced a unique method of masonry construction. Without the benefit of metal tools, they impeccably smoothed the surfaces of their stones, joining them in highly irregular, interlocking courses. While the widespread use of stone was due partly to its availability from the mountains,

of resources. The victims helped to stave off the final annihilation predicted in the Aztec ritual calendar. Directly in front of the Great Temple, they purposely built a cylindrical platform temple devoted to Quetzalcoatl, the god who had abandoned the Aztecs and promised a vengeful return that would bring their end. When the bearded Cortés arrived with a fleet of eighteen caravel ships, guns, fanfare, and mounted steeds, he appeared to the Aztecs as the likeness of the dreaded deity, fulfilling the prophecy of the demise of Moctezuma's realm.

Stones of the Inca: From Agricultural Terraces to Cut-Stone Memorials

During the same period of Aztec ascendancy over Mexico, the Inca assembled much of South America into a larger, better-organized empire. Their territory stretched 4,000 km (2,485 miles) between the Andes Mountains and the Pacific coast, comprising modern Ecuador, Peru, Bolivia, and Chile. Through both war and diplomacy, the Inca absorbed the other cultures of the region. Steeped in religious and ideological dictates, the kings and their courts fostered a highly articulated monumental architecture.

Although the word "Inca" has come to represent the entire culture, it literally referred to the king as the son of the solar deity Inti. The Inca ruled an empire they called *Tahuantinsuyu* with a form of theocratic socialism, scrupulously managing the distribution of surplus and the location of the population. They structured the entire society on multiples of ten, units that could be easily counted. Inca officials made assessments using knots of colored twine known as *quipu*. Their decimal records comprehended clusters from 10 to 10,000 households. The *quipus* served as a tool for not only commandeering a portion of the agricultural output due to the state but also calculating the percentage of time each individual owed as forced labor. This surfeit of workforce explains the Incas' impressive output of public works, the Inca invested the material with profound religious connotations. According to their legends, the first Inca, Manco Capac, who reigned at the end of the twelfth century, was turned to stone upon his death. Other cultures that used cut stone, such as the Egyptians and the Greeks, carved it as a means of achieving greater volumetric purity of a pyramid or a colonnaded temple. The Incas used stone more as an end in itself. Somewhat like the designers of the Indian rock-cut temples (see Section 6.3) and those who built the great shrine of Zimbabwe in southern Africa (see Section 9.3), the Inca used stone as a fetish, a thing capable of possessing a spirit. Like the petrified body of the first Inca, stone was sacred.

The cut-stone masonry in the Inca capital of Cuzco was the finest in the empire, indicating the city's elevated religious status. The city's name meant *omphalos*, or "navel," of the world, and the Incas' supremely hierarchical and efficient government radiated from this central point. While small compared to Tenochtitlán, Cuzco served almost exclusively as a stage for the theocratic rituals of the state. The Inca resisted the concept of cities, preferring to keep the population scattered in agricultural villages. Only courtiers, priests, secretaries, and the necessary artisans and servants of the court lived in the capital. The rulers distributed the commoners of Cuzco among hundreds of agricultural villages in the valley.

Pachacuti Yupanqui (r. 1438–1471), "the world transformer," rebuilt Cuzco during the 1440s. This coincided with the doubling of the size of the empire after the conclusion of the war with the Chimu people of the north. The grid-based Chimu capital of Chan Chan, reserved exclusively as a royal compound for that culture's king and nobility, served as a model for restructuring the Inca capital. Pachacuti designed Cuzco in the shape of a puma, a feline divinity (Fig. 10.3-10). The jagged outcrop of Sacsahuamán represented the head; the central ceremonial plaza of Huacaypata the belly; and the Temple of the Sun, or Coricancha, at the confluence of two small rivers, the tail. This zoomorphic pattern recalls the geoglyph creatures left by the Nazca.

While built of orthogonal, or **cancha**, blocks, Cuzco did not follow a perfect grid. Fine examples of the tradition of walled urban blocks have survived in Ollantaytambo, 70 km north of Cuzco, built by Pachacuti during the same years as Cuzco. A solid high wall divided each of the *cancha* blocks into two courts (Fig. 10.3-11a,b). The small pavilions set on the four sides of each court exploited the external wall for support. The corners of the courts were usually left empty for planting kitchen gardens. One entered the windowless rooms through trapezoidal doorways, which served as built-in braces against earthquakes. The central pavilion shared a **party wall** and roof with the neighboring house behind it. Steep gables held the beams and purlins supporting the thatch roofs.

The *canchas* in Cuzco were similar to those of Ollantaytambo, only double or triple the scale. Some typical walls can still be admired on the Street of the Sun, now called Loreto Street. The road extended only 3 m (9.8 ft) across, while the walls rose 5 m (16 ft) on a battered incline, an empirical solution to seismic dangers. The unrelieved elevations, more than 100 m (328 ft) in length, extended as regular courses of cushion-shaped rustication that would have been the envy of Florentine palace builders. The fine stonework indicated the special functions of these blocks: one served as the Acllahuaci, a royal harem compound for the Virgins of the Sun, the other as the Amarucancha Palace, built for Pachacuti.

Each of the succeeding Inca built a palace in Cuzco upon assuming power. The walls of these palaces often included trapezoidal niches, a special sign of sacredness. After the death of the patron, the palace was maintained as if he were still alive. Courtiers washed and dressed his mummy on a daily basis and carried it in a sedan chair to public ceremonies. These ghostly palaces surrounded the great ceremonial plaza of Huacaypata, the Terrace of Leisure. A huge open space, similar in scale to the Rynek Główny in Kraków, it was covered in a thick layer of white sand, a half-meter (2 ft) deep. The sand came from the beaches of the Pacific, a distance of over 400 km (248 miles), and pilgrims deposited votive objects of gold and silver in its depths. In the midst of the plaza, a gilded platform known as the *ushnu* served as a podium for the reigning Inca to stand amid the mummies of his ancestors. The *ushnu* represented the sun, and forty-two radial lines extended from this point to over 300 holy shrines in the city. Thus, despite the orthogonal alignments of the city blocks, Cuzco also had a transcending radial pattern.

Figure 10.3-9 Tiahuanaco, Bolivia. Sunken Court, twelfth century.

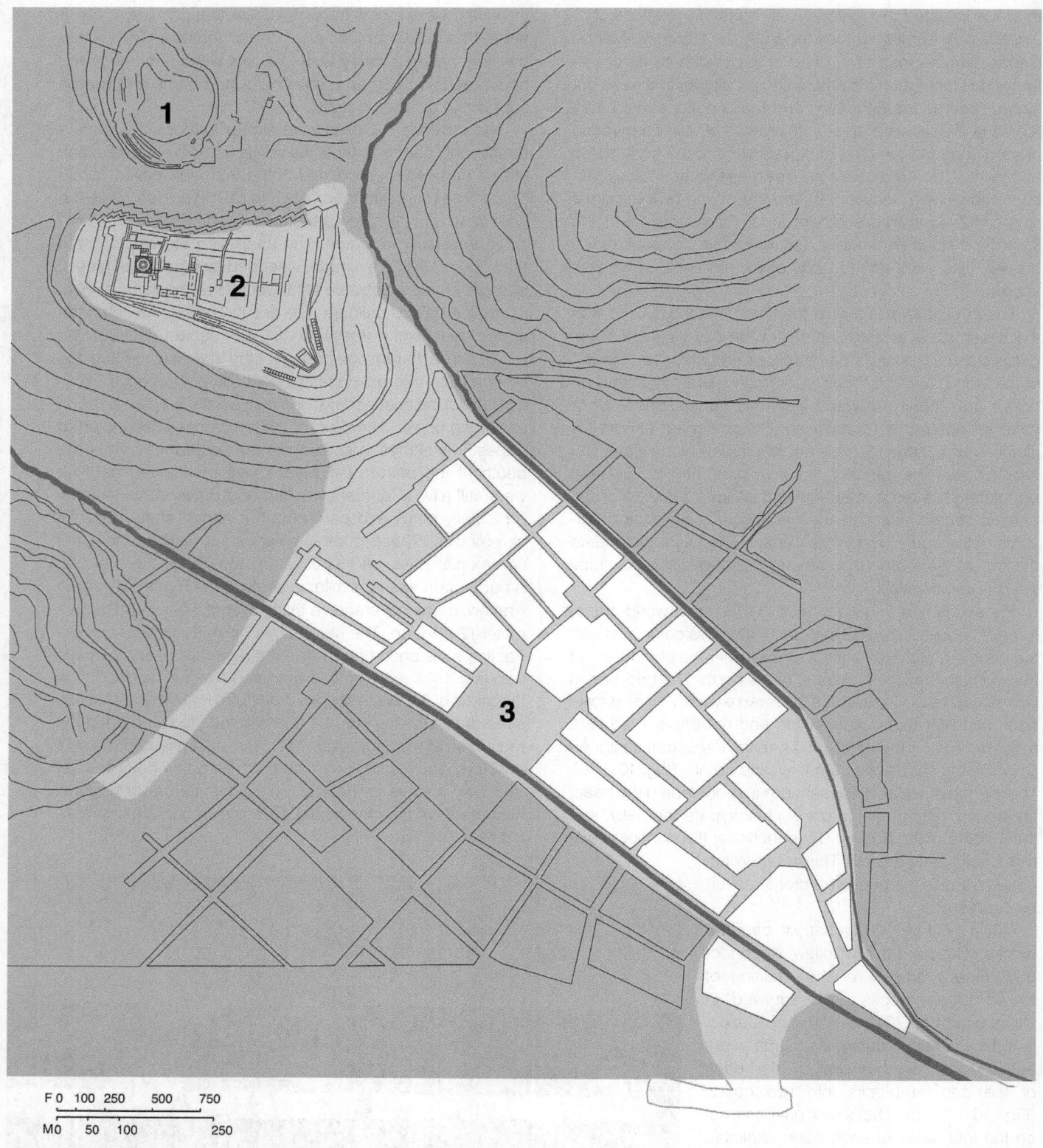

F 0 100 250   500   750

M 0   50 100   250

Figure 10.3-10 Cuzco, Peru. City plan, in shape of puma: (1) Inca Throne; (2) Sacsahuamán Temple; (3) Huacaypata Square.

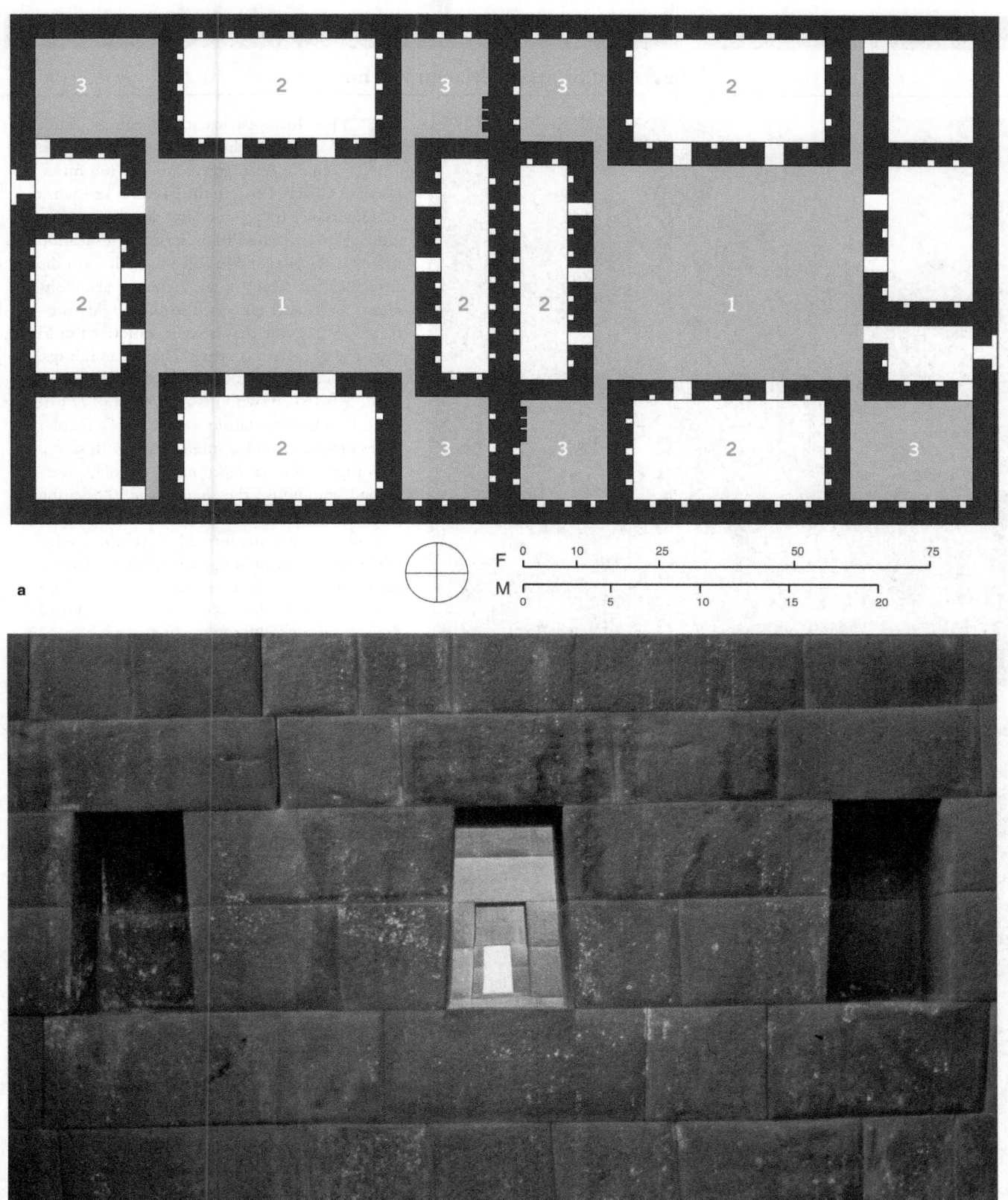

F / M scale: 0 10 25 50 75 / 0 5 10 15 20

a

b

Figure 10.3-11 Ollantaytambo, Peru. (a) Plan of typical *cancha* block, fourteenth century, showing (1) the two courts; (2) pavilions; and (3) corner gardens. (b) Walls showing the precision of Inca masonry.

The Sacred Stones of Machu Picchu

The Inca Pachacuti Yupanqui built Machu Picchu ("old mountain"), a remote royal town 110 km (68 miles) north of Cuzco, Peru, in the 1460s. Like Pienza in Renaissance Italy—and built during the exact same years—Machu Picchu served as a vacation town for the Inca and fulfilled in built form the Inca ideal of social order. After its abandonment, the citadel remained so thoroughly protected by a ravine that it went unnoticed until the early twentieth century. The 143 buildings, built for a camp of 1,000, stood dramatically in a saddle between two hills at 2,743 m (8,777 ft) altitude. The town fabric was made of a regular series of walled *canchas* interspersed with sacred buildings. The extraordinary rotated, heel-shaped monolith, the *Intihuatana* ("hitching post of the sun"), functioned as a sundial and solar observatory and formed the southern edge of a gently terraced, longitudinal plaza. Among the tombs one finds the peculiar genius of Inca masonry where the carvers seamlessly joined the natural rock outcrop to cut-stone blocks.

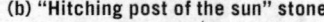

(a) Machu Picchu, Peru, 1460s.
(b) "Hitching post of the sun" stone.

Inca Masonry

The builders of Sacsahuamán dragged the huge stones from a quarry 4 km (2.5 miles) away without the benefit of the wheel. The teams must have included thousands of workers putting in their tribute time. The knobs used for securing the hoist ropes can still be seen on some of the stones. To dress these stones into their cushiony, smooth shapes required a special labor-intensive technique of repeatedly bouncing hard black river flints against their surfaces until the desired shape and texture were achieved. The peculiar intertwining of the courses of masonry resulted from propping irregularly sized blocks on top of each other and then dressing them *in situ* to fit. The builders adjusted each stone to fit to the next.

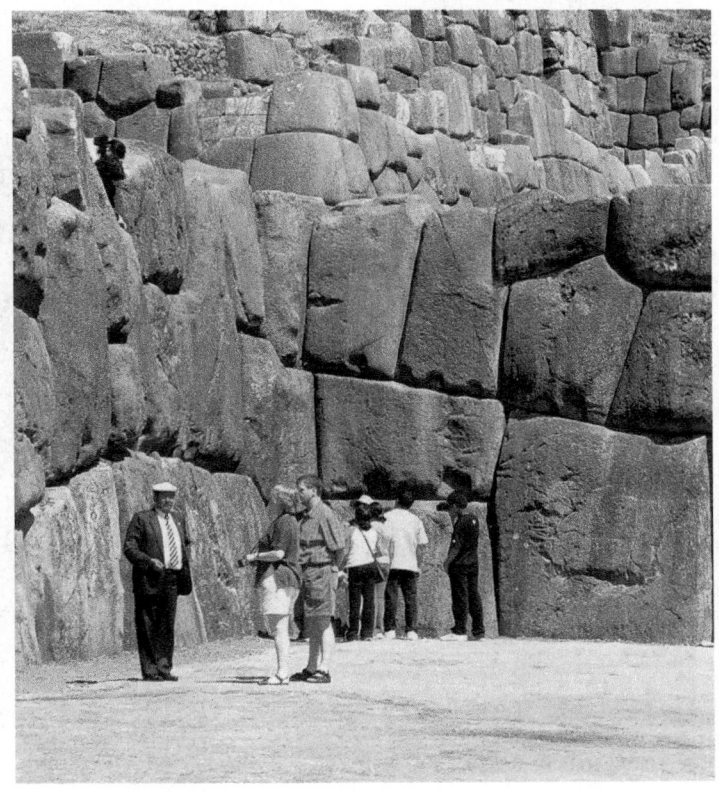

Cuzco, Peru. Cut stone from Sacsahuamán, 1460s.

The most impressive work of Inca masonry remained the hillside site of Sacsahuamán overlooking the city (Fig. 10.3-12). Some of its stones were as large as 9 × 5 m (30 × 16 ft), weighing more than 300 tons. Although often referred to as a "fortress" and used as one by the Spanish during their conquest, Sacsahuamán undoubtedly functioned as a cult site. The long northern flank looking away from the city rose on a succession of three levels with twenty irregularly placed sawtooth bastions. Their rounded corners created a spectacular rippling elevation. This redented pyramid faced a theatrical esplanade where thousands could congregate for festivals. A series of platform altars, known as the Inca Throne, were cut into the domical rock facing the undulating walls. The base of the hill, looking toward the city, sheltered a series of warehouses to store the surplus of the empire. As in many ancient cultures, this major cult site was part fortress, part silo.

How Cortés in Aztec Mexico and Francisco Pizarro (ca. 1471–1541) in the Inca Empire of *Tahuantinsuyu* overcame these highly organized and heavily populated lands with small bands of steel-clad soldiers, a few guns, trumpets, and horses baffles the imagination. The Spanish invaders thinly veiled their materialist motives with a sense of duty to God and king while setting in motion one of the greatest tragedies of human history: the disappearance in less than a century of millions of indigenous American peoples, reduced through violence and disease to a fraction of their former number. As with most ancient peoples, every action of the Aztecs and Incas corresponded to profound religious meanings. Their struggle with ambitious European adventurers, who imported such technological improvements as the great sailing ships, cannons, guns, and armor, led to a clash of mentalities. The contact between Europe and the Americas thus represents the turning point for modernity. The victory of the pragmatic moderns began to shift the focus of architecture away from a cosmological center to other priorities geared to the individual, political goals, and social pathologies.

Figure 10.3-12 Cuzco, Peru. Partial view of redented walls of Sacsahuamán Temple compound, fourteenth to fifteenth century.

Further Reading

Bauer, Brian S. *Ancient Cuzco: Heartland of the Inca*. Austin: University of Texas Press, 2004.

Burger, R. L., and L. C. Salazar. *Machu Picchu: Unveiling the Mystery of the Incas*. New Haven, CT: Yale University Press, 2004.

Chappell, Sally A. Kitt. *Cahokia: Mirror of the Cosmos*. Chicago: University of Chicago Press, 2002.

Clendinnen, Inga. *Aztecs*. New York: Cambridge University Press, 1991.

Fiedel, Stuart J. *Prehistory of the Americas*. Cambridge, UK: Cambridge University Press, 1987.

Knight, Alan. *Mexico: From the Beginning to the Spanish Conquest*. Cambridge, UK: Cambridge University Press, 2002.

Moctezuma, Eduardo Matos. *The Great Temple of the Aztecs: Treasures of Tenochtitlán*. London: Thames & Hudson, 1988.

Nabokov, Peter, and Robert Easton. *Native American Architecture*. New York: Oxford University Press, 1989.

Neitzel, Jill E., ed. *Pueblo Bonito: Center of the Chacoan World*. Washington, D.C.: Smithsonian Institution Press, 2003.

Protzen, Jean-Pierre. *Inca Architecture and Construction at Ollantaytambo*. New York: Oxford University Press, 1993.

Townsend, Richard. *The Aztecs*. London: Thames & Hudson, 2000.

Young, B. W., and M. L. Fowler. *Cahokia: The Great American Metropolis*. Urbana: University of Illinois Press, 2000.

↗ Visit the free website **www.oup.com/us/ingersoll** to view chapter outlines and study questions; Google Maps showing the location of key sites; links to UNESCO World Heritage Sites; and essays on topics that cross time and culture.

1500–1600

CHAPTER

11

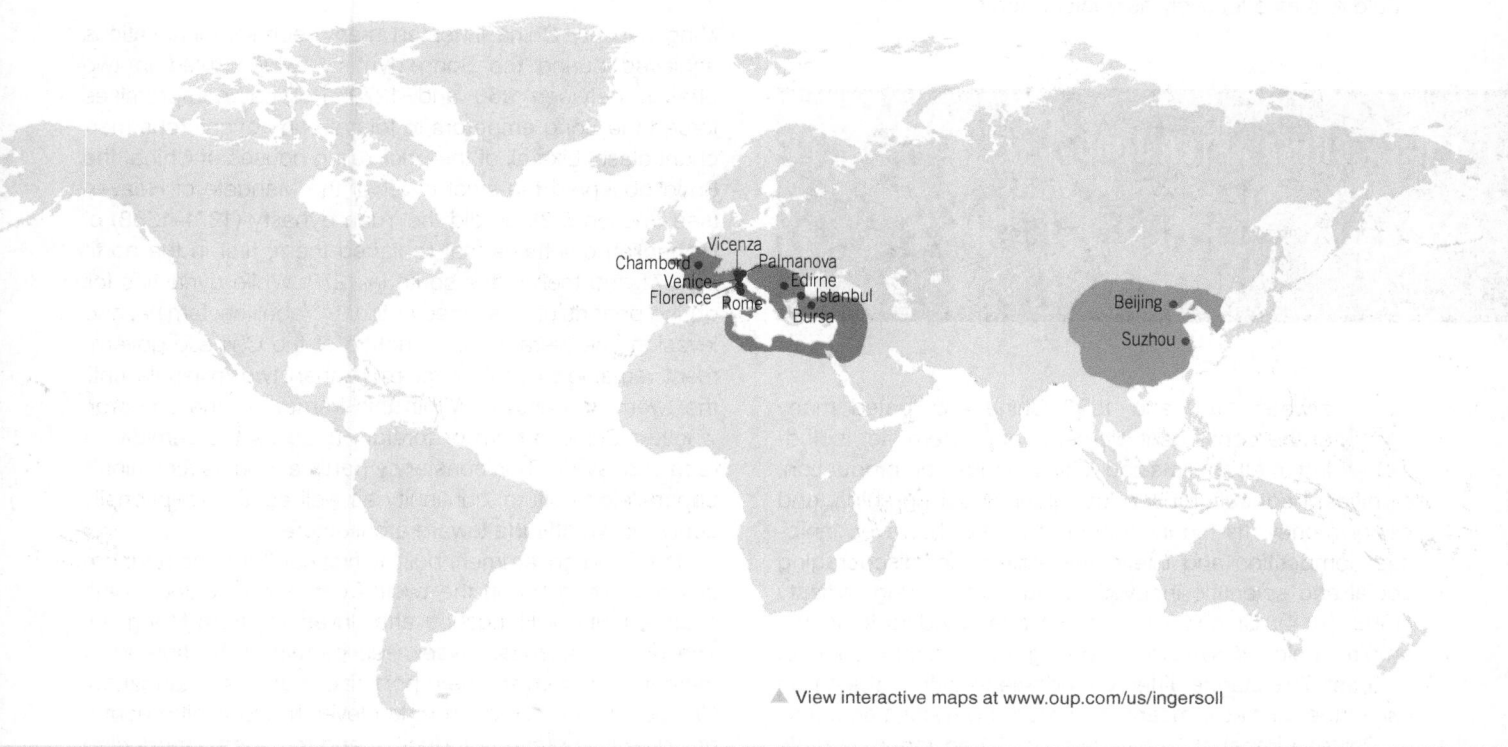

▲ View interactive maps at www.oup.com/us/ingersoll

Since the second century BCE, China had maintained a relatively stable imperial system with periodic ruptures and changes in dynasties, including a century of rule by Mongolian outsiders. In the aftermath of the Black Death, the Ming dynasty benefited from progressive technical achievements developed during earlier dynasties such as paper money, the printing press, gunpowder, and the Grand Canal, while exercising extreme cultural and political conservatism. During the fifteenth and sixteenth centuries the Ming emperors created the Forbidden City in Beijing as a permanent realization of the Mandate of Heaven. China's limited understanding of Europe and the Mediterranean came through Portuguese and Spanish traders and Italian missionaries. In Europe great contrasts arose during the sixteenth century among the emerging nation-states of France and Spain, the contentious Italian city-states, and the northern countries affected by the Protestant movement. The Ottoman Empire introduced a further threat to the region by claiming most of the Islamic territories of the eastern and southern Mediterranean while advancing through the Balkans to Central Europe. Most of these European regimes, including that of the Turks, revived the ancient Roman rhetoric of empire. The popes in Renaissance Rome attempted to restore their power with new imperial displays at the Vatican Palace and New St. Peter's. The kings of Spain and France followed suit with works such as the convent of El Escorial (see Section 12.2) and the Château de Chambord. Only the Ottoman sultans, however, achieved true imperial status through their efficient military and bureaucratic system. They erected great domed mosques with spiky minarets, vaulted markets, luxurious baths, and impressive walls throughout their territories, producing a tangible idea of an Islamic empire that could rule as effectively as ancient Rome.

11.1 CHINA AFTER 1000
The Mandate of Heaven Made to Last

Between 1100 and 1500 China anticipated many of the constituent elements of modern life, including metropolis-sized cities, industrial production, significant agricultural surplus, gigantic sailing ships, and paper money. Its highly centralized state, however, inhibited competition and intellectual enterprise, discouraging social and scientific innovation. During the Ming dynasty (1368–1644), China's ruling class attempted to keep the empire a closed system, repeating the cultural models of the past. This stance differed fundamentally from the Italian use of the past as a means of surpassing historic sources.

Chinese imperial architects reproduced the immutable scheme of the Mandate of Heaven, a system of theological and political hierarchy. The Ming dynasty, however, exhibited one important difference from earlier dynasties: it built its structures to last. Due to their use of stone and brick construction, many Ming projects have remained essentially intact.

As much as the imperial regime proved inflexible, certain members of its civil service, the scholar-officials, succeeded in designing an alternative order. In the wealthy city of Suzhou many retired administrators laid out superb gardens, designing their landscapes like paintings. They pursued an underlying strategy of indirect access, creating meandering paths and constantly changing points of view.

The scholar gardens in Suzhou posed a subtle critique in built form of the strict hierarchical order of the Mandate of Heaven in Beijing.

The Prelude to Ming China: Mercantile Society and Foreign Influences

Ming dynasty China inherited many technical innovations achieved during the Song dynasty, which ruled in two phases between 960 and 1279. Political compromises forced the Song emperors to tolerate an adventurous merchant class. Like all of the prior ruling houses of China, the Song observed the strict order of the Mandate of Heaven (see Section 5.2), as did the Yuan dynasty (1271–1368) of Mongolian chieftains that replaced them, first in the north in 1271 and then in the south in 1279. While dynasties fell during periods of weakened authority, rebellion, famine, and invasion, the hierarchical structure of the Chinese government remained constant for more than two millennia until the twentieth century. Within this framework the emperor, whether Chinese-born or foreign, ruled as the semidivine "son of heaven." This constancy partly accounts for China's unparalleled cultural continuity as well as its exceptionally conservative attitude toward architecture.

The Song government built its first capital in the northern city of Kaifeng but in the twelfth century relocated to the southern city of Hangzhou after invasions from Mongolia. The dynasty's military weakness permitted the spread of mercantilism from southern port cities such as Guangzhou. Chinese merchants during the eleventh and twelfth centuries greatly improved production and transport, introducing large multiple-mast ships known as "junks" for long-distance voyages and inventing technological wonders such as the magnetic compass and the astrolabe. The increasing international demand for Chinese tea, silk, and porcelain led to mass production of these goods on a scale similar to that seen in the late-eighteenth-century factories of the European Industrial Revolution. Some enterprises employed up to 500 workers in a single warehouse. Three centuries before Johannes Gutenberg, the Chinese invented movable type for printing books to satisfy the growing literacy of the bureaucratic and merchant classes. With the introduction of printed paper currency the Song state greatly facilitated the flow of goods and capital.

1406–1420

Yongle emperor Chengzu builds Forbidden City in Beijing

Ming dynasty initiates Tiantan, Altar of Heaven, in Beijing

1406–1420

1433

Ming Dynasty sponsors "treasure fleet" expedition to the Straits of Hormuz

While merchants prospered during the Song period, the central authority became unstable, and the dynasty finally fell to internal threats and the Mongolian invaders of the mid-thirteenth century. Genghis Khan (ca. 1162–1227) united the Mongols with the Tatars, Turks, and other nomadic peoples of Central Asia to conquer the largest territory yet to be ruled by a single regime. The four resulting "khanate" states stretched from Indonesia through China, across the vast arid lands of the Silk Road, to include Persia, most of Russia, and the edges of Europe in Poland and Hungary. The Mongols behaved mercilessly toward those who opposed their cavalry but once in power fostered amnesty. The so-called *Pax Mongolica* promoted tolerance for different cultures and the liberalization of trade, from which the rulers skimmed off a 10% tribute tax.

Khubilai Khan (1215–1294), a grandson of Genghis, owed part of his successful command of China to the use of gunpowder, invented by the Chinese during the late Song period. He planned the new capital of Khanbaliq, known in Chinese as Dadu (now Beijing), with a Chinese architect, Liu Bingzhong, who drew on the *Kaogongji* (*Book of Rites*), used for the construction of imperial Chinese capitals since the second century BCE. As a nomad, Khubilai had few preconceptions about architecture and sought to win over his Chinese subjects by adhering to their customs. His architect planned Dadu as a literal reproduction of the *wangcheng* diagram, a grid of three north–south streets and three east–west streets, with a large space for the palace in the center. The only contradiction to its orthogonal grid came with the insertion of an informal lake that passed from the west through the center to the south, skirting the imperial palace. The builders of Dadu piled the earth extracted from the moats and the expansion of the lake onto the artificial Coal Hill, directly behind the palace on the north, which, according to *feng shui* masters, conserved the positive *qi* forces.

Khubilai's capital grew rapidly into a large, multiethnic metropolis with three concentric sets of walls surrounding the outer city; an intermediary administrative city; and, at the core, the palace. The outer "Tatar" walls covered half the area of eighth-century Tang Chang'an (see Section 7.2) but a space over twice the extent of ancient Rome. The main streets were many times the width of streets in medieval Europe. The Mongols encouraged foreign merchants and tolerated a great variety of religious practices, including

RELIGION, PHILOSOPHY, FOLKLORE

Feng Shui and Indirect Access

Feng shui, which literally means "wind–water," is the ancient method of Chinese geomancy used since the fourth century BCE for the siting and orientation of tombs, buildings, and cities. Important works during the Ming dynasty (1368–1644), such as the imperial tombs at Changling, were constructed with the participation of a *feng shui* master. The underlying goal of Chinese geomancy is to favor the forces of *qi*, or cosmic breath. A south-facing orientation for buildings, with protective mountains to the north and a river flowing to one side as a conduit for the spirit, are considered the most favorable circumstances. Human-made constructions, such as the Coal Hill, built as the northern closure for the Forbidden City in Beijing, can also encourage the presence of *qi*. The tradition of oblique entries and routes with indirect access, found in all of the gardens of Suzhou from this period, relates to the *feng shui* criterion that the flow of negative energy be contained.

Nestorian Christianity, Islam, and Buddhism, whose followers freely built halls of worship and monasteries. The emperor favored Vajrayana Buddhism, practiced in Tibet and Mongolia, and in 1277 sponsored the Baita, the White Pagoda, at the Miaoying Monastery. The Tibetan monk A'nige (1224–1306) designed the bell-shaped *stupa*, or *dagoba*, bringing with him from Nepal a large contingent of *lamas*, Buddhist monks, for its construction. The foreign-inspired tower, built in brick and covered in white plaster, dominated the skyline of Dadu and remains the only architectural trace of the Yuan dynasty's city.

Despite Khubilai's efforts to imitate the traditional Chinese imperial structure, the Yuan dynasty of the Mongols had divided interests, loyal to the confederacy of the khanates in the steppes as well as the Chinese state. The Yuan emperors continued to live in yurts, despite having built conventional Chinese palaces in Dadu. The dynasty began to flounder after Khubilai's death in 1294 and by the mid-fourteenth century had lost control as a result of numerous rebellions and the scourge of the Black Death. Dadu fell without resistance to the founder of the next dynasty, Ming

▼ **1510**

Retired bureaucrat and poet Wang Xiancheng builds Artless Administrator's Garden in Suzhou

▲ **1440–1550**

Ming Dynasty rebuilds and augments the Great Wall of China

Emperor Jiajing rebuilds Tiantan (Altar of Heaven) complex in Beijing

▲ **1530**

▼ **1556**

Portuguese traders set up permanent base in Guangzhou (Canton), China

Figure 11.1-1 Ming China. A painted silk showing Chinese officials, including the alleged architect Kuai Xiang, in front of the Forbidden City, ca. 1500 CE.

Taizu (r. 1368–1398), who in 1366 destroyed and cordoned off the city.

Ming Beijing: The Permanent Mandate of Heaven

The first Ming emperor shunned Dadu, preferring to keep his capital in the southern city of Nanjing. The next important ruler, Chengzu (r. 1402–1424), who called his reign *Yongle* ("Perpetual Happiness"), came to power through a coup d'état, ousting Ming Taizu's designated heir. His decision to return to Khubilai's city, renaming it *Beijing* ("the northern capital"), allowed him to make a clean start, creating for himself an atmosphere of legitimacy, free of the political conflicts remaining in Nanjing. The northern base also served better to monitor the periodic Mongolian raids that continued after the fall of the Yuan dynasty.

Chengzu constructed Beijing over the remnants of Khubilai's abandoned capital. The red walls of the imperial palace marked its center, while the vast gardens for the imperial temples defined its edges. The Forbidden City (*Zijin cheng*) (Fig. 11.1-1), begun by Chengzu at the outset of the fifteenth century, served as the exclusive district of the emperor, accessible only to court officials. The walled enclave fit into the outline of Khubilai Khan's earlier palace, measuring 960 × 760 m (3,150 × 2,493 ft). Its walls overlooked a moat as broad as the Grand Canal in Venice. Its major palaces and courtyards lined up along a central axis in strict symmetry, while the perimeter hosted hundreds of minor buildings for members of the court more casually distributed on orthogonal alignments. The scale and symmetry of the central areas of the Forbidden City achieved an order similar to that seen in the walled compounds of the Khmer built two centuries earlier in Cambodia (see Section 8.1). The resemblance may not be accidental, as one of Chengzu's architects, Ruan An, surveyor of the city's water works, came from Annam in Southeast Asia.

The grandeur of the Ming imperial setting came less from mass and monumentality than from the vast emptiness of its open courts. The negative space surrounding the relatively small palace structures instilled a sense of awe. The sequence passed through the double barrier of Tiananmen ("Gate of Heavenly Peace") to a half-kilometer, granite-paved boulevard. To the east lay the Taimiao Temple to the imperial ancestors and to the west the Temple to Soil and Grain, both of which were traditionally placed in front of the ruler's palace. The colossal *Wumen* ("Meridian Gate") (Fig. 11.1-2) interrupted the path with its *U*-shaped forecourt, which extended on a broad platform over the moat. Beyond this point only members of the court and those with official business could proceed.

The imperial palace extended over a series of seven large courtyards on the central axis and dozens of smaller courts to either side. A laterally placed colonnaded hall raised on a platform dominated each court. In the first court on the main axis one crossed the Golden River, a gracefully curving, marble-clad canal. Beyond this lay the Outer Court (Fig. 11.1-3a), a vast assembly space, 10,000 m² (107,639 ft²) in area, planned as a site where thousands of courtiers could appear on ritual occasions such as coronations, imperial birthdays, and New Year celebrations. In the middle of the court a pyramidal platform ascended on three gradual terraces to a succession of three ceremonial halls, or *gongs*, which seemed to hover above the space in a linear sequence. In plan the platform formed a longitudinal *I* shape.

The first structure, the Hall of Supreme Harmony (11.1-3b), was the largest wooden structure in China, 70 × 37 m (220 × 120 ft) and 37 m (120 ft) high, yet remained smaller than comparable halls from other cultures, such as the ancient Roman basilicas or the contemporary European public palaces. Behind it stood the Hall of Middle Harmony, one-tenth smaller and perfectly square in plan. Surrounded on all sides by an open colonnade, delicate lattice windows defined its inner chamber as a more intimate throne room. The emperor would rest there before carrying out ceremonies in the larger hall in front. The third structure, the Hall of Preserving Harmony, stood one bay smaller in each direction than the front hall but appeared otherwise identical. It served as a site for minor festivals.

Figure 11.1-2 Beijing. *Wumen*, the Meridian Gate, of the Forbidden City, fifteenth century.

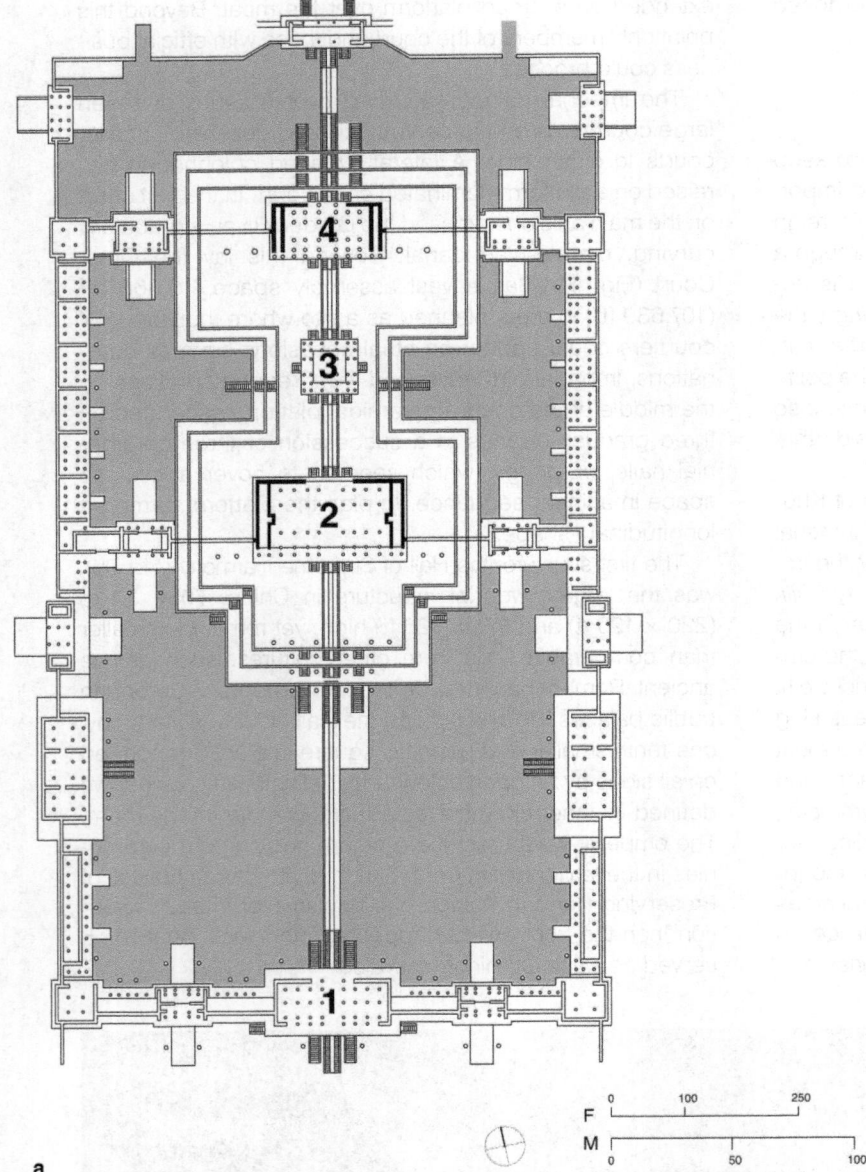

Figure 11.1-3 Beijing. (a) Plan of Outer Court of the Forbidden City, showing (1) the vaulted gate; (2) Hall of Supreme Harmony; (3) Hall of Middle Harmony; (4) Hall of Preserving Harmony, fifteenth century. (b) View of the Hall of Supreme Harmony.

Most of the architectural solutions of the Ming came from the typological and proportional recommendations of the *Yingzao Fashi* (*State Building Standards*) manual. The double-eaved roofs of the two main halls corresponded to the type and proportions recommended in the treatise, with the lower eave flaring out over a porch. Most of the large buildings in the Forbidden City, including those above the gates, repeated this style of double-eave roofs, which indicated high status. Further status was conveyed by the concave crests of the **hipped roofs** and upturned eaves made possible by the internal support of the branch-like *dougong* brackets. One variation from the typical solution of colonnaded buildings occurred in the main halls, which had a central bay wider by one-half and end bays narrower by one-half. The Ming style of brackets differed from earlier *dougong* interlocking brackets, using flat, colorful, wing-like supports to join the columns to the rafters.

The designers of the Forbidden City assembled its major structures from a kit of parts that, along with the universal color scheme, guaranteed cohesion despite hundreds of different buildings. They rendered the walls in deep red plaster and gave the roofs golden-glazed cup tiles. The tiny terra-cotta figures lining the crests of the roofs represented legendary creatures such as lions, dragons, and men riding roosters and served as talismans, meant to drive away evil from the structure (Fig. 11.1-4). Eleven figures sat on each of the crests of the Hall of Supreme Harmony, while the other pavilions had nine, seven, five, and so on, indicating their decreasing importance. Most of the wooden and ceramic elements of the principal structures of the Forbidden City built in the fifteenth and sixteenth centuries have been replaced, but the seventy-two wooden columns inside the Hall of Supreme Harmony rest on the original sixteenth-century marble bases. The granite, marble, and brick masonry used throughout this building on the lower levels ensured the imperial buildings a new fireproof permanence not known in other Chinese capitals.

Beyond the Outer Court, the Inner Court for the imperial residence repeated the grand ceremonial landscape at half the scale. Between the two oblong halls, the front reserved for the emperor and the rear for the empress, stood the

Yingzao Fashi: The Chinese Architectural Manual

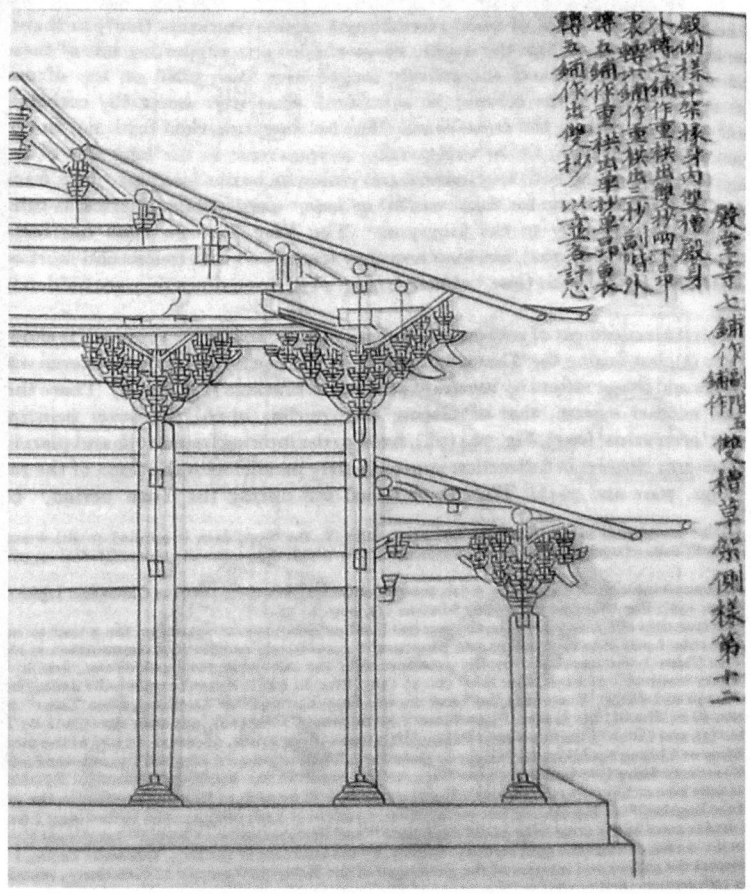

Around 1100, the Song dynasty sponsored the publication of the extraordinary architectural manual the *Yingzao Fashi* (*State Building Standards*), among the earliest printed Chinese books. The author, the dynasty's minister of construction, Li Jie, focused solely on practical information. Unlike the Roman author Vitruvius and the Italian Renaissance treatise writers, he avoided questions of history, society, and interpretation. Li Jie brought together in his manual the official knowledge of building types and proportions, explaining how to calculate proportions, how to design the bay structures of standard building types, how to estimate labor costs, and which materials to use. The modular system he proposed for giving dimensions to timber members, known as *caifen*, allowed for the thorough standardization of a structure's parts. The manual's finely drawn illustrations, noteworthy for their precision, show details such as the pieces of mortise-and-tenon wooden joinery, the arrangement of interlocking *dougong* brackets, the interwoven patterns of painted decorations, and the eight grades of modular scales of buildings. Some of the earliest uses of section drawings demonstrate the relationship of the brackets to the rafters.

Ming China. Page from the *Yingzao Fashi* treatise, 1100.

Figure 11.1-4 Beijing. Forbidden City, guardian figures on the crest of the roofs.

Figure 11.1-5 Beijing. Forbidden City, a concubine courtyard, sixteenth century.

Hall of Union, a superb architectural conceit celebrating royal intercourse. Aside from his nuptial duties, the emperor was expected to enjoy the company of a multitude of concubines, who numbered more than 100 by the sixteenth century. Organized like an army into five ranks, the concubines occupied the dense courts to either side of the Inner Court (Fig. 11.1-5). In these intimate enclosures the concubines cultivated music and literature in the company of maids. The role of concubine presented one of the few means of upward mobility for women during this period. Families groomed their daughters for the role from childhood, forcing them from infancy to have minute, doe-like bound feet, which made them useless for any other activity such as farm labor. Women with bound feet walked as if on tiptoes, elegantly, slowly, and painfully.

Court eunuchs comprised another large contingent residing within the Forbidden City. They did the heavy labor, kept order, and maintained the complex sexual relations of the imperial palace. Because of their castration, these men were presumed to have neither familial ambitions nor lust for the imperial concubines and maids. By the sixteenth century they numbered over 70,000. Unless they worked as guardians, the eunuchs lived in barrack-like buildings on the edges of the compound.

Scholar-officials represented a third significant group using Beijing's imperial palace. They spent long years studying the classic texts of Confucianism, Daoism, and Chinese history, and if they successfully passed the state civil service examination, they could gain a tenured position in the empire's bureaucracy. The government usually dispatched the scholar-officials far from their homes to avoid conflicts of interest. Thousands served the emperor in Beijing, but despite the high status of direct participation in the Forbidden City, working there was not without risks, as court intrigue and espionage on the part of the eunuchs frequently led to the indictment of scholar-officials for treason or corruption. Unlike concubines and eunuchs, the scholar-officials resided outside the Forbidden City, in what later became known as **hutongs**, long alleys set in gridded blocks, to the east of the palace. They lived with their families in narrow *siheyuan* courtyard dwellings made of modest assemblies of small pavilions within a perimeter wall. All buildings not belonging to the emperor were uniformly colored gray with gray roof tiles, creating a remarkably homogeneous setting in contrast to the vibrant crimson and gold of the Forbidden City.

Chengzu also initiated the Ming dynasty's necropolis at Changling, 45 km (27 miles) northwest of Beijing. Here, the Hall of Eminent Favor appeared as a near replica of the Forbidden City's Hall of Supreme Harmony, like a parallel world for the spirit. One approached the Ming tombs through a beautifully carved granite *pailou*, a five-bay square arch derived from the Indian Buddhist *torana* gates. The Spirit Path, lined with thirty-six pairs of granite statues, depicted a dream world of giant camels, elephants, horses, and men. The 6.5 km (4 mile) path toward Chengzu's burial mound repeated the same distance from the gate of the outer city of Beijing to the Hall of Supreme Harmony as a conscious reference to the imperial city.

The Ming dynasty suffered a succession crisis at the beginning of the sixteenth century, resulting in the crowning of an underage prince, Zhengde. The court eunuchs easily manipulated the boy-emperor, encouraging him toward debauchery, until he died in an alcoholic stupor before reaching age thirty. After Zhengde another young emperor, named Jiajing ("admirable tranquility," r. 1521–1567), took

the throne. Enjoying one of the longest reigns of the Ming dynasty, he developed into a controversial tyrant. His interest in Daoism and alchemy led him into major ideological conflicts with the Confucius-based Mandarin elite.

Motivated by theological zeal, Jiajing rebuilt the Tiantan, or Altar of Heaven, in Beijing. Initially conceived for Chengzu in the 1420s, it occupied a site in the outer city larger than the Forbidden City and served the same function as the Mingtang temple of earlier dynasties, requiring the emperor to perform ceremonies during the two yearly solstices to ensure optimal conditions for agriculture. Jiajing restructured the compound in the 1530s by surrounding the ritual areas with an enormous wooded estate and enclosing the site with a concentric set of inner and outer horseshoe-shaped walls (Fig. 11.1-6a). The emperor's major ritual

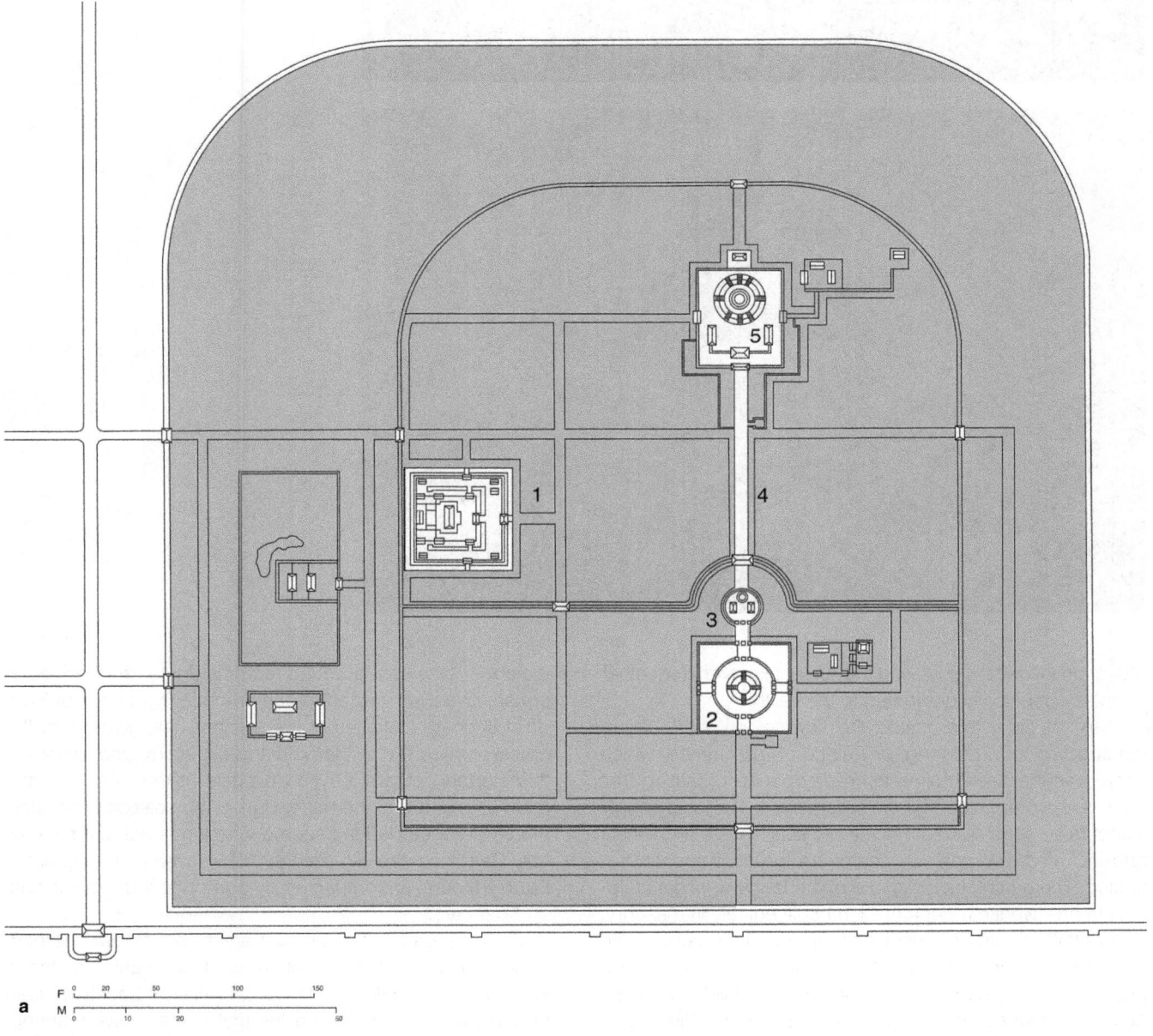

Figure 11.1-6 Beijing. (a) Plan of Tiantan: (1) Palace of Abstinence; (2) Earthly Mount; (3) Vault of Heaven; (4) ramped thoroughfare; (5) Dasi Hall. (b) and (c) See next page.

Figure 11.1-6 Beijing. (b) View of Tiantan, showing triple terrace of the Earthly Mount, 1540s. (c) Dasi Hall, rebuilt in 1540s.

alteration involved separating the Altar of Heaven from other temples specifically dedicated to the earth.

West of the altars, inside the first set of walls, Jiajing constructed the Zhaigong, or Palace of Abstinence, which served as the base for the three-day period of fasting that occurred in preparation for the ceremonies. The increasingly insecure emperor placed it inside two sets of walls and moats and included 160 garrison chambers for his personal protection. The central hall was one of the few residential buildings in pre-twentieth-century China built entirely in masonry.

Tiantan's central sequence of three shrines began with the Earthly Mount (Fig. 11.1-6b), a triple terrace of ascending circular stages, ringed by marble balustrades and accessed by four stairways radiating in the cardinal directions. The circle in Chinese cosmology signified heaven and the square, earth. Each of the three major shrines involved a

dialogue between a round central figure and an outer square one. Reminiscent of the ambulatory spaces of Buddhist shrines, multiples of the number nine, symbol of the emperor, recurred in the balustrades, stairs, and pavers of this stepped pyramid, with 36 posts at the top, 72 in the middle, and 108 at the base. During the solstice ceremony, the emperor carried the sacred wooden tablet of the Heavenly Deity from the silo-like Vault of Heaven to the top of the Earthly Mount, accompanied by burnt offerings, musicians, and dancers.

After the Earthly Mount the Tiantan axis followed a long, bridge-like thoroughfare that ramped up slightly, connecting to the Dasi Hall (Fig. 11.1-6c), or Hall of Sacrifice, used to make a burnt offering on the first moon of every spring. A rectangular set of outer walls framed the circular platform, which at the eastern edge contained kitchens and a slaughter pavilion for sacrifices and to the north a pavilion for the tablets of the heavenly spirits. The cylindrical hall rose 37 m (118 ft) and was unique in type, capped by three diminishing levels, each skirted with a broad apron of eaves supported by complex brackets. The closest thing to a dome in China, its form derived from Buddhist pagodas. The interior of the Dasi Hall offered a soaring void structured on cantilevered brackets. Neither crossbeams nor columns assisted in its support. Although all the roof tiles today are uniformly blue, originally they were blue at the top, gold at midlevel, and green below, signifying heaven, earth, and the myriad things of nature.

The Tiantan ensemble constitutes one of the world's most memorable religious settings, yet very few people ever gazed upon it until the twentieth century. Like the Forbidden City, it stood apart as a well-guarded enclave for the exclusive use of the emperor and his retinue. Its formal vocabulary of circles, squares, and the grand axis branded the landscape with the certitude of imperial hierarchy, a scene reserved for the Mandate of Heaven alone.

The Scholars' Gardens of Suzhou:
The Art of Indirect Access

The magnificent axial settings of Beijing reproduced the urban and architectural models of Chinese imperial tradition. The other cities of China, however, were denser, less rigidly structured, more pragmatic, and subject to quick changes. One of the better preserved of these urban areas, the southern city of Suzhou, reached its prime in the sixteenth and seventeenth centuries during the Ming dynasty and in many ways developed as a counterpoint to the capital. Instead of relying on a grand central axis, its urban pattern was full of diverted paths and detours, and in place of a single tyrant's domain, there were dozens of delicate gardens, each designed by a different patron and stocked with small lakes, shady pavilions, and fantastically shaped rocks. The city's structure appeared like a rationalized version of Venice: fourteen canals running east–west and six north–south, with streets lining one side of the canals and nearly 300 stone bridges. Most of the intersections of the straight streets jogged, leaving T-shaped or zigzag junctions. This alternative order came from a rhetorical love of indirect access.

Suzhou in the sixteenth century had a population of over a half-million, twice as large as any European city of the time. It commanded a territory laced with canals that connected the fertile Shanghai peninsula to the Grand Canal. The city's good climate derived from its proximity to the eastern shore of Lake Tai, one of the deepest lakes of China and the source of the spectacular eroded rocks (tai hu) that served as prized items of contemplation in the scholars' gardens. Because of the high crop yield of its well-watered fields and the availability of easy transport for commercial exchange, the region surrounding Suzhou became the wealthiest of the country. While imperial authority did not allow Chinese cities to develop with political autonomy, Suzhou possessed some of the characteristics of a European city-state, including an exchange economy, a large merchant class, high educational standards, and a subtle resistance to imperial authority. Rather than making direct attacks on the inflexible central government, this critique appeared indirectly, in the form of withdrawal from political life to the private garden. The design of the gardens of Suzhou produced the highest expression of a different method of Chinese design and, thus, an alternative to the hierarchical order of Beijing.

Most civil servants did not take their exams until age thirty. The rewards of the work that followed these exams proved so lucrative that many retired after only a decade of service. As Suzhou became one of the principal places for training scholar-officials, those who succeeded often returned, either to teach or to cultivate their literary and artistic interests in good company. At least twenty substantial scholars' gardens, each with its own literary name, were wedged between the city's regular patterns of courtyard houses and canals. The smallest, Wang Shi Yuan (the Net Master's Garden), originally built in the twelfth century, was rebuilt in successive campaigns from the fifteenth to the eighteenth century. Its title referred to a famous Daoist literary trope: the nets for catching fish are like the words used for arriving at meaning. The metaphor implies that one can never quite express meaning with words. The Net Master's Garden was one of the few scholars' gardens attached to a residence; usually, the scholar-officials conceived these sites as getaways from the home. The gardens never had a single itinerary. In the Net Master's Garden one could leave the rooms of the house on three different paths to explore the series of enclosed landscapes. In each case the entry required one to make an oblique turn (Fig. 11.1-7a).

The word for "landscape" in Chinese came from a combination of the characters for water and mountain. The term corresponds to the artifice of the Net Master's Garden, where a small, irregularly shaped lake set up the studied compositions of tai hu rocks. One passed through pavilions for studying, for taking tea, and for painting. A nonhierarchical system of crooked galleries (lang) skirted the lake, and as one continued, different, unexpected views emerged. The open pavilions, or tings, all had names and occupied special viewing platforms—one hexagonal ting, named "Moon Arriving and Breeze Coming," rose three steps above the path to jut into the lake for multiple points of view (Fig. 11.1-7b,c). The moods of the different courtyards differed according to the amount of vegetation, water, and paving they contained, as well as the placement of tai hu rocks (Fig. 11.1-7d).

Wang Xianchen (1479–1559), a censor during the reign of the debauched boy-emperor Zhengde, built the largest of the Suzhou gardens, the Zhuo Zheng Yuan, or Artless Administrator's Garden, in 1512. Its title made a subtle joke about the difficulties of serving at court during that period, referring to an old adage that "gardening is the only form of administration suited to the artless." The allegory may have been intended to refer to the patron's retreat from Beijing in the wake of the replacement of the chief scholar-officials by the young emperor's eunuchs. After his departure Wang

Figure 11.1-7a Suzhou, China. Net Master's Garden (Wang Shi Yuan), thirteenth–seventeenth centuries.

Hall from Which One Looks
at the Pines and Contemplates
the Paintings

Pavilion of the
Accumulated Void (Library)

Lake

Pavilion of the
Clouds and Moon

Halls of
the house

Nursery for potted plants

"Barrier of Clouds" Hall

Figure 11.1-7 Suzhou, China. (b) Different shapes of *ting* pavilions, demonstrating the love of variety. (c) Net Master's Garden, *ting*. (d) *Tai hu* rock formation.

Figure 11.1-8 Suzhou, China. Artless Administrator's Garden (Zhuo Zheng Yuan), variegated struts on a ting window, 1512.

visitors. The pergola from the western terrace framed the view to the North Pagoda, situated a few blocks away, an example of *jeijing*, a "borrowed landscape" that contributed to the painterly quality of the immediate garden. Both Japanese and English gardens later exploited a similar concept.

The scholar-officials conceived sites for nonhierarchical experiences in their gardens, allowing visitors to discover them a bit at a time. Both the design of the pathways and the gardens' political symbolism remained indirect. While it may have been inappropriate to imitate the emperor's axial landscapes, the obvious negation of this tradition served as a subtle statement of disaffection. Every change of direction in the scholars' gardens offered a new point of view, while the imperial landscapes unfolded with relentless uniformity. The charm of these gardens proved so powerful that in 1796 Emperor Qianlong, upon abdicating his throne after a sixty-year reign, added a Suzhou-style garden behind the Inner Court of the Forbidden City. Its ponds, galleries, randomly placed pavilions, and contorted *tai hu* rocks aspired to the irregular compositions of the retired scholar-officials who had taken their liberties in Suzhou.

Further Reading

Heng Chye Kiang. *Cities of Aristocrats and Bureaucrats: The Development of Medieval Chinese Cityscapes*. Honolulu: University of Hawai'i Press, 1999.

Johnston, R. Stewart. *Scholar Gardens of China: A Study and Analysis of the Spatial Design of the Chinese Private Garden*. Cambridge: Cambridge University Press, 1991.

Keswick, Maggie. *The Chinese Garden: History, Art and Architecture*. Edited by A. Hardie. Cambridge, MA: Harvard University Press, 2003.

Mote, W. *Imperial China, 900–1800*. Cambridge: Cambridge University Press, 1999.

Needham, Joseph, and Robin D. S. Yates. *Science and Civilization in China*. Vol. 5, *Chemistry and Chemical Technology*. Part 6, *Military Technology: Missiles and Sieges*. London: Cambridge University Press, 1994.

Skinner, G. William, ed. *The City in Late Imperial China*. Stanford, CA: Stanford University Press, 1977.

Yinong Xu. *The Chinese City in Space and Time: The Development of Urban Form in Suzhou*. Honolulu: University of Hawai'i Press, 2000.

Xianchen turned his wealth and imagination toward a place where he could exercise an artful control over the landscape, resulting in a design that tactfully contradicted the rigid parameters of the Forbidden City.

Like the Net Master's Garden, the Artless Administrator's Garden had a southern orientation. One passed through multiple courts while visiting over forty pavilions (Fig. 11.1-8), each of which had a name inspired by a landscape. A large lake had evocative islands, while zigzag bridges served the smaller ponds. The plentiful water came from springs on the site and drained out to the canals. *Tai hu* compositions awaited the visitor in intimate courts. In the farthest court, the Pavilion of the Mandarin Ducks, a stunning interior streaked with the bright blue of tinted glass awaited

11.2 THE OTTOMAN EMPIRE
A Culture of Local Symmetries

The Ottoman Turks descended from the nomadic tribes of the Central Asian steppes. They settled in western Anatolia and during the fourteenth century pieced together a large state with ambitions to revive the power of the ancient Roman Empire. Their commitment to urban culture led to the foundation of magnificent mosque compounds that usually included a tomb, a bath, a religious school, and a soup kitchen (*imaret*). Ottoman architects created a strong sense of internal order by placing a dome over each bay of their important buildings. The symmetry of their mosque enclaves and public markets stood in great contrast to the otherwise irregular patterns of their cities.

From the early Ottoman capital on the Asian side of the Bosporus in Bursa, their legions moved to the European side, first settling in Edirne and then taking Constantinople in 1453. They conquered the territories of the Byzantines, which lay partly in Asia and partly in Europe, in order to propose a new Roman Empire for Islam. Architecture played an important role in this effort, demonstrating the regime's authority, efficiency, and love of order. The Byzantine masterpiece, the church of Hagia Sophia, exerted a commanding influence on the design of Ottoman mosques. Both the sultans and their architects aspired to equal or surpass the great church. Mimar Sinan, the state architect from 1538 until his death in 1588, and author of over 300 projects executed during the long and fruitful reigns of Süleyman I and his son Selim II, perfected an Ottoman method of design as assured and recognizable as that of the ancient Romans.

The Prospect of a Muslim Roman Empire: Royal Mosques and *Imarets*

From the fifteenth to the eighteenth century the Ottoman Turks reigned as the leading power of the Mediterranean. They became prodigious builders in the effort to control a vast empire. The Turks in Anatolia often went by the name of "Rum," and in their conquests they consciously aspired to Roman precedents. Like the ancient Romans, they maintained a well-organized military to oversee the construction and maintenance of public works. The impressive infrastructure projects carried out by the Ottoman army, such as the new walls of Jerusalem, the Süleyman Bridge at Büyükçekmece, and the Mağlova aqueduct, rivaled those of the Romans. The Ottomans promoted a rich urban life as well, building markets, baths, and great religious complexes. They crowned their cities with cascading domes and spiky "pencil" **minarets**, while organizing public buildings, such as the markets and the charitable hospices, or *imarets*, into

self-contained symmetrical compositions set adrift in an otherwise casual fabric of winding streets lined with wooden or half-timber houses. Ottoman urbanism varied according to the cultural and historic context: On the periphery of well-established cities such as Damascus, Aleppo, and Tunis, Ottoman planners built new structures that did not interfere with existing ones. In Istanbul and Edirne, they frequently displayed a desire for local symmetry, in which only the parts of a larger whole remained in geometric harmony.

The Turks came from ancient nomadic stock and developed their own written language. From the steppes of Central Asia they moved to Southwest Asia as mercenaries and slaves, first in the service of the Abbasids and then in service of the Seljuks. By the tenth century most of the Turkish tribes had converted to Islam. The founder of the Ottoman dynasty, the great military chieftain Osman I (1258–1326), settled his people in northwestern Anatolia during the thirteenth century (Fig. 11.2-1). Most of the region had been devastated by the raids of Ghengis Khan a few generations earlier, which gave the Turks a distinct advantage. By the fourteenth century they had absorbed their Muslim and Christian neighbors on the Anatolian peninsula, subsequently known as Turkey.

Osman's son Orhan chose the Byzantine spa town of Bursa as his capital in 1326. From here his clan swept over the lands of the Byzantine Empire in Asia Minor and the Balkans. At the end of the fourteenth century the Ottomans relocated the capital to Adrianopolis (renamed Edirne) to be in Europe. During the next half-century they literally engulfed Constantinople, which fell in 1453. Their political goal of achieving peace and justice through a universal world government dominated by the Islamic faith became a Turkish variation of Charlemagne's *Renovatio Romanae Imperii* (see Section 8.3). Once they possessed the city of Constantine, they attempted to launch a new Roman Empire, while among Muslims they gained respect as the new protectors of the shrines in Mecca, Medina, and Jerusalem.

Ottoman architects initially relied on architectural models from the Anatolian region, synthesizing the vaulted masonry of Armenian churches, the beehive domes of Seljuk tombs, and Persian arcades. The Orhan Gazi **Camii** (*camii* is the Turkish word for mosque), built in Bursa in 1339 overlooking the central markets, followed the basic reverse-*T* plan of early Ottoman royal mosques. It served exclusively as a place for the sultan's court. The entry facade had a five-bay porch, made with pointed arches. The masonry resembled Byzantine craft, with alternating bands of brick and limestone similar to Roman *opus mixtum*. One entered the short sides of the arcade through pointed biforium arches (Fig. 11.2-2), closer in style to Christian than to Muslim buildings. An octagonal fountain house for ablutions stood in the garden on-axis with the central bay of the porch. Inside, two central domes covered an axial prayer hall leading to the *mihrab* (the niche oriented toward Mecca), while the minor domes on the sides covered auxiliary rooms.

The reverse-*T* mosque type reappeared in many other royal structures in Bursa (Fig. 11.2-3), including the Yeşil

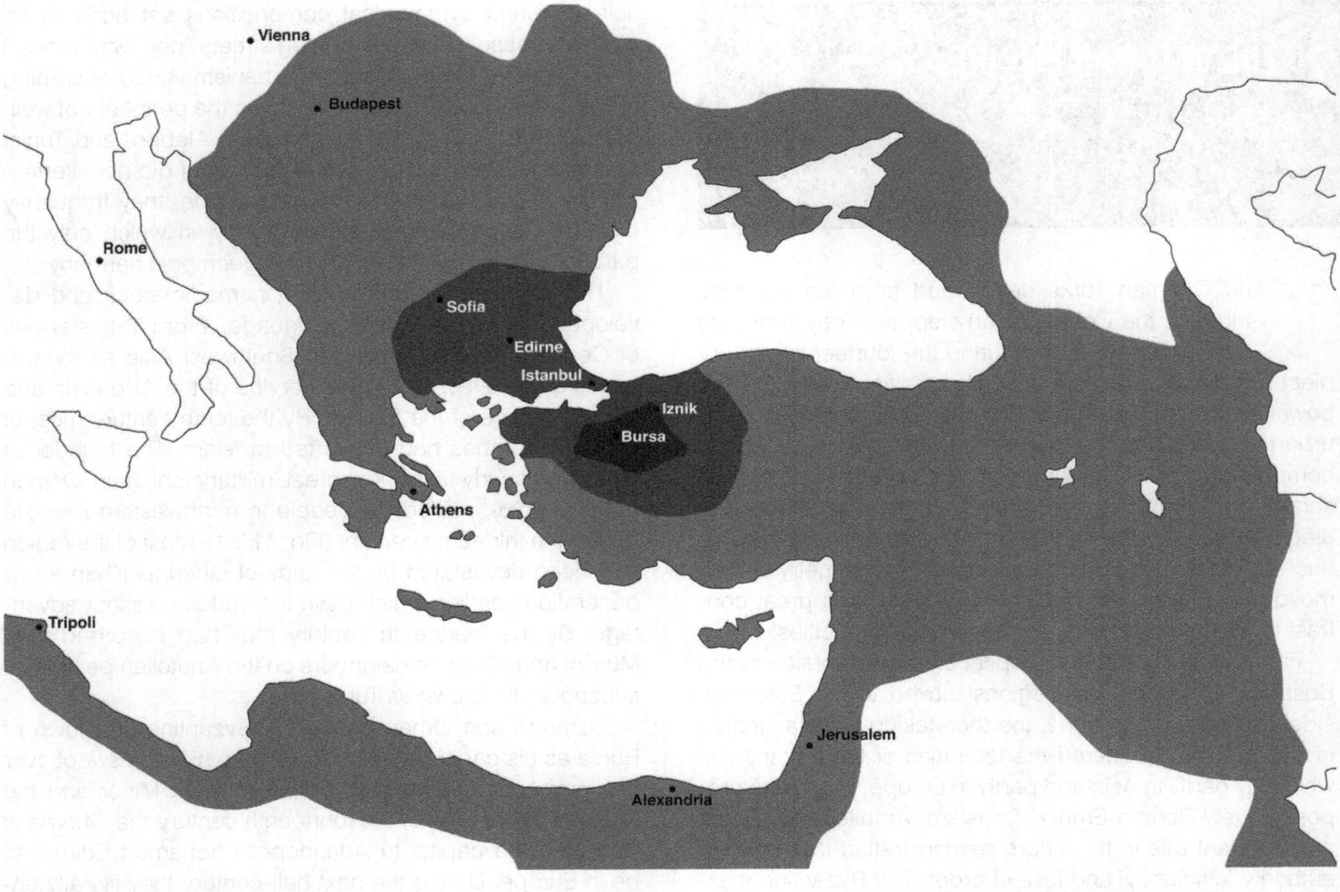

Figure 11.2-1 **The spread of the Ottoman Empire: black, ca. 1300; dark gray, ca. 1500; gray, ca. 1700.**

Camii, or Green Mosque, built in the early fifteenth century for Mehmed I (r. 1413–1421) a half-kilometer east of the fortress. The designers clad this *camii* with beautifully rendered **ashlar blocks** of marble. Unlike the eccentric details of Orhan's mosque, they matched all of the elements proportionally and repeated them serially. The interior of Yeşil Camii at first seemed like a palace with a foyer and stairs leading to the second level, where comfortable rooms remained separated from the prayer hall. The sultan looked down from the loggia to the domed spaces of the prayer hall, set on-axis with the *mihrab*. Such a gesture to royal hierarchy resembled Byzantine protocol. Upper clerestory

windows glazed with green and blue panes brought filtered light into the mosque, while delicate *muqarnas* articulated its niches. The impressive reveals of the side windows extended 2 m (6.5 ft) deep, providing intimately scaled residual chambers for reading the Quran and other sacred texts.

The Yeşil Camii belonged to a unique type of charitable religious compound introduced by the Ottomans during the fourteenth century. These complexes usually included a *camii* (mosque), a **turbe** (tomb of the donor), one or more *madrasas* (religious colleges), a **hammam** (bath), and a public soup kitchen, or *imaret*, which gave its name to the institution (Fig. 11.2-4a,b). Sometimes they also included a hospital or

TIME LINE

▼ 1420

Yeşil Camii completed in Bursa for Mehmed I

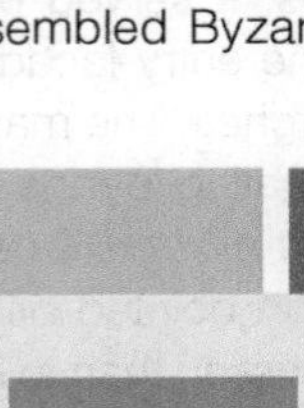

Mehmed II, Fatih the Conqueror, takes Constantinople

▲ **1453**

▼ 1459

Mehmed II begins Topkapi Palace in Istanbul

Mehmed II demolishes Constantine's Apostoleion in Istanbul to build Fatih Camii and imaret

▲ **1463**

Figure 11.2-2 Bursa, Turkey. Orhan Gazi Camii, biforium entry, 1339.

a *tekke* for dervish monks. Over time the term *imaret* became so closely associated with the soup kitchen that scholars in the twentieth century introduced a new term, **külliye**, to signify the overall community functions of the complex. The Ottoman *imaret* served as a site for the expression of Muslim benevolence to appease the populace. Through pious religious conduct and good works of welfare they promoted Islam and Ottoman governance. As the institution evolved, the *imarets* became centers of well-defined neighborhoods, held together through family bonds, shared professions, or places of origin. The earliest examples in Bursa were casually distributed over a sloping terrain. Each Ottoman sultan by tradition created a foundation, or *waqf*, that financed and administered an *imaret* complex in his name, preserving his memory for posterity. Much like Christian monasteries, the *waqf* possessed extensive revenue-producing estates.

The great congregational mosque of Bursa, the Ulu Camii, differed in type from the reverse-*T* royal mosques. It followed the hypostyle model used by the Abbasids in Baghdad, with the unique difference of setting shallow hemispherical domes over each bay. Built under Mehmed I's father, Bayezid I (r. 1389–1402), at the end of the fourteenth century, it stood in the thick of the city overlooking the markets, about 200 m (656 ft) west of the Orhan Gazi Camii.

The square bay with a rounded dome became the standard unit of Ottoman architecture, repeated in palaces, hospitals, schools, baths, mosques, and even the impressive commercial structures of Bursa. The silk market, or Koza Han (Fig. 11.2-5), constructed in 1491, extended as a rectangular court with two levels of arcades surrounding

▼ 1521

Süleyman I conquers Belgrade, taking control of all of the Balkans

Sinan builds the Şehzade Camii in honor of the death of Süleyman I's heir in Istanbul

▲ 1543

▼ 1558

Sinan completes Süleymaniye Camii in Istanbul

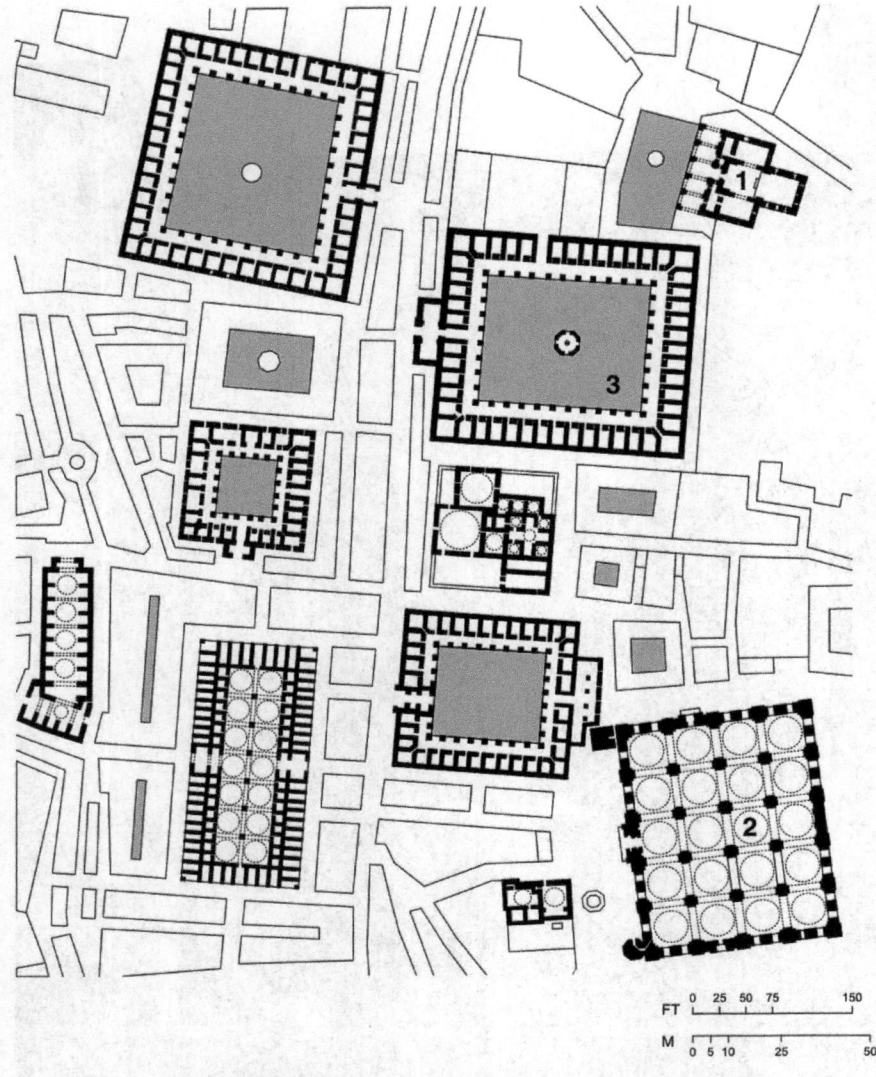

Figure 11.2-3 Bursa, Turkey. The early Ottoman capital: (1) Orhan Gazi Camii, 1339; (2) Ulu Camii, 1400; (3) the Koza Han, or Silk Market. The other rectangular buildings with courts are *hans*, or markets.

a domed treasury. The upper level had cupolas over each bay. The symmetrically organized public buildings of the early Ottoman capital conveyed the idea of a new, efficient political order.

Constantinople Becomes Istanbul

The Ottoman goal of creating a legitimate Islamic Roman Empire required the capture of Constantinople. During the millennium since its foundation, Constantine's city, despite periodic faltering, had remained an unmatched source of authority as the Greek-speaking heir to the Roman Empire. Byzantine art, architecture, and ritual life influenced places as diverse as Damascus, Kiev, Venice, and Córdoba. By the fourteenth century, however, it had dwindled to a small city-state with perhaps as few as 50,000 residents. Hemmed in by the Ottomans, Constantinople succumbed in 1453 after a fifty-two-day siege to Mehmed II (r. 1451–1481), known as *Fatih*, the Conqueror.

While Ottoman officials continued to call the metropolis the "city of Constantine," a new name, "Istanbul," derived from the Greek phrase "to the city," took hold in the vernacular. Fatih declared a general amnesty for non-Muslim ethnic groups to quickly repopulate his capital, allowing Greek, Armenian, Jewish, and Italian traders to return and form communities, or *millets*, governed by their own laws. To stimulate merchant activity, he founded the markets of Kapali Çarşi, which, like the Koza Han in Bursa, had square bays capped with rounded, lead-covered domes. The *bedestan*, a fortified compound for luxury goods, rose slightly taller than its predecessor in the midst of 3,000 shops. Istanbul's population doubled in two decades and by the end of the sixteenth century had returned to over a half-million, making it once again the largest city in Europe.

The young sultan absorbed the cultural and technical innovations of Italy and apparently commissioned a portrait from the Venetian painter Gentile Bellini. His fortifications both before and after the siege of the capital showed the influence of Italian engineering. The round towers of Rumeli Hissar (Fig. 11.2-6),

▼ **1571**

Coalition of Spain, Venice, and papal Rome defeats Ottoman navy at Battle of Lepanto

Nurbanu (Venetian Cecilia Venier-Baffo) indirectly rules Ottoman Empire as queen mother for a decade

▲ **1574**

▼ **1609**

End of the long war between Hapsburg Austria and Ottomans

Sultan Ahmed Camii (Blue Mosque) begun in Istanbul

▲ **1609**

a

F 0 10   25   50   75
M 0   5   10   25

Figure 11.2-4 Bursa,
Turkey. (a) Plan of Yeşil
Camii complex: (1) Yeşil
Camii; (2) Yeşil Turbe, tomb
of Mehmed I (3) madrasa;
(4) *hammam*, or thermal
bath; (5) *imaret*, or soup
kitchen. (b) Yeşil Turbe.

b

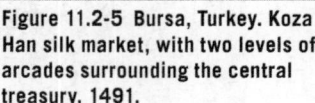

Figure 11.2-5 Bursa, Turkey. Koza Han silk market, with two levels of arcades surrounding the central treasury, 1491.

Figure 11.2-6 Istanbul. Mehmed II's fortress of Rumeli Hissar, built according to Italian architectural criteria, ca. 1450.

The young sultan considered the majestic Hagia Sophia to be his great prize and quickly converted the venerable Palatine church into a royal mosque, adding a minaret (to which three others were added during the next century). He inserted into its eastern apse a *mihrab*, slightly askew from the main axis, to point correctly to Mecca. Inspired by the great Byzantine church, Mehmed II commissioned Atik Sinan (not to be confused with Mimar Sinan) to build a new mosque with an extensive *imaret* complex, the Fatih Camii, in 1463 (Fig. 11.2-7a,b). That the new mosque and tombs displaced the ruins of the Apostoleion, Constantine's Church of the Holy Apostles and imperial tomb site, carried great political significance. In his eagerness to acquire the imperial power of Constantine, the young sultan used the title *kayser-i Rûm*, or "caesar of Rome," and beginning with his reign, Istanbul experienced a conscious revival, an Ottoman renaissance parallel to that occurring to the west. Fatih's new mosque rose over the city with a grand hemispherical dome only a few meters less in diameter than that of Hagia Sophia. Beneath its fenestrated drum a semidome stepped down to the east, while the northern and southern aisles were capped with

the fortress he constructed on the Bosporus to intercept Christian naval support to the Byzantines, and the star-shaped fort of Yedikule, built at the Golden Gate after the conquest of Constantinople, responded to the development of weapons fired by gunpowder. Fatih's secret weapon, the cannon known as "Orban," took the name of the Hungarian engineer who designed it. The new forts had thicker walls with polygonal bastions capable of supporting cannons.

three smaller rounded domes. Two slender minarets stood at the front corners of the mosque. It incorporated a rectangular forecourt, covering approximately the same area as the interior. Small cupolas topped each bay of the court's arcades, and ancient granite columns supported pointed arches. The voussoirs alternated red and white masonry, repeating the familiar pattern of *ablaq* (see Section 7.1). In the cemetery garden behind the mosque, Fatih prepared his octagonal *turbe* and that of Gulbahar, the mother of his heir.

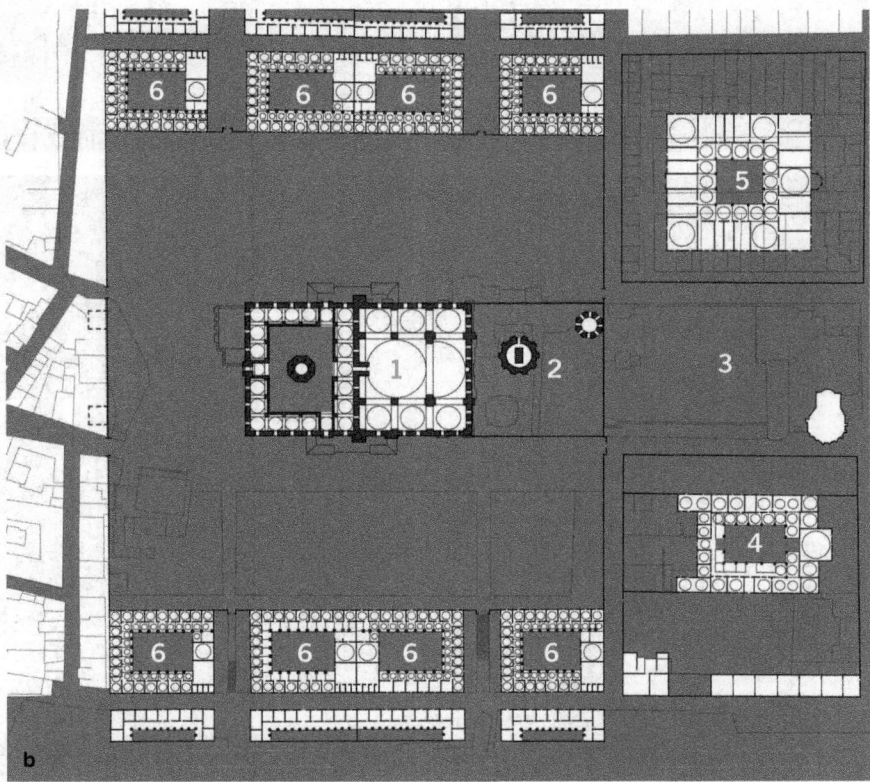

Figure 11.2-7 Istanbul. (a) Melchior Lorich's view of Fatih Camii, produced prior to the mosque's reconstruction, in 1559. (b) Plan of Fatih's *imaret*. (1) Fatih Camii; (2) cemetery with *turbes* of Fatih and his wife; (3) garden (later an extension of cemetery); (4) hospice and kitchens; (5) hospital; (6) *madrasas*.

The Fatih Camii occupied the center of a vast, perfectly square plaza. Its scale, roughly 200 m (656 ft) per side, approximated that of the great courts of the Forbidden City in Beijing. The barrel vaults of earlier Byzantine cisterns served as the foundation for the terraced complex. On the north and south sides stood sets of eight *madrasas*, in perfect bilateral symmetry, serving as spaces for the study of canonical law, or *sharia*. Beyond the walls of the precinct to the east lay two smaller walled areas for hospitals (staffed with Jewish doctors and divided into Muslim and non-Muslim sectors), thermal baths, stables, kitchens, and hospices. Fatih intended the *imaret* as a gift to the people to demonstrate the benefits of the Ottoman peace. He invited his subjects for a three-night stay, using the plaza as a campsite. The kitchens prepared meals for over 1,000 people per day.

In 1459, Mehmed II decided to move from his palace in the center of the city to a new one at the extreme tip of the peninsula, where the acropolis of the ancient Greek city of Byzantium once stood. The resulting Topkapi Saray complex offered a more secluded residence, with fortified walls surrounding a hilly, wooded park. The sultan's private realm appeared the antithesis of European palaces: willfully asymmetrical, spreading out more like a garden than a building. The scattering of its parts, its strong connection to natural features, and its framed views of Bosporus landscapes made Topkapi closer to a Chinese scholar's garden than to the geometrically coordinated Italian palazzo.

Topkapi was organized on a succession of three courts that were added to and elaborated throughout the sixteenth and seventeenth centuries, a process of development that partly explains its piecemeal character. The Imperial Gate, like an Ottoman triumphal arch, stood a few steps from the apse of Hagia Sophia. From here one took an oblique path that passed amid randomly placed trees past the church of Hagia Irene, which was transformed later into an armory, and various freestanding pavilions to the Middle Gate, which resembled a Byzantine triumphal entry, flanked by delicate octagonal towers with pencil-point turrets. Beyond this point only the sultan was permitted to remain on horseback, and only those with official business were granted entry. The imperial hierarchy gathered for formal ceremonies in this Court of Processions, a roughly trapezoidal expanse planted with tall plane trees. Fatih's architect, Murad Halife, wrapped the edges of the court with an arcade of pointed arches, using ancient columns capped with freshly sculpted *muqarnas*-style capitals.

The most important political space in Topkapi, the **Diwan**, or Council Hall, jutted into the northwest corner of the courtyard (Fig. 11.2-8a,b). It comprised a succession of three domed halls, skirted by an unassuming *L*-shaped **portico**. Rebuilt in the mid-sixteenth century, the Diwan served as a space for official meetings and the daily administrative assembly of the viziers, the chief administrators of the realm.

Behind the Diwan lay the *harem*, an intricate collection of small courts and densely packed chambers on

Figure 11.2-8 Istanbul. (a) Model of Topkapi. (b) Portico surrounding the Diwan at the northwest edge of the court, 1480–1560.

The Harem of Topkapi and the Reign of Women

Fatih's harem was radically restructured in the sixteenth century during the long reign of Süleyman I. Süleyman I's favorite concubine, the Ukrainian-born Roxelana, or Hürrem (1500–1558), insisted that the sultan marry her and allow her to live in the harem with her children. He commissioned an apartment for her needs. This initiated a period that some court historians dubbed the "reign of women." A second influential concubine, Nurbanu (1525–1587), a Venetian named Cecilia Venier-Baffo, was the first to be recognized as *valide sultan*, or "queen mother." In the 1580s she was awarded a large apartment with a courtyard inside the harem. Nurbanu convinced her son Murad III (r. 1574–1595) to add to the northern corner of the harem his *L*-shaped apartment with three double-height rooms whose domes glimmered with golden mosaics. The sultan's favorite concubines were awarded small apartments, while the lesser ones lived in a dormitory, sleeping ten to a couch, surveilled by Ethiopian eunuchs in crowded, prison-like conditions. The Tower of Justice, where the Diwan intersected with the harem, was begun under Fatih as a treasury and added onto during the 1520s. The current upper story, with Italian mannerist details, was added in the nineteenth century.

Istanbul. (a) Topkapi harem court. (b) New quarter for the sultan built in the harem for Murad III, ca. 1580.

three levels that served as the residence for the sultan's concubines. The convent-like atmosphere of the harem hints at Fatih's ulterior intention for building Topkapi. In this controlled environment, away from the center of the city, he could guide both female and male slaves in a grand social experiment: the creation of an ideal Ottoman society of obedient, well-instructed, foreign-born slaves. The army abducted young women and boys from their families before puberty, educated them in the Turkish language, and converted them to Islam. As they matured they remained beholden to the paternal authority of the sultan.

During the sixteenth century the harem housed as many as 150 women, guarded by both white and black eunuchs. If impregnated, the concubine moved back to the Old Palace, where at least another 1,500 women were being groomed for service. If she gave birth to a son who was acknowledged by the sultan, the court sent the concubine and child to a province, where the child was educated as a prince and military leader, to eventually compete with his half-brothers for power.

Enslaved boys trained as pages lived in the last court of Topkapi, entered through the tent-like Gate of Felicity

Figure 11.2-9 Istanbul. Topkapi, Gate of Felicity, the entry to the final court of the sultan's private residence and the Enderun College for pages, 1480s.

outset, of the conflicts of interest typical of hereditary aristocracies.

Sinan and the Challenge of Hagia Sophia

Sinan (1490–1588), the greatest architect of the Ottoman renaissance, came from this mass of young slaves and rose to prominence during the reign of Süleyman I (r. 1520–1566). Under the *devshirme* system, he was inducted into the honor guard to assume a role of authority. This practice derived from a long tradition of slave militias in Islamic governments, by whom the Turks themselves had often been captured. Beginning in 1512, every five years the imperial army seized new boys from among the non-Islamic communities of the empire to be converted and trained for the elite military corps, which in its prime had 15,000 members. The best among them were sent to the Enderun school at Topkapi. The cadets wore white caps, and their name in English, "Janissaries," derived from the word *Yeniceri*, or "new troops."

The Ottoman military played an overarching role in the administration of the empire and included the state architects of the Hassa Mimarlar Ocagi (Imperial Body of Architects). Sinan, sometimes referred to as Hoca Sinan (the Younger), or Mimar Sinan (the architect), emerged as the most prolific and accomplished architect of the age, responsible for over 300 projects throughout the realm, including mosques in Aleppo and Damascus and magnificent infrastructure works, such as the Mağlova aqueduct. He commanded a team of sixty to seventy assistants and developed a design method in which no two works were identical, yet all belonged to the same family through rational geometry and repeated architectural elements. In Istanbul alone he authored twenty-two major mosques and *imarets*, transforming the city's fabric into a glittering patchwork that juxtaposed impressive monumental enclosures studded with billowing cupolas and marble-clad minarets alongside neighborhoods of narrow streets and densely packed wooden houses. Sinan came from a Greek family living in the Anatolian hinterlands. He gained the title of Architect of the Abode of Felicity at the relatively late age of forty-seven. During long years of military campaigns, including invasions of Iraq, the Balkans, and southern Italy, he witnessed a variety of design solutions and gained thorough command of engineering through the production of bridges and transport ships. He accumulated wide knowledge of structure, composition, and decoration while serving as an

(Fig. 11.2-9). The portal's broad awnings and umbrella dome recalled the tensile structures found on the battlefield. Fatih used the gate for official appearances to the court. The Court of the Male Pages functioned as the *Enderun*, the Ottoman school of government. While the courtyard followed perfect orthogonal alignments, each of its elevations carried a different style of arcade and roof type, including an arcade with rounded arches and northern Italian capitals. A mosque jutted obliquely into the court from the western range, aimed toward Mecca.

The Privy Chamber, the sultan's private apartment, protruded into the northwestern corner of the Court of the Male Pages. Its six interconnected rooms and open verandahs looked away from the court toward fountains that cascaded down the north slope. In these relatively tiny structures, the low horizontal bands of windows that did away with the solidity of the wall became an extension of the ground plane. The couches responded to this horizontal conception of interior space, connecting the view to the gardens.

Most of the surrounding halls in the Court of the Male Pages served as dormitories and school buildings for as many as 500 slave boys, who underwent a fourteen-year training period at the Enderun, the institution that produced the Ottoman equivalent of the Mandarin civil servant. Like the concubines, the pages received an excellent education. The court eunuchs monitored their comportment. The rules required absolute silence outside of class time, forcing the boys to resort to sign language to communicate. The uncanny silence of Topkapi, imposed even during state dinners, created an extra level of social distance. The boys of merit became the empire's elite class of viziers, who administered the empire, and often women of the harem or daughters of the sultan were allotted to them as wives. Fatih's system of training obedient slaves as his "family" produced a ruling class that appeared free, at least at the assistant to his predecessor, Acem Alisi, designer of most of Süleyman I's additions to Topkapi.

Sinan's earliest commissions in Istanbul came from two female clients in the 1530s: the powerful Hürrem, wife of Süleyman I and mother of Selim II, and her daughter Mihrümah, who was much favored by Süleyman and married to the grand vizier Rüstem Pasha. The *imaret* in honor of Hürrem, the Haseki Hürrem complex, was constructed on a site in the western part of the city where the road branched off from the Mese toward the Golden Gate. Sinan covered the mosque with a single hemispherical dome and designed the hospital, an institution specifically for women, with an unusual octagonal court. The two *imarets* built in honor of Mihrümah (the earliest across the Bosporus in Üsküdar, built in 1546, and the second at the northwest Edirne Gate of the Theodosian walls) also occupied remote sites in the city but were very prominent within their landscapes. The latter, the Mihrümah Camii, built in the 1560s, carried one of Sinan's most intrepid domes, a hemispherical cupola stretching 20 m (65 ft) in diameter and rising 37 m (121 ft) from a square plan on massive octagonal piers

without flying buttresses. Working from a similar mindset to that of the Gothic master builders, Sinan attempted to eliminate the weight of bearing walls, allowing great expanses of fenestration under the four grand supporting arches, which were subtly pointed for greater strength, nearly parabaloid in shape. The dazzling luminosity of the interior, especially the *qibla* wall with six levels of stain glass windows, rivals Ste.-Chapelle (see Section 9.2).

Sinan's first work for Süleyman I, the Şehzade Camii (the Prince's Mosque, 1543–1548), offered his earliest challenge to surpass Hagia Sophia (Fig. 11.2-10a–d).

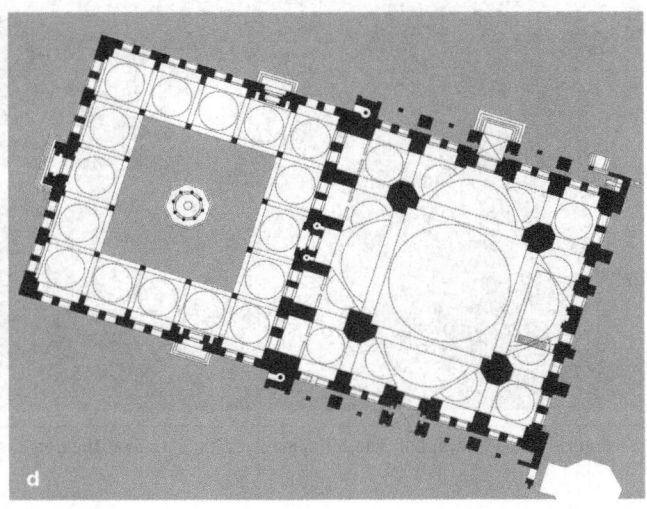

Figure 11.2-10 Istanbul. Şehzade Camii, 1540s. (a) Exterior. (b) Interior courtyard, or *sahn*. (c) Dome. (d) Plan.

The sultan dedicated the mosque and its *waqf* to his designated heir, Mehmed, the first-born of his union with Hürrem, who had just died mysteriously at age twenty-one. The pyramidal massing of the central dome, supported by eight flying buttresses, cascaded to four semidomes, flanked by four buttress towers and terminating in four smaller domes at the corners. It looked onto a perfectly square forecourt for the fountain house, isometric in area to the mosque. From this early masterpiece Sinan would expand on a structural and decorative language for the construction of dozens of other mosques.

At the height of his power, Süleyman I commissioned his own royal mosque, the Süleymaniye (Fig. 11.2-11). Here Sinan explicitly emulated the composition of Hagia Sophia, setting a central dome flanked on the east and west sides by semidomes. Similar to his design of Şehzade Camii, he supported the dome with flying buttresses and strengthened the perimeter with four octagonal buttress towers at the corners of the dome. Like Gothic pinnacles, these towers served as counterweights over the four piers that carried the major loads of the dome. The two sets of minarets, the taller inner ones with three balconies, the outer ones with two, harmonized with the pyramidal massing of the dome. On the two sides without semidomes the walls of the arched elevations were punctured by three rows of windows, similar

to those of the Mihrümah Camii. Unlike Hagia Sophia the lateral wings of the Süleymaniye were united with the central nave to create a single grand space animated by the play of light coming from multiple fenestrations and shimmering tiles.

The Süleymaniye's *imaret* occupied the true center of Istanbul, looming over the port district of the Golden Horn. While it covered slightly less area than Fatih's complex, it had a similar layout, with the mosque dominating a vast terraced space, 150 × 200 m (492 × 656 ft). Seven *madrasas* held the edges, each with a square courtyard. The complex became the prime center of learning in the Ottoman Empire, leading to Süleyman's moniker of *Kanuni*, the "Lawgiver." A variety of entries from different levels brought one into the orderly precinct surrounding the mosque. The collection of hospices, kitchens, baths, and a hospital found there, each separated by a side street or stair, contributed to the complex's overall sense of porosity. Süleyman guaranteed the same welfare services enjoyed at Fatih's *imaret*, offering camping privileges and serving 1,000 meals each day. Behind the dome of the mosque Sinan installed the founder's *turbe* and that of Hürrem. Süleyman's tomb, an octagonal domed structure with a colonnaded verandah, became one of the city's major cult sites, served by gardeners, incense keepers, janitors, and 134 Quran readers. Just

Figure 11.2-11 Istanbul. The Süleymaniye, looming over the port district of the Golden Horn, Sinan, 1550s.

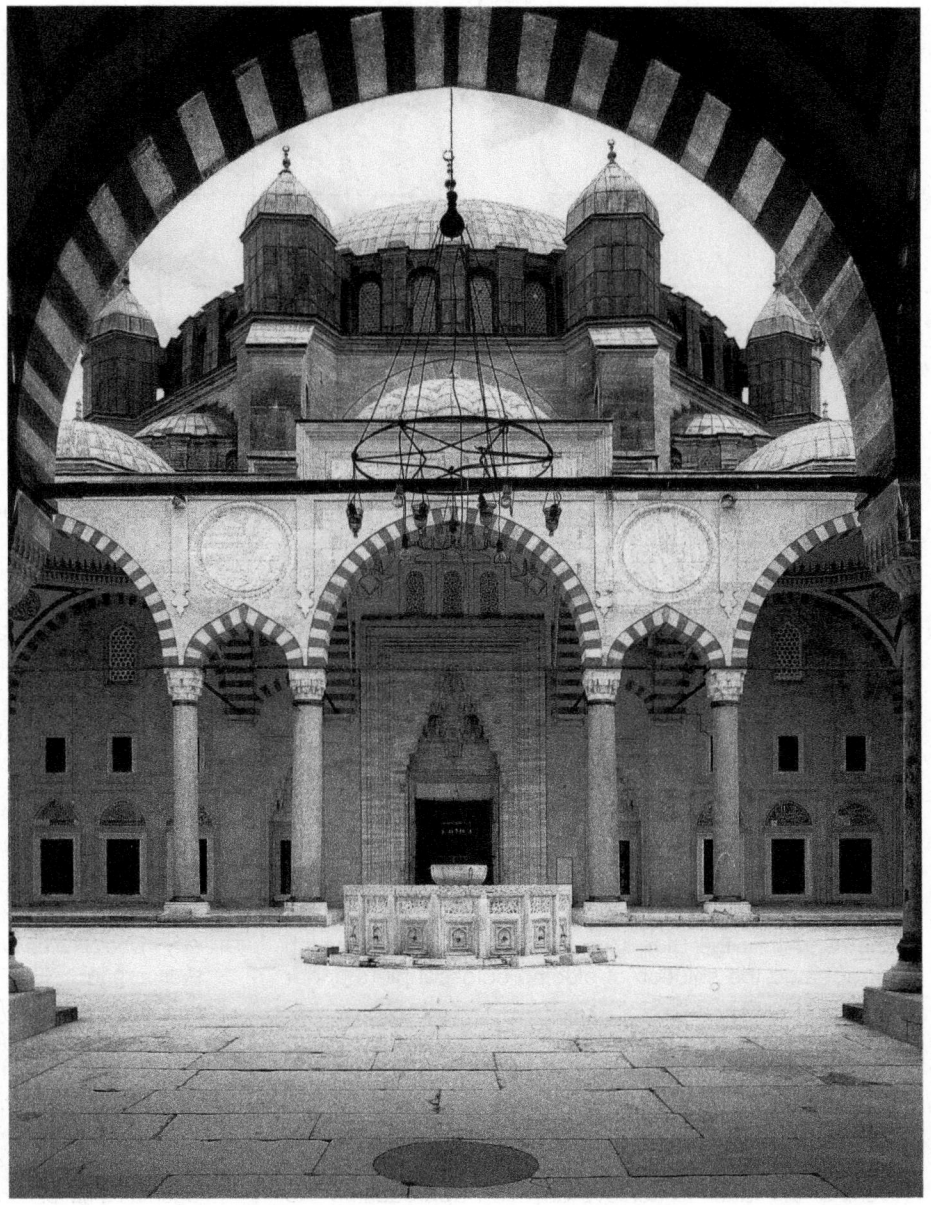

Figure 11.2-12 Edirne, Turkey. The Selimiye complex, alternating small and large arches, Sinan, 1570s.

outside the northwestern corner of the Süleymaniye precinct, Sinan prepared a triangular site for his own residence and tomb. The latter structure included a fountain house at the corner and a stele topped with a turban marking his grave, attesting to his extraordinary status.

If the economy of the Ottomans remained healthy throughout the sixteenth century, the credit went mostly to the well-trained viziers, graduates of the Enderun palace school, who also excelled as patrons for major works of architecture. Süleyman's favorite, Rüstem Pasha, became an imperial son-in-law. As grand vizier he commissioned Sinan to create the Rüstem Pasha Camii, begun in 1561, the year of his death, and completed by his widow, Mihrümah. Set on a steep, crowded site overlooking the Golden Horn port, with little room for a courtyard, the mosque was raised

one story above grade, giving it an arcaded terrace two bays deep in lieu of a court. Sokollu Pasha, who succeeded Rüstem Pasha as grand vizier, likewise married a daughter of a sultan and through his wife's influence commissioned Sinan to design an even more impressive *imaret* on a steep hillside overlooking the Marmara Sea. The mosque's central dome rose on a fenestrated drum set over a hexagon. Two small semidomes to either side pushed obliquely to the edges. The building's blue tiles from Iznik, tinted windows, and uninterrupted interior contributed to a dynamic yet coherent whole.

Sinan built his largest mosque, the Selimiye (Fig. 11.2-12), in Edirne during the 1570s for Süleyman's successor, Selim II (r. 1566–1574). The dome spread slightly larger than that of Hagia Sophia, and the minarets were among

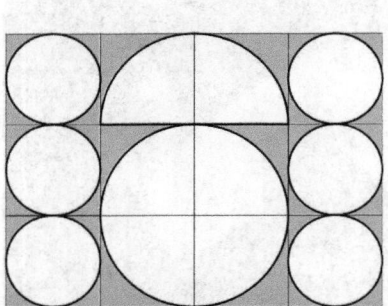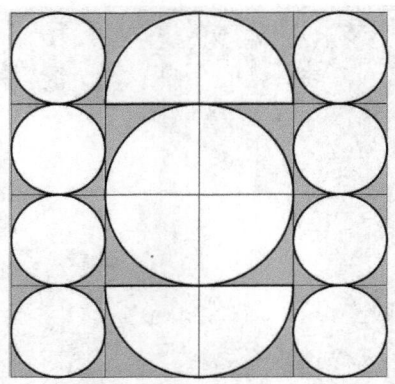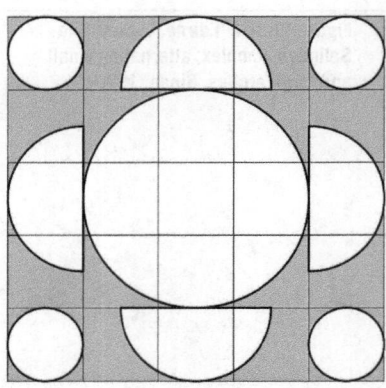

Figure 11.2-13 Ottoman method of subdividing space around a central dome. After the taking of Constantinople by Fatih in 1453, Ottoman architects practiced variations on the great vaulted structure of Hagia Sofia, extending semidomes from a central dome. Left: Mehmed II's Camii, a central dome with one semidome and flanks lined with small domes, 1460s. Center: Bayezid II Camii, a central dome with two semidomes (similar to Hagia Sophia) and flanks lined with small domes, ca. 1520. Right: Sinan's Şehzade Camii, a central dome with semidomes on all four sides and smaller domes at the corners, ca. 1535.

the tallest of all Islam. Sinan designed the *mihrab* as a semienclosed chamber covered with a semidome, reminiscent of the mosques of al-Andalus (see Section 8.2). The eight piers rose as single, colossal columns at the corners of the octagonal drum supporting the dome. Sinan articulated the facade in the courtyard with an alternating rhythm of wider and narrower bays, intimating a kind of Ottoman mannerism. The rhythmic alternation of bay widths was continued by Sinan's successor, Mehmed Agha (ca. 1540–1617), one of the architects of Sultan Ahmet Camii, or the Blue Mosque, begun in 1609, which also repeated the solution of placing colossal piers under the dome (Fig. 11.2-13).

In one of his three autobiographies Sinan made no secret of his obsession with Hagia Sophia:

Architects in Christian countries may rank themselves above Muslims in technical skills, owing to the failure of the latter to achieve anything approaching the dome of Hagia Sophia. This assertion of insurmountable difficulty has wounded the author of these writings. However, with God's help and the Sultan's mercy, I have succeeded in building a dome for Sultan Selim's

mosque which is four ells greater in diameter and six ells higher than that of Hagia Sophia.

By perfecting the Ottoman architectural method, Sinan assisted a new empire in acquiring the order and grandeur of those of the past.

Further Reading

Celik, Zeynep. *The Remaking of Istanbul: Portrait of an Ottoman City in the Nineteenth Century.* Seattle: University of Washington Press, 1986.

Freely, John. *Istanbul: The Imperial City.* New York: Viking, 1996.

Goodwin, Godfrey. *A History of Ottoman Architecture.* London: Thames & Hudson, 1971.

Gunay, Reha. *Sinan: The Architect and His Works.* Istanbul: Yapi Endustri Merkezi, 1998.

Necipoğlu, Gülru. *The Age of Sinan: Architectural Culture in the Ottoman Empire.* London: Reaktion Books, 2005.

——. *Architecture, Ceremonial, and Power: The Topkapi Palace in the Fifteenth and Sixteenth Centuries.* Cambridge, MA: MIT Press, 1991.

Rogers, J. M. *Sinan.* London: I. B. Tauris, 2006.

11.3 PAPAL ROME
The Fountainhead of Renaissance Classicism

The architecture of ancient Rome suggested to Italian architects of the sixteenth century a system of symmetry, harmonious proportions, and decorative columns, which they either copied or struggled to improve. In Rome the popes sponsored a talented group of artists and architects, including Donato Bramante, Raphael, Antonio da Sangallo the Younger, and Michelangelo, who played with the language of classicism in designing statements of the Catholic Church's power. Their projects for churches, streets, palaces, and **villas** promoted the city's pilgrim trade with the collateral effect of improving the dynastic situations of papal families.

The rise of the Protestant movement of Martin Luther and other religious reformers contributed to a temporary lull in the brilliant cultural advances that the papacy had made during the first two decades of the sixteenth century. In 1527 the Sack of Rome by renegade soldiers, one-third of them Protestants, brought the city to its knees. This catastrophic event had two major consequences for architecture. First, in reaction to the mobile cannon, it encouraged the formulation of new theories of fortification and urban design. Second, many of the designers of papal Rome emigrated to other cities, taking with them the Roman language of classical architecture. The illustrated treatises of Sebastiano Serlio and Andrea Palladio, published in northern Italy, popularized the new design method and style of papal Rome, profoundly influencing the taste for classical architecture in other European countries and eventually the Americas.

The Papal Restoration: The Destruction and Redesign of St. Peter's

Over the centuries the ancient city of Rome had dissolved into a shadow of its old self. Despite the efforts of popes and religious institutions to bolster the city's livelihood through church building, the effects of invasions and floods combined with the disinvestment by the landowning classes contributed to its drastic shrinkage. Contentious feudal interests kept the streets periodically convulsed with anarchy. The Roman Forum reverted to a grass-covered cattle market known as Campo Vaccino. The popes abandoned Rome during most of the fourteenth century to reside in Avignon, France. Their return to Rome during the first half of the fifteenth century opened the way for the Papal Restoration, which was devoted to rebuilding both the urban fabric and the primacy of the Catholic Church. The Renaissance, or rebirth, of classical culture that originated with the merchants

of Tuscany migrated to Rome to assist in the rebirth of the city as a magnificent capital.

The ideologues of the Papal Restoration introduced highly theatrical papal ceremonials, luxurious costumes, and triumphal architectural settings to boost the image of the pope as a charismatic ruler. Pope Nicholas V (r. 1447–1455) underlined the key role of architecture in this enterprise when he proposed the sponsorship of "great buildings, seemingly made by God." He initiated the grandest project of the age, the demolition and rebuilding of Old St. Peter's in 1452. Rather than restore the millennial basilica, he proposed to start over and create a new image for the institution. In 1450 he ordered the Florentine architect Bernardo Rossellino (see Section 10.1) to demolish and rebuild the apse. Half a century later, his successors returned in earnest to demolish the entire church, including Nicholas V's apse, to make way for a great domed structure.

During the late fifteenth century papal authority combined their spiritual mandate for the leadership of Christendom with the temporal power to rule one of the largest realms in Italy. The Papal States stretched from the borders of Milan to those of Naples. Pope Alexander VI (Rodrigo Borgia, r. 1492–1503) and his ambitious son, Cesare Borgia (ca. 1475–1507), attempted to politically unify the peninsula under a single ruler. Cesare's military pragmatism paralleled his father's bold approach to urbanism in Rome, where he sponsored Via Alessandrina, the first straight street of the Papal Restoration. In 1499 papal planners plowed a straight, 800 m (2,625 ft) long avenue through the Vatican Borgo district between Castel Sant'Angelo and St. Peter's, requiring significant demolitions, including the removal of an ancient pyramid. While the new street officially served as a route for pilgrims for the jubilee year of 1500, it doubled in the same year as the triumphal route for Cesare's return from his victories in Romagna. The military advantage of the road for troop movement became apparent to all.

Via Alessandrina served as the site for a few of the most advanced classical palaces in Rome (Fig. 11.3-1). At the street's midpoint one of Alexander VI's closest friends, Adriano Castellesi, in 1501 began work on a new palace, a project that coincided with Alexander's appointment as a cardinal. Palazzo Castellesi (today Giraud-Torlonia), completed in 1521, differed from earlier cardinals' palaces built in Rome, which were fortified with towers and crenellations (as at Palazzo Venezia, built by Francesco del Borgo in 1455–1468). The new cardinal's block-like palace, as tall as the street was wide, offered the model of urban scale and elegance for the rest of the new street, and embodied a Florentine ideal of civic beauty. Smooth ashlar rustication at the base and paired Corinthian pilasters on the upper two stories articulated the seven bays of its travertine facade. A projecting cornice of delicately carved brackets capped the whole. The pilasters, round-headed windows, and cornices, although combined differently, imitated details found on the Colosseum.

The facade of Palazzo Castellesi greatly resembled the Cancelleria, begun a decade earlier but not finished

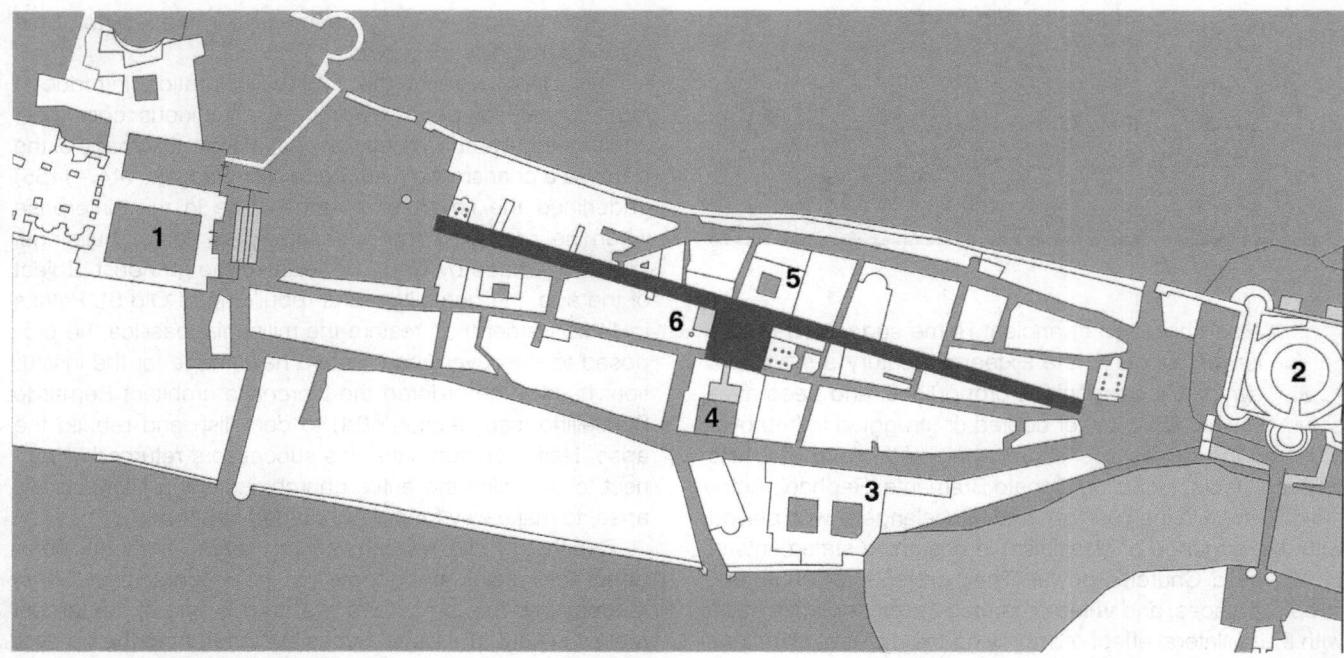

Figure 11.3-1 Rome. Via Alessandrina, papal Rome's first straight street and site of several classical palaces in Rome, 1500: (1) St. Peter's; (2) Castel Sant'Angelo; (3) hospital of Santo Spirito; (4) the Penitenzieria; (5) Palazzo Adriano Castellesi; (6) Palazzo Caprini.

until 1513. Its patron, Cardinal Raffaele Riario, was the administrator in charge of the construction of Via Alessandrina, and his structure no doubt influenced Castellesi, who used nearly identical decorations. The broad, travertine facade of the Cancelleria (Fig. 11.3-2a) spread more than twice the width of Castellesi's palace, concealing a church that occupied nearly half of its volume. The secular prospect of the palace virtually swallowed the church. In the Cancelleria's courtyard (Fig. 11.3-2b) two levels of arcades rose on ancient granite columns taken from a nearby ruined theater. To solve the corner problem, when two planes in an arcaded courtyard converged on a single column, the designers used intersecting piers, similar to those used in the ducal palace of Urbino, which gave an extra sense of support (see Section 10.1).

When Riario's cousin Giuliano della Rovere became Pope Julius II (r. 1503–1513), he attached the new papal coat of arms to the left edge of the Cancelleria's facade. Julius, the only pope to personally lead troops into battle, proved himself to be as aggressive a patron as the tyrant

princes of northern Italy or the sultans in Istanbul. For his imperially scaled projects he relied on the architect Donato Bramante (1444–1514), newly arrived in Rome in 1499 after having worked for Ludovico Sforza, the tyrant of Milan. In Milan Bramante designed the tribune and dome of Santa Maria delle Grazie and the oblong piazza of Vigevano, one of the largest and most orderly public spaces in Italy, which he surrounded with regular arcades.

Bramante's first documented commissions in Rome coincided with the opening of Via Alessandrina. In 1501 he designed Palazzo Caprini (Fig. 11.3-3), which sat perpendicular to Palazzo Castellesi. The two-story palace carried heavy rustication at the base of its five-bay facade, allowing for the placement of two small shops to either side of the central portal. Bramante articulated the **piano nobile** with the unprecedented use of paired Doric half-columns and a correct Doric frieze containing triglyphs and metopes worthy of the ancients. He set the windows in temple-like **aedicules**, each with a **balustrade** at the base and a triangular **pediment** on top. In contrast to the planar quality

▼ **1420**
Papal court returns to Rome after seventy years in France

Constantinople captured by the Ottomans and becomes Istanbul, the Ottoman capital
▲ **1453**

▼ **1492**
Spanish ships led by Christopher Columbus cross the Atlantic to the Caribbean island of Hispaniola

Pope Alexander VI's son Cesare Borgia begins his conquest of Romagna
▲ **1499**

▼ **1500**
Via Alessandrina, the first straight street of papal Rome, constructed

Figure 11.3-2 Rome. (a) Cancelleria, containing the Church of San Lorenzo in Damaso, 1489–1516. (b) See next page.

of Palazzo Castellesi, Bramante's facade showed palpable depth, its columns and balustrades generating beautiful contrasts of light and shade.

In 1502, the Spanish monarchs Ferdinand and Isabella commissioned Bramante to build a small domed shrine in the cloister of the hillside church of San Pietro in Montorio. This Tempietto (Fig. 11.3-4) resembled an ancient round *tholos*-type temple. Its central plan suited its purpose as

a martyrium, commemorating the alleged site of St. Peter's crucifixion. The sixteen granite columns of the porch carried a Doric entablature, with sculpted metopes depicting the symbolic attributes of St. Peter. Bramante diverged from the ancients by placing a balustrade above the entablature and adding a very tall drum to support the hemispherical cupola. These ideas had a lasting impact on church design. The plan of the Tempietto, with niches scooped from the

Bramante's Tempietto in Rome commissioned by king and queen of Spain

▲ 1501

▼ 1506

Julius II begins demolition of Old St. Peter's for Bramante's New St. Peter's in Rome

Bramante begins Belvedere Court in Rome

▲ 1508

▼ 1517

Martin Luther publishes *95 Theses* against papal Rome, fomenting the Protestant Reformation

Sack of Rome by renegade troops of Charles V

▲ 1527

Figure 11.3-2 The Cancelleria. (b) Court.

exterior alternating with niches on the interior, revealed a new taste for **plasticity**. Although the building appears monumental in photographs, its cell stretches only 4.5 m (15 ft) across, large enough for a handful of people to gather comfortably. Bramante intended the domed memorial to be enclosed by a concentric colonnade of proportionally larger columns, which would have established an organic relationship between container and contained.

In 1506 Bramante took charge of the most important project of the century, the demolition and rebuilding of the Constantinian basilica of St. Peter's. Both architect and patron intended New St. Peter's to represent the Papal

Restoration. The pope also decided that a wing of the church should be large enough to accommodate his grand tomb. The displacement of old by new paralleled Mehmed II's decision to replace Constantine's Apostoleion with the Fatih Camii. Drawing inspiration from the great works of antiquity, Bramante hoped to pitch a hemispherical dome like that of the Pantheon on top of the grand coffered vaults seen in the Basilica of Maxentius. Like the Tempietto, New St. Peter's was to follow a concentrically ordered central plan. The central dome would sit on a drum girded by a ring of columns, and four smaller domes would step down to the outer corners, which in plan resembled the fractal order of

▼ **1534**

Newly installed Medici dynasty commissions Fortezza da Basso to control Florence

Jacopo Sansovino begins La Zecca (the Mint) and Library of San Marco in Venice

▲ **1536–1537**

▼ **1536–1546**

Michelangelo develops plan for Campidoglio in Rome

Michelangelo presents his design of the dome of St. Peter's

▲ **1560**

▼ **1563**

Conclusion of the Council of Trent and onset of the Counter-Reformation

Figure 11.3-3 Rome. Palazzo Caprini on Via Alessandrina, Donato Bramante, 1501. Engraving by Antoine Lafrery, mid-sixteenth century.

a snowflake. The only precedents for this break from the conventional basilica were early Christian martyria such as Santa Costanza and Santo Stefano Rotondo (see Section 6.1). The five-dome scheme proved closer to Byzantine quincunx plans, such as St. Mark's in Venice, and even bore some resemblance to the central-plan designs of Ottoman mosques. Although Bramante supervised the foundations, his project languished and underwent four major redesigns during a century of construction (Fig. 11.3-5).

Julius requested that Bramante undertake another grand project at the same time, a structure that would provide a bridge between the Vatican palace and the Belvedere Villa to the north. Bramante's scheme ran long parallel wings lined with arcades on either side of terraced gardens (Fig. 11.3-6). To negotiate the sloping topography of the Belvedere Court, he inserted two tiers of grand steps that stretched across its width. The first served as seating for theatricals and tournaments. The second revived the ancient type of bifurcated stairs known from the Temple of Fortune at Palestrina. In the rounded exedra at the end of the axis Bramante borrowed another ancient conceit: a stairway with a dozen convex steps that came to a circular landing and continued beyond with a dozen concave steps. To relieve the monotony of the long walls of the upper court, he used **rhythmic trabeation**, a flattened version of the theatrical order of ancient theaters and arenas, like a series of linked triumphal arches. The imperial pretensions of the Belvedere Court went far beyond both the real power of Julius and the appropriate imagery of a pope as servant of God. It also exceeded Bramante's skill as an engineer, and after two decades part of the eastern wing, the only one that had been completed, collapsed. The next generation of papal architects completed it in 1562.

The Sack of Rome and the Development of Angled Bastions

The project of New St. Peter's and the imperially scaled works of Julius II triggered the metamorphosis of Rome. Bramante's *all'antica* style inspired numerous churches and palaces. After the death of both Julius in 1513 and his architect a few months later, the new pope, the Florentine Leo X (Giovanni de' Medici, r. 1513–1521), proved an equally ambitious patron. Son of Lorenzo the Magnificent, Leo was the youngest, wealthiest, and most jovial person ever to be elected to the office. He shifted the focus of papal policy from warfare to culture: "If God has granted us this office, we should enjoy it." The prime patron of the University of Rome, Leo spread his patronage to music, hunting, cuisine, and theatricals.

Palladio designs Villa Rotonda near Vicenza

▲ 1566

▼ **1577**

Palladio begins Il Redentore in Venice, after the plague of 1575

Sixtus V and Domenico Fontana build network of straight streets terminated by obelisks in Rome

▲ **1585–1590**

▼ **1590**

Giacomo della Porta completes dome of New St. Peter's in Rome

Figure 11.3-4 Rome. Bramante's Tempietto (San Pietro in Montorio), sponsored by Ferdinand and Isabella of Spain, 1502.

The new pope turned to Raffaello Sanzio (Raphael, 1483–1520), Bramante's young countryman from Urbino, to fill the role of the master. Raphael even moved into Palazzo Caprini as a gesture of continuity and designed a near replica of it, the Palazzo Vidoni-Caffarelli, in 1518. Although previously known for such painted works as the *School of Athens* (Fig. 11.3-7), a wondrous simulation in fresco of the planned interior of Bramante's New St. Peter's, Raphael now took charge of the construction of the project. Responding to the liturgical critique of the central plan of Bramante's scheme, he revised the layout into a longitudinal basilica.

Raphael also began work on a magnificent villa for Leo's cousin, Cardinal Giulio de' Medici, on a hill overlooking the city a few kilometers north of the Vatican. Now called Villa Madama, it remained unfinished, but even in its partial state, this first grand cardinal's villa displayed the pursuit of Bramante's new plasticity. The completed half of its circular court and the vaulted loggia looking toward the terraced gardens used strictly classical language, with thickened piers and half-columns flanked by deep niches. The architects conceived the complex of hanging gardens, a fishery, and a grand stable as a single architectural whole in strict symmetry. Ideally, Villa Madama would have included a replica of an ancient theater with a rounded *cavea* and a colonnaded *scenae frons*, to be carved into the slope above the circular courtyard.

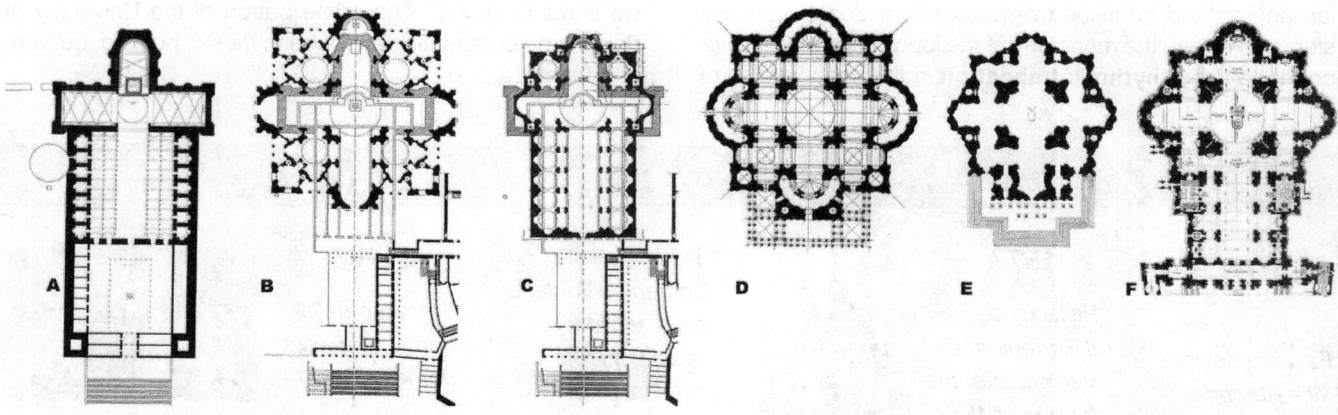

Figure 11.3-5 Rome. Evolution of plans for New St. Peter's: (A) Nicholas V and Rossellino, 1452. (B) Julius II and Bramante, 1506. (C) Leo X and Raphael, 1516. (D) Clement VII and Peruzzi, 1522. (E) Pius IV and Michelangelo, 1560. (F) Paul V and Maderno, 1610.

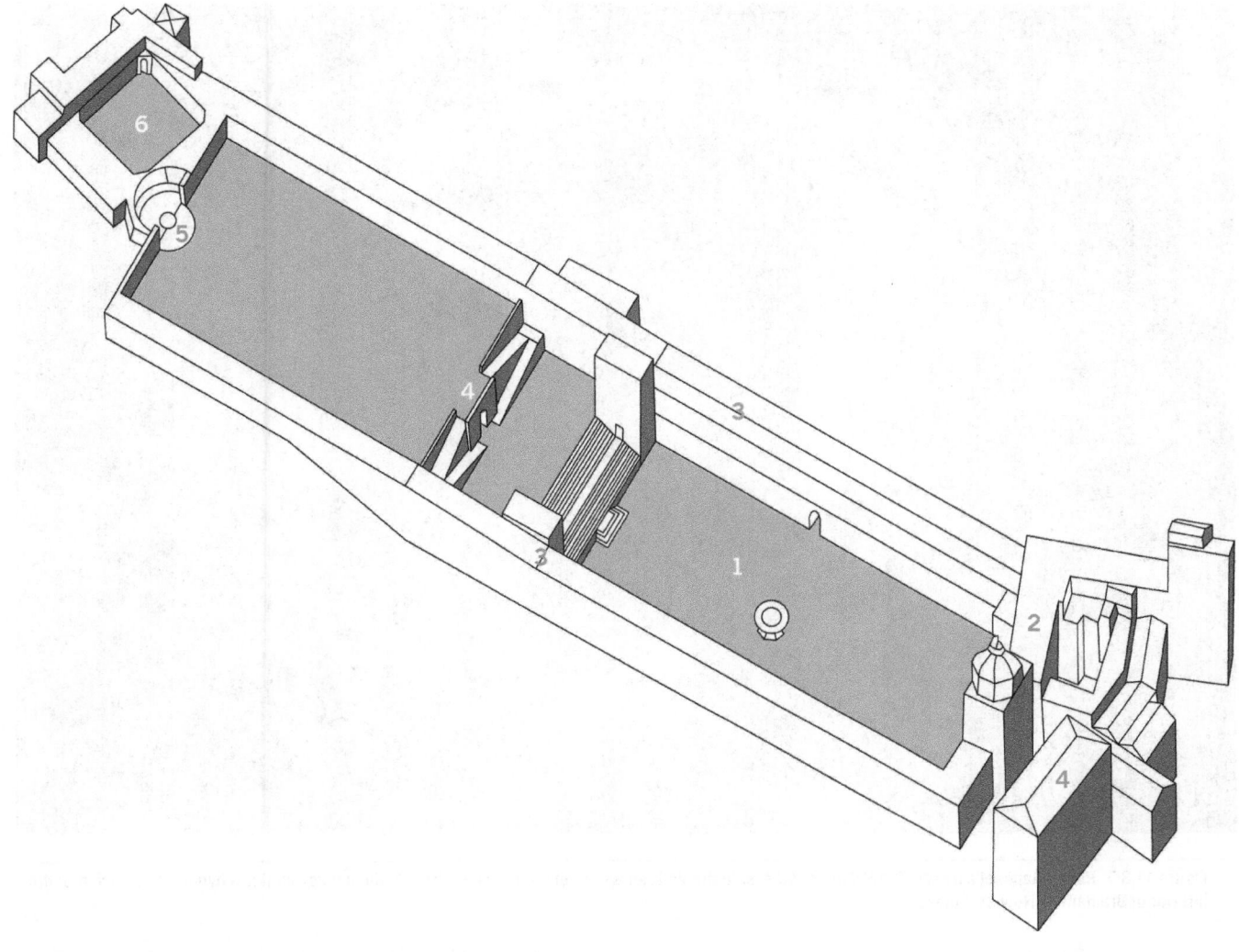

Figure 11.3-6 Rome. Bramante's 1507 scheme for the Belvedere Court, showing: (1) Sistine Chapel; (2) papal palace initiated by Nicholas V, 1450; (3) parallel wings designed as passageways to the Belvedere Villa; (4) bifurcated stairs separating lower from upper courts; (5) niche with convex and concave steps; (6) Belvedere Villa, added by Innocent VIII, 1487.

The worldly pursuits of the papal court in Rome inspired widespread discontent with the church abroad. In 1517 Martin Luther (1483–1546) published his *95 Theses* denouncing the abuses of the papal government. Among his complaints he singled out Bramante's project for New St. Peter's: "Why does the pope, whose wealth today is greater than the wealth of the richest Crassus, build the basilica of St. Peter with the money of poor believers rather than with his own money?" From his isolated position at the castle church of Wittenberg in northern Germany, Luther spread his message thanks to the printing press. After the publication of the Gutenberg Bible in 1452, the new technology of movable type became indispensible to the growth of the Protestant movement. For the first time ordinary people could read the holy texts for themselves, including Luther's new translation of the Bible into German. The Protestant Reformation spread to Switzerland among the followers of Ulrich Zwingli in Zurich and Jean Calvin in Geneva. The church in Rome took nearly half a century to formulate a coherent response,

the Counter-Reformation, which resulted in new rules, the bureaucratic treatment of the sacraments, and a spate of church building.

During this period of religious turmoil, the political rivalry of France's François I and Spain's Emperor Charles V turned Italy into an international battlefield. After the devastating Battle of Pavia, which concluded in 1525 with over 10,000 casualties, large contingents of Charles V's army mutinied. Footloose German and Swiss mercenaries, many of them Protestants intent on punishing Rome, joined them. Leo X's cousin Giulio de' Medici, now Pope Clement VII (r. 1523–1534), failed to deter the renegades, who swept into Rome in 1527 and held the city in terror for nine months. The pope remained a hostage inside Castel Sant'Angelo while the invaders abused and extorted the city's inhabitants. Since the fifth century Rome had suffered numerous invasions, but this event has remained in popular memory *the* Sack of Rome—not just an attack on the city, but a blow to the moral authority of the papacy.

Figure 11.3-7 Rome. Raphael's fresco *The School of Athens*, in the Vatican apartment of Julius II, 1510. In the background is a hypothetical vision of the interior of Bramante's New St. Peter's.

Figure 11.3-8 Florence. Fortezza da Basso, built to protect the new Medici regime by Antonio da Sangallo the Younger, 1534.

The Sack of Rome had a direct impact on the political situation in Florence, where the republican faction restored the commune and expelled the papal governor. After the conclusion of the Sack, the pope gained the support of the emperor and dispatched troops in 1529 to take back Florence. With the emperor's support the pope installed a young nephew as the first Medici duke of Florence. In 1534 the new regime commissioned Antonio da Sangallo the Younger (ca. 1484–1546) to secure the city's western flank with the Fortezza da Basso (Fig. 11.3-8), a pentagonal fortress similar in scale to Castel Sant'Angelo. That Sangallo directed the lookout tower of the keep toward the city and not away from it indicated to the Florentines that this polygonal military apparatus served more to control them than to defend them from outside aggressors. Unlike the tall curtain walls used in the fourteenth-century defenses of Florence, the new walls sat relatively low and sloped, with a mass of earth behind them to absorb the blows of cannon fire. The **angled bastions**, shaped like arrowheads, served as shooting platforms, taking their shape from the lines of fire. Sangallo clad the tall keep with elegant faceted rustication studded with balls and diamonds, two emblems frequently used by the Medici family.

During his career as Italy's most esteemed military architect, Sangallo proposed an ideal city in a polygonal shape with radiocentric streets. He designed a version of it for the areas surrounding Castel Sant'Angelo in Rome in the 1540s, creating a system of radiating straight streets, including the three-prong trident of Piazza di Ponte. Toward the end of the century, Venice sponsored the fullest realization of the radial plan for the garrison town of Palmanova (Fig. 11.3-9). Its star shape, laid out by the military engineer Giulio Savorgnan, allowed troops to move quickly from the fortress in the center to the angled bastions at the points of a nine-sided system of walls. Sangallo's refinement of the angled bastion influenced the rest of Europe in the replanning of cities against the threat of mobile cannons. Unlike the classical conventions used by Renaissance architects for other programs,

Peruzzi's Theaters

The revival of ancient theater under Leo X led to the exquisite perspective sets of Baldassare Peruzzi (1481–1536). For the production of *La Calandria* given in the Vatican courtyard in 1514, Peruzzi designed a three-dimensional frame of contemporary buildings around a painted scrim with a *capriccio* view of Rome showing the Colosseum, the Pantheon, Castel Sant'Angelo, the Vatican obelisk, and the Torre delle Milizie in a single vision. A few months later the same architect designed a temporary theater for the Campidoglio. He designed the theater, one of the first efforts to revive the ancient type, within a rectangle as a *U*-shaped series of bleachers oriented to a stage entered from doors to either side. This unitary vision for the space no doubt inspired the remaking of this piazza during the latter half of the century. Serlio in his famous architectural treatise described in detail how he constructed a temporary wooden theater with seating, stage, and the three classical sets: the tragic scene with fancy palaces, the comic scene with a mix of storefronts and bawdy houses, and the satiric scene of an idyllic natural landscape.

Figure 11.3-9 Palmanova, Italy. Aerial view of city, ca. 1590.

Chambord: François I's Italianate Utopia

he contest to control Italy between François I (1494–1547) and Emperor Charles V (1500–1558) during the first half of the sixteenth century led both monarchs to import the Roman style of architecture to their respective courts. The French king's lifelong project, the Château de Chambord, was much more of a symbol of power and taste than a place to live. Attributed to an Italian, Domenico da Cortona, construction began in 1519 during the period that the king hosted Leonardo da Vinci (1452–1519), who is thought to have been the true designer. Set in the midst of a wooded park, Chambord's four-square plan was rigorously symmetrical, like the castles of Milan and Pavia, cities that were claimed by François I in the 1520s but lost at the Battle of Pavia. The round corner towers, rather than appearing to be fortified, had Roman-style pilasters articulating each of their three levels. A church was tucked into one of them. The cruciform hall led to a double-helix staircase at the center, two intertwined spirals that permitted one person to ascend without crossing the path of a second person descending. Da Vinci made drawings of a similar system. While the elevations of Chambord appeared severe, its roofscape burst into a riotous assembly of steeply pitched cones, ornate dormer windows, and over 200 sculptural chimneys in the French manner.

a

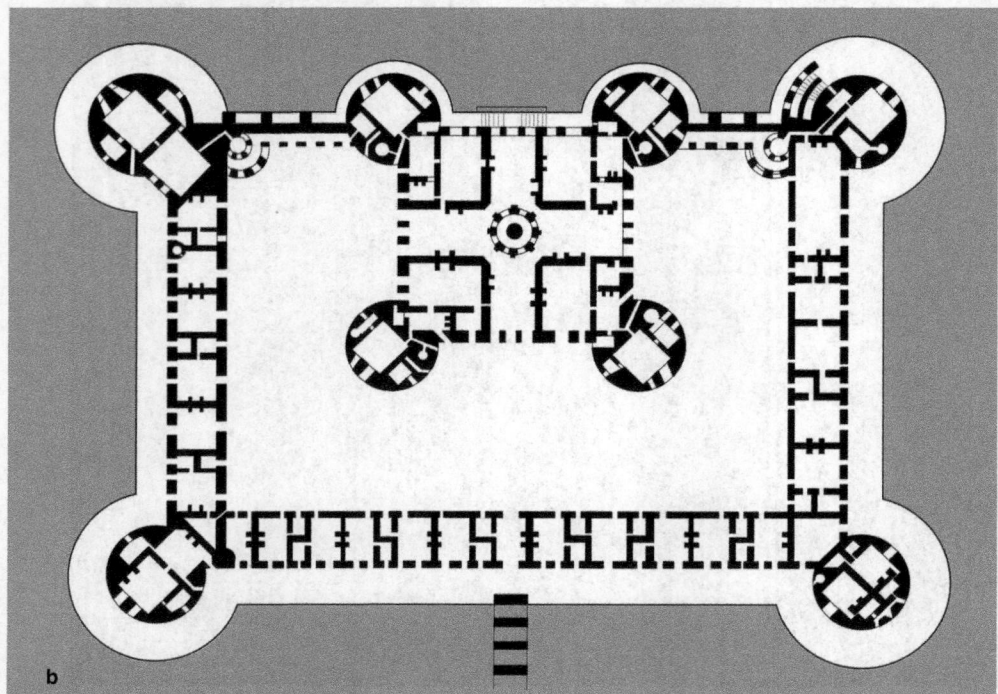

b

Chambord, France. (a) François I's Château de Chambord, built with the participation of Italian designers, 1519–1547. (b) Plan.

the formal research into military architecture after the Sack of Rome inspired wondrous sculptural masses intended as pragmatic answers to the problem of defense.

Mannerism: Making and Breaking the Rules of Classical Architecture

The Sack of Rome unleashed an artistic diaspora. Many artists and architects, including Jacopo Sansovino, Giulio Romano, Baldassare Peruzzi, and Sebastiano Serlio, fled Rome either shortly before or after the Sack. Sansovino went to Venice, where he became the state architect. Romano, expelled from Rome in 1524, became the court architect for the Gonzaga dynasty in Mantua. The sackers tortured Peruzzi before he returned to his hometown of Siena to take charge of fortifications. Serlio, who had served as Peruzzi's assistant, went to Venice, where he began to publish a fully illustrated treatise on architecture. His books spread as quickly among architects as Luther's tracts did among Protestants. Serlio clarified in visual terms the rules of classical architecture but also welcomed the possibility of "inventions," or infractions of the rules, that in the hands of his colleagues became known as "mannerism."

Shortly after the Sack, Sansovino (born Jacopo Tatti, 1486–1570) became *proto*, or state architect, in Venice and worked on numerous public projects surrounding the city's political center, introducing the architectural idiom of papal Rome. In each project he employed a standard system of classical elements that he enriched with an invention, or variation, such as the rusticated Doric half-columns on the *piano nobile* of the Zecca (the Mint, 1536-1556) (Fig. 11.3-10). For the Library of San Marco (1537–1591) (Fig. 11.3-11), Sansovino's greatest civic project, he planned a uniform facade for the western side of the Piazzetta facing the ducal palace. The ground-floor arcades appeared like a narrow version of the bays of the Colosseum, with an elegantly carved Doric frieze. On the upper story Sansovino made concessions to Venetian practice, eroding the wall with tall fenestration. The tightly packed triumphal arch motif between the piers became known as a **serliana**, popularized in Serlio's treatise.

Sebastiano Serlio (1475–1554), a frequent companion of Sansovino, lived in Venice during the 1530s, where he began publishing his *Five Books of Architecture*. Unlike Alberti, he wrote in Italian and provided copious illustrations integrated with the text as a means of teaching professionals the principles of classical architecture. He based his theory on *disegno*, analysis through drawing. Beginning with point, line, and plane, he presented the basic concepts of descriptive geometry and proportions, as well as methods of orthographic projection. Serlio enumerated tangible rules for the classical orders, lining up the five column types on a single page (Fig. 11.3-12). He noted their differences by presenting the number of modules per height of each: the Tuscan 1:6, the Doric 1:7, the Ionic 1:8, the Corinthian 1:9, and the Composite 1:10. In Book Three of his work he charmed

Figure 11.3-10 Venice. La Zecca (the Mint), Sansovino, 1536–1556, with top story added by Vincenzo Scamozzi, 1580s.

Figure 11.3-11 Venice. Library of St. Mark's, opposite the ducal palace, begun by Sansovino in 1537 and completed by Scamozzi in the 1580s.

his readers with plans, elevations, sections, and details of the famous buildings of ancient Rome, including the Pantheon, the Colosseum, the Basilica of Maxentius, the Arch of Constantine, the Baths of Diocletian, and other lesser-known works. Amid the antiquities he integrated three works by Bramante, the Tempietto, the Belvedere Court, and New St. Peter's, as modern exemplars worthy of the ancients.

Serlio based many of his drawings on those of Baldassare Peruzzi (1481–1536). Peruzzi returned to Rome in the mid-1530s to design his final project, the Palazzo Massimo alle Colonne (1533–1536), for a noble Roman family whose houses had been destroyed during the Sack. The uncanny curve of the facade (Fig. 11.3-13a) made reference to the curved walls of the ancient Odeon Theater near the site. The unusual loggia on the ground floor evoked the houses of the republican past that had included open ceremonial spaces at their entries (Fig. 11.3-13b). The windows of the *piano nobile* rested on top of the ground level's entablature, but those of the upper two stories floated strangely in a field of ashlar rustication without **string courses** to mark the floor divisions. With every design choice Peruzzi exercised a knowing flexibility with the rules of classical composition.

Another of Serlio's acquaintances, Giulio Romano (born Giulio Pippi, 1499–1546), moved to Mantua after being indicted in Rome for his pornographic illustrations to accompany Pietro Aretino's erotic sonnets. He came to serve the dowager marquise Isabella d'Este (1474–1539), one of the most independent women of the age, but found a more indulgent patron in her son, Federico Gonzaga II (1500–1540). The newly instated duke had grown up in the court of Julius II in Rome as a political hostage at the same time that Romano was working as an apprentice to Raphael on paintings in the Vatican palace. In 1525 Gonzaga and Romano developed the program for Palazzo Te, situated on an island just outside the western walls of the city. Romano's frescoes give a hint of its purpose: in one room there were portraits of the marquis's horses and in other rooms, mythological scenes of orgies. Here, Gonzaga kept a large stable of racehorses and dallied with his mistress away from the

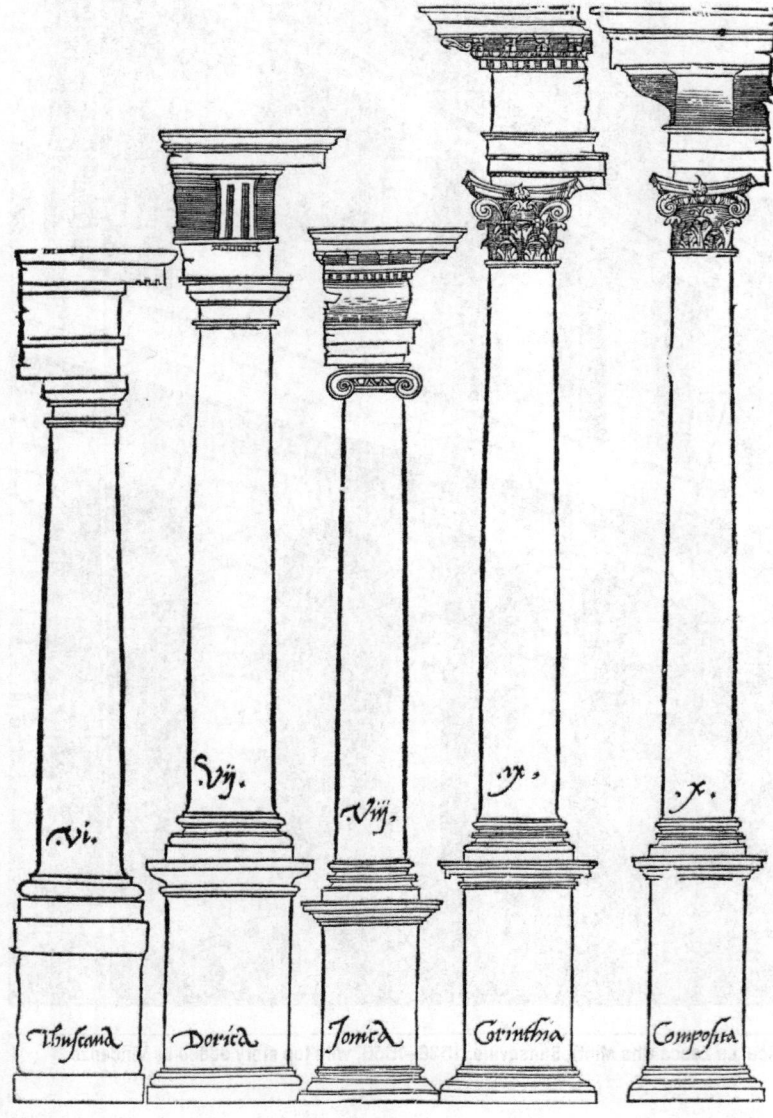

Figure 11.3-12 The five canonical classical orders, Sebastiano Serlio, 1540s. Left to right: the Tuscan, the Doric, the Ionic, the Corinthian, and the Composite.

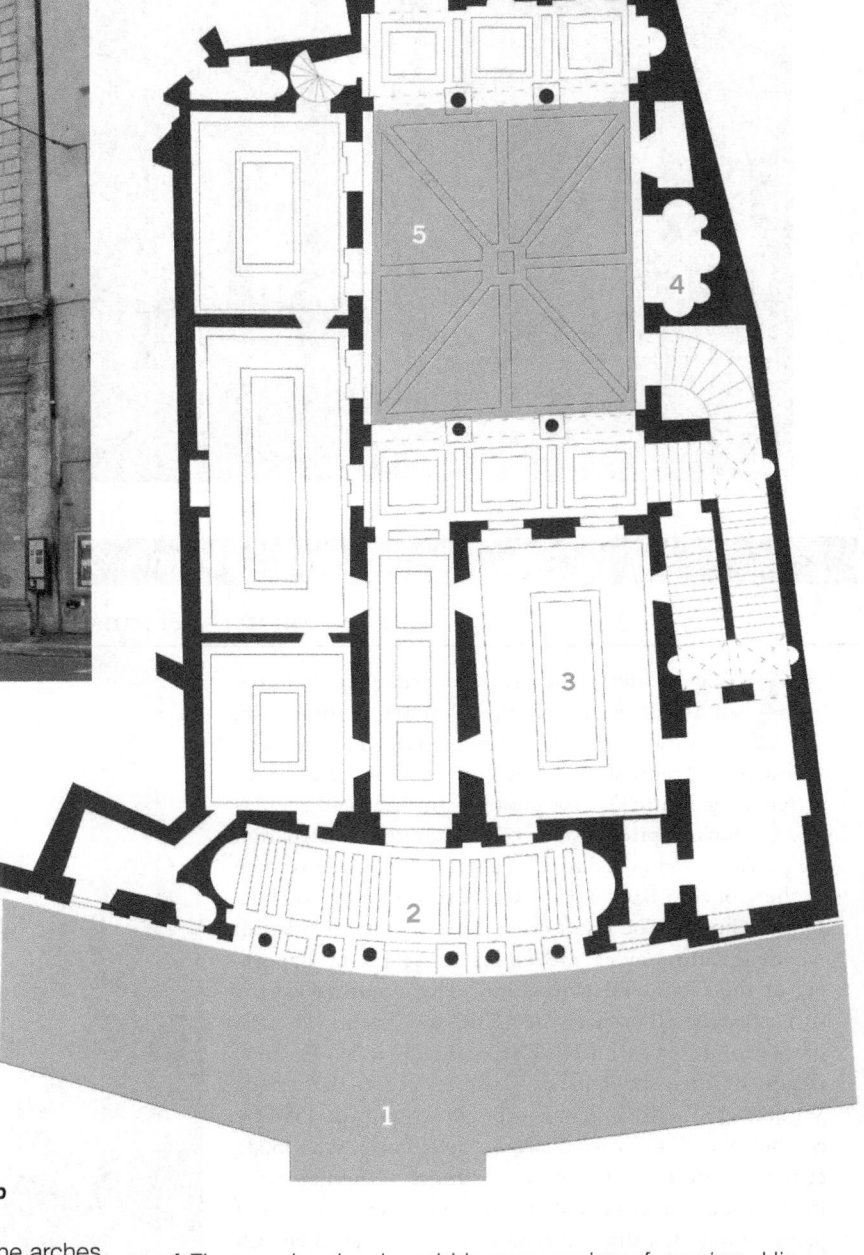

Figure 11.3-13 Rome. (a) Palazzo Massimo alle Colonne, Baldassare Peruzzi, 1532. (b) Plan, showing: (1) Via Papale; (2) convex colonnade, open to the street; (3) office of the patron; (4) nymphaeum; (5) courtyard; (6) rear entry from small piazza.

scrutiny of his mother. Romano articulated the exterior with a **colossal order** of Doric pilasters that rose two stories to the cornice. Under the conventional Doric entablature he spaced the pilasters irregularly, some in pairs and others set at wider intervals. The rear facade overlooking the fishery also contained willful anomalies. The arches of the center three bays rested on clusters of four columns, like the ancient *tetrakionion* of Palmyra, and to either side the four bays were articulated by *serlianas* in rhythmic trabeation. As the arches reached the outer edges the spacing became syncopated, with paired pilasters replacing single columns. Romano saved his most witty invention for the courtyard elevations: here, he let the triglyphs of the Doric entablature slip between the half-columns, as if falling into ruin (Fig. 11.3-14). The conventions of classical architecture that Romano brought from Rome served as rules that he could not resist subverting.

The painter Giorgio Vasari (1511–1574), whose *Lives of the Most Excellent Painters, Sculptors, and Architects* (published in both 1550 and 1568) established the notion of stylistic progress in the arts, identified mannerism as the willful divergence from the classical norm. As court painter and architect

of Florence he developed his own version of *maniera*. His work for Cosimo I de' Medici, grand duke of Tuscany, included transforming the old public palace, Palazzo Vecchio, into a ducal residence, while inserting next to it the Uffizi, the largest urban renewal scheme of sixteenth-century Italy. Vasari's design for the Uffizi combined the majesty of an outdoor arcaded piazza with the intimacy of a palace courtyard (Fig. 11.3-15a,b). He artfully integrated new with old, discreetly incorporating a series of medieval structures, including a church, a medieval tower house, the city's mint, and the Loggia dei Lanzi. The bays of the ground floor of the Uffizi rhythmically alternated niched piers with three-bay colonnades rendered in gray *pietra serena*, the local sandstone

Figure 11.3-14 Mantua, Italy. Giulio Romano's Palazzo Te, courtyard facade with slipping triglyphs, 1525–1540.

RELIGION, PHILOSOPHY, FOLKLORE

The Counter-Reformation Church

After decades of debates and delays, the Church of Rome produced the Counter-Reformation, its answer to the Protestant Reformation. The Council of Trent, which met between 1545 and 1563, scripted the church's new program of rules and regulations, which inspired a wave of new church construction for parish churches and new educational institutions, such as the Collegio Romano in Rome, to create propaganda for the church. The Jesuit order, followers of the Spanish fanatic Ignatius Loyola, proved the most militant supporters of the Counter-Reformation. Their mother church in Rome, the Church of the Gesù, was financed by the grandson of Pope Paul III, Cardinal Alessandro Farnese. Begun by the accomplished classicist Jacopo Barozzi da Vignola (1507–1573), it was brought to term in 1584 by Michelangelo's follower Giacomo della Porta, who made critical changes to the facade, nesting a triangular pediment inside of a segmental one. The Gesù's two stories of paired pilasters, a slight variation on Serlio's ideal church facade, published in 1540, became the model for many Counter-Reformation churches. On the interior the designers eliminated the side aisles, giving the nave a more auditory function, as in Protestant churches. While simplifying the plan, the followers of Loyola advocated intensifying the decoration. Loyola recommended that followers concentrate on a picture of a Christian mystery to improve their faith and obtain divine inspiration.

Rome. Il Gesù, mother church of the Jesuit order, facade by Giacomo della Porta, 1584.

used in Florentine courtyards. At the end of the space Vasari inserted a triumphal arch opening a view to the river and above it a *serliana* framing a statue of the patron.

Palladio: The Mason who Learned Latin

The greatest master of the Roman rules of classical architecture, Andrea Palladio (1508–1580), was born in Padua and worked most of his life in Vicenza and the Veneto, the northeastern region of Italy. Like Serlio, he published a fully illustrated treatise in Italian, *I quattro libri dell'architettura* (*Four Books on Architecture*, 1570), in which he explained the conventions of the classical orders and the typologies to which they could be applied. In contrast to Serlio, Palladio used mostly his own work as examples. His scrupulously detailed annotations on measurements advanced the theory of classical architecture as a comprehensive system of harmonious proportions, similar to the laws of harmony in music. In his palaces, villas, and churches, Palladio's common sense as a builder led to a clear correspondence between interior and exterior forms.

Palladio's development as a humanist fits the early twentieth-century architect Adolf Loos's definition of the architect as "a mason who has learned Latin." Coming from the building trades, he entered the world of architecture under the protection of Gian Giorgio Trissino in Vicenza, who gave him the name "Palladio" and grounded him in ancient literature and history. As a result of their expeditions to Rome in the 1540s, Palladio published a guidebook to the city. His career took off in 1548 when he won the commission to restructure the Basilica of Vicenza. The great medieval council hall, modeled on Padua's Palazzo della Ragione (see Section 9.1), had partly collapsed in 1496. Palladio's project, which kept him on the city's payroll throughout his life, wrapped the existing structure in a classical two-level portico close in spirit to the facade of Sansovino's Library of St. Mark's. The spaces between each of the white marble piers were much broader, however, allowing Palladio to insert prominent *serlianas* on both levels (Fig. 11.3-16).

In 1540 Palladio collaborated with Giulio Romano on Palazzo Thiene in Vicenza and during the next two decades designed numerous palaces for the leading noble families of the city. At first he relied on the facade solutions of Bramante and Raphael in Rome. At Palazzo Porto Festa (1550) he made a base with ashlar rustication and the *piano nobile* with Ionic half-columns

framing aedicular windows with alternating segmental and triangular pediments. He dreamed of reviving the Roman *domus* type as described by Vitruvius, proposing a four-column vaulted atrium at the entry that led into a colonnaded court. In the same years he designed Palazzo Chiericati (Fig. 11.3-17) for a noble patron who was much involved in municipal affairs and bartered with the city to acquire a bit of public property for his loggia with the proviso that it would remain open to the public. The palazzo indeed seems more like a public building than a residence, with a continuous open loggia on the ground floor, raised on a base of three steps overlooking a public piazza. At the juncture of the colonnade and the side elevation Palladio inserted an arch, a transitional device he invented to articulate the structural difference between column and wall.

Palladio earned his greatest fame from his villas, positioned like temples to agriculture on the estates of Venetian nobles (Fig. 11.3-18). He justified the use of the pedimented temple front by reasoning that the ancients derived the temple type from the house. For Villa Emo at Fanzolo, begun in 1559, he set a raised central block with a temple front between two low arcades, or *barchesse*, that terminated with dovecote towers for pigeons. He increased the villa's monumentality by propping up the central block one story and extending a majestic, three-tiered ramp to reach it. The four columns of the temple front framed a deep porch set into a smooth cubic volume.

Most of the plans of Palladian villas conformed to a nine-square grid and seemed almost like churches, with grand central halls around which smaller rooms clustered (Fig. 11.3-19). Palladio gave Villa Foscari (1560), or the Malcontenta, a vaulted cruciform central hall. The facade facing the river carried a grand Ionic temple front reached by **dog-leg stairs** on either side. He stripped the decoration off the rear elevation, leaving only a trace of the front pediment

Figure 11.3-15 Florence. (a) Uffizi, housing thirteen offices for tax farmers and guilds and combining the majesty of an outdoor arcaded piazza with the intimacy of a palace courtyard, Giorgio Vasari, 1560. (b) See next page.

Figure 11.3-15b Florence. Plan of the Uffizi.

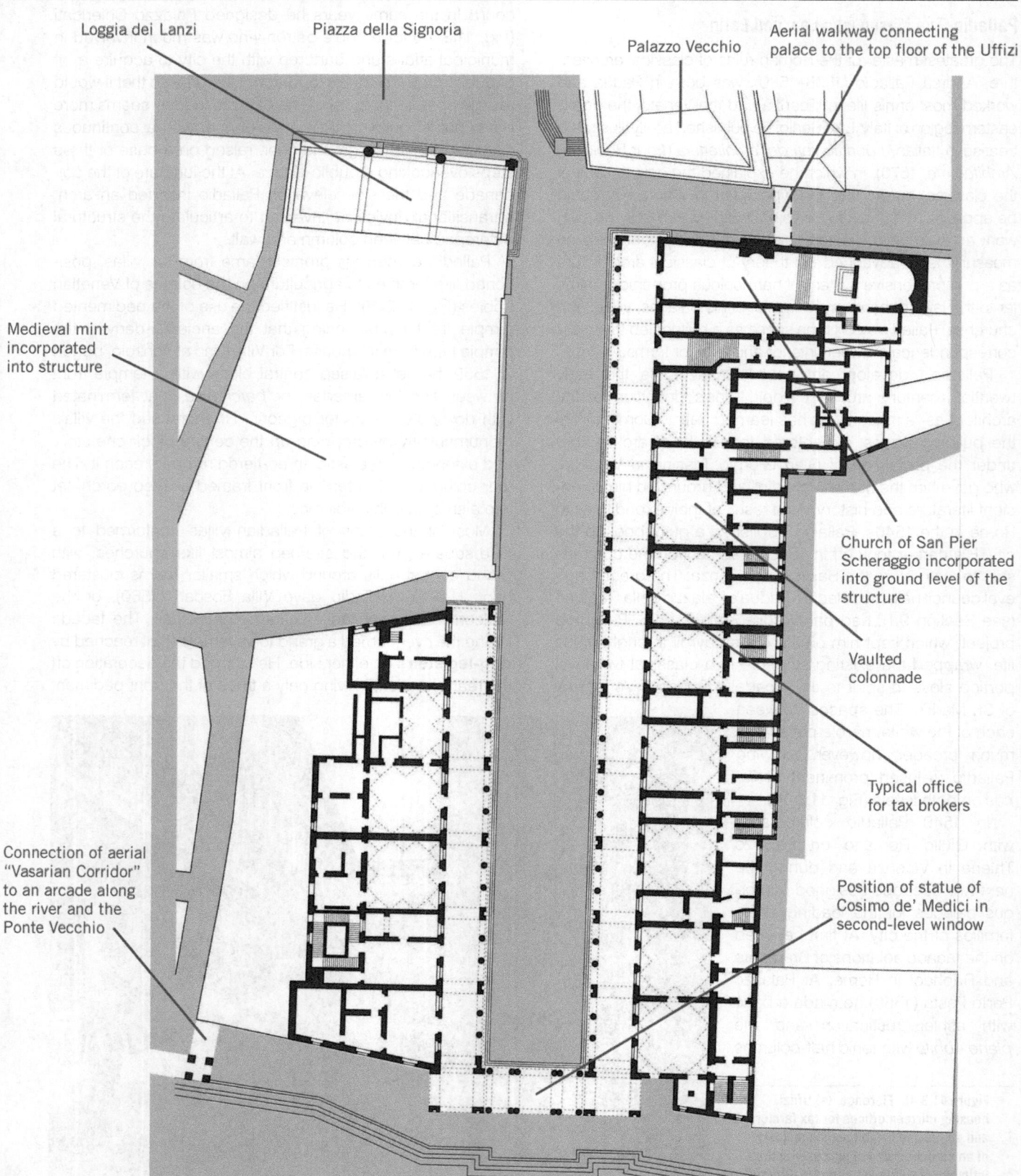

Loggia dei Lanzi

Piazza della Signoria

Palazzo Vecchio

Aerial walkway connecting palace to the top floor of the Uffizi

Medieval mint incorporated into structure

Church of San Pier Scheraggio incorporated into ground level of the structure

Vaulted colonnade

Typical office for tax brokers

Connection of aerial "Vasarian Corridor" to an arcade along the river and the Ponte Vecchio

Position of statue of Cosimo de' Medici in second-level window

Figure 11.3-16 Vicenza, Italy. Andrea Palladio's renovation of the municipal basilica, 1548–1589.

as an outline, breaking its hypotenuse with a rounded three-part **thermal window**. This unexpected type of fenestration, borrowed from vaulted Roman baths, brought more light into the interior and became one of Palladio's favorite mannerisms.

Palladio built Villa Rotonda (Fig. 11.3-20) on a hill a few kilometers east of Vicenza for the wealthy bachelor Paolo Almerico. The patron, who had been forced to abandon his career as a priest in Venice because of an accusation of homicide, had worked in the papal court in Rome at midcentury. He retired in solitude to his estate in Vicenza in 1564. The villa's cubical structure, perfectly symmetrical in all directions, radiated six-column Ionic temple-front porches on all four elevations. At the center of the nine-square plan Palladio capped the double-height **rotunda** with a hemispherical dome. To use such a form, usually reserved for churches, appeared to vindicate the patron's frustrated career as a cleric. On the porches, Palladio used the same low side arches found at Palazzo Chiericati to connect the colonnaded temple fronts to the walls of the villa.

Palladio's domed villa served as a rehearsal for the design of a church, and during his final decade he gained commissions for several religious structures in Venice. He designed the monastery and church of San Giorgio Maggiore and the votive church of Il Redentore (Fig. 11.3-21) in the 1570s but did not survive to see their completion. Palladio's churches followed conventional basilical plans. He innovated by adding thermal windows

Figure 11.3-17 Vicenza, Italy. Palazzo Chiericati, a private residence composed like a public palace, Palladio, 1550s.

on the sides for better day lighting, and for the facades he invented a variation on the classical temple front, overlaying a smaller-scaled temple front on the taller central one. The orders on the facade related in an organic manner to those articulating the interior. The colossal columns of the nave reappeared in the central temple front, while copies of the shorter pilasters of the side chapels flanked the lower temple front on the facade. At Il Redentore the use of a stilted dome with flanking minaret-like campaniles evoked the Eastern precedents of Venice, perhaps inspired by Sinan's

mosques in Istanbul, well known to the principal sponsor of the church, Marc'Antonio Barbaro, who during his years in Istanbul enjoyed a friendship with Grand Vizier Sokollu, patron of the Ottoman master.

During the last year of his life Palladio designed a theater for the Olympic Academy of Vicenza, a humanist organization to which he and many of his clients belonged. The concept of Teatro Olimpico (Fig. 11.3-22a,b) brought together in a single vision Palladio's universe. The *cavea* for the seating was half of a lateral oval that fit into a preexisting

Figure 11.3-18 Fratta Polesina (Rovigo), Italy. Villa Badoer, Palladio, ca. 1554–1563.

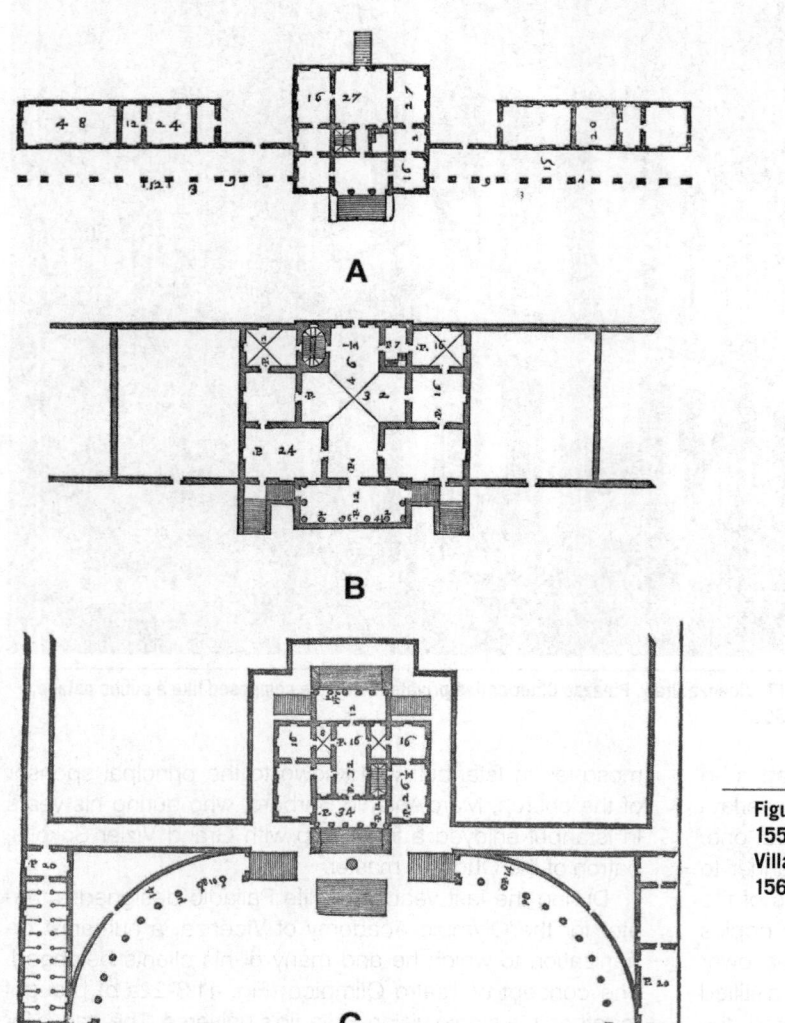

A

B

C

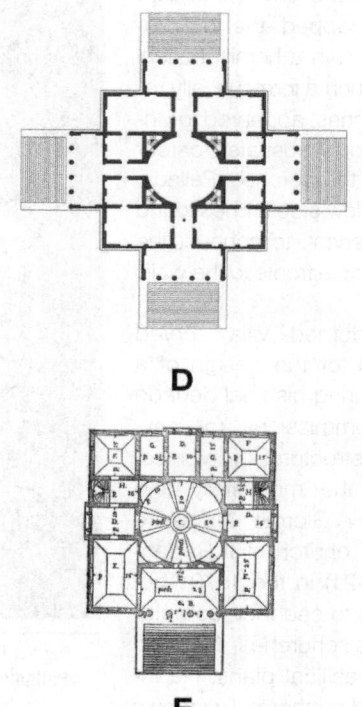

D

E

Figure 11.3-19 Plans of Palladian villas: (A) Fanzolo, Villa Emo, 1558; (B) Malcontenta, Villa Foscari, 1559; (C) Fratta Polesina, Villa Badoer, 1554–1563; (D) Villa Rotonda (today Valmarana), 1566–1585; (E) Rocca Pisani (by Scamozzi), 1578.

Figure 11.3-20 Vicenza, Italy. Villa Capra, or La Rotonda, built by Palladio for Paolo Almerico, 1565.

Figure 11.3-21 Venice. Church of Il Redentore, Palladio, 1570–1590.

a

b

Perspective scene

Scenae frons

Cavea

Figure 11.3-22 Vicenza, Italy. (a) Teatro Olimpico, Palladio and Scamozzi, 1585. (b) Plan.

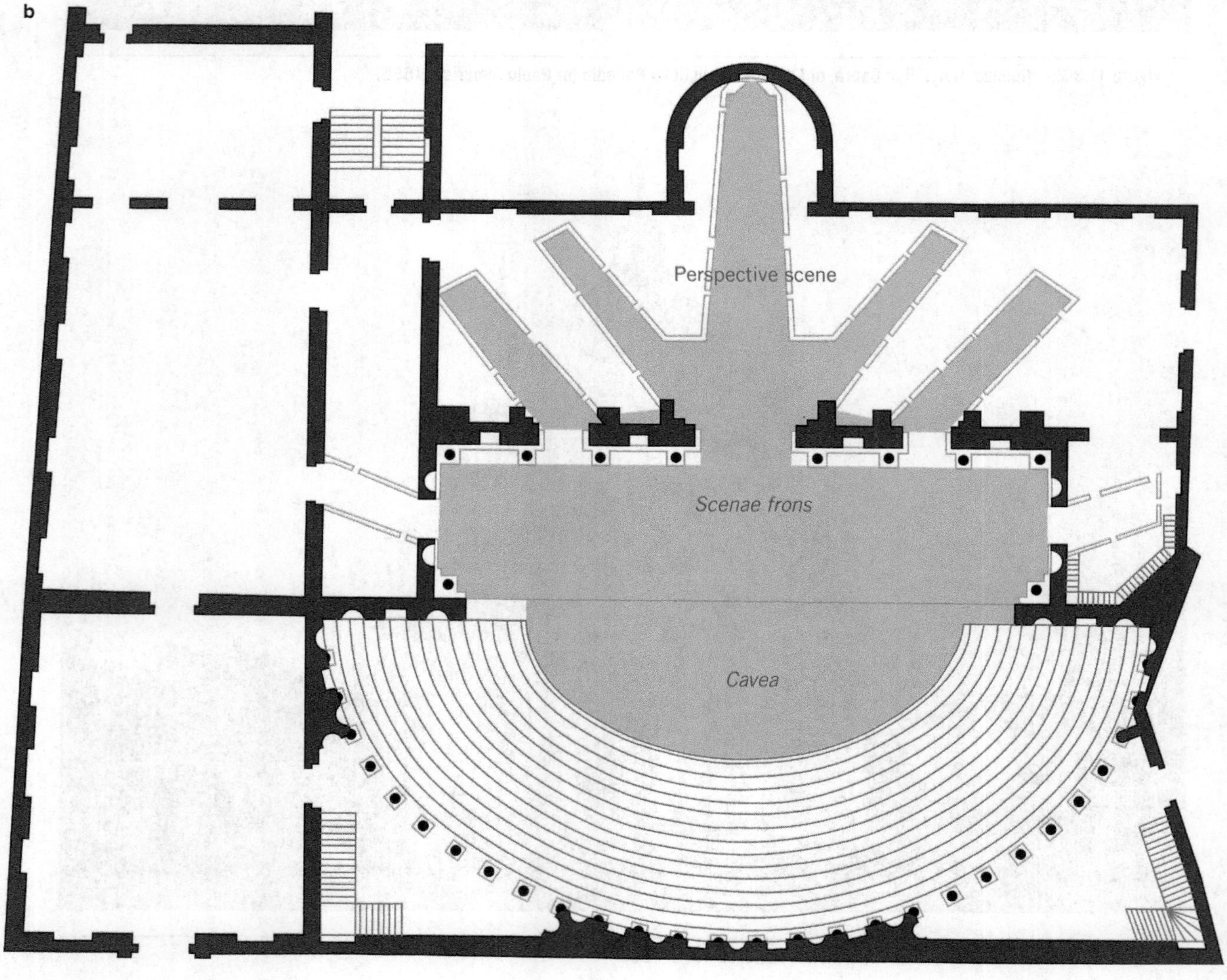

Figure 11.3-23 Florence. New Sacristy of San Lorenzo, site of Medici tombs, Michelangelo, 1518–1540s.

volume, the top range articulated with a curved colonnade and toga-clad statues. For the scene building he proposed a triumphal arch with three openings, behind which straight streets radiated with three-dimensional, forced-perspective facades. Scamozzi completed the project in 1585, embellishing the scene buildings with a vision that tempted the audience to imagine a miniature version of Palladio's Vicenza, full of the classical improvements he had built for many of the members of the academy.

Michelangelo, Architect: The Restless Imagination

Although Michelangelo Buonarroti (1475–1564) often denied being an architect, he designed some of the most influential projects of papal Rome, including the Campidoglio and

much of New St. Peter's. Michelangelo's architecture was full of provocative contradictions. He approached the classical elements of design with the same disturbing search for plasticity and strange proportions seen in his sculptures. Aside from an unbuilt facade for San Lorenzo in Florence (1516), his first major architectural project was the New Sacristy for the same building (1519–1534) (Fig. 11.3-23), commissioned by Leo X as a mausoleum for the first Medici dukes. Here, he placed elements that corresponded to Brunelleschi's Old Sacristy next to completely new inventions. Between the gray Corinthian pilasters, he inserted pronounced marble aedicules that seemed to be bursting out of the planar composition. He broke their segmental pediments with T-shaped recesses, a highly plastic impulse that undermined classical norms.

Figure 11.3-24 Florence. Ricetto, entry to Laurentian Library at cloister of San Lorenzo, Michelangelo, 1523–1540s.

In the foyer, or *ricetto*, of the Laurentian Library (1523–1565) (Fig. 11.3-24) in the cloister of San Lorenzo, Michelangelo intervened with a shocking change of scale. One enters counteraxially into a shaft-like space roughly 10 × 10 m (33 × 33 ft) and 14 m (46 ft) high to find the area mostly occupied by a triple cascading stair. Michelangelo further upset expectations of how classic architecture should be by pushing the lower sets of paired columns into deep pockets in the walls, while pulling their supporting consoles in front of them. He tapered the vertical supports of the aedicular niches, making them look like human shins. Light entered mysteriously through upper clerestories. As with his sculptures, Michelangelo molded space to provoke strong emotional reactions.

Michelangelo left Florence definitively in 1534 for Rome, to work for Pope Paul III (Alessandro Farnese, r. 1534–1549). He concentrated mostly on painting and sculpture until the death of Antonio da Sangallo the Younger in 1546, when he assumed the role of chief papal architect. Michelangelo harbored a legendary dislike for Sangallo, whom he considered unable to draw the human body. For Michelangelo, *disegno*, which meant both drawing and design, derived from the study of human nudes, and he treated architecture as an analogue to the body. Among his first tasks was the completion of Palazzo Farnese (Fig. 11.3-25). Begun by Sangallo in 1517 and doubled in size after 1534 when Cardinal Farnese became Pope Paul III, it surpassed the dimensions of the nearby Cancelleria. Palazzo Farnese became the new standard for a dignified aristocratic residence. Sangallo, esteemed for his practicality, developed a standard kit of parts for architectural elements such as consoles, aedicular windows, and pediments. He kept costs down by putting rusticated **quoins** on the corners and leaving the rest of the walls in a relatively cheap brick bond. The major design attention was given to the vaulted vestibule, lined with Doric columns and niches, Sangallo's interpretation of the atrium of an ancient *domus*. The three-level arcades of the square courtyard, 30 m (98 ft) per side, recalled the arched piers and half-columns of the Colosseum. For Paul III, Sangallo carved a grand piazza from the neighboring fabric, animating the space with two fountains, colossal granite tubs taken from the Baths of Caracalla. Michelangelo's alterations to Sangallo's project included jacking up the cornice 3 m (10 ft) and doubling its depth to make it more imposing. He also widened the central window above the entry, added a huge coat of arms, and broke the pediments of the aedicules of the top-floor windows, a move that generated a sense of restlessness.

Michelangelo's design for the Campidoglio began as a sculptural project in 1537, when Paul III asked the artist to relocate the equestrian statue of Marcus Aurelius from the Lateran area to the Capitoline Hill. After 1546, however, Michelangelo embarked on the total redesign of the site of Rome's communal government, transforming it from an unpaved, irregular space adjacent to the thirteenth-century church of the Aracoeli into a magnificent outdoor sculpture gallery (Fig. 11.3-26). Rather than change the skewed orientation between the existing Senators' Palace and the Palace of the Conservators, he left the oblique alignment and inserted a third palace with a facade identical to that of the Palace of the Conservators to enforce the symmetry as a trapezoid. To boost the central position of the Senators' Palace, he added a grand bifurcated stair and rebuilt the campanile in a central position, while lining the upper two stories of the facade with colossal Corinthian pilasters. He used the same pilasters on the piers of the other two palaces and inserted at less than half their size full columns carrying the ground-floor entablatures of the porticoes. The new Campidoglio seemed like a permanent stage set in which ancient statues performed a pageant. The horse tamers flanking the top of the ramped stairs welcomed the visitor up the hill. The imperial equestrian statue at the center commanded the scene from a gently mounded oval paved with an intricate starburst pattern. On the same axis the figure of Roma sat in the niche under the stairs of the Senators' Palace holding symbols of justice, while the two ancient river gods to either side lounged at the foot of the stairs. Lining the balustrades of the three facades, a series

Figure 11.3-25 Rome. Palazzo Farnese, begun by Sangallo in 1525, expanded after the election of Pope Paul III (Farnese), and taken over by Michelangelo in 1546.

CAPITOLII·SCIOGRAPHIA·EX·IPSO· EXEMPLARI·MICHAELIS·ANGELI·BONAROTI·A·STEPHANO·DVPERAC·PARISIENSI·ACCVRATE·DELINEATA
ET·IN·LVCEM·AEDITA·ROMAE·ANNO· SALVTIS·ꝏDLXIX

Figure 11.3-26 Rome. The Campidoglio, an oval set in a trapezoid, surrounded by unified facades, Michelangelo, 1537–1610 (star-shaped paving realized in 1940). Depiction by Étienne Dupérac, 1568.

of tiny, toga-clad figures looked on like a chorus of ancient senators. Not completed until the early seventeenth century, the piazza conveyed a strong sense of hierarchical authority, when in fact the only power left to city administrators concerned the budget for Carnival.

The colossal pilasters at the Campidoglio later migrated to Michelangelo's greatest architectural effort, the completion of New St. Peter's. There, he wrapped the rear apses of the church with a thick layer of paired Corinthian pilasters that negotiated the contours of constantly shifting wall planes (Fig. 11.3-27). At the joints between the facets he clustered shadow pilasters like the wrinkles of the skin at the joints of human limbs. He thickened the walls of the apse to help buttress the immense load of the dome. The numerous aedicules functioned as relief arches for the structure. With the constantly turning surfaces and the syncopated rhythm of the pilasters and their shadow pilasters, Michelangelo completely reinvented the distributive logic of classical architecture.

The 42 m (137 ft) diameter of St. Peter's dome (Fig. 11.3-28) required considerable buttressing. Sangallo had proposed to support the base of the dome with two layers of arcaded piers around the drum, which would have hidden the dome on the exterior. Sinan had solved the same problem by using radiating flying buttresses that stepped down from the drum

to the outer walls aided by four counterweight towers over the piers that absorbed diagonal thrusts. With the empirical good sense of a sculptor, Michelangelo restored the clean hemispherical profile of the dome, borrowing some technology from Brunelleschi. The double-shelled dome rose on ribs to a crowning lantern. He ringed the drum with solid, spur-like buttresses, hidden behind pairs of engaged Corinthian columns. The sixteen ribs arched up to the lantern, where colonnaded buttresses reappeared at half-scale. Two flanking domes, one-third the size of the cupola, were installed by Jacopo da Vignola and Pirro Ligorio before the completion of the central dome, creating an effect similar to the cascading compositions of Sinan. Giacomo della Porta (1532–1602) completed the cupola in 1593, giving it a slightly taller, more pointed shape for stability. Although Michelangelo hoped to keep Bramante's idea for New St. Peter's as a central-plan church, the nave was later extended by Carlo Maderno (1556–1629) as a longitudinal basilica. Maderno unveiled the facade in 1614, which at short range blocked the view of the dome. Seen from a distance, however, the new dome enriched the Roman skyline and gave it a fresh sense of artistic superiority. The confidently mannered use of classical architecture projected the desired authority of the Counter-Reformation church to restore Rome's role as the spiritual leader of the city and the world.

Figure 11.3-27 Apse of St. Peter's, showing colossal pilasters and rippling shadow pilasters, Michelangelo, 1560s.

Figure 11.3-28 Rome. View of St. Peter's with completed dome, Michelangelo and della Porta, 1588–1593.

Cardinals' Gardens and Papal Urbanism

Rome's growing network of linked axes coincided with the invention of the formal Italian garden. The villas built for Cardinal d'Este at Tivoli and Cardinal Montalto next to Santa Maria Maggiore in Rome represented microcosms of a desired urban order. The antiquarian-architect Pirro Ligorio (1520–1583) began the gardens of Villa d'Este for Cardinal Ippolito d'Este II (1509–1572) after the latter's appointment as governor of Tivoli in 1550. The grand axis of the garden intersected several cross-axes leading to geometrically arranged subspaces and a collection of surprising outdoor piazza-like enclosures, making the layout resemble that of a small city, made mostly of natural materials. The major cross-axis, the Allée of 100 Fountains, connected two theatrical spaces: on the east, the Fountain of the Tiburtine Sybil, framed by an annular tunnel formed by sheets of water; to the west, *Rometta*, a miniaturized Rome, similar to a stage set, beyond which could be seen the real Rome.

Upon election as pope, Sixtus V ordered his architect, Domenico Fontana (1543–1607), to treat the rest of the city like an extension of his garden. Fontana placed the Moses Fountain like a triumphal arch at the juncture of Sixtus's new aqueduct and Strada Pia (an axis built for Pius IV in the 1560s). Fontana raised the obelisk in front of St. Peter's, one of the great technical feats of the age, and planted three other obelisks as goals at the end of new straight avenues: one at the trident of Porta del Popolo, another at the Lateran, and a final one at Santa Maria Maggiore. The long, straight avenues, built to help pilgrims move about the edges of the city, passed through mostly unsettled districts and, to maintain the third dimension, were lined with high garden walls.

Although the religious function of the Sistine plan of Rome appeared its most obvious intention, the pope had several modernizing objectives in reordering the city as well. He prepared a new market between the ruins of the Baths of Diocletian and Santa Maria Maggiore, right behind his villa, with his new axes connecting the city's edges to this new commercial space. Fontana drew up plans to transform the Colosseum into a silk factory to create jobs for the chronically unemployed citizens of Rome. Although the papal planners planted the mulberry trees needed for silk production, they never began work on the factory. The new avenues of the Sistine plan also served an ulterior purpose: wealthy residents, who in late-sixteenth-century Rome acquired carriages as status symbols, now had thoroughfares to show off their vehicles. While the linking of straight avenues in papal Rome subsequently inspired the planning of many modern cities, the modernity proposed by Sixtus V and Fontana in the form of production sites and markets remained stifled by the city's chronic inertia. Aside from Rome's impressive construction of buildings and public spaces, the city adhered almost exclusively to a service economy. The classical facades, straight streets, cupolas, and shaped piazzas supplied a glamorous theatrical setting for attracting religious revenues and the pilgrim trade.

(a) Tivoli. Villa d'Este, designed by Pirro Ligorio for Cardinal Ippolito d'Este II, 1560s. Painting based on an etching by Étienne Dupérac, sixteenth century. (b) See facing page.

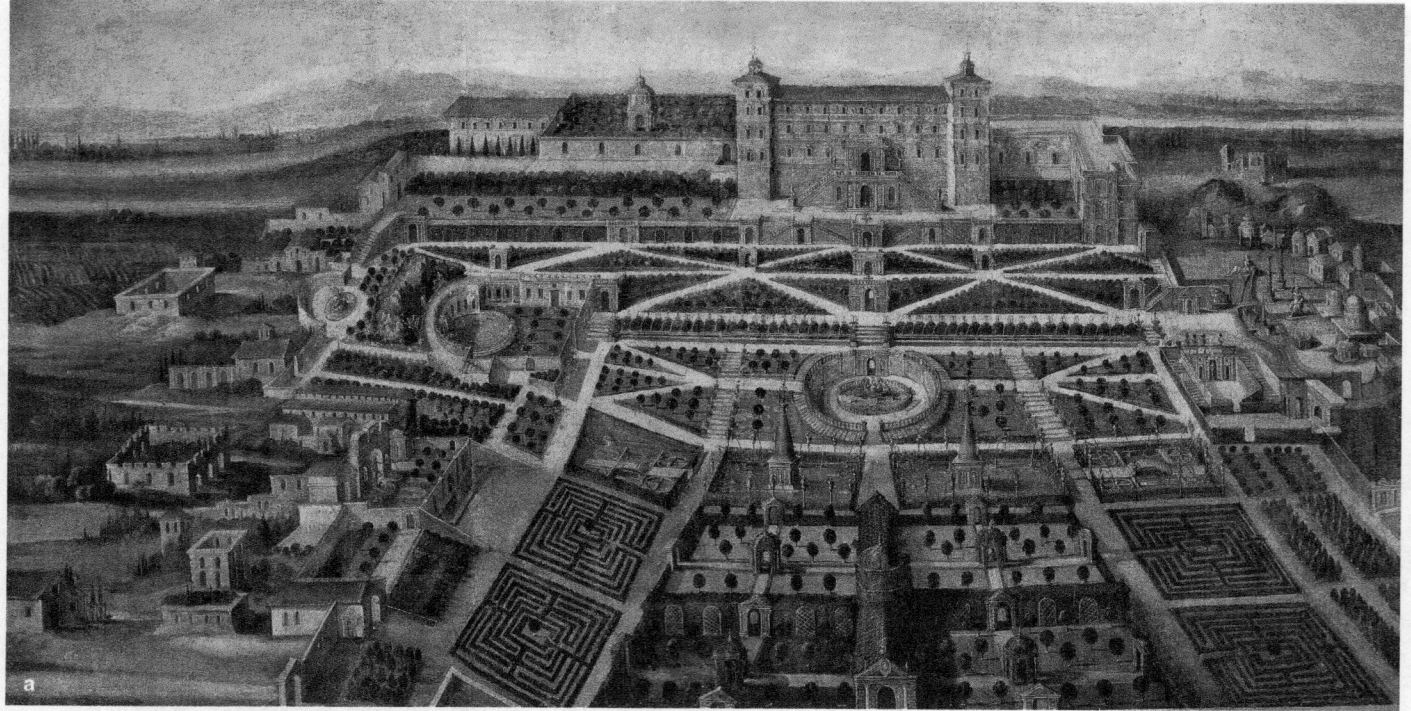

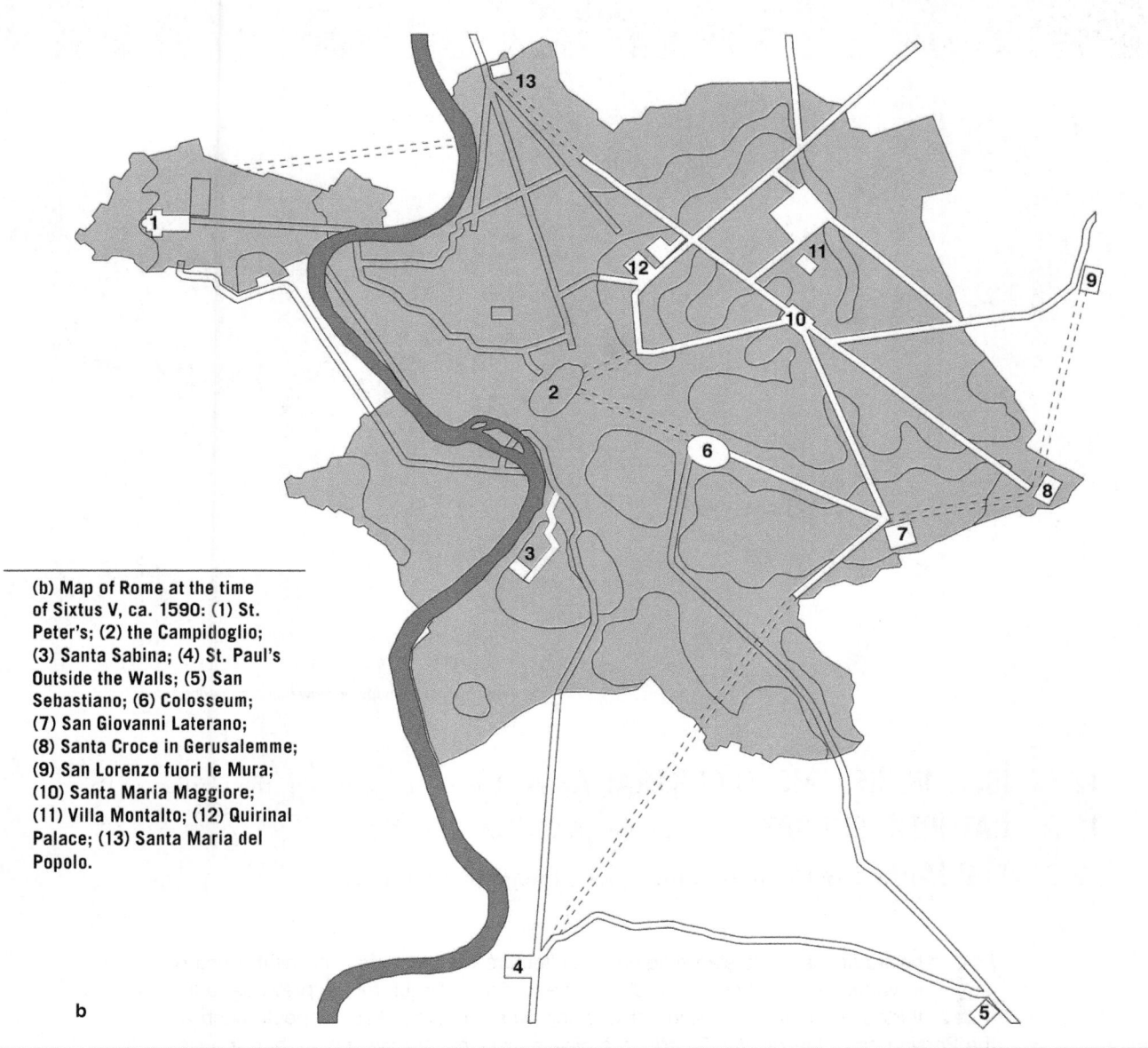

(b) Map of Rome at the time of Sixtus V, ca. 1590: (1) St. Peter's; (2) the Campidoglio; (3) Santa Sabina; (4) St. Paul's Outside the Walls; (5) San Sebastiano; (6) Colosseum; (7) San Giovanni Laterano; (8) Santa Croce in Gerusalemme; (9) San Lorenzo fuori le Mura; (10) Santa Maria Maggiore; (11) Villa Montalto; (12) Quirinal Palace; (13) Santa Maria del Popolo.

b

Further Reading

Ackerman, James. *Palladio*. London: Penguin, 1966.

Boucher, Bruce. *Andrea Palladio: The Architect in His Time*. New York: Abbeville Press, 1998.

Bruschi, Arnaldo. *Bramante*. London: Thames & Hudson, 1973.

Hollingsworth, Mary. *Patronage in Sixteenth Century Italy*. London: John Murray, 1996.

Howard, Deborah. *Jacopo Sansovino: Architecture and Patronage in Renaissance Venice*. New Haven, CT: Yale University Press, 1987.

Lotz, Wolfgang. *Architecture in Italy, 1500–1600*. Revised by Deborah Howard. New Haven, CT: Yale University Press, 1995.

Millon, H., and V. M. Lampugnani. *The Renaissance: From Brunelleschi to Michelangelo*. New York: Rizzoli, 1997.

Partridge, Loren. *The Renaissance in Rome, 1400–1600*. London: Calmann & King, 1996.

Pepper, Simon, and Nicholas Adams. *Firearms and Fortifications: Military Architecture and Siege Warfare in Sixteenth-Century Siena*. Chicago: University of Chicago Press, 1986.

Steenbergen, Clemens, and Wouter Reh. *Architecture and Landscape: The Design Experiment of the Great European Gardens and Landscapes*. Munich: Prestel, 1996.

↗ Visit the free website **www.oup.com/us/ingersoll** to view chapter outlines and study questions; Google Maps showing the location of key sites; links to UNESCO World Heritage Sites; and essays on topics that cross time and culture.

CHAPTER 12

1600–1700

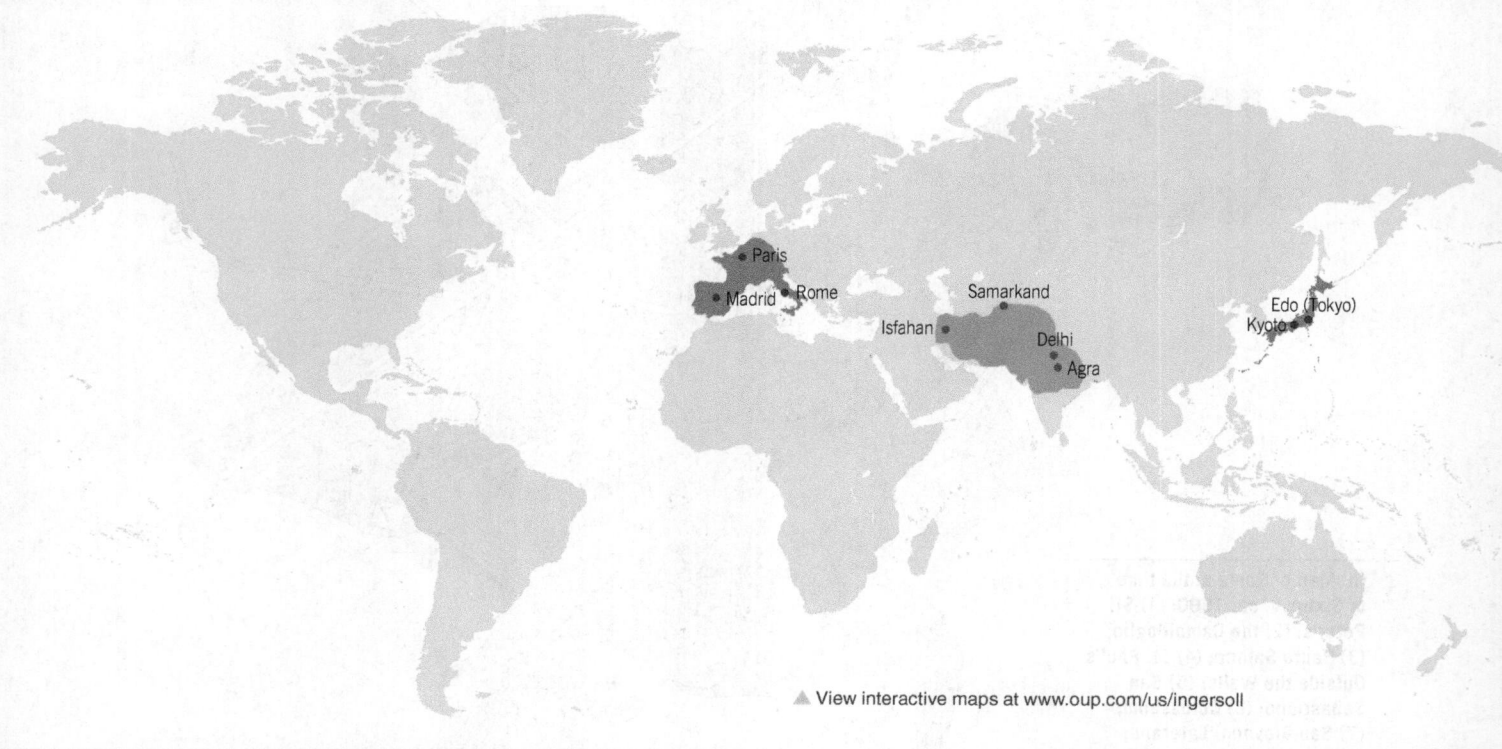

▲ View interactive maps at www.oup.com/us/ingersoll

12.1 ISLAMIC REALMS IN CENTRAL ASIA: The Dome of Power, the Garden of Paradise

12.2 CATHOLIC EUROPE: The Settings of Absolutism

12.3 EDO JAPAN: Isolation from the World, Integration with Nature

The traditions of Persian religious architecture matured after the ninth century in various political contexts. During the period of Seljuk rulers, previous to the thirteenth-century invasions of Genghis Khan, characteristic aspects such as the Persian arch, the *pishtaq* facade, the nine-square *hasht bihisht* plan, and the tile-clad bulbous dome were perfected in such works as the old Friday Mosque of Isfahan. Timur, the upstart conqueror who emulated the conquests of the khans, attempted to create a Persian-style capital in Samarkand (Uzbekistan), importing Persian architects for the task. When the Safavid dynasty reclaimed most of Persia during the late sixteenth century, Shah Abbas I began the process of doubling the size of his capital of Isfahan and transforming it into an immense garden city, with a grand *maydan* plaza, a new Friday Mosque, and a grand fountain-lined boulevard for the villas of the aristocracy. His example stimulated the Mughal court in India, successors to Timur, who preserved Persian customs, architecture, and language while attempting to assimilate characteristics of the Indian context. Through their funerary monuments built from the late sixteenth to the mid-seventeenth century, the Mughals provided visions of paradise comprehensible to all faiths. During the same period in Europe Louis XIV of France dominated the political scene. He relocated the court to the palace of Versailles outside

Paris, where he sponsored a grand landscape of symmetry and perspectival control. The papal court in Rome, although much less powerful, supplied the precedents for the pompous style used in France. Through elaborate costumes, wigs, facial makeup, fancy carriages, and ever more decorative settings, the protagonists of this age created a highly theatrical lifestyle. In papal Rome Gian Lorenzo Bernini perfected this trend in the arts, a process that culminated in the great "theater" of the piazza at St. Peter's. Life at the French court developed into a daily recital, with architectural backgrounds conceived as stage sets for court rituals. In Japan, which during the same period cut itself off from all contact with the rest of the world, a similar crossover from theater to court life occurred. The *shoguns*, who had consolidated the aristocratic rule of the archipelago by the beginning of the sixteenth century, played out their roles both within their palaces and in the Noh theaters attached to them. In their palaces, monasteries, and gardens the Japanese pursued an uncanny asymmetrical order, the complete contrary of the axial symmetry of Isfahan and Versailles.

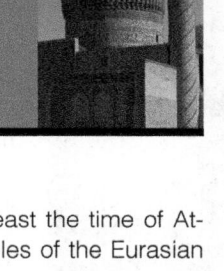

12.1 ISLAMIC REALMS IN CENTRAL ASIA
The Dome of Power, the Garden of Paradise

For nearly a millennium, since at least the time of Attila's invasions, the nomadic peoples of the Eurasian steppes had seemed more intent on destroying monuments than constructing them. Beginning in the fifteenth century, however, the descendants of these Turkic and Mongolian cavalries distinguished themselves as patrons of grand domes and exquisite gardens. Relying on the architectural traditions established several centuries earlier in Persia, they created new monumental settings in the thinly populated region ranging from western Iran to Uzbekistan and northern India.

First the Timurid dynasty in Uzbekistan, followed by the Safavids in Iran and then the Mughals in India, sponsored shining cities with bulbous domes and towering minarets. Unlike Europe or China, where printed treatises aided the transmission of architectural types and styles, this Persian renaissance relied on itinerant professionals to design the magnificent new mosques, *madrasas*, and tombs of these metropolises. In each geographic context local builders contributed decorative motifs and construction practices to the Persian types. The nomadic rulers, who at first preferred to continue living in their yurts, eventually yielded to the conventions of more permanent forms of architecture. As they consolidated their political power, they commissioned domes and gardens that conveyed compelling visions of paradise to legitimate their rule.

The Persian Renaissance: From the Timurids to the Safavids

Most of the territories between the Mesopotamian delta, the Eurasian steppes traversed by the Silk Road, and the Indus valley came under Muslim rule during the first two centuries of Islam. From the tenth to thirteenth century the Ghaznavids and the Seljuks, Turkish warrior dynasties from the steppes, established a pattern of nomadic outsiders taking control of territories and converting to Islam. Without a built tradition of their own, they sponsored monuments based on longstanding Persian traditions. Similar to the Norman kings in medieval Sicily, these nomadic rulers relied on local artisans for their art and architecture. They generally encouraged an autonomous Persian culture, which resulted in outstanding literary works, such as the *Shahnamé*, the great Persian epic by Ferdowsi, written around 1000 in Farsi. The Seljuks enriched the local building traditions with new programs, including more articulated public spaces and more prominent funerary monuments. Their broad, **iwan**-shaded courts and massive cupolas provided models for later nomadic conquerors.

During the early thirteenth century the nomadic leader Temujin (1162–1227) became the "Universal Ruler," or, in the local language, Genghis Khan. He unleashed his Mongolian hordes throughout the entire region, slaughtering millions, destroying irrigation systems, and devastating much of the architectural patrimony of cities such as Baghdad and Samarkand. The Great Khan and his immediate successors did not convert to Islam, nor did they create monuments. After three generations, however, most of the khanate ruling class had become Muslim. Once settled and committed to Islam, the dynasties that subsequently rose throughout the region, such as the Timurids, the Safavids, and the Mughals, sponsored large cities with magnificent gateways, palaces, formal gardens, and funerary cupolas of colossal dimensions. Islam provided them with conventional programs for building mosques, *madrasas*, and mausoleums. Frequently, the conversion of nomads from the steppes resulted in the development of unorthodox religious tendencies, such as the promotion of Sufi mystics in Samarkand, the privileging of the Shiite sect in Iran, and the attempted synthesis of Islam with Hinduism in northern India.

After the decline of the khanate descendants of Genghis, Timur (r. 1370–1405), often referred to as Tamerlane (Timur the Lame), a general of Mongolian–Turkic origin, succeeded in conquering most of Central Asia. A ruthless leader, he assembled an empire that stretched from Baghdad to Delhi. Unlike the khans, who after their conquest offered a kind of *Pax Mongolica*, promising clemency, tolerance, and the development of infrastructure, Timur preferred more intimidating methods of rule. Famous for his cruelty, he is known to have beheaded thousands of resisters without mercy. During the siege of Isfahan in 1387, he constructed a series of gruesome pyramids out of the skulls of his victims.

Timur progressed from building with the body parts of his victims to constructing great cities in masonry. The ancient city of Samarkand became his showcase capital. Like the

Figure 12.1-1 Samarkand, Uzbekistan. Great Mosque of Bibi-Khanym, early fifteenth century.

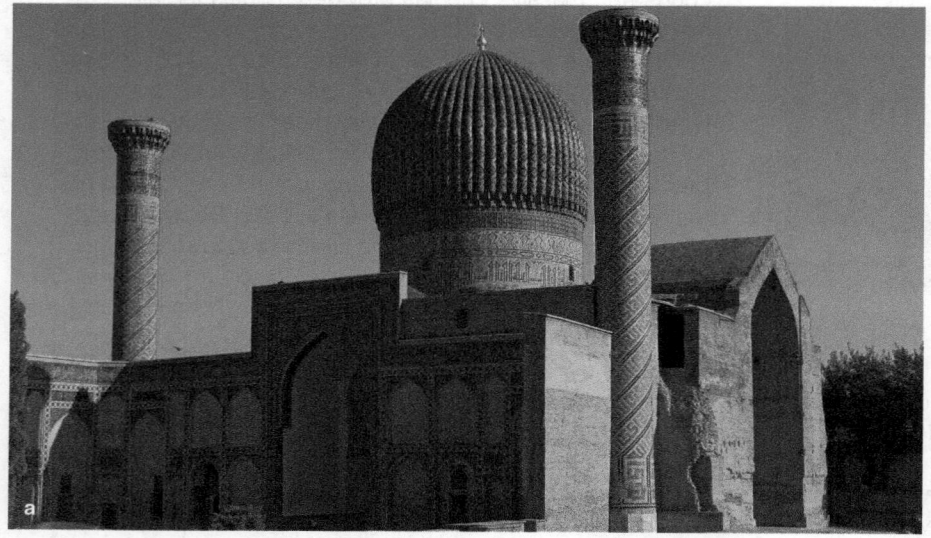

Figure 12.1-2 Samarkand, Uzbekistan. (a) Gur-é-Amir, dome over Timur's tomb, early fifteenth century. (b) See facing page.

of the fifteenth century, Timur commissioned the Great Mosque of Bibi-Khanym (Fig. 12.1-1), named after his great-uncle's most prestigious wife, who traced her lineage directly to Genghis Khan, allowing Timur to claim the status of son-in-law to the khan. The construction of the mosque also served as a way to celebrate the recent addition of northern India to his empire. Indian elephants dragged hundreds of marble columns across Afghanistan for use in the mosque's hypostyle prayer hall. Each corner of the outer walls of the Bibi-Khanym complex carried a slender minaret, marking off an area slightly larger than that of the Great Mosque of Córdoba. Timur relied on Persian architects to reproduce the traditional sacred court. Each side focused on a **pishtaq**, a deep *iwan* arch, flanked by two thin minarets. The facade of the mosque concealed a tall, stilted dome clad in green ceramic tiles. The architects decorated the domes behind the minor *pishtaqs* with corrugated ribs, coated in blue and green glazed tiles.

At the other end of the city Timur planned his mausoleum with the Persian architect Mohammed al-banna al-Isfahani during the year of his death, 1405. The dome over his tomb, the Gur-é-Amir (Fig. 12.1-2a,b), dominated a square court, which had cylindrical minarets at each corner. To its east stood the Madrasa of Muhammad Sultan, Timur's favorite grandson, who died a year before the emperor. To the west rose a domed **khanqah**, a special monastic building for a mystic brotherhood, similar to the *tekke* built for dervishes in Ottoman Turkey. Pilgrims still visit Timur's mausoleum, as next to his tomb lies the grave of the mystic saint Sayyid "Umar, the 'Master of Baha' ud-Din Naqshband." The Naqshbandi Sufi brotherhood originated the monastic *khanqahs* of the region. A slender pole, like those used for the graves of nomads in the steppes, marked the saint's tomb.

khans, he preferred to live in a portable yurt set in a park outside the city, but this did not inhibit him from creating a city palace, religious monuments, and a magnificent covered market street to impress the people. During the first years

TIME LINE

▼ **1501**

Safavid dynasty established in Tabriz by Ishmail I

Mughal dynasty established in Delhi by Babur

▲ **1526**

▼ **1566**

Akbar begins the Red Fort in Agra

Humayun's tomb built in Delhi

▲ **1565–1572**

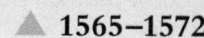

Most of the significant fifteenth-century projects in Sa-markand, including the completion of Timur's tomb, were planned by Ulugh Beg (1393–1449), the founder's grand-son, who served as governor of the city for thirty years

before commencing his brief tenure as emperor in 1447. A studious man known for his command of mathematics and the sciences, Ulugh Beg sponsored the Great Observatory on the outskirts of the city. He also initiated a monumental

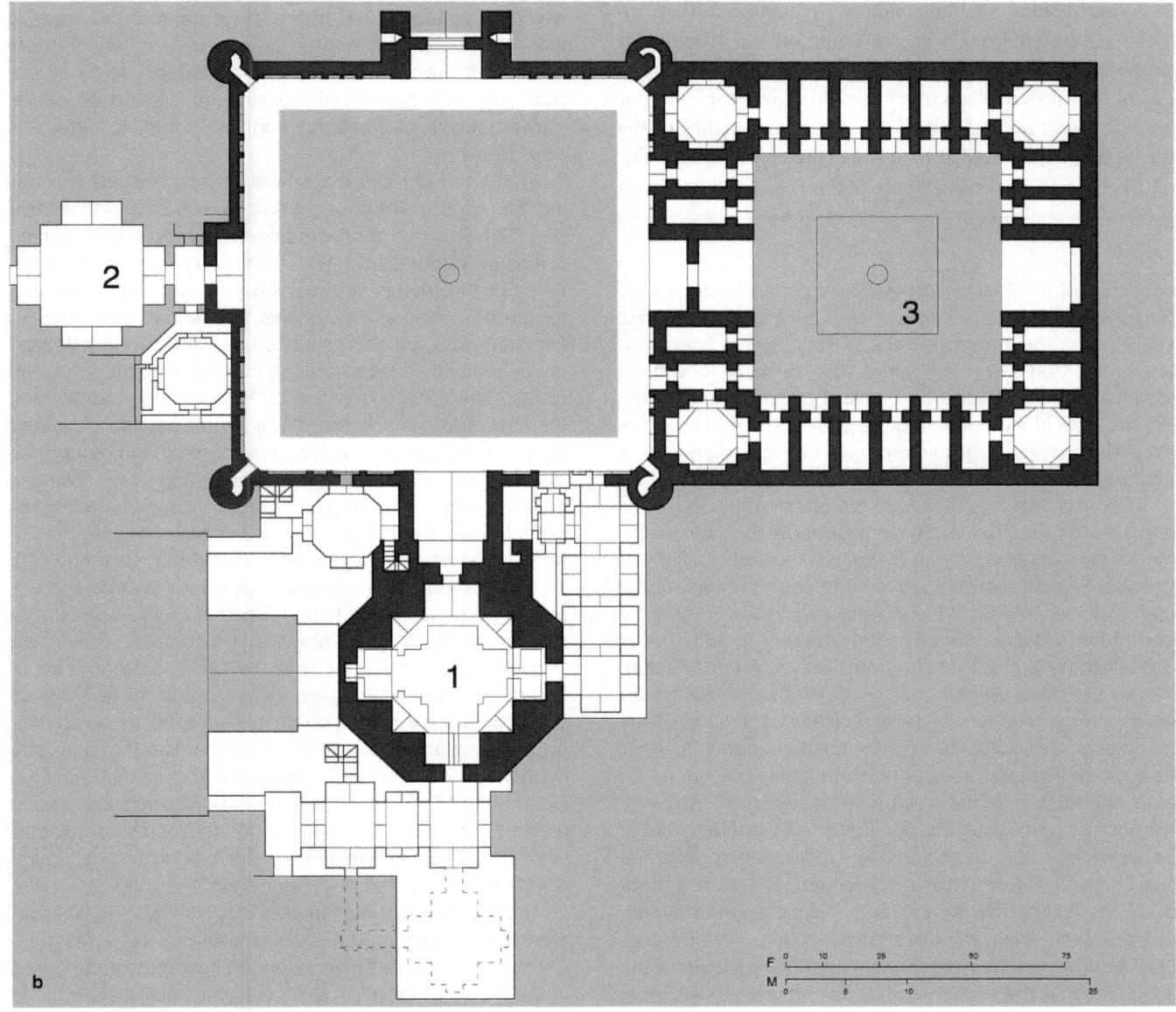

Figure 12.1-2 Samarkand, Uzbekistan. (b) Plan: (1) mausoleum of Timur and Sayid 'Umar; (2) *khanqah* for dervish-like monks; (3) *madrasa*.

The Persian Arch

The Persian arch is a pointed arch that spreads to wide, rounded sides. Unlike a simple rounded arch that can be generated from a center point on the baseline or a simple pointed arch that has two centers, the Persian arch is drawn from four different fulcrums to yield different pitches for its upper and lower parts. Most of the domes and arches of the Timurid, Safavid, and Mughal monuments were made this way. Figure 12.1-3 shows a prime example of the Persian arch.

collection of *madrasas*, arranged symmetrically around the Registan **plaza** at the midpoint of Timur's covered market street. Here, the Timurid regime in Beg's words attempted to promote "the duty of every true Muslim, man and woman, to strive after knowledge." A colossal *pishtaq* and column-like minarets at the edge of the facades framed each of the three sides of the Registan, a project that took more than a century after the patron's assassination to complete.

While the Timurids borrowed directly from the Persians, using Persian designers and craftspeople for their monumental projects, the Safavid dynasty in Iran, which claimed genuine Persian origins, tried to keep pace with the monumental achievements of the invaders from the north. At the end of the sixteenth century Shah Abbas I (r. 1587–1629) relocated the Safavid capital from Qazvin in northwestern Iran to the more central position of Isfahan. While his architects repeated many of the typical architectural solutions for palaces and religious buildings used throughout Central Asia, Shah Abbas's projects fit into a highly original urban plan attributable to the Lebanese philosopher, architect, astronomer, and poet Shaykh Baha' ad-Din (1547–1621). Between them, patron and architect more than doubled the size of the city, treating it as a single immense garden. Their additions included the new imperial palace, a vast **maydan**, at the end of which was the shah's mosque, two new covered bridges, and a garden district for the palaces of the aristocracy. As the shah's urbanization program took shape, some Safavid courtiers began to refer to Isfahan as "half of the world," meaning the part of the empire that the emperor could directly control. By 1670 the Persian capital allegedly counted 1 million residents, larger than Istanbul, Paris, or London.

Shah Abbas began his urban renewal by restructuring the center of Isfahan, enlarging the Old Maydan next to the **Masjid**-e-Jami, or Great Friday Mosque (Fig. 12.1-3), to which he also made additions. He expanded the court of the earlier Seljuk mosque of the eleventh century, framing it with four *iwans* articulated with abnormally large *muqarnas*. The enlargement of the mosque pushed its edges outward, making its external contours completely irregular (Fig. 12.1-4).

Within the old city the shah's planners rebuilt a winding 3.5 km (2 mile) covered *suk*, known as the Qaisariya (Fig. 12.1-5), which connected the area of the Masjid-e-Jami to the newly urbanized center. At the entry a caravansary donated by the shah in 1601 served as an inn and storehouse for the privileged silk merchants. Its geometrically regular, two-story arcaded court supplied the model for the dozens of new caravansaries built along the sinuous path of the *suk*. Despite the shifting direction of the street, the regularity of the new buildings and the comfort of the vaulted passages gave the city center a strong sense of order and dignity.

The new palace, Naqsh-i Jahan ("Map of the World"), consisted of a series of geometric gardens in a walled compound nearly as large as the existing city. Similar to the Ottoman precedent of Topkapi in Istanbul (see Section 11.2), its grounds included kitchens, quarters for guards and eunuchs, and a secluded harem. Each of Shah Abbas's successors added a new pavilion to the complex. During the 1640s his immediate heir built the Chihil Sutun, or Hall of Forty Columns, for formal receptions, one of the few original buildings of the compound that has survived. Its porch rose on twenty elongated wooden columns, recalling the lofty hypostyle halls of ancient Persepolis. The Hasht Bihisht, or Hall of Eight Paradises, built in 1670, followed the classic nine-square grid plan, with octagonal rooms at the corners and square rooms in between looking onto a central double-height domed hall (Fig. 12.1-6).

Nearby, the Ali Qapu palace rose six stories, with an elongated upper loggia looking over the New Maydan. Official guests were taken to the top floor to be entertained in the music room (Fig. 12.1-7), a grand hall capped with folded *muqarnas* made of wood and papier-mâché, reminiscent of those in the Friday Mosque. The immense open

1611

Persian-born Nur Jahan, wife of Akbar's heir, indirectly rules India for more than a decade

Shah Abbas I builds new Friday Mosque in Isfahan

1611–1630

1632

Shah Jahan builds the Taj Mahal in Agra

Shah Jahan deposed and kept under house arrest in the Red Fort of Agra

1659

space of the New Maydan spread more than triple the area of St. Mark's **Square** in Venice, enclosed by uniform two-story porticoes for shops and businesses. A 2 m (6.5 ft) wide canal and rows of plane trees skirted the plaza's perimeters to help cool the area, while the center was surfaced in sand for the polo tournaments popular at the time. No comparable formal space existed in other Islamic cities, excepting the Hippodrome in Istanbul.

To the west of the palace compound, Shah Abbas and Shaykh Baha' ad-Din inserted their most innovative urban feature, the park-like axial boulevard of Chahar Bagh Avenue, 110 m (360 ft) wide. The street took its name from the typical geometrically ordered Persian garden of paradise, which was divided into four quadrants. The words for the earliest Persian gardens—*pairi* (enclosed) and *daeza* (walls)—led to the word "paradise" picked up by the Greeks and spread to other cultures. Chahar Bagh's sequence of fountains and geometrically planted trees extended for 3 km (1.8 miles) on either side of the magnificent new Si-o-se Pol Bridge of thirty-three arches, built in 1602 (Fig. 12.1-8). Small interconnected chambers lined the bridge, providing a shaded pedestrian path. A second, even more impressive covered bridge furnished with sluice gates, the Pol-e Khaju, was built downstream fifty years later. The shah's palace enclave stood at the north end of the Chahar Bagh axis, while his suburban villa, Abbasabad Chahar Bagh, stood at the southern end on the other side of the bridge. The landscape designers planted the Chahar Bagh with eight rows of *chenar*, Persian plane trees, and ran a marble-lined water channel down its center, interrupted every 300 m (984

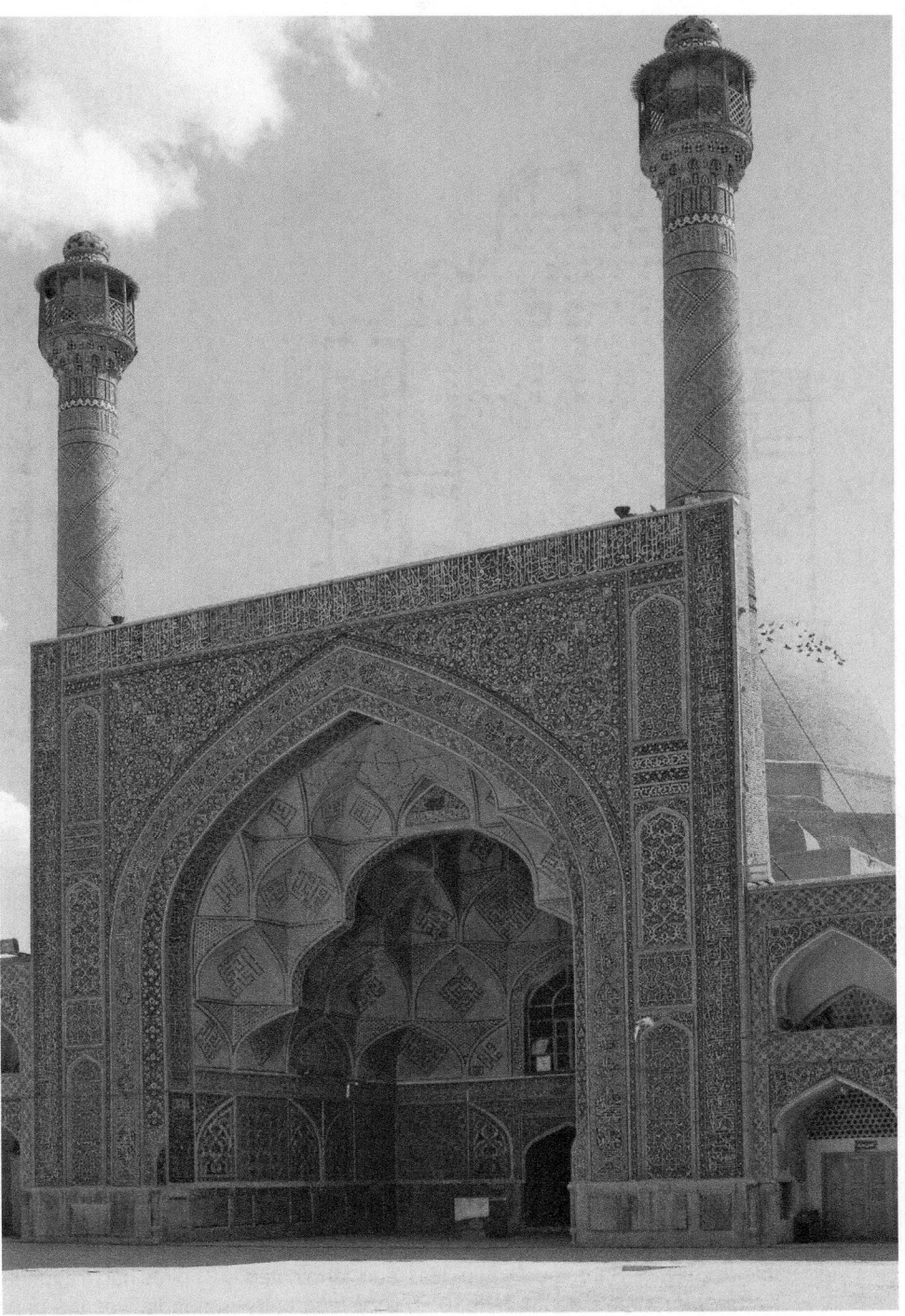

Figure 12.1-3 Isfahan, Iran. Masjid-e-Jami, the old Friday Mosque, begun in the eighth century, rebuilt in the eleventh century, and expanded by the Safavids in the sixteenth century.

ft) by large geometric pools. To either side of this refreshing axis the upper echelons of Abbas's court built walled gardens for their villas.

Two bulbous domes peered over the cornices of the New Maydan: one belonged to the Shaykh Lutfallah Mosque (Fig. 12.1-9a–c) on the east, and the other to the Masjid-i Shah Mosque on the south (Fig. 12.1-10). The great square imposed such a dominant geometric order on the area

that both of the new mosques were forced to rotate 45° to respect the southwest *qibla*. This dramatic shift enforced the distinction between secular and sacred space. The Shaykh Lutfallah Mosque was named for an exiled Shiite mystic favored by the court. It was designed by Shaykh Baha' ad-Din and was reserved for the exclusive use of the shah, his court, and his harem, who accessed the prayer hall from an underground passage beneath the Maydan.

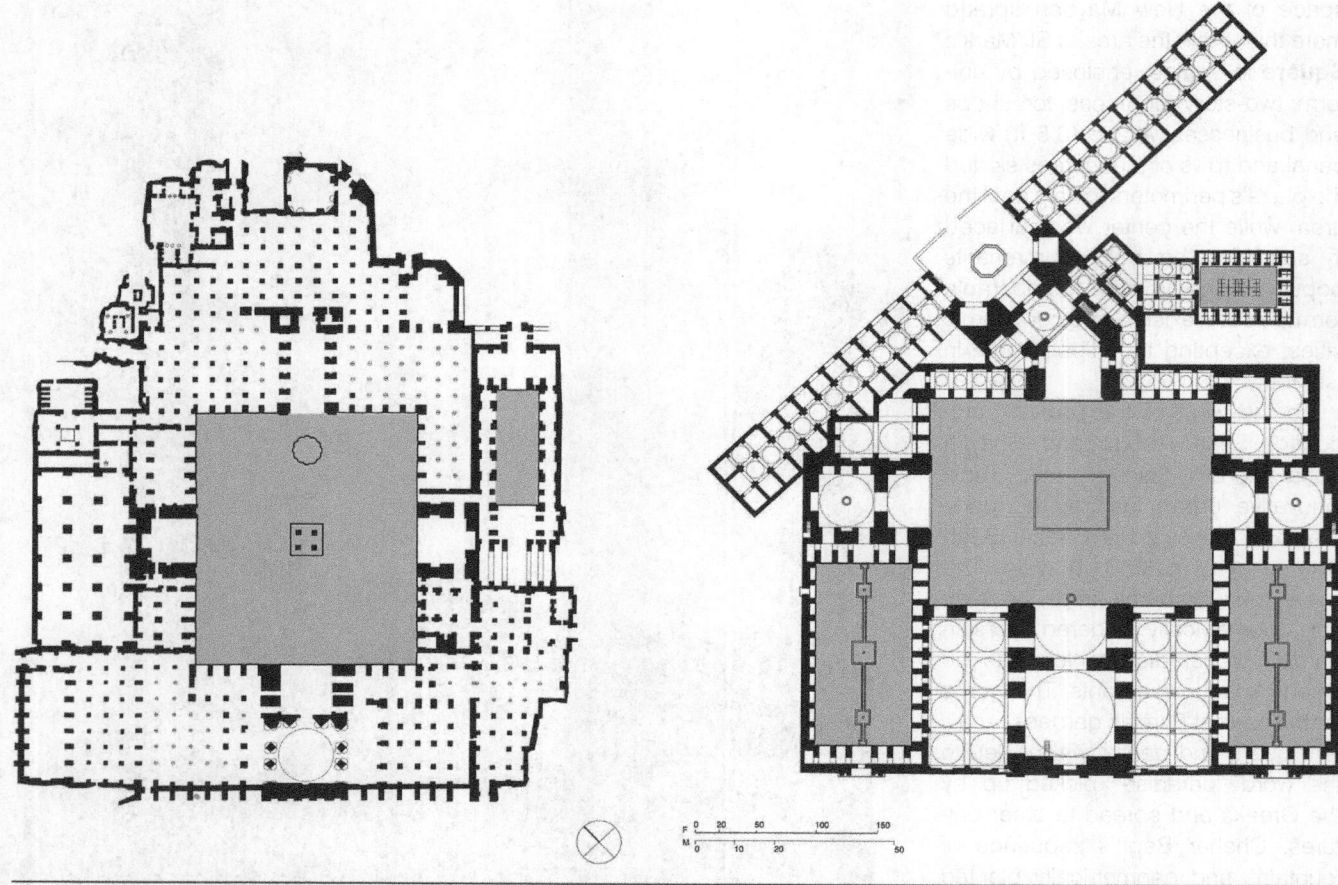

Figure 12.1-4 Isfahan, Iran. Left: Plan of the Great Mosque in the old city, eleventh–sixteenth centuries. Right: Plan of Shah Abbas I's mosque, 1530. Both are arranged around courtyards.

Begun in 1603, the *pishtaq* entry rose above the two-level arcades and looked directly across to the Ali Qapu Gate. The entry sequence resembled a labyrinth in plan, skirting the dome on a diagonal and making two right-angle turns in order to enter the domed prayer hall facing the *qibla*. Like the domes in Samarkand, the Lutfallah dome rose on a tall drum with a double shell to increase its visibility across the city. The mosque's interior and exterior tile work was among the finest achieved under the Safavids and included poems by the architect.

Construction began on the Masjid-i Shah Mosque, attributable to Shaykh Baha' ad-Din, in 1611 and terminated a year after the patron's death in 1630. The *pishtaq* entry porch appeared like a triumphal gate, its *iwan* pushing deep into a five-sided cove that sheltered a refreshing octagonal pool. Two slender minarets accentuated its verticality. The minarets served more for decoration than for communication, as the *muezzin* used a booth pitched on top of the western side of the inner court for calls to prayer. The axis shifted diagonally as it penetrated the mosque's rectangular *sahn*, each side of which had a central *pishtaq* flanked by two-story porticoes. The short sides contained *madrasas*, each served by independent rear gardens. The *pishtaq* into the mosque's prayer hall stood higher than the entry facade, contributing to the effect of a mounting succession

of planes leading to the great bulbous dome, 52 m (170 ft) high and 25 m (82 ft) in diameter. The dome's oblique orientation allowed its gracefully swelling form to be viewed in full profile as the glimmering emblem of Safavid power and the city's greatness.

The Mughal Empire: Islam Tinged with Indian Diversity

The Mughal dynasty in India experienced a parallel history to the Safavids in Iran between the early sixteenth and the mid-eighteenth centuries. The governments of the two empires had frequent, usually friendly, exchanges, and Mughal India was the principal foreign trading partner of Iran, providing the latter with cloth and foodstuffs. The Persian cultural influence on India was so strong that Farsi prevailed as the official language of the Mughal court. Iran offered refuge and support to the Mughals during their exile in the mid-sixteenth century, and Mughal emperors in turn married Persian princesses and offered Persian courtiers the highest positions in the Indian administration. Persian architectural models and motifs infiltrated India, where they mixed with the strong traditions of both Hindu and Islamic precedents.

As rulers of one of the most populous and ethnically diverse regions of the world, the Mughals relied on the power

Figure 12.1-5 Isfahan, Iran. Plan of city for Shah Abbas I, late sixteenth century.

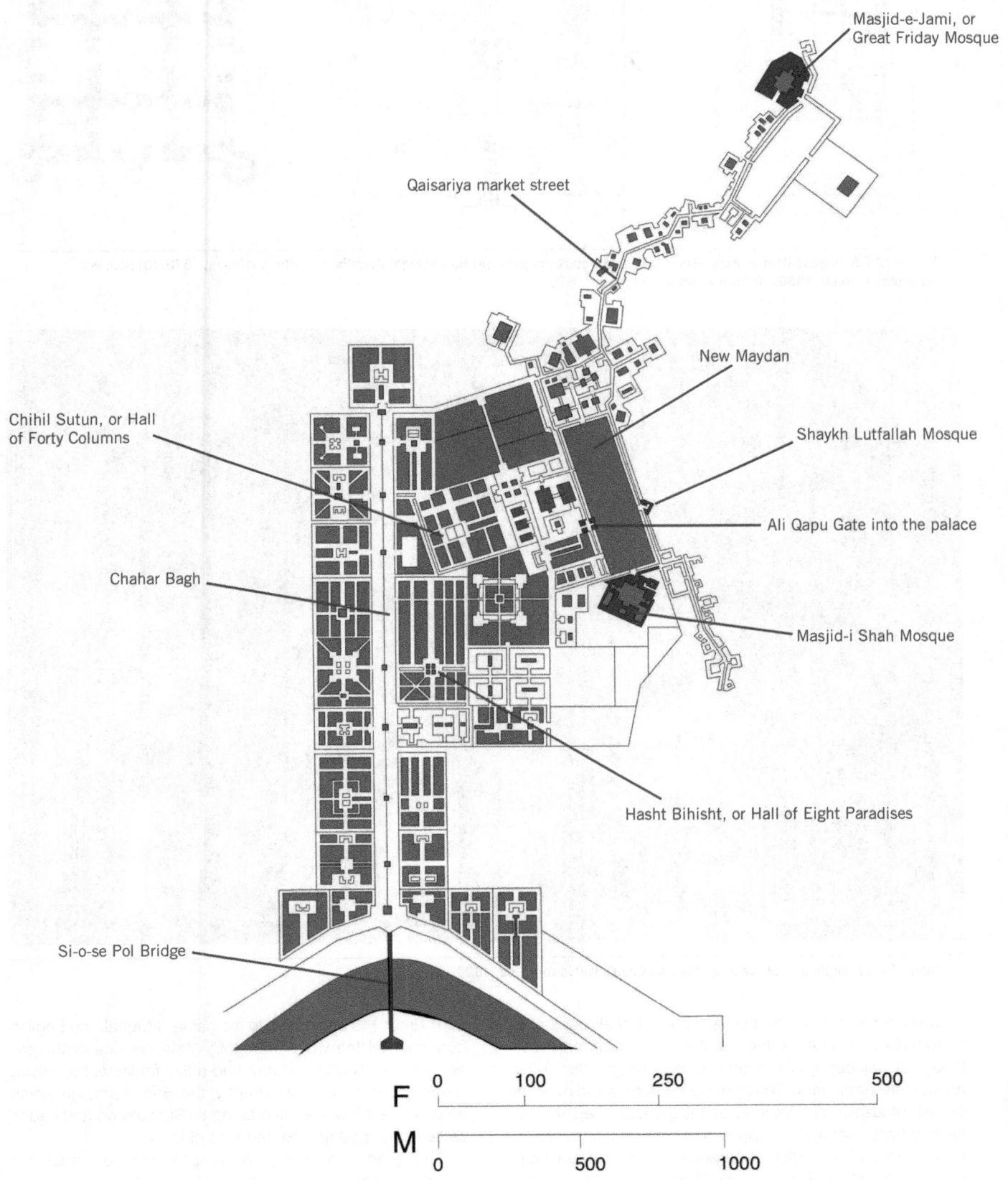

Masjid-e-Jami, or Great Friday Mosque

Qaisariya market street

New Maydan

Chihil Sutun, or Hall of Forty Columns

Shaykh Lutfallah Mosque

Ali Qapu Gate into the palace

Chahar Bagh

Masjid-i Shah Mosque

Hasht Bihisht, or Hall of Eight Paradises

Si-o-se Pol Bridge

F 0   100   250   500

M 0   500   1000

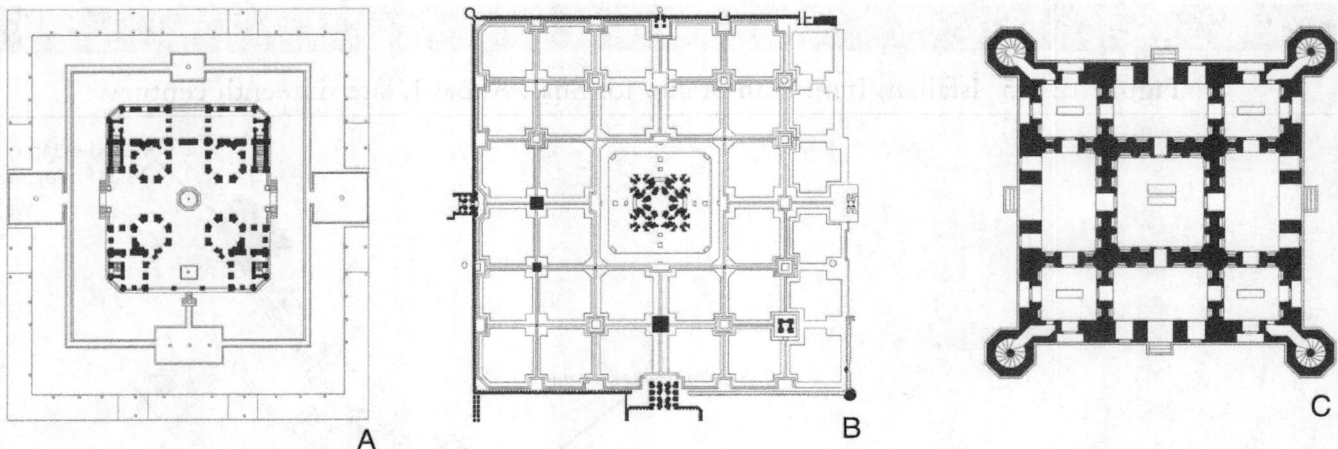

A

B

C

Figure 12.1-6 Islamic Central Asia. *Hasht bihisht* **structures in plan: (A) Hall of Eight Paradises pavilion, Isfahan, 1670; (B) Humayan Mausoleum, Delhi, 1560s; (C) Itimar-ud-Daulah, Agra, 1628.**

Figure 12.1-7 Isfahan, Iran. Ceiling of the Ali Qapu's music room, ca. 1620.

of monuments to transmit their authority. In their capitals of Lahore, Delhi, and Agra they erected impressive fortresses, mosques, palaces, gardens, and some of the grandest funerary complexes on earth. The shimmering domes and minarets of their mausoleums, set in luxuriant gardens lined with reflecting pools, geometric hedges, fruit trees, and flower beds, offered a wondrous vision of paradise. The first Mughal emperor, Babur ("the Lion," r. 1526–1530), descended directly

from Timur. His origins led to the name "Mughal," an English corruption of the word "Mongol." While not one of the dynasty's great builders, Babur had a flair for literature, writing an action-packed autobiography, the *Baburnama*, in which he described how he failed to regain Samarkand and had to settle for the bad air and bad food of Delhi.

The grand Mughal projects commenced under his grandson, Akbar ("the Great," r. 1556–1605), who with the

Figure 12.1-8 Isfahan, Iran. Si-o-se Pol (Thirty-Three-Arch) Bridge, also known as Allahverdi Khan Bridge, connecting the planted avenue of Chahar Bagh to the villas on the other side of the river, 1602.

Tomb of Humayun (Fig. 12.1-11), built for his father in Delhi between 1562 and 1571, established a new scale and order for Indian architecture. The commission began with Humayun's widow, Hamida Banu Begum, who enlisted for its execution the Persian architects Mirak Mirza Ghiyath and Sayyid Muhammad from Herat. Among the few designers of this period in India known by name, these two architects also achieved fame as poets. Political goals clearly motivated the large scale of the mausoleum, which was intended to show that Babur's line overshadowed other dynastic claims to India.

The Tomb of Humayun commands a vast *chahar bagh*, a walled paradise garden, 300 × 300 m (984 × 984 ft). The architects ran stone-lined water channels, representing the legendary rivers of paradise, to divide the park into four quadrants and set the mausoleum in the center. A palatial structure built in red sandstone with white trim, it rose on an immense square plinth surrounded with shady niches. A Persian-style bulbous dome crowned the structure. Another Persian idea, the **hasht bihisht** nine-square plan, served as the basis for both the layout of the gardens and the plan of the mausoleum. The great cupola rose above the cenotaphs in the central square. The surrounding eight squares connected radially to the central domed space. Hindu influences appeared on the parapets of the roof,

which carried decorative **chhatris**, domed kiosks raised on four or more columns, unknown to Islamic architecture but with a long heritage in India (see Section 6.3). These puffy lanterns were borrowed from the gabled aedicules where statuary was placed on Hindu temples. The endowment of the Humayun complex served benevolent social functions similar to those of the *imarets* of the Ottomans, employing 300 *hafiz* (Quran readers) and hosting a *madrasa* and a welfare kitchen.

To defend the Mughal regime against internal and external threats, Akbar constructed a series of fortress-palaces. The most important, the Red Fort in Agra (Fig. 12.1-12), begun in 1566, spread as large as a city, within 2.5 km (1.3 miles) of walls. The tawny red masonry of its gateway and the *zenana*, or women's palace, resembled the *rajput* forts of the local non-Muslim aristocracy, such as the fortress of Gwalior. Akbar absorbed elements of different sources, attempting to integrate the best from India's diverse ethnicities into a syncretic culture. This effort included marrying a Rajput (Hindu) princess, who became mother of his heir.

In 1569, after the birth of his first son and heir, Akbar established a religious memorial, a *khanqah*, devoted to Shaykh Salim, a holy man of the Chishti cult (the Indian version of Sufism) who had foretold the event. For its location he chose a hillside at Sikri, 37 km (23 miles) southeast of Agra, the

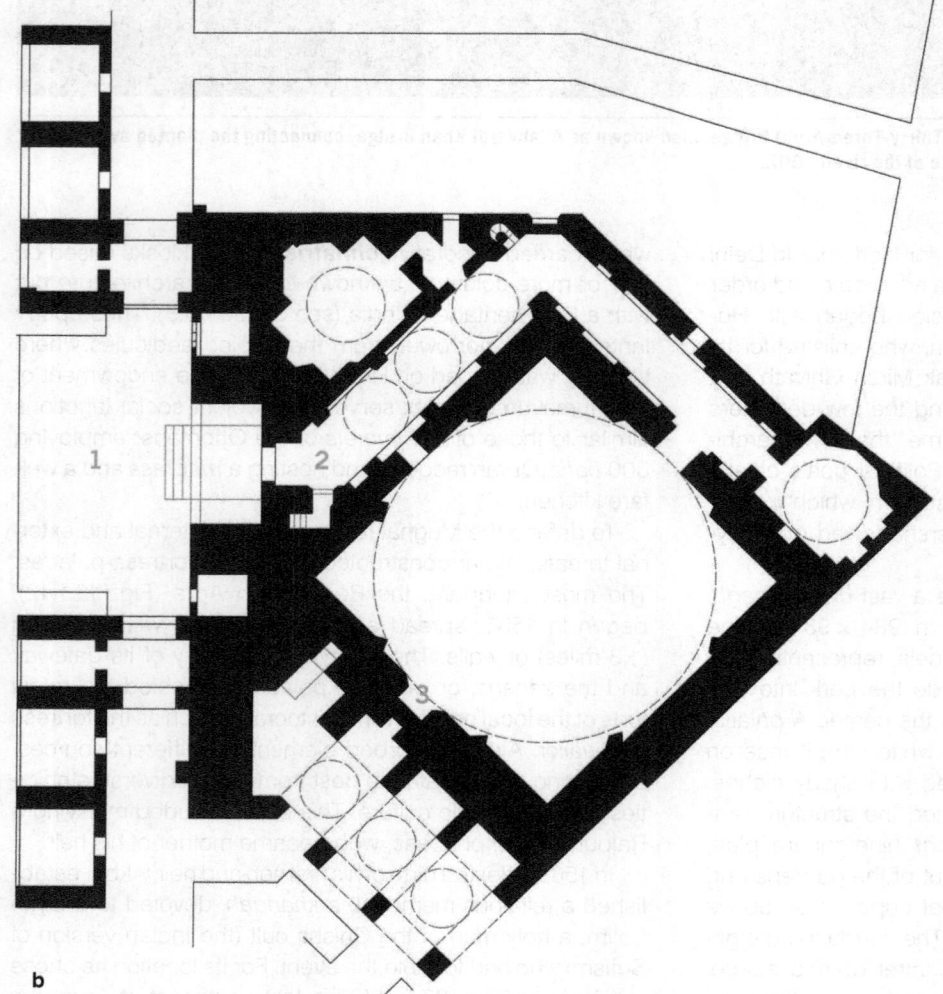

Figure 12.1-9 Isfahan, Iran.
(a) Lutfallah Mosque, Shaykh Baha'
ad-Din, 1603. (b) Plan, showing:
(1) *iwan* entry from New Maydan;
(2) secret tunnel entry for women
from the royal harem; (3) *mihrab*.
(c) See facing page.

Figure 12.1-9 Isfahan, Iran. Lutfallah Mosque. (c) Tile work.

Figure 12.1-10 Isfahan, Iran. View of New Maydan to the Masjid-i Shah, ca. 1620.

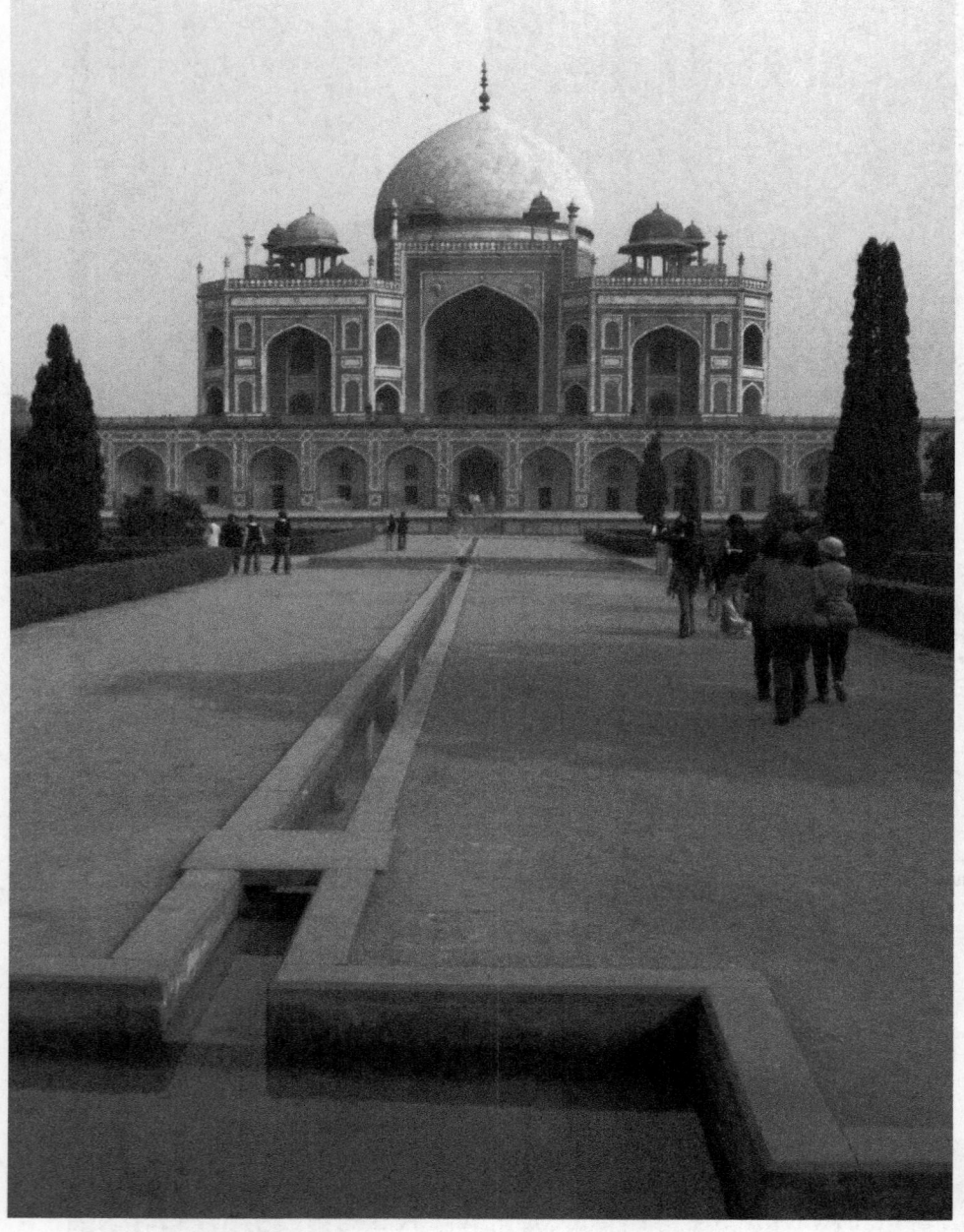

Figure 12.1-11 Delhi, India. Tomb of Humayun, Mirak Mirza Ghiyath and Sayyid Muhammad, 1560s.

a lake, which later dried up. The Great Mosque and the imperial palace occupied an acropolis in the center, following a strict east–west alignment (with the *qibla* direction pointing west toward Mecca). The streets and buildings below the hill ran on a northeast–southwest grid, diagonal to the upper precinct. In front of the gate, between the palace and the lake, Akbar's planners set three square caravansary compounds for foreign traders, similar in scale to those at Isfahan.

The white marble dome of the mausoleum of Shaykh Salim sat at the religious core of Fatehpur Sikri, in the court of the Great Mosque. It still attracts pilgrims. Perforated marble screens, known as *jalis*, graced its elevations, giving the interiors a golden glow of mottled light. One entered the mosque complex on the south through the colossal Buland Darwaza (the Sublime Gate) (Fig. 12.1-14). Its formidable *pishtaq* rose at the summit of a pyramidal set of red sandstone stairs, looking over the city like a triumphal arch; indeed, its construction was financed by Akbar's military campaigns to the west. The arch carefully asserted its religious purpose through white marble inscriptions quoting the Quran. Beyond the threshold, the cornice of the gate stepped down three levels, each lined with rows of bell-like *chhatris*, to adjust to the lower scale of the court. The Great Mosque opened to the court with a rhythmic series of arches set at alternating widths like the rhythmic trabeation of Italian mannerists (see Section 11.3). In the center the *pishtaq*, with its graceful Persian-arched *iwan*, concealed the central of three domes.

quarry site for the exquisite rust-colored sandstone used on the Red Fort. Four years later, after his conquest of the Gujarat area to the southwest, the emperor decided to expand the project into a new capital city, which he named Fatehpur Sikri (Fig. 12.1-13), meaning "victory." He impressed craftspeople from the conquered Gujarat region to build his ideological testament. Although Akbar used the new city for only fifteen years, he built it with no expense spared as a permanent imperial setting. Like Pienza or Machu Picchu (see Sections 10.1 and 10.3), the monumental district of Akbar's capital served as a short-lived utopian experiment. The town layout roughly fit into a rectangle, bordered on three sides by fortifications. The northwest flank opened to

The palace complex at Fatehpur Sikri (Fig. 12.1-15), although detached from the mosque, followed the same orientation and implied many religious connections. The eastern half of the palace served the king and his administrators, while the more intimate western half housed the *zenana*, or women's quarters. Each of the palace's individual parts obeyed perfect symmetry even as they were distributed diagonally as a series of broad terraces in staggered positions. In the eastern zone the unusual composition of interlocking terraces permitted continuous oblique views across the separate sectors of the vast expanse.

Akbar commissioned several unique structures to put himself on display to the public. An elevated platform

Figure 12.1-12 Agra, India. Red Fort, begun by Akbar, 1560s.

Figure 12.1-13 Fatehpur Sikri, India. The *sahn* courtyard of the mosque. The large *iwan* on the left is the entry of the mosque; the white structure in the center is the tomb of Shaykh Salim, 1580s.

(Fig. 12.1-16) in the throne room gave onto a window of appearances, known as the *jharoka*, for the daily ceremony of showing himself to his people. On the courtyard side, this platform overlooked the Anup Talao pool, a square tank with four cross-axial bridges leading to a central island platform, where Akbar would appear to his court, shaded by silk umbrellas. North of this terrace, a slightly lower terrace served as the site for an exceptional structure, the Diwan-i Khas (Fig. 12.1-17), a cubic two-story volume capped with tall *chhatris* that accentuated each corner and ornate

Hindu-style brackets supporting the balconies. Inside, a single column capped with a cluster of thirty-six radiating brackets as tall as the column's shaft occupied the double-height space. It supported a circular platform reached by four diagonally placed catwalks. Akbar allegedly sat on top of the column to preside over religious debates. Although careful to portray himself as a devout Muslim, he invited a series of spiritual leaders, including Hindus, Sikhs, Zoroastrians, Jews, Jains, and Jesuits, to participate in these debates, leading to the proposal of a new "Religion of God,"

Figure 12.1-14 Fatehpur Sikri, India. Buland Darwaza (Sublime Gate), 1570s.

Din-i Ilahi, over which he presided as the divinely sanctioned arbiter.

In the western zone of Akbar's palace rose a five-level pyramidal structure, the Panch Mahal. Structured on a hypostyle grid, it looked like a steel-frame high-rise. The *jali* screens that once sheathed the structure have disappeared, leaving it as open as a scaffold. From the top stories the women of the *zenana* could catch the breezes coming off the lake and peek into Akbar's courtyard through the screens.

Akbar's heir, Jahangir ("World Conqueror," r. 1605–1627), was at one point opposed to his father's authority but in retrospect praised him. Once in power, he took a background position, leaving much of the empire's administration to his wife, Nur Jahan ("Light of the World," 1577–1645), a widow of Persian origin whom he married in 1611. Assisted by her father and brother, she took command of the government and proved to be a gifted

---

CONSTRUCTION, TECHNOLOGY, THEORY

The Great Central Asian Observatories

Ulugh Beg's scientific quests led to the construction in 1420 of the Great Observatory of Samarkand, a three-story cylindrical structure 48 m (157 ft) in diameter, slightly broader than the Pantheon in Rome. He set his study center on a hill outside the city before knowledge of telescopes. Although only the foundations and the underground stone-lined arc used to register astronomical alignments remain, the observatory apparently contained a large crescent bisected by a staircase. Three centuries later Jai Singh II modeled his superb observatories, the so-called Jantar Mantar in Delhi and Jaipur, on this earlier scientific adventure.

Delhi, India. Jantar Mantar, astronomical observatory, seventeenth century.

Figure 12.1-15 Fatehpur Sikri. India. Palace plan, 1570s.

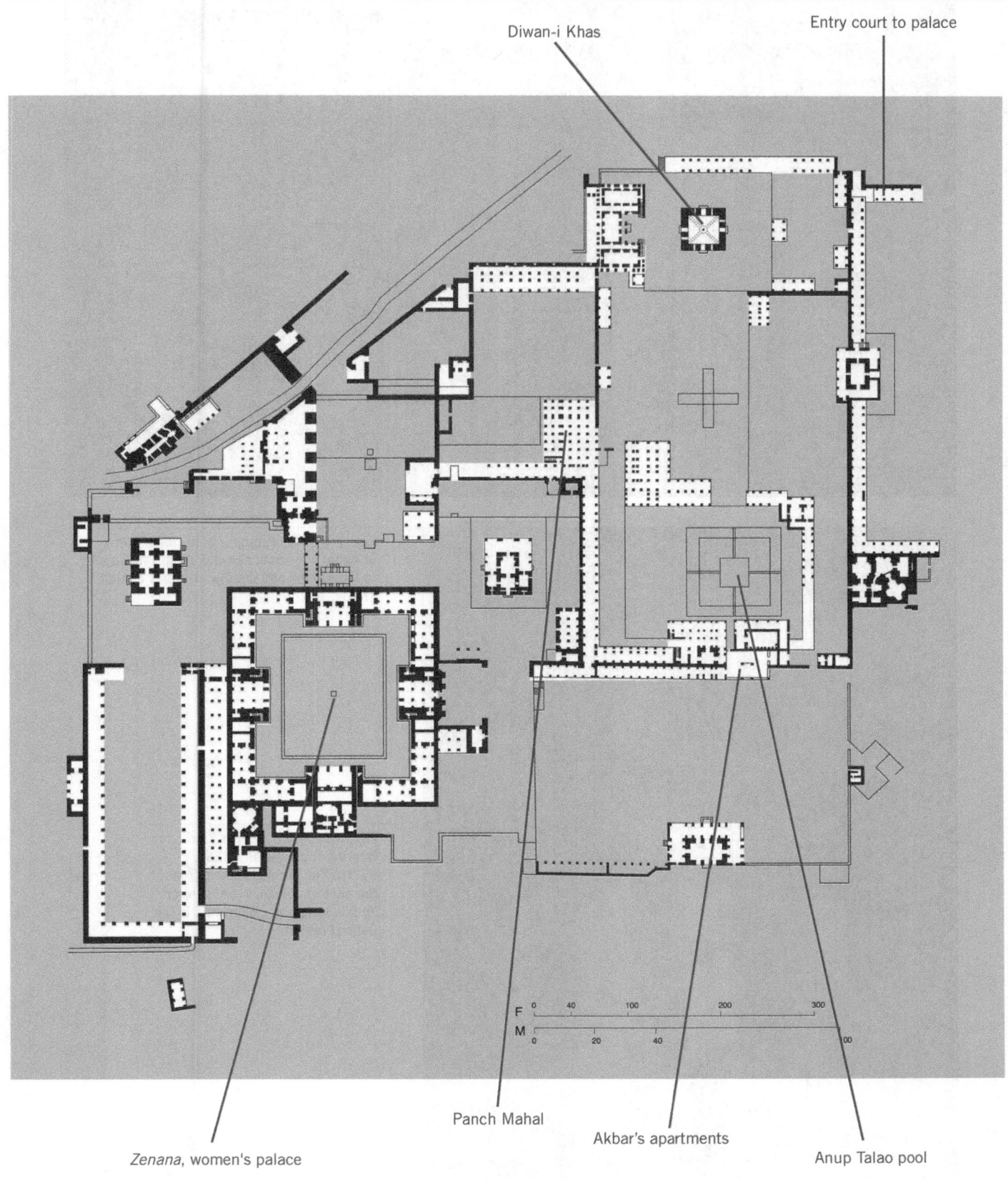

Diwan-i Khas

Entry court to palace

Panch Mahal

Akbar's apartments

Anup Talao pool

Zenana, women's palace

Figure 12.1-16 Fatehpur Sikri, India. View of Akbar's terrace, showing Anup Talao pool in foreground and the Diwan-i Khas behind, 1570s.

Figure 12.1-17 Fatehpur Sikri. Interior of the Diwan-i Khas, 1570s. The brackets rising from the central column were inspired by Jain religious monuments in the Gujarat region.

Figure 12.1-18 Agra, India. I'timad-ud-Daulat, tomb built for Nur Jahan's Persian parents, 1628.

minister of finance. Although confined to the *zenana*, Nur Jahan presided over political appointments and economic policies dealing with foreign trade. She amassed considerable personal wealth. Aside from her political role she wrote poetry, designed carpets and clothes, and as a patron of architecture had no equal at this time. Aside from the immense platform tombs she designed for Jahangir and herself, plus several civil works near Lahore, her most inspired project was the beautifully proportioned tomb and gardens of I'timad-ud-Daulat, built for her parents in Agra (Fig. 12.1-18). Sited across the river from the Red Fort, she had the mausoleum clad completely in white marble and decorated with elaborate intarsia of precious stones in floral patterns. Her project initiated the tradition of Mughal tombs with minarets at each corner of the volume.

The greatest Mughal builder, Shah Jahan ("Ruler of the World," r. 1628–1658, d. 1666), the grandson of Akbar and stepson of Nur Jahan, took an active interest in all aspects of design. During his reign the empire reached its zenith in economic terms, and he spent lavishly, rebuilding most of the internal structures of the Red Fort at Agra in white marble (Fig. 12.1-19). In Delhi he founded an analogous Red Fort, known as Shahjahanabad. Shah Jahan sponsored works in an unconventional style, parallel to European mannerism, using columns shaped like drooping balustrades, bulging cupolas, and scalloped arches. He introduced the roof type with down-curved eaves, borrowed from Hindu temples in Bengal. All of his favorite stylistic devices appeared in the small Najina Masjid of 1637 (Fig. 12.1-20), the mosque for the court women inside the Red Fort of Agra. Three jewel-like marble domes crowned its porch.

Figure 12.1-19 Agra, India. Shah Jahan's new terrace in the Red Fort with scalloped arches and Bengali roofs, 1630s.

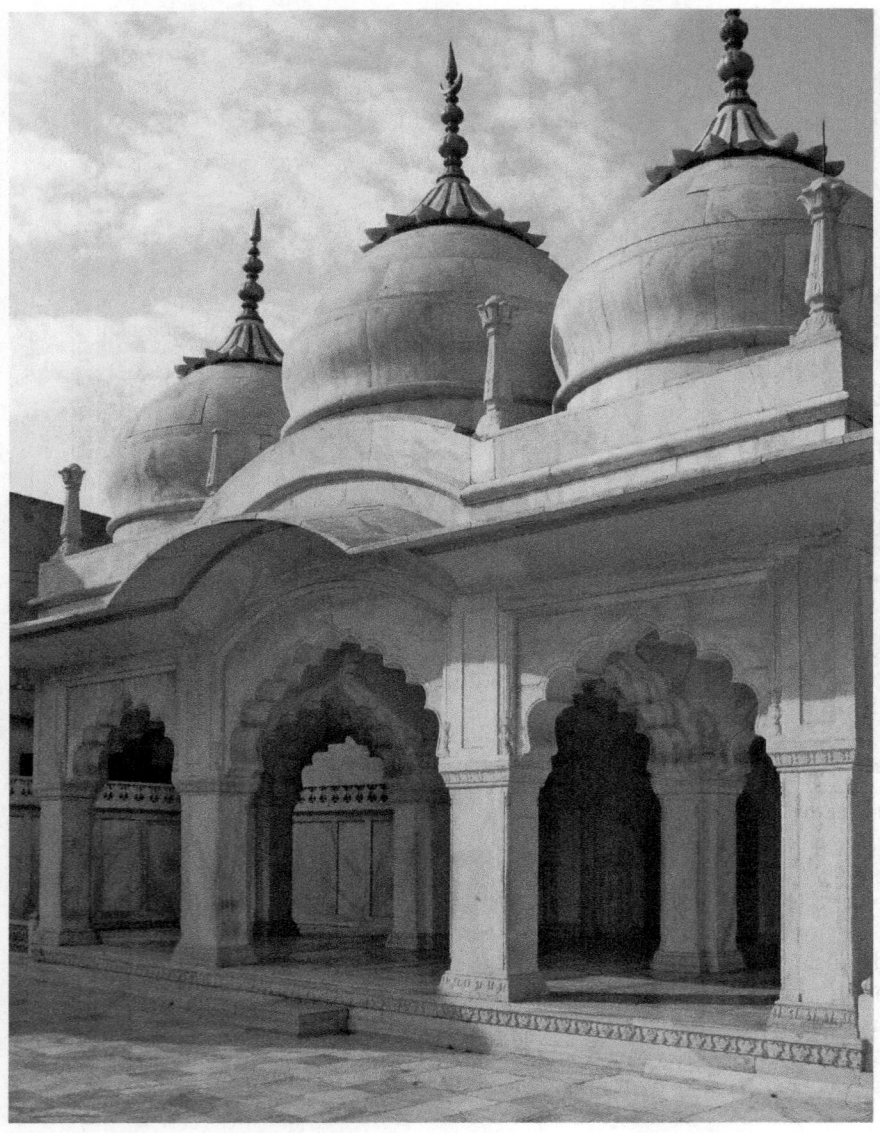

Figure 12.1-20 Agra, India. Najina Mosque, known as the "Ladies Mosque," inside the Red Fort, showing the flamboyant style of Shah Jahan, 1637.

Another important woman in the Mughal court, Shah Jahan's wife, Mumtaz Mahal ("Palace Favorite"), inspired the Taj Mahal (Fig. 12.1-21), properly known as Rauz-i Munavvara, or "Illuminated Tomb." Mumtaz, niece of Nur Jahan, died at age thirty-eight giving birth to her fourteenth child. Construction on the tomb began in 1632 and took twenty years to complete. The probable architect, Ustad Ahmad Lahouri, a Persian born in Lahore, also worked on the design of Shahjahanabad in Delhi. The monument's soaring white profile overlooked the Jamuna River in the southeastern suburbs of Agra, downstream from the Red Fort. The Taj Mahal included its own village, known as Mumtazabad, in the southern area in front of the gate. Once an orderly landscape of caravansaries, shops, and rental properties that provided revenue for the maintenance of the complex, it is now overrun with spontaneous development.

One entered the complex through a grand *pishtaq* built in red sandstone and decorated with white marble intarsia. Its *iwan* framed a view of the dome in the distance and opened to a conventional *chahar bagh* garden, about the same size as that of the Humayun complex. Four cross-axial channels met at a central square fountain that caught reflections of the dome. At the end of the north–south axis, set on a solid white plinth, the marble-clad

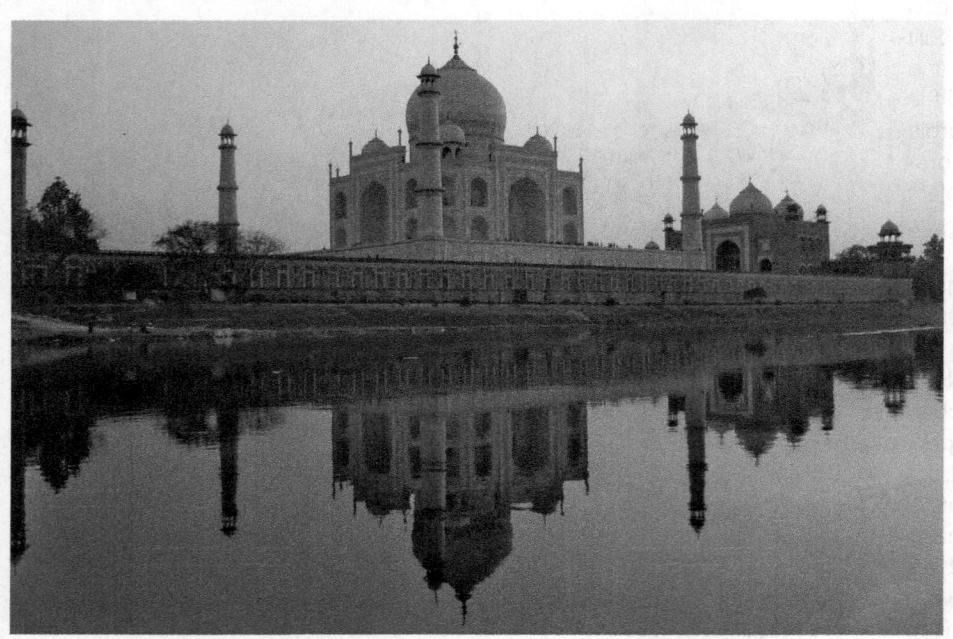

Figure 12.1-21 Agra, India. Taj Mahal, view from the river, with the mosque on the right, 1632–1652.

The Plan of Shahjahanabad, Delhi

Shah Jahan moved the Mughal capital to Delhi in 1639, creating the new fortified city of Shahjahanabad, now known as the Red Fort. Delhi had been settled since 1000 BCE, and was preceded by eight other cities, including Din Panah, used by earlier Mughal rulers. Compared to Akbar's Fatehpur Sikri, Shahjahanabad followed a regular, symmetrical plan. The overall figure was an elongated octagon, 820 × 492 m (2,690 × 1,614 ft). The important palace structures straddled the eastern wall overlooking the river, while the internal areas adhered to

a cross-axis lined with shops for the **bazaar** and covered with high vaults on the Persian model.

A square market plaza occupied the intersection of the two major streets. Beyond this a larger plaza opened to the public ***diwan*** audience hall, where the emperor could be seen framed by baluster columns in the *jharoka*. About 60,000 people, half of them connected to the army, lived inside the palace-fortress. Outside Shahjahanabad's walls stretched a semicircular city for another 400,000, with a single grand east–west axis leading to the fortress gate.

Delhi, India. Plan of Shahjahanabad, 1630s, showing: (1) principal gate to the city; (2) protected market; (3) the *diwan*, where the sultan held court; (4) palace and harem area.

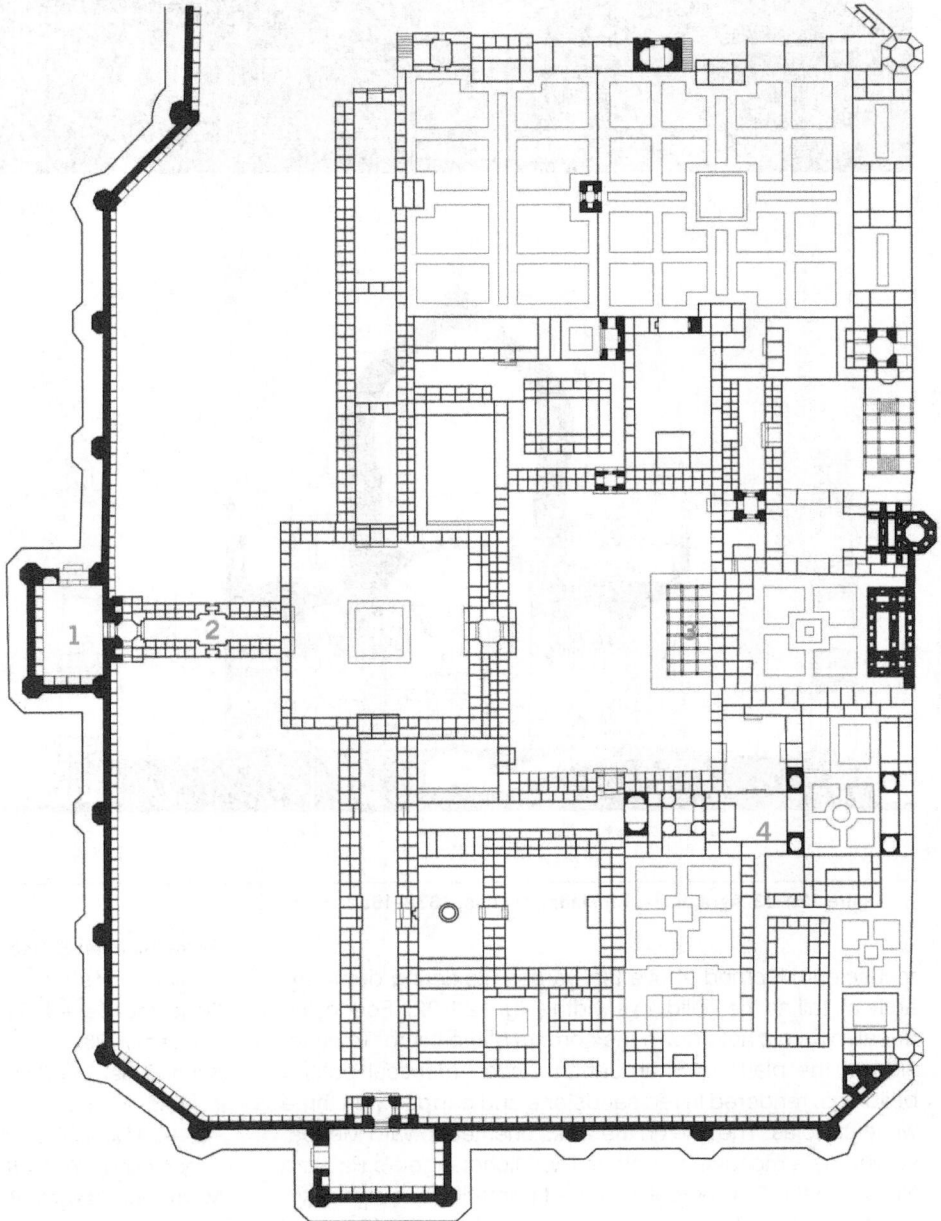

**Figure 12.1-22 Agra, India.
Taj Mahal, 1632–1652.**

desired for New St. Peter's, but with considerably more mass. The plan of the ground floor reveals that the interior was designed with more wall *poché* than voids. While the Taj Mahal appeared to be a solid stone structure, it was built entirely in brick and then clad in smooth, almost seamless, gray-veined white marble. Exquisite black and red intarsia in floral patterns framed its edges. The designers elegantly resolved the problem of allowing the dome to be seen over the volume of the building by raising it on an extra-tall drum (Fig. 12.1-23). The inner dome reached a height of 25 m (82 ft) as a near hemisphere, while the great bulbous shape of the outer dome soared more than twice that height, surrounded on four sides by octagonal *chhatris*.

In 1658, Shah Jahan's son deposed and imprisoned him, forcing the builder of the Taj Mahal to live under house arrest in the comfort of the *zenana* of the Red Fort in Agra. From the balconies under the curved Bengal roof that he had added to the palace at the beginning of his reign, the deposed emperor passed his final eight years in contemplation of his grandest creation, its dome reflected in the river, a vision of a perfect world that would eventually serve as his own final resting place.

Further Reading

Asher, Catherine B. *Architecture of Mughal India*. Cambridge: Cambridge University Press, 1992.

Blake, Stephen P. *Half the World: The Social Architecture of Safavid Isfahan, 1590–1722*. Costa Mesa, CA: Mazda, 1999.

Degeorge, Gérard. *Samarkand, Bukhara, Khiva*. Paris: Flammarion, 2001.

Koch, Ebba. *The Complete Taj Mahal and the Riverfront Gardens of Agra*. London: Thames & Hudson, 2006.

———. *Mughal Architecture: An Outline of Its History and Development (1526–1858)*. New York: Oxford University Press, 1991.

Moynihan, Elizabeth B. *Paradise as a Garden in Persia and Mughal India*. New York: George Braziller, 1979.

Tillotson, Giles. *Mughal India*. London: Penguin, 1991.

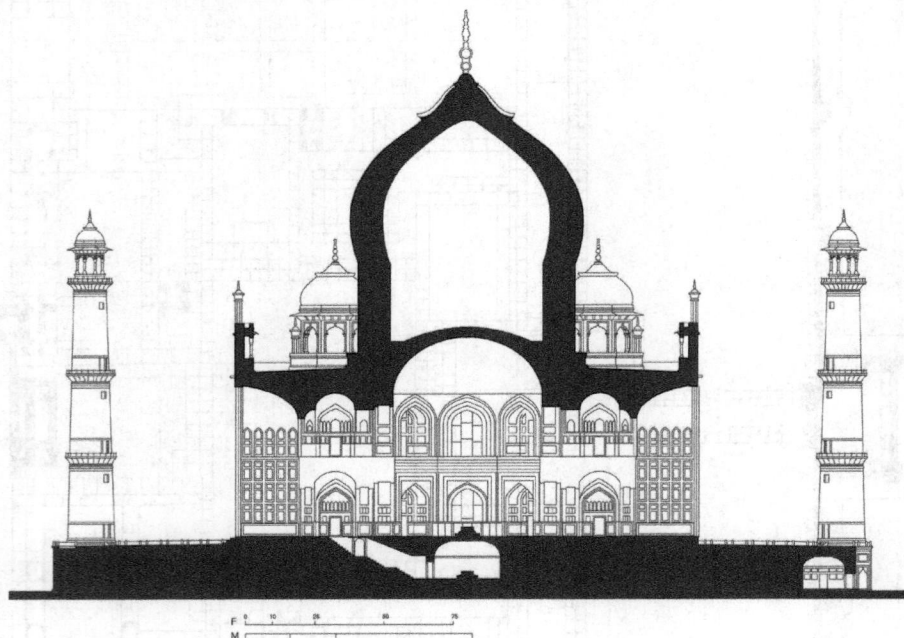

Figure 12.1-23 Agra, India. Taj Mahal, section, 1632–1652.

mausoleum loomed above the garden, its flaring dome exactly as tall as the building's width (Fig. 12.1-22). Four cylindrical minarets held down the corners of the plinth. To either side of the platform Shah Jahan placed identical oblong buildings, rendered in red sandstone and capped with three white cupolas. The one on the west, oriented toward Mecca, served as a mosque; the other, like Michelangelo's Palazzo Nuovo on the Campidoglio, served primarily for symmetry.

The plan of the mausoleum repeated the *hasht bihisht* scheme, achieving the kind of central plan that Bramante

12.2 CATHOLIC EUROPE
The Settings of Absolutism

While political power often jumped from one region to another, leadership in design did not necessarily follow. Spain and France became the dominant powers in Europe during the seventeenth century, but the architectural models continued to come from Italy. The Roman Catholic Church remained central to the culture of the three regions, launching the Counter-Reformation in 1563 at the conclusion of the Council of Trent to undermine the Protestant Reformation. The expanded activities of the Counter-Reformation church included the founding of new religious orders, the training of missionaries, new bureaucratically run parish structures, an increase of rituals and sacraments, and the construction of numerous religious colleges and churches. Above all, Catholicism promoted a theatrical approach to religion to stimulate the enthusiasm of the faithful, a strategy that encouraged the great urban set pieces designed in Rome by Bernini and his colleagues.

Spain prided itself on being "the most Catholic nation," and, as if to prove it, Philip II built the Escorial monastery as his preferred residence during the late sixteenth century. France vied with Spain as "the very Christian nation" and for much of the first half of the seventeenth century allowed cardinals to run the country. When Louis XIV assumed power in 1661, he established the model of absolutist power, drawing on papal protocol, including elaborate costumes, ceremonies, and scenery, to reinforce his authority. His palace and vast gardens at Versailles served as the ultimate theatrical setting for the projection of the illusion that the monarch controlled the entire world.

Habsburg Spain: The Catholic Mandate for Classical Rigor

In an age characterized by theatricality and decorative excess, the aesthetics of the Habsburg dynasty in Spain during the late sixteenth and early seventeenth centuries offered an austere counterpoint. The court dressed in black with stiff white collars and became famous for its sober comportment. Spain's national unity had been achieved during the previous centuries as a result of the religious crusade against the Islamic occupants of the south. The resulting military structure clung to its "divine mission." In the late sixteenth century the Habsburgs exerted claims to widespread territories including Italy, Austria, Germany, Burgundy, and the Netherlands, emerging as the dominant military power in Europe. The wealth accruing from Spanish possessions both in Europe and in the newly colonized regions of the Americas raised the level of well-being in many Spanish cities, particularly the port of Seville.

Charles V, the Holy Roman emperor (r. 1519–1556) and the first Habsburg king of Spain (r. 1516–1556), brought the region to the apex of its power. A few years before his demise he decided to make amends after a lifetime of battles and abdicated the throne, retiring to a monastery. His son and successor, Philip II (r. 1556–1598), moved the capital from Valladolid to the relatively small town of Madrid, where he could remain free of the feudal politics of the past. Like his father, who had commissioned Diego de Sagredo to translate Vitruvius, the new king favored the classical style of early sixteenth-century Rome and requested a Spanish translation of Sebastiano Serlio's treatise. He developed his greatest architectural project, the monastery of San Lorenzo at Escorial, 50 km (31 miles) north of the new capital. While Philip II sponsored several other palaces and gardens and renewed the plazas and public buildings in a few major Spanish cities, he clearly intended the severe and well-balanced design of the Escorial to serve as an antidote to the Alhambra and a manifesto of his ideological goals. Contrary to the mannerist flamboyance found in Italy, he proposed the *estilo desornamentado* ("undecorated style"). He believed that the use of correct classicism in architecture encouraged correct attitudes in both religion and government.

Philip conceived the Escorial with his father as a site for dynastic burials. Planning for the complex began in 1559, the year of Charles V's death, under Juan Bautista de Toledo (1515–1567), who had worked with Michelangelo on the plans for the dome of St. Peter's. The Italian-trained architect designed the convent's gridded plan (Fig. 12.2-1), allegedly a conceit representing St. Lawrence's symbol of the grill. The convent's area was roughly equal to that of the Süleymaniye in Istanbul. Like the great mosque and the subsidiary buildings of its *imaret*, the Escorial followed a complex program, starting with a grand domed church in the center, a royal mausoleum, a monastery for 100 monks, a religious college, a palace for the king's court, the royal apartments, a hospital attached to the southwest corner, a grand plaza, and three blocks of office buildings surrounding the convent on the north and one block on the west.

The construction of the Escorial began in 1563. After the death of Juan de Toledo in 1567, his assistant, Juan de Herrera (1530–1597), took charge of the design, working closely with the king to create a distinctive, pure style. Built of solid blocks of granite, a type of stone difficult to carve with subtle details, the structure's facades were stripped to a bare minimum, leaving the impression of austere grandeur. The southern prospect presented a long unbroken plane, overlooking terraced gardens and a fishery (Fig. 12.2-2). Its forty-six bays repeated the same design relentlessly, without variation, more like a penal institution than a luxurious palace.

For the western entry facade, Herrera prepared a more articulated central portal, similar to the standard church facade presented in Serlio's treatise: two levels of colossal paired half-columns, the lower set supporting a Doric entablature and the narrower upper level joined by simple volutes to Ionic orders

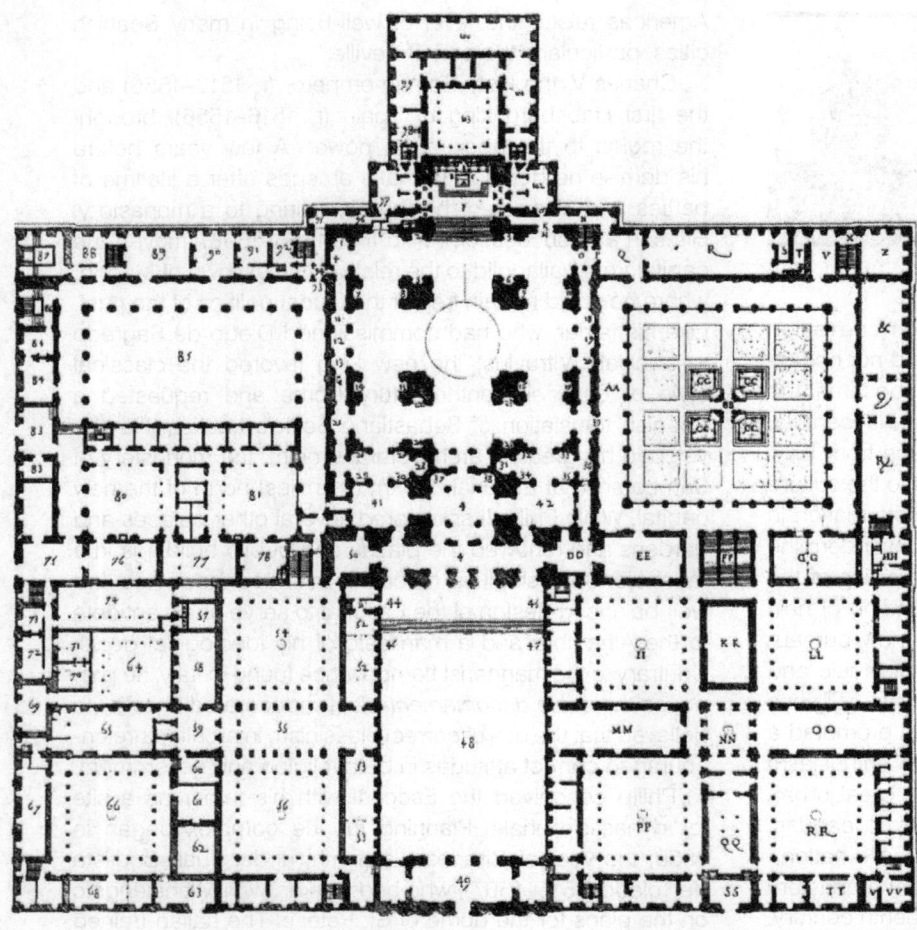

Figure 12.2-1 San Lorenzo de El Escorial, Spain. Plan of El Escorial by Juan de Toledo and Juan de Herrera, 1567–1590. The convent was divided by the large court and church in the center. The cruciform corridors to the left and to the right of the central court were for a religious college and the monks' cells, respectively. The royal courtiers used the court on the upper left, and the king had a suite and small court behind the apse of the church. His bedroom was to the right of the apse, with a window that opened to the altar.

carrying a conventional triangular entablature. The architect reserved the most decorative aspect of the exterior for the roofs above the corner towers: steeply pitched, slate-covered pyramids topped with pointed spires, built by Flemish carpenters in the style of Burgundian castles. This roof type, so unlike the low-pitched Mediterranean tiled roofs of Spain, became the signature element of the Habsburg dynasty's projects and a vestige of their ill-fated claims to northern Europe.

The entry into the Escorial led to a long court, the Royal Patio (Fig. 12.2-3). On the left stood the seminary and on the right the convent, each subdivided by long wings arranged in cruciform and enclosing four square courts. The church, flanked by two bell towers, faced the entry with a second facade, this one carrying a broken pediment. The Jesuit friar Juan Bautista Villalpando later published a treatise (1596–1604) in which he reasoned that the Vitruvian principles of the Escorial were sanctioned by the biblical descriptions of the Temple of Solomon. Indeed, statues of the biblical kings David and Solomon graced the entry to the Escorial's church. The church's square central plan capped by a dome imitated Bramante's and Michelangelo's preferred design for St. Peter's in Rome. The dome rose on a tall drum articulated by paired columns separated by arches. The elaborate Habsburg crypt, the new burial site for the royal family, lay directly beneath the altar. Philip II and the architects of the Escorial established a new vision of Catholic order, markedly distinct from the ornate Gothic and *mudéjar* styles of the recent Spanish past. While they clearly drew from Roman classicism and Serlio's treatise, the clean lines of the Escorial's *estilo desornamentado*, its uncompromised symmetry, and the rational order of the whole surpassed the Italian models.

Juan de Herrera, and after him Francisco de Mora and his nephew Juan Gomez de Mora, brought a similar sense of order and minimal decoration to numerous royal and municipal projects. After a 1561 fire in Valladolid, the king ordered the rebuilding of the Plaza Mayor as a clean rectangular void with uniform arcades. Its proportions of 2:3 were repeated in the Plaza Mayor in Madrid, Philip II's most significant public project, which Herrera initiated in 1590 (Fig. 12.2-4a,b). Set in a sloping part of the town, the plaza was leveled and enclosed by regular arcades. Unlike Italian precedents, it lacked a major monumental focus. The king paid

---

TIME LINE

▼ **1559**

El Escorial royal monastery planned near Madrid

Protestant Henri IV converts to Catholicism as king of France

▲ **1589**

▼ **1604**

Henri IV sponsors Place des Vosges in Paris

Henri IV assassinated in Paris

▲ **1610**

▼ **1616**

Marie de' Medici builds Cours la Reine

for the only building of distinction, the Pana-
deria, or bakery, which had classical half-
columns at its base and was set off from
the other houses by turrets with Habsburg
roofs. The facades of the other buildings,
completed during the first half of the seventeenth century, followed a uniformly severe
style, with four floors of regularly placed windows above the ground-floor arcades. Like
the *sahn* of a mosque, the Plaza Mayor appeared internally coherent but did not relate
to the alignments of existing streets running
into it. Successive royal plazas in Spanish
cities, such as Salamanca, adopted a similar approach of cutting a square out of the
existing fabric of the city.

The strict order of the plazas at Valladolid and Madrid served as guides for the
production of public spaces in Spanish
colonial towns. As early as 1573, the king
applied these models to the American
colonies in the "Laws of the Indies," which
specified, "Around the (central) plaza . . .
there shall be porticos, for these are of
considerable convenience to the merchants" (see Section 13.3).

Philip II's "Christian classicism" fixed the image of Spain
as a disciplined and orderly state. Despite the modernizing circumstances connected to Spain's development, in
particular the pragmatic organization of its maritime and
military activities, Spanish culture remained essentially theocratic. The Inquisition suppressed any ideas or individuals
suspected of having a connection to Protestantism, and the
state discouraged competitive economic activities. Spain's
commitment to religion and endless involvement in territorial disputes, however, inhibited its economic development.
The king's ideal of a divine mission became an unflagging
obsession: his bedroom in the Escorial included an interior
window that allowed him a direct view from his bed to the
altar in the church.

The Paris of Henri IV: Pieces of Urban Order

France competed with Spain throughout the sixteenth and
seventeenth centuries to secure the position of Europe's

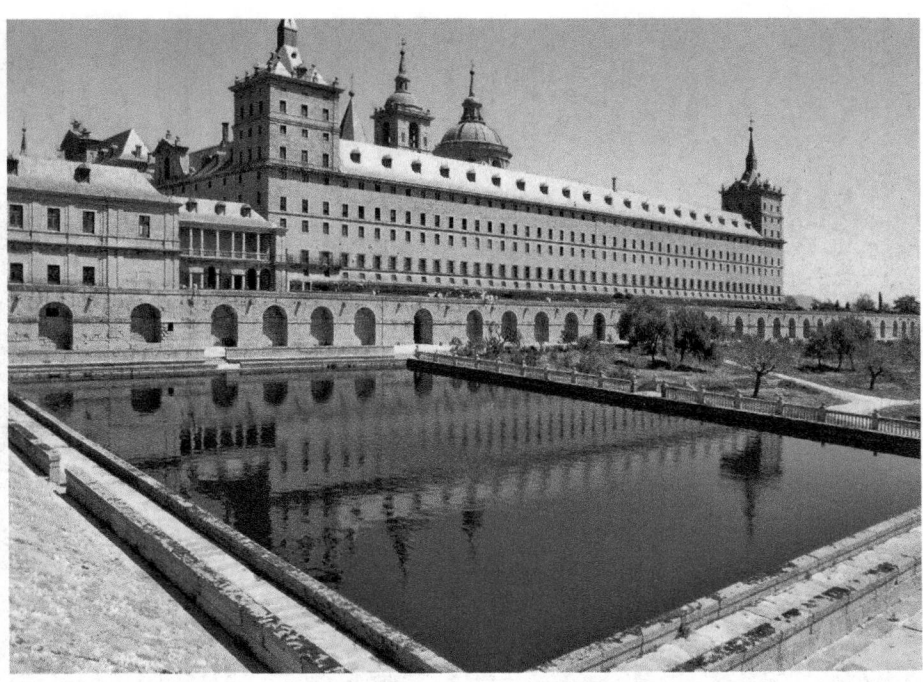

Figure 12.2-2 San Lorenzo de El Escorial, Spain. Convent/palace of El Escorial, Juan de Toledo and Juan de Herrera, 1567–1590.

major power. Four times as populous as Spain, with about
20 million people in 1600, its wealth derived from the great
fertility of its land and an abundant workforce. During most
of the second half of the sixteenth century France was torn
by civil wars between Protestants and Catholics. Henri IV
(r. 1589–1610), heir to the French throne, was an avowed
Protestant but in 1593 converted to Catholicism in the interests of national unity. In his own words, "Paris [a Catholic stronghold that held out against him] is worth a mass."
During his reign France became increasingly centralized
and surpassed Spain in political and economic importance.
As France's fortunes rose, the king began to replan Paris as
the symbol of a dynamic state.

Paris in 1600 remained one of the largest but worst-kept
cities in Europe, with an estimated population of 350,000
and no decent streets or urban spaces. Henri IV's renewal
program included the rebuilding of the royal precinct of the
Louvre; the quadrupling in size of the four-square castle;
and the enlargement of the long gallery that ran to the Tuileries, a château with formal gardens built a generation

1617 — Cardinal Richelieu made regent of France

1642 — Cardinal Mazarin named regent of France during youth of Louis XIV

Borromini begins Sant'Ivo della Sapienza in Rome — 1642

1657 — Bernini designs oval piazza for St. Peter's in Rome

Vaux-le-Vicomte château inaugurated for French finance minister Fouquet — 1661

earlier outside the city walls. More importantly, the king initiated work on two grand public spaces that aimed to economically stimulate the growing merchant and artisan sectors. For the general well-being of the city he completed a new bridge begun four decades earlier by his predecessors, still known as Pont-Neuf, at the western tip of the Île de la Cité. Its unprecedented width of 28 m (92 ft) established a new scale for the city's thoroughfares. At its midspan he attached the triangular Place Dauphine, a geometric space initially lined with unified facades. Henri IV also founded a major plague hospital, as large as the new Louvre, on the northern edge of Paris, just outside the city walls, in an effort to contain the perennial health hazard.

Unlike Philip II, Henri IV had fewer preconceptions about architecture. He privileged functionality over style. The most important of his interventions, the **Place** Royale (now known as Place des Vosges), began as a commercial project associated with a silkworks factory in 1604. The state hoped to stimulate the productive capacity of the city and create employment. Plans called for the north side of the square to contain the workshops, while the other three **ranges** were to contain nine four-bay houses each. The planners proposed the three-story house type as suitable for merchants and wealthy artisans but too small for upper-class dwellers. Henri IV and his chief finance minister (or *grand voyer*), the Duke of Sully, made gifts of the lots to political supporters in the hopes that the project would be developed on a consensual

Figure 12.2-3 San Lorenzo de El Escorial, Spain. El Escorial, view from the King's Courtyard to the facade of the basilica, Toledo and Herrera, 1567–1590.

▼ **1662**

Louis XIV begins transformation of château of Versailles into the symbol of the state

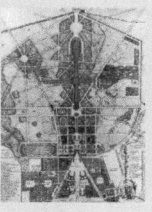

Franco-Dutch War

▲ **1672**

▼ **1679**

Louis XIV inaugurates Les Invalides military hospital in Paris

Figure 12.2-4 Madrid. (a) Plaza Mayor, begun by Herrera, 1590s, finished by Francisco de Mora, 1630s. (b) Detail of seventeenth-century map of Madrid, anonymous.

basis. After only three years, however, the developers removed the silk factory from the program and combined several of the properties into larger floor plans for aristocratic palaces (Fig. 12.2-5a). Despite these changes in the internal arrangements of the lots, each facade respected the building code for uniform materials and windows, resulting in a uniquely harmonious public space framed by vaulted arcades (Fig. 12.2-5b).

Similar in scale to Madrid's Plaza Mayor, the Place des Vosges lent itself to use as a stage for royal ceremonials and tournaments but remained a secular space for residences without a monumental focus. Only the central pavilions of the south and north ranges, developed by the king himself, used classical pilasters, but even that distinction appeared slight. The elevations surrounding the square were dressed with a combination of vertical strips of stone rustication mixed with simple brick bond. By the end of the seventeenth century the square's predominantly aristocratic clientele had attempted to exclude the lower classes from using the public space by transforming it into a gated garden open only to those with a key.

In 1610, at the height of his power, Henri IV was assassinated. His widow, Marie de' Medici, in 1614 installed an equestrian statue as a memorial on the tip of the island, astride the two halves of the king's new bridge, looking toward the Place Dauphine. The queen, as regent, continued her own architectural agenda, commissioning Salomon de Brosse (1571–1626) in 1615 to build the Luxembourg Palace (Fig. 12.2-6) on the southern edge of the city. The two wings projecting toward the gardens served the queen

The Planted Boulevard

Marie de' Medici imported from the gardens of Florence the idea of the broad, tree-lined *allée* planted with full-grown, symmetrically placed linden trees. Her promenade in Paris, built in 1616 on the banks of the Seine as the Cours la Reine, served a similar function as the Chahar Bagh Avenue in Isfahan, offering an orderly and well-shaded place for strolling. Like the straight streets in Sixtus V's Rome, the queen's planted avenue became the prime parade ground for aristocratic carriages, which could not easily circulate in the more densely packed quarters of the city. In the 1660s, when Louis XIV replaced the walls of Paris with tree-lined avenues, this new type of street acquired the name "**boulevard**," deriving from a Dutch word for "bastion."

Paris. Cours de la Reine, planted boulevard sponsored by Marie de' Medici for carriage travel, 1616.

Figure 12.2-5 Paris. (a) Place des Vosges (originally Place Royale), 1604–1610. Engraving from the Turgot map of Paris, 1739. (b) Place des Vosges.

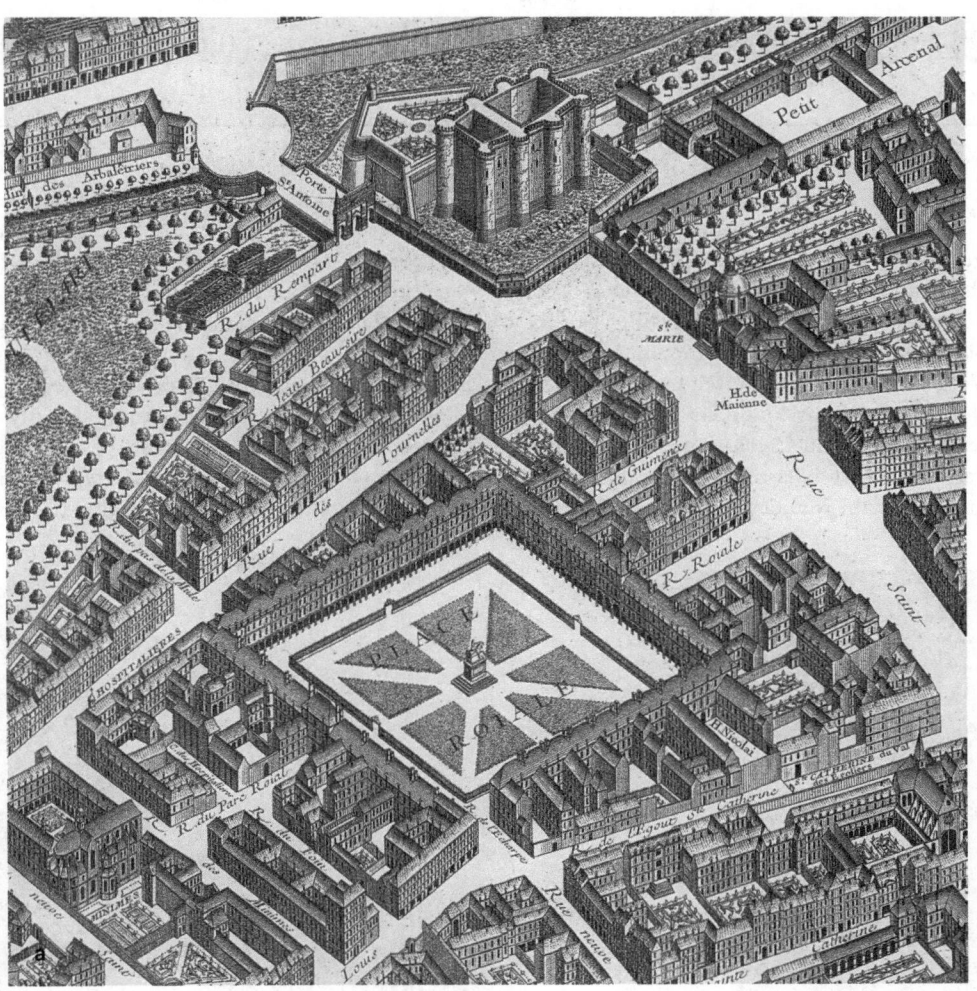

The French *Hôtel*

The Parisian aristocratic house type differed from the townhouse type that surrounded the Place des Vosges. Now called the *hôtel particulier* to distinguish it from an inn, it required a large, deep site, setting the central dwelling block, or *corps de logis*, between court and garden. One of the best examples of the type, Hôtel de Sully, was built adjacent to the southwest corner of Place des Vosges in 1624 and acquired by Henri IV's right-hand man, the Duke of Sully, in 1634. The street facade, designed by Jean Androuet du Cerceau, presented a classical single-story gate lined with balustrades and flanked by two-story wings crowned with rounded pediments. One passed through the *porte-cochère* entry into the courtyard. A stable for a dozen horses occupied this front area, while the *corps de logis* stood as the principal facade overlooking the court.

The French *hôtel* type differed from the block-like Italian palazzo in that it usually adjusted to the site rather than commanding it. The Hôtel de Beauvais, built for Catherine Henriette Bellier in the 1650s by André Le Pautre, squeezed gracefully into an extremely irregular site. In this case the *corps de logis* stood directly above the *porte-cochère*, while the horseshoe-shaped court gave the illusion of symmetry. To maximize the tight space, the architect used the stables tucked into the rear as the base for a small hanging garden.

Paris. (a) Hôtel de Sully, 1630s. (b) and (c) See facing page.

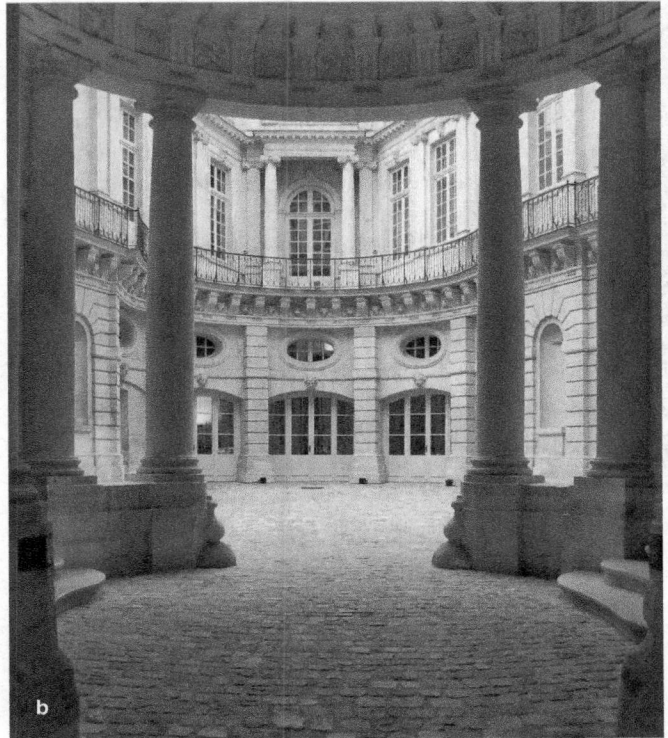

Paris. (b) Hôtel de Beauvais,
Louis Le Pautre, 1650s.

Paris. (c) Hôtel de Beauvais, plan.

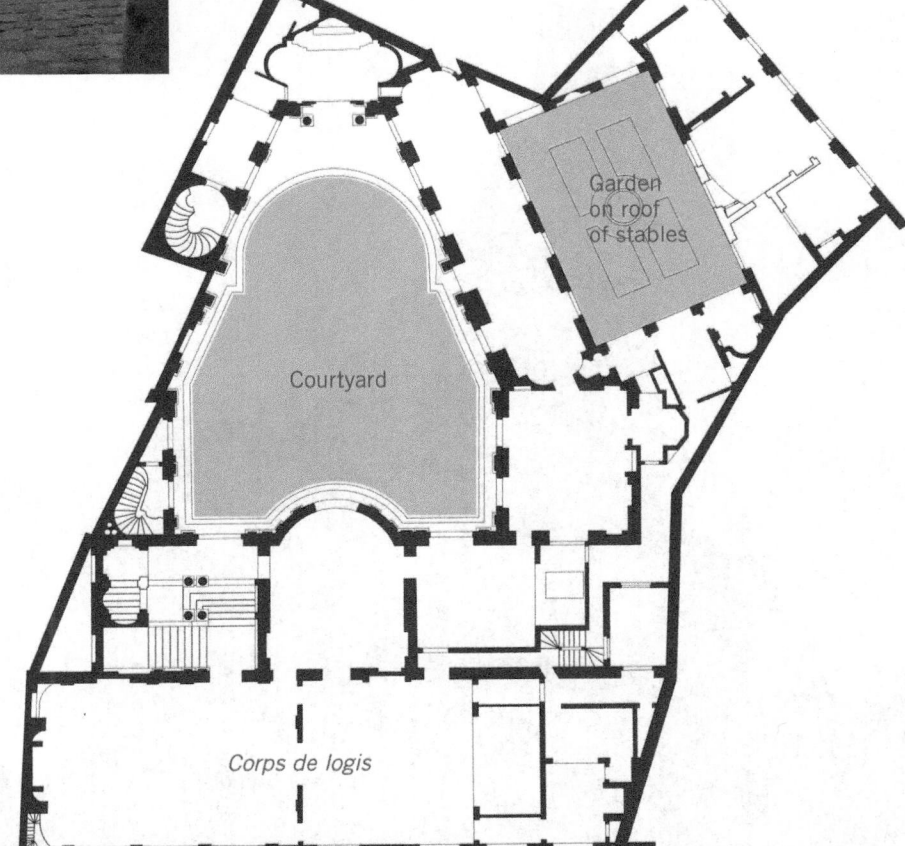

Figure 12.2-7 Paris. St. Étienne-du-Mont, 1490–1626.

Figure 12.2-6 Paris. Luxembourg Palace, garden facade, 1615.

and her estranged son, Louis XIII, respectively. The rusticated columns of the facade and the large geometrically planned gardens with marvelous fountains evoked the feeling of the Boboli Gardens behind the Pitti Palace in Florence, where the queen had spent her childhood.

A political movement surrounding Louis XIII ousted Marie de' Medici as regent of France in 1617, and after considerable struggle, the queen went into exile. The sixteen-year-old king entrusted the management of the state to Cardinal Richelieu (1585–1642), who for two decades prevailed as the most powerful patron in France. The cardinal used state money to rebuild his family's feudal estate, creating a château attached to the new town of Richelieu. Designed by Jacques Lemercier (1585–1654), the new town was double the area of Montpazier, with a grand square at each end—one for the cathedral, the other for the market. In Paris the cardinal had Lemercier build an immense palace, now called the Palais-Royal, next to the Louvre. Although the palace, along with its theater and gardens, was completely rebuilt after a fire in the late eighteenth century, the layout of its rectangular ranges, enclosing roughly 100 × 200 m (328 × 656 ft), represented one of the most orderly components of the city.

Cardinal Richelieu did not share Henri IV's religious tolerance and actively persecuted Protestants. His promotion of Catholicism as the state religion led to the founding of over seventy new religious institutions in Paris during the seventeenth century. Most of the new ecclesiastical buildings looked to the classical style of Renaissance Rome. The late Gothic church of St. Étienne-du-Mont (Fig. 12.2-7), begun in the fifteenth century and finished in 1626, carried a facade that reflected this transition. On the ground level a classical temple front presented rusticated half-columns and a triangular pediment, above which rose a second level with two classical niches and a broken segmental pediment enclosing a Gothic wheel window. A steep gable crowned the facade and included an Italian-style window frame with a broken pediment, concealing the structure of Gothic ribbed vaults and flying buttresses that lay behind it.

The rebuilding of the University of Paris, the Sorbonne, proved Cardinal Richelieu's principal architectural legacy. Construction began in 1626 and included the addition of a church for the cardinal's tomb. The Roman-trained Lemercier designed the church according to Serlio's model of a two-level facade articulated with Corinthian half-columns below, pilasters above, and subtle volutes connecting the two stories. Finished in 1645, three years after the patron's death, the church of the Sorbonne launched the first hemispherical dome of the Parisian skyline. While the Gothic vaults and crocket-laden spires that originated in the Île-de-France had for centuries signified the highest expression of religious architecture for the rest of Europe, these new Parisian churches, marked by classical columns and rounded domes, confirmed the models of papal Rome and the Counter-Reformation as the new source of architectural authority.

Figure 12.2-8 Paris. Val-de-Grâce, François Mansart and Jacques Lemercier, 1646.

Louis XIV and Versailles: The Mirror of Absolute Rule

During the long reign of Louis XIV (r. 1643–1715), the quintessential absolutist ruler, the intellectual and technical bases for the modernization of Europe emerged. Rational organization, scientific principles, and, above all, coordinated bureaucracies supplied new means for organizing society. The king, with the support of superb engineers, expanded the French army into the largest and best-managed fighting force in Europe. France enacted national strategies in which the protection of the state, rather than individual cities, became the chief goal. Perhaps the most modern aspect of Louis XIV's reign came with his use of various types of media to establish the mythical image of the Sun King, the radiant center of an omnipotent state. Through stagecraft involving costumes, choreography, literature, and scenery, the king's every action became a performance. His life provided a narrative for the entire nation to follow.

Another cardinal/prime minister dominated the first two decades of Louis XIV's seventy-two-year reign. Cardinal Mazarin (Giulio Mazzarini, 1602–1661), an Italian diplomat trained in Rome, gained the confidence of both Cardinal Richelieu and the future king's mother, Queen Anne of Austria, during the 1630s. After the death of Richelieu in 1642, followed by that of Louis XIII a year later, Mazarin assumed Richelieu's role as prime minister. His previous connection to the Barberini family of Pope Urban VIII in Rome heavily influenced his taste. The cardinal stayed abreast of the latest artistic trends in Rome, sending his agents to acquire hundreds of works of art. He aspired to involve Gian Lorenzo Bernini (1598–1680) in the production of great works for France, including an equestrian statue of Louis XIV proposed for the steps leading to the French church of Trinità del Monte in Rome. In 1646 Mazarin commissioned one of the most ornate church facades in Rome, Santi Vincenzo e Anastasio, by Martino Longhi the Younger. Its rippling triple portico overlooked the Trevi Fountain.

Mazarin's Roman taste influenced many projects in Paris. The convent church of Val-de-Grâce (Fig. 12.2-8), begun in 1645 and finished two decades later, appeared the most Roman of the new Parisian churches. Built for the convent sponsored by the queen mother, where she kept her own apartments, the design by François Mansart and Jacques Lemercier reflected Mazarin's enthusiasm for the facades of

Figure 12.2-9 Paris. Collège des Quatre-Nations (now Institut de France), Louis Le Vau, 1660s.

Giacomo della Porta and Carlo Maderno in Rome. Like the Jesuit church of the Gesù in Rome (1573), the grand volutes of the Parisian church made a graceful transition from the wider lower level to the upper story. Shadow pilasters and niches framed the Corinthian columns of the entry porch, and the dome, with its tightly packed crown of colonnaded buttresses girding the tall drum, appeared a polite miniaturization of the dome of St. Peter's.

Like Richelieu, Mazarin financed a major educational institution, the Collège des Quatre-Nations (now known as Institut de France) (Fig. 12.2-9), which focused on a domed church intended for use as his mausoleum. The crafty cardinal intended the benevolent program of his project to serve as a ploy to divert attention from the corrupt practices that led to his great wealth. The college accommodated forty students from four different linguistic groups in areas recently acquired by France and also included a riding academy and a public library. Despite Mazarin's interest in importing the greatest artists of Rome, after his death his executors appointed to complete the project the leading architect of Paris, Louis Le Vau (1612–1670), who in the same years was remodeling the Louvre directly across the river. The college's final design of 1662, executed a year after the patron's death, introduced a lateral oval dome and concave side wings that reflected the fluid curves then fashionable in Rome. The balustrades along the parapets gave the facade a clean profile, while behind them lurked the only traces of French character: steep roofs with **dormer** windows.

Le Vau pursued this new spatial freedom in the design of the château of Vaux-le-Vicomte (12.2-10a–c), built for the

a

Figure 12.2-10 Maincy, France. (a) Vaux-le-Vicomte, Le Vau and André Le Nôtre, 1656–1660. (b) and (c) See facing page.

royal minister of finance, Nicolas Fouquet, in 1656–1661. The overall plan bears a striking resemblance to the plan of the Collège des Quatre-Nations: a central oval dome flanked by concave wings. Aside from its variety of interior spaces, the marvel of Vaux-le-Vicomte lay in the formal gardens designed by André Le Nôtre (1613–1700). They step down in terraces behind the château as a geometric progression of topiaries, boxwood hedges, basins, and parterre beds set in lace-like patterns known as *broderies*.

The oval salon at Vaux-le-Vicomte, with its pilastered, double-height interior, functioned like an indoor courtyard for large receptions to view the garden. Fouquet planned the most famous of these occasions, a three-day event in 1661, to flatter the young Louis XIV. Instead, it precipitated Fouquet's comeuppance: the king, both envious of and indignant at such a conceited display of luxury, had the minister thrown into jail

Figure 12.2-10 Maincy, France. (b) Oval salon, Le Vau. (c) Plan of the *corps de logis*, showing: (1) the vestibule; (2) saloon; (3) antechambers; (4) chambers; (5) cabinets.

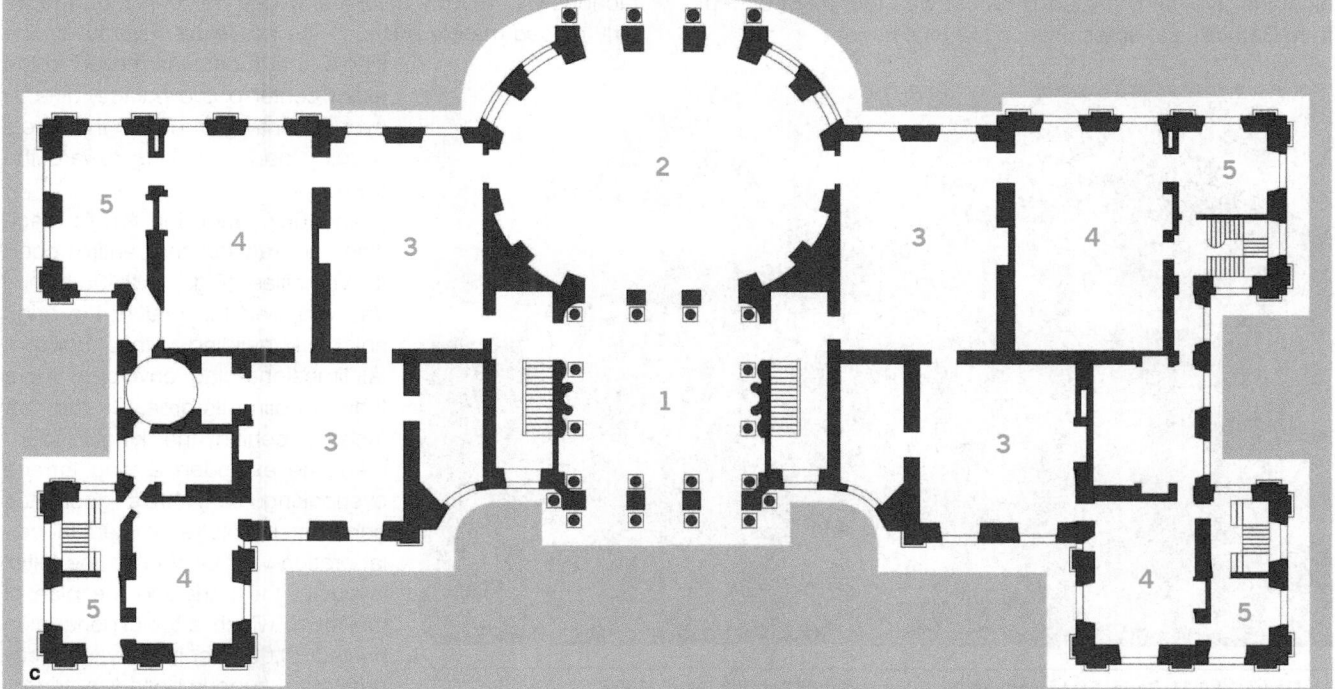

three weeks later on charges of embezzlement. He then co-opted Fouquet's team of designers to work on the largest project of seventeenth-century Europe, the transformation of the small hunting château of Versailles into a grand royal enclave.

Behind the incarceration of Fouquet lurked the power of a new breed of court official, Jean-Baptiste Colbert, an assistant to Mazarin who under Louis XIV became the state's most indispensable bureaucrat and public servant. From the time of his assumption of power in 1661 until his death in 1687 Colbert put the finances of the state in order and organized a veritable propaganda machine to glorify the king. He guided France from a state with an inefficient feudal economy into a dynamic international power by increasing state intervention and bureaucracy on all levels. Among his efforts to limit imports and increase exports he founded the state-run Gobelins factory in 1667 for the production of tapestries and luxury furnishings. During the 1660s he also added new fields to the French academies of letters and art founded by Richelieu and Louis XIII to improve the quality of the state's arts and sciences. The academy of architecture influenced the practice of architecture by turning it toward a new rationalism tinged with the awareness of Roman stylistic movements. As superintendent of buildings, Colbert challenged the appointment of Le Vau to oversee the Louvre project, favoring the use of competitions to obtain a happy medium between the extremes. In 1665 he invited Italy's most coveted artist, Gian Lorenzo Bernini, to Paris to design the east facade of the Louvre (12.2-11). While Bernini's first design sympathized with the original project by Le Vau, placing an oval figure at midspace, his third design proved more severe, offering a flat expanse with rhythmically placed colossal pilasters on the corner towers and half-columns on the central block. The flatness of the cornice line, typical of Italian palaces, was the only concept from Bernini's schemes used in the final project.

After Colbert rewarded Bernini and sent him back to Rome, Le Vau returned to work on the facade with a team that included the finance minister's close friend Claude Perrault (1613–1688). Perrault practiced as a physician and was a respected natural scientist, becoming a leading member of the French Science Academy. Among other distinctions he translated Vitruvius into French. In the debate between the "ancients," who insisted on copying the models of the past, and the "moderns," who used empirical methods to arrive at solutions, he defended the latter. His notion of modern architecture did not exclude classical solutions but demanded they derive from common sense and rationality instead of dogma. Perrault, collaborating with Le Vau and the painter Charles Le Brun, achieved a harmonious synthesis for the east facade of the Louvre: a central block with a central pediment, corner towers marked with paired pilasters, and between these slightly protruding volumes screens made of colossal pairs of Corinthian columns.

As the Louvre was reaching completion, Louis XIV (Fig. 12.2-12) decided to escalate his plans for Versailles. The program of the new royal palace, built 17 km (10 miles) west of Paris, became the young king's personal contribution to the Sun King myth. The move to Versailles kept him safe from the dangers of the city center while serving as a means of disciplining the nobility, who were now obliged to live within its isolated confines. The palace occupied the center of a stellated pattern, which radiated on one side into the adjacent town of Versailles and on the other into the geometric terraces of a vast park that extended beyond the horizon as a metaphor of absolutist control. Le Vau designed the first expansion of Versailles in 1662, creating a series of volumes flanking the U-shaped Marble Court. The additions spread laterally to accommodate kitchens and stables, ministries and offices. The architect ennobled the modest brick facades with marble columns, gilded balconies, and regularly placed marble busts on the two levels. Eventually, the king's apartment was moved to the exact center of the palace, directly over the entry porch, with three sets of tall windows looking toward the town.

In 1667, after the king's decision to transfer the entire court to Versailles (Fig. 12.2-13a,b), Le Vau wrapped the rear of the original brick building with a horizontal limestone-clad envelope, more than doubling its area. On the rear facade, behind the king's apartment, he extended a long terrace overlooking Le Nôtre's geometric gardens. Le Nôtre worked in collaboration with Le Vau on the initial layout of the park and the plan of the town, which after a generation hosted 30,000 people. Over the city grid they superimposed a trident

Figure 12.2-11 Paris. East facade of the Louvre, Claude Perrault, et al., 1667.

radiating from the Marble Court. Versailles received another significant expansion in 1678–1687 from Jules Hardouin-Mansart (1646–1708), who added lateral wings to both sides of the main block, more than tripling the length of the rear facade to 670 m (2,200 ft).

By the end of the seventeenth century, about 1,500 nobles and their retinues lived in the palace at Versailles. Like the Escorial, but without its religious premise, the palace became an immense social experiment that incorporated hundreds of apartments with kitchens, dining halls, billiard rooms, a theater, and a church. In the central block of the rear facade, Hardouin-Mansart enclosed the terrace with a brilliant gallery for strolling, lined with seventeen full-length mirrors. He converted the exterior into a pure volume articulated with pilasters and three protruding Ionic porches supporting sculptures.

Louis XIV believed the gardens of Versailles (Fig. 12.2-14) had greater importance than the architecture of the palace and personally composed a guidebook for visiting them. Le Nôtre set the gardens on a primary east–west axis that extended across a terrace with two flanking basins, stepping down through a grid of parterres. The central axis continued down a grassy *allée* to the 2 km (1.2 mile) long Grand Canal, which disappeared into the western horizon. The perspective effect of looking from the palace gave the impression of an ever-widening, infinite landscape governed by strict laws of symmetry and proportion. In effect, as one moved off the central axis into the **bosquets** and secret gardens,

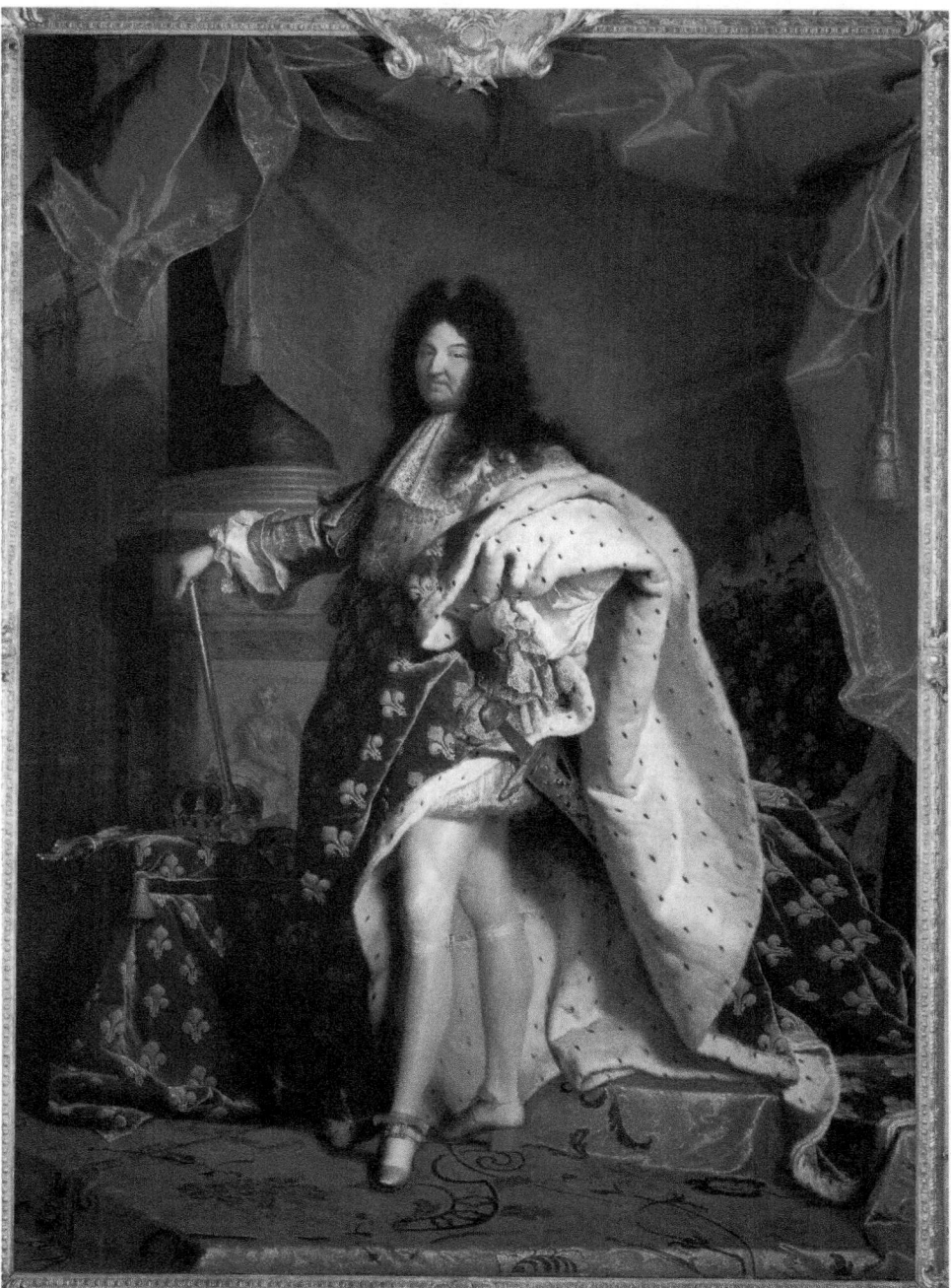

Figure 12.2-12 Louis XIV, painted by H. Rigaud, 1701.

the overall symmetry relaxed and gave way to local symmetries that structured the secondary areas. Directly south of the first terrace spread the garden of the Orangerie, where gardeners cared for hundreds of orange trees, one of which was brought to the king's bed each morning so that he could personally pick the fruit. The cruciform Grand Canal proved large enough for testing the prototypes of the royal French navy. The gardens required massive amounts of water, leading to the construction of an industrial-scale water pump 5 km (3.1 miles) to the north at Marly. The king also began a huge aqueduct at Maintenon to supplement the water supply.

Once settled at Versailles, Louis XIV rarely returned to Paris. Colbert, however, encouraged some major urban improvements. In 1685 a private sponsor, the Maréchal de la Feuillade, began the Places des Victoires, a round plaza intersected by six radiating streets just north of the Palais-Royal. Hardouin-Mansart designed the facades with arches for shops at the ground level and Ionic pilasters articulating the upper two stories for apartments. Above the cornices the roofs had dormer windows that extended the rentable space vertically for two or three more stories. This sort of habitable roof, although not invented by either Hardouin-Mansart or his uncle François Mansart before him, has acquired the

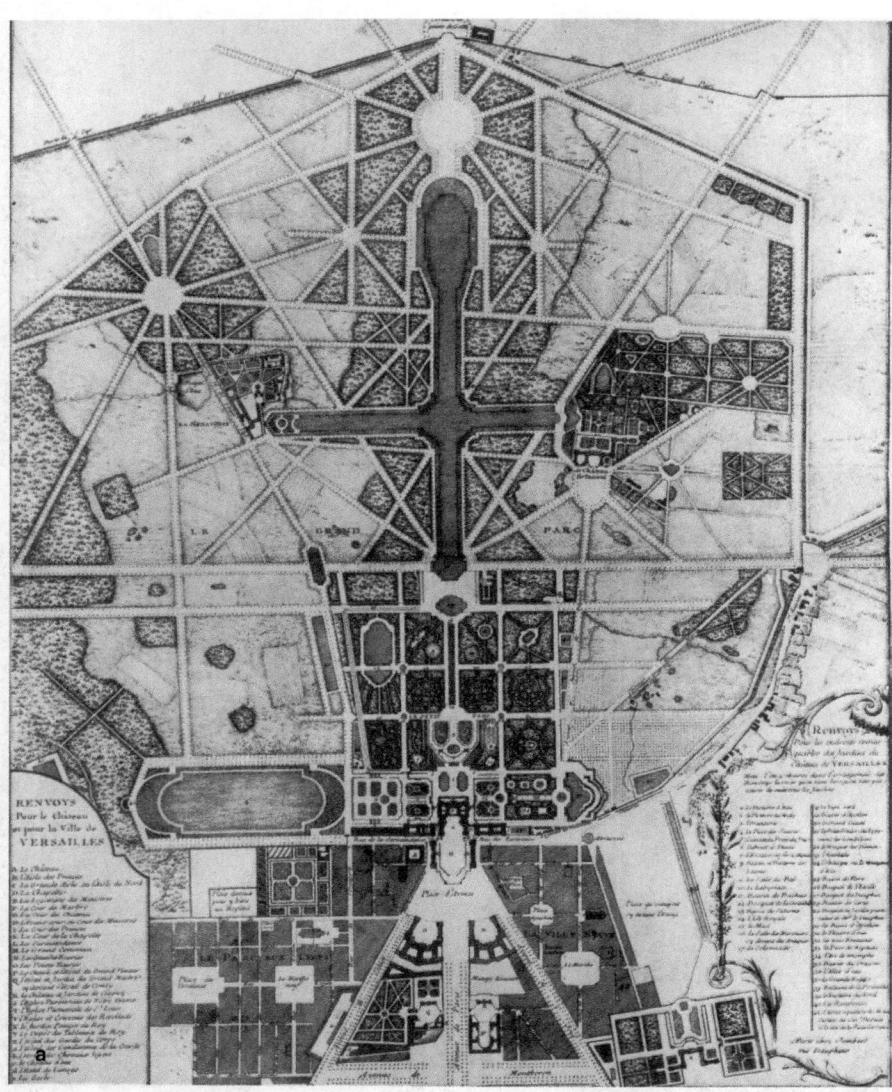

Figure 12.2-13 Versailles, France.
(a) Plan showing expansion of hunting
château into Louis XIV's grand royal
palace, Le Vau and Le Nôtre, 1660–1680.
Engraving by Abbé Delagrive, Paris,
1746. (b) Marble Court.

Figure 12.2-14 Versailles, France. The Apollo Basin, Le Nôtre, 1680s.

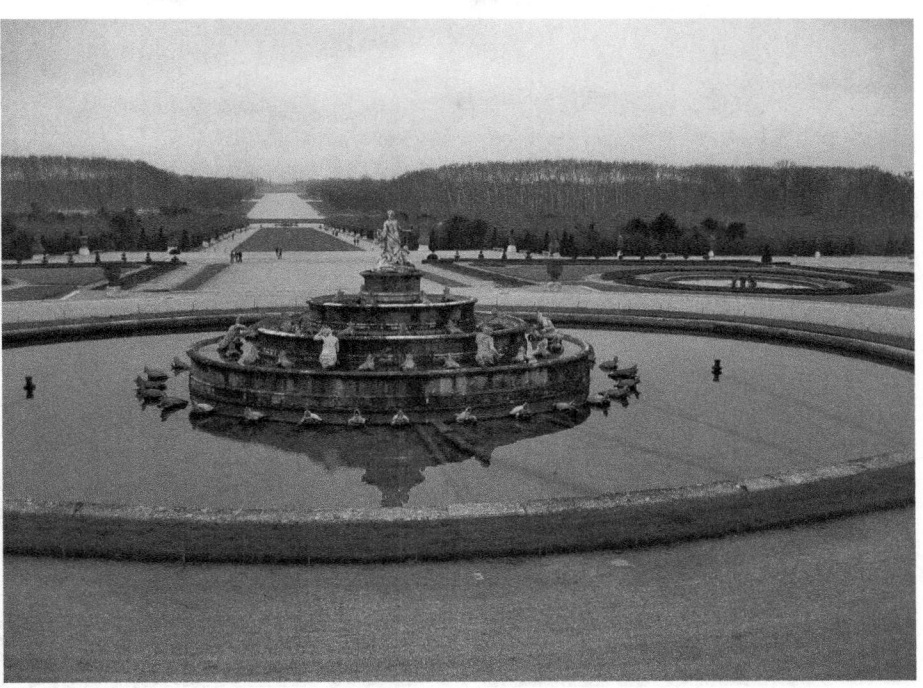

name **mansard roof** in his honor. The royal architect inserted a second square to the west of the Palais-Royal in 1699, a decade after Colbert's death. Place Louis-le-Grand (now Place Vendôme), a rectangle with beveled corners, accommodated the large-scale *hôtel particuliers* of the nobility, which fit behind the uniform facades to appear like a single large palace rather than a series of houses.

The equestrian statue of Louis XIV at Place Louis-le-Grand sent a message of the military commitment of the regime. France's army during this period was transformed into a modern, bureaucratic system without parallel, and the great military theorist Sébastien Le Prestre de Vauban (1633–1707) provided an equally systematic approach to the defense of the state, using models at 1:600 scale to communicate with his engineers. Starting with the refortification of Lille in 1667 (Fig. 12.2-15), he designed the fortifications of 130 cities on France's frontiers. He built some ex-novo, such as the octagonal-shaped Neuf Brisach, but in most cases, such as the magnificent walls stepping up the hill of Belfort, he adapted to existing urban and topographic conditions. In addition to the Italian angled-bastion fort, he introduced *V*-shaped rippling mounds, or **ravelins**, outside the walls as further interruptions to attackers in the field.

France's wars came at great human cost. To reward his armies, Louis XIV founded in 1669 the first great military hospital in Europe, Les Invalides (12.2-16a,b), built specifically to house 6,000 disabled veterans returning from the king's military campaigns. The hospital spread on a grid of square courts, covering an area larger than the Escorial. Hardouin-Mansart took over the project's design from the initial architect, Libéral Bruant, and added to the existing longitudinal church a second church with a grand dome. The plan of the domed church of Les Invalides repeated the nine-square layout of the *hasht bihisht*, or "eight paradises," plan of Mughal tombs such as

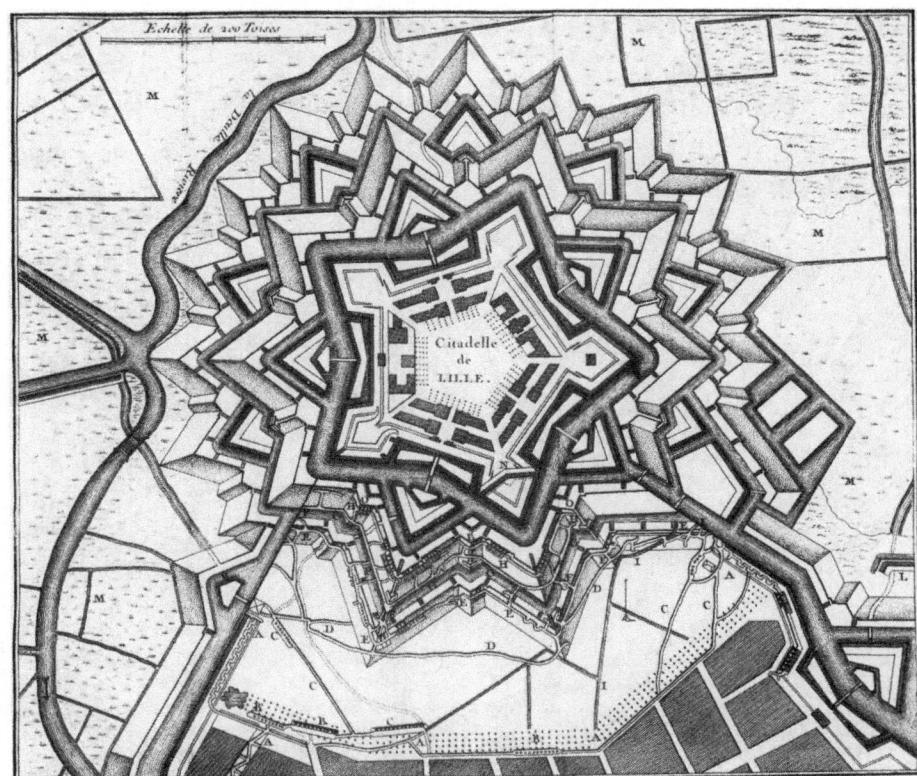

Figure 12.2-15 Lille, France. New fortress with *ravelins* at edges, Sébastien Le Prestre de Vauban, 1708.

the Taj Mahal. Learning from the problem of St. Peter's in Rome, where the dome cannot be seen behind the facade, the royal architect added an extra attic above the tall drum to boost its height above the four stories of the hospital to 100 m (328 ft). On the skyline of Louis XIV's Paris, the gilded cupola of Les Invalides, set off by its grand planted

Figure 12.2-16 Paris. (a) Les Invalides, dome of the church with double drum, Jules Hardouin-Mansart. 1669. (b) Turgot map of grand esplanade to the river.

esplanade facing the river, proved the most visible monument of the age. The hospital constituted a social project of considerable scope, serving as a gesture of compensation for the strain that Versailles put on the national economy. It remained a testament to the modern, bureaucratic approach to warfare, sheltered under the reassuring dome of the Roman church.

Bernini's Rome: Theatricality versus Complex Geometry

At Versailles Louis XIV confronted daily life as a series of scripted events, from the audience held for the *petit lever* upon awakening to that for his nightly retiring, or *grand coucher*. The luxurious satin costumes of his courtiers, their powdered wigs, and the extensive use of makeup by both men and women contributed to a sort of permanent masquerade. Such a theatrical way of life originated with papal protocol in Renaissance Rome. Although by the seventeenth century the city had lost its political relevance, it continued to influence the culture of Europe, especially in terms of the visual arts. There, spectacles abounded: fireworks spewed from atop Castel Sant'Angelo for formal entries and festivals, processions filled the streets several times a week with bright costumes and ephemeral decorations, and Carnival produced a rich repertoire of triumphal carts, races, and masks. Papal architects redesigned most of the major spaces of seventeenth-century Rome as theatrical displays, using coordinated architectural elements, cascading fountains, and sensuous statues.

Gian Lorenzo Bernini dominated this scene as the greatest sculptor of the age and Rome's most sought-after architect. He also excelled as a director of spectacles for the Roman stage, writing, directing, acting, and, not least, designing the sets. His theatrical background showed clearly in the design of the Cornaro Chapel (Fig. 12.2-17) inside the church of Santa Maria della Vittoria in 1647. The altar thrust forward like a proscenium between paired columns. St. Teresa of Avila floated on a cloud, her mouth trembling in ecstasy, while a smiling angel poised nearby with his arrow pointed at her heart. To charge the sculptures with the illusion of movement, Bernini introduced a stage device: indirect lighting from a chimney-like light trap. On either side of the chapel he placed life-like sculptures of members of the Cornaro family, as if they were observing the saint's performance from box seats in a theater.

One of Bernini's stage sets anticipated the construction of the twin churches at Piazza del Popolo (12.2-18), where a trident of streets converged at Rome's northern entrance. The idea for this fanciful propylaia began as a temporary decoration for the 1655 entry of Queen Christina of Sweden, Rome's most prized convert to Catholicism. Carlo Rainaldi (1611–1691), under Bernini's supervision, eventually made this setting permanent in the 1660s using two seemingly identical churches to frame the trident of streets. The churches had identical temple-front porches but in fact differed slightly because of the varying sizes of their sites: one carried an oval dome, while the other was circular in plan. This illusionistic frame for the northern entry into Rome mixed scenography with urban design.

For the design of the piazza of St. Peter's (Fig. 12.2-19), Bernini returned to the most cherished theatrical structure of antiquity, the oval space of the Colosseum. Begun in 1657, it stretched 200 m (656 ft) across, matching the area of the ancient arena. The planners conceived the oval-shaped piazza as a space to accommodate the international crowds of thousands who came to receive papal blessings. The design integrated the old entrance into the Vatican palace north of the facade and the obelisk placed

Figure 12.2-17 Rome. Sta. Maria della Vittoria, Cornaro Chapel, depicting St. Teresa of Avila and patrons as if in box seats, Gian Lorenzo Bernini, 1645.

Figure 12.2-18 Rome. Piazza del Popolo, twin churches, Bernini and Carlo Rainaldi, 1660s.

Figure 12.2-19 Rome. Piazza of St. Peter's, Bernini for Pope Alexander VII, 1657. Print by Giovanni Battista Falda, 1665.

by Sixtus V into a sequence that moved from the great oval to a trapezoidal space that flared onto Carlo Maderno's facade.

Bernini derived the oval of the piazza of St. Peter's from two intersecting circles, joined as an *ovato tondo*. He wrapped the edges with colossal, semicircular canopies made of stark Tuscan columns four rows deep. The density of the 300 travertine columns created a strong sense of enclosure. At the apex points of the piazza, however, their radial alignments produced a theatrical effect: like

Figure 12.2-20 Rome. (a) Sant'Andrea al Quirinale, Bernini, 1660s. (b) Interior.

a curtain opening on stage, one could see straight through the wings to the city beyond. The statues of the saints lining the balustrades encouraged the crowd to identify with the early Christian martyrs allegedly fed to the lions in the Colosseum.

Bernini's most talented and difficult colleague, Francesco Borromini (1599–1667), worked on his earliest architectural project, the colossal bronze **baldacchino** over the high altar of St. Peter's, begun in 1625. The spiraling columns referred specifically to the twisting "Solomonic" columns believed to have been in the Temple of Jerusalem. As produced in bronze at such a colossal scale, the columns of the baldacchino exuded a sense of galvanizing energy. Borromini executed all of the architectural drawings for the ten-story structure, an early sample of his passion for complex geometric forms.

While Bernini appeared affable and comfortable with the courtly life of his patrons, Borromini proved withdrawn and socially inept. Their diverging attitudes toward architecture became like the distinction of shadow from substance: Bernini always respectful of conventions, within which he created spectacular effects; Borromini obsessed with ever more intricate geometries that pushed beyond conventions. The contrast became clear in the projects executed by the two architects for two churches set on the same street skirting the Quirinal Palace. Bernini built the church of Sant'Andrea al Quirinale in a relatively brief period from 1658 to 1665 for a wealthy cardinal to serve members of the powerful Jesuit order. Borromini designed the monastery of San Carlo alle Quattro Fontane, known as San Carlino, in 1634 for the poor friars of the Discalced Trinitarians, working without fee. The complex remained incomplete at his death in 1667.

Bernini set Sant'Andrea back slightly from the street, with a low, concave wall (Fig. 12.2-20a). The facade used the typical architectural language of late-sixteenth-century mannerism: two colossal Corinthian pilasters supported a well-proportioned pediment. The only novelty appeared in the semicircular porch that seemed to have dropped down from the clerestory of the same shape. The plan followed a lateral oval, which drew one's attention to pairs of chapels on either side. Bernini framed the central altar with a proscenium-like aedicule flanked with pairs of luxurious carnelian marble columns. The interior presented a reduced version of the Pantheon,

Figure 12.2-21 Rome. (a) San Carlo alle Quattro Fontane, also known as San Carlino, Francesco Borromini, begun 1638. (b) Interior.

with the addition of marvelous sculpted figures that flitted around the rim of the lantern as if hailing St. Andrew as he ascended on a cloud through the broken pediment over the altar (Fig. 12.2-20b). Aside from the sculptural performance and the fancy materials, Bernini attempted neither a complicated nor a disquieting composition.

Borromini worked in a different way at San Carlino (Fig. 12.2-21a,b), which from the facade to the interior conveyed a haunting sense of unfamiliarity. He undulated the two-story entry porch, curving the colonnade in, then out, and then in again, while placing deep niches and smaller columns in the bays. As one entered, the axis shifted 5° from a perpendicular alignment but remained imperceptible as a result of the strange, flowing configuration of the interior. Instead of the luxurious marble and golden light of Bernini's church, Borromini's interior was made of modest, whitewashed plaster. The upper zone of the cupola rested on a longitudinal oval, similar in shape to the *ovato tondo* of St. Peter's Piazza. The vaulting contained a sponge-like set of coffers that diminished in size as they reached the lantern. The lower register undulated between framing columns like the ground floor of the facade. Borromini's drawings demonstrate that the overall structure of San Carlino's interior derived from two equilateral triangles placed back to back to make a diamond and two circles placed within the triangles. The semicircular shape of the main altar and entry niche repeated the circumference of these circles, while the flat arcs of the side chapels duplicated the curve of the oval made from joining the two circles. What initially appeared incoherent in fact belonged to a complex geometric system.

Borromini, a provincial from a small town on Lake Lugano in Switzerland, remained an outsider in Rome, working mostly for modest religious institutions. He lived alone, spending most of his time working and reworking the drawings for his projects. For the small church of Sant'Ivo alla Sapienza (the chapel of the University of Rome) (Fig. 12.2-22a,b), begun in 1642, he created a composition based on two superimposed equilateral triangles, in this case rotated to form a six-point star. He lopped off the acute corners of the star, replacing them with convex piers, and added semicircular apses to each of the sides. The drum rose as six rounded lobes to support a pumpkin-shaped dome—a type of vault that had not been used since Hadrian's Villa. To counteract the bulges of the cupola, he scooped out the lantern above with six concave indentations. The Sapienza's arcane iconography included collections of three, inspired by the mystery of the holy trinity; the star of David, representing the basis of Judeo-Christian thought; and, crowning the lantern, a fantastic ziggurat-like spiral that ascended to a flaming crown. The imagery implied that

Figure 12.2-22 Rome.
(a) Sant'Ivo alla Sapienza,
lantern on dome, Borromini,
1640s. (b) Plan drawn by
Sebastiano Giannini, 1720.
The star-shaped church sits
at the end of the long court
of the University of Rome.

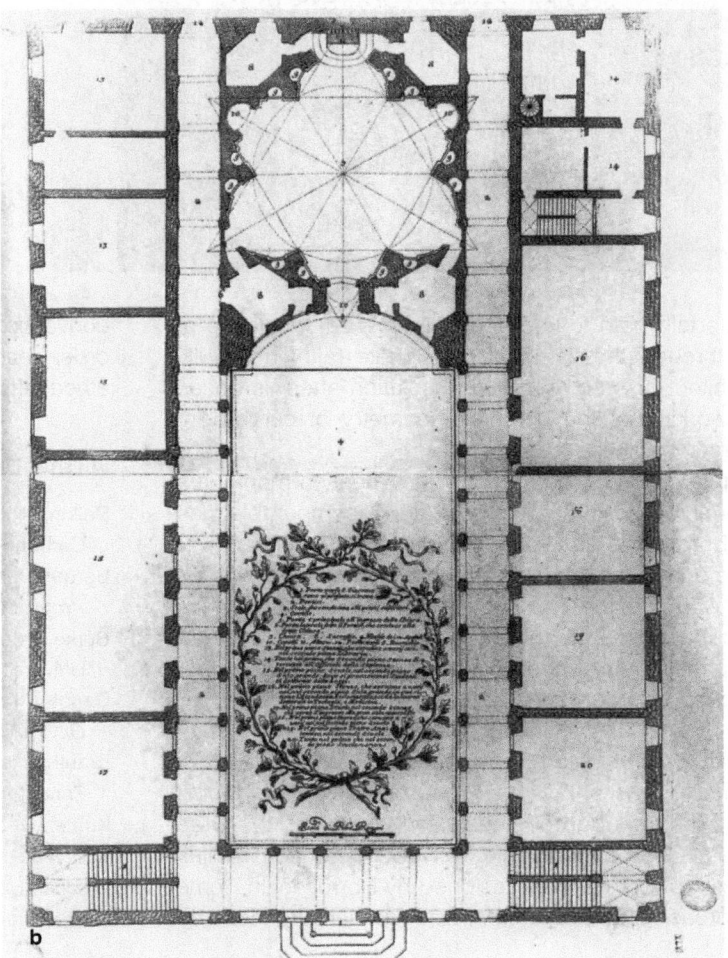

Figure 12.2-23 Turin. Chapel of the Holy Shroud, Guarino Guarini, 1660s.

the uncertain path to knowledge (*sapienza*) would be attained through the flame of passionate faith, much like the architect arriving at a design solution after his obsessive reworking of the complex geometry of curves and countercurves.

Despite several imitators, only the Theatine monk Guarino Guarini (1624–1683) demonstrated a comparable mastery of Borromini's geometric complexity. Guarini had lived in Rome during the 1640s at the precise moment Borromini began work on the two aforementioned churches. Two decades later, in Turin, he attempted a similar crescendo of interpenetrating geometric figures in the domes added to the church of San Lorenzo and the Chapel of the Holy Shroud (Fig. 12.2-23). Guarini even hoped to terminate the latter with a spiral lantern, in homage to Borromini. His use of interlacing basket-like ribs in the dome of San Lorenzo suggested knowledge of Andalusian works like the Great Mosque of Córdoba but could well have come from rethinking the strapwork ceilings designed by Borromini in Rome. The approach of both Borromini and Guarini surpassed the

conventions of classicism to explore a new type of spatial order based on geometric criteria that reached beyond theatrical effects.

Further Reading

Ballon, Hillary. *The Paris of Henri IV: Architecture and Urbanism.* Cambridge, MA: MIT Press, 1991.

Berger, Robert W. *A Royal Passion: Louis XIV as Patron of Architecture.* Cambridge: Cambridge University Press, 1994.

Burke, Peter. *The Fabrication of Louis XIV.* New Haven, CT: Yale University Press, 1992.

Dennis, Michael. *Court and Garden: From the French Hotel to the City of Modern Architecture.* Cambridge, MA: MIT Press, 1986.

Krautheimer, Richard. *The Rome of Alexander VII.* Princeton, NJ: Princeton University Press, 1985.

Kubler, George. *Building the Escorial.* Princeton, NJ: Princeton University Press, 1982.

Wilkinson-Zerner, Catherine. *Juan de Herrera: Architect to Philip II of Spain.* New Haven, CT: Yale University Press, 1993.

12.3 EDO JAPAN
Isolation from the World, Integration with Nature

Unlike the far-flung empires of Central Asia and the European nation-states, seventeenth-century Japan, after a brief period of international exchanges, developed in near-total isolation. As a reef of islands off the Asian mainland, Japan's geographic position left it naturally cut off. After the 1639 *sakoku* edict, which sealed its borders to foreigners, Japan became one of the few modern instances of an autarchic, or self-sufficient, society.

Despite its remoteness, Japan shared many patterns of patrimonial culture and politics with other parts of the world. It had acquired much of its formal and technical culture from mainland Asia. Yet during the Edo period, Japanese designers pursued a truly unique approach to architecture, rejecting symmetry as the first organizing principle. As the Tokugawa clan consolidated Japan's political power in the early seventeenth century, the design of palaces, temples, and tombs exhibited an unprecedented openness to natural features, attempting to integrate architecture with the order of nature rather than pursuing the autonomous dictates of geometry.

The Shogunate and the Proliferation of Feudal Castles

At the end of the sixteenth century, after several centuries of recurring civil wars, Japan achieved national unity under a succession of powerful military leaders, or *shoguns*. Oda Nobunaga (1534–1582), Toyotomi Hideyoshi (1536–1598), and finally Tokugawa Ieyasu (1542–1616) brought an end to feudal disputes. The last established a long-term hereditary dynasty. Since the twelfth century the role of the Japanese emperor had been limited to a religious function, while the country's political power had been dissipated among the *daimyo*, the 262 feudal lords of Japan. From their number a supreme military leader, or *shogun*, periodically gained sway through his valor in the field. The term for the *shogun*'s power, *bakufu*, referred to the multitude of tents belonging to his loyal knights, or *samurai*. During the second half of the sixteenth century, the *shoguns* turned away from tents and the ephemeral wooden structures that had previously characterized Japanese dwellings to build permanent symbols of their authority, castles with rustic stone bases and multilevel towers, known as **tenshu**.

Although only twelve *tenshu* have survived, the *shoguns* and their followers built nearly 100 such structures in the brief period between 1576 and 1634. These imposing towers, pitched on prominent topographic outcroppings, appeared quite unlike the compact medieval castles of Europe. Their form recalled the tiered structure of pagodas, with a tapering series of wide eaves stacked six or seven levels above a battered masonry foundation. Japanese military architects developed this new defensive structure after the introduction of firearms by Portuguese traders in the mid-sixteenth century: the raised masonry base and the plastered walls proved less susceptible to fire and offered better protection from gunfire. They perforated the walls with loopholes on the first three levels and on the upper levels added projecting boxes from which defenders could drop stones and fire on attackers. The wheeled cannon, which influenced the streamlining of fortifications in Europe and Asia, did not enter Japanese warfare until the nineteenth century. This may help to explain the fanciful treatment of ruffled layers of eaves and multiple gables in the upper ranges of the *tenshu*.

Nobunaga built the first great *tenshu* in 1576 at Azuchi, on Lake Biwa, east of the imperial capital of Heian, now called Kyoto. Although his enemies destroyed the castle after the leader's assassination in 1582, the stone base remains and the design can be tenuously reconstructed from literary sources. It sat on a 22 m (72 ft) high pyramidal foundation made of cyclopean stones. During its three years of construction Nobunaga's *tenshu* required thousands of laborers to transport giant stones from distant quarries and place the hundreds of interlocking pieces into a sloped platform. Five levels of wood and plaster terraces rose from the two-story base. The third floor covered an area about half the footprint of Palazzo Farnese. The master builder, Okabe Mataemon, famous for his shipbuilding endeavors, designed the wooden levels. From the rectangular base each level of the interconnected wood frames diminished in area like a pagoda. Mataemon inserted an octagonal chamber at the sixth level and above it a square belvedere with an elaborate hipped roof.

The first four levels of Nobunaga's *tenshu* enclosed a cavernous atrium, like the hollow spaces inside of Buddhist temples that sheltered the colossal statues of the Buddha. The patron intended the religious association and, despite his political persecution of several Buddhists sects, placed a Buddhist *stupa* at the bottom level of the building as the symbolic basis of his power. Nobunaga, known as much for his culture as for his military prowess, ordered that a platform be cantilevered into the atrium space at the second level as a stage for the performance of the highly formalized Noh theater. He positioned his audience hall adjacent to the stage on the same level. As at European courts, the frequent performance of theater became a ritual that paralleled the increased role-playing required of elites.

Hideyoshi, the military strongman who succeeded Nobunaga in 1582, came from peasant stock, which prevented the emperor from granting him the title of *shogun*. Only a person of the knightly samurai class qualified for such a designation. As if to compensate for his lack of legitimacy, Hideyoshi staged military and architectural projects on a grand scale. To take the pressure off internal disputes, he organized the invasion of Korea, with devastating effects for that country. From Korea he then plotted to invade China but settled for diplomatic compensations. His enthusiasm for architecture, painting, theater, and ritual, along with his policies of international military intervention, led to the construction of new castles for his family and shrines that honored him as a deity. Hideyoshi succeeded in forging national unity through force and then imposed drastic policies. At the same time that he declared the abolition of slavery, he also declared that no one outside of the samurai class could carry weapons—and thus ensured that a peasant like himself would never be able to rise up the social ladder. To dramatize this policy, he seized the arms of the peasants, melting them down to cast a colossal statue of the Buddha.

Hideyoshi built two castles similar in style to Nobunaga's Azuchi, the largest in Osaka and a second, known

as Fushimi, on the Momoyama Hill at the edge of Kyoto. Neither castle survived into the seventeenth century, although both were reconstructed in concrete in the late twentieth century. Among his most overt acts of cultural politics, Hideyoshi commissioned a luxurious dwelling, the Jurakudai Palace in Kyoto, as an environment suitable to receive the emperor and share in the legitimacy of the imperial persona. Although the Jurakudai Palace was later destroyed, an extant screen painting depicts its layout as a zigzag pattern. The roofs had flaring eaves set with gold-leafed tiles. Hideyoshi performed in Noh plays, some written about his own life. Like Louis XIV, he blurred the line between art and life. He also became a master of the tea ceremony and courted the participation of the saintly tea master Sen no Rikyu (1522–1591), a Zen Buddhist who had served Nobunaga. The *chanoyu* tea ceremony of Rikyu required a particular, ascetic environment and encouraged

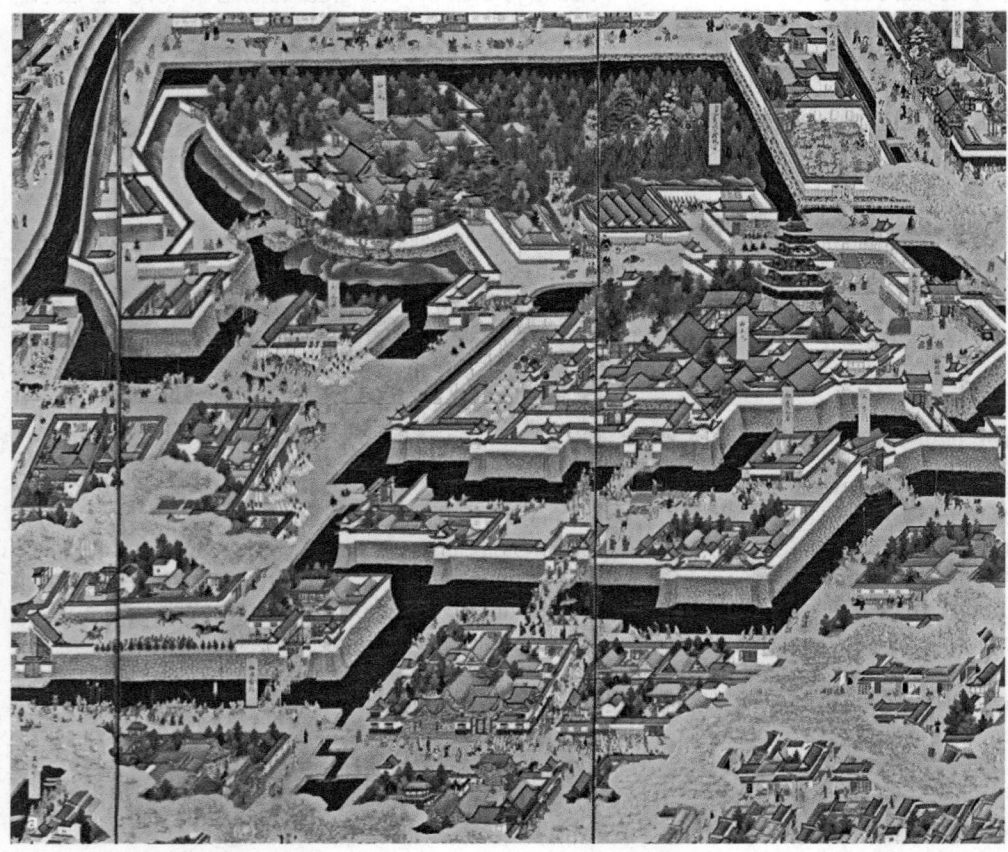

Figure 12.3-1 Edo (Tokyo), Japan. (a) Detail from the *Edozu byobu* panels, showing *tenshu* of Ieyasu in the city center), ca. 1620. (b) See facing page

 1582

Hideyoshi leads Japanese invasion of Korea, attempts to invade China

Tokugawa Ieyasu establishes definitive shogunate in Japan, moves capital to Edo (Tokyo)

 **1600**

 **1610**

Himeji tenshu *built in Kobe*

the self-effacing attitude known as **wabi-sabi** (rustic simplicity), in which the purity of design and protocol became a form of heightened consciousness. The aesthetic of the tea ceremony influenced the restrained treatment of state halls as clean, planar environments.

The final *shogun* to complete the unification of Japan, Tokugawa Ieyasu, initially withdrew his patronage from the imperial city of Kyoto and transformed the small fishing village of Edo (Fig. 12.3-1a,b), now known as Tokyo, into a capital city. Here, he created a formidable fortified enclave. His *tenshu* rose 60 m (197 ft), and though twice rebuilt, it finally succumbed to the Meireki fire of 1657, which devastated 80% of the city. Part of the castle's base survived, but its likeness can only be reconstructed from the drawings made by the architect Kora Munehiro (1574–1646) in 1638 and the beautiful twelve-part screen painting panorama of Edo, the *Edozu byobu*.

The *Edozu byobu* shows the core of the city, which after three generations had grown to a population of half a million. According to its depiction the *tenshu* rose high above the rest of the fabric, surrounded by two inner moats and dozens of palace structures. A bridge connected the rear of the enclave to a secluded palace compound for the *shogun*'s family members, set in a large, thickly forested park. Ieyasu obliged the *daimyo* nobles to construct an outer moat of 15 km (9.3 miles) circumference and 50 m (164 ft) width, a task that nearly bankrupted them. While other Japanese capital cities followed a grid, Edo's moat took a spiral pattern. Similar to Louis XIV at Versailles, Ieyasu attempted to control the nobility by obliging them to build a palace in his capital and spend every other year in residence there. Allegedly, over 60% of Edo's territory in the seventeenth century was occupied by these obsequious residences, but today only two fragments of gardens from this age remain intact.

Figure 12.3-1 Edo (Tokyo), Japan. (b) Map of spiral pattern of Edo, where courtiers were obliged to build near the Tokugawa stronghold in the center.

Tokugawa dynasty builds Ninomaru Palace in Kyoto

▲ **1625**

▼ **1639**

Sakoku policy forbids all contact between Japan and other countries

Katsura Rikyu villa completed on the outskirts of Kyoto

▲ **1660**

Himeji Castle (Fig. 12.3-2a,b), west of Kobe, offers the largest and best preserved of the *tenshu* type, built during the first decade of the seventeenth century by Ikeda Terumasa (1565–1613), a trusted ally of the Tokugawa clan. The lofty upturned eaves of its five levels combined with the concatenation of alternating cusped and *A*-shaped gables, and the whiteness of its plastered elevations led to its name, the "white heron." Three smaller towers surrounded the central tower, stepping down to meet a labyrinthine series of walls guarded by eighty-four gatehouse towers. The builders created the masonry base with the same labor-intensive drywall technique of interlocking pieces used at Azuchi. A 6 km (3.7 mile) moat encapsulated the irregular contours of the castle's two knolls. The builders structured the upper stories of Himeji with mortise-and-tenon wood beams joined to two vertical masts, extending the entire height of the structure like a spine. The construction method, which performed well under seismic stress, resembled the structure of trees, which usually withstand earthquakes.

RELIGION, PHILOSOPHY, FOLKLORE

Zen Buddhism in Japan

Zen Buddhism entered Japan through Chinese missionaries in the twelfth and thirteenth centuries. In the classic memoir of Zen wisdom *Tale of a Ten Foot Square Hut*, written by Kamo no Chōmei in 1212, one finds an intimation of this philosophy's essential law of nature, a concept close to that propounded by Epicurean philosophers in ancient Greece: "The river flows on without cease yet its waters are never the same." The monk's discussion of his hut is reminiscent of the nineteenth-century American transcendentalist Henry David Thoreau's diary of building a cabin at Walden Pond (see Section 16.2). The economy of these huts and their modest simplicity led both authors to a sense of oneness with nature. The *wabi-sabi* (rustic simplicity) aesthetic of teahouses and minimal stone gardens derived from such a sensibility.

Kyoto became the center of the Zen Buddhist movement, as the philosophy had great appeal to the aristocratic level of Japanese society. The most important Zen monasteries, such as Daitokuji (where Sen no Rikyu lived) and Nanzenji, sat close to the city, on hilly sites with woods that favored the contemplation of natural features.

Kyoto. Kogetsudai (moon-viewing platform), with Ginkaken-ji (Silver Pavilion) in the background, begun in 1465 and rebuilt 1615.

RELIGION, PHILOSOPHY, FOLKLORE

Wabi-Sabi and the Japanese Teahouse

The tea ceremony, or *chanoyu*, like many important cultural forms in Japan, was initially imported from China but developed into an autonomous form of entertainment for the upper classes. Japanese intellectuals prized the teahouse for its minimalism, achieved according to the theory of design known as *wabi-sabi*, "rustic simplicity." Contrary to the symmetry and strict order of European and Persian architectures, Japanese designers cultivated the imperfect, impermanent, and incomplete.

The famous tea master Sen no Rikyu allegedly prepared the miniscule Taian Teahouse at the Myokian Temple near Kyoto to receive the *shogun* Hideyoshi in 1582. The teahouse fit into a square, 3 m (10 ft) per side. The master entered on the north through the narrow kitchen and then passed into the perpendicular anteroom transitional space. From here he turned to open a sliding door onto the two *tatami* mats of the tearoom, where he received the guest. The guest entered from the south under a protective porch through a 72 cm (28 inch) high crawl space. He looked directly to a *tokonoma* alcove placed on-axis to the entry, which made the space seem larger. The pitched ceiling above the guest's position enhanced the spatiality of the room. On the master's side of the room at the interior corner stood a small hearth cut into the floor for boiling the water for tea. Most of the building materials were left in an unprocessed state to convey the rustic ideal—the window in the anteroom, for instance, was cut from the plaster, revealing the bamboo wattles as a shade.

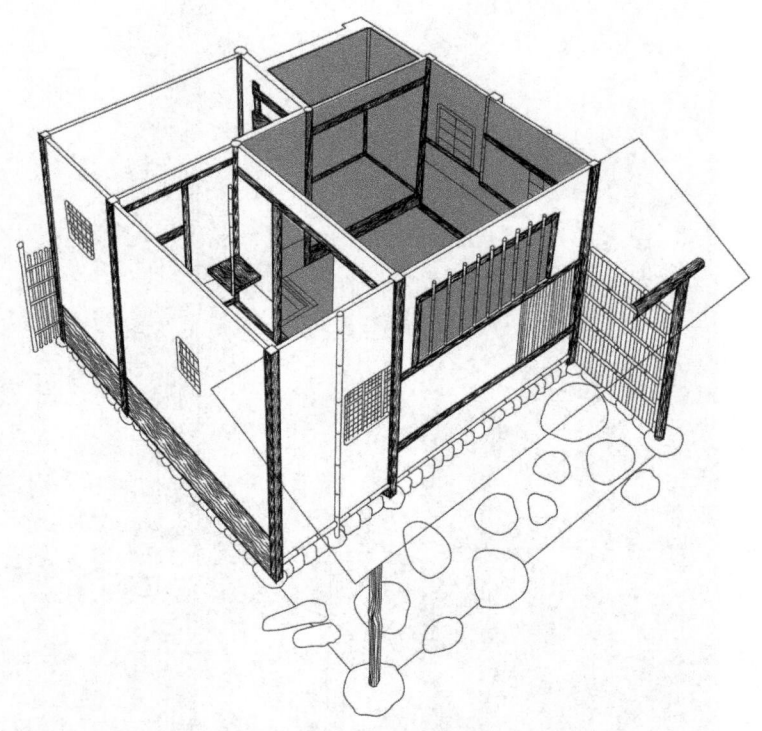

Kyoto. Taian Teahouse, Myokian Temple, plan, 1580s.

In 1615, after quelling the final resistance from the heir to Hideyoshi, Ieyasu promulgated a law against building castles and had many of them destroyed. While the new castles built for the Tokugawa served to send the message of the *shogun*'s power, he attempted to limit competition, forbidding the *daimyo* to possess more than one castle per region. In this same spirit of vigilance his grandson Iemitsu enacted the policy of *sakoku*, the closing of the borders of Japan in the late 1630s. This interdict against foreign influence, be it Asian or European, endured for more than 250 years. The Japanese only permitted Dutch and Chinese merchants to come to an island near Nagasaki to trade, mostly in armaments.

The Japanese Exception: To Privilege Asymmetrical Order

Aside from the strikingly original formal solution of the *tenshu* towers built during the sixteenth and seventeenth centuries, the Japanese ruling class cultivated a unique palace type, which displayed their authority horizontally in the midst of well-groomed parks. In earlier periods the typical Japanese palace, known as a *shinden*, had derived from Chinese precedents (Fig. 12.3-3). It featured an oblong reception hall surrounded by porches. The palace compounds in imperial Kyoto occupied one or more orthogonal patches of the grid plan and were surrounded by thick earthen walls and, in some cases, a moat. Inside the enclosure the landscape appeared natural. The park usually included a free-form lake with one or more islands in the south, and the porches of the palace extended to offer views to the lake.

During the Edo period the new palace type, the **shoin**, broke definitively from Chinese precedents. Often, the composition followed the "flock of wild geese" plan, a staggered series of pavilions on an oblique axis, connected by enclosed verandahs. Since the rooms did not adhere to a central axis, their redented zigzag disposition increased the linear exposure to external landscape elements. The Ninomaru Palace in Kyoto, built for Ieyasu in 1610 and enlarged in 1626 by his grandson Iemitsu, remains the most

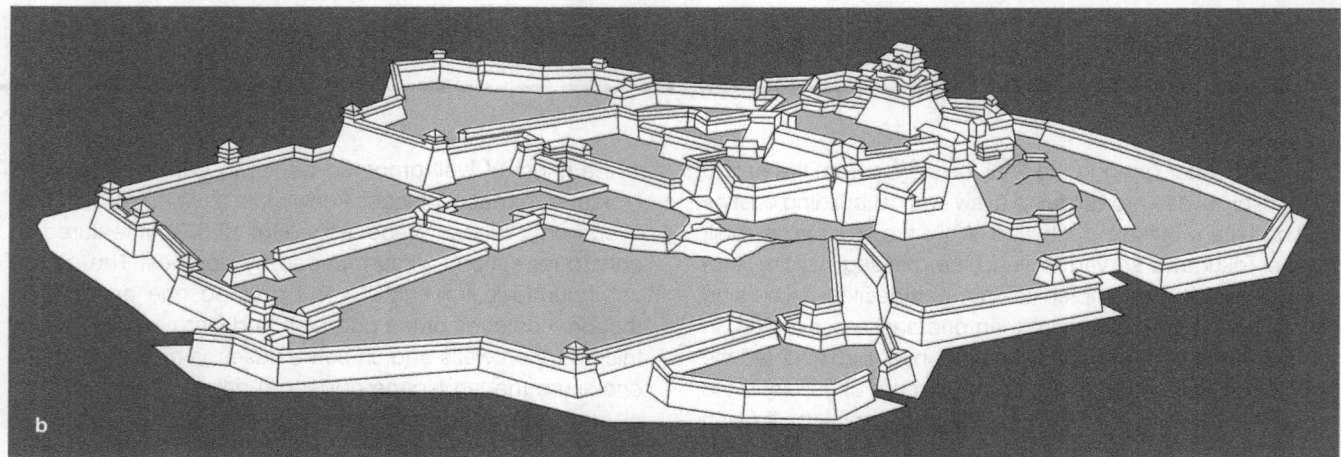

Figure 12.3-2 Kobe, Japan. (a) Himeji (White Heron) *tenshu*, built for an ally of the Tokugawa clan, ca. 1610. (b) *Tenshu* axon.

influential and best preserved of the *shoin* type. In the effort to maintain his quasi-regal status, Ieyasu planned his *shoin* palace as a suitable environment to receive the emperor, a function similar to that of Hideyoshi's erstwhile Jurakudai Palace. While the *shogun* kept his court in Edo, the maintenance of a palace in the emperor's city of Kyoto served to symbolically grant him imperial sanction. The palace occupied one corner of the Nijo Castle block, a 400 × 500 m

(1,312 × 1,640 ft) estate that held down the northwest quadrant of the grid of the ancient capital, in opposition to the northeast site of the emperor's Gosho Palace. Ieyasu's complex included a five-story *tenshu*, destroyed by lightning in the eighteenth century, and several other buildings that have since disappeared.

All of the constituent parts of the Ninomaru Palace (Fig. 12.3-4a,b) related to a geometric module, but its

Figure 12.3-3 Kyoto. Reconstruction of Hojujiden, a Chinese-inspired *shinden*-type palace, tenth century.

composition remained asymmetrical, with five pavilions staggered on a diagonal. One entered off-axis through the covered vestibule on the far southeast corner of the first volume and proceeded laterally through enclosed verandahs on the southern and western perimeters of the halls. Operable sliding shutters opened the corridors to the privileged views of the lake and gardens. The verandahs linking the five halls had floorboards that purposely squeaked as one passed, to alert the occupants of any intruder.

The *shoin* type took its name from the built-in writing desk that would have been placed in a niche in the principal rooms. Next to this niche one always found a formal alcove (**tokonoma**) with a painted scene, much like a theatrical backdrop for the appearance of the patron. To the side of the alcove stood shelves mounted in a staggered pattern. The lateral walls in these chambers were made of sliding panels (*fusuma*) decorated with paintings. In each of the main halls of the Ninomaru Palace the niche for the desk jutted into the verandah on the west, sheathed by translucent paper **shoji** screens that infused it with a special glowing light, as ethereal as the illumination from Bernini's light traps. Natural scenes painted in a stylized manner by court painter Kanō Tan'yū (1602–1674) covered the walls. He depicted trees and animals abstractly against gold-leaf backgrounds to pick up the light. With its gold leaf–painted panels, gilded coffered ceilings, and polished hardwood frames, the hall exuded the deep luster of a lacquered box.

The *shogun* reserved the fourth hall, the *Ohiroma* (Fig. 12.3-5), for the reception of the emperor. Here, Kanō decorated the *tokonoma* alcove with a solitary twisted pine

tree, the symbol of enduring authority. The pavilion was subdivided into an *L*-shaped sequence enclosed by painted *fusuma* panels that could be opened toward the minor servant spaces. The first area of the sequence served as a foyer on the east, from which those allowed to enter made a right turn to be seated in the lower area of the two-level hall. For formal receptions the *shogun* sat on the upper level of the north end of the hall in front of the alcove painting, cross-legged on a slightly raised mat. This rear half of the room stood 0.5 m (1.6 ft) above the front half, creating a tangible court hierarchy.

One could read the modular order of the Ninomaru Palace pavilions by counting the number of their **tatami** floor mats. Designers used *tatami* in most traditional Japanese buildings, from the *minka* house type for peasants to the small teahouse to the pleasure districts' brothels. Roughly 1 × 2 m (3.2 × 6.5 ft), the size of a sleeping space, the straw-woven floor pads, lined with black silk hems, provided a universal unit of measurement and proportion. Like the classical column in European architecture, *tatami* mats conveyed a sense of measurement through the analogy with the human body, in this case prone rather than standing. One perceived the order and proportion of rooms in terms of their number of mats. The double area of the *Ohiroma* reception hall held ninety-six *tatami*, while the flange space of its foyer held forty-six.

Ninomaru Palace's ceremonial spaces also resembled the play spaces of Noh theater, which took as their most common backdrop a lone pine tree. The Noh stage at Ninomaru jutted off the verandah at the southern end of the *Ohiroma*, almost like a mirror of the great hall. Japanese

Figure 12.3-4 Kyoto. (a) Ninomaru
Palace, within the Nijo Castle
compound, 1616–1636. (b) See
facing page.

compound with a temple and mausoleum that encouraged the worship of the defunct leader. While the designers treated the prayer halls with restraint, they loaded the gateways with gilded decoration and eaves that supported a complex series of multiple brackets.

Not to be outdone by his predecessor, Ieyasu planned for the worship of his spirit at the Tosho-gu shrine at Nikko (Fig. 12.3-6a,b), 50 km (31 miles) west of Tokyo. Built by his son and rebuilt in 1634 by his ambitious grandson, the dozens of buildings at the shrine stepped up a wooded slope, with the entry gates ranking among the most ornate buildings ever conceived in Japan. The celebrated master builder Kora Munehiro designed the most important parts of the Nikko shrine. In his role as the *bungo*, the *shogun*'s superintendent of public works, he prepared the *Shomei* treatise, similar to the Chinese *Yingzao Fashi*, to demonstrate how to use the proportions of wooden members to make credible cost estimates. His drawings illustrate the earliest use of the conventions of plans, elevations, and sections in Japan.

The Tosho-gu shrine at Nikko avoided strict symmetrical order as a result of its steep site. The two major decorative buildings, the Yomeimon Gate and the Karamon Pavilion, formed a glimmering passage toward the inner sanctuaries. An oblique stairway with several bends led to the tomb of Ieyasu, where a relatively restrained stone pagoda stood on an octagonal base like those used in statues of Buddhist saints. Despite the charged decoration of the complex, with its multiple brackets, ornate sculptures, cusped eaves, and delicate metalwork, the relation of the buildings to the landscape recalled the Shinto reverence for the divinity of nature.

rulers unwittingly paralleled the theatricality of the courts of absolutist Europe: the more the central authority attempted to exert control, the more it resorted to creating theatrical ceremonies and spaces for the enactment of obedience.

While the details of the interior of the Ninomaru Palace in Kyoto would have appeared serene and minimal, designers during the Edo period also resorted to decorative excess. The burial sites of the *shoguns* attracted the most elaborate structures. The tradition began with Hideyoshi, who left instructions to treat his soul as a divinity. During the first years of the seventeenth century his widow, the regent Yododono (1565–1615), one of the few female protagonists in Japanese history, sponsored the Toyokuni shrine on the outskirts of Kyoto. She prepared a Shinto-inspired

Figure 12.3-5 Kyoto. Ninomaru
Palace, *Ohiroma* hall with decorated
niche, 1616–1636.

Figure 12.3-4b Kyoto. Ninomaru Palace, with an asymmetrical "flock of geese" plan, 1616–1636.

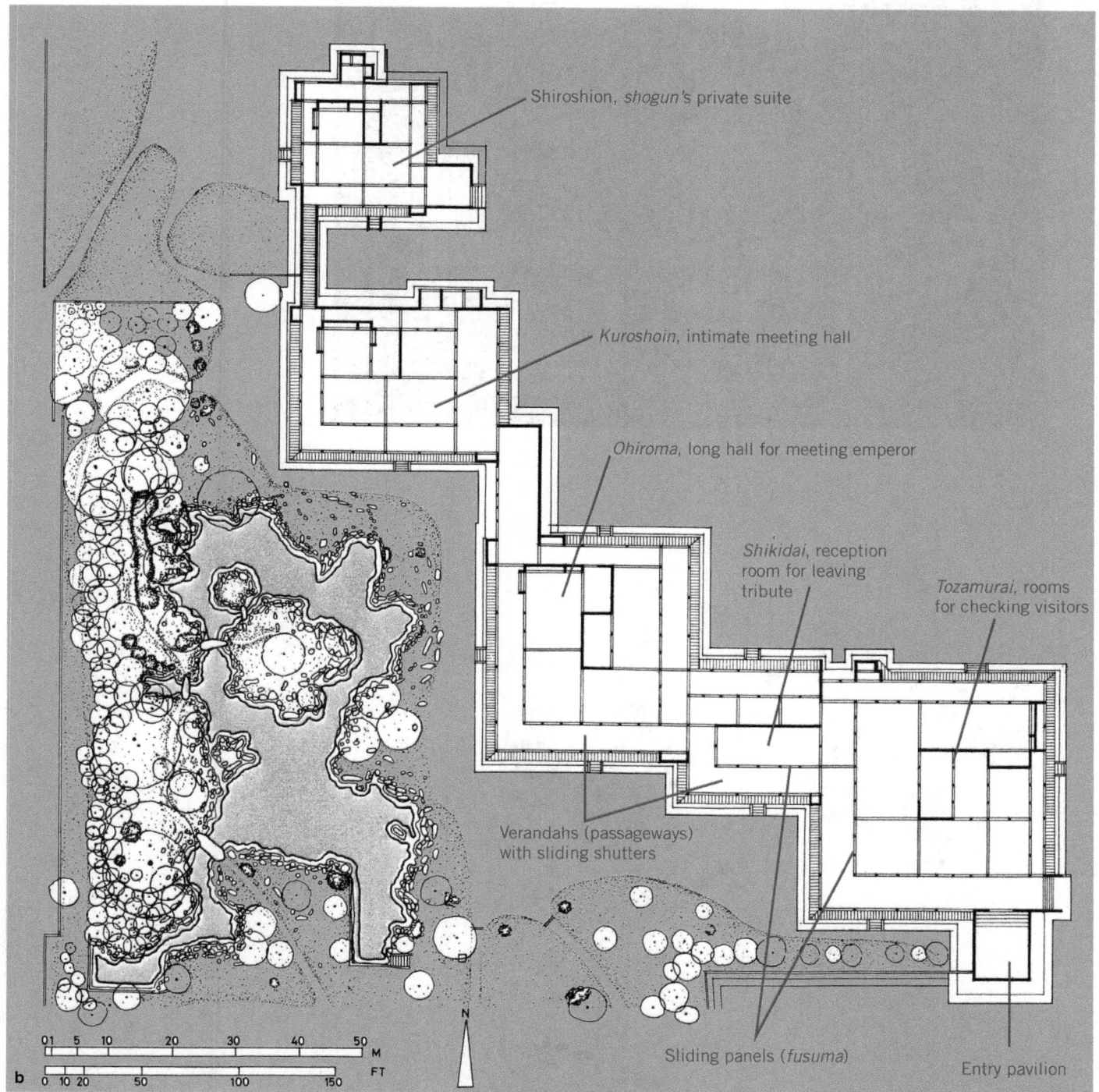

Shiroshion, *shogun's* private suite

Kuroshoin, intimate meeting hall

Ohiroma, long hall for meeting emperor

Shikidai, reception room for leaving tribute

Tozamurai, rooms for checking visitors

Verandahs (passageways) with sliding shutters

Sliding panels (*fusuma*)

Entry pavilion

b

Dry Gardens and Borrowed Landscapes

While André Le Nôtre in seventeenth-century France "forced" natural ingredients into abstract patterns on perspectival axes, the designers of Japanese gardens reached a more acute level of artificiality in their recreations of nature. In the two major types of gardens seen in Japan at this time, the "stroll" garden and the enclosed "dry" garden, designers molded natural ingredients into miniature representations of nature. The most famous byproduct of this trend, the dwarf *bonsai* tree, was trained through pruning and root crimping

Figure 12.3-6 Tokyo. (a) Nikko necropolis for Tokugawa, Yomeimon Gate, 1630s. (b) Plan showing asymmetrical layout.

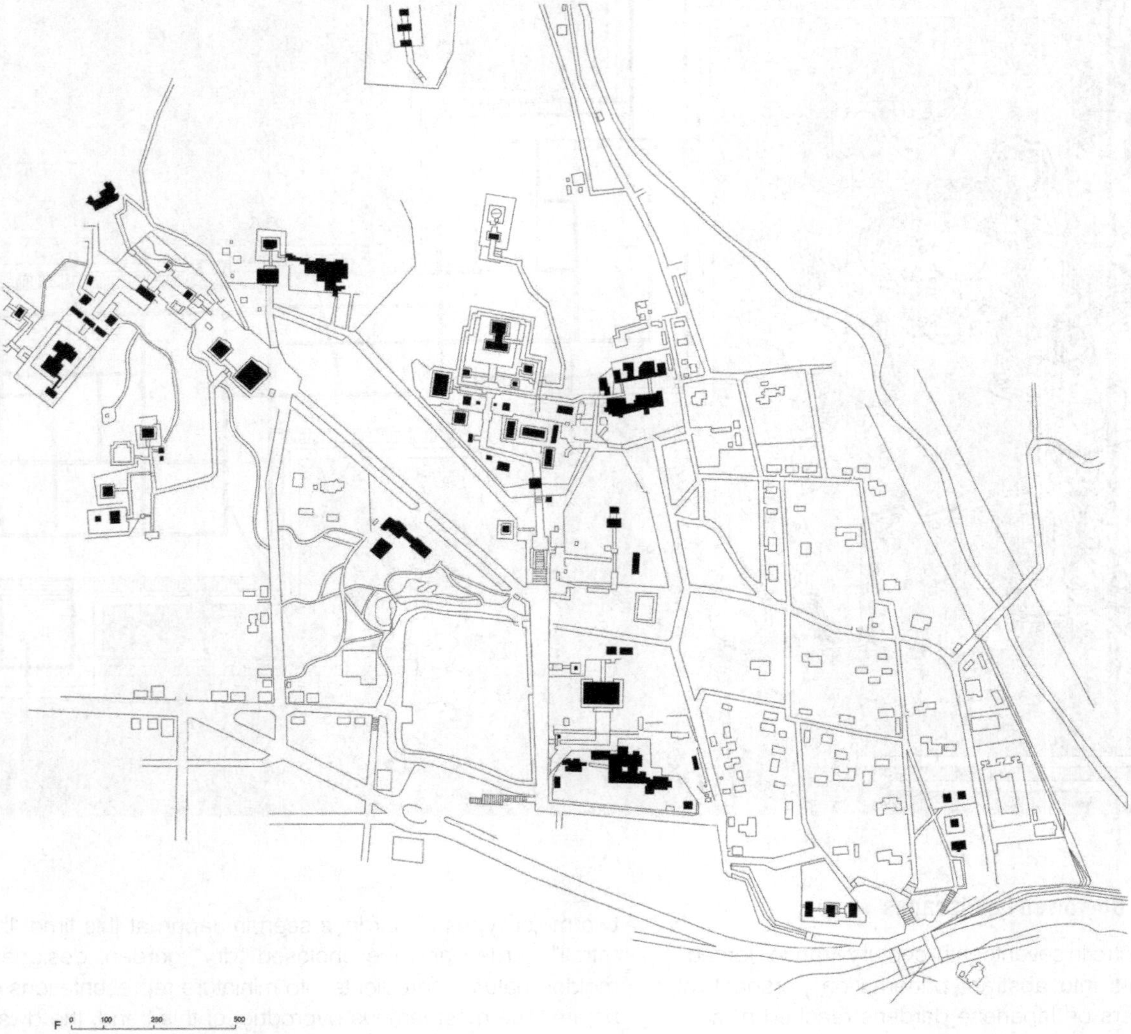

b

F 0   100   200   500

M 0   50   100   250

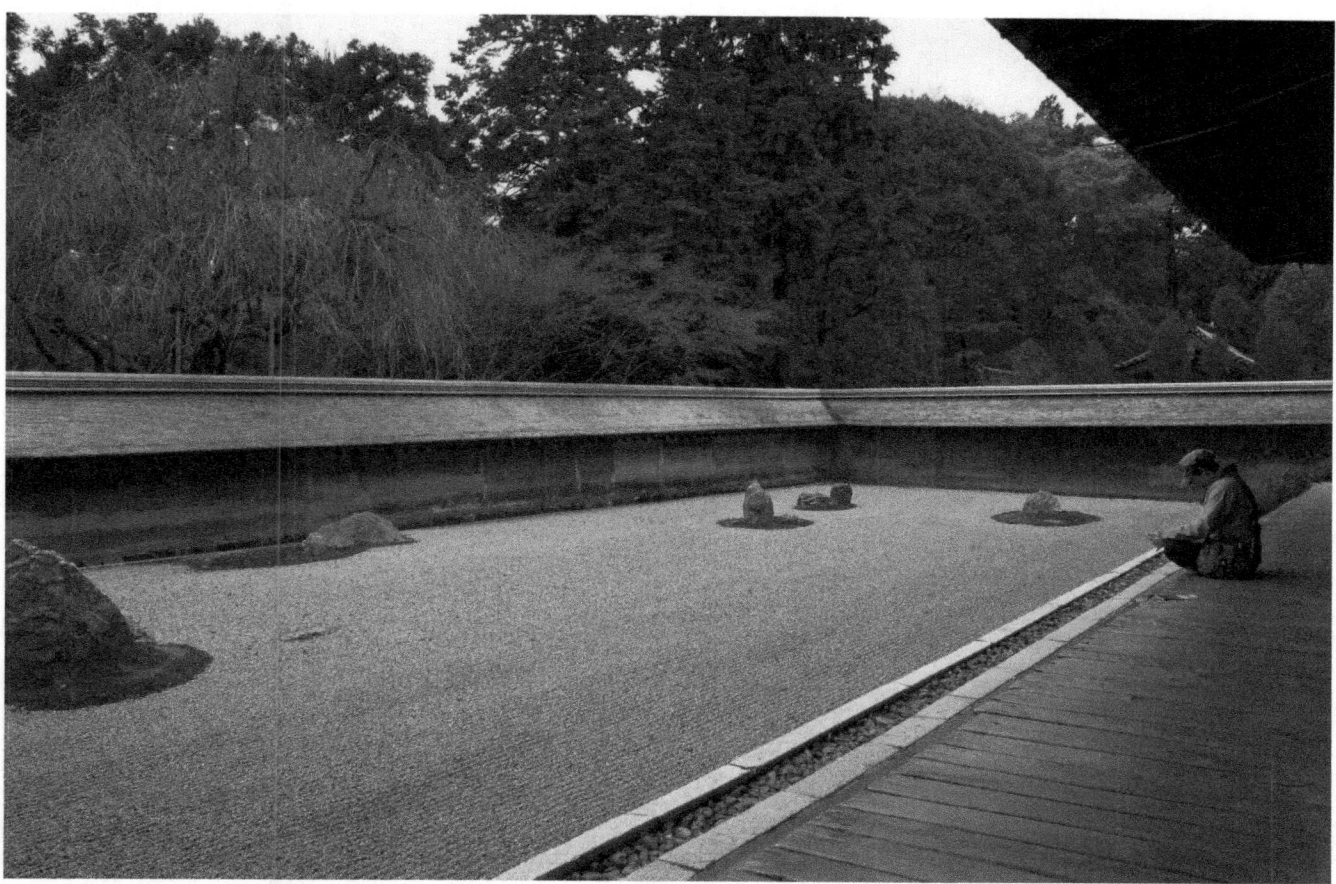

Figure 12.3-7 Kyoto. Ryoanji Zen temple, *karesansui* dry garden, early sixteenth century.

into a miniature version of a large tree. The great gardens of Edo period Japan served either as settings for the aristocratic palaces or as places of contemplation in Buddhist monasteries. As in the Chinese scholars' gardens of Suzhou (see Section 11.1), their designers avoided axial alignments, setting up itineraries with frequently changing points of view. Zen Buddhism, which focused on enlightenment through meditation, inspired a new taste for controlled natural settings, which added a more sophisticated understanding to the indigenous Shinto respect for the phenomenal landscape.

The Nanzenji monastery became the most influential Zen center in Japan. Important patrons competed to sponsor its gates, palaces, temples, and gardens. Hideyoshi rebuilt the main temple and Buddha hall in 1597, while Ieyasu soon after tried to obscure the importance of these works by donating the immense ornamental gate. The Tokugawa clan replaced many of the works paid for by Hideyoshi, such as the palace for the emperor and the main convent. During the Edo period patrons donated more than sixty subsidiary temples, or *tatchus*, around the principal temple, and most of them included a garden.

Kobori Enshu (1579–1647) designed the most famous gardens at Nanzenji. He descended from a samurai father entrusted with building castles for Ieyasu and inherited one of them, a bequest that gave him *daimyo* status. Somewhat like Leon Battista Alberti in fifteenth-century Italy, Enshu stood on

equal ground with his aristocratic patrons. He designed the additions to the Ninomaru Palace in Kyoto under Iemitsu in the mid-1620s. Aside from his talent in architecture and garden design, Enshu gained notoriety as a master of the tea ceremony. He had studied with Furuta Oribe, the successor to Sen no Rikyu, and at Nanzenji he designed several teahouses and gardens in the restrained style of the great master.

The Zen garden often appeared as a prelude to the teahouse and served as a form of poetic discipline confined to an enclosed site, suitable for meditation. Instead of offering direct exposure to nature, it served as a metaphorical artifact, a way of portraying the qualities and forces of nature. The enigmatic *karesansui*, "dry gardens," made of raked white pebbles and rough stones, represented landforms amid the waves of bodies of water. The stone garden of Ryoanji in Kyoto (Fig. 12.3-7), built in the early sixteenth century, defined the type: a walled court filled with white pebbles raked into wavy rills, with fifteen stones placed at irregular intervals, symbolic of islands or dragons. Enshu's *karesansui* gardens at Nanzenji also included shrubs. Here, he demonstrated his mastery of **shakkei**, or "borrowed landscapes," in which the foreground comprised a miniaturization of mountains and forests while beyond the wall one perceived real mountains and forests in correspondence.

Katsura Rikyu (Fig. 12.3-8a,b), a villa on the southwest side of Kyoto, built from 1620 to 1660, displayed the austerity

Figure 12.3-8 Kyoto. (a) Katsura Rikyu, built for Prince Toshihito, 1620–1660. (b) Detail.

and ingenuity of the teahouses of Rikyu and Enshu. Similar to the Ninomaru Palace, it followed the *shoin* plan, with a jogging sequence of four rectangular volumes wrapped with verandahs on the south and west, where they overlooked the lake. The project began in 1620 under Prince Hachijo Toshihito (1579–1629), the brother of Emperor Goyozei and advisor to Emperor Gomizuno-o. The latter was the same emperor received at Ninomaru Palace by Ieyasu in 1615. He abdicated the throne in 1629, the year of his uncle's death, and lived the rest of his long life as a Zen Buddhist monk. The Zen aesthetic motivated the design of the villa of Toshi-hito, his close associate. The patron's son, Noritada, continued the project of Katsura Rikyu with the financial support of the *shogun* until his death in 1662.

The designers of Katsura Rikyu left the timbers of the structural frame in their raw, unplaned state to exhibit the wear of time. The wooden posts that raised the villa 1 m (3.3 ft) above grade rested directly on rough stones. Translucent *shoji* panels divided the interior, permitting flexible reconfigurations of the central spaces. At the most privileged point of the villa, the "moon-viewing space," the white *shoji* screens of the interior slid open to a vision of the lake, the woods behind, and the path to the bamboo platform at the edge of the lake for observing the heavens at night.

Around Katsura Rikyu's lake the visitor encountered isolated teahouses that further demonstrated the Zen sensibility. The Shokin-tei (Fig. 12.3-9), standing on the island farthest from the palace, was the most memorable, its plaster walls decorated with blue and white rectangular checkers and in the midst of the tearoom a wonderfully gnarled tree trunk sustaining a partition panel. To reach the teahouses, one passed through the stroll garden with its different bridges: one in wood, one a solid piece of stone, and one with miniature towers. Combinations of mosses, shaped hedges, and dwarf trees framed the views. Some of the compositions around the lake represented famous landscapes. The gardens of Katsura Rikyu, executed with extraordinary restraint and modesty, provided an elite clientele an artful reenactment of the natural world, developed amid Japan's willful seclusion from the rest of the world.

Further Reading

Coaldrake, William H. *Architecture and Authority in Japan.* London: Routledge, 1996.

Naito, Akira. *Edo: The City that Became Tokyo.* Translated by H. Mack Horton. Tokyo: Kodansha International, 2003.

Nishi, Kazuo, and Kazuo Hozumi. *What Is Japanese Architecture?* Translated by H. Mack Horton. San Francisco: Kodansha International, 1983.

Figure 12.3-9 Kyoto. Katsura Rikyu, detail of the Shokin-tei teahouse, 1620–1660.

Nitschke, Gunther. *Japanese Gardens: Right Angle and Natural Form.* Cologne, Germany: Taschen, 2003.

Young, David, and Michiko Young. *Introduction to Japanese Architecture.* Singapore: Periplus Editions, 2004.

↗ Visit the free website **www.oup.com/us/ingersoll** to view chapter outlines and study questions; Google Maps showing the location of key sites; links to UNESCO World Heritage Sites; and essays on topics that cross time and culture.

CHAPTER 13

1700–1750

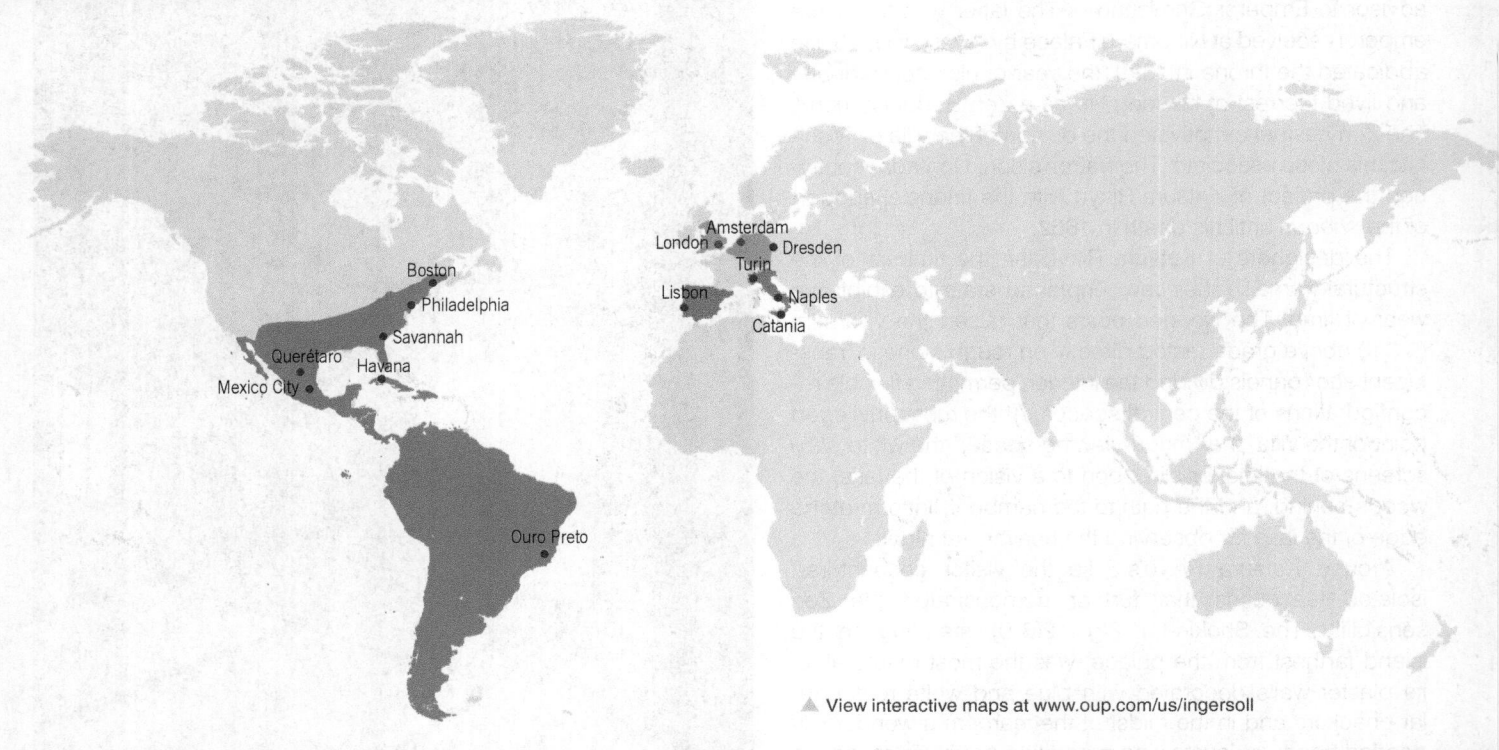

Amsterdam
London • • Dresden
Turin
Lisbon • • Naples
Catania
Boston
Philadelphia
Savannah
Querétaro Havana
Mexico City
Ouro Preto

▲ View interactive maps at www.oup.com/us/ingersoll

13.1 PROTESTANT EUROPE: An Architecture of Essentials

13.2 THE DIFFUSION OF THE BAROQUE: Life as Theater

13.3 THE AMERICAN COLONIES: Domination and Liberty on the Grid

Since the mid-sixteenth century, the religious division of Europe into Protestant and Catholic areas had exerted profound effects on the region's political and cultural structures. During the seventeenth and eighteenth centuries Holland and England, which had a predominance of Protestants, produced republican parliamentary monarchies, while the largely Catholic societies of Portugal, Spain, France, and parts of Germany submitted to "absolutist" monarchies. The monochromatic austerity of Dutch church interiors stood in direct opposition to the colorfully ornate rococo altars of churches in cities such as Seville and Munich. In Sicily, following the great earthquake of 1693, local architects, inspired by the curves and countercurves of Baroque Rome, designed exceptionally animated churches and public squares. This trend toward curvilinear and organic shapes, also found in northern Italian cities like Turin, came to a halt in the mid-eighteenth century, a reversal seen most forcefully in the rigorous classical geometry of the Reggia of Caserta. While the riches of Portuguese and Spanish colonial holdings in the Western Hemisphere helped sponsor grand churches, convents, and palaces, such colonial cities as Mexico City, Havana, and Ouro Preto also produced analogous monuments, incorporating into them the creative details of local craftspeople. The colonies of Protestant countries, in what became New England, built more austere works, following an ethic of expedient serviceability. Utility, within the framework of classical and vernacular precedents from Europe, became the chief criterion in the Anglo-American quest for an appropriate architectural language.

13.1 PROTESTANT EUROPE
An Architecture of Essentials

When Martin Luther launched his campaign against the church of the popes in Rome in 1517, architecture figured among his complaints. He railed against the great expense lavished on St. Peter's. During the rest of the century, as the various strains of Protestantism developed, a critical position emerged on architectural design. The Calvinists and Lutherans abjured the showiness and theatricality of Catholic churches, preferring austere, undecorated buildings. Calvinists in seventeenth-century Amsterdam kept their halls of worship whitewashed and unadorned. By 1700 the facades of the houses of wealthy Dutch merchants lining the city's major canals had conformed to an obvious code of republican moderation under which everyone seemed equally well-off. The modest exteriors, however, often concealed luxuriously appointed interiors.

In late-seventeenth-century England, the Anglican Church assumed a different attitude, nearly identical to that of the Roman Catholic Church. While refusing to acknowledge the spiritual leadership of the pope and allowing their priests to marry, Anglicans retained most of the Catholic ceremonies. The Church of England continued to use the great cathedrals of the past and built new ones in grand style. Christopher Wren designed fifty new churches after the 1666 Great Fire of London, borrowing heavily from the Catholic precedents of Rome and Paris. With the rise of the Whig faction in Parliament after 1700, however, liberal patrons insisted on the use of simple, planar volumes in emulation of Andrea Palladio, rejecting the complex, curving forms of Wren. This shift to a neutral, inconspicuous architecture reflected the Protestant agenda for a secular society that treated religion and private life as personal matters of conscience.

The Dutch Republic: An Alternative to the Grand Manner

In 1700 Europe stood roughly divided into Catholic countries in the south (Portugal, Spain, France, Italy, and Austria) and Protestant countries in the north (England, Switzerland, many of the German states, Holland, Denmark, and Sweden). While the two sides shared common Christian beliefs, Protestants rejected the pope's claim to be their spiritual leader. Once free from papal authority, most of the reformed churches focused on the individual's relationship to the divine and downplayed collective ceremonies and ecclesiastical hierarchy. Early Calvinists, for instance, selected their own ministers directly from the congregation. Quakers needed no ministers at all. Most Protestant sects rejected the cults of the saints and generally purged their churches of statues and images. Like the Cistercian monks of the twelfth century (see Section 8.3), adherents to the sects that emerged during the Reformation stripped away expressions of luxury from their places of worship.

During the age of absolutist monarchies, the small, predominantly Protestant country of the Netherlands emerged with a political system derived from the medieval merchant-run city-states: a republic composed of a federation of seven provinces. The Dutch Union took root in 1579 during the struggle against Habsburg Spain and produced modern Europe's earliest parliamentary democracy. Similar to Venice, Holland's embrace of republicanism derived from its large class of shipping entrepreneurs. Canals for transporting goods in barges to warehouses laced the important trading cities of Delft, Amsterdam, and Rotterdam. The shipping industries generated great fortunes and international corporations, such as the East India Company, founded in Amsterdam at the beginning of the seventeenth century. As the major importer of Asian goods, the Netherlands soon accumulated the largest pool of financial assets in the world. The state-sanctioned Wisselbank offered the lowest lending rates in Europe, attracting numerous foreign investors. Despite their great wealth, the Dutch magnates never flaunted their status in public, preferring the code of republican moderation. Thus, they usually commissioned unpretentious houses.

The United Provinces of the Netherlands rebelled against Spain in 1568, but only the northern half succeeded in winning independence. For much of the latter half of the seventeenth century the Dutch republic was locked in conflict with France as a result of the expansionist policies of Louis XIV. While Sébastien Le Prestre de Vauban deployed his network of fortified cities along the northeast border of France, Baron Menno van Coehoorn (1641–1704) designed a similarly scaled series of defenses for the Netherlands. His masterpiece, Bergen-op-Zoom, built in the south in 1700, survives only as a plan, but his small fortress town of Naarden, 20 km (12.4 miles) east of Amsterdam (Fig. 13.1-1), remains intact, boasting a belt of angled bastions surrounded by two rings of canals. The Dutch, with 70% of their territory below sea level, understood the advantages of water as a defensive resource against invading armies and in times of siege purposely flooded the land to confound their enemies.

The great port of Amsterdam developed into the most powerful and tolerant city of the Dutch Union. It directed some of its formidable mercantile wealth toward social investments in education, orphanages, hospitals, and workhouses. Visitors, such as the English essayist John Evelyn (1620–1706), marveled at the absence of poverty and apparent social equality among its inhabitants. The city's oligarchic elite appeared virtually indistinguishable from the

Figure 13.1-1 Naarden, the Netherlands. Fortress town by Baron Menno van Coehoorn, ca. 1700.

common people, and the citizens enjoyed unprecedented access to their governing representatives. While the majority of Dutch residents were Protestants, the Netherlands fostered a previously unseen level of religious tolerance, permitting Jews, Catholics, and all variety of Protestants the equal right to worship. More out of commercial interest than moral conviction, Amsterdam welcomed people of all faiths, even Catholics, encouraging them to build churches. The Jewish synagogues of Amsterdam rivaled the Calvinist churches in their scale.

As Amsterdam's economy grew, it sponsored an exceptional expansion plan, initiated in 1613 and concluded around 1700 after three phases of development (Fig. 13.1-2a). The planners looked to the precedents of the three-canal

addition to Antwerp and the three-canal scheme for an ideal Dutch town by Simon Stevin (ca. 1548–1620) (Fig. 13.1-2b). Instead of following straight lines, however, they wrapped the three new tree-lined canals around the old city core, like the rings of an onion or the section of a tree. Unlike radiocentric schemes, such as Versailles, Amsterdam's plan yielded consistently oblique views, intentionally rejecting grand axes and monumental backdrops. This lack of formal hierarchy corresponded to the Protestant ethic of social balance without putting on display the privileges of wealth and power.

The churches in Amsterdam pursued the reverse of the decorative excesses of Baroque Catholicism. At first, Dutch Protestants retrofitted existing Catholic churches, such as the late Gothic Nieuwe Kerk in Amsterdam (Fig. 13.1-3a,b),

TIME LINE

▼ **1581**

Foundation of the Republic of the Seven United Netherlands

Great Fire of London

▲ **1666**

▼ **1668**

Amsterdam Stadhuis completed

Daniel Stalpaert designs the central-plan Oosterkirk in Amsterdam

▲ **1670**

stripping the sculptures and paintings from the old buildings and whitewashing their piers and walls. The new order dismantled lavish altars, choirs, and rood screens, and instead of focusing on an ornate altar at the end of the nave, its followers favored a centrally placed pulpit, capped with a broad wooden sounding board. The liturgical program shifted from processional to auditory needs, which preferenced the central plan. Under this new program churchgoers gathered about the pulpit and the movable altar as the minister, a member of the community, conducted the service. Dutch genre painters Pieter Jan Saenredam and Emanuel De Witte described with clinical accuracy the new openness and casual atmosphere of the interiors of seventeenth-century Dutch churches, showing men with their hats on, a few accompanied by their dogs!

The earliest new churches in Amsterdam, the Zuiderkerk (1606) and Westerkerk (1620), both designed by the city architect Hendrik de Keyser (1565–1621), conformed to longitudinal plans. Rather than taking their names from saints, the Calvinist churches of Amsterdam acquired generic names based on geography. De Keyser, who had worked his way up the building trades, took his style from mannerist pattern books that featured balustrades and decorated gables. He designed relatively austere interiors, marked only with simple classical columns and pilasters. To each of his churches de Keyser added a distinctive steeple, arranged in three or four tiers of engaged columns with a bulbous crown on the top, breaking the monotonous skyline of the city. He achieved a conceptual breakthrough

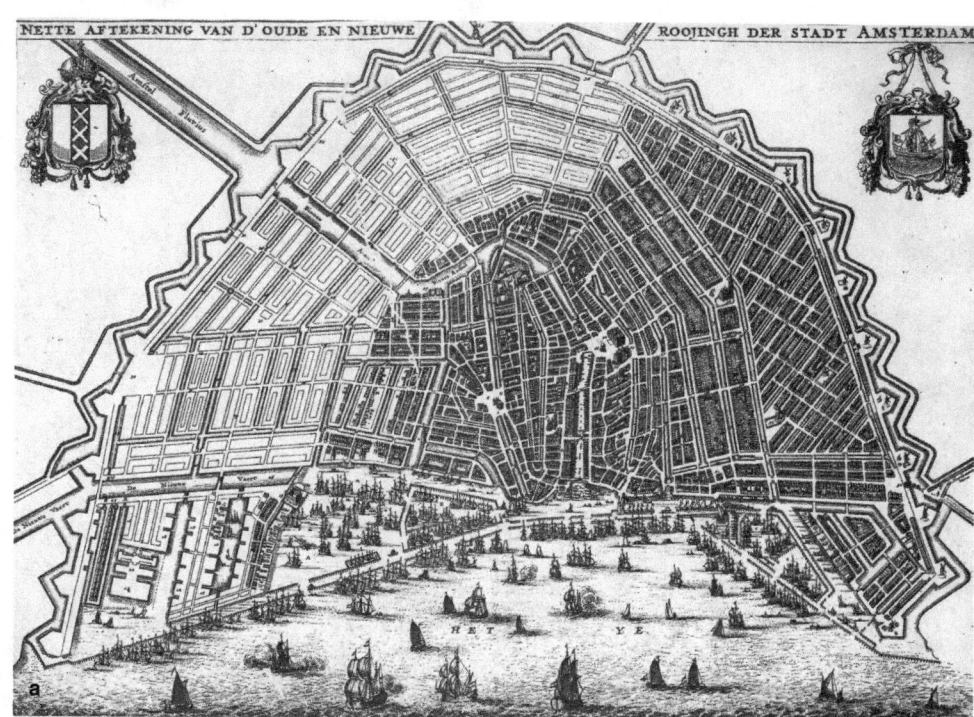

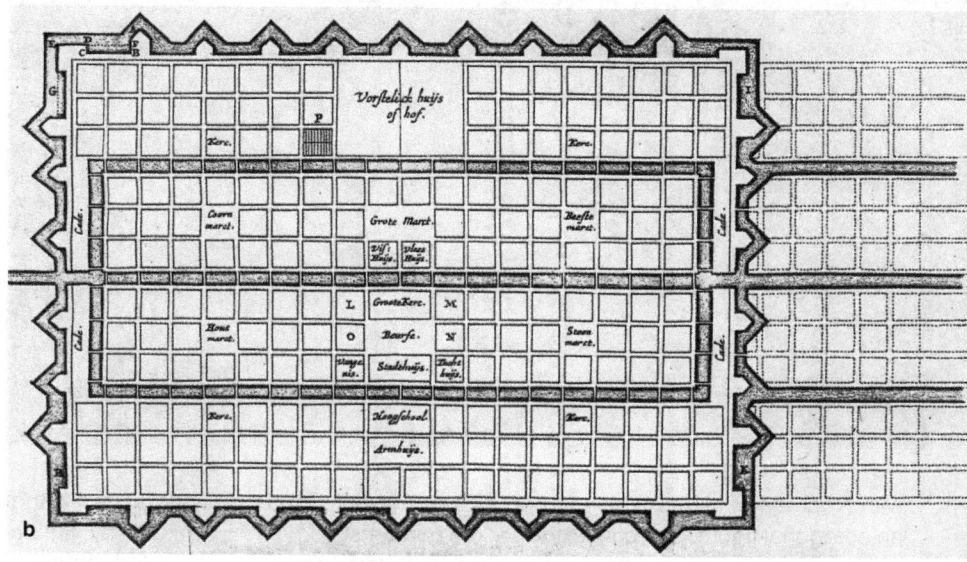

Figure 13.1-2 (a) Amsterdam. Plan of the city, I. B. Homanns, 1717. (b) Plan for ideal Dutch town, Simon Stevin, 1590.

▼ 1670–1700

Final section of Amsterdam's concentric plan filled out

Christopher Wren's St. Stephen, Walbrook, completed in London

▲ 1680

▼ 1688

England establishes a constitutional monarchy

Christopher Wren's St. Paul's in London completed after thirty years

▲ 1708

Figure 13.1-3 Amsterdam. (a) Nieuwe Kerk, showing whitewashed interior and wooden pulpit with sounding board. Painting by Emanuel de Witte, 1657. (b) See facing page.

A second generation of classically grounded Dutch architects was led by Jacob van Campen (1595–1657), who came from a privileged intellectual background. His Nieuwe Kerk in Haarlem (1645) perfected de Keyser's central-plan church, fitting the Greek cross into a perfectly square volume. The interior appeared luminous and unadorned, with four colossal Ionic piers supporting a groin vault over the central crossing. The Oosterkerk (1670) in Amsterdam, designed by van Campen's assistant Daniel Stalpaert (1615–1676), followed the same plan, articulating the facade with two levels of pilasters that broke down its mass. The Lutheran congregation of Amsterdam commissioned the most literal "auditorium" plan from Adriaan Dortsman (1636–1682), who began work on the structure in 1682. The architect joined a circular plan to an outer half-circle ambulatory, similar to a stage with a rounded *cavea*. The Lutheran Church also stood out as the only domed church in the city.

During the same period, Amsterdam hosted the construction of several large synagogues, the first in Europe to be built as freestanding monuments. The Esnogo, or Portuguese Synagogue (Fig. 13.1-5), designed in 1671 by Stalpaert with Elias Bouman (1636–1686), resembled the city's central-plan churches, perfectly square in plan. A wooden barrel vault ran down the center nave, flanked by two barrel-vaulted aisles with galleries for the

with Noorderkerk (1620), planned on a **Greek cross** within an octagonal figure. The pulpit stood at the northeast corner of the crossing. This central-plan auditorium better served the Calvinist service and exerted wide influence in Holland, England, and Germany (Fig. 13.1-4).

1717

Colen Campbell publishes *Vitruvius Britannicus*

James Gibbs designs St. Martin-in-the Fields in London

1721

1725

Lord Burlington creates the epitome of English Palladianism at Chiswick

Figure 13.1-3 Amsterdam. (b) Oosterkirk, Daniel Stalpaert, 1670.

women. The exterior conformed to the "severe style" of other Dutch religious buildings, presenting tall brick volumes with subdued articulation. The white-frame windows constituted the building's only decorative aspect.

Although Calvinists discouraged worldliness, late-seventeenth-century Amsterdam flourished as the leading market of consumer goods in the world. This contradiction was captured in the understated facades of the houses on the three new canals (Fig. 13.1-6), which concealed the sumptuous lifestyles of the great merchant families. Amsterdam's building plots remained relatively narrow, 8.5 m (27 ft) wide by 60 m (192 ft) deep, and even after the municipality attempted to encourage larger houses by preparing larger lots, speculators would acquire two lots and divide them into three properties. Pragmatic considerations often prevailed over aesthetic ones, and most of the facades in Amsterdam tilted forward slightly over the street to support a crane at the apex of the gable, conceived as a way to haul furniture or goods through the buildings' windows without damaging the facades.

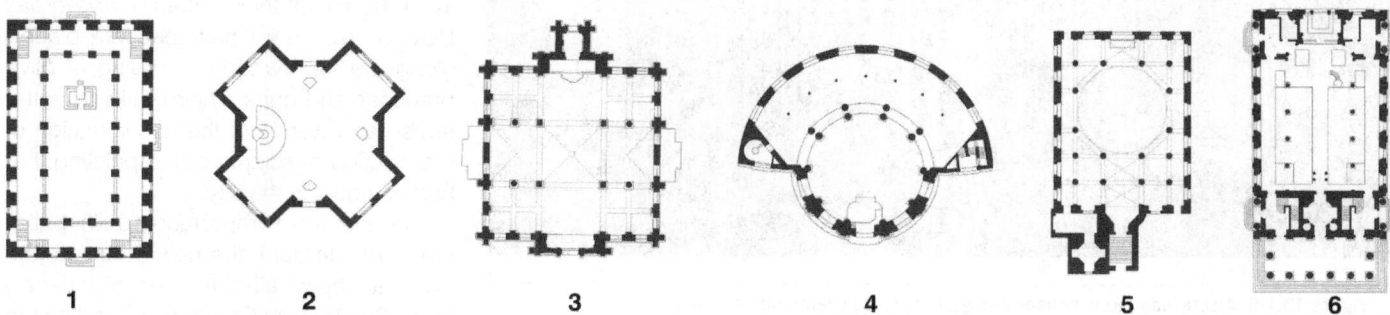

Figure 13.1-4 Plans of early Protestant churches: (1) Paris, Temple of Charenton, Salomon de Brosse, 1623; (2) Amsterdam, Noorderkerk, Hendrik de Keyser, 1620; (3) Amsterdam, Oosterkerk, Daniel Stalpaert, 1670; (4) Amsterdam, Lutheran Church, Adriaan Dortsman, 1682; (5) London, St. Stephen, Walbrook, Christopher Wren, 1680; (6) London, St. Martin-in-the-Fields, J. Gibbs, 1721.

different, with steep gables and narrow windows that created their own symmetry. The modest brick elevations occasionally carried pilasters and rusticated window frames, reserving their greatest expression of individuality for the *gevel*, the articulated gable, decorated with scrolls, balls, balusters, swags, urns, and inscriptions.

Van Campen perfected his classical pilaster style at his Mauritshuis (Fig. 13.1-7), a freestanding townhouse in the Hague built in 1633 for the governor of Holland's short-lived colony in Brazil. The rear facade of the cubical volume overlooked a canal and carried a mannerist composition of six bays of colossal two-story Ionic pilasters capped by a pediment over the four central bays, motifs that the artist-architect perfected after his return from Italy. Like a Palladian villa, the plan of Mauritshuis adhered to perfect symmetry, with a large entry hall leading to a great hall at the rear.

Justus Vingboons (1620–1698) designed a grander version of van Campen's pilaster style for the sandstone-clad facade of the Trippenhuis in Amsterdam. Built in 1662 as a double house for two brothers who had made their fortune as arms dealers, it was one of the few truly palatial buildings in Amsterdam. Instead of the typical Dutch gable, a classical pediment covered the central three bays, uniting the two houses while leaving an ambiguous bay of windows in the center at the dividing point between them. The Tripp brothers established a near monopoly on munitions, running their business like a modern multinational corporation, and dared to declare in the pediment their slogan, *Ex bello pax* ("Out of war we will have peace"), placed alongside the symbolic crossing of olive branches and guns. Their profits from the arms trade went into the accumulation of a collection of sculpture and painting that had no equal in the city.

For the most important public building of Amsterdam, the new Stadhuis (the City Hall, now called the "Royal Palace") (Fig. 13.1-8a), van Campen insisted on the

Figure 13.1-6 Amsterdam. Row houses and gables, late seventeenth century.

Some of the wealthier families acquired two lots for a single house, allowing for a grander facade. Despite Amsterdam's conformity of scale, every facade looked severe pilaster style. Conceived in 1648 and finished nearly twenty years later, the palace rose as one of the largest secular buildings in seventeenth-century Europe, a four-square volume almost twice the size of Palazzo Farnese in Rome. Two levels of Corinthian pilasters and a central pediment articulated the blocky limestone exterior in a subdued version of Italian classical style. A cupola rose over a central belvedere, probably the first dome used on a nonreligious public building, taking the privilege of crowning the city away from the church.

Amsterdam had four elected burgomasters, who served two-year terms. They occupied offices in the seven-bay central wing under the pediment. The Burgerzaal, the great hall in the center of the building, covered a 40 × 20 m (128 × 64 ft) area, with four tiers of windows on its long sides (Fig. 13.1-8b). The Stadhuis belonged to the tradition of medieval public palaces, built in direct competition with the sixteenth-century town hall of Antwerp. Its exterior encased the anonymous workings of the republic's bureaucracies, including the Wisselbank, the state bank, which became one of the most important European lending institutions. Imposing yet modest, Amsterdam's city hall volleyed a Protestant response to the excesses of Versailles.

Wren's London: After the Great Fire

Architecture in England around 1700, while conditioned by some of the same factors that influenced Holland, such as Protestantism and mercantilism, proved less stylistically coherent. The landed aristocracy and monarchy, which aspired to the absolutism of France, stood at odds with the fundamentalist Puritan movement among English

The French Huguenots' Protestant Temple of Charenton

The French Calvinists, known as "Huguenots," built their "temple" in Charenton-le-Pont, a suburb a few kilometers to the southeast of Paris, in 1607. After its destruction by fire, the Huguenot architect Salomon de Brosse, assisted by Jean Thiriot, built a new church on the model of an ancient basilica. A rectangular box with tall windows but no exterior decoration, the interior presented a large, well-lit auditorium with a small altar in the west, ringed by an upper gallery. Although it was destroyed in 1685, the temple influenced the design of English churches, such as St. Paul's at Covent Garden, and many American churches.

Protestants. Political and religious conflicts in seventeenth-century England resulted in the beheading of Charles I; a civil war; the short-lived, Puritan-dominated republic of Oliver Cromwell; the Restoration of the pro-French, pro-Catholic Stuart monarchy; and the "Glorious Revolution" for a constitutional monarchy led by Protestants in 1688. While the English court and aristocracy looked to France and Italy for ostentatious models, the Puritans introduced an austere countertendency, strongly objecting to the corrupting influence of theater. During their moment of political

The Dutch House and Feminine Order

Dutch houses accommodated small, nuclear families averaging 4.7 members, with only one or two servants. While women in the Netherlands did not participate in society politically, they achieved more respect than their counterparts in other European countries. Dutch laws expressly forbade wife beating. Portraits of married couples by artists such as Frans Hals showed wives as valued friends and equal partners in the domestic realm. Pieter de Hooch in the 1660s portrayed Dutch interiors as a feminine realm with a strong sense of cleanliness and order. The act of housekeeping represented a moral imperative that became a cultural fetish. The flip side of this unusual respect for women at home, however, proved to be the equally extraordinary sex industry of Amsterdam's port district.

Pieter de Hooch, *At the Linen Closet*, 1663.

Figure 13.1-7 The Hague, the Netherlands. Mauritshuis, Jacob van Campen, 1633.

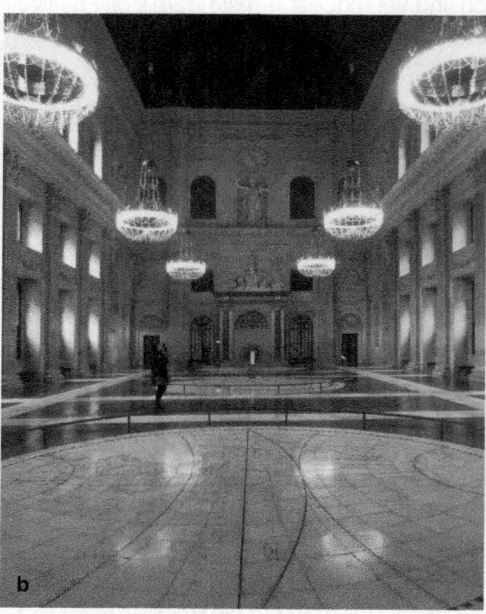

Figure 13.1-8 Amsterdam. (a) Stadhuis (later Royal Palace), van Campen, 1648–1668. (b) The Burgerzaal.

ascendancy in the 1640s, they commanded the destruction of the theaters of London, including the circular Globe Theater used by William Shakespeare.

Despite the Puritan undercurrent in England, Christopher Wren (1632–1723) succeeded in creating a remarkable local variation of Roman classicism during the Restoration of the 1660s. The domed profile of his greatest project, St. Paul's Cathedral, although strictly Protestant in its identification, could easily pass for a sibling of St. Peter's in Rome. Wren's approach to architecture derived from observing the works of Jules Hardouin-Mansart and Louis Le Vau in France while gaining secondhand knowledge of Gian Lorenzo Bernini and Carlo Rainaldi in Italy. During the same period he also became aware of the central plans of Dutch Protestant churches.

Previous to Wren, the most successful classical projects in England came from the hand of Inigo Jones (1573–1652),

the surveyor general of the king's works, who had traveled at least twice to Italy. His Queen's House in Greenwich (Fig. 13.1-9), a cubic pavilion with planar facades, captured the simple proportions of Palladio's early villas. Built under James I (r. 1603–1625) in 1616, it served as the hinge of Wren's Royal Naval Hospital, his grandest Baroque endeavor, built at the end of the century.

During the 1630s Jones designed Covent Garden Square (Fig. 13.1-10), London's first coordinated urban plan. His assistant, the French architect Isaac de Caus, a Huguenot living in exile, may have influenced him to include arcades similar to those of the Parisian square of Place des Vosges (see Section 12.2). Jones referred to St. Paul's, his small church on the west side of the square, as "the grandest barn in England." Although later transformed beyond recognition, Covent Garden initiated a much-repeated model

Figure 13.1-9 Greenwich, London. Queen's House, Inigo Jones, 1616.

Figure 13.1-10 London. Covent Garden, Inigo Jones, 1630s.

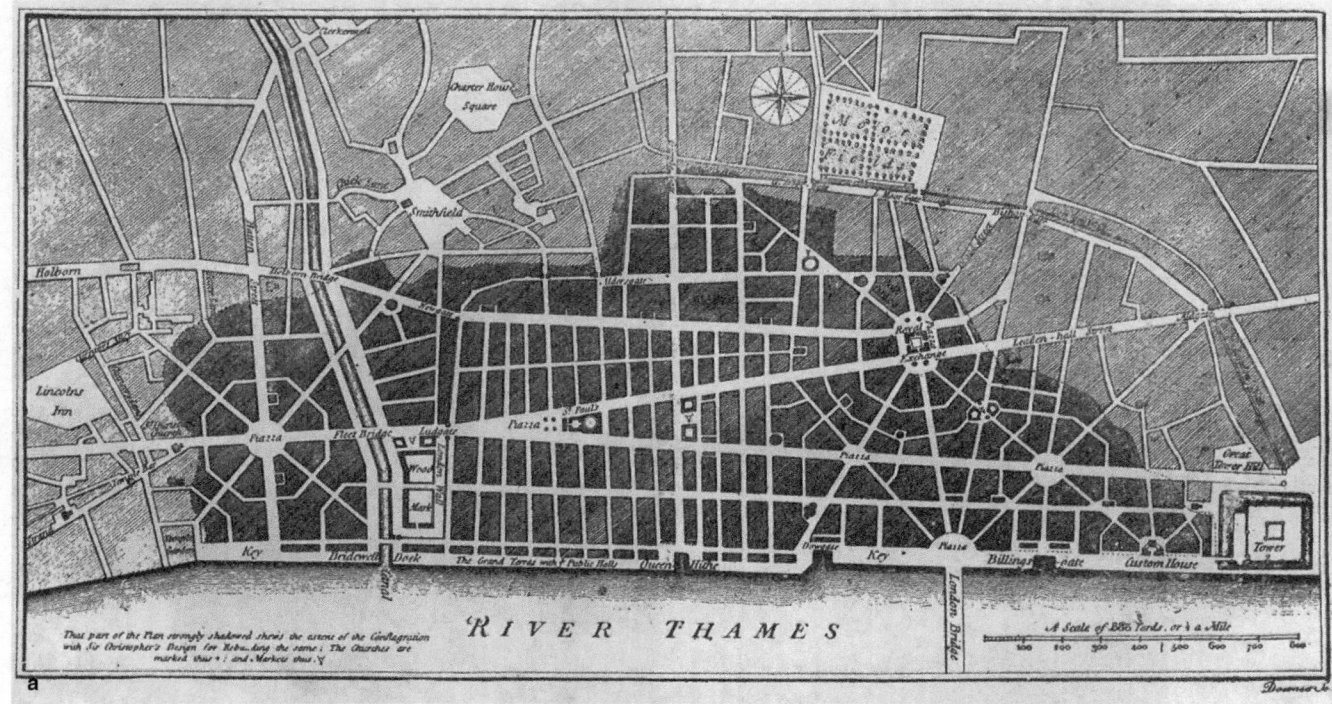

a

b

Figure 13.1-11 London. (a) Christopher Wren's unexecuted plan, 1667. (b) The Monument, Wren, 1670.

of development in London, by which an individual patron commissioned a formal square surrounded by rows of coordinated houses to create a patch of marketable order.

Wren, a polymath with wide interests, began his career as a professor of astronomy at Oxford but acquired greater prominence as a designer after the Great Fire of London of 1666. He eventually obtained the office of surveyor general. While mindful of the classical orders and the laws of symmetry, his background in the sciences led him to pursue empirical methods and experiments in form. Wren's plan for rebuilding London after the Great Fire combined a series of wide, straight axes with radiocentric districts (Fig. 13.1-11a). If it had been followed, the scheme would have generated one of the most complicated street systems in Europe, with St. Paul's as a wedge dividing two forking boulevards, leading to three interlinked octagonal starbursts. While Wren's plan came to nothing, he succeeded in creating a permanent reminder of the Great Fire, known simply as "The Monument" (13.1-11b), a fluted Doric column 61.5 m (202 ft) high, which cast its shadow on Pudding Lane, where the fire began. In this and many of his projects during the 1670s and 1680s, he was assisted by fellow scientist and designer Robert Hooke (1635–1703).

As surveyor general, Wren took charge of the reconstruction of fifty churches destroyed by the fire while working on his lifetime project of St. Paul's, which underwent several major redesigns. Wren's parish churches, of which two dozen survive, occupied irregular sites crowded by adjacent structures. While at ground level he limited their external display, he gave each a distinctive steeple, surpassing the elegance of de Keyser's belfries in Amsterdam. Wren recast the idea of the Gothic spire using classical details assembled idiosyncratically. The steeple of St. Mary-le-Bow (1680) (Fig. 13.1-12) displayed great originality: set on a square base, it rose to a cylindrical tempietto with Corinthian columns supporting radially aligned volutes that swirled up to sustain a smaller tempietto crowned by an obelisk. The new steeples added to London's skyline a fantasy world of miniature temples, triumphal arches, bulging urns, and soaring obelisks.

The interiors of Wren's London churches attest to his compositional skill, combining known types in novel ways. He churned out schemes that ranged from barrel-vaulted basilicas with and without galleries to Greek crosses made with cross-vaults to domed cores capping a nave. Like the Dutch, Wren preferred the acoustics of a central plan, commenting that Catholics "hear the Murmur of the Mass, and see the Elevation of the Host, but ours are to be fitted for the Auditories." Although he never traveled to Holland, his collaborator, Hooke, had been there, and the scheme of Nieuwe Kerk in Haarlem and Oosterkerk in Amsterdam reappeared in several Wren churches, where a Greek cross was fitted into a

Figure 13.1-12 London. St. Mary-le-Bow, steeple, Wren, 1680s.

square. In 1672 Wren designed his most important parish church, St. Stephen, Walbrook (Fig. 13.1-13), the church of the lord mayor; it presented a Greek cross in a square room surmounted by a 20 m (66 ft) diameter dome. The superimposition of a circle of eight arches over the cruciform layout of the galleries resulted in stunning spatial interpenetration.

The plan of St. Stephen influenced Wren's Greek cross scheme in his second design for St. Paul's (Fig. 13.1-14a,b), also begun in 1672. Wren produced the intermediary "warrant design" with a pagoda-like spire over a small dome. His final design for the dome proved more conventional in form while more innovative in structure. It rested on a ring of

Corinthian columns, recalling Donato Bramante's proposal for the dome for St. Peter's, and was built in three layers: an interior hemispherical dome over the crossing, a concealed conical dome to support the lantern, and a hemispherical exterior dome. As built, the church reverted to the longitudinal basilica type, with the choir as long as the nave. Construction began in 1676 and dragged on for thirty years, paid for with the income from the coal tax. Wren changed the front facade from a colossal temple front to a two-level colonnaded loggia with towers at each end, reprising the imaginative piling of columns on his steeples for parish churches.

At either end of London Wren created majestic esplanades open to the Thames River for veterans' hospitals,

Figure 13.1-13 London. St. Stephen, Walbrook, Wren, 1672–1680.

Figure 13.1-14 London. (a) St. Paul's Cathedral, Wren et al., 1680–1710. (b) See facing page.

Figure 13.1-14 London. (b) St. Paul's Cathedral, section.

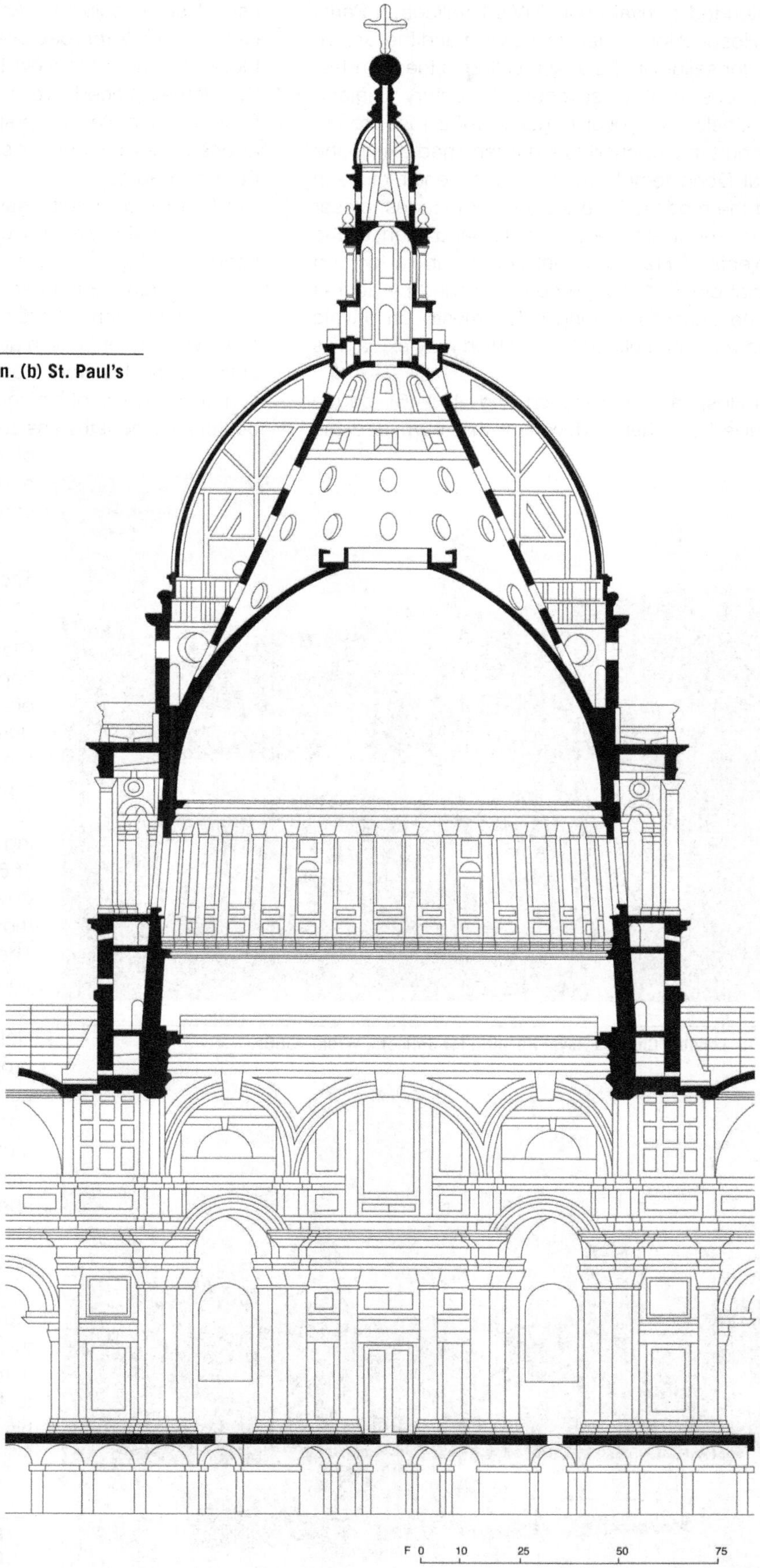

b

F 0   10   25   50   75

M 0   5   10   25

institutions intended to rival Louis XIV's Invalides in Paris. The Chelsea Hospital for soldiers in the west and the Greenwich Hospital for sailors in the east resulted in the grandest formal landscapes in all of seventeenth-century England (Fig. 13.1-15). Chelsea Hospital, begun in 1682, rose around a *U*-shaped court that opened to a garden-lined axis to the river. Colossal Doric temple fronts at the center of each wing relieved the modest three-story brick facades, closer in spirit to the frugal architecture of Holland than to the luxurious projects of France. A belvedere cupola loomed over the central block. Although commissioned by decree of the king, the project's funding relied mostly on private donations and a tax on soldiers' pay, which may explain its modest style.

The Royal Hospital in Greenwich (Fig. 13.1-16), begun in 1694, received a richer endowment that permitted the use of stone columns. Assisted by Nicholas Hawksmoor (1661–1736), Wren deployed paired ranges of colonnaded blocks to frame the view toward the Queen's House. The two domes placed over the corners of the opposing colonnades animated a perspectival view from the river that appeared as engaging as the twin cupolas at Piazza del Popolo in Rome.

Wren's monuments gave London a new urban scale commensurate with the city's advancing political status. London during the first half of the eighteenth century surpassed all other European cities, with its population growing from a half-million in 1700 to 900,000 fifty years later. Wren's style went out of fashion at the turn of the century, and later critics found his work "too pagan," leading to the demolition of seventeen of his churches during the late nineteenth century. He nonetheless succeeded in forging a new image of the city, with glistening domes and steeples that invited comparisons with those of Rome and Paris.

The English Country House: Architecture and Ideology

Classical style acquired ideological implications with the ascendance of the Whig faction in England during the first two decades of the eighteenth century. The Whigs represented the liberal opposition to Tory conservatives, orchestrating the bloodless Revolution of 1688–1689, which converted the government into a constitutional monarchy based on a bill of rights. They ousted the Stuart dynasty and then invited William III, the *stadthouder,* or prime minister, of Holland, to reign as their king, thus promoting a Protestant regime and consolidating business ties between London and Amsterdam. The Whigs' moment of maximum power came with their installation of the German-speaking and easily manipulated George I (r. 1714–1727) of Hannover as the English monarch.

The most influential Whig ideologue of the early eighteenth century, Anthony Ashley Cooper, the third Earl of Shaftesbury, objected to the complex style of Wren and his followers, advocating a simpler

Figure 13.1-15 London. Chelsea Royal Hospital for Soldiers, Wren, 1680s.

Figure 13.1-16 London. Greenwich Royal Hospital for Sailors, Wren and Nicholas Hawksmoor, 1690s.

style that would represent the Protestant and anti-French tendency. His two-volume tract *Characteristics of Men, Manners, Opinions, Times* (1708) became the backbone of English liberal protocol, debunking Catholic notions such as original sin, pleading for the republican value of moderation, and proposing that the landed aristocracy become well-educated "virtuosi" with a feeling of collective responsibility for the nation. He steered his contemporaries toward the architecture of Palladio and Inigo Jones as superior models of good taste and economy. As frequently occurred in the arts, however, categories based on ideology became easily blurred, and the precepts of Palladio influenced the followers of Wren as much as Wren's ideas infiltrated the work of the English Palladians.

Wren's younger assistant, Nicholas Hawksmoor, continued his master's line of research, designing six churches in a second campaign for new churches in London between 1711 and 1733. His St. Mary Woolnoth, begun in 1716, offered a new degree of sophistication for church exteriors. He lined the side elevations with three rusticated niches, in each of which he pulled out a convex Ionic aedicule in the dynamic manner of Francesco Borromini.

Hawksmoor's major competitor in church construction, James Gibbs (1682–1754), had trained to be a Catholic priest and spent five years in Rome working under Bernini's successor, Carlo Fontana. Gibbs's most influential design, St. Martin-in-the-Fields on Trafalgar Square (1721) (Fig. 13.1-17a,b), presented a relatively pure composition of a Pantheon-style temple front supporting a steeple. Countless imitations of this solution appeared in England and its colonies during the next two centuries. Inside he suspended a wood and plaster barrel vault from the roof trusses to reduce the load on the slender columns of the aisles, allowing a great diffusion of light into the galleries. A large *serliana* window (known to the English as a "Palladian" window) lit the **chancel** wall. It remains no small irony that the designer of this quintessentially Protestant church lived privately as a Catholic.

In 1699 Hawksmoor entered an informal partnership with the well-connected playwright John Vanbrugh (1664–1726), a union that yielded Castle Howard and Blenheim Palace, the two grand country houses that touched off the Neo-Palladian reaction. Vanbrugh belonged to the major Whig club, where he encountered

Figure 13.1-17 London. (a) St. Martin-in-the-Fields, James Gibbs, 1720s. (b) Interior.

his clients, and as a well-traveled intellectual aspired to the monumental landscapes of Vaux-le-Vicomte and Versailles. He relied on Hawksmoor's experience to carry out his ideas. Castle Howard, begun in 1700, employed the *U*-shaped forecourt of the French prototypes, with spaces for stables on one side and kitchens on the other. The central block rose twice as tall as the long side wings, accentuated by colossal pairs of Doric pilasters. The architects crowned the triple-height entry hall with a cupola, set on a tall octagonal drum, giving the space the dramatic uplift of the crossing of a central-plan church.

Vanbrugh and Hawksmoor created an even grander assembly of classical motifs for Blenheim Palace, near Oxford, begun in 1704 (Fig. 13.1-18). Intended as both an aristocratic residence and a national monument, the estate took its name from the small Bavarian town where the Duke of Marlborough had won a resounding victory over the French. The architects designed the lengthy approach as a triumphal route that crossed a massive three-arched bridge before rising to the palace gate. They built up the massing around the *U*-shaped forecourt to climax at a colossal temple-front entry porch. Perched above the pediment, they stacked a second pediment, pierced with a clerestory that illuminated the grand entry hall. Vanbrugh described the animated roofscape of Blenheim, with its collection of urns, volutes, and sculptural chimneys, as "castle-airs." He arranged the rear facade with spoils from the duke's battles, including a 30-ton bust of Louis XIV brought back from Tournai. Although the project suffered from many disagreements, including the Crown's unwillingness to pay and Vanbrugh's resignation after a dispute with the widowed

duchess, Hawksmoor stayed on to complete the grandest country house in England.

The countertrend to the Baroque extravagance of Vanbrugh and Hawksmoor took shape after the publication of the first Neo-Palladian treatise, *Vitruvius Britannicus* by Colen Campbell (1676–1729), in 1717. While opposed to the style of Blenheim, the author felt obliged to include an engraving of it in his work because of its national significance. Campbell did not hesitate, however, to exclude the work of his rival, James Gibbs, a fellow Scot and a Catholic. The text and the majority of examples in the treatise reflected Shaftesbury's call for a style suited to an enlightened Protestant gentry. On the merits of his book, Campbell quickly gained commissions for country manors, including Houghton Hall (1722) for the Whig prime minister, Sir Robert Walpole, who by now proved more powerful than the king. Gibbs, who had been ostracized by the Palladians, eventually had his revenge when he was commissioned to complete Houghton Hall and stacked Baroque cupolas over the corner towers. Gibbs also surpassed Campbell in his well-received *Book of Architecture*, published in 1728. He stocked his text with hundreds of his own designs, many of which seemed more Palladian than those of the Palladians.

In the 1720s the Neo-Palladian movement coalesced around the person of Richard Boyle, Lord Burlington (1695–1753), who under the protection of his widowed mother embodied the essence of the Whig virtuoso. A cultivator of musicians, artists, and designers, he dabbled in all of the arts, including architecture. Although Gibbs initially began the rebuilding of Burlington House in London, the young lord convinced his mother to hire Campbell to finish

Figure 13.1-18 Oxfordshire, England. Blenheim Palace, John Vanbrugh and Hawksmoor, 1704.

Figure 13.1-19 London. Chiswick, Lord Burlington and William Kent, 1725.

the project. The new architect cribbed the facade from Palladio's Palazzo Iseppo Porto in Vicenza, which he knew from the *Four Books of Architecture*, which had just been published in English in 1715.

Burlington also retained Campbell for his villa at Chiswick (Fig. 13.1-19) but in 1725 grew dissatisfied with the scheme and decided to design the project himself with the help of the painter William Kent (1686–1748). While Campbell had proposed a near replica of Palladio's Villa Rotonda, Burlington's design came closer to Vincenzo Scamozzi's Rocca Pisani at Lonigo (1573): a cubic base supporting an octagonal drum fed by thermal windows and capped by a dome. On the front facade he placed a pedimented porch over a rusticated base, and on the rear he carved out a series of three Palladian windows (*serlianas*) in recessed arches. The three chimneys on either flank rose as obelisks. Burlington combined various classical motifs into a hybrid that related as easily to the style of Vanbrugh as it did to that of Palladio. The double set of bifurcated stairs at the entry and the French-style gallery on the back of the house contradicted the idea of Palladian simplicity.

Burlington's protégé, Kent, had spent ten years training as a painter in Italy. His career as a designer commenced

in Burlington's garden at Chiswick and continued when he obtained, with Burlington's backing, the commission for his first major project, Holkham Hall (Fig. 13.1-20a), in 1734. As Campbell would have done, Kent placed a pure temple-front porch in the center of the main block, terminating the volume with corner towers before stepping down to four lower side wings. He pulled these lower volumes away from the main block as separate pavilions, giving the whole a crab-like layout. One wing served the kitchen, another the chapel, a third the family's bedrooms, and the last guest rooms. As in most of the great country houses, the bedrooms in the central block served as a suite for royal visits. While Kent attempted to imitate the clean volumes of Palladio, his love of decoration led him to place *serlianas* at the corner bays of the central block and to vary the window styles on the side wings. In the Marble Hall (Fig. 13.1-20b) he created one of the most theatrical spaces of any of the great English country houses: a double-height room wrapped on the second level by a narrow colonnade made of dappled marble shafts, leading to an apsidal stair, behind which rose a smaller apse. Despite the Whig rhetoric of Neo-Palladian simplicity, such theatrical gestures and luxurious fittings did not correspond to an orthodox "Protestant" style.

Figure 13.1-20 Norfolk, England. (a) Holkham Hall, William Kent, 1734. (b) The Marble Hall.

Further Reading

Downes, Kerry. *The Architecture of Wren*. New York: Universe Books, 1982.

Girouard, Mark. *Life in the English Country House*. New Haven, CT: Yale University Press, 1978.

Gray, Robert. *A History of London*. New York: Taplinger, 1978.

Kuyper, W. *Dutch Classicist Architecture: A Survey of Dutch Architecture, Gardens and Anglo–Dutch Architectural Relations from 1625–1700*. Delft, the Netherlands: Delft University Press, 1980.

Rykwert, Joseph. *The First Moderns: The Architects of the 18th Century*. Cambridge, MA: MIT Press, 1980.

Schama, Simon. *The Embarrassment of Riches: An Interpretation of Dutch Culture in the Golden Age*. Berkeley: University of California Press, 1988.

Summerson, John. *Architecture in Britain, 1530–1830*. New York: Penguin, 1970.

13.2 THE DIFFUSION OF THE BAROQUE
Life as Theater

The style associated with Bernini and Borromini in mid-seventeenth-century Rome struck many critics as bizarre, or "baroque." The theatricality of the Baroque, as the style came to be called, corresponded to the Catholic Church's promotion of religious faith as an emotional experience. The embracing curves of the facades, the thrust of the engaged columns, the luxurious swirls of decorations, and the dramatic placement of sculptures attempted to inspire the passionate involvement of the faithful.

Roman Baroque spread to the farthest reaches of the Italian provinces and to the rest of Catholic Europe. Royal courts throughout Europe attempted to lure Italian designers versed in the theatrical style of Rome, while patrons and designers from north of the Alps descended into Italy for the Grand Tour. Many governments and aristocratic sponsors maintained artists in Rome to perfect their knowledge of ancient, Renaissance, and Baroque styles. The cross-pollination of Roman styles and provincial settings often produced highly original expressions, such as the flamboyant churrigueresque in Spain or the organic style of rococo decoration in France and Germany.

Using theatrical tactics, Baroque designers reshaped disparate urban pieces into coherent compositions. This task went beyond the re-creation of religious structures to address greater issues of urban form. From Sicily to Turin, from remote parts of Bavaria and Austria to Lisbon and Seville, the design of public spaces, churches, and palaces in the mid-eighteenth century made a virtue of excess. While scenographic decoration piled up to the point of obfuscating the clarity of structure, Baroque designers often clarified the connections between disjointed parts of cities through their decorative interventions.

Carlo Fontana and the Diffusion of Roman Baroque in Italy

Despite Rome's diminished role in European politics, it remained the primary art school for the rest of Europe. National academies, following the example of the French Academy, began to send scholars and artists to the city to study both ancient and modern art and architecture. Artistic leadership passed from the generation of Bernini, da Cortona, Rainaldi, and Borromini to Carlo Fontana (1638–1714), who trained dozens of successful architects working in Italy and abroad, including Filippo Juvarra, James Gibbs, Matthaus Daniel Pöpplemann, and Johann Lucas von Hildebrandt. Rome attracted many of the more culturally adventurous aristocrats of Europe, including Queen Christina, Catholicism's most celebrated convert. After abdicating the throne of Sweden in 1654, she spent most of the next three decades in Rome, commissioning Fontana to retrofit a theater inside the old prison of Tor di Nona. Leading tastemakers such as England's William Kent and Austria's Johann Bernard Fischer von Erlach exploited their Roman experience as the touchstone for their careers. The Rome of Fontana unleashed the Baroque sensibility across most of Europe.

Two of Fontana's most important works in Rome stood at opposite ends of the social scale. His 1675 facade for the high-profile church of San Marcello al Corso (Fig. 13.2-1) added a new treasure to Rome's collection of glamorous

Figure 13.2-1 Rome. San Marcello al Corso, Carlo Fontana, 1670s.

Figure 13.2-2 Rome. Piazza San Ignazio, apartment buildings, Filippo Raguzzini, 1720s.

Silentium because its inmates observed the rule of absolute silence.

Filippo Raguzzini (1680–1771), one of the few architects in Rome not closely associated with Fontana's circle, designed a highly original series of apartment buildings at Piazza San Ignazio (Fig. 13.2-2), begun in 1725. He arranged the piazza and its surrounding alleys like a stage set, broken into a five-part composition based on overlapping concave curves. A four-story apartment building, triangular in plan, faced the church directly across the piazza, while the streets pushed obliquely behind it, shaping the flanking buildings into polygonal figures. Raguzzini eroded each of the corners with concave curves, creating oval voids between the buildings. This bizarre composition may have been a ploy to lure taste-conscious clients to live in Rome's first rental apartments.

The Rome of Fontana exerted a strong impact on planning and design in southeastern Sicily after the catastrophic earthquake of 1693. The major city in the region, Catania, was restructured into a model city with broad, straight streets and regularly placed piazzas. The young architect in charge of the plan of Catania, Giovanni Battista Vaccarini (1702–1768), although born in Sicily, had trained in the studio of Fontana's son in Rome. During the 1730s Vaccarini brought Roman Baroque style to the city and the region using the abundant supply of lava stone in combination with white limestone trim for the major buildings of the Piazza del Duomo. He articulated the cathedral facade (Fig. 13.2-3) with a dynamic series of engaged columns canted at different angles. The openness of rebuilt Catania displayed a new approach to disaster planning, with straight axes ranging from 12 to 20 m (39 to 65 ft) in width, about

sacred spaces. Here he layered three concave planes, framed with pairs of columns and pilasters, a composition that generated many imitations. On the other side of the river he initiated one of Europe's first large-scale penal institutions, the Ospizio di San Michele, in 1691. Conceived as a reform school and workhouse for delinquent children and indigent elders, it was popularly known as the

---

 1693

Great earthquake
of Sicily

*Blenheim Palace
begun by Vanbrugh
and Hawksmoor*

 1704

 1714

Conclusion of the War
of Spanish Succession

*King João V begins
the convent of Mafra,
Portugal's equivalent
of El Escorial*

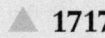 **1717**

The *Silentium*

Carlo Fontana's Ospizio di San Michele set a new standard of reform architecture. When completed by Ferdinando Fuga in the 1740s, it stretched nearly 400 m (1,312 ft) along the bank of the Tiber River. San Michele represented one of the first efforts to use architecture as a means of conditioning the behavior of those identified as a social problem. Inmates were sworn to absolute silence, leading to the prison's moniker: *Il Silentium*. Built around a series of courts, the wings of the building converged on a central-plan church. The typical wing contained a three-level open hall lined with a dozen small cells on each side reached by canti-levered balconies. This basilica scheme allowed easy surveillance, anticipating some of the aspects of the Panopticon prison proposed a century later by Jeremy Bentham (see Section 14.3).

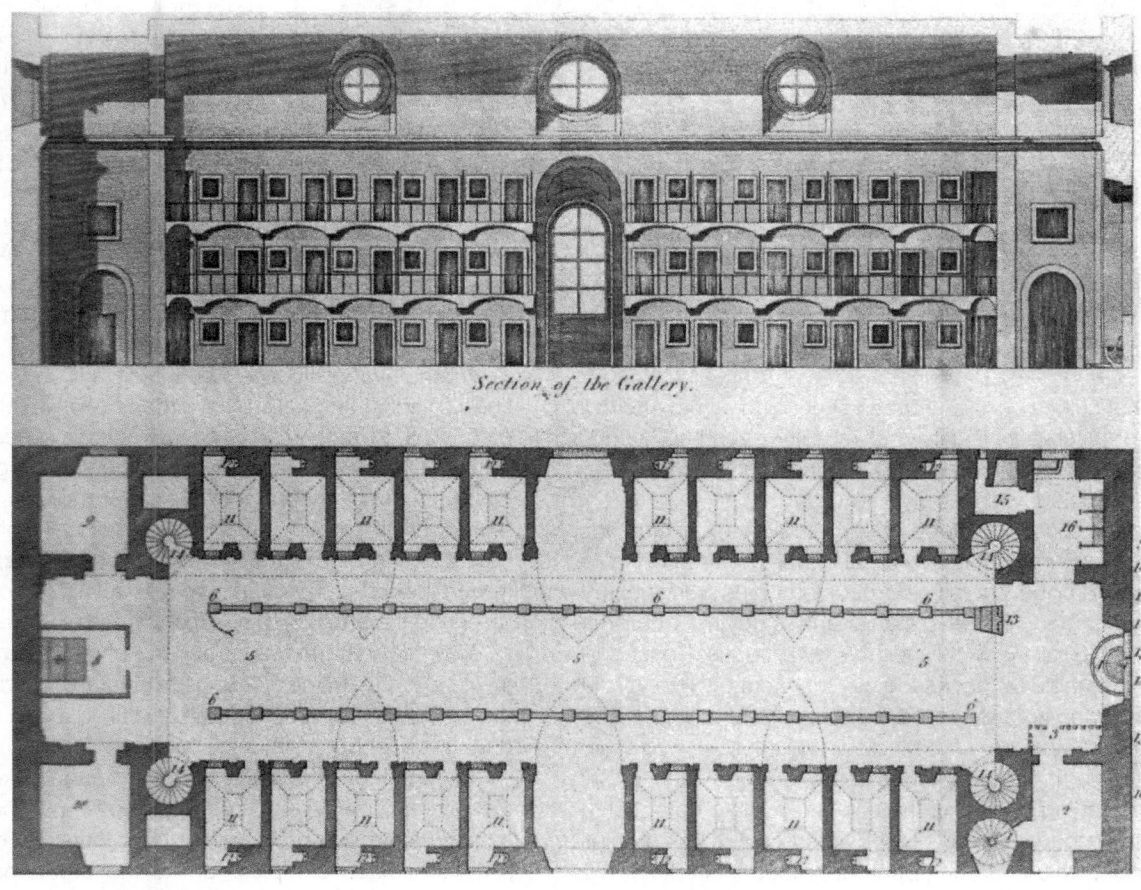

Rome. Plan and section of Ospizio di San Michele, Fontana, 1690s.

▼ **1720s**

Sicilian city of Noto
rebuilt on a new site

*Dukes of Savoy commission
Baroque castle of Stupinigi
by Filippo Juvarra near Turin*

▲ **1729**

▼ **1743**

*Neumann builds
Vierzehnheiligen
pilgrimage church
near Würzburg*

Figure 13.2-3 Catania, Sicily. Cathedral, Giovanni Battisti Vaccarini, 1736.

The most accomplished of Fontana's students, Filippo Juvarra (1678–1736), also came from Sicily but gained an international reputation, bringing him commissions from as far away as Portugal. He had been ordained a priest in Messina before moving to Rome in the first years of the eighteenth century, where he distinguished himself as a set designer, famous for spectacular perspective scenes. Like the Galli-Bibbiena clan, he perfected the *scena vedute per angolo* scene, which extended the perspective obliquely to two vanishing points, giving the impression of unfathomable depth.

twice that of the normal European street of the time. After two major disasters, fire safety and mobility became Catania's functional criteria for street building, leading to an emphasis on unobstructed, wide, straight roads.

Another local architect of the Sicilian reconstruction, Rosario Gagliardi (ca. 1698–1762), never ventured to Rome, learning Baroque curves and countercurves from observing Vaccarini's work in Catania and studying published sources. He in turn published his own treatise, based on his considerable output as the city architect of Noto, a town that had been transferred from a steep hill to a gently sloping site. In Ragusa and Modica (Fig. 13.2-4), Gagliardi built his two most memorable works, both devoted to San Giorgio. Setting both churches on steep sites, he accentuated the cascading thrust of their convex stairs. His greatest innovation, which had no apparent precedent in Sicily, was to incorporate the campanile into the facade, recalling the churches by Hawksmoor and Gibbs in London. He thrust the front portal forward as a single unit on a convex curve, with four tiers of ascending colonnades.

When Juvarra arrived in Turin in 1715, he worked on fitting projects into Italy's most orderly city, which had been planned with regular **arcaded** streets by Ascanio Vitozzi and the Castellamonte family of architects during the seventeenth century. Juvarra added sixteen palaces to the city's fabric while correcting the alignments of many of the streets. His facade for one of the twin churches in Piazza San Carlo turned the arcaded square into a special point of reference, reversing the effect of the twin churches at Porta del Popolo in Rome so that one saw the Turin churches while leaving the city center. In the 1720s he added a Baroque facade to the medieval Palazzo Madama and filled it with a luminous, double-switchback staircase.

Juvarra began his greatest project for the Dukes of Savoy, the villa of Stupinigi, in 1729 (Fig. 13.2-5a,b), boosting this small hunting lodge on the southern outskirts of Turin into a major palace complex. Unlike the broad prospects of Versailles, the layout of Stupinigi followed an expanding and contracting plan, looking from the air like the great claws of a lobster. Its central wing rose on an *X*-shaped plan, opening at the crux onto a triple-height oval salon. From here the

---

Vanvitelli displays rational classicism in royal palace of Caserta near Naples

▲ 1750

▼ 1755

Lisbon destroyed by an earthquake and tsunami

Replanning of Lisbon by Marquis de Pombal on rational principles

▲ 1760

Figure 13.2-4 Modica, Sicily. Church San Giorgio, Rosario Gagliardi, 1740s.

wings extended around a hexagonal forecourt, which opened to a concatenation of ovals, terminating in a grand crescent.

Despite similar programs, nothing could have been further from Juvarra's Stupinigi than the royal palace for the king of Naples, built at Caserta a generation later (Fig. 13.2-6). Its architect, Luigi Vanvitelli (1700–1773), son of the Dutch landscape painter Gaspar van Wittel, trained with Fontana's son before entering the papal office of works. After building several projects in Rome and the Papal States, he gained the commission in 1750 to design the Reggia of Caserta for Charles of Bourbon, the king of Naples. As son of the king of Spain and great-grandson of Louis XIV, the patron desired a complex that would be a mixture of the Escorial and Versailles, on a site 33 km (20 miles) north of Naples. Here, he intended to establish an ideal administrative city free from the troubles of one of Europe's most populous and disorderly cities. One approached the palace on a 10 km (6 mile) axis that terminated in a grand oval forecourt lined with service wings, similar in scale and shape to the piazza of St. Peter's in Rome. The sober facades of Caserta avoided curves and bizarre theatrics, signaling the end of Baroque plasticity. Vanvitelli divided the great block of the Reggia into four courtyards, alluding to the style and type of the Escorial and other Spanish palaces dear to the patron. Against this rigorously classical backdrop Vanvitelli inserted a wonderfully kinetic staircase, resembling the perspective scenes seen on the Baroque stage. It rose on switchbacks to the upper landing, terminating under a dome. He extended the garden along a breathtaking axis of water that stepped down the mountainside (Fig. 13.2-7). At its base a waterfall served as the setting for the sculptural reenactment of the transformation of Endymion into a stag. While Vanvitelli worked on Caserta for the rest of his life, his patron left Naples in 1758 to succeed to the Spanish throne.

Central Europe after the Thirty Years' War: Grandeur beyond One's Means

During the seventeenth century the Thirty Years' War between the Catholic Holy Roman emperors and the Protestant lords of the many minor states of Germany inhibited the architectural production of Central Europe. The region was also threatened by the Ottomans on the eastern borders of the Habsburg Empire until 1683. With the increased

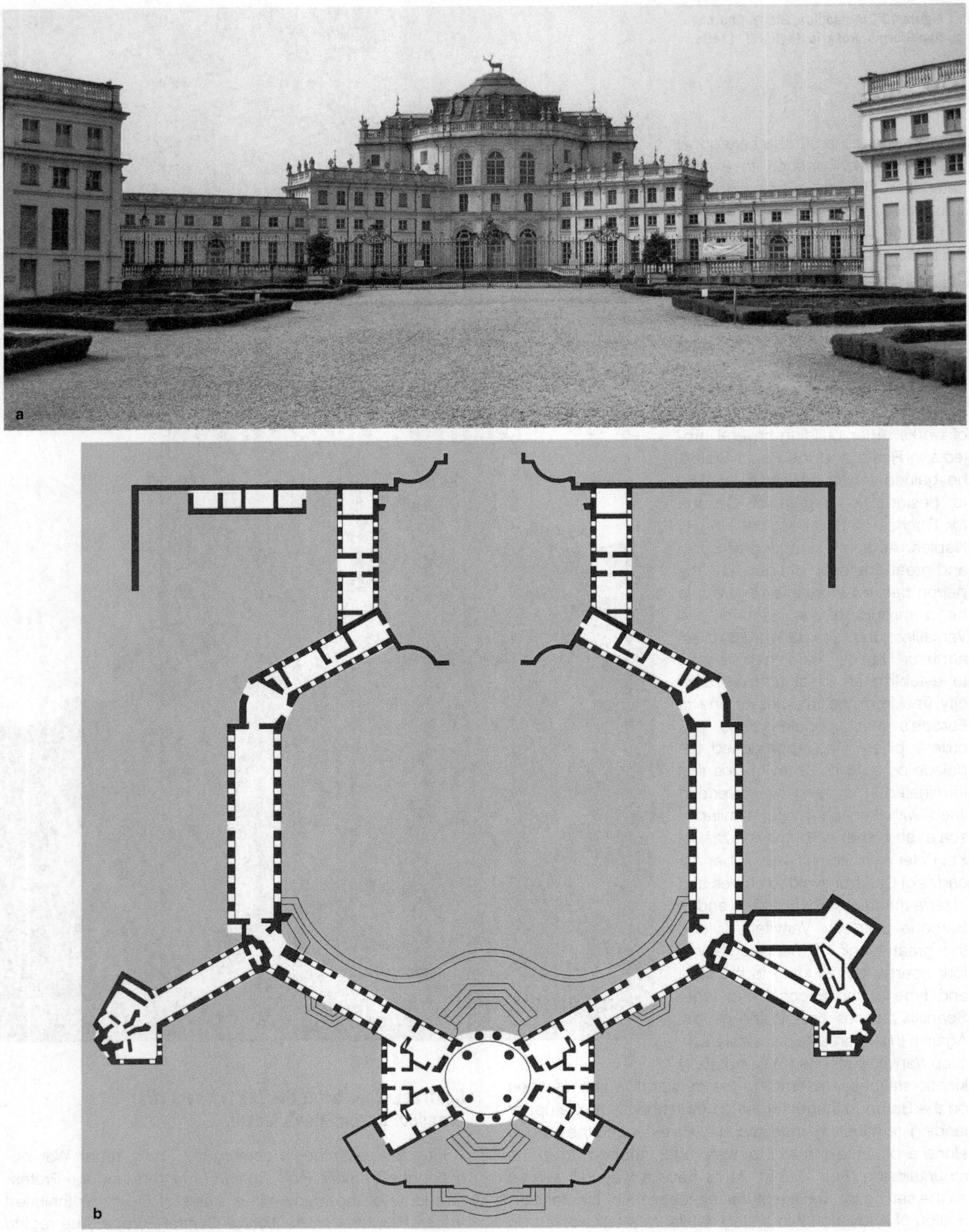

Figure 13.2-5 Turin, Italy. (a) Palazzo Stupinigi, Filippo Juvarra, 1720s. (b) Plan showing the main hall as a domed oval intersected by an X-shaped configuration of rooms.

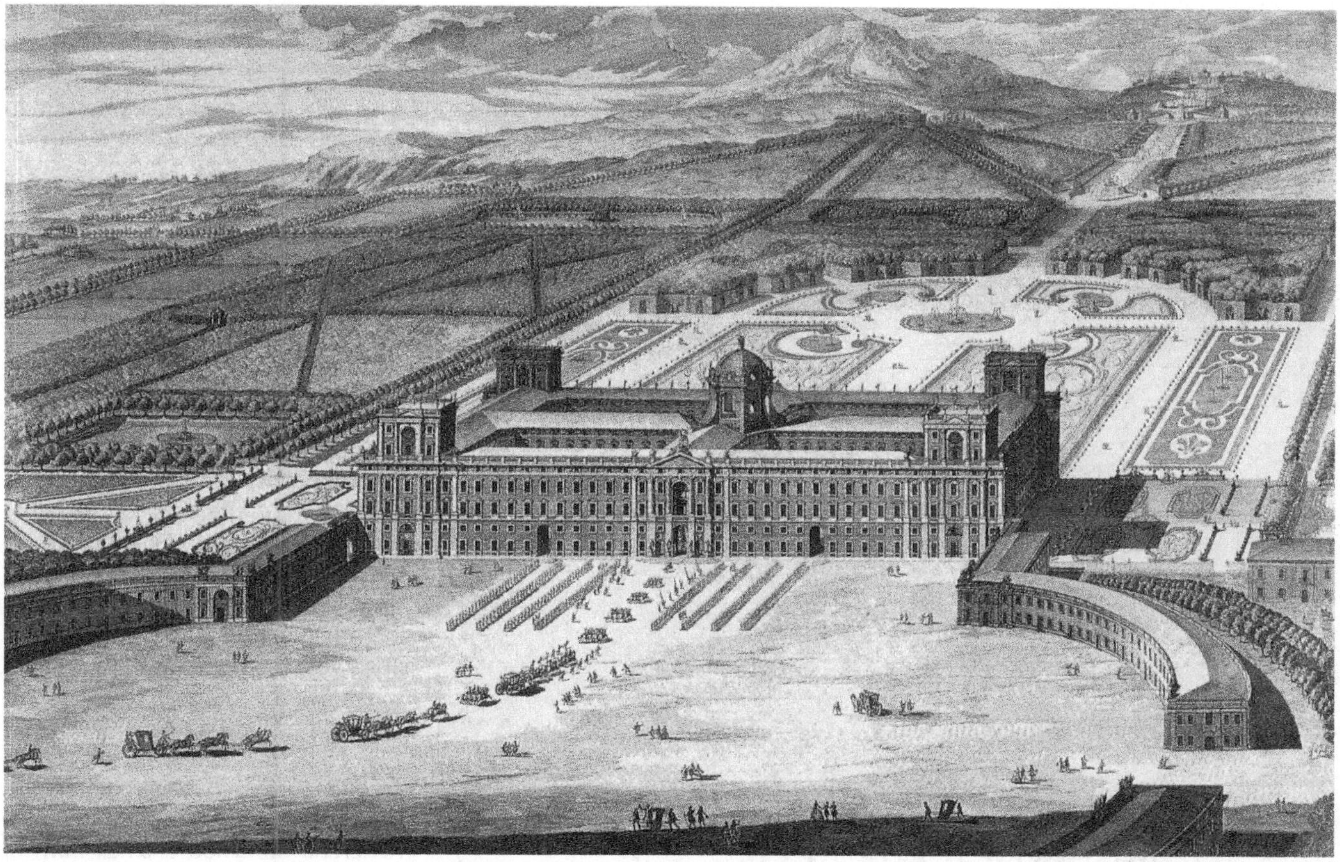

Figure 13.2-6 Caserta, Italy. Luigi Vanvitelli's engraving of La Reggia, built as the court residence for the king of Naples, 1750s.

stability after the resolution of these two conflicts, a wave of building activity swept the region, leading to grand urban schemes, immense palaces with formal gardens, and spectacular convent churches. In some cases the ambitious projects also led to financial ruin.

While local variations of Baroque style emerged throughout Central Europe, Italian designers, some from the Italian canton of Switzerland and the Lombardy region and others from Rome, exercised enormous influence over the area's architectural development. Francesco Caratti in Prague, Filiberto Lucchesi in Vienna, and Gaetano Chiaveri in Dresden established a new scale of practice in these capitals while transmitting Roman architectural language to them. Chiaveri, the architect of the Hofkirche in Dresden in the 1730s, came from the milieu of Fontana. His church, which resembled the churches of Gagliardi

Figure 13.2-7 Caserta, Italy. La Reggia, fountain of Endymion at the base of the cascades, Vanvitelli, 1750s.

in Sicily, incorporated the campanile into the convex entry bay. Such a Catholic-looking church in Protestant Dresden came from the desire of the patron, Augustus the Strong, the elector of Saxony, who had converted to Catholicism in order to inherit the throne of Poland in 1697. The new church stood in front of the royal residence and the Zwinger Court, offering a viable alternative to the impressive Lutheran cathedral of Frauenkirche, begun ten years earlier.

This latter church, built in Dresden from 1726 to 1743, seemed more Baroque than its Catholic competitor. The stone-clad, bell-shaped dome of Frauenkirche (Fig. 13.2-8) rose as an elongated bulb to the exceptional height of 95 m (312 ft), framed by ornate, diagonally placed turrets at the corners. The plan by Georg Bähr (1666–1738), an architect who had made his way up from the carpentry trades, satisfied the Protestant program for better auditory relations, stacking five tiers of galleries around a central plan like the box seats in a theater.

The grandeur of Versailles inspired many imitations in Central Europe, such as the castle-town of Karlsruhe (Fig. 13.2-9), founded in 1715 by Margrave Karl Wilhelm of Baden-Durlach. Jacob Friedrich von Batzendorf prepared the plan that hinged thirty-two radiating avenues on the Y-shaped palace. The palace was rebuilt in masonry in 1752 with the addition of a ten-story octagonal observatory in the rear. The front wings opened on a 60° spread toward the houses of the city, while 75% of the rays extended into formal gardens and the hunting park behind the residence. Despite its grand plan, Karlsruhe remained a small town of fewer than 4,000 people.

In Vienna Johann Bernhard Fischer von Erlach (1656–1723) also dreamed of surpassing Versailles with his initial plan in 1690 for Schönbrunn Palace for the Habsburg emperor. He envisioned the arrival sequence as three ramping terraces through two historiated columns, making tangible the Habsburg emblem of the columns of Hercules. The project proved both too extravagant and highly impractical, as it did not allow a direct path to the oval entry court. A decade later, faced with budget cuts, Fischer replaced the terraces and ramps with a more modest rectangular entry court that led directly to a grand bifurcated stair.

Born into a family of artists, Fischer received a grant in the 1670s from Prince Eggenberg to train in Rome, where he spent fifteen years. His talent as a draftsman and connoisseur of historical models from around

Figure 13.2-8 Dresden, Germany. Frauenkirche, Georg Bähr, 1720s, destroyed in World War II and reconstructed 2002.

Figure 13.2-9 Karlsruhe, Germany. Radial plan, Jacob Friedrich von Batzendorf, 1715–1750s. Bildstelle der Stadt Karlsruhe.

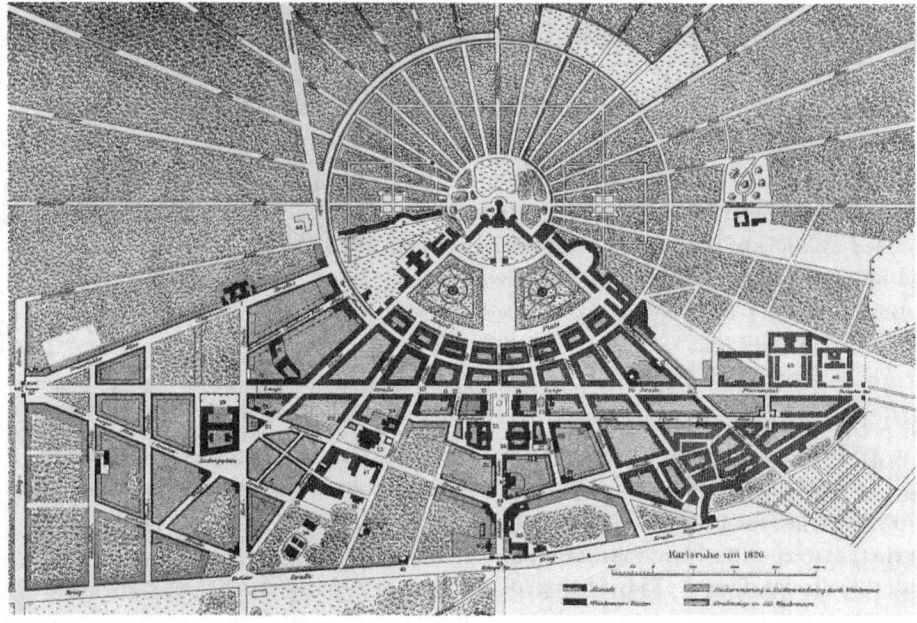

CONSTRUCTION, TECHNOLOGY, THEORY

Fischer's *Atlas of Architecture*

In 1721, Fischer published his extraordinary treatise *Entwurff einer historischen Architectur (A Plan of Civil and Historical Architecture),* which in five years went through several editions, including two English translations. He had prepared these "sketches" while employed as tutor to the crown prince. Aside from renderings of the seven wonders of the ancient world, he supplied images of the Parthenon in Athens, the Temple of Solomon, lesser-known Roman buildings such as Diocletian's palace at Split, and a section entitled "Of Some Arab and Turkish Buildings as Well as about Modern Persian, Siamese, Chinese and Japanese Architecture." Despite his noble cross-cultural intentions, most of the scenes of this architectural atlas were fantasies based on verbal reports.

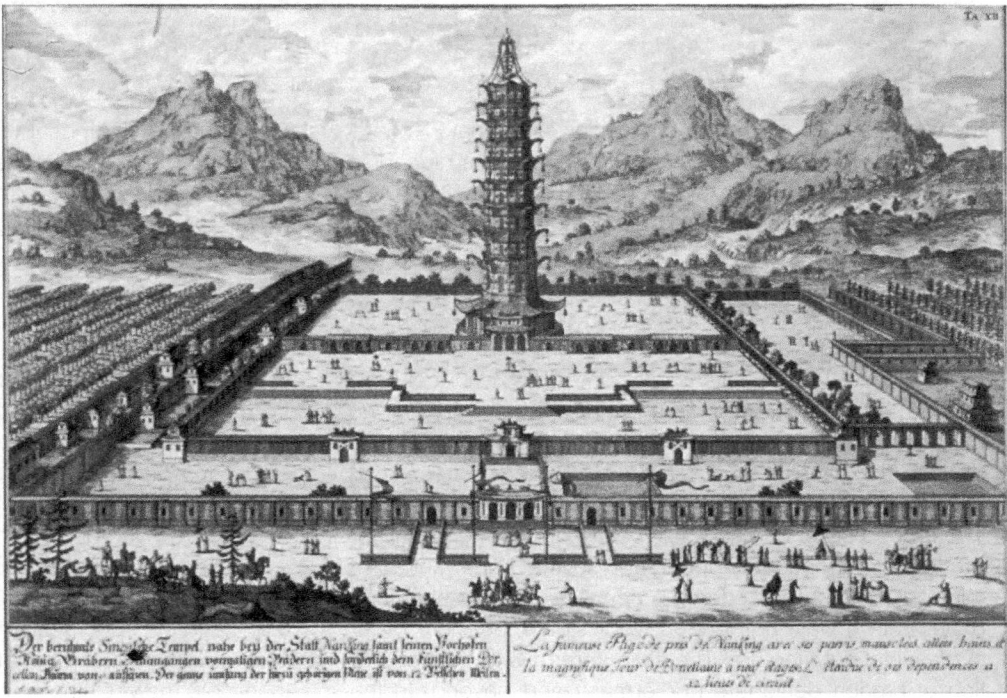

Pagoda in China from the *Atlas* of Fischer, 1721.

Of Bodies Bearing Buildings: Atlantids

The *caryatids*, sculptures of young women used to prop up the side porch on the Erechtheion in Athens, offered the most renowned example of sculptural bodies used as architectural supports (see Section 4.2). By the eighteenth century the muscular atlantids (inspired by the giant Atlas who held up the world in Greek mythology) had become a widespread motif for entries and stairways. Michelangelo's painted figures in the Sistine Chapel (1510) inspired others to bring such a corporeal vision to architecture. The Milanese sculptor Leone Leoni (1509–1590) popularized the use of this ancient type by placing eight colossal figures on the pilasters of his own house in Milan in 1565, with the ulterior motive of advertising his talent.

Fischer and his great rival in Vienna, Johann Lucas von Hildebrandt (1663–1745), frequently used atlantids in place of columns at entries and staircases. In Hildebrandt's largest project in Vienna, the Belvedere Palace, he even put atlantids at the tips of pilasters in place of capitals. At the entry to the central block he set large figures to bear the load of the vaults in front of the principal stair. The imagery alluded to the ability of powerful patrons to subjugate the bodies of their subjects.

Milan, Italy. Casa degli Omenoni, an early use of atlantids on an urban palace, Antonio Abondio and Leone Leoni, ca. 1565.

---

the world led to important commissions in Vienna. Fischer's scholarly interest in multiple cultural sources surfaced in his final work in Vienna, the Karlskirche (Fig. 13.2-10), a votive church designed after the plague of 1713 and finished posthumously by his son Joseph Emmanuel. Its tall oval dome and side belfries with bulging crowns resembled other Baroque works, but the placement of two historiated columns to either side of a classical temple-front entry appeared like archaeological infusions. The twin columns evoked the Habsburg emblem but also alluded to the two spiral columns at the entry to the Temple of Solomon.

After the conclusion of the War of Spanish Succession in 1714, French influence increased in Central Europe. The rococo style, named after *rocaille*, the French word for grotto rock formations, appeared in several important commissions. The rococo offered a new appreciation of natural patterns in a way that tended to dissipate the clear order of classical architecture. The style spread with the emigration of French designers to Germany and beyond. In the Spiegelsaal (Mirror Room) in the Amalienburg Pavilion

(1734) of the Nymphenburg Castle of Munich, the French designer François Cuvilliés the Elder (1695–1768) created an atmosphere of riotous movement through the flashing of mirrors and the sweeping gestures of gilded vegetal details (Fig. 13.2-11). Such decorative excess corresponded to the size and complexity of the powdered wigs worn at this time by the aristocrats using these interiors.

The rococo mode of decoration reached its apex in the work of Balthasar Neumann (1687–1753). Neumann rose from the crafts and traveled to Italy and Vienna as a military engineer during the first years of the eighteenth century. Under the patronage of the Schönborn dynasty of prince-bishops, he spent much of his career working on the grand Residenz of Würzburg, begun in 1715, a project that nearly exhausted the region's resources. He worked out the city's geometric plan, the palace's great halls, the theatrical staircase, and the spectacular Hofkirche.

During the first half of the eighteenth century more than 200 new Catholic churches appeared in Bavaria, most of them on remote sites connected to monasteries

Figure 13.2-10 Vienna. Karlskirche, Johann Bernhard Fischer von Erlach, 1720s.

or pilgrimage shrines. Neumann designed his masterpiece, the pilgrimage church Vierzehnheiligen (1743) (Fig. 13.2-12a), on a hilltop site where a vision of the fourteen "helping" saints was said to have occurred. He treated the facade with restraint, the entry bay slightly bulging between two tall bell towers, recalling Carolingian westworks (see Section 8.3). The interior glistened with colored marbles, undulating balconies, angels flitting in mid-air, and strands of sinuous rococo ornament. The scintillating effects of the sculptural decorations almost obscured the complexity of the curves and countercurves that shaped the nave. Neumann invented a system for his interiors in which he played a series of ovals against stiff outer walls, like internal organs contained within the skin of a body (Fig. 13.2-12b). The inner shell billowed into rounded plaster vaults supported by colorful columns. The succession of intersecting ovals was analogous to the layered musical fugues of Johann Sebastian Bach.

The Iberian Metamorphosis of Colonial Gold

Portugal and Spain were the first European countries to benefit from shipping exploits across the Atlantic. The western-oriented ports of Lisbon and Seville flourished as the largest and wealthiest cities of their respective countries. During the sixteenth century, profits from the spice trade of India, the slave trade of Africa, and eventually the cash crops of the Americas financed the creation of a series of substantial convents and palaces on the Iberian Peninsula,

Figure 13.2-11 Munich. Amalienburg Pavilion at Nymphenburg Castle, Mirror Room, François Cuvilliés, 1734.

endowed with taxes on the imports. By the eighteenth century two distinct styles had emerged: one a severe version of the classicism of the Italian Renaissance and the other an ornate mix of late Gothic, Baroque, and *mudéjar* motifs. Italian designers had been imported to Spain since the sixteenth century as court favorites, and their influence showed in the two most important royal commissions of sixteenth-century Spain: the monastery of the Escorial and the palace of Charles V at the Alhambra (see Section 12.2). Italians showed up in Portugal a bit later, in the late seventeenth and early eighteenth centuries. Despite the Italian influence, an Iberian Baroque style evolved into its own expression,

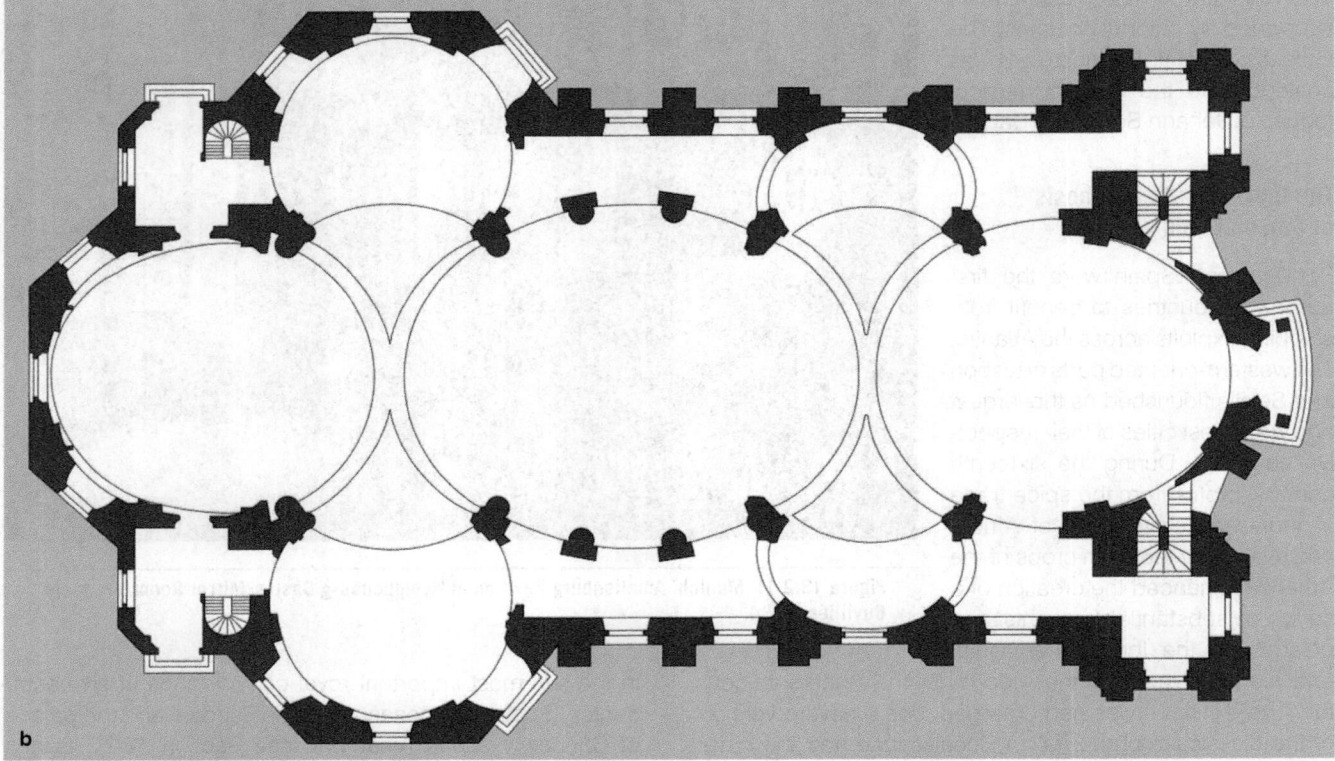

Figure 13.2-12 Vierzehnheiligen. (a) Pilgrimage church, Balthasar Neumann, 1740s. (b) Plan showing the concatenation of ovals from the narthex to the nave, the side altars, and the main altar.

indulging in piles of ornament and gilded details. The incredibly ornate **retable** screens that crowded the altars in churches such as San José in Seville, designed around 1760 by Cayetano de Acosta (1709–1778), seemed like glowing deposits of bullion from the New World.

While the Bourbon dynasty commissioned Juvarra and his assistant, Giovanni Battista Sacchetti (1690–1764), to return to the severe style of the Escorial for the new palace of La Granja near Segovia and the Royal Palace in Madrid, a more expressive style came from local designers working outside of royal patronage. Francisco Hurtado Izquierda (1669–1725), working mostly in Granada, designed the Sagrario of both the Cartuja Convent and its associated cathedral. His system of reverberating decoration included spiraling Solomonic columns and framing elements with staggered cusps cut into them. He also popularized the use of **estipites**, columns or pilasters that taper downward to intermediate chunks of rustication. Leonardo de Figueroa (1650–1730) worked in a similar manner in Seville. His church of San Luis, begun in 1699, loaded the pink facade with spiraling Solomonic columns, anticipating their use on the interior, where they ascended like flames from smooth columns to articulate the oval space of the nave. The repetition of swirling columns created a vibrating vista toward the densely loaded *retable*. Figueroa also infused the central portal of the Colegio de San Telmo (Fig. 13.2-13), built in 1722, with the complex decoration usually reserved for the altar.

Figure 13.2-13 Seville, Spain. Colegio de San Telmo, Leonardo de Figueroa, 1722.

Spanish Baroque was often called **churrigueresque**, after three brothers—José Benito, Joaquin, and Alberto Churriguera, born in Barcelona in the 1660s and 1670s and mostly known for their *retables* executed in Madrid and Salamanca. Their work proved more sober than that of contemporaries such as Pedro de Ribera, whose cluttered packing of decorations on the steeple of Salamanca best represented the term "churrigueresque." Fernando de Casas y Novoa (ca. 1690–1749) completed the facade of Santiago de Compostela (Fig. 13.2-14), arguably Spain's most important church, in churrigueresque style in the 1740s. The stacks of decorative elements formed vertical bands that blended well with the Gothic structure.

While Spain had a greater overall population than Portugal, Lisbon prevailed as the largest city on the Iberian Peninsula, with over 150,000 inhabitants in the eighteenth century. Here, the expression of colonial wealth occurred in two phases. The first, during the time of King Manuel I (r. 1495–1521), corresponded to the initial growth of trade with Asia and Africa. Vasco da Gama (1469–1524), the mariner who secured the route around the African cape to India, was awarded a magnificent tomb in the narthex of the grandest work of sixteenth-century Portugal, the Jeronimite Monastery at Belem. The church's design, with a nave and two aisles of equal height, resembled a German *hallenkirche*, while the intricate web vaults aspired to the flamboyant

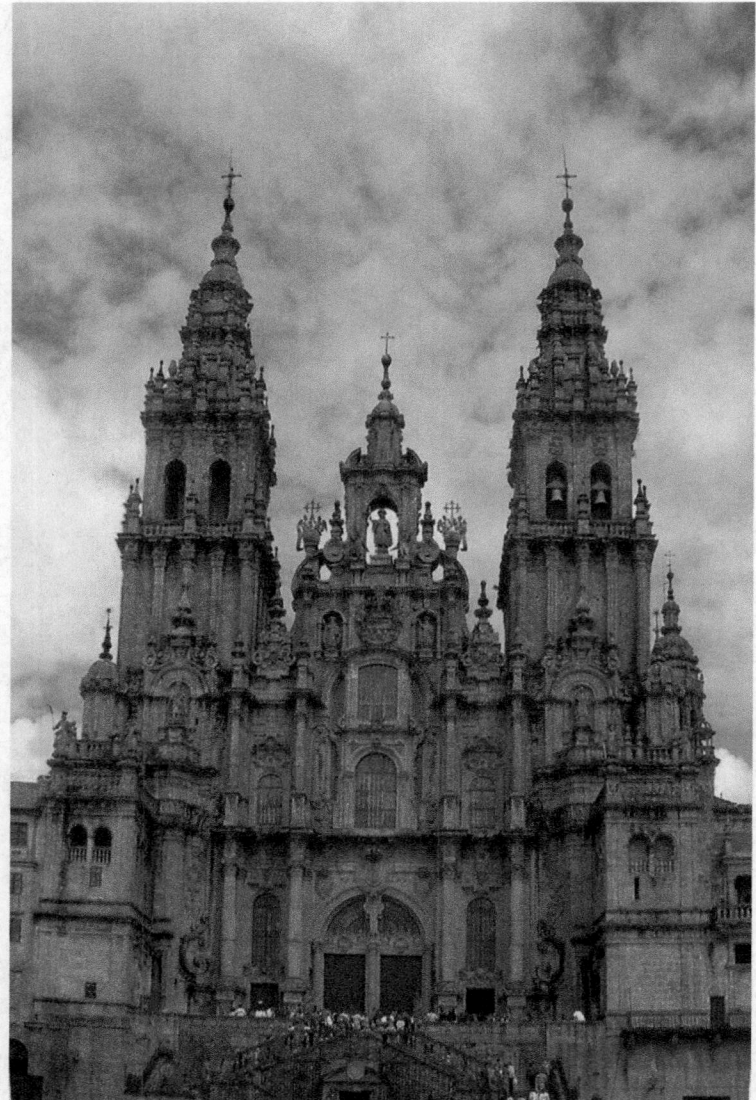

Figure 13.2-14 Galicia, Spain. Santiago de Compostela, facade, Fernando de Casas y Novoa, 1720s.

French Gothic of the time. The luxurious details at Belem, which included fancifully chamfered corners and lace-like frames for the arches, were financed by skimming off 20% of the taxes on goods from the route to India. A spiraling cone dotted with balls crowned each of the piers, while carvings of crocodiles, seashells, African *putti*, and exotic plants indicated the overseas origin of the convent's wealth.

The second phase of Portuguese splendor occurred during the early eighteenth century, after Brazil returned to Portuguese control. King João V (r. 1706–1750), known as the "Magnanimous," took advantage of the new influx of wealth, claiming 20% of the income from the gold mines discovered in Minas Gerais, Brazil. This windfall gave him both exceptional leverage as a patron of the arts and autonomy from the Portuguese nobility. Inspired by the Spanish court, João V hoped to obtain the services of famous Italian designers such as Juvarra and Vanvitelli. The king proved so keen on having an authentic Italian building in Portugal that he commissioned the latter to design and build the church of Sao Rocco in Rome and ship it to Lisbon to be reassembled piece by piece in 1747.

For the largest project in Portugal, the monastery-palace of Mafra (Fig. 13.2-15), 30 km (19 miles) north of Lisbon, João V hired a well-trained German, Johann Friedrich Ludwig, known as "Ludovice" (1670–1752). Ludovice had worked in Rome for ten years under Andrea Pozzo and produced a design close to the style of Fontana. The initial project was begun in 1717 as an ex-voto in thanks for the birth of the king's male heir and served as a convent for a dozen Franciscans.

During the next decade the program escalated into an immense complex rivaling the Escorial, with a grand cathedral, a palace, a monastery for 300 friars, and Portugal's largest library. Like Versailles, Mafra dominated a small town that spread below it on three radiating streets. The 220 m (722 ft) enfilade of the upper story of the palace passed from the king's tower on the north through the benediction loggia of the church to the queen's tower on the south. The magnificent dome over the crossing of the palace church made Mafra the grandest ecclesiastic space in Portugal. The decorators slathered

Figure 13.2-15 Mafra, Portugal. Monastery-palace of Mafra built for João V by Ludovice, 1720s.

Portuguese *Azulejos* Cladding

Portugal's local Baroque architects produced ornate *retables* similar to those seen in Spain and often covered church interiors and porticoes with blue and white *azulejos* tiles. Used as protective wainscoting, the tiles came to typify Portuguese architecture, used not only on churches but also to cover the facades of entire buildings. The *azulejos* derived from Chinese porcelains, and until 1710 the Portuguese imported them from Dutch artists for works such as the convent church of Madre Deus in Lisbon. The city of Porto hosts several churches clad with *azulejos*, such as San Ildefonso, built in 1710–1730.

Porto, Portugal. San Ildefonso, *azulejos* tiles as cladding, 1710–1730.

the interior with pink and gray marble and sculptures by prominent Roman artists. Over 45,000 workers contributed to its construction, leading to the consumption of a great portion of the state's income from Brazil.

Some of Portugal's colonial wealth went toward the public good, such as the impressive aqueduct of Aguas Livres (1729–1748), which served Lisbon. Responding to the progressive interests of the Enlightenment, the king attempted to encourage local industry and sponsored workshops for the production of metals and ceramics. Ludovice worked in the 1720s as one of the designers for a special act of social patronage, the library, belfry, and grand Ionic portico at the University of Coimbra, a program gathered around a magnificent terraced court that overlooked the city. Aside from a few investments in infrastructure and education, Portugal's colonial gold went toward the production of magnificent churches, such as the pilgrimage church of Bom Jesus near Braga in the north of Portugal (1727), poised at the summit of seven terraces.

Further Reading

Blunt, Anthony, ed. *Baroque and Rococo: Architecture and Decoration*. London: Paul Elek, 1978.

Boscarino, Salvatore. *Sicilia Barocca: Architettura e città, 1610–1760*. Rome: Officina Edizioni, 1997.

Braunfels, Wolfgang. *Urban Design in Western Europe: Regime and Architecture, 900–1900*. Translated by K. Northcott. Chicago: University of Chicago Press, 1988.

DaCosta Kaufmann, Thomas. *Court, Cloister and City: The Art and Culture of Central Europe, 1450–1800*. Chicago: University of Chicago Press, 1995.

Kubler, George, and Martin Soria. *Art and Architecture in Spain and Portugal and Their American Dominions*. Harmondsworth, UK: Penguin, 1959.

Portoghesi, Paolo. *Roma Barocca*. Bari, Italy: Edizione Laterza, 1997.

Tobriner, Stephen. *The Genesis of Noto, an Eighteenth-Century Sicilian City*. Berkeley: University of California Press, 1982.

13.3 THE AMERICAN COLONIES
Domination and Liberty on the Grid

The resettlement of the Western Hemisphere by European colonialists resulted at once in the crass exploitation of people and resources and unparalleled experiments in political and religious freedom. From the sixteenth to the eighteenth century, as newcomers claimed lands, built cities, and tapped resources, the indigenous populations of the Americas ended up either enslaved or devastated by diseases. Despite the idealism of some of the European efforts to start over in a new land, colonization inevitably caused the displacement and ruin of native-born peoples.

Spain, Portugal, France, Holland, and England all established colonies in the Americas, producing a variety of political orders that ranged from the reproduction of feudal hierarchy in New Spain to self-managed commonwealths in New England. Europeans brought their architecture with them: the Spanish built palaces with colonnaded courtyards; the Dutch built tall, narrow houses with decorative gables; the English built cottages with half-timbers. Even those who came against their will, the African slaves, contributed architectural knowledge, reviving the long "shotgun" house type with shady verandahs. In areas such as Mexico and Peru, where large indigenous populations survived, the local crafts amalgamated with European types.

Most of the new towns in the Americas followed orthogonal grids. While the grid of Mexico City acquired stone palaces and block-sized convents, resulting in a fabric larger and more orderly than that of any city in Spain, the grid of a Puritan settlement such as New Haven, Connecticut, remained village-scaled and sparsely built, with small wooden houses set back from the streets. Despite these differences in scale, the grid served in all cases as a game board for working out the social order of the American colonies.

Spanish Cities in the Western Hemisphere: Fulfilling the Law of the Indies

European colonialism had its quickest and boldest success in Mexico, known also as "New Spain." A generation after the Spanish "Contact," the surviving members of the native population converted to Christianity. Scores of planned settlements decorously sheltered the tiny Spanish minority and urbanized the largely pastoral *indios*. By 1700, the colonial power had restructured the Mexican landscape into a network of thriving cities, served by sophisticated hydraulic works and crowned by domed cathedrals. A viable society capable of housing and employing millions, the Spanish colony established mining and manufacturing towns while keeping in check the transient and nomadic tribes that lived at the edges of the territory.

The Spanish settlers, rude soldiers of fortune, claimed land and indigenous slaves through *encomienda* grants. Each owner commanded several hundred slaves. The Catholic Church sent religious missionaries, who founded over 400 independent, self-supporting monastery towns. These friars frequently took up the cause of the mistreated *indios*: Fra Bartolomé de las Casas in particular denounced the appalling injustices of the colonizers to the king, demanding, "Tell me by what right of justice do you hold these Indians in such a cruel and horrible servitude?"

Toward the end of the sixteenth century the viceroys reformed the *encomienda* system into a feudal organization of *hacienda* estates with poorly paid *peóns* compelled to work the land. Despite the friars' sympathy for indigenous peoples, they launched a campaign to eliminate all traces of native religions, destroying the native temples as "houses of the devil." They erected new monasteries and cathedrals on top of ancient platforms, such as the church at the summit of the ancient pyramid of Cholula. At the Augustinian convent of Acolman, native artisans left traces of Aztec culture in the capitals of the cloister's columns. A decade after Cortés transformed Tenochtitlán into Mexico City, the Virgin of Guadalupe appeared miraculously to a Nahuatl-speaking convert, helping to secure native loyalty to the new religion.

Orthogonal planning had deeper roots in pre-Contact Mexico than in Spain, and native geometric schemes offered a ready source for the layout of these new towns. Puebla, founded in 1531, took the coordinates and dimensions of

▼ **1636**
Harvard, the first university in North America, founded in Cambridge, Massachusetts

William Penn founds Philadelphia on grid plan
▲ **1668**

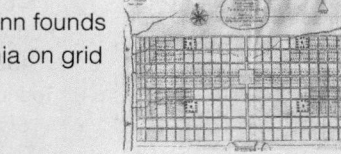

▼ **1690**
Gold discovered in Minas Gerais, Brazil

RELIGION, PHILOSOPHY, FOLKLORE

The Virgin of Guadalupe

In 1531 Juan Diego, a native recently converted to Catholicism, encountered a miraculous vision of the Virgin Mary about 4 km (2.5 miles) north of Mexico City. Calling herself by a word that sounded like "Guadalupe," which in the Nahuatl language meant "corn goddess trampling a serpent," the hill took that name and became the most important pilgrimage site in the Western Hemisphere. The Virgin first appeared at a well, or *pocito*, and during a second appearance, she ordered Juan Diego to gather the roses growing on the hill into his *sarape* and take them to the archbishop. When he opened his cloak in front of the archbishop to let the roses fall to the ground, a magnificent portrait of the Virgin appeared, the first miracle of the New World. The basilica to house the image was rebuilt by Pedro de Arrieta in the early eighteenth century. One of his assistants, a native of Guadalupe, Francisco Guerrero y Torres, went on to design the Baroque settings of El Pocito chapel (1777), a shrine to the well of the Virgin, placing a steep dome clad in blue and white Puebla tiles over an oval plan. Two subdomes covered the entry and the altar, which inside rose on flamboyant spiraling columns.

Mexico City. Chapel of El Pocito, Francisco Guerrero y Torres, 1777.

Palace of the
Inquisition built
in Mexico City

▲ 1710

▼ **1733**

*Ideal city of Savannah
begun in South Carolina*

American
colonies present
the Declaration
of Independence

▲ 1776

▼ **1810**

Mexico declares
independence
from Spain

its orthogonal plan from the grid of the nearby indigenous city of Cholula. Whatever the source of the colonial grid, the Spanish urbanization of Mexico proceeded methodically, similar to the colonial planning of the ancient Greeks and Romans or the medieval *bastide* builders. In 1573, after the settlement of hundreds of gridded towns in the Spanish American territories, the colonial administrators codified the practice of urbanism in a set of 148 articles, known as the "Laws of the Indies." These articles recommended straight, wide streets, laid out "using cord and ruler." The central plaza was to be surrounded by arcades and measure one and a half times as long as wide, the oblong shape working better for festival games. That the plan of Caracas, Venezuela, initiated in 1578, corresponded perfectly to that of towns such as Oaxaca in Mexico and Mendoza in Argentina, built a generation before the Laws of the Indies, demonstrates that the legislation summarized nearly fifty years of successful town-planning practice.

Mexico City remained the privileged capital of New Spain. The first metropolis of the colonial settlements, it enjoyed administrative rights over Cuba, Guatemala, and other nearby Spanish territories. Cortés's surveyor, Alonso Garcia Bravo (1490–1561), designed the city's plan in the 1520s to replace the ruins of the Aztec capital of Tenochtitlán (see Section 10.3). Its *traza*, or grid, followed the orthogonals of the native city. The Spanish initially segregated the indigenous residents from the European colonialists, sending them to the neighboring town of Tlatelolco to the north. By 1700 Mexico City appeared larger and better served than any city in Spain, with broad paved roads, sewers, and aqueducts. The major square, the Zócalo, measured 240 m (768 ft) per side, exceeding the dimensions recommended in the Laws of the Indies and more than twice the size of the Plaza Mayor in Madrid. The Cathedral of Mexico (Fig. 13.3-1),

designed in 1573 by the Spanish-born architect Claudio de Arciniega (1527–1593), dominated the northern edge of the plaza, in imitation of the cathedrals of Segovia and Salamanca. Its construction and considerable redesign continued throughout the seventeenth century. As the largest church in the Western Hemisphere, the cathedral covered an entire city block, with two bell towers, a vaulted nave sustained by massive buttresses, and a grand dome. In 1748 Lorenzo Rodriguez of Granada (1704–1774) added an adjacent chapel, the Sagrario Metropolitano, using a Greek cross plan, and clad it with a highly ornate churrigueresque facade.

An independent Mexican style appeared in many settlements, such as the wealthy frontier town of Querétaro, 200 km (124 miles) north of Mexico City. Amid the conventional palace and convent types set on the city's orthogonal plan one could find delightfully eccentric details. The external buttresses of the church of Santa Rosa de Viterbo (1727) (Fig. 13.3-2a) connected the body of the church with a novel series of colossal volutes. In the convent cloister of the same church, built a few decades later and attributed to the local architect Ignacio Mariano de las Casas (1719–1771), the arches on the second level dipped in the center to assume an unconventional *M* shape. The same architect designed the nearby convent of San Augustin in the 1730s, using grotesque totem-like figures on the piers of the cloister (Fig. 13.3-2b). The breasts of these figures blended surreally with geometric scrolls.

In the early eighteenth century, Querétaro embarked on an impressive work of infrastructure: the seventy-four-arch aqueduct of La Cañada. Juan Antonio de Urritia y Arana, marquis of Villa del Villar, representing a new breed of Mexican public servant, devised, built, and partly paid for the new public work. The aqueduct fed a great round basin sustained with battered sides and scrolled buttresses. The water emptied into ten public fountains built in the city's plazas and diffused further into sixty private fountains for religious settlements and large private houses. The marquis sponsored one of these residences in the center of town in 1756 as a gift to his wife. Although discreet on the exterior, the arches of its inner courts indulged in fanciful scalloped motifs. The strong sense of municipal autonomy expressed by the aqueduct and other public projects made Querétaro the epicenter of the Mexican movement for independence that took root in the early nineteenth century.

Pedro de Arrieta (ca. 1690–1738), born and educated in Mexico, emerged as the colony's most original designer during the eighteenth century. He built numerous churches in Mexico City and became the "maestro mayor" of the cathedral. At the Palace of the Inquisition

Figure 13.3-1 Mexico City. Cathedral, Claudio de Arciniega, begun in 1573.

Figure 13.3-2 (a) Querétaro, Mexico. Santa Rosa de Viterbo, Ignacio Mariano de las Casas, 1727. (b) Cloister of San Augustino, de las Casas, 1720s.

(Fig. 13.3-3) he introduced an exquisite break from the typical patio-type palace. He wrapped the exterior with the conventional dark red *texontle* stone and strapped windows, but instead of placing the entry midblock, he put it at the corner, chamfering the edge. One entered on a diagonal into the square patio to find that the architect had removed the columns at the corners. Contrary to the Renaissance practice of thickening the corner, he offered a marvelously counterintuitive solution, taking away support where one would expect to find it doubled. The playful style of the building belied the repressive function of the Inquisition, a religious institution that imprisoned suspected heretics and brought them to trial in the Zócalo in a ceremony known as *auto-da-fé*. The confession of heretical beliefs that occurred during this ceremony concluded with the public immolation of the accused, evoking the tradition of human sacrifice that

Figure 13.3-3 Mexico City. Palace of the Inquisition, Pedro de Arrieta, 1710s.

had supposedly been suppressed by the civilizing process of European colonization.

The African Diaspora to the Antilles, Brazil, and Beyond

Slave labor became one of the most ingrained economic factors in the European colonization of the Americas, generating tragic consequences. In Mexico, the Spanish ruthlessly enslaved the *indios*, treating them as property belonging to the land. In many of the new territories the natives either fled or perished in epidemics of European viruses such as smallpox. Rough estimates propose that 60%–90% of the indigenous people of New Spain vanished during the sixteenth century. With fewer natives to exploit, the Europeans drew on the African slave market. They imported people from the Benin region to work the labor-intensive sugarcane crop and the mines of the Antilles Islands in the Caribbean. The new colonies benefited from the vernacular design solutions and carpentry skills of peoples such as the Yoruba and those from Benin, who introduced the bungalow type surrounded by shady verandahs and louvered shutters.

The Atlantic slave trade commenced in the fifteenth century with the Portuguese voyages to the East Indies that circumnavigated Africa. The islands off the coast of West Africa—Madeira, the Azores, Cape Verde—became the first European colonial outposts and eventually the stepping stones for exchange between continents. Portuguese merchants introduced African slaves acquired from local slave traders on the African coasts to the Americas to sustain the labor-intensive sugar plantations and gold-mining operations established there. The English, French, Dutch, and Danish joined the Portuguese slave traders in the following century. Initially the taskmasters took the slaves from the Senegal–Gambia River area of Western Africa and the Gold Coast at the mouth of the Volta River to Italian-style island fortresses, such as Gorée, off the coast of Senegal. However, as the demand for slaves increased, the Portuguese moved farther south, creating a major dispatching colony on the island of San Tomé. By the seventeenth century the trade in humans had expanded to 50,000 per year, resulting in more than 12 million Africans being sold by other Africans to the European traders over four centuries. In some cases, during the Middle Passage across the Atlantic, the slave masters forced up to 400 people to lie in stacks in the hold of a ship like cargo, deprived of food, drink, and sanitation. An estimated 15% did not survive the journey. Those who did were stripped of their dignity, starting with the loss of their names.

Over half of the slaves arrived to work the sugar plantations of the Antilles owned by the Spanish, French, Dutch, and English. Hispaniola (now Santo Domingo), the site of Columbus's first landing, was divided into a Spanish colony on the eastern side of the island and a French settlement, Saint Domingue (now Haiti), on the west. By the eighteenth century Africans outnumbered Europeans in Haiti by more than ten to one. The plan of Le Cap-Français obeyed a near-perfect grid, with the central Place d'Armes overlooked by a cathedral and a polygonal fortress on the hill. Left to their own

for housing, the Africans produced clusters of huts similar to their erstwhile villages, giving the most design attention to the storehouse, the cooking house, and the small temple, later associated with the voodoo cult. The boxy houses, with front porches and thatch made of tropical leaves, recalled structures built by the Yoruba people in Nigeria. In the later eighteenth century, enslaved peoples adopted house types from English pattern books arriving from the United States. In Port-au-Prince the designers of the Old Cathedral, begun in 1720, copied Renaissance models, loading a simple two-level facade with pilasters and scrolls and capping it with a cupola belfry on the front. After the revolution of 1802, which resulted in the independent African American state of Haiti, intense sugar production and slave traffic relocated to neighboring Cuba.

Wary of pirates and local rebellions, Europeans built fortresses in the region. On Haiti alone the French built forty such structures, using the criteria of Vauban. The Spanish planted as many Italian-inspired forts on Santo Domingo, Puerto Rico, and Cuba. Fortresses with angled bastions of cut stone, such as the Castillo de San Felipe de El Morro (Fig. 13.3-4) in San Juan, Puerto Rico, begun in 1591 by Juan de Tejada and the Italian engineer Battista Antonelli (1547–1616), compared admirably with their European models. Antonelli also designed the angled bastions of the fortress of Los Tres Reyes del Morro in the 1590s at the mouth of the harbor of Havana, Cuba, a port that became the principal entrepôt for ships going between New Spain and Seville. The polygonal fortress at the mouth of the harbor served as the city's highest architectural expression until the construction of the cathedral in 1748.

The Portuguese colony of Brazil imported the largest number of slaves, over 4 million in total, leading to an exceptional amalgamation of European and African culture. Due to the unstable political situation of Portugal during the seventeenth century and a brief interval of Dutch rule in Brazil, the colony developed with considerable autonomy compared to its Spanish rivals. After the discovery of gold in 1693 in the Minas Gerais area, the mountain town of Vila Rica, now called Ouro Preto, emerged as Brazil's colonial showplace. Unlike the other colonial powers, the Portuguese did not build cities on the grid but left the street system casual and additive. During the eighteenth century Ouro Preto received twelve new churches, along with several significant palaces and civic institutions, many of them designed by Portuguese architect Manoel Francisco Lisboa. His son, Antônio Francisco Lisboa, or Aleijadinho (1730–1814), born to an African slave mother, designed and decorated San Francisco de Assis da Penitência (1766–1794) (Fig. 13.3-5). There, he created a naive variation of European Baroque types, representing a synthesis of races and cultures.

The British sugar islands of Barbados and Jamaica, although relatively small, brought enormous consequences for the North American mainland. From 1627 on, Barbados, in the southern Antilles, served as the first American island on the itinerary of the slave ships traveling from Africa to the colonies. It briefly succeeded as the first profitable British

Figure 13.3-4 San Juan, Puerto Rico. El Morro fortress, Juan de Tejada and Battista Antonelli, begun 1591.

colony, a distinction that quickly faded. Although the first two generations of settlers relied on the labor of indentured servants, African slaves were imported to the island beginning in 1650 and by 1712 made up 75% of the population. Soil depletion from overintense planting and deforestation reduced the island's yield capacity, and by the end of the eighteenth century Barbados had become a bit player in the sugar market, yielding its position to Jamaica, which imported ten times as many Africans. The first bona fide architect in Barbados, Sir Thomas Robinson, arrived there as governor (1742–1747) and brought Palladianism to the scene, evident in the design of Government House in Bridgetown. Europe's insatiable demand for sugar and tobacco, new consumer commodities of dubious nutritional value, encouraged all of the Antilles islands to overwork both the land and the slaves, leading to ecological devastation and a future of political unrest.

Palladian Plantations in the American South

The English settlements in North America varied from corporate enterprises modeled on the East India Company to small, idealistic communities founded by religious reformers.

The southern colonies developed as a series of agricultural estates, relying on African slaves. Rather than settling in cities, the southern colonists spread across the land and in some cases sponsored great mansions of architectural distinction, modeled on the English gentry's manor houses. The initial workforce in the British colonies was composed of indentured servants, generally poor Caucasians who promised several years of labor in exchange for transatlantic passage. After the 1660s, however, it became increasingly difficult to find people who would come of their own free will. To fill the gap, southern estate owners in Virginia, the Carolinas, and the ex-French colony of Louisiana imported African slaves by way of Barbados and other ports in the Antilles to work the large plantations of tobacco, rice, and cotton. By the time of the outbreak of the American Civil War in 1861, the southern states possessed about 2.5 million slaves. Like the wealthy aristocrats of ancient Rome, the important landowners kept hundreds of slaves.

The first English colony in mainland North America took root in Virginia's marshy Tidewater area of Chesapeake Bay. In 1607 the Virginia Company, a joint-stock enterprise under royal charter, founded Jamestown some 20 km (12.4 miles) inland of the Atlantic. The small capital was

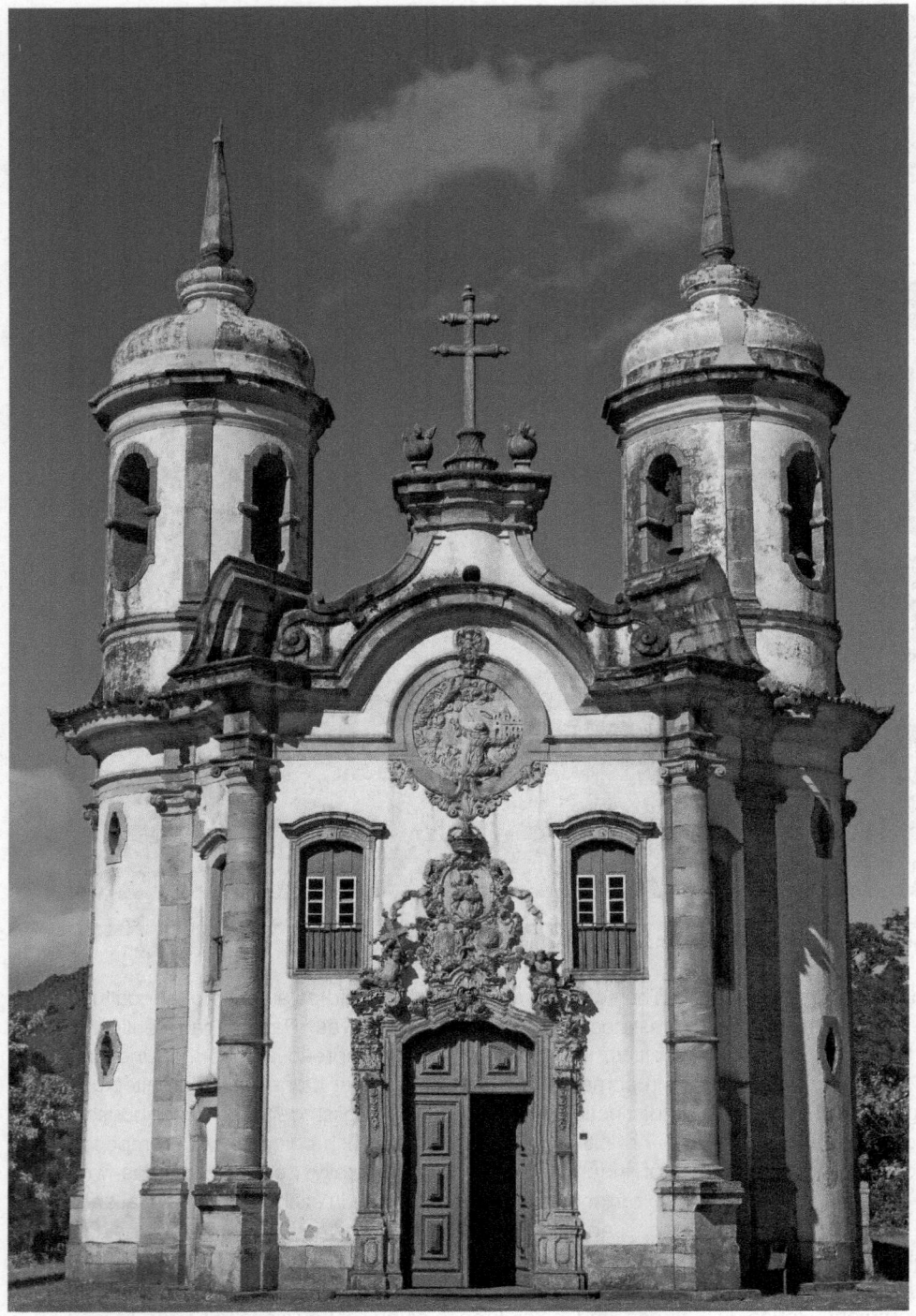

Figure 13.3-5 Ouro Preto, Brazil. San Francisco, Aleijadinho, begun 1766.

manner, the only regulation being a 7 km (4 mile) minimum distance one from the next. The cash crop of tobacco led to immense fortunes. In 1698 the colony attempted to renew its urban efforts by moving the capital to Williamsburg, a site on high ground midway between the York and James Rivers. Although intended as a small city for 2,000 people, Williamsburg received a grand plan (Fig. 13.3-6a,b). The central avenue, Duke of Gloucester Street, stretched 30 m (98 ft) across, wider than any street in England at this time. It connected the College of William and Mary to the new capital, which looked onto a large square 150 m (480 ft) per side. A market square stood at the crux of the main axis, with a secondary axis leading south to the courthouse, the Powder House, and the parish church. A second intersection opened to a grand planted esplanade foregrounding the Governor's Palace. The generous spaces and abundant greenery of Williamsburg seemed closer to the layout of Baroque gardens than to existing urban models. Despite its ambitious plan, the city remained underpopulated, and when the capital was moved farther inland to Richmond in 1780, it fell into permanent decline.

William Byrd II (1674–1744), who designed the grid plan of Richmond, had spent two decades in England before returning to Virginia. In the mid-1720s he began to rebuild his family's estate at Westover, transforming it into one of the great plantation houses of Virginia. His son, William Byrd III, rebuilt it after a fire in 1749 with a mixture of the common sense of colonial vernacular brick houses and the sophisticated style of English country houses. Like the modest homes of the region, he embedded the chimneys into the lateral walls but also added high-style windows with segmental transoms, classical pilasters, and a **broken pediment** over the entry in imitation of the mansions of the British aristocracy. His contemporary Thomas Lee (1690–1750), the acting governor, followed suit in 1730 with the mansion of Stratford Hall (Fig. 13.3-7a). While smaller than Westover, it appeared more monumental. The Lee mansion rested on a raised basement made

poorly sited and inconsequential to the colonial economy that developed around the plantations. Although the term "plantation" initially referred to colonial urban settlements, it came to signify the landscape of an agricultural estate with a big house and a collection of secondary buildings, including one-room shacks to house the slaves. Most of the early plantation houses related better to the river than to the roads, and the estates sprawled in a fairly chaotic

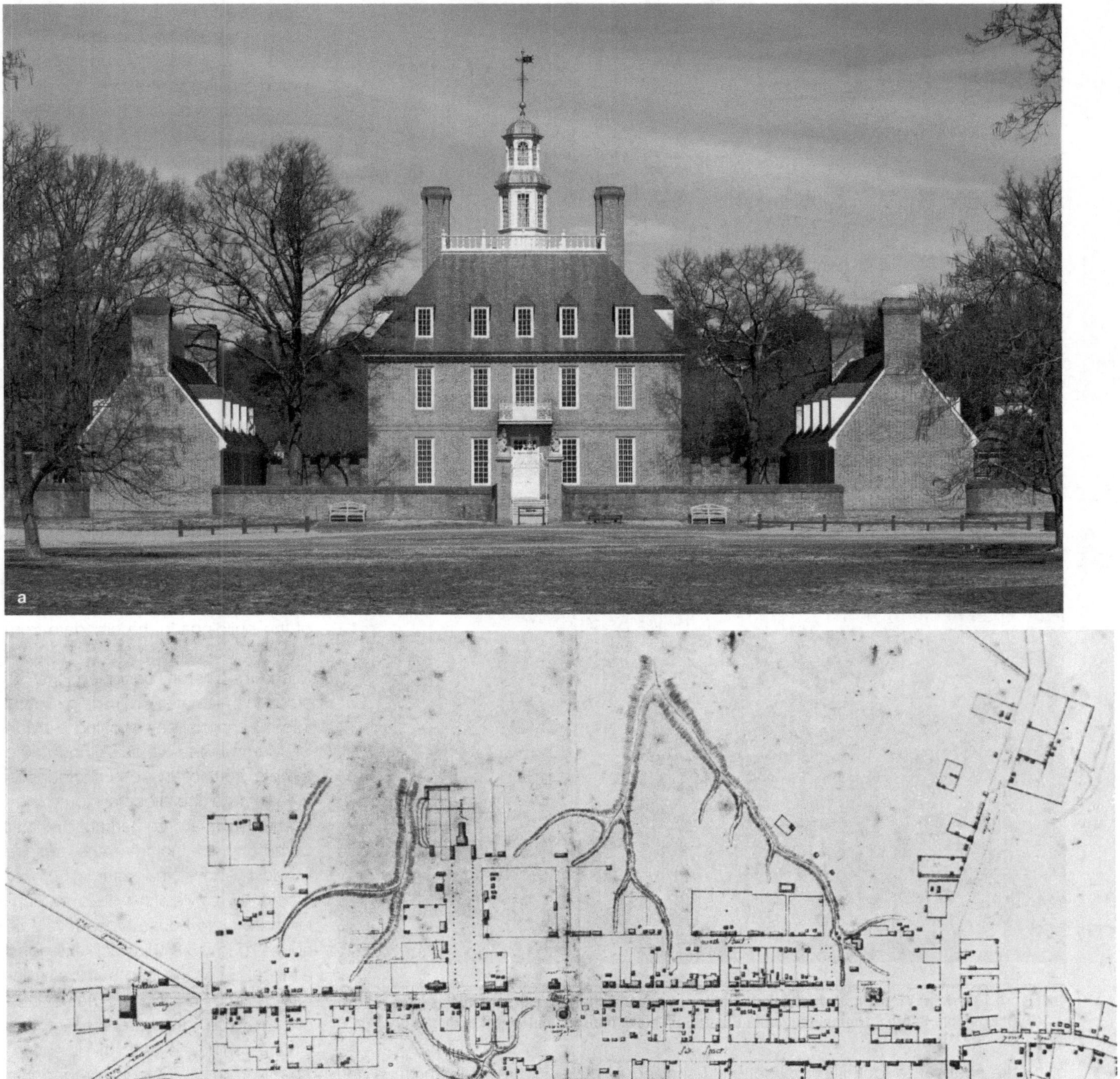

Figure 13.3-6 Williamsburg, Virginia. (a) Reconstructed Governor's Palace, ca. 1700. (b) City plan, attributed to Governor Nicholson, 1698.

Figure 13.3-7 (a) Virginia. Stratford Hall, plantation house built for Governor Thomas Lee, 1730s. (b) Charleston, South Carolina. Magnolia Plantation, slave houses, mid-eighteenth century.

clear Neo-Palladian manner. Shirley, commissioned by Elizabeth Hill in 1738, had a two-story temple-front porch looking to the river, similar to the depiction of Villa Pisani in Palladio's treatise. A series of outbuildings, arranged symmetrically, created an orderly forecourt, while a dozen wooden duplexes for more than 100 slaves stood a fifteen-minute walk from the big house. John Tayloe II (1721–1779) borrowed the design for Mount Airy (1758) (Fig. 13.3-8) from Gibbs's treatise. This "gentleman's house" likewise had a series of outbuildings arranged symmetrically around a forecourt.

Over half of the slaves sold in North America passed through the slave market of Charleston, South Carolina, which became the only sizable city in Great Britain's southern colonies. By the mid-eighteenth century half of the city's population of 12,800 descended from African origins. Most of the buildings in the city date from after the devastating fire of 1740. St. Michael's Church, designed in 1752, stood in the center, protruding slightly into the main street, evoking Gibbs's St. Martin-in-the-Fields. Although the temple front of the church today is smaller and the steeple stouter, the interior appears remarkably similar to the original, including the *serliana* window above the altar. The city blocks were filled in with a particular three-story house type, or "single house" (Fig. 13.3-9), which extended a lateral porch the length of the structure to help mitigate the hot, humid climate. Often, the entry stair into the Charleston house led to this linear verandah. The type derived partly from West African precedents as they filtered through the Antilles.

of bricks shaped to look like rustication. *I*-shaped in plan, the two side wings were soldered to the central block with grand tetrapylon chimneys. The entry stair flared out dramatically from the central block. Houses for the plantation's more than 100 slaves remained sufficiently far from the "big house" not to be seen (Fig. 13.3-7b). The sole surviving example of such structures, a well-built duplex, was made in cut stone with a central chimney wall dividing the two units.

Of the 40,000 plantations in the American South, only about 5% qualified as manorial estates. These larger plantations possessed nearly half of the region's slaves. As the intensity of slave labor increased, so did the sophistication of the architecture of the big houses. The mansion houses of Shirley and Mount Airy on the James River exhibited a

The French intended their colonial efforts in Canada and Louisiana to be urban but likewise had difficulty filling up their cities. By 1718, the year of the founding of New Orleans, the chain of forts, trading posts, and towns that comprised New France stretched from the Great Lakes to the Gulf of Mexico. The French founded numerous cities that went undeveloped, such as Louisbourg, the main fortress town in Canada, which followed the patterns of Vauban's fortified cities, and Detroit, which imitated the *bastides* of southwest France. The most common French plan, however, seen in Montréal, St. Louis, and New Orleans, set a narrow linear grid along a river, with a central *place d'armes* close to the water's edge.

Figure 13.3-8 Virginia. Mount Airy, built for John Tayloe, 1758.

Figure 13.3-9 Charleston, South Carolina. Typical "single house" with lateral verandah, eighteenth century.

The Plan of Savannah: The Brief Reign of Utopia

South of Charleston, the prison reformer James Oglethorpe founded the settlement of Savannah, Georgia, in 1733. Intended as a haven for poor settlers and ex-convicts, he designed it as a self-sufficient society, a model agriculturally based town without slavery or alcohol. The grid of wards, each 183 m (604 ft) per side, with forty regular lots surrounding a planted square for public buildings, provided the basic social unit. New wards were added as the town grew. By the mid-nineteenth century Savannah had long lost its idealistic social premises: slavery was introduced in 1752, and Oglethorpe's moral criteria, such as temperance, were abandoned. The ward system of the plan miraculously survived to cover a total of twenty-four orderly neighborhoods, achieving an extraordinary balance between public and private space.

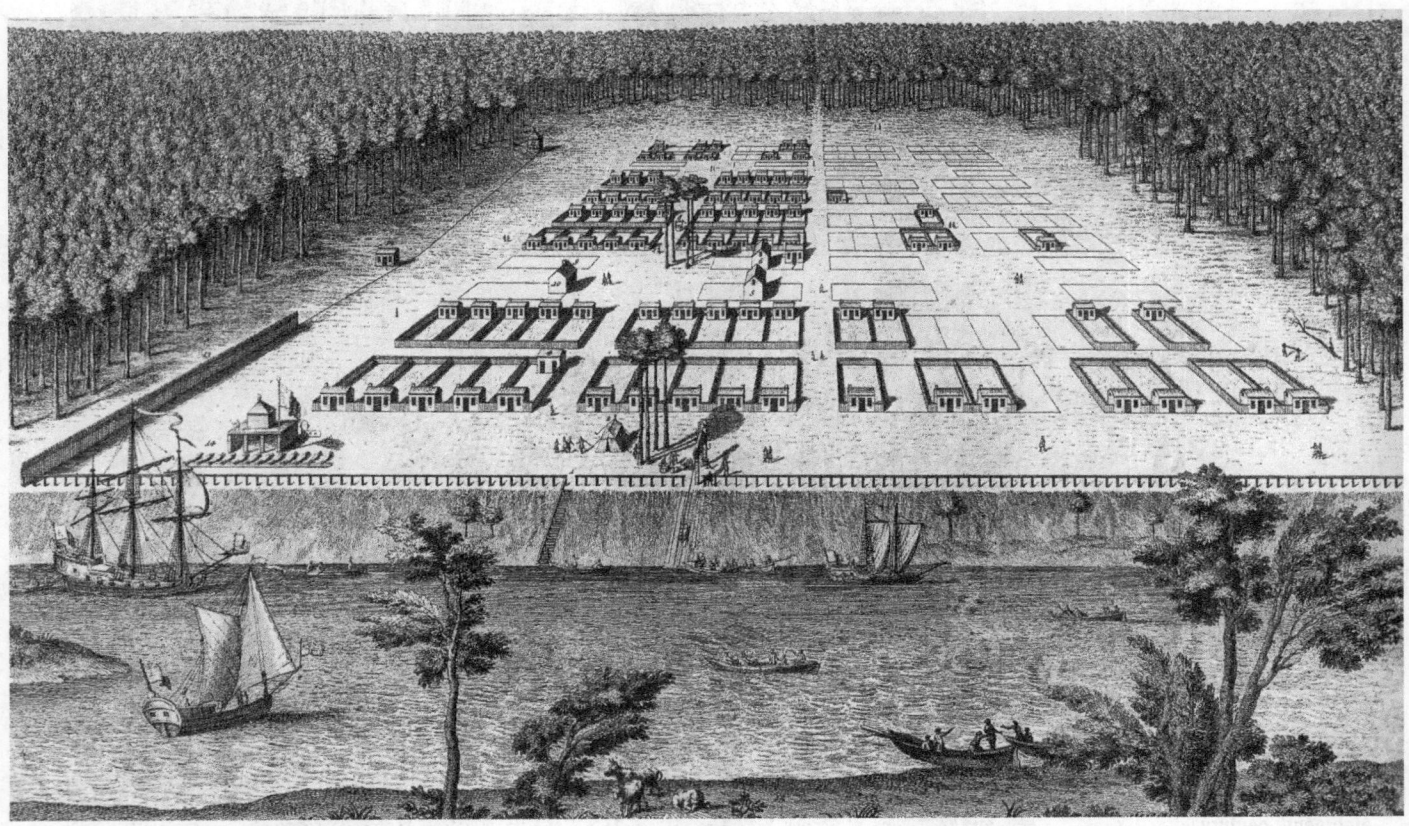

Savannah, Georgia. View of city, Peter Gordon, 1734.

In France's southern colonies the typical house, in both town and country, featured an elevated first floor and a colonnaded verandah that wrapped all the way around it to trap shade and cool breezes. Charles Dickens described the porches as "tumbledown galleries." The French plantation houses in Louisiana, such as the Parlange Plantation (Fig. 13.3-10), built in the 1750s, shared the British admiration for Palladian rigor. Regularly spaced classical columns supported the deep verandahs on two levels, offering the optimal passive ventilation for the hot, humid climate. Until the emancipation of the region's slaves in the mid-nineteenth century, the large plantations of the southern colonies supported hundreds of residents, associated craftspeople, and retainers, comprising significant economic and productive units distinct from the cities.

The Protestant Ideal in New England: A City on a Hill

The fragmented topography and colder climate of New England favored small, agriculturally oriented townships. The Puritans, religious radicals who considered the Church of England too close to Catholicism, founded the earliest towns. Even after the development of substantial ports, such as Boston and Newport, and the emergence of a merchant class, the Puritan towns continued as discrete communities. If the plantations in Virginia sprawled randomly along the waterways without need of urban centers, the New England towns sprawled in a different manner, leaving inordinately large spaces between the houses and allowing generous setbacks from the streets. Every family's house stood on its own, producing the antithesis of the dense European street.

At the heart of the Puritan migration lay a religious covenant. Governor John Winthrop in 1630 declared the wish that the region's first colony become "like a city on a hill," referring to the theological ideal of creating a parallel to Jerusalem. Each township was seen as existing under a commission from God. The righteousness of strict Puritans often led to an exclusive, quasi-theocratic atmosphere, culminating in the Salem witch trials of 1692. Their towns, founded between 1620 and 1650, remained intentionally small and self-sufficient, with each village possessing all the skills necessary to sustain a closed community. The town of Sudbury, Massachusetts, founded in 1638 by English tenant farmers, reproduced the farm life of southern England. The first

Figure 13.3-10 Louisiana. Parlange Plantation, built for French nobleman Vincent de Ternant, 1750s.

twenty-two houses followed a patchy, linear pattern on a gently undulating main street, with each house standing in the midst of a large, narrow lot. At midpoint the planners placed the Sudbury Meeting House as the political, educational, and religious focus of the town. South of the main street they marked off a **common**, a large pasture equal in size to all of the land of the houses combined. The settlers divided the lands in town and in the country according to merit, with the size of each allotment reflecting either the relative amount

each member had contributed to the initial expense of the enterprise or the extent of each member's personal property. Puritan class hierarchy also appeared in the organization of the meetinghouse, in which the most prominent people were placed closest to the pulpit.

Some of the Puritan towns, such as Cambridge, Massachusetts, founded in 1631, used a grid (Fig. 13.3-11a). The future university town's roughly drawn blocks appeared peculiarly small, averaging 30 m (96 ft) per side. By contrast,

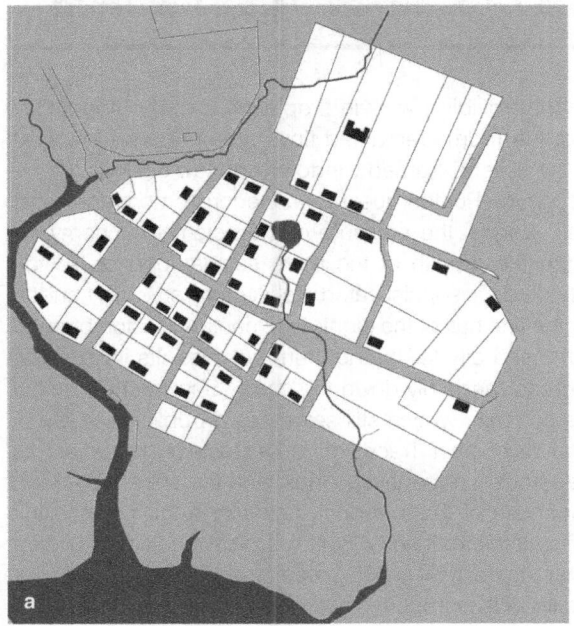

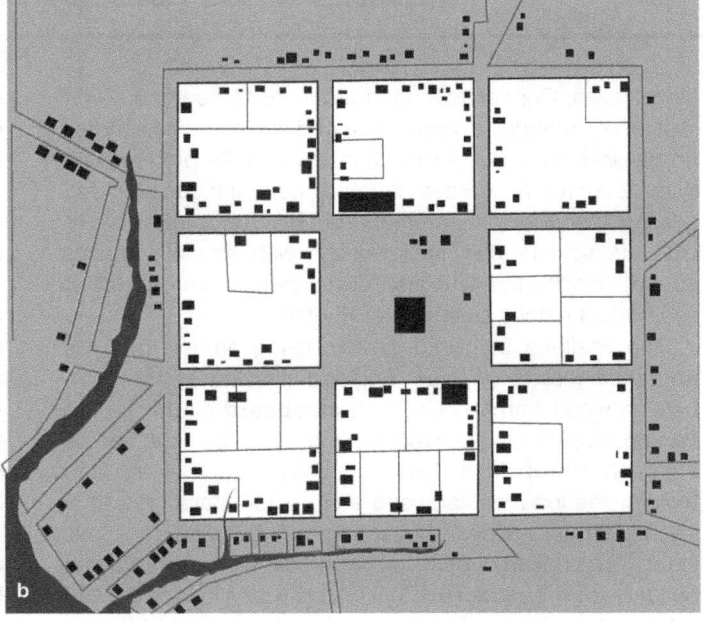

Figure 13.3-11 Colonial America. Two Puritan towns based on a grid. (a) The dense grid of Cambridge, Massachusetts, seventeenth century. (b) The diffused pattern of New Haven, Connecticut, seventeenth century.

The Puritan Meetinghouse

The Puritans called the physical symbol of their covenant a "meetinghouse" rather than a church to avoid associations with Catholics and Anglicans. The Old Ship Meetinghouse in Hingham, Massachusetts, built in 1681, corresponded to the Puritan ideal of a four-square hall with the pulpit accessible to all. The hipped roof with a central steeple raised on an open-truss structure with curved struts recalled the frame structure of a ship.

Hingham, Massachusetts. Old Ship Meetinghouse, 1681.

New Haven, Connecticut, founded in 1637, seemed a correction of Cambridge, with a pure grid of nine equal squares and blocks ten times larger than those of its predecessor (Fig. 13.3-11b). New Haven's voided central block provided a large space for the common, roughly 300 m (960 ft) per side. Its settlers built their houses with ample setbacks so that despite the precision of the grid, the urban fabric seemed as patchy as the linear Puritan towns.

The Puritans built expediently, using timber from the abundant forests. In New England this led to the "saltbox," a wood frame house with **clapboard** cladding. The Parson Capen House (1680s) (Fig. 13.3-12), set on the common of Topsfield, Massachusetts (near Salem), and built for the local pastor, used a structure similar to that of the half-timber houses of east England, but with horizontal clapboards nailed directly to the vertical studs. The Puritan builders also abandoned the thatch roof for cleaner and safer cedar shingles. The second story of the Parson Capen House cantilevered slightly over the first, while its massive brick chimney in the center gave the house its only hint of opulence, providing walk-in fireplaces on both floors. The scale of the rooms remained tiny, an impression enforced by the small, lead-framed windows and low ceilings.

Despite the Puritan quest for a theocratic commonwealth of small villages, the pressure of the colonial economy encouraged the growth of the more secular port of Boston, which hosted the sophisticated architectural styles of London. During the first half of the eighteenth century Boston became the command city for the northern colonies. Its initial urban core spread randomly down the soggy Shawmut Peninsula. A large common, which still serves as a public park, lay on the outskirts of town. Traces of Puritan taste remained at Paul Revere's house, a modest saltbox, and the sober Old South Meetinghouse of 1729, a brick box with a thick, monolithic steeple over the front entry. Boston's initial municipal building, the Town House, built in 1657, resembled medieval European town halls, with an open ground floor for public assemblies and an upper room for closed meetings and archives.

As Boston grew, it diversified. By 1700 it had a population of 15,000. Brick structures became more common, and two works in particular, Faneuil Hall and King's Chapel, exhibited the arrival of classicism. The wealthy merchant Peter Faneuil founded the building named after him in 1740 as an open market on the ground floor with an assembly room above. The English painter John Smibert (1688–1751), a resident of Newport, designed the hall as a two-story longitudinal structure, with three by nine bays. Smibert placed classical pilasters between the open arcades and the upper windows. Charles Bulfinch rebuilt and expanded Faneuil Hall after it burned down in the early nineteenth century, adding four bays and a third story (Fig. 13.3-13).

King's Chapel (Fig. 13.3-14), designed in 1749 by Peter Harrison (1716–1775) as the first non-Puritan religious structure in Boston, had a

Figure 13.3-12 Topsfield, Massachusetts. Parson Capen House, the saltbox type house, 1680s.

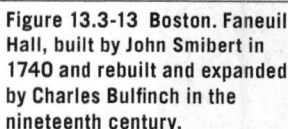

Figure 13.3-13 Boston. Faneuil Hall, built by John Smibert in 1740 and rebuilt and expanded by Charles Bulfinch in the nineteenth century.

Figure 13.3-14 Boston. King's Chapel, Peter Harrison, 1749.

Figure 13.3-15 Newport, Rhode Island. Redwood Library, Harrison, 1748–1750.

strong aesthetic impact on the city. Harrison demonstrated his professional skill through scale and materials, constructing the chapel with beautifully cut granite blocks. He derived the concept from Gibbs's St. Martin-in-the-Fields, capping the broad Ionic porch with a flat balustrade instead of a pediment. Although planned, the steeple was never built over the square tower.

Harrison, who had trained in England and possessed the largest collection of architectural books in the colonies, settled in the more tolerant colony of Rhode Island. He built his most charming works in Newport, a port city that rivaled Boston. For the Athenaeum, a learned society founded by the philosopher Bishop Berkeley during his short residence in Newport, Harrison designed the Redwood Library in 1748–1750 (Fig. 13.3-15). Sited on a hill, the four columns of its Doric temple front offered the most accurate and creative use of classical architecture yet seen in

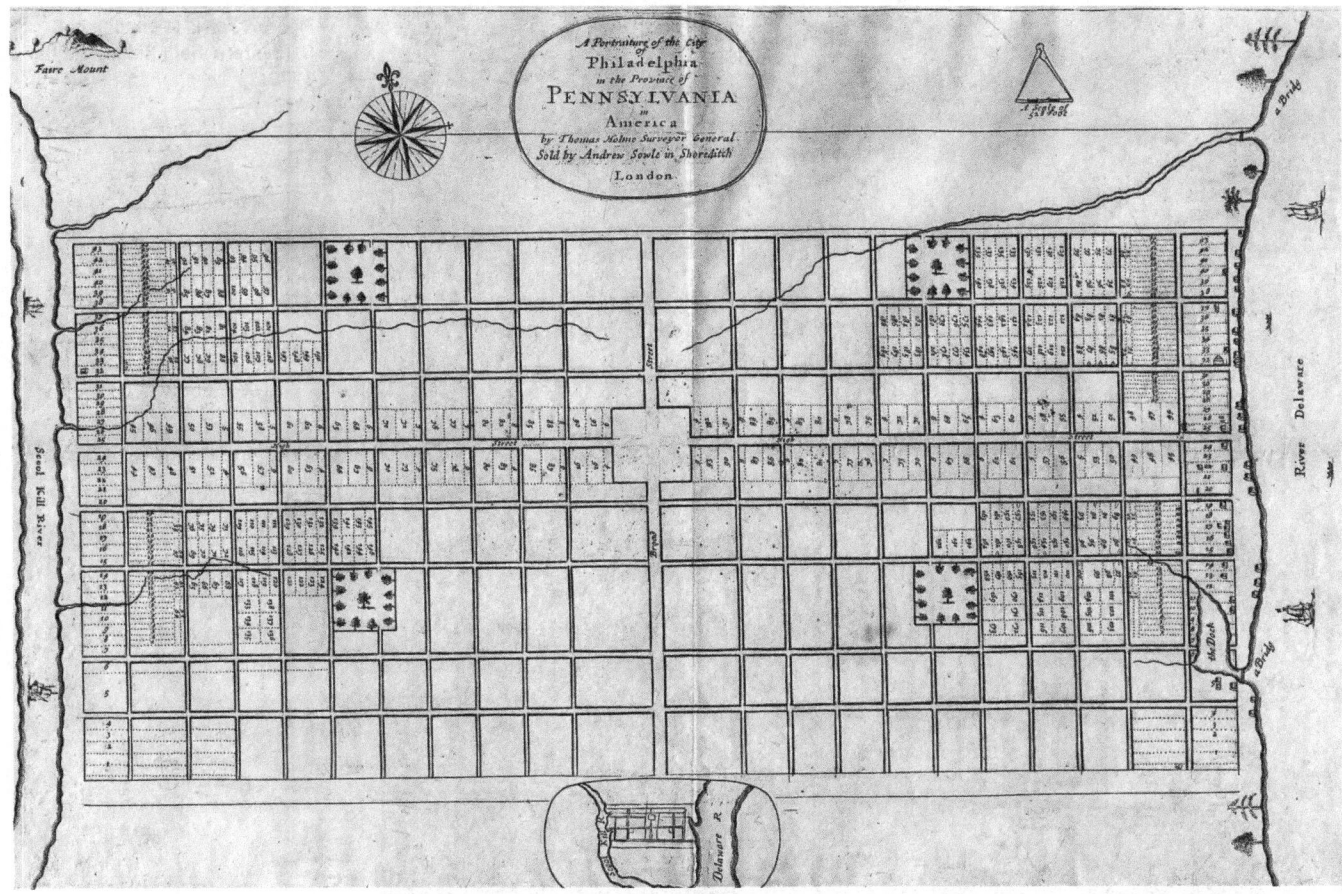

Figure 13.3-16 Philadelphia. William Penn's plan, drawn by Thomas Holme, late seventeenth century. From Lowber, Ordinances of the City of Philadelphia, 1812.

the American colonies. Nearby he designed one of the earliest Jewish synagogues in America, the Touro Synagogue of 1763. Like the Portuguese Synagogue in Amsterdam, it stood on its own, a nearly square, barrel-vaulted hall flanked by side aisles with upper galleries. The Ionic entry porch represented the only decoration of its pure volume.

After a brief effort to settle New York and Pennsylvania, the Dutch abandoned colonial North America in the 1660s, leaving the flat coastal plains of New Jersey and Pennsylvania open to British settlement. Here, the prominent Quaker statesman William Penn (1644–1718) planted his model city of Philadelphia in 1681 (Fig. 13.3-16). He worked out the plan of the grid with the surveyor Thomas Holme, clearly influenced by Richard Newcourt's plan for post–Great Fire London. Penn's plan provided extremely wide streets, 33 m (105 ft) across, and regularly placed plazas. He hoped the settlers would build manor houses on large lots and leave plenty of planted space surrounding them to produce a "green country towne." Instead of spreading on the grid between the two rivers, however, Philadelphia grew laterally along the waterfront. Speculators produced dense blocks of row houses, such as those at Elfreth's Alley, similar to the dense housing of London. Philadelphia's population by the mid-eighteenth century had risen to 25,000, making it the second-largest English-speaking city after London.

While Penn's ideal for a spacious city went unrealized, his Quaker mandate for a tolerant society endured. The Quakers made up 20% of Philadelphia's population and declared themselves strict pacifists. They were the first to condemn American slavery. Benjamin Franklin (1706–1790), an editor, scientist, and political figure, moved to Philadelphia to enjoy its liberal atmosphere. Born in Boston and apprenticed to his brother as a printer, he set up his own print shop in Philadelphia and became the leading essayist of the colonies. After the publication of "Experiments and Observations in Electricity" in 1751, he achieved European renown. His importance to architecture came indirectly, as the inventor of the iron stove, the lightning rod, and the Franklin streetlamp. He also exerted influence on patronage, as a founding member of many urban institutions, including a subscription library, a fire department, the University of Pennsylvania, the American Philosophical Society, and the Philadelphia Hospital, all of which commissioned stout brick buildings with unexceptional Georgian details.

The most important building of the city, the State House (now known as Independence Hall), site of the Liberty Bell, included one of Franklin's patented lightning rods on its belfry. Franklin hired Robert Smith (1722–1777), the first trained architect working in Philadelphia, to design his house, which was later demolished. Smith soon after proved his worth on

Figure 13.3-17 Philadelphia. Carpenters' Hall, Robert Smith, 1770s.

the design of the Carpenters' Hall (Fig. 13.3-17), a structure created for the builders' guild, and composed a trade manual for the Carpenter's company guild. He organized the hall on a Greek cross plan and finished it just in time for the first assembly of the Continental Congress of 1774, a precursor to the American Revolution that broke out in 1776. The grid of Philadelphia, even though greatly compromised in its realization, became the laboratory for American liberty, encouraging the radical solution of modern democracy as a deterrent to the oppression of patrimonial regimes.

Further Reading

Berlin, Ira. *Many Thousands Gone: The First Two Centuries of Slavery in North America*. Cambridge, MA: Belknap Press, 1998.

Gasparini, Graziano. *Formacion Urbana de Venezuela Siglo XVI*. Caracas, Venezuela: Armitano Editores, 1991.

Gelernter, Mark. *A History of American Architecture: Buildings in Their Cultural and Technological Context*. Hanover, NH: University Press of New England, 1999.

Meinig, D. W. *The Shaping of America*. Vol. 1, *Atlantic America, 1492–1800*. New Haven, CT: Yale University Press, 1986.

Reps, John. *Town Planning in Frontier America*. Columbia: University of Missouri Press, 1980.

Segal, Ronald. *The Black Diaspora: Five Centuries of the Black Experience Outside Africa*. New York: Noonday Press, 1995.

Weismann, Elizabeth Wilder. *Art and Time in Mexico: Architecture and Sculpture in Colonial Mexico*. New York: Icon Editions, 1985.

Visit the free website **www.oup.com/us/ingersoll** to view chapter outlines and study questions; Google Maps showing the location of key sites; links to UNESCO World Heritage Sites; and essays on topics that cross time and culture.

1750–1800

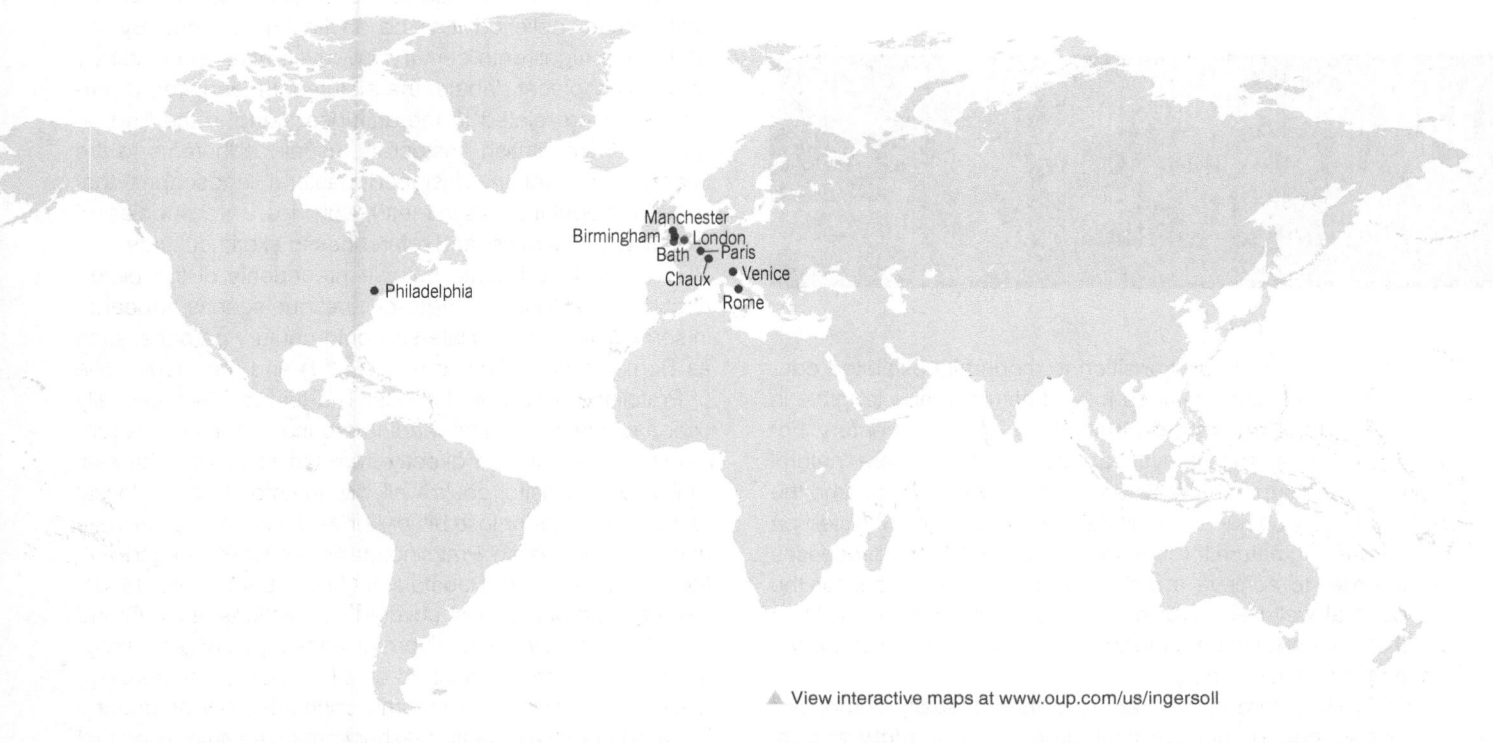

Manchester
Birmingham London
Bath Paris
Chaux Venice
Rome

Philadelphia

▲ View interactive maps at www.oup.com/us/ingersoll

14.1 THE PICTURESQUE: Landscapes of the Informal, the Exotic, and the Sublime

14.2 ENLIGHTENMENT EUROPE: Theory, Revolution, and Architecture

14.3 INDUSTRY AND PUNISHMENT: Factories and Warehouses, Prisons and Workhouses

During the latter half of the eighteenth century the primary conditions of modernity—including mobilization for political emancipation, the rapid development of technology and industry, and exponential demographic expansion of cities—appeared in parts of Europe and North America. Manchester, England, evolved from an inconsequential hamlet into the booming epicenter of technical advances and labor struggles, while Paris spawned the great political debates that eventually led to the overthrow of the *ancien régime* of absolute monarchy. The publication of Diderot and d'Alembert's *Encyclopedia*, begun in 1751, launched the quest for universal knowledge for all people as the basis of a new, ethical society. The investigations of philosophers in London, Paris, and Rome inspired many theoretical works about architecture, from the rigorist concepts of Laugier and Lodoli to the fantasies of Piranesi and Boullée. In England the rise of the liberal Whig faction accompanied the emergence of the picturesque aesthetic, which seemed to complement empirical attitudes. The casual order of the English gardens celebrated the ideal of "nature" as a transcendent value. Piranesi in Rome explored the parallel phenomenon of the sublime in his majestic re-creations of antiquity and gloomy visions of prisons. In Paris a generation of architects, inspired by the new social and political agendas of the *Encyclopedia*, created ambitious utopian projects as solutions to social problems. The new conditions of industrial society in Manchester and London, which included slum dwellings, alcoholism, and degeneracy, inspired a reform movement for prisons and workhouses that culminated with the Panopticon, a building conceived as a surveillance machine.

14.1 THE PICTURESQUE
Landscapes of the Informal, the Exotic, and the Sublime

The European transition to modernity exhibited contradictory attitudes toward nature, made tangible in the **English gardens** of the eighteenth century. For some, the return to a mythical state of nature, where "natural man" had supposedly lived in relative equality, became the key to new social and political attitudes. Others insisted on surpassing nature through the use of mechanical processes in order to achieve a higher level of development for the general well-being. As a technically sophisticated artifact that appeared to be a product of nature, the English garden embodied this contrast.

English gardeners referred to their casually composed landscapes of nonclassical order as the **picturesque**. Rejecting the symmetry of classicism, they organized their gardens piece by piece, setting up separate components to be discovered and never allowing a vision of the whole. The practitioners of the picturesque preferred shaping the land in sinuous, organic patterns. In this scheme buildings no longer dominated the scene but deferred to it as passive elements. In the sequence of non-axial English gardens one came across exotic fragments, such as fake classical ruins, Gothic towers, and Chinese pagodas, placed like quotations from other times and distant cultures. This naturalized landscape echoed the quest for a society based on a broader knowledge, if not control, of other peoples. It also could reflect, however, the ideal of natural law as the source of human liberty.

The English Garden and Empirical Thinking

During the seventeenth and eighteenth centuries the term "picturesque" signified a variety of things. It could refer to a landscape that looked like a painting of nature or to a space designed like a setting for a narrative action. The French attributed the idea to the English and vice versa, while others believed it to be an Italian concept. By the end of the eighteenth century, however, after much literary and philosophical debate, the picturesque acquired a precise meaning related to the attitudes found in the English garden. Here, British aristocrats, usually adherents to the liberal Whig faction, designed pastoral landscapes that exalted irregularity, asymmetry, surprise, rare species of plants, artificial ruins, and references to exotic cultures.

Italy produced some notable precedents of the picturesque English garden. Proto-picturesque scenes appeared in some of the region's late-sixteenth-century gardens, such as Bomarzo near Orvieto (Fig. 14.1-1) and the Medici villa of Pratolino outside of Florence. The first rambled casually over a ravine, with paths winding around dozens of allegorical sculptures carved directly from the stones on the site. At Bomarzo a visitor could walk into the mouth of a colossal rock-cut monster or lose his or her sense of orientation in an uncanny tilted house. Pratolino, designed for Francesco I de' Medici by Bernardo Buontalenti (1531–1608) in the 1570s, became one of the most coveted destinations of the Grand Tour through Italy. There, informal landscapes of great irregularity and surprise branched off either side of the garden's grand axis. A series of randomly connected basins drained into a pond with a gigantic washerwoman, an automaton that whipped up froth in the water. Both Bomarzo and Pratolino anticipated the themes of informality, otherness, and terror explored in the eighteenth-century English garden.

English theorists of the picturesque looked to the paintings of Claude Lorrain (1600–1682), a French artist who lived most of his life in Rome. He depicted dramatic landscapes with stark contrasts, composed on sinuous lines, using evocative ruins as points of interest. Lorrain's paintings became so popular with British aristocrats that when they traveled to Italy on the Grand Tour they brought with them a small, tinted convex mirror, the so-called Claude glass, to look at the landscapes with the same perspective taken in his paintings.

Picturesque taste delighted in exotic cultures, distant in either time or space. Landscape designers inserted pavilions

1740
John Wood and son begin Bath Circus, England

Stowe Gardens created in Buckingham, England, as the laboratory of the picturesque

▲ **1740**

1749
Strawberry Hill begun near London

RELIGION, PHILOSOPHY, FOLKLORE

The Picturesque and Natural Law

The development of the picturesque accompanied the rise of empiricism in philosophy. English scientists during the seventeenth century, such as Francis Bacon, Isaac Newton, and Robert Boyle, shifted their method from relying on a priori knowledge to assessing evidence that could be observed and tested by the senses. Newton's close friend and fellow scientist John Locke (1632–1704) wrote the definitive philosophical discussion of empiricism in his *Essay Concerning Human Understanding* (1689). Here, he demonstrated the value of inductive reasoning and logic based on the observation of nature. Locke worked for the first Earl of Shaftesbury, founder of the Whig Party, and tutored his son, the third Earl of Shaftesbury, who in turn provided the theoretical voice of the Palladians. The English garden that took shape next to Palladian mansions corresponded to Locke's investigation into the logic of nature, natural rights, and natural man. The philosopher's injunction that every sensible man should cultivate his own garden served at once as a metaphor for being true to one's sensory experiences and as a mandate for the picturesque landscapes being built by his Whig contemporaries.

Wiltshire, England. Stourhead gardens, bridge, and Pantheon, Henry Flitcroft, 1741–1772.

Edmund Burke publishes *A Philosophical Enquiry into the Origins of Our Ideas of the Sublime and the Beautiful*

▲ 1756

▼ **1764**

William Chambers's Kew Gardens Pagoda built in London

John Wood the Younger begins the Royal Crescent at Bath, England

▲ 1767

▼ **1811**

John Nash's Regent Street provides picturesque cross-axis in London

Figure 14.1-1 Orvieto, Italy. Bomarzo, garden of the monsters, 1560s.

into their gardens as Greek, Roman, Gothic, and Persian **follies**. The knowledge of other cultures filtered slowly into European culture as a consequence of mercantile and colonial exploits. As a result of the maritime success of the East India Companies of the Dutch, English, and Danish, the European elite acquired masses of Chinese porcelain, wallpaper, and lacquered furniture. In 1685 William Temple (1628–1699) coined the term **"sharawaggi"** to indicate his understanding of the Chinese alternative to the Western notion of beauty. He described Chinese aesthetics as a "beauty that shall be great and strike the Eye, but without any order or disposition of parts" after reading descriptions of China by the sixteenth-century Jesuit missionary Matteo Ricci and observing Chinese scroll paintings. Chinese follies began to appear in English gardens during the mid-eighteenth century. William Chambers (1723–1796), the only European architect to have traveled to China during this period, built the most ambitious one, the Pagoda of Kew Gardens, in 1762 (Fig. 14.1-2). The octagonal structure rises 50 m (164 ft) on ten levels and still elicits a shock of incongruity.

Not long after Chambers built his pagoda in London, the Qing emperor Qianlong (r. 1735–1796) made additions to the Summer Palace gardens in Beijing (Fig. 14.1-3) using European motifs as exotic curiosities. He commissioned Jesuit missionaries to create a European-style maze and six Baroque pavilions with curving stone eaves. These European follies, destroyed in the mid-nineteenth century during the Boxer Rebellion, stood in the midst of the kind of Chinese garden that had inspired the concept of sharawaggi.

A third characteristic of the picturesque was its aspiration to the sublime, a concept that philosopher

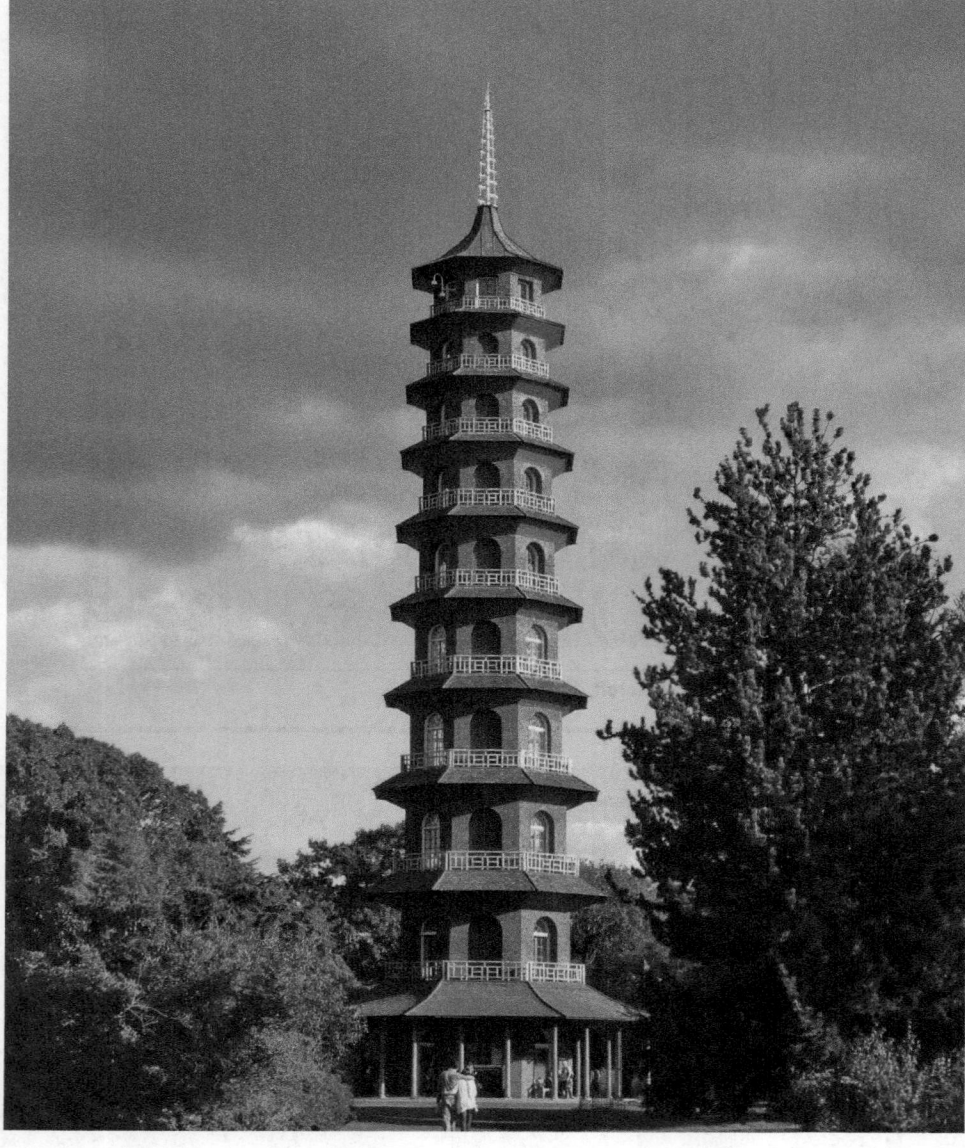

Figure 14.1-2 London. Kew Gardens, the Pagoda, William Chambers, 1764.

Architectural Orientalism

The literary critic Edward Said defined "Orientalism" in 1978 as the Western tendency to treat non-Western cultures as exotic and subordinate. Garden follies, such as the pagoda at Kew Gardens, were among its first expressions. The villa of Sezincote, which was renovated in 1803 in a pseudo-Mughal style for a retired functionary of the East India Company, appeared like a souvenir brought back from a strange land. The scalloped arches superficially resembled those of the pavilions of the Red Fort in Agra, while the central cupola imitated the shape of Mughal domes but was built of wood covered with copper.

Following the example of Sezincote, the Prince of Wales decided in 1815 to orientalize the Royal Pavilion in Brighton. John Nash added to the existing structure a riotous collection of domes, cones, and mock minarets. To support the billowing forms, which were pure set design, Nash used innovative cast-iron frames. The cast-iron columns in the pavilion's kitchen imitated slender palm trees. The heterogeneous blend of styles from India and China appeared as capricious as carnival decorations, representing the Western fantasy of Asian cultures. The Royal Pavilion's construction coincided with the East India Company's conquest of Bengal and the advent of England's imperial dominance of India.

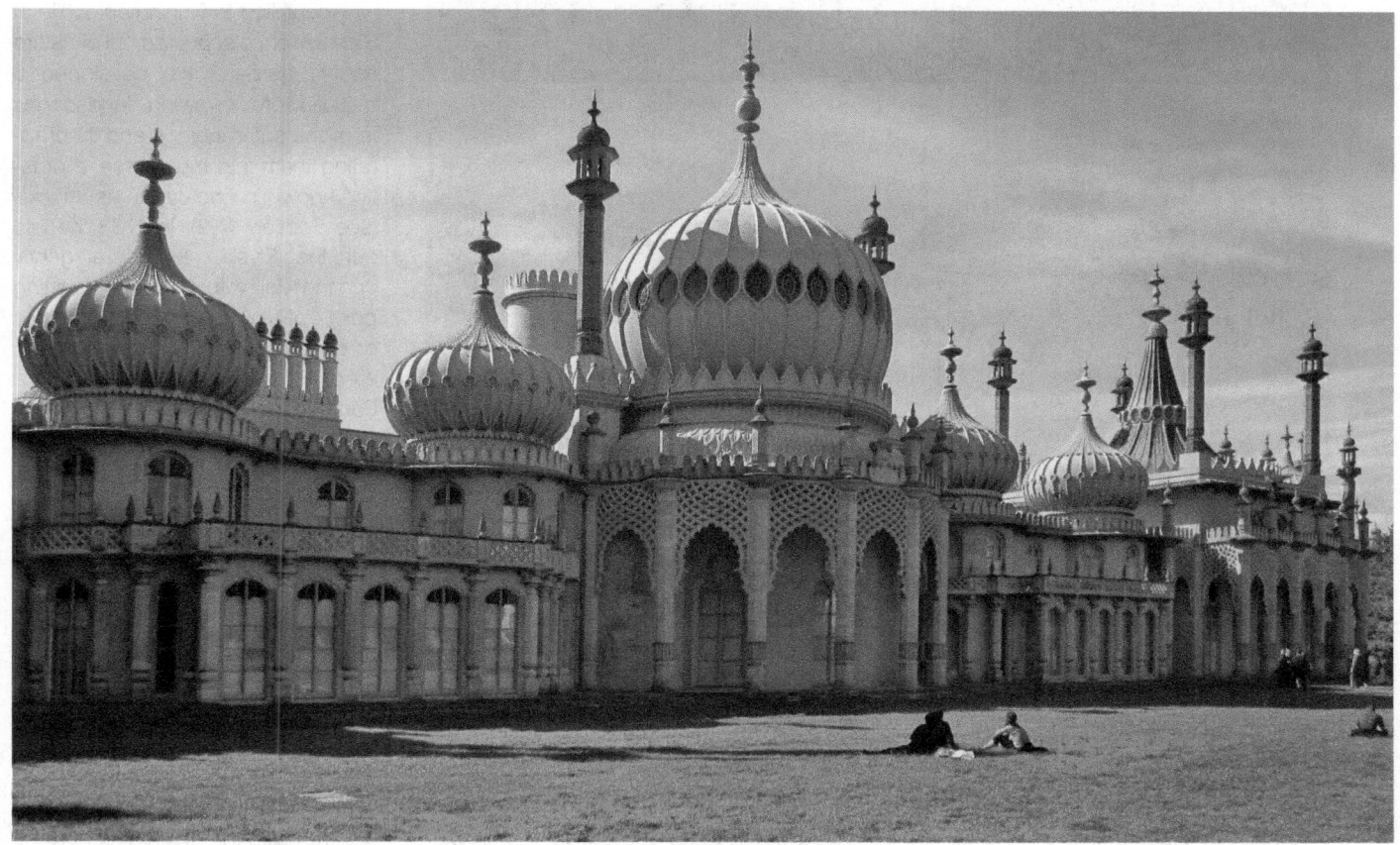

Brighton, England. Royal Pavilion, John Nash, 1815.

George "Bishop" Berkeley (1685–1753) called "an agreeable kind of Horror." The pleasant shock of encountering a rushing waterfall or a steep mountain gorge moved Edmund Burke, in his *Philosophical Enquiry into the Origins of Our Ideas of the Sublime and the Beautiful* (1756), to theorize an alternative aesthetic to harmonious beauty. At its core he placed "terror, the common origin of all that is sublime." The gardens at Stourhead, designed between 1741 and 1772 by the patron Henry Hoare the Younger and his architect

Henry Flitcroft (1697–1769), evoked the sublime through daunting passages into deep grottoes, surprise encounters with classical tempiettos hidden in the woods, and oblique vistas across the lake.

The contrived informality of the English garden accompanied the ideological turn to the basic formality of Palladian architecture, hatched in the same political milieu of Whig virtuosity. Lord Burlington in the gardens of Chiswick attempted to shed the strict geometry of French-inspired models. The

Figure 14.1-3 Beijing. View of Summer Palace maze with European follies built for Emperor Qianlong, 1780s.

and the patron's taste, however, Bridgeman dabbled in asymmetrical compositions that responded to the irregular lay of the land. In the interests of including the distant surroundings into the views from his gardens, he introduced the *ha-ha*, a moat-like depression that concealed a fence for keeping grazing animals from entering the garden. Although first used in France, the *ha-ha* became a standard feature of the English garden.

According to Burlington, while at Stowe, Kent discovered "all of nature as his garden." He developed a method of borrowing landscapes from the surroundings and incorporating them into the views—a practice known in Edo Japan as *shakkei* (see Section 12.3). In 1733, he laid out the Elysian Fields, a gently curving dell with constantly shifting points of view and no straight lines or geometric paths. At the base he erected a rusticated **crescent** as a Pantheon, with niches for statues of British worthies. Not far from here, Gibbs inserted his Palladian Bridge, a miniature version of Palladio's unrealized Rialto project. He also created an enigmatic triangular pavilion rendered in Gothic details, known as the Temple of Liberty (1741–1747), drawing from the symbols and secret rituals of the Freemasons.

The final gardener at Stowe, Lancelot "Capability" Brown (1716–1783), arrived in 1741. Combining a strong technical background in horticulture with the aesthetics of Kent, he perfected the conceit of making nature look more natural. Brown

Figure 14.1-4 Buckingham, England. Stowe Garden, the Palladian bridge, James Gibbs et al., 1740s.

gardens at Stowe House in Buckingham (Fig. 14.1-4), designed for the prominent Whig politician Richard Temple, Earl of Cobham, became a laboratory for picturesque experimentation. Begun in 1718 under John Vanbrugh, the gardens received additions from many famous architects, including William Kent and James Gibbs. During the next three decades, various architects installed dozens of garden follies, placed randomly in pastoral settings. Vanbrugh brought with him the gardener of Blenheim, Charles Bridgeman (1690–1738), who initially treated Stowe as a formal, geometric garden. As he became acquainted with the site

went on to design more than 200 English gardens, including the revision of the grounds of Blenheim. Through his widespread practice he contributed as much as literary critics to the diffusion of picturesque taste. Brown's nickname referred to his talent for enhancing the capabilities already present in a natural setting. He specialized in turning streams into lakes with sinuous shores and encircling his gardens with winding paths, along which one found oblique vistas from one destination to the next.

Stowe's mixture of naturalism and exotic follies from other times appealed to exponents of the French Enlightenment.

The philosopher Jean-Jacques Rousseau (1712–1778) visited the site during his exile in 1766 and enshrined the English garden in his theory of the liberty of natural man. In one of his novels, *Julie, ou la nouvelle Héloise*, he described a fictional English garden that one of his admirers, Louis-René Girardin, attempted to reproduce at Erménonville between 1766 and 1776. It included a temple to philosophy that imitated the round Temple of Sibyl at Tivoli, purposely designed in a state of decomposition as a mock ruin, and a Gothic tower dedicated to Henri IV's mistress, Gabrielle. Girardin prepared a rustic hermit's cottage by the lake as a residence for Rousseau, who moved there in 1778. The philosopher died in this setting during the same year, prompting the patron to place a sarcophagus for Rousseau in a ring of poplar trees on an island in the lake—a romantic isle of the dead.

Figure 14.1-5 Versailles, France. Palace of Versailles, *hameau* of Marie-Antoinette, Richard Mique, 1778–1785.

The German prince Leopold III Friedrich Franz of Anhalt-Dessau (1740–1817) dutifully copied Rousseau's funeral island at Wörlitz Gardens near Dessau. His enthusiasm for Rousseau and the English garden inspired him to quote from other gardens as if they were literary texts. He traveled with his architect, Friedrich Wilhelm von Erdmannsdorff (1736–1800), to Stowe and then to Italy for the Grand Tour. After their return they stocked Wörlitz with such conventional follies as tempiettos, a Chinese garden, and a Gothic house but in the 1790s introduced truly novel features: a miniature Mount Vesuvius with a replica of the villa of volcanologist William Hamilton and a small-scale version of the first cast-iron bridge at Coalbrookdale. Aside from pursuing literary interests, Prince Leopold promoted his estate as a laboratory for progressive agricultural techniques, encouraging the general public to visit it as a public park.

Rousseau's polemical texts, which celebrated the superior freedom of the noble savage and natural man, reached the highest levels of French society. His theories inspired Queen Marie-Antoinette to transform a remote corner of the park of Versailles into a peasant village, or *hameau* (Fig. 14.1-5). Between 1778 and 1785 she directed the court architect Richard Mique to build twelve peasant houses, informally grouped around a curving pond. The structures, dressed in modest half-timber and roofed with tiles or thatch, served as working parts of a farm, which included a mill with a waterwheel, a dovecote, and barns for milking cows. Some of the rustic facades, however, concealed the aristocratic comforts of a boudoir, a billiard room, and a ballroom. Within this contrived version of the return to nature lurked the seeds of the French Revolution. Set against the classicism of Versailles, Marie-Antoinette's dabbling in the picturesque raised the question of equal rights as a key aspect of the state of nature, a concept that eventually toppled the *ancien régime* and cost the queen her head.

The Picturesque in Architecture and Urbanism

The theory of the picturesque pertained initially to landscape design, but by the mid-eighteenth century it had infiltrated the practice of architecture and urbanism. In its broadest sense picturesque design integrated buildings with a natural setting as elements of the landscape. In 1794 Sir Uvedale Price published his *Essay on the Picturesque*, explaining the principles of roughness, variety, and irregularity. He cited the roofscape at Blenheim (see Section 13.1) as an example of the style in architecture. Gothic architecture, which only a few generations earlier had offended good taste, acquired new prominence because of its irregular massing and eccentric details.

Horace Walpole (1717–1797), the bachelor son of an important Whig prime minister, used thoroughly picturesque criteria to create Strawberry Hill (Fig. 14.1-6a,b). This "little Gothick castle" appeared like an overgrown folly, with towers, crenellations, lancet windows, and spires. Begun in 1749, the construction of Strawberry Hill continued over the course of three decades, with the advice of several architects, including the classicist Robert Adam (1728–1792). Walpole kept the plan purposely irregular, an elongated *L* shape with numerous projecting bays, and coined the term "serendipity" to indicate the chance combination of disparate things. No two rooms repeated the same shape. The ceiling of the long gallery, designed for his collection of paintings and busts, imitated the fan-vault ceilings of

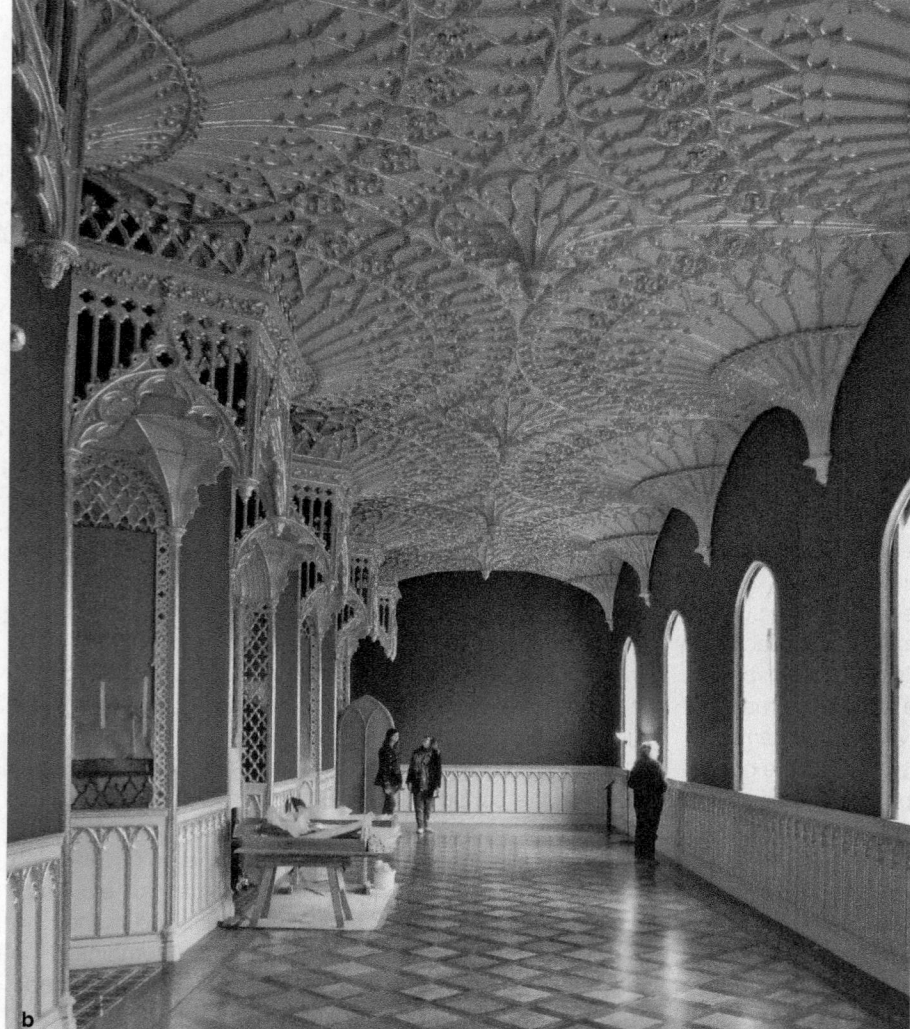

Figure 14.1-6 Twickenham, England.
(a) Strawberry Hill, Horace Walpole
with Robert Adam, 1749–1780.
(b) Interior.

Westminster Abbey. Other details came from Ely Cathedral. In 1767 Walpole published a Gothic novel, *The Castle of Otranto*, a literary parallel to his architectural enterprise. The bizarre combinations of Strawberry Hill and its superb collection of artworks eventually became such a tourist attraction that toward the end of his life the patron felt obliged to move to a nearby cottage and charge entry fees to visitors of his castle.

Walpole's exploit inspired an even grander Gothic fantasy, William Beckford's (1760–1844) Fonthill Abbey (Fig. 14.1-7), designed in 1795 by James Wyatt (1746–1813). Like Walpole, Beckford was an eccentric bachelor. He studied architecture with one of England's leading classicists, William Chambers. He too wrote a Gothic novel, *Vathek*, in French and proved to be an even more ambitious collector than his predecessor. Twenty of his paintings, by such artists as Raphael, Titian, and Bellini, became the pride of London's National Gallery. Beckford began building Fonthill Abbey as an addition to a garden folly on his father's estate next to a conventional Palladian villa. His folly soon burgeoned into the size of a cathedral, overshadowing his father's mansion. He borrowed details from disparate sources, including lacy window motifs from the late Gothic convent of Batalha in Portugal. The two long side wings served as picture galleries. At the crossing of the cruciform plan an octagonal belfry rose 84 m (275 ft), taller than most of the Gothic cathedrals. Attached volumes sprouted irregularly off the four wings. The tower collapsed twice during construction, and the third version also fell in 1826, a few years after Beckford sold the estate. His project exhausted the family fortune, which came from the slave trade and sugar plantations in Jamaica. The ruin of the mock abbey seemed a fitting conclusion to a picturesque extravaganza.

Richard Payne Knight (1750–1824) and Uvedale Price, the two most influential theorists of picturesque design during the late eighteenth century, also built Gothic-inspired residences. Payne Knight's Downton Castle near Ludlow in 1774 appeared like a Gothic castle with crenellated towers. His mentor, Price, pursued the theory of the picturesque in his own gardens and, in 1795, commissioned John Nash (1752–1835) to design Castle House at Aberystwyth, Cardiganshire. A year later Nash formed a partnership with Humphrey Repton (1752–1818), who succeeded Capability Brown as the most prestigious landscape designer in

Figure 14.1-7 Wiltshire, England. Fonthill Abbey, built for William Beckford by James Wyatt, 1790s; the tower collapsed in 1836.

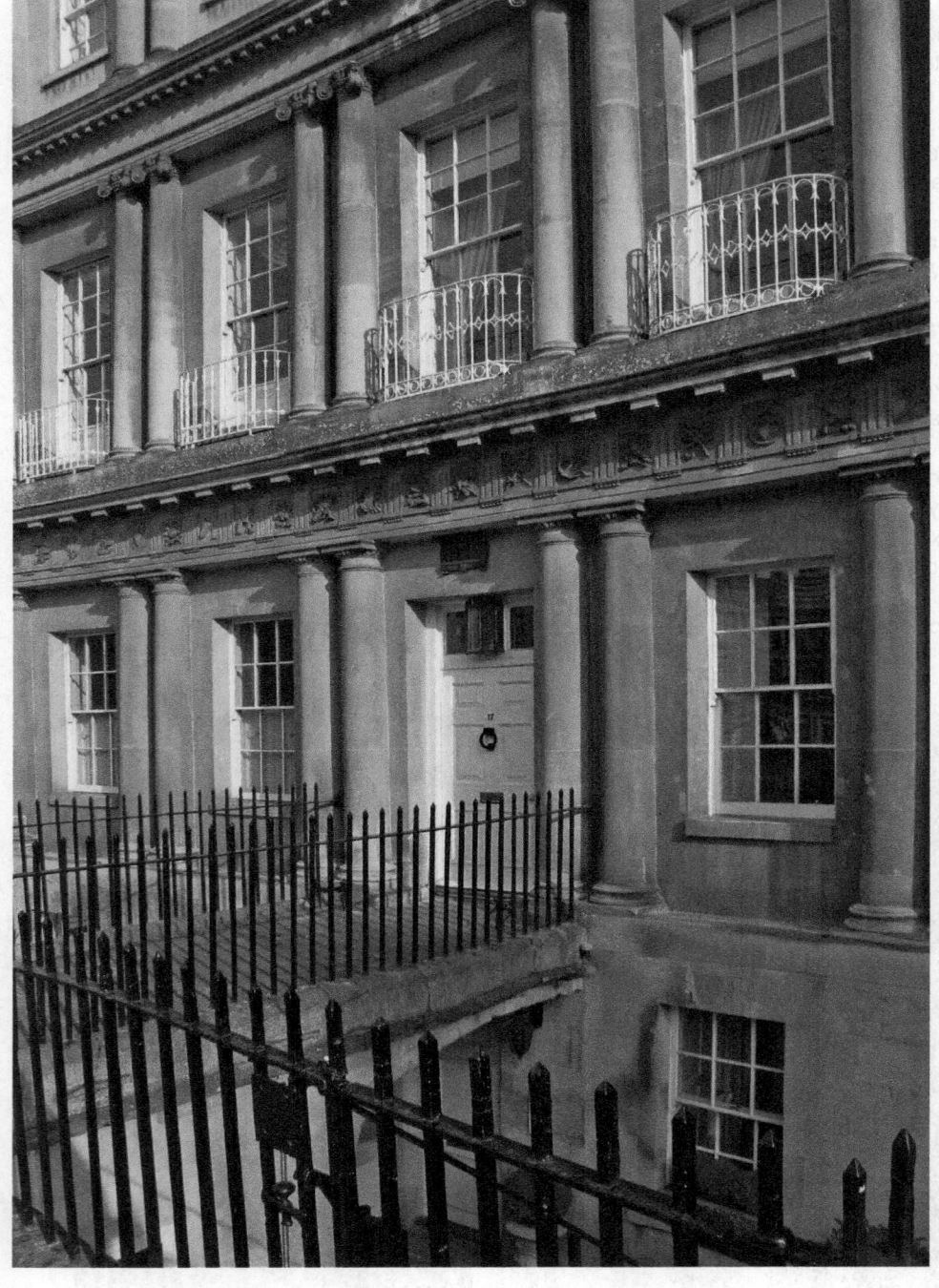

Figure 14.1-8 Bath, England. Circus, John Wood the Elder, 1740s.

astonished critics by their diversity of styles, as varied as a collection of follies in an English garden.

The picturesque design method influenced architecture by blending buildings into the landscape as subordinate parts of a greater whole. At the resort town of Bath this concept began to influence urbanism. The initial expansion plan for this small spa town in the west of England followed a grand classical vision. At Queen's Square the planner John Wood the Elder (1704–1754) imitated the Palladian urban squares of London, with each side comprising a series of row houses behind a single palace-like facade with a temple front in the center. As the city expanded, however, he increasingly exposed the urban fabric to natural features. In his final project, Bath **Circus** (Fig. 14.1-8), he arranged thirty-three row houses around a planted circular plaza. Like a Roman arena turned inside out, the three stories of its colonnaded facades looked onto a broad public garden.

Bath's turn to the picturesque matured with Wood's son, John Wood the Younger (1728–1782), who attached the Royal Crescent to one of the three radiating streets of the Circus (Fig. 14.1-9a,b). Like an ancient arena cut in half, the thirty row houses of the crescent formed a semi-ellipse open to a grassy landscape that swept down to the Avon River. This unique combination of urban density and rural openness aspired to the relationship of the great **manor** houses to their parks. John Palmer (1738–1817) added the last significant section of Bath, Lansdown Crescent, in 1789. These undulating terraces, set high above the Royal Crescent, alternated concave and convex contours, following the lay of the land. William Beckford moved to these residences after selling Fonthill Abbey. He later moved farther up the hill and in his garden built yet another tower, this time with classical columns. The late-eighteenth-century projects at Bath, in their effort to connect to the natural landscapes that surrounded them, offered novel urban solutions that

the picturesque mode. Together they designed Luscombe Castle, Devon, for the banker Charles Hoare in 1800 as an integrated vision of buildings and landscapes. Nash placed the rambling volumes in sympathy with the curving hollow of a glen and enlivened the exterior with mock Tudor windows and decorative crenellations. At Cronkhill, Shropshire (1802), Nash and Repton created an asymmetrical Italian farmhouse, inspired by a painting of the Roman countryside by Claude Lorrain. Like the porches of *shoin* palaces in Japan, the *L*-shaped verandah wrapped around the south side, opening the house to vistas. Nash and Repton

Figure 14.1-9 Bath, England. (a) Royal Crescent, John Wood the Younger, 1770. (b) Aerial view of Bath Circus and Crescent.

had many analogies to the housing blocks of the nineteenth and twentieth centuries.

The picturesque planning in Bath influenced the greatest urban project of early-nineteenth-century London: Regent Street (Fig. 14.1-10a,b). Intended as an answer to Napoléon's Paris, John Nash conceived this street in the early 1800s as a glamorous spine, or royal mile, for the prince regent, the future George IV (r. 1820–1830). The project took twenty years to complete and involved hundreds of buildings for commerce, culture, and residence,

financed by a multitude of speculative developers, including the architect himself. Regent Street connected the royal enclave at St. James Park to the newly acquired Regent's Park, intended as the site of a royal summer residence. Starting at the steps of Carlton House Terrace, the new street pushed axially to Piccadilly Circus. Here, it followed the curving "quadrants," colonnades that Nash designed and financed. The next stretch directed its axial focus toward Nash's All Souls Church, with its round tempietto porch and obelisk spire.

Figure 14.1-10 London. (a) Regent Street, the Quadrant, John Nash, 1820. Engraving by T. Shepherd, 1828. (b) See facing page.

While the subtle bends in Regent Street kept the new thoroughfare from disturbing the fancy squares of the West End, its shifting viewpoints were similar to those experienced in the sinuous paths of a picturesque garden. At the end of the sequence the curving facades of Park Crescent funneled out to the park. Here, Nash placed grand row houses with sham classical facades—thirty-unit palaces similar in scale to those at Bath Crescent, and overlooking the informal landscape of Regent's Park. On the upper edges of the park he built two proto-suburbs, Park Village East and Park Village West (Fig. 14.1-11), with planted lanes for dozens of single-family "villas." Each house had an open verandah and a dovecote tower, articulated in slightly different styles, anticipating the layout and house types of Anglo-American suburbs. Nash transposed picturesque ideas from the remote estates of the gentry to the heart of the metropolis, establishing a vibrant alternative to the rigid classical approach to urban space on the continent.

Further Reading

Cunliffe, Barry. *The City of Bath.* New Haven, CT: Yale University Press, 1987.

Mansbridge, Michael. *John Nash: A Complete Catalogue.* New York: Rizzoli, 1991.

Olsen, Donald J. *Town Planning in London: The Eighteenth and Nineteenth Centuries.* New Haven, CT: Yale University Press, 1982.

Figure 14.1-11 London. Regent's Park East, villas of Park Village West, Nash, 1820s.

Figure 14.1-10b London. Plan of Regent Street, Nash, 1820.

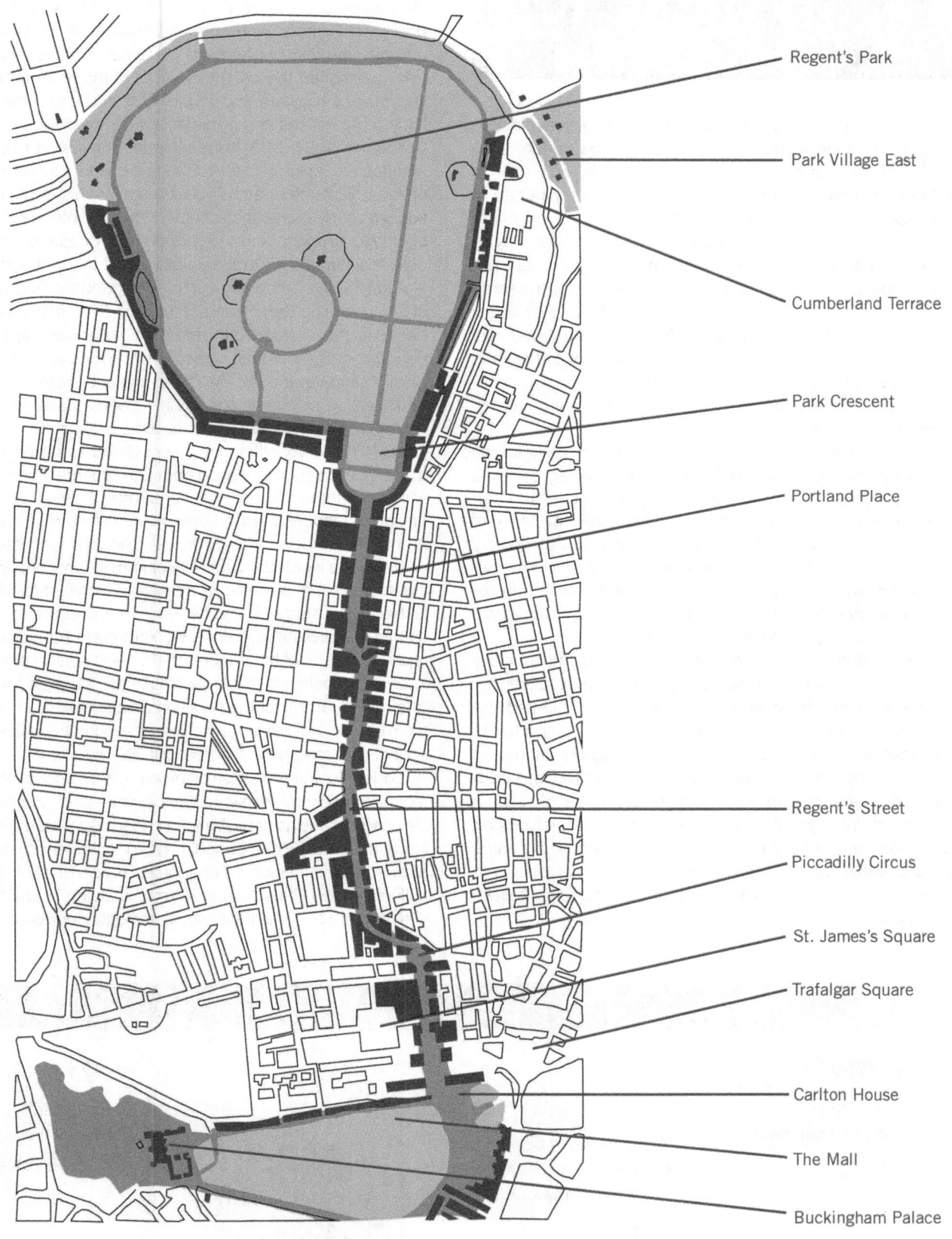

Regent's Park

Park Village East

Cumberland Terrace

Park Crescent

Portland Place

Regent's Street

Piccadilly Circus

St. James's Square

Trafalgar Square

Carlton House

The Mall

Buckingham Palace

14.2 ENLIGHTENMENT EUROPE
Theory, Revolution, and Architecture

While designers often have difficulty explaining their work, buildings cannot be made without a theory of order, assembly, and use. In mid-eighteenth-century Europe, however, theory began to diverge from practice. Intellectuals with little or no experience as builders now expounded on the correct way to make architecture. The philosophers of the European Enlightenment, in their pursuit of epistemology and search for ultimate causes, kindled new theoretical debates about architecture. The major dispute arose between those who favored a Greek origin of architectural knowledge and those who supported an Etruscan–Roman line. Archaeology became an essential ally in the debate among French, English, and Italian scholar-architects.

With the publication in Paris of Diderot and d'Alembert's *Encyclopedia* from 1751 to 1765, the bitter disagreements among architects over questions of style shifted to wider theories about the social role of architecture. The utility of buildings as instruments in the transformation of society led to a new interest in programs for theaters, schools, hospitals, factories, and prisons. Throughout the cities of pre-revolutionary Europe the practical ideas of the *Encyclopedia* stimulated proposals for social reform.

The enduring burden of unfair taxes and the arbitrary application of justice under absolutist regimes ultimately outweighed efforts at reform and eventually sparked the French Revolution of 1789. The architectural response to the Revolution was initially ephemeral. Designers attempted to create scenes that could represent the power of popular sovereignty over the antiquated structures of religion and the divine right of kings. Revolution had been assisted by theory, and theory from this time on became a central pursuit within culture. Instead of leading to a revolution in architectural form, however, it led back to yet another revival of classicism.

Meta-architecture: Theory before Practice

During the mid-eighteenth century a debate emerged in the field of European architecture in reaction to the flamboyant curves and loaded decoration of Baroque and rococo design, with those who opposed such style focusing on a return to the first principles of classical architecture. Theorists questioned the ornamental use of the orders, the spirited play of pilasters and applied columns, and the errant folding of cornices and pediments. For Abbé Jean-Louis de Cordemoy (1631–1713), a French priest interested in religious architecture, columns served the first builders as working elements of structure and should return to this original function. His early eighteenth-century inquiries into the sincerity of Gothic structure and the proportional beauty of classical columns inspired a fundamentalist strain in European architectural theory. Cordemoy and others found the Roman style of Gian Lorenzo Bernini and Francesco Borromini untenable because they treated the orders as nonstructural, applied decoration. These critics recommended returning to the clear, columnar architecture of the ancient Greeks.

Those who championed the Greeks became known as "rigorists." The most extreme among them, Carlo Lodoli (1690–1761), a Venetian monk, considered architecture to be a science. His stance derived from Enlightenment philosophy, which sought to interpret the world through reason and empirical evidence. Although Lodoli never published the treatise he had prepared in the 1750s, his followers synthesized its contents. He insisted on the duty of form to function, applying the same sort of scientific principles to architecture used by Galileo in his study of physics. Lodoli proposed that nothing should be visible that is not a working part of a building. As reported by one of his students, he argued against aesthetics in favor of function and representation. By the latter he meant "the individual and total expression which results from the way the material is disposed according to geometric–arithmetic–optical rules to achieve the purpose intended."

Lodoli pioneered the use of the adjective "organic" in architecture to describe the sympathy between form and function. He used the design of the Venetian gondola to make his point. Naval architecture had periodically led to the improvement of architectural technology, a phenomenon seen in such diverse cultures as the Phoenicians, Normans, Dutch, and Chinese. With Lodoli it became the specific analogue for the economic

TIME LINE

ca. 1750

Beginning of the European Enlightenment

Ange-Jacques Gabriel wins competition for Place Louis XV (Place de la Concorde) in Paris

▲ **1750**

1751

Denis Diderot publishes first volumes of the *Encyclopedia*

fit of form to function. Many later theorists (including the nineteenth-century American Henry Greenough, Le Corbusier, and Renzo Piano) have used a similar maritime conceit. One rare example of the application of Lodoli's proto-functionalist theory can be found in the windowsills of the Venetian convent of San Francesco in Vigna (Fig. 14.2-1), which droop in the center, like a stress diagram of the compressive strength needed for a span. Despite Lodoli's proto-functionalist position, he accepted the use of classical orders, preferring the Doric and Tuscan, the more elementary columns used for working structures.

Yet another cleric, Abbé Marc-Antoine Laugier (1713–1769), espoused a fundamentalist line in his *Essay on Architecture* (1753) with the slogan "Never lose sight of the primitive hut." Laugier saw the origins of architecture as rooted in nature, combining the tradition of Vitruvius's primitive hut with Rousseau's "natural man." The single illustration in his treatise showed a structure improvised over four tree-trunk columns that supported pitched branches in the form of a gable with a pediment (Fig. 14.2-2). Laugier advocated the use of Greek, columnar architecture, which he never knew firsthand, insisting that "the less the wall appears the more beautiful the work will be, and when it does not appear at all the work will be perfect." He insisted that construction and decoration should coincide and condemned the Baroque use of applied pilasters, broken pediments, spiral columns, and curving entablatures.

Figure 14.2-1 Venice. Cloister of San Francesco in Vigna, Lodoli's proto-functionalist windowsills, 1750s.

Ange-Jacques Gabriel designs Petit Trianon for Louis XV's mistress, Mme. de Pompadour

▲ **1760**

▼ **1774**

Claude-Nicolas Ledoux begins Royal Saltworks at Chaux

Death of Louis XV

▲ **1774**

Figure 14.2-2 Frontispiece by Charles Eissen for Abbé Laugier's treatise on architecture, *Essai sur l'architecture*, 1753.

Laugier also launched a sweeping critique of urbanism: "Our towns are still what they were, a mass of houses crowded together haphazardly without system, planning, or design." He suggested treating the city with the same bold method as the geometric French garden: cutting a straight path through the thick woods.

The theoretical appeals to reason and first principles of Lodoli and Laugier, both of whom had little working knowledge of architecture, inspired a generation of scholars to undertake archaeological expeditions to ancient ruins to document architecture's origins. They diverged into camps of pro-Greek and pro-Roman supporters. On the Greek side were James Stuart (1713–1788) (Fig. 14.2-3a) and Nicholas Revett (1720–1804), English amateurs sent to Greece by an aristocratic club known as the Society of Dilettanti. After several years of taking measurements they published the first of four volumes of the *Antiquities of Athens* in 1762. In 1754, shortly after Stuart and Revett departed from Athens, their French competitor, the academician Julien-David Leroy (1724–1803), arrived there. Leroy succeeded in publishing his findings on Greek antiquities four years before the English study. More imaginative but less accurate, the French scholar drew hypothetical reconstructions of ruined buildings, such as the Propylaia in Athens (Fig. 14.2-3b). This in turn provoked a struggle between the dogmatic interest in historical artifacts and the use of antiquities as creative stimuli.

Johann Joachim Winckelmann (1717–1768), who became chief curator of the papal collection of antiquities in the 1760s, prevailed as the champion of the Greek way. The German scholar considered the masculine purity of

---

1783

Victor Louis redesigns Palais Royal for apartments, cafés, and shops

United States approves the Bill of Rights and a democratic constitution

▲ 1783

1789

French Revolution begins in Paris

Jacques-Germain Soufflot's Panthéon completed in Paris

▲ 1792

1793–1794

Reign of Terror in France leads to execution of Louis XVI and Marie Antoinette

Figure 14.2-3 (a) Hagley Hall, Doric folly by James Stuart, 1760s. (b) Reconstruction of the Propylaia in Athens, 1758, from Julien-David Leroy's *Les ruines des plus beaux monuments de la Gréce*, 1770.

Napoléon crowns himself emperor and publishes his Civil Code of laws

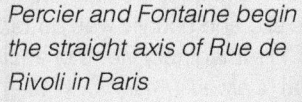
1804

▼ **1801**
Percier and Fontaine begin the straight axis of Rue de Rivoli in Paris

Jean-Francois-Thérese Chalgrin's Arc de Triomphe in Paris

▲ **1808–1832**

Piranesi's *Carceri* and the Sublime

Piranesi published his etchings of fantasy prisons, the *Carceri d'invenzione*, in two different editions in 1745 and 1761. His visions conveyed an ultimately negative message of architecture as inherently repressive. He depicted sinister atmospheres crowded with the drawbridges and catwalks of a visual maze without exit. Piranesi's prisons captured the metaphysical position of the sublime, a beauty stimulated by terror.

Giovanni Battista Piranesi's drawbridge scene, from *Carceri*, 1762.

Greek art in the age of Pericles as the apex of artistic development. In his *Geschichte der Kunst des Alterthums* (*The History of Ancient Art*) (1764), he classified and distinguished between the art movements of the past, establishing the historicist method still in use. He described the artistic progression from Paestum to the Parthenon, followed by the decline of good taste at Palmyra and Baalbek, where the focus on decoration compromised good proportions.

In contrast, Giovanni Battista Piranesi (1720–1778), a Venetian-born architect, fervently advocated the superiority of Roman culture. Piranesi insisted that the Roman way developed independent of Greece through Etruscan precedents. His position improved with the systematic excavations of Herculaneum and Pompeii from 1738 to 1756, which revealed the great variety of Roman architecture. Piranesi, who like Leroy worked mostly as a graphic artist and educator, represented a new category of professional, the meta-architect, whose production remained primarily in

the imaginary realm of printed media. His beautifully crafted etchings and engravings described both archaeological reconstructions and theoretical fantasies. In a publication of 1743 he explained his resignation to paper architecture: "The truth is that today we see no buildings as costly as . . . the Forum of Nerva, an Amphitheatre of Vespasian, a Palace of Nero; nor have Princes or private citizens appeared to create any; no other option is left to me, to any other modern Architect, than to explain his own ideas through drawings."

In hundreds of perspective *vedute* (views) of ancient and modern Rome, Piranesi demonstrated with maniacal detail a propulsive kind of architecture that seemed to have grown from its site and usually was dotted with plants growing on it as well. His imaginary views of ancient settings and his metaphysical *Carceri* (*Prisons*, 1745–1761) offered a brooding kinesthetic vision of a spatial flow up stairs, under bridges, and into chasms bounded by colossal masonry structures. At a time when profuse decoration seemed contrary to good taste, Piranesi lavished it everywhere. His one proviso: decoration should always be framed—a mandate that led to the placement of *passe-partout* edges on all his architectural elements. The facade of his only completed building, the renovation of the Roman church of Santa Maria del Priorato of 1764–1766, exuberantly illustrated this framing strategy.

During his early years in Rome Piranesi collaborated with Giambattista Nolli (1701–1756) on the Nolli Map (Fig. 14.2-4), published in 1748, in which they perfected the graphic conventions of two-dimensional "figure-ground" representation. The density of the Nolli Map inspired Piranesi's delirious cartography of the ancient Campus Martius (1762) (Fig. 14.2-5), in which he reimagined the fabric of ancient Rome made entirely of monuments. Among his fictional projects, the plan for the Magnifico Collegio (1750) proposed an extravagant radiocentric scheme with concentric rings of chambers connected by stairs to the great hall under a central cupola. This redundant concatenation of geometry came curiously close to the mounded sequences of Angkor Thom (see Section 8.1) and remained as complex and full of curves as late Baroque architecture.

Despite the crypto-Baroque style of his work, Piranesi gained the respect of many of the advocates of rational design. No one could equal his archaeological knowledge. His analytical presentations, such as his plates dedicated to the Emissarium (1761), the water collector for the ancient aqueducts, provided a treasure trove of layered information (Fig. 14.2-6). Piranesi directly influenced several of the most important architects of the next generation in France and England, including Leroy, Jacques-Germain Soufflot, Charles de Wailly, Robert Adam, and William Chambers. Indirectly, through his evocative prints, he touched almost every distinguished architect of the late eighteenth century. With Piranesi the meta-architect became the protagonist of architectural theory.

The *Encyclopedia,* a Mandate for Progress

The *Encyclopedia* (*Encyclopédie ou dictionnaire raisonné des sciences, des arts et des métiers*), directed by Denis Diderot (1713–1784) and co-edited during its first five years by the mathematician Jean-Baptiste d'Alembert (1717–1783), represented the central intellectual project of the European Enlightenment. Compiled in Paris between 1751 and 1765 and published sporadically over the course of thirty years, it brought together a comprehensive, up-to-date knowledge

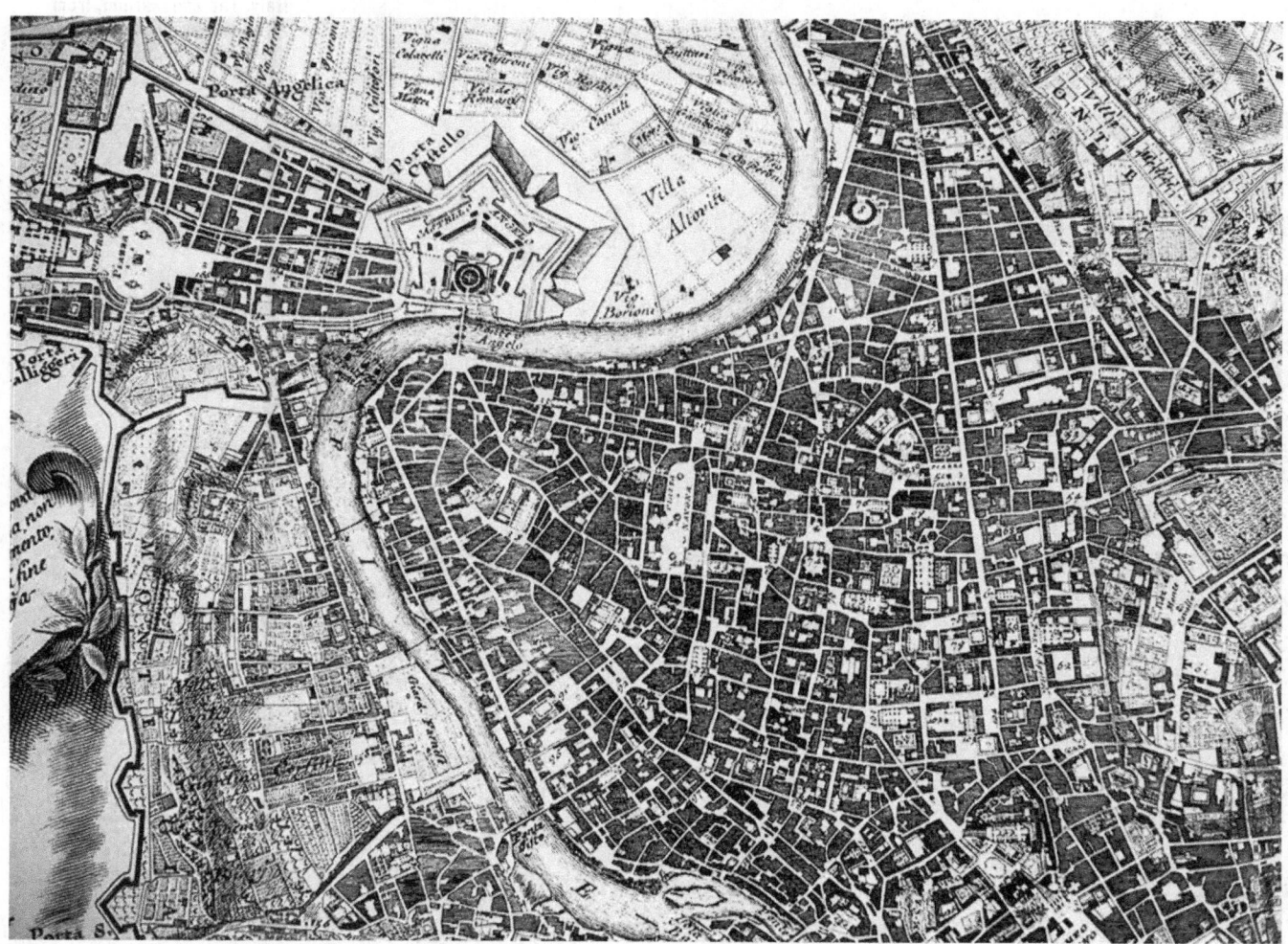

Figure 14.2-4 Detail of the map of Rome by Giambattista Nolli, assisted by Piranesi, 1748.

Figure 14.2-5 Rome. Reconstruction of Campus Martius from Piranesi, *Il Campo Marzio dell'Antica Roma*, 1762.

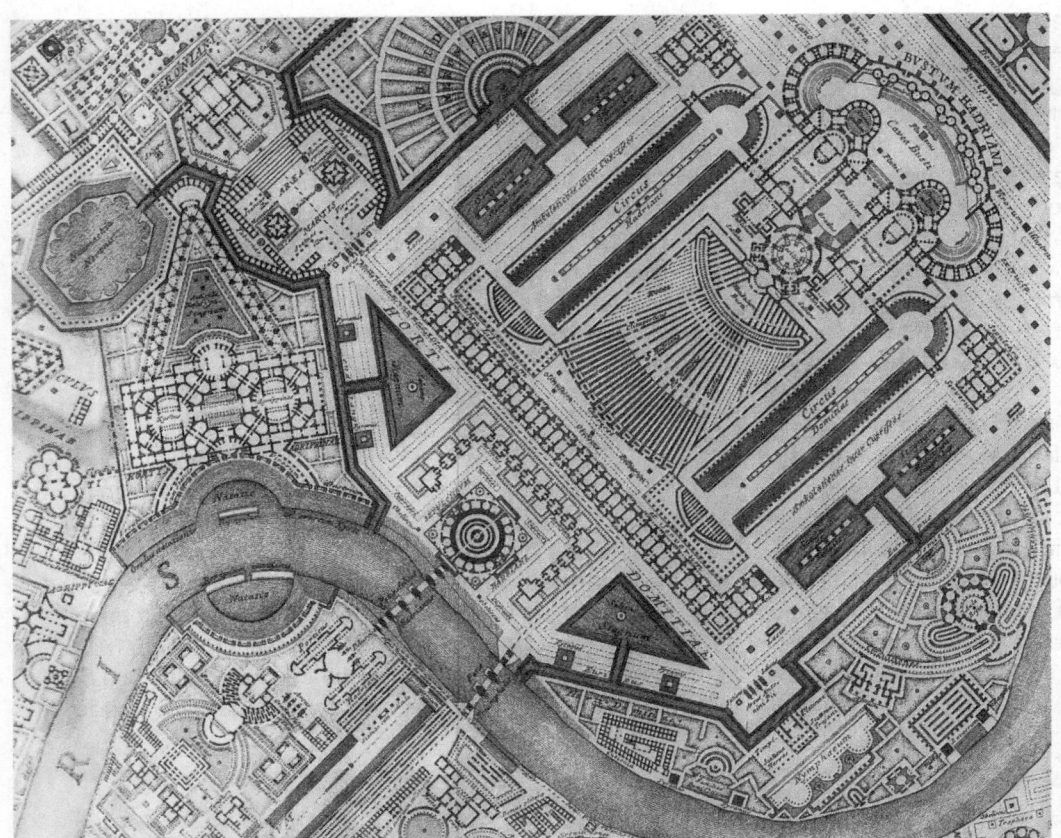

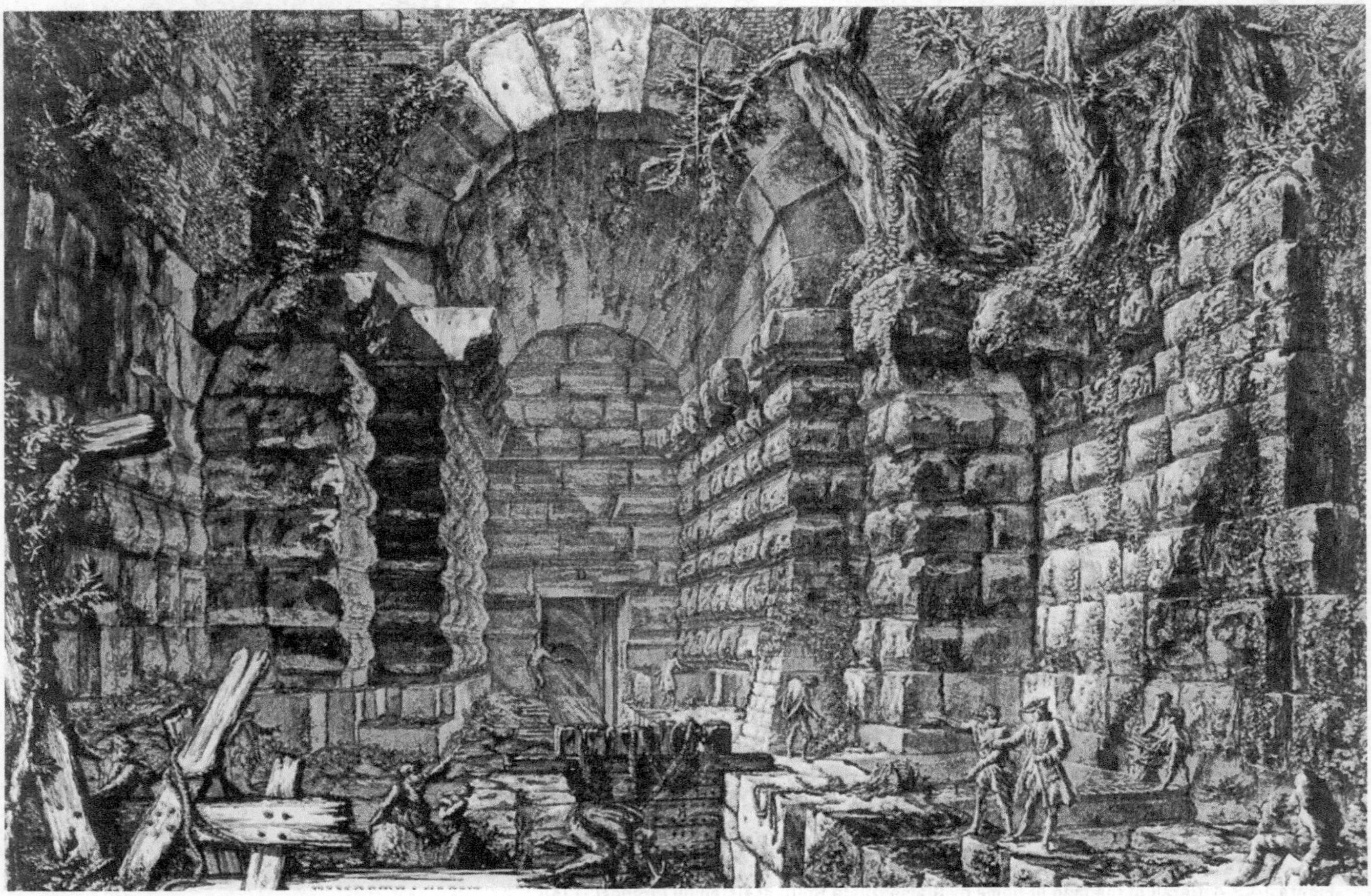

Figure 14.2-6 Lake Albano, Italy. The Emissarium, from Piranesi, *Descrizione e Disegno dell'Emissario del Lago Albano*, 1762.

base for the sciences and the arts that grounded Europe's emerging modernity. Separate volumes with thousands of analytical illustrations describing a new world of technical and social progress supplemented the 72,000 articles of the *Encyclopedia* (Fig. 14.2-7). From the text's details on the production of glass and the workings of the steam engine to historical views on the role of commerce, the medical profession, and the basis of law, Diderot imposed the criterion of rationality to transcend the received notions, taboos, and superstitions of the past. His critical perspective presented a threat to the religious and authoritarian tenets of the *ancien régime*, which periodically attempted to suppress the publication. While the articles on architecture had none of the theoretical polemics found in Piranesi's texts, the description of programs for social institutions and working environments greatly widened the scope of architecture to embrace its role as a public good.

Jacques-François Blondel (1705–1774) wrote most of the *Encyclopedia*'s entries on architecture. Although sympathetic to rococo interiors, Blondel admired the clarity of the works of late-seventeenth-century French architects such as Claude Perrault and Jules Hardouin-Mansart (see Section 12.2). He espoused a rational theory of architecture based on the good economic sense of fitting form to function, maintaining that architectural beauty came from good proportions rather than excessive decoration. "The architect should begin with the naked mass and be content with this, before trying to add ornament," he declared. As the founder of the first independent school of architecture, Blondel exerted enormous influence in the field, teaching many of the same architects who visited Piranesi in Rome. In one of his few built works, the Hôtel de Ville at Metz (1764), Blondel exercised a Spartan attitude, close to the severity of Dutch public buildings. He rendered the facade without columns or pilasters, using a minimum of relief in the striated bands of rustication along the arcuated base. He tucked the only sculptural ornament into the pair of pediments above the protruding entry blocks. Squared-off insets framed the windows without fancy moldings.

The work of his contemporary Ange-Jacques Gabriel (1698–1782), the court architect of Louis XV, corresponded closely to Blondel's pitch for a return to classic purity. The facades of Gabriel's twin blocks on the new square dedicated to Louis XV (now known as Place de la Concorde) (Fig. 14.2-8) recalled the second-story colonnades of Perrault's facade of the Louvre. Despite such clarity, Voltaire criticized Place de la Concorde for its lack of utility in a city that needed better circulation and basic services such as public markets. The square served only as a celebratory

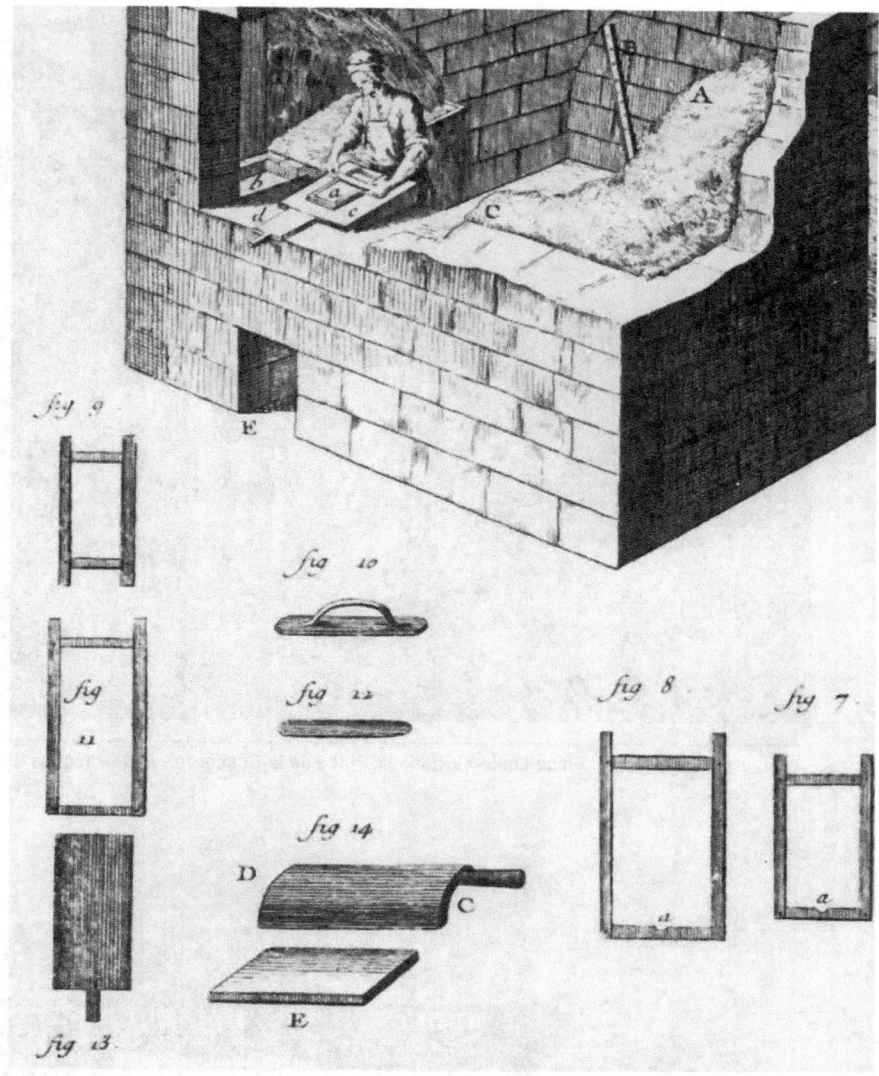

Figure 14.2-7 Illustration of masonry techniques from Diderot and d'Alembert, *Encyclopedia*, 1751–1765.

space for an equestrian statue of the king. During the French Revolution's years of terror, this royal esplanade acquired an unexpectedly grisly function as the site of the guillotine for public executions.

Gabriel built his most renowned work, the Petit Trianon (Fig. 14.2-9), in the 1760s in the park of Versailles for Louis XV's official mistress, Madame de Pompadour (1721–1764). The pavilion read as a crisp, cubic volume, with each of the three visible facades articulated with a different organization of colossal Corinthian pilasters and half-columns. Madame de Pompadour, a great beauty admired for her artistic talent as a singer and painter, dominated the formation of taste as one of several powerful female patrons in prerevolutionary France.

Madame de Pompadour also influenced the promotion of her younger brother, Marquis de Marigny (1727–1781), to the role of state building superintendent in charge of several key projects of the age. Somewhat like Burlington, the young marquis went to Turin and Rome in 1749 on the Grand Tour to improve his taste. His retinue included an art critic

Figure 14.2-8 Paris. Place Louis XV (today's Place de la Concorde), Ange-Jacques Gabriel, 1750s.

Figure 14.2-9 Versailles, France. Petit Trianon, built for Mme. de Pompadour, Gabriel, 1760s.

CONSTRUCTION, TECHNOLOGY, THEORY

The Panthéon and Iron Reinforcing

Soufflot used a large amount of concealed iron to reinforce the structure of Ste.-Geneviève, later named the Panthéon. He attempted to synthesize the empirical knowledge observed in the structure of Gothic buildings with the classical ideal, reducing the structural components to a minimum. Like Cordemoy, he desired to make structure visible. Metal components, however, represented a different category of structure from masonry; like bones in a body, he believed, the iron reinforcing bars should not show in the finished product. The corrosion of the metal, however, later caused problems for the structure.

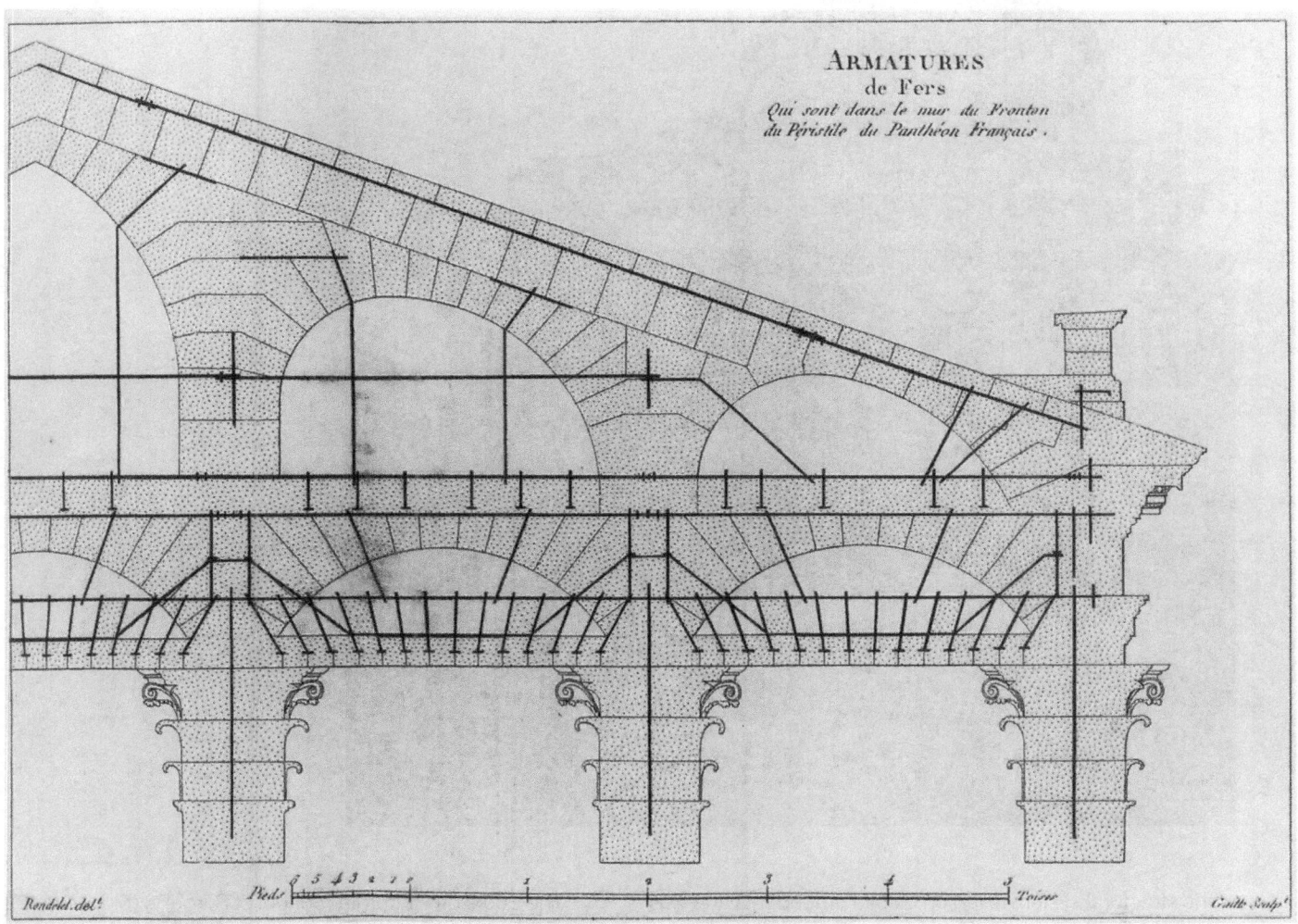

Paris. Ste.-Geneviève, section of temple-front porch showing iron reinforcing, Soufflot, 1757–1792.

and the architect Jacques-Germain Soufflot (1713–1780), who remained his lifelong friend. To Soufflot went the most important commission of the age, the church of the patron saint of Paris, Ste.-Geneviève (also known as the Panthéon) (Fig. 14.2-10). He desired to return to the sensible structural principles that could be abstracted from the great buildings of the past. Begun in 1757, Soufflot's project for the church underwent several major design changes influenced by research into Gothic structure. Soufflot based the Corinthian columns of the temple-front porch on those of the recently documented Temple of Venus at Baalbek and let them rise taller than those of the Pantheon in Rome.

The plan of the Parisian Panthéon resembled that of St. Mark's in Venice, a quincunx arrangement with a high central dome and side domes over the four arms of a Greek cross (Fig. 14.2-11). The pendentives of the domes funneled down perilously to meet the support of single colossal Corinthian columns at each corner. The astounding lightness

of the structural system relied on Gothic precedents and was assisted with hidden iron reinforcing rods. Soufflot achieved the sort of synthesis that Piranesi advocated, taking the grace of Hellenistic decoration, the magic of Gothic structure, and the flow of Byzantine vaulted spaces while discreetly inserting modern industrial techniques. The dome's triple-shell structure and the ring of columns around its drum derived from Wren's solution for St. Paul's in London. Like its model, an inner conical dome added support for the lantern. At the completion of Ste.-Geneviève in 1792, the revolutionaries renamed the church the Panthéon, converting the somber, rusticated crypt into a burial ground for the heroes of the new French republic, many of them authors of the *Encyclopedia*.

The École de Chirurgie (School of Surgery) (Fig. 14.2-12), begun in 1769 by Jacques Gondoin (1737–1818), captured the spirit of the *Encyclopedia*. A student of Blondel, with a four-year scholarship to the French Academy in Rome, Gondoin devoted his career almost entirely to this single project, planned with the advice of the king's surgeon. The building came to signify a modern, scientific commitment to medicine. Instead of using an enclosing wall for the facade, Gondoin lined the street with a magnificent Ionic colonnade that allowed views from outside into the school's courtyard. The columns blended into a triumphal arch entry. On-axis stood a colossal Corinthian temple front, behind which lay the hemispherical anatomy theater. The effect of mixing

Figure 14.2-11 Paris. Ste.-Geneviève (Panthéon), interior, Soufflot, 1757–1792.

the two orders at different scales resembled the layering of Palladio's church facades and marked the difference of scale between the full-volume theater and the two stories of the rest of the school. The semicircular *cavea* of the theater seated 1,200 in its eight tiers. A coffered half-dome with a grand oculus introduced superb top lighting into the space of performance. Like Soufflot, Gondoin used the columns of classical architecture as working parts of the structure. His school expanded the role of architecture to express a new

social agenda with singular practicality. The architect had hoped to add a new prison facing the school, to provide cadavers for dissection in the theater.

The proliferation of grand public theaters indicated societal changes afoot before the Revolution. In 1767 Marigny commissioned Charles de Wailly (1730–1798), a pupil of both Blondel and Piranesi, to build a new theater for the Comédie-Française (later called the Odéon) with Marie-Joseph Peyre (1730–1785). They set the theater's pure

Ledoux's Female Clients

The architect Claude-Nicolas Ledoux first came to public attention in 1770 as a result of the house he designed for Mademoiselle Guimard, a diva at the Royal Ballet, who requested that a small theater be included in her *hôtel particulier* in Paris. At the entry to the house's main block, the architect placed an Ionic screen of columns in front of a scooped-out exedra, producing delightful deep shadows. The left door led to a stair, the central to a bathroom, and the right into the oval foyer. From here one followed a sequence of two salons, the first intercepted by the cross-axis of the grand dining hall, a double-height room lined with Ionic columns. Financed by her lovers, the house was eventually lost by Guimard due to her sponsors' economic misfortunes. Ledoux designed a second noteworthy project for an even better-placed female client, Madame du Barry (1743–1793), the official mistress of Louis XV after the death of Madame de Pompadour. For her he designed a pavilion at Château Louveciennes similar in function to the Petit Trianon.

Paris. Facade of Mlle. Guimard's house, Claude-Nicolas Ledoux, 1770. From Ledoux, *l'Architecture.*

rectangular volume behind an austere Doric frontispiece of eight colossal columns. On the flanks they placed arcades as a shelter where servants could wait while their masters went to the performances. The perfectly square vestibule opened to stairs on either side. The circular auditorium intersected the projecting thrust stage, a shape that the authors acknowledged was perfect as geometry but flawed in terms of viewpoints. Like Soufflot's Panthéon, the Odéon was conceived as a complete urban setting, framed by a semicircular, *cavea*-shaped plaza.

Victor Louis (1731–1800) designed in Bordeaux the largest and best conceived of all prerevolutionary theaters. The architect had connections with the world of theater through his wife, the famous singer Marie Bayon, who performed for Diderot's birthday in 1770. From 1772 to 1780 he conceived the Grand Theatre as a perfect rectangular block with a severe Corinthian portico for its frontispiece (Fig. 14.2-13). The arcades along the flanks hosted the theater's café and restaurant. Louis insisted on generous space for circulation, reserving almost half of the area as social space. One

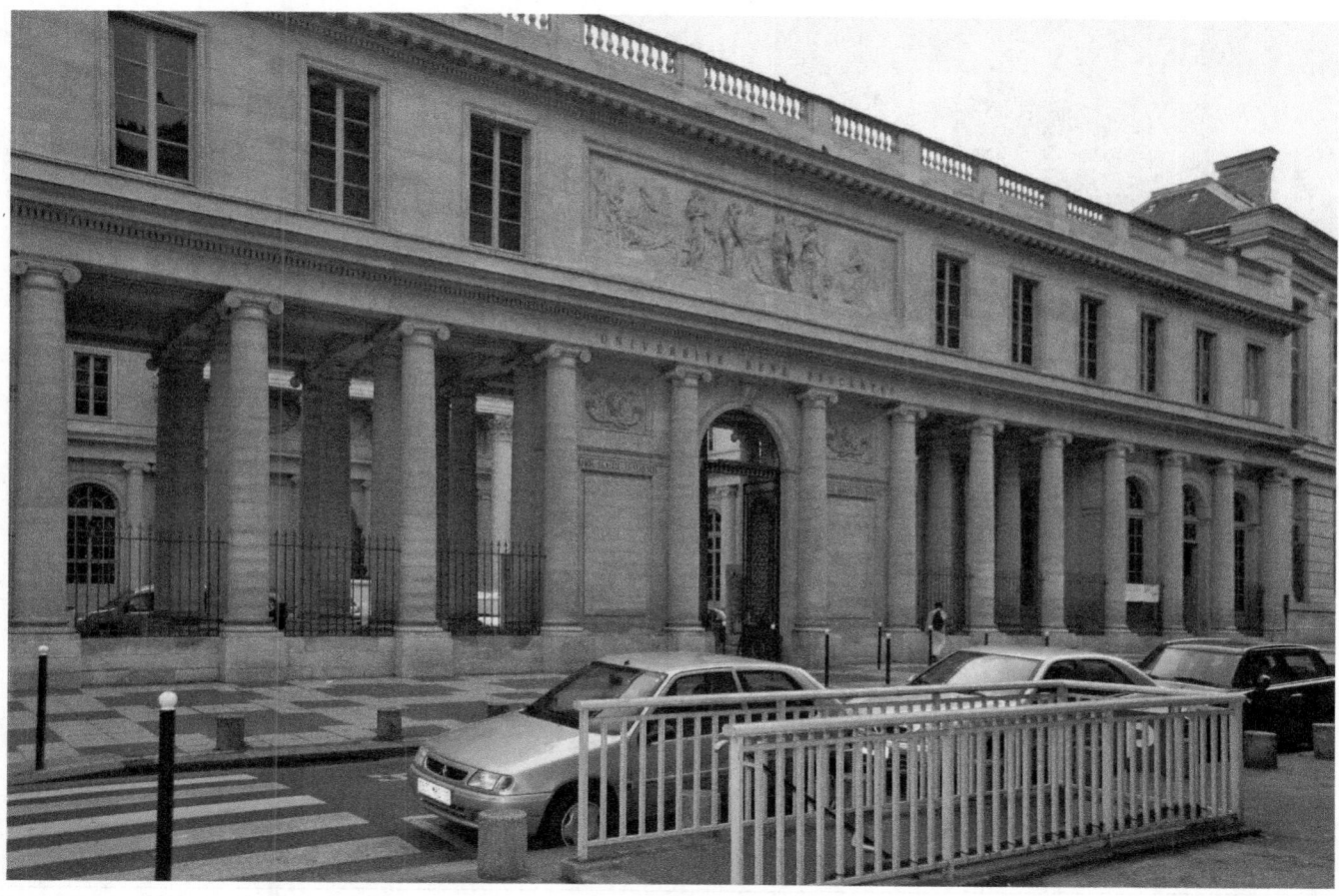

Figure 14.2-12 Paris. École de Chirurgie (medical school), Jacques Gondoin, 1769.

passed through the columns of the foyer into a triple-height atrium laced with a grand stair and upper loggias for interacting with the crowds. He covered the atrium with a novel twelve-part groin vault and inserted a second, smaller theater above the foyer for ballet performances. The principal auditorium followed a circular plan surrounded by a ring of colossal columns. Between them he boldly cantilevered the boxes, using concealed iron braces to help support the structure.

During the 1780s Louis also designed the Comédie-Française theater for the northwest end of the Palais-Royal in Paris. He tucked the foyer of this much smaller theater under the slope of the auditorium seating. In the interest of fireproofing and strength, the architect suspended the vaulted ceiling from iron girders, among the first ever used in a public building. The Comédie-Française was the crowning ingredient of the speculative venture of the architect and the owner, the Duke of Chartres, to expand the Palais-Royal as a series of arcades for 145 shops with three-story townhouses above (Fig. 14.2-14). Behind the palace and the theater the long court stretched 200 m (656 ft) around a formal garden, accessible to visitors. When the renovated Palais-Royal opened in 1783, it offered a new model of bourgeois life with a combination of theater, gardens, commerce, and housing. In the cafés under its arcades the rallying cries

for revolution first sounded in 1789. The Palais-Royal's mix of commerce and culture enlarged the social base of the formally planned spaces of the city, increasing the enfranchisement of civic participants.

Citizen Architect: From Reform to Revolution

The spirit of the *Encyclopedia* stimulated the demand for theaters, markets, schools, hospitals, and places of production. It advanced the notion that architecture could improve society and led to a raft of real and ideal projects for reform. While the aristocrats of the *ancien régime* hesitated to accept the modernizing agenda presented by Diderot and his authors, a large movement for reform grew, often sustained by secret liberal societies such as the Freemasons. On the eve of the French Revolution, enlightened architects proposed radical projects as realizations of an architecture in the public interest.

The work of Claude-Nicolas Ledoux (1736–1806) embodied the Enlightenment ideals of reform and justice advocated by Diderot and Voltaire. Trained as an engraver and for several years a student at Blondel's school, Ledoux did not have the advantage of a scholarship to Rome. He learned classical architecture from observing buildings in Paris and flipping through the treatises of Sebastiano Serlio

Figure 14.2-13 Bordeaux, France. Grand Theatre, Victor Louis, 1780s.

Figure 14.2-14 Paris. Palais Royal courtyard, remodeled by Victor Louis during the rebuilding of the Comédie Française, 1780s.

Ledoux's major public projects came through the Ferme Générale, the Royal Institute of Tax Farmers. Inspired by the physiocrats, a group of economists and philosophers who maintained that all wealth and goodness were derived from working the land, the architect designed the Saline de Chaux, the royal saltworks, on a rural site near the eastern border of France. The project went into production between 1773 and 1779. In a theater-like composition, Ledoux arranged the factory sheds and director's house as a proscenium stage addressing the hemicycle arrangement of workers' dwellings and support buildings (Fig. 14.2-15). The Director's House (Fig. 14.2-16a), the tallest structure, stood out with a colossal temple front made of chunky rusticated columns. Ideally it would have included a chapel at its summit, underlining

and Palladio. His designs ranged from fancy residences to social institutions to industrial estates. During his last years, no longer able to work because of his close association with the deposed monarchy, he produced a treatise on architecture that described the utopian projects he believed would lead to a better-managed society.

Figure 14.2-15 Chaux, France. Saline de Chaux, ideal view of the saltworks, Ledoux, 1770–1800. From Ledoux, *l'Architecture considérée sous le rapport de l'art, des moeurs et de la legislation*, 1804.

the director's moral authority. Ledoux's "theater of industry" provided radial surveillance from this central point to the dwellings of the workers, and just in case the workers attempted to run away, the compound was surrounded by a wall and a moat. This attention to security was likewise an effort to protect the valuable product from thieves. The architect hoped to improve the living standards of the workers by giving them collective housing. Each building served four family units gathered around a central kitchen with a grand hearth to provide food and heating for all. To dramatize the salt-processing functions at Chaux, Ledoux created a grotto-like entry, with ground-floor windows sculpted as jars spouting crystalline substances (Fig. 14.2-16b).

Long after the termination of Ledoux's contract at Chaux, he returned to the plan for this partially realized settlement as the basis for a utopian society. In his imaginary campus the barrel-makers lived in a house decorated with concentric rings, the charcoal burners had a pyramidal building mimicking industrial chimneys, and the director of the riverworks lived in a dam-like house with a waterfall running through its center. His scheme for the Oïkéma (Fig. 14.2-17), a house of pleasure for initiating young men into the world of sex, proved both subtle and overt: the plan resembled an erect penis but could be perceived only from an aerial perspective. Such literal indications of function led Ledoux's

critics to accuse him of designing **architecture parlante**, or "talking architecture." While he imagined novel institutions for Chaux, he also created an unprecedented kind of urban layout: beyond the compact oval at the center of his ideal settlement, he scattered the buildings loosely, surrounding them with ample gardens. The resulting green city downplayed axial alignments and appeared almost as picturesque as an English garden. His plan embodied the physiocrats' ideal of reconnecting the citizens to the land.

In Ledoux's other royal project managed by the Ferme Générale, the *barrières* (tollhouses) in the tax wall surrounding Paris, the architect attempted to provide a rational building system for a much-detested function. The sixty tax stations, begun in 1784 on the eve of the French Revolution, appeared like a collection of garden follies. Each one carried a different combination of elements chosen from an almanac of mannerist motifs found in the treatises of Serlio and Palladio. The shared elements included rusticated columns, *serlianas*, temple fronts, rhythmic trabeation, rotundas, and tempiettos. William Beckford, while visiting Ledoux, accompanied him to Freemason ceremonies and described the tollhouses as having a "massive sepulchral character more like the entrances of a necropolis." When the Revolution broke out in 1789, the mob destroyed a few of the *barrières*, but most of them survived until the demolitions in the 1860s for Georges-Eugène Haussmann's urban

Figure 14.2-16 Chaux, France. (a) Saline de Chaux, Director's House and factories, Ledoux, 1770–1800. (b) Representation of salt formations.

Figure 14.2-17 Chaux, France. Plan of the Oïkéma, for the sexual education of young men, from Ledoux, *l'Architecture*, 1804.

Figure 14.2-18 Paris. *Barrière* at La Villette, Ledoux, 1780s.

In his treatise Ledoux illustrated the theater's auditorium reflected in an enormous eye (Fig. 14.2-19), signifying that equally good views could be obtained from all seats. During the Revolution, the Jacobins indicted Ledoux as an *architecte du roi* (royal architect) and thus enemy of the revolution. The architect defended his role as a citizen architect, explaining the nonhierarchical design of the Theater of Besançon as a "republican theater built during the despotism." While this defense saved him from the guillotine and he was eventually released from prison, it ended his career, pushing him to withdraw into his utopian research.

The Revolution was kinder to Ledoux's contemporary Étienne-Louis Boullée (1728–1799), who spent most of the 1780s drawing fantastic projects on a superhuman scale. Some of Boullée's designs adhered to real programs, such as the call for a cemetery outside the walls of Paris and competitions for a new royal library (Fig. 14.2-20a). Others were pure acts of imagination, including the colossal sphere proposed as Newton's **cenotaph** (1784) (Fig. 14.2-20b), in which he projected the exterior as the sphere of the planet and the interior as the sphere of the universe, pierced with stars. Boullée's fascination with funerary architecture allowed him to explore pure form, which he called "the architecture of shadows." In one of his tomb projects he literally projected a Doric temple front as shadows, the negative spaces cut out of the plane. Like Piranesi, Boullée explored forms that went beyond style and conventions. He rejected decoration to investigate the idea of "character," or the effects on the emotions of colossal scale and shadow-casting mass. For the architectural competitions organized during the Revolution, Boullée designed an immense National Palace, with a stark, unrelieved facade decorated solely with an inscription of the "Rights of Man," as defined by the revolutionary convention in 1792.

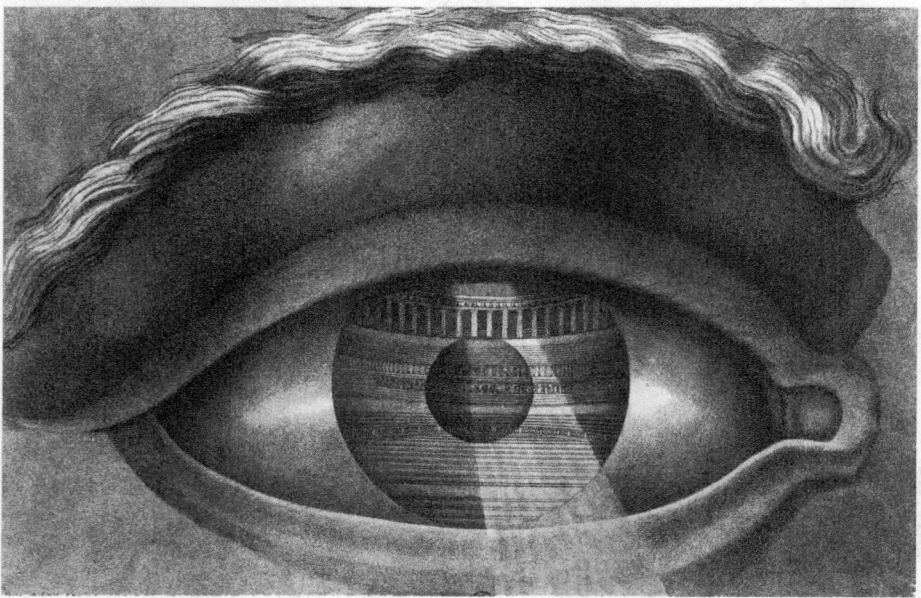

Figure 14.2-19 Besançon, France. Illustration of the Theater of Besançon, from Ledoux, *l'Architecture*, 1804.

plan (see Section 16.1). Of the four that remain, the Rotunda at La Villette has the most monumental allure. Overlooking the Ourcq canal, it rises as a massive cylinder articulated by a ring of linked *serlianas* and, capped by a Doric entablature, easily could be mistaken for an imperial mausoleum (Fig. 14.2-18).

As a civic architect, Ledoux achieved his greatest success with the Theater of Besançon, designed in 1775 and opened ten years later. The auditorium broke substantially from contemporary models by stepping up in grades like a Roman theater, eliminating the privileged tiers of box seats. At the top level a ring of Doric columns supported the ceiling.

During the chaotic first years of the French Revolution the building industry languished. Paris witnessed more destruction than construction, including the symbolic attacks on

Figure 14.2-20 (a) Paris. Rendering of proposed royal library, Étienne-Louis Boullée, 1780s. (b) Rendering of proposed cenotaph for Newton, Boullée, 1780s.

FÉDÉRATION GÉNÉRALE
au Champ de Mars,

DES FRANÇAIS,
le 14 Juillet 1790.

Figure 14.2-21 Paris. Champs de Mars, Festival of Federation, Charles Monnet, 1790.

Ledoux's *barrières* and the demolition of the Bastille prison. Most of the revolutionary projects were designed either for fictional competitions or as ephemeral works of propaganda. Events such as the Festival of Federation (Fig. 14.2-21), held on July 14, 1790, to celebrate the first anniversary of the Revolution, brought a new kind of mass participation to urban space. More than a million people, arranged in orderly rows of troops, turned out for the celebration. They filed across the Champs de Mars through a colossal triumphal arch toward a central four-square mounded altar to swear allegiance to the new republic. Around the same time the painter Jacques-Louis David (1748–1825) became a fervent republican with a grudge against the Academy of the *ancien régime*. He joined the radical wing of the Jacobins that ordered mass executions during the Terror. In 1794 he supervised the neo-pagan Festival of the Supreme Being, set on a picturesque hill with the Tree of Liberty at its summit, and in the same year organized the *Plan des Artistes*, an unexecuted plan to build straight streets in Paris for better circulation.

Disillusioned by the Jacobins and punished for his participation in their movement, David later turned to Napoléon Bonaparte (r. 1799–1815) as his ideal revolutionary

hero. Napoléon swept to power using the rhetoric of the French Revolution to become the dictator of an empire. By the first years of the nineteenth century he had begun to commission large public projects. After crowning himself emperor in 1804, he set his trusted architects Charles Percier (1764–1838) and Pierre-Francois-Leonard Fontaine (1762–1853) to construct the seemingly endless series of identical blocks of arcaded apartment houses on Rue de Rivoli (Fig. 14.2-22). This project resulted in the first straight street through the center of Paris.

Napoléon's dictum that "what is big is always beautiful" characterized his attitude toward architecture. His planners proposed a vast network of highways around Europe, including a tunnel cut through Mont Blanc, as well as major revisions to the urban form of Paris, Milan, and Rome. The Napoleonic projects, such as the Bourse Building of 1805 by Alexandre-Théodore Brongniart (1739–1813), an immense peripteral cube (now altered), and the peripteral Church of the Madeleine, begun by Ledoux's pupil Alexandre-Pierre Vignon (1763–1828) in 1806 as the Temple to the Glory of the Great Army, were completed long after Napoléon's demise. Both the twelve-column temple front of the Chamber of

Figure 14.2-22 Paris. The arcaded Rue de Rivoli, Charles Percier and Pierre-Francois-Leonard Fontaine, begun 1805.

Deputies by Bernard Poyet (1742–1842), begun in 1808, and the ten-story Arc de Triomphe by Jean-Francois-Thérese Chalgrin (1739–1811) (Fig. 14.2-23), at the terminus of the Champs Élysées, reached completion more than two decades later.

The French Revolution initiated a process of emancipation and social progress that engaged architects to design solutions for social problems. Most of their efforts remained on paper or went toward propaganda. Despite Napoléon's transformation of the goals of the Revolution into a new manifestation of despotism, the revolutionary principles of "liberty, equality, and fraternity" entered into the public architecture of France and influenced the rest of the world as a progressive challenge to premodern order.

Further Reading

Braham, Allan. *The Architecture of the French Enlightenment*. Berkeley: University of California Press, 1980.

Etlin, Richard. *Symbolic Space: French Enlightenment Architecture and Its Legacy*. Chicago: University of Chicago Press, 1994.

Harrington, Kevin. *Changing Ideas on Architecture in the* Encyclopédie, *1750–1776*. Ann Arbor, MI: UMI Research Press, 1985.

Pérez-Gomez, Alberto. *Architecture and the Crisis of Modern Science*. Cambridge, MA: MIT Press, 1983.

Rykwert, Joseph. *The First Moderns*. Cambridge, MA: MIT Press, 1980.

———. *On Adam's House in Paradise: The Idea of the Primitive Hut in Architectural History*. Cambridge, MA: MIT Press, 1972.

Vidler, Anthony. *Claude-Nicolas Ledoux: Architecture and Social Reform at the End of the* Ancien Régime. Cambridge, MA: MIT Press, 1990.

———. *The Writing of the Walls: Architectural Theory in the Late Enlightenment*. New York: Princeton Architectural Press, 1987.

Wilton-Ely, John. *Piranesi as Architect and Designer*. New Haven, CT: Yale University Press, 1993.

Figure 14.2-23 Paris. Arc de Triomphe, Jean-Francois-Thérese Chalgrin, 1805–1832.

14.3 INDUSTRY AND PUNISHMENT

Factories and Warehouses, Prisons and Workhouses

In England, during the same period as the revolutionary awakening of the middle class in France and the colonists in America, an equally convulsive change occurred in the realm of production. The so-called Industrial Revolution found its epicenter in Manchester and the Lancashire region of northern England, which were favored by an excellent coal supply to run steam engines and good connections to a national canal system. The area also possessed an abundant supply of cheap labor, in particular young women and children, to work the machines of the great textile mills.

During the rapid social transformations of England's industrialization, two new building types took hold: the factory and the prison. So similar were the problems of controlling workers and prisoners that the reformer Jeremy Bentham proposed his **Panopticon** as an architectural solution that could work for both. Industrialized production led to the development of a dynamic consumer society and an expanded middle class. It also precipitated the emergence of new forms of human degradation, seen in the slum tenements of Manchester. As mechanization increased, the course was set for human-made environmental problems on a larger scale than had ever been known. Modernization had arrived, and from the outset it represented a mixed blessing.

Manchester, Machines, and the Factory System

The transition to industrialism was not exactly a revolution, as it did not involve one group overthrowing another. Yet what occurred in late-eighteenth-century England proved even more powerful than a revolution, and the effects of the factory system of production accompanied by the development of monopoly capitalism produced profound and irreversible changes to the social, urban, and environmental order in both England and the rest of the world. While the authors of the *Encyclopedia* in France discussed modernity's theoretical premises, pragmatic English industrialists put them into action, often with brutal consequences. Industrial architecture radically altered the scale and fit of buildings into the urban fabric.

Life expectancy rose dramatically once the British applied such new technologies as the steam engine and cast iron to agriculture, mining, cloth production, and transportation. For the first time in history—except rare situations like ancient Rome, Venice, and Amsterdam—the majority of the population no longer toiled in the fields. Chronic unemployment, however, accompanied this technical progress, and the peasants migrated from the countryside to the workshops and poorhouses of the cities. One city in particular, Manchester, in northwest England, exhibited the extremes of the new industrialized society: at one end a growing class of clever entrepreneurs and inventors, and at the other the unlettered mass of workers. From a small feudal town of fewer than 20,000 in 1770, it burgeoned into a major trading center with factories and warehouses. By 1853, the year that Manchester became legally incorporated as a city, it counted more than 250,000 inhabitants, making it the second-largest English city after London. Located near an abundant supply of coal, Manchester was well connected to the national canal system and only a short haul to the port of Liverpool. Its lack of a municipal government or guilds gave industrialists free rein with trade and labor regulations. The industrial innovations that began in rural settings quickly converged on Manchester, crowding its canals and riverbanks with an austere collection of cotton mills. While mill owners at rural factories commonly provided workers accommodations, in Manchester they left the workers to fend for themselves, leading to the growth of the first industrial slums, appallingly overcrowded blocks without services. Families lived ten persons per room, and often beds were rented for eight-hour shifts. Manchester expanded without a plan, and the questions of water and sewage were left to private interests. The factories spewed filth into the waterways, and the soot of the steam engines, running twenty-four hours per day, clouded the atmosphere with a vile haze. The air and water pollution soon reached critical levels.

A key factor in England's transition to industrialism, its impressive national canal system, began as a private venture near Manchester in the mid-eighteenth century. The canal

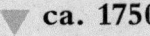 **ca. 1750**

Beginning of the Industrial Revolution

John Howard publishes *State of Prisons*, leading to prison reform

 **1779**

Boulton and Watt introduce the commercial steam engine in Birmingham, England

▲ **1777**

Iron Bridge of Coalbrookdale, England

▲ **1779**

builders produced a network that stretched hundreds of kilometers across the entire island. Their venture promoted the pragmatic ideal that engineering and technology, combined with imagination, could overcome the irregularities and barriers of nature.

None of the constituent ingredients of the Industrial Revolution originated in Manchester. James Watt (1736–1819) patented the key technical improvement of the age, the steam engine with pistons, in Glasgow in 1765. He commercially produced steam engines at Matthew Boulton's foundries in Birmingham fifteen years later. Abraham Darby (1678–1717) perfected another essential ingredient, mass-produced cast iron, using a new process of coal-based coke instead of wood-based charcoal in Coalbrookdale, a town about 50 km (31 miles) west of Birmingham. In 1779 his grandson, Abraham Darby III (1750–1791), produced the first monument to the structural capacity of cast iron, the Iron Bridge of Coalbrookdale (Fig. 14.3-1), designed with the architect Thomas Farnolls Pritchard (1723–1777). Five round arched ribs, each made from two monolithic cast-iron pieces bolted at the top, stretched between stone abutments to support a span of 30 m (98 ft). The builders added 800 stabilizing struts of cast iron, assembled with the mortise-and-tenon joints of carpentry. The Iron Bridge developed cracks almost as soon as it opened yet persevered as the mythical harbinger of a new age of technology. Thomas Telford (1757–1834) improved on its design in a second iron bridge built a decade later at nearby Buildwas. He used less than half the amount of iron to span a crossing 10 m (33 ft) wider. The Sucerland Bridge, built in 1793–1796, showed a further innovation, with the ribs of the single arch constructed from many cast-iron panels bolted together to act like the voussoirs of a masonry arch. The patent for this system belonged to the Anglo-American revolutionary Thomas Paine (1737–1809).

Figure 14.3-1 Coalbrookdale, England. The Iron Bridge, Abraham Darby III and Thomas Farnolls Pritchard, 1779.

Telford emerged as the first great bridge builder of the age. A Scottish stonemason who briefly worked for Robert Adam in London, he became one of the principal protagonists of the Industrial Revolution while working as the superintendent of the Ellesmere Canal between Liverpool and the pottery factories of Stoke-on-Trent. His spectacular Pontcysyllte Aqueduct over the River Dee (Fig. 14.3-2), designed in 1795 and opened in 1805, spanned a valley of more than 300 m (984 ft) with a nineteen-arch masonry structure that carried a 4 m (13 ft) wide cast-iron trough made of interlocking pieces. Telford defied nature by pitching the aerial waterway 40 m (131 ft) over the river valley. His masterpiece, the Menai Suspension Bridge of 1819 (Fig. 14.3-3), connected Anglesey Island to the Welsh mainland. For this first large suspension structure Telford attached sixteen chain cables made from iron bars to the two limestone piers, spanning 176 m (577 ft). He combined pragmatism and grace to reveal the superb tensile capacity of iron. While iron tie-bars had been used since the time of Brunelleschi's dome, they had never appeared so dominant or visible. Telford endowed the masonry abutments with picturesque

▼ 1790

Jeremy Bentham proposes the Panopticon as an architectural solution to control behavior

Thomas Telford's Menai Suspension Bridge, Wales

▲ 1819

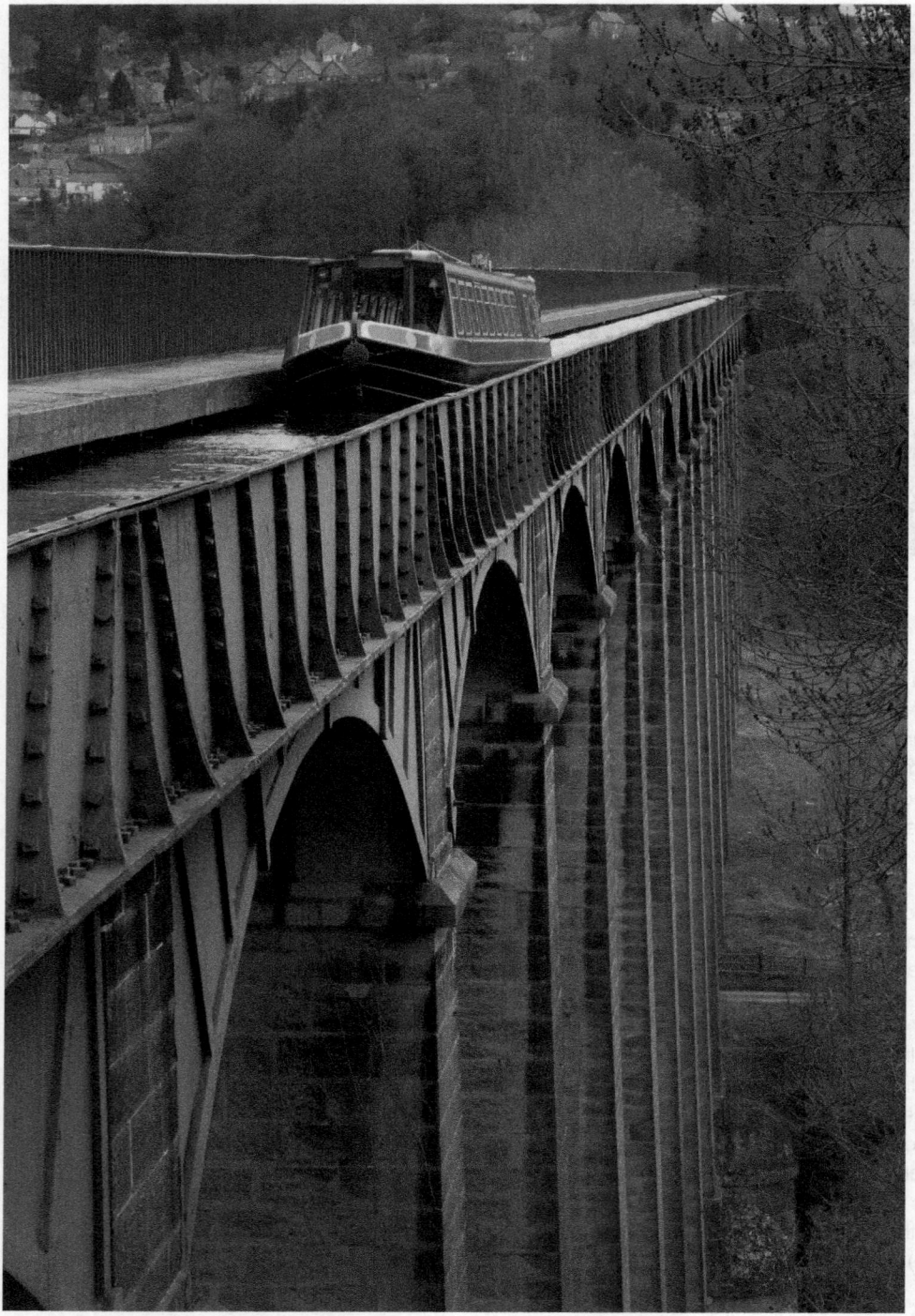

Figure 14.3-2 East Wales. Pontcysyllte Aqueduct on the Llangollen Canal, Thomas Telford, 1795–1805.

tiratoi sheds that lined the Arno in fourteenth-century Florence, set the precedents for this type. However, the factory, as the new unit of industrial production in England, integrated industrially produced materials and machines with buildings. The English factory type surpassed the height and breadth of all other urban structures except cathedrals.

The patronage for industry outside of England usually remained the exclusive right of a sovereign, which partly explains why other nations' factories often resembled palaces. Ledoux's industrial compound at Chaux was only one of many royal enterprises in France organized like grand châteaux. The engineer Pierre Toufaire (1739–1794) built the cast-iron foundry at Le Creusot for Louis XVI a few years before the French Revolution, relying on the technical advice of British industrialist William Wilkinson. The compound followed a palace plan, with a *U*-shaped court and a segmental pediment above the central block. The Spanish royal sponsorship in 1728 of the Fábrica de Tabacos of Seville (Fig. 14.3-4)—the cigarette factory that employed the fictional Carmen in Bizet's famous opera—produced a two-story facade similar to a Baroque palace. Its vast hypostyle masonry structure, punctured with various courtyards, covered an area about one-third larger than the Great Mosque of Córdoba and just slightly smaller than the Escorial.

In England a new class of industrial entrepreneurs sponsored, and occasionally designed, the factories, often resulting in severe, utilitarian buildings. In 1765 Benjamin Wyatt II created the building for Boulton and Watt's Soho Manufactory in Birmingham, which produced the first steam engines. Although it initially looked like a palace, with a Palladian thermal window and Doric columns at its entry, as the factory grew, pragmatic needs compromised its formal order, leading to the construction of many appendages and added courtyards. Likewise, the initial structure of the 1768 Etruria pottery works in Burslem founded by Josiah Wedgwood (1730–1795) followed classical organization, with a central pediment over the entry block and a rotunda at each end.

massing and decorated the metal surfaces with molded filigree. These gestures to architectural niceties did little to hide the bridge's unprecedented scale and explicit use of industrial materials.

Industrialization exploited the new materials of advanced engineering to yield a new building type, the factory, a multistory rectangular box with abundant fenestration. Earlier industrial buildings, such as the rope-making halls of the seaports of Venice and Amsterdam and the wool-dying

Figure 14.3-3 Isle of Anglesey, Wales. Menai Suspension Bridge, Telford, 1819.

Figure 14.3-4 Seville, Spain. Royal Tobacco Factory, Ignacio Sala, 1728.

Figure 14.3-5 Derby, England. Silk factory, John Lombes, 1721.

Like Lombes, he employed several hundred workers in each of his factories, many of whom were children. For these early, semirural factories the owners supplied long barrack housing for the workers.

Arkwright's ex-partner Jedediah Strutt (1726–1797) built several cotton mills in the town of Belper, near Derby, with his engineer son, William Strutt. In response to the devastating fire that destroyed the Albion Mills in London in 1791, they introduced the first **fireproof construction** mill a year later, using segmental-vault brick ceilings and cast-iron columns (Fig. 14.3-6). The West Mill, which still stands today, rose six stories. They ran a single row of iron columns the length of its interior production halls, designing them with a cruciform section, a significant conceptual break from the traditional cylindrical form. To fireproof the wooden beams, they embedded them in brick vaults and covered them with plaster. Strutt's factories used a mixture of waterwheels and steam engines, placed in separate sheds adjacent to the production halls.

The final improvement to the design of the factory type came with the Ditherington flax mill (Fig. 14.3-7), built for a team of business associates in 1796. One of the partners, Charles Bage (1751–1822), designed the structure. He inserted a grid of cast-iron beams joined to the slender cast-iron columns, resulting in a

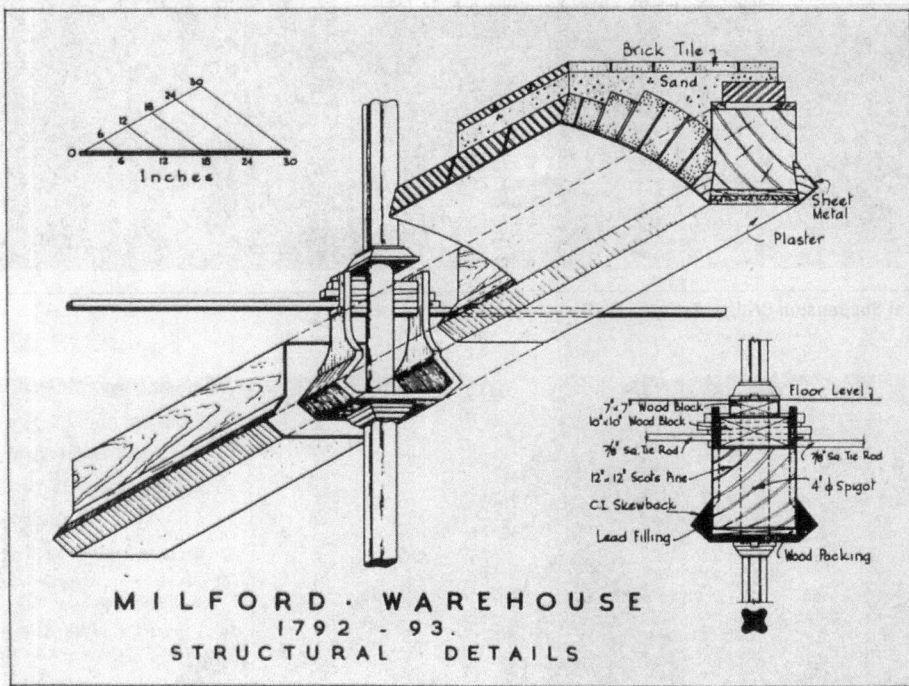

MILFORD · WAREHOUSE
1792 - 93.
STRUCTURAL DETAILS

Figure 14.3-6 Belper, England. Factory design, with structural cast-iron columns and fireproof ceilings, Jedediah and William Strutt, 1792.

John Lombes (1693–1722) introduced the first box-type factory in 1721 in Derby (Fig. 14.3-5), about 100 km (62 miles) south of Manchester. It housed his waterwheel-driven silk mill in a six-story parallelepiped with flat parapets masking the pitched roof. Lombes employed 300 workers to produce silk using a process that he had plagiarized from Italian silk makers. Based on Lombes's model, Richard Arkwright (1732–1792), the inventor of the "water frame" technique for driving cotton looms, built several large mills in the Derby area. His Masson Mill at Cromford, built in 1783, stood as a stripped-down, utilitarian block, with a single gesture to classical decoration—a central row of *serlianas*.

thin metal skeleton. At the advice of the younger Strutt, Bage placed the columns at 3 m (10 ft) intervals and gave them a cruciform section. The columns gently flared with entasis to resist buckling, and the beams thickened on their undersides where they needed more strength, resulting in the inverted-*T* beam. Bage split the capitals of some of the columns into a *U* shape so that the crankshafts of the looms could pass through them. His ingenious series of pragmatic structural solutions unwittingly fulfilled the functionalist precepts of Lodoli.

Arkwright built the first of the big cotton mills of Manchester in 1782. During the next twenty years nearly 100 mills appeared to compete with his. In 1799 Boulton and Watt built the Philips and Lee mill at Salford, a town that had fused with Manchester's northwestern edge. Here, they introduced hollow iron columns, which also served as heating conduits. The imposing bulk of the new factory structures, along with their homeliness, marked a disturbing rupture from earlier urban prospects. Visitors recoiled from the overwhelming bluntness of the factories. These raw buildings, rude and expedient, soon became the source of the greatest concentrations of capital in Europe. While visiting Manchester in 1826 architect Karl Friedrich Schinkel drew a quick sketch of the crowded conditions on the Rochdale Canal, including the eight-story McConnel and Kennedy Mill, which at its height employed 1,500 workers. Nearly two decades later another German visitor, Friedrich Engels (1820–1895), was inspired to po-

Figure 14.3-7 Ditherington, England. Flax mill, showing cruciform-section columns with hollow capitals for placing crankshafts, Charles Bage, 1796.

litical activism after encountering the environmental horrors and social injustice of Manchester, which to him represented "the grim future of capitalism and the industrial age."

Severe crowding, unfair labor conditions, lack of sanitary infrastructure, and air pollution were among the many urban pathologies that plagued Manchester as the vanguard of modernity. Women made up more than half of the city's industrial workforce, while at least 15% were under the age of fourteen. The inhumane conditions led to forms of resistance. Reformers compiled the first report on the exploitation of children, the "unknown, unprotected, and forgotten," in 1795. Frustrated laborers joined the Luddite movement, which began vindictive attacks on industrial equipment in 1811 as a direct assault on the unfairness of the new factory system. The trade union movement became a more effective means of struggle, leading to organized strikes. The first socialist league took root in Manchester. The French essayist Alexis de Tocqueville (1805–1859) best captured the jarring contradictions of industrial Manchester after his visit in 1835: "From this foul drain the greatest stream of human industry flows out to fertilize the whole world. From this filthy sewer pure gold flows. Here humanity attains its most complete development and its most brutish; here civilization works its miracles, and civilized man is turned back almost into a savage."

Building Character: The Birth of the Penitentiary

While the Industrial Revolution produced great wealth, it also encouraged widespread pauperism. The poor who could no longer make a living from the land ended up in the cities. Unable to find employment, they often turned to crime or welfare. As industry expanded, places of incarceration,

prisons and workhouses, appeared in the effort to contain the growing numbers of indigents and social misfits. For Piranesi the prison provided an allegorical vision of the sublime, the terrifying beauty of claustrophobic dungeons. For the leaders of industrial society, however, the design of the prison became an urgent mission, inspiring the development of various strategies of confinement. The penitentiary joined the factory as a new building type that facilitated the inauguration of the industrial age.

Prior to the late eighteenth century, the judicial officials of Europe improvised their prisons in the foundations and attics of castles. The fourteenth-century fortress of the Bastille in Paris served this purpose and was destroyed during the French Revolution as a symbol of injustice. Filarete, in his fictional city of Sforzinda (1460) (see Section 10.1), proposed to eliminate the death penalty and build a more humane prison on a hospital-like model for long-term inmates. The Venetian republic sponsored the first structure designed specifically as a prison, the Prigioni Nuove ("New Prisons") (Fig. 14.3-8a), built in 1589 next to the ducal palace. The architect, Antonio da Ponte (1512–1595), masked the severe rustication and barred windows of the block with an arcaded palatial facade for the offices of justice looking toward the Grand Canal. The courtyard of the Prigioni Nuove was severe, made of stripped-down mass and square windows cut uniformly into the stone elevations without moldings, the sort of structural honesty that appealed to Lodoli. The ornate Bridge of Sighs (Fig. 14.3-8b), designed by da Ponte's nephew Antonio Contino, connected the upper story of the new prison to the judicial chambers in the ducal palace. Its capricious crest of reverse-curve scrolls offered a profound contrast to the austere style of

Figure 14.3-8 Venice. (a) New Prisons, Antonio da Ponte, 1580s. (b) Bridge of Sighs, Antonio Contino, 1650.

the prison. The architect divided the passage into a path for those entering and another for those leaving to avoid contact between the two.

A greater improvement on prison design came from the maritime republic to the north, the Netherlands, which founded "houses of correction" at the end of the sixteenth century. The movement for these workhouses began in Amsterdam with the Rasphuis for men (1596) and the Spinhuis for women (1597). The burghers proposed these institutions as a means of encouraging the redemption of the prisoner through forced labor: sawing logs and making dyes from wood shavings for the men, spinning and weaving for the women. The monumental gate of the Rasphuis in Amsterdam carried on its frontispiece an image of two chained captives on either side of a figure representing punishment. Below the figures a triumphal cart carried the logs used in the jail.

Reformers in England adopted the workhouse concept at Bridewell Prison, named after a London palace used as a prison. The workhouses were intended to train and employ indigents but by the eighteenth century had become places of drudgery. The Poor Laws, instituted in 1601 and amended many times, by the mid-eighteenth century had generated about 2,000 workhouses, caring for over 100,000 inmates. The goal of helping poor people to produce goods while getting them back into society, however, gained little support and led to the institutionalization of the poor in degrading circumstances.

The great prison reformer John Howard (1726–1790) documented the deplorable conditions of European prisons at the time of the Enlightenment. Having managed a county jail while serving as a high sheriff, he was enraged by local conditions and sought better models of prisons elsewhere. After traveling all over Europe, he published the *State of Prisons in England and Wales* in 1777, followed by *An Account of the Principal Lazarettos in Europe* in 1789, denouncing the unsanitary, lightless environments and dehumanizing treatment of prisoners. Howard provided analytical engravings in the style of the *Encyclopedia*, showing plans and sections of prisons. His positive examples included the *Silentium* of San Michele in Rome (1703–1735) (see Section 13.2) and the Ackerghem Prison in Ghent, Belgium (1772–1775), both of which were supplied with solitary cells, which in Howard's words "separate the young from the old, and force them both, in solitude, with labour and low diet, to make experiment how far their natural strength of mind can support them under guilt and shame and poverty."

Empress Maria Teresa of Austria sponsored the Ghent prison in her program of reform. The four rows of cellblocks followed a radial design. Most of the institutions of incarceration built for the Habsburgs in this period used radial plans, including the Narrenturm insane asylum in Vienna, built in 1784 (Fig. 14.3-9). Each cell of the round tower of Narrenturm had space for two beds and a corner sink set

Figure 14.3-9 Vienna. Narrenturm insane asylum, 1780s.

in a radial pattern around annular corridors. A chapel occupied the center of its circular court.

George Dance the Younger (1741–1825) designed the Newgate Prison in London as the major English prison of Howard's time. Finished in 1778, it was rebuilt only two years later after being burned down in a riot. Howard attempted to influence its design and program, but the administrators quickly abandoned his suggestion of solitary cells in favor of collective halls and chained prisoners. The architect put most of his effort into the front facade, creating an imposing mass with heavily rusticated elements in the style of the firewall surrounding the imperial fora in Rome. The only windows appeared in the central administration block. Chains carved in the frieze over the front gate indicated the prison's unreformed method of confinement. The rusticated facade offered a grim backdrop for public executions. Rather than creating a program for rehabilitation or moral instruction, Newgate reverted to the use of intimidating iconography and repression, close in spirit to the brooding visions of Piranesi.

Howard died of typhus in 1790 while inspecting prisons in Crimea and thus never returned to England to build his ideal prison. His ideas shaped those of other reformers, however, such as William Blackburn (1750–1790), who built the Liverpool Gaol in 1785–1789 on the model of the Ghent prison. Its six radiating wings had corridors lined with individual cells to separate the prisoners. Jeremy Bentham (1748–1832) became Howard's most influential follower. He included prison reform as part of his theory of utilitarianism, or "the greatest good for the greatest number." In 1791 Bentham published a treatise on the model prison, the Panopticon, and spent most of his time and money during the next two decades trying to get it built. The radial plan derived from an experimental workhouse built in 1786 by his brother Samuel in Russia. Like the Narrenturm in Vienna, the cells of Bentham's ideal project radiated around a cylinder. Instead of being enclosed on their inner walls, the cells opened to the center so that the prisoner in solitary confinement could be observed behind an iron grille from a central control booth. The inmates could not see if anyone occupied the booth or not, and thus, the building created a feeling of "invisible omniscience." Bentham envisioned stepped rows of seats for daily prayer services between the supervisor's core and the cells. He intended the Panopticon as a machine for surveillance, leading to its name, meaning the "all-seeing place." This conception introduced a new psychological dimension into architectural theory, which the late-twentieth-century philosopher Michel Foucault considered an insidious proposal for social control.

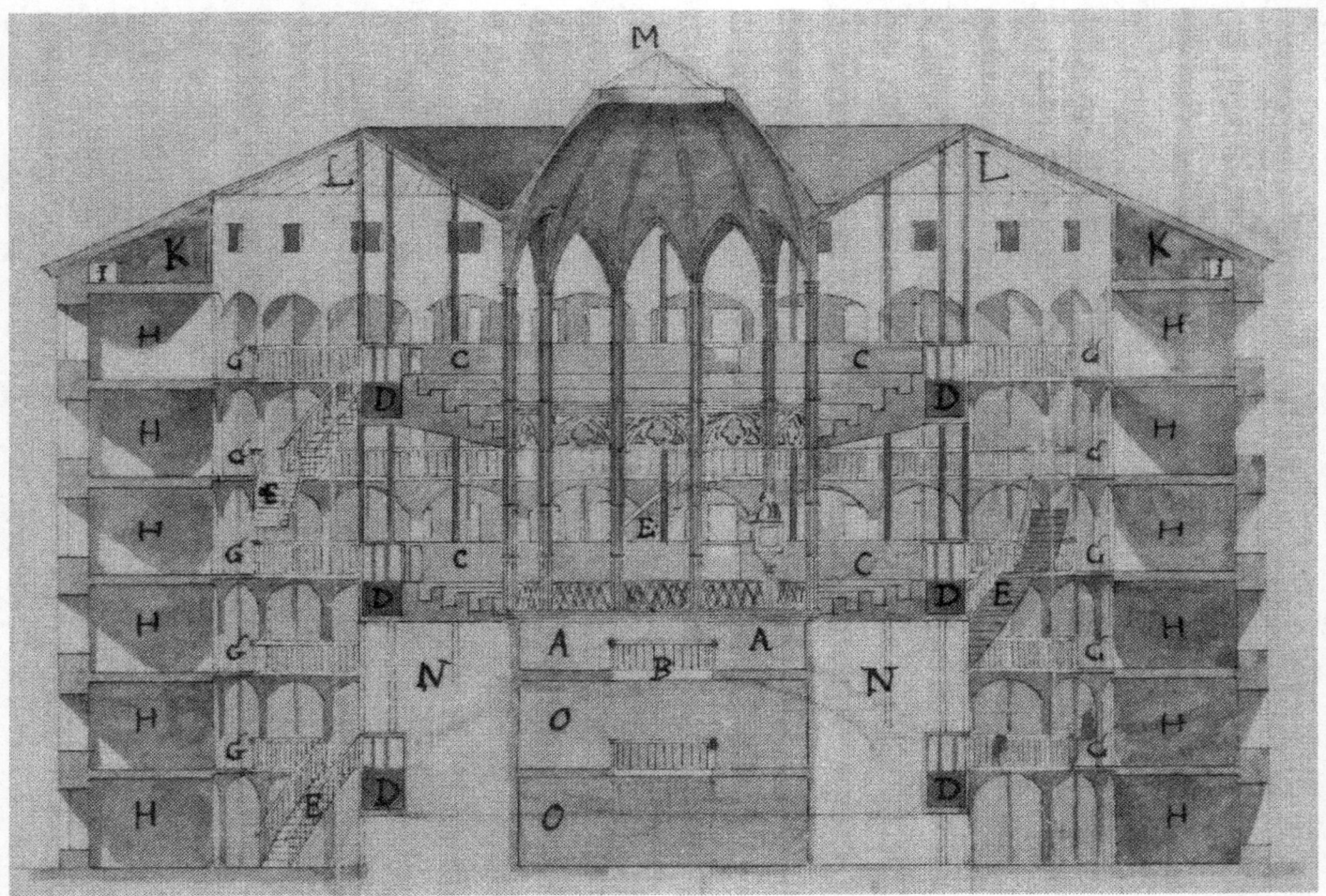

Figure 14.3-10 England. Jeremy Bentham's design for the Panopticon, 1790.

The Panopticon presumed that people would behave properly if they thought they were being watched.

Bentham believed his invention suitable for innumerable disciplinary situations, such as schools, hospitals, asylums, workhouses, and factories. As he put it, "Morals reformed—health preserved—industry invigorated—instruction diffused—public burdens lightened—economy seated, as it were, upon a rock—the Gordian knot of the Poor Law not cut, but untied—all by a simple idea in Architecture!" He patented the Panopticon (Fig. 14.3-10), a structure that would have been supported on slender cast-iron columns and roofed by a glazed ceiling, but he never saw it constructed.

That Bentham proposed the Panopticon for the design of factories reveals the disciplinary problems of the workplace. Many depictions of the early factory work halls show supervisors carrying whips. William Strutt sponsored the sole application of Bentham's idea to industry in the Round House, added in 1803 to his collection of factory buildings at Belper (Fig. 14.3-11). To visually control the workers inside the cylindrical structure, Strutt placed a central revolving supervisor's chamber on a swivel driven by the wind.

When the British government finally settled on its model prison, it bypassed Bentham's idea of surveillance in favor of structures for solitary confinement. The models for the British institution came from the United States, where the Quaker-inspired "Philadelphia system" fostered works such as John Haviland's Cherry Hill Prison, or Eastern Penitentiary (Fig. 14.3-12a,b). The seven radiating wings of the original structure of 1821 had a single story, and each prisoner remained in solitary silence in isolated cells with a small garden. The guards controlled the corridors by a system of angled mirrors. The cells contained a private sink and toilet. The model British prison at Pentonville, built in 1840 by Joshua Jebb (1793–1863), repeated the radiating layout and solitary cell with services. The model was also used in Manchester at Strangeways Prison, built by Alfred Waterhouse (1830–1905) in 1868 as a perfect radial figure with six arms, leading to a twelve-sided polygonal tower in the center.

Bentham's philosophy demonstrated the contradictions of modernity. He proposed at once to liberate and to repress. While he dreamed of the model place of confinement, he also campaigned for most of the great liberal causes that became the basis of modern social emancipation. Bentham published pamphlets against slavery and in support of the separation of church and state, the freedom of the press, women's rights, animal rights, divorce, and the decriminalization of sodomy. He encouraged the founding of London University so that not only the privileged with connections to the Anglican Church could receive a higher education. Yet alongside his goal of maximizing freedom, he remained obsessed with the penitentiary and punitive

Figure 14.3-11 Belper, England. Industrial application of the Panopticon at factory, Round House, William Strutt, 1790s.

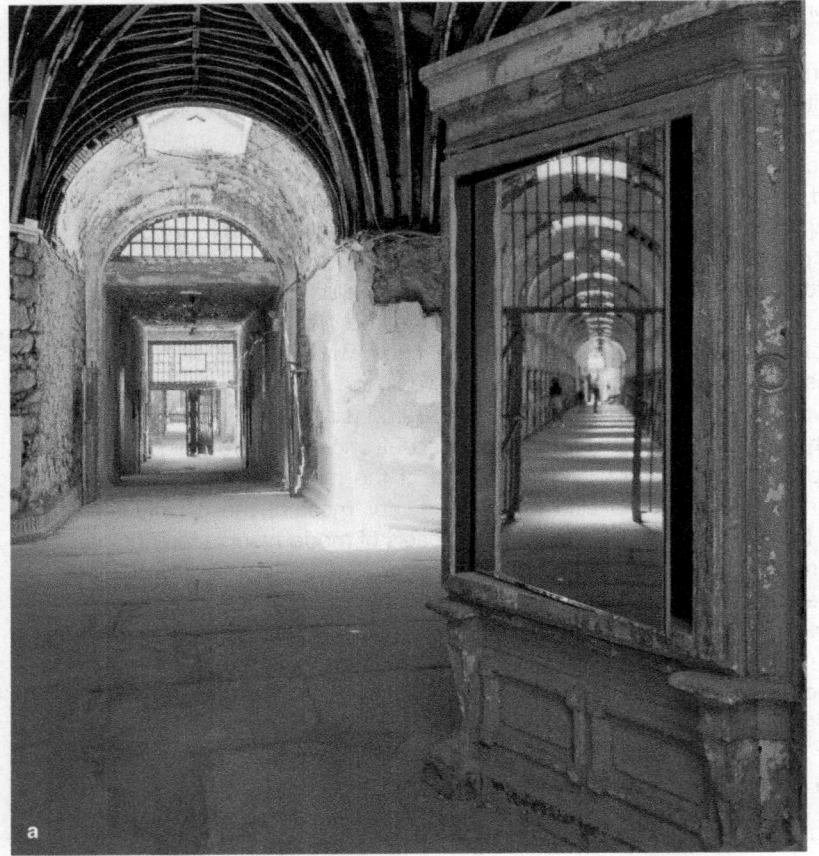

surveillance. Bentham could not imagine happiness for the greatest number without his design for the control of the misfits.

Further Reading

Bender, John. *Imagining the Penitentiary: Fiction and the Architecture of Mind in Eighteenth-Century England*. Chicago: University of Chicago Press, 1987.

Foucault, Michel. *Discipline and Punish: The Birth of the Prison*. Translated by A. Sheridan. New York: Random House, 1977.

Marcus, Steven. *Engels, Manchester, and the Working Class*. New York: W. W. Norton, 1974.

Markus, Thomas A. *Buildings and Power: Freedom and Control in the Origin of Modern Building Types*. London: Routledge, 1993.

Pevsner, Nicholaus. *A History of Building Types*. Princeton, NJ: Princeton University Press, 1976.

Semple, Janet. *Bentham's Prison: A Study of the Panopticon Penitentiary*. Oxford: Clarendon Press, 1993.

↗ Visit the free website **www.oup.com/us/ingersoll** to view chapter outlines and study questions; Google Maps showing the location of key sites; links to UNESCO World Heritage Sites; and essays on topics that cross time and culture.

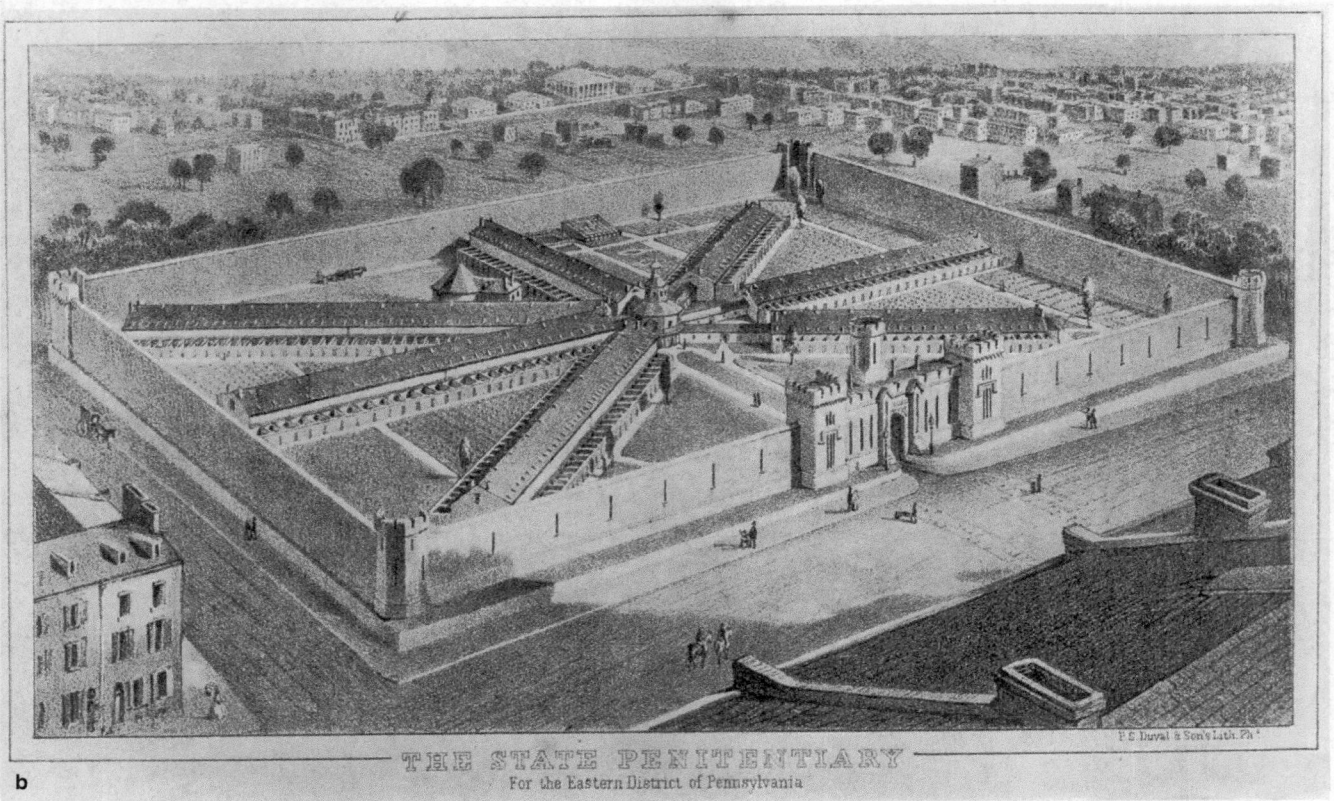

Figure 14.3-12 Philadelphia. (a) Cherry Hill, Eastern Penitentiary, John Havilands, 1821. (b) Plan.

1800–1850

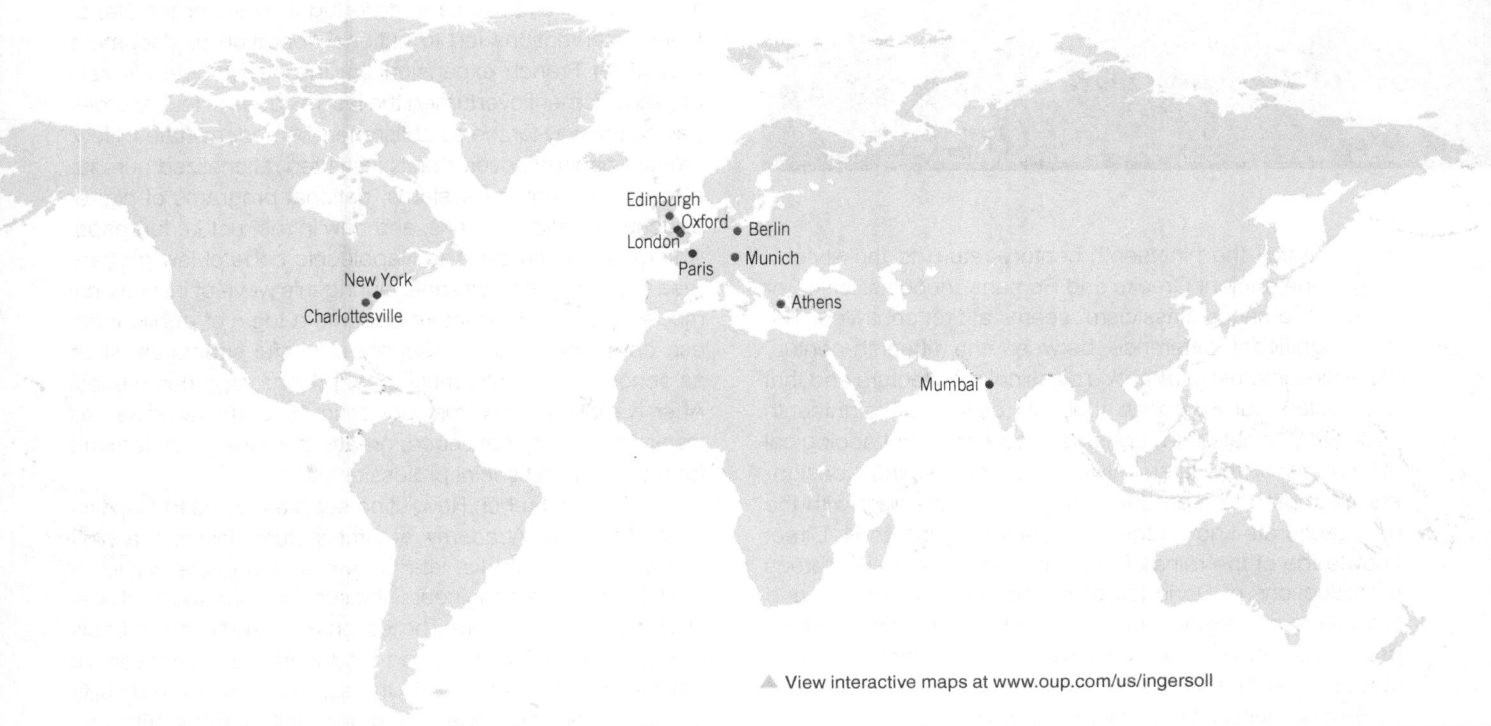

▲ View interactive maps at www.oup.com/us/ingersoll

15.1   AFTER THE REVOLUTION: The Ideological Uses of Neoclassicism

15.2   THE GOTHIC REVIVAL: Antimodern and Proto-Nationalist

15.3   THE NEW IRON AGE: The Spread of Metal and Glass Technologies

The nineteenth century opened with Napoléon Bonaparte's clamorous efforts to impose the principles of the French Revolution on the rest of Europe, establishing dependent states within a hypothetical European empire under French rule. During the same period the British extended their colonial interests throughout the world, mostly through mercantile relationships. In a variety of political contexts, the rational system of Greco-Roman classicism suited the call for clarity and utility and soon began to represent nationalist agendas, ranging from Napoléon's program of empire building to the American call for republicanism and the goals of the Prussian and Bavarian monarchies. The revival of Gothic style appeared soon after, proposed by some as the antidote to the dehumanizing effects of industrialism and by others as the correct national style. In France the interest in Gothic style derived from efforts to preserve the state's medieval historic patrimony. Viollet-le-Duc focused attention on the structural ingenuity of medieval buildings as an inspiration for modern architects of the industrial age. The industrial production of such building materials as cast iron and large panes of glass led to the possibility of lightweight and transparent ferrovitreous structures. While proposed initially for working structures, such as train sheds and hothouses, the ferrovitreous solution, used in the construction of the Crystal Palace for the 1851 International

Exhibition in London, resoundingly demonstrated the virtues of industrial technologies, bringing a new level of efficiency to the question of utility in architecture.

15.1   AFTER THE REVOLUTION
The Ideological Uses of Neoclassicism

To call the nineteenth-century return to the style of the ancient Greeks and Romans "neoclassicism" or "Romantic classicism" seems at first contrived. The only significant difference between the fifteenth-century Florentine interest in *all'antica* classical architecture and that of neoclassical European theorists of the late eighteenth and early nineteenth centuries was the archaeological awareness of the later revival. Post-Renaissance designers attempted to reproduce images from the past with the more accurate knowledge of documentary sources. Direct knowledge of the ruins of ancient Greece led to numerous reproductions of Doric temples. The ruins of Pompeii and Herculaneum, excavated in the mid-eighteenth century, produced a new vision of classical interiors, influencing attitudes toward furniture and decoration.

Beyond questions of style, what made neoclassicism different from earlier classical revivals was its social and technical context. Both the French Revolution and the Industrial Revolution generated new motivations for the embrace of classical architecture. The emancipatory aims of the first favored a universal architecture accessible to all, and the economic demands of the second required expedient assembly and standardization. Replicas and variations of the Parthenon, the Propylaia, the Maison Carrée, and the Pantheon proliferated among the new institutions of the growing cities of France, England, Germany, Russia, and the United States. Despite differing ideological intentions, by the mid-nineteenth century neoclassicism had become one of many possible styles in the panoply of historical revivals, vying with Neo-Gothic, Neo-Romanesque, and even the neo-Hindu of colonial India.

"Utility Circumscribes Everything": From Durand's Rationalism to Nationalism

Napoléon exported the discourse of the French Revolution to the rest of Europe through aggressive military campaigns. His wars attracted the support of republican sympathizers in Belgium, Switzerland, Italy, Germany, Poland, and, to a lesser extent, Spain and Portugal. Whether the Napoleonic interventions led to national liberation or became a pretext for French expansionism, the new emperor's self-aggrandizement overturned the last residues of feudal order, paving the way for the establishment of modern states. New, French-inspired governments instituted rationalized bureaucracies; efficient tax systems; national programs of higher education; national banks; and new infrastructure for roads, water, and sanitation. The Napoleonic code of law guaranteed the rights of all citizens. During this wave of institutional modernization, architecture became a topic of public interest, concerned with the supply of useful structures, such as schools, hospitals, museums, prisons, and cemeteries. After Napoléon's fall from power in 1815, these advances toward modernity continued, greatly increasing the demand for technical and social professionals.

In 1793 the French Revolution suppressed Jean-Baptiste Colbert's Royal Academy of Architecture, favoring a new school of public works, later known as the École Polytechnique. Primarily for engineers, the school promoted a rational approach to architecture. The lessons of Jean-Nicholas-Louis Durand (1760–1834) provided the theoretical foundation for the creation of buildings with the same sense of universality as the Napoleonic Code. Rather than following the Vitruvian triad of *firmitas–utilitas–venustas* (solidity–utility–beauty), Durand proposed a new formula: economy–simplicity–convenience (Fig. 15.1-1). He wrote, "It is obvious that to please has never been the purpose of architecture. Public and private utility, the well-being and the maintenance of individuals and society, that is the aim of architecture."

As an assistant to Étienne-Louis Boullée, Durand conserved much of his master's rational geometry. The younger architect objected, however, to the primacy of "character," or a building's emotional impact. While Boullée produced breathtaking projects of unrelieved mass, his disciple attempted to eliminate such effects in his program for pragmatic, standardized plans. Although Durand and his associate Louis-Michel Thibault consistently won the major

1740–1786

Reign of Frederick II (the Great) of Prussia

Somerset House built by William Chambers in London

▲ 1776

1780s

Brandenburg Gate built by Carl Gotthard Langhans in Berlin

Jean-Nicholas-Louis Durand presents his compositional method in *Précis des leçons d'architecture données à l'École polytechnique*

▲ 1802–1805

competitions that took place during the Revolution, this success did not lead to built works. Their winning entry for a "temple to equality" in 1794 (Fig. 15.1-2) showed Boullée's influence in the rendering of a pure volume charged with the sort of symbolic qualities that Durand later rejected. The unbuilt project set a small peripteral temple on a stepped base and achieved a crisper delineation of its profile with square, rather than round, columns. Each of the front six columns carried a human head as a capital and an inscription devoted to a virtue promoted by the new revolutionary society of equals: wisdom, economy, work, peace, courage, and prudence. Following Boullée, the young designers proposed to literally write the building's message on the facade.

In *Précis des leçons d'architecture données à l'École polytechnique* (1802–1805), Durand presented his compositional method of reducing all **types** and forms to a series of standardized parts that fit into a basic proportional grid. He proposed his universal matrix, which simplified the modular systems of the Greeks and Romans without reference to styles or historical sources. Durand urged architects to avoid imitation, concentrating on rational production. He considered decoration and symbolism auxiliary to basic design. He thus analyzed the famous buildings of the past in terms of a universal grid. Although he avoided the topic of new materials, Durand insisted that the structural logic of simple forms and the spatial relationships

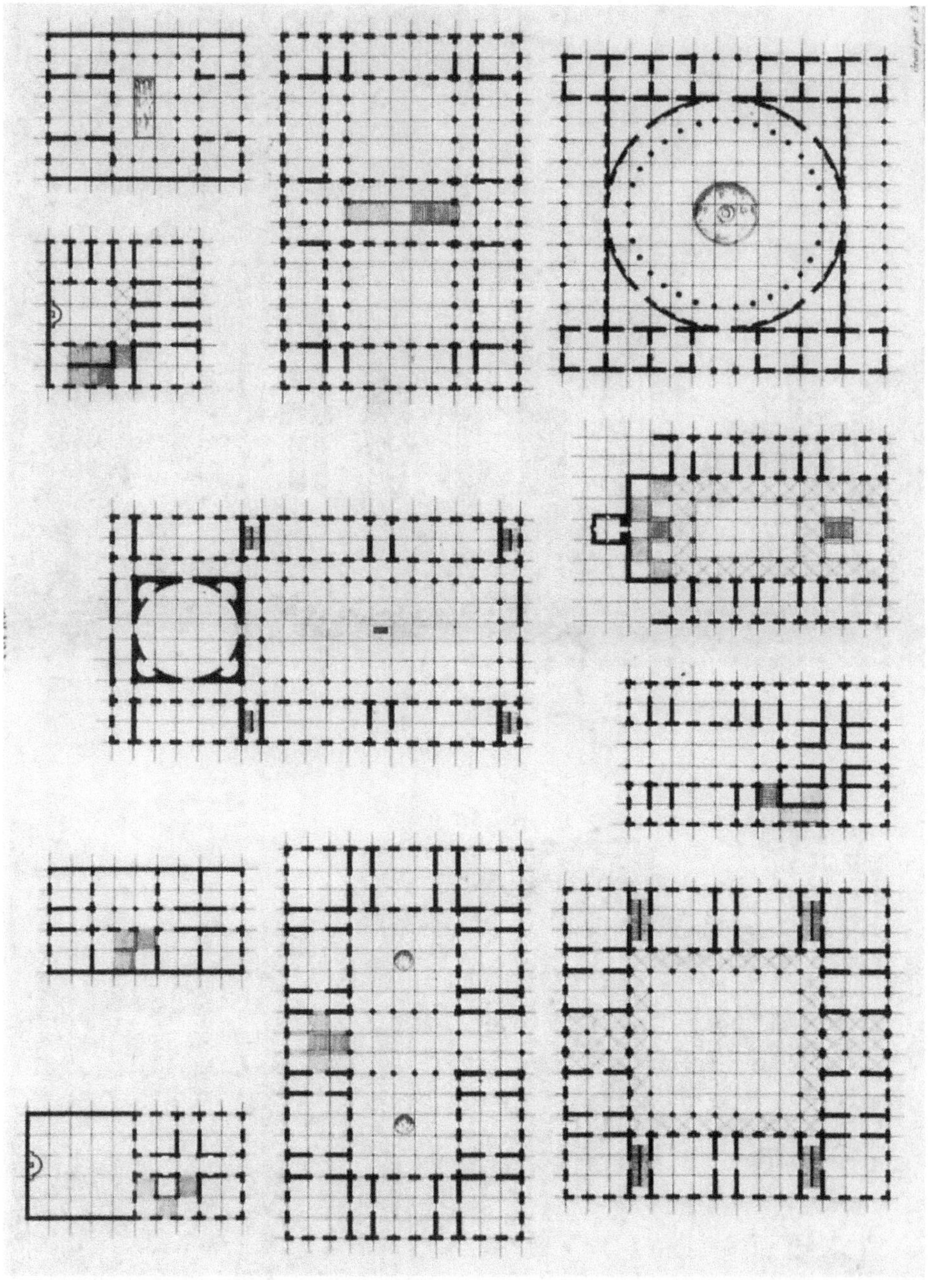

Figure 15.1-1 Postrevolutionary France. Jean-Nicholas-Louis Durand's universal grid applied to plans of different types, from *Précis des leçons d'architecture données à l'École Polytechnique*, 1802–1805.

▼ **1803**

Thomas Jefferson hires Benjamin Henry Latrobe as surveyor of public buildings in Washington, D.C.

John Soane begins his house in London

▲ **1810**

▼ **1815**

Napoléon defeated at Waterloo

Karl Friedrich Schinkel appointed director of Prussian Building Commission in Berlin

▲ **1816**

▼ **1816**

Leo von Klenze begins first project for Ludwig I of Bavaria, the Glyptothek Museum, in Munich

obtained through rational method saved time and money. His ideal of creating an expedient, standardized system in the interests of economy appeared analogous to the approach outlined in the twelfth-century Chinese manual *Yingzao Fashi* (see Section 11.1), which standardized building parts and compositional solutions.

While Durand's utilitarian method corresponded to Napoléon's efforts to rationalize the military, the bureaucracy, and the planning agencies, it exerted wide influence beyond France, particularly in Prussia, the best-organized and most enlightened of the semiautonomous territories of Germany. Its capital, Berlin, grew from two small castle towns into an orderly city during the seventeenth century and by the time of Frederick II, the Great (r. 1740–1786), prevailed as both the center of a great military power and a beacon of tolerance. Frederick, as an enlightened monarch, was committed to the coexistence of religions and the abolition of torture and slavery. Voltaire described Frederick's Berlin as "Sparta by day and Athens by night." The city's gridded additions hooked up to the broad planted boulevard of Unter den Linden, which served as the military parade ground. The western expansion included three major gates, each served by a differently shaped plaza: one square, one octagonal, and the most southerly circular. The accomplished classicist Carl Gotthard Langhans (1732–1808) came to Berlin toward the end of

Figure 15.1-3 Berlin. Brandenburg Gate, Carl Gotthard Langhans, 1780s.

Thomas Jefferson begins the campus for University of Virginia

1817

▼ **1823**

Karl Friedrich Schinkel begins Altes Museum in Berlin

Otto I, son of Ludwig I of Bavaria, named first king of modern Greece

▲ **1833**

▼ **1833**

Washington Monument begun in Washington, D.C.

Figure 15.1-4 Berlin. Project for a monument to Fredrick the Great, Friedrich Gilly, 1797.

the eighteenth century to design a theater and added a decorative gate to the square plaza. His Brandenburg Gate (Fig. 15.1-3) shows how much German architects had absorbed the lessons of French architecture during the time of the *Encyclopedia*. The composition of the six-column Doric portico flanked symmetrically by lower colonnaded structures evoked Julien-David Leroy's depictions of the Propylaia in Athens.

Langhans joined David Gilly (1748–1808), an architect from a French Huguenot family, as codirector of royal works. Berlin welcomed the Huguenots after the repeal of the Edict of Nantes in 1685 had forced them to abandon France. Gilly founded the city's first architectural school. His son, Friedrich Gilly (1772–1800), spent time in revolutionary Paris, where he studied the unbuilt projects of Boullée. His 1797 proposal for a monument to Frederick the Great (Fig. 15.1-4) became the cornerstone of German neoclassical architecture. Although never constructed, its bold massing of a pyramidal series of terraces supporting a stark Doric temple inspired many imitations.

After Gilly's untimely demise, his good friend Karl Friedrich Schinkel (1781–1841) attempted to complete some of the young architect's unfinished projects. Schinkel traveled to Rome and Sicily to gain firsthand knowledge of ancient buildings, producing cold, analytical drawings of panoramic scenes that delineated every minimal detail. After the end of the Napoleonic Wars, he served for two decades as the city architect of Berlin, adding key public buildings that defined the city's character as both orderly and civil. Schinkel did not design with Durand's universal grid, but his approach to public projects followed a personal code of classical

standards close to the rationalist method. The first of his urban works, the Neue Wache (Fig. 15.1-5), begun in 1816, served as a guardhouse on Unter den Linden. Its program and prominent urban position glorified the use of military criteria for the design of Berlin. Schinkel wedged the six-column Doric **temple front** between two unrelieved masses so that it appeared like a fragment from the base of Gilly's unbuilt monument.

The following year, Schinkel rebuilt the Schauspielhaus theater (Fig. 15.1-6a) on Gendarmenmarkt, a few blocks away from the guardhouse. He reused the six Ionic columns from Langhans's original porch, creating a temple front at the top of a broad stair. He broke down the rest of the mass of the theater with rows of tall, narrow windows, which brought daylight into the circulation spaces and gave the structure an unusually open feeling. Inside, Schinkel indulged his calling as a set designer, often creating the scenes for operas performed there (Fig. 15.1-6b).

Figure 15.1-5 Berlin. Neue Wache, Karl Friedrich Schinkel, 1817.

Figure 15.1-6 Berlin. (a) Schauspielhaus, Schinkel, 1818. (b) Schinkel's set design showing a perspective scene featuring the theater set between the twin churches of Gendarmenmarkt Plaza, from *Sammlung architecktonischer Entwürfe*, 1819–1840.

In 1822 Schinkel began building Berlin's first museum, now referred to as the "Old," or Altes, Museum (Fig. 15.1-7a,b), on the river island facing the royal palace across the Lustgarten plaza. The eighteen columns of its Ionic portico recalled Boullée's colonnaded project for a public library, while the plan of long galleries framing a central pantheon-like rotunda seemed cribbed from a plan for a museum published by Durand in 1805. Schinkel's Altes Museum proved more complex than either source, however, neither following the dictates of a square grid nor forcing all of the rooms into perfect symmetrical relations. As one of the first great public museums, its colonnade offered a genuinely inviting *stoa* as a frame for a new, enlightened society.

As the most influential professor of architecture in Berlin, Schinkel preached a message similar to Durand's dictum that "utility is the fundamental principle of all building." He nonetheless pursued a less dogmatic approach to design. His interests in new materials and historical styles brought variety to his work. After a trip to England, where he observed the utilitarian brick and iron factories of Manchester, Schinkel designed Berlin's Bauakademie School of Architecture in 1831. The only one of his buildings that strictly followed a

Figure 15.1-7 Berlin. (a) Altes Museum, Schinkel, 1822. (b) Plan.

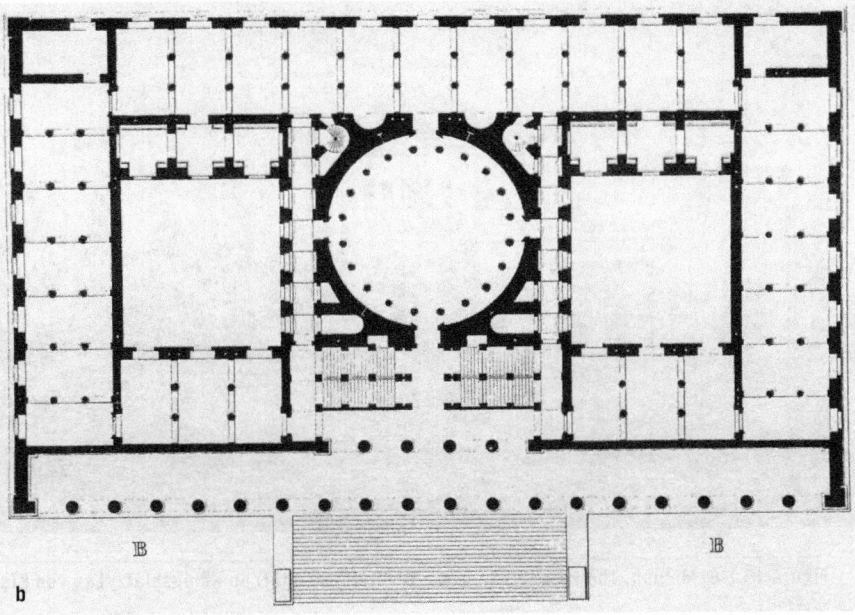

Durand-like square grid, the school also related to the point-loaded structures of British warehouses, built on a skeleton of cast-iron columns. The roofs sloped down from the parapets to an internal courtyard, like a Pompeian *atrium*, leaving the outside squared off as a crisp cube. Schinkel clad the four-story exterior in red brick with terra-cotta trim, lining the contours of each of the nine piers per side with yellow bricks. Like a cross between an Italian palazzo and a Manchester factory, the Bauakademie represented a utilitarian synthesis of past and present. Schinkel not only taught in the building but resided there in an apartment on the top floor for the rest of his life.

In Munich, the capital of the new state of Bavaria, Leo von Klenze (1784–1864) played a similar role to that assumed by Schinkel in Prussia. He had trained in Berlin with Friedrich Gilly and, after a tour of antiquities in Italy, moved to Paris to study under Durand. There, he met his future patron and fellow admirer of all things Greek, Ludwig I of Bavaria (r. 1825–1848). Klenze's first project in Munich, the Glyptothek Museum for plaster casts of famous ancient sculptures (Fig. 15.1-8), begun in 1816, closely adhered to Durand's models of galleries, covered by a succession of shallow domes and cross-vaults.

In 1825, as soon as his patron came to power, Klenze, along with a rival court architect, Friedrich von Gärtner (1791–1847), began creating a series of iconic buildings for state and municipal institutions inspired by the great works of ancient Greece and the Italian Renaissance. Munich acquired an Athenian-style propylaia, an imitation of Palazzo Farnese, a copy of the Loggia dei Lanzi, and a portico inspired by Brunelleschi's Foundling Hospital. The new facade of the Residenz, or royal palace, copied the massing of Palazzo Pitti while borrowing pilasters from Palazzo Rucellai. Klenze began his most original work, the Alte

Pinokothek (Old Picture Gallery) in 1825. The top-lit galleries provided the paintings with optimal illumination. His success on the project led to the commission for the Hermitage Museum in St. Petersburg from 1839 to 1851.

In the midst of the transformation of Munich, Ludwig I's eighteen-year-old son ascended to the throne of post-Ottoman Greece as that country's first elected monarch, Otto I (r. 1832–1862). The image of Athens, at this point a small town with a dense medieval fabric dotted with tiny Byzantine churches and ancient ruins, did not correspond to the German neoclassicist ideal of the classical city. Ludwig dispatched both Klenze and Gärtner in 1834 to make proposals for the new capital. Schinkel was also consulted, but Klenze objected to his scheme to place the new royal palace on the Acropolis behind the Parthenon. Klenze's new plan for Athens, based on an earlier proposal by local architects Stamatios Kleanthis (1802–1862) and Eduard Schaubert (1804–1860), situated the city's institutional structures, including the royal palace, on a triangular perimeter of modern boulevards that circumscribed the old city. Between 1840 and 1880 Athens acquired a dozen neoclassical buildings for modern institutions, including a city hall, parliament (Fig. 15.1-9), university, and archaeology museum. The resulting city appeared more "classical" than ancient Athens ever had.

Neoclassicism as Institutional Style: The British Isles

After England established its union with Scotland in 1707 and added Ireland in 1801, the British Isles became known as the "United Kingdom" and soon emerged as the dominant economy of the world. British military and maritime strength, following more than a decade of struggle with France, eventually prevailed over Napoléon in 1815. During

Figure 15.1-8 Munich. The Propylaia and the Glyptothek (right) on Königsplatz, Leo von Klenze, 1820s.

Figure 15.1-9 Athens. View to the neoclassical parliament, plan by Klenze, 1840–1880.

the first two decades of the century British business inter-ests took command of an international network of exchange whose interests ranged from the distribution of the indus-trial products of Manchester to the import of raw cotton from India, sugar from Barbados, and slaves from West Africa, to the smuggling of opium into China. The managers of the East India Company became the de facto government of India, protected by British soldiers. During the rest of the nineteenth century, the same sort of enterprise led to British colonization of half of Africa and half of Asia. When com-bined with the territories of Australia and Canada, these do-minions comprised the largest empire, in both population and land area, in the history of the world.

Despite such power, the public architecture of the British Isles appeared unsubstantial in comparison to other leading European countries. During the late eighteenth and early nineteenth centuries, with the United Kingdom's increas-ing imperial status, its leaders in the major cities of London, Dublin, and Edinburgh began to commission orderly clas-sical envelopes for institutional settings. New universities, museums, and government offices gave a public face to the empire. William Chambers, through his *Treatise on Civil*

Architecture (1759), defined the use of classical architec-ture for public buildings in late-eighteenth-century England. Born in Sweden to Scottish parents, Chambers served in his youth as a dependent of the East India Company and traveled extensively, visiting Asia three times. He won early distinction in 1750 for his exotic follies, the "House of Con-fucius," and the ten-story pagoda in Kew Gardens, soon after publishing a pamphlet on Chinese architecture (see Section 14.1). Influenced by both Giovanni Battista Piranesi in Rome and Jacques-François Blondel in Paris, Chambers assumed the title "architect of the king's works" in 1760. This led to his project for Somerset House (1776–1796) (Fig. 15.1-10), the major statement of institutional architec-ture in eighteenth-century London. Approximating the scale of the Louvre, this huge complex for government offices had a long central wing overlooking the riverbank. The rus-ticated base showed the architect's debt to Piranesi, while the decoration of the central block with a temple front and rounded cupola looked to French classicism. In one of the minor courtyards of Somerset House, Chambers set aside space for the Royal Academy, at which he served as the first professor of architecture.

Figure 15.1-10 London. Somerset House, William Chambers, 1776–1796.

a triumphal arch, freely inspired by the Arch of Constantine, with a hemispherical domed space based on the Pantheon. At Osterley Park, finished in 1780, he used the Greek Ionic order for the house's free-standing entry portico. Adam drew the greatest praise for his stunning interiors, which cited motifs found in Palmyra, Hadrian's Villa, the palace of Diocletian at Split, and the Acropolis in Athens. His Etruscan-style dressing room at Osterley Park evoked Piranesi's fantasies.

Adam's largest project in London, the Adelphi Terrace, begun in 1774, repeated the solution of Somerset House in site and scale, setting a long prospect on the Thames. Prepared as a speculative endeavor for apartment houses, with a lower level of warehouses to be leased to the government, the project failed as a result of financial ruin during the English economic depression that followed the American Revolution. Adam exerted more influence on public architecture in his native Edinburgh, where toward the end of his career he returned to design a series of important public buildings: the Register House for the state archives, with a temple front and **saucer dome**, and the University of Edinburgh, with a Doric triumphal arch entry. He also built a cylindrical mausoleum for his friend, the philosopher David Hume. Adam designed Charlotte Square for Edinburgh's New Town, a new, low-density suburb to the north of the original town, begun in 1767 on a plan by James Craig (1739–1795). Adam's addition furnished an elegant terminus for the central axis of

Figure 15.1-11 Derbyshire, England. (a) Kedleston Hall, begun by James Paine, 1760s, finished by Robert Adam, 1770s. (b) See facing page.

Chambers's chief rival in London, Robert Adam (1728–1792), came from a Scottish family of architects. He spent several fruitful years in Rome under the guidance of the French connoisseur Charles-Louis Clérisseau, who introduced him to Piranesi. Endowed with an accomplished archaeological perspective on ancient works, Adam created an original style by combining and imitating rather than copying classical models. For the garden facade at Kedleston Hall (1760–1770) (Fig. 15.1-11a,b), he united

the 30 m (98 ft) wide George Street. Each of the perimeter elevations appeared as a single palace. The northern side, only partly finished at the time of Adam's death in 1792, contained nine three-bay townhouses.

The generation that followed Adam in Edinburgh pursued a more orthodox classicism, aspiring to the ancient scale of Athens. Calton Hill became a simulacrum of the Acropolis, with a partial reconstruction of the Parthenon, built in 1822, serving as a national monument to celebrate

Figure 15.1-11b Derbyshire, England. Plan of Kedleston Hall, begun by James Paine, 1760s, finished by Robert Adam, 1770s.

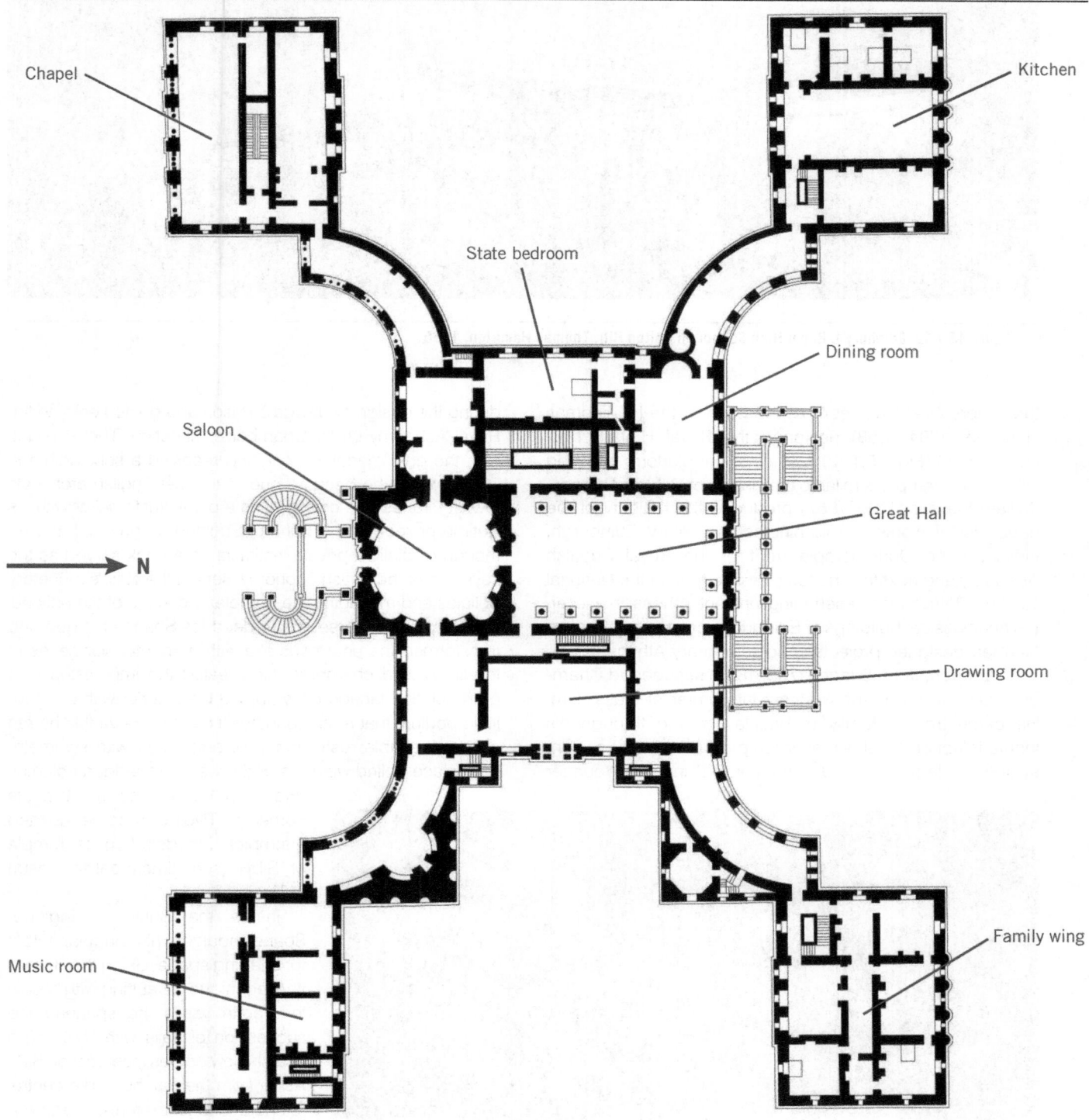

Chapel

Kitchen

State bedroom

Dining room

Saloon

Great Hall

N

Drawing room

Family wing

Music room

Figure 15.1-12 Edinburgh. Royal High School on Calton Hill, Thomas Hamilton, 1825.

the victory over Napoléon. At the base of the hill Thomas Hamilton (1784–1858) designed the Royal High School (1825–1829) (Fig. 15.1-12) as a classical platform crowned with a Doric temple, similar to the visions of Gilly and Klenze. William Playfair (1790–1857) produced the majority of the neoclassical works in mid-nineteenth-century Edinburgh, including the Doric temple front of the Royal Scottish Academy and next to it the Ionic temple front of the National Gallery. Rather than resembling ancient Athens, however, the neoclassical buildings of Edinburgh looked more like the German-designed projects of contemporary Athens.

In London, John Soane (1753–1837) succeeded Chambers and Adam as the greatest interpreter of classicism. He came from a family of bricklayers and through his innate talent and tireless research produced a magnificent synthesis. He apprenticed with George Dance the Younger during the design of Newgate Prison and gained entry to the Royal Academy under Chambers's direction. There, Soane won the gold medal in 1777 and received a scholarship to Rome, where he became one of the last English architects to visit Piranesi. He emerged as a public tastemaker with his lifetime project for the Bank of England, begun in 1788. Although officially a private institution, the bank served as the keystone of the British economy, setting the state's monetary policies and managing the complex workings of the national debt. Over the course of four decades Soane enlarged and transformed the enormous site with a spectacular series of top-lit, vaulted chambers. He created the impression of a grand unified facade by wrapping the exterior with a monolithic podium that reached to head height. Above this he ran an impenetrable rusticated wall, articulated with symmetrically placed blind windows and rows of embedded columns (Fig. 15.1-13). At the most acute corner, or Tivoli Corner, he inserted a tempietto, modeled on the Temple of Sibyl (sometimes called Vesta) in Tivoli.

Inside the Bank of England, Soane indulged his singular talent for shaping space. Using the Byzantine technique of vaulting with hollow terra-cotta vases, he spanned the succession of halls with light vaults and shallow domes (see Section 6.2). Aside from the Pantheon-like central rotunda, Soane preferred segmental arches, which gave the domes of the other halls a graceful saucer shape. He borrowed the idea of layered ceilings from Roman Baroque churches in order to diffuse daylight from central lanterns. Clerestories

Figure 15.1-13 London. Bank of England, John Soane, 1788–1830, depicted as ruins by Joseph Michael Gandy.

Figure 15.1-14 London. Soane House, John Soane, ca. 1810.
(a) Section by Michael Gandy. (b) Facade.

on the perimeter and lanterns in the center illuminated the great rotunda and the six counting halls, while classical columns and melancholy caryatids supported the upper lanterns.

During the same years of the bank's construction, Soane designed his own house on the square of Lincoln's Inn Fields. The Soane House (Fig. 15.1-14a) became a laboratory for architecture, a fantastic assembly of caryatids, saucer domes, and light traps in which the master displayed his collection of plaster casts of classical sculpture and architectural *spolia*. Soane treated the facade of his house with a minimum of decoration, emphasizing mass rather than classical details. In 1812 he added a thin screen of white Portland stone that jutted out 0.5 m (1.6 ft) as a loggia for the three central bays (Fig. 15.1-14b). The facade's planar, stripped-down classicism anticipated the style of early twentieth-century Viennese secession (see Section 17.3), breaking from the strict neoclassical work of his contemporaries.

As a professor at the Royal Academy for thirty years, Soane used his house to teach students about form, space, and iconography. Magnificent watercolors by his collaborator Joseph Michael Gandy (1771–1843) captured the interior's tumultuous jumble of fragments animated by concealed light sources. The Breakfast Room (Fig. 15.1-15), set in the center of the house, offered a manifesto for interior space: intimate yet expansive. A central lantern ushered light into its ocher segmental dome, while convex mirrors in the pendentives and smaller mirrors lining the arches further diffused the light. A skylight over the flanking corridor brought in additional illumination, giving the tiny room an uncanny grandeur.

Although Soane gained the commission for the House of Lords at Westminster in the 1790s, the project languished, owing both to the economic difficulties of the state during the Napoleonic Wars and to professional rivalries. London's major public buildings, such as William Wilkins's (1778–1839) National Gallery (1832) (Fig. 15.1-16) and Robert Smirke's (1780–1867) British Museum (1823–1848), went to the next generation of architects, trained by Soane. Like the generation that followed Adam in Edinburgh, these younger architects concentrated more on reproducing correct classical forms than on achieving original spatial effects. Such neoclassical works in London, Dublin, and Edinburgh eschewed invention in favor of conforming to the universal

Figure 15.1-15 London. Soane House, Breakfast Room, John Soane, ca. 1810.

and rational language of classicism in the effort to create an image of authority and justice for the British Empire.

American Classicism: The Correct Style for Democracy

The spread of the British Empire began in the seventeenth century with the settling of America, but here the colonial power's imperial authority encountered its first setback. After the American Revolution, known to the English as the War of American Independence (1775–1783), the thirteen colonies on the Atlantic seaboard became an independent federal republic. During the colonial period Americans generally relied on vernacular builders without the assistance of trained architects, but around 1800 professionals began to work regularly in Boston and Philadelphia. They largely followed the neoclassical models of their ex–mother country

but, because of the fledgling republic's alliance with France during the war, also looked to French models for pure forms and geometric planning. The new nation realized some of the most striking neoclassical landscapes of the age, including the new capital of Washington.

Charles Bulfinch (1763–1844) of Boston established the first American architectural practice after the conclusion of the war. He came from a wealthy family and went to Europe on the Grand Tour. His designs in the 1780s for Tontine Crescent and the Federal Street Theater imitated the manner of Robert Adam. For the State House (Fig. 15.1-17), his most significant public building in Boston, built in 1795–1797, Bulfinch consciously emulated Chambers's Somerset House. While the exterior displayed a poorly coordinated mix of materials, with a stout brick body beneath a gilded wooden cupola, the interior chamber for the House of Representatives offered a new type

Figure 15.1-16 London. National Gallery, William Wilkins, 1832.

of expansive space, somewhat like Soane's bank interiors, with segmental arches and a plaster and lathe saucer dome suspended from the ceiling.

Coming from a practice as an engineer and architect in London, Benjamin Henry Latrobe (1764–1820) brought a new level of professionalism to American architecture. In his first commission in Virginia, the State Penitentiary in Richmond, he achieved one of the most innovative prisons of the age (see Section 14.3). Soon after, he designed the Bank of Pennsylvania (1798–1800) (Fig. 15.1-18), a freestanding volume with Ionic temple fronts at both ends. This project established the temple type as an appropriate form for American banks. He set a central dome over the rotunda, the first true masonry vault in the United States, in a design that referred to Soane's Bank of England. Latrobe surpassed this accomplishment at the Baltimore Cathedral (also known as St. Mary's) (Fig. 15.1-19), the first Roman Catholic cathedral in the United States, in 1806–1818. The church carried a 21 m (69 ft) diameter saucer dome with an ornate coffered ceiling. In Philadelphia Latrobe further demonstrated his skill as an engineer by lifting drinking water from the river and pumping it to a central distribution point at the center of the city, housed in a pure cube capped with a tall dome.

Figure 15.1-17 Boston. State House, Charles Bulfinch, 1795.

No one cared more about developing a national architecture than Thomas Jefferson (1743–1826), the principal author of the American Declaration of Independence and an amateur architect. His comment that "the Genius of architecture seems to have spread its maledictions over this land" launched the challenge to improve American taste while building the new republic. Jefferson had unique opportunities to guide

Figure 15.1-18 Philadelphia. Bank of Pennsylvania, Benjamin Henry Latrobe, 1800.

Figure 15.1-19 Baltimore. St. Mary's Cathedral, Latrobe, 1806.

architectural policy, having served as governor of Virginia, secretary of state under George Washington, vice president, and finally third president of the United States. He both advised Bulfinch during his European tour and hired Latrobe for his first job in Virginia, giving him the brief for the Richmond penitentiary. Jefferson taught himself about architecture through the treatises of Andrea Palladio and James Gibbs, and his knowledge matured while serving as ambassador to France from 1785 to 1789. There, he engaged the services of Clérisseau, the same architect who had been Robert Adam's mentor, to catch up on the current works of Ange-Jacques Gabriel, Claude-Nicolas Ledoux, Jacques Gondoin, and others.

While in Nîmes, Jefferson experienced an architectural epiphany in front of the Maison Carrée, a small Roman temple of the republican period (see Section 5.1). He claimed to have gazed on it for hours, "like a lover at his mistress." With Clérisseau he prepared a model based on the temple to serve as the new Virginia state capitol building in Richmond (Fig. 15.1-20). While a bit of the design was lost in translation—with two levels of windows set between the pilasters, the capitals changed to the more simple Ionic instead of Corinthian order, and the construction of columns without flutes— the essence of the temple type remained, and officials had to fit the various functions of government into the pure volume of Jefferson's temple.

Jefferson's final project, the "academical village" of the University of Virginia (Fig. 15.1-21a),

CONSTRUCTION, TECHNOLOGY, THEORY

Jefferson's Monticello: The Prototypical American House

Jefferson began his study of architecture in 1768 while designing his own house, Monticello, on an agricultural estate he inherited near Charlottesville, Virginia. At first he relied on Palladio, creating a two-story temple-front entry porch. He sited the house on a slope so that the rooms of the second floor opened directly to the upper level of the rear garden. He tucked the service functions of storage rooms and kitchens into ground-level wings that spread in a *U* shape around the garden. In 1809, after his tenure as president, Jefferson doubled the size of Monticello, adding its octagonal dome. His enthusiasm for the French use of *poché* led him to place his bed in the 2 m (7 ft) thickness of the wall between his study and his dressing room, making it accessible to both spaces. Jefferson invented a series of domestic gadgets for his villa, including a dumbwaiter to bring food from the lower-level kitchens, triple-hung windows that allowed one to walk through them like doors, and bookshelves that could double as packing cases. Monticello became the primordial American house, representing at once stability and creativity, respectful of European traditions yet pragmatic in its emphasis on comfort and incorporation of effort-saving inventions.

Charlottesville, Virginia. (a) Monticello, garden facade, Jefferson, 1768–1809. (b) Jefferson's plan before final expansion, 1772.

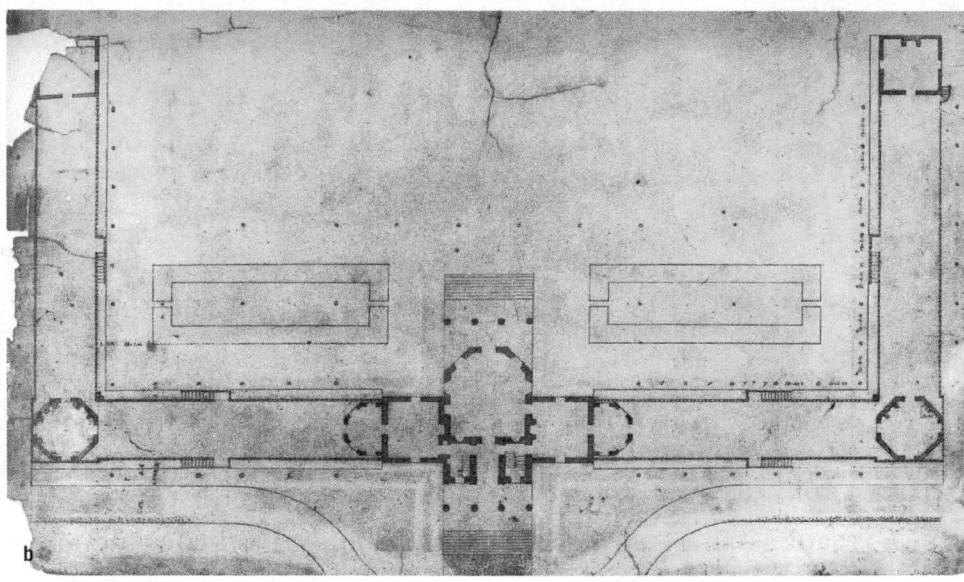

Figure 15.1-20 Richmond. Capitol building, Thomas Jefferson and Charles-Louis Clérisseau, 1785–1798, back wings added early twentieth century.

demonstrated his progress as an architect. Among the first state universities in the country, it became a model of secular education. Here, with Latrobe's advice, he built a Pantheon at half scale at the head of a grassy mall flanked by interlinked colonnaded pavilions. The rotunda housed the library (Fig. 15.1-21b), while ten subsidiary pavilions, five on each side of the great lawn, served as professors' residences and classrooms. Each pavilion became part of an encyclopedia of classical architecture, articulated with a different variation of the Roman orders. The students lived in the rooms under the porticoes that framed the 200 m (656 ft) esplanade that stepped down three terraces toward the open landscape. Behind each of the faculty pavilions, Jefferson enclosed a formal garden and kitchen yard within serpentine walls (Fig. 15.1-21c). He found these undulating walls more economical since they required only a single thickness of brick. Outdoor toilets were discreetly placed on the

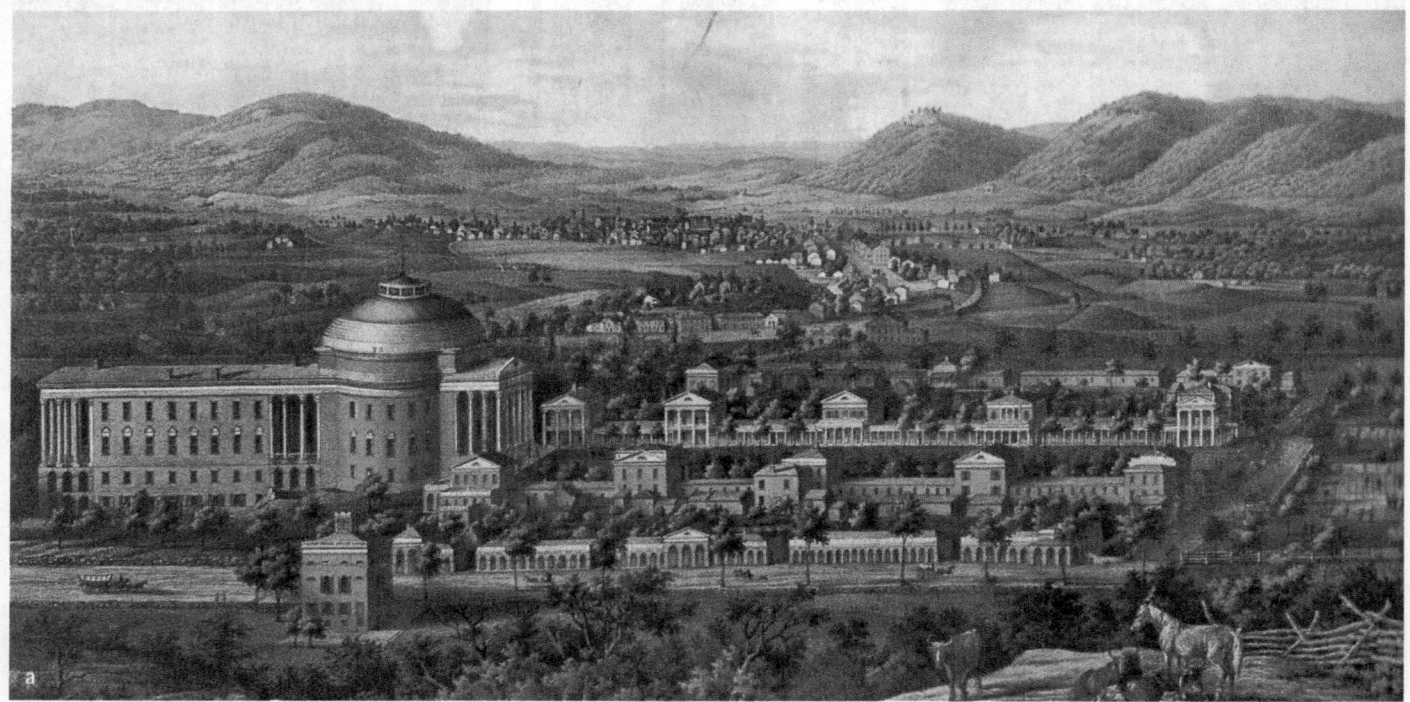

Figure 15.1-21 Charlottesville, Virginia. (a) View to the University of Virginia, Jefferson et al., begun 1817. Painting by Casimir Bohn, 1856. (b) and (c) See facing page.

perimeters. Brick colonnades linked the outer ranges beyond the garden to six independent "hotels," the refectories for student meals. The smaller rooms under the porches housed African slaves, who remained a constant factor in the Virginian economy until the conclusion of the American Civil War in 1865. While Jefferson spoke publicly against slavery and attempted to create a law for its abolition in Virginia, both at the campus and at his villa he accepted the practice, owning over 200 slaves himself.

Jefferson's orderly rural setting for the University of Virginia reflected the same physiocratic philosophy that inspired Ledoux in the planning of Chaux. He even left an homage to the French architect in the last pavilion of the western range, the niched entry of which imitates Mademoiselle Guimard's

Figure 15.1-21 Charlottesville, Virginia. (b) University of Virginia library, begun 1822. (c) Serpentine wall, ca. 1822.

hôtel particulier in Paris. Jefferson's ideal of an ethical republic based on freedom of speech and religious tolerance required universal education. Beyond this he dreamed of an enlightened society of gentleman farmers like himself. In 1785 he convinced Congress to enact the National Land Ordinance, resulting in the continental grid between the Appalachians and the Mississippi River. This pragmatic land division, based loosely on the Roman system of **centuriation**, provided for the equitable division of land for small farms, resulting in square townships measuring 10 km (6 miles) per side. The townships were subdivided into thirty-six smaller sections, which were then broken up into standard plots for settlers. Four sections were reserved for future public functions. County roads tended to follow the grid, as did the structure of the new towns. Thus, despite differences in terrain, most of America became part of a grand orthogonal design.

The plan of Washington, D.C., appeared as the stunning exception to this rule (Fig. 15.1-22). Here, Jefferson made a preliminary grid plan for the triangular site on the Potomac chosen by President George Washington. Washington, who had surveyed the layout of several prerevolutionary cities, including the nearby town of Alexandria, desired something grander, however, and appointed Major Pierre Charles L'Enfant (1754–1825) to the job. Son of a court painter at Versailles, L'Enfant arrived from France with Lafayette as a volunteer to fight in the Revolutionary War and became a prized aide to Washington. His 1791 plan for the capital evoked the great geometric gardens of the age of absolutism, such

as Versailles, with diagonal avenues crisscrossing a basic grid. These diagonal boulevards were exceptionally broad, comprising a roadway, double rows of trees, and a setback, for a total width of 48 m (158 ft). L'Enfant positioned the Capitol Building, the president's palace, the national bank, and a nondenominational church as terminating goals for the boulevards, reasoning that the great distances between them would allow the city to fill out in even growth.

The American capital's plan surpassed the princely ambitions of Baroque capitals such as Berlin and St. Petersburg. The ideological implications of its bold hierarchy, however, appeared in contradiction to the egalitarian intentions of America's nascent democracy. Although L'Enfant was dismissed in 1792, replaced by Andrew Ellicott (1754–1820), the Baroque order of the plan was retained. The great diagonal of Pennsylvania Avenue connected the two major buildings, the White House and the Capitol Building, both designed by amateur architects, James Hoban (1758–1831) and William Thornton (1759–1828), who won the competitions for their respective designs. During Jefferson's administration, Latrobe was appointed surveyor of public buildings to improve these two structures and the Naval Yard.

Little of Latrobe's efforts survived the destruction of the city by the British during the War of 1812, excepting the porches of the White House. His influence continued, however, through the work of his former assistant, Robert Mills (1781–1855), who during the 1830s produced a number of classical set pieces. Mills attempted to establish the proper classical

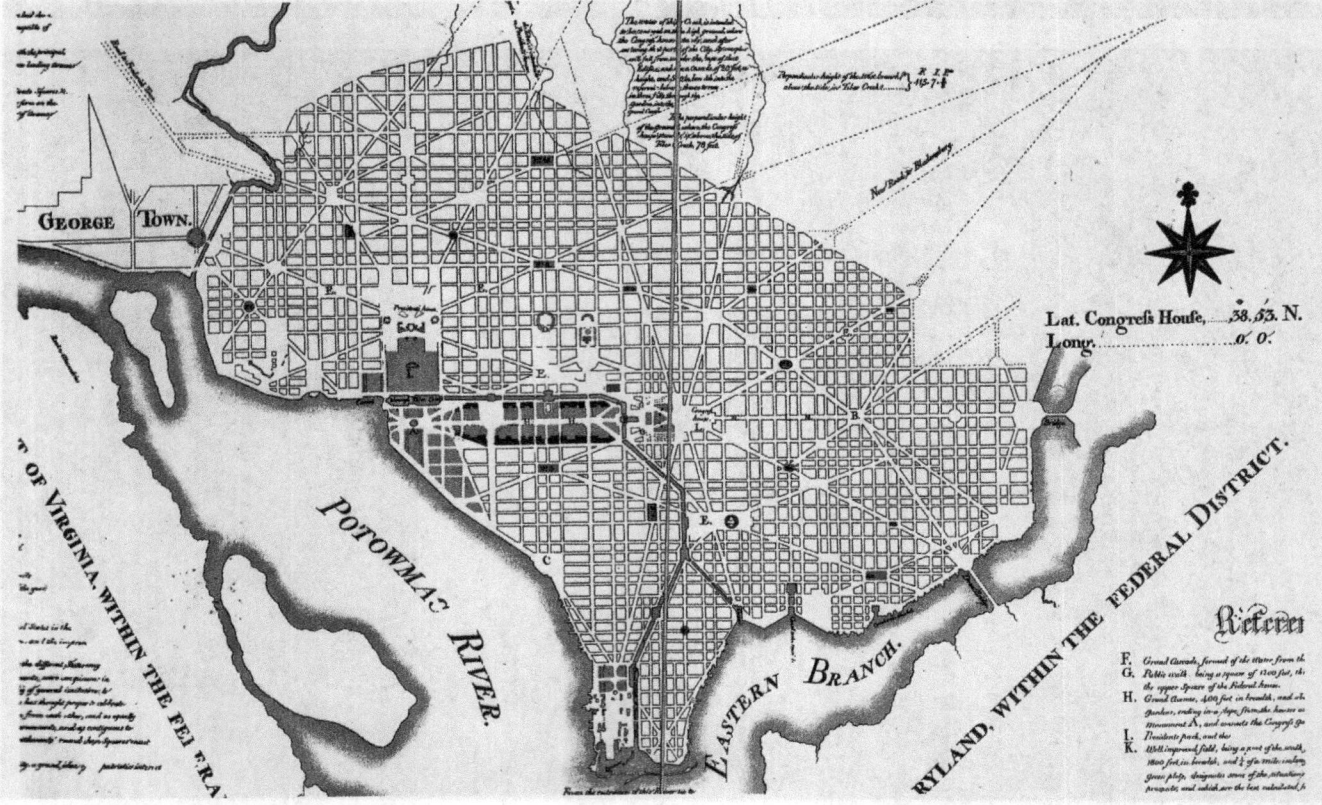

Figure 15.1-22 Washington, D.C. Plan, Pierre Charles L'Enfant, 1791, revised by Andrew Ellicott, 1792.

Figure 15.1-23 Washington, D.C.
(a) Treasury Department, Robert Mills,
1834. (b) Capitol Mall and Washington
Monument, Mills, 1833–1884.

scale for Pennsylvania Avenue with the long Ionic colonnade of his fireproof Treasury Building (1836) (Fig. 15.1-23a), while his project for the colossal obelisk of the Washington Monument (Fig. 15.1-23b), which won an 1836 competition, proved worthy of the sublime visions of Boullée. Partly constructed of stones sent from all over the country and from the rest of the world, the great spike reached completion in 1884, giving the city a monumental pivot. Rising 170 m (558 ft), its pure form triangulated between the major sites of Washington while serving as a shining beacon for the new nation.

Further Reading

Collins, Peter. *Changing Ideals in Modern Architecture, 1750–1950.* Montreal, Canada: McGill-Queen's University Press, 1965.

Durand, Jean-Nicolas-Louis. *Précis of the Lectures on Architecture.* Edited by A. Picon. Los Angeles: Getty Research Institute, 2000.

Hitchcock, Henry-Russell. *Architecture: Nineteenth and Twentieth Centuries.* New York: Penguin Books, 1977.

Hobsbawm, E. J. *The Age of Revolution, 1789–1848.* New York: Mentor Books, 1962.

Ruffinière du Prey, Pierre de la. *John Soane: The Making of an Architect.* Chicago: University of Chicago Press, 1982.

Snodin, Michael. *Karl Friedrich Schinkel: A Universal Man.* New Haven, CT: Yale University Press, 1991.

Villari, Sergio. *J. N. L. Durand (1760–1834): Art and Science of Architecture.* New York: Rizzoli, 1990.

15.2 THE GOTHIC REVIVAL
Antimodern and Proto-Nationalist

In nineteenth-century Europe, political revolutions and industrial transformations abruptly cut people off from their architectural traditions. In response, architects produced quotations of earlier styles, conceived as **revivals** rather than continuations. Various forms of the revival of Greco-Roman style, under way since the fifteenth century, competed with a return to Gothic style in the middle of the eighteenth century. The variety of medieval revival styles that took hold in mid-nineteenth-century Europe corresponded to a desire to recuperate the lost crafts and values of a simpler and presumably more humane premodern society.

The return to Gothic occurred alongside the development of a new academic understanding of medieval styles, inspired by the ambitious restorations of monuments. Revival styles also carried strong nationalist connotations both at home and in contexts far removed from European style periods, such as the Americas and Asia. Rather than stimulating a return to traditional building practices and medieval community formation, however, the revival styles tended to remain on the surface, as symbolic gestures to supplement the drive toward modernity.

Medievalism: Idealizing the Other Past

In 1773 the young German humanist Johann Wolfgang von Goethe (1749–1832) praised the Gothic manner of Strasbourg Cathedral as the material expression of the German genius in the essay "On German Architecture." Although Goethe later professed more admiration for the rational forms of classical architecture, designing for his garden in Weimar a sphere atop a cube as a statement of his aesthetic ideal, his early celebration of a nonclassical style signaled the awakening interest in medieval architecture that appeared in Germany, France, and England during the first half of the nineteenth century.

German intellectuals after the fall of Napoléon championed Gothic style as a form of resistance to the neoclassical projects of the French. In 1815 Schinkel proposed a Gothic cathedral on the outskirts of Berlin to commemorate the Wars of Liberation as "the soul-stirring style of ancient German architecture." While Schinkel built only a small Gothic aedicule on a hill in Kreuzberg, the Gothic revival took root elsewhere in Germany. In 1832 construction was resumed on Cologne Cathedral (Fig. 15.2-1) after three centuries of inactivity. Its completion in 1880 coincided with the formation of the modern state of Germany, unified under the Prussians, and the grand Gothic pile became a symbol of the new nation.

An even stronger movement for Gothic revival emerged in England at about the same time, with similar nationalist undertones. The emergence of the style coincided with the maximum extension of the British Empire, which reached its zenith during the reign of Queen Victoria (r. 1837–1901). Victoria's German husband Prince Albert (1819–1861) was an active promoter of industry and the arts. While England had seen several earlier dalliances with Gothic revival during the eighteenth century, such as Strawberry Hill and Fonthill Abbey, a concerted movement for the Neo-Gothic took root in the 1830s. Its success came partly from the tireless propaganda efforts of Augustus Welby Northmore Pugin (1812–1852) and partly from the fundamentalist religious movements under way simultaneously in Cambridge and Oxford.

Pugin came from a French Huguenot family but converted to Catholicism in 1835, convinced of the moral superiority of the society that built the pre-Reformation medieval churches. In his polemical tract *Contrasts* (1836), he juxtaposed images of premodern and modern life to show the greater harmony of medieval cities, dominated by church institutions, compared to modern factory towns, pitting the courtyard of a charitable parish church against a radiocentric workhouse (Fig. 15.2-2). Pugin built more than twenty Catholic churches during the 1840s, from the large cathedral of St. Chad in Birmingham to his own parish church at Ramsgate. At the small church of St. Giles at Cheadle he revived the **rood screen** separating the altar from the nave and encrusted the interior with carved and painted decorations. Pugin, while most concerned with decoration, theorized in terms close to those of Durand about the structural

TIME LINE

 1812

Luddite movement against the machines of the Industrial Revolution in England

East India Company gains control of Bengal

 1815

 1837

Queen Victoria begins sixty-three-year reign over British Empire

Neo-Gothic Houses of Parliament begun in London

1840

virtue of the Gothic in his 1841 treatise *The True Principles of Pointed or Christian Architecture*. He claimed, "First, that there should be no features about a building which are not necessary for convenience, construction or propriety; second, that all ornament should consist of enrichment of the essential construction of the building."

Neo-Gothic style reached the pinnacle of British nationalism with the rebuilding of the Houses of Parliament (Fig. 15.2-3) in perpendicular Gothic style. After the destruction by fire of the Palace of Westminster in 1834, Parliament launched a competition for their reconstruction, specifying that the style of the new structure must be either Gothic or Tudor. The judges felt that classical styles would offend the adjacent Gothic and Tudor structures, but they also hoped to avoid associations with the style of recent American government buildings. Charles Barry (1795–1860), the gifted designer of the neoclassical Royal Institution in Manchester (1824), won the competition with the assistance of Pugin, who was generally excluded from major public projects because of his religious sympathies but spent his final decade almost exclusively occupied with the Parliament's decoration. While Barry's plan appeared as rational as any of Durand's gridded schemes for institutions, the elevations carried regularly spaced perpendicular Gothic panels and the three towers were placed asymmetrically above the roof. After completing the basic structure

Figure 15.2-1 Cologne, Germany. Cathedral, finished 1880.

▼ **1843**

Labrouste's Bibliothèque Ste.-Geneviève begun in Paris

All Saints, Margaret Street, begun in London

▲ **1849**

▼ **1857**

India converted into British colony after Indian Rebellion

Victoria Terminus built in Gothic style in Bombay

▲ **1878**

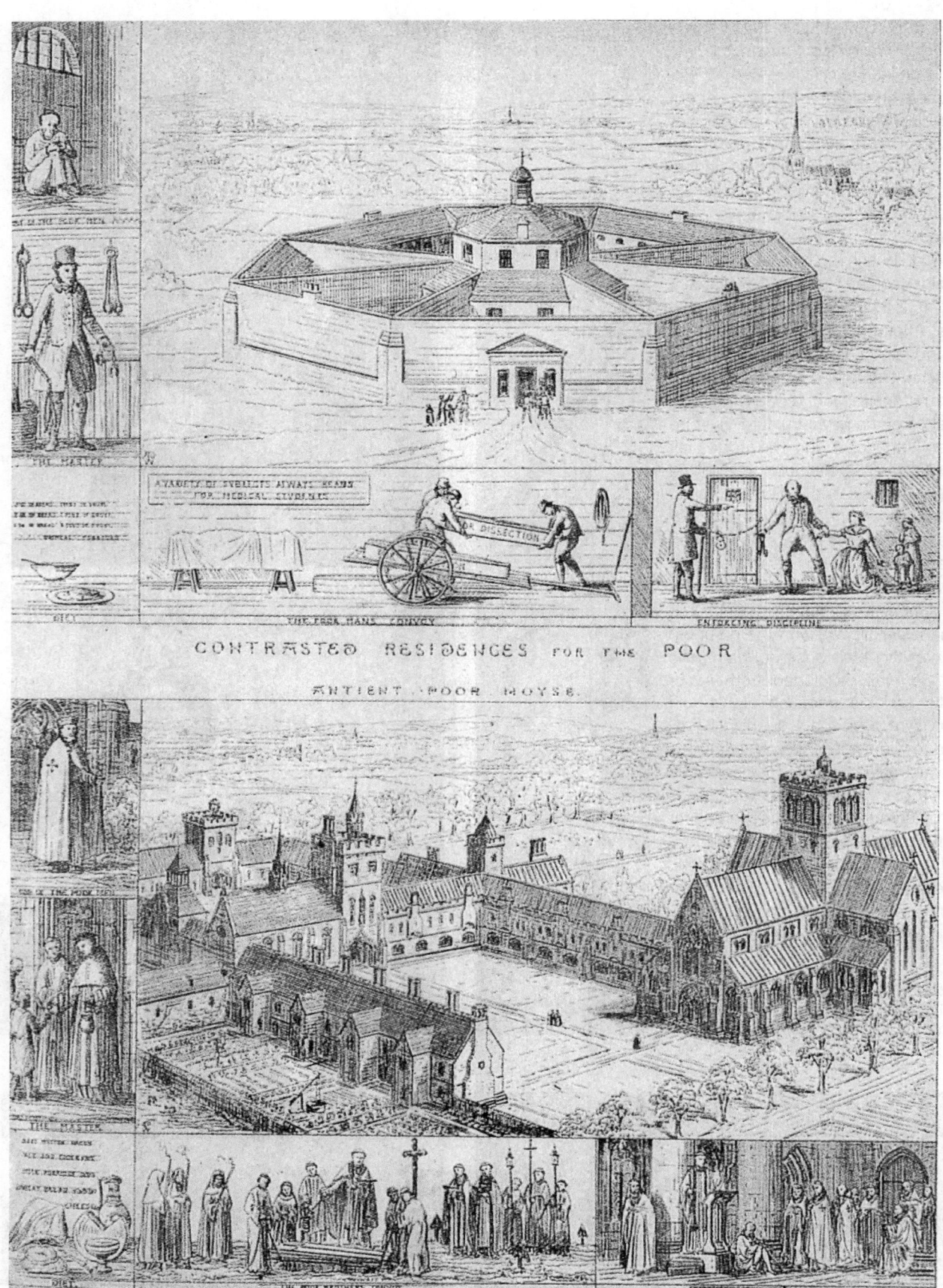

Figure 15.2-2 England. Rendering showing the superiority of medieval convent welfare to the modern workhouse, from Augustus Welby Northmore Pugin, *Contrasts*, 1836.

Figure 15.2-3 London. Houses of Parliament, Charles Barry and Pugin, 1840s.

in 1844, Barry insisted that Pugin have complete control of the decorative details, a task he executed with maniacal attention, literally losing his sanity in the process.

The Camden Society in Cambridge and the Oxford Movement of High Anglicans shared Pugin's zeal for Gothic style, but from a different religious point of view. Their journal *The Ecclesiologist* became a prime forum to promote both Neo-Gothic architecture and the idea of reforming society through religion. The debates on the return to Gothic in England had repercussions in America as well. Richard Upjohn (1802–1878), an expatriate British architect who fully ascribed to Pugin's principles, completed his crocket-studded pinnacles of Trinity Church on Wall Street in New York in 1846 (Fig. 15.2-4).

In London, the Camden Society commissioned William Butterfield (1814–1900) to design All Saints, Margaret Street, in 1849 as a manifesto of their ideals. The architect discreetly inserted the church into a dense block near Regent Street, its five-story facades alternating black, yellow, and red bands of brick as a means of making decoration out of structure (Fig. 15.2-5a). The vicar's apartment and dorms for the choirboys faced the street, blending into the scale and color of the context. The church lay behind a *U*-shaped courtyard set off by a gabled gateway. One entered the church obliquely through a side aisle, since

Figure 15.2-4 New York City. Trinity Church, Richard Upjohn, 1840s.

the nave ran counteraxial to the court. Thus, the space opened up as one turned toward the soaring arches of the interior and the higher vaults above the altar (Fig. 15.2-5b). Moving toward the altar, the chromatism of All Saints intensified, with decorations ranging from chevron brick patterns to contrasting marbles and terra-cotta tiles.

The influential art critic John Ruskin (1819–1900) admired All Saints, Margaret Street, and shared *The Ecclesiologist*'s conviction that the votive nature of Gothic ornament strengthened community. In *The Seven Lamps of Architecture* (1849) and *The Stones of Venice* (1853), Ruskin popularized northern Italian Gothic and proposed a Gothic revival as a program of social

reform. His campaign pleaded for the dignity of labor and pride in well-crafted artifacts. Hyperbolic in his praise and blame, he left no doubt about the ethical superiority of medieval architecture. He condemned classicism as "base, unnatural, unfruitful, unenjoyable, and impious. Pagan in its origin, proud and unholy in its revival, paralyzed in its old age . . . an architecture invented as it seems to make plagiarists of its architects, slaves of its workmen, and sybarites of its inhabitants."

Like Pugin, Ruskin admired Gothic decoration but believed it should always be integrated with structure so as not to hide or mystify it. In the "Lamp of Truth" he championed the structural honesty of the flying buttresses of

Figure 15.2-5 London. (a) Facade of All Saints, Margaret Street, William Butterfield, 1849. (b) Interior.

Beauvais Cathedral versus the superfluous pinnacles and buttresses added for scenic effect in later cathedrals. His call for a return to medieval craft and his splendid sketches inspired numerous architects, in particular the Irish firm of Deane & Woodward, designers of the University Museum in Oxford (Fig. 15.2-6), built between 1855 and 1860. During the prolonged absences of architect Benjamin Woodward (1816–1861), Ruskin took charge of the project. The architects designed the front wing with northern Italian biforium windows while placing a central tower like that seen in Flemish medieval town halls. Beyond the entry one came upon an astounding central court, with a glazed roof supported on a system of wrought-iron columns and pointed arches. While the designers resorted to materials of the Industrial Revolution, they did not permit the architectural elements to be mass-produced. Each iron piece was carved by hand with filigree, and each of the capitals depicted a different species of flora. The glass roof imbued the space with a transparency that exceeded the dematerialization of Gothic cathedrals.

Many of the most important public buildings of the Victorian age were produced in neomedieval styles. Alfred Waterhouse designed several Neo-Gothic projects in Manchester, such as the grandiose City Hall of 1868. George Edmund Street (1824–1881), perhaps the greatest enthusiast of the Neo-Gothic, wrote pamphlets to influence the programs of public buildings in the style. He was finally rewarded for his efforts with the rebuilding of the Law Courts (Fig. 15.2-7), one of the largest public buildings in London, in the late 1870s. Neo-Gothic style reached its maximum diffusion in the works of George Gilbert Scott (1811–1878), whose office produced hundreds of projects. These included restorations of Gothic churches, the huge Gothic tabernacle for the Prince Albert Memorial (1863) in Hyde Park, college structures at Cambridge and Oxford, train stations, and international commissions, such as the city hall of Hamburg and university buildings in Bombay. Victorian Gothic, which began as a spiritual movement intended to redeem society from the ills of industrialism, became less a social remedy than a fashion statement, encompassing the modern functions of commercial and state projects.

European Revival Styles in India: The Gothic Raj

The British commenced commercial activities in India in the early sixteenth century, but imperial control of the region began two centuries later, coincident with the decline of the Mughal Empire (see Section 12.1). They used the East India Company to set up governing institutions and the Indian Civil Service. As they became more settled, the British sponsored a series of impressive public buildings, first executed in neoclassical styles and later in Neo-Gothic, to represent their claim to the Raj, or rule over Indian territory.

John Ruskin's *Seven Lamps of Architecture*

Ruskin advocated the revival of a crafts-based culture for the spiritual redemption of industrial society. In *The Seven Lamps of Architecture* (1849) he charted a moral campaign for architecture to overcome the materialist orientation of his times. His "lamps" represented the flickering of meaning communicated by true architecture. In the "Lamp of Sacrifice" he proposed that labor and craft demonstrated belief, while utility was much less important than the sincerity of the act of making. The other lamps—Truth, Power, Beauty, Life, and Obedience—shone as agents of a total process that led to Memory: "When we build, let us think that we build forever. . . . For, indeed, the greatest glory of a building is not in its stones, nor in its gold. Its glory is in its Age, and in that deep sense of voicefulness, of stern watching, or mysterious sympathy, nay, even of approval or condemnation, which we feel in walls that have long been washed by the passing waves of humanity."

Pisa, Italy. Palazzo Agostini, watercolor by John Ruskin, 1840s.

The first British governor in India, Warren Hastings (1732–1818), recommended in 1773 that the British "adapt our Regulations to the Manners and Understandings of the People, and the Exigencies of the Country, adhering as closely as we are able to their ancient uses and Institutions." This sympathetic policy lapsed under subsequent governors, and later colonists invariably preferred to establish racially segregated cities. At their first town of Madras (today Chennai), founded on the southeast coast in 1639, a walled fortress protected the "White Town" from the area for indigenous residents, called the "Black Town."

In Calcutta, the first capital city of British India, the East India Company sponsored a series of classical buildings and monuments in the "White Town" during the first decade of the nineteenth century. A Doric town hall by Colonel John Garstin accompanied the Ochterlony Monument (1828), a 50 m (164 ft) high Doric column commemorating one of the company's generals during the period of conquest. The sprawling Government House by Charles Wyatt (1758–1819) stood out as the most conspicuous building of early colonial Calcutta. Wyatt, a military engineer, descended from a distinguished architectural dynasty in England—his uncle James, aside from building the ill-fated Gothic extravaganza of Fonthill Abbey, designed several country houses on a par with the works of Robert Adam. Charles Wyatt chose Adam's Kedleston Hall, a project that had been supervised by another uncle, Samuel Wyatt, as his model for Calcutta. Like the American imitations of Neo-Palladian and neoclassical works, Government House lost something in translation, especially in the carving of its capitals and the treatment of its interior spaces. It nonetheless provided an image of authority, to the point that several Indian *maharajas* imitated its classical details for their own residences.

Figure 15.2-6 Oxford, England.
Oxford University Museum,
Deane & Woodward, with the
assistance of John Ruskin, 1855.

Figure 15.2-7 London. Law Courts,
George Edmund Street, 1870s.

On the western coast of India, Bombay (today Mumbai), the only deepwater port in the region, was taken by the British in 1661 but remained relatively unimportant until their conquest of the interior in the 1820s. The walled compound of its "White Town" covered the tip of an island, 18 × 6 km (11 × 3.7 miles), which was greatly expanded through landfills during the first half of the nineteenth century. As in Calcutta, a military commander, Colonel Thomas Cowper, established the initial colonial presence, placing a Doric temple front on Bombay's Town Hall in 1820. The new structure served both as a site for government functions and as a cultural center, with a library and a museum. The Doric columns were carved in England and shipped to Calcutta. The addition of *jhilmil* hoods over the windows introduced a local vernacular remedy for the torrid climate.

In 1857, after widespread rebellions, the British parliament officially dismissed the East India Company and took formal control of the colony. As India's gateway to the rest of the world, Bombay became the most important city. Still relying on the company's military engineers, the imperial government sponsored a series of grand projects. Rather than Doric temple fronts, however, the leaders opted for Neo-Gothic pinnacles, which, with the completion of the Houses of Parliament, had become the new national style. Compared to European classicism, which had the virtue of simplicity, the Gothic details of such projects as the Public Works Office by Colonel Henry St. Clair Wilkins (1828–1896), begun in 1869, appeared truly incongruous within the Indian context. Nevertheless, over a dozen large Neo-Gothic structures appeared in downtown Bombay between 1870 and 1900, most of them government-sponsored. The most prominent Victorian practitioner of the style, George Gilbert Scott, designed three buildings for the university. His Rajabai Tower resembled a Flemish town hall, while the library combined a colonnade and upper terrace inspired by the Doge's Palace in Venice, with a spiral stair turret (Fig. 15.2-8).

In 1878 Frederick William Stevens (1847–1900) designed the Victoria Terminus (now called Chhatrapati Shivaji Station) (Fig. 15.2-9), the city's most extravagant Gothic pile. The station celebrated colonialism as a new world of

Figure 15.2-8 Mumbai. University of Mumbai (previously Bombay), George Gilbert Scott, 1870s.

technological improvement draped in an antiquated foreign style. The exuberant exterior carried a high masonry dome with ribs sprouting crockets. Prominent gargoyles radiated from the base of the dome, while **oriole** turrets rose from the corners of its towers. The arches alternated pink and white voussoirs sheltering many different scales and styles of fenestration. Ruskin's vision of Venice inspired the polychrome masonry and pointed arches. Although the ornate details came from European Christian heritage, they had a strange sympathy with the decorative attitudes of Rajput palaces

British colonialists were not alone in using revival styles in Victorian India. One of the semiautonomous Rajputs, Ram Singh, the maharaja of Jaipur, engaged Colonel Samuel Swinton Jacob (1841–1917) as his engineer for a series of public works. They focused most of their attention on the Albert Hall Museum (Fig. 15.2-10), set in a new public park begun in 1876 and, like the Victoria Terminus, completed for the 1887 jubilee of Victoria's reign. The patron insisted that the style attempt a synthesis of British and Indian motifs to demonstrate his support of the colonial regime. The museum's plan followed the Western museum type, a circuit of galleries on two floors surrounding a double-height hall. Swinton Jacob articulated the tiers with a fanciful combination of Mughal *chhatris* and Palladian windows. During the years of Albert Hall's construction, the same patron insisted on using only local styles for the expansion of his private palace in the city's center, drawing a clear line between his endorsement of the colonial power and his autonomous realm.

The French Invention of Architectural Heritage

Not until the arrival of industrialization did Europeans begin to feel alienated from their architectural past. Pragmatic and utilitarian attitudes rapidly changed the landscape, obliterating many historical contexts. The addition of modern infrastructure required the demolition of countless medieval buildings without a second thought for their cultural significance. During the first half of the nineteenth century, many Europeans began to lose contact with their continuous traditions of making cities and buildings. The more they became involved with modern life, with its quickened pace and industrial materials, the more historic monuments came to be seen as unique and unrepeatable works of a lost world. This sense of disconnect inspired the concept of architectural heritage and generated theories of restoration for the preservation of built artifacts.

Figure 15.2-10 Jaipur, India. Albert Hall, Samuel Swinton Jacob, 1876.

and Hindu temples. Stevens went on to attempt a synthesis of European Gothic with local motifs. His Municipal Corporation Building, finished in 1893, blended Venetian arches with bulbous cupolas that converted the details from Mughal tombs into an Indo-Saracenic style. He emblazoned the front gable with a prophecy of Bombay's leadership: *Urbs Prima in Indis* (the first among Indian cities).

In France during the 1830s the battle for the conservation of historic buildings, especially those of the medieval past, came to public attention through the polemics of the novelist Victor Hugo (1802–1885). Hugo's grand tapestry of fifteenth-century Paris, *Notre-Dame de Paris* (*The Hunchback of Notre-Dame*, 1831), abounded with architectural observations and moralizations about the role of great buildings. He exposed both the lamentable condition of historic buildings and the contemporary decline of architectural expression as a result of the mechanical processes of modernity. In the chapter "This Will Kill That," Hugo delivered a breathtaking panorama of the entire history of architecture, explaining how monuments once functioned as the supreme vehicle of human thought but, since the fifteenth-century introduction of the printing press, had lost their communicative advantage. Hugo considered Gothic the most vital expression of the people, while everything produced after 1500 evoked "the last dotage of a decrepit grand art falling back into infancy before it dies." His pamphleteering and loving depiction of the medieval context of Notre-Dame inspired the French state to create an agency for architectural heritage in 1830 to catalogue and review the condition of the country's significant monuments. The chief commissioner, the novelist Prosper Mérimée, motivated by Hugo's ideas, ordered the restoration of numerous Romanesque and Gothic churches, including Notre-Dame in Paris.

Whereas the English fantasized about a return to tradition as a means of redeeming society from the effects of industrialization, the French considered historic monuments as representations of the past, distinct from the processes of modern life. This difference became clear in the two cultures' contrasting opinions about how to restore historic buildings. Ruskin, in the "Lamp of Memory," took the extreme position that any alteration of a historical work constituted an unpardonable offense to the past. Thus, one should only maintain what already existed, allowing a work to show its age. The French, in contrast, believed that historic buildings should be consolidated, cleaned, conserved, and in some cases completed. The most important French professional involved in the debate, Eugène-Emmanuel Viollet-le-Duc (1814–1879), carried out aggressive restorations of medieval monuments. He repaired and completed the ruins of the fortified city of Carcassonne (1852–1879), adding gray slate roofs instead of the documented terracotta tiles. While the hilltop castle town appeared more harmonious, the restored version differed greatly from the thirteenth-century original.

Viollet-le-Duc began his most important commission, the restoration of Notre-Dame in Paris, in 1844. With his partner Jean-Baptiste Lassus (1807–1857), he patched up the damaged areas and cleared away previous restorations. They also added new elements that did not exist in the historic structure, such as a spire over the crossing with a statue of the architect himself on top and a new sacristy. Viollet-le-Duc favored idealized restoration rather than historical accuracy. He insisted that "restoration: both the word and the activity itself are modern. To restore a building is not to repair or rebuild it, but to re-establish it in a complete state which may never have existed at any given time."

The Gothic revival in France did not lead to the creation of new buildings in historic styles but rather to interventions into old buildings to make them whole and more convincingly Gothic. Viollet-le-Duc restored over 200 structures, taking particular pride in those that were Gothic, the style that he believed best represented the French nation. He professed that the French vernacular genius had led to the invention of the pointed arch and the flying buttress. Although he showed few scruples about substituting more durable materials for the originals, he objected to using modern materials, such as iron, in premodern buildings. In his ten-volume treatise *Dictionnaire raisonné de l'architecture française du XIe au XVIe siècle* (*The Dictionary of French Architecture*) (1854–1868), Viollet-le-Duc offered a tool for historic architecture comparable to Diderot's *Encyclopedia*. His subsequent theoretical explorations proposed a new architecture based on modern materials that would benefit from principles found in Gothic structure and decoration. Viollet-le-Duc's 1856 design for a concert hall, for example, showed a skeletal application of wrought-iron structural members (Fig. 15.2-11).

Although Viollet-le-Duc's own buildings appeared unremarkable and did not indulge in extensive use of iron, his theories of a new structural rationalism greatly affected younger designers. He wrote: "If we would invent that

Figure 15.2-11 France. Proposal for a market hall using wrought iron structural members, Eugène-Emmanuel Viollet-le-Duc, 1850s.

Figure 15.2-12 Paris. Library of Ste.-Geneviève, upper floor with cast-iron columns, Henri Labrouste, 1843–1850.

woven skeleton of metallic members in the design of large free-span interiors but was unable to realize any projects until the twentieth century.

Henri Labrouste (1801–1875) came closer to Viollet-le-Duc's ideal with his library, the Bibliothèque Ste.-Geneviève (Fig. 15.2-12), begun in 1843 and finished in 1850. Although grounded in classicism within the Beaux-Arts system, he remained critical of received models. Having served as atelier master for Lassus, Labrouste was well acquainted with Viollet-le-Duc and had served as Victor Hugo's consultant on architecture for "This Will Kill That." The exterior of his Bibliothèque Ste.-Geneviève recalled the inscribed facades proposed by Boullée and Durand and bore no relation to Gothic design or structure. An oblong box, articulated with flattened, partially blind arcades, its spandrels carried the names of 810 authors, carved in chronological order. Inside, Labrouste combined innovative cast-iron frames with masonry piers and arches. He structured the upper reading room on a central row of slender cast-iron columns that supported twin fireproof barrel vaults made of plaster-covered metal lattices. The bookcases stepped up on two levels into the hollows of the perimeter arches. Large clerestories brought in light from above to create a luminous space. By combining traditional masonry and modern materials without concealing the structure, he fulfilled Viollet-le-Duc's goal of structural rationalism.

Further Reading

Blau, Eve. *Ruskinian Gothic: The Work of Deane and Woodward, 1845–1861*. Princeton, NJ: Princeton University Press, 1982.

Choay, Françoise. *The Invention of the Historic Monument*. Cambridge: Cambridge University Press, 2001.

Davies, Philip. *Splendors of the Raj: British Architecture in India, 1660 to 1947*. London: John Murray, 1985.

Hearn, M. F., ed. *The Architectural Theory of Viollet-le-Duc*. Cambridge, MA: MIT Press, 1990.

Leniaud, Jean-Michel. *Viollet-le-Duc, ou les délires du système*. Paris: Éditions Mengès, 1994.

Stanton, Phoebe. *Pugin*. New York: Viking Press, 1971.

architecture of our own times . . . we must certainly seek it no longer by mingling all the styles of the past, but by relying on novel principles of structure." Louis-Auguste Boileau (1812–1896), for instance, used cast-iron columns in a Gothic style for the church of St.-Eugène in Paris (1854) in order to economize, gaining the master's disapproval for the use of one material to simulate another. Anatole de Baudot (1834–1915), who for many years worked as Viollet-le-Duc's assistant, developed numerous proposals for the use of a

15.3 THE NEW IRON AGE
The Spread of Metal and Glass Technologies

Until the nineteenth century, architects chose from a limited palette of building materials, ranging from locally obtained wood to mud and stone. Brick and ceramics proved the most highly processed materials, baked in local kilns. The Industrial Revolution introduced into buildings large quantities of iron and glass, materials often shipped from faraway foundries. The increasing use of iron and glass revolutionized traditional construction methods, inspiring great feats of enclosing or traversing space. Not since the Roman perfection of concrete construction had building technology so radicalized structural possibilities.

The development of these **ferrovitreous** techniques spread from functional structures—such as factories, warehouses, and train sheds—to commercial buildings and even monumental works such as Labrouste's library. Designers wove webs of iron and glass between structures to create covered galleries. The new lightweight systems of spanning with iron proved cheaper, stronger, and more fire-resistant than methods that relied on wood or stone. Tension became a heroic new factor in large-scale design, best seen in the astounding **suspension bridges** built for rail travel. The pragmatic and calculating engineer, both a destroyer and a creator, emerged as the new protagonist in design. Tension, once a secret method of vernacular construction in nomadic societies, now returned to serve an increasingly mobile society that sought to shrink distances and accelerate time.

Industry in the Service of Commerce: From the Arcades to the Crystal Palace

Although architects had used metal in buildings since the ancient Greeks in the sixth century, it usually remained hidden as a supplement to structure. Occasionally, bronze, copper, or lead served as a roofing material. While most architects found exposed iron unseemly, during the nineteenth century it became increasingly difficult to ignore its structural potential. Iron proved cheaper than stone and more resilient. It could withstand fire better than wood. The casting process led to the prefabrication of iron components in bulk that could be shipped to a site for ready-made assembly. After experiments with structure were carried out in the Lancashire factories, iron became a desirable option as a light, strong, and relatively fire-resistant material.

The first nonindustrial uses of ferrovitreous structures that combined iron and glass appeared in commercial settings and garden hothouses in France and England during the early nineteenth century. In Paris in 1813 François-Joseph Bélanger (1744–1818) replaced the spectacular wood and glass cupola of the Halle au Blé, which had been destroyed by fire, with a glass dome on an iron frame, covering a diameter as large as that of the Pantheon in Rome. The building remained essentially a masonry structure, with its industrial components only visible from the interior court (Fig. 15.3-1).

While this early ferrovitreous dome had no immediate imitators, another building type that relied on iron and glass coverings—the *passage*, or arcade—became widespread in Paris. These top-lit alleys cut through the middle of long blocks, presenting continuous display windows for shops and cafés. The first arcade, the Passage du Caire, opened in 1798 during Napoléon's campaign in Egypt. Like a covered *suq*, it inserted a pedestrian path through several blocks to connect to the busy commercial street of St. Denis. By the mid-nineteenth century Paris had more than 150 arcades. Among them, the **Galerie** Vivienne (1823) (Fig. 15.3-2) stood out as a work of architecture and not just the use of leftover space. There, François Jean Delannoy created a truly elegant atmosphere, harmonizing the internal facades and shop windows with patterned mosaic pavements, overhead glass roofs on metal struts, and a central crystalline cupola.

The Parisian arcades generated copies throughout Europe and the Americas. A prominent arcade with Ionic portals appeared in Providence, Rhode Island, as early as 1828. In Brussels the architect-developer Jean-Pierre Cluysenaer created one of the most sophisticated of the type, the Passage St. Hubert (1836–1847), spanning wide halls with glass barrel vaults. He inscribed the motto *Omnibus Omnia* ("Everything for Everyone") over the entry of this precursor of modern consumerism. The twentieth-century literary critic Walter Benjamin (1892–1940) considered the arcades emblematic of the contradictions of modern bourgeois existence. Their tawdry solicitations of glamour promoted the consumerist phantasmagoria, where fashion, commodity fetishism, escapism, disorientation, gambling, prostitution, and social introversion contributed to the illusion of well-being in the modern metropolis.

The Parisian arcades began to lose their economic importance in the 1860s with the appearance of the first department stores. Now the variety of merchandise scattered in the arcades was gathered into a single grand masonry envelope served by a central, top-lit atrium space that reproduced an arcade-like environment for the spectacle of consumerism. The Au Bon Marché store built by Louis-Charles Boileau, with the assistance of the engineer Gustave Eiffel (1832–1923), treated Paris to a spectacular cast-iron atrium. Its cascading stairs opened to four floors of balconies for shoppers to display themselves to others (Fig. 15.3-3).

The arcades built in newly unified Italy during the 1870s introduced a larger scale, becoming triumphant symbols of a new secular society. The Galleria Vittorio Emanuele II in Milan (Fig. 15.3-4), begun in 1863 during the period of Italian unification, covered a four-block area connecting the

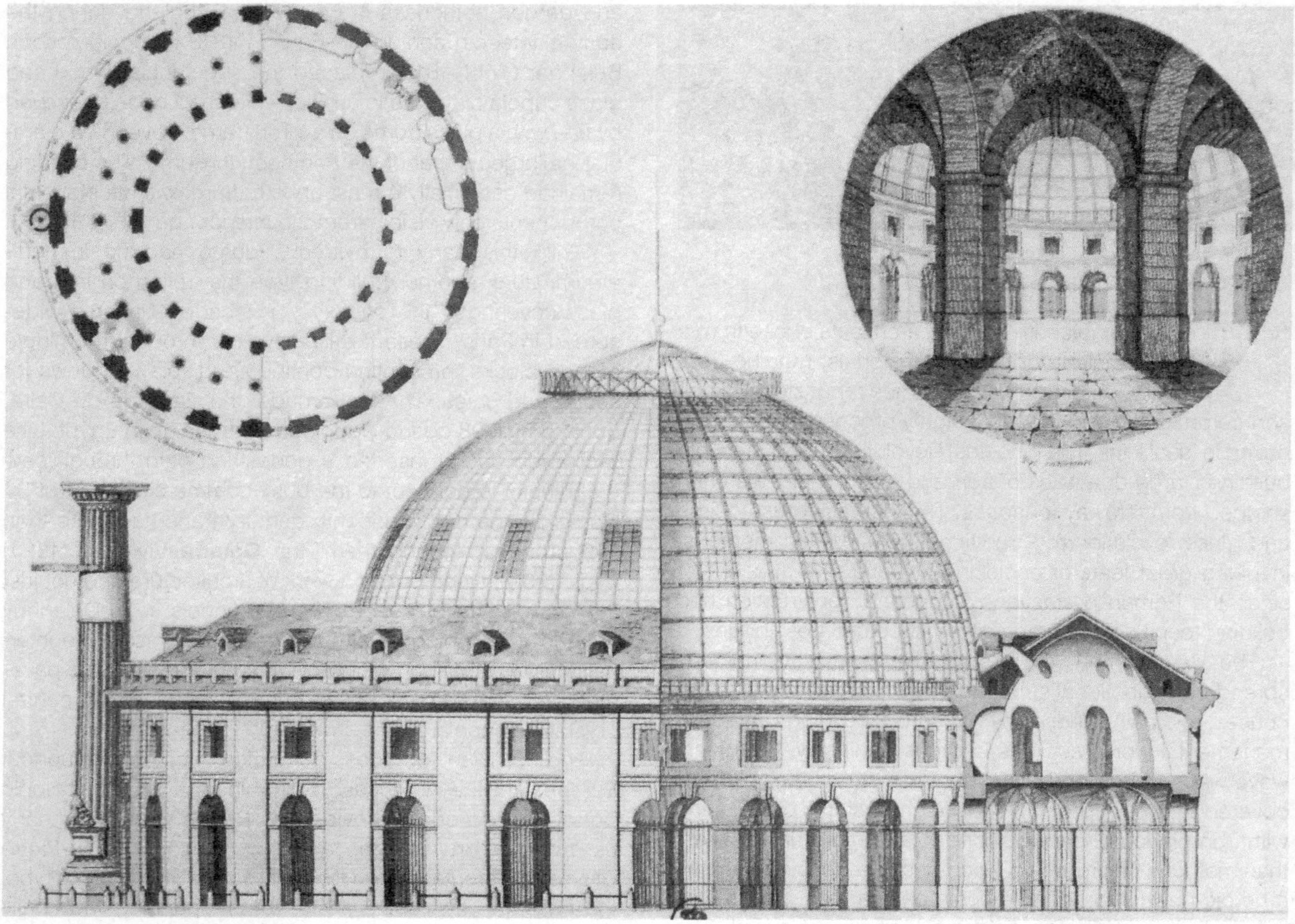

Figure 15.3-1 Paris. Halle au Blé, as rebuilt by François-Joseph Bélanger, 1813.

city's two major public spaces. The architect, Giuseppe Mengoni (1829–1877), designed the cruciform plan with ferrovitreous vaults culminating in a central glass cupola over the crossing. Financed by a British consortium, the Galleria included a mixture of two levels of retail, three levels of office space, and residential units above the glass vaults. All the major cities of Italy built their own version of Milan's Galleria in order to participate in this new expression of national progress.

The Milan Galleria remained at heart a masonry structure with a glass roof. The second solution for the ten sheds of Les Halles, the central wholesale market in Paris adjacent to the Halle au Blé, finally broke from this reliance on masonry exteriors. Victor Baltard (1805–1874) initially designed the market halls as a series of masonry shells covered with iron and glass roofs, but in 1853 he abandoned the masonry exteriors altogether, creating completely ferrovitreous skeletons (Fig. 15.3-5). Émile Zola (1840–1902) set his novel *The*

TIME LINE

1823

*François Jean Delannoy's
Galerie Vivienne in Paris*

*Joseph Paxton
builds Crystal Palace
for International
Exhibition in London*

1851

1855

*Victor Baltard's Les Halles, wholesale
markets, completed in Paris*

Figure 15.3-2 Paris. Galerie Vivienne, François Jean Delannoy, 1823.

Belly of Paris (1873) in the new markets. One of the characters points to Les Halles and paraphrases Victor Hugo, "This will kill that, iron will kill stone, the time is drawing near."

The idea for completely transparent iron and glass structures originated in England, where the landscape architect John Claudius Loudon (1783–1843) popularized the design of glass-covered iron vaults through numerous pamphlets. After experimenting with curvilinear hothouses in his own garden, Loudon created the two-tiered dome of the Palm House at Bretton Hall in 1827. A low outer ring of masonry and an interior circle of cast-iron columns supported the cascading bell-shaped dome. The wrought-iron sashes,

said by Loudon to be inspired by nomadic tents, proved exceptionally lightweight. He supplied steam heat from a hypercaust system that vented through the reveals between the upper and lower vaults. The majestic Palm House at Kew Gardens (Fig. 15.3-6a,b), built from 1844 to 1848 by Decimus Burton (1800–1881), testified to the durability and beauty of such new ferrovitreous structures.

Joseph Paxton (1801–1865) copied the section of his friend Loudon's "campanulated house" to build the Great Conservatory at Chatsworth (1836), where he served as chief gardener. Instead of a central plan, he extruded the bell shape on a rectangular basilical plan. Paxton also

Louis-Charles Boileau (with assistance from Gustave Eiffel) designs Au Bon Marché department store in Paris

▲ **1869**

▼ **1883**

Brooklyn Bridge completed in New York City

Forth Bridge begun near Edinburgh

▲ **1883**

Figure 15.3-3 Paris. Au Bon Marché, the grand staircase, Louis-Charles Boileau and Gustave Eiffel, 1867.

developed a more sophisticated roofing system based on some of Loudon's theories, using pleated glass, or ridge-and-furrow, construction. He folded the plane of the roof in a chevron pattern to both strengthen the structure and channel the water runoff more directly. The pleated roof brought in beneficial morning and evening sunlight while resisting the perpendicular rays of the harsh midday glare. The hollow, cast-iron columns of the interior doubled as drainpipes. Paxton also standardized the cast-iron parts so that they could be mass-produced and convinced the glass manufacturer to fabricate larger panes, 1.3 m (4 ft) long, reducing the number of struts needed to hold the glass. His "Great Stove" fulfilled a singularly Orientalist brief, housing the patron's rare tropical flora—orchids, bananas, and palms brought back from colonial India. In 1849 Paxton built a second hothouse with vertical walls to protect the same patron's greatest horticultural trophy, the gigantic *Victoria regia* water lily from the Amazon. The Lily House required a heated pool with a deep soil bottom to simulate the jungle conditions that allowed the lily's leaves to spread 2 m (6.5 ft) in diameter. Using the steam, glass, and iron of industry, Paxton created a virtual climate machine, with pipes heating the water, waterwheels that kept the water from stagnating, and mechanical vents that opened when needed. He patented the roof of the Lily House, which integrated the ridge-and-furrow panel system with grooved joists that functioned as gutters to carry the water runoff to crossbeams with larger gutters.

Figure 15.3-4 Milan. La Galleria, Guiseppe Mengoni, 1863–1878.

The Lily House served as the prototype for Paxton's design of the Crystal Palace, the most innovative ferrovitreous structure of the century. Designed to house the Great Exhibition of the Works of Industry of All Nations of 1851, the Crystal Palace (Fig. 15.3-7a) took its place among the largest structures ever built, longer than the Palace of Versailles and as tall as a Gothic cathedral. It embodied the utilitarian spirit of modern industry, built without masonry, almost exclusively of standardized components of iron and glass (Fig. 15.3-7b). Prince Albert stated at the inauguration that Paxton's structure clearly demonstrated the secret of the new industrial age: the division of labor.

Paxton set the enormous frame into limestone footings and followed a 7.3 × 7.3 m (24 × 24 ft) structural bay, which determined the layout of the 13,000 exhibition spaces. The site for the World's Fair in Hyde Park included a grand elm tree that could not be removed or damaged, and Paxton, whose structures until this point had been exclusively for hothouse plants, gladly created an envelope with a central barrel-vaulted transept to include the tree in the project. With an ingenuity similar to that exhibited by Brunelleschi (see Section 10.1), Paxton used the structure as a scaffold during construction. The grooved gutters in the ceiling joists served as rails for the aerial carriage of the glazers, pulled across the ceiling as they put the glass panels into place. Like the gardener's hothouses, the Crystal Palace exuded tremendous thermal energy. Despite the vents at the base and top of the structure and copious fountains distributed

Figure 15.3-5 Paris. Les Halles, interior, Victor Baltard, 1845–1855.

in the nave, Paxton had to add canvas tarps to shield the folded glass roof during the summer months.

Over 6 million people visited the Crystal Palace during its eighteen-month showing. While it attracted extremes of praise and blame, most critics recognized it as a turning point for architecture. New construction methods and materials had engendered a new aesthetic. Ruskin condemned its brittle, undecorated facades, yet the majority of commentators remained in awe. The great shed's sheer, glistening exterior conveyed the promise of utilitarianism, the greatest good for the greatest number. To modulate the harshness of the interior, Owen Jones (1809–1874), a leading theorist of the decorative arts, coordinated the colors applied to the structural members (Fig. 15.3-8).

The exhibitions ranged from displays of industrial machines, such as turbines, power looms, and McCormick's reaper, to handicrafts from colonial dependencies in India, Australia, and New Zealand. Pugin fashioned a Gothic display, while sixty individual countries sent exhibitions of their decorative arts. On the grounds nearby Prince Albert sponsored the construction in brick of a model four-plex structure for workers' housing. The great ferrovitreous shell of the Crystal Palace provided a stage for the prowess of the British Empire—dominator of world markets, vanguard of industry, and ruler of both huge colonial populations and the local working class.

The Architectural Response to Railways

The Crystal Palace proved too radical to have an immediate impact on architecture. While a smaller cruciform version of it appeared for a similar exposition in New York City in 1853, the techniques of mass production and lightness were confined to temporary structures. Architects desired to gain the structural advantage of iron skeletons but feared their insubstantial appearance. In 1857, when Sydney Smirke (1798–1877) designed a ferrovitreous cupola to cover the new Reading Room in the court of the British Museum (designed by his brother Robert), he went to great pains to disguise the metal with a type of *papier-mâché*, making it look like masonry.

England's most daring ferrovitreous buildings accompanied the advent of new infrastructures for the railways. Rail carriages pulled by horses had been used since the sixteenth century, usually for industrial purposes. The first railway for a steam-driven engine, a 40 km (25 miles) course used for the transport of goods, began operation in 1825 between Stockton and Darlington. Five years later a 60 km

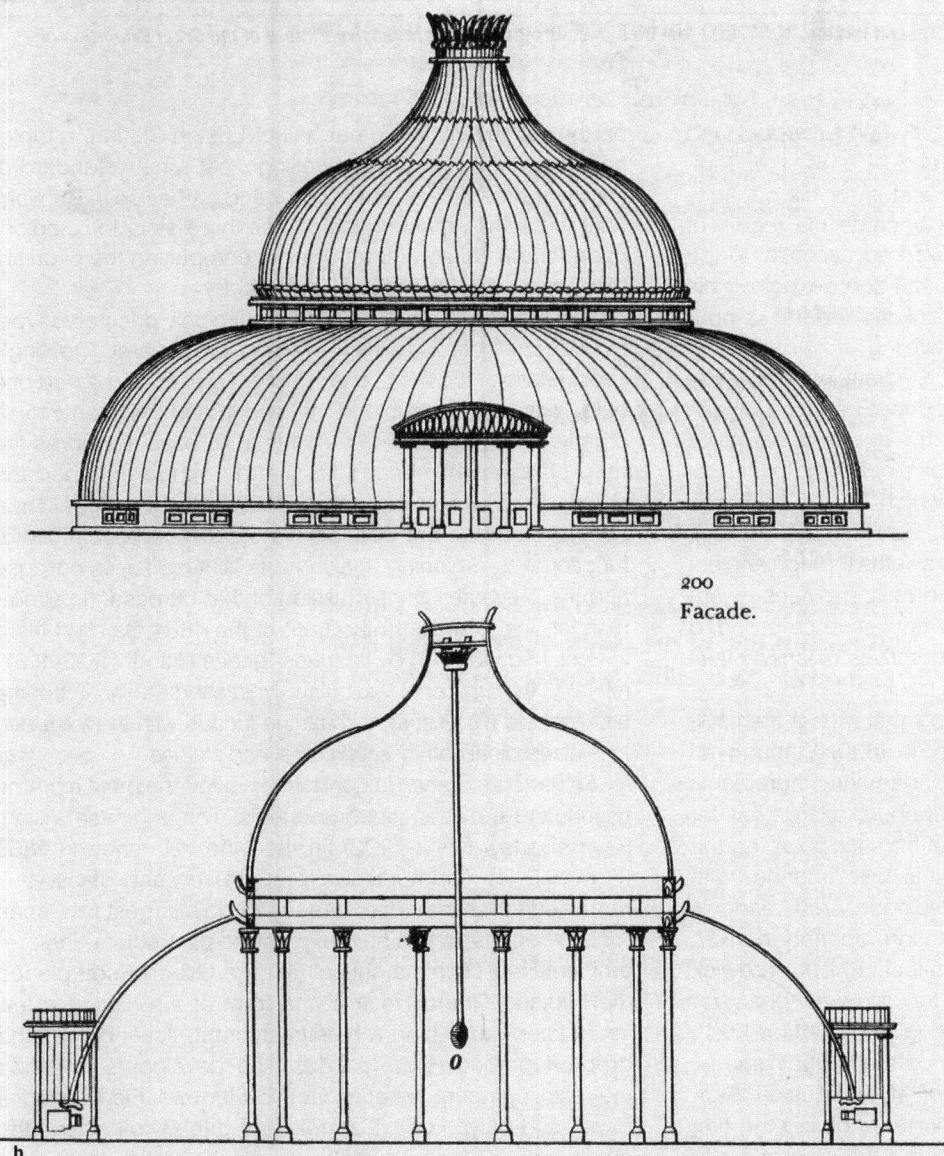

200
Facade.

O

Figure 15.3-6 (a) London. Kew Gardens, Palm House, Decimus Burton, 1844–1848. (b) England. Bretton Hall, Palm House, John Claudius Loudon, 1827.

Figure 15.3-7 London. Crystal Palace, Joseph Paxton, 1851. (a) From Dickinson Brothers, *Comprehensive Picture of the Great Exhibition of 1851*, 1854. (b) See facing page.

(37 mile) passenger line opened between Liverpool and Manchester. George Stephenson (1781–1848), the engineer behind both, assumed heroic status for his capacity to overcome natural obstacles. He became the model of the engineer-entrepreneur who proved so essential to the business of early railways. Stephenson soon exported his services to Belgium and Sweden. To keep the tracks on a relatively flat course required the leveling of hills, digging of tunnels, and bridging of vales. The violent imperatives of railway infrastructure led the philosopher Friedrich Wilhelm Nietzsche (1844–1900) to call it the agent of "creative destruction." Engineers ruthlessly eliminated both natural and urban settings to lay tracks, which by the 1850s in England alone covered more than 10,000 km (6,213 miles). An army of tens of thousands cut raw swaths through ancient hills—brutally fording, tunneling, and raising pylons where rural churches and princely country houses once brooded over the land. Stephenson's iron locomotives belched black clouds as they rattled along parallel tracks (Fig. 15.3-9).

Stephenson established the world's first proper train station, Crown Street Station in Liverpool, in 1830. Although not much to look at, it possessed the fundamental ingredients of the new type, including a drop-off court, a large hall for the ticket office, a waiting area, a platform for boarding the trains, and a covered train shed—in this case, spanned with a pitched timber roof. Stephenson also sponsored London's first example of the type, Euston Station, opened in 1837. He hired a classically trained architect, Philip Hardwick (1792–1870), to design the station for his Birmingham-to-London line. The engineer, Charles Douglas Fox (1840–1921), designed the utilitarian wrought-iron roofs of the train sheds. Hardwick's colossal Doric propylaia at the Euston Arch marked the entry to the drop-off court, becoming the first monument to railway travel. It reoriented the idea of a city gate to a central position within the city rather than a point

on the perimeter. The great hall of Euston Station, a triple-height atrium with coffered ceilings, set a new standard of luxury and elegance. At the other end of the line in Birmingham the same architect designed a three-story Ionic colonnade for the Curzon Street Station, completing the circuit of modern travel with ancient iconography.

While the station hall evolved into a highly decorated type, the train shed became one of the most functionalist. The King's Cross Station (1851) by Lewis Cubitt (1799–1883) proved one of the only stations to blend the facade and the shed into an organic composition. The arcades at its base served as the drop-off site, while enormous thermal windows traced the shape of the two ferrovitreous barrel vaults of the train shed behind them. Cubitt justified his stark facade with proto-functionalist reasoning, claiming its "fitness for its purpose and the characteristic expression of that purpose." In similar manner, the **lunette** on the front of the 1864 Gare du Nord in Paris (Fig. 15.3-10) by Jacques-Ignace Hittorff (1792–1867) revealed the functional vault of the train shed behind it, but the architect did his best to animate the facade with the full repertoire of classical cornices, columns, and statues.

St. Pancras Station in London exhibited the most extreme disjuncture between its components. The engineer William Henry Barlow (1812–1902) finished the train shed in 1868 (Fig. 15.3-11). Its impressive wrought-iron and glass vault remained for several decades the world's largest free-span roof. In contrast to this pure expression of structure, the pre-eminent Neo-Gothic architect George Gilbert Scott placed the Midland Grand Hotel at the front of the station a few years later, combining a hotel/restaurant, ticket office, and drop-off portico (Fig. 15.3-12). The developers intended the resulting riot of Venetian Gothic windows, Flemish clock tower, and polychromatic turrets and gables to improve the area's reputation as a poor slum, and the station became a national symbol.

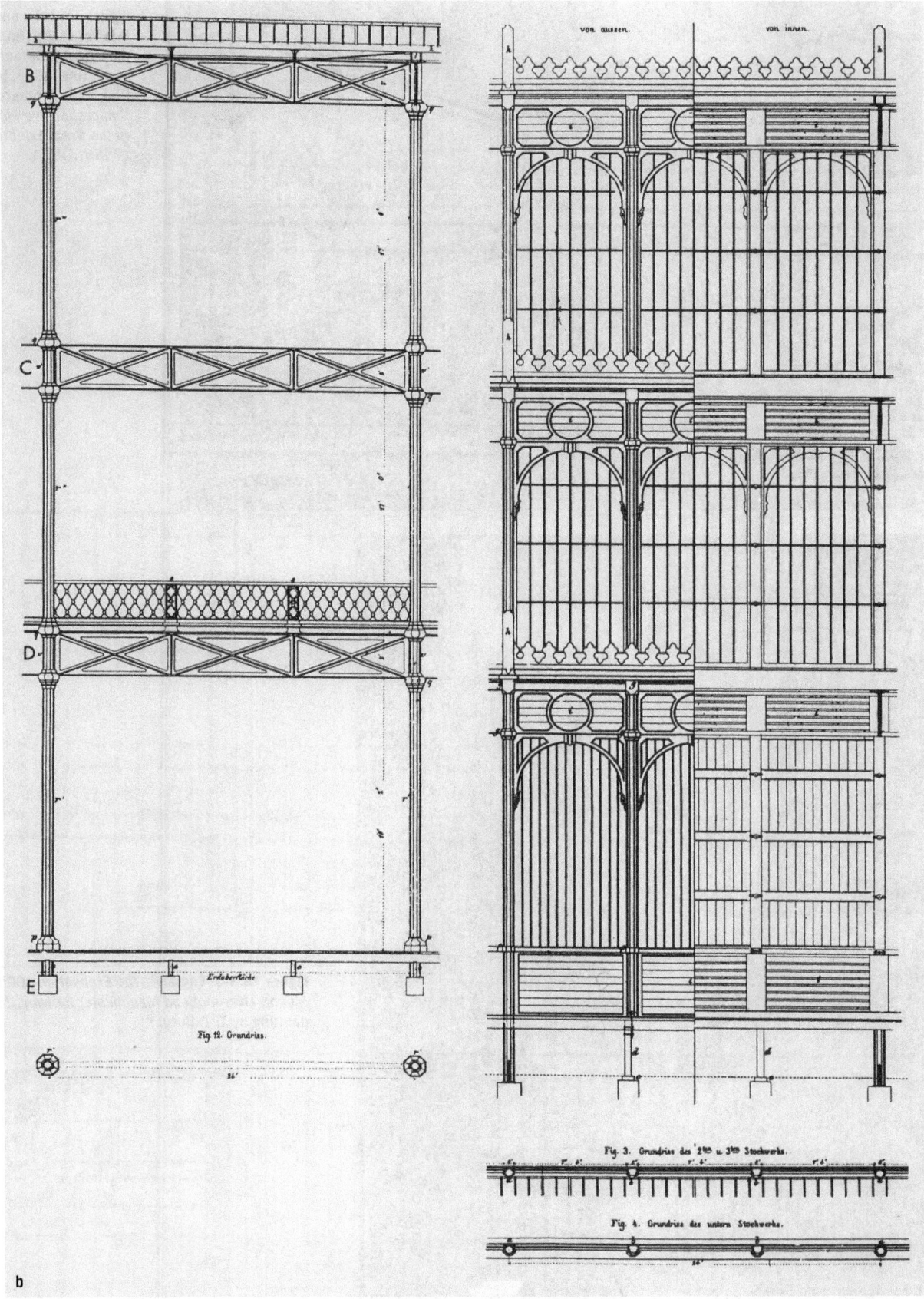

Figure 15.3-7 London. Crystal Palace, Joseph Paxton, 1851. (b) Details of mass-produced cast-iron facade, from Dickinson Brothers.

Figure 15.3-8 London. Interior of Crystal Palace during International Exhibition, 1851, from Dickinson Brothers, *Comprehensive Picture of the Great Exhibtion of 1851*, 1854.

Figure 15.3-9 England. *The Excavation of Olive Mount, Liverpool and Manchester Railway*, 1831, painting by T. T. Bury.

Figure 15.3-10 Paris. Gare du Nord, Jacques-Ignace Hittorff, 1860s.

Figure 15.3-11 London. St. Pancras Station train shed, William Henry Barlow, 1868.

Figure 15.3-12 London.
St. Pancras, Neo-Gothic hotel,
G. G. Scott, 1868.

The greatest advances in iron construction commenced with Stephenson's long-span bridges for his railways. His posthumously completed Britannia Bridge of 1850 over the Menai Strait, located within view of Telford's suspension bridge (see Section 14.3), introduced another kind of national symbol. To guarantee the stability of the bridge and absorb the lateral forces of moving trains, he created a long, wrought-iron tube with a rectangular section that pierced through three masonry pylons. Each section spanned 150 m (492 ft), resulting in an elevated tunnel. Stephenson's method proved both conservative and empirical: he intended the tall piers to carry the chains of a suspension bridge, but the tubes proved to be strong enough without this extra support.

Stephenson's friend and rival, Isambard Kingdom Brunel (1806–1859), took greater risks. From 1825 to 1841 he worked with his father installing the Thames Tunnel, the first underwater tunnel in the world. The 396 m (1,300 ft) tube served initially as a route for carriage travel and later for the subway system. His father invented the tunneling shield, a device that kept the water back as the workers dug the shaft. The operation used steam engines to drive the pumps and the cutting blades that removed the soil from the river bottom. Brunel lived up to the role of the cigar-smoking entrepreneur of the railways and steamship lines, designing bridges, stations, and huge iron steamships. Following Stephenson's example, he founded a railway company (the Great Western) and built such projects as the Box Tunnel near Bath, the longest tunnel in the world when completed in 1841. His Paddington Station in London rose on three vaults carried by wrought-iron arches. Brunel created his most adventurous structure for the Royal Albert Bridge in Saltash (Fig. 15.3-13), Cornwall, begun in 1855 and finished shortly before his death. For that structure he returned to the concept of wrought-iron tubes, placing two lengths between the short stone pylons above the train deck in the shape of segmental arches. He then mirrored the arches around the horizontal axis under the tracks, creating eye-shape forms. To stabilize the bridge, he dropped suspension cables from the top arches to the deck. Brunel spanned a similar distance as Stephenson's Britannia Bridge, but with only half as much material and at half the cost.

Brunel trained in France, where engineers tended to gain a better theoretical base for analyzing the forces acting on metal structures. The greatest among them, Gustave Eiffel, likewise became an entrepreneur, owning a factory for iron components. He started his career designing an iron railway bridge with web **trusses** in Bordeaux

Figure 15.3-13 Saltash, England. Royal Albert Bridge, Isambard Kingdom Brunel, 1859.

in 1858 and, after building numerous iron bridges in various countries, brought his work to a climax with the world's tallest structure, the tower that took his name for the 1889 Exposition in Paris. Eiffel felt confident in his calculations, always factoring in wind pressure as a major force. He perfected a system of delicate iron webs, used on such structures as the Maria Pia Viaduct over the Duoro River in Porto (1877) (Fig. 15.3-14). Its masonry foundations supported towers of wrought-iron girders that formed a central crescent arch, spanning a record-breaking 160 m (525 ft). Eiffel used the bridge's structure as a scaffold for lifting prefabricated sections into place. The arch's form resembled an elegant stress diagram, deep and narrow at the central summit and flaring outward at the hinged bases.

Eiffel's diagrammatic type of structure prepared the way for the consummate work of web construction, the Forth

Figure 15.3-14 Porto, Portugal. Maria Pia Viaduct, open web trusses, Eiffel, 1877.

Bridge near Edinburgh (Fig. 15.3-15), designed by Benjamin Baker (1840–1907) in 1883. Using structural steel, Baker raised three tapering towers of hollow steel tubes and then

Open Web Trusses

Wrought iron and steel are both strong in tension. Systems of open web struts, organized into triangular, folded, or crisscross patterns, can be made from either material into skeletal trusses that have the depth of beams without the mass. When a flat truss is extended laterally, it becomes a space truss, or space frame, of the sort used on bridges. The common truss is made of diagonal members, the Pratt truss has crossed members, the bowstring truss is a common truss shaped into an arch, and the Vierendeel truss uses squares instead of diagonal members.

cantilevered the arches from these pyramidal piers. To his numerous critics who objected to such a stark structure he replied that "fitness was the fundamental condition of beauty."

Most of the great bridges of the first age of the railways traversed rural settings. America's greatest bridge builder, John Augustus Roebling (1806–1869), an émigré from Germany with a strong theoretical background, built his first internationally recognized suspension bridge in the wilderness near Niagara Falls in 1852. He innovated by using cables of woven steel instead of iron chains, which led to greater stability. Like the other famous engineers, he started his own manufacturing business. He mass-produced the cables, thus ensuring his fortune. Roebling's final project addressed a completely urban situation, the most intense urban setting in the United States, joining Brooklyn to the southern tip of Manhattan Island. Although he died in an accident in 1869, the very year that construction on the Brooklyn Bridge began, his son, Washington Roebling (1837–1926), and his son's wife, Emily Warren Roebling (1843–1903), brought the project to completion in 1883. The structure of the Brooklyn Bridge mixed an open-joist system for the deck with a suspension system hung from two monumental masonry towers. Nearly 2 km (1.3 miles) long, the central span stretched 486 m (1,594 ft). The stone towers with their lancet arches evoked the cathedrals of medieval Europe, while the steel cables spoke of the power of modern technology. Roebling's bridge was neither as light nor as economical as Eiffel's and Baker's structures yet represented a major cultural breakthrough. It became at once an emblem of America's modernity and an icon of national pride. The quality of the Brooklyn Bridge, functional yet representational, raised infrastructure to the highest art of the new Iron Age.

Figure 15.3-15 Edinburgh. Forth Bridge, steel tube structure, Benjamin Baker, 1883.

Emily Warren Roebling's Brooklyn Bridge

Only three years after his father's untimely death, Washington Roebling became afflicted with caisson disease, or "the bends," a nervous disorder suffered by miners. Partially paralyzed and unable to speak, Roebling relied on his wife, Emily Warren Roebling, to carry out the completion of the Brooklyn Bridge. At first she acted as her husband's emissary, but soon she directly supervised construction. Gifted in mathematics, she became thoroughly literate in engineering computations and budgetary matters. Emily Warren Roebling abandoned engineering after the completion of the bridge and acquired a law degree to become one of the leaders of the women's suffrage movement.

New York City. Brooklyn Bridge, John Augustus Roebling, Washington Roebling, and Emily Warren Roebling, 1869–1883.

Further Reading

Billington, David P. *The Tower and the Bridge: The New Art of Structural Engineering*. Princeton, NJ: Princeton University Press, 1983.

Kohlmaier, Georg, and Barna von Sartory. *Houses of Glass: A Nineteenth-Century Building Type*. Translated by J. C. Harvey. Cambridge, MA: MIT Press, 1986.

Williams, Rosalind. *Notes on the Underground*. Cambridge, MA: MIT Press, 1990.

Visit the free website **www.oup.com/us/ingersoll** to view chapter outlines and study questions; Google Maps showing the location of key sites; links to UNESCO World Heritage Sites; and essays on topics that cross time and culture.

1850–1890

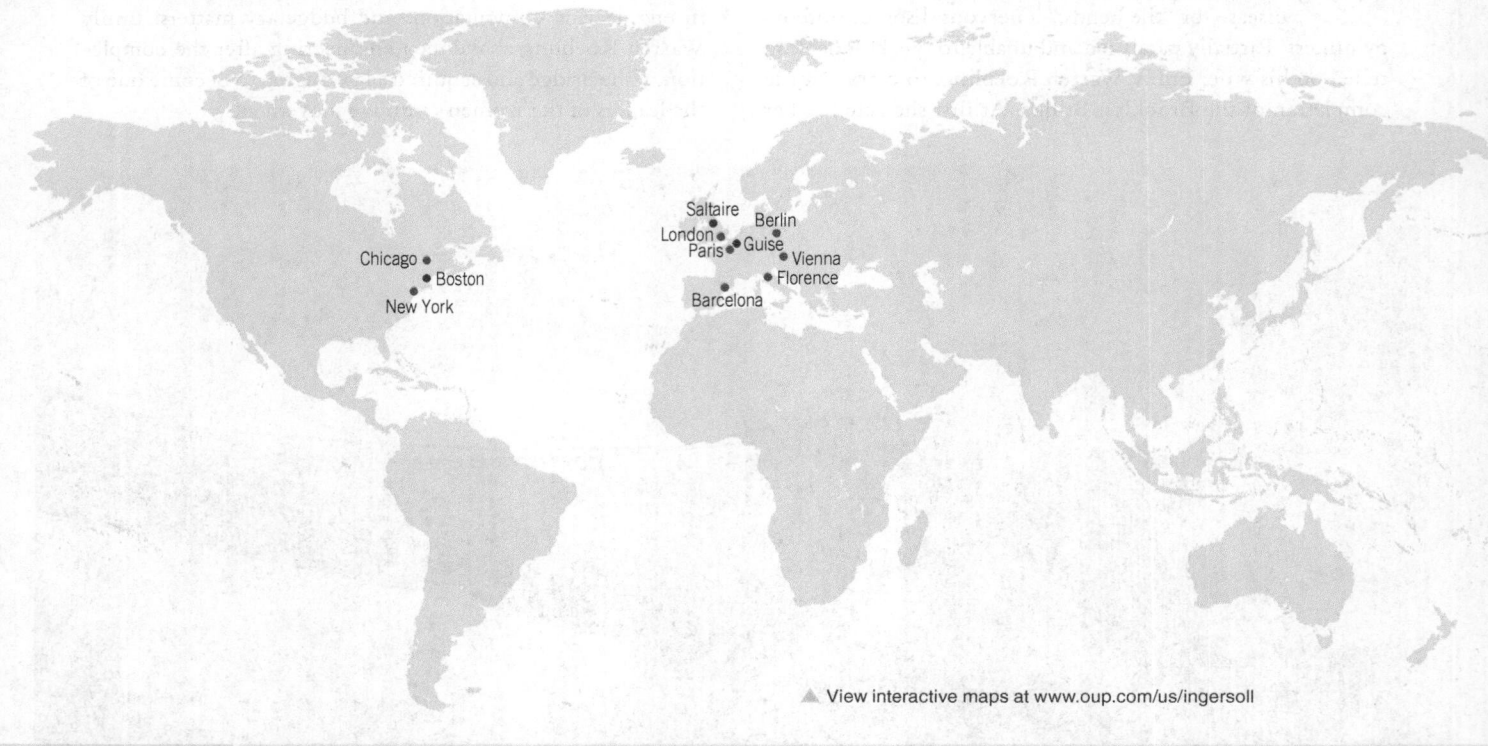

Saltaire
Berlin
London • • Guise
Paris • •
Chicago • Vienna
• Boston • Florence
New York Barcelona

▲ View interactive maps at www.oup.com/us/ingersoll

16.1 THE RISE OF THE METROPOLIS: Urbanism and the New Scale of Architecture

16.2 LIFESTYLES AND HOUSE FORM: Apartments, Row Houses, Bungalows, and Utopias

16.3 THE BEAUX-ARTS: Eclecticism and Professionalism

The dramatic increase in the size of industrial cities during the nineteenth century spawned regular conflicts related to labor, disease, transportation infrastructure, housing, and public space. While London emerged as the first great metropolis of modernity, Paris produced the strongest urban models as a result of planner Baron Haussmann's demolition and rebuilding of large sections of the city using technocratic criteria of transportation on broad boulevards, efficient sewerage, a renewed water supply, and grand public parks. In Vienna planners replaced the old fortifications around the historic city with the Ringstrasse in the effort to stay apace with France. Cerdá's 1859 plan for Barcelona, a grand linear grid made of standard blocks, proposed an efficient model for the new industrial metropolis that allowed ample green spaces. As the cities expanded, new building types appeared. Train stations became important references in the new fabric, while multilevel apartment buildings began to densify city blocks. The row house type, preferred in Anglo-American contexts, resulted in a more horizontal urban expansion, while the single-family dwelling consumed even greater amounts of land per person. Socialists and utopians proposed collectivist alternatives, such as the Familistère at Guise in France. Amid the great urban transformations, architects attained a new level of professionalism. The Beaux-Arts School in Paris provided the model for international architectural education, inspiring innumerable projects with eclectic combinations of classical, Baroque, and medieval architectural styles applied to rational plan organization. In the United States the Beaux-Arts influence spawned an "American Renaissance," best illustrated by the classical extravaganza of the White City at the 1893 Chicago Columbian Exposition.

16.1 THE RISE OF THE METROPOLIS
Urbanism and the New Scale of Architecture

Modernity and the metropolis nurtured each other. During the boom periods of industrial development, the cities of Europe and America grew beyond recognition. Their dramatic growth was the result of both a lowered mortality rate and mass immigration. Newcomers from the countryside arrived in trainloads in the central cities of Europe, while ocean liners transported millions of impoverished Europeans to ports across the Atlantic. London accumulated over 1 million inhabitants in the early nineteenth century and continued to double in size every fifty years. Paris caught up by midcentury and by 1900 had a population of 3.3 million. Berlin grew ten times its size to a population of 1.5 million by the 1890s. Chicago, which in 1850 had fewer than 40,000 residents, reached the same size as Berlin at century's end.

This new scale of population growth inevitably affected the form and governance of cities. As they grew higher and wider, they required more comprehensive planning and social services. *Metropolis*, the Greek word for "mother city," came to signify an urban core surrounded by widely spread subsidiary settlements. The industrial metropolis grew too large to cross on foot, inspiring new forms of transportation, such as omnibuses and streetcars. London introduced the first underground railway in 1863 and established the prototype for a layered city with service functions below grade. Crime and health problems accompanied urban overcrowding, inspiring new health, police, and prison systems and improved infrastructures for sewer and water management. Technical progress generated new architectural types, such as office buildings, train stations, large hotels, and department stores. Rapid immigration, expedient housing solutions, and the anonymous culture of mass society contributed to the success of the new industrial metropolis while resulting in an unexpected consequence: a city of strangers.

Haussmann's Paris: The Dawn of the Technocrat

After the impressive transformation of London's Regent Street during the first half of the nineteenth century (see Section 14.1),

European cities experienced a wave of metropolitan-scale planning. By midcentury Paris commanded the center of attention, revealing the most dramatic urban changes. There the modern practice of urbanism, a mixture of technical, social, and aesthetic ideas for the design of large cities, took hold on a comprehensive scale. During the relatively liberal reign of Louis-Philippe (r. 1830–1848), planners began to widen and straighten the city's streets, architects refined the form of institutional buildings, and engineers increased the city's water and sewerage capacity. After the revolt of 1848, which toppled the restored monarchy, the government of the Second Republic chose the nephew of Napoléon Bonaparte as president. Louis-Napoléon, the "prince-president," had spent most of his life as an exile in such cities as Munich, Milan, New York, and London. His travels made him a staunch supporter of the technological marvels of the liberal state. During his third year as the legally elected president, he staged a *coup d'état* that left him in power for another eighteen years. As Emperor Napoléon III (r. 1852–1870), he vowed that France's Second Empire would complete the task of modernization begun by the first Napoléon.

To achieve his goals, Napoléon III appointed the resourceful technocrat Georges-Eugène Haussmann (1809–1891) as the all-powerful prefect of the Seine, granting him the title of "baron." The new emperor dashed a series of colored lines over the map of Paris, indicating the boulevards he would like to open to clarify the structure of the city; and his chief administrator took care of the rest, coordinating matters of demolition, water supply, sanitation, transportation, and public debt. Together they executed an unprecedented urban renovation, transforming most of Paris from an overcrowded city of narrow, damp streets into a clean, well-lit metropolis of broad, tree-lined boulevards and public parks.

Haussmann came from a Protestant family in Alsace and had studied law in Paris. As prefect of Bordeaux he acquired sound experience with the technical dimensions of infrastructure. He also revealed a talent for deficit financing. During his two decades of power in Paris, he proudly referred to his design method as *éventrement*, or "disemboweling." He proposed "surgical" interventions involving costly expropriations and massive demolitions to obtain a healthy ensemble of level and paved tree-lined streets, perfectly aligned apartment buildings, asphalt sidewalks, underground water mains, sewers, and gaslights. Starting with the Île de la Cité, the oldest and densest quarter of Paris, Haussmann proceeded to operate systematically on what he considered the "sick" city. By 1860, all that remained standing on the island were the newly restored monuments; the Cathedral of Notre-Dame (see Section 9.2), now set off by a plaza forty times larger than the original **parvis**; the Ste.-Chapelle, now enveloped by the new Palace of Justice; and the triangular Place Dauphine. The rest of the island carried tangible expressions of the new regime's priorities for hygiene and security: the new Hôtel-Dieu hospital and the central police headquarters. The demolitions also eliminated the homes of more than 14,000 residents, most of

Figure 16.1-1 Paris. (a) Buttes-Chaumont Park, built over a dump site, Jean-Charles Adolphe Alphand, 1860s. (b) See facing page.

his seventeen years in office he built two major aqueducts, which finally freed Paris from relying on the river for its water. He further improved the city's hygiene with the installation of eleven sewer trunk lines that dumped effluents farther downstream at Asnières. Newly constructed buildings had to conform in plan and elevation to these lines in order to plug into the complex network of drains and water mains. The hydraulic engineers who constructed this infrastructure used the innovative constructional material of ferroconcrete, a cement-based mixture stiffened with metal mesh, invented by François Coignet (1814–1888). Paris's new clean water supply reduced the threat of the waterborne disease of cholera, which in 1849 had taken the lives of 20,000.

Hygiene also motivated Napoléon III's planners to multiply 100-fold the number of public gardens in the city, creating new parks for both its wealthy and its poor sections. The most expensive, the Parc des Buttes-Chaumont (Fig. 16.1-1a,b), occupied an old gypsum quarry that had been turned into a dump site in the city's poorest neighborhood. In addition, Haussmann's program yielded seventy schools, two hospitals, nine military barracks, and seven markets.

them destitute, compelling them to move to shantytowns on the outskirts of Paris. Haussmann's technocratic strategies intended to clean up the city both physically and socially, resulting in the first substantial case of urban gentrification, by which the new rich uprooted the poor from the center of the city.

Haussmann's most substantial interventions, the 140 km (87 ft) of aqueducts and a major network of sewers, remained out of sight beneath the new boulevards. During

The 150 km (93 mile) network of new Parisian boulevards remained Haussmann's most conspicuous achievement

TIME LINE

 1848

Revolutions in many European countries; publication of Marx and Engels's *Communist Manifesto*

Baron Haussmann directs public works for Paris

▲ **1851–1869**

▼ **1852**

Louis-Napoléon Bonaparte, president of France, takes power as emperor of the Second Empire

After more than two centuries Japan ends policy of isolation

▲ **1854**

▼ **1855**

Earthquake, tsunami, and fire destroy Edo (Tokyo)

Figure 16.1-1 Paris. (b) Engraving from Adolphe Alphand, Les Promenades de Paris, 1873.

(Fig. 16.1-2). He gave the streets coherent facades and a uniform square section of roughly 18 m (59 ft) from building to building. The wider streets, such as Avenue Foch, which stretched 130 m (427 ft) from side to side, carried broad flanks of full-grown trees, leaving in the center the standard 18 m (59 ft) width for the carriage route. Haussmann privileged Boulevard Sebastopol as the new north–south crossing with the Rue de Rivoli. To economize, he ran the new street through the middle of the block rather than widening an existing street, spending two-thirds less on expropriation than he would have if he had borne the cost of purchasing the street frontage. He struck the new street from the riverbank to the Gare de l'Est. The traffic strategy of connecting the seven major train stations with wide boulevards made underground connections unnecessary until 1900.

Napoléon III made no effort to hide the regime's political motives for carving broad boulevards across the eastern districts of Paris, where rioting and the erection of barricades had become popular traditions. The tree-lined Boulevard Richard Lenoir, which covered a 2 km (1.2 mile) stretch of the St. Martin Canal, eliminated a major impediment to military deployment in that part of the city. Lucrative real estate speculation and tax incentives spawned the frenetic renewals that turned Paris into a chaotic building site for nearly thirty years. As a means of popular appeasement, the regime offered a public works program, keeping about one-third of the population at work on demolitions and construction.

Aside from their hygienic and military objectives, both Napoléon III and Haussmann aspired to architectural

▼ **1858**

Creation of Ringstrasse plan for Vienna

▲ **1858**

Olmsted and Vaux's Central Park begun in New York City

French add Vietnam and much of Southeast Asia to their colonial holdings

▲ **1859**

▼ **1859**

Cerdá produces plan for Barcelona of linear grid with open blocks

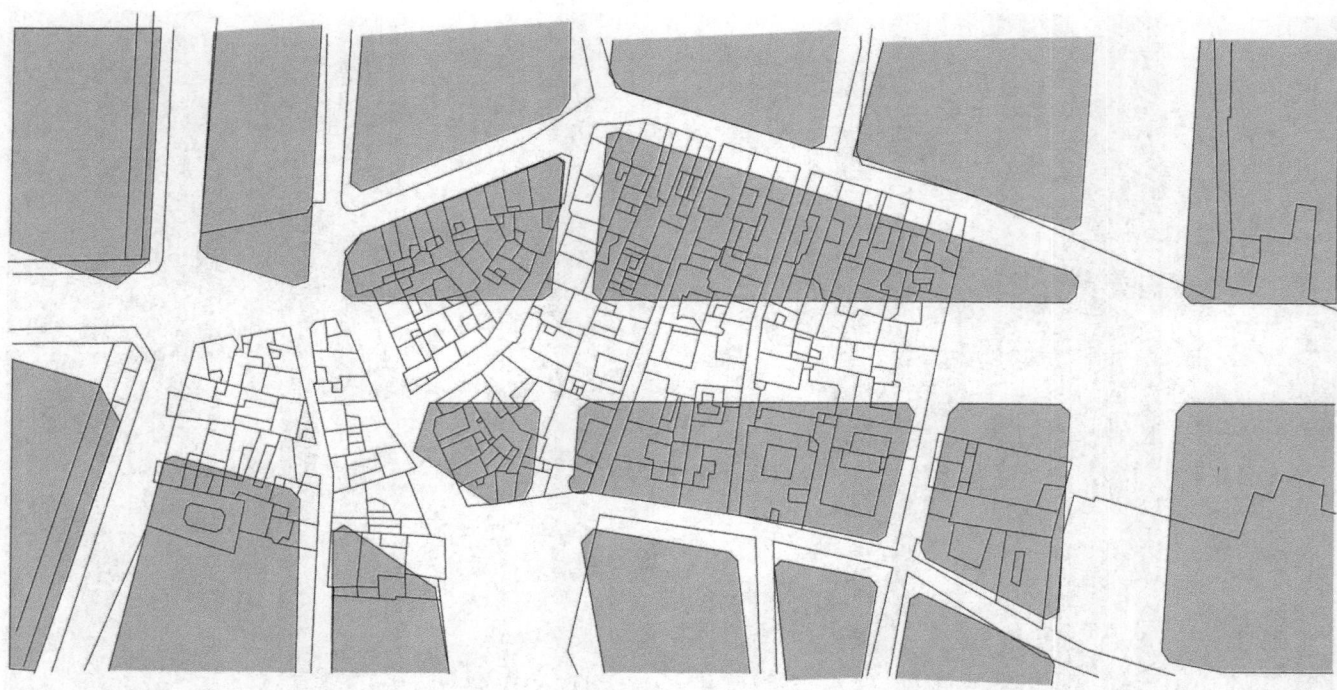

Figure 16.1-2 Paris. Map showing a detail of Georges-Eugène Haussmann's interventions, 1855–1860. The gray areas represent the new blocks built over the demolished medieval fabric, which was replaced by the 22 m (70 ft) wide Boulevard St. Michel and its new apartment buildings, shown in white.

greatness. They shared a preference for the clean lines of French Renaissance buildings but also encouraged the spread of eclectic styles. They insisted that major plazas be surrounded with coordinated facades, such as those designed by Jacques Hittorff for the twelve radiating avenues at Place de l'Étoile (now Place Charles de Gaulle) that framed the Arc de Triomphe. Haussmann tried to align his new boulevards to monuments at the end of perspective corridors for aesthetic pleasure.

Haussmann drew upon a gifted batch of professionals from different camps in the Parisian architectural debate. The great restoration expert Eugène-Emmanuel Viollet-le-Duc, a personal friend of Empress Eugénie, represented one extreme that placed more value on structural expression than on decoration. He was commissioned to restore the medieval castle of Pierrefonds as the imperial couple's private retreat. Most of the projects of the Second Empire, however, went to the studio masters of the École des Beaux-Arts, who, unlike Viollet-le-Duc, insisted on classical composition

and fanciful decoration. The emperor chose the classically trained Louis-Tullius-Joachim Visconti (1791–1853) to design the first important monument of the Second Empire, the completion of the Louvre-Tuileries compound for the imperial residence, various ministries, and the celebrated museum. After the untimely death of Visconti, the project was completed by Hector-Martin Lefuel (1810–1880). He cleared the slum dwellings from the outer court and decorated the new wings with sculptural window frames, colossal scrolls, and steep, three-level mansard roofs (Fig. 16.1-3). The bombastic elaboration of the dormers and the bulging mansards on the central pavilion became widely copied icons of the Second Empire style.

Despite Napoléon III's authoritarian bent, he endorsed liberal, secular culture. He favored the new Opéra, rather than a church, a palace, or a triumphal arch, as the institution to represent his re-gime. Haussmann allotted the Opéra a prime position at the end of a broad axis struck obliquely from the new wing of the Louvre. He set it in a

▼ **1861–1865**

American Civil War causes 600,000 casualties

Empress Dowager Cixi gains control of Chinese state

▲ **1861**

Italians achieve national unity

▲ **1861–1870**

▼ **1863**

London begins building first underground rail system

Transcontinental railway built across United States

▲ **1869**

▼ **1869**

Suez Canal built by French company to connect Red Sea to Mediterranean

Adolphe Alphand's Urban Landscapes

Haussmann brought from his team in Bordeaux the gifted engineer Jean-Charles Adolphe Alphand (1817–1891) to oversee the design of major new parks and planted boulevards. Adolphe Alphand pursued picturesque design principles rather than French formal precedents, reshaping the Bois de Boulogne with a rushing waterfall and creating an enchanted island connected to the rest of the park with iron bridges at Buttes-Chaumont. With the landscaper Jean-Pierre Barillet-Deschamps, he determined the section of the new Parisian boulevards, insisting on the installation of full-grown trees to give them formal definition. In this enterprise he was joined by Gavriel Davioud (1824–1881), one of the few important architects of the time not associated with the Beaux-Arts, who designed the street furniture, kiosks, and outdoor urinals for the principal landscape projects. After Haussmann's demise and the fall of the Second Empire, Adolphe Alphand continued as director of public works. He celebrated the urban design of Paris in his treatise *Les Promenades de Paris* (1873).

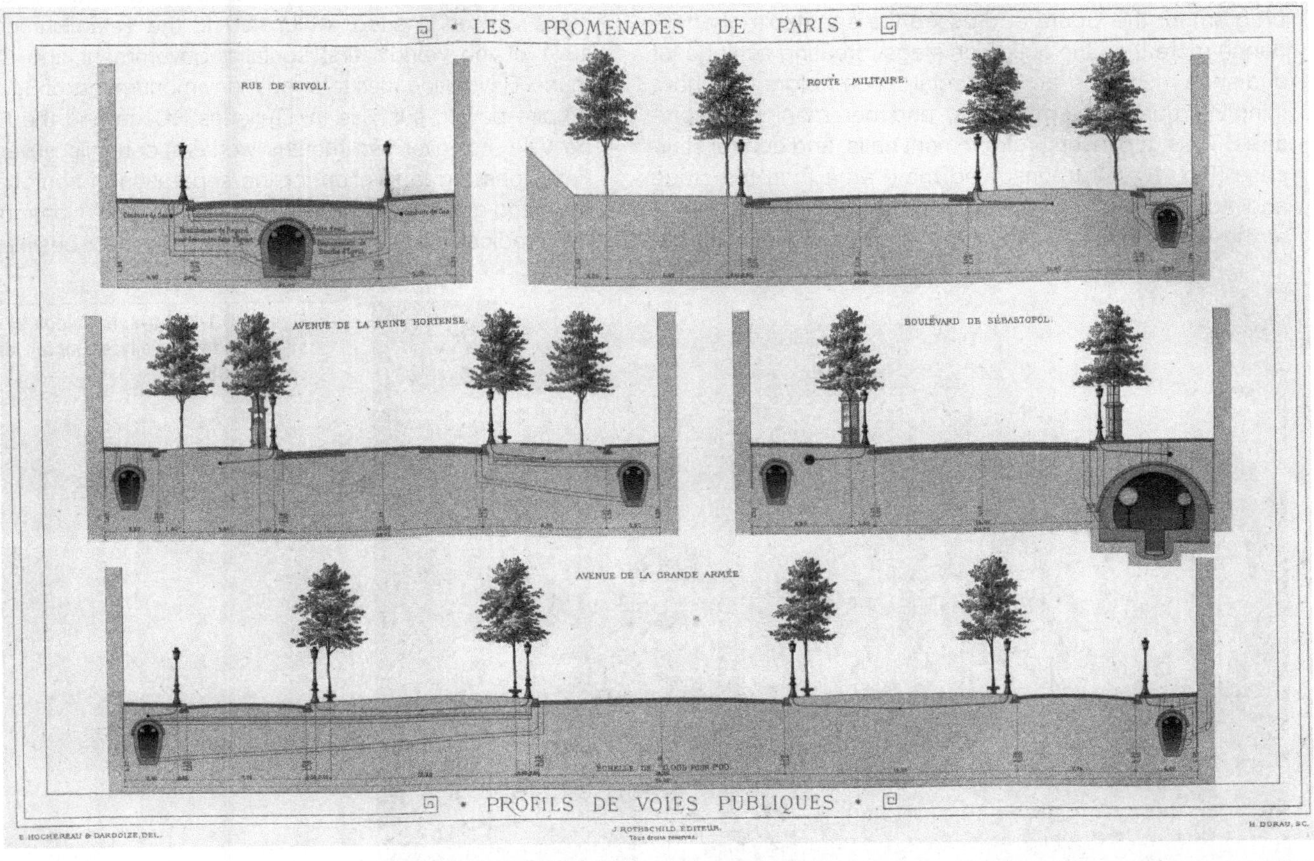

Paris. Section of Parisian boulevards. From Adolphe Alphand, *Les Promenades de Paris*, 1873.

1871

Franco–Prussian War places Paris under siege and leads to German national unity

1870–1871

Two-month communist government of La Commune in Paris

Great Chicago Fire

1871

1892–1895

Freud introduces theories of mental health in Vienna

Burnham & Root's Reliance Building in Chicago

1893

diamond-shaped square in which all of the surrounding facades utilized the same colossal pilasters (Fig. 16.1-4a). The young Beaux-Arts architect Charles Garnier (1825–1898) won the competition for the Opéra's design in 1861, pursuing the reverse of Viollet-le-Duc's theory of structure as decoration. He artfully concealed the theater's structural iron frame with polychromatic stone cladding. For the front facade he created a synthesis of Claude Perrault's paired columns on the Louvre and Michelangelo's colossal porticoes on the Campidoglio. Above the roof, he pitched a bulging, copper-clad dome as a crown for the auditorium seating. The exterior dome rose independently of the interior vaulted ceiling, soaring about twice its size, leaving a huge void that served no other purpose than to conceal the shaft for drawing up the immense chandelier during performances. Garnier's program for the Opéra addressed the spectacle of attendance more than the action on stage, creating settings for audience members' arrival, socialization before the show, mingling during intermissions, and ceremonious departures. Thus, the foyers, refreshment halls, and central staircase (Fig. 16.1-4b) consumed more area than the stage and auditorium. The convergence of the various entries at the triple-height atrium of the grand staircase put the well-to-do on display. In the subscribers' lobby below the auditorium Garnier embedded mirrors into the columns to pick up the light and allow those in fancy dress to check their attire before ascending the curvaceous staircase. Because of two earlier assassination attempts while the emperor was on his way to a theater, the design included a separate *porte-cochère* on the western flank for the imperial entry, leading to a grand suite with a dining hall. Napoléon III fell from power before the theater's completion and did not survive to see it open in 1875.

The gentrified city of the Second Empire, where the lower classes could no longer afford the rents, generated a popular backlash. Haussmann, indicted on charges of embezzlement, left office in 1870. The emperor abdicated a few months later after his failure to stop the Prussians from invading France. A rent strike organized by lower-class women ensued, which led to the establishment in 1871 of the world's first socialist government, the Commune. Revolutionaries torched many monuments of Second Empire power, such as the Tuileries Palace and the Hôtel de Ville. For over two months workers' councils governed Paris, passing legislation for the separation of church and state and granting women the right to vote. The Commune's most radical law permitted workers to take over businesses

Figure 16.1-3 Paris. Napoléon III's additions to the Louvre, Hector-Martin Lefuel, 1855.

▼ 1894

Pullman strike spreads from Chicago to most of the United States

Sullivan publishes "The Tall Office Building Artistically Considered"

▲ 1896

▼ 1900

New York City population reaches 3.4 million, up from 60,000 in 1800

Gilbert's Woolworth Building built in New York City

▲ 1913

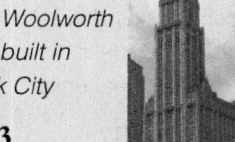

Figure 16.1-4 Paris. (a) Façade of 1859 the Opéra, Charles Garnier, 1875. (b) Grand staircase.

that had been abandoned by their owners. The outraged bourgeoisie, which had profited from Haussmann's renewals, backed the subsequent siege of the Commune by the national guard. While the Communards ultimately lost and were systematically executed, they held eastern Paris for a few weeks by erecting barricades across some of Haussmann's new boulevards. Ironically, the thoroughfares intended for easy troop movement proved the rebels' best defense.

The Ringstrasse and the Linear Grid: Tearing Down the Walls of European Cities

Haussmann's urban surgery in Paris represented an extreme case of "creative destruction," admired throughout Europe but never matched. The replanning of Vienna, capital city of the Habsburg Empire, provided an equally influential alternative. Rather than expropriating properties to build new streets throughout the city, Austrian planners exploited the state-owned space of the eighteenth-century fortifications, using their *glacis* to create a grand 800 m (2,560 ft) wide girdle around the historic city. They developed the Ringstrasse area (Fig. 16.1-5) for blocks of bourgeois apartments and as sites for modern institutions, including a theater that could compare with Garnier's in Paris in splendor. Real estate speculators acquired the public land to build high-rent apartment blocks, generating profits used to finance the new public buildings. The incentives of thirty-year tax breaks ensured that most of the apartments were constructed ahead of the monuments. Beyond this elite ring spread Vienna's growing industrial suburbs and lower-class districts. Rather than restructuring the entire urban territory, the Ringstrasse strapped a belt of modernity between the city's historic core and its industrial periphery.

As with Haussmann's boulevards, defense strategies partly motivated the creation of the Ringstrasse. The same revolutionary forces that had shaken Paris in 1848 emerged in Vienna as well, leading to calls for better internal security. The Ringstrasse plan set aside ample sites for military barracks. Its central tree-lined boulevard, 56 m (180 ft) wide, permitted unobstructed troop movement while providing a grand parade route. Emperor Franz Joseph (r. 1849–1916), while defending the conservative values of monarchy and Catholicism, attempted

Figure 16.1-5 Vienna. Ringstrasse, ground map showing the new streets, begun 1858.

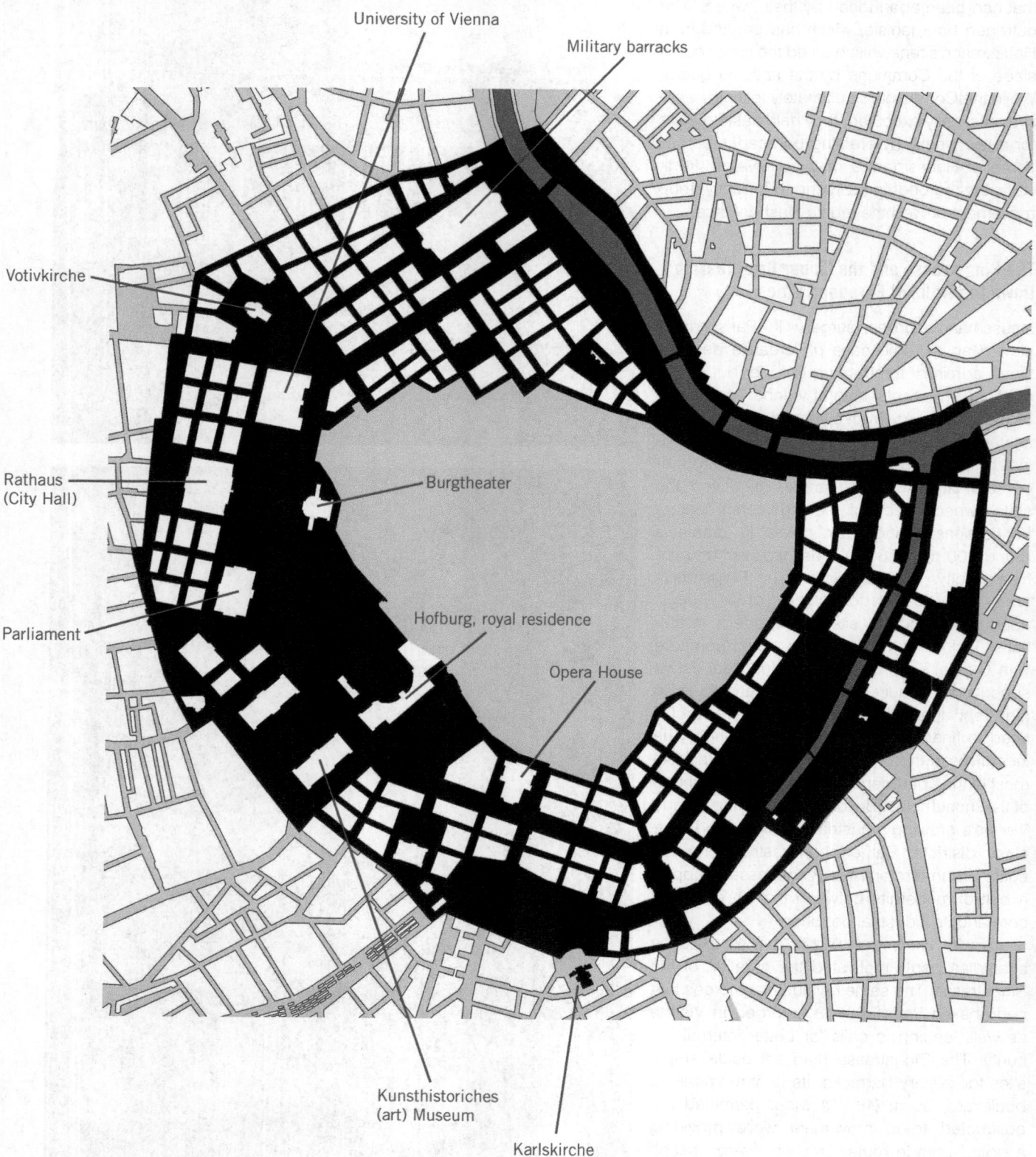

to accommodate the same liberal interests that pressured Haussmann. He granted Vienna the right to become a self-governing municipality in 1850, and the Austrian state became a constitutional monarchy in 1860. Two years earlier, Ludwig Förster, Eduard von der Nüll, and August von Siccardsburg won the 1858 competition to plan the Ringstrasse. Working on a **tabula rasa**, an empty slate, they plotted the positions of freestanding institutional structures, each designed in a different neo-historical style.

The Votivkirche, the first in the parade of new public buildings on the Ringstrasse, rose on the northwest edge as a stunning twin-towered Neo-Gothic cathedral. Designed by local architect Heinrich von Ferstel (1828–1883), it commemorated the emperor's survival of an assassination attempt in 1853. It also served both as a garrison church for the nearby barracks and as a pantheon for Austria's great men. The only other religious structure on the Ringstrasse, Johann Bernhard Fischer von Erlach's Karlskirche of a century and a half earlier (see Section 13.2), stood far to the east on the outer edge of the *glacis*. Otherwise the content of the new ring remained resoundingly secular.

Construction began on the rest of the Ringstrasse's two dozen institutional structures in the 1870s. Using an approach somewhat like that adopted for Ludwig I's Munich, the planners chose a distinct style from the historical repertoire for each building to subtly convey information about its functions. The City Hall, or

Figure 16.1-6 Vienna. New City Hall, Friedrich von Schmidt, ca. 1880.

Rathaus (Fig. 16.1-6), by the German Neo-Gothic master Friedrich von Schmidt (1825–1891), had soaring spires and pinnacles borrowed from medieval Flemish town halls. Theophilus Hansen (1813–1891), a Danish architect who had participated in the neoclassical makeover of Athens, designed the Parliament (Fig. 16.1-7a), placing a classical temple between two lower wings to allude to ancient Greek democracy. The Burgtheater for dramatic arts (Fig. 16.1-7b) stood directly in front of the Rathaus across a 200 m (656 ft) deep plaza. Gottfried Semper (1803–1879), the leading German theoretician of the age, with his local associate Karl Freiherr von Hasenauer, designed the theater in a Neo-Baroque style, hoping to match Garnier's display of

architectural sumptuousness at the Opéra in Paris. Semper also prepared a plan for the Culture Forum, proposing a building with parallel wings connecting to the imperial palace. The complex would have been linked by triumphal arches across the central boulevard of the Ringstrasse to twin museums for art and natural history. While only half finished, the project rivaled the scale of the expanded Louvre. As in Paris, Vienna's core was gentrified, with new palace-like apartment blocks for the well-to-do serving to frame the new institutional buildings.

While the modernity of the Ringstrasse satisfied Vienna's bourgeoisie, it troubled the urban planner Camillo Sitte (1843–1903), who found it lacking in human scale and urban

Figure 16.1-7 Vienna. (a) Parliament, Theophilus Hansen, ca. 1880. (b) Burgtheater, Gottfried Semper, ca. 1870.

beauty. He felt the huge voids between the new buildings induced "agoraphobia," the fear of entering public places. Sitte was influenced by the new science of psychology that emerged during the years that Sigmund Freud (1856–1939) introduced his theories of mental health in Vienna. The architect proposed a return to the enclosed public spaces of preindustrial Europe. To make his case he designed alternative solutions for the Ringstrasse, framing the voids around the Votivkirche and the Parliament with new buildings (Fig. 16.1-8).

Barcelona likewise tore down its walls in 1858 but encouraged the creation of a much more comprehensive plan. The well-traveled engineer Ildefonso Cerdá (1815–1876), who held various political positions during his lifetime, proposed an immense linear grid as a coordinated enlargement, or *Ensanche*, of the historic core (Fig. 16.1-9a,b). Heavily influenced by the proto-socialist literature of France, he admired the technical improvements of Haussmann's Paris but rejected its elitism. Cerdá proposed the addition of 50 km² (19.3 mi²) of square blocks derived from hygienic and sociological criteria. His streets spread on a 20 m (66 ft) width-to-cornice section and crossed at diamond-shaped intersections formed by the **chamfered** corners of the blocks. The broad streets and diamond-shaped plazas guaranteed a nonhierarchical fabric for a great democratic city. Several other Spanish cities, including Madrid and Pamplona, followed Barcelona's example, adding *Ensanche* grids in the 1870s. They tended, however, to suffocate the center by wrapping the new districts around it rather than creating a linear grid.

In Italy, which achieved national unification during the 1860s, urbanism became a major consideration. To prepare Florence as the country's interim capital, Giuseppe Poggi (1811–1901) created Italy's first comprehensive master plan. Between 1865 and 1870, the city tore down its walls and created a planted ring boulevard for a series of blocks, some of them with chamfered corners, that wrapped around the core. Poggi's most original contribution, the hillside park leading up to Piazzale Michelangelo, offered a grand terrace with a breathtaking panorama of the city. The architect also proposed a major Haussmann-like demolition of a swath through the historic center that remained unrealized. Two decades later, however, a group of speculators succeeded in convincing the city council to tear down half the historic center in the name of public hygiene and security. The new owners of the area displaced its poor residents and a few anarchists to rebuild the Mercato Vecchio district (Fig. 16.1-10a) with Neo-Renaissance-style buildings for banks, department stores, and expensive hotels. A colossal triumphal arch integrated with a double-height **arcade** at its core (Fig. 16.1-10b) signaled the victory of unrestrained gentrification: 6,000 poor residents were evicted, and of the original 1,093 property owners, only 63 remained after the demolitions.

When the capital of Italy moved to Rome in 1870, the walls of that city were maintained almost completely intact. Only the symbolic breach of Porta Pia was opened to let the troops of the new nation storm the papal city. Alessandro Viviani immediately prepared a master plan of Rome, revised in 1883. The plan elicited a critique from Baron Haussmann, however, who surprisingly advised the Romans to leave the center untouched and build a new administrative city outside the historic walls. No one in Rome had the sort of authority he had enjoyed, however, and much of the city's development followed real estate interests,

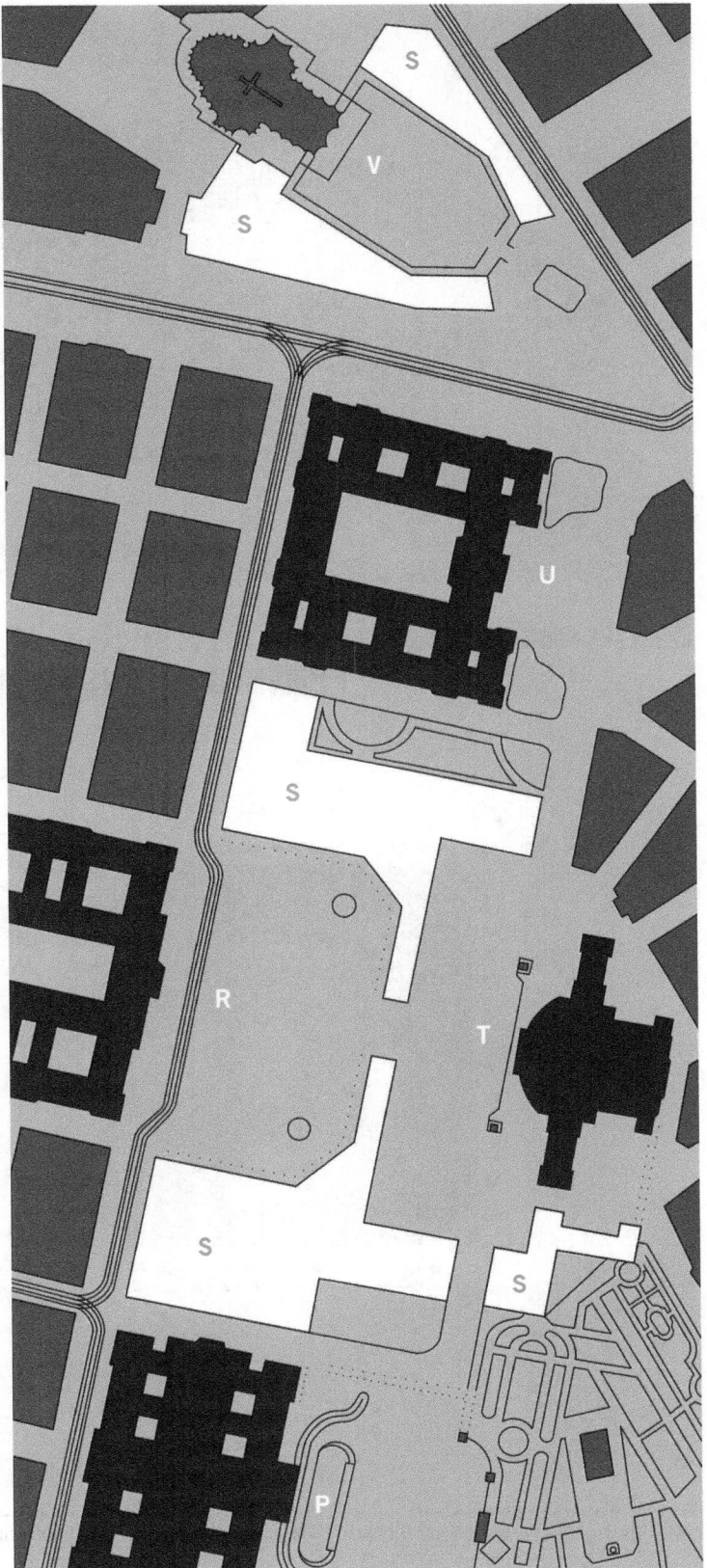

Figure 16.1-8 Vienna. (a) Proposal to enclose the spaces of the Ringstrasse, Camillo Sitte, 1890s, showing (S) buildings proposed by Sitte to help redimension the public spaces; (V) Votivkirche; (U) university; (T) Burgtheater; (R) Rathaus (City Hall); (P) Parliament.

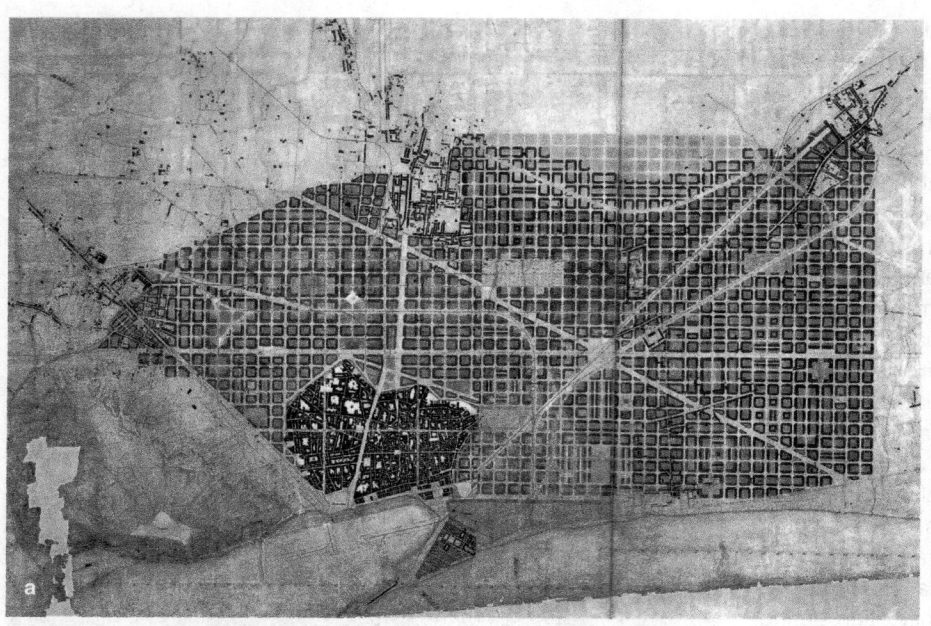

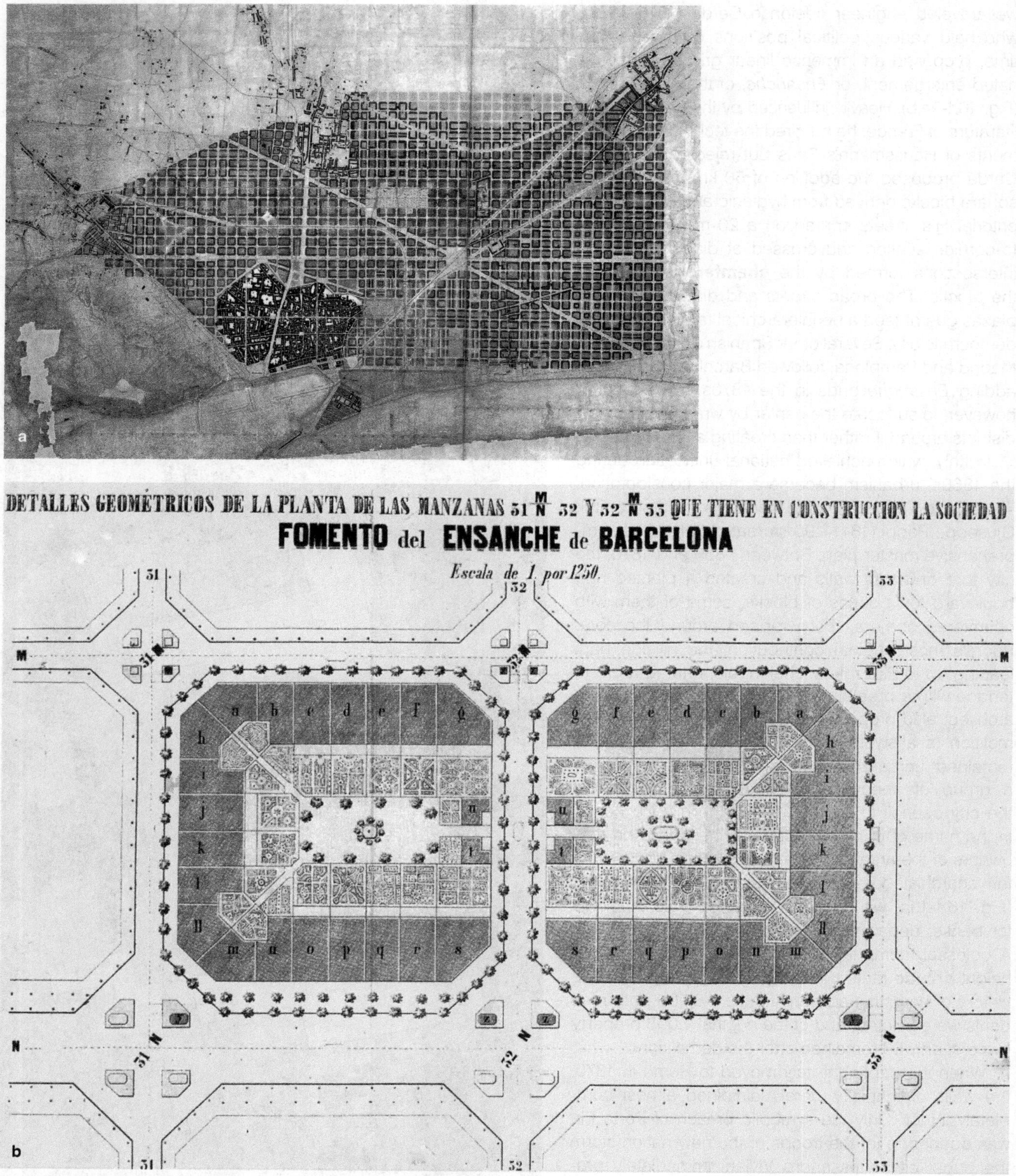

DETALLES GEOMÉTRICOS DE LA PLANTA DE LAS MANZANAS 51 M/N 52 Y 52 M/N 53 QUE TIENE EN CONSTRUCCION LA SOCIEDAD
FOMENTO del ENSANCHE de BARCELONA
Escala de 1 por 1250.

Figure 16.1-9. Barcelona. (a) City plan, Ildefonso Cerdá, 1859. (b) Block structure.

which pulled growth in all directions. Amid the confusion, an innovative piecemeal method of renewing historic districts emerged in Rome. Rather than disemboweling the center, the planners suggested *diradimento*, or "weeding." They

focused on Corso Vittorio Emanuele II (1884–1910), which, like Regent Street in London, snaked its way through the historic fabric. They selectively tore down parts of the historic context while leaving, or tactfully transposing, the most

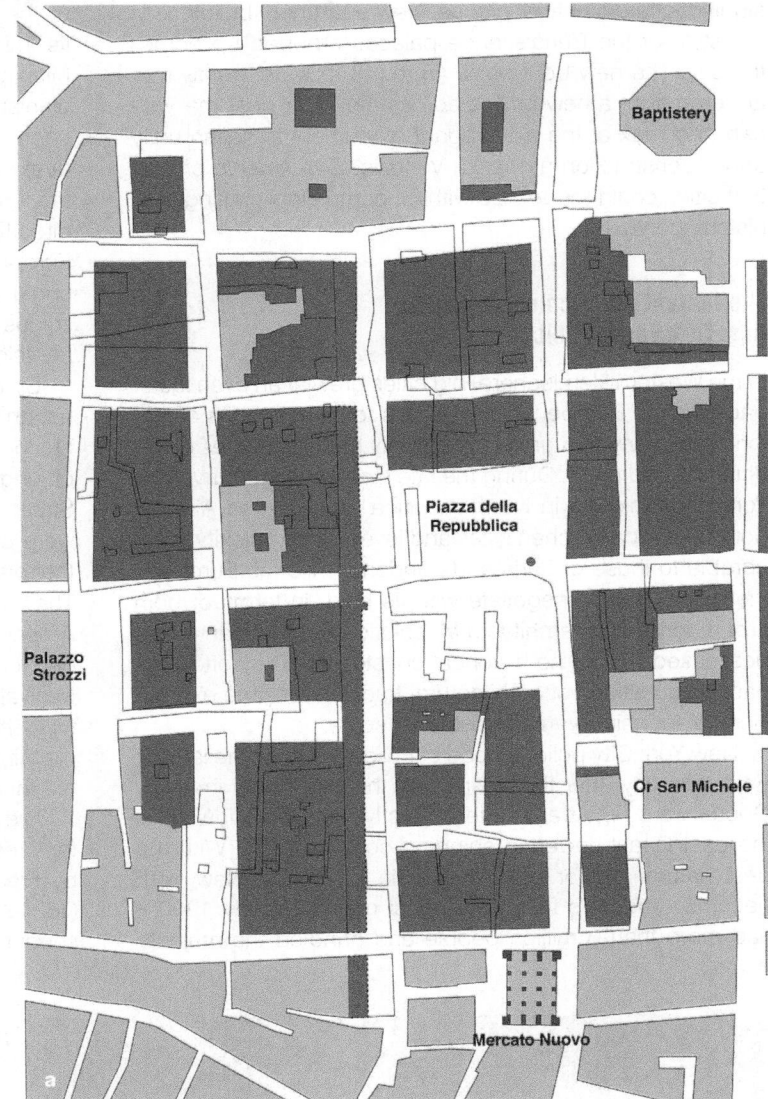

Figure 16.1-10 Florence. (a) Demolition of the Mercato Vecchio historic center, 1890s; white outlines indicate original buildings, mostly from the medieval period, that were demolished; light gray indicates buildings that were left standing; dark gray indicates new, replacement buildings. (b) Triumphal arch at Piazza della Repubblica.

significant architectural pieces. New apartment buildings in the style of the Renaissance palaces cropped up across the city. The new boulevard, 15 m (48 ft) wide, gently meandered from a new bridge across the Tiber near the Vatican to climax at the extravagant monument to Italian unity under construction at Piazza Venezia. *Diradimento* proved that cities could modernize without completely erasing their historic context.

The Instant American Metropolis: New York versus Chicago

In the Western Hemisphere, big cities grew at an even faster pace than in Europe. They had less to lose in terms of historic patrimony and grew on relatively blank stretches of undifferentiated grids. During the late nineteenth century, New York and Chicago in North America and Buenos Aires in South America reached sizes and levels of complexity comparable to those of Paris and London. While the European metropolis had to negotiate with its past, in terms of both urban form and architectural solutions, American cities possessed almost no historical constraints. They often bypassed questions of architectural tradition for pure expressions of technique and unrestricted scale.

New York City pulled ahead of Philadelphia as the largest American city after the opening of the Erie Canal in 1825. Goods were now transported directly from the Midwest to the East Coast, lowering shipping costs by 95%. With the best natural harbor on the Atlantic seaboard, New York became America's first and largest metropolis. By 1900 it had more than 3 million people and handled the majority

of the country's imports and exports, as well as most of its immigrants. Chicago, on the southwest shore of Lake Michigan, grew in synchronicity with New York as the pivot of inland shipping and train transport. The two cities fed on each other's success while developing a strong architectural rivalry. Each tried to surpass the other in the race for the world's tallest building. In New York, which dealt more directly with Europe, architects consistently acknowledged European heritage while using new technologies to achieve ungainly heights. Chicago architects remained less conscious of historical sources, developing a more direct expression of construction as an alternative "American" style.

By the end of the nineteenth century the island of Manhattan had become the densest city in the world. It spread out on the 1811 Commissioners' Plan, a uniform grid of oblong blocks covering an 80 km² (31 mi²) area above 14th Street (Fig. 16.1-11). While the twelve north–south avenues were exceptionally wide, stretching 30 m (98.4 ft) across, the planners neglected to set aside much open space. They permitted a single, irregular street, the ancient Native American trail of Broadway, to move obliquely against the grid, causing occasional triangular gaps in the urban fabric. Motivated by real estate interests, the commissioners justified the logic of the rigid repetition of oblong blocks by claiming that "straight sided and right angled houses are the most cheap to build and most convenient to live in."

The only relief to Manhattan's relentless grid came with the creation of Central Park (Fig. 16.1-12a), designed in 1857 by Frederick Law Olmsted (1822–1903) and Calvert Vaux (1824–1895). The strict orthogonal frame of dense blocks surrounded this immense 340 hectare (840 acre) green

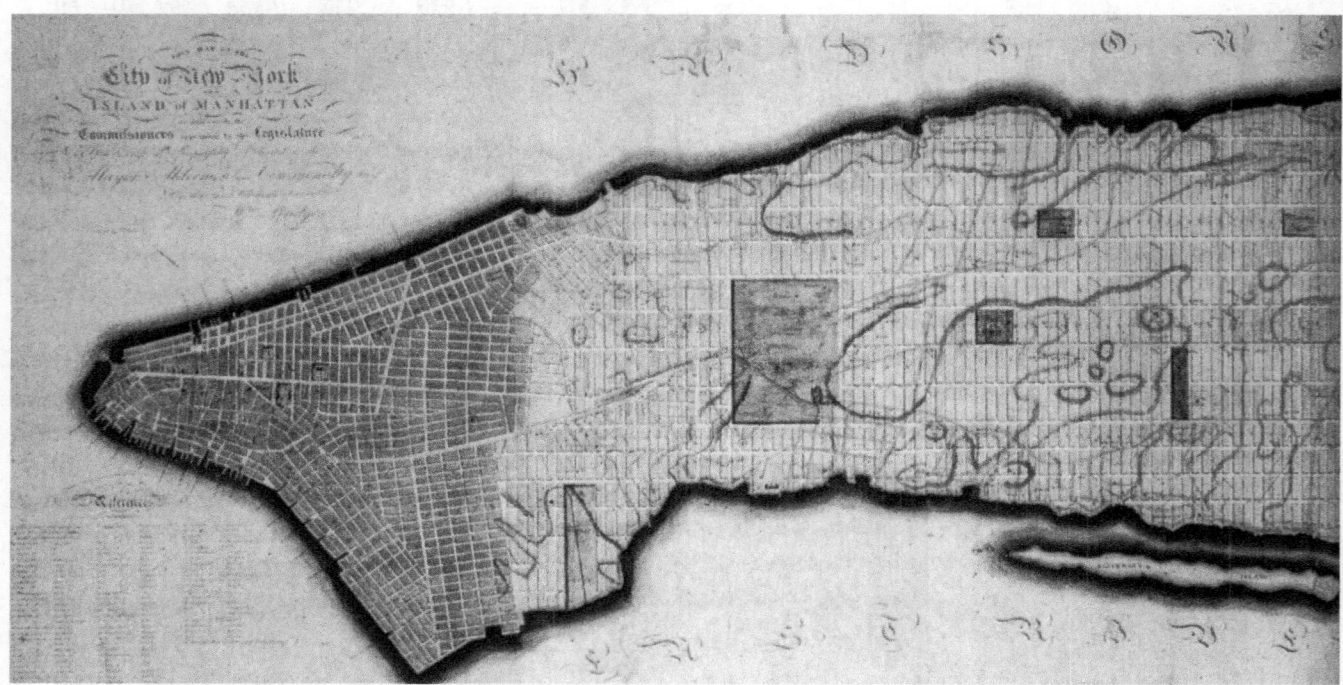

Figure 16.1-11 New York City. Commissioners' Plan, a uniform grid from 14th Street north, 1811. The Central Park area was moved and enlarged in the 1850s.

Figure 16.1-12 New York. (a) Central Park, Frederick Law Olmsted and Calvert Vaux, 1860s. (b) The park's Gothic bridge.

space. The designers, inspired by the casual organization of English picturesque gardens, replenished the barren site by importing thousands of tons of soil and trees. To enhance Central Park's artificially obtained naturalness, Olmsted introduced a system of separated traffic on different grades so that carriages could cross the park without disturbing strollers (Fig. 16.1-12b). Unlike the Bois de Boulogne, which extended off the western edge of Paris, Central Park stood in the midst of New York's blocks like a captured patch of wilderness. The stark contrast truly energized the edges of the park.

From 1861 to 1865 the Civil War held American urban development in check. While the northern states of the Union were partly industrialized, resulting in new forms of injustice, the southern states of the Confederacy continued their agrarian economy, relying on slave labor. Many of the founding fathers, such as George Washington and Thomas Jefferson, had been slave owners, and much of Washington, D.C., including the Capitol Building, was constructed by slave labor. Slavery nonetheless remained an untenable contradiction of the democratic principles of liberty outlined in the American Constitution. After the British and French promulgated laws against slavery at the outset of the nineteenth century, abolition became a major theme among America's moral leaders. The ensuing Civil War caused the deaths of over 600,000 Americans, many of whom were victims of new military technologies, such as Richard Gatling's machine gun and the first submarines. Abraham Lincoln's 1863 Emancipation Proclamation provided the moral imperative for the Union armies, leading to the liberation of over 4 million African American slaves, who after the conclusion of the war began to migrate to New York and Chicago.

The Union victory in 1865 stimulated the productivity of the northern metropolises. Manhattan filled out as its transportation systems improved. At first only the very wealthy with carriages could live uptown, where they built enormous mansions on Fifth Avenue above 42nd Street. Those built for the heirs of the shipping and railway tycoon Cornelius Vanderbilt I (1794–1877), the wealthiest man on earth, approached the scale and luxury of French châteaux. McKim, Mead & White, the most successful Beaux-Arts architectural firm of the age, built one of the last remnants of this period of plutocratic splendor, the Villard Houses on Madison Avenue (Fig. 16.1-13). Designed in the 1880s for a railroad magnate, the block of six townhouses wrapped around a U-shaped court, forming a unified whole with the look and details of an early sixteenth-century Italian Renaissance palazzo. The original owner, sensitive to objections from New Yorkers who believed that the immense complex served a single family, decided to move out before the building's completion, a clear sign of the social conflicts that were brewing at the turn of the century.

New York's middle-class commuters initially spread across the East River to the neighboring city of Brooklyn. Before the completion of the Brooklyn Bridge in 1883, they reached the downtown office district by a twelve-minute ride on the Fulton Ferry between Brooklyn and Manhattan. By the 1860s, the loud and invasive elevated rail lines had replaced the horse-drawn streetcars, allowing downtown office workers to live farther uptown. In 1869, the same year that the Transcontinental Railway opened, Vanderbilt created Grand Central Terminal, New York's major transit node. Rather than designing the building as a direct expression of the iron and glass structure of the train sheds, Vanderbilt's architects opted for an exterior reminiscent of Napoléon III's additions to the Louvre in Paris, with tall, billowy mansards. The architectural firm of Warren and Wetmore rebuilt the station in 1904 as a multilevel complex dominated by an immense vaulted hall worthy of a Roman bath (Fig. 16.1-14a,b).

In Chicago one reached the sixty-block Loop district by elevated rail. The configuration of the suburbs ranged from casual to regimented. Oak Park, where Frank Lloyd Wright (1867–1959) undertook his first works, followed a typical grid. In 1869 Olmsted, fresh from his work on Central Park, designed the suburb of Riverside without a grid, deliberately curving streets despite the level topography to "suggest and imply leisure, contemplativeness and happy tranquility" (Fig. 16.1-15). He imported thousands of trees to give the prairie a more forested look. Despite these charms, the developer went bankrupt in 1874, preventing the area from filling in as planned.

One of Chicago's suburbs, Pullman, became the country's most admired company town. Built 15 km (9.3 miles) south of the Loop on the western shore of Lake Calumet, it offered an important package

Figure 16.1-13 New York. Villard Houses, McKim, Mead & White, 1880s.

Figure 16.1-14 New York.
(a) Grand Central Terminal,
Warren and Wetmore, 1904.
(b) Interior.

of civic services. In the mid-1880s the young architect Solon S. Beman (1853–1914) prepared 1,700 high-quality brick row houses for the workers of the Pullman Palace Car Company factories. The settlement possessed religious, educational, and athletic facilities and an attractive plaza overlooked by a grand covered market, the Pullman Arcade. The houses were among the first to be served by indoor plumbing. During the economic slump of 1893, however, Pullman resorted to layoffs, forcing the majority of the company's 4,000 workers to move to lower-rent districts.

To protest the company's paternalistic policies, the workers organized one of the most widely supported strikes in American labor history, leading to violent conflicts and the demise of Pullman's urban experiment.

As New York and Chicago expanded laterally toward the suburbs, their downtowns took off in the vertical dimension. Tall, awkward structures for offices, hotels, wholesale and mail-order companies, and apartments came to characterize the American metropolis. The introduction of the safety elevator, designed by Elisha Otis (1811–1861) for New York's

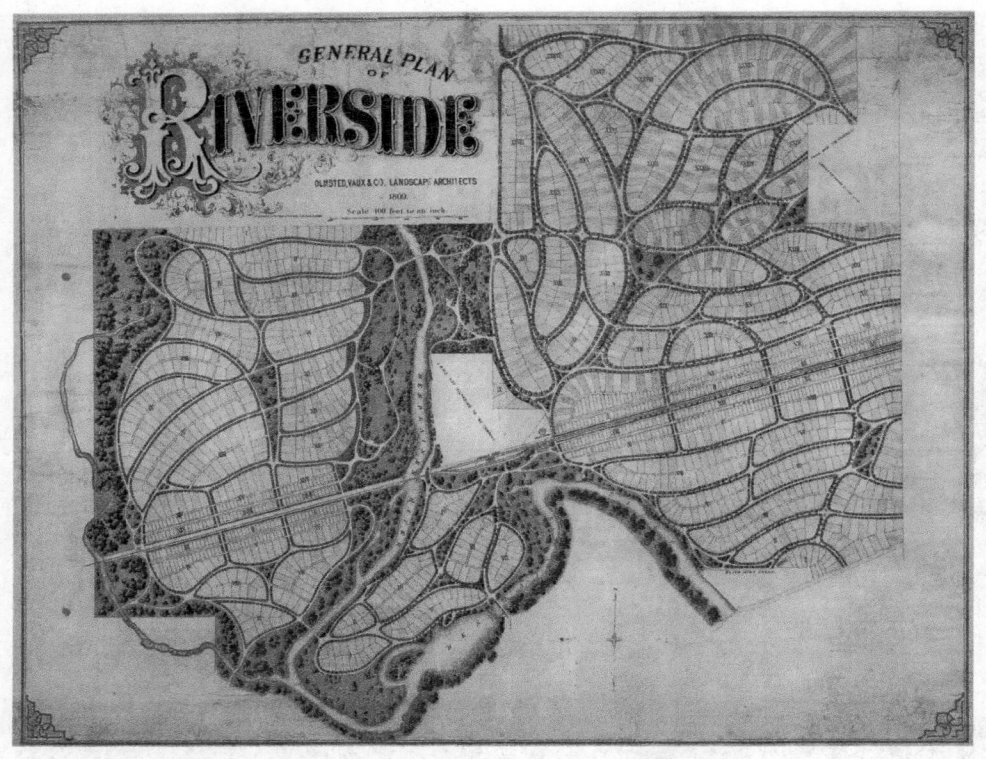

Figure 16.1-15 Riverside, a picturesque suburb of Chicago, Olmsted, 1870s.

version of the Crystal Palace in 1854, became an essential factor in the move toward taller buildings. During the 1870s, New York broke beyond the six-story norm with several belfry-like towers. The novelist Henry James saw the skyline of Lower Manhattan as "extravagant pins in a cushion already overplanted." The eastern edge of City Hall Square attracted three of the most ostentatious examples of such structures, each designed to publicize a competing newspaper. George B. Post (1837–1913) designed two distinct sixteen-story towers in 1889, the New York Times Building and the World Building, to either side of the 1875 New York Tribune Building by Richard Morris Hunt (1827–1895). To his building, Hunt added thick buttresses to support a masonry structure, placing a three-story clock tower over the narrow entry bay. To surpass the image of this campanile, Post raised a gilded dome over the World Building (Fig. 16.1-16a), where the

Figure 16.1-16 New York. (a) World (Pulitzer) Building, George B. Post, 1890. (b) Tribune Building, Richard Morris Hunt, 1875–1903.

owner, Joseph Pulitzer, kept his office. In 1903 the *Tribune* reacted by adding nine more floors to its original building, using innovative steel-frame technologies (Fig. 16.1-16b).

The Great Fire of 1871 in Chicago consumed one-third of the city's mostly wooden structures. Thus, the new tall buildings that replaced them were designed as solid, fireproof volumes with scant reference to European styles of decoration. During the 1880s William Le Baron Jenney (1832–1907), who trained as an engineer in France and rose to the rank of major in the Union Army's corps of engineers, perfected the structural solutions of high-rises. In his Leiter Store (1879) (Fig. 16.1-17), a seven-story department store, he mixed a cast-iron structure with external masonry-bearing walls to achieve an extremely light, nearly skeletal solution. Behind the piers he placed cast-iron columns, which allowed him to make intervals wide enough for three **sash windows**. In his second Leiter Store (finished 1891), Jenney replaced the iron with a much stronger steel frame.

The Chicago metal-frame structure attained aesthetic maturity with the Marshall Field Wholesale Store of 1885, designed by the Boston architect Henry Hobson Richardson (1838–1886). He clad the elevations with rusticated blocks, pink granite on the slightly battered ground floor and gray limestone on the seven stories above. The diminishing scale of the building's arches, with one at the lower register, two in the middle, and four in the attic, conveyed

Figure 16.1-17 Chicago. Leiter Store, William Le Baron Jenney, 1879.

CONSTRUCTION, TECHNOLOGY, THEORY

American Mass-Produced Buildings

During the boom years of the United States's "instant metropoles," pragmatic engineers invented mass-produced systems of construction. In Chicago Augustin Taylor perfected the manufacture of iron nails and in the 1830s patented the **balloon-frame** system, based on a thin skeleton of precut wooden joists joined by machine-made nails. The cladding of panels and shingles, or other light materials such as tin, was nailed to the frame. A prefabricated balloon-frame building could be shipped great distances and assembled quickly by a pair of carpenters.

The American inventor James Bogardus (1800–1874) introduced another method of mass-produced construction in New York City with his 1850 patent for cast-iron facades. He perfected a system of joining prefabricated metal piers with half-columns and arches. His cast-iron facades for warehouses and businesses once characterized the district of Lower Manhattan.

New York. Edgar Laing Stores, a cast-iron frame building by James Bogardus, 1850s.

Figure 16.1-18 Chicago. Reliance Building, Burnham & Root, 1893.

the functionalist purity of Roman aqueducts. Topped with a flat cornice and supported by brackets, the Marshall Field Store immediately drew comparisons with the severe rusticated facades of fifteenth-century Florentine palaces.

After Jenney's introduction of steel-frame construction in the late 1880s, Chicago's sparsely decorated, box-like structures overtook those of New York as the tallest in the world. The firm of Burnham & Root designed the sixteen-story Monadnock Building in 1891 as one of the last Chicago high-rises to rely on exterior-bearing wall construction. Its massive canted-brick walls spread 2 m (7 ft) thick at the base. Two years later the same office designed the fifteen-story Reliance Building with a steel frame (Fig. 16.1-18). Instead of the 2 m (7 ft) thickness that diminished in depth from floor to floor, the exterior walls stood as uniformly thin, nonbearing curtains made of horizontal bands of broad **Chicago windows** and white terra-cotta spandrel panels. The point-loaded system of the steel skeleton carried the loads. The broad eaves of the Reliance Building added a crisp outline to its boxy profile, but otherwise the architects made little effort to give the tower historical associations.

Americans started calling tall buildings "skyscrapers" after Louis Sullivan (1856–1924), one of Chicago's leading architectural practitioners, wrote the first theoretical gloss on the type. He realized that with the structural possibilities offered by the steel frame, architects could stop imitating historic masonry precedents and strive toward a new state

of tectonic purity in which "form ever follows function." In his 1896 essay "The Tall Office Building Artistically Considered," Sullivan reasoned that the skyscraper needed a basement, placed out of view, for storage and machinery; a two-story base for commercial activities; a shaft made of an indiscriminate number of stories for identical offices; and an attic for mechanicals and ventilation. Adler & Sullivan's Wainwright Building in St. Louis (Fig. 16.1-19), finished in 1894, a ten-story tower clad in red terra-cotta panels, corresponded closely to his analytical description. The only contradiction appeared in the structural bays expressed on the facade: the architects added extra nonstructural mullions, doubling the number of bays and increasing the impression of verticality.

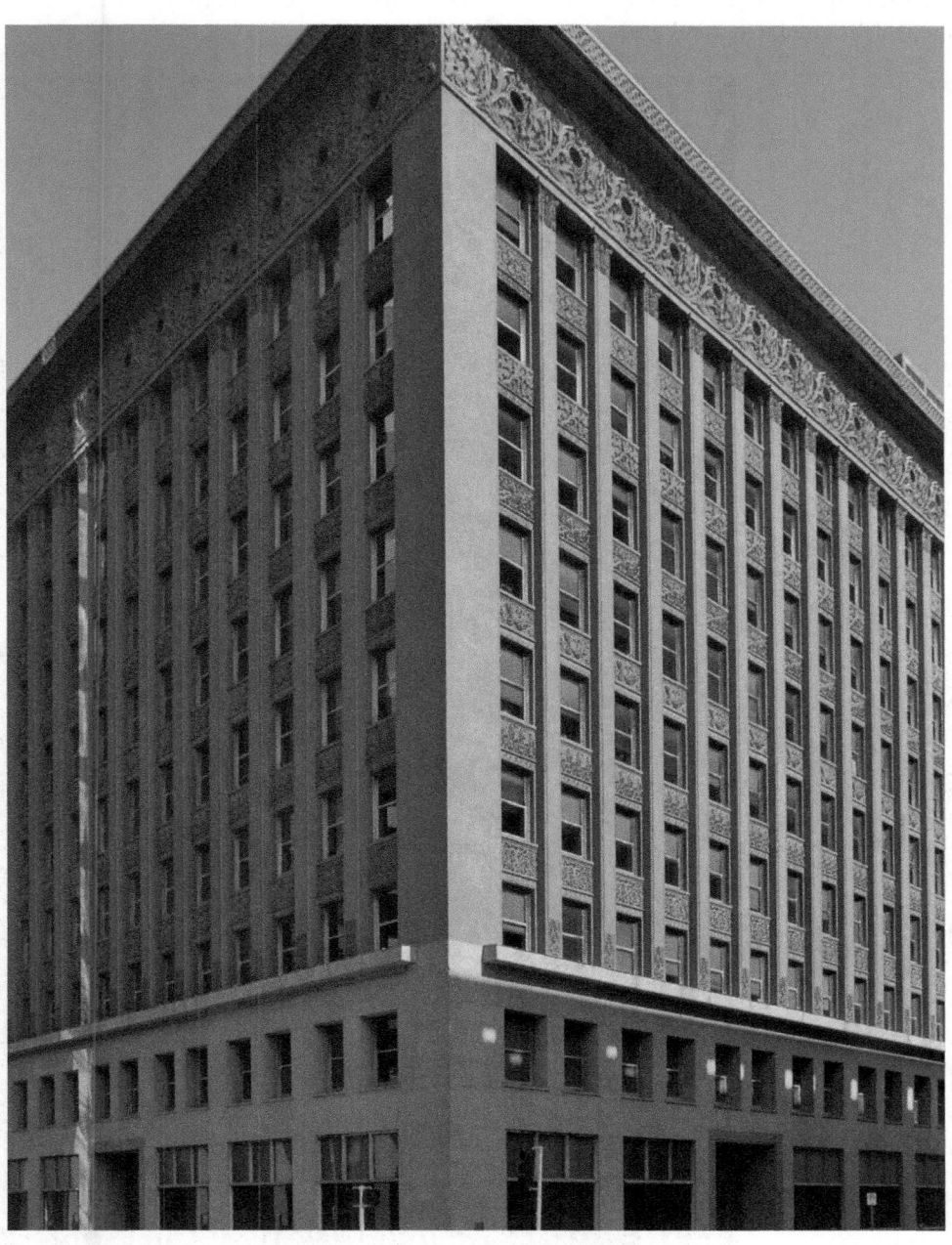

Figure 16.1-19 St. Louis. Wainwright Building, Adler & Sullivan, 1894.

Chicago School Techniques for Tall Buildings

During the 1880s architects in Chicago began using steel-frame structures, reducing their reliance on masonry for support. The great department stores became the most eager clients of this technology, seeking to maximize space while minimizing costs and reducing fire hazards. While the Marshall Field Wholesale Store by Richardson figured among the last great masonry structures, the second Levi Z. Leiter Store by Jenney demonstrated the lightness of the new steel-frame structures. Richardson's rusticated facade seemed the opposite of Jenney's delineated structural grid.

Sullivan exploited the new structural techniques for his Schlesinger & Mayer Building (until recently the Carson, Pirie, Scott Department Store). Begun in 1899, it became a testament to lightness. The elevations eliminated all excess surfaces, protecting the grid of steel structure with terra-cotta cladding. Chicago windows, made with a large central pane flanked by smaller, operable bays, filled the voids between the columns and the beams, leaving more glass than wall. Sullivan lavished the bottom two floors with ornate cast-iron filigree.

Chicago. Steel-frame structures. (a) Carson, Pirie, Scott Department Store (now the Schlesinger and Mayer Building), Louis Sullivan, begun 1899.

(b) Detail of cast-iron filigree.

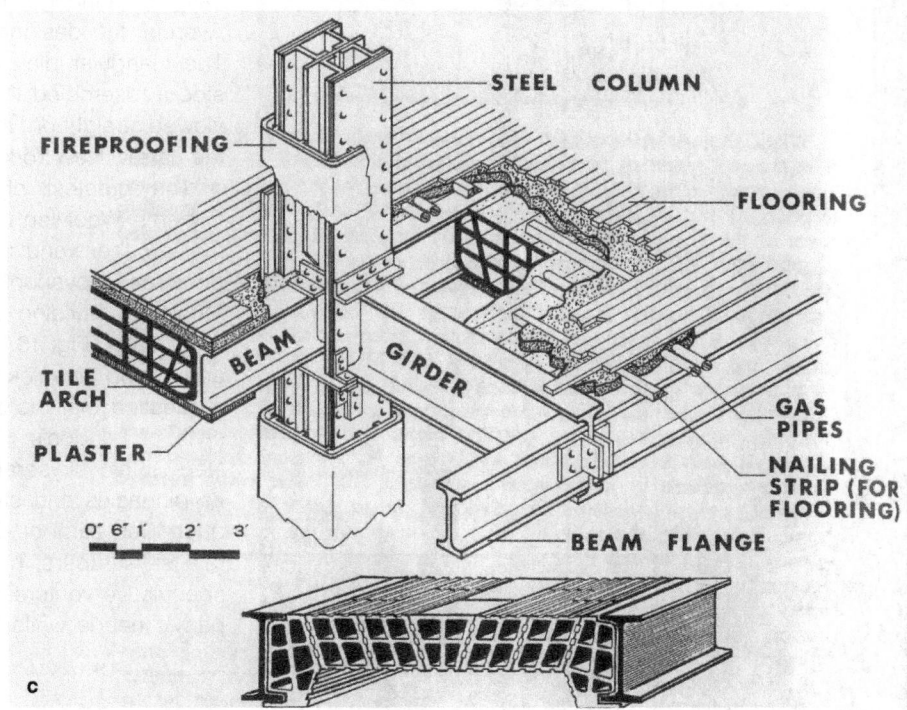

(c) The Chicago system.

Figure 16.1-20 Chicago. Auditorium Building, Adler & Sullivan, 1890.

With the completion of Adler & Sullivan's Auditorium Building in 1890 (Fig. 16.1-20) and Burnham & Root's twenty-two-story Masonic Building in 1892, Chicago boasted the two tallest buildings in the world. During the economic crisis of 1893, however, the city planning department imposed a ten-story height limit, which kept Chicago out of the race for ever-higher towers with New York. Chicago architects had to go to New York to realize their potential for producing tall buildings. In 1903 Daniel Burnham's office produced the twenty-three-story Fuller Building, known as the "Flatiron" Building because of its wedge shape (Fig. 16.1-21). Located on a triangular site where Broadway intersected Fifth Avenue, the designers extruded the entire block upward. The triangular plan generated a massive slice. From the side it resembled the tall, boxy buildings of Chicago, but viewed straight on, the rounded, prow-like corner related to the narrow New York belfries.

The greatest of such campanile-like towers, Cass Gilbert's Woolworth Building of 1913 (Fig. 16.1-22a), remained the world's tallest office building for nearly two decades. It overlooked City Hall Park facing the 40-story Municipal Building by McKim, Mead & White, finished a year later (Fig. 16.1-22a,b). The patron conceived it as an advertising gimmick for his chain of "five and dime" stores, requesting that the architects produce the building in the style of London's Houses of Parliament. He obtained a Neo-Gothic skyscraper clad in white terra-cotta panels. Its pinnacles and stepped-up massing earned the sobriquet "Cathedral of Commerce." As with almost all corporate skyscrapers, he financed the Woolworth tower as a speculative venture, requiring only two floors for his company's needs while leasing the other fifty-three for profit.

Figure 16.1-21 New York. Fuller (Flatiron) Building, Daniel Burnham, 1903.

Figure 16.1-22 New York. (a) Woolworth Building, Cass Gilbert, 1913. (b) Manhattan Municipal building (now David Dinkins Municipal Building), McKim, Mead & White, 1907–1914.

The late-nineteenth-century American metropolis imposed few regulations and required even less urban coordination, which encouraged the development of an audacious and often brutal environment of severe contrasts. There, self-interest tangibly prevailed over the collective well-being.

Further Reading

Fishman, Robert. *Bourgeois Utopias: The Rise and Fall of Suburbia*. New York: Basic Books, 1987.

Jordy, William. *American Buildings and Their Architects*, vol. 3. New York: Anchor Books, 1972.

Landau, Sarah B., and Carl Condit. *Rise of the New York Skyscraper, 1865–1913*. New Haven, CT: Yale University Press, 1996.

Loyer, François. *Paris Nineteenth Century: Architecture and Urbanism*. Translated by C. L. Clark. New York: Abbeville Press, 1988.

Pinckney, David. *Napoleon III and the Rebuilding of Paris*. Princeton, NJ: Princeton University Press, 1958.

Schorske, Carl E. *Fin-de-Siècle Vienna: Politics and Culture*. New York: Vintage Books, 1981.

Upton, Dell. *Architecture in the United States*. New York: Oxford University Press, 1998.

16.2   LIFESTYLES AND HOUSE FORM

Apartments, Row Houses, Bungalows, and Utopias

Until the mid-eighteenth century urban residents in Western countries used two basic categories of common dwellings. Families lived either in detached houses that could be extended horizontally or in row houses that could be expanded vertically. Exceptions appeared mostly outside of Europe, such as the circular Hakka compounds in southern China and the Anasazi pueblos. Very poor families regularly improvised shelters either in vertical tenements or in shanty clusters.

The apartment type, a five- to six-story structure with several family dwellings on each floor, appeared in Europe during the eighteenth century, first as units within a subdivided palace and then as a vertically stacked alternative to row houses. Apartment buildings increased the potential density of urban sites to become the dominant building type of most nineteenth-century metropoles.

Homeowners in England and the United States, however, offered strong resistance to vertical living. Rather than fantasizing about a palatial apartment, the Anglo-American middle classes dreamed of either living in a wider row house or, better yet, owning a detached dwelling or bungalow. Both alternatives allowed for a small garden.

The social upheavals that accompanied industrialization inspired a variety of utopian alternatives to the standard house forms. Social reformers envisioned collective dwellings based on cooperative services. While few of the utopian communities survived, their aim of finding more efficient, socially responsible ways of living led to the development of the theory of "housing" for planned neighborhoods with services.

Vertical Living: The Apartment Block

The modern apartment building emerged amid the crowded housing circumstances of eighteenth-century Paris. The increased density of the city led to speculative projects for five- and six-story structures with shops and storage on the ground floor and mezzanine, two or three floors of rental units immediately above, and one or two more stories of attic space tucked under steep mansards with dormer windows for the servants (Fig. 16.2-1). The model for the apartment building indeed may have descended from France's grandest palace, the château of Versailles, which was subdivided into several hundred apartments for the courtiers of the Bourbon kings. The market for vertically stacked units by the 1780s allowed Victor Louis to restructure the great court of the Palais Royal as a series of fancy apartments over arcaded shops. As the type became more socially acceptable, the late-eighteenth-century building legislation of Paris determined its profile, limiting the cornice lines to a height of 17.5 m (56 ft).

The bourgeois apartment, or *maison de rapport*, corresponded to the new rituals of polite society. Once a week, the family received regular guests in its "salon" for music, reading, and gossip. The units usually included a large salon, a small salon, and a dining room, separated by double doors that could open to accommodate large numbers during salon day. The regularly spaced tall windows on the front facade of the building served the major social rooms. The kitchen with pantry and two or three bedrooms overlooked the rear court with smaller windows. The toilets and baths fit into the *degagements*, residual spaces between the major rooms, using internal plumbing run through the walls. A typical Parisian apartment had four or five chimney flues for fireplaces, stoves, and kitchens. Central heating was introduced at the end of the nineteenth century.

As one's status on the social scale diminished, so did the number of rooms in one's apartment. The smallest workers' flat in Paris, for instance, had one or two bedrooms and a kitchen–dining area, with the kitchen sometimes set in an alcove. These units shared toilet facilities in an access hall. At the turn of the century, several charitable institutes produced models of ideal workers' apartments. Those designed by Auguste Labussière provided entries from a large internal courtyard to reduce the feeling of overcrowding. He placed collective bathing and laundry services in the basement. Poor urban dwellers usually limited their bathing to once per month.

Parisian apartment buildings frequently consumed an entire city block, offering a new scale of urban composition. Until this time, most streetscapes had included a wide variety of widths and cornice heights, from the two-bay Gothic

1840–1846

Brook Farm, Massachusetts, utopian experiment in communal living

Davis builds his Llewellyn Park suburb near New York City

1858

1859

Godin begins socialist Familistère in Guise, France

The Model Tenement in New York

The Danish immigrant Jacob Riis (1849–1914) documented the pathetic conditions of New York's tenements in his 1894 exposé *How the Other Half Lives*. Similar to the efforts of private philanthropists in nineteenth-century London, various citizens' organizations in New York attempted to change the building codes and stimulate the production of better housing for the working class. Ernest Flagg proposed in 1894 that tenements be decongested into a square plan set on four lots, 30 × 30 m (98 × 98 ft), permitting the addition of a large court and guaranteeing cross-ventilation for all units. The New Law of 1901 forbade the minimum 8 m (26 ft) lot width.

The East River Houses by Henry Atterbury Smith (1909) were among the few projects built for low-income tenants using Flagg's idea of courtyard blocks. Flagg started his own development company to build ideal tenement blocks using fireproof steel and concrete construction, a few of which still stand on 10th and 42nd Streets. Small developers generally feared the extra costs implied by the new legislation, and most of the courtyard apartments that did get built went to middle-class tenants.

New York. Tenement, from Jacob Riis, *How the Other Half Lives*, 1894.

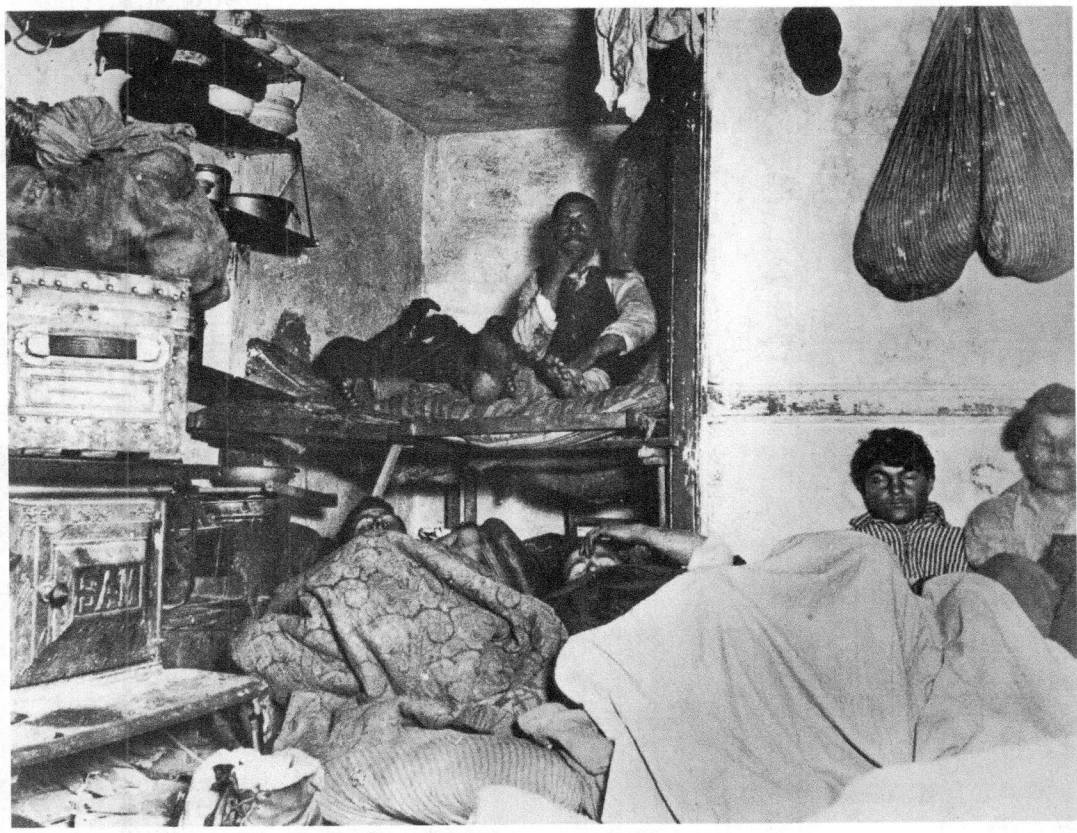

▼ **1882**

Hardenbergh's Dakota residence hotel built in New York City

Tenement House Act leads to Ware's competition-winning "dumbbell" scheme

 1879

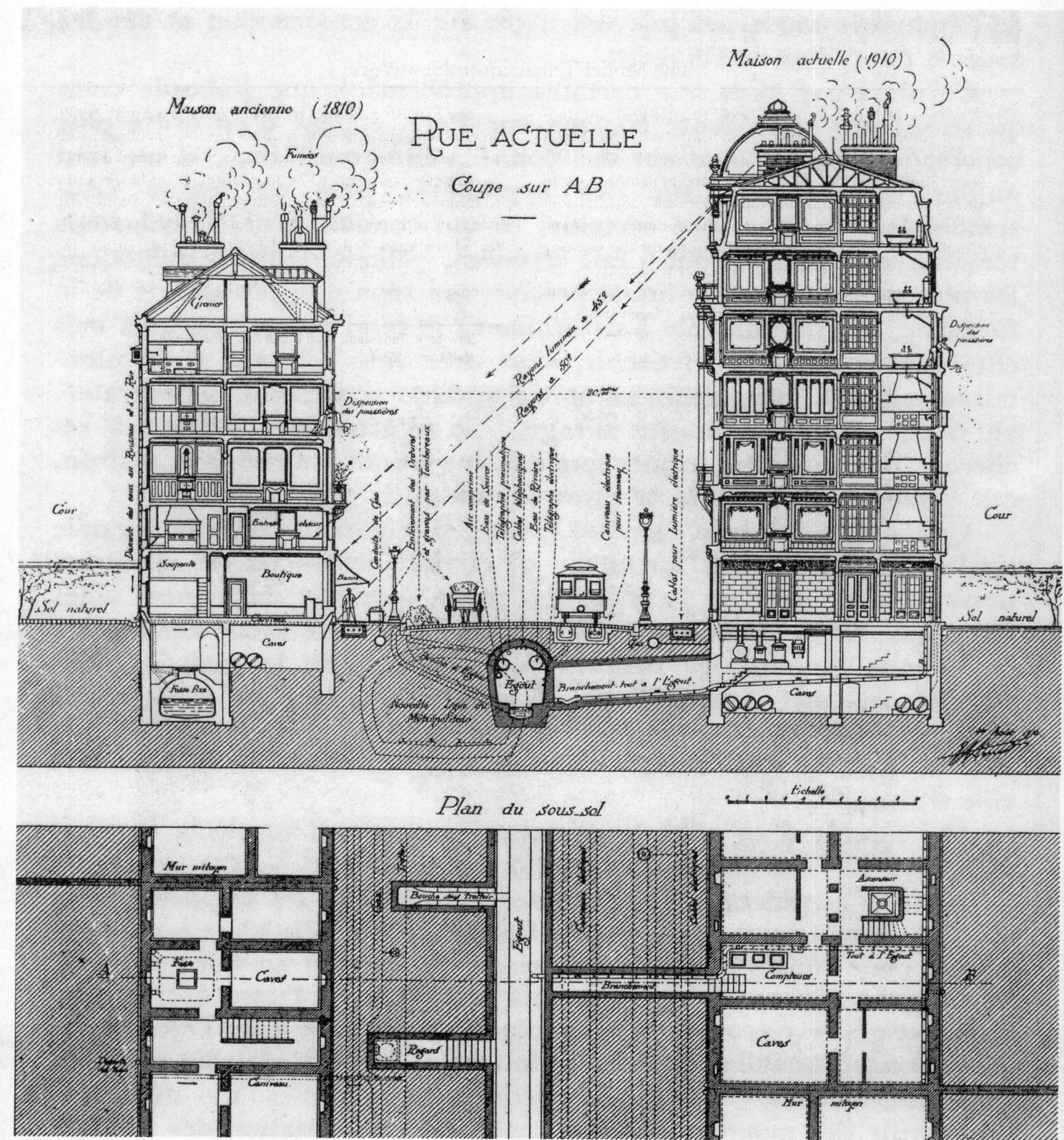

Figure 16.2-1 Paris. Analysis of the apartments on Parisian streets in 1810 and in 1910, Eugène Hénard, 1903.

Figure 16.2-2 Comparison of original apartment plans. (A) Vienna, *Mietpalast*, 1870s. (B) Berlin, *Mietkaserne*, 1880s. (C) New York, the Dakota, 1882. (D) New York, Mills House, 1898.

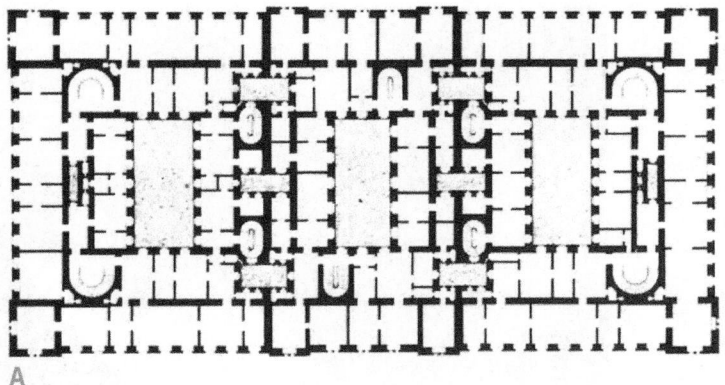

A

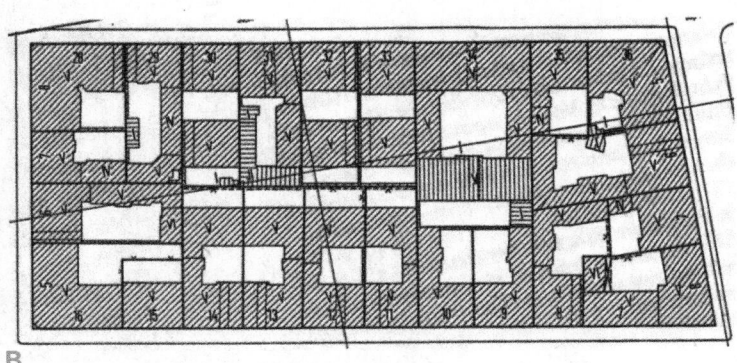

B

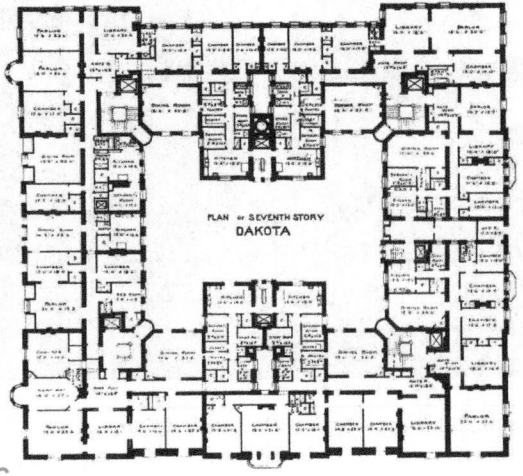

C

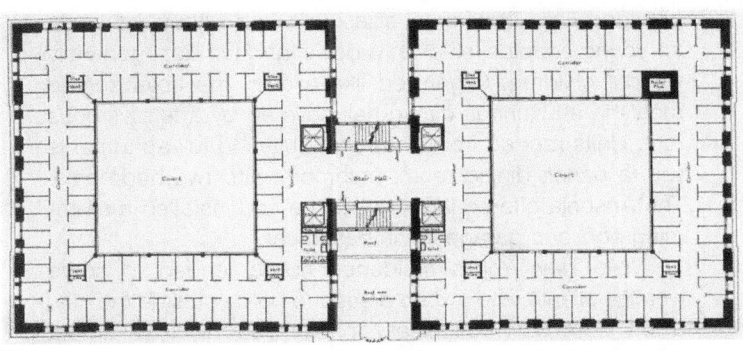

D

lots of medieval houses to the broad, multiple bays of Renaissance palaces. François Mansart's unified elevations at Place Vendôme, built at the end of the seventeenth century, provided an influential model for the emergent apartment block (see Section 12.2). Planners down through Haussmann encouraged developers to create continuous facades, articulated with an apron of cast-iron balconies on the level of the *piano nobile*. A setback on the sixth floor added variety and diminished the scale.

In Vienna the new apartments in the Ringstrasse district followed similar criteria (Fig. 16.2-2). The *Mietpalast*, literally "rental palace," fit into large unified blocks that looked like independent palaces with luxurious facades (Fig. 16.2-3). Theophilus Hansen devised the *Gruppen zinhuis* as an integral block articulated with domes marking the corners of the central zone. While appearing as a single building, it could be subdivided into eight separately owned, multiple-unit properties, each with its own stair and court, permitting small-scale speculators to enter the real estate market.

Apartment blocks became the basic unit for the substantial expansion of late-nineteenth-century Berlin following the Hobrecht Plan of 1858–1862. The plan structured new districts, such as Kreuzberg and Charlottenburg, with large, contiguous apartment blocks. The planners intended the increased size of the blocks to supply more space for interior courts and greenery. But while the building codes limited the cornice heights and stipulated that courtyards be a minimum of 36 m² (385 ft²), they made no restrictions on density. Consequently, the blocks filled up with a multitude of inner courts. While the *Mietpalast* type gracefully lined the principal streets, these buildings concealed the more densely packed *Mietkaserne* (Fig. 16.2-4), or rental barracks, which sometimes had a sequence of as many as five internal courts. These rear courts quickly degenerated into overcrowded slums kept out of public view.

The prejudice against the apartment type in England and the United States came from its associations with the poor, who lived in dense, vertically stacked "flats." On the confined island of Manhattan, however, apartments began to replace row houses in the 1870s. The Dakota (Fig. 16.2-5), designed in 1882 by Henry Janeway Hardenbergh (1847–1918), stood as an isolated, castle-like volume near the edge of Central Park. Its patron was a director of the Singer Sewing Machine Company and desired a housing development for people from three different income brackets. The ground floor included a restaurant, a ballroom, and guestrooms for visitors.

New York developers created a series of residence hotels during the last quarter of the nineteenth century for significant numbers of wealthy and middle-class people

Figure 16.2-3 Vienna. Typical *Mietpalast*, 1870s.

who desired seasonal lodging. The eighteen-story Ansonia, built in 1904 by developer W. E. D. Stokes (1852–1926), provided units of different sizes, with and without kitchens, for young couples, singles, widows, and families, generally without children. Organized like a club, the hotel served meals in a luxurious dining hall covered by a ferrovitreous roof. Units ranged from two-room suites to full apartments with a parlor, dining room, bathroom, and two bedrooms. The Ansonia offered laundry service and installed a swimming pool and garage in the basement.

While New York's residence hotels tended to serve wealthy clients who owned a second home outside the city, a few were built specifically for the poor. In 1898 Ernest Flagg (1857–1947), a reform-minded Beaux-Arts architect,

designed the Mills House (Fig. 16.2-6), a pair of twelve-story, palace-like blocks joined by a glazed lobby and stair tower as a single room–occupancy hotel for working-class bachelors. It included a dining hall, library, lounge, bathhouse, and other social amenities.

The mass of poor folk in industrial cities around the world lived in crowded **tenements**, multiple-story walk-up flats (Fig. 16.2-7). In late-nineteenth-century New York over two-thirds of the population was packed into 80,000 buildings. The five- and six-story rectangular shoeboxes that comprised the tenements filled the entire lot, separated by thin party walls. The internal rooms received no direct daylight or air. Such small flats reproduced the crowding and squalor experienced earlier in the industrial slums of Glasgow and

Figure 16.2-4 Berlin.
Mietkaserne, courts of rental
barracks, 1880s.

**Figure 16.2-5 New York. The Dakota
residence hotel, Henry Janeway
Hardenbergh, 1880s.**

Figure 16.2-6 New York. Mills House, a bachelor hotel, Ernest Flagg, 1898.

Manchester. Entire families lived in single rooms without services. The 1879 Tenement House Act attempted to require that buildings provide more exposure to light and air, leading to James Ware's competition-winning "dumbbell" scheme. Named after its *I* shape, the design specified two front and two back units for each floor and cut out a 0.5 m (1.6 ft) wide gap on either side of a central core for the stairwell and toilets. By 1900 the majority of New York's tenements followed the dumbbell scheme, which did little to remedy the overcrowding problem. Their undecorated brick elevations presented a Spartan dignity to the street. The addition of zigzagging iron fire escapes and iron-framed rooftop water towers gave the structures pragmatic forms of articulation.

Lateral Options: Row Houses

The row, or **terrace**, house emerged in English-speaking countries and parts of northern Europe as the alternative to vertically stacked apartments. Terrace housing got its name from the section of the lot that stepped down from street level to rear gardens, or "terraces." The units usually met the contour of the street with a uniform building line and were separated from each other by party walls. The bylaws of nineteenth-century English cities prescribed a minimum of open space between the houses and the back of the property, ranging from 4 to 7 m (13 to 22 ft). Ideally, half of the lot was allotted for open space. The width of the units usually allowed three window bays, equivalent to 8 m (26 ft), but poor neighborhoods often had only two. Each unit had an entry stoop, a basement, and two or three upper stories, rarely rising to a fourth. In 1900, 87% of the British population lived in row houses, and in the first important American colonial cities, such as Boston and Philadelphia, they were the dominant dwelling type. Until the mid-twentieth century the new cities in Australia and New Zealand likewise preferred English-inspired row houses.

Since Roman times the European urban fabric had evolved as rows of houses sharing party walls. The modern

Figure 16.2-7 New York. Former tenements in Lower Manhattan with fire escapes, late nineteenth century.

version of the terrace house type, however, reflected the different standards that had emerged after the Great Fire of London in 1666. The enterprising Nicholas Barbon (1640–1698), a graduate of the medical school of Utrecht University in Holland, returned to England after the fire and developed several hundred row houses, influenced no doubt by Dutch examples. In his widely circulated books he laid out the principles of laissez-faire economics, privileging the role of construction. In *Apology for the Builder, or a Discourse Showing the Cause and Effects of the Increase of Building* (1685), he explained how the building industry stimulated the economy. Aside from producing speculative housing, Barbon organized one of the first fire insurance companies and operated his own fire brigade to protect his interests. Little remains of his cheaply built houses, excepting the layout of Red Lion's Square, his largest single development. Barbon's typical unit stood three bays wide and

four stories high, with access to a small backyard garden. The kitchen, storage, and servants' spaces occupied the lowest level, partially sunk below the street level but at grade with the garden. Above this he provided a dining room and parlor, two bedrooms on the next floor, and servants' rooms in the attic.

The architectural handbooks of William Halfpenny and Batty Langley, published in the early eighteenth century, encouraged the standardization of house building in London. They influenced the development of entire streets, planned by a single speculative builder, lined with nearly identical terrace houses, mass-produced by bricklayers and carpenters working in the construction trades. London expanded in patches from the sequential subdivision of aristocratic estates. Each subdivision usually focused on a planted square that served the fancier houses. The Duke of Bedford's Bloomsbury estate, for instance, yielded Bedford

Catharine Beecher and the Proto-Feminist Dwelling

Many theories of female liberation took root within the movement for American abolitionism. While Catharine Beecher (1800–1878) laid out a program for reform in her *Treatise on Domestic Economy* (1841), her sister, Harriet Beecher Stowe (1811–1896), published *Uncle Tom's Cabin*, which garnered immense sympathy for the Union. Beecher intended to empower women in the home through increased efficiency and the elimination of unnecessary labor. The new American house would not need servants. Her books came with plans for rationalizing domestic space, featuring kitchens that had the ergonomic logic of factories. Melusina Fay Peirce went further in promoting the emancipation of American women, proposing kitchenless houses and collectivized housework. The New York residence hotel, if it could be rendered into a self-managed cooperative with child-care services, supplied the model of a way of life that could free women.

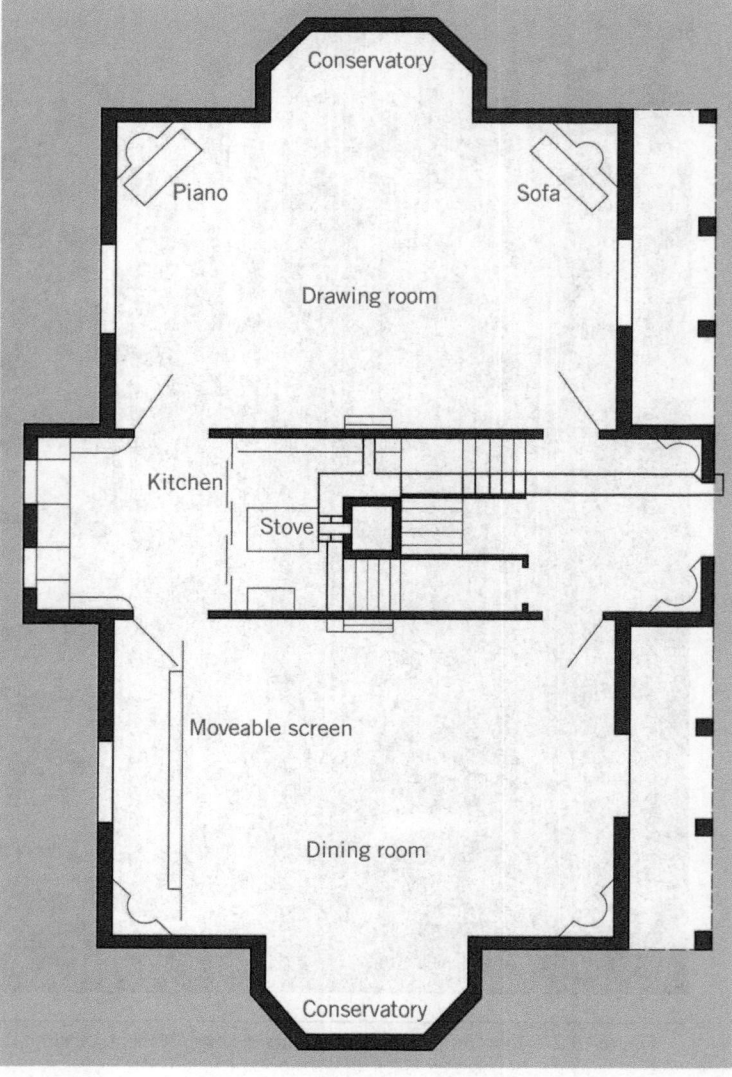

Catharine Beecher's optimal house plan, the so-called Christian House, from *The American Women's Home*, 1869. Note there is no fireplace, only a Franklin stove serving radiators.

Square and Bloomsbury Square, lined with row houses that shared the same cornice and looked as if they belonged to a single palatial structure. In contrast to the rental palaces on the continent, English row house "palaces" maintained horizontal, rather than vertical, divisions. In mid-nineteenth-century London the contractor Thomas Cubitt (1788–1855) built the most important row houses. Aside from carrying out the construction of public projects such as the new royal residence of Buckingham Palace, Cubitt produced entire sections of the city, such as Belgravia, with orderly streets and squares lined with classical porches (Fig. 16.2-8).

The row houses of London's poor presented a completely different atmosphere (Fig. 16.2-9). Densely packed in the eastern sections of the city, they rarely had rear gardens and, with their lack of light and air, shared the same

problems of the New York tenements. Many of the earliest rows of workers' housing stood back-to-back. The units lined narrow blocks without a yard between them, and thus all of the walls, except the entry elevations, were party walls. The municipality outlawed such cramped conditions during the mid-nineteenth century.

In 1851 the enlightened industrialist Titus Salt (1803–1876) attempted to improve the conditions for workers at Saltaire. This early company town offered a more hygienic and sober environment for the employees of Salt's new alpaca weaving factory north of Bradford. Salt had served as head constable and mayor of Bradford in the 1840s and observed directly the degeneration of the working class living in back-to-back units. For Saltaire he commissioned the firm of Lockwood and Mawson to build over 800 units during a twenty-year

Figure 16.2-8 London. Belgrave Square, Thomas Cubitt, 1840s.

Figure 16.2-9 London. Gustave Doré's vision of the city's row house slums, 1870s.

Figure 16.2-10 Saltaire, United Kingdom. Town dominated by Salt's Mill, as seen from a nearby hill, 1851–1870s.

period (Fig. 16.2-10). The company constructed solid stone structures, eliminating the basements. Each dwelling had two rooms below and two above and was set in a long row, with a small garden and service alley in the back separating it from the other units. The town offered a restaurant, public baths, a library, a school, a church, retirement homes, and a large park with playing fields and allotment orchards. Salt eliminated taverns from the plan, proposing sports as a better diversion for workers. Throughout the nineteenth century, English efforts to improve the living conditions of the poor focused almost exclusively on the row-house type.

The Detached Single-Family House: Villas and Bungalows

During the late nineteenth century, in the industrial cities, the extended family became increasingly less practical. The nuclear family, consisting of a married couple and their children, became the norm in Anglo-American culture and, with it, detached dwellings surrounded by gardens away from the city. Well-to-do Londoners since the eighteenth century had kept a townhouse for city life and a small country villa for weekend retreats from the city. The second house became known as a "bungalow," after the modest camp buildings built for colonists in India. Often built using technologies of mass production, the bungalow provided a cheap and expedient solution for a single-story house surrounded by porches. The Anglo-American suburbs that sprang up along the new train lines were typically filled with villas and bungalows. The railroad entrepreneurs who established these lines often doubled as developers of the surrounding commuter suburbs.

While the wealthy had always owned country estates, the poorest members of European society usually lived on the urban fringes. The *terrains vagues* that surrounded

Paris abounded with shanty dwellings. In London during the 1790s, members of the Evangelical movement established the first upper-middle-class suburb for nuclear families at Clapham Common. Here, seventy-two like-minded families built single-family detached houses with ample gardens around a large park. The men commuted to the city in the horse-drawn omnibus, while the women and children stayed behind in the villas, protected from the pernicious distractions of the city, with its promiscuous street life, theaters, pollution, and poverty. The leader of the community, William Wilberforce (1759–1833), wrote the British law for the abolition of slavery in 1807 (extended to the colonies in 1833). He idealized the single-family villa as the proper setting for giving children a moral education, hygiene, and the beneficial influence of nature. While its founders had high moral expectations for their community, Clapham Common also pioneered the trend of class segregation, resulting in cities that were as divided as the White and Black Towns in colonial India.

The earliest English suburbs followed the architectural examples of John Nash's Park Villages, built on the eastern and western edges of Regent's Park in London in the 1820s. The rising middle class appreciated Nash's mixture of styles, ranging from castle-like to Italianate to Tudor half-timber, preferring each house to be distinct from the next. Gothic villas became fashionable with the pattern books of the landscape architect John Claudius Loudon (see Section 15.3). His *Encyclopedia of Cottage, Farm, Villa Architecture* (1834), written with his wife, Jane Webb Loudon (1807–1858), illustrated small-scale, single-family houses in the interest of improving middle-class standards of dwelling. To protect one's investment from depreciation, Loudon recommended settling in neighborhoods where everyone belonged to the same class.

RELIGION, PHILOSOPHY, FOLKLORE

Thoreau's Cabin on Walden Pond

In 1845, while the rest of American culture attempted to leave behind colonial simplicity to create ornate buildings and grand urban settings, Henry David Thoreau (1817–1862) retreated to Walden Pond to build a small cabin and live off the land. He intended his exercise in self-reliance to challenge the conformism by which "the mass of men lead lives of quiet desperation." Thoreau built his tiny dwelling on a site owned by his mentor, the philosopher Ralph Waldo Emerson (1803–1882), spending the negligible sum of $28 for its construction. Thoreau described in minute detail the joinery and craft that went into making his one-room, rectangular cell, built with wooden planks and covered with a pitched roof, and extolled the comfort of living within one's means. His proposition for a functionalist architecture based on minimized needs seemed almost as radical as his proposals for nonviolent resistance to political authority.

Concord, Massachusetts. Reconstruction of Thoreau's cabin at Walden Pond, 1845.

Joseph Paxton, a decade before his great exploit of the Crystal Palace (see Section 15.3), laid out the planned suburb of Victoria Park, south of Manchester. Its roads gently curved according to picturesque principles, leaving occasional public gardens at their intersections. He set each of the houses behind a prominent wall to guarantee privacy. The factory owners of Manchester desired prominent, castle-like houses in which the master of the house had a suite that included a library, a study, and a billiard room, and his wife had her boudoir, parlor, and sitting room. The children received their own spaces for a nursery and playroom, while the servants navigated the buildings through concealed corridors connected to the cellar and attic. The segregational nature of Victoria Park became obvious in comparison to the infamous Manchester suburb known as Little Ireland, about a kilometer (0.6 mile) away. Here, immigrants lived in back-to-back rows in utmost squalor. Friedrich Engels, researching the condition of the working class, witnessed "heaps of refuse, offal, and sickening filth . . . everywhere interspersed with pools of stagnant liquid." He concluded that the occupants "must surely have sunk to the lowest level of humanity."

Bedford Park, designed in London in the 1870s by the Scottish-born architect Richard Norman Shaw (1831–1912), did not have a park of its own but attracted its clientele through a unique, romantic style that conveyed the idea of comfort. Shaw's Queen Anne style mixed charming aspects of historic vernaculars while avoiding reference to the pretentious high styles of the past. The houses in Bedford Park (Fig. 16.2-11) stood close to the street rather than hidden

behind walls. Shaw gave them a sense of privacy through asymmetrical massing. He also enlivened the elevations with projecting elements, such as entry porches, **bay windows**, overhanging upper stories, ornamented gables, and massive chimneys. The interiors featured inglenooks around the fireplaces and window seats, with walls encrusted in decorative patterns.

The moral premise of the British detached dwelling influenced house building in the United States, Canada, Australia, and New Zealand. Americans already had the ideals of Puritan villages and William Penn's "green country town" as precedents. An early planned suburb, Llewellyn Park, in New Jersey, 20 km (13 miles) from Manhattan, was built by Llewellyn S. Haskell in the 1850s, with the architect Alexander Jackson Davis (1803–1892). In 1842 Davis illustrated the highly influential publication of *Cottage Residences* by landscape architect Andrew Jackson Downing (1815–1852). Like Loudon, Downing proposed modest villas in different styles, favoring the Gothic. At Llewellyn Park (Fig. 16.2-12), Davis designed medieval fantasies with round, crenellated towers and pointy roofs, including his own Gothic cottage of Wildmont. The influential abolitionist preacher James Miller McKim acquired one of Davis's Gothic cottages. McKim, father of one of America's most accomplished Beaux-Arts architects, Charles McKim (1847–1909), rejected the nuclear family model, combining his family with the Garrison family.

Charles McKim and his future partner Stanford White (1853–1906) had both worked at different stages in the New York office of Henry Hobson Richardson, the most influential

Figure 16.2-11 London. Bedford Park, Richard Norman Shaw, 1870s.

Figure 16.2-12 Llewellyn Park, New Jersey. Wildmont, Alexander Jackson Davis, 1870s.

American architect of the late nineteenth century. Before they embarked on a career of grand institutional structures, they helped Richardson create some of the most beautiful American versions of the Queen Anne style. White took charge of the William Watts Sherman House in Newport, Rhode Island (1874) (Fig. 16.2-13). He composed it asymmetrically, like the works of Richard Norman Shaw, letting the prominent chimneys and half-timber walls protrude from a skin of tightly placed cedar shingles.

On their own, McKim and White designed dozens of patrician villas in the shingle style. With the William G. Low House of 1886 (Fig. 16.2-14) they achieved a genuinely monumental solution. Under a vast, pediment-like pitched roof they arranged an open sequence, this time in symmetry around a central axis. They subordinated the L-shaped verandah and bay windows within the broad triangular volume. The rear elevation, with its great expanse of brown shingles, evoked the formal dignity of an early Doric temple.

Figure 16.2-13 Newport, Rhode Island. Watts Sherman House, Henry Hobson Richardson firm, 1874.

Figure 16.2-14 Bristol, Rhode Island. William G. Low House, McKim, Mead & White, 1887.

The innovative approach to the Low House showed how the program for the detached single-family dwelling inspired the American architectural imagination.

The Utopian Challenge: Collectivist Alternatives

The nineteenth-century metropolis disrupted the social fabric of urban life. It introduced the unsettling speed of modern transport and the annoying pollution of coal-burning factories. It spawned alienation through the proximity of so many strangers and their glaring class differences. The oppressive conditions of the poor led to frequent riots in such places as Manchester, Berlin, and New York. In response, socialists like Robert Owen (1771–1858), a factory owner, advocated the collectivization of human needs, especially housing. He founded the company town of New Lanark in Scotland in 1816 and dreamed of the day when the workers would own the factory themselves. Charles Fourier (1772–1837) in Lyons independently formulated a theory of socialism, dreaming of a much more libertarian outcome. In 1848, the year of widespread revolutions, Karl Marx (1818–1883) and Friedrich Engels published the *Communist Manifesto*, urging the working class to rise up in the name of socialism because they had "nothing to lose but their chains." By the time of the Paris Commune of 1871, socialism had become a project that could not be ignored. In America, Edward Bellamy (1850–1898) in his utopian novel *Looking Backward* (1888) foresaw a technocratic socialist society that would succeed in equitably distributing the wealth of a wonderfully productive populace. The work ranked as the third-best-selling U.S. book of the nineteenth century and generated innumerable Bellamy clubs.

Utopian socialism usually involved some notion of collective housing. In the movement's foundational text, Thomas More's *Utopia*, written in 1516, the mythical island on which the action unfolded contained many small cities that were not allowed to grow beyond a set number of 20,000 inhabitants. More described the basic social unit of each utopian city as a street lined with thirty houses, each for a family of ten to sixteen people. No one in Utopia could own his or her house, and residents were obliged to move every ten years to avoid the development of a sense of proprietorship. Each family took responsibility one day a month for feeding and serving the neighborhood. More, who had lived for several years in a Carthusian monastery, transferred the monastic experience of collective eating and dwelling to his ideal neighborhood unit.

Owen published his first treatise on socialism in 1817 and eight years later organized the socialist colony of New Harmony in Indiana. Stedman Whitwell drew the ideal plan of New Harmony with Neo-Gothic details, much like the scholastic quadrangles of Oxford and Cambridge. For Owen, 1,200 people constituted the ideal community size, with each family allotted a four-room row house looking onto the central quad. In the middle stood the public kitchen, dining hall, and schools. Owen's socialist colony, which abolished money and private property, disbanded after four years as a result of incompatible members. Despite New Harmony's failure as a community, it left behind Indiana's first public library and the first public grammar school in the United States. The town remained the homestead of Owen's children, who became influential in politics and science. Owen's heirs ironically became pillars of American capitalism as the founders of Standard Oil.

Fourier's project for socialism, first published in 1808, called for the formation of like-minded groups to work together as a "phalanx." In a weekly magazine published in the 1830s he specified that the ideal phalanx should have 1,600 members and live cooperatively in a single building, or *phalanstery*. He wrote detailed descriptions of this building, which would possess all of the functions of a little city. In shape it resembled the palace of Versailles, only double its size. He reserved the ground floor for vehicles and services, while a glazed three-story gallery acted as an interior street, connecting the entire complex so that one need never go outside. The various sizes and qualities of apartments suited the 108 categories of persons hypothesized by Fourier. The attic level served as a visitors' hostel, while public dining halls and libraries occupied central locations. He imagined nurseries for the children on the mezzanine level, which was considerably shorter than the other levels. As a self-sustaining society the phalanx would run industries, isolated in a separate wing, and enjoy boisterous ballrooms for entertainment.

Fourier's liberational philosophy, which he called "passional attraction," celebrated female independence, permitted open relationships, and condoned homosexuality. He proposed organized prostitution for those who were unable to have relationships. His social ideals of a harmoniously integrated, cooperative society strongly appealed to idealistic Americans before the Civil War. Dozens of phalanxes cropped up at midcentury. Reverend George Ripley (1802–1880) founded the most famous, Brook Farm, in West Roxbury, Massachusetts, in 1840. Its members included the novelist Nathaniel Hawthorne and the proto-feminist journalist Margaret Fuller, members of the literary circle of Ralph Waldo Emerson. The Brook Farm commune lasted six years, constructing several buildings around the original farm, but did not survive the economic setback of a devastating fire. In 1855 Victor Considerant, a direct collaborator of Fourier and designer of the original phalanstery, established La Réunion a short distance from the center of modern Dallas. Although the commune attracted 250 European settlers, severe weather conditions ruined the first year's agricultural harvest, and the settlers disbanded five years later.

One of Considerant's backers, the industrialist Jean-Baptiste-André Godin (1817–1888), established the most successful Fourierite community. Upon relocating his ironworks factory to the small town of Guise in northeastern France in 1859, he built a reduced version of the phalanstery, which he called the Familistère (Fig. 16.2-15). He

Figure 16.2-15 Guise, France. (a) Plan of the Familistère, Jean-Baptiste-André Godin, 1859–1890, from Godin, *Solutions Sociales*, 1871. (b) Interior of the Familistère housing, 1883.

linked three courtyard buildings around a *U*-shaped entry court and provided the interior atrium courts with cast-iron balconies and glass roofs. Godin's Familistère had a certain Panoptic quality, since everyone could see everyone else as they came and went on the cast-iron balconies. Each of the 350 families in the Familistère of Guise lived in a four-room flat. Although Godin opposed matrimony, the workers tended to prefer traditional family structure. The housing blocks faced three lower buildings, with the central one for the theater and the schools, the one closest to the factory for the kitchens and collective meals, and the last for workshops, a club, and the bakery. A communal bathhouse and laundry with an indoor swimming pool stood next to the bridge leading to the factory. In 1880 Godin's company, famous for its cast-iron kitchenware, stoves, and bathtubs, became a cooperative, owned and managed by the workers. Unusually for the time, many women took management positions. Godin transformed the concept of the paternalistic company town into a unique outpost of worker autonomy. When the socialist novelist Émile Zola came to visit, however, he proved less impressed by the social justice of the Familistère than by its regimented boredom.

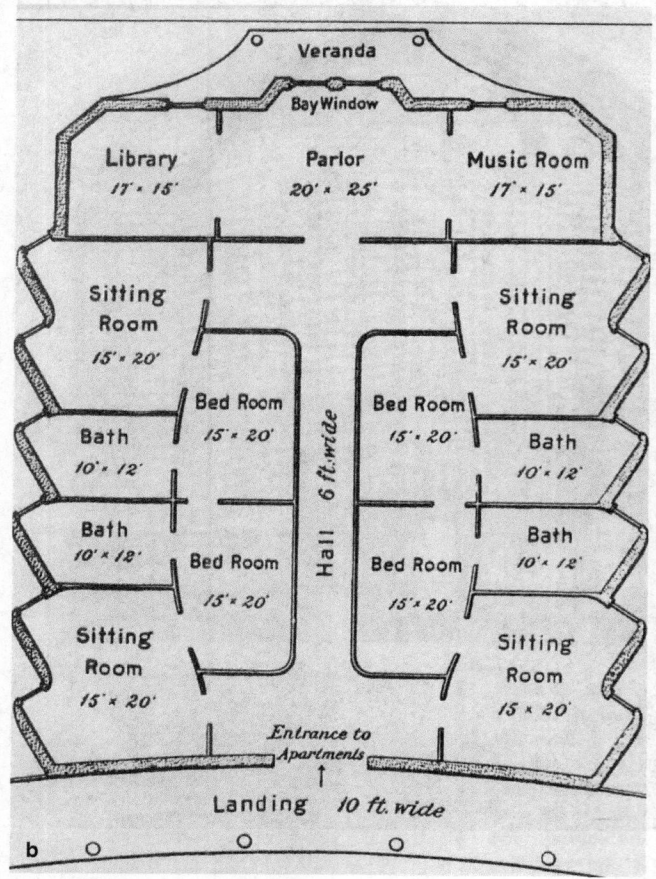

Figure 16.2-16 (a) United States. Utopian scheme for America, King Camp Gillette, from *The Human Drift*, 1894. (b) Apartment plans, 1894.

While Godin's architecture did not exert much influence, his thought that "the social progress of the masses is subordinated to the progress of the social provisions of architecture" became central to architectural theory in the early twentieth century. The American inventor of the safety razor, King Camp Gillette (1855–1932), proposed a more ambitious utopian settlement, likewise set in isolated, glass-roofed buildings (Fig. 16.2-16a). Published in 1894, his work *The Human Drift* outlined a grandiose, authoritarian scheme run by a benevolent state corporation that coerced the entire nation to live in a single rigidly planned metropolis. The hexagonal grid of Gillette's city resembled a giant beehive. Each of the thirty-story apartment cylinders stood in its own park. Like New York residence hotels, Gillette's units eliminated kitchens (Fig. 16.2-16b) in favor of collective meals eaten in the domed void of his crystal palaces. Other towers, set between the dwelling compounds, served as sites for education, recreation, and food preparation. Like Godin, Gillette designed the urban and architectural models of his theoretical world of progress convinced that form determined behavior, a utopian premise that influenced many housing projects of the next century.

Further Reading

Hayden, Dolores. *The Grand Domestic Revolution: A History of Feminist Designs for American Homes, Neighborhoods, and Cities*. Cambridge, MA: MIT Press, 1981.

Muthesius, Stephan. *The English Terraced House*. New Haven, CT: Yale University Press, 1982.

Scully, Vincent, Jr. *The Shingle Style*. New Haven, CT: Yale University Press, 1971.

Stern, R. A. M., G. Gilmartin, and J. Massengale. *New York 1900: Metropolitan Architecture and Urbanism, 1890–1915*. New York: Rizzoli, 1983.

Wright, Gwendolyn. *Building the Dream: A Social History of Housing in America*. Cambridge, MA: MIT Press, 1981.

16.3 | THE BEAUX-ARTS
Eclecticism and Professionalism

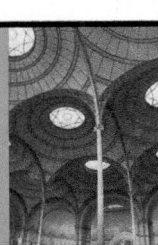

Almost every major public building in nineteenth-century France showed the influence of the École des Beaux-Arts. The school taught the principles of classical architecture, favoring symmetrical composition in plan and facade, rational layouts for circulation, and the clear expression of the hierarchy of functions. It also encouraged profuse decoration, inspired by mixing the most admired motifs of the past. Beaux-Arts style appeared truly eclectic, amalgamating elements from different styles in the effort to fit into the historic city while creating something new. Although the term "eclectic" subsequently acquired negative connotations, it originally referred to the good intentions of synthesis, an attempt to combine the best of everything. But rather than leading to what philosopher Victor Cousin (1792–1867) called "the good, the true, and the beautiful," it often led to awkward hybrids.

By the end of the nineteenth century, as the Beaux-Arts style began losing support in Europe, it gained significant momentum in the United States during the boom period of the "American Renaissance." American Beaux-Arts architects trained in Paris influenced the formation of professionals for several generations. They produced exquisite public buildings that imitated the scale of ancient Rome and Second Empire Paris while supplying the great monopoly capitalists with suitably grand statements of their new status. So closely did American Beaux-Arts architects identify with their patrons that they began to organize their offices on the corporate model, creating a new level of professionalism.

Beaux-Arts Eclecticism: Something for Everyone

The French Revolution eliminated Jean-Baptiste Colbert's Royal Academy as an elitist institution, and for a generation the new schools of engineering, such as Jean-Nicholas-Louis Durand's employer, the École Polytechnique, served as the primary institution for the preparation of architects. The Academy reappeared in 1819 during the restoration of the monarchy as the École des Beaux-Arts. It resuscitated the **atelier** system, in which students worked in the studio of a senior patron and younger students aided the older ones to prepare projects for the Prix de Rome competition. The winners of this prize continued their education for several years in Rome, researching works of the classical past and preparing magnificent analytical drawings. The Beaux-Arts method began with the concept of the **parti**, the basic organizing principles of circulation and room layouts. In addition to this commitment to compositional order, the major

contribution of Beaux-Arts design concerned the creation of appropriate style and decoration.

In 1863 Viollet-le-Duc attempted the equivalent of a coup d'état at the École des Beaux-Arts to reform its curriculum. He objected to classical style and the atelier system, desiring to foster a less hierarchical and more focused mastery of technical knowledge. Viollet-le-Duc planned to open up the institution to a broader range of students and teachers, considering the atelier system incestuous and incapable of reflecting the progress being made in other fields. His didactic program, based on the careful analysis of structure and nature, opposed the traditional study of the canonical works of classicism. Viollet-le-Duc's lessons in architectural history met with open rebellion from the students and teachers, including the followers of Charles Garnier, and his reforms languished. Despite this initial unpopularity, Viollet-le-Duc's theories greatly influenced most practitioners of the period, helping to destabilize the orthodoxy of classicism.

Julien Guadet (1834–1908), the chief theorist at the Beaux-Arts during the latter part of the century, popularized canonical buildings as "everything which has remained victorious in the struggle of the arts, everything that continues to arouse universal admiration." Thus, while a proper academic education must begin with classical buildings like the Parthenon, he believed that it should also include such works as Hagia Sophia and the cathedral at Chartres. Guadet endorsed **eclecticism** as the combination of the best aspects of different styles into a contemporary style. The design of the Beaux-Arts school buildings illustrated the evolving eclecticism of the times. Félix Duban (1797–1870) began rebuilding the school in 1832. In a move evocative of John Soane's house in London, he stocked the corridors with fragments of historical architecture from the architectural museum and copies of Renaissance paintings and sculptures as spoils to be studied. The facade of the central building (Fig. 16.3-1) emulated Roman Renaissance style, with its base borrowing the Cancelleria's ashlar rustication and the upper story with bays borrowing from the Belvedere Court at the Vatican. If the trip to Rome remained the chief goal of the program's curriculum, the school gave students a foretaste of what to expect.

Twenty years later Duban added the facade to the new wing of the school on Quai Malaquais in a truly eclectic style. He again used classical half-columns to mark each bay but between them inserted broad segmental arches for the studio windows and crowned every other bay with a pronounced beef-eye window. In 1867 he enclosed the main courtyard of the earlier building with a ferrovitreous vault (Fig. 16.3-2a). His use of exposed iron supports resembled the innovative work of his friend Henri Labrouste at the new reading room of the Bibliothèque Nationale, where a grid of slender metal columns held up billowing domes, each with a glazed oculus (Fig. 16.3-2b). In both cases the architects used modern ironwork discreetly for interior situations, while the framing structure of the whole remained clearly legible in classical masonry.

The eclecticism of Beaux-Arts graduates led to creative combinations rather than classical rigor. The facade of the

Figure 16.3-1 Paris. École des Beaux-Arts, second phase, Félix Duban, 1867.

Figure 16.3-2 Paris. (a) École des Beaux-Arts, court, Duban, 1867. (b) See facing page.

▼ **1861–1875**

Garnier's Opéra built in Paris

Dollmann's Neuschwanstein begun in Bavaria for Ludwig II

▲ **1872**

▼ **1873**

Richardson's Trinity Church begun in Boston

Abadie's Sacré-Coeur begun in Paris

▲ **1874**

Palais des Beaux-Arts in Lille (Fig. 16.3-3), designed in 1885 by Edouard Bérard (1843–1912), featured a colorful assembly of classical and Baroque elements that rivaled Garnier's Opéra. Each bay thrust forward as an independent aedicule. Léon Vaudoyer (1803–1872) created one of the most extreme combinations of different historical styles in the new cathedral in Marseilles (1852–1893) (Fig. 16.3-4). Finished by his successor, Henri-Jacques Espérandieu, Ste.-Marie-Majeure evoked Roman, Romanesque, Renaissance, and Byzantine precedents. The polychrome exterior of *ablaq*-like alternating bands of green and white limestone dominated the whole. Like most eclectic works, the cathedral evoked a feeling of disjointedness in its contradictory references to different historical styles.

In Paris the church of Sacré Coeur (Fig. 16.3-5), soaring above the hill of Montmartre, offered a coherent yet incongruous vision. Begun in 1874 as a monument of national atonement for the offenses committed against the Catholic Church during the revolt of the Commune, it reached completion after much protest in 1919. The architect, Paul Abadie (1812–1884), took Viollet-le-Duc's principles of creative restoration to extremes. At his reconstruction of the medieval church of St. Front in Périgueux (1850–1884), he added a cluster of elongated domes similar to those at Sacré Coeur, causing great controversy for this mystification of the original. While consistent with the Greek cross plan of St. Front, Abadie's domes were pure invention with no basis in historical fact. They vaguely recalled the dome of Pisa's cathedral, but their solid stone construction and needle-like lanterns seemed closer to Indian *stupas* than to Byzantine cupolas. The similar domes of Sacré Coeur covered an ancient gypsum quarry that had been used by the Communards as an arms deposit and a place of execution, where the bishop of Paris and many of the rebels met their end during the repression of their movement. The church's remarkable whiteness came from a peculiar type of travertine that continually exuded calcite, contributing to its uncanny, dazzling presence on the Parisian skyline.

Beaux-Arts eclecticism spread beyond France. Perhaps the best-known, and certainly the most exuberant, expression was the monument in Rome to Italy's first king, Victor Emmanuel II (r. 1861–1878). Known as the "Vittoriano" (but also called by many nicknames, such as the "Wedding Cake" and the "Typewriter"), the formally named Altar of the Country terminated the new boulevard also named after

Figure 16.3-2 Paris. (b) National Library, reading room, Henri Labrouste, 1865.

the king, presenting one of the most emphatic backdrops in the history of urbanism (Fig. 16.3-6). Although the first round of the competition held for its design went to French architect Paul-Henri Nénot (1853–1934), the second, held in 1882, went to Count Giuseppe Sacconi (1854–1905), who proposed a piece of unrestrained scenography. Meant to upstage Michelangelo's Campidoglio, which stood directly behind it, the Vittoriano's grand, 40 m (128 ft) wide stairway led up forking paths to three terraces, past the equestrian

1882

Sacconi's "Vittoriano" monument begun in Rome

Statue of Liberty erected in New York Harbor

▲ 1886

1888

Boston Public Library begun by McKim, Mead & White

Burnham's White City plan for the Columbian Exposition in Chicago

▲ 1893

Figure 16.3-3 Lille, France. Palais des Beaux-Arts, Edouard Bérard, 1885.

Figure 16.3-4 Marseilles, France. Ste.-Marie-Majeure, Léon Vaudoyer, 1852–1893.

Figure 16.3-5 Paris. Sacré Coeur, Paul Abadie, 1874–1919.

statue of the king, to a concave screen of columns crowned by bronze quadrigas at each end. The choice of the stridently white Brescia marble in contrast to the typically warm colors of Rome augmented the monument's struggle with the site, making it among the most memorable, and ridiculed, works of the nineteenth century.

Ludwig II of Bavaria (r. 1864–1886), grandson of the patron of Munich's historicist monuments, became one of the most enthusiastic sponsors of eclecticism. The young king chose as his architect Georg Dollmann (1830–1895), the son-in-law of the earlier king's architect, Leo von Klenze. Ludwig presided over his kingdom as an extremely

well-read romantic with a passion for the operas of Richard Wagner (1813–1883). He brought Wagner to Munich and bankrolled all of his later works, including the Bayreuth opera house. Unlike Garnier at the Opéra in Paris, Wagner left the exterior of his theater unadorned, chiefly concerned with the illusions on the stage. Ludwig II desired to live in a world of such Wagnerian illusions, programming a series of permanent stage sets for his bizarre, solitary way of life. In an age when the military function of castles had long vanished, he built three. At Linderhof (1870), a Baroque pavilion decorated with rusticated columns and atlantids in the style of Fischer (Fig. 16.3-7a), he devoted the decoration of the

Figure 16.3-6 Rome. Altar to the Nation, or the "Vittoriano," Giuseppe Sacconi, 1882–1932.

interior to the life of Louis XIV of France. In the woods behind the palace, he commissioned his prized setting, the Grotto of Venus, where a small interior pond evoked the first act of Wagner's *Tannhauser*. Ludwig's most ambitious castle, Neuschwanstein (Fig. 16.3-7b), loomed above the ancient family castle of Hohenschwangau, where he had spent much of his childhood. Inspired by Viollet-le-Duc's creative restoration of Pierrefonds, he built a turreted collage of thirteenth-century fortresses on a knoll overlooking a waterfall. Each of the great halls displayed scenes from Wagner's operas, while the throne room, with its gilded vault, seemed worthy of Charlemagne. Having nearly bankrupted the state with his architectural obsessions, Ludwig's ministers had him declared insane, provoking his probable suicide. In an explanation of his creative excesses he touched upon one of the fundamental regrets of industrialism: "It is essential to create such paradises, such poetic sanctuaries where one can forget for a while the dreadful age in which we live."

Ludwig remained a harmless aesthete, afraid of ruling any place outside of his own gardens. Another monarch of the time, Leopold II of Belgium (r. 1865–1909), proved as prodigious a builder but also extremely dangerous. His reign began as the foundations were being laid for the Palace of Justice in Brussels, built between 1866 and 1883. Much like the Vittoriano in Rome, this immense pile of marble sat on a knoll overlooking its city. It came to represent the relatively new kingdom of Belgium, founded in 1831. Joseph Poelaert (1817–1879), as municipal architect, usurped the competition process to impose his own design. Trained at the Beaux-Arts in Paris, Poelaert followed a typically

foursquare *parti*, placing a tall dome at the central crossing of a large grid of cross-axial wings. The project ran fifteen times over budget, an infraction permitted by the guarantee of the king. As the scaffolds were being removed in Brussels, Leopold II set out on one of the most heinous acts of imperialism in modern history, the founding of the Congo Free State. In 1885 he declared the Congo his private property, a territory eighty times the size of Belgium. As a result of his brutal exploitation of the people to increase his profits from the rubber plantations, millions of Congolese died from mistreatment and cruelty, leading to the world's first international sanction for human rights abuses.

Eclectic architects attempted to make something new from something old. The leading French critic, César Daly (1811–1894), pointed out in 1853, however, the inadequacy of such **historicism** to properly represent the industrial age. "In the architecture of the future," he wrote, "we shall have arches, vaults, beams, pillars, and columns, as in ancient architectures, but we shall also have an aesthetic principle which will bear the same relationship to past principles as a locomotive bears to a stagecoach."

The American Renaissance

By the end of the nineteenth century, the United States produced over one-third of the world's industrial output. The unparalleled wealth this generated, much of it controlled by entrepreneurial families such as the Vanderbilts, led to a flourishing of high-style architectural patronage, frequently called the "American Renaissance." In the effort to

a

Figure 16.3-7 (a) Linderhof, Bavaria. Peacock Pavilion, Georg Dollmann, 1870s. (b) Bavaria. Neuschwanstein, Dollmann, 1870s.

b

compensate for their lack of a past, Americans not only acquired warehouses full of historic artworks and furniture but in some cases imported entire structures from Europe. They dispatched Beaux-Arts-trained architects to reproduce the glories of the Old World in such unlikely settings as uptown Manhattan and rural North Carolina.

Richard Morris Hunt, the first American trained at the Beaux-Arts in the 1840s, worked several years for Lefuel on the additions to the Louvre complex. He founded an office in New York in 1857 and introduced a new level of professionalism into American architecture. Hunt took on a wide range of projects, creating rows of buildings with cast-iron facades, the first belfry-like high-rises, the first French-inspired apartment buildings, and, at the end of his career, the cavernous vaulted halls of the Metropolitan Museum. He ran his office like a Parisian atelier, training his assistants using Beaux-Arts methods. As the favorite architect of the heirs of Cornelius Vanderbilt I, Hunt created several Fifth Avenue mansions, the marble-clad Renaissance palace of the Breakers in Newport, and, grandest of all, the Biltmore, in Asheville, North Carolina (Fig. 16.3-8). Begun in the late 1880s for George Washington Vanderbilt (1862–1914) on a 32 km² (12.3 mi²) estate as large as a feudal duchy, the Biltmore rivaled the delusions of grandeur produced for Ludwig II in Bavaria. Hunt borrowed the slate-covered mansard roofs and the projecting octagonal staircase from the châteaux of the Loire valley. Among the Biltmore's 250 rooms one found an indoor swimming pool and a bowling alley. The scale and erudition of Hunt's projects demonstrated that although America did not possess the heritage of Europe, it had the resources to simulate it.

Hunt also designed the rusticated base for the Statue of Liberty (Fig. 16.3-9), a 93 m (305 ft) high copper-clad colossus erected in 1886 by the French academic Frederic Auguste Bartholdi. The statue rose on an iron structural frame conceived by Maurice Koechlin (1856–1946), chief engineer of Gustave Eiffel, who in turn received advice from Viollet-le-Duc. Sitting at the mouth of New York's harbor, Liberty overlooked the stately vaulted halls built on Ellis Island in 1892 to receive, quarantine, and document over 20 million immigrants before allowing them to enter the United States. As a colossus that surpassed all those of antiquity, the Statue of Liberty communicated the hopes of the new world of democracy while combining the innovations of metal framing with the antiquated style of the Beaux-Arts.

Hunt's studio at one time included the Philadelphia architect Frank Furness (1839–1912). Rather than pursuing the Beaux-Arts ideal, Furness turned toward the sort of Yankee individualism advocated by his father, a Unitarian minister and a leading abolitionist with strong ties to the literary circle of Ralph Waldo Emerson, Henry David Thoreau, and Walt Whitman. While grounded in the rational planning principles of his master, Furness explored a language of truly disquieting hybrids. He designed the Pennsylvania Academy of Fine Arts with George Watson Hewitt (1841–1916) (Fig. 16.3-10), completed in time for the Centennial Exposition of 1876 in Philadelphia. Inspired by Ruskin's descriptions of medieval Venetian architecture, Furness attempted to capture the compressive strength of the stout granite columns of the Doge's Palace at the museum's entry by placing stubby columns that seemed to carry all of the overwhelming mass of the granite porch. The flanking bays carried a collage

Figure 16.3-8 Asheville, North Carolina. Biltmore Estate, Richard Morris Hunt, 1880s.

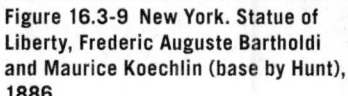
Figure 16.3-9 New York. Statue of Liberty, Frederic Auguste Bartholdi and Maurice Koechlin (base by Hunt), 1886.

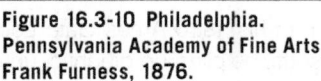
Figure 16.3-10 Philadelphia. Pennsylvania Academy of Fine Arts, Frank Furness, 1876.

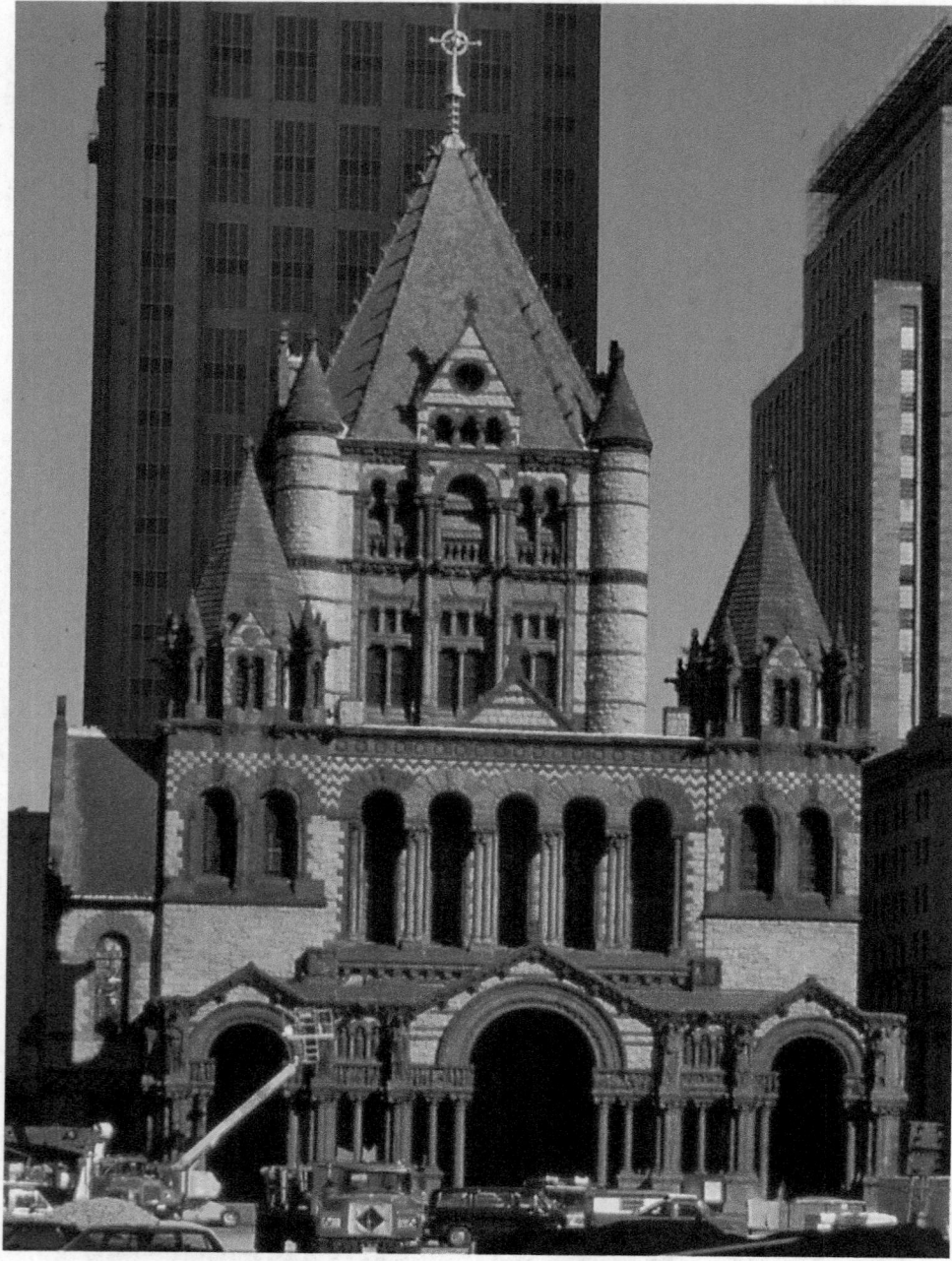

Figure 16.3-11 Boston. Trinity Church, Henry Hobson Richardson, 1873.

of fragments, including a Doric entablature with outsized metope friezes placed above outsized triglyphs. The side elevations appeared even more shocking, presenting one of the first explicit displays of iron beams on a nonindustrial structure. In this building Furness achieved Viollet-le-Duc's predictions of active metal structure.

Henry Hobson Richardson improved on Furness's attempt to transform medieval European motifs into a uniquely American style. Born in New Orleans and initially trained in Boston, Richardson studied for six years at the Beaux-Arts in Paris, working in the studio of Jacques Hittorff, the apostle of architectural polychromy. Like Furness, Richardson found that dense arrangements of medieval masonry conveyed a sense of place. Most of his works stood on magnificent

plinths of granite rustication. In his 1880 Ames Gate Lodge in North Easton, Massachusetts, he piled up gigantic, unrendered boulders as if the building were an accident of nature. Richardson's earliest public works, such as Trinity Church in Boston (1873) (Fig. 16.3-11), exhibited a colorful patching together of beloved Romanesque elements—the central tower was cribbed from the cathedral of Salamanca and the front porch from St.-Gilles-du-Gard (see Section 8.3). In later projects, such as the Allegheny County Courthouse in Pittsburgh (1886), he dispensed with quotations and delivered the raw essence of Romanesque massing and masonry.

Richardson's polychromatic use of rough stone as an expression of America's own mineral resources fostered many imitators in the United States and Canada. He even had admirers in Europe, such as the Finnish architect Eliel Saarinen (1873–1950). Throughout the midwestern states, many late-nineteenth-century county courthouses, universities, and churches aspired to Richardsonian Romanesque. Works like the University of Wichita, Kansas, designed by the firm of Proudfoot and Bird, and James Riely Gordon's Ellis County Courthouse in Waxahachie, Texas (Fig. 16.3-12), vaunted solid, colorful courses of granite and limestone masonry as if to compensate for America's lack of a medieval past.

Richardson's studio employed all three partners of McKim, Mead & White, the major Beaux-Arts practice in late-nineteenth-century America. Established in 1879, the latter office completed more than 900 projects, ranging from mansions to men's clubs to office towers to state capitols to university campuses. The young architects' first major public project, the Boston Public Library (Fig. 16.3-13), begun in 1888, clearly showed their familiarity with Paris. Set on Copley Square across from Richardson's Trinity Church, the library seemed to quicken the pace in the evolution of historicist styles, moving from neomedieval to Neo-Renaissance. The architects borrowed the *parti* of Labrouste's Ste.-Geneviève library and expanded it into a cubic palace with an arcaded courtyard based on the Cancelleria in Rome. They avoided re-producing Labrouste's most interesting invention, however, the exposed cast-iron structure holding up the vaults of the reading room. A single barrel vault embossed with classical coffers enclosed the Boston library's reading room. They tucked its iron supports behind plaster casing. The library introduced a new level of grandeur to American public buildings, with features such as the bifurcated, marble-lined stairway.

McKim, Mead & White joined six other Beaux-Arts firms to create the classical vision of the "White City" at the 1893 World's Columbian Exposition in Chicago. Daniel Burnham (1846–1912) coordinated the master plan following a campus design by Frederick Law Olmsted (Fig. 16.3-14). At one end of the oblong lagoon rose a dome by Richard Morris Hunt, pushing a level above the rest like a cathedral, and at the other end stood a colossal gilded statue with arms outstretched, representing the republic. The imagery seemed more imperial than republican, creating a fantasy environment that recalled the grand projects of Trajan and Hadrian. The facades evoked ancient splendor, wrapped in cheap veneers of wood and plaster painted uniformly white. The interiors of the structures used ex-posed wrought-iron web frames. Like the colonial settlements in India, the White City in Chicago referred not only to the color of the buildings but to race. The exposition's Court of Honor was placed as the climax of evolutionary progress, distinct from the more casually sited "villages" and side-shows of what the planners considered less evolved cultures, such as Java, Turkey,

Figure 16.3-12 Waxahachie, Texas. Ellis County Courthouse, James Riely Gordon, 1890s.

Cairo, and Dahomey (Benin). Japan sponsored the Ho-o-den Temple, the most authentic of the ethnic exhibitions, a wooden temple built *in situ* by Japanese craftspeople. It exerted a pro-found influence on the interior space and wooden details of the works of Frank Lloyd Wright and other young architects who attended the fair. The white protagonists of the White City proposed to the nonwhites excluded from the classical Court

Figure 16.3-13 Boston. Public Library, McKim, Mead & White, 1888.

Figure 16.3-14 Chicago. The "White City," as realized for the 1893 Columbian Exposition, master plan by Daniel Burnham, 1893.

Figure 16.3-15 San Francisco. City Hall, Arthur Brown, 1907.

of Honor a civilizing mission of electricity, machinery, and education. The Women's Building, by twenty-one-year-old Sophia Hayden Bennett (1868–1953), America's first female graduate in architecture, stood far from the Court of Honor but used a similar vocabulary of Renaissance details. While clearly a breakthrough for women as members of the world of professionals, the content of its exhibitions reiterated the theme of progress as the white man's mission.

Burnham emerged as America's major architectural protagonist after the 1893 fair. His office became a model for the profession. Like the corporate clients he served and mingled with—he even married the daughter of one of them—Burnham applied new management methods, effectively turning his office into a corporation in 1891. D. H. Burnham and Company at its height had 180 employees, who worked in teams with a proper division of labor. While this system tended to depersonalize the design process, it guaranteed a steady supply of standardized, high-quality projects such as office towers and city plans. Burnham's coordination of landscape, infrastructure, and facades at the Chicago Fair inspired the **City Beautiful** movement among citizens' groups and planners, leading to such grand renewal efforts as the 1901 McMillan Plan for Washington, D.C., and the 1907 Civic Center for San Francisco (Fig. 16.3-15).

Figure 16.3-16 Chicago. City plan, Burnham, drawn by Jules Guerin, 1909.

Burnham also prepared an ambitious Parisian-style plan for Chicago in 1909 (Fig. 16.3-16).

Like McKim, Mead & White, Burnham's firm tended to wrap the instruments of technical progress, such as the 1903 Union Station in Washington, D.C., in classical attire. As the demand for the Chicago-based architect's services increased throughout the country, he opened subsidiary offices in New York and San Francisco. Burnham allegedly preached, "Make no little plans; they have no magic to stir men's blood and probably themselves will not be realized. Make big plans; aim high in hope and work, remembering that a noble diagram once recorded will never die." Such sentiments made him the perfect choice to develop the plans for the United States' first colonial adventure in the Philippine Islands. His vision for Manila in 1904 appeared like an extension of the White City in a tropical setting.

Further Reading

Bergdoll, Barry. *European Architecture, 1750–1890.* New York: Oxford University Press, 2000.

Hines, Thomas. *Burnham of Chicago: Architect and Planner.* New York: Oxford University Press, 1974.

Hitchcock, Henry-Russell. *Architecture: Nineteenth and Twentieth Centuries.* New York: Penguin, 1977.

Rydell, Robert W. *All the World's a Fair: Visions of Empire at American International Expositions, 1876–1916.* Chicago: University of Chicago Press, 1984.

Wilson, Richard Guy. *McKim, Mead & White.* New York: Rizzoli, 1983.

↗ Visit the free website **www.oup.com/us/ingersoll** to view chapter outlines and study questions; Google Maps showing the location of key sites; links to UNESCO World Heritage Sites; and essays on topics that cross time and culture.

CHAPTER
17

1890–1920

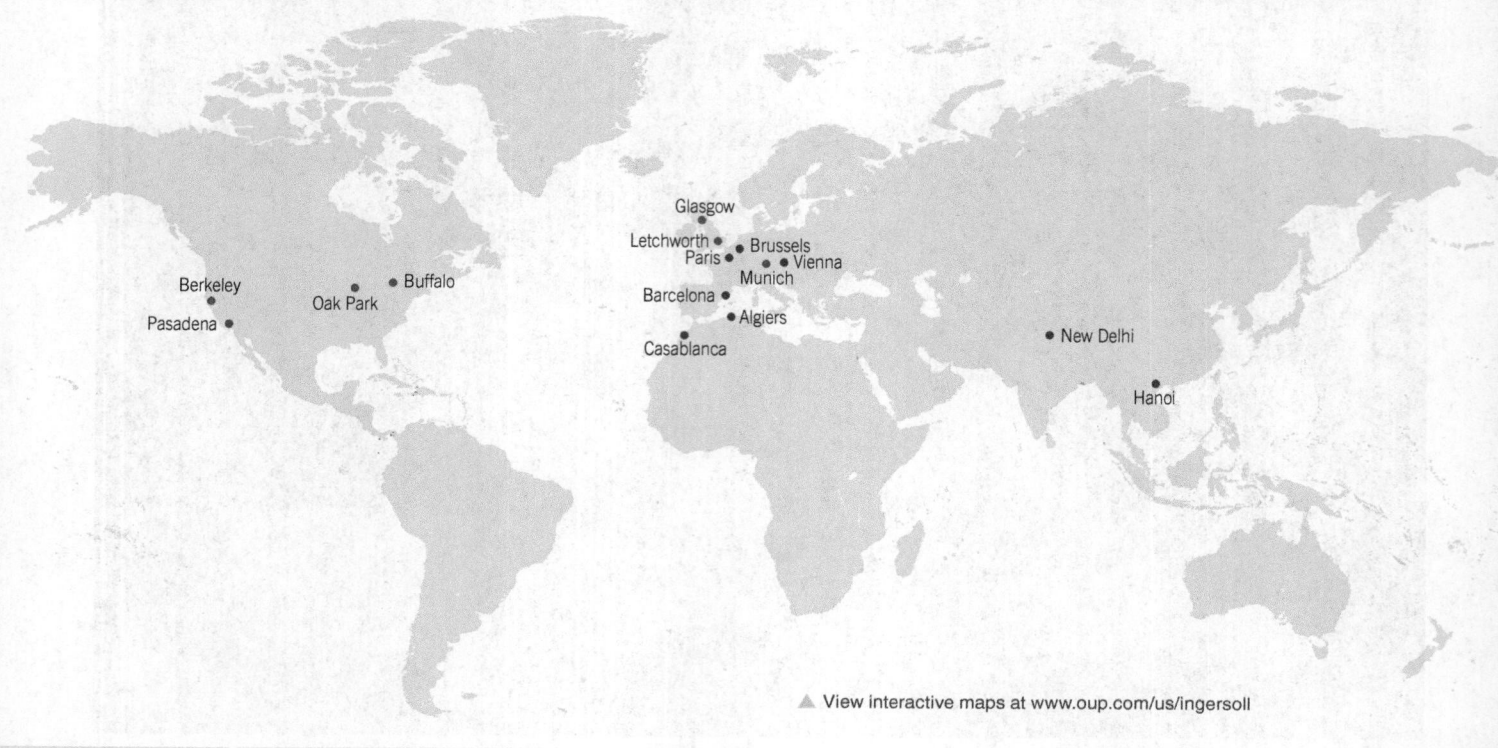

▲ View interactive maps at www.oup.com/us/ingersoll

17.1   **ARTS AND CRAFTS:** Design and the Dignity of Labor

17.2   **THE TWILIGHT OF WESTERN IMPERIALISM:** Monuments to the White Man's Burden

17.3   **ART NOUVEAU AND THE SEARCH FOR MODERN FORM:** Architecture without Precedents

Toward the end of the nineteenth century, reformers in many of the developed nations proposed design solutions to counteract industrialism's negative effects, such as pollution, urban decay, and human degradation. Within an overall socialist outlook that sought to build a society based on mutual benefits, some advocated a return to the guilds of preindustrial towns, while others desired industrial solutions that broke radically from historic urban contexts, combining new technology with collectivist lifestyles. The Garden City emerged as an ideal to correct the crowding of the metropolis. While the leaders of the Arts and Crafts movement advocated a return to medieval-scale communities based on local exchange, the proponents of Art Nouveau attempted to create a new language of design, full of the dynamism of natural forms but open to modern technology and free of references to the past. As the class struggles of industrialized cities intensified, the colonial holdings of Western countries reached their farthest extent. After the First World War, the United Kingdom imposed a majestic imperial vision on New Delhi as the last gasp of imperial control, while the French in Algeria and Morocco attempted to create parallel societies of indigenous residents and colonialists.

17.1 ARTS AND CRAFTS
Design and the Dignity of Labor

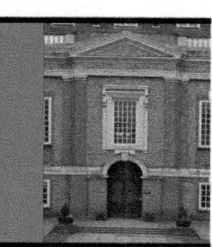

At the turn of the twentieth century, not everyone welcomed such Beaux-Arts piles as the White City built at the Chicago Expo of 1893. The influence of art critic John Ruskin, who reviled the classical orders, extended far beyond the mid-nineteenth-century Gothic revival. He condemned the moral decline of industrial society, which denied the satisfaction of craft to the worker. His descriptions of the skill and toil of medieval cathedral builders, selflessly carving stone and tooling wood, inspired several generations to seek a return to handicrafts. One of Ruskin's greatest converts, William Morris, proposed an artistic and political program that exalted the dignity of the craftsperson while advocating community-based forms of socialism. In the British Isles, idealistic craftspeople, architects, and artists, inspired by Ruskin and Morris, united into guild societies.

The Arts and Crafts movement in England reached maturity during the last two decades of the nineteenth century. Architects attempted to free themselves from historical high styles by emulating vernacular buildings. Planners, inspired by Ebenezer Howard's theory of controlled urban growth, promoted Garden Cities as the alternative to the sprawling industrial metropolis. The Arts and Crafts movement spread to other European countries as well and greatly influenced design in the United States, Australia, and even colonial India. The German Werkbund, through its publications and exhibitions, surpassed the English concept of a craft guild to form a substantial national syndicate for the promotion of design quality. Despite the strong aesthetic influence of the Arts and Crafts movement, it never came close to reforming society into crafts-based socialist communities.

From Medievalizing Guilds to Garden Cities

At the turn of the nineteenth century, the United Kingdom remained unchallenged as the greatest industrial and colonial power in the world. Its overextended empire, on which the "sun never set," produced great fortunes while generating bitter internal conflicts, ranging from class antagonism and racism to disputes over environmental catastrophes. The exploitation of the working class at home paralleled the plunder of the colonies abroad. Liberals campaigned for more technical progress and greater welfare spending as solutions to social problems, while conservatives advocated paternalistic munificence in dealing with disaffected workers and colonials. The English Arts and Crafts movement took shape within this turbulent ideological atmosphere. Through the example of John Ruskin (see Section 15.2), who founded St. George's Guild in the 1870s, a grassroots effort attempted to circumvent industrialism and return to handicrafts. Numerous craft guilds, including the Arts and Crafts Exhibition Society of 1888 and the 1907 Women's Guild of the Arts, sprang up. Perhaps for the first time since Neolithic cultures women assumed important roles as designers. The movement found its voice in the 1860s with William Morris (1834–1896), who, following Ruskin, declared, "Art is mankind's expression of his joy in labor."

In 1859 Morris married Jane Burden, the favorite model of the Pre-Raphaelite brotherhood of painters. They decided to build Red House (Fig. 17.1-1) at Bexleyheath, Kent (now part of London), where they could live communally with their young friends. Morris collaborated on the design with the architect Philip Webb (1831–1915), resulting in a house that served as a manifesto of the Arts and Crafts ethic. Red House appeared rustic without making specific historical references. It signaled the revival of regionalist vernacular sympathies, sometimes called the "English Free Style." Built in modest red brick with high-pitched red tile roofs, the plan followed a casual L shape, with a prominent stair tower at the inner juncture. Morris and Webb purposely made the windows in different styles and sizes, some rounded and

Figure 17.1-1 Bexleyheath, London. Red House, Philip Webb, 1860.

Figure 17.1-2 Brockhampton, England. All Saints Church, William R. Lethaby, 1901.

others set in pointed arches, placing them randomly where they were needed, rather than following a prescribed geometric order. Morris's experience of crafting the interior and its furnishings with his wife and friends motivated him to set up a business in handicraft goods in London. He and his family abandoned Red House after five years, moving to central London, close to his company's workshops.

Red House launched Webb's career and inspired many talented architects, including Richard Norman Shaw (see Section 16.2), Arthur H. Mackmurdo (1851–1942), William R. Lethaby (1857–1931), and Charles F. Annesley Voysey (1857–1941). Mackmurdo, one of the founders of the Century Guild in 1882, campaigned for a synthesis of the arts and social reform. His early work resembled the Queen Anne vernacular of Shaw, with a penchant for half-timbering and bay windows, while later buildings proved more severe and stripped down. Ultimately, Mackmurdo's excursions into the minor arts of wallpaper and silverware, which he presented with swirling motifs, took precedence over his architectural projects. Lethaby worked as Shaw's chief draftsman for ten years and helped found the Art Workers' Guild in 1884. His

approach shifted from Queen Anne motifs to pure volumes, seen in All Saints Church, Brockhampton, constructed in 1901–1902 (Fig. 17.1-2). Its steep, pointed-vault ceiling, made of concrete and covered with thatch, conveyed the essential qualities of a medieval church without referring to any recognizable historical style.

Voysey apprenticed with a follower of Augustus Pugin but on his own attempted to escape from historical styles. In his own house, the Orchard, built in 1900 at Chorley Wood, he used white, roughcast plaster to unify the elemental volumes into a broad range, framed between the peaks of two flattened gables. Voysey's crisp lines and horizontal compositions corresponded to the shingle-style houses of McKim, Mead & White of the same period (see Section 16.2). He repeatedly placed battered buttresses at the corners of his houses, giving them an extra stout and sturdy look while allowing him to open large portions of the walls for rounded bow windows.

Edwin Lutyens (1869–1944), the most successful architect to emerge from the English Free Style of the Arts and Crafts milieu, was also the first to betray it. His early

TIME LINE

▼ ca. 1859
Beginning of Arts and Crafts movement in England

Mackintosh begins Glasgow School of Art
▲ 1897

▼ 1898
Howard inspires Garden City movement

Wright builds Larkin Building, an open-plan office, in Buffalo, New York
▲ 1904

Figure 17.1-3 Godalming, England. Munstead Wood, Edwin Lutyens and Gertrude Jekyll, 1896.

houses, like those by Shaw and Webb, derived from the broad vernacular type. For more public commissions, however, Lutyens considered the Beaux-Arts approach more appropriate. His career took off after meeting the versatile landscape designer Gertrude Jekyll (1843–1932) in 1893. Their mutual interest in the teachings of Ruskin and Morris led to an intensely creative partnership. They first designed her family's properties in Godalming, about 40 km (25 miles) south of London. Lutyens also designed Jekyll's house, Munstead Wood, in 1896 (Fig. 17.1-3) and created a series of country houses in the area for her relatives and friends. The formal influence of Jekyll's gardens led to an integration of geometric compositions with stray bits of historical iconography.

The Scottish architect Charles Rennie Mackintosh (1868–1928) also came from the Arts and Crafts movement. Mackintosh worked exclusively in and around the industrial port of Glasgow, which at this time was considered the United Kingdom's "second city," though it still remained culturally on the margins. A gifted draftsman and painter, he trained with local firms, working in eclectic styles, but preferred the Free Style. With fellow architect Herbert McNair (1868–1955), he joined forces with the Macdonald sisters, Margaret (1865–1933) and Frances (1874–1921), to create a guild-like Arts and Crafts group known as "The Four." Together they forged a synthesis of the arts, combining architecture with furniture, textiles, and stained glass. Margaret, whom Mackintosh married in 1900, conceived the decoration of his later works. Mackintosh's major project, the Glasgow School of Art, was begun in 1897. The school's director, Francis Newbery (1855–1946), advocated the Arts and Crafts approach and desired a utilitarian atmosphere of well-lit studios to accommodate woodcarving and stained glass production. The resulting structure was functional, but with strong hints of handicraft. Mackintosh's wife carved the door frame with an elaborate emblem of growth over the entry, but the rest of the facade appeared remarkably plain, interrupted only by spindly iron brackets on the windows that resembled Margaret's paintings of elongated roses (Fig. 17.1-4a). The addition of the library wing in 1907 created a more animated elevation, with the stacking of three bay windows that stretched the entire height of the upper

▼ **1906**

San Francisco
earthquake and fire

Werkbund founded
in Munich

▲ **1907**

▼ **1907**

*Greene & Greene's Gamble House
built in Pasadena, California*

Figure 17.1-4
Glasgow, Scotland.
Glasgow School of
Art, Charles Rennie
Mackintosh, 1897–
1907. (a) Detail of
entrance facade.
(b) See facing page.

stories, revealing the double height of the central nave of the reading room behind them (Fig. 17.1-4b).

Mackintosh designed Hill House in Helensburgh (Fig. 17.1-5), 40 km (25 miles) northwest of Glasgow, for the publisher Walter Blackie. He stated that its abstract volumes did not resemble either "an Italian Villa, an English Mansion House, a Swiss Chalet, or a Scotch castle. It is a Dwelling House." Stripped down and covered in white roughcast plaster with projecting bays, Hill House followed an irregular L-shaped plan with staggered massing. True to the Arts and Crafts approach, its forty windows were differently shaped and asymmetrically placed.

During the 1880s Morris began to campaign for socialism, briefly adhering to Karl Marx's communist position and later adopting a more reformist theory. He preached that beauty was a right regardless of class, yet his handcrafted books, textiles, wallpapers, and furniture could be afforded only by an elite clientele. This contradiction did not discourage Morris from taking ever more anticapitalist positions. In

his utopian novel *News from Nowhere* (1890), he described a cooperative alternative to the metropolis. "Suppose people lived in little communities," he wrote, "among gardens and green fields, so that you could be in the country in five minutes' walk, and had few wants, almost no furniture, for instance, and no servants, and studied the (difficult) arts of enjoying life, and finding out what they really wanted: then I think one might hope civilization had really begun." Such a vision corresponded to the Garden City proposed by Ebenezer Howard (1850–1928) (Fig. 17.1-6). Howard moved in the same socialist circles as Morris and proposed the "social city" as a means of controlling urban growth and maintaining human dignity. In his book *Tomorrow, a Peaceful Path to Real Reform* (1898), he advocated more efficient land use through a self-sufficient network of small cities separated by greenswards for forests and agriculture.

The Garden City Society convened in the early years of the twentieth century at the two most enlightened company towns of the age, Lever Soap Company's Port Sunlight and

1911–1929

New Delhi, India, designed by Lutyens and Baker

Behrens builds AEG Turbine Hall in Berlin

▲ **1908**

Werkbund Theater built by van de Velde in Cologne

▲ **1914**

1919

Julia Morgan begins Hearst Castle, in San Simeon, California

Figure 17.1-4 Glasgow School of Art. (b) Stacked library windows.

Cadbury Chocolate's Bournville, both built in the 1890s. Lever sponsored 800 units of worker housing in Craftsman style, providing the residents with an array of public buildings, including an art gallery, a cottage hospital, schools, a concert hall, an open-air swimming pool, a church, and a temperance hotel. The row houses by the firm of Grayson & Ould exhibited clear Arts and Crafts sympathies (Fig. 17.1-7).

The young architects Raymond Unwin (1863–1940) and Barry Parker (1867–1947) won the competition to design Letchworth, the first Garden City based on Howard's theory. They adhered to the Arts and Crafts movement and designed both workers' settlements and middle-class houses in the manner of Voysey. The name "Garden City" proved to be slightly misleading; their plan of 1903 was relatively dense, with a Baroque layout of radiating streets set around a central core for public buildings. Nevertheless, at twelve units per acre, more than half of the land of each block remained free for gardens or setbacks. They also set aside large parcels as parkland or commons, and a greensward as the city's frontier. Unwin and Parker designed many of the town's first structures, including their own residence, Glade House, in the Free Style. Howard moved into the Homesgarth Cooperative, a set of thirty-two apartments arranged around a *U*-shaped commons with a central kitchen and dining hall for its members. While Letchworth was only 54 km (33 miles) north of London, it attracted only a few Arts and Crafts workshops and failed to reach a population of more than 5,000.

In 1907, soon after the founding of Letchworth, the social reformer Henrietta Barnett (1851–1936) engaged Unwin to design the Hampstead Garden Suburb in London. Although it contradicted Howard's theory of autonomous, self-supporting Garden Cities, the plan included many of the formal and social ideas begun at Letchworth. Barnett, coauthor of *Praticable Socialism* (1888), had done charitable work in the slums of London and was keen on maintaining a broad mix of incomes in the suburb. For the design of the central

Figure 17.1-5 Helensburgh, England. Hill House, Mackintosh, 1901.

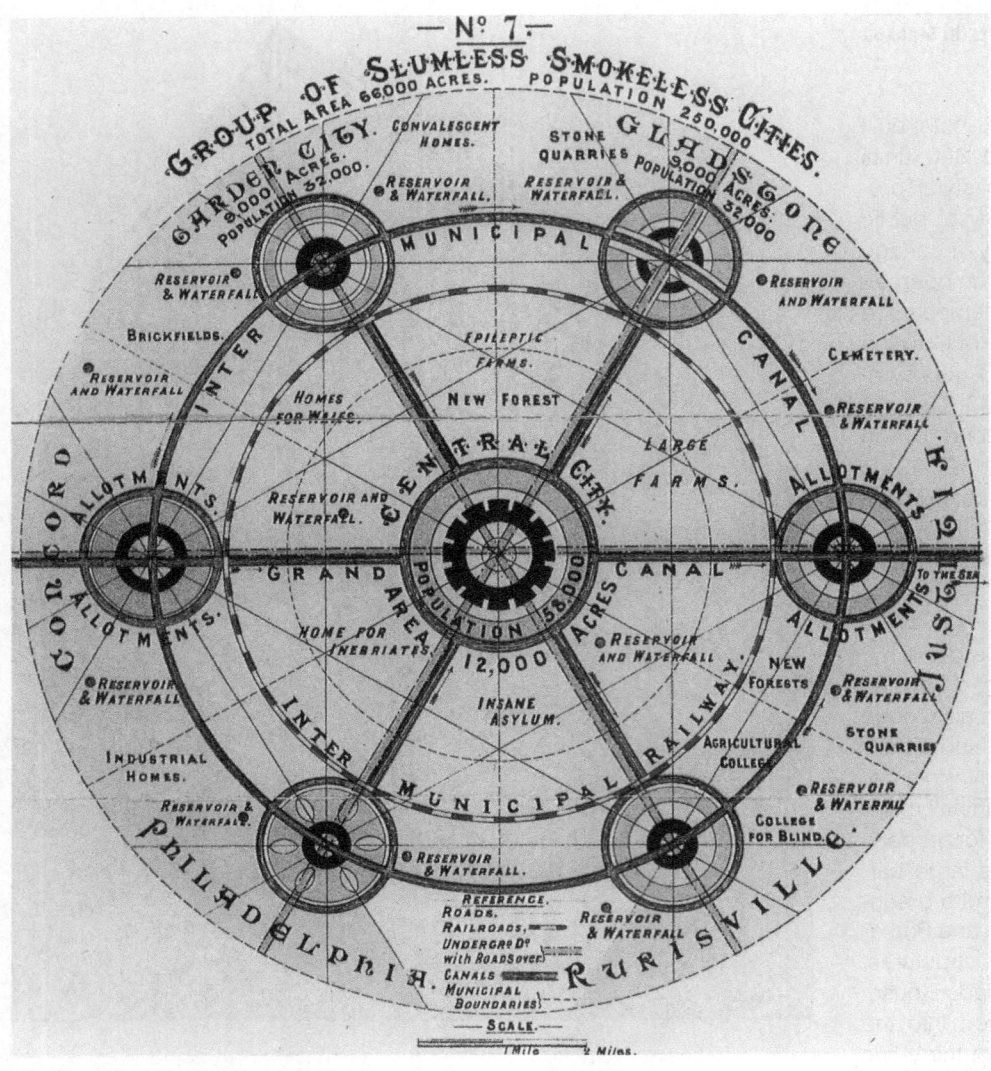

The Birth of the Superblock

Unwin experimented with ways to obtain more open space per person in row-house blocks. His studies showed that if the block was enlarged, eliminating half of the public streets, it resulted in more open space per unit, which he proposed be distributed as allotments or parks. The idea of an expanded block, which later in the century became known as the "superblock," led him to introduce cul-de-sacs, dead-end access roads, into the block. His plans for the Bird's Hill and Pixmire estates at Letchworth demonstrate how the land of the interior of the block could be efficiently distributed among the units while pushing heavy traffic to the block's perimeter.

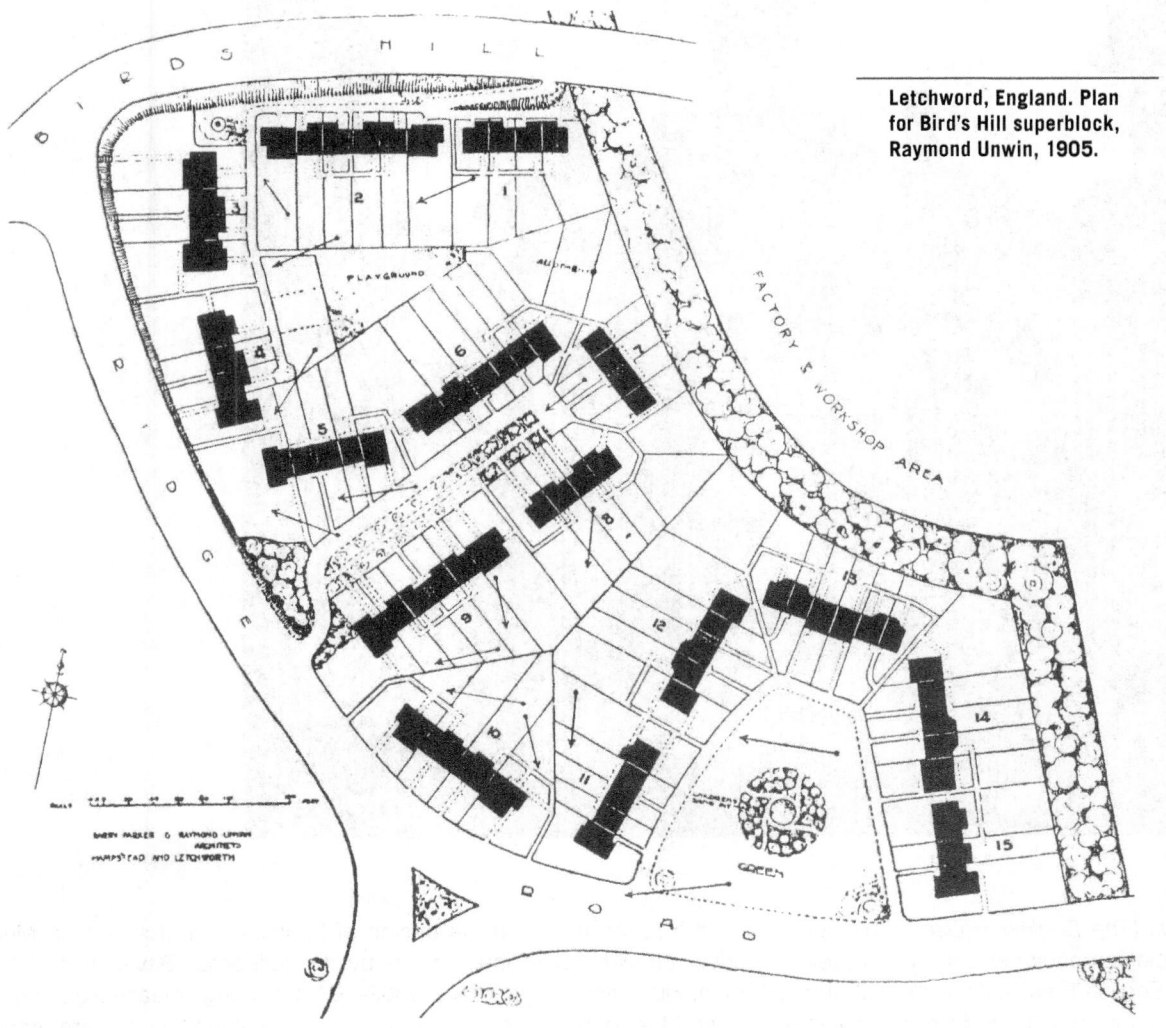

Letchword, England. Plan for Bird's Hill superblock, Raymond Unwin, 1905.

square Unwin deferred to Lutyens, who set twin churches and the Hampstead Institute (Fig. 17.1-8) on a formal trident. Lutyens here made one of his first assays into classical order, returning to the ornamental and compositional style of Christopher Wren and James Gibbs (see Section 13.1). The institute, clad with pilasters and capped with a Wren-like belfry, provided classrooms, a library, and a concert hall.

Although the forces of speculation eventually compromised the social vision of Hampstead, Unwin continued to propose Garden City plans, which led the next generation to advance the greenbelt theory for the Greater London Regional Planning Committee. While the Arts and Crafts aesthetic had by then subsided, the premise of a coordinated set of Garden Cities endured.

The German Werkbund: From *Heimatstil to Typisierung*

The English Arts and Crafts movement had a strong appeal for German designers. Hermann Muthesius (1861–1927), after a seven-year sojourn in England, wrote *Das englische*

Haus (*The English House*, 1904), promoting the return to simple vernacular styles. He built several houses emulating the English Free Style in the suburbs of Berlin. His enthusiasm for the Arts and Crafts movement inspired the foundation of the German Werkbund, which attracted a similar roster of utopians, idealists, and socialists. Instead of rejecting industrialism and commerce, however, it became a concerted effort to reform such processes. Unlike the English guilds made of small, withdrawn groups, the Werkbund evolved into a significant national organization with more than 1,500 members. Its internal debates gave expression to various positions, ranging from the folksy *Heimatstil*, or love of regional vernaculars, to the eccentric promotion of art for art's sake, seen in the *Jugendstil*.

The Werkbund was founded in Munich in 1907 in response to Muthesius's condemnation of eclectic and historicist taste in the design of furniture and architecture. Muthesius was later joined by the influential Bavarian architect Theodor Fischer (1862–1938). Although clearly a defender of regional styles, Fischer was one of the first modern architects to use a rational system of concrete construction, seen in his high school at Elisabethplatz in Munich (1902–1904) (Fig. 17.1-9) and the Garrison Church at Ulm (1908–1911).

Aside from the Werkbund's English sources, the German movement relied heavily on the artistic output of the Wiener Werkstätte, founded in Vienna four years earlier by Josef Hoffmann (1870–1956) and Kolo Moser (1868–1918). The Viennese designers fought a similar battle as that pitched in England against academic styles. Hoffmann's projects for furniture, such as his *Sitzmachine*, or machine for sitting, an adjustable bentwood armchair, brought a new level of abstraction to modern design.

Tony Garnier and the Industrial City

Tony Garnier (1869–1948) of Lyons won the Prix de Rome in 1899 and, during his tenure in Rome, introduced a strong social criterion into the work of Beaux-Arts research. He presented in 1901 a graphic reconstruction of ancient Tusculum as an urban, rather than a formal, system. At the same time he began developing his ideas of modern urbanism in drawings for a contemporary industrial city, finally published in 1917 as *Une Cité Industrielle*. Like Ebenezer Howard, he imagined a low-density urban pattern for habitation based on linear rail transportation. He zoned the industrial functions downwind and toward the river port and anticipated a power source in a hydroelectric dam upstream. The center of Garnier's city lacked religious institutions. Instead, it had a clock tower and a grand assembly hall with an octagonal roof, inscribed with socialist quotes from Émile Zola's novel *Travail* (*Work*). Garnier rejected the romantic style of English Garden Cities, proposing flat-roofed concrete buildings with terraces and pergolas set in shady gardens.

Throughout his career Garnier produced pieces of Lyons that corresponded to his initial scheme, including the Gerland Stadium, the slaughterhouses, the États-Unis housing district, and the Grange Blanche Hospital, all of which were planned before World War I but not brought to term until the end of the 1920s. The hospital, organized as symmetrically planned pavilions connected by underground tunnels and set in parkland, best represents the pleasant human scale of his industrial city.

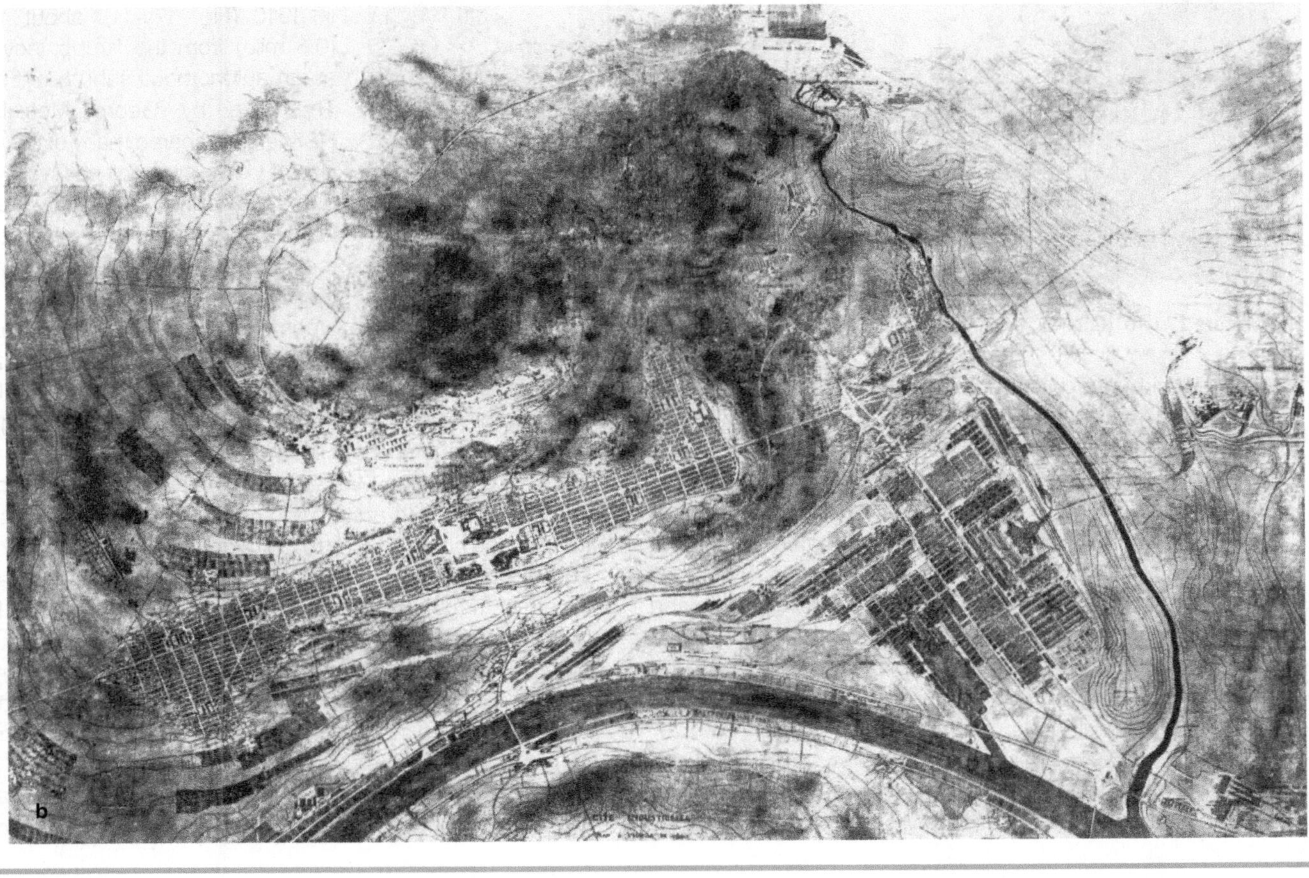

(a) Tony Garnier's low-density housing. (b) Garnier's plan for The Industrial City, 1917.

Figure 17.1-9 Munich. Elisabethplatz High School, Theodor Fischer, 1902.

Figure 17.1-10 Hellerau, Germany. Jaques-Dalcroze Institute, Heinrich Tessenow, ca. 1910.

designed additional houses in a more essential style. The streets of Hellerau curved gently, with planted setbacks, close to Unwin's prototypes. Schmidt brought the Swiss educator and musician Émile Jaques-Dalcroze (1865–1950) to Hellerau to establish the school of eurhythmic dance and music. Heinrich Tessenow (1876–1950) designed the institute housing the school (Fig. 17.1-10) and, like Lutyens at Hampstead, insisted that public buildings follow the clear hierarchy of classicism. Tessenow's stripped-down temple front became the focus of the Hellerau community. In the tympanum he placed a *taijitu*, the yin/yang symbol of harmony.

Margarethe Krupp (1854–1931), the recently widowed heiress of the great armaments and steel company, organized Germany's other significant Garden City at the beginning of the twentieth century. She began her company town of Margarethenhöhe in 1910 (Fig. 17.1-11), about 1 km (0.6 mile) from the Krupp factories, as an autonomous suburb of Essen. The plan by Georg Metzendorf (1874–1934) shared many of the qualities of Unwin's urbanism. Over 3,000 duplex dwellings lined the narrow lanes. The gables and dormers of the roofs came from folk housing. While Metzendorf pursued a variety of plan types, he gave Margarethenhöhe an overall unity by coating the buildings with gray, roughcast plaster, a trick borrowed from the English Free Style. The white columns on the porches and green window trim and shutters produced a sense of continuity from block to block. The Market Square related to the tradition of civic squares, with a strong formal axis between the market hall and the hotel. A 200 m (656 ft) deep greensward of woods engulfed the entire settlement, reinforcing its separate identity from the surrounding districts of suburban Essen. While Margarethenhöhe remained an isolated experiment in the industrialized Ruhr valley, Metzendorf's assistant, Richard Kauffmann (1887–1958), took his experience of Garden City planning to Palestine. During the 1920s he executed 160 rural settlements for the idealistic Jewish settlers of the Zionist movement.

Peter Behrens (1868–1940) assumed great importance in the Werkbund as the chief designer for AEG, the major

The Werkbund gained practical experience from Karl Schmidt (1873–1948), who founded his handicrafts factory, the Deutsche Werkstätten für Handwerkskunst, in 1898. Like Muthesius, Schmidt traveled through England during the 1890s, absorbing ideas from the Arts and Crafts and Garden City movements. In 1909 he relocated his factory to Hellerau, on the northwest edge of Dresden, where he employed over 500 people. After reading Howard's book on Garden Cities, he commissioned his brother-in-law, Richard Riemerschmid (1868–1957), one of the founders of the Werkbund, to design his company town as the first Garden City outside of England.

Hellerau became a mirror of Werkbund positions. While Riemerschmid designed the factory, marketplace, and several duplex houses in the *Heimatstil*, Muthesius and Fischer

Kibbutzim and Richard Kauffmann

In Palestine during the 1920s, the Zionist colonists established a series of agricultural collectives, the *kibbutzim*, and cooperatives, the *moshavs*. Richard Kauffmann was commissioned by the Jewish Agency to prepare the plans for the new settlements. His first project for the *moshav* of Nahalal literally transposed Howard's radiocentric Garden City diagram to the Middle East. He oriented each house toward the central civic structures while fanning the lots of cultivatable land into the wedges. Kauffmann soon after abandoned such geometric ideas as too inflexible. He organized most of his *kibbutzim* plans as superblocks, one for the dwellings and social buildings and one for the working structures. This approach separated the wheeled traffic and the sounds and smells of the agricultural work from the living areas. The dwelling areas of his *kibbutzim* were accessed by pedestrian paths and felt as tranquil as college campuses. The only large building, a dining hall for meals and meetings, occupied a central position, while the small cabins for the collective's members stood in staggered positions on the edges of the green. The strong socialist ideology of the *kibbutz* movement led to the unique social experiment of raising the children collectively in nurseries, separating them from their biological parents. *Kibbutzim* proved to be highly productive and became the economic and political backbone of the future state of Israel in 1948.

Palestine. Nahalal Moshav (collective), Richard Kauffmann, 1920.

German manufacturer of electronic goods. Prior to his transfer to Berlin in 1907, he worked at the utopian arts community of Mathildenhöhe in Darmstadt, designing the theater and his own house. In Berlin, the enlightened industrialist Emil Rathenau (1838–1915) of AEG hired Behrens to coordinate the design of products, graphics, factories, and housing. Behrens sought a coherent industrial aesthetic derived from essentials. This approach led to the magnificent AEG Turbine Hall of 1908 (Fig. 17.1-12a), often described as the temple of industry. The factory's immense open interior was lined with tapering steel girders tied to pin joints at the bases (Fig. 17.1-12b). Parallel tracks ran the length of the hall to carry

Figure 17.1-11 Margarethenhöhe, Essen, Germany. Typical street of workers' housing, Georg Metzendorf and Richard Kauffmann, 1910.

a mobile gantry for lifting and moving the turbines during assembly. Behrens capped the short facade with a polygonal pediment of six facets. A central bay of steel sash glazing jutted slightly forward on the same plane as the pediment, leaving rusticated piers at the corners. He placed each of the three letters of the AEG logo inside a hexagon that fit into a larger hexagon, implying the industriousness of a beehive.

Although Behrens came from the decorative *Jugendstil* milieu, his new role in industry led to a more functionalist attitude. In 1913 Muthesius, impressed by the AEG products and buildings, introduced a new objective to the Werkbund called *Typisierung*, meaning the standardization of ideal types for better-crafted production. Many of his colleagues, including Behrens, were outraged by the impersonal implications of such a strategy. The artistic faction replied that artists should be free to follow their imaginations and not be constricted by the pragmatic considerations of industrial standards. The debate culminated at the 1914 Werkbund Exhibition in Cologne. While Behrens resorted to classicism for the facade of the Festhalle, his ex-assistant, Walter Gropius (1883–1969), pursued the search for essentials in two buildings, the Model Factory (Fig. 17.1-13) and the Machine Hall. The former made clear references to Frank Lloyd Wright's horizontal roof style, while the latter, a steel-framed hall, evoked the clean rationalism of Behrens's Turbine Hall.

Other buildings at the fair included a *Heimatstil* village, Fischer's Neo-Baroque octagonal cupola for the main

exhibition hall, and two eccentric works that served as manifestos of artistic freedom: the shimmering cupola of the Glass Pavilion (Fig. 17.1-14), made of diamond-shaped facets of glass by Bruno Taut (1880–1938), and the sinuously curved Werkbund Theater, by Henry van de Velde (1863–1957). Taut became architectural advisor to the German Garden City Society, while van de Velde served as director of the School for Applied Arts in Weimar, the institution later transformed by Gropius into the Bauhaus. While no one at this point agreed on *Typisierung*'s full significance, Muthesius's invitation to clarify the works of industry and improve its places of production held the Werkbund together despite its members' wide-ranging stylistic attitudes.

The American Craftsman Movement and the California Lifestyle

The works of Ruskin and Morris deeply affected the development of architectural language in the United States. Gustav Stickley (1858–1942), in emulation of Morris, established a furniture company in Syracuse, New York, where he produced his "Mission"-style tables and chairs. He began publishing *The Craftsman* magazine in 1901 and for fifteen years spread the ideas and styles of the Arts and Crafts movement across America. Aside from advertising his own wooden furniture, Stickley ran articles on Native American crafts, Japanese joinery, socialism, contemporary architecture, and Garden

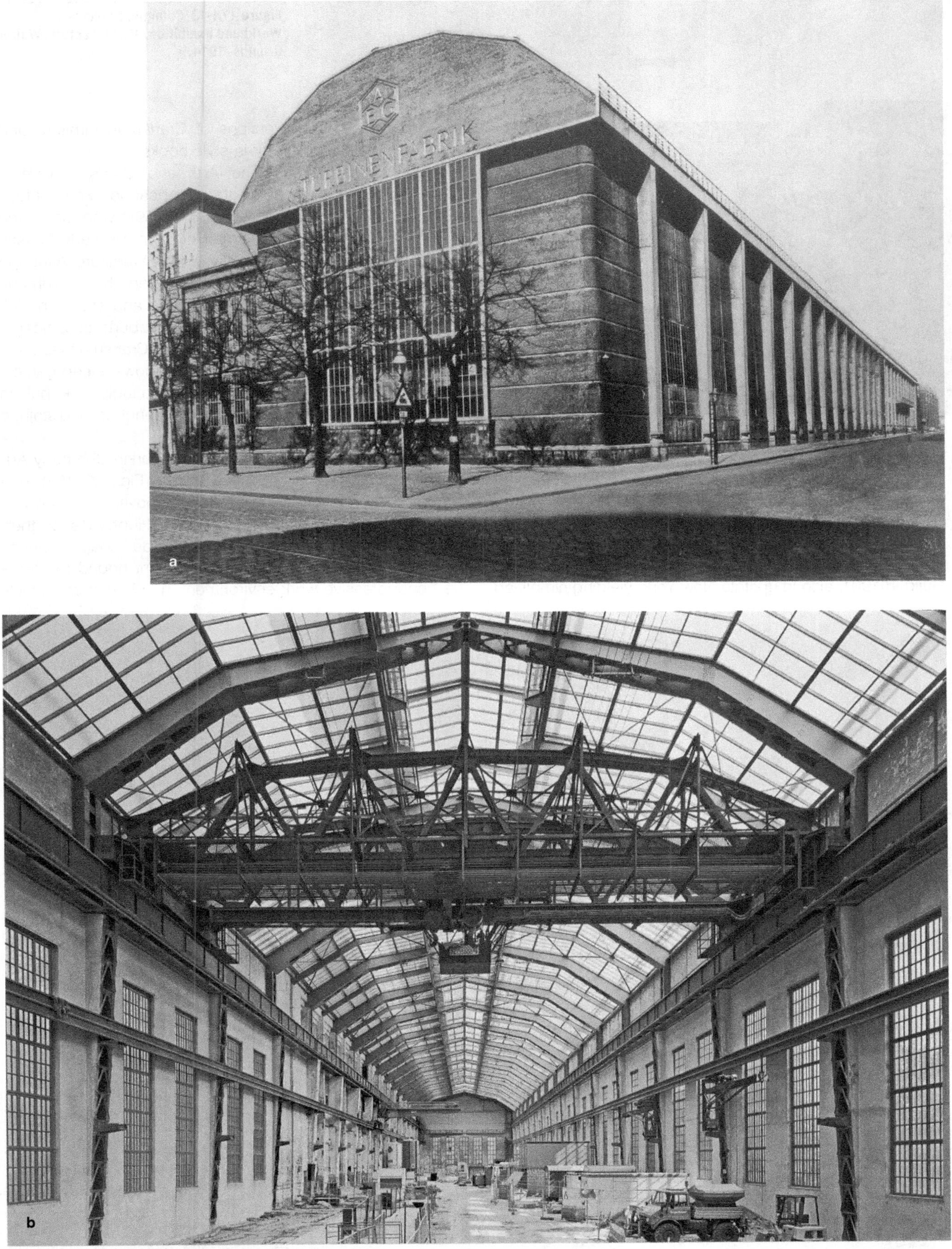

Figure 17.1-12 Berlin. (a) AEG Turbine Hall, Peter Behrens, 1908. (b) Interior.

Figure 17.1-13 Cologne, Germany. Werkbund Exhibition, Model Factory, Walter Gropius, 1914.

versions of Craftsman furniture and Morris-style books.

The Arts and Crafts movement held great appeal for Frank Lloyd Wright (1867–1959), who used the Craftsman ethic in his early houses and bulky, wooden furniture. Although he later repudiated the movement, the Wright house and studio in Oak Park (1889), a suburb of Chicago, contained typical Craftsman features, such as bow windows, steep gables, a fireplace with an inglenook, built-in cupboards and benches, and stained glass windows.

Cities. Raymond Unwin frequently contributed articles. *The Craftsman* also published house designs by well-known architects as well as plans for self-build bungalows. Stickley for a brief period attempted to manufacture economic prototypes through his own building company. His example inspired Elbert Hubbard (1856–1915) to found the Roycrofters Guild in 1901, also in upstate New York, yielding simplified

Wright's first large-scale work, the Larkin Company Administration Building in Buffalo (1904) (Fig. 17.1-15a), had a direct connection to the Craftsman movement, as it was commissioned by Darwin C. Martin, Hubbard's brother-in-law. Wright's project for the mail-order soap company revolutionized the office type. The client hoped to create a nonoppressive work environment, rich in cultural stimuli.

Figure 17.1-14 Cologne, Germany. Werkbund Exhibition, Glass Pavilion, Bruno Taut, 1914.

Figure 17.1-15 Buffalo, New York. (a) Larkin Company Administration Building, exterior, Frank Lloyd Wright, 1904. (b) Interior, atrium for the secretarial pool.

Wright put the circulation and bathrooms in the corner towers, somewhat like a medieval fortress. The offices in the side wings had parapets overlooking the central atrium, where the mass of the secretarial pool was located (Fig. 17.1-15b). An organ for noontime recitals loomed over the north end of the five-story atrium, inscribed with the message "Honest labor needs no master, simple justice needs no slaves." Many of the features that are taken for granted in contemporary office buildings originated here, including the open-plan office, built-in file cabinets, radiant floor heating, air-conditioning, steel furniture, and wall-hung toilets.

Wright culled ideas from the English Arts and Crafts but diverged from Ruskin's resistance to the machine. In his essay "The Art and Craft of the Machine" he at once praised the possibilities of the machine and new materials while condemning the banality of mass production. In 1905, to replace a wooden structure that had just burnt down, Wright designed the Unity Temple in Oak Park (Fig. 17.1-16a,b) using the unprecedented industrial technique of **reinforced concrete** walls. This approach lowered the building's cost and improved fire safety while permitting a grand span over the nave. As with the Larkin Building, he tucked the services into the four corner towers.

Wright's design breakthrough came at the turn of the century with a series of houses done in the Prairie style, characterized by horizontal volumes and low-pitched roofs with deep eaves. His culminating work in this manner, the Frederick C. Robie House of 1906–1909, sat on a tight urban site. To protect it from the street, he set it on a platform and sheltered it with inordinately wide projecting eaves (Fig. 17.1-17a), using concealed steel joists to sustain their cantilever. Long banks of "light screens" rather than ordinary sash windows connected the interior and exterior. Inside, the major social spaces flowed together, rotating asymmetrically around the massive hearth (Fig. 17.1-17b). The grooved patterns in the wooden ceilings, built-in furniture, and leaded windows were completely integrated with the plan of the house in an effort to "eliminate the decorator."

Many of the best Craftsman-inspired architects in the United States moved to California at the turn of the century. Among them was Irving Gill (1870–1936), who shared some of the same background as Wright, having worked briefly in Chicago for Louis Sullivan. Gill moved to San Diego in 1893, where he picked up on the local Mission style. He developed an abstract language of flat-roofed buildings with planar facades and long, steel-sash windows that went far beyond the Free Style's attempt to shed historic associations. His masterpiece, the Dodge House in West Hollywood, built in 1915 (demolished in 1965), presented a cascading sequence of pure volumes punctured by broad, asymmetrically placed windows (Fig. 17.1-18). While Gill's exteriors appeared severe, his interiors revealed the Craftsman love of built-in wooden furniture and inglenook fireplaces. He pioneered the use of tilt-up concrete walls in projects such as the La Jolla Women's Club of 1912 and perfected the Los Angeles "bungalow court" type as an alternative to single-block, multiple-unit housing. In 1919 he built the Horatio West Court using reinforced concrete walls fitted with internal moisture barriers to protect against the humidity of the nearby ocean. The stepped massing resembled the *pueblos* of the Southwest, while subtle shifts in the layouts of the units allowed for optimal exposure to views of the ocean.

Stickley's *Craftsman* promoted the modest bungalow type, a small house framed by shade-giving verandahs, as the ideal American home. He frequently published examples built by the Greene brothers, Charles Sumner (1868–1957) and Henry Mather (1870–1954). The Greenes moved from Boston to California in the same year as Gill, bringing with them the experience of working for the successors of Henry Hobson Richardson. They also arrived stimulated by the Ho-o-den Temple at the 1893 Chicago Expo. Like Wright, they were fascinated by Japanese brackets, bundled beams, and joinery without nails—not to mention the open plan. A sequence of spaces that could be modulated by sliding panels became one of their principal strategies of organization. Among the thirty houses designed by Greene and Greene in Southern California before World War I, the Gamble House of 1907 (Fig. 17.1-19) remained their masterpiece. Built for one of the heirs of the Procter & Gamble soap company, it seemed more a villa than a bungalow. Raised on a rough brick base, the porches were shaded by spreading roofs, supported by Japanese-inspired rafters that protruded beyond the eaves. The exceptional craftwork required the architects to train the workers themselves. They left no hard edges in the entire house, artfully sanding and polishing the corners of every wooden joist. The Greene brothers avoided using metal nails, preferring highly burnished mortise-and-tenon joints, protruding dowel pegs, and occasional cast-iron bands to strap the timbers together. The stunning stained glass panels in the front door, produced by the Tiffany Company, recalled the painted screens depicting twisted pine trees in the *tokonoma* alcoves of *shoin* palaces in Kyoto (see Section 12.3). The art glass also indicated that although the Gamble House aspired to the simple life of the bungalow, it possessed unrestrained luxury.

The San Francisco Bay Area cultivated many original thinkers and designers at the turn of the century. In Berkeley, the University of California attracted a large number of idealists and activists, many of whom belonged to the Hillside Club, a group with similar objectives to Howard's Garden City Society. As nature lovers, many of them organized their homes with outdoor sleeping porches, took long hikes, and followed exotic diets of nuts and berries. The Beaux-Arts-trained architect Bernard Maybeck (1862–1957) arrived in Berkeley in 1890, bringing with him his own eccentricities, such as a desire to dress up for medieval pageants. Most of his early houses were bungalows for fellow Hillside Club colleagues. He built a house for the club's chief ideologue, Charles Keeler (1871–1937), author of *The Simple Home* (1905), who captured the essence of the group's ideal, writing that the house should be "landscape gardening around a few rooms for use in case of rain." Unfortunately, Keeler's

Figure 17.1-16 Oak Park, Chicago. (a) Unity Temple, Wright, 1904. (b) Interior.

Figure 17.1-17 Hyde Park, Chicago. (a) Robie House, with wide projecting eaves, Wright, 1906–1909. (b) Interior.

Figure 17.1-18 West Hollywood, California. Dodge House, Irving Gill, 1915.

Figure 17.1-19 Pasadena, California. Gamble House, Greene and Greene, 1907.

house and many of Maybeck's best efforts burned down in the 1923 fire.

In 1895 Maybeck began working for one of the greatest patrons of the age, Phoebe A. Hearst (1842–1919). Widowed in 1891, she inherited the proceeds of the largest mining fortune in America. As a regent of the University of California, she played a key role in programming and financing a new Beaux-Arts plan for the campus. Maybeck, the university's first professor of architecture, assembled the brief for the campus competition and designed several of its buildings. Hearst also put Maybeck in charge of her most extravagant project, the storybook castle of Wyntoon in northern California. Begun in 1902, the castle was vertically massed on seven levels around a prominent stair tower constructed using local boulders and capped by steep, clay-tile roofs.

Set in a misty redwood forest on the banks of the McCloud River, Wyntoon Castle approached the operatic manner of Ludwig II's Neuschwanstein (see Section 16.3).

Maybeck's eclectic desire to integrate folk wisdom with historic sources was best expressed in the First Church of Christ Scientist (1909) (Fig. 17.1-20). Here, he incorporated Craftsman vernacular, Japanese-style trellises, Gothic tracery, and modern steel-sash windows with reinforced concrete construction. The plan was almost perfectly square at grade but became a Greek cross at the level of the clerestories. The impressive free span of the interior was achieved by intersecting, wood-framed Vierendeel trusses that sprang diagonally from four concrete piers. The iron tie-rods were concealed behind the wooden casing. Flamboyant Gothic tracery, painted red and gold, filled in the structural gaps. Like

Figure 17.1-20 Berkeley, California. First Church of Christ Scientist, Bernard Maybeck, 1909.

Maybeck's Craftsman houses, the Christian Science church wove the indoors with the outdoors, using deep eaves, pergolas laced with wisteria vines, and generous porches.

Maybeck encouraged one of his best students, Julia Morgan (1872–1957), to go to the Beaux-Arts in Paris. She not only became the first woman to finish the program but went on to enjoy a prolific career, designing over 700 buildings. Morgan also trained as an engineer and was among the first architects to build houses and public buildings with reinforced concrete. At the outset of her career she worked with Maybeck on several campus buildings. While Maybeck was completing the Christian Science church, she was busy a few blocks away building St. John's Episcopal Church (1910). With its open-truss redwood rafters and shingle siding, it remained her lasting tribute to the Craftsman style. Phoebe Hearst supported Morgan while she was studying

in Paris and in 1913 hired her to design the Asilomar Conference Center (Fig. 17.1-21) for the Young Women's Christian Association (YWCA) at a coastal nature preserve south of Carmel. Here, Morgan repeated the exposed redwood structure of her church, integrating it with a local stone base and a monumental fireplace made of cyclopean boulders. She organized the campground with long, wooden tent buildings set on an elevated boardwalk, consistent with the Craftsman love of outdoor living.

Morgan designed numerous women's institutions, including a YWCA in Oakland that contained an internal court based on the cloister of Bramante's Santa Maria della Pace in Rome and another YWCA in San Francisco's Chinatown that incorporated Chinese-style roofs and windows. Phoebe Hearst's son, the media baron William Randolph Hearst (1863–1951), became Morgan's greatest client for historical

Figure 17.1-21 Carmel, California. Asilomar Conference Center, Julia Morgan, 1913–1930.

Figure 17.1-22 Russian River, California. Wyntoon, Bear House, Maybeck and Morgan, 1902–1930s.

fantasies. She designed first the Mission-style headquarters of his newspaper in Los Angeles; then a series of additions to Wyntoon, including the Bear House (Fig. 17.1-22); and finally the lifetime project of the "Enchanted Hill" at San Simeon, or Hearst Castle.

Hearst Castle dominated a ranch about 200 km (120 miles) south of San Francisco. The project began in 1919 and evolved as the patron acquired artistic and architectural treasures from different periods of European history. Morgan modeled the twin bell towers on a Spanish Baroque church (Fig. 17.1-23a), while inside she reproduced a doge's salon,

a French Renaissance hall with a François I mantelpiece, and a Gothic hall hung with *palio* banners from Siena. On one of the terraces, she pieced together ancient *spolia* to create a pseudo-antique temple overlooking an oval swimming pool (Fig. 17.1-23b). During the height of construction in the 1920s, Morgan spent every weekend at San Simeon, where she commanded a force of 100 craftspeople who carved stone and wooden details that would blend with the historical artifacts. Clearly, she favored earnest craftsmanship, but at Hearst Castle she shed the modest Craftsman ideals to satisfy her patron's ambition to possess the past.

Further Reading

Boutelle, Sara Holmes. *Julia Morgan, Architect*. New York: Abbeville Press, 1988.

Buder, Stanley. *Visionaries and Planners: The Garden City Movement and the Modern Community*. New York: Oxford University Press, 1990.

Campbell, Joan. *The German Werkbund: The Politics of Reform in the Applied Arts*. Princeton, NJ: Princeton University Press, 1977.

Cardwell, Kenneth H. *Bernard Maybeck: Architect, Artisan, Artist*. Santa Barbara, CA: Peregrine Smith, 1977.

Crawford, Alan. *Charles Rennie Mackintosh*. London: Thames & Hudson, 1995.

Hall, Peter, and Colin Ward. *Sociable Cities: The Legacy of Ebenezer Howard*. New York: John Wiley and Sons, 1998.

Longstreth, Richard. *On the Edge of the World: Four Architects in San Francisco at the Turn of the Century*. Berkeley: University of California Press, 1983.

Quinan, Jack. *Frank Lloyd Wright's Larkin Building: Myth and Fact*. New York: Architectural History Foundation, 1989.

Stansky, Peter. *Redesigning the World: William Morris, the 1880s, and the Arts and Crafts*. Princeton, NJ: Princeton University Press, 1985.

Woodbridge, Sally. *Bernard Maybeck: Visionary Architect*. New York: Abbeville Press, 1996.

Figure 17.1-23 San Simeon, California. (a) Hearst Castle, twin bell towers, Morgan, 1919–1940. (b) Pastiche of Roman temple at the outdoor pool.

17.2 THE TWILIGHT OF WESTERN IMPERIALISM
Monuments to the White Man's Burden

During the nineteenth century, several modern European nations with parliamentary governments converted most of Asia and Africa into dependent colonies, imposing their rule through military might. The British poet Rudyard Kipling (1865–1937), born in colonial India, excused this offense to the sovereignty of nations as a civilizing mission, calling it the "white man's burden" in his 1899 poem of that name. The colonizers, convinced of their technical and moral high ground, not to say their racial superiority, transferred the technologies of progress—such as modern infrastructures, communications technologies, and hygienic services—to their holdings in the hopes of imposing their own culture and gaining profit.

The British ruled India, the largest and most important colony, while France grabbed most of Southeast Asia and significant areas of the Maghreb and West Africa. Western powers overran sub-Saharan Africa by the turn of the century. Southwest Asia, which the Ottomans had ruled for four centuries, was divvied up into French and British "protectorates" at the conclusion of World War I. The other major colonial powers included Portugal, Holland, Germany, and Italy. The United States took the Philippines in 1903, and Japan annexed Korea in 1910. Colonial architects created their boldest expressions during the first three decades of the twentieth century. Initially they relied on Beaux-Arts models but often introduced imagery or types based on local traditions, attempting to demonstrate authority while showing sympathy for indigenous cultures. Western imperialism left behind an ambitious monumental imprint that evoked the contradictory legacy of both gift and theft.

Colonial India: British, but also Native

British colonialism, whether in the Americas or in India, began as private enterprise. In 1639 the Honorable East India Company (HEIC) constructed its first fortified camp at the port of Madras (today Chennai) on the southeast coast of India, which ushered in three centuries of colonial engagement. The company's architectural interventions ranged from conventional neoclassical buildings to Gothic revival to romantic adaptations of the so-called Indo-Saracenic style. The HEIC, easily confused with the British state, exerted monopolistic authority over trade between England and Asia, raising its own army to protect its interests. One of the company's most lucrative, but dubious, enterprises included the export of opium from India to China, which led to major armed conflicts and the taking of Hong Kong in 1842 as an English colonial port. By the mid-nineteenth century the anomaly of a Western, profit-driven corporation presiding over most of India had become increasingly difficult for both the British and the Indians to tolerate. The first Indian War of Independence in 1857, known to the British as the "Indian Mutiny," convinced Parliament to dismiss the HEIC as governors of India and take direct control of the territory as an official colony.

After nearly a half-century of accommodation, the British inserted into the heart of each of its major colonial cities significant new monuments to convey the regime's intention to stay. Near the fortress of the capital city of Calcutta (today Kolkata) they placed a grand pile of white marble, known as the Victoria Memorial (1906–1921) (Fig. 17.2-1), in honor of the queen/empress. The viceroy of India, Lord Curzon, coached the architect William Emerson (1843–1924) to design the British equivalent of the Taj Mahal, a monument so intransigent that it would embody the full impact of the "white man's burden." Curzon requested that it also be executed in Western style since Calcutta was "a city of European origin and construction." The program included offices, libraries, and a museum, and when finished, the Victoria Memorial carried the fifth-largest dome in the world, raised on a drum like those of St. Peter's and St. Paul's and ringed with sumptuous buttress scrolls reminiscent of Santa Maria della Salute in Venice. Emerson placed four minor domes at the base of the drum and four towers to mark the outer edges of the complex. The monument, set in lush gardens with reflecting pools, so clearly represented Western imperialism that it still attracts the rage of protesters.

During the second half of the nineteenth century, Bombay (today Mumbai) surpassed Calcutta as India's leading port.

Figure 17.2-1 Kolkata (Calcutta). Victoria Memorial, William Emerson, 1906–1921.

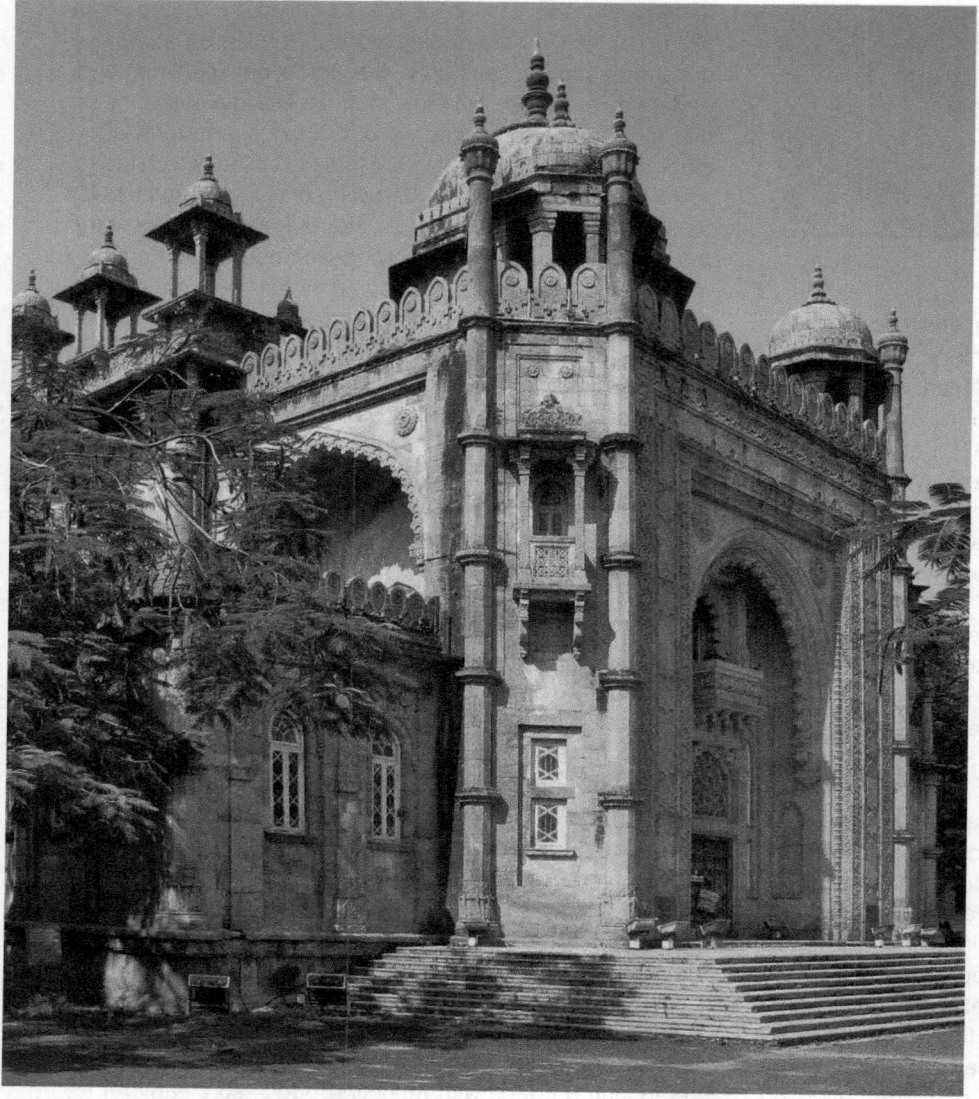

Figure 17.2-2 Madras, India. Victoria Memorial Hall (today Chennai National Museum), Henry Irwin, 1906–1909.

art schools. Rudyard Kipling's father, John Lockwood Kipling (1837–1911), came to India in 1865 to direct the art school in Lahore. Inspired by Ruskin's exaltations of craft, he initially embraced the Indian Gothic revival. Later, he advocated that Indian handicrafts be quarantined from industrial processes. Such esteem for craft accompanied the regionalist work in Jaipur of Colonel Samuel Swinton Jacob (see Section 15.2). In 1890, Swinton Jacob published *Jeypore Portfolio of Architectural Details*, with over 300 plates of beautifully delineated Indian motifs. His research inspired the Orientalist eclecticism at Bikaner, where he designed the Lalgarh Palace for the local maharaja.

Colonial designers attempted to synthesize European building types with local motifs, creating a unique Indo-Saracenic style. In Madras the students of the local art school reproduced Orientalist details on Western institutional buildings, best seen in the Victoria Memorial Hall, now the Technical Institute (1906), by Henry Irwin (1841–1922) (Fig. 17.2-2). The architect clad the structure in red sandstone and borrowed the *chhatris* and pointed merlins from Fatehpur Sikri (see Section 12.1), a place that previously had no connection to this southern port.

George Wittet (1878–1926) brought the Indo-Saracenic style to a climax in Bombay. His Prince of Wales Museum (1909) carried an immense concrete dome ringed with cusped tracery. His Gateway of India (Fig. 17.2-3) reproduced the Roman triumphal arch type with Indian

Colonial architects studded the city with dozens of Gothic revival structures as an alternative to the neoclassical style (see Section 15.2). Doubts about using the Gothic in India encouraged many designers to adopt Orientalist styles, resulting in an eclectic revival of Oriental rather than Western traditions. The emergence of this approach coincided with the arrival of the Arts and Crafts movement in India through the

TIME LINE

 1830

France begins colonization of Algeria

Avenue de l'Imperatrice (now Che Guevara) built by French in Algiers

▲ **1856–1870**

 1857

France begins colonial annexations in Southeast Asia

France colonizes Tunisia

▲ **1880**

Figure 17.2-3 Bombay. Gateway of India, George Wittet, 1911–1928. To its left is the Taj Mahal Hotel, built by Indian architect Sitaram Khanderas Vaidasentr for the Indian entrepreneur Jamsedji Tata in 1903.

iconography. First built in ephemeral materials at a dockside position for the arrival of King George V and Queen Mary in 1911, it was rebuilt during the 1920s in stone. The arch ultimately served as the ceremonial backdrop for the departure of the British troops when the United Kingdom formally relinquished the colony in 1948.

During King George's 1911 visit, the colonial administration decided to relocate the capital from Calcutta to Delhi. The founding of New Delhi inspired a grandiose expression of authority. The Royal Institute of British Architects recommended the appointment of Lutyens as chief architect, and he was assisted by his old friend Herbert Baker (1862–1946), who had worked for over a decade in South Africa. Swinton Jacob was also included in the design team as the consultant for Indian details. Lutyens and Baker, however, believed that classical style would convey the proper imperial expression and that they should "not pander to sentiment and all this silly Moghul-Hindu stuff." They placed the monumental core of government buildings at the center of a vast east–west axis and laid out the rest of the city on a complex hexagonal grid.

The plan appeared to be a vindication of Christopher Wren's unrealized plan for London after the Great Fire of 1666 (see Section 13.1). The central axis of New Delhi, nearly 300 m (985 ft) wide and ten times as long, stretched between the isolated All India Arch War Memorial, dedicated in 1931 to the victims of World War I, and the imposing dome of the Viceroy's House (Fig. 17.2-4), finished two years earlier. While the central axis resembled the Mall in the 1902 McMillan Plan for Washington, D.C., the rest of the plan, with its radiating streets, came closer to the urbanism of the Hampstead Garden Suburb, where Lutyens had

▼ **1899–1901**
Boxer Rebellion breaks out against foreign influence in China

Doumer Bridge built by Eiffel Company over Red River near Hanoi, Vietnam

▲ **1902**

▼ **1903**
United States colonizes the Philippines

France annexes Morocco as a "protectorate"

▲ **1907**

▼ **1910**
Japan annexes Korea

CULTURE, SOCIETY, GENDER

Cecil Rhodes's Total Plan for Africa

Herbert Baker came to India from South Africa after serving under one of the British Empire's greatest colonial masterminds, Cecil Rhodes (1853–1902). Rhodes excelled as both a politician and an entrepreneur, founding the De Beers Diamond Company. During the 1890s, he annexed the lands between South Africa and Lake Victoria with hopes of taking the entire continent in the name of England. Until 1964 the modern states of Zambia and Zimbabwe carried his name, as Rhodesia. Rudyard Kipling often visited Rhodes's Groote Shur estate and clearly found there the essence of the "white man's burden." Rhodes boasted that the British "are the finest race in the world and the more of the world we inhabit the better it is for the human race." Inspired by John Ruskin's beliefs on the duty of the British elite, which he encountered at Oxford, Rhodes dedicated his fortune to founding a secret society that would help England to rule the entire world and, thus, establish world peace. Although today his clandestine homosexuality would qualify him as a member of a minority, he exercised a notorious lack of consideration for other minorities, indigenous peoples, and Indian émigrés. Rhodes financed Baker's tour of the Mediterranean to inspire him to introduce classical works to South Africa. This resulted in the 1905 Rhodes Memorial, a U-shaped Doric altar lined with stone lions overlooking Cape Town. In 1909 Baker began work on the South African Union's government complex in Pretoria. He planned a domed parliament building at the summit of the hill to dominate an axis flanked by symmetrically placed secretariats, each crowned with a cupola. While the central dome went unbuilt, the composition clearly prefigured the arrangement of the Viceroy's House and the symmetrical secretariats in New Delhi.

Figure 17.2-4 New Delhi. Axis to the Viceroy's House (on left), Edwin Lutyens and Herbert Baker, 1920.

Habous district built outside of Casablanca, Morocco, by Laprade

▲ 1917

▼ **1928**

Gateway of India completed in Bombay

Laprade's Museum of Colonial Arts constructed in Paris

▲ 1931

Figure 17.2-5 Canberra, Australia. Plan for the capital city, Walter Burley Griffin and Marion Mahony Griffin, 1912.

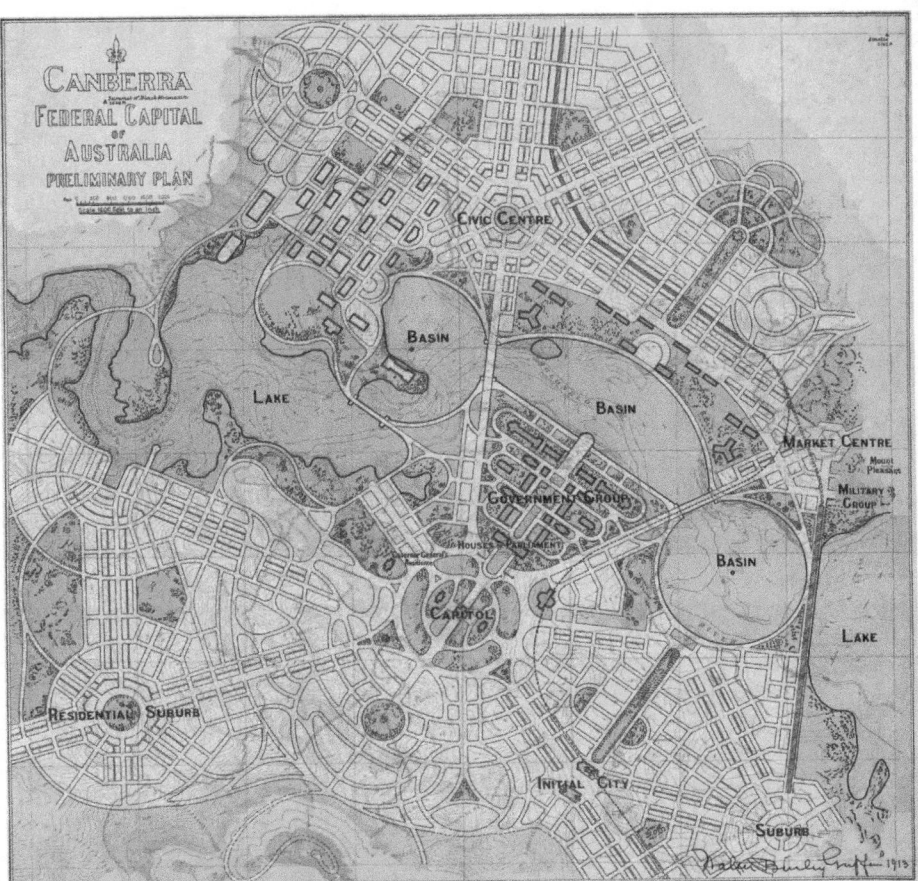

recently worked. The detached villas and bungalows, with generous setbacks on tree-lined streets, were organized in hierarchical order according to status and race. The low density of the new capital was as extreme as the crowding of Old Delhi surrounding Shahjahan's Red Fort.

Both Lutyens and Baker adhered to racist tenets of colonial ideology. Lutyens wrote that the realization of the grand classical axis of New Delhi would "only be possible now under a despotism. . . . Hurrah for despotism!" An alternative to tyranny motivated the plan for Canberra, Australia, during the same years. American designers Walter Burley Griffin (1876–1937) and his wife, Marion Mahony Griffin (1871–1961), both of whom worked for several years with Frank Lloyd Wright in Chicago, won the competition to design the capital of the newly unified Australian dominion in 1912 (Fig. 17.2-5). Their scheme proposed a series of radiating star shapes without a strong hierarchy. A lake interrupted the only prominent axis. They specifically avoided references to classical columns, domes, and the grand axis, seeking more direct expression of functions, which they believed to be a consequence of democracy.

While colonial despotism in India allowed the capital to be completed in fifteen years, Canberra's construction dragged on until the late 1980s. However, the British regime in India ultimately failed, while parliamentary democracy in Australia has endured. Despite Lutyens's objection to the Indo-Saracenic style, the viceroy insisted that New Delhi's designers include the Orientalist details of *chajja*, or diagonally projecting stone eaves; *jali* screens of drilled stone; and *chhatris* so that Indians would be flattered. Lutyens detested these gestures to folklore but went one further by ringing the drum of the dome of the Viceroy's House with stone railings like those surrounding the Great Stupa at Sanchi, evoking Buddhist iconography in a country where Buddhism had long since been eradicated.

The European colonists' obsession with style carried relatively little interest for Indians, who worried more about taxes and home rule. Their greatest leader, Mohandas (Mahatma, "the great soul") Gandhi (1869–1948), had also been inspired by Ruskin—not in his appeal to the British genius for rule, but in his praise of the virtues of small-scale socialist communities, described in *Unto This Last* (1860). Gandhi came to South Africa during the same years that Baker worked there for Cecil Rhodes, serving as a lawyer defending immigrant Indian workers. While in South Africa he founded the Phoenix Settlement in 1895, a collective farm that operated without distinctions of class or race, directly in contrast to Rhodes's hierarchical ideals for British imperialism.

Upon returning to India, Gandhi organized the Sabarmati Ashram in 1917 near Ahmedabad. From this monastic settlement his movement for nonviolent resistance to colonialism took root. The buildings of the ashram were constructed without iconographic embellishment, following the vernacular models of long, mud-wall sheds with wooden-pole porches. Gandhi's community pursued a self-reliant, crafts-based lifestyle. Everyone had the responsibility to weave his or her own clothes. Gandhi's importance for maintaining peace during the British Raj was such that he was the first Indian official invited to the Viceroy's House after its completion in 1929. He entered under the grand Pantheon-like dome dressed in a humble *dhoti* tunic that he had woven himself, a silent reproach to the vanity of the imperial trappings.

The French in North Africa and Indochina: The Strategy of Associationism

France possessed the second-largest colonial network at the turn of the twentieth century. Modern French colonialism began in 1830 with the seizing of Algeria, followed by the absorption of Tunisia in 1880 and the annexation of Morocco during the first decade of the twentieth century. France also attempted to keep up with British colonialism in Asia, maintaining a trading port in southern India. During the late

Figure 17.2-7 Notre Dame d'Afrique, Jean-Eugène Fromageau, 1858–1872.

Figure 17.2-6 Algiers. Port embankments and boulevard with porticoes that imitate the Rue de Rivoli, Charles-Frédéric-Henri Chassériau, 1860s.

Paris to build new boulevards, an analogous process began in Algiers (in Arabic, *El-Jazair*) with the clearing of a major plaza next to the city's most visible mosque, the white-domed Mosque of the Fisheries. The colonial planners demolished the Ottoman walls and in the late 1850s inserted a magnificent Parisian-style boulevard on top of the new fortified embankments (Fig. 17.2-6). Avenue de l'Imperatrice (later Avenue Che Guevara) reproduced the uniform arcades of Rue de Rivoli. The grand ramps and deep arches of the embankment's prominent retaining walls rose 20 m (64 ft) above the port, providing one of the world's most dramatic urban waterfronts.

In the first French addition to Algiers, straight European-style streets were extended from the southern edge of the *casbah*, where the Theater of Algiers (1853), the first important public building built by the colonial power, became the first sign of the expansion. Charles-Frédéric-Henri Chassériau (1802–1896), chief architect of the embankments, designed the theater in French Renaissance style, placing it as the axial focus of a square plaza. Thus, the regime imposed a secular monument that was as essential to French bourgeois culture as it was alien to the Algerians, launching the program to structure a segregated society.

Jean-Eugène Fromageau (1822–1897) designed the first major church of the Algerian colonists, Notre-Dame d'Afrique (1858–1872) (Fig. 17.2-7), on an isolated hill 2 km (1.2 miles) north of the *casbah*. Beneath its Neo-Byzantine domes ran an inscription that captured the divided mentality of the colonists: "Our Lady of Africa pray for us and for the Muslims." At the end of the century, as French Algeria gained greater stability, Albert Ballu (1849–1939) converted the seventeenth-century Ketchaoua Mosque into the Cathedral of Algiers. This intrusion into the southern edge of the *casbah* signified a direct effort to displace local power, and in 1962, at the termination of the Battle of Algiers, the structure was immediately reconverted into a mosque.

Throughout the nineteenth century, the French exhibited a strong Orientalist taste in the fine arts and literature, best represented in the harem paintings by Eugène Delacroix (1798–1863). French architects, however, avoided Oriental vernaculars until around 1900. By this time European settlers, who included French, Spanish, Italians,

nineteenth century the French absorbed most of Southeast Asia into the colonial confederation of Indochina. From the outset they attempted to give more structure to their colonies than the British, resulting in a strong urban vision. While the grand manner and formal plan of New Delhi proved an exception to British practice, they were generally the rule for the French. Their professional planners, many of them trained at the Beaux-Arts, realized in the colonies the sort of coordinated plans worthy of Georges-Eugène Haussmann's transformation of Paris (see Section 16.1).

Algeria, located directly across the Mediterranean from Marseilles, became the most prominent French colony. Never a harmonious endeavor, France's colonial adventure there was upset by frequent rebellions and climaxed in the Battle of Algiers during the decolonization of the 1950s and 1960s. At the same time that Haussmann was demolishing and Jews, had become the dominant presence in Algiers. Neo-Moorish buildings began to appear during the first decade of the twentieth century, when Célestin-Auguste-Charles Jonnart (1857–1927) became governor of Algeria. He actively promoted the construction of new public buildings for Muslims, such as the Médersa Thaâlibyya religious school by Henri Petit, a domed structure evoking Mamluk style. Jonnart encouraged Neo-Moorish cladding for state buildings, such as the Prefect's Office and the Central Post Office (Fig. 17.2-8), both finished around 1910 by Jules Voinot. These projects featured stilted domes, horseshoe arches, and flowery merlins lining the parapets but seemed strangely out of place. Like the British Indo-Saracenic style, the Neo-Moorish buildings of Algiers transposed a pseudo-ethnic iconography onto European building types.

The French occupation of Morocco began in 1907 under Louis-Hubert-Gonzalve Lyautey (1854–1934), a key ideologue of colonial policy. Fresh from assisting Jonnart in Algiers, Lyautey had spent two decades in the military administrations of Vietnam and Madagascar. He proposed "associationism" as the correct strategy for pacifying colonial dominions, insisting that France conserve the local cultures and their ruling hierarchies so that they could "associate" with a parallel European administration. Thus, he installed a puppet regime in Morocco, making the brother of the deposed sultan the titular monarch. As resident-general of the colony from 1912 to 1925, Lyautey imposed the French standard of modern urbanism, hiring Henri Prost (1874–1959) to create comprehensive master plans for nine cities, including Casablanca, Rabat, and Fez. Lyautey and Prost left the traditional *medinas* untouched, while using *cordon sanitaires*, or hygienic greensward, to keep the indigenous population separate from the Europeans. The ancient urban centers remained formally independent enclaves on the fringe of the geometrically organized additions of broad, radiating boulevards.

Lyautey considered the Neo-Moorish movement in Algeria to be "romantic bad taste." He encouraged designers in Morocco to be more like the Normans in medieval Sicily: "We are the architects and Morocco furnishes us with artisans." As governor, he established the colonial capital in the small royal city of Rabat, leaving the larger port city of Casablanca as the commercial and industrial hub. In 1918 he created the Résidence de France, or governor's compound, in Rabat, with a collection of ministries lining a curved drive. Its large estate with formal gardens stood directly across the major boulevard from the sultan's royal palace, leaving no doubt about the symmetry of rule. The new European district focused on the train station, east of the historic *medina*. By creating a distinction between the modern and the traditional city, Lyautey not only segregated races but repeated a practice that had been typical in North African cities, in which the ruling dynasties always lived separated from the ruled (see Section 7.1). His architect, Albert

Figure 17.2-8 Algiers. Central Post Office, Jules Voinot and M. Toudoire, 1907–1910.

Laprade (1883–1978), combined a Beaux-Arts plan with a square courtyard based on the traditional Moroccan *riad* (see Section 8.2). Contrary to local custom, he surrounded the palace with open arcaded terraces. Laprade used smooth, planar surfaces while including a trace of Marinid style in the treatment of the tiled roofs and arches raised on slender marble columns. The terraces overlooked French geometric gardens with views to the distant ruins of Chella.

During the same years, on the outskirts of Casablanca, Laprade designed the Habous district for a new royal palace (Fig. 17.2-9), as the sultan had not previously had a residence in that city. Abutting the garden walls of the palace, he created a "new *medina*" for 250 modest indigenous houses. The courtyard houses revived the traditional *riad* scheme, partly to indulge the romantic taste of Orientalist fantasies but mostly as a political strategy: "Peasant, port workers, and factory laborers," Laprade wrote, "can trade their goods, pray, and amuse themselves without impinging on the European town." The narrow streets with arched gateways abstracted the architectonic qualities of the Moroccan *medina* while including modern plumbing and services.

Lyautey's ideal synthesis of local and European styles reached maturity in Casablanca in the administrative buildings constructed in the early 1920s around the Place Administrative (now Place des Nations Unies), the major new square in Casablanca. The new buildings included Joseph Marrast's Law Courts (Fig. 17.2-9a), Adrien Laforgue's Post Office (Fig. 17.2-9b), and the Casablanca City Hall by Marius Boyer (1885–1947). Critics referred to their pure volumes and minimal use of traditional Moroccan decoration as "Arabisance."

Boyer went on to refine the style in dozens of commercial projects, such as the Asayag housing block, a series of ten-story apartment towers built in 1932. Using reinforced concrete frames and industrial steel-sash windows, he abandoned all pretense of traditional iconography to pursue a Moroccan version of functionalist architecture. By the end of the 1930s, the European district of Casablanca appeared a white modernist city of abstract towers. The stunning Sacré-Coeur Cathedral, begun in 1930 by Paul Tournon (1881–1964), stood on the edge of the Place Administrative as the proud beacon of a new architectural language. Its brilliant white twin towers and light concrete vaults eluded the historicism of both colonized and colonizers to achieve a Moroccan *Moderne* style.

The French colonies in Asia experienced a similar, if slower, transmission of architecture and urbanism. France followed the British example of setting up "treaty ports" and concessions in Asian cities such as Shanghai. Its colonial

Figure 17.2-9 Casablanca. Habous "indigenous" district, Albert Laprade, 1917.

CONSTRUCTION, TECHNOLOGY, THEORY

Moroccan *Moderne*

Many talented French, Italian, and Moroccan architects built surprisingly modern mid-rise towers, exclusively for European clients, during the 1920s and 1930s. Marius Boyer produced dozens of white towers in Casablanca, such as the Asayag project, using abstract forms derived from structure and function. The planar walls with deep sunshades and small apertures built on concrete frames became a commercial vernacular, free of sentimental gestures to local vernaculars. Paul Tournon designed the culminating monument of Moroccan *Moderne*, the Sacré-Coeur Cathedral of Casablanca, begun in 1930 and finished in 1952.

Casablanca. (a) Asayag Apartments, Marius Boyer, 1930. (b) Sacré-Coeur Cathedral, Paul Tournon, 1930–1952.

annexations in Southeast Asia began in 1857 and by the end of the century included Vietnam, Laos, and Cambodia, which it controlled as the colonial federation of Indochina. Saigon (today Ho Chi Minh City) served as the first capital of French Southeast Asia. While the new City Hall and Opera House seemed like caricatures of European eclecticism, the Governor's Palace (1890) by Alfred Foulhouz stood as a competent essay in classicism.

In 1887 the colonial administrators moved the capital north to Hanoi. Aside from the construction of an incongruous Neo-Gothic cathedral (Fig. 17.2-11) and a grand opera house (Fig. 17.2-12), the only exceptional European work was the Eiffel Company's cast-iron Doumer Bridge (now Long Bien). Built in 1902, it stretched 1,600 m (5,120 ft) over the Red River, connecting Hanoi to Haiphong.

In 1923, following the example of Lyautey's urban restructuring of Morocco, the governor of French Indochina established a technical office for planning. He hired one of Prost's colleagues from the Musée Social, Ernest Hébrard (1875–1933), to work on the considerable urban problems of hygiene and circulation in the Asian colonies. Hébrard, a winner of the Prix de Rome, brought a strong Beaux-Arts

Figure 17.2-10 Casablanca. (a) Law Courts, Joseph Marrast, 1923. (b) Post Office, Adrien Laforgue, 1920.

Figure 17.2-11 Hanoi, Vietnam. Cathedral of St. Joseph, 1880s.

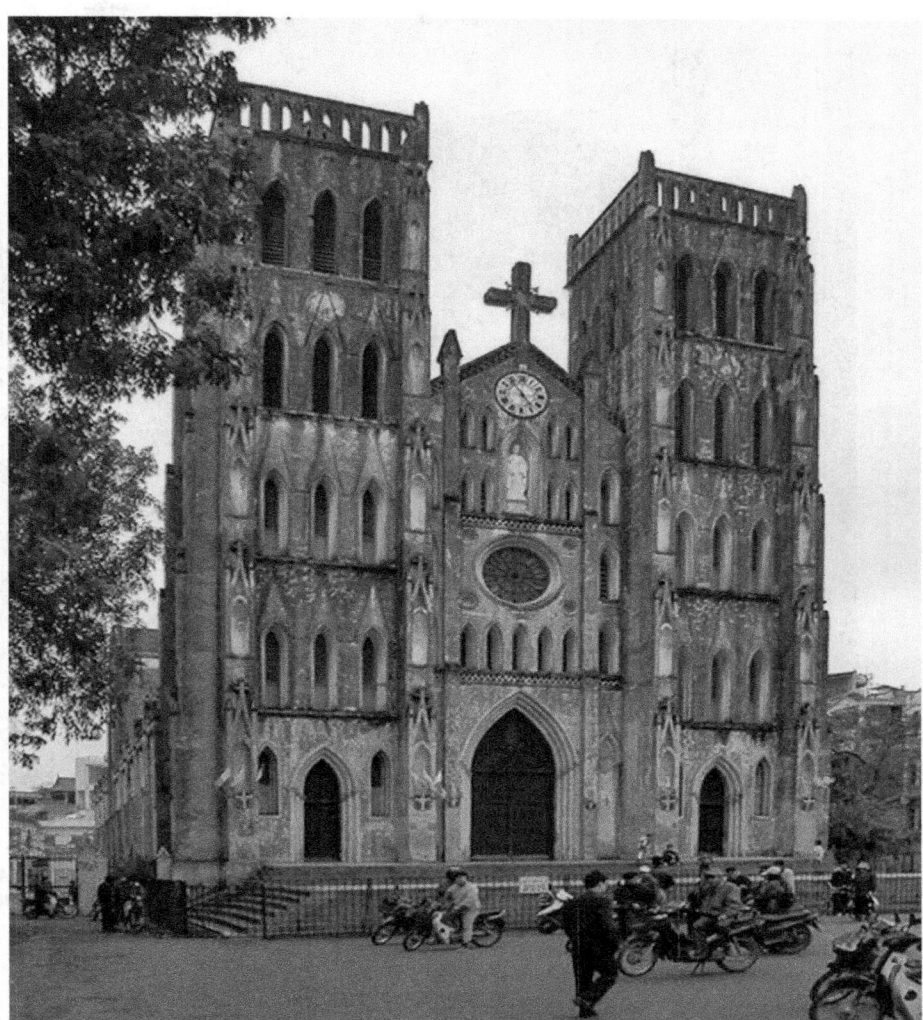

background to the task. His experience included the design of the grandiose utopian scheme of Hendrik Christian Andersen for a World Center of Communication, published in 1913. Hébrard's colonial office created comprehensive plans for Saigon, Hanoi, Haifong, Phnom Penh, and the vacation hill-town of Dalat. Once the plans were drawn he attempted to synthesize Asian and European styles in numerous projects. The Lycée Petrus Ky in Saigon, built in 1925, served as a model school for training Vietnamese children according to European criteria. Its verandahs and breezeways copied the local solutions for mediating the climate without resorting to the brackets, curved roofs, or other indicators of Asian iconography.

French colonial planning never equaled the commanding monumental vision of Lutyens's and Baker's New Delhi. The urban schemes of Prost and Hébrard were outgrown almost at the moment of their layout. Informal shanties rose faster than streets could be built. One of the last attempts to salvage Western imperialism as a positive contribution came in 1931 with the immensely popular International Colonial Exposition in Paris. Over 30 million people visited its reconstructions of the temple of Angkor Wat and the Great Mosque of Djenné, which itself had only recently been rebuilt. The director of the event was none other than Lyautey, who engaged Laprade to design the major exhibition hall as a Museum of Colonial Arts (now called Palais de la Porte Dorée) (Fig. 17.2-13a). A porch of tall, slender piers protected Albert Jannio's golden reliefs encrusting the entire front elevation (Fig. 17.2-13b). Jannio densely packed representations of exotic animals, colonial products, merchant ships, and scantily clad subject peoples from around the colonial world, who presumably had learned to coexist in "association" with the well-dressed French colonists. Such a loaded vision of imperialism conveyed a retrospective message that the "white man's burden" had become too heavy to carry.

Figure 17.2-12 Hanoi, Vietnam. Opera, V. Harley Broyer and Francois Lagisquet, 1880s.

Figure 17.2-13 Paris. (a) Museum of Colonial Arts, porch of slender piers, Laprade, 1931. (b) Detail of reliefs.

Further Reading

Abu-Lughod, Janet. *Rabat: Urban Apartheid in Morocco*. Princeton, NJ: Princeton University Press, 1980.

Celik, Zeynep. *Urban Forms and Colonial Confrontations: Algiers under French Rule*. Berkeley: University of California Press, 1997.

Cohen, Jean-Louis, ed. *Alger: Paysage Urbain et Architecture, 1800–2000*. Paris: Les Éditions de L'imprimeur, 2003.

Cohen, Jean-Louis, and Monique Elab. *Casablanca: Colonial Myths and Architectural Ventures*. New York: Monacelli Press, 2002.

Davies, Philip. *Splendours of the Raj: British Architecture in India, 1660 to 1947*. London: John Murray, 1985.

Dwivedi, Sharada, and Rahul Mehrotra. *Bombay: The Cities Within*. Bombay: India Book House, 1995.

Metcalf, Thomas R. *An Imperial Vision: Indian Architecture and Britain's Raj*. Berkeley: University of California Press, 1989.

Morris, Jan. *Stones of Empire: The Buildings of the Raj*. Oxford: Oxford University Press, 1983.

Rabinow, Paul. *French Modern: Norms and Forms of the Social Environment*. Chicago: University of Chicago Press, 1995.

Sonne, Wolfgang. *Representing the State: Capital City Planning in the Early Twentieth Century*. Munich: Prestel, 2003.

Wright, Gwendolyn. *The Politics of Design in French Colonial Urbanism*. Chicago: University of Chicago Press, 1991.

17.3 ART NOUVEAU AND THE SEARCH FOR MODERN FORM

Architecture without Precedents

Aside from the Arts and Crafts movement and the attempts of Western architects to "Orientalize" their projects in the colonies, there existed another, more radical alternative to Beaux-Arts classicism and eclectic styles. The Art Nouveau movement emerged in rebellion to academic approaches to design. Some of its major exponents, including Mackintosh and Antoni Gaudí, originated in the Arts and Crafts, while others, like Henry van de Velde and Peter Behrens, came from avant-garde circles in the fine arts. While Arts and Crafts rejected the imitation of historical styles but extolled tradition, finding transcendent truth in regional craft production, the theorists of Art Nouveau advocated a clean break from the past to find a new formal language appropriate to modernity. The Eiffel Tower's appearance in 1889 as a raw expression of structure represented the first liberating act of this movement.

Artists and architects, eager for new sources, turned to nature for inspiration, abstracting mineral formations, botanical sinews, and marine life. Their works expressed movement, sensuality, and playfulness. The tendency of Art Nouveau designers to privilege decoration and aestheticism eventually provoked moralistic reactions. Adolf Loos in "Ornament and Crime" criticized their efforts to design and decorate everything as a pathological sign of decadence that induced an atmosphere of oppression. While Art Nouveau did not last for more than a decade, its vigorous challenge to the academic styles cleared the way for avant-garde positions to emerge in the design fields. The search for newness became a way for architects to adjust to modernity.

The Newness of Art Nouveau: Exposed Structure, Whiplash Lines, and Social Reform

Art Nouveau appeared at the end of the nineteenth century as an intense, but short-lived, eruption in the arts. It originated in the provincial settings of Brussels and Nancy, before finding its major point of diffusion in Paris. Although best known by its French name, it reemerged in different regional variations as *Jugendstil* in Germany, *Secession* in Austria, *Stile Liberty* in Italy, and *Modernisme* in Spain. The stem-like cast-iron awnings installed in 1900 at the Paris Métro stations by Hector Guimard (1867–1942), with lamps like sprouting buds and graphics like sinuous tendrils, expressed the dynamic spirit of the new style. The Art Nouveau aesthetic dominated the Paris Exposition Universelle of the same year. As if to combat the resurgence of academic classicism at the 1893 Chicago World's Fair, Art Nouveau channeled a widespread feeling of rebellion among young artists and designers. Their work, however, remained mostly within the confines of the elite; indeed, their chief patronage came from luxury commercial enterprises, such as department stores. Thus, despite Art Nouveau's radical premises and the involvement of many of its protagonists with campaigns for social reform, it ultimately resembled changes in clothing fashions.

The arrival of Japanese prints and handicrafts in the Western world after Japan revoked its strict isolationist policy in 1854 influenced painters such as James McNeill Whistler (1834–1903) and Edouard Manet (1832–1883), who became eager collectors and promoters of "Japonisme." This in turn affected the applied arts, yielding the fanciful glassware by Émile Gallé (1846–1904) in Nancy. The flatness and abstraction found in the work of Japanese printmaker Katsushika Hokusai (1760–1849) inspired the graphic art of Jan Toorop (1858–1928), Aubrey Beardsley (1872–1898), and Henri de Toulouse-Lautrec (1864–1901).

Toulouse-Lautrec in his lithographic posters captured another aesthetic stimulus: the sensational effects of the American modern dancer Loïe Fuller (1862–1928). Her manipulation of undulating silk veils became the highlight of the Folies Bergère cabaret during the 1890s (Fig. 17.3-1). The dynamic whiplash motifs used in the graphics and architectural decorations of the period shared the liberating verve of Fuller's dancing. She presided over her own pavilion at the 1900 Paris Expo, designed by Henri Sauvage (1873–1932). Its curvaceous facade mimicked the movement of her silken gowns.

In Brussels an anti-academic association of artists gathered around the painter James Ensor (1860–1949) and in 1884 began exhibiting as "Les XX." Their promotion by Octave Maus and his magazine *Art Moderne* influenced the taste of progressive patrons, most of whom belonged to the Masonic Lodge of Philanthropic Friends and supported the Social Democratic Party. The young architect Victor Horta (1861–1947), in league with this group of artists and patrons, asked, "Why can't architects be independent and audacious like the painters?" In 1892, the year he began to teach at the Open University in Brussels, his colleague Emile Tassel asked him to design his house. Tassel, a professor of descriptive geometry, traveled widely and liked to entertain. Horta described the house as a portrait of the patron, an erudite bachelor who lived with his grandmother. The facade at first appeared discreet, symmetrically organized around a protruding bow window. The capitals of the stout stone columns of the mezzanine, however, carried the novelty of an exposed iron entablature. Most of the upper story was articulated with iron mullions, unprecedented in domestic buildings of the day. Inside, a molded wrought-iron structure with sinuous botanical forms bore the central stair (Fig. 17.3-2). Magnificent swirling patterns of interlacing tendrils appeared in the mosaic floors of the foyer, continued in the painted decoration of the walls, and wrapped around the metal structure of the railings. Every aspect of the house,

Figure 17.3-1 Loïe Fuller, protagonist of the whiplash aesthetic, 1900.

from door handles to furniture to stained glass windows, contributed to an integrated system of decoration and structure. The Tassel House embodied the aesthete's vision of a modern environment free of references to the past.

One of the painters of Les XX, Henry van de Velde, followed Horta's style of organic interiors to become the most sought-after Art Nouveau decorator in Europe. Van de Velde, like William Morris, built his own house as a demonstration of his aesthetic and founded a handicrafts company to produce his designs. In 1895, he built Bloemenwerf House in Uccle, a suburb of Brussels, for his new bride,

integrating the design of the hardware, wallpaper, fabrics, furniture, and even his wife's gowns, the so-called reform dress, into a total work. Van de Velde created three rooms in 1897 for Samuel Bing's Maison de l'Art Nouveau in Paris, achieving the fullest realization of the whiplash style. The rooms were reinstalled in Munich (Fig. 17.3-3) and Dresden, where they caused a sensation, leading to van de Velde's move to Germany in 1900, where he became the catalyst of *Jugendstil*. As the first director of the Kunstgewerbeschule, founded in Weimar in 1905, he led the break from historicist approaches to design.

TIME LINE

▼ **ca. 1880s**

Beginning of
Art Nouveau

*Gaudí takes on
lifetime project of
La Sagrada Familia
Cathedral in Barcelona*

▲ **1883**

▼ **1889**

*Eiffel Tower and Galerie
des Machines built for
World Exhibition in Paris*

Horta's Maison du Peuple and Fin-de-Siècle Socialism

At the beginning of the twentieth century, even those who ascribed to the most decadent "art for art's sake" position, such as Oscar Wilde, declared themselves socialists. Throughout the nineteenth century various socialist theorists, from communist revolutionaries to reformist social democrats, offered solutions to human problems that religion could no longer supply. Most socialists agreed that the accumulation of capital in the hands of a few was unfair. All people needed access to health care, education, and housing, which could be achieved through the equitable redistribution of wealth. Socialist organizations met to debate questions of collectivization and methods of political transition.

In Brussels Horta completed one of the most significant works of Art Nouveau, the Maison du Peuple (House of the People), for the Social Democratic Party. His four-story structure served a complex program of café, bookshop, offices, library, clubrooms, and a large meeting hall for 1,700 people. The undulating shape of the facade came from its irregular site at the intersection of a circular plaza. While Horta avoided using ornamental details that might be condemned as decadent decoration, he exposed the iron mullions, painted red, to do the work of articulation. The meeting hall's undulating ceiling was supported on curved web trusses, which corresponded to the acoustical model proposed at Wagner's Bayreuth opera house. Lining the parapets were the names of socialist heroes, including Karl Marx and Pierre-Joseph Proud'hon, printed like brand names on placards. At the Maison du Peuple the progressive theories of socialism, based on workers' rights, found correspondence in an architecture that had been freed from historical references.

Brussels. Maison du Peuple, Horta, 1896.

1895

Oscar Wilde convicted of sodomy and imprisoned

Horta designs Tassel House in Brussels

1892

Olbrich's Secession House built in Vienna

1898

1900

Paris Métro system stations designed by Guimard

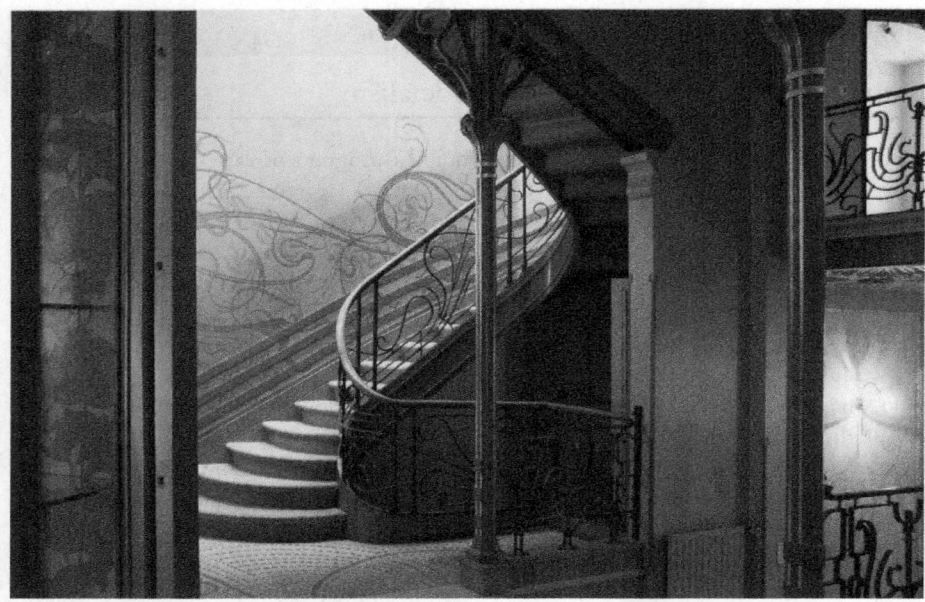

Figure 17.3-2 Brussels. Tassel House, detail of Art Nouveau staircase, Victor Horta, 1892.

Figure 17.3-3 Writing desk and chair ("Diplomat Desk"), Henry van de Velde, 1897–1898. Van de Velde's style of organic interiors made him the most sought-after Art Nouveau decorator in Europe.

While there were hints of Gothic tracery and rococo floral patterns in Art Nouveau, the Parisian architect Frantz Jourdain (1847–1935), designer of the Samartaine department store, championed the style as a way to liberate architecture from historic precedents. His contemporary, Hector Guimard, visited Brussels in 1893 and quickly altered his designs for the Castel Beranger housing project in Paris, completed in 1898. Instead of the neomedieval details he had originally intended, he applied sinuous patterns inspired by Horta. The exposed-metal structure of his Métro stations in Paris (Fig. 17.3-4) indulged in botanical imagery akin to that of the Tassel House stairway.

Other designers, such as Georges Chedanne (1861–1940), created a more abstract version of the style related to Eugène-Emmanuel Viollet-le-Duc's theory of structural rationalism (see Section 15.2). In his iron and glass facade for the 1903 *Parisien* newspaper headquarters on Rue de Réamur he exposed vertical iron buttresses that flared out at the top story like branches, supporting cantilevered bay windows (Fig. 17.3-5).

Because of its novel ornamentation and strong connection to major turn-of-the-century department stores, Art Nouveau appeared to be a fashion phenomenon. Most of its adherents, however, were sincere believers in socialism and social reform. Jourdain belonged to a philanthropical society that promoted the efforts of Henri Sauvage, one of the major Art Nouveau designers, to create affordable housing alternatives. Sauvage's first experiments in 1903 at Rue Trétaigne provided a reinforced concrete–frame structure for a mix of units for married and single workers, with services such as a meeting hall, a library, a restaurant, and a rooftop garden. This project led Sauvage

▼ 1905

Gaudí's Casa Milà
built in Barcelona

Hoffmann's Palais Stoclet
built in Brussels

▲ 1905

▼ 1909

Loos's Goldman & Salatsch
store, now known as
"Looshaus," built in Vienna

CONSTRUCTION, TECHNOLOGY, THEORY

The Eiffel Tower and the Galerie des Machines

Frantz Jourdain celebrated the two great technical achievements of the 1889 Paris Exposition Universelle, the Eiffel Tower and the Galerie des Machines, as the auguries of the new style for modernity. Eiffel's younger assistant, the Swiss engineer Maurice Koechlin (1856–1946), conceived the former structure as inclining curves corresponding to the diagram of wind resistance. Except for the nonstructural arches added by Koechlin's colleague Stephen Sauvestre at its base, which served to signal the entryway to the Champs de Mars fairgrounds, every one of the 18,000 prefabricated iron struts contributed to the tower's optimal strength. While critics on the "Committee of 300" (one critic for each of its 324 meters) condemned it as a modern Tower of Babel, the Eiffel Tower became a manifesto of teleology, or the idea that "form follows function." Once in place, however, the only function the tower truly served was symbolic, becoming one of the few modern structures to acquire instant iconic value, signifying both Paris and France.

Several decades later, when, according to contract, it was to be dismantled, a use was found for the Eiffel Tower as the world's tallest radio antenna.

The other spectacular demonstration of the engineer's prowess, the Galerie des Machines, proved more useful for architects as a lesson in covering space. Set at the opposite end of the Champs de Mars, the 400 m (1,280 ft) long hall struck Jourdain as "a work of art as beautiful, as pure, as original, as elevated as a Greek temple or a cathedral." The architect Charles Dutert (1845–1906) and engineer Victor Contamin (1840–1893) created a pointed ferrovitreous vault supported on pairs of curved trusses, tied to pin joints at the base, and locked together at the apex by a third pin joint. While the Eiffel Tower attained the world's then greatest height, the Galerie des Machines covered the largest span, at 115 m (370 ft). As with the Crystal Palace, the designers made no effort to conceal the building's structure on either the interior or exterior. The raw ironwork became its decoration.

Paris. (a) Eiffel Tower, Maurice Koechlin, 1889. (b) Galerie des Machines, Charles Dutert and Victor Contamin, 1889.

Figure 17.3-4 Paris. Métro station, Hector Guimard, 1900.

to develop a new apartment typology, the *gradins*, or the vertical setback block. He produced a small demonstration on Rue Vavin in 1912, in which each floor stepped back to leave a terrace above the previous floor, thus allowing daylight to penetrate into the street (Fig. 17.3-6). Ideally, the type would cover an entire block, its stepped section creating a pyramidal void on the interior for collective services. The collectivist social conscience behind Sauvage's housing represented the most original aspect of Art Nouveau.

National Liberation and the Search for the Appropriate Style of Modernity

The whiplash aesthetic of Art Nouveau spread throughout the world by means of poster art, product packaging, and the diffusion of applied art products, such as lamps and jewelry sold by such artisan-entrepreneurs as the American Louis Comfort Tiffany (1848–1933). The architecture of Art Nouveau, however, usually absorbed regional characteristics. The designs of the Italian architect Raimondo d'Aronco (1857–1932), who began working in Istanbul in 1893 as the court architect of the sultan, combined the undulating botanical motifs of Art Nouveau with late Ottoman pointed cupolas.

In Helsinki Eliel Saarinen and his colleagues participated in the Arts and Crafts colony at Hvittrask. After visiting Paris in 1900 to build a pavilion based on Finnish vernacular at the International Exposition, they dropped all historical references. The Helsinki Station, built between 1904 and 1914, showed a new effort to develop a formal language free of precedents, deriving decorative value from the rippling outlines of structure. This architectural approach echoed the

search for a modern national identity, in the context of Finland's liberation from Russia.

Jože Plečnik (1872–1957) trained in Vienna and worked in Prague before returning to his native Ljubljana in 1921, where he attempted to foment a national Slovenian style in his designs for markets, bridges, and a church on the edge of town, where he lived like a monk. His grandest creation, the National Library (1930–1941) (Fig. 17.3-7), took shape in the center of the city, with such eccentric details as randomly placed patches of rustication and a single colossal Ionic column reaching from the bottom to the top floor in front of the bank of windows.

Similar efforts to break from academic styles cropped up in many peripheral situations, usually in the company of national liberation movements. Prague, which was still reluctantly a part of the Austro-Hungarian Empire at the beginning of the twentieth century, became the center of a peculiar movement in the applied arts and architecture, roughly based on the Cubism of Georges Braques (1882–1963) and Pablo Picasso (1881–1973). In 1908 the Cubists shocked the art world in Paris with collages and paintings that dismembered elements of still-life compositions and reassembled them with syncopated rhythms. When Czech artists such as Josef Čapek (1887–1945) came to Prague, they applied the Cubist aesthetic of fragmentation and angular extrusion to design. Czech Cubism centered around the Group of Plastic Artists founded in 1911, who, inspired by van de Velde's example, sought to produce total interior environments. They sent a room of angular furniture and objects to the Werkbund Exhibition at Cologne in 1914 coordinated by Josef Gočár (1880–1945). The apartment block on Premislova Street by his colleague Josef Chochol

Figure 17.3-5 Paris. *Le Parisien* offices, Georges Chedanne, 1903.

(1880–1956), however, demonstrated that Czech Cubist architecture was generally limited to the decoration of facades (Fig. 17.3-8). The faceted style brought vitality to the elevations of Prague buildings without requiring custom treatment of windows or doors, but it did not have much relation to the interior spaces or to construction methods.

In the Netherlands Heinrich Berlage (1856–1934), who had studied with Gottfried Semper in Zurich and was heavily influenced by the structural theories of Viollet-le-Duc, led the Dutch search for a new language of architectural expression. With the Koopmansbeurs Stock Exchange built in Amsterdam from 1898 to 1903 (Fig. 17.3-9), he provoked an anti-academic trend. His project showcased both the attempt to use modern construction methods and the desire to integrate the plastic arts into architecture. The horizontal layout of the Stock Exchange recalled the

Auguste Perret and Modern Concrete Construction

Auguste Perret (1874–1954), working with his brother Gustave Perret (1876–1952), developed the techniques of construction with François Hennebique's reinforced concrete, patented in 1897. Perret understood concrete construction as the continuation of the rationality of classicism, leading him to build with structural grids. At the Rue Franklin apartments (1902–1904), he clad the skeletal frame with terra-cotta insets. In his industrial works, such as the 1919 Esder Factory, he left the frame exposed. For economic reasons, he left the columns and vaults of the 1922 church of Notre Dame de Raincy in raw concrete, with stunning effects.

Figure 17.3-6 Paris. Rue Vavin *gradins*, or vertical setbacks, Henri Sauvage, 1912.

Figure 17.3-7 Ljubljana, Slovenia. National Library, Jože Plečnik, 1930.

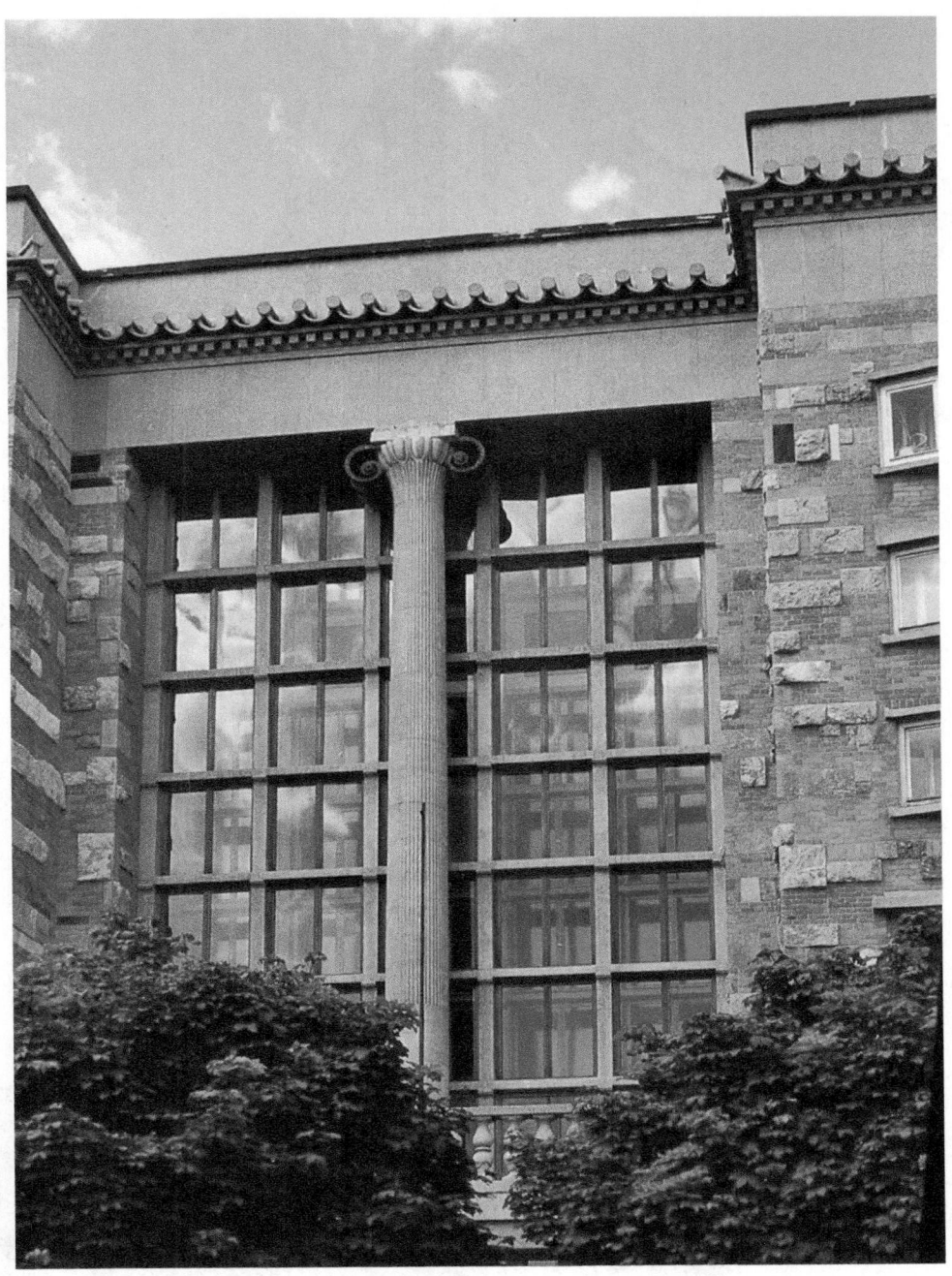

Figure 17.3-7 Ljubljana, Slovenia. National Library, Jože Plečnik, 1930.

Neo-Romanesque volumes of Richardson, but the decorative details displayed Art Nouveau flourishes, including ceramic panels by Toorop (1858–1928), one of the first graphic artists to use the whiplash motif.

As chief planner of the extension of south Amsterdam, Berlage influenced the attitudes of the next generation of designers, who participated in building one of the world's first extensive programs of social housing (Fig. 17.3-10). The architects of the Amsterdam School designed hundreds of units of municipally financed, low-cost housing between 1914 and 1925, using remarkably expressive details. They treated the hardware, windows, gables, and street corners as customized, artistic statements close to the spirit of Art

Nouveau. The most inventive among them, Michel de Klerk (1884–1923), aspired to the personalized designs of the English Arts and Crafts. His 1914 Ship housing estate for the cooperative society Eigenhaard took its name from a slender, mast-like steeple that stood at the head of the triangular plot for 102 units. While the interiors were rationally organized, the exteriors included a wide variety of differently shaped and tapered windows, undulating walls, and sculptural doorways.

By far the strongest regional variation of Art Nouveau occurred in turn-of-the-century Barcelona. During the late nineteenth century the literary *Renaixença* movement promoted the romantic quest for an autonomous Catalan

Figure 17.3-8 Prague. Neklanova apartments, Josef Chochol, 1913.

Figure 17.3-9 Amsterdam. Koopmansbeurs Stock Exchange, Heinrich Berlage, 1898–1903.

Figure 17.3-10 Amsterdam. Social housing, Eigenhaard Ship housing estate, Michel de Klerk, 1914–1920.

culture, which deeply affected the arts. At first, this movement produced an emphasis on neomedieval fantasies inspired by Viollet-le-Duc and Ruskin, resulting in the plan for a Neo-Gothic cathedral set amid the unbuilt blocks of Cerdá's *Ensanche*. The design of the Sagrada Familia (Fig. 17.3-11), although begun in 1882 by Francisco de Paula del Villar i Lozano (1828–1901), was taken over the following year by his young assistant, Antoni Gaudí (1852–1926). It remained his lifelong project and a register of his artistic development from a medievalizing craftsperson to the inventor of unprecedented organic forms.

Gaudí's breakthrough came through his friendship with the wealthy textile heir Eusebi Güell (1846–1918), who in 1886 commissioned a palace in the Gothic quarter of Barcelona that rivaled the Tassel House, exploiting the architect's love of parabaloid arches and vaults. The foyer rose three stories to a beehive-inspired vault and included a gilded cabinet/chapel with an organ for religious ceremonies that when combined with the frescoes, swirling ironwork, and mosaics became a paroxysm of art, music, religion, and architecture. Gaudí populated the roof with the first of his celebrated colorful tile-clad chimneys. Güell's fortune originated from a textile factory, but in 1901 he founded a cement factory, the products of which went into the production of Gaudí's eccentric Park Güell, intended as a social center serving an English-style Garden City suburb. Only two of the sixty houses planned were built, with one serving as the house of the architect and his niece until 1912. On the slopes of the park Gaudí experimented with reinforced concrete, producing an uncanny hypostyle of primitive Doric columns for a covered market hall. On its roof terrace he wove a spectacular parapet of undulating benches encrusted in *trencadís*, mosaics composed from broken colored tiles, coordinated by his assistant and successor Josep Maria Jujol (1879–1949).

Gaudí's organic manner, known locally as *Modernisme*, filtered into the renovation of a townhouse called the Casa Batlló, begun in 1905. He created bulges on the flat facade, using bone-like formations to support the bow windows. On the roof he capped the apartment house with a waving sweep of green tiles,

Figure 17.3-11 Barcelona. Sagrada Familia Cathedral, Antoni Gaudí, 1882.

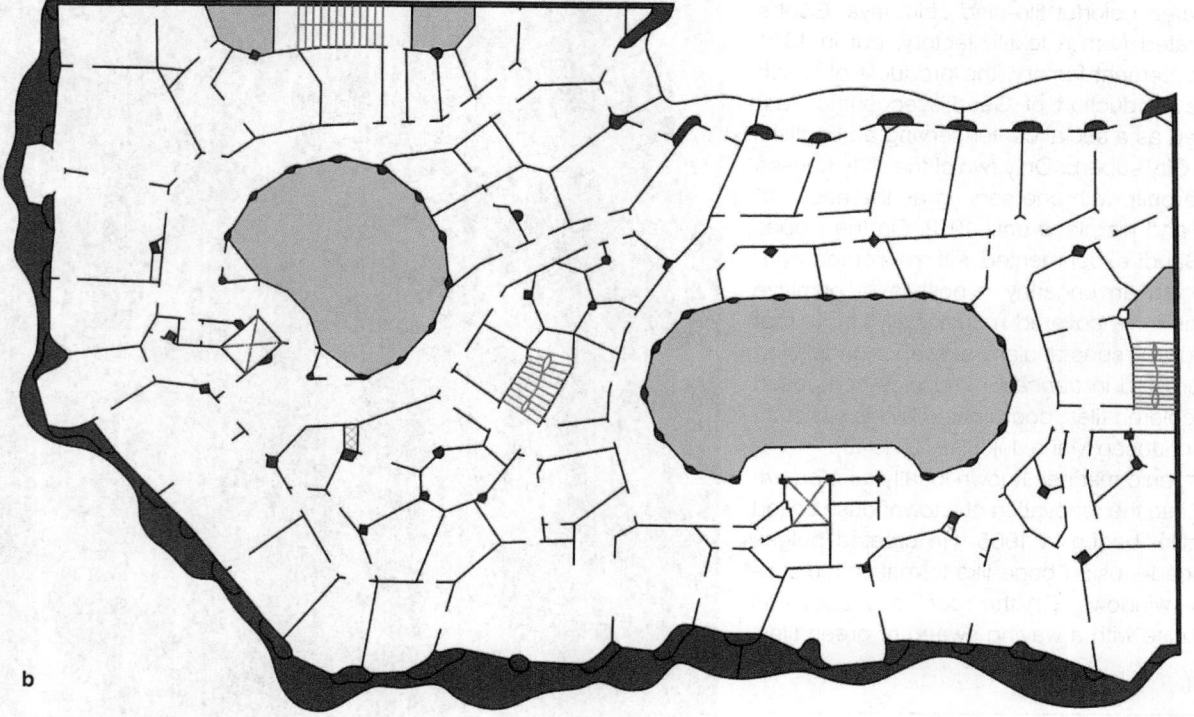

Figure 17.3-12 Barcelona. (a) Casa Milà, Gaudí, 1905. (b) Plan of eight apartments, with no right angle used anywhere. (c) See facing page.

Figure 17.3-12 Barcelona.
(c) Roofscape of Casa Milà.

like the scaly spine of a dragon, which served as a metaphor of Catalan independence.

Between 1905 and 1907 Gaudí brought his passion for undulating surfaces to a climax in the Casa Milà (Fig. 17.3-12a), a large apartment complex on one of the most prominent corners of Cerdá's *Ensanche*. Despite his skill with concrete, Gaudí preferred to build in stone, and the block is commonly known as *La Pedrera*, or the quarry. The warped surfaces appeared like a parasitical deformation of Cerdá's rational imprint. Gaudí categorically avoided right angles on the facade and in the plan (Fig. 17.3-12b). No two rooms had the same shape. The exterior rose like an eroded cliff, dotted with dark caves. Kelp-like iron balustrades spilled over the shelves of its balconies. The undulating roof served as a theater for anthropomorphic chimneys, twisting like a legion of helmeted knights, ready to defend Gaudí's "modern" cave dwellers (Fig. 17.3-12c).

In late-nineteenth-century Vienna, the word "modern" acquired an entirely different meaning. Otto Wagner (1841–1918), who had worked with the leading eclectic architects of the Ringstrasse, attempted in the early 1890s to create a style suited to the changes of modern life. He proposed in *Modern Architecture* (1896) that the "architecture of the future will be based on utility alone." He envisioned a *Groszstadt*, a continually expanding high-density city with regularly spaced parks for relief. Wagner's association with Art Nouveau became evident in his greatest encounter with utility, the major infrastructural planning for the Viennese *Stadtbahn* subway system, begun in 1894. This project entailed the design of tunnels, fifteen bridges and viaducts, thirty-six stations, and 45 km (30 miles) of level

track. While Wagner's stations appeared more reserved than those of Guimard in Paris, their decorative ironwork and mosaics belonged to the whiplash aesthetic. The pair of pavilions at the Karlsplatz Station (Fig. 17.3-13) used an ingenious frame of wrought-iron mullions to fasten white marble panels inlaid with gilded floral decorations. They illustrated Wagner's definition of "modern" architecture as an art generated from "the lines of load and support, the panel-like treatment of surfaces, the greatest simplicity, and an energetic emphasis on construction and material." Wagner applied this system to a larger-scale project, the Postal Savings Bank, built in Vienna from 1903 to 1912. Here, he clamped thin sheets of granite cladding into place with aluminum nubs, which then became the facade's principal ornament.

In 1897 the dissident younger generation of Vienna, many of whom worked for or were taught by Wagner, gathered around the painter Gustav Klimt (1862–1918), whose erotic paintings had scandalized the bourgeoisie and given youthful impetus to the Secession movement. The following year Wagner's assistant, Josef Maria Olbrich (1867–1908), built the Secession House near the Karlsplatz Station. Financed by the prominent industrialist Karl Wittgenstein, father of the philosopher Ludwig, the hall carried the inscription "To each age its art, to art its freedom," advertising its purpose as a venue for avant-garde art and design. In line with Wagner's demand for a modern break from academic styles, the Secession House diverged from the Art Nouveau love of undulating lines and irregular spaces, proving as orthogonal and symmetrical as a classical temple, with stylized foliage clustered into squared-off shapes at the junctures of the facade (Fig. 17.3-14). The central entry

Figure 17.3-13 Vienna. Karlsplatz Station, Otto Wagner, 1898.

Figure 17.3-14 Vienna. Secession House, Josef Maria Olbrich, 1898.

Figure 17.3-15 Darmstadt, Germany. Ernst Ludwig Exhibition Hall at Mathildenhöhe, Olbrich, 1904.

element stepped back from two blank, horizontal wings to thrust up four pylons that carried a sphere of gilded laurel leaves. The foliated ball was Olbrich's alternative to a dome.

Impressed with Olbrich's exploit, the grand duke of Hesse, Germany, coaxed him and the painter Peter Behrens to join the utopian adventure of Mathildenhöhe at Darmstadt. From 1899 until his death in 1908, Olbrich had free rein to build over a dozen structures of the artists' colony, most of which adhered to the planar language of his teacher. The Wedding Tower and the Ernst Ludwig Exhibition Hall (Fig. 17.3-15) illustrated the prominent role of artists in the colony, its archway encrusted with golden mosaics and two colossal figures, a David-like boy and an Athena-like girl, on the steps. Olbrich even produced a model worker's residence, similar to the prototypes planned by Heinrich Tessenow.

Josef Hoffmann, Olbrich's colleague in Wagner's office, excelled as the premier designer of furniture for the Wiener Werkstätte. In 1905, a wealthy Belgian patron lured Hoffmann to Brussels, the home of Art Nouveau, to build the Palais Stoclet (Fig. 17.3-16). There, he further explored the planar language of Wagner, using smooth marble panels to create a composition of crisply defined volumes outlined with bronze, brocade-like frames. His patron also commissioned Klimt to prepare a 14 m (46 ft) long mosaic backdrop for the dining room. The architect coordinated all of the furnishings and decorations as a total design effort. The cubic sequence of the exterior culminated in a tower that stepped up to a platform supporting four heroic figures that surrounded a laurel-leaf dome evoking the Secession House in Vienna.

The attempt by the Art Nouveau generation of designers to control all aspects of design and infuse every centimeter of surface with art inspired the Viennese architect and critic Adolf Loos (1870–1933) to write his 1908 diatribe "Ornament and Crime." Considering the movement alongside the tattooed inhabitants of New Guinea and the graffiti scrawled in public toilets, Loos maintained that the more evolved a society, the less it needed decoration. "The day will come," he chided, "when the furnishing of a prison cell by the court decorator Schultz or by Professor van de Velde will be

Figure 17.3-16 Brussels. Stoclet Palace, Josef Hoffmann, 1905.

considered to be an aggravation of the penalty." As an antidote he offered the Museum Café in Vienna, an interior he had designed near the Secession House in 1899. Its minimal decoration earned the space the nickname the "Nihilist Café." Instead of specially designed furniture, he insisted on standard cane chairs and left exposed electrical conduits as decorative patterns. Loos reduced the language of his houses to white plastered boxes with a few apertures, such as the 1926 Müller House in Prague (Fig. 17.3-17a,b). He argued that a house should not be designed as a work of art but as a place to hang works of art. The section of his houses, however, revealed a complex series of level changes, what Loos called *Raumplan*, for which he used a relatively open plan while giving the impression of divisions between rooms.

In 1910 Loos built his most prominent example of restraint, the Goldman & Salatsch store, now known as

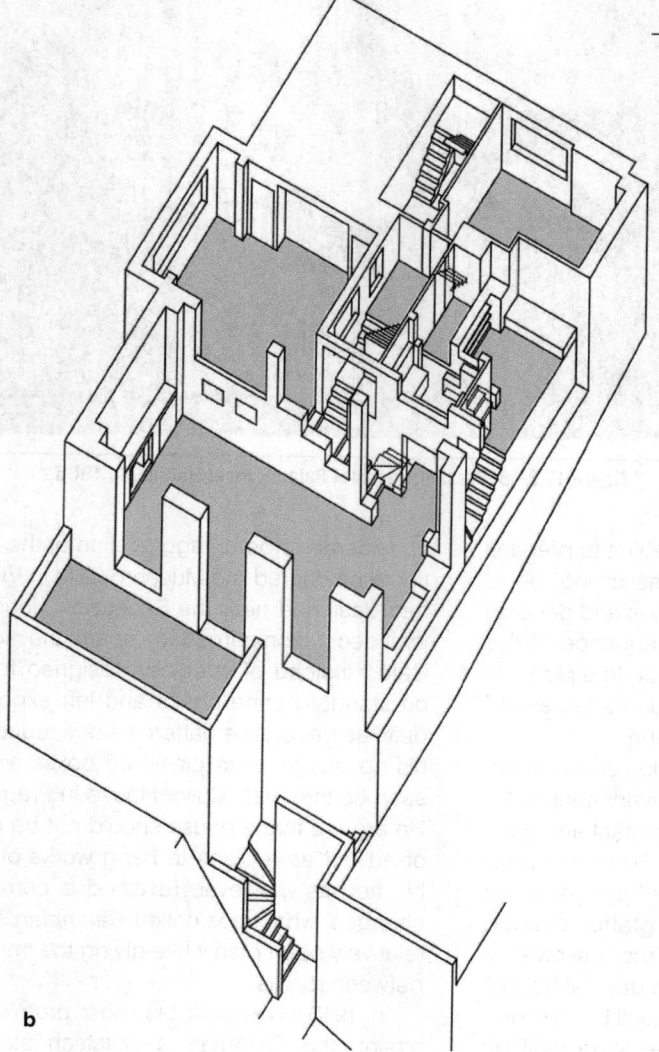

Figure 17.3-17 Prague. (a) Müller House, exterior, Adolf Loos, 1926. (b) Axon, showing *raumplan*.

a

b

**Figure 17.3-18
Vienna. Goldman
& Salatsch (today
Looshaus), Loos,
1909.**

Looshaus (Fig. 17.3-18), across from Vienna's imperial palace. Here, he allowed the materials themselves to serve as the ornament, rendering the four structural columns at the entry and the street level in luxurious green *cipollina* marble while leaving the upper four stories unadorned and treating the windows as simple rectangular apertures within walls of smooth plaster. Through rational composition, understatement, and refined materials, Loos struggled against the excesses of signification produced by both those obsessed with history and those who wanted to free themselves from history through applied art.

Further Reading

Ballilari, D., and E. Godoli. *Istanbul 1900*. Florence: Octavo, 1995.

Britton, Karla. *Auguste Perret*. New York: Phaidon, 2001.

Clausen, Meredith L. *Frantz Jourdain and the Samaritaine: Art Nouveau Theory and Criticism*. Leiden, the Netherlands: E. J. Brill, 1987.

Frampton, Kenneth. *Studies in Tectonic Culture: The Poetics of Construction in Nineteenth and Twentieth Century Architecture*. Cambridge, MA: MIT Press, 1995.

Sembach, Klaus-Jürgen. *Art Nouveau, Utopia: Reconciling the Irreconcilable*. Cologne, Germany: Benedict Taschen, 1991.

↗ Visit the free website **www.oup.com/us/ingersoll** to view chapter outlines and study questions; Google Maps showing the location of key sites; links to UNESCO World Heritage Sites; and essays on topics that cross time and culture.

1920–1940

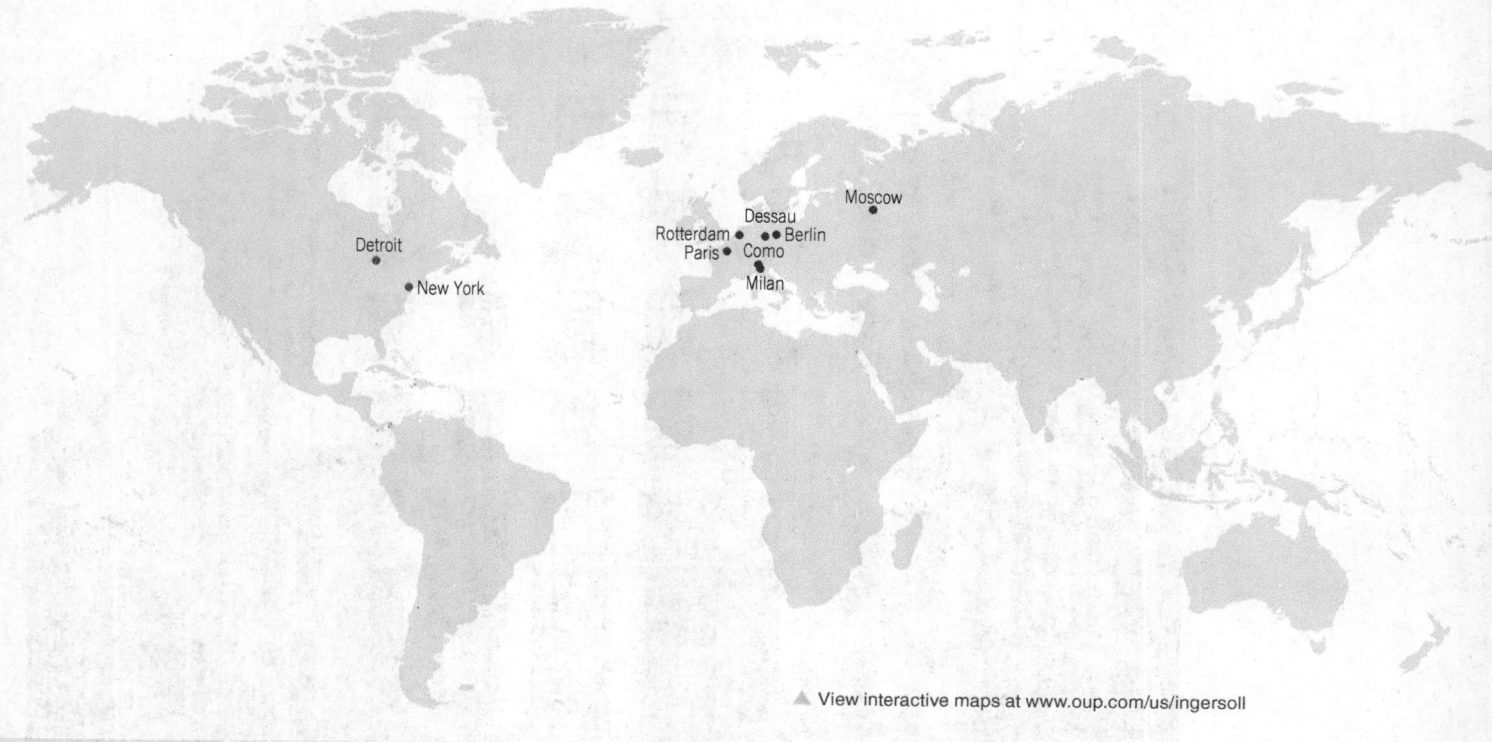

▲ View interactive maps at www.oup.com/us/ingersoll

18.1 **AMERICAN SKYSCRAPERS AND AUTOMOBILES:** Mass Production Meets Individualism

18.2 **EUROPEAN MODERNISMS:** A Dialogue between Form and Function

18.3 **TOTALITARIAN SETTINGS IN MODERN EUROPE:** Architecture as Propaganda

In the race toward industrial development, Americans felt fewer ties to existing contexts and social relations than their counterparts across the Atlantic. They seemed comfortable with the quick changes of mechanization, from the use of elevators in tall buildings and subway systems to the profusion of automobiles and their mass production in factories. Manhattan and Chicago sprouted dozens of office towers, radically changing the urban scale. In Detroit Henry Ford perfected the automobile assembly line and at the same time offered workers better hours and conditions. The automobile soon insinuated itself into American culture as the central item of consumerism, leading individuals to consume greater quantities of resources. European Modernists remained enchanted by the American break from the past, celebrating the nation's grain silos, skyscrapers, and automobiles as a new basis of beauty. Le Corbusier, the Bauhaus, and the Dutch and Russian avant-gardes produced critical urban visions inspired by the American precedents. After 1929, as the global economic situation deteriorated into capitalism's worst economic crisis, totalitarian regimes in Italy, Germany, and other countries swept to power, proposing a return to grand imperialist settings to complement their ideologies of control.

18.1 AMERICAN SKYSCRAPERS AND AUTOMOBILES
Mass Production Meets Individualism

Until the twentieth century the scale of architecture related primarily to the human body. Even such colossal structures as the pyramids at Teotihuacán and the dome of the Taj Mahal corresponded to a landscape determined by human footsteps. During the first three decades of the twentieth century, however, Americans astounded the world with a new kind of scale related to machines and mechanical production. Tall buildings pushed several times above the traditional seven-story height, fragmenting the skylines.

At the same time, elevated highways directed toward the suburbs broke down the lateral dimensions of the urban fabric. American builders, pushed by a new breed of corporate executive, ruthlessly tore apart skylines and urban edges without concern for traditional scale or historic contexts. Their tools of construction became the hydraulic lift elevator, the steel frame, reinforced concrete, and the internal combustion engine. Cliff-like skyscrapers and fast motorcars took command of the environment. The wild dynamism of the streets and buildings of New York and Chicago came as the consequence of the expedient and unregulated world of deficit financing and rampant real estate speculation that unleashed the catastrophic global economic depression of 1929.

Manhattanism and the Crisis of Capitalism

Skyscrapers, structured on steel girders and equipped with high-speed elevators, became America's most important contribution to architecture. They reached maturity during the period that the United States pulled ahead as the world's leading industrial power. While the devastations of World War I (1914–1918) left the industrial powers of Europe in tatters, American industries thrived. The booming economy of the 1920s encouraged the financing of dozens of skyscrapers in New York and Chicago, and at least one crowning tower appeared in every major American city. This rash of tall buildings included the forty-story City Hall Building in Los Angeles, the forty-two-story Cathedral of Learning in suburban Pittsburgh, and the fifty-two-story Terminal Complex in central Cleveland. The tower soaring over the Nebraska State Capitol Building (1922) (Fig. 18.1-1), set in the prairie flatlands

Figure 18.1-1 Lincoln, Nebraska. State Capitol, Bertram Goodhue, 1922.

of Lincoln, became an emblem of the new type. Its designer, Bertram Goodhue (1869–1924), the creator of exquisite Neo-Gothic and Neo-Byzantine schools and churches, realized that the innovative techniques and unprecedented scale of the skyscraper demanded a new architectural language. He stripped away historical references from the upper shaft of the capitol building and let the stepped massing and vertical lines of the structure define the building's style.

Most high-rise projects designed at the beginning of the 1920s still relied on some form of historicist detail to accentuate their verticality. The winning entry to the 1922 Chicago Tribune Tower Competition, by Raymond Hood (1881–1934) and John Mead Howells (1868–1959), carried a crown of flying buttresses on its eight-story Neo-Gothic pinnacle (Fig. 18.1-2). The newspaper dispatched a traveling exhibition to major American cities featuring the winner and many of the 265 competition entries for "the most beautiful skyscraper in the world." While skyscrapers had yet to be built in Europe, several European architects, including Walter Gropius, proposed the most daring solutions, completely eliminating decoration from their structures.

In New York, the convergence of mass transportation, real estate speculation, advertising, deficit spending, and architectural ambitions intensified the growth of a dense, vertical city. The 1916 **Zoning** Law was precipitated by the completion in 1915 of the Equitable Building, by the firm of Graham, Anderson, Probst & White (the successor to Burnham's firm). As the world's largest office building, it reproduced the area of the lot it stood on thirty times. Municipal authorities imposed the limit of the "floor area ratio" of 12:1 on future buildings and proposed five different prescriptions for the heights of street facades that varied according to the type of street. This trend, later called "Manhattanism," was characterized by the step-back of the massing of commercial towers, driven more by the market than by aesthetic considerations. While not limiting the overall height of buildings, the law imposed setbacks at regular intervals to allow an angle of daylight into the street, resulting in the ziggurat profiles of New York skyscrapers during the 1920s. The 1926 Paramount Building on Times Square by Rapp & Rapp offered a diagrammatic example of the rule, with thirty-three stories stepping back seven times before reaching a crowning clock tower and illuminated orb.

Raymond Hood, a Beaux-Arts-trained architect, was among the first to respond to the 1916 Zoning Law in search of a distinctive New York skyscraper style. His twenty-three-story American Radiator Building of 1924 became a model of stepped massing (Fig. 18.1-3a). He clad the steel frame in black bricks to reduce the contrast between the dark window hollows and the walls. The golden finials capping each structural bay repeated in miniature the geometry of the tower's stepped forms. Many of Hood's projects were presented in perspective views by the gifted draftsman Hugh Ferriss (1889–1962). Like Piranesi, Ferriss created sublime visions, but instead of seeking inspiration from the past, he probed into the future, extrapolating forms generated by the 1916 Zoning Law into ziggurat profiles with zigzag decorations (Fig. 18.1-3b).

The serrated patterns encouraged by the Zoning Law culminated in the two tallest skyscrapers of what came to be known as the Zigzag Moderne style, the seventy-seven-story Chrysler Building (Fig. 18.1-4) by William Van Alen (1883–1954) and the eighty-six-story Empire State Building by Shreve, Lamb & Harmon, both begun in the fateful year of 1929, a few months before the stock market crash triggered the Great Depression. The Chrysler Building indulged in lively geometric decorations, including a seven-tiered starburst steeple. Such details as hubcaps in the friezes and corner gargoyles derived from the hood ornaments of the Chrysler automobile enhanced the tower's role as advertising.

By the end of the decade Hood had refined his skyscraper palette with his design for the 1929 Daily News Building, in which he pursued a more functionalist approach. He eliminated superfluous decorative details and used staggered massing and contrasting materials to create style. Vertical stripes of smooth, gleaming white brick cladding over the structural piers alternated with black and red window and spandrel shafts. Instead of a crowning pinnacle, the slab-like tower ended in an unadorned flat top. Only the thirty-four-story PSFS Building in Philadelphia (Fig. 18.1-5), begun in the same year by Swiss émigré William Lescaze (1896–1969), the new partner of George Howe (1886–1955), surpassed Hood's functionalism. The architects built the six-story plinth as a streamlined, highly polished, granite-clad corner, with shops on the ground floor and the banking hall in a grand, double-height space above, reached by one of the world's first escalators. They articulated the twenty-six-story shaft with exposed structural piers on the broad sides and pushed out the short

---

TIME LINE

▼ **1908**

Ford establishes assembly-line factory near Detroit, Michigan

Ford's opens New Shop factory in Highland Park, Michigan

▲ **1909**

▼ **1914–1918**

World War I involves most European nations and the late-entry United States

▲ **1929**

Stock market crash in New York spurs global economic depression

▼ **1929**

Van Alen's Chrysler Building begun in New York City

CONSTRUCTION, TECHNOLOGY, THEORY

Eliel Saarinen's Skyscraper City

The runner-up design for the Tribune Building competition, by Finnish architect Eliel Saarinen, had a greater influence than the winner on the taste for step-back massing and clustered geometrical ornament derived from the tower's structure. In 1923 Saarinen left Finland for Chicago, where he proposed an ideal urban solution for the skyscraper city. In his unbuilt project for a forty-story, ziggurat-like tower he envisioned a large enclosed plaza framed by two levels of shops. He layered the complex with a plinth, submerging fast automobile traffic and parking below grade, while leaving slower streets for pedestrians above. Saarinen imagined the skyscraper as a means to combine modern infrastructure and civic space.

Chicago. Project for the Grant Hotel, Eliel Saarinen, 1923.

northern side with a slight cantilever. Juxtaposed to this skeletal tower stood a solid tower for circulation and services on the south. The building terminated with flat roofs, one serving as a restaurant terrace, where the obliquely set "PSFS" logo concealed the mechanicals. Among its many innovations, the PSFS Building contained one of the first air-conditioning systems and an escalator in its banking hall.

By 1920 New York had surpassed London, Tokyo, and Paris as the biggest city in the world, becoming the fulcrum of world capitalism. The Stock Exchange on Wall Street set

Rockefeller Center designed by Associated Architects in New York City

▲ **1930–1939**

▼ **1936**

Wright's Fallingwater built in Bear Run, Pennsylvania

Wright's Johnson Wax Building built in Racine, Wisconsin

▲ **1939**

Figure 18.1-2 Chicago. Tribune Tower, Raymond Hood and John Mead Howells, 1922–1925.

had been overconfident in their belief in eternally expanding markets, backed by overly lenient lending policies. While construction continued on several of the tallest towers, including the Empire State Building, some sites abruptly shut down.

At the outset of the Great Depression, when economic gloom inhibited most development, several of the protagonists of Manhattanism collaborated on their most audacious project, Rockefeller Center (Fig. 18.1-6). Construction began in 1930 and terminated in 1939, just as the crisis was waning. Financed by America's wealthiest tycoon, John D. Rockefeller, Jr. (1874–1960), the project employed a significant portion of New York's construction industry. Unlike other Manhattan skyscraper projects, it was conceived as a set of coordinated buildings with the same kind of civic attention that Eliel Saarinen had envisioned for Chicago. Hood coordinated a consortium of several firms, known as the "Associated Architects," including the technical office of Reinhard & Hofmeister, Harvey Wiley Corbett (1873–1954), and the young Wallace K. Harrison (1895–1981) (see Section 19.1). They configured the three-block site with a central tall tower and three midsized towers, flanked by a few lower buildings. To break up the long Manhattan blocks, they introduced a private cross street and a generous open plaza. Although the project began as the home for the Metropolitan Opera House, its program evolved into a series of fourteen rent-producing office buildings for large corporate clients, and after the Opera withdrew, the builders inserted Radio City Music Hall into the rear of the site, creating an immense theater with 6,000 seats.

the pace of global financial markets, and the city's bristling landscape of towers expressed the aggressive, often cutthroat, competition of American business. The credit crisis that devastated the economy in November 1929 was partly the result of overproduction. Major industries, particularly automobile manufacturing and real estate development,

The RCA Building, a seventy-story giant at the center of the complex, followed the example of Hood's Daily News Building as a series of stepped-back slabs ending in a flat top. The narrow two-bay width of each slab ensured good access to natural light and ventilation. The privately sponsored shopping concourse at its base sloped gently down to a sunken

Figure 18.1-3 New York. (a) Tower of the American Radiator Building, Hood, 1924. (b) Sketch of 1925 pyramidal massing for high-rises according to the 1916 zoning ordinance, from Hugh Ferriss, Metropolis of Tomorrow, 1929.

plaza, presided over by a gilded statue of Prometheus. A reflecting pool picked up the summer light and in the winter was transformed into an ice-skating rink. To glorify the entrance, the patrons hired the Mexican muralist Diego Rivera (1886–1957) to create a fresco, but because of its controversial political content, which included a portrait of Vladimir Lenin (1870–1924), the leader of the Bolshevik Revolution, they replaced it with a more generic work. As if to counteract the ideological threat, Rockefeller installed a plaque overlooking the plaza with his capitalist creed: "I believe in the supreme worth of the individual."

In a city characterized by brutal contrasts in scale and style, Rockefeller Center appeared homogeneous and humanely scaled. All of the different structures respected a standard bay system based on the widths of vertical piers and were uniformly clad in tan-colored sandstone.

Figure 18.1-4 New York. Chrysler Building, William Van Alen, 1929–1931.

A marvelous new type of privately owned public space emerged by integrating infrastructure, including a subway connection, an underground area for truck loading, and an 800-car parking garage, with entertainment facilities, shops, and offices. Manhattanism achieved a remarkable work of civic richness despite its speculative origins.

following the recommendations of efficiency expert Frederick Winslow Taylor (1856–1915), author of *Principles of Scientific Management* (1911). By timing actions, observing the amount of wasted movements, and training workers to do a single task, Taylor streamlined production practices around the standardization of piecework. While workers resented this infringement on their individuality, factory owners and managers embraced Taylor's efficiency methods, eager to reap rewards from the increased productivity.

By the time Henry Ford (1863–1947) decided to build his first automobile factory in Detroit, Taylorism had taken root. Ford's significant innovation, the assembly line, permitted the systematic flow of materials and products along mechanical conveyor belts, borrowed from the meatpacking plants of Chicago. Albert Kahn (1869–1942) designed the initial Ford factory, or Old Shop, at Highland Park (1908–1910) as a long, four-story concrete-frame box, completely glazed, with steel-sash bays. His only nods to art were the projecting cornice, the brick towers at the corners, and the Ford Motor Company sign on the roof. The well-lit open lofts of the interior permitted the assembly line to sort materials on conveyor belts. As workers joined pieces, they sent them through voids cut between the floors until the process reached the heavier stage of work on the chassis, conducted at ground level. Ford's New Shop, built next door in 1914, improved the delivery between levels by leaving a six-story void in the center for a mobile gantry.

Ford revolutionized the market for automobiles with the Model T, transforming what had been a luxury item into one that the middle class could afford. The mass production of a single optimal model cut the price more than 50% during the first five years of production. By 1920 the Model T accounted for over half of the automobiles made in the world, and Ford, as an inventor and entrepreneur, appeared the demiurge of industrial capitalism.

Albert Kahn, Ford's architect, also worked for most of his competitors, building the factories and office buildings of

Detroit, Ford, and the Assembly Line

Beyond Manhattan and Chicago, Detroit accumulated the greatest collection of skyscrapers during the 1920s. As the hub of the powerful automobile industries, it hatched the scientific management of Taylorism, the assembly lines of Fordism, and the marketing strategies of Sloanism. The boost these developments gave to mass production ushered in a consumer society. By 1925, one in five Americans owned an automobile, and at least one-third of the national economy depended on its production.

During the late nineteenth century many American industrialists reorganized their factories as integrated systems

Figure 18.1-6 New York. Rockefeller Center, Associated Architects, 1929–1939.

Packard, Chrysler, and General Motors. Kahn's office designed more than 2,000 factories in the United States. Like Ford, Kahn was a self-made man, working his way up as the son of an immigrant Jewish rabbi from Germany. He applied the methods of mass production to design, breaking down tasks into the same sort of division of labor found in the factories, with departments for management, design, field supervision, specifications, and engineering services. By the 1930s, Kahn ran the largest architectural office in the world, employing about 400 workers. Despite its impersonal scale, Kahn's office remained a family enterprise, dependent on his four brothers. One brother, Julius, specialized in engineering and patented the Kahn System of Reinforced Concrete used on all of their projects. Another brother ran the foreign export sector, which in the 1930s built over 500 factories in the Soviet Union that produced the Fordson tractor, which made Ford as much of a hero in Russia as Lenin.

European Modernists admired Kahn's factories as the direct expression of function. For Gropius in 1913, and Le Corbusier and others soon after, American factories and grain silos represented the unconscious monumental output of American pragmatism. Kahn did not share their enthusiasm for the use of the factory aesthetic in public or commercial projects and, when designing office buildings, applied the Beaux-Arts manner of McKim, Mead & White. Likewise, he believed that industrial structures should not be conceived as autonomous works of art because of the frequent changes required by industry. His own most widely admired industrial structure, the 1922 Ford Glass Plant for making windshields, underwent significant alterations over the years. It sat on part of Ford's River Rouge compound, south of Detroit, which had the new advantage of transportation access to the river. The factory site involved more than 100,000 workers in a horizontal flow of production, dispersed among a series of oblong, single-story structures. Five rail tracks dispatched the sorted

raw materials from the canal to specific production buildings and the 1 km (0.6 mile) long High Line warehouse. Distinct from the other production halls, the Glass Plant shone like a crystal, clad in continuous steel-sash **glazing** and capped with butterfly monitors. The four smokestacks for its blast furnaces stood like a colossal colonnade in front of the structure.

American urban life changed dramatically with Ford's democratization of the automobile, leading to widened streets, stoplights, parking garages, service stations, traffic jams, rampant suburbanization, and over 30,000 automobile-related deaths per year. In the meantime, as the internal combustion engine spread, emitting lethal quantities of carbon dioxide, the air quality of American cities began to decline. Ford, as the protagonist of automobile culture, actively campaigned against the growth of large cities such as New York and Chicago. "We shall solve the city problem by leaving the city," he announced and proposed his Model T as the means to do so. Ford recommended combining

Figure 18.1-7 Clinch River, Tennessee. Norris Dam, built for the TVA by Roland Wank, 1933.

agriculture and industry on rural sites and attempted to lead a program for industrial and urban decentralization in connection with the U.S. Army's plan to build a dam at Muscle Shoals, Tennessee, in 1922. While Ford's program for rural development never materialized, a decade later it resurfaced under the Tennessee Valley Authority (TVA). This government agency inserted a series of dams along the Tennessee River, spanning seven southern states from Tennessee to Alabama. Managed by President Franklin Delano Roosevelt's Public Works Administration as a means to curtail unemployment, the TVA applied regional planning to handle such issues as hydroelectric power, flood control, reforestation, the development of new rural towns, and highways. The TVA's chief architect, Roland Wank (1898–1970), a Hungarian émigré trained by Viennese Secession masters, arrived in New York in 1924. He designed his first independent project, the 1933 Norris Dam (Fig. 18.1-7), with the technical advice of Albert Kahn. The dam included lookout plazas at either end of a road spanning its crest. Wank articulated his concrete buildings with alternating horizontal and vertical patterns embossed by the wooden formwork. This use of rusticated concrete became a precursor for Brutalism, popularized by Le Corbusier, who visited Norris Dam in 1947. From 1933 until the program's conclusion in 1944, Wank designed seven dams and numerous service structures, combining monumental unity with the decorative details of Zigzag Moderne.

The economic crisis of the Great Depression partly resulted from Ford's failure to comprehend mass markets. While he excelled in flexible methods of production, he remained inflexible about his product. He conceived the Model T in 1908 and still insisted on its production in 1926. The company had sold over 15 million identical black cars during two decades, but by the end of the 1920s Ford's sales had plummeted 30%, resulting in massive layoffs in the factories. Ford's chief rival, Alfred P. Sloan, Jr. (1875–1966), the vice president of General Motors (GM), introduced styling and packaging as new sales strategies. Consumers could now choose Chevrolets and Cadillacs in many different styles and colors. Sloan also initiated "research and development" to stimulate technological improvements. Two of GM's improvements, leaded gas and the coolant Freon, while initially solving efficiency problems, spawned disastrous environmental consequences for future generations. Sloan converted the automobile industry to the "science" of marketing, which became as important to automotive design as technological changes. His move from Detroit to offices in Rockefeller Center during the 1930s indicates how important communications became in the recovery from the Great Depression.

From New York City Sloan guided one of GM's most successful publicity stunts, the Futurama exhibition, staged in the GM Pavilion, at the 1939 World's Fair in New York City (Fig. 18.1-8). Stage designer Norman Bel Geddes (1893–1958) created a major set piece—a silvery, curving volume that simulated the aerodynamic teardrop shapes used for automobile bodies. Once inside, the visitor sat on a conveyor belt, just like an assembly line, and traveled through a vision of the American city twenty years hence, depicted in animated scale models. Bel Geddes predicted for 1960 a country dominated by automobiles, served by fourteen-lane freeways and grand interchanges set amid skyscrapers. At the exit one encountered a full-scale mockup of an urban intersection served by aerial walkways overlooking motionless cars. The Futurama exhibition glorified the automobile's impact on the American city, which by plan or by default became a scattered landscape of urban sprawl.

Frank Lloyd Wright: The Hero of Usonia

During the Great Depression, Frank Lloyd Wright reemerged with a series of stunning Modernist projects. Like Ford, he detested the metropolis and, several years before the Futurama exhibition, produced sketches and models of Broadacre City, a vision of a decentralized urban future. Wright returned to Thomas Jefferson's notion that every American deserved an acre of land. If this rural ideal could be enacted, the city would begin to disappear. In 1935 he exhibited Broadacre City, his antidote to New York, in the

The Radburn Plan

Radburn, New Jersey (1929), was planned as an experimental suburb of New York City, promoted by the Regional Planning Association of America, whose most prominent member was the critic Lewis Mumford (1895–1990). Somewhat like Frank Lloyd Wright's campaign to decentralize urban growth, the plan, devised by Clarence Stein and Henry Wright, revived Ebenezer Howard's Garden City concept for the American automobile suburb in an effort to conserve land as it was being developed. Only partially completed, the 500 detached houses of Radburn were distributed around cul-de-sacs set in a superblock. Instead of facing the roads, the front porches stood on the rear of the buildings, where they opened to a collective park that connected to other cul-de-sacs. The landscape designer, Marjorie Sewell Cautley, created an internal path that tucked under the automobile roads so that children could walk from their homes to school or the shops without encountering automobiles.

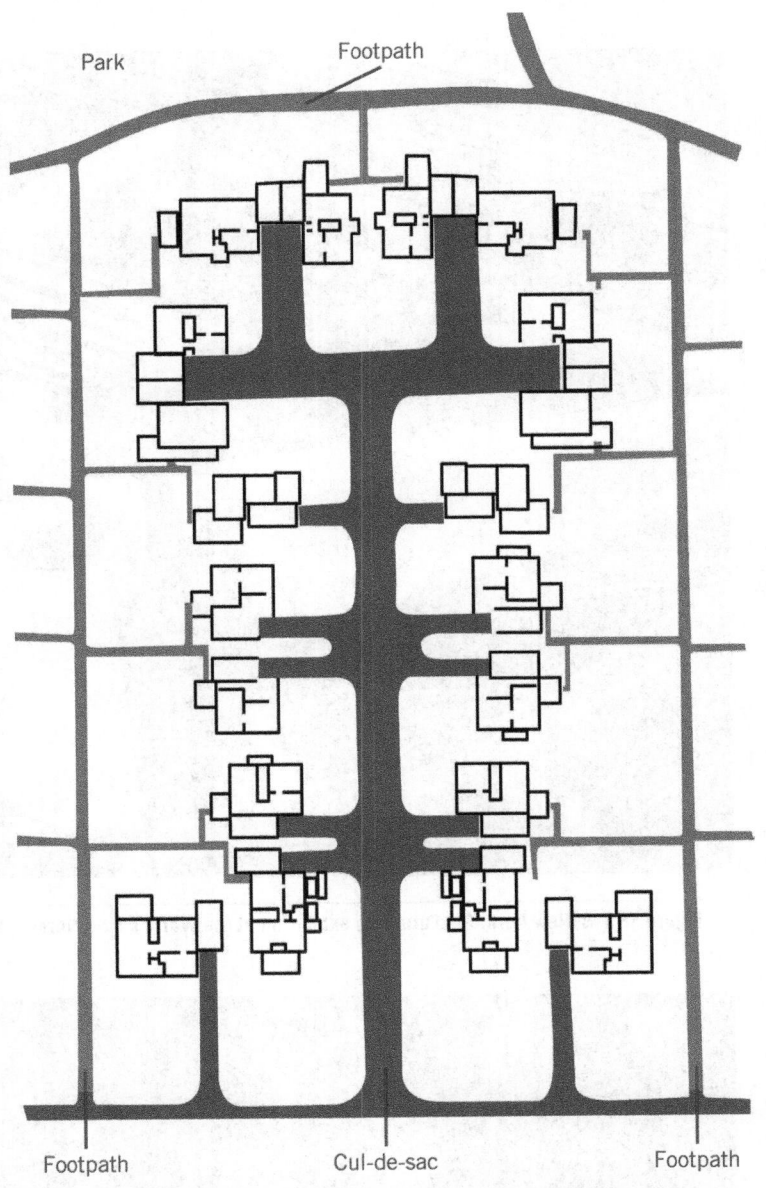

Radburn, New Jersey. Cul-de-sac, Clarence Stein and Henry Wright, 1929.

heart of that city at Rockefeller Center. He dreamed of a network of freeways and individual air travel that would allow the city to be "everywhere and nowhere." All of Wright's later works belonged to this rural vision, from his affordable houses to the great corporate headquarters for Johnson Wax to the brook-side exploit of Fallingwater. The one exception, the Guggenheim Museum on Fifth Avenue, faced the great natural void of Central Park. He designed its upwardly spiraling swirl in defiance of New York's rigid "boxment."

Wright renamed the country "Usonia," short for the United States of North America, and called his affordable houses "Usonian," intending them as the architectural equivalent of

the Model T. Unlike European solutions to low-income housing, which with rare exceptions involved large, multiple-unit structures, Wright insisted on the detached dwelling and the value of American individualism. He designed several prototypes that could be assembled by their owners and built twenty-eight examples during his last two decades. The first Jacobs House (1936) (Fig. 18.1-9a,b) near Madison, Wisconsin, cost $5,500, about half the price of a typical single-family house at that time. Its *L*-shaped plan presented the closed side to the street and the open side, lined with tall windows, to a backyard terrace. Wright clustered services in a brick core that included a concrete cellar, a hearth, the kitchen, and the bathroom. He eliminated radiators by putting heating coils in the concrete paving. The living room and dining niche fit into one wing, while the two small bedrooms and a study filled a staggered row along the other. Stiffer masonry elements supported two levels of flat wooden roofs and shouldered the light sandwich walls made of horizontal board-and-batten panels nailed to either side of a balloon frame. A band of clerestories accentuated

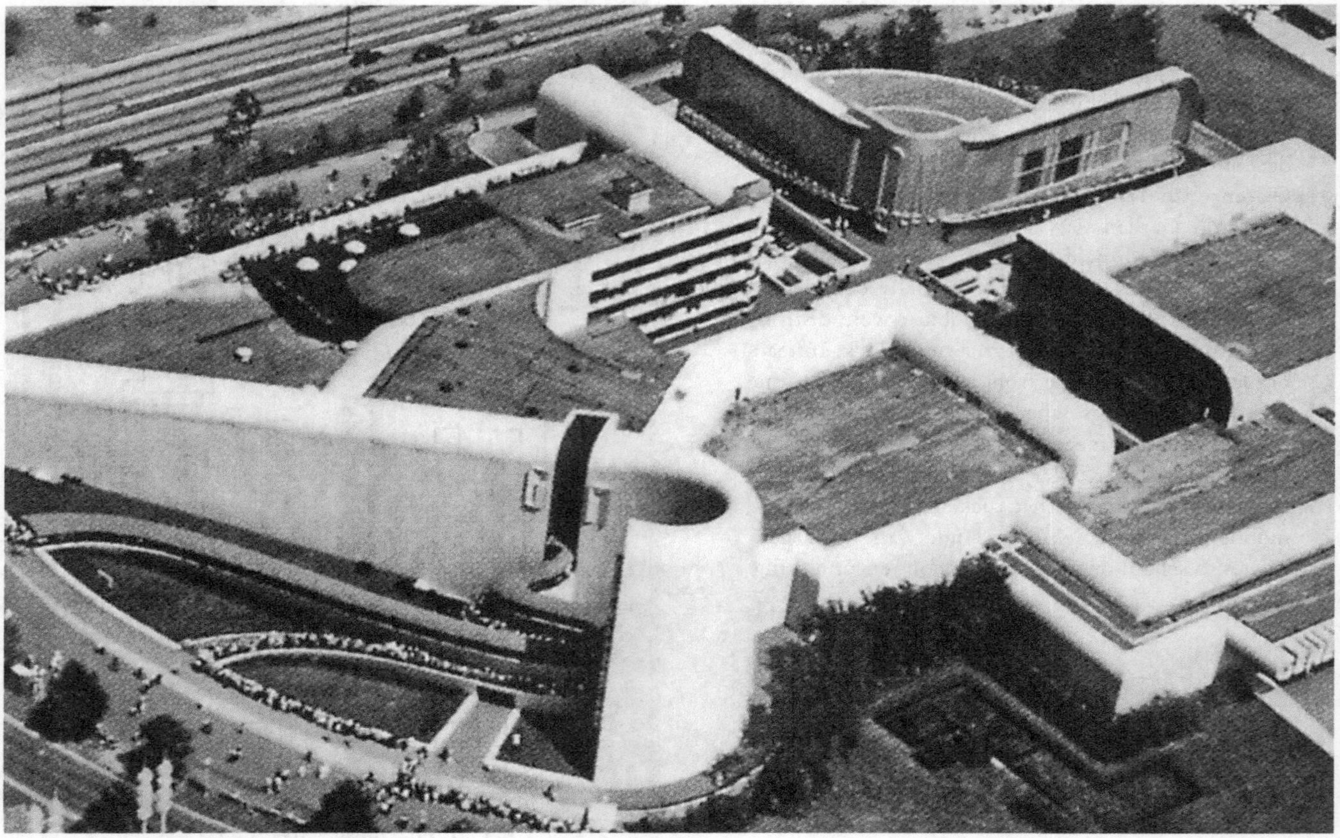

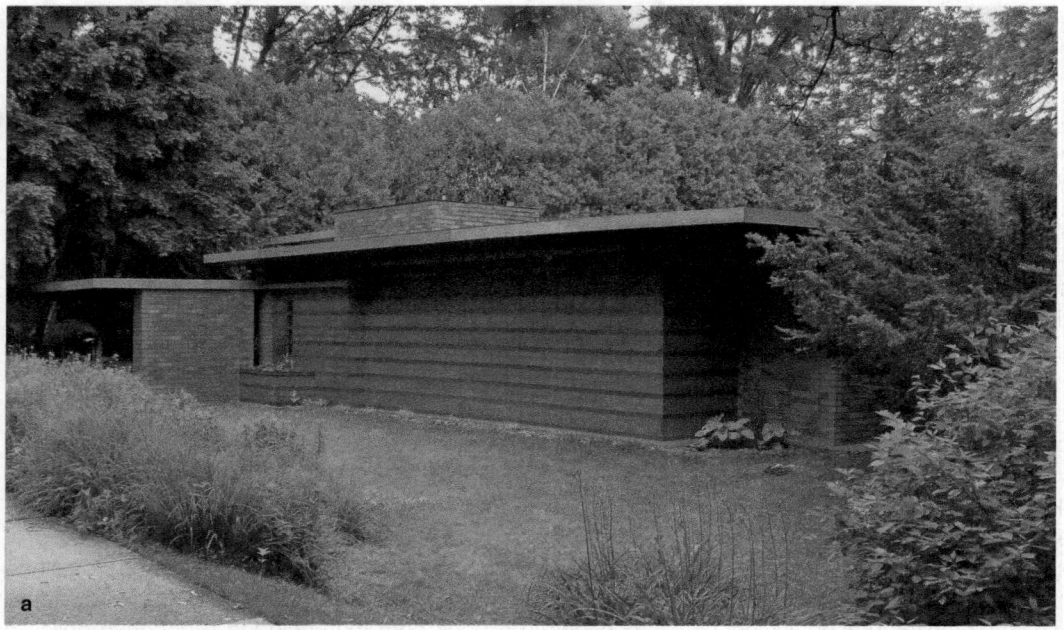

Figure 18.1-8 New York. GM Futurama exhibition at the World's Fair, Norman Bel Geddes, 1939.

a

Figure 18.1-9 (a) Madison, Wisconsin. First Jacobs House, Frank Lloyd Wright, 1936. (b) See facing page.

Figure 18.1-9b Plan, first Jacobs House, Wright, 1936.

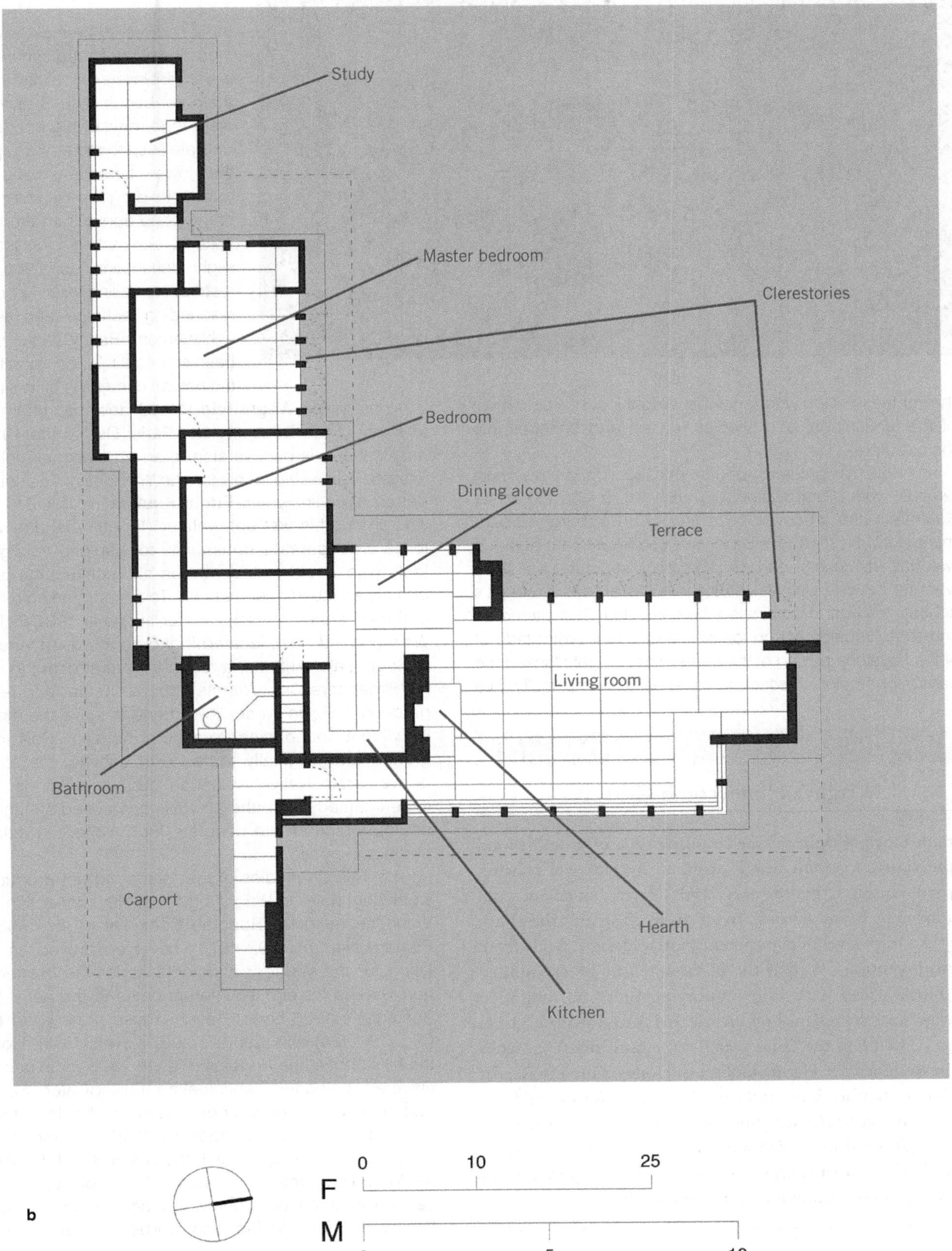

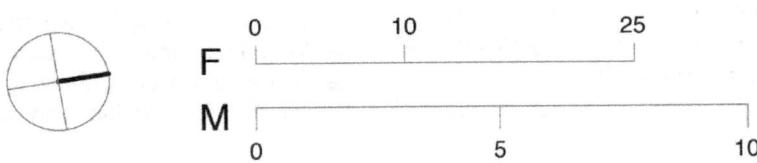

Study

Master bedroom

Clerestories

Bedroom

Dining alcove

Terrace

Living room

Bathroom

Hearth

Carport

Kitchen

F

0 10 25

M

0 5 10

b

three shelves of the rocky surroundings. These reinforced concrete trays were cantilevered from the mass of the core, bending up at their perimeters to form waist-high parapets. A delicate suspended stairway pierced the lower terrace, inviting brave guests to dip into the chilly waters of the pond above the waterfall. Despite the contracting errors that led to slight deflections, corrected during restoration, Fallingwater appeared a resounding technical and aesthetic achievement. Rarely had a building been so beautifully incorporated with the natural conditions of its site.

the lightness of the wooden walls. Wright incorporated most of the furnishings, bookshelves, desks, and benches into the structure.

In 1936, Wright also began construction on his most famous work, Fallingwater (Fig. 18.1-10), a villa for Edgar Kaufmann, the art-collecting owner of a Pittsburgh department store. Nestled in a bend of a country stream above a waterfall, its luxury and extraordinary structural solutions went far beyond Usonian prototypes. As always in Wright's houses, the hearth dominated the core. Here, it sheltered an immense fireplace set on top of live rock that protruded out of the flagstone paving of the living room. Wright stacked the broad, buff-colored concrete terraces asymmetrically, like

In his youth Wright had turned down Burnham's offer to study at the Beaux-Arts in Paris. During the 1930s he established his own version of an educational atelier, the Taliesin Fellowship, at his farm in Wisconsin. The son of the patron of Fallingwater, Edgar Kaufmann, Jr. (1910–1989), was among his first apprentices. Wright intended Taliesin to be a cooperative community for aspiring young architects who would collaborate on his architectural projects and his agricultural endeavors. To escape the cold months of the north he created a winter studio in 1937 at Taliesin West (Fig. 18.1-11), located in the open desert landscape of Scottsdale, Arizona, a resort town that came to resemble Broadacre City. With its cabaret theater and terraced gardens, Taliesin West allowed one to leave the metropolis without abandoning its cultural benefits. Built into the ground and originally roofed with canvas, the structure derived from Native American dugout buildings. Wright experimented with battered walls composed of huge local boulders stuffed into concrete form works that left them partially exposed.

CONSTRUCTION, TECHNOLOGY, THEORY

Wright's Honeycomb Grid

Frank Lloyd Wright pursued another type of order beyond the classical system. Partly inspired by Japanese culture, partly inspired by the Arts and Crafts movement, and mostly moved by his own stubborn efforts to go against the grain, he brought a high level of experimentation to design. Aside from numerous inventions, such as the ill-fated textile block (hollow cement blocks laced with iron reinforcing rods), he sought to break away from the reliance on orthogonal plans by using a hexagonal grid. In 1936, the same year that he built the first Jacobs House, he designed the Hanna House, or Honeycomb House, for a professor at Stanford University in California. Wright laid out the house in an overall *L* shape but subdivided it with a hexagonal grid, which allowed more flexibility in the placement of minor walls and built-in furnishings. The fireplace at the juncture of the two wings stepped down to a hexagonal pit.

The Taliesin studios of the 1930s did not produce any significant heirs to Wright's genius. His connection to two Viennese émigrés, Rudolph Schindler (1887–1953) and Richard Neutra (1892–1970), however, proved as stimulating for the younger architects as for the master. Both had worked for him at different times in the early 1920s. Schindler's 1926 Lovell Beach House at Newport Beach (Fig. 18.1-12a) and Neutra's 1927 Lovell Health House in the hills above Los Angeles (Fig. 18.1-12b) both used cantilevered balconies, anticipating Fallingwater. Schindler had studied with Adolf Loos before arriving in Chicago in 1914. He moved to Los Angeles in 1919 to oversee Wright's projects. On his own he built the Lovell Beach House as a reinforced concrete frame made of five hollowed-out vertical planes that were poured in place. He left the ground floor open for parking and barbeques and placed a double-height loft above. Four small rooms, reached by the third-floor balcony, opened to a semienclosed, cantilevered sleeping porch. Wright inspired such touches as built-in furnishings.

Neutra also had studied with Loos and worked briefly for Erich Mendelsohn (1887–1953) in Berlin before moving to Chicago. Wright hired him in 1923, but he stayed only six months before joining Schindler in Los Angeles. The same client who had engaged Schindler to produce the Beach House, Dr. Philip Lovell, commissioned Neutra a year later to build his principal residence in Los Angeles. Rather than using a concrete structure, Neutra designed the Health House with a steel frame, which took only

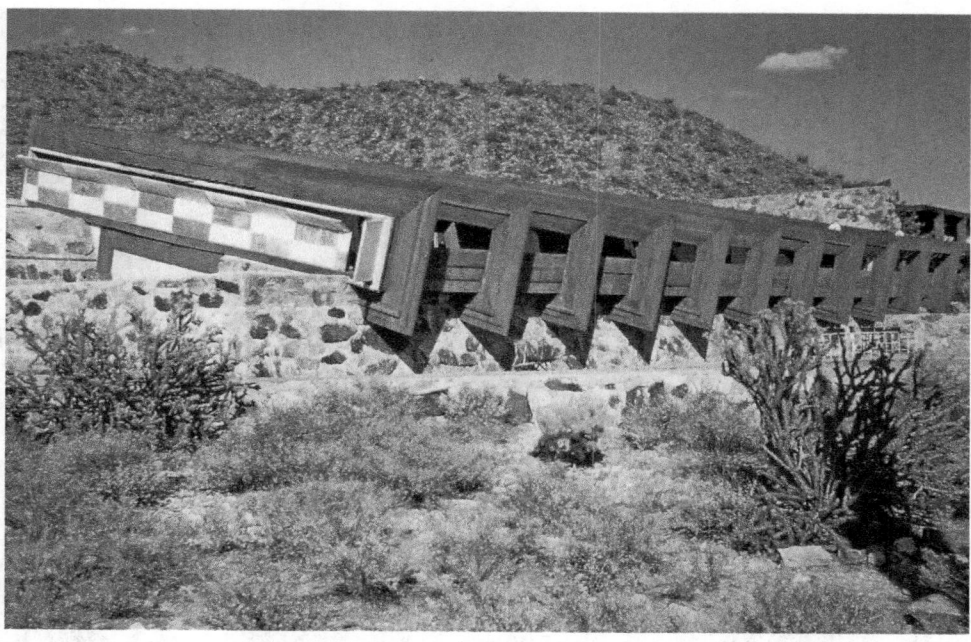

Figure 18.1-11 Scottsdale, Arizona. Taliesin West, Wright, 1930s.

forty hours to assemble. The steel-sash windows and metal panels of the living room were effortlessly joined to the prefabricated structure. Some of the walls were made with gunnite, another innovative technique by which concrete was sprayed onto a wire mesh. The strength of the steel frame allowed Neutra to cantilever the upper stories and use a relatively open plan. To underline the perfection and efficiency of Health House's machine-made minimalism, he lit the main staircase with headlights from the Ford Model A.

One of Wright's largest projects, the Johnson Wax Building in Racine, Wisconsin (1936–1939) (Fig. 18.1-13), demonstrated his creative struggle between the Craftsman's desire to design every aspect of a structure and the allure of working with modern technology. The new administrative building flanked the company's factories and warehouses in a small town 100 km (60 miles) north of Chicago. Like the Larkin Building of three decades earlier, the building unfolded as a variation of the Panopticon (see Section 14.3), a single, windowless hall oriented to a balcony from which the owner could observe the employees. Wright invented a hollow column based on the structure of cactus plants, with which he achieved the atmosphere of a great hypostyle mosque. These "dendriform," or tree-like, columns rose from a 23 cm (9 inch) diameter at the base to a lily pad disk at the ceiling 6 m (20 ft) wide. A filigree of curving glass-tube skylights fit into the gaps of the ceiling. The experimental Pyrex tubes of the skylights fulfilled Wright's desire to synthesize craft and industry. Unfortunately they leaked without mercy owing to cracked caulking. Likewise, his tubular furniture, including the notorious three-legged "suicide" chair, greatly challenged the workers' comfort.

Wright preached that form and function were one, yet his final act at Johnson Wax, the addition of the fourteen-story

Research Tower in 1944 (Fig. 18.1-14), upset the balance in favor of form. The concept came from Wright's five-year sojourn in Japan, where he observed the sections of tall pagodas. He proposed a tower based on the structure of a tree, forging deep, taproot foundations and placing the services in the central shaft. In this way, the floors could be cantilevered like the branches of a tree, permitting open-plan spaces and a nonbearing free facade. While ingenious as a structural solution, the inflexible vertical arrangement of the Research Tower proved impractical for scientists, who preferred open lofts for easy communication and constant adaptation. The tower could also not accommodate fire escapes and was eventually closed. Function got the better of the Research Tower, which, although it proved conceptually satisfying, lacked enough flexibility to be changed. The tower remained a beautiful but useless pendant.

Further Reading

Alofsin, Anthony, ed. *Frank Lloyd Wright: Europe and Beyond.* Berkeley: University of California Press, 1999.

Banham, Reyner. *A Concrete Atlantis: U.S. Industrial Building and European Modern Architecture, 1900–1925.* Cambridge, MA: MIT Press, 1986.

Bucci, Federico. *Albert Kahn: Architect of Ford.* New York: Princeton Architectural Press, 1993.

Cohen, Jean-Louis. *Scenes of the World to Come: European Architecture and the American Challenge, 1893–1960.* Paris: Flammarion, 1995.

Koolhaas, Rem. *Delirious New York.* New York: Rizzoli, 1978.

Lipman, Jonathan. *Frank Lloyd Wright and the Johnson Wax Buildings.* New York: Rizzoli, 1986.

a

Figure 18.1-12 (a) Newport Beach, California.
Lovell Beach House, Rudolph Schindler, 1926.
(b) Los Angeles. Lovell Health House, Richard
Neutra, 1927.

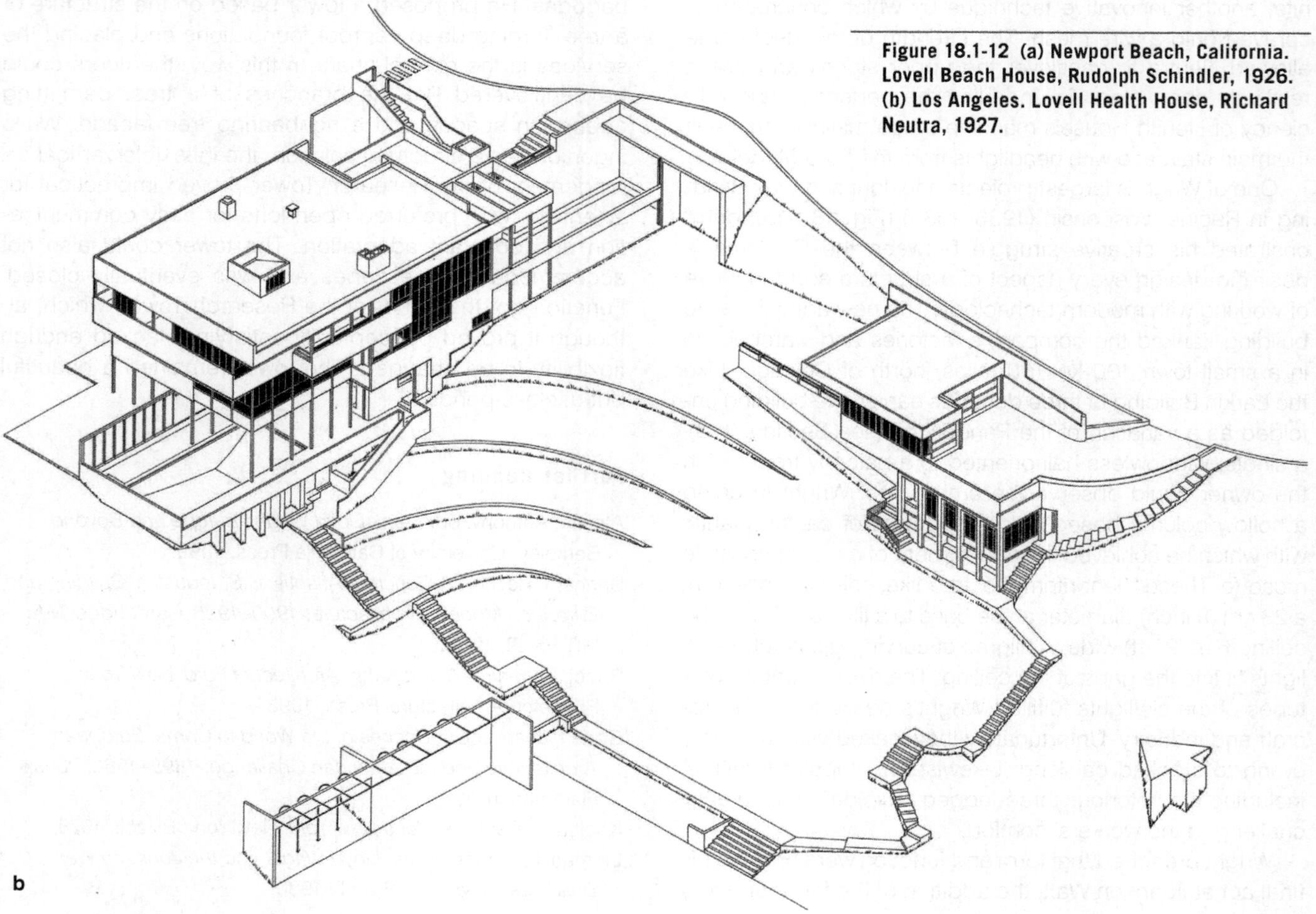

b

Figure 18.1-13 Racine, Wisconsin. Johnson Wax offices, Wright, 1939.

Figure 18.1-14 Racine, Wisconsin. Johnson Wax Research Tower, Wright, 1944.

Longstreth, Richard. *City Center to Regional Mall: Architecture, the Automobile, and Retailing in Los Angeles.* Cambridge, MA: MIT Press, 1997.

Muschamp, Herbert. *Man about Town: Frank Lloyd Wright in New York City.* Cambridge, MA: MIT Press, 1983.

Sergeant, John. *Frank Lloyd Wright's Usonian Houses: Designs for Moderate Cost One-Family Homes.* New York: Whitney Library of Design, 1984.

Stern, Robert A. M., Gregory Gilmartin, and Thomas Mellins. *New York 1930.* New York: Rizzoli, 1987.

Storrer, William Allen. *The Frank Lloyd Wright Companion.* Chicago: University of Chicago Press, 1993.

Willis, Carol. *Form Follows Finance: Skyscrapers in New York and Chicago.* New York: Princeton Architectural Press, 1995.

Wright, Gwendolyn. *USA: Modern Architectures in History.* London: Redaktion Books, 2008.

18.2 EUROPEAN MODERNISMS
A Dialogue between Form and Function

"Modern architecture" can mean two different things. In its most general sense "modern" refers to a period of time close to the present. But during the first half of the twentieth century many artists and architects used the same word to signify a break from the past. Such avant-garde movements as Cubism, Futurism, Expressionism, Dadaism, Neo-Plasticism, and Constructivism led to artistic and architectural works of great formal novelty. Many artists crossed into the field of architecture, where they could pursue the concepts of abstraction on a larger scale.

Le Corbusier, the de Stijl movement in the Netherlands, the Russian revolutionaries, and the members of the Bauhaus school all designed projects that still shock in their bold detachment from traditions. By the end of the 1920s, however, the Great Depression and new political calls for order encouraged a stricter functionalist approach. This New Objectivity focused on the utilitarian aspects of mass housing and urban planning, resulting in a generic "Modernism" later known as the "International Style," a sensible application of standardization with little pretense to the avant-garde.

Le Corbusier: Machines for Living in and Cities for Machines

Le Corbusier (born Charles-Édouard Jeanneret, 1887–1965), a Swiss-born French designer, became the most influential Modernist architect of the twentieth century. In *Toward an Architecture* (1923), he launched a campaign against the academy. Not since the treatises of Sebastiano Serlio and Andrea Palladio had a book exerted such a strong impact on the practice of architecture. "The house," he wrote, "will no longer be this solidly-built thing which sets out to defy time and decay. . . . It will be a tool as the motor-car

is becoming a tool." If Ford's methods were applied to architecture, he contended, they would yield a "machine for living in."

Le Corbusier, however, should not be categorized exclusively as a harbinger of machine-age aesthetics. His life contained many contradictory strains. As a design student in the watchmaking town of La Chaux-de-Fonds he eagerly read John Ruskin as well as Owen Jones's *Grammar of Ornament* (1857). Seized by the mission of the Arts and Crafts movement, the young Le Corbusier and his school friends built a chalet in rusticated stone, plaster, and wood. Their 1907 Villa Fallet appeared the antithesis of Modernism, with the steep, hipped roofs of the Swiss vernacular and decorated balcony railings and **sgraffito** surfaces. They used abstractions of the *sapin* pine as the recurring theme and carved the corners of the eaves to represent icicles.

During the construction of Villa Fallet Le Corbusier followed Ruskin's steps in Tuscany, where he visited the fourteenth-century Carthusian monastery of La Certosa at Galuzzo, outside Florence. Here, he discovered the monk's cell with a small private garden, which he came to see as "the solution to workers' housing." For the rest of his life he returned to this basic *L*-shaped unit. At La Certosa each cell looked beyond its garden wall to the greater landscape of the surrounding hills, dotted with beautiful patches of vineyards and olive orchards. The cells were entered from an arcaded cloister that was collectively used, resulting in a compact yet open atmosphere.

Before World War I, Le Corbusier explored the most progressive trends in design, working for brief periods for Auguste Perret in Paris and Peter Behrens in Berlin. From Perret he learned the structural advantages of reinforced concrete frame construction, used to build the master's studio and apartment at 25 Rue Franklin. In Behrens's office he became acquainted with the rational industrial organization of the AEG factories. Le Corbusier also spent time in the Garden City of Hellerau, went to Hampstead Garden Suburb in London, and visited Tony Garnier in Lyons to discuss his zoning model of the Industrial City. In 1915 he prepared a small treatise on urbanism that proposed to soften the rigid grid pattern of his hometown using Camillo Sitte's method of human-scaled enclosed spaces.

Due to legal disputes over his projects in Switzerland, Le Corbusier moved definitively to Paris in 1916. There, he joined the avant-garde painter Amédée Ozenfant (1886–1966)

TIME LINE

1917
Bolshevik Revolution in Russia establishes first Communist regime and the foundation of the Soviet Union

November Revolution in Germany suppressed
1918

1920
Tatlin proposes Constructivist tower in Moscow

Le Corbusier publishes *Toward an Architecture*
**1923**

1925
Steiner completes Second Goetheanum in Dornach, Switzerland

in formulating Purism, a critique of the Cubism of Braque and Picasso. They also founded the journal *L'Esprit nouveau*, published irregularly from 1920 to 1925. Le Corbusier, who never legally registered in France as an architect, opened an office in 1922 with his cousin Pierre Jeanneret (1896–1967), who was licensed to practice. They experimented with the industrial aesthetic in one of their first projects, the 1923 Ozenfant House (Fig. 18.2-1), using a serrated monitor roof like a factory and industrial steel-sash windows for his friend's north-facing studio.

From the outset, Le Corbusier championed the use of reinforced concrete. In 1914, while still in La Chaux-de-Fonds, he submitted a patent with an engineer friend for the Dom-Ino method of concrete construction, based on a grid of columns supporting horizontal slabs. In contrast to Perret's concrete frames, the columns of this point-loaded system were recessed from the wall planes and thus in plan resembled Dom-Ino tokens. The Dom-Ino model inspired Le Corbusier's 1926 design manifesto, the "Five Points of a New Architecture." Intended as the antithesis to masonry construction in general and to academic architecture in particular, his new rules offered a means of "liberating" foundations, thick walls, vertical windows, and pitched roofs. With the Dom-Ino system one had the option of a free ground plane, a free facade, a free plan, long windows, and a rooftop garden.

Le Corbusier best fulfilled the "Five Points" in his most famous house, the Villa Savoye (Fig. 18.2-2a–c), built between 1928 and 1931 at Poissy, a suburban town 15 km (10 miles) northwest of Paris. Set in the midst of a large wooded site, the flat box on stilts conveyed a feeling of rupture from the architecture of the past, as powerful as the shock of Cubist paintings, yet with a pure volumetric starkness that evoked a Greek temple. The curved, glazed wall of the ground floor receded behind *pilotis*, rows of slender white poles that made the upper story

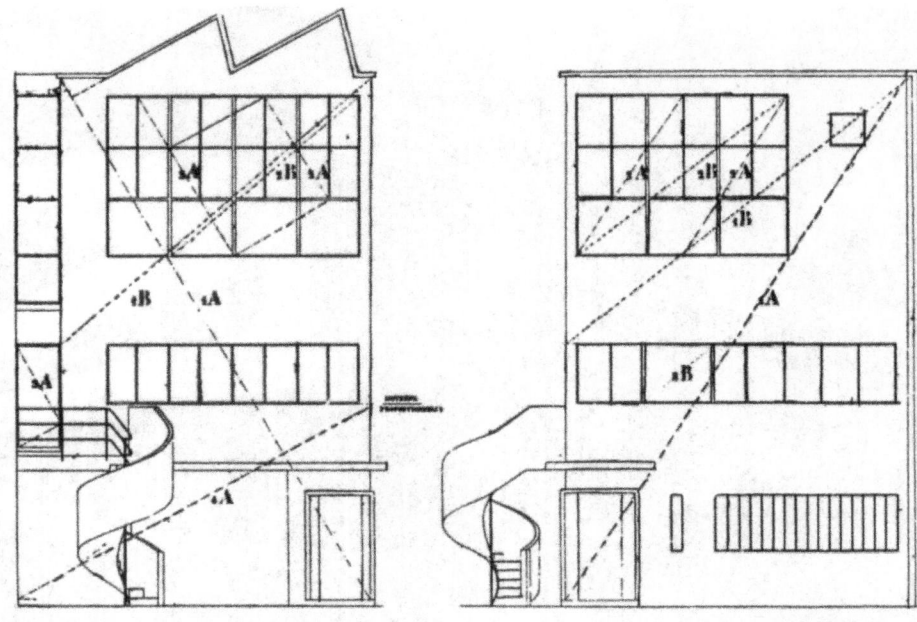

Figure 18.2-1 Paris. Ozenfant House, Le Corbusier and Pierre Jeanneret, 1923.

seem to hover in the air. Unlike classical buildings, Villa Savoye had an uneven number of columns on each side. Long bands of windows on the second floor extended the length of the facade, exaggerating its horizontality. The rounded parapets on the third level served as sculptural tokens of the free plan within and were used as a protective solarium oriented to the south. Le Corbusier structured the sequence of spaces on a meandering itinerary that he dubbed the "architectural promenade." Like the constantly changing point of view in a picturesque garden, movement up the ramps yielded surprising oblique vistas. Formally, Villa Savoye lived up to Le Corbusier's dictum that "Architecture is the masterly, correct, and magnificent play of volumes assembled in the light." Technically, however, it proved a disaster, impossible to heat and plagued with severe leaks and humidity. The clients eventually abandoned the house.

Like Frank Lloyd Wright, Le Corbusier considered architecture a redeeming mission. Unlike his American counterpart, however, his ideal vision of society involved collective solutions for urbanism and housing. For the 1925 Exposition Internationale des Arts Decoratifs, the event that gave

Gropius moves Bauhaus to Dessau, Germany, and builds new building

▲ 1925

▼ 1926

Stalin assumes power in Soviet Union

Le Corbusier designs Villa Savoye in Poissy, outside Paris

▲ 1928

▼ 1929

Mies van der Rohe designs German Pavilion in Barcelona

Figure 18.2-2 Poissy, France. (a) Villa Savoye, exterior, Le Corbusier and Jeanneret, 1928–1931. (b) Comparative plans of three levels of Villa Savoye (top) and three levels of Melnikov House in Moscow, 1927 (bottom). Le Corbusier used a point-loaded structure of reinforced concrete; Melnikov built his house with thick brick walls. Each was interested in the open plan with a rooftop terrace. (c) See facing page.

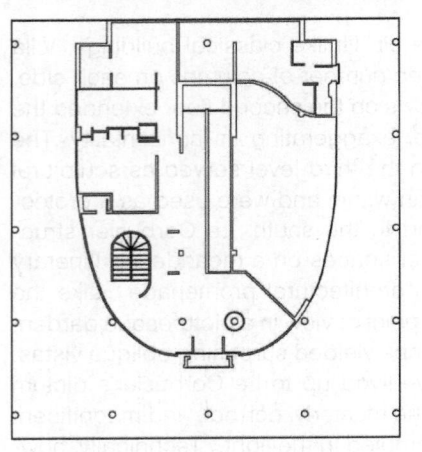
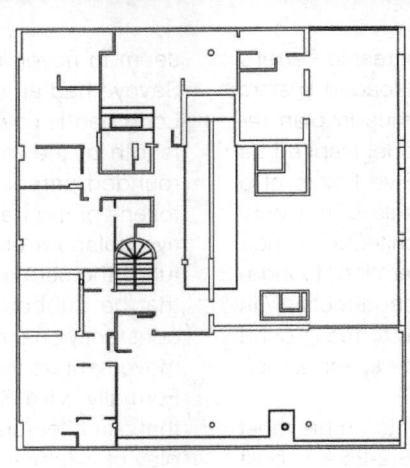
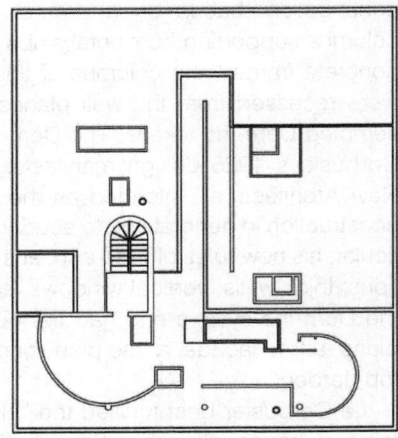

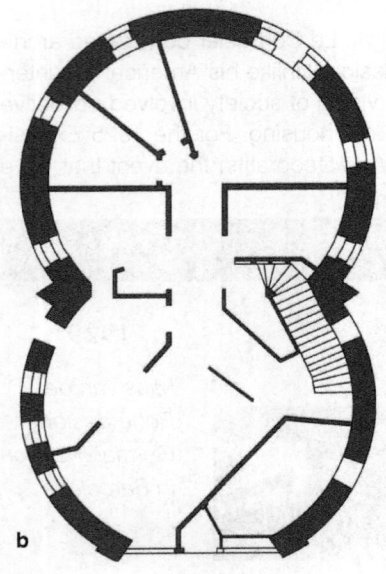
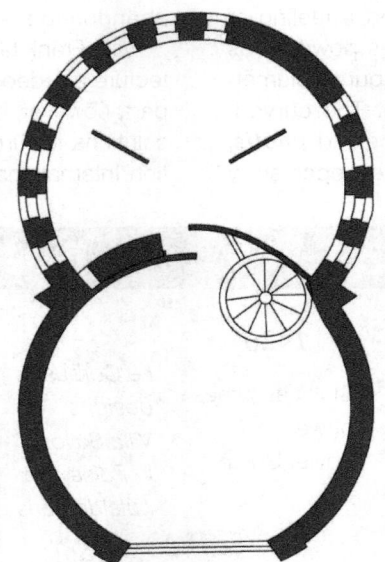
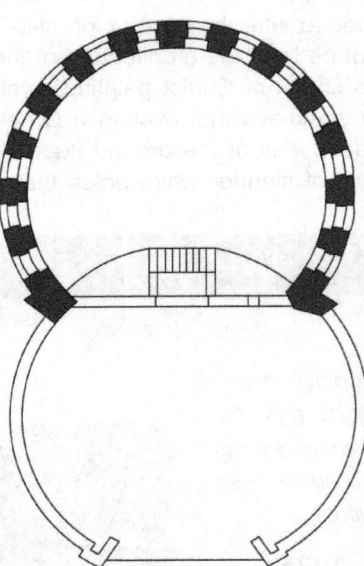

Figure 18.2-2 Poissy, France. (c) Service stair, Villa Savoye.

the Art Deco style its name, Le Corbusier and his friends prepared the Esprit Nouveau Pavilion (Fig. 18.2-3). This full-scale mock-up of his ideal apartment-villa provided a Modernist version of the Carthusian monk's cell. The *L*-shaped unit offered a double-height living space, like an artist's loft, and a double-height terrace.

The Esprit Nouveau prototype was intended to fit into twelve-story blocks set around a park-sized central court. Attached to the pavilion Le Corbusier included two models of his ideal city based on these blocks. Like the Futurama exhibition, Le Corbusier imagined the future city dominated by transportation infrastructures. In the mandala-shaped "City for Three Million Inhabitants" (Fig. 18.2-4), he arranged the blocks in redented patterns to either side of a twelve-lane highway. In the center he proposed a multilevel plinth as a transportation node, with a landing pad on top and a train station below. He surrounded the plinth with a cluster of forty-story cruciform skyscrapers. His theory of vertical urbanism, which he later named the Radiant City, increased the density of the urban area while offering a greater amount of open space, presenting an open fabric of tall buildings in isolated park settings that signaled the "death of the street."

Futurism and the City

The precedent for Le Corbusier's urban vision came from Italian Futurism. The "Futurist Manifesto," published in Paris in 1909 by the poet Filippo Marinetti (1876–1944), celebrated the violent and transitory nature of the machine age. Marinetti, a master of nihilistic hyperbole, proclaimed that "a roaring motor car, which seems to run on machine-gun fire, is more beautiful than the Victory of Samothrace." In his diatribes against the past he celebrated war as the world's only instrument of hygiene. His young protégé, Antonio Sant'Elia (1888–1916), attempted to envision an architectural interpretation of Futurism in *La Città Nuova* (*The New City*) of 1914. While Sant'Elia's style appears in retrospect an unthreatening variant of the Viennese Secession movement, the content of his urban vision was more jarring, emphasizing a tumultuous new city of untamable mechanical regeneration. His manifesto on Futurist architecture described a city of speed, full of constantly moving cranes and lifts, "an immense building yard" that never stopped remaking itself.

La Città Nuova (The New City), Antonio Sant'Elia, 1914.

Figure 18.2-3 Bologna, Italy. Reconstruction of L'Esprit Nouveau Pavilion, Le Corbusier, 1925.

While few in the 1920s completely endorsed Le Corbusier's ideal city, it became immensely influential two decades later during post–World War II reconstruction. His ideas were widely diffused by the Congrès Internationale d'Architecture Moderne (CIAM), an organization founded in 1928 in solidarity with Le Corbusier, whose winning entry to the 1926 League of Nations Competition in Geneva had been unfairly disqualified. The CIAM's conventions helped to promote such urban solutions as slab housing and tower-in-the-park neighborhoods.

Despite his international influence, Le Corbusier obtained few opportunities in Europe to realize his ideal Radiant City.

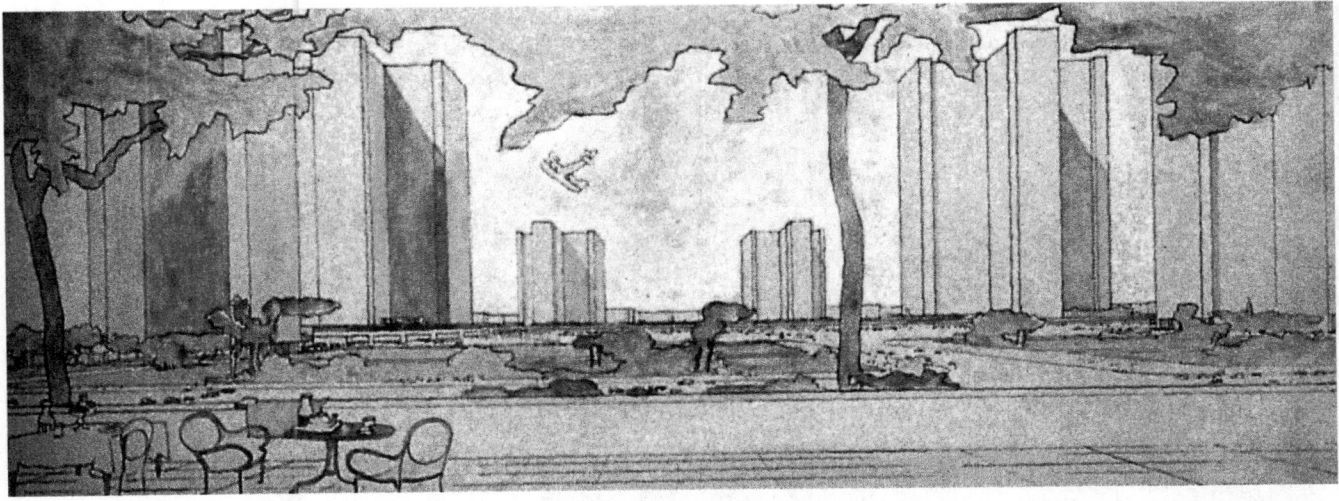

Figure 18.2-4 "Contemporary City for Three Million Inhabitants," from Le Corbusier's *Vers une architecture*, 1922.

One of his only large projects, the 1947 Unité d'Habitation in Marseilles (Fig. 18.2-5a), served as reconstruction housing for about 1,600 people. Like Wright, Le Corbusier never completely abandoned the Craftsman ideal. While he intended the Unité as a model of prefabrication, he gave it many artisan touches, from the formwork and reliefs embossed in the crude concrete (a style soon to be labeled "Brutalism" after *béton brut*, or raw concrete, but also referring to the neo-primitive *art brut* movement) to the molded wooden door handles to the wading pool and sculpted mounds on the roof terrace for the children's playground. The transverse section of the Unité showed its greatest innovation for mass housing: by eliminating a public corridor on alternate floors, the two-story apartments crossed over from one side to the other, gaining an increase in natural light and cross-ventilation (Fig. 18.2-5b). In this instance Le Corbusier returned to the *L*-shaped unit not in plan but in section. The units remained small and narrow without divisions between rooms. Like a ship, they were fitted with built-in furnishings, such as a row of shelves between the kitchen and living room, which created a sense of spatial separation. A bookcase-parapet overlooking the double-height living room helped to isolate the open loft of the parents' bedroom. A sliding door that doubled as a blackboard separated the two children's rooms.

The original working-class inhabitants for whom the Unité was planned disliked the apartments because of the strange kitchens and cabin-cruiser bathrooms. Later residents, however, who tended to be teachers, intellectuals, and artists, thrived in its open loft spaces and embraced its eccentric details. The Unité combined innovative technologies, such as garbage disposals, with rough, neo-primitive details, like the stumpy "legs" at the building's base. In all of his later projects—in particular the dolmen-like pilgrimage church of Notre Dame du Haut at Ronchamp, completed in 1954 (Fig. 18.2-6)—Le Corbusier attempted to integrate the primitive with the modern. Rather than the sleek prisms of machine-age precision of which he dreamed during the 1920s, in the end he preferred rugged surfaces that hinted at a connection to the origins of architecture.

The Bolshevik Revolution and Revolutionary Formalism

Le Corbusier's *Toward an Architecture* concluded with the enigmatic image of a briar pipe as an artifact of industrial standardization and the invective "Architecture or revolution, revolution can be avoided." By this he meant that if the housing question were treated with the same machine-made logic as the pipe, social pressures would be eliminated. The revolution he feared was the 1917 Bolshevik Revolution in Russia, led by Vladimir Lenin. Little did Le Corbusier suspect that the resulting Soviet Union would commission his largest project of the 1920s, the Centrosoyuz Administration Building, designed in 1928 and completed in 1936. Few observers anticipated Russia's transformation into the center of the international revolutionary movement for socialism, and fewer still expected the artistic innovations that accompanied the revolution. But from this backwater of underdevelopment, an alternative political order took root and eventually came to govern one-third of the world's population for most of the twentieth century. In its early years, Communism's demand for a "new man" inspired a nascent avant-garde that rode the wave of political upheaval.

Russian architecture before the revolution lacked modernization. It ranged from historicist religious works by Konstantin Thon (1794–1881), such as the Cathedral of Christ the Savior, built in Moscow between 1839 and 1883, to imitations of European academic styles by Ivan Fomin (1872–1936). The GUM market hall on Red Square in Moscow remained among the few relatively modern constructions. Built in 1893, it contained 1,200 shops in a grand interior arcade. Although the exterior was draped with eclectic elevations, it rose on an innovative steel frame with glass vaults and reinforced concrete interior bridges designed by Vladimir Shukhov (1853–1939).

Prior to the revolution, the poet Vladimir Mayakovski (1893–1930) instigated a Russian version of Futurism.

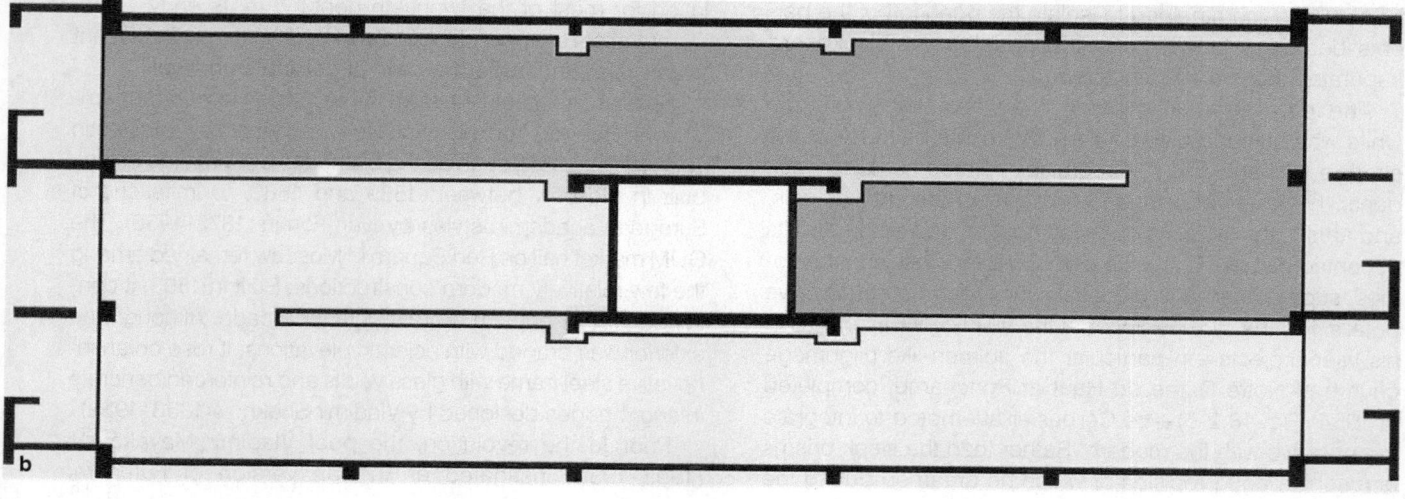

Figure 18.2-5 Marseilles, France. (a) Unité d'Habitation, Le Corbusier, 1946–1952. (b) Section, showing the innovative double-height space and cross-ventilation permitted for each apartment. Elevators stopped at every other floor.

Maison de Verre

The Maison de Verre, set in a courtyard in Paris, achieved a much higher technological level than the works of Le Corbusier. Pierre Chareau (1883–1950) designed it in 1928 for the celebrated gynecologist Dr. Jean Dalsace, who maintained consulting offices on the ground floor. Its upper two stories contained a double-height loft for his famous salon for artists and left-wing intellectuals. Chareau, with the help of the Dutch architect Bernard Bijvoet (1889–1979), devised an ingenious crutch of steel girders to hold up the fourth-floor apartment, which by law could not be demolished, during the removal and reconstruction of the lower floors. This approach led to a series of industrial choices, including the glass bricks that covered the two courtyard facades and gave the house its name. Other advanced technologies included rubber tile floors, perforated metal wall partitions, and mechanical light fixtures. Every detail, while inspired by standardized industrial products, required expensive custom fabrication.

Paris. Maison de Verre, Pierre Chareau, 1931.

A small avant-garde movement produced two of the greatest innovators in the trend toward nonrepresentational, or abstract, art: Kazimir Malevich (1878–1935) and Wassily Kandinsky (1866–1944). While Malevich's Suprematism juxtaposed elemental geometric forms, Kandinsky explored the dynamic interpenetrations of unusual shapes. Both artists inspired formalist movements in the quest for an appropriate art that was launched after the October Revolution.

For architects the ensuing civil war during the Russian Revolution and the uncertain economy led to few commissions. Many joined the planning teams in St. Petersburg and Moscow after the 1918 decree for the socialization of land. Fomin's group in St. Petersburg favored "proletarian classicism," while the team assembled by Ivan Zholtovsky (1867–1959) and Alexei Shchusev (1873–1949) in Moscow proved more open to a younger avant-garde and to abstraction. In both cases the models for urbanization derived from Ebenezer Howard's Garden City. With the state now the majority landowner, the provision of greenbelts and satellite cities seemed more likely.

The few public works designed immediately after the revolution insisted on the academic tradition. After removing dozens of tsarist sculptures, the Soviet government installed new statues to Bolshevik heroes, designed in a similarly academic style. Vladimir Tatlin (1885–1953), founder of Constructivism, objected to such an anomaly and attempted to challenge the revolution's conservative approach in his project for the Monument to the Third International, exhibited in Moscow in 1920 (Fig. 18.2-7). Tatlin's 6 m (20 ft) high scale model portrayed an open webbed-iron structure taller than the Eiffel Tower that coiled two spirals around a tilted mast. The metal frame served to support a stack of four glazed volumes: a cube at the base, a triangular prism in the middle, and a cylinder at the top with a small sphere above. Intended as a meeting place for a world government, each volume would rotate at a different rate—once a year, once a month, and once a day, respectively. This dynamic composition, which used construction to convey symbolic ideas, struck Mayakovski as "the first monument without a beard." Tatlin's Constructivism inspired an aesthetic of industrial materials assembled in dynamic compositions of interpenetrating forms.

Although Tatlin's tower went unbuilt, the engineer of GUM, Vladimir Shukhov, constructed a magnificent transmitting

Figure 18.2-6 Ronchamp, France.
(a) Notre Dame du Haut, exterior,
Le Corbusier, 1954. (b) Interior.

tower in Moscow two years later (Fig. 18.2-8). The Moscow Tower soared 160 m (410 ft) on a stack of five gently curving hyperboloid shafts, the iron mesh of which served as its own scaffold during construction. While not intentionally Constructivist in composition, the tower acquired iconic status in the skyline as a triumph of modern Russian technology. Shukhov's tower made significant improvements to Eiffel's system in terms of lightness and economy. It was one of twenty built in the Soviet Union on similar principles, helping to open the way toward the acceptance of the inherent beauty of raw structure.

Although Lenin remained unsympathetic to the artistic avant-garde movements, his minister of culture, Anatoly Lunacharsky (1875–1933), offered support to teachers and students at the new design school, the Vkhutemas, founded in Moscow in 1920. Within the school, splinter associations such as ASNOVA (Association of New Architects) and OSA (Organization of Contemporary Architects) sustained ferocious debates between abstract formalism and rationalist functionalism. Two of the school's more influential teachers of Constructivism were women: Lyubov Popova (1889–1924) and Varvara Stepanova (1894–1958). Both began in graphics and moved to practical design for textiles. They also ventured into theater, designing costumes and three-dimensional sets as abstract dynamic constructions. Stepanova created a skeletal "acting apparatus" for

Figure 18.2-7 St. Petersburg. Model for a tower dedicated to the Third Communist International, Vladimir Tatlin, 1920, from Ivan Puni, *Tatlin*, 1921.

the 1922 play *The Death of Tarelkin*. One of the first built works of Constructivism, it juxtaposed contrasting geometric shapes made of exposed lumber joists.

Western Europe became aware of the Constructivist aesthetic through El Lissitzky (1890–1941). As a graphic artist he pursued the Suprematist abstractions of Malevich, while in his three-dimensional *Prouns* he explored the dynamic Constructivist theory of Tatlin. A frequent visitor to Paris, Zurich, and Berlin, he organized exhibitions and publications to promote avant-garde Soviet art and architecture. In 1923, with the help of Dutch architect Mart Stam (1899–1986), Lissitzky proposed the *Wolkenbügel* ("cloud hanger"), a flattened version of a skyscraper, which he recommended placing as a series on the external ring of Moscow (Fig. 18.2-9). Rather than a tower, he envisioned a long, *U*-shaped loft for two levels of offices that cantilevered

over a trio of four-story shafts. His design left the ground plane free while spreading the volume laterally. He claimed the *Wolkenbügel* represented an anticapitalist solution, driven by a desire to keep the land open to the public rather than to speculation.

The most prolific and individualistic of the Russian avant-garde architects, Konstantin Melnikov (1890–1974), ran a studio at Vkhutemas and gained international fame in 1925 as the designer of the Soviet Union Pavilion at the Art Deco exhibition in Paris. There, he divided the rectangular site with two triangular volumes linked by a diagonal staircase and sheltered by folded crisscross panels. Unadorned except for a suspended hammer-and-sickle emblem, the walls ran flush wooden planes with steel-sash fenestration from floor to ceiling. The two roofs dipped in contrasting single pitches. Melnikov's pavilion offered a more dynamic

Figure 18.2-8 Moscow.
Transmitting tower, Vladimir
Shukhov, 1924.

spatial expression of Modernism than the one displayed by Le Corbusier.

During the late 1920s Melnikov built six of the thirty Soviet workers' clubhouses in Moscow, which became emblematic of the state's commitment to the development of a proletarian culture that could replace the role of churches. He gave each an original style while carefully making their functions legible on the exteriors. The facade of his Rusakov clubhouse for the Union of Municipal Workers sprouted three cantilevered wings of seating divided by two glazed shafts for circulation. The design intimated that the three halls could be used independently or opened into a single theater.

Melnikov built his own house in 1927, a sign that the state's collectivizing policies had softened. While conceived as a prototype, he created one of the most hybrid formal explorations of the age as a personal manifesto against bureaucratic functionalism (Fig. 18.2-10). He composed the house as two interlocking cylinders. The silo-like volumes provided an inherently strong shape and a maximum area per wall surface. The nonbearing wooden partitions on the interior could be easily rearranged for either

Figure 18.2-9 Project for the *Wolkenbügel* (cloud hanger), El Lissitzky and Mart Stam, 1923.

individual or collective needs. Melnikov clustered the services for cooking and bathing in radiating rooms on the ground floor and put the sleeping area in a mezzanine that opened to a double-height living space above. Half a story above in the opposing cylinder he set a second double-height space for his studio, with a stair leading to a rooftop terrace. The external walls were constructed of thick brick masonry laid on a hexagonal grid pattern, which allowed the architect to punch dozens of hexagonal windows into his studio walls. On the front facade he cut a glazed slice through the cylinder and capped it with an entablature inscribed with his name. Such blatant self-promotion led to Melnikov's ostracism within Soviet architecture.

Moisei Ginzburg (1892–1946) promoted a more functionalist line in his 1928 Narkomfin prototype housing block (Fig. 18.2-11). Most of the units were designed without kitchens, as the whole was intended as a "social condenser," concentrating cooking, child care, and laundry in collective spaces. While the Soviet government permitted private houses, subjecting them to less severe regulations, apartment buildings had to conform to the *Kommunalka* policy: any apartment of more than one room was to be shared by more than one family. This policy led to the idea of open-plan apartments with lofts instead of room divisions so that the unit would be registered as a single room. While the social condenser may have seemed a good economic idea, the forced collectivization it engendered encouraged the reverse of social condensation. Ginzburg followed Le Corbusier's Five Points, creating a long concrete structure

Figure 18.2-10 Moscow. House and studio, Konstantin Melnikov, 1927.

raised above the ground level on columns, with strip windows extending the length of the five-story elevations. Conversely, Le Corbusier, who visited the project in 1928, may

Rudolph Steiner's Anthroposophy and Spiritual Functionalism

Whether the philosopher Rudolph Steiner (1861–1925) knew of Taut's Crystal Chain or not, he realized a veritable *Stadtkrone* on the outskirts of Basel during the same years the architects of the chain were exchanging letters. Steiner, born in Croatia and educated in Vienna, moved among the literary and artistic avant-gardes of Munich. He broke from the spiritual movement of Theosophy in 1912 to found the Anthroposophical Society. An expert on Goethe's color theory; the biographer of Friedrich Nietzsche; and defender of Ernst Haeckel (1834–1919), the originator of the theory of ecology, Steiner put forward the earliest proposal for an ecological lifestyle. At his community in Dornach, near Basel, he trained his followers in biodynamic agriculture and pursued a theory of architecture based on organic relationships, which he called "spiritual functionalism." Reasoning that nature did not produce right angles, he designed crooked and curved windows, doors, and roofs for more than a dozen structures. His central project, the Goetheanum, begun in 1913, a great double-domed theater made entirely of carved wood, opened for theatricals and spiritual events in 1919. After its destruction by arson in 1922, Steiner used the insurance money to build a fireproof replacement, one of the first nonindustrial, monolithic structures to be built in reinforced concrete. The second Goetheanum, finished in 1928, took on the faceted shapes found in nature, fulfilling the aesthetic ideals of the Expressionist *Stadtkrone*.

Dornach, Switzerland. Goetheanum, Rudolph Steiner, 1919 (rebuilt 1928).

have borrowed from Ginzburg the section for the Unité, which placed corridors on alternate floors, allowing the double-story units to cross from one side to the other.

Narkomfin was an elite project, intended for employees of the Ministry of Finance. The **penthouse** went to the minister of finance, Nikolai Milyutin (1889–1942), the leading proponent of "disurbanism," the Soviet theory of the linear city (Fig. 18.2-12). His proposal that industry, services, and housing follow a linear flow came close to Ford's assembly-line concept, applied to urban life. To keep the socialist city from the overcrowding, environmental degradation, and alienation of the capitalist city, he envisioned development that spread in a scattered fashion along the lines of mass transportation. In 1930 Milyutin proposed a linear city scheme for the new steelworks factory town of Magnitogorsk, arranging bands of industry closest to the

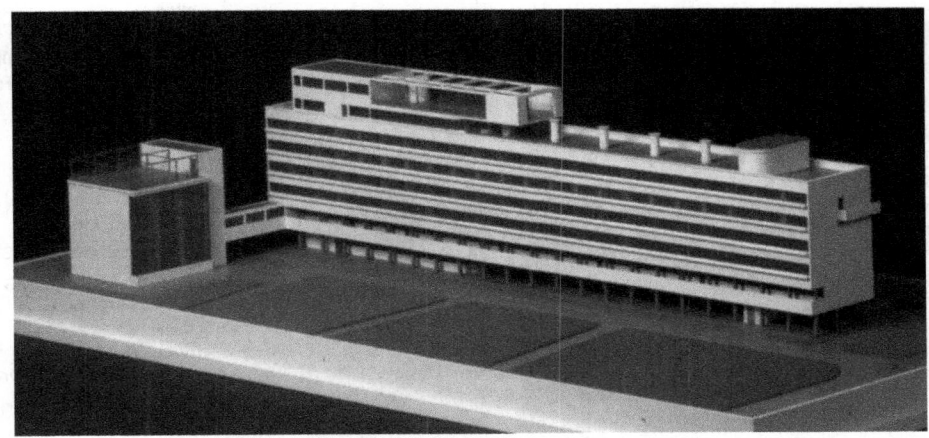

Figure 18.2-11 Moscow. Project for Narkomfin housing, Moisei Ginzburg, 1928.

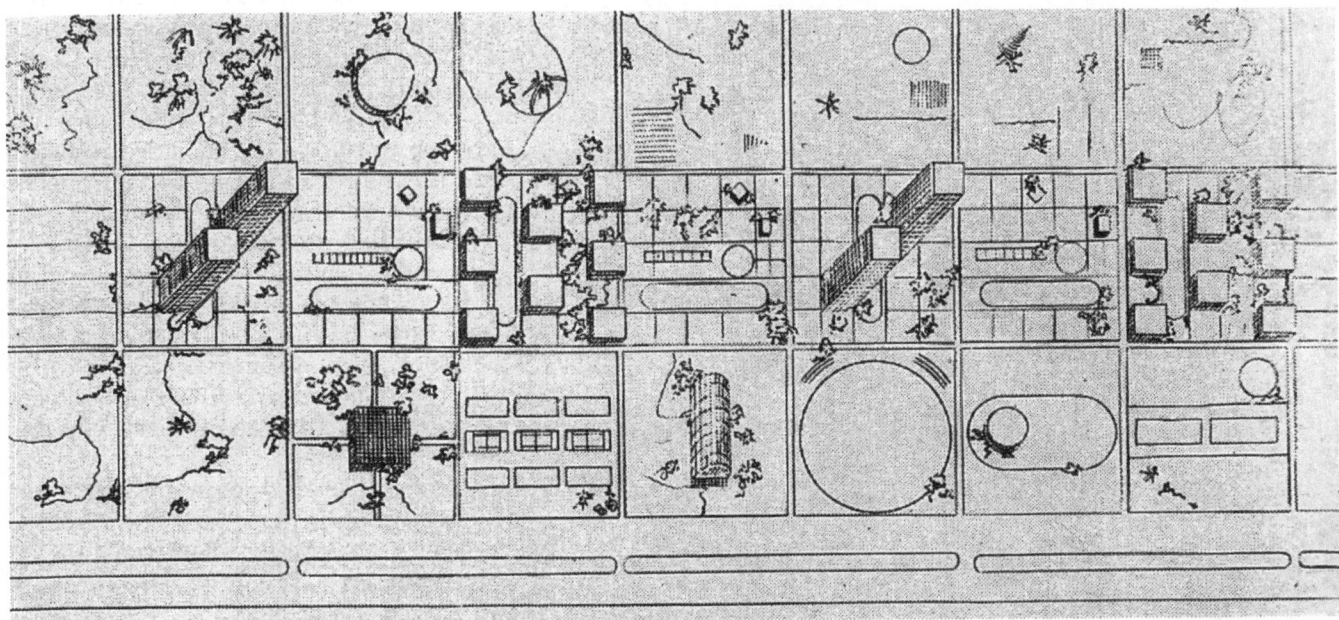

Figure 18.2-12 Scheme for Soviet linear city, inspired by Nikolai Milyutin, Ivan Leonidov, 1928.

rail lines, a greenbelt strip to conceal the highway, a band of residences and services, and a final strip for a natural park along the water feature. Disurbanism, however, devoted even less attention to public space than the ideal cities of either Frank Lloyd Wright or Le Corbusier. Milyutin assumed that residual parks would satisfy social needs.

As Joseph Stalin (1879–1953) consolidated his control over the Soviet government during the late 1920s, the development of Magnitogorsk became central to the First Five-Year Plan for industrializing Russia. Stalin's henchman, Lazar Kaganovich (1893–1991), converted the GUM stores in 1928 into an immense office building for the Five-Year planners. While Kaganovich orchestrated some of the most despised policies of Stalin's regime, including the 1932 famine in the Ukraine and the purges of the party, he gained notoriety as the organizer of the Moscow metro system, which was originally named after him. He gave it a decidedly anti-Modernist style, decorating the stations with classical pilasters and chandeliers

reminiscent of tsarist palaces. Under Stalin, a new conformist mentality discouraged the impractical, formalist works of Constructivism.

When the major competition of the age, for the design of the Palace of the Soviets, was announced in 1931, the shift in taste was already clear. Kaganovich personally oversaw the dynamiting of Thon's church of Christ the Savior to clear the site. Le Corbusier, who misinterpreted the cultural climate in Moscow, sent a film of his model, an homage to Tatlin, in which the main auditorium was suspended from a freestanding parabolic arch. Ginzburg designed a more discreet figure, an immense glazed dome. The winning project, by Boris Iofan (1891–1976), catered to the official return to academic styles. Iofan had trained in Rome, and his plan showed the influence of the Vittoriano monument (see Section 16.3). His design rose above the river on a broad, colonnaded terrace, stepping up on five levels to a round, ten-story office tower, which he proposed to cap with a realistic statue of Lenin

Figure 18.2-13 Paris. The crowning figures on top of the Soviet Pavilion at the World's Fair, Boris Iofan, 1937.

The Bauhaus: From Expressionism to New Objectivity

Most early twentieth-century political theorists believed that Germany, not Russia, would produce the first socialist state. It had the strongest labor unions and the most developed left-wing culture. After losing World War I, Germans felt shaken to their roots and ready for radical change. A socialist revolution indeed occurred in November 1918. Two months later, however, with the cooperation of the Social Democratic Party, the state crushed the revolt, resulting in the martyrdom of Rosa Luxemburg (1870–1919) and Karl Liebknecht (1871–1919), the leaders of the Spartacus movement. This intense moment of political uncertainty coincided with an explosion of artistic exploration, including the founding of the Bauhaus, a state design school that became the most influential matrix of Modernist design in Germany.

The Spartacus movement attracted numerous architects, who joined the *Arbeitsrat für Kunst* (Worker's Council for the Arts) and later the *Novembergruppe*. Some members, including Bruno Taut, Walter Gropius, and Hans Scharoun (1893–1972), participated in the "Crystal Chain," an exchange of utopian letters. Throughout 1919 Taut theorized on the "dissolution of cities," proposing a collectivized version of a rural utopia. His drawings often depicted the *Stadtkrone*, a city crown, as the spiritual center of socialist communities (Fig. 18.2-14). Scharoun's version of the *Stadtkrone* spewed colored lights from an artichoke-shaped glass structure. After this brief period, Scharoun alone continued the Expressionist research of the Crystal Chain.

Figure 18.2-13 Paris. The crowning figures on top of the Soviet Pavilion at the World's Fair, Boris Iofan, 1937.

extending his arm in a gesture of comradeship, similar in scale to New York's Statue of Liberty. While Iofan's palace got no further than the foundations, which were later transformed into a public swimming pool, his Soviet Pavilion at the Paris World's Exposition of 1937 gave a foretaste of its scale and style. A stepped tower lined with classical cornices served as a pedestal for two giant statues: a male worker thrusting a hammer that intersected a female peasant's outstretched sickle (Fig. 18.2-13). This return to realism completely contradicted the formal experimentation of Melnikov's earlier pavilion and signaled the suppression of the Soviet avant-gardes.

Although Erich Mendelsohn (1887–1953) did not participate in the Crystal Chain, he belonged to the radical groups of 1919. More than any other designer he captured the Expressionist aesthetic in his astronomical observatory dedicated to Albert Einstein (1879–1955) in Potsdam. The organic shapes of the Einstein Tower, built between 1919 and 1921 (Fig. 18.2-15), evolved from Mendelsohn's "trench sketches," made while serving during World War I. The tower appeared to be made of molded concrete but above the foundations was mostly brick covered in plaster. He used molded cement to create the scooped insets of the windows and the dynamic bulge of the base.

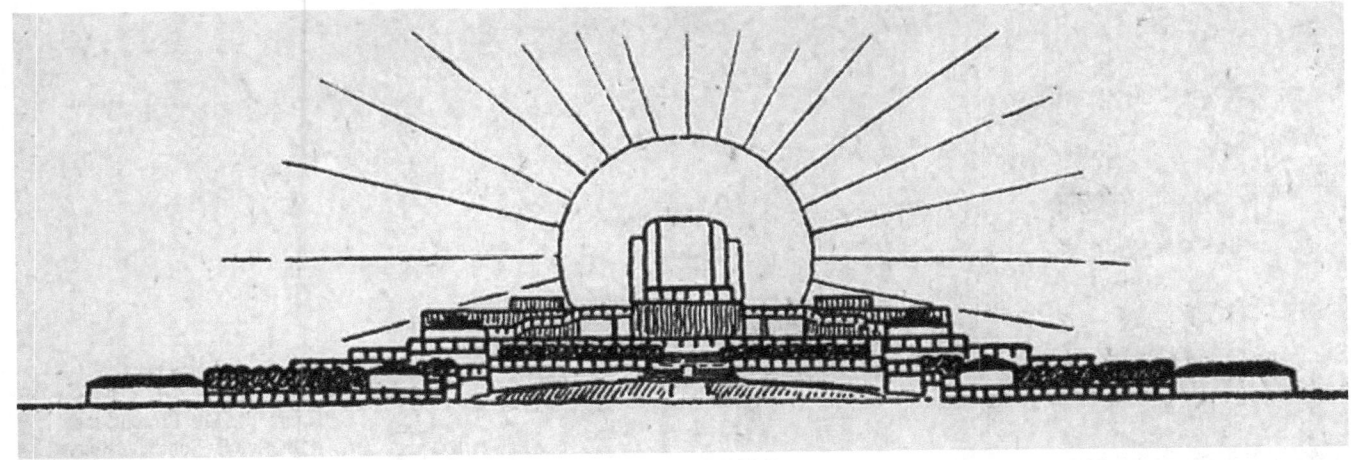

Figure 18.2-14 Germany. *Stadtkrone*, Bruno Taut, 1919.

Even Ludwig Mies van der Rohe (b. Ludwig Mies, 1886–1969), known later for his disciplined geometry, participated in this brief season of Expressionism. In 1921 he designed a twenty-story skyscraper for the Friedrichstrasse competition in Berlin, proposing a glass-sheathed shard that in plan looked like three leaves attached to a circular stem. In a second design done for his own research, he imagined a tower wrapped by an undulating curtain wall on a butterfly-shaped plan. While shear curtain walls became part of Mies's mature architectural language, the eccentric biomorphic shapes of Expressionism never reappeared.

In 1919, as the Crystal Chain letters were being written, Walter Gropius became the first director of the Bauhaus in Weimar. The new school replaced the Arts and Crafts academy previously directed by Henry van de Velde, himself a precursor of Expressionism. Gropius proposed the Bauhaus as a first step toward the "cathedral of the future," which many interpreted as the "cathedral of socialism." The school's first curriculum did not include architecture, and the teachers came mostly from the arts. Expressionism dominated the curriculum as a result of the influence of the mystic Johannes Itten (1888–1967). This changed with the visit of Dutch theorist Theo van Doesburg (1883–1931) in 1921, after which the Bauhaus moved toward more Rationalist formal concepts.

Van Doesburg published the avant-garde journal *De Stijl*, founded in Rotterdam in 1917, and promoted the abstract aesthetic of Piet Mondrian (1872–1944). Mondrian's *Nieuw-Beelding*, or Neo-Plasticism, relied entirely on primary colors, flat planes, and orthogonal geometry, arranging contrasting color fields into dynamic compositions. Van Doesburg pursued the theory

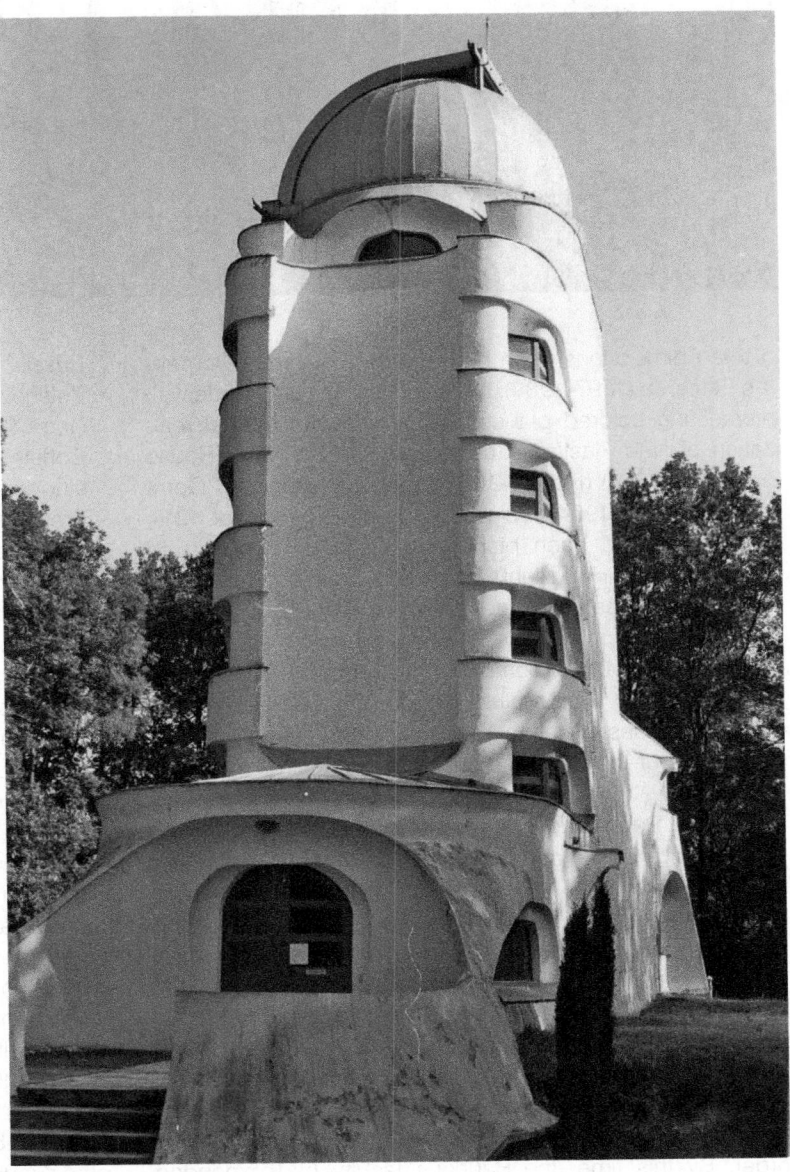

Figure 18.2-15 Potsdam, Germany. Einstein Tower, Erich Mendelsohn, 1919–1921.

Figure 18.2-16 Utrecht, the Netherlands. Schröder House, Gerrit Rietveld, 1924.

in three dimensions. With his architect colleague Cornelis van Eesteren (1897–1988), he proposed housing made with intersecting colored planes. The fullest architectural realization of Neo-Plasticism came with the Schröder House in Utrecht (1924) (Fig. 18.2-16) by furniture designer Gerrit Rietveld (1888–1964). As with his red/blue chair of 1917, Rietveld colored each plane and element in the house independently. His client and future collaborator, Truus Schröder, requested a house without walls, and Rietveld organized the upper story as an open space that could be subdivided into three rooms with differently colored, sliding wooden planes. At Gropius's school the clearest expression of Neo-Plasticism emerged in the 1923 designs for the furnishings of the director's office, conceived as intersecting planes.

The first Bauhaus exhibition was held in 1921 in Berlin at Sommerfeld House, which the students and faculty built for a lumber merchant. They made it of logs and decorated it as a romantic holdover from the Arts and Crafts. The second Bauhaus exhibition, however, produced Haus am Horn, a prototype house built near the school in Weimar in 1923 that broke significantly from the past. The structure's flat roofs, steel-sash windows, and planar surfaces retained none of the handcrafted Expressionist angles of Sommerfeld House. The interiors appeared bright, airy, and flat; the furnishings skeletal and geometric; the kitchen a model of ergonomic order. By this time, the Bauhaus faculty had expanded to include the Swiss painter Paul Klee (1879–1940); the

Russian painter Kandinsky, whose brand of abstraction the Bolsheviks now condemned as decadent; László Moholy-Nagy (1895–1946), a Hungarian designer sympathetic to Constructivism; and Oskar Schlemmer (1888–1943). Gifted students, such as Herbert Bayer (1900–1985) and Marcel Breuer (1902–1981), became catalyzing members of the design studios. Bauhaus posters emulated Constructivism, with dynamic abstract compositions made from squared-off letters and numbers. The purging of Expressionism at Haus am Horn resulted in one of the first examples of *Neue Sachlichkeit*, New Objectivity, in Germany. The exhibition so irritated the right-wing city authorities, who associated the style with Bolshevism, that Gropius and his school were forced to leave Weimar.

The transfer of the Bauhaus to Dessau in 1925 allowed Gropius to design a new Bauhaus building as a manifesto of Modernism (Fig. 18.2-17). While its glazed front elevations closely resembled a factory, the dynamic pinwheel of its three major wings belonged to Constructivism. The school's asymmetry resulted from its program, which placed workshops in the glazed wing, architecture studios in the wing with banded windows, and student housing in a five-story tower with a balcony for each room to the rear. A bridge lined with administrative offices spanned the driveway to connect the two teaching areas, while a lower canteen hall led back to the student residences. Breuer designed the tubular furnishings, including the still-popular Wassily armchair.

Figure 18.2-17 Dessau, Germany. The Bauhaus, Walter Gropius, 1926.

In 1927 Gropius appointed Hannes Meyer (1889–1954), a Swiss exponent of New Objectivity, as instructor of the Bauhaus's first architecture course. A year later Gropius left the school and Meyer became director. Meyer pushed the school away from formal concerns toward a more materialist interpretation of design. His tenure was marred by severe political conflicts, partly triggered by his own affiliations with the Communist Party. The clashes resulted in Meyer's forced resignation in 1930. He moved to the Soviet Union, along with Ernst May (1886–1970) and other leftist architects, the following year.

The last director of the Bauhaus, Mies van der Rohe, had shown left-wing sympathies as the designer of the 1926 Monument to Rosa Luxemburg and Karl Liebknecht in Berlin. After the conflicts that surrounded Meyer, he chose to close the school for several months, expelling the most radical students. At the time of his appointment he had just completed his two most lyrical projects, both conceived with interior designer Lilly Reich (1885–1947). The first, the temporary German Pavilion at the Barcelona Exposition of 1929 (reconstructed in 1983) (Fig. 18.2-18), offered an uncompromised statement of minimalism. He treated each of its staggered planes, including the flat roofs, using independent materials: travertine paving, large panes of green tinted glass, a light box of frosted glass, outer walls of green Tinian marble, and inner walls in book-matched butterfly patterns of rose-veined onyx. Shining chrome-covered columns with a cruciform section stood out against the planes, while the sole occupants of the maze-like space were two broad-seated Barcelona chairs for the king and the queen and a bronze statue of a nude in the patio pond.

Mies carried over many ideas, such as the chrome-plated columns, from the pavilion in Barcelona to the Tugendhat House in Brno, Czechoslovakia (1930) (Fig. 18.2-19a,b). The clients, a wealthy Jewish couple, allowed him fairly free rein to create elegant, flowing spaces. He constructed one of the freestanding planes of black onyx, while setting

Figure 18.2-18 Barcelona. German Pavilion, Ludwig Mies van der Rohe, 1929 (reconstructed in 1983 by M. Sola-Morales).

off the dining area from the main living room with a curved *séparé* in veined ebony. The use of floor-to-ceiling panes of glass wrapping around the salon created a sense of integration with the landscape.

Steeped in his profession and interested mostly in making good buildings, Mies attempted to deflate the Bauhaus's political issues. He hired the art critic Ludwig Hilberseimer (1885–1967) as the master of the housing studios. In 1924 Hilberseimer had produced a terrifying vision of the city of the future that he called the *Hochhausstadt*, or High-Rise City, a scene of tall slabs connected at the fifth-floor level with aerial walkways (Fig. 18.2-20). He envisioned an unrelenting city of chilling uniformity, where no blade of grass

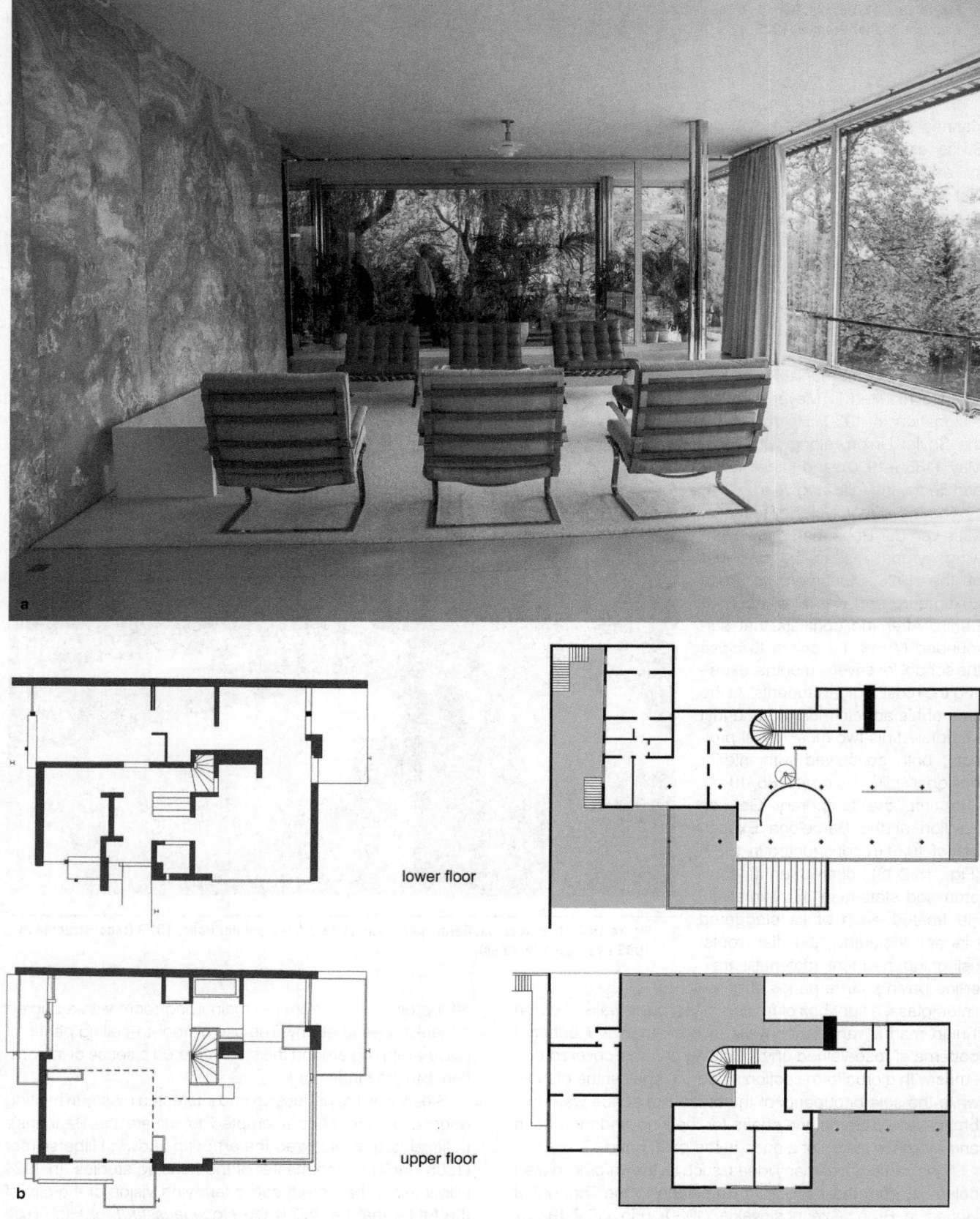

Figure 18.2-19 Brno, Czech Republic. (a) Tugendhat House, view of living room, Mies van der Rohe, 1930. (b) Comparative plans of Schröder House in Utrecht by Rietveld (left) and Tugendhat House in Brno by Mies van der Rohe (right).

Figure 18.2-20 Germany. View of the 1924 Vertical Metropolis, from Ludwig Hilberseimer's *Groszstadt Architektur*, 1927.

would ever grow. At the Bauhaus, however, he altered his approach, coaching the students to develop a Modernist version of the Garden City for low-rise urbanization plans made up of densely placed, *L*-shaped units. The Bauhaus came increasingly under attack as the Nazi Party gained power, and in 1932 the school was closed once again. Mies briefly reopened it in Berlin as a private institution, hoping to be free of political struggles. But a year later, after the Gestapo tried to bar Kandinsky, a Russian Jew, and Hilberseimer, an exponent of Marxism, for racial and political reasons, the Bauhaus came to an end.

Further Reading

Banham, Reyner. *Theory and Design in the First Machine Age.* London: Architectural Press, 1960.

Blau, Eve. *The Architecture of Red Vienna, 1919–1934.* Cambridge, MA: MIT Press, 1999.

Droste, Magdalena. *Bauhaus, 1919–1933.* Cologne, Germany: Taschen, 1991.

Frampton, Kenneth. *Studies in Tectonic Culture: The Poetics of Construction in Nineteenth and Twentieth Century Architecture.* Cambridge, MA: MIT Press, 1995.

Ikonnikov, Andrei. *Russian Architecture of the Soviet Period.* Translated by L. Lyapin. Moscow: Raduga, 1988.

Khan-Magomedov, Selim O. *Pioneers of Soviet Architecture.* New York: Rizzoli, 1987.

Moos, Stanislaus von. *Le Corbusier: Elements of a Synthesis.* Cambridge, MA: MIT Press, 1979.

Nerdinger, Winfried. *Walter Gropius.* Berlin: Bauhaus Archive, 1985.

Sommel, Flora. *Le Corbusier: Architect and Feminist.* New York: John Wiley & Sons, 2004.

18.3 TOTALITARIAN SETTINGS IN MODERN EUROPE
Architecture as Propaganda

World War I (1914–1918) shook up and redistributed much of Europe. Old empires, including the Habsburg and the Ottoman, vanished overnight. Italy and Germany, both only recently unified, stood in ruins. Faced with demands for a return to order and fearful of another Bolshevik Revolution, Italy in 1922 gave way to an authoritarian government run by the Fascist Party and its charismatic leader, Benito Mussolini. A decade later Germany followed suit, with the rise of Adolf Hitler's Nazi Party. Spain also fell to a military dictatorship in 1936, as had Portugal in 1932.

While totalitarian governments used censorship, police repression, and terrorist techniques to eliminate opposition, they projected a benevolent public image, celebrating the virtues of motherhood and family values. Amid the crisis in world capitalism after 1929, they boasted of bureaucratic efficiency, full employment, and harmonious national unity. The architects of Fascist Italy and Nazi Germany created grand assembly spaces and monumental public buildings as propaganda. They returned to building on a colossal scale, using piles of masonry in inflated classical style to express the durability of the military regimes. As their economies worsened the authoritarian regimes turned their aggression beyond internal foes to weaker countries, provoking World War II and precipitating greater ruin for Europe.

Italian Fascism: Between Modernism and Totalitarianism

Although Italy fought on the winning side of World War I, its economic and political fabric was left devastated. In 1922 the black-shirted members of the Fascist Party undermined the parliamentary process. They symbolically marched on Rome to demonstrate their disenchantment with the ailing republic. Three years later, following the assassination of opposition leader Giacomo Matteotti, Benito Mussolini (1883–1945) proclaimed himself dictator, creating the twentieth century's first military regime. He called this new rule "totalitarianism," signifying a political system in which the majority of citizens adhered to state ideology. The Fascist Party restructured the trade unions as an extension of the state, while the government appointed civic officials, eliminating elections. The press was strictly censored, opposition parties were outlawed, and their leaders beaten and jailed. Women were considered mostly in terms of their maternal reproductive function or else in private as prostitutes. Architecture assumed an important role in promoting the Fascist state.

Using mass media and bureaucracy, Mussolini projected the image of Italy as a great corporate state that was both technologically advanced and protective of the conservative values of the family. His movement revived the Roman motif of the *fascio* bundle of sticks, bound with the *littorio* axe, to symbolize the strength of the people under a single leader. Fascism thrived on uniforms, symbols, songs, and children's camps to promote a compelling vision of national identity. The careful censorship of radio, newspapers, and cinema removed any negative messages about Fascism while fostering Mussolini's personality cult. *Il Duce*, "the leader," became ubiquitous, appearing at every ground-breaking, bicycle race, and military parade, ready with a stirring speech for all occasions.

Fascism revitalized Italian architecture as a grand frame for Mussolini's exploits. Early in the century Italy had produced a single, highly influential flicker of avant-garde culture with the Futurists. Urged on by Filippo Marinetti's celebration of the destructive beauty of machines and war, however, many of the Futurists, including the promising architect Antonio Sant'Elia, lost their lives as combatants in World War I. Around 1920, Milan hosted another movement in the arts, the *Novecento*, or twentieth-century, style. Painters such as Mario Sironi (1885–1961) and Giorgio de Chirico (1888–1978) stripped their scenes to simple geometric representations of large volumes and shadow-filled voids that anticipated a new architectural taste for pure monumentality. Giovanni Muzio (1893–1982), the most influential of the *Novecento* architects, designed Ca' Brüta, a two-block apartment complex in Milan in 1919 (Fig. 18.3-1). Unlike the Futurists, who attempted to break with the past,

▼ **1922**

Mussolini and the Fascist Party gain control of the Italian government

Muzio's Ca' Brüta, sign of the Novecento style, built in Milan

▲ **1922**

▼ **1924**

Asplund's Stockholm Public Library begun

Weissenhof settlement in Stuttgart built by Modernist architects for the Werkbund

▲ **1927**

▼ **1932**

Terragni begins Casa del Fascio in Como

Muzio stylized historic architecture. In Ca' Brüta he increased the sense of mass by flattening the niches, half-columns, pediments, and balustrades of Renaissance classicism until they resembled tracings on a bloated figure. A gigantic triumphal arch, flattened and stripped of all decoration, stretched between the two volumes of the complex. Muzio's superhuman scale and inflated classicism became the foundation of the official Fascist style.

The *Novecento* style influenced one of the first major Fascist public projects, the Foro Mussolini by Enrico Del Debbio (1891–1973), begun in 1928 on the northern outskirts of Rome (Fig. 18.3-2). Emulating an ancient imperial forum, the architect arranged a group of sports halls and a stadium around an obelisk and

Figure 18.3-1 Milan, Italy. Ca' Brüta, Giovanni Muzio, 1919–1922.

a mosaic-paved plaza. The mosaics repeated the name "Duce" and depicted military emblems and airplanes. Del Debbio coated the stout volumes of the two buildings in red plaster and laced them with thin vestiges of white columns and broken pediments. Double-height, muscle-bound male nudes lined the parapets of the stadium. Luigi Moretti (1907–1973) designed the obelisk dedicated to Mussolini with staggered vertical setbacks like a miniature Manhattan skyscraper.

The dictator's biographer and mistress, Margherita Sarfatti (1880–1961), influenced the aesthetic policy of Fascism's early years. A prominent Jewish intellectual, she had been central to the success of the *Novecento* movement in Milan. In the late 1920s, however, she was dropped from the dictator's life. Thereafter, the prominent academic architect Marcello Piacentini (1881–1960) became the major power broker. His 1928 scheme for Piazza della Vittoria in Brescia (Fig. 18.3-3) served as the model of Fascist planning. A large section of the historic city underwent the process of *sventramento*, or disemboweling, to be replaced by a rigid

space lined with colossal public buildings, including Italy's first skyscraper, which stretched thirteen stories. Piacentini carefully repeated historic types, such as loggias and campaniles, and used familiar materials, such as travertine and banded masonry. At the same time, he inflated the structure's scale and stripped down its facades to the essentials.

While Piacentini borrowed freely from *Novecento* style, he also recognized the innovative work of younger Rationalist architects. The Gruppo 7, founded in 1926 in Milan and inspired by Le Corbusier and the Bauhaus, attempted to create an Italian version of functionalism. The group's first experiment was the Novocomum apartment block in Como (Fig. 18.3-4), completed in 1929 by Giuseppe Terragni (1904–1942). Its cylindrical, glazed corners evoked the Constructivist workers' clubs, while its bands of long windows followed Le Corbusier's invitation to liberate the plan and facade.

Terragni's masterpiece, the Casa del Fascio (Fig. 18.3-5), built as the party headquarters in Como between 1932 and 1936, presented a stylization of the Renaissance palazzo

Figure 18.3-2 Rome. Foro Mussolini, Modernist obelisk dedicated to Mussolini, Luigi Moretti, begun 1928.

Figure 18.3-3 Brescia, Italy. Piazza della Vittoria, Marcello Piacentini, 1928.

Figure 18.3-4 Como, Italy.
Novocomum apartment block,
Giuseppe Terragni, 1929.

Figure 18.3-5 Como, Italy. Casa
del Fascio, Terragni, 1932–1936.

Fascist Summer Camps

In 1936, one of Piacentini's assistants, Giuseppe Vaccaro, built the audaciously functionalist AGIP Colonia Summer Camp at Cesenatico on the Adriatic coast. The complex belonged to a group of summer "colonies" run by the state for the indoctrination of Fascist youth. The camps accommodated hundreds of children aged eight to fourteen, who spent a month or two away from the city to engage in gymnastics, sing Fascist songs, and breathe the healthy sea air under the strict supervision of nurses and guards. Vaccaro's building rose on *pilotis*, allowing an easy flow from the back lawns to the beach. He scored the three levels of its oblong box-like dorms with deep, shaded, banded windows.

Cesenatico, Italy. **AGIP summer camp, Giuseppe Vaccaro, 1936.**

overlooking a large open piazza facing the apse of the cathedral. By stripping away all iconography and leaving only a luminous geometrical puzzle, Terragni, a devout Fascist, hoped to convey the rather antithetical ideal of transparency to the party. He used the reinforced concrete frame as an open structure to layer translucent planes of glass bricks. The classical symmetry of the seven-bay facade was upset by the decision to treat five bays as a cage of rectangular sunscreens and the right two bays as a completely blank zone for political posters. The glazed atrium took the place of a courtyard, spanned by deep concrete beams and glass-brick ceilings that sent glowing light in all directions. On the left of the entry foyer Terragni installed a black marble altar to the Fascist martyrs.

Italian Rationalism began to push the boundaries of Fascist style after the results of several public competitions. The new Santa Maria Novella Station in Florence (Fig. 18.3-6), the competition for which was won by Giovanni Michelucci (1891–1990) and his students, opened in 1934. Built in reinforced concrete and clad with Florentine brownstone, it combined familiar materials to produce unprecedented formal results. Michelucci composed the exterior

Figure 18.3-6 Florence. Santa Maria Novella train station, Giovanni Michelucci et al., 1932.

with balanced asymmetry. He wrapped the base with broad bands of glazing and pulled vertical bands of translucent onyx over the ticket hall. A flat glass ceiling cantilevered on steel beams brought light to the circulation space in front of the train platforms, adding a new dynamism to the ferrovitreous solutions of the past. Luxurious marble pavers with brass insets enhanced the station's charm. Mussolini, who preferred straightforward variations on classicism, was forced to respond to the controversial new station in a major speech, declaring that Italian architecture could be both Fascist and modern.

The Fascists felt ambivalent about cities. While the regime feared them as dangerous and subversive, the dictator longed to have the largest city in the world as a point of pride. Mussolini thus extended Rome's territory and boosted its monumental role while simultaneously pursuing anti-urban policies. He hoped to reduce the size of large cities by building a series of new towns for agricultural resettlement. He began with the rebuilding of his own hometown, Predappio, and sponsored the planning of eleven new Fascist towns. The most successful, Sabaudia (1932–1934) (Fig. 18.3-7a,b), was designed by Gino Cancellotti, Eugenio

Montuori, Luigi Piccinato, and Alfredo Scalpelli. Set near the coast at Monte Circeo, its growth was limited by the natural borders of an artificial lake on one side and a new national forest on the other. The architecture was consistently Rationalist, with flat roofs, banded windows, and smooth planes, while the layout evoked the ideals of Ebenezer Howard's Garden City.

In 1936 Mussolini declared the Italian Empire, having invaded Ethiopia the year before with air raids. Italian troops were dispatched to repress the independence movements in the existing colonies of Albania and Libya. After signing the 1936 friendship pact with Nazi Germany, Mussolini defined the two states' new partnership as the "Axis," invoking classical order and imperial scale. Plans formulated by the two military regimes included the linking of Germany's 4,000 km (2,485 miles) of Autobahn with Italy's project for 3,000 km (1,864 miles) of *autostrada*.

The change in attitude became palpable during the planning of the greatest of all Fascist projects, the World Exposition for Rome (EUR), set for 1942 (Fig. 18.3-8). Piacentini initially engaged only Rationalist designers to work on his master plan for a site 3 km (1.8 miles) west of

Figure 18.3-7 Sabaudia, Italy.
(a) City center, Gino Cancellotti,
Eugenio Montuori, Luigi Piccinato,
and Alfredo Scapelli, 1932–1934.
(b) Aerial view.

the city walls. The first schemes in 1937 included glass and steel high-rises and cloverleaf intersections reminiscent of Le Corbusier's Radiant City. As the plan evolved, however, travertine was prescribed for all buildings, and the over-blown columns and arches of *Novecento* style returned as bombastic signifiers of empire. Muzio was awarded an important segment of the monumental district, the twin ex-edras at its entry. Two major monuments, the Palace of Italian Civilization and the Congress Hall, loomed at either end of the first cross-axis. On the former, a thick travertine shell of six levels of crisply etched arches encased a 50 m (164 ft) cube of glass and steel curtain walls. Known colloquially as the "Square Colosseum," it stood high on a plinth reached by a majestic three-tiered staircase. The arches served as efficient, if extravagant, *brise soleils*.

At the other end of the cross-axis, Adalberto Libera (1903–1963) produced the Congress Hall (Fig. 18.3-9a,b), a building dominated by a monolithic square shaft and capped by a vault made of segmental arches. Broad columns framed the entry, masking a glass and steel curtain wall. A podium jutting out of the middle of the facade, intended to hold a sculpture, cast an evocative deep shadow. Libera, who was among the original Rationalists in Milan, treated the rest of the structure as a simple hangar-like box. He clad it with alternating courses of marble masonry and at the hooded short ends placed metallic frames to carry broad planes of glass. The Congress Hall's flat roof provided an enormous garden terrace for outdoor meetings. World War II put a halt to the planned EUR, leaving a setting of superhuman scale for a phantom empire. Its ponderous

---

CULTURE, SOCIETY, GENDER

Casa Malaparte: The Individual versus the Regime

In 1938 the writer Curzio Malaparte (born Kurt Suckert, 1898–1957) built the Casa Malaparte, a rusty-colored, oblong box perched above the crashing surf on a jagged outcrop of the island of Capri. Initially a strong supporter of Fascism, Malaparte participated in the 1922 March on Rome. He nursed an increasingly critical view of the regime, however, as an internationally respected journalist and diplomat. In 1933 he was exiled to the Sicilian island of Lipari for his outspoken criticism of Mussolini and Hitler but, thanks to friends in high places, remained relatively free to roam.

Malaparte first commissioned Adalberto Libera to design his house on Capri in 1937 but completed the design by himself, adding an inverted pyramidal stair to the rooftop terrace, which included a white, curved solarium. He created an austere, refectory-like salon in the form of a pure white box with a stone floor, lit by two long windows. Benches ran along the walls looking toward a pyramidal fireplace that had an uncanny window inside the hearth. Next to his bedroom was the room of *la favorita*, his mistress of the moment. Malaparte's hermitage yielded one of modern Italy's most extreme statements of architectonic purity, starkly prismatic inside and out. The house remained an individualist's expression of resistance both to the regime and to the strictures of society. He continued his defiance by leaving the villa to the People's Republic of China in his will.

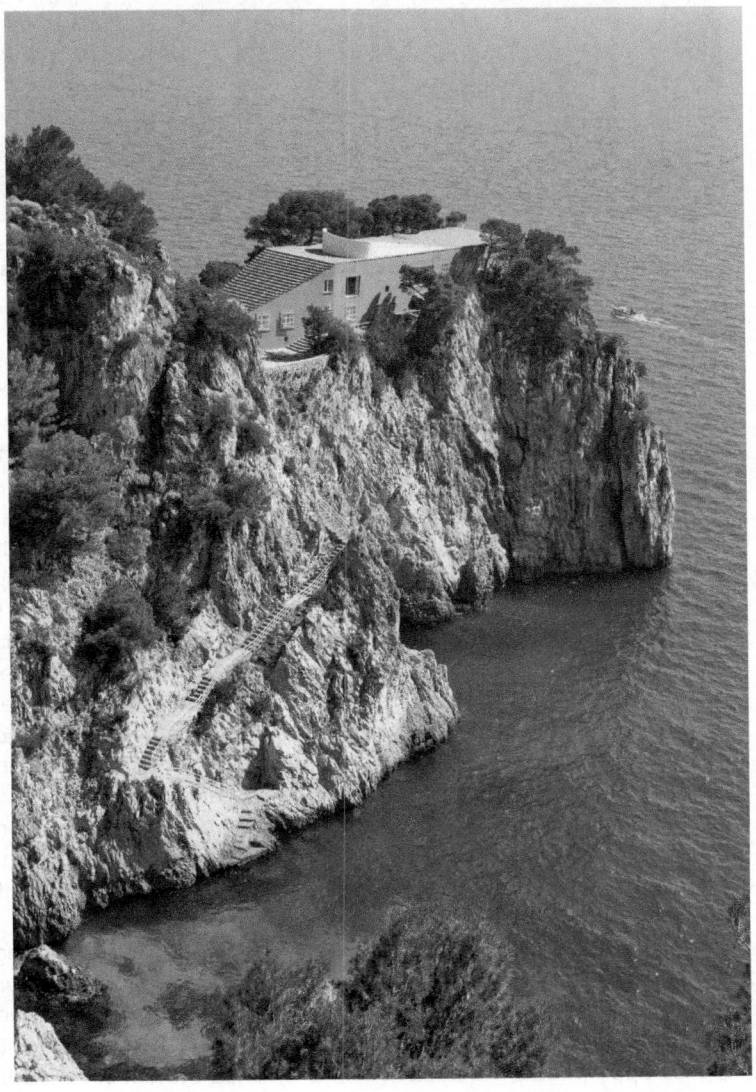

Capri. Casa Malaparte, Adalberto Libera and Curzio Malaparte, 1938–1943.

Figure 18.3-8 Rome. EUR, Palace of Italian Civilization, G. Guerrini, E. La Padula, and M. Romano, 1942.

structures appealed to antiquity in their cladding and proportions while remaining modern at their core.

Nazi Germany: Millennial Classicism for the Master Race

Fascism attracted wide acceptance until 1936, when the Italian regime broke international treaties. In the Depression years, it promised new hope for capitalism by eliminating labor conflicts and maintaining the loyalty of businesses to the state. The future dictator of Germany, Adolf Hitler (1889–1945), was inspired by Mussolini's success. Hitler, a destitute Austrian artist who in his youth failed to gain admission to Vienna's academy, joined right-wing fringe groups in Munich after World War I. He was arrested in 1923 for terrorist tactics of the sort used by the early Fascists and sent for a brief period to jail. Shortly after, he published his political credo, *Mein Kampf* (*My Struggle*, 1925), and as a frustrated architect made plans for a triumphal arch bigger than the one in Paris and the world's greatest dome, which would cover all of the German community. When a few years later he assumed the role of *Führer*, a direct translation of *Duce*, he covered Germany with flags of his own design, featuring a rotated swastika in a circle on a red field. Nazi ideologues appropriated the ancient Jain and Hindu symbol of good fortune as their logo for the master race. To the Italian

formula for totalitarianism Hitler added maniacal efficiency laced with more emphatic cruelty and racism. The Nazis also sponsored children's summer camps and, for the enemies of the state, dreadful concentration camps.

During the early 1930s the brown-shirted members of the Nazi movement staged violent acts of intimidation against minorities. They detested the Jews as the most successful capitalists and most prominent socialists. Taking advantage of the 1933 terrorist attack on the Reichstag, the German parliament in Berlin, Hitler's party took control of the government on a law-and-order platform. The Nazis, working on the Fascist model, soon eliminated freedom of the press, trade unions, and political parties while engaging architects and designers to execute grand projects of propaganda.

After the military regime took power, proponents of academic classicism gained wide support, as did the defenders of *Heimatstil*, the vernacular of the homeland. The rural settlements sponsored by the regime, such as Ramersdorf by Guido Harbers (1934) and Schottenheimsiedlung near Regensburg (1934), were built with pitched roofs and farm-style typologies (Fig. 18.3-10). Hitler's cultural policies condemned Modernism in the arts as "degenerate" and poorly suited to national values. The Modernist flat roof became a frequent subject of ridicule and source of racist slurs, called "Oriental" and "nomadic." Anti-Modernist critics

Figure 18.3-9 Rome. (a) EUR, aerial view, 1943. (b) Congress Hall, Adalberto Libera, 1942.

Figure 18.3-10 Regensburg, Germany. Schottenheimsiedlung (now Konradsiedlung-Wutzlhofen), Nazi-era model of *Heimatstil* housing that returned to the local vernacular, 1934.

dubbed the 1927 Weissenhof settlement an "Arab village" (Fig. 18.3-11), and functionalist architecture came to signify "cultural Bolshevism."

At the outset of the regime, the Nazi hierarchy seemed more concerned with scale than style, and throughout the decade functionalist projects continued to be built using modern construction materials such as steel and reinforced concrete. Werner March's Olympia Stadium for the 1936 Olympics in Berlin, while encrusted with Nazi insignia, appeared a thoroughly modern project. Hitler pursued his ideal architecture in Munich, where his favored architect, Paul Troost (1878–1934), designed symmetrical additions to Leo von Klenze's Königsplatz (Fig. 18.3-12) (see Section 15.1). The new buildings included the Führerbau, a palace for the

dictator's offices, and a matching building across from it. Troost inserted between the two palaces twin tempiettos, the square *Ehrentempels*, as open-air memorials to Nazi martyrs, each framed with twenty-four square Doric columns. Upon Troost's sudden death, his wife, Gerdy Troost (1904–2003), brought the projects to term and remained an intimate of Hitler. In 1938, she published the influential book on Nazi architecture *Das Bauen in Neuen Reich* (*Construction in a New Reich*).

Some of the formal ideals of the new nationalist style derived from the National Romantic movement in Scandinavia. Gunnar Asplund (1885–1940) at the Stockholm Public Library (1924–1928) (Fig. 18.3-13) combined classical models with abstract geometry, placing a stark cylinder

Figure 18.3-11 Weissenhof Siedlung, Germany. Duplex, Le Corbusier, 1927.

Figure 18.3-12 Munich. Königsplatz, twin temples and Führerbau added to Leo von Klenze's space by Paul and Gerdy Troost, 1934–1938.

Figure 18.3-13 Stockholm. Public Library, Gunnar Asplund, 1924–1928.

above a cube. While his intentions were closer to the democratic ideals of Étienne-Louis Boullée than to totalitarianism, the stark symmetrical volumes held great appeal for those seeking a powerful national style.

In 1935 Hitler chose Albert Speer (1905–1981), a student of Heinrich Tessenow, as the new state architect. The young architect began his interventions in Nuremberg, a city that had acquired special prominence for the Nazis as the site of their annual party rally (Fig. 18.3-14). In the Marsfeld district on the southern outskirts of town he laid out the Grosse

---

CONSTRUCTION, TECHNOLOGY, THEORY

Nazi Concentration Camps

In 1933, during the first year of the Nazi regime, Hitler's henchman Heinrich Himmler set up the initial work camp for political prisoners at Dachau, outside of Munich. From there a system of hundreds of slave labor camps was established throughout Germany and later in the countries appropriated by Germany, including Poland, Austria, and Italy. The camps followed rigid planning guidelines, with industrial buildings isolated behind a wall to one side and long row buildings behind another wall for the dormitories. The administrative complex faced the rows as a U-shaped series of long wings.

The largest camps, like Dachau, housed more than 5,000 prisoners. During the last three years of World War II they were transformed into death camps to facilitate the "Final Solution" for the complete elimination of the Jews, announced by Hitler in 1942. Jews from all over Europe were sent in railroad boxcars by Nazi soldiers to be scientifically processed in holding camps and dispatched to the extermination camps in Poland, where they were usually executed in gas chambers.

Strasse, a 40 m (128 ft) wide parade axis paved with huge granite slabs, for the marching formations of thousands of troops. At the cross-axis he placed on one side the German Stadium, modeled on the ancient stadium in Athens, and opposite it the *Zeppelinfeld*, with its marble-clad tribune, inspired by the Altar of Pergamon (see Section 4.2). During Hitler's annual harangues, the disciplined soldiers stood at attention in perfect rows. In 1937 Speer added to this monumental setting the "Cathedral of Light," an ephemeral nave made of 130 anti-aircraft Klieg lights. He shot the lamps into the sky at regular intervals in crossed patterns, producing a spectacle intended to enhance the religious fervor of these rallies in support of the *Führer* as a messiah figure. Farther down the parade axis, the Congress Hall, designed by Ludwig Ruff (1878–1934) and his son Franz (1906–1979), an immense simulation of the Colosseum, was planned to hold 100,000 but remained half finished at the outbreak of World War II. The granite panels of its facade represented flattened, stylized variations of the classical model, similar to the late Fascist style of Piacentini.

Speer reserved his greatest attention for the new plan of Berlin, begun in 1938 (Fig. 18.3-15). He hoped to realize Hitler's dream of the world's biggest triumphal arch and largest dome on a new north–south axis run through the Tiergarten. As with EUR, the plan was intended for an international exposition to be held in 1950, when the city's name would be temporarily changed to "Germania." At the same time that munitions were being built up and young Germans drafted into Europe's largest army, Hitler revealed his architectural goal: "Our task is to build a 1,000-year nation with a 1,000-year historical and cultural heritage for the future lying ahead of our fair-born 1,000-year city."

Hitler's headquarters, the new *Reichskanzlei*, or New Chancellery (Fig. 18.3-16), stood out as one of the few buildings realized for the Berlin plan. It had an inordinately long, narrow plan, like the great temple compounds in ancient Thebes (see Section 3.2). While the exterior blended with the three-story surroundings of Leipzigerplatz, the scale of the interiors proved pharaonic. The route to Hitler's office extended more than 300 m (984 ft), passing through five control spaces. The austere Doric columns and pilasters rose double height. The great gallery, covered completely in marble, gave evidence of the building's great expense. Hitler's subterranean bunker lay a short walk away in the garden.

Speer's big plans for Hitler's Berlin remained mostly as scale models, as the military buildup took precedence over architecture. His own role evolved in 1942 from court

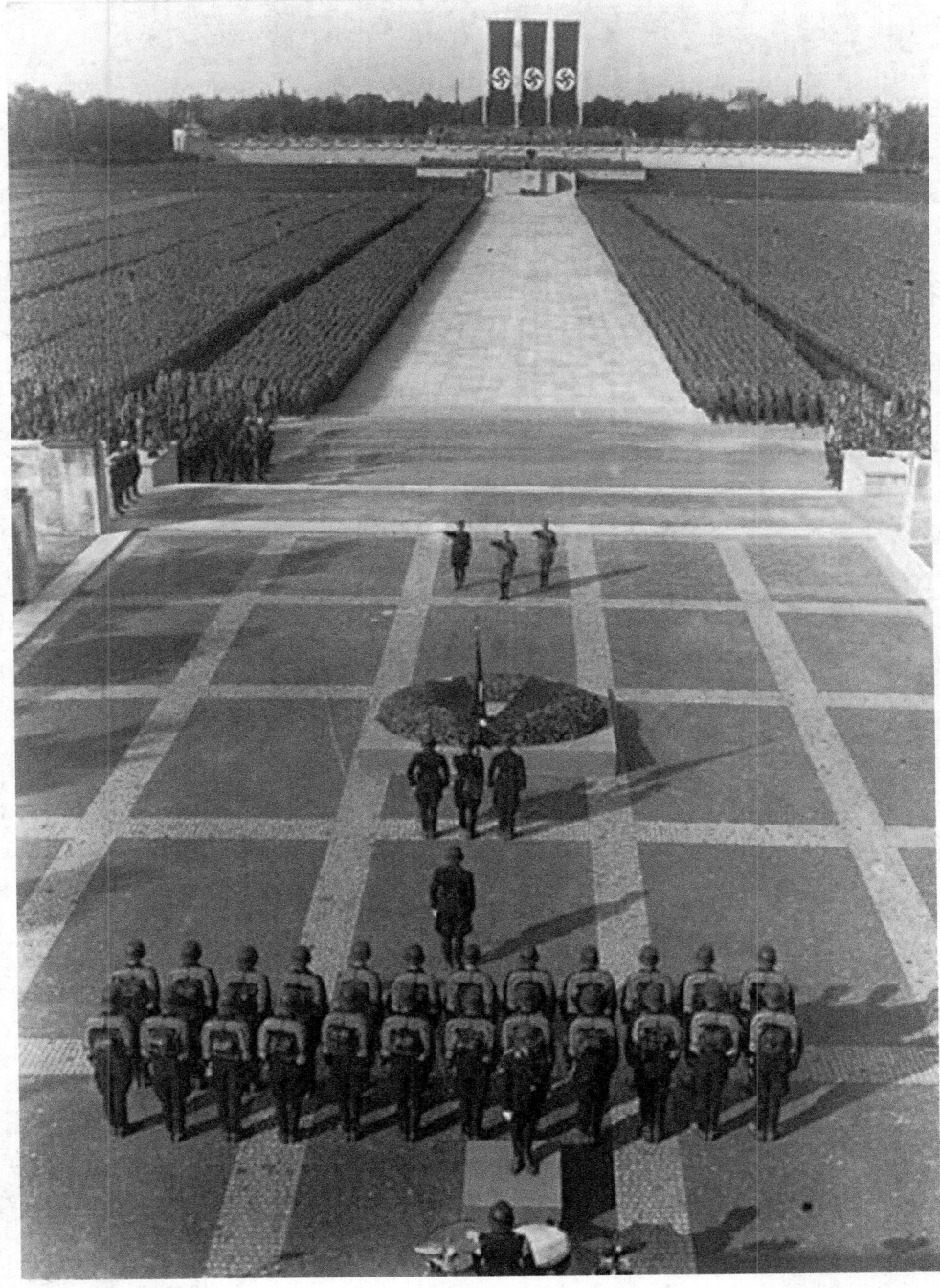

Figure 18.3-14 Nuremburg, Germany. *Zeppelinfeld* **building, Albert Speer, 1930s.**

architect to minister of armaments. After the Germans invaded Poland in 1939, they had little time for culture. The Nazis used foreign conscripts as forced labor to build up the eastern defenses of Germany and expanded their system of concentration camps, confining enemies, dissidents, and those considered to be racially inferior. The initial "work" camp at Dachau near Munich served as a detention site for political prisoners during the first year of the regime in 1933. On its iron gates the Nazis inscribed the insidious slogan *Arbeit macht frei*, "Work makes you free." The administration

occupied a *U*-shaped complex at the head of four rows of long, narrow, wooden barracks. Although many of the prisoners were Jewish, their crimes at this point were political. In 1935 the arrests began to include Jehovah's Witnesses, homosexuals, and immigrants, and three years later came the crackdown on Jews and gypsies. After Dachau over 150 more camps were built, and with the annexation of Poland in 1938, still more added, including the notorious death camp of Birkenau at Auschwitz. While many deaths and perfidious medical experiments took place in the German camps, the

Figure 18.3-15 Berlin. Model of Nazi plan for central city, Speer, 1938.

Figure 18.3-16 Berlin. New Reichskanzlerei for Hitler's offices, Speer, 1938.

Nazis preferred to send their victims to Poland rather than have them exterminated on German soil. Of the more than 6 million murdered by the regime, 1 million were killed with cyanide gas at Birkenau, the victims of an industrial and bureaucratic approach to mass murder.

Genghis Khan and Timur probably carried out greater slaughters, and horrendous acts of racist terror have included the extermination of indigenous Americans and the Middle Passage of 15 million African slaves to the Western Hemisphere. Yet the Holocaust perpetrated by the Nazis has proved the most diabolical instance of genocide in history. The Nazis applied Taylorism to extermination to fulfill their goal of the systematic and scientific elimination of fellow Europeans. Only a few years earlier Jews had in every way held equal status with non-Jews in Germany; the most successful architect in Berlin during the 1920s, for instance, was Erich Mendelsohn. Defense of a notion of homeland could never justify such wholesale contempt for the dignity of life. The bitterness instilled by the Holocaust and World War II brought an unforeseen consequence for architecture, clearing away everything that hinted at *Heimat*, the celebration of regionalism, or monumental classicism. Although hardly worth the sacrifice in human lives, the war made the world safe for Modernism.

Further Reading

Ciucci, Giorgio. *Gli architetti e il Fascismo: Architettura e città, 1922–1944*. Turin, Italy: Einaudi, 1989.

Helmer, Stephen D. *Hitler's Berlin: The Speer Plans for Reshaping the Central City*. Ann Arbor, MI: UMI Research Press, 1985.

Kostof, Spiro. *The Third Rome, 1870–1950: Traffic and Glory*. Berkeley, CA: University Art Museum, 1973.

Lane, Barbara Miller. *Architecture and Politics in Germany, 1918–1945*. Cambridge, MA: Harvard University Press, 1985.

Scarrocchia, Sandro. *Albert Speer e Marcello Piacentini: L'Architettura del totalitarismo negli anni trenta*. Milan: Skira, 1999.

Taylor, Robert R. *The Word in Stone: The Role of Architecture in the National Socialist Ideology*. Berkeley: University of California Press, 1974.

Visit the free website **www.oup.com/us/ingersoll** to view chapter outlines and study questions; Google Maps showing the location of key sites; links to UNESCO World Heritage Sites; and essays on topics that cross time and culture.

CHAPTER 19

1940–1970

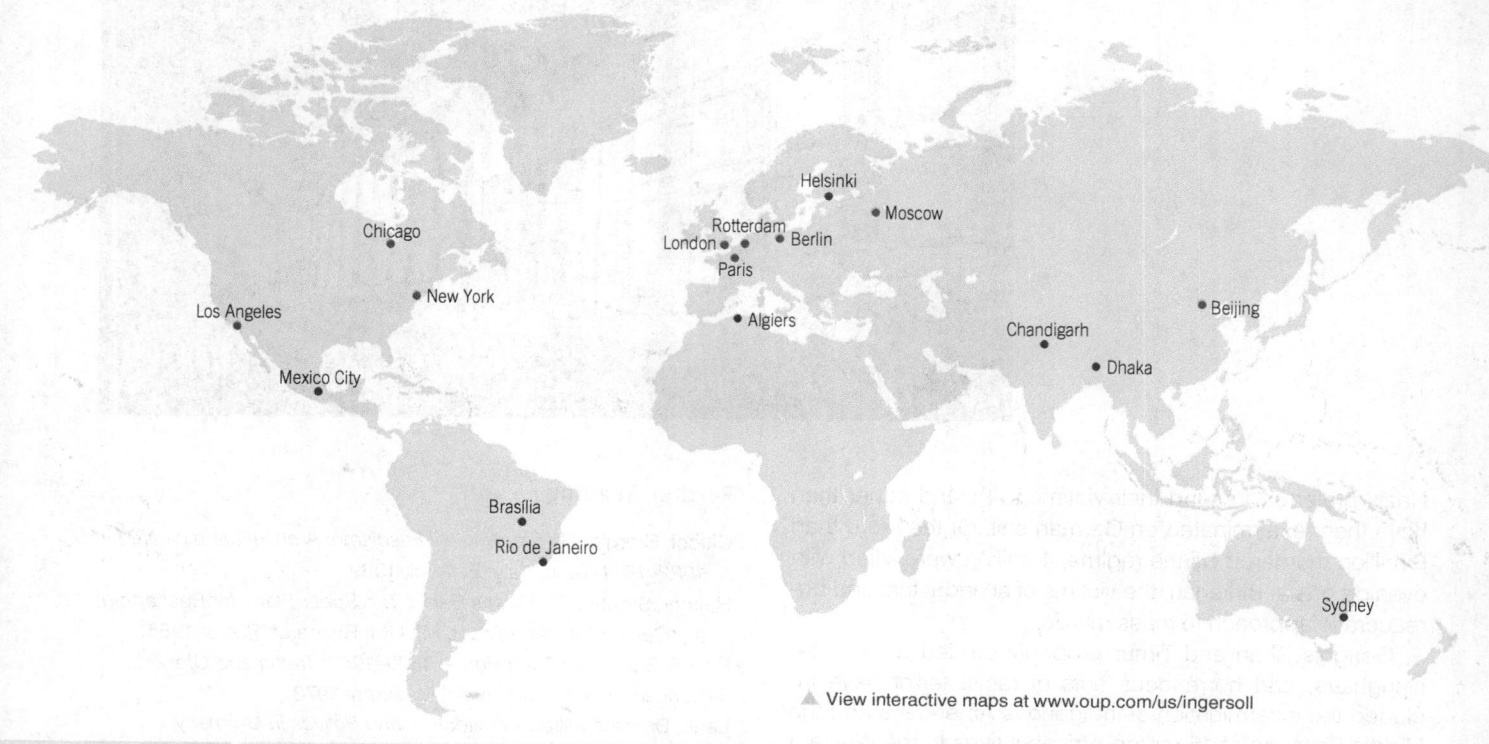

▲ View interactive maps at www.oup.com/us/ingersoll

19.1 THE INTERNATIONAL STYLE AND THE ADVENT OF THE WELFARE STATE:
Modernism Becomes Conventional

19.2 THE BIRTH OF THE THIRD WORLD: Experiments in Postcolonial Architecture

19.3 THE EXPRESSIONIST RESURGENCE: Hybrids amid Mass Culture

The reconstruction of the cities devastated during the aerial bombardments of the Second World War led to a widely accepted application of planning. Large housing settlements and new towns were built in most European countries, reinforcing the structure of the welfare state that guaranteed the health, education, and housing of entire populations. The United States, while relatively untouched by wartime destruction, carried out sizable plans to demolish city centers in the name of urban renewal. The prefabricated concrete panel building and the glass and steel box offered expedient solutions that derived from the minimalist aesthetics of the International Style. Variations of this Modernist approach appeared throughout the world as icons of postcolonial liberation. Universities in Mexico City and Caracas, the new capital cities of Brazil and India, and national banks and public buildings in recently liberated African countries aspired to the clarity and transparency of such modern structures as the United Nations headquarters building in New York City, often producing structures ill-suited to the demands of the climate. As the International Style spread, many architects attempted to combat its banality by exploring Expressionist or organic forms. Hybrid monumental solutions using grand curved shapes and nonorthogonal geometry appeared at university campuses, government centers, museums, and airports, providing a monumentality that broke from the rigidity of mass-produced boxes as well as from the forms of the past.

19.1
THE INTERNATIONAL STYLE AND THE ADVENT OF THE WELFARE STATE
Modernism Becomes Conventional

While the fighting of World War I remained primarily confined to Europe, World War II brought catastrophe to almost every continent. Aerial bombardments pulverized Le Havre, Coventry, London, Berlin, Dresden, Warsaw, Novgorod, Milan, Tripoli, Benghazi, Mandalay, Tokyo, Hangzhou, Darwin, and Honolulu. The first atomic bombs annihilated Hiroshima and Nagasaki. Extreme acts of cruelty, such as the systematic genocide of 6 million European Jews and the governmental sacrifice of millions of Russians, assumed diabolical proportions, still difficult to comprehend or pardon. The war claimed more than 35 million lives in Europe alone, more than half of them civilians. Reconstruction proceeded at a steady pace in Europe and Japan, while the United States, which emerged from the conflict relatively unscathed, surged ahead to build the world's dominant economy.

In most European countries social democratic planning for the welfare state guided the reconstruction effort, leading to the production of new towns, large housing estates, and highway systems. Architects generally avoided monumentality and classicism, disenchanted with the bombastic exploits of Rome and Berlin before the war. For both practical and ideological reasons, they favored the simple, undecorated solutions of functionalism. The International Style, which before the war was seen mostly in avant-garde projects for flat-roofed white boxes with pure planes and long windows, became the canonical solution for reconstruction. The glazed slab of the United Nations secretariat and the stark steel grids designed by Ludwig Mies van der Rohe appeared at the high end of this approach, while the prefabricated concrete panel construction used for mass housing deferred to the low-income needs of the nascent welfare state.

The Postwar Culture of Planning and the Mandate for Neutrality

At the conclusion of World War II (1939–1945), the United States was the only major industrial power still standing. Leadership in architecture thus quite naturally drifted across the Atlantic. Many of the same European Modernists who during the first decades of the twentieth century had idealized America's uninhibited industrialism moved there before, during, and after the war. Walter Gropius and Marcel Breuer landed at Harvard in 1937. Other Bauhaus teachers—Ludwig Mies van der Rohe, Ludwig Hilberseimer, and László Moholy-Nagy—went to Chicago. Erich Mendelsohn,

whose work had been significantly influenced by a visit to the United States in 1924, spent his final decade in San Francisco. America suddenly found itself host to a significant number of key expatriate architects, who initially influenced education more than construction.

The notion of a coherent International Style was anathema to most exponents of Modernism, who like Le Corbusier held that "styles are a lie." When Gropius published a survey of modern architecture as *International Architektur* (1925), he was alluding to the Socialist International and not to style. The formalization of *the* International Style came from two American art historians, Henry-Russell Hitchcock (1903–1987) and Philip Johnson (1906–2005), who in 1932 mounted an exhibition on modern architecture at the Museum of Modern Art in New York. Through the title of their catalogue, *The International Style*, they sidestepped political and social connotations and imposed a stylistic orthodoxy: undecorated volumes, flat roofs, banded fenestration, and asymmetrically ordered white planes. Although not popular before World War II, the International Style suited the needs of reconstruction Europe. It likewise fit the new pragmatism of American corporations. Technical elements such as steel frames, prefabricated concrete walls, and plate glass became widespread signifiers of progress throughout the world.

Postwar architects resumed activity with a reverence for planning. The impressive results of the Five-Year Plans in the Soviet Union, the nationalization of industries and transportation in Fascist Italy and Nazi Germany, and New Deal agencies such as the Tennessee Valley Authority in America encouraged a culture of planning. During the buildup of the American military-industrial complex, large corporations began working for the government to produce munitions, aircraft plants, food, and temporary housing. The greatest triumph of American planning, the Manhattan Project for the atomic bomb, coordinated 130,000 individuals in over thirty different locations on research and production. In 1942, anticipating European reconstruction, Le Corbusier published a manual for planning, the *Charter of Athens*, based on the 1933 Congrès Internationale d'Architecture Moderne (CIAM) convention held on a cruise ship that sailed from Marseilles to Athens. He outlined the principles of functional zoning, isolating housing, recreation, work, and circulation as the four functions of architecture, each deserving of a separate solution. In the same year his Spanish colleague Josep Lluis Sert (1902–1983), who moved to New York in 1939 and in the 1950s served as the dean of Harvard's Graduate School of Design, published *Can Our Cities Survive?*, a fancifully illustrated explanation of the Charter of Athens that was widely circulated in America. Its emphasis on programming, housing, circulation, and the abstract diagrams of planning tended to downplay formal issues in architectural design.

The founding of the United Nations (UN) in 1945 represented one of the major acts of postwar planning. The new organization for maintaining world peace generated a key architectural project of the era, the UN headquarters

Figure 19.1-1 New York. United Nations headquarters, Wallace K. Harrison et al., 1947–1952.

in New York City (Fig. 19.1-1). Le Corbusier arrived in the United States in 1946 as the French delegate to the UN site-selection committee. A year later he was retained as one of ten members of the international design team, under the supervision of Wallace K. Harrison (1895–1981). The nascent peacekeeping organization proposed this collaborative design effort as a demonstration of international cooperation, what Harrison referred to as the "workshop for peace." Despite the ideal of teamwork, Le Corbusier dominated the process, and the final design synthesized his scheme with that of the young Brazilian architect Oscar Niemeyer (1907–2012). The resulting oblong tower, connected to a low-slung auditorium, stood in the midst of a large hanging garden, offering a clear contrast to the typical hemmed-in density of the blocks of Manhattan. The glazed slab of the Secretariat tower became an instant icon of modern technology. The innovative curtain walls used double layers of green-tinted thermopane glass, requiring the insertion of copious air-conditioning equipment into the bands of the grilled mezzanines on the sixth, sixteenth, twenty-eighth, and thirty-ninth floors.

The culture of planning in the United States culminated in the urban renewal program, the offspring from the marriage of the 1949 Housing and Urban Development Act and the 1956 Highway Act. While the first was intended to stimulate affordable housing alternatives and the latter to improve

TIME LINE

 1945

Hiroshima and
Nagasaki destroyed
by U.S. atomic bombs

United Nations
founded

 1945

 1946

United Kingdom approves
New Towns Act and initiates
development of ten cities

*Harrison leads team
of ten architects in
design of United
Nations headquarters
in New York City*

 1947

interurban connections, taken together they led to slum clearance for downtown highway construction. The success of the Golden Triangle project in Pittsburgh (1943–1949) served as the prototype (Fig. 19.1-2). There, planners replaced a decaying industrial slum in the city center with aluminum-clad, cruciform highrises designed by New York architect Irving Claven. These towers in the park seemed like replicas of Le Corbusier's Radiant City (see Section 18.2). Urban renewal produced *tabula rasa* demolitions, flattening city centers and low-income neighborhoods to prepare the way either for Modernist corporate headquarters or for traffic interchanges. Thus, the United States, which had suffered war damage only in Hawaii, experienced the equivalent of the bombed-out sites of European and Japanese reconstruction. Those who had feared that planning would lead to communism could rest assured

Figure 19.1-2 Pittsburgh. Golden Triangle, Irving Claven, 1943–1949.

that the interests of business came first. Only a tiny portion of the nearly half-million poor families displaced by urban renewal obtained access to public housing options.

From 1950 to 1966, entire sections of American downtowns were bulldozed, usually at the expense of poor and ethnic neighborhoods, resulting in new business and government enclaves, such as San Francisco's Embarcadero Center, Boston's Government Center, Philadelphia's Society Hill, and Albany's Empire State Plaza (Fig. 19.1-3). Harrison designed the project in Albany to provide Governor Nelson Rockefeller with an improved version of the UN project. To clear freeway access to a massive parking plinth, 9,000 poor Jewish and Italian residents were displaced. Empire Plaza's marble-clad terrace was lined with slender towers and punctuated by an egg-shaped auditorium. While urban renewal promised to revive city centers, it ultimately had the reverse effect, creating cloistered office environments occupied only during business hours. The community advocate Jane Jacobs (1916–2006), who in 1961 launched

a successful campaign against urban renewal, denounced such plans: "This is not the rebuilding of cities. This is the sacking of cities."

Only a fraction of America's housing stock was the result of direct government subsidies. Many of the most distinguished examples were built for the war effort, such as MacKie and Kamrath's Dutch-inspired Allen Parkway Village in Houston (1942) (Fig. 19.1-4a). While there were noteworthy federal housing projects in San Francisco and New York, subsidized housing became better known for its catastrophes. The failed Pruitt-Igoe project (Fig. 19.1-4b) near downtown St. Louis became the scapegoat for the American program of social housing. Due to the practice of racial segregation in Missouri, the initial plan in 1951 set aside half of the eleven-story slabs for African Americans and half for whites. After a 1954 Supreme Court ruling mandated desegregation, most of the white tenants left. The buildings were soundly built but never properly finished because of budget delays. They contained numerous design

▼ **1947–1953**

Stalin's planners create seven skyscrapers in a ring around Moscow

Israel recognized as independent state

▲ **1948**

▼ **1949**

Mao Zedong leads Communist revolution for the foundation of the People's Republic of China

Eames Case Study house built in Pacific Palisades, California

▲ **1949**

Figure 19.1-3 Albany, New York. Empire State Plaza, Harrison, 1965–1978.

flaws, such as elevators that stopped every third floor and ambiguous social spaces that became crime havens. The absence of maintenance, services, and transportation contributed to the poor general environmental and social malaise. Twenty years after the project's construction, public officials decided to blow up its thirty-three buildings, inspiring a distrust of modern planning for the next few decades.

The U.S. government spent more on financing the loans of the Federal Housing Authority than on social housing. This policy channeled welfare to middle-class homeowners rather than poor renters, on the theory that the benefits of privately owned housing stock would "trickle down" to the poor. In Los Angeles, John Entenza (1905–1984), the publisher of *Arts & Architecture*, attempted to improve middle-class taste

through the Case Study Houses program. Between 1945 and 1963, he matched sponsors with architects to produce twenty-eight prototype houses. Charles Eames (1907–1978) and his wife Ray (1912–1988) designed the most famous of the lot, the Eames House in Pacific Palisades, California (1949) (Fig. 19.1-5), for which they assembled a kit of metal parts and panels ordered from industrial catalogues. They set up a double-height loft like a nomadic structure, open to a luxuriant garden. Two other houses produced by Craig Ellwood (1922–1992) made superb use of steel-frame technology and frosted glass planes. Most of the Case Study Houses relied on a consistent Modernist vocabulary of flat roofs, box-like open plans, suspended planes of glass, and **exoskeletal** pergolas.

▼ **1952**

Barbican Centre begun in London (completed 1986)

Khrushchev assumes power in Soviet Union after death of Stalin

▲ **1953**

▼ **1956**

United States approves National Interstate and Defense Highways Act

Stalinallee begun in East Berlin

▲ **1956**

▼ **1957**

Soviet Union's *Sputnik* space program launches first satellite into outer space

The Modernist box could not compete with the ranch house, however, which, with its low-pitched roofs, looked more like the conventional idea of a house (Fig. 19.1-6). Cliff May (1909–1989), a leading designer of ranch houses in California, proposed in his 1958 book that the type derived from Spanish colonial patio houses. The undecorated wood-frame structure with broad, low-pitched roofs proved flexible to the dweller's needs. Sliding plate-glass windows opened to the rear patio, serving a casual indoor–outdoor lifestyle.

Private developers became the real planners in postwar America. Builders such as William Levitt (1907–1994) mass-produced simplified versions of the ranch house and the New England saltbox type, producing thirty houses per day. Somewhat like Henry Ford's rationalization of the automobile industry, Levitt built his "tract home" through a piece-work process. This allowed him to produce a house at half of the normal market price. The first Levittown opened in 1947, 30 km (18.5 miles) east of Manhattan on Long Island, attracting over 80,000 residents. Its low density, setbacks, cul-de-sac roads, and the absence of civic or commercial services discouraged an urban lifestyle. In all, Levitt and Sons built 140,000 houses and played a major role in marketing the American Dream (Fig. 19.1-7). Instead of European-style, government-owned blocks of prefabricated concrete housing, the United States, through its subsidized loan programs, encouraged the construction of partially prefabricated detached houses, which opened the floodgates to suburban **sprawl**.

When God Was in the Details: The Minimalism of Mies van der Rohe

Ludwig Mies van der Rohe, more than any other Modernist émigré working in the United States, set the standard of elegance for the International Style after World War II. His refinement of a deceptively simple language of steel-frame structures and sheer glass walls encouraged a new cult of restraint, conveyed in the slogan "Less is more." To modern architecture he brought both the solemnity of the ancient Doric temple and the lightness of a Japanese *shoin* palace. Mies, having failed to receive commissions from the Nazi patronage system, left Berlin for Chicago in 1938 to head the school of architecture at the Armour Institute, soon after renamed the Illinois Institute of Technology (IIT). Like many

European Modernists, his prewar work had been limited to small private commissions and exhibitions, but once in the United States, he received commissions for over 100 large-scale projects, many of them public buildings.

Mies planned a new campus for IIT and during his twenty-year tenure developed it into a disciplined landscape of minimalist urban order. Set in a rundown district of south Chicago, a neighborhood with mostly poor, African American families, the school received federal funding for its *tabula rasa* slum-clearance efforts, anticipating the urban renewal program by a few years. Beginning in 1939, Mies prepared a symmetrical arrangement of low, flat boxes set in large green spaces, using an 8 m (26 ft) module based on the standard size of American classrooms. Mies proposed a set of essential materials and clear structural principles to achieve an austere vision of modernity. His universal grid for the campus's ground plane and elevations seemed like a return to Jean-Nicholas-Louis Durand's rational system, but without classical columns (see Section 15.1). When Frank Lloyd Wright reviewed the plan, he commented disparagingly that it seemed like "a new classicism."

The earliest of Mies's twenty-two buildings at IIT resembled industrial structures, reflecting the institution's scant wartime budget. The Mineral and Metal Research Building, finished in 1943 (Fig. 19.1-8), appeared as unassuming as a factory, a steel-frame structure clad with a tan brick wall at ground level and above this a taut, gridded skin of oblong steel-sash windows. Chicago safety codes required interior steel columns of multistory buildings to be covered with fire-retardant concrete. Mies responded by cladding the concrete casements of the columns with black steel plates. Throughout the campus, all of the rolled steel members were painted pitch black, establishing a uniform language of large glass planes and black frames.

At the conclusion of World War II, Mies met two of his most important clients in Chicago, one a real estate developer and the other an independent professional woman interested in the arts. Herbert Greenwald (1916–1959), a well-educated young man who had trained to be a rabbi before going into business, commissioned Mies for a series of speculative and government-subsidized projects. The resulting designs seemed like siblings of the IIT campus. At the Lakeshore Drive Apartments (1948) (Fig. 19.1-9) in Chicago, Mies set two twenty-six-story rectangular boxes perpendicular to each other, dressing them with the same

Mies van der Rohe and Johnson's Seagram Building built in New York City

▲ **1958**

▼ **1961**

Construction of Berlin Wall, symbol of Cold War

Martin Luther King, Jr., leads civil rights march in Selma, Alabama

▲ **1965**

▼ **1969**

U.S. *Apollo* space program lands man on the moon

Figure 19.1-4 (a) Houston, Texas. Allen Parkway Village, MacKie & Kamrath, 1942. (b) St. Louis, Missouri. Pruitt-Igoe housing, Minoru Yamasaki, 1951–1956 (demolished 1971).

Figure 19.1-5 Pacific Palisades, California. Eames House, Charles and Ray Eames, 1949.

I-beam mullions on fully glazed elevations used at the university.

Mies enlisted his old Bauhaus colleague Hilberseimer to design another Greenwald project, Lafayette Park (1956), a superblock of mixed-scale housing in Detroit. They arranged sets of single-story courtyard houses, long rows of two-story apartments, and three isolated apartment towers in a traffic-free park, producing a setting reminiscent of the openness of the Radburn model (see Section 18.1). The apartments remained racially and economically mixed,

one of the few successful subsidized projects in the United States.

Dr. Edith Farnsworth (1903–1977), Mies's other important postwar client, commissioned a small country retreat. The Farnsworth House (1946–1951) (Fig. 19.1-10) in Plano, Illinois, an hour's drive west of Chicago, stood in a clearing by the frequently flooded Fox River. Mies raised it 1.5 m (5 ft) above the ground plane on a set of eight exoskeletal steel I-beam columns, which he painted white—the only divergence in his portfolio from painting steel members

Figure 19.1-6 Walnut Creek, California. Typical California ranch house, inspired by Cliff May, 1960s.

Figure 19.1-7 Bel Air, Maryland. Typical "colonial" model house built by Levitt and Sons, 1961.

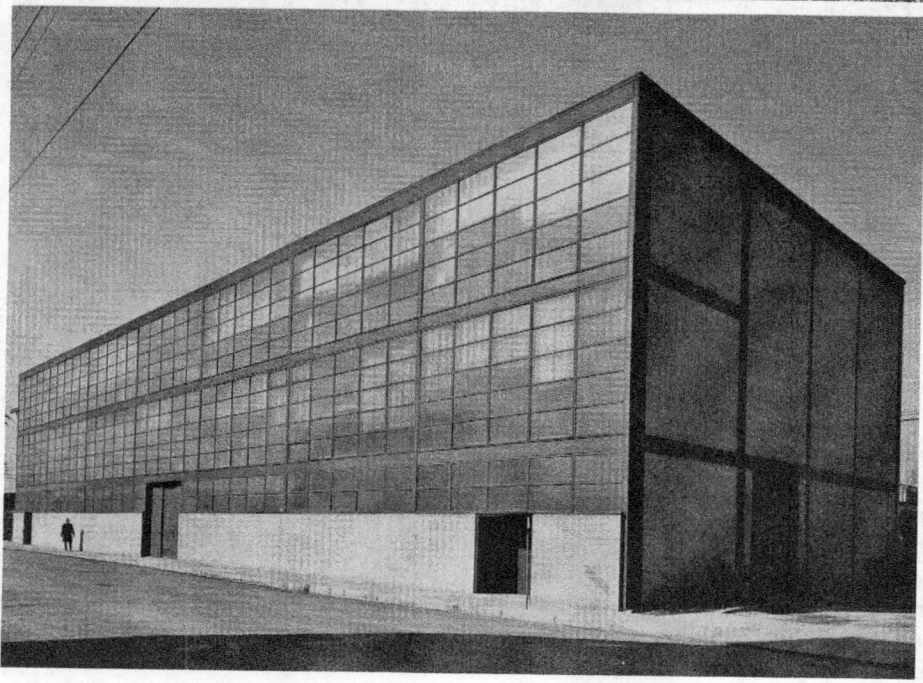

Figure 19.1-8 Chicago. Illinois Institute of Technology, Mineral and Metal Research Building, Ludwig Mies van der Rohe, 1943.

Figure 19.1-9 Chicago. Lakeshore Drive Apartments, Mies van der Rohe, 1948.

black. He set a travertine terrace landing in a staggered position facing the river. The stairs continued to a covered porch, which occupied one of the three bays of the volume. Sheer glass elevations enclosed the other two bays, interrupted only by a lone entry through a floor-to-ceiling double door. Mies's bold concept resulted in a completely transparent house contained in a single oblong room. He divided the interior with a long rosewood-paneled volume, containing a fireplace, and two bathrooms to either side. He tucked the kitchen into a linear counter, running the length of the rear side of this island. The patron's bed abutted the short side of the rosewood block but, like all of the

house's functions, remained completely exposed to view. Farnsworth's difficulty adjusting to the house led to a bitter lawsuit against the architect for cost overruns, the impossibility of heating the structure in the winter or cooling it in the summer, lack of storage and mosquito screens, and an absence of privacy either inside or out. She lost her case and was cruelly humiliated by suggestions that she had commissioned the house to acquire the sexual favors of the architect. After attempting to cope with what she called her "Miesconception" for twenty years, she sold the house and moved to Italy, where she lived in seclusion, translating the poetry of Eugenio Montale.

Figure 19.1-10 Plano, Illinois. Farnsworth House, Mies van der Rohe, 1946–1951.

Figure 19.1-11 New Canaan, Connecticut. Glass House, Philip Johnson, 1949.

in solid brick walls containing the bedrooms—as private as the initial house was exposed.

Johnson assisted Mies on his only work in New York City, the Seagram Building (Fig. 19.1-12), begun in 1956 with the advice of the patron's daughter, Phyllis Lambert (b. 1927). The curtain walls of its thirty-eight-story steel and concrete–framed structure were articulated with characteristic Miesian I-beam mullions, which in this case were cast in precious bronze. The dark tower with its sepia-tinted glazing contrasted with the bright, travertine-clad foreground plaza that covered more than half the site.

Mies produced Crown Hall (1950–1956) (Fig. 19.1-13) as his final contribution to the IIT campus. Designed for the architecture school, it presented a single, columnless hall as an essay in "universal space." He suspended the roof and curtain walls from an exoskeletal system of 4 m (13 ft) deep steel trusses attached on either end to steel columns. Not since flying buttresses appeared on the apse of St. Denis had such an ingenious method been invented for using external structure to liberate interior space from structural mass. As with the Farnsworth House, the completely exposed interior presented the constant challenge of how to adapt specific functions to universal space.

Despite its obvious defects, the Farnsworth House inspired imitations. Philip Johnson's Glass House (1949) (Fig. 19.1-11) in New Canaan, Connecticut, though completed almost two years earlier, can only be judged in terms established by Mies's model. Johnson, an independently wealthy connoisseur, became one of Mies's greatest promoters and built his house in homage. Rather than being raised off the ground, the Glass House rested on a thin brick base. A handrail skirted the four glass elevations on the interior, which each had floor-to-ceiling doors, allowing cross-ventilation. Like Wright, he gathered the services into a cylindrical brick core, with a fireplace on one side and bathroom on the other. A counter to the left of the entrance served as a kitchen but was used more for cocktails in this consummate bachelor's pad. Overlooking his Glass House, about 20 m (66 ft) away Johnson added a guesthouse rendered

The New National Gallery (1962–1968) (Fig. 19.1-14) in Berlin, Mies's final work, poised a massive roof plane made of steel coffers over eight columns. In a process that lasted only nine hours, he engaged hydraulic jacks to lift the prefabricated roof in place and hinge the columns to it. The cruciform columns stood like colossal intersected I-beams and tapered subtly from bottom to top, a refinement worthy of the Parthenon. The sublime void of the interior, while full of religious expectations, posed significant problems for museum display. The overexposed hall retroactively became a prime location for site-specific installation art, with more traditional exhibitions relegated to the basement.

Mies's frequently quoted statement "God is in the details" indeed reflected his understanding of architecture

Mies's I-Beam Mullions

Mies introduced a modern form of pilaster made from I-beams on many of the IIT buildings, such as the 1945 Alumni Memorial Hall. He set these vertical **mullions** to mark the divisions of walls and large plate-glass windows. The I-beams became the chief decorative element on Mies's elevations, analogous to Alberti's use of classical pilasters in Renaissance Florence (see Section 10.1). They had no specific structural purpose, except to offer some resistance to shear forces. To turn the corners of the major buildings, he created an indentation for a square concrete pier covered by a bent steel plate, to which he welded I-beam mullions set perpendicular to each other.

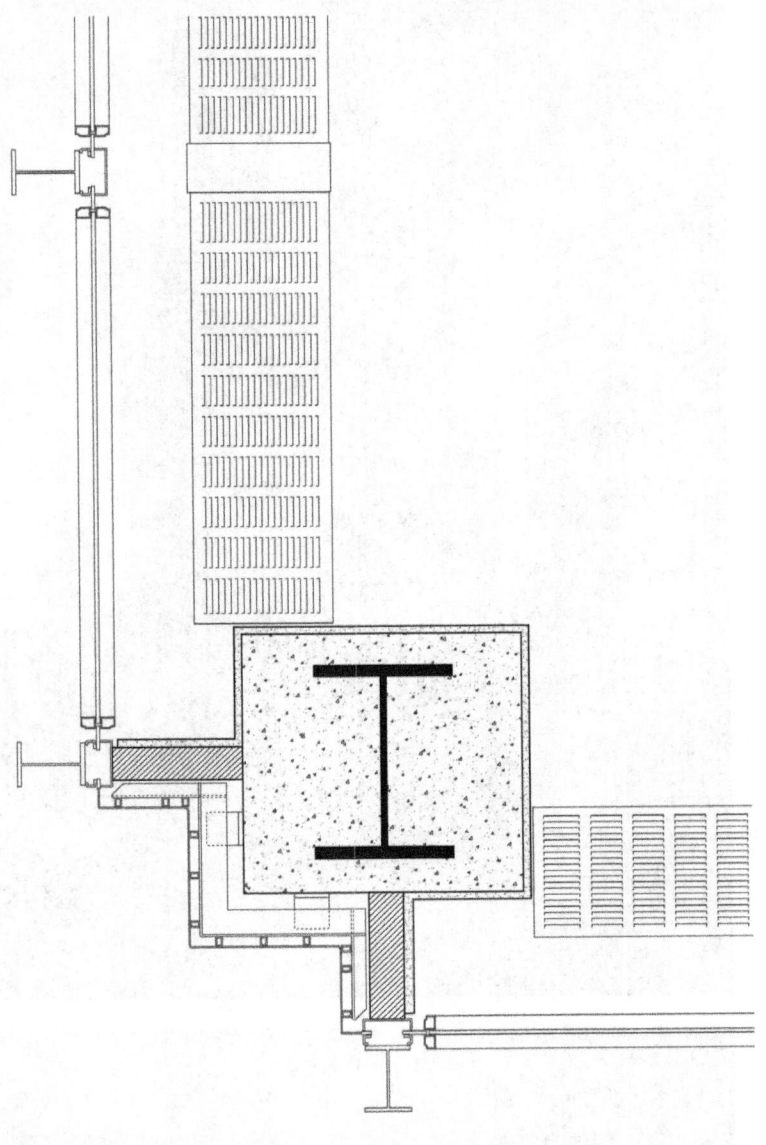

Plan of typical corner pier on a Miesian building, with I-beam flanges set counteraxially like pilasters.

as a theological quest that promised spiritual redemption through the reduction of form to a few well-conceived elements. Through the lightness of structure, the freedom of his plans, and the purity of his details, he attempted to create a modern version of monastic minimalism. He often used the expression *Beinahe nichts*, "almost nothing," to describe the challenge of design. And while such cult-like restraint may have caused some problems for the users of his buildings, it resulted in a compellingly vacant beauty to which functions had to adapt. Mies's homily of minimalism, however, became increasingly alien to the agents of American consumerism, which promoted "almost everything."

Reconstruction Europe: New Towns and Social Housing

The welfare, or social, state took root in late-nineteenth-century Europe with the appearance of guaranteed national pension funds. In 1936 Sweden inaugurated the first comprehensive system of pensions, unemployment insurance, and universal health care that served as a model for other countries after the war's end. Housing soon became an important aspect of welfare. As early as the 1920s large municipal housing estates occupied the edges of cities in Holland, Germany, and Austria. Postwar Germany and England, where over 30% of the dwellings had been destroyed, sponsored mass housing estates as large as entire towns.

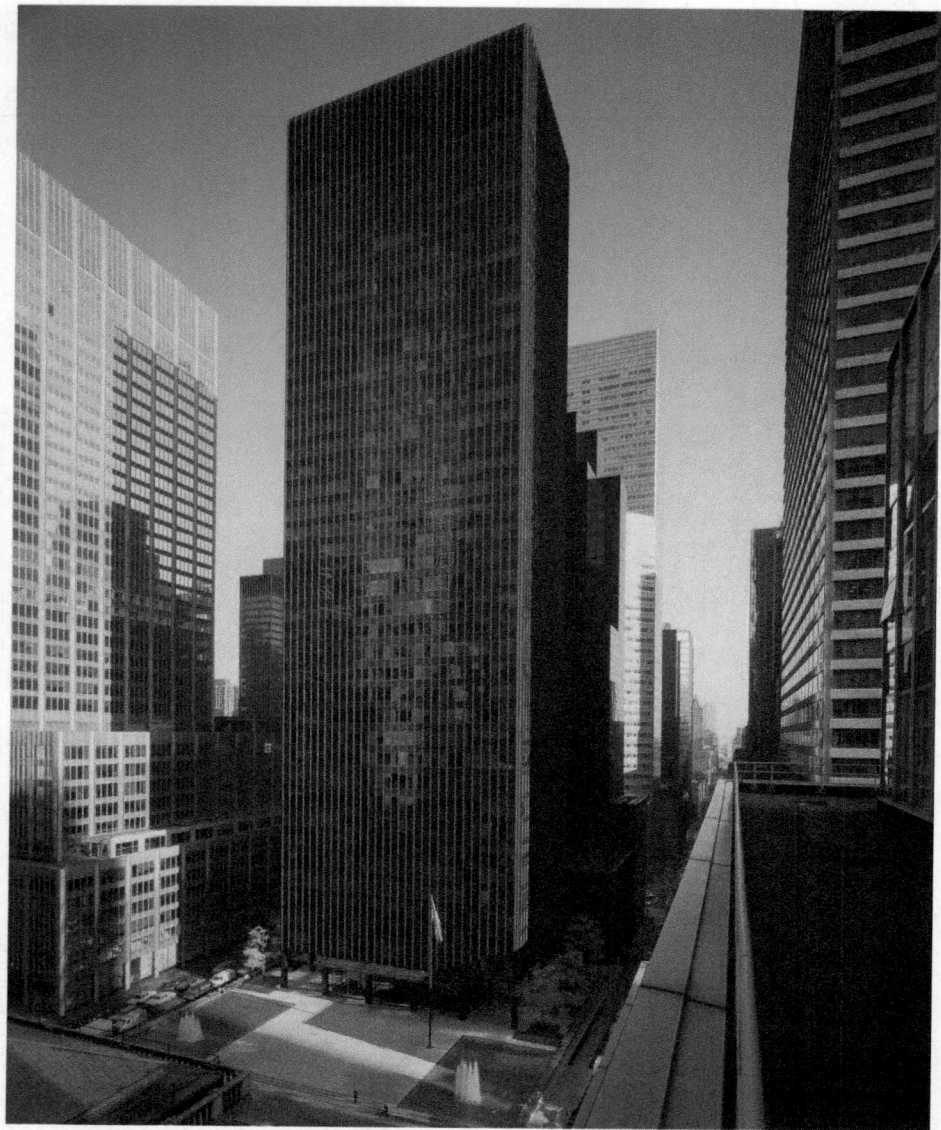

Figure 19.1-12 New York. Seagram Building, Mies van der Rohe and Johnson, 1956–1958.

Figure 19.1-13 Chicago. Illinois Institute of Technology, Crown Hall, Mies van der Rohe, 1950–1956.

Rotterdam was the first city destroyed by aerial bombardments during World War II. It also was the first to respond with a reconstruction plan. Shortly after the bombing in May 1940, a group of civic leaders and architects convened in the Van Nelle tobacco factory, the icon of Dutch New Objectivity designed by Johannes Brinkman (1902–1949) and Mart Stam (1889–1986) in 1926. They acknowledged that despite the tragedy, the German blitz had provided an unexpected *tabula rasa* that could be used as an opportunity for creating a more efficient city center (Fig. 19.1-15). The head of planning, Cornelius van Traa (1889–1970), proposed to wipe out old property lines and rebuild the center from a 55% building-to-space ratio to a 35% ratio.

The Rotterdam plan kept a fairly even mix of uses in the center—apartments, shops, offices, and small artisan studios—while eliminating heavy industries through zoning restrictions. The principal avenues of the rebuilt center were six lanes across, three times as wide as the old streets. Jakob Bakema (1914–1981) and Jo van der Broek (1898–1978) designed the central

Figure 19.1-14 Berlin. New National Gallery, Mies van der Rohe, 1962–1968.

shopping street, the Lijnbaan, as a four-block-long pedestrian concourse lined with two-story shops, trees, benches, and pergolas (Fig. 19.1–16). Set behind this loomed fifteen-story apartment towers, "like parents watching over their children at play." Completed in 1953, the Lijnbaan provided

Figure 19.1-15 Rotterdam, the Netherlands. *Tabula rasa* after aerial *Blitzkrieg*, 1940.

Figure 19.1-16 Rotterdam, the Netherlands. Lijnbaan shopping street, Jakob Bakema and Jo van der Broek, 1953.

a much-admired model for separating pedestrian from vehicular traffic.

Dutch cities expanded during the postwar reconstruction with spacious suburban housing estates. The social housing program culminated in the construction in 1962–1971 of Bijlmermeer (Fig. 19.1-17), a southern district of Amsterdam, designed by municipal architect Siegfried Nassuth (1922–2005). Its 40,000 units constituted the largest housing estate in Europe. The nine-story bar buildings followed a honeycomb grid, which seen from the air projected an astounding beehive pattern over the land. The prefabricated slabs rose on piers above grade, allowing pedestrians to filter through hexagonal courts to parklands, playgrounds, and lakes. Bijlmermeer suffered from many of the same problems as

Figure 19.1-17 Amsterdam. Model of Bijlmermeer, Siegfried Nassuth, 1962–1971.

Pruitt-Igoe: lack of services, poor transportation connections, no maintenance, and racial discrimination. Its biggest design flaw was the placement of the garages along the elevated highway, forcing the residents to walk more than 500 m (1,640 ft) to their apartments. Instead of being accessed from streets and plazas, the units were entered from long corridors, which became frequent sites for rapes and muggings. Many of Bijlmermeer's blocks were torn down in the 1990s and replaced with low-rise alternatives, with parking adjacent to the units.

Postwar Britain enacted the New Towns Act of 1946 to govern its process of reconstruction. In all, the United Kingdom built twenty-eight new towns in two phases housing a combined population of 2.2 million during the Labour governments of 1947–1951 and 1961–1970. In postwar London, municipal or "Council" housing adopted the high-rise models of Le Corbusier for such projects

as the forty midrise slabs of Churchill Gardens Estate (1955) (Fig. 19.1-18a) by Powell & Moya. After repeated critiques of the blandness of the first new towns, such as Harlow (1947), the planners of Cumbernauld (1956) (Fig. 19.1-18b) near Glasgow attempted to give the urban center a strong architectural character. Chief architect Hugh Wilson produced a grand hooded figure for a high-density civic core, detailed

Figure 19.1-18 (a) London. Churchill Gardens, Powell & Moya, 1955. (b) Cumbernauld, Scotland. Civic center for new town, Hugh Wilson, 1960s.

in Neo-Brutalist exposed concrete, but its monumentality failed to generate vitality.

The Barbican Centre (1952–1975) (Fig. 19.1-19) appeared the most heroic of British reconstruction programs. The 16 ha (40 acre) site in central London became a **megastructure** raised over a parking plinth and set off from the streets. The thirteen towers held more than 2,000 units that connected to a grand internal landscape, laced with aerial causeways and Mughal-style water gardens. The enclave, designed by Chamberlain, Powell, and Bon, contained three theaters, a concert hall, cinemas, schools, and convention spaces. Its interior circulation proved so complex that yellow lines were taped to the pavement to help people find their way.

France produced the widest variety of formal solutions for postwar public housing, from straightforward functionalist bars to explosive starbursts. Auguste Perret pursued a conservative plan in 1948 for rebuilding Le Havre (Fig. 19.1-20), which had been heavily bombed during the war. Using a standard concrete frame grid, he increased the city's density while widening its streets but basically left the port's original fabric intact. His major monumental contribution, the church of St. Joseph, completed in 1954, the year of his death, soared above the seven-story fabric of the reconstructed area like an Art Deco skyscraper.

In contrast, Le Corbusier advocated large, isolated structures set in open plazas, seen in his 1946 unbuilt plan

---

CONSTRUCTION, TECHNOLOGY, THEORY

Dutch Structuralism and the Layered Grid

The Dutch architect Aldo van Eyck (1918–1999) visited sub-Saharan Africa in the early 1950s, an experience that inspired his research on built form as the articulation of community. In his 1960 Amsterdam Orphanage he staggered spaces on a grid, allowing for overlap between different socializing areas. His plan for Buikslotermeer in 1962 continued the investigation of a layered grid, an approach that later was dubbed

"Dutch Structuralism," not to be confused with the literary and philosophical movement of French Structuralism. Van Eyck's assistant, Piet Blom, designed the 1962 project for "Noah's Ark," an interlocking layered grid, which was presented at the Team X meeting of 1964. The layered grid also turned up in Le Corbusier's 1964 project for the Venice Hospital, and the firm of Candilis-Josic-Woods used it as the basis of Frei Universität in Berlin (1970).

Amsterdam. Orphanage and school, Aldo van Eyck, 1960.

Figure 19.1-19 London. Barbican Centre, courtyard, Chamberlain, Powell, and Bon, 1952–1975.

for St. Dié in the east of France. Aside from the Unité d'Habitation in Marseilles (see Section 18.2), he received little work in reconstruction France. His only significant urban commission came from the resistance leader Eugène Claudius-Petit (1907–1989) to add a new quarter to the industrial town of Firminy. Le Corbusier's plan for Firminy-Vert (1954–1965) (Fig. 19.1-21) included a stadium, a cultural center, and a Unité housing block. Its cone-shaped church was not completed until 2006.

While the French government snubbed Le Corbusier, his theories of urbanism and mass-produced housing dominated planning procedures. By the mid-1950s, France had become the largest sponsor of public housing in the world, producing 200,000 units per year. Large estates, the *Grands Ensembles*, such as the Parisian suburb of Sarcelles,

housed up to 100,000 people but offered little civic space and few services. Since the bureaucratic restrictions on such housing units were inflexible, architects put most of their design energy into the composition of the whole. Émile Aillaud (1902–1988) designed Les Courtilières (1955–1960)

Figure 19.1-20 Le Havre, France. City center with church of St. Joseph in center, Auguste Perret, 1950–1956.

Figure 19.1-21 Firminy-Vert, France. Church of St. Pierre, Le Corbusier, 1954–1965, completed by Jose Oubrerie, 2006.

at Pantin outside Paris as a serpentine figure set in a park. The office of Candilis-Josic-Woods proposed a branch-like plan for Toulouse-Le Mirail (1961) (Fig. 19.1-22a,b) to house 100,000, reversing the **figure-ground** pattern of the old city on a terrain of comparable size.

The anonymity of the large slab projects led many French architects toward what they called *recherche combinatoire*, the search for ways of stacking prefabricated units to leave interstitial social spaces and rooftop gardens. Jean Renaudie (1925–1981) created the most expressive of such combinations, such as the 1969 star-shaped project at Ivry (Fig. 19.1-23a). These efforts to create variety with standard units ran parallel with the Habitat 67 project by Moshe Safdie (b. 1938), three spectacular mounds of interlocking prefabricated apartments built for the 1967 Expo in Montréal, Canada. The roof of each unit became a terraced garden for the unit above it (Fig. 19.1-23b).

In 1965 France enacted the *Schéma Directeur* master plan for five new towns near Paris, hoping to siphon off the growth of the city center. The area of Cergy-Pontoise (1969) was greater than that of Paris, with about one-tenth the density. The new towns accompanied the construction of France's grandest urban project, La Défense (Fig. 19.1-24), a business district set at the head of the axis of the Champs-Elysées. Planned in 1958, it evoked the multilayered plinth at the center of Le Corbusier's 1922 Contemporary City, serving as an infrastructural node with a three-level platform for

a high-speed rail station, a subway connection, and parking for 32,000 cars. The upper deck of the plinth served as a site for shops and a pedestrian concourse, skirted by two dozen office towers. While intended to generate a French Manhattan, the high overhead of the first generation of La Défense left the buildings half empty, turning the atmosphere ghostly and windswept. Correctives began in the 1980s, including the colossal squared-off Arche de la Défense, designed in 1983 by the Danish architect Johann Otto von Spreckelsen (1929–1987), which gave a formal cap to the plinth. During the 1990s La Défense's rules for density were relaxed, increasing its number of offices and apartments while attracting greater commercial vitality. The architecture of the welfare state attempted both to assist urban recovery and to stimulate the economy of postwar Europe. Sometimes the good intentions fell flat and degenerated into anomalous urban conditions that required major redesign or even demolition, but in general, as at La Défense, the welfare state established the outline of Europe's urban future.

The Eastern Bloc: From Socialist Realism to the *Plattenbau*

While the formal inventions of Russian Constructivism exerted considerable impact on the development of twentieth-century avant-gardes in the West, the Soviet government actively discouraged the movement. As early as the

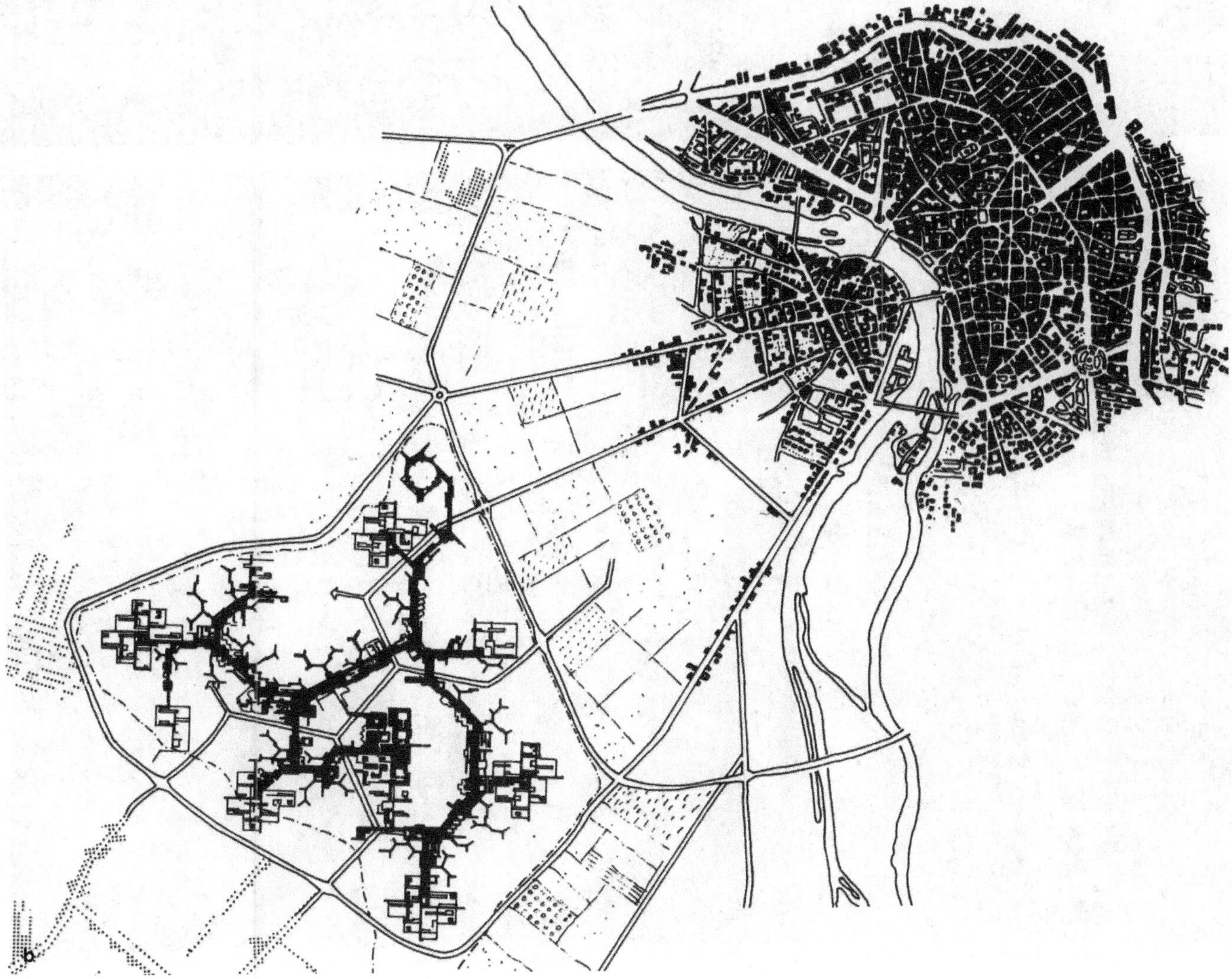

Figure 19.1-22 Toulouse-Le Mirail, France. (a) Housing estate, Candilis-Josic-Woods, 1961. (b) Plan.

Figure 19.1-23 (a) Ivry, France. Jean Renaudie, 1969. (b) Montréal. Habitat 67, Moshe Safdie, 1967.

Figure 19.1-24 Paris. La Défense, showing the squared-off Arche de la Défense, Johann Otto von Spreckelsen, 1983.

mid-1920s an internal debate about **functionalism** versus formalism led to the suppression of the most creative exponents of Constructivism. One brilliant emerging talent, Ivan Illich Leonidov (1902–1959), never gained a commission. In many ways the Soviet building industry, slow to make the transition to concrete and steel technologies, enforced conservative attitudes. As Joseph Stalin consolidated his grip on the Communist Party at the end of the 1920s and Lazar Kaganovich began his subway stations, Soviet taste in the arts turned from abstraction to historicism. Stalin's regime promoted the policy of Socialist Realism, insisting in 1934 that art had to be (1) "proletarian" and accessible to the workers; (2) typical, showing scenes of everyday life; (3) realistic and representational; and (4) supportive of the aims of the Soviet state and the Communist Party. While this program mostly concerned painting and sculpture, it led to a decorative Neo-Renaissance style in Soviet architecture.

The paintings and sculptures of Socialist Realism depicted heroic workers, angelic uniformed children, and happy farmers living in the perpetual glow of the rising sun. Favorite scenes included Vladimir Lenin leading the revolution and Stalin as a benevolent father figure giving blessings over Soviet abundance. The architecture of Socialist Realism embraced the return to historical motifs. The prime example in Moscow came from Ivan Zholtovsky (1867–1959), a classically trained architect, whose 1934 apartment house on Mokhovaya Street (now called Zholtovsky House) presented a row of colossal engaged Corinthian columns, inspired by Andrea Palladio's Loggia del Capitaniato in Vicenza. He innovated on the type by inserting fully glazed steel-sash bays in the interstices. Zholtovsky's turn to the Italian Renaissance inspired the rebuilding of Gorky Street, which was widened from 16 to 50 m (52 to 164 ft). Italianate façades coordinated by Arkady Mordvinov (1896–1964) lined

this new boulevard, named after the author Maxim Gorky (1868–1936), whose 1908 novel *Mother* inspired the theory of Socialist Realism. Karo Alabyan (1897–1959), editor of *The Architecture of the USSR*, designed a star-shaped plan for the Red Army Theater (1936–1940) (Fig. 19.1-25). That the star could only be perceived in plan and that such a shape proved highly impractical for a theater did not discourage his pursuit of political iconography.

The bulk of Socialist Realist architectural projects were built after the war. For Stalingrad (today Volgograd), which was devastated during one of the key battles of World War II, Alabyan designed a new monumental core, inserting a grand set of symmetrical stairs (Fig. 19.1-26a) flanked by classical pavilions that cascaded down to the river. The colossus *The Motherland Calls!* by Yevgeny Vuchetich (1908–1974) (Fig. 19.1-26b), an 85 m (278 ft) woman holding an upraised sword, offered a terrifying vision of maternal fortitude as Stalingrad's alternative to the Statue of Liberty. The center of Kiev, capital of the Ukraine, likewise gained a new monumental core of classical pergolas, which seemed a cynical compensation for the state-induced famine that the region underwent as a result of Stalin's policies.

Socialist Realism came to a climax with Stalin's proposal of a ring of skyscrapers, the *vysoltki*, for Moscow that could vie with the symbols of modernity in capitalist countries. The style of the towers came from early twentieth-century works in Liverpool and New York, in particular New York's Municipal Building by McKim, Mead & White. Eight projects were planned, but only seven were constructed, at great sacrifice to the economy. One, the main building of Moscow State University (Fig. 19.1-27), designed by Lev Rudnev (1885–1956), who replaced Boris Iofan, was completed in 1953 and built by the inmates of a *gulag* camp for political prisoners. Its central spire rose 240 m (768 ft), allowing it

Figure 19.1-25 Moscow. Red Army Theater, Karo Alabyan, 1936–1940.

Figure 19.1-26 Stalingrad (now Volgograd). (a) Stairs, Alabyan, 1950s. (b) The colossus *The Motherland Calls!*, Yevgeny Vuchetich, 1963–1967.

Figure 19.1-27 Moscow. State University, Lev Rudnev, 1953.

to reign as the tallest building in Europe for over three decades. The plan spread symmetrically into four centripetal wings like Kent's Holkham Hall (see Section 13.1), producing a complex of enormous volume with over 5,000 rooms for housing the professors and students. The central spire lifted a red star as its pinnacle, while four minor towers carried Baroque crowns and clocks. Mordvinov's Hotel Ukraina (1953) stood almost as high and for many decades remained the tallest hotel in Europe, with over 1,500 rooms. Moscow's *vysoltki* were greatly overbuilt in terms of steel because of a lack of local experience with high-rise construction.

As the Soviet Union extended its control over the Eastern Bloc countries, it exported the towering complexes as signs of colonial influence. Poland, which suffered the largest percentage of casualties during World War II, losing 6 million of its inhabitants, entered the Soviet sphere in 1952. Rudnev designed the Palace of Culture and Science (1952–1955) (Fig. 19.1-28) in Warsaw, a simulacrum of his university, as a "gift from the Soviet people."

Poland received another architectural "gift" from the Soviet Union during the early 1950s, the new town of Nowa Huta ("New Steel Mill") (Fig. 19.1-29a,b), located 10 km (6 miles) east of Kraków. The town accompanied the Soviet establishment of a large steel plant in a region that lacked both iron and coal. Nowa Huta was given a classical plan, with a trident converging on a grand esplanade, somewhat like Karlsruhe, but without the focus of a central palace. The designers neglected to include a church, prompting the predominantly Catholic residents to surreptitiously build one as an act of defiance.

The most ambitious application of Socialist Realist architecture appeared in East Berlin with Stalinallee (now Karl-Marx-Allee) (Fig. 19.1-30). Egon Hartmann (1919–2009) created the master plan, but the historicist style was set by Hermann Henselmann (1905–1995), who designed the tempiettos and classical arcades at Strausberger Platz and Frankfurter Tor. Between 1951 and 1956 Hartmann and Henselmann coordinated the grand boulevard, which was 90 m (295 ft) wide and lined with eight-story housing blocks. Stalinallee included a major hotel, outdoor cafés, and the Modernist Moskova cinema. The Soviet-backed

Figure 19.1-28 Warsaw. Palace of Culture and Science, Rudnev, 1952–1955.

government completed construction on the second phase, resorting to prefabricated slab buildings, in 1961, the same year they installed the Berlin Wall, which divided East Berlin from West Berlin for nearly thirty years.

Nikita Khrushchev (1894–1971), as chief party official in Moscow in the early 1950s, attempted to compensate for Stalin's misplaced priorities. Socialist Realist architecture catered to the bureaucratic elite and contributed relatively little to the needs of mass housing. There was actually less space per person in the Soviet Union by the time of Stalin's death in 1953 than there had been before. In 1955, after assuming the role of party president, Khrushchev exposed Stalin's crimes, including the purge of thousands, the *gulag* prison camps, and the state-induced famine in the Ukraine that killed millions in the mid-1930s. He released a policy statement, "On the Liquidation of Architectural Excess,"

Figure 19.1-29
Kraków. (a) Nowa
Huta, central
esplanade, 1950s.
(b) Plan, with
the steel factory
located 1 km
(0.6 miles) to
the east.

a

b

effectively putting an end to Socialist Realist decoration while endorsing the *Khrushchyovka*, the Russian prefabricated concrete panel blocks. Vitaly Lagutenko (1904–1967) introduced a concrete panel system hung on concrete frames in 1947, used first for buildings with ornamented facades and later for the anonymous ***Plattenbau*** (panel building), seen in the latter half of the apartments along Stalinallee.

The Soviet Union exerted a strong influence on China at the outset of the 1949 revolution led by Mao Zedong (1893–1976). The early architectural transformations of Beijing responded to Stalin's Socialist Realism. Mao's planners tore down the Ming walls surrounding the city center to build ring roads. In front of Tiananmen Gate they laid out an immense 40 ha (99 acre) plaza, the largest public space in the world. Flanking the space rose two major

institutions: the Great Hall of the People (1959), designed by Zhang Bo; and the National Museum of China (1958), by Zhang Kaiji (1912–2007). The latter architect had worked for Palmer and Turner in Shanghai, the major Beaux-Arts office in China before the war, and his museum design approximated European models of spatial organization more than the nearby Chinese models in the Forbidden City.

A colossal portrait of Mao already hung over the Tiananmen Gate, and a year after his death a grand mausoleum was placed opposite the gate (Fig. 19.1-31). Hua Guofeng, Mao's successor, supervised the monument's construction to mark the conclusion of the decade-long Cultural Revolution, which had sent leading professionals like Zhang Kaiji to do janitorial jobs in the name of proletarian justice. The new monument indicated a return to Chinese sensibilities

CONSTRUCTION, TECHNOLOGY, THEORY

Plattenbau and Prefab Housing

The *Plattenbau* technique of prefabricated concrete panel construction took its name from postwar East German public housing projects but was introduced by the Dutch in the 1920s and used in several prewar Social Democratic housing estates, such as Ernst May's *Siedlungen* in Frankfurt and Gropius's Torten project in Dessau. Although *Plattenbau* became characteristic of Eastern Bloc suburbs, where the same plan was reproduced in hundreds of different cities, yielding environments of crushing uniformity, it was also developed in most Western European countries. Constructed using a "dry" technique, as opposed to the wet technique of formwork concrete, *Plattenbau* structures were much easier to assemble, especially during the forbidding conditions of the Russian winter. While lacking in urban niceties, *Plattenbau* remained a desirable alternative to slums and barracks.

Petržalka, Bratislava, Slovakia.
The most extensive use of
Plattenbau, 1970s.

Figure 19.1-30 Berlin (then East Berlin). Stalinallee (now Karl-Marx-Allee), Hermann Henselmann et al., 1951–1956.

Figure 19.1-31 Beijing. Mao's mausoleum at Tiananmen Square, 1977.

as a stylization of the order of the Hall of Supreme Harmony inside the Forbidden City (see Section 11.1). Its double roof spread flat instead of being pitched, and its twelve columns were square instead of round. The interstices, narrower at the ends and wider in the center, repeated those of the Ming-era hall. Like the Pantheon in Rome or the Padana in Persepolis, Mao's mausoleum incorporated materials from all over the country: granite from Sichuan, porcelain plates from Guangdong, pine trees from Yan'an, earth from quake-stricken Tanshan, colored pebbles from Nanjing, quartz from the Kunlun Mountains, pine logs from Jiangxi, and rock samples from Mount Everest. Over 700,000 people participated in its construction as a testament of Chinese autonomy from both its capitalist and its communist rivals.

Further Reading

Evenson, Norma. *Paris: A Century of Change, 1878–1978*. New Haven, CT: Yale University Press, 1979.

Friedman, Alice T. *Women and the Making of the Modern House: A Social and Architectural History*. New York: Harry N. Abrams, 1998.

Jordy, William. *American Buildings and Their Architects: The Impact of European Modernism in the Mid-Twentieth Century*, vol. 4. Garden City, NY: Doubleday, 1972.

Mumford, Eric. *The CIAM Discourse on Urbanism, 1928–1960*. Cambridge, MA: MIT Press, 2002.

Ockman, Joan. *Architecture Culture, 1943–1968*. New York: Rizzoli, 1993.

Riley, Terrence. *The International Style: Exhibition 15 and the Museum of Modern Art*. New York: Rizzoli, 1992.

Schulze, Franz. *Mies van der Rohe: A Critical Biography*. Chicago: University of Chicago Press, 1985.

Shanken, Andrew. *194X: Architecture, Planning, and Consumer Culture on the American Home Front*. Minneapolis: University of Minnesota Press, 2009.

Smith, Elizabeth A. T., ed. *Blueprints for Modern Living: History and Legacy of the Case Study Houses*. Cambridge, MA: MIT Press, 1989.

Wagenaar, C., and M. Dings. *Ideals in Concrete: Exploring Central and Eastern Europe*. Rotterdam, the Netherlands: NAi Publishers, 2004.

Wall, Alex. *Victor Gruen: From Urban Shop to New City*. Barcelona: Actar-D, 2005.

World War II undermined international colonial systems. The Third World emerged as a new political category, comprising former colonies on the brink of industrialization. While the British left India in relative peace at the end of 1947, the French did not relinquish Algeria until 1962, after a bitter war. The African colonies below the Sahara took the longest to gain independence. First Ghana won statehood in 1957, then three dozen other independent African countries followed suit during the next ten years. Jawaharlal Nehru, the first prime minister of India, coined the term "Third World" to signify the developing countries that fell outside of the two predominant economic models: capitalist America and Europe and the communist Eastern Bloc led by the Soviet Union. By 1970, the majority of the world's population lived in the Third World.

Most of Latin America had been independent since the nineteenth century but shared the conditions of postcolonialism because of slow development and continuing economic subordination to the industrialized countries. Postcolonial culture originated among writers and artists in Latin America as a form of resistance to outside domination and reappeared in many other Third World contexts. In some countries postcolonial architects returned to indigenous models as a way of showing their independence, a trend that became more prevalent at the end of the twentieth century. Quite often, however, postcolonial architects attempted to demonstrate that they could produce versions of the International Style that were just as good as or better than the models coming from more advanced economies. Third World countries often imported a technically progressive architecture to display their commitment to a new standard of development as a choice rather than an imposition.

Latin American Modernism: New Rhythms and a Culture of Resistance

Latin America, which comprises all of the former colonies of Spain and Portugal in the Western Hemisphere, nurtured several strains of Modernism, producing some of the most inspired architectural compositions of the mid-twentieth century. Although most Latin American countries gained independence shortly after Napoléon's 1808 invasion of Spain, the new ruling elites tended to behave much like the colonialists before them, exploiting a large population of peasants or, in the case of Brazil, slaves. Sustained by conservative militaries, they imported architecture and technology from England, the United States, and France, resulting in the cultural and political sluggishness so masterfully described by Gabriel García Márquez in his bittersweet novel *One Hundred Years of Solitude* (1967). A genuine discourse of postcolonialism did not arise until the Mexican Revolution of 1910–1920, when revolutionaries such as Pancho Villa (1878–1923) and Emiliano Zapata (1879–1919) brought the aristocratic class of landholders to its knees. Other Latin American countries measured their cultural independence against Mexico's achievements.

The last Mexican dictator, Porfirio Díaz (1884–1911), who had ruled off and on from 1876 until 1911, relied on France for culture and the United States for technology. He had little interest in acknowledging Mexican traditions or the rights of the poor. He commissioned such architectural novelties as the Palacio de Bellas Artes (Palace of Fine Arts) (Fig. 19.2-1), a white marble extravaganza with Art Nouveau touches designed by the Italian Adamo Boari (1863–1928). Although begun in 1904, the European-style opera house took thirty years to complete owing to its faulty foundations and the interruptions of the revolution. The muralists Diego Rivera (1886–1957), David Alfaro Siqueiros (1896–1974), and José Clemente Orozco (1883–1949) decorated the interior with revolutionary iconography. In 1933 Rivera reproduced there the same scene that had been eliminated from the atrium of Rockefeller Center the previous year, showing Lenin at the crossroads of social and technical development.

The drive for a postcolonial culture of resistance, a movement that sought to be both modern and regenerative of local traditions, began with Mexico's revolutionary muralists. José Vasconcelos, Minister of Education from 1921 to 1924, encouraged these artists to create a new awareness of Mexican cultural identity as the "cosmic race." Although the minister's taste in architecture stopped at Mexican colonial styles, he introduced a key transformative concept, *mexicanidad*, or Mexican-ness. He sponsored the work of archaeologists and anthropologists to codify the formal traditions of Mexico from the ancient cult sites to Indian crafts to colonial-era *haciendas*.

Mexican architects attempted to convert the models of European Modernism into distinctly Mexican expressions. The path led from the muralists to the architects: Juan O'Gorman (1905–1982), an architect who also worked as a muralist, designed the Rivera-Kahlo Studios (Fig. 19.2-2) in 1929 with a sawtooth monitor roof and a full wall of industrial sash windows similar to those seen at Le Corbusier's Ozenfant House in Paris of 1922 (see Section 18.2). He painted the taller of the two planar volumes rusty red for Rivera and the smaller box *azul añil*, indigo blue, for his wife, the Surrealist painter Frida Kahlo (1907–1954). While conforming to the utilitarian language of European Modernism, O'Gorman conceived the Rivera–Kahlo Studios in a new way, with bright planes of color. He fenced in the lot with a surreal wall of tall, columnar cactus plants.

The Mexican economy grew significantly during World War II as a result of its state-owned oil companies. As in

Figure 19.2-1 Mexico City. Palacio de Bellas Artes, Adamo Boari, 1904–1932.

most Third World situations, the university emerged as the key project to signal a national commitment to progress and well-being. The new Ciudad Universitaria (University City) (Fig. 19.2-3), built in a southern suburb of Mexico City between 1950 and 1954, involved over 150 architects and engineers in a grand Modernist project, coordinated by Mario Pani (1911–1993) and Enrique del Moral (1906–1987). The University City proved a breakthrough, a large project that most people recognized as both Modernist and Mexican. O'Gorman initially proposed a stepped pyramid for the central library but was discouraged from such an overtly historicist gesture. His final design, conceived with Gustavo Saavedra and Juan Martinez de Velasco, stacked a massive box clad with exuberant stone mosaics above a two-story transparent base. The central panel narrated pre-Columbian cosmology, with two large circles that suggested the goggle-eyed Aztec rain god Tlaloc.

The campus planners encouraged a synthesis of Modernist architecture with revolutionary decoration, hoping to achieve *integración plastica* (the synthesis of the arts). University City served as the testing ground for most of the important Modernist

Figure 19.2-2 Mexico City. Rivera–Kahlo House and Studios, Juan O'Gorman, 1929.

Figure 19.2-3 Mexico City. Ciudad Universitaria, administration tower by Mario Pani, library by O'Gorman et al., 1950s

artists and architects of Mexico. Pedro Ramírez Vazquez (1919–2013) went on to design the Anthropology Museum (1964) (Fig. 19.2-4), with its gigantic umbrella fountain cooling the court, and the Guadalupe Cathedral (1965). Teodoro González de León (1926–2016), who worked in Le Corbusier's studio during the 1930s, later designed the National Theater (1978). The university also attracted the expatriate German Modernists Max Cetto (1903–1980) and Matthias Goeritz (1915–1990).

Luis Barragán (1902–1988), the most famous Mexican Modernist, was missing from this roster. Only a few years earlier he had designed and developed the suburban subdivision of El Pedregal, adjacent to the campus. Barragán came from a wealthy landowning family whose property had been expropriated during the land reforms of the revolution and, unlike the other Mexican Modernists, felt no sympathy for the left. While his Modernist contemporaries worked mostly on public projects with social goals, Barragán worked as both an architect and a developer of wealthy suburbs. He perfected his own version of *integración plastica*, setting brightly colored planes into interlocking compositions with fragments of folk culture. A detail in the Barragán House (1947–1957), the wooden stair that cantilevered from the freestanding wall in his living room, reveals his knack for amalgamating modern and vernacular forms. In the glowing

Figure 19.2-4 Mexico City. Anthropology Museum, Pedro Ramírez Vazquez, 1964.

interiors of the Tlalpan Chapel of the Convent of las Capuchinas (1953–1960) (Fig. 19.2-5), a work that Barragán anonymously financed with his own fortune, he transformed

▼ **1956–1960**

President Kubitschek commissions construction of Brasília, Modernist capital of Brazil

Nkrumah declares Ghana's independence from Britain, sparking wave of African liberation

▼ **1959**

Pouillon builds social housing in Algiers

Le Corbusier joins team to plan and build Chandigarh, capital of Punjab, India

▲ **1951**

▲ **1957**

Figure 19.2-5 Mexico City. Tlalpan Chapel of the Convent of las Capuchinas Sacramentarias, Luis Barragán, 1953–1960.

a rudimentary box with an oblique wall, a hidden light source, and a gold-leaf altarpiece into a truly mystical setting.

Barragán mistrusted modern building technologies, preferring wood to iron and brick to reinforced concrete. What made his work modern was its formal abstraction, the juxtaposition of colored planes, and the creation of interpenetrating spaces. At the plaza of Las Arboledas, one of his suburban developments, he created a stunning Neo-Plastic space by juxtaposing a long trough of water at knee level with a freestanding white plane (Fig. 19.2-6). The great court serving the house and stables of the Egerstrom House juxtaposed pink, red, and brown planes against the refreshing pool fed by an overhead spout. While Barragán confessed to there being no political motives behind his turn to Modernism, his works conveyed the essence of postcolonial sensibility, integrating Modernist abstraction with the colors and spatial types of the indigenous past.

The other major economies of Latin America—Venezuela, Brazil, Argentina, and Chile—aspired to the modernity of developed countries but experienced perennial cycles of poverty, corruption, and military overthrow. Most South American countries at one point or another yielded to a variation of Italy's Fascist regime. Populist dictators in Argentina, Venezuela, and Brazil attempted to create the atmosphere of patriotic enthusiasm, corporate partnership between government and industry, and a nationalist vision of the social state. Architecture served as propaganda.

Until the Great Depression of 1929, Argentina possessed the strongest economy in Latin America, closely connected to the markets of England, the United States, and France. The center of Buenos Aires followed Beaux-Arts models designed by European-trained architects. Its boulevards resembled those of Paris, lined with tall apartment buildings capped

Figure 19.2-6 Mexico City. Las Arboledas, El Bebedero Fountain, Barragán, 1957–1962.

Figure 19.2-7 Buenos Aires. Kavanaugh Building, Sanchez, Lagos, y de la Torre, 1930–1933.

with mansard roofs. The last expression of the Argentinean desire to keep up with foreign fashions came with the twenty-nine-story Kavanaugh Building by the architectural firm Sanchez, Lagos, y de la Torre (Fig. 19.2-7), an impeccable Art Deco skyscraper worthy of Manhattan, completed in 1933.

During the 1920s French planners, such as Jean-Claude Nicolas Forestier (1861–1930) in Buenos Aires and Donat-Alfred Agache (1875–1934) in Rio de Janeiro, introduced new standards of modernity to urbanization. They were followed by Le Corbusier in 1929, whose trip to South America attained mythical status in the history of Latin American Modernism. His tour led from Buenos Aires through Uruguay to Brazil. His dreams of conquest were inflated by his first flight in an airplane, resulting in sketches for colossal mega-structures laid over the topography of Montevideo, São

Paulo, and Rio de Janeiro. Le Corbusier proposed a plan for São Paulo that vertically extruded a *cardo* and *decumanus* as twenty-story viaducts. The structure would serve as a scaffold for housing, while the highway on top would provide an expeditious route from the suburban hills to the center. The impact of Le Corbusier's lectures about the integration of art, urbanism, and architecture changed the way in which Brazilians saw their structures.

In 1935 Lúcio Costa (1902–1998) won the competition to construct the Ministry of Education and Health, or MES (Fig. 19.2-8), the key project of the populist dictator Getúlio Vargas (r. 1930–1945). Costa had grown up in France and previously designed in the Beaux-Arts manner. In 1930, however, he began working for the Russian émigré Gregori Warchavchik (1896–1972), the only architect in South America Le Corbusier considered modern enough to be

including ground-level walls dressed in *azulejos* tiles and luscious roof gardens planted in swooping curves. Niemeyer invented the operable shutters in the *brise soleils*.

In the postwar period Reidy became director of public housing and designed the serpentine Pedregulho project in Rio de Janeiro (1947–1955) (Fig. 19.2-9). At the top of the sloping terrain he placed a seven-story, 260 m (853 ft) long block that followed the sinuous contours of the site more or less like Lansdown Crescent at Bath, but without the classical details (see Section 14.1). Unlike the alienating circumstances of most social housing, the planners integrated Pedregulho with schools, a gym, a pool, a band shell, shops, and a laundry as complimentary services to those who paid rent.

During the 1940s Niemeyer and Burle Marx remained active at Pampulha, a new luxury suburb set on an artificial lake south of Belo Horizonte. Niemeyer, perhaps influenced by the bold, flowing forms of Burle Marx's gardens, abandoned the orthogonal rigidity of the International Style to create sensuous curves. The little church of São Francisco (1943) sat on the shore as a graphic gesture, with four parabaloid humps, the tallest serving the extended nave. Niemeyer anchored the entry with a campanile that tapered downward like an inverted obelisk. He introduced even more sensuous curves in the canopy at the outdoor café of the dance hall, ingeniously balancing the roof on a single row of staggered columns, positioned with the dynamism of a rumba line.

The patron of Pampulha, Juscelino Kubitschek (1902–1976), served as mayor of Belo Horizonte during the 1940s. In 1956 he won the presidential election of Brazil with the campaign promise of "50 years of progress in 5." To dramatize his program, he called on his friend Niemeyer to collaborate on the design of a new capital city, Brasília. The site in the desolate scrublands of the geographic center of Brazil was to have an artificial lake, just like Pampulha.

included in the CIAM. Vargas's minister of culture, Gustavo Capanema (1900–1985), played a role similar to that of Vasconcelos in Mexico, pushing for a solution that would be both modern and Brazilian. He hoped to change the image of Brazil from a relaxed and backward country to a leader of social and technical progress. The MES building, constructed between 1937 and 1943, became the incubator of Brazilian Modernism, involving the talents of Costa's assistants Oscar Niemeyer and Affonso Reidy (1909–1964) and landscape designer Roberto Burle Marx (1909–1994). To ensure the project's Modernist credentials, Costa invited Le Corbusier back to Brazil to participate in the design. The concept of a freestanding slab on a landscaped block and the architectural elements of *pilotis*, *brise soleils*, and rooftop gardens were the French master's contribution to the project, while the realization of the details was Brazilian,

Niemeyer's friend and mentor Costa won the competition for the Plano Piloto master plan of the city, proposing a simple diagram somewhat like a bow and arrow. The pattern took shape as a gently curved, linear city running 12 km (7.5 miles) on a north–south axis, interrupted by a central cross-axis of a 200 m (656 ft) wide mall for the government institutions. Niemeyer designed the monumental buildings on a scale that surpassed the great axial landscapes of both Washington, D.C., and New Delhi. He lined each side of the mall with ten-story slab buildings for the various ministries and terminated the axis with a gigantic plinth. The pure shapes of the Senate building dome and the saucer on the Chamber of Deputies were balanced by a pair of thin, thirty-story towers behind the plinth. Although produced by a democratic government, the austere remoteness of the monumental core of Brasília fit perfectly the representational needs of the military dictatorship that took power from 1964 to 1985 (Fig. 19.2-10).

Kubitschek remained a hero for most Brazilians, as he made good on his promises, stimulating

technical progress, setting up an independent automobile industry, and building the brilliant set piece of Brasília in just three years. To do so, however, he nearly bankrupted the country. At the opening ceremonies for the city in 1960 the president reminded his constituents of why it had been worth the effort, as they "imported neither architects nor town planning experts to design Brasília . . . and the laborers who erected it, from the contractor down to the 'candango' . . . were all our own people." Brazil became the first

Figure 19.2-9 Rio de Janeiro. Pedregulho, Affonso Reidy, 1947–1955.

Figure 19.2-10 Brasília, National Congress complex (Senate and Chamber of Deputies), Oscar Niemeyer, 1962.

Lina Bo Bardi

Lina Bo Bardi (1914–1992), one of the major protagonists of Brazil's sensual form of Modernism, was born in Milan and worked for a period of time with Gio Ponti before moving to Brazil in 1946 with her husband, the art curator Pietro Maria Bardi (1900–1999). Her Glass House of 1951 was as transparent as Mies's Farnsworth House but was carefully sited on a slope, allowing protected spaces. In 1957 she designed one of the major cultural institutions of Brazil, the São Paulo Museum of Art. She suspended the longitudinal glass box from two immense exoskeletal concrete beams supported like a table on four legs, dramatically painted red. The solution left a vast open ground plane as a shaded sculpture garden. As a woman Bo Bardi occupied a class of her own in the realm of Brazilian design, rarely bonding with other professionals but much loved by the popular sector, especially for one of her final projects, a social center improvised in an abandoned concrete factory.

São Paolo. São Paolo Museum of Art, Lina Bo Bardi, 1957–1968.

instance of a Third World country that turned the tables and took the lead in architecture.

Indian Independence and the Absorption of Modernism

The public buildings of colonial India surpassed the scale of those in the mother country. New Delhi remained the grandest classical landscape ever conceived in the British Empire, while the University of Bombay, the Victoria Museum in Madras, and the Victoria Monument in Calcutta provided magnificent urban set pieces. After the state was granted independence at midnight on December 31, 1947, the new government felt no immediate need for additional architectural expressions, as most of India's institutions had already been anticipated by the colonial administration. The new parliament simply occupied Edwin Lutyens's capital buildings.

The question of postcolonial architecture did not arise until India split into five states: India, East Pakistan (now Bangladesh), West Pakistan (now simply Pakistan), Burma, and Ceylon (now Sri Lanka). The painful process of relocating Muslims to West Pakistan and Hindus and Sikhs to India resulted in the new northern province of Punjab, which remained without an administrative city. Its capital, Chandigarh, became the most famous of nearly 300 new towns built in India. The government of Jawaharlal Nehru (r. 1947–1964) intended it to represent a commitment to modernity and serve as a means of stimulating Indian architectural talent through contact with accomplished foreign professionals.

As in Brazil, the stimulus for modern Indian architecture proved to be Le Corbusier, who in all made twenty-two trips to India. The French master, his cousin Pierre Jeanneret, and the English couple Maxwell Fry (1899–1987) and Jane Drew (1911–1996) were hired in 1950 to design Chandigarh. Le Corbusier, now in his sixties, had finally gained the patronage he so eagerly sought throughout his career. His client, Nehru, seemed more progressive in his thinking than

The Cuban Art Schools

The creation of the Cuban National Art Schools, built in Havana a few years after the Cuban Revolution (1961–1965), proved a unique postcolonial exploit. Fidel Castro (1926–2016) and Che Guevara (1928–1967), the leaders of the Cuban Revolution, decided while playing a round of golf that the bourgeois golf course would make the perfect setting for the schools. They invited the young Cuban architect Riccardo Porro (b. 1925), assisted by two Italian architects, Vittorio Garatti (b. 1927) and Roberto Gottardi (1927–2017), to create buildings appropriate for a revolutionary culture. Inspired by the African heritage of colonial Cuba, Porro and his colleagues created curvilinear forms in brick and glass inspired by folk art. Unfortunately, as the five complexes were nearing completion, Cuba underwent a major ideological shift in response to its greater dependence on the Soviet Union. Much as Constructivism had been undone during an earlier period in Russia, the fluid forms of the campus were condemned as decadent expressions of individualism.

Havana, Cuba. School of Plastic Arts, Riccardo Porro, 1965.

the architect. By the 1950s, Le Corbusier had misgivings about technical progress, whereas Nehru was an enthusiastic technocrat, betraying Gandhi's anti-industrial grassroots principles by founding a series of technical universities and promoting modern industries. Nehru hoped Chandigarh would rise "unfettered by the traditions of the past, a symbol of the nation's faith in the future."

The plan of Chandigarh followed a loose grid of seventy superblocks, called "sectors," each roughly 1,200 × 800 m (3,937 × 2,625 ft), similar in scale to the *superquadras* of Brasília. Each sector had its own internal circulation and easy pedestrian connections. A beautifully maintained linear park system ran through the central sectors, terminating at the capital district. Here, Le Corbusier personally designed the monuments to sit facing each other across a broad esplanade. Without romanticizing his efforts, he attempted to create a modern Indian architecture. His Orientalism differed from the Indo-Saracenic style of Colonel Samuel Swinton Jacobs and the British colonialists in that he translated local forms into his own idiom. For the High Court he stylized the Mughal divan, an open hypostyle hall, with a series of see-through concrete vaults raised on flanges. He then slipped into this horizontal frame a triple-height main court under the two end bays on the left and, to the other side of the three-bay causeway, the eight smaller double-height courtrooms. He articulated the facades with deep *brise soleils* arranged in staggered patterns like gigantic versions of *jalis*, or perforated screens. A switchback ramp moved between the two sides of the causeway, reviving the architect's notion of the architectural promenade.

Le Corbusier considered the Assembly Building a vindication of his exclusion from the executive design committee for the UN headquarters. He proudly noted that the budget for the entire city cost half of what had been spent on the UN. As a rebuke of the classical portico, he set eight concrete fins to sustain a colossal rounded gutter, which channeled the roof's runoff water into a reflecting pool at the corner of the terrace. He punched irregular apertures through the fins to give them kinetic relief. The roofscape carried sculptural forms inspired by the Jantar Mantar observatory in Delhi (see Section 12.1). Instead of a dome, he placed a tapered concrete cylinder over the lower chamber, evoking the hyperboloid profile of the cooling towers at power plants. The concrete horns on the roof alluded to the sacred cows found on Indian streets. Next to it a tilted pyramid rose over the upper chamber. He packed the offices into the three perimeter walls surrounding an interior hypostyle hall, dimly lit from upper clerestories. In his first sketch for the capital district of Chandigarh, Le Corbusier drew a tall skyscraper for the Secretariat overlooking the public halls but, owing to a shortage of steel,

turned the tall building on its side, as a seven-story horizontal skyscraper for the bureaucratic offices. Between the Assembly Building and the High Court (Fig. 19.2-11a) he planned the never-realized Governor's Palace, for which there was no longer any need, to be capped with a colossal scoop, an inversion of Lutyens's dome. Two decades after Le Corbusier's death, the Monument to the Open Hand (Fig. 19.2-11b), which he had conceived as a symbol of Nehru's Third World movement of nonaligned nations, subject neither to capitalism nor to communism, was added to the edge of the capital complex as a weather vane overlooking the lake.

During his first trips to India Le Corbusier encountered the wealthy industrialists of Ahmedabad, who commissioned five buildings, including the Mill Owner's Association, a museum, and a house for Manorama Sarabhai (Fig. 19.2-12). The Sarabhai family had been influential in the independence movement, sponsoring Gandhi's ashram in Ahmedabad in the 1920s. Of all Le Corbusier's works, the Sarabhai House, completed in 1956, proved the most comfortable, while the Mill Owner's Association proved the least habitable. He structured the Sarabhai House on a series of ten **Catalan vaults**, supported by brick-clad concrete walls and covered with a sod roof for thermal insulation. The staggered wall divisions on the interior provided a relatively free plan, making light and air easy to control and serving as a model of passive solar design.

Le Corbusier exerted an immense impact on the emerging architectural profession in India: several of

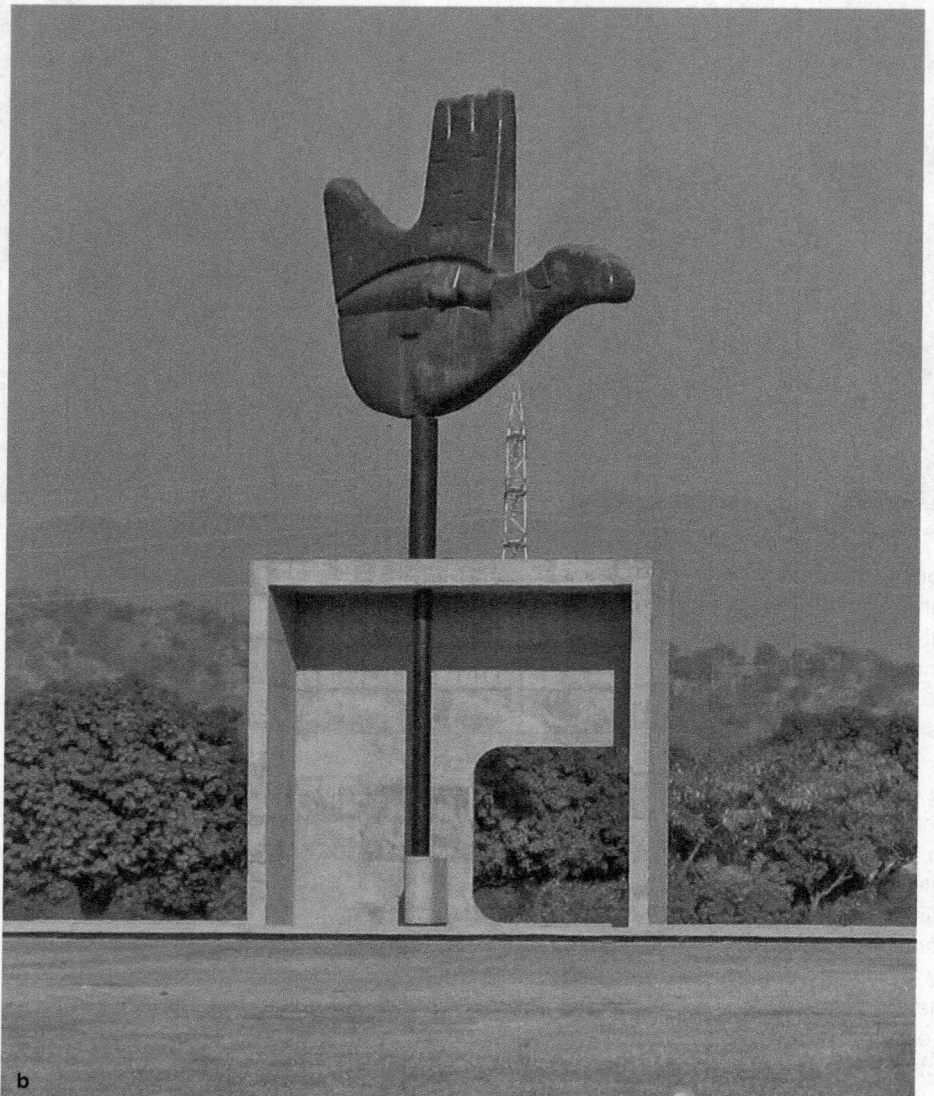

Figure 19.2-11 Chandigarh, India.
(a) Capitol and Palace of Justice, Le Corbusier, 1952–1960.
(b) Monument to the Open Hand, Le Corbusier, completed 1987.

Figure 19.2-12 Ahmedabad, India. Sarabhai House, Le Corbusier, 1956.

the children of his clients became architects, and many of the designers who worked on Chandigarh continued to pursue his ideals in the town's school of architecture. Balkrishna V. Doshi (b. 1927) worked in the master's studio in Paris for four years before returning to supervise sites in Chandigarh and Ahmedabad, where he set up his own office in 1956 and created a foundation for low-income housing solutions. Doshi's most important early work, the School of Architecture in Ahmedabad (Fig. 19.2-13), completed in 1968, showed a close affinity for the brick walls and cooling devices of the Sarabhai House.

While Delhi and Bombay were more important economically and politically, Ahmedabad, because of its progressive patronage, became the matrix of modern Indian architecture. One of India's most important practitioners, Charles Correa (1930–2015), who trained at the Massachusetts Institute of Technology (MIT), got his breakthrough commissions here. In 1963 he designed the Smarak Sangrahalaya memorial to Gandhi (Fig. 19.2-14a,b), a series of open-air and enclosed pavilions adjacent to Gandhi's modest residence at Sabarmati Ashram, where he practiced a crafts-based lifestyle from 1917 to 1930. Correa approached the site as an architectural landscape based on a checkerboard grid. He defined the modules with thick brick corner piers linked by reinforced concrete beams that doubled as gutters and clustered the tile-clad pyramidal roofs in various combinations to cover open verandahs and small exhibition spaces. Operable wooden slats helped to avoid the use of glass.

Figure 19.2-13 Ahmedabad, India. School of Architecture, Balkrishna V. Doshi, 1968.

Like Doshi, Correa began research on low-income housing, resulting in the 1973 project for squatters in Bombay (now Mumbai), which was laid out on a similar checkerboard plan with four one-room units under a single pyramidal roof and a small open court attached to each unit. He developed this idea further in a sites-and-service project at Belapur (1986) in New Bombay, where he devised units that could be expanded according to need. While designing for the poor, Correa also created in 1970 the twenty-seven-story Kanchanjunga Tower (Fig. 19.2-15a,b) for luxury housing in the center of Bombay. The concrete structure rose on a square plan and had notches cut rhythmically from its corners that revealed double-height verandahs. The tower achieved Le Corbusier's dream of the apartment-villa, or, in this case, the skyscraper-bungalow. All of the units had stepped sections and extended over 200 m² (2,152 ft²) in area. Correa made no secret of his infatuation with ancient

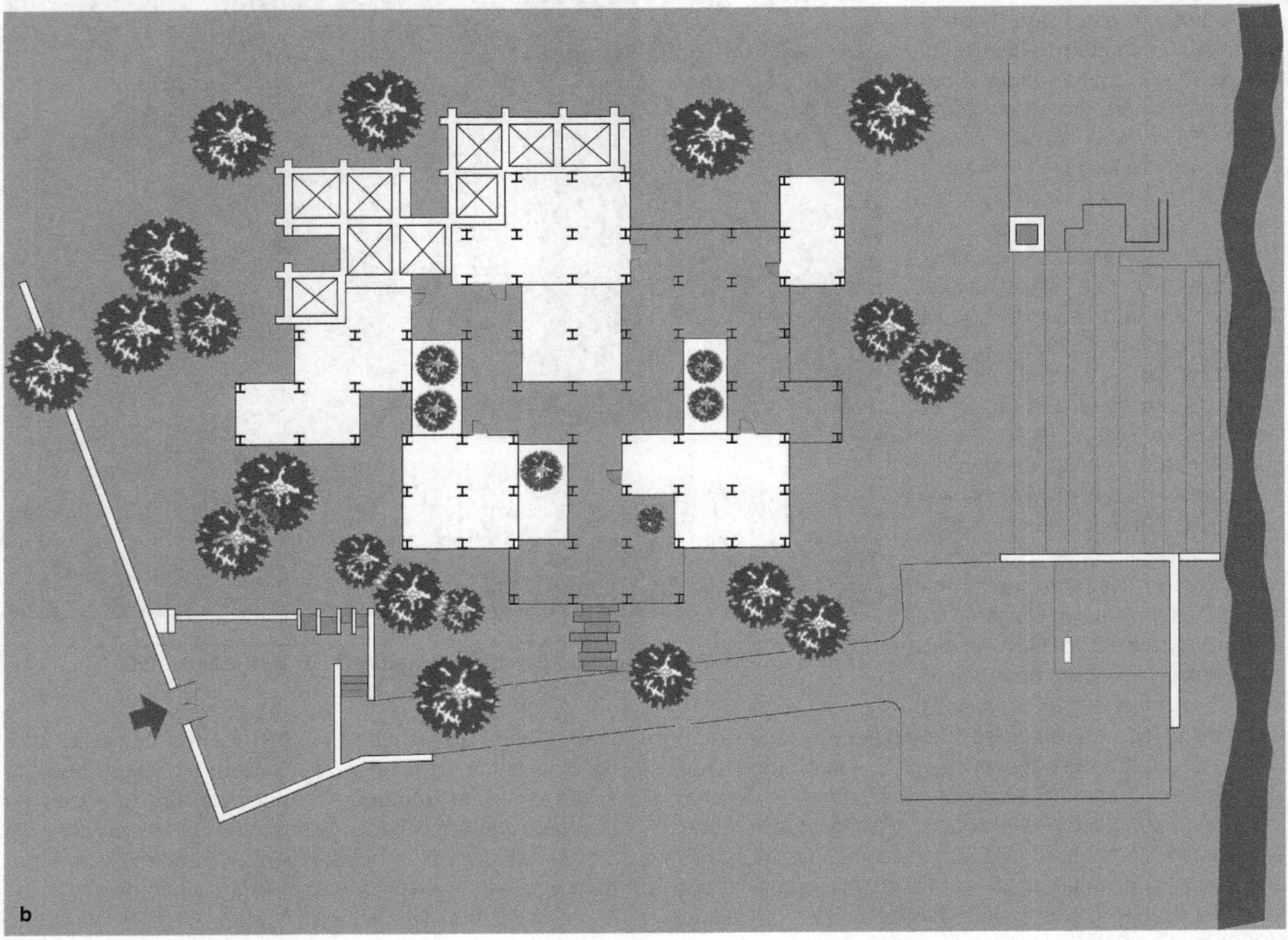

Figure 19.2-14 Ahmedabad, India. (a) Smarak Sangrahalaya memorial, Charles Correa, 1963. (b) Plan.

Figure 19.2-15 Mumbai.
(a) Kanchanjunga Tower, Correa, 1970.
(b) Plan, with stepped sections shown in different shades of gray.

Hindu geometry, returning to the mandala grid of the *Vastu Purusha* as his base, trying to strike a balance between the appropriate technology and cultural continuity.

Raj Rewal (b. 1934) demonstrated a similar interest in ancient geometry. Like all of the important postcolonial Indian architects, he studied abroad before starting his practice, working for Michel Ecochard (1905–1985) in Paris. He first gained recognition for a radical structure, a series of reinforced concrete **space frames** for the Exhibition Complex of New Delhi, begun in 1972. While the truncated pyramids appeared to be made with metal members, he used hand-poured concrete to make the thin struts of the polyhedron trusses. Rewal's Nehru Memorial Pavilion in New Delhi, also built in 1972, set a redented mandala plan on an artificial mound. He recuperated traditional abstract forms while exploiting the maximum technical possibilities of reinforced concrete construction, creating deep cuts for natural light and columnless spans within the mound. In India, more than in other Third World countries, modern architecture was able to conserve its connection with historical traditions, partly because of the impressive breadth of the culture's historic patrimony and partly because of the slow pace of development it experienced.

Postcolonial Africa and the False Promises of Modernism

During the "scramble for Africa" at the end of the nineteenth century, European nations divided the continent into forty

colonial states. Britain and France governed the largest number of colonies, while Portugal, Spain, Belgium, Italy, and Germany all staked their claims to smaller areas. The African colonies were the last to free themselves from European dominance, obtaining independence during the period of 1957–1964 (Fig. 19.2-16). The initial optimism of the new African states was usually accompanied by competent International Style projects for universities, hospitals, and government buildings. The countries of postcolonial Africa aspired to continue the development of technical progress while forging new national identities. With few exceptions, however, the independent states of Africa degenerated into political turmoil. Corruption, military coups, dictatorships, and even genocide have plagued the continent since the mid-1960s, greatly hindering planned urban development and discouraging patronage for architecture.

The cities of North Africa were more settled than the rest of Africa, built on a strong Islamic base that had endured for over a millennium. The French, starting in Algiers, consistently imposed a strong colonial image on their holdings that separated the European from the indigenous city (see Section 17.2). In 1953, as the Algerian independence movement gained force, the new mayor of Algiers, Jacques Chevallier, attempted to appease colonial discontent with the construction of decent housing. He appointed Fernand Pouillon (1912–1986) of Marseilles as the city's chief architect with the intention of improving the lot of squatters living in *bidonvilles* (tin can cities), who comprised up to 30% of the population. Pouillon immediately produced 1,600 units during his first year. Although he used a Modernist style, he preferred to build in masonry and was a keen observer of local techniques. He achieved a new variation of the shady, vaulted *suq* with his Diar el-Mahçoul Market (1955), making it modern by using parabolic vaults arranged in cross-axial sequences. His 200 Colonnes (Climat de France) (Fig. 19.2-17) in 1959 provided one of the twentieth century's grandest visions of subsidized housing. Pouillon inserted into the western hills an immense oblong block for 5,000 residents. Its courtyard recalled the scale of both the Palais-Royal in Paris and the Maydan-I Shah in Isfahan. The colossal freestanding colonnade, built of white square piers three stories high, lined the courtyard, adding intense shadows and a strong formal unity. Although France lost its hold on Algeria in 1962, Pouillon's work lived up to the mayor's mandate to guarantee the "triumph of human dignity, of French liberties, and of the future of French-Muslim civilization."

The wave of independence struggles that swept sub-Saharan Africa began in the small West African country of Ghana, the wealthiest

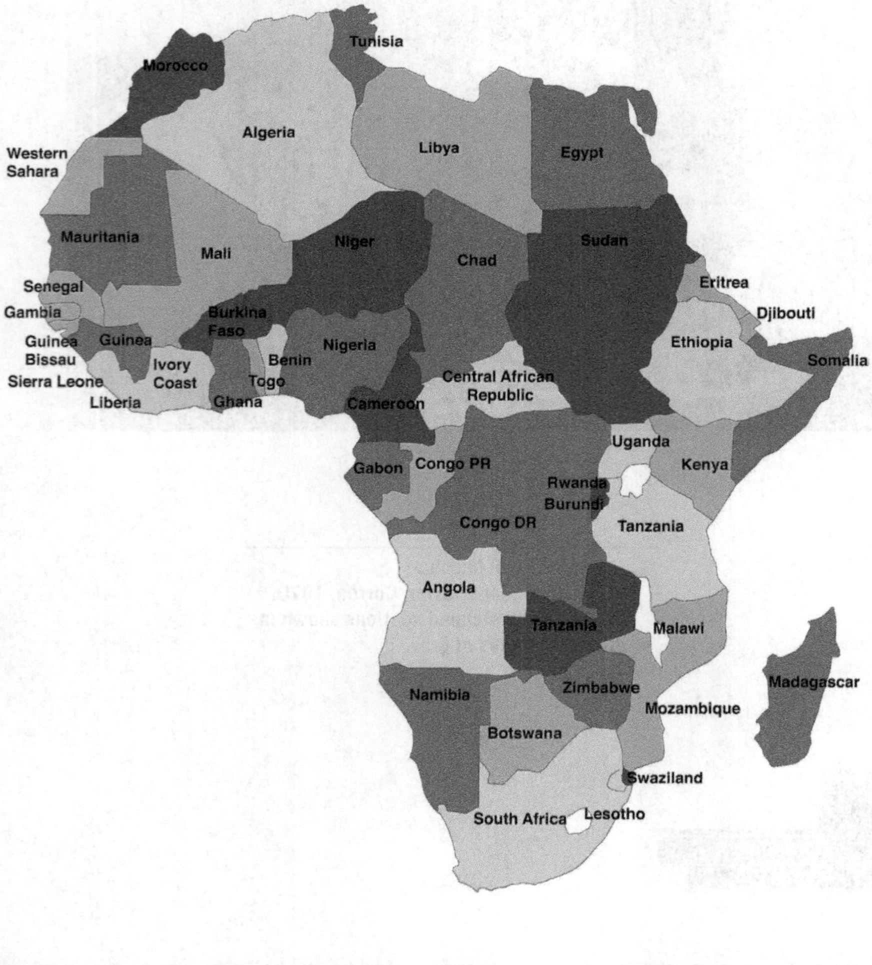

Figure 19.2-16 Postcolonial Africa.

Figure 19.2-17 Algiers. Climat de France social housing project, Fernand Pouillon, 1959.

and best developed of the British colonies. A triumphal arch erected at the port of Accra marked the state's year of independence, 1957, alongside the promise of Kwame Nkrumah (1909–1972) for "freedom and justice." Nkrumah militated for pan-African unity, aspiring to a socialist vision of universal well-being and human rights. Schools, hospitals, and government buildings were on his agenda, while housing came later. Because of the lack of locally trained professionals, both independent Ghana and nearby Nigeria, which became independent in 1960, relied on the British for their institutions. James Cubitt (1914–1983) became one of the most prolific and inventive of these "import" architects, working primarily in Ghana. There he designed schools and universities, including the University of Kumasi (later named after Nkrumah) (Fig. 19.2-18). He gave the new nation's major school for science and technology a superbly innovative laboratory in 1965, structured on exoskeleton columns supporting wide *V*-shaped beams that sheltered clerestories for light and air.

Fry and Drew, who, previous to their stint at Chandigarh, had worked in colonial Africa, returned in the mid-1950s to design several university campuses, including the University of Nigeria at Ibadan. Here, they explored the use of screens, louvers, causeways, deep eaves, and other methods of passive cooling. With their new partner Denys Lasdun (1914–2001), they designed the aluminum-domed museum in Accra, which they prefabricated and shipped from England. They gave the Cooperative Bank in Accra a gridded facade made of operable louvers, which started a trend for similar buildings, such as the Cooperative Bank of Western Nigeria in Ibadan (Fig. 19.2-19). Kenneth Scott, another important British architect working in Africa, built a house for himself in Accra inspired by Villa Savoye but equipped with cooling strategies to accommodate the tropical climate of Ghana. His library in Koforidua, Ghana, proved a model of restraint, using a grid of slender steel

Figure 19.2-18 Accra, Ghana. University of Kumasi (later Nkrumah) laboratories, James Cubitt, 1965.

columns with gaps in the bookshelf walls to obtain diffused light.

France's former colonies, such as Senegal, Côte d'Ivoire, and Cameroon, turned to French professionals for help. One building, the Palais du Grand Conseil d'Afrique (1950–1956), built in Dakar, Senegal, by Daniel Badani (1914–2006) and Pierre Roux-Dorlat, remained a symbol of French colonial nearsightedness. Intended as the clearinghouse for a federation of French holdings in Africa, most of which would be lost shortly after the building was completed, it became independent Senegal's National Assembly. CIAM delegate Michel

Figure 19.2-19 Accra, Ghana.
Cooperative Bank, Maxwell Fry and
Jane Drew, 1956.

projects in postcolonial Africa, the new capital city of Abuja in Nigeria, begun in 1980 (Fig. 19.2-21a,b). He oriented the strong axis of the gridded city toward an astounding geological phenomenon, the Aso Hill, a single dome-shaped rock that rises straight up 200 m (656 ft). Aside from this natural feature, the architecture appeared as a collection of concrete and glass scaffolds with rounded corners, typical of Tange's style but with little sympathy for local traditions. While many of the outer areas of Abuja have been built, the plan for the unrealized central district has been recently revised by the office of Albert Speer, Jr.

After the great expectations of the 1960s, the prospects for architecture in most of Africa grew dim. Cities like the Democratic Republic of Congo's Kinshasa (the former Léopoldville of Belgian Congo) grew by a factor of ten between 1940 and 1960, and today Lagos, Nigeria, vies for the most populous city in the world, with over 21 million inhabitants. The majority of its inhabitants reside in self-built *bidonvilles* without adequate transportation, water, or sewerage. The alarming demographic increases, coupled with endemic health crises and food shortages, have left the region with limited resources for great architecture. During the late twentieth century Africa became one of the biggest consumers of arms, and military overthrows occurred with alarming regularity. Chronic hunger and political instability have left little room for serious building.

Figure 19.2-20 Casablanca. Ben Sliman Hospital, Jean-François Zevaco, 1958.

Ecochard (1905–1985) designed the Federal University in Yaoundé, Cameroon (1962–1969), while Roland Simounet (1927–1996), fresh from designing vaulted hillside housing in Algiers, built the dormitories of the Tanarive University in Malagasy Republic (later part of Madagascar). By far the most original designs came from the Moroccan-born architect Jean-François Zevaco (1916–2003), whose Ben Sliman Hospital in Casablanca, Morocco (Fig. 19.2-20), exuded vibrant Expressionist tendencies.

The Japanese architect Kenzo Tange (1913–2005) produced plans for the last of the great International Style

Further Reading

Bednarek, Nicola. *Cruelty & Utopia: Cities and Landscapes of Latin America.* New York: Princeton Architectural Press, 2005.

Benton, Tim, ed. *Le Corbusier: Architect of the Century.* London: Arts Council of Great Britain, 1987.

Brillembourg, Carlos. *Latin American Architecture, 1929–1960: Contemporary Reflections.* New York: Monacelli Press, 2004.

Casciato, Maristella, and Stanislaus von Moos. *Twilight of the Plan: Chandigarh and Brasilia.* Mendrisio, Switzerland: Academia di Architettura, 2007.

Figure 19.2-21 Abuja, Nigeria. (a) Revision of Kenzo Tange plan of the 1980s by Albert Speer, Jr., 2011. (b) Aso Hill, the dome-shaped rock that provides a central axis for Abuja.

Hassan Fathy's Return to Vernacular Construction

The greatest theoretical critique of postcolonial African architecture came from an Egyptian, Hassan Fathy (1900–1989), who recognized the economic and environmental advantages of returning to traditional building techniques, especially in rural situations. Instead of the concrete and glass of the International Style, he advocated handmade adobe. His chance to experiment came in 1946, when the Egyptian government decided to evict the residents of Gourna, near Luxor, so that the site could be controlled by archaeologists. Fathy was commissioned to build New Gourna, and he hoped to effect a social transformation by teaching the residents self-build construction techniques and other crafts to improve their economy. He rediscovered the pitched-brick technique of making vaults without falsework and reintroduced the *malqaf*, or wind-catcher flue, used in most of the Mamluk palaces of Cairo (see Section 9.1).

Fathy proved that traditional houses built in mud cost a fraction of those built in concrete and worked better with the climate. The government withdrew its support from the project in 1953, however, and although the school, the mosque, the theater, and a few houses had been completed, most of the residents of New Gourna eventually left, going back to their old trade of tomb robbing. The buildings were articulated with delicate grilles and capped with smooth vaults, but their beauty was not enough to sustain the desired political and social evolution.

New Gourna, Egypt. Mud-pitched vaults of the mosque, Hassan Fathy, 1946–1953.

Çelik, Zeynep. *Urban Forms and Colonial Confrontations: Algiers under French Rule*. Berkeley: University of California Press, 1997.

Correa, Charles. *Housing and Urbanisation*. London: Thames & Hudson, 1999.

Elleh, Nnamdi. *African Architecture: Evolution and Transformation*. New York: McGraw-Hill, 1997.

Fraser, Valerie. *Building the New World: Studies in the Modern Architecture of Latin America, 1930–1960*. London: Verso, 2000.

Fry, Maxwell, and Jane Drew. *Tropical Architecture in the Dry and Humid Zone*. New York: Robert E. Krieger, 1964.

Holston, James. *The Modernist City: An Anthropological Critique of Brasília*. Chicago: University of Chicago Press, 1989.

Loomis, John. *A Revolution of Forms: Cuba's Forgotten Art Schools*. New York: Princeton Architectural Press, 1998.

Meredith, Martin. *The State of Africa: A History of Fifty Years of Independence*. London: Free Press, 2006.

Prakash, Vikramaditya. *Chandigarh's Le Corbusier: The Struggle for Modernity in Postcolonial India*. Ahmedabad, India: Mapin, 2002.

Segre, Roberto. *América Latina fin de Milenio: Raíces y perspectivas de su arquitectura*. Havana, Cuba: Editorial Arte y Literatura, 1999.

Underwood, David. *Oscar Niemeyer and the Architecture of Brazil*. New York: Rizzoli, 1994.

Zanco, Federica, ed. *Luis Barragán: The Quiet Revolution*. Milan: Skira, 2001.

19.3 THE EXPRESSIONIST RESURGENCE

Hybrids amid Mass Culture

Expressionism appeared for a brief moment in architecture after the First World War, yielding a small group of highly individualistic, biomorphic designs. Mendelsohn's Einstein Tower and Rudolph Steiner's Goetheanum were among the few realizations of the style. After World War II, however, at the moment when the International Style reached its widest diffusion, questions of artistic invention and monumentality began to pull at the edges of functionalism. In 1954 Le Corbusier shocked the architectural establishment with the unveiling of Notre-Dame du Haut at Ronchamp. Its thick, rough walls and irrational curves evoked the primitive energy of a prehistoric dolmen. During the same period Frank Lloyd Wright, who for many decades had promoted "organic architecture," took revenge on the grid of New York with his Guggenheim Museum. Its inverted spiral ramp, designed in 1943 but not constructed until 1956, contradicted the rigid orthogonality of the International Style. These idiosyncratic works acted as a prelude to an international exploration of Expressionist forms and organic shapes, which broke from the commonsense solutions of functionalism. The one-off, hybrid nature of the forms required custom-made assembly, contradicting the economic logic of the prefabricated, rational products of mass culture.

European Organic Architecture: Between Rationalism and Intuition

The Expressionist trend in the arts descended from the organic forms of Art Nouveau, exemplified in such works as Gaudí's Casa Milà (see Section 17.3). It gathered momentum among the artistic and spiritual avant-gardes in Munich and Berlin before the First World War and continued into the early 1920s with the eccentric projects of the Crystal Chain and Russian Constructivism. After World War II, Expressionist architecture reappeared in Europe and America like an afterthought. While the International Style provided an apparently dull but sensible theory for modern architecture, Expressionism's pursuit of unfamiliar forms and sensual effects offered an enviable monumentality.

In Finland the turn to organic forms occurred a decade earlier. Alvar Aalto (1898–1976) prevailed as the leading Finnish protagonist of functionalism, using pure planes, strip windows, and no decoration, but from the outset he favored a picturesque approach to composition in his projects. At the Paimio Sanatorium (1928–1933) he arranged the wings of a tuberculosis hospital into a free composition of obliquely set slabs, seeking the optimal exposure to sunlight in the midst of the woods. A decade later he and his wife Aino Marsio-Aalto (1894–1949) designed the Villa Mairea (Fig. 19.3-1) for

Figure 19.3-1 Noormarkku, Finland. Villa Mairea, Aino Marsio-Aalto and Alvar Aalto, 1938–1939.

Figure 19.3-2
Säynätsalo, Finland.
(a) Civic Center, Aalto,
1952. (b) See facing
page.

friends in Noormarkku. The structure's terrace, upper pop-out windows, and entry canopy assumed free forms, like parasites attaching themselves to the rational *L*-shaped plan. The architects celebrated raw materials, from fieldstones to birch saplings, as a kind of honest decoration. An organic cavity scooped out of the mantelpiece in the living room allowed a ray of light to penetrate the chamber from a side window. They added a log structure covered with a sod roof for the sauna, connecting it to the main house by a causeway of industrial-style white *piloti*.

In 1952, Aalto completed the town hall of the small factory town of Säynätsalo (Fig. 19.3-2a,b). Located on an island on the northern shore of Lake Päijanne, the four wings of the complex crowned an artificial hill, opening on the southern side to let grassy steps cascade down from a central court. Inspired by medieval Siena, Aalto built all of the volumes in brick and placed a campanile with a single-pitch roof at the entry. The designers spanned the council chamber with wooden joists supporting tree-like branching rafters. The gracefully laced leather straps around the door

handles demonstrated a personalization of the details that most involved human interaction.

Aalto designed several churches for which he solved the problems of structure and program with rational design but developed the forms through intuition. His unorthodox approach resulted in a functionalist Expressionism, best seen in the three-lobe body of the Church of the Three Crosses at Imatra (1959) and the House of Culture (1958) (Fig. 19.3-3), built for the Finnish Communist Party, in Helsinki. The bulging, brick-clad elevations of the latter corresponded to the rounded acoustical hall inside.

The Danish architect Jørn Utzon (1918–2008) emerged as one of Aalto's most talented assistants. After training in Copenhagen, he went to Stockholm during the war and then to Helsinki, where he worked for Aalto. His wanderings included a year in Morocco, where he designed housing, and another in Mexico, where he studied the ancient ceremonial platforms. After building an open-plan house for himself near Copenhagen, Utzon won the competition to design the Sydney Opera House in 1957 (Fig. 19.3-4). His scheme

TIME LINE

 1952

Aalto completes town hall at Säynätsalo, Finland

Le Corbusier builds church at Ronchamp
▲ 1954

1957

Jørn Utzon wins competition for Sydney Opera House (Utzon resigns ten years later; project completed 1972)

**Figure 19.3-2
Säynätsalo,
Finland. (b) Plan.**

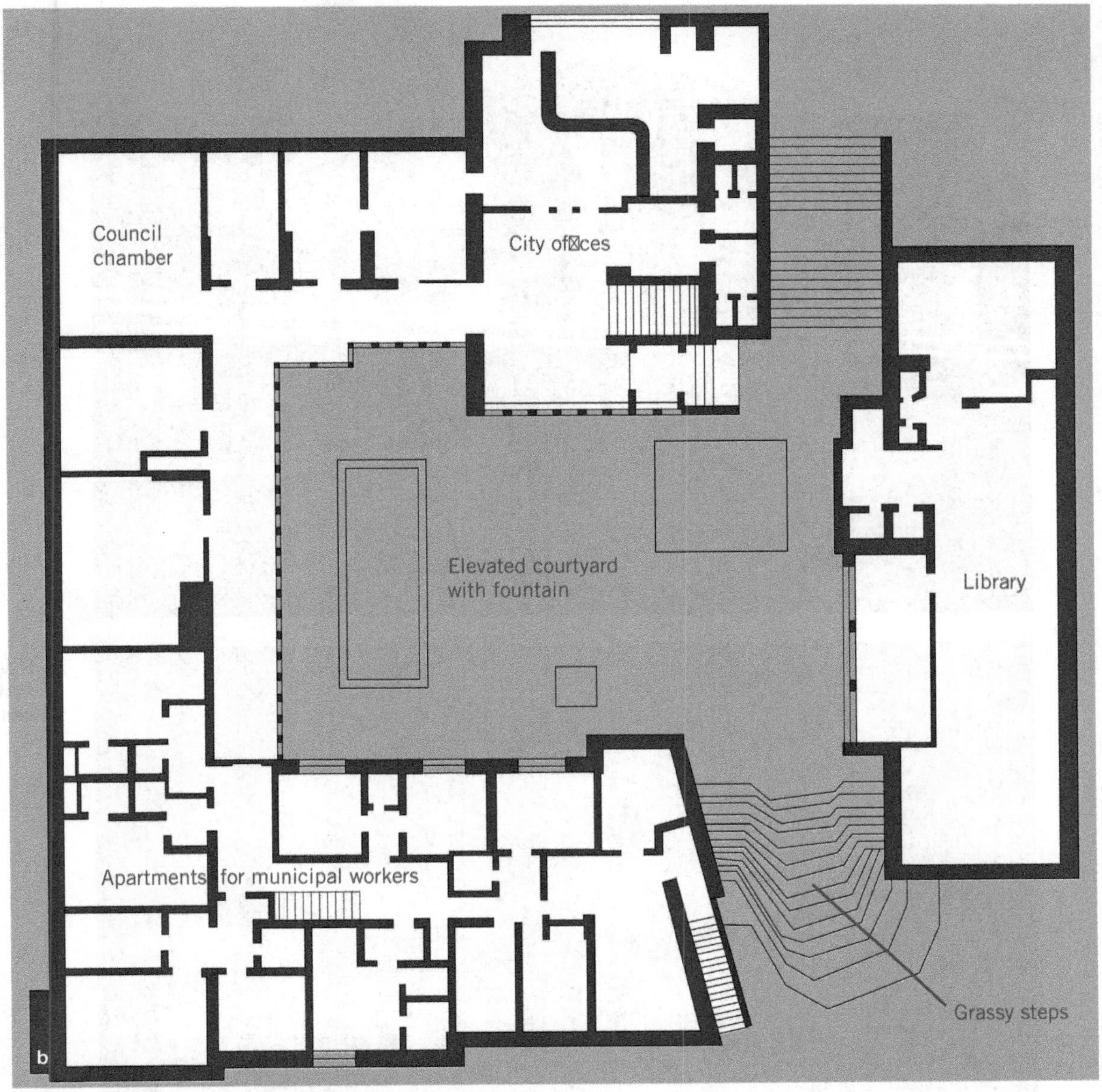

Council chamber

City offices

City offices

Elevated courtyard with fountain

Library

Apartments for municipal workers

Grassy steps

b

for the two theaters rose over a platform jutting into the bay. Each hall was capped by triple-hooded vaults, whose billowing forms suggested crashing surf and sailing ships. The Anglo-Danish engineer Ove Arup (1895–1988) took the basic form and structure of Utzon's unprecedented shells and treated them as hinged segments of a sphere, sustained by folded internal ribs. The team designed both the ribs and the tiled panel coverings in precast post-tension concrete,

Wright's
*Guggenheim
Museum opens
in New York City*

1959

1962

Kahn begins
*capital complex
of Dhaka,
Bangladesh
(finished 1984)*

Saarinen's TWA
*terminal opens at
Idlewild (now John
F. Kennedy) Airport,
New York City*

1962

1972

Kahn's Kimbell
*Museum completed
in Fort Worth, Texas*

Figure 19.3-3 Helsinki. House of Culture, Aalto, 1958.

Figure 19.3-4 Sydney, Australia. Opera House, Jørn Utzon, 1957–1972.

manufactured on site. Construction began in 1963, but Utzon resigned in 1966 under pressure concerning cost overruns of more than 1,000%. He nonetheless left behind a work of organic monumentality that became synonymous with Sydney and the most unabashed Expressionist vision yet realized.

Utzon's major work in Denmark, the suburban church in Bagsværd (1976) (Fig. 19.3-5), a northern suburb of Copenhagen, proved a more subtle example of Expressionism. It appeared on the exterior like an anonymous industrial shed, clad with horizontal concrete panels. Inside, the ceilings, suspended from the roof, descended as curved concrete vaults that seemed to swirl like great unrolled pieces of fabric. The curves of the ceilings captured the diffused

light from the upper clerestory, creating an atmosphere of blanched mystery.

In postwar Germany the International Style prevailed as a safe alternative to the visions of the Nazi past. In Berlin, however, Hans Scharoun, one of the survivors of the Crystal Chain of 1919, acquired an important role in the reconstruction of the city. Scharoun never abandoned his earlier Expressionist style, which characterized his two stunning additions to the Culture Forum in the Tiergarten: the Philharmonie, a tent-like concert hall (1956–1963) (Fig. 19.3-6), and, across the way, the horizontal volumes of the Staatsbibliothek (1964–1978), the city's principal library. Scharoun shaped the interiors of both buildings

Figure 19.3-5
Copenhagen. Bagsværd
Church, Utzon, 1976.

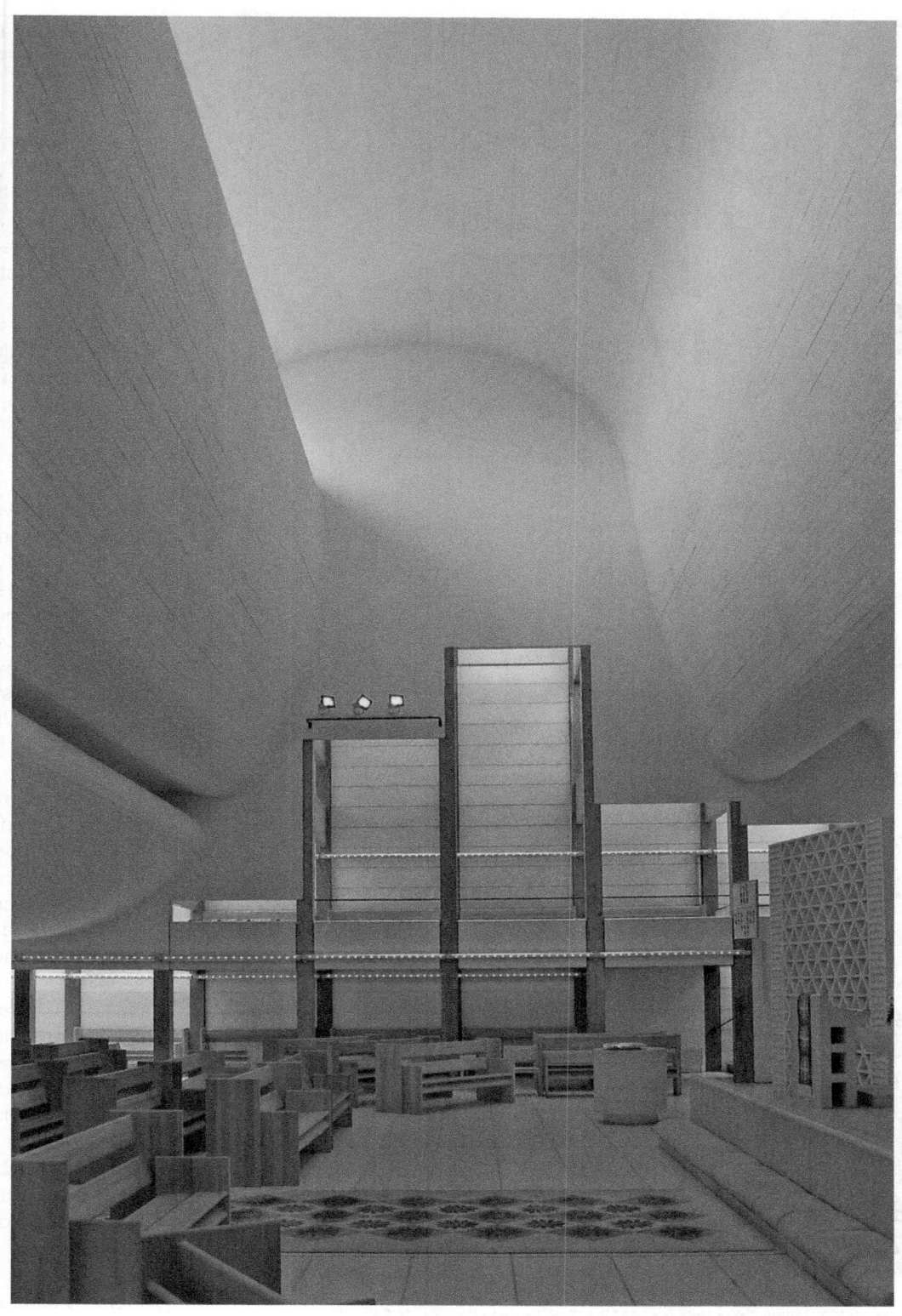

through the dynamic intersection of angled surfaces, so that as one moved through the spaces the perspectives constantly changed.

Scharoun's Expressionism responded to the call for an antitotalitarian monumentality. A similar reaction surfaced in post-Fascist Italy. The office of BBPR, led by Ernesto Rogers (1909–1969), designed the picturesque Torre Velasca, completed in Milan in 1958 (Fig. 19.3-7). Its profile resembled a medieval campanile, with the top six stories for apartments cantilevered on brackets set 1 m (3.5 ft) from the lower twenty levels of offices. Rogers's rival, Gio Ponti (1891–1979), always a more unorthodox designer, completed the smooth Pirelli Building, the world's tallest concrete structure, in the same year. Its sheer volume tapered

Figure 19.3-6 Berlin. Tiergarten Culture Forum, Philharmonie, Hans Scharoun, 1956–1963.

at San Giovanni dell'Autostrada (1964) (Fig. 19.3-8), by Giovanni Michelucci, a church set on the edge of the new freeway outside of Florence. The base of the church appeared primitive and grotto-like, with bulging stone walls. The architect even installed a dolmen near the entry with a dedication to those who lost their lives building the road. The copper-clad roof swooped up like a tent and on the south side took the shape of a drooping catenary curve, like a sheet hung out to dry. The interior was laterally oriented, with tilting concrete masts that branched out to hold the great vault in place.

Among the post-Fascist generation of Italian architects, Carlo Scarpa (1906–1978) best appropriated Wright's theory of organic architecture. Most of his work involved exhibition design and the reworking of existing historic structures, such as the Castelvecchio Museum (1964) in Verona. In the Brion tomb, however, begun in 1968 for an important industrialist family in the country cemetery of San Vito d'Altivole near Treviso (Fig. 19.3-9), Scarpa realized his most complete vision of form, wrapping the existing cemetery with an L-shaped precinct that unfolded like a picturesque park. The entries were mysterious and indirect, leading to such follies as a water pavilion with concrete panels raised on bronze crutches and placed at eye level to obstruct one's view. He rendered the entire environment in porous concrete and frequently used redented moldings, which sometimes pushed into the walls and sometimes protruded from them. Idiosyncratic decorations abounded, including bubble-like disks, linked circles, and single lines of multicolored mosaic tiles. Behind the thick battered walls of the cemetery, Scarpa carried out his battle against the conformity and banality of the International Style and mass culture.

Figure 19.3-7 Milan. Torre Velasca, BBPR office, Ernesto Rogers, 1958.

on its short sides into a thin lozenge shape, so that when seen from the side it nearly disappeared.

The prominent anti-Fascist critic Bruno Zevi (1918–2000) promoted Expressionism through his Association of Organic Architecture. His relentless campaign prepared the way for the most complete realization of organic expression

Abstract Expressionism: American Misfits

One of Frank Lloyd Wright's final works, the Solomon R. Guggenheim Museum in New York (Fig. 19.3-10), opened in 1959, a few months after his death. Its inverted spiral captured the new wave of Expressionist forms in American art

Nervi, the Artful Engineer

The engineer of the Pirelli Building, Pier Luigi Nervi (1891–1979), created some of the most dynamic structures of the age. His Palazzetto dello Sport (1957), built in Rome for the 1960 Olympics, extended a grand concrete dome over a radiating series of Y-shaped exposed buttresses. For the Burgo paper factory (1963) in Mantova, Nervi used the concept of the suspension bridge to hang the ceiling of the work hall, leaving an enormous free span on the interior.

Rome. Palazzetto dello Sport, built for the 1960 Olympics, Pier Luigi Nervi, 1957.

and architecture. By this time American corporations had become the dominant economic power, imposing a rigid standardization in architecture that reflected the moral and political conformism of the postwar period. In contrast, the New York art market promoted the enormous canvases of Abstract Expressionism. The wildness and colossal scale of the "action" paintings by Jackson Pollock (1912–1956) covered entire gallery walls. Both he and Mark Rothko (1903–1970) conceived enormous paintings as rooms. While Abstract Expressionism made a virtue of liberation from the strictures of representation, it remained willfully void of political content.

Amid the diffusion of corporate architecture and the Abstract Expressionist movement, Eero Saarinen (1910–1961) absorbed influences from both directions. Trained in his father's crafts-based design school at Cranbrook Educational Community near Detroit, he pursued a teamwork approach to design, seeking a synthesis of the arts. While Saarinen

produced some of the most orthodox International Style buildings for corporate clients, beginning with the General Motors Technical Center in Warren, Michigan (1948–1956), he also created some of the most hybrid forms of the twentieth century. His first formal breakthrough came in 1947 with the competition to design the Jefferson National Expansion Memorial in St. Louis, which he won with a 192 m (630 ft) stainless steel–clad catenary arch. From here he pursued Expressionist conceits in university settings, beginning at MIT in 1950 with the segmental vault of the Kresge Auditorium, an immense triangular concrete canopy heroically anchored to three pin joints. The bulging theater accompanied the cylindrical Kresge Chapel, clad in clinker bricks. Deceptively simple, the differently sized arches at the base hinted at the irregular wavy walls of the interior. At the Ingalls Hockey Rink (1958) (Fig. 19.3-11) at Yale University, Saarinen created the most dynamic structure in the country, a stingray-shaped roof designed like a cabled bridge.

Figure 19.3-8 Florence. San Giovanni dell'Autostrada, Giovanni Michelucci, 1964.

Figure 19.3-9 Treviso, Italy. San Vito d'Altivole, Brion tomb, Carlo Scarpa, 1968.

Figure 19.3-10 New York. Guggenheim Museum, Frank Lloyd Wright, 1943–1959.

Figure 19.3-11 New Haven, Connecticut. Ingalls Hockey Rink, Eero Saarinen, 1958.

Regularly placed steel cables were hung from a single longitudinal concrete arch to support the thin covering of wood and copper.

Saarinen created his most effusive designs for airports. With the TWA building at Kennedy Airport in New York and Dulles Airport in Chantilly, Virginia (just outside Washington, D.C.), both completed the year after the architect's untimely death in 1961, he captured the fluid forms explored in Mendelsohn's trench sketches from half a century earlier. The flamboyance of the bird-like TWA terminal (Fig. 19.3-12a,b) suited the company's owner, the controversial tycoon Howard Hughes (1905–1976), who attempted to outflank Pan Am in

the contest for international air travel dominance. The terminal's four segmental vaults swept up from twisted branching trunks, leaving the interior as a unified, undulating space. Curving bridges led to the upper ticketing level, while undulating stairs flowed down to the baggage claim area. The electronic schedule boards rose languidly on lily-shaped pedestals. Despite the TWA terminal's fluid shapes and its superb metaphor for flight, its fixed forms were singularly inappropriate for the constantly changing needs of the flight industry and soon proved to be obsolete.

Saarinen's Dulles Airport (Fig. 19.3-13) had better luck: its grand concrete canopy, suspended from a series of

Figure 19.3-12 New York.
(a) TWA terminal, Saarinen,
1956–1962. (b) See facing page.

a

outward thrusting piers that punched through the catenary curve of the roof's surface, left more space for adaptation. The concave glazed walls between the piers, like reverse bow windows, served multiple entries, while on the lower rear side they indicated docking points. Among Saarinen's technical innovations were the mobile lounges, which transported passengers from the terminal to the aircraft out in the field. A single vertical element, containing the monumental downspout from the roof, interrupted the grand hall. Unlike the TWA terminal, Dulles was easily expanded, doubled to thirty bays during the 1980s.

Few American architects during the 1950s rivaled Saarinen's sculptural exploits. Only Marcel Breuer, Gropius's erstwhile partner from the Bauhaus, commanded a comparably fluid vocabulary of molded concrete forms and, after Saarinen's demise, garnered some of the most interesting commissions. For St. John's University Church in Collegeville, Minnesota (1956–1961) (Fig. 19.3-14), he designed massive curving legs to hold up a vertical plane carrying the cross and the carillon bells. Across the plaza, at the Alcuin Library (1966), Breuer laid a waffle slab ceiling on a colossal trunk-like column with spreading branches rendered in Brutalist concrete. At the Whitney Museum in New York City (1966), he eroded the ground level to bring daylight to the glazed

café, set below grade. The three granite-clad gallery levels stepped up and cantilevered over the entry bridge. A single polygonal window protruded provocatively toward Madison Avenue.

Some of the leading architects of the Expressionist resurgence trained at Harvard's Graduate School of Design under Gropius and Breuer during the 1940s, including Paul Rudolph (1918–1997) and I. M. Pei (b. 1917). Rudolph's 1963 Art and Architecture Building at Yale University vied with Pei's 1973 Herbert F. Johnson Museum of Art at Cornell University in Ithaca, New York, in the effort to express programmatic functions through form. In Boston Pei's partner Henry Cobb (b. 1926) designed the ill-fated Hancock Tower (1976), which rose sixty stories as a sheer prism in mirror glass. A rhomboid in plan, it evoked the abstract quality of Mies's 1922 Friedrichstrasse project. Owing to faulty detailing, however, the tower became one of the most problematic high-rises in history, with the shear wind factor peeling off some of its glass panels. After this demeaning exploit Pei regained legitimacy with the addition in 1978 of the East Building to the National Gallery in Washington, D.C. (Fig. 19.3-15). Its plan of two staggered triangles produced sculptural plasticity, with monolithic acute corners dressed in pink Tennessee marble incised with deep fissures.

**Figure 19.3-12 New York.
(b) Interior of TWA terminal.**

**Figure 19.3-13 Washington, D.C.
Dulles Airport, Saarinen, 1961.**

Figure 19.3-14 Collegeville, Minnesota. St. John's University Church, Marcel Breuer, 1956–1961.

Figure 19.3-15 Washington, D.C. National Gallery, East Wing, I. M. Pei, 1978.

Many Expressionist works in America were produced in marginal situations. Bruce Goff (1904–1982), an acolyte of Frank Lloyd Wright, was heavily influenced by Native American culture. He pursued unconventional forms using exotic materials in the relative obscurity of Norman, Oklahoma. His Bavinger House (1955) (Fig. 19.3-16), built with his students for an artist and his family, wrapped a spiral sequence of spaces around a central steel mast borrowed from the local oil rigs. The structure mixed light steel and glass elements with rough stonework. Goff embedded glass gullets into the stone walls to give them sparkle. Although the house was essentially a single room, the two turns of the spiral divided the spaces into distinct zones for quiet contemplation. Like so many Expressionist works, the Bavinger

House was a heroic effort to resist mass culture and thus remained a hybrid gesture.

Louis I. Kahn: Servant and Served

The early work of Louis I. Kahn (1901–1974) gave no hint that he would emerge as the most significant architect of the mid-twentieth century. The son of poor Jewish immigrants from Estonia, he grew up in Philadelphia, attended public schools, and studied architecture with the Beaux-Arts master Paul Philippe Cret (1876–1945), for whom he later worked. During the Depression Kahn designed low-income housing and neighborhood plans. He formed a partnership in the 1940s with the German functionalist

Figure 19.3-16 Norman, Oklahoma. Bavinger House, Bruce Goff, 1955.

Oscar Stonorov (1905–1970), specializing in housing and planning. Kahn was best known in bureaucratic circles for his planning activities and in the earliest meetings for the UN project was considered as a possible designer. In 1950 he won a fellowship to the American Academy in Rome and a year later received his breakthrough commission for the Yale University Art Gallery. From a designer mostly geared toward solving social issues, he blossomed into a consummate form maker. The antiquities of Rome taught him an essential lesson: "A good building makes a good ruin," a dictum that led him to cherish the importance of mass. Kahn remained committed to the goals of Modernism yet open to the works of the past, especially the grand vaulted spaces of the Romans and the massive fortress towers of medieval Europe. His mature works combined structural innovation and modern programs with a historically tinged language of monolithic form and deep shadows.

Like Saarinen, Kahn advanced his formal ideas through connections with educational institutions, which offered more adventurous patronage than private clients. Both architects were strongly involved with Yale: Kahn taught there from 1947 to 1957, and Saarinen was hired to be dean of the school of architecture the year of his death. Both also built two important works there. As a teacher, Kahn seemed to be teaching himself as much as his students and became famous for his enigmatic aphorisms, such as "Ask a building what it wants to be."

Kahn's most enduring lesson, that structures should be composed in terms of "servant and served spaces," first appeared in his work of the mid-1950s. At the Bath House for the Jewish Community Center in Trenton, New Jersey (Fig. 19.3-17a,b), a cluster of pavilions with pyramidal roofs, the U-shaped corner piers functioned as both structure and containers for services such as storage, stairways, and toilets. In all of his subsequent projects he treated the working structure as the vessel of "servant" functions in order to liberate the "served" space.

For the Richards Medical Research Laboratories at the University of Pennsylvania (1956–1964), Kahn set the three square towers in a pinwheel configuration around a central mast that contained the elevators and bathrooms. The solid, brick-clad, turret-like appendages in the middle of each side of the towers functioned as ventilation shafts and stairways for the seven-story labs. He inserted exposed mechanical conduits into the ceiling's grid of post-tension concrete trusses, again integrating structure and service. Contrary to standard research labs, which were organized as a series of horizontal rooms along a double-loaded corridor, Kahn imagined a series of large, open rooms stacked vertically. The laboratory's lack of privacy, bad acoustics, heat buildup, and glare, however, sparked hostility from some of its users, whose work was inhibited by the "served" spaces.

In 1959 Kahn met the creator of the polio vaccine, Jonas Salk, who desired a similar program for the Salk Institute in La Jolla, California (Fig. 19.3-18a,b). Salk wanted a place where he "might also invite Picasso." Learning from the experience of the Richards Labs, Kahn proposed an ingenious system of loft-like laboratories, with services tucked into mezzanines made from 3 m (10 ft) deep **Vierendeel trusses** spanning the workspace. The loft space of the labs could be subdivided easily according to spatial needs, while an open causeway connected them to secluded towers with wood-paneled studies, where resident professors could retreat for privacy. He set the towers on solid fins of concrete with facets bent 45°, allowing each office

Figure 19.3-17 (a) Trenton, New Jersey. Jewish Community Center, Bath House, Louis I. Kahn, 1956. (b) Plans for Kahn's buildings: Trenton Bath House (left); Parliament Building, Dhaka, Bangladesh (center); and Kimbell Museum, Fort Worth, Texas (right).

a view to the Pacific Ocean. The two identical wings of the Salk Institute enclosed an elevated court in stark travertine that appeared like a sacred *temenos*, to which the Mexican architect Luis Barragán suggested adding a narrow ribbon of water in homage to the Alhambra. The skin-like smoothness of the institute's poured-in-place concrete walls came from using formwork lined with polyurethane. The monolithic elevations, with their chiseled seams and button-like pocks placed every half meter (2 ft), resembled ashlar rustication. The abstract, sculptural quality of Kahn's solids and voids corresponded to the Expressionist search for form without

precedents, while the regularity of the plan adhered to the traditions of classical order.

The residues of Kahn's Beaux-Arts background reappeared in the *U*-shaped plan of the Kimbell Art Museum (Fig. 19.3-19), built on the edge of Fort Worth, Texas, in 1972. The patrons desired a modern style, but with the atmosphere of a palace-type museum, such as the Frick Collection in New York. While using a relatively free plan, Kahn created the impression of enclosed, room-like spaces by laying top-lit vaults over the galleries. He modulated the light of the interior by inserting three courtyards, one of which

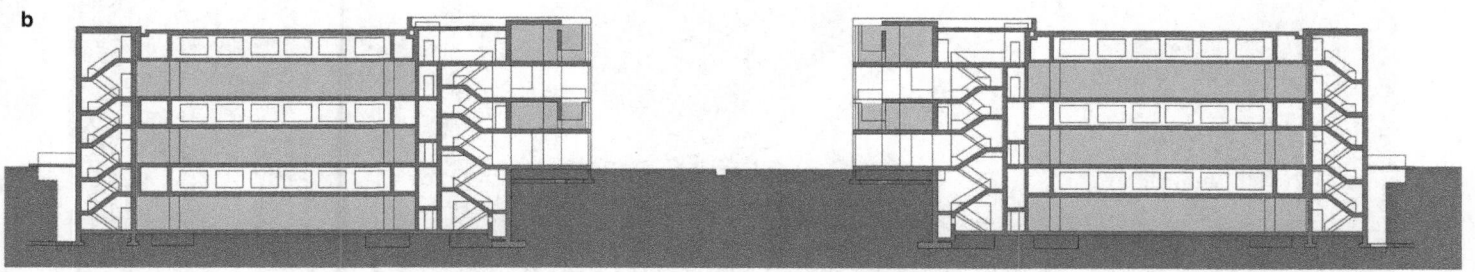

Figure 19.3-18 La Jolla, California. (a) Salk Institute for Biological Sciences, Kahn, 1959–1965. (b) Section, with servant spaces white and served space shaded light gray.

opened to the office court on the lower level. As if to disarm suspicions of historicism, the vaults of the Kimbell derived from the uncommon cycloid curve, which was slightly flatter than a circular arch, and structurally behaved as beams. With the engineer August Komendant (1906–1992), Kahn developed the idea to span the 32 m (102 ft) spaces with post-tension concrete vault-shaped beams. This approach permitted them to cut zenith skylight slots into the apex, where normally a vault would need a keystone. Plexiglass hoods protected the apertures from the elements, while perforated aluminum baffles hung under them to rebound daylight onto the smooth concrete surfaces. Between the Kimbell's vault/beams, Kahn placed 2 m (7 ft) wide, aluminum-clad, flat channels as "servant" spaces carrying the air ducts and conduits in their hollows. These secondary flat ceilings created a syncopated order, visible on the side elevations, like the rhythmic trabeation of *serliana* arches (see Section 11.3). Kahn further clarified the structural, rather than the iconographic, nature of the linked arches with the oddly shaped clerestories under each vault beam, which appeared as thin strips pinched toward their apex: the nonbearing travertine wall was a regular arch, while the

Figure 19.3-19 Fort Worth, Texas. (a) Kimbell Art Museum, Kahn, 1966–1972. (b) Interior foyer.

Figure 19.3-20 Ahmedabad, India.
Indian Institute of Management, Kahn,
1962–1974.

concrete above was a flattened cycloid arch. Without quoting historical sources, the Kimbell achieved resonance with classical traditions while attaining an uncommon synthesis of Modernist structural and programmatic innovation.

Like Le Corbusier, Kahn obtained his dream commissions in postcolonial India. In both the campus for the Indian Institute of Management in Ahmedabad (1962–1974) (Fig. 19.3-20) and the capital complex of the Sher-e-Bangla Nagar (City of the Bengal Tiger) in Dhaka, Bangladesh (1962–1984), he indulged in monumental landscapes. Considering the lower standard of concrete construction, he resigned himself to brick masonry structures with occasional concrete members for long spans. In Ahmedabad his clients came from the same circle that had hired Le Corbusier a decade earlier; Doshi, whose office supervised construction, was instrumental in Kahn's selection. Anant Raje (1929–2009), who had been a student of Kahn's in Philadelphia, completed the majority of the campus buildings, interpreting and elaborating his teacher's numerous incomplete designs. The architects gave the campus, set on a barren 26 ha (65 acre) site in the suburbs of Ahmedabad, the feel of a densely packed medieval city. Many of the brick walls were battered at the base, with prominent buttresses. Some elevations had tapered buttresses set between two segmental window slits, appearing like gigantic faces. When Kahn asked the brick what it wanted to be, it responded "an arch," and he explored a form that had been anathema for most Modernists. He made the arches modern by combining them with white concrete transoms with inflected impost corners. He also cut out grand circles from some of the elevations, exposing a second layer of elevations behind. Setting a building within a building worked as a strategy for passive cooling and glare control.

Kahn pursued the theme of buildings within buildings on a grander scale at Dhaka. Here, the committee for the new capital complex had been unable to obtain the services of Le Corbusier and, on the advice of the Yale-trained architect

Muzharul Islam (1923–2012), invited Kahn to carry out the task. His patron, Field Marshal Ayub Khan, seized control of East Pakistan in a military coup in 1958, promising to restore East and West Pakistan, which were separated by 1,600 km (960 miles), to democracy under Islam. Initially, Kahn was also hired to design the executive complex of Islamabad in West Pakistan, a project that was later abandoned. For the legislative capital in Dhaka he was given a huge site adjacent to, and as large as, the airport. Steeped in visions of Mughal grandeur, such as the Red Forts of Agra and Delhi, he proposed monumental groups as "citadels," one for the National Assembly (Fig. 19.3-21) and the other for the "institutions," meaning schools, museums, a national library, and markets. He separated the two citadels with a V-shaped lake, alluding to the water-bound nature of the country, which has the world's lowest water table and hosts the delta of the Ganges and several other rivers. Kahn reasoned that the earth that would be removed to form the lake would serve to mound up the sites of the surrounding buildings and protect them from frequent floods.

Construction on the capital buildings of Dhaka began in 1968 but halted in 1971, when East Pakistan declared independence from West Pakistan, taking the name "Bangladesh." The new country, substantially weakened by the war for independence and natural disasters, periodically resumed construction. To this day Bangladesh remains one of the most overpopulated and poorest countries in the world, occasionally ruled by military governments or single-party regimes, yet somehow Kahn's idea for a commanding citadel of democracy, one of the grandest visions of government ever conceived, reached completion in 1982. Kahn dressed all of the secondary structures set around the lake in thick brick walls, reserving concrete for the central structure of the National Assembly as evidence of modernity. The preindustrial process of its construction involved thousands of workers, mostly women, who transported fresh concrete in baskets on their heads to pour into the slip forms.

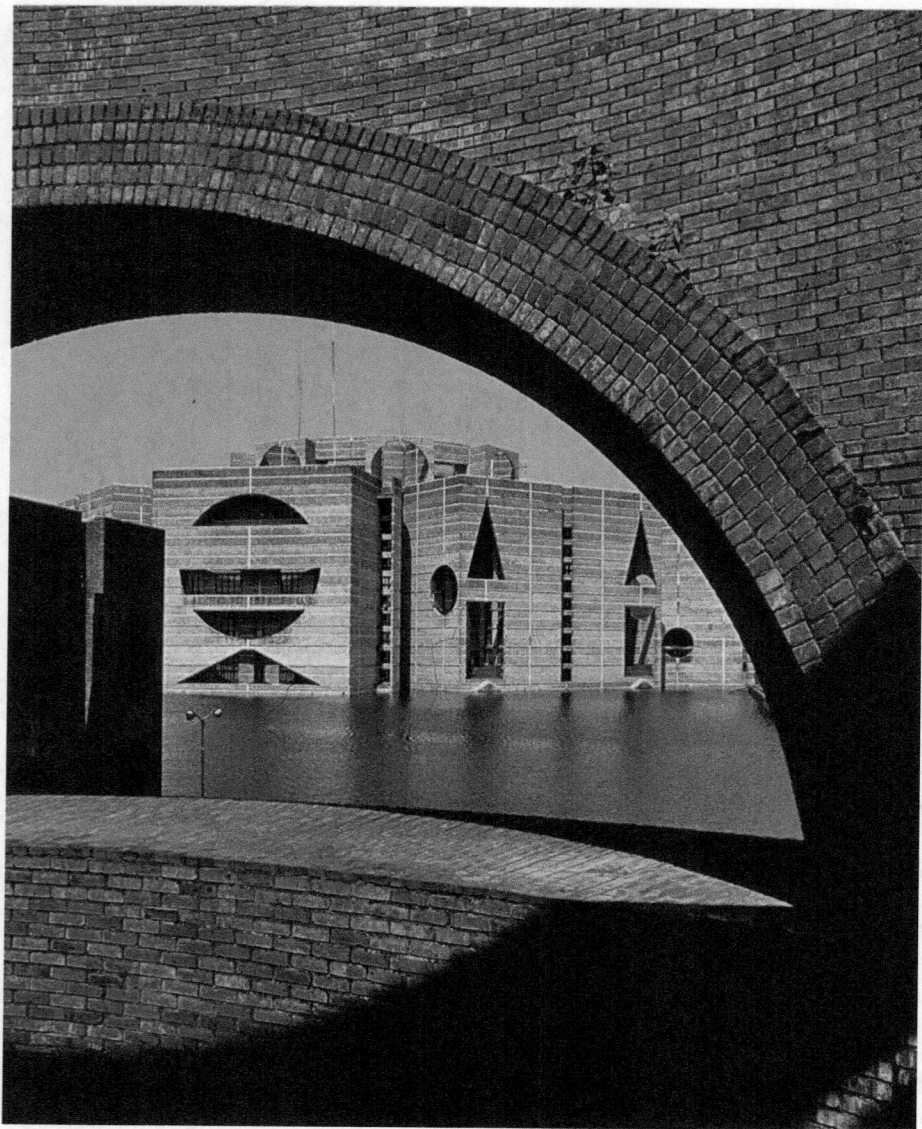

Figure 19.3-21 Dhaka, Bangladesh. View through a "citadel" arch to the National Assembly, Kahn, 1962–1983.

This slow process of production led to an ingenious variation on *ablaq* in which the limit of each day's pour was marked by the placement of marble strips, leaving a panel-like surface of 1.5 m (5 ft) bands.

Seen across the broad brick platform of the southern approach, the rounded and squared apses of the National Assembly appeared like a medieval castle studded with bastions (Fig. 19.3-22), while in plan it evoked a rotated *hasht bihisht* nine-square scheme (see Section 12.1), with the eight subspaces set symmetrically around a central void. The clients requested a dome over the assembly hall, but Kahn preferred a flattened octagon of radiating Vierendeel trusses to cap the structure, like a gigantic prayer wheel above the auditorium. He created a barbican entry with rounded turrets and skewed it slightly so that the prayer hall on the upper level conformed to the southwest *qibla* to Mecca. Throughout the project, Kahn cut out colossal figures—circles, rectangles, and elongated triangles—from the outer walls, revealing a second layer of inner walls. The dark gaps left by these hollows resembled the shady reveals of diwan arches in Persian *pishtaqs* but also hearkened back to other times and places, such as the entry to the Treasure House of Atreus at Mycenae or Étienne-Louis Boullée's projects for an architecture of shadows.

Kahn's National Assembly seems nothing short of a miracle, overcoming an incredible set of contradictions: designed by an American architect with a strong Jewish identity for a country committed to Islam; constructed with extremely primitive means but achieving a technically sophisticated structure; planned for the highest expression of democratic participation in a country that often reverted to autocracy; and full of historical resonances from Europe and Asia while hoping to express liberation from the past. Kahn may not have conceived of his work as the essence of postcolonialism, but those who paid for it did. The chance to step back from the advanced technology of America and rethink a lifetime of formal intuitions led to a masterpiece of transcultural synthesis.

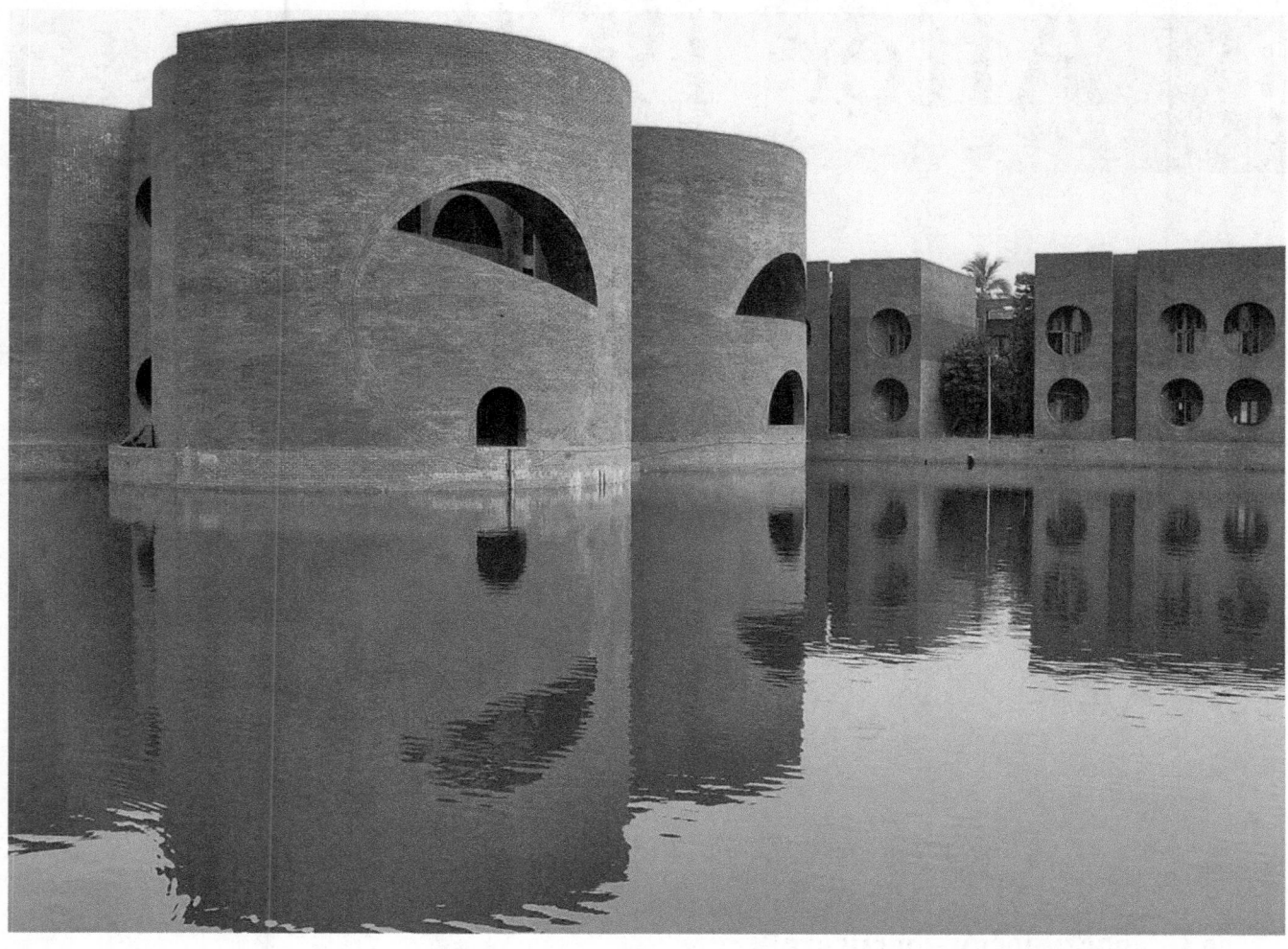

Figure 19.3-22 Dhaka, Bangladesh. View from the hostels to the Assembly, Kahn, 1962–1983.

Further Reading

Brownlee, David B., and David G. De Long. *Louis I. Kahn: In the Realm of Architecture*. New York: Rizzoli, 1991.

Goldhagen, Sarah Williams. *Louis Kahn's Situated Modernism*. New Haven, CT: Yale University Press, 2001.

Loomis, John. *Revolution of Forms: Cuba's Forgotten Art Schools*. New York: Princeton Architectural Press, 1999.

Marcus, Mette, ed. *Jørn Utzon: The Architect's Universe*. Copenhagen: Louisiana Museum, 2008.

Merkel, Jayne. *Eero Saarinen*. London: Phaidon, 2005.

Nerdinger, Winfried, ed. *Alvar Aalto: Toward a Human Modernism*. New York: Prestel, 1999.

Olsberg, Nicholas, ed. *Carlo Scarpa Architect: Intervening with History*. Montreal: Canadian Centre for Architecture, 1999.

↗ Visit the free website **www.oup.com/us/ingersoll** to view chapter outlines and study questions; Google Maps showing the location of key sites; links to UNESCO World Heritage Sites; and essays on topics that cross time and culture.

After 1970

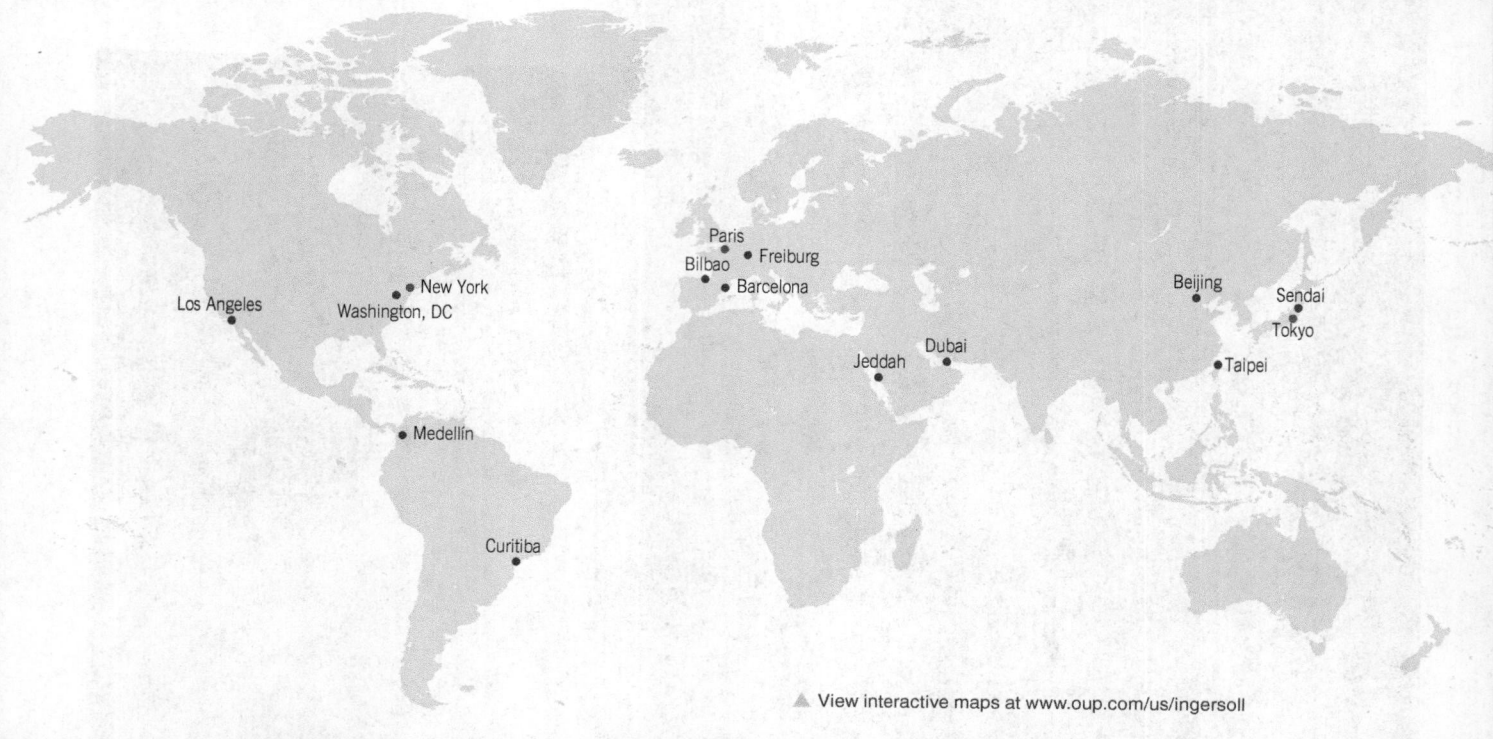

▲ View interactive maps at www.oup.com/us/ingersoll

During the tumultuous 1960s, with constant protests against nuclear weapons, wars, racism, sexism, and environmental abuses, the International Style and Modernism attracted criticism as part of the problem. Many proposed the development of a "people's architecture" that would be easier to build, comprehend, and care for as an alternative. In some cases communities programmed and built projects for themselves. In others they demanded better integration of structures with the environment. Most notably, many Postmodern architects returned to recognizable historical iconographies while using a high degree of irony. Despite widespread community movements, global corporations continued to expand their control over the environment, usually sidestepping political processes. After the first oil embargo of 1973, instead of sparking a turn to restraint, the use of nonrenewable carbon fuels escalated. Skyscrapers and multilane freeways appeared in boom cycles, encircling the planet from Houston to Shanghai to Lagos to Dubai. By the mid-1980s the environmental consequences of nearly two centuries of high-entropy practices had become evident with the documentation of the ozone hole over Antarctica and the measurable increase in world temperatures caused by greenhouse gases. A new name, the Anthropocene, indicated that the current geological period was determined by human interventions, and many designers, prompted by the ecology crisis, sought inspiration from landforms, while most became engaged in the challenge of creating sustainable environments.

20.1 POSTMODERN MOVEMENTS
Populism, Radicalism, and Irony

During the 1960s, mass social movements shattered the complacency of European and American cities. Protests raged in the streets against such issues as nuclear weapons and the war in Vietnam. In the United States racial discrimination provoked violent riots. Interest groups, which ranged from industrial workers, students, civil rights activists, ecologists, feminists, and sexual minorities, fought for social justice, while many designers turned to nonhierarchical approaches, such as populism, neo-vernacularism, and contextualism. The discontent culminated in 1968, when police and military forces brutally swept students and protestors off the streets of Paris, Rome, New York, Chicago, Berkeley, and Prague.

The generation of 1968 generally advocated a "people's architecture" involving participatory design. The more radical groups returned to the attitudes of Futurism, proposing ephemeral scaffolds equipped with advanced technology and electronics as a means to liberate society from the oppressive effects of permanent structures. The widespread influence of linguistic theories encouraged the revival of forms that everyone could understand, analogous to Pop Art's recourse to comic books and advertising. Postmodernist architects created ironic combinations of types and images from the past. Perhaps the greatest irony was that despite its progressive origins, Postmodernism, with its attention to imagery, proved more conservative both socially and technically than the Modernist architecture it challenged.

People's Architecture

By the end of the 1950s, the theoretical armature of the Congrès Internationale d'Architecture

Moderne (CIAM) had begun to collapse as the top-down urbanism and architecture of Modernism became more of a problem than a solution. In 1954 the younger dissident members of CIAM founded Team 10 as a critique of the Athens Charter's insensitivity to community and urban context. They condemned functional zoning as incapable of generating socially complex urban environments. In America Jane Jacobs led the resistance to urban renewal and, by extension, the debunking of the International Style. Her struggle inspired the development of participatory methods of planning geared toward saving the architectural and social fabric of such neighborhoods as Manhattan's Greenwich Village and Boston's North End. A new category entered architectural theory: the "user." The respect for users led to sociological surveys of needs and desires, stimulating architects to explore a "people's architecture."

Eero Saarinen (see Section 19.3) pioneered the application of sociology to architecture in the planning of Stiles and Morse Colleges (1958) (Fig. 20.1-1) at Yale University. As part of the planning process students filled out questionnaires, and the architect's office tabulated the users' responses with computers, creating charts to map such variables as privacy and community, color and texture, openness and protection, and style. The users' information led Saarinen to propose a New Brutalist version of collegiate Gothic, the

Figure 20.1-1 New Haven, Connecticut. Stiles and Morse Colleges, Eero Saarinen, 1958.

preferred style of the students. He embedded large stones as aggregate in his shear concrete walls, mixing the notions of handmade and machine-made structure. Each of the rooms had a slightly different shape, fitting into long curving wings that opened to courtyards. The interiors mixed a taste for comfortable modern furniture with inglenooks and bay windows. The Sardinian sculptor Costantino Nivola (1911–1988) carved decorative pieces from the same concrete used in the construction to infuse the project with the medieval sense of craft and participation.

The inability of functionalist architects to fulfill urban and social needs sparked calls for popular participation in the design process. In 1962 the Dutch architect N. John Habraken (b. 1928) proposed the "supports" method, advocating a flexible approach to mass housing based on fixed structural frames and infrastructure combined with adaptable infill determined by the users. His concept influenced the development of many universities, public housing estates, and even shantytowns. The postwar "baby boom" led to the expansion of university campuses during the 1960s as the number of students quadrupled in both the United States and Europe. Lucien Kroll (b. 1927) orchestrated one of the first applications of Habraken's theory at the Memé project, a building for the medical faculty at Woluwé-St-Lambert (Fig. 20.1-2), begun in 1968 on the outskirts of

Brussels. The students acted as the client, choosing an architect sympathetic to radical causes. Kroll designed the structure and infrastructure of the complex using standard architectural techniques but asked the users to design the customized infill. The students responded with a chaotic placement of walls and windows. Kroll and the students molded the concrete forms of the metro stop into fungus-like, undulating patterns and gave the outdoor spaces surreal organic details. While Memé satisfied the demands of student activism of the 1960s, its chaotic elevations and homely interior finishes failed to bring comfort to the next generation. The naive iconography of people's architecture became a relic of the evanescent taste of the radical occupants who had since moved on.

The Austrian painter Friedensreich Hundertwasser (b. Friedrich Stowasser, 1928–2000) proposed a similar sort of colorful disorder. In 1958 he published a polemic against modern architecture, *Verschimmelungs Manifest gegen den Rationalismus in der Architekur* (*The Mould Manifesto against Rationalism in Architecture*), complaining that standardized design dehumanized life. After two decades of campaigning, he succeeded in convincing the Viennese municipality to fund his organic version of social housing, in which every occupant would have a unit that was a personal statement of color and vegetation. He built the Hundertwasserhaus (1983–1986), a low-income social housing project, pro bono, content to prove his point. The elevations, like his paintings, proffered bright and contrasting colors, bits of ceramic tiles, rounded corners, and gilded domes. No two units were alike, and the floor levels remained intentionally uneven. He planted the roof terraces with trees and let ivy spread freely from floor to floor in the effort to integrate construction and natural growth. During the final

Figure 20.1-2 Brussels. Woluwé-St-Lambert, Memé medical building, Lucien Kroll, 1968.

1961 Jane Jacobs publishes *The Death and Life of the Great American City*

Habraken publishes *Supports* **1961**

1966 Venturi publishes *Complexity and Contradiction*

Rossi publishes *The Architecture of the City* **1966**

1967 Summer of Love youth movement occurs in San Francisco

Historic Preservation

In 1963 public outrage at the demolition of New York City's Pennsylvania Station, McKim, Mead & White's masterful reworking of the Baths of Caracalla completed in 1910, bolstered the growing American movement for historic preservation, leading to the National Historic Preservation Act of 1966. From San Francisco to Savannah, neighborhood groups documented and saved districts of nineteenth-century Victorian houses that had been slated for demolition under urban renewal (see Section 19.1). Preserving historic patrimony also became a significant agenda in most European cities after the 1969 demolition of Les Halles in Paris. The new appreciation of historic buildings and urban fabric inspired theories of contextualism, leading to designs for infill projects that maintained the scale and rhythm of the existing urban fabric. It also prepared the way for the popularity of the Postmodern revivals of historic iconography.

New York. Pennsylvania Station, McKim, Mead & White, 1910, demolished in 1963.

Culmination of international student and worker protests

▲ 1968

▼ **1970**

Osaka, Japan, Expo features Japanese Metabolism by Tange et al.

Kurokawa's Nagakin Capsule Towers built in Tokyo

▲ 1970

▼ **1971**

Rossi's San Cataldo Cemetery built in Modena, Italy

decade of his life Hundertwasser designed several large projects, including the Waldspirale (2000) in Darmstadt, Germany, a multicolored apartment house that climbed as a layered spiral to a twelve-story tower. A forest of trees and shrubs covered the roof as it spiraled up to an onion-shaped cupola, offering a fairy-tale setting.

During the late 1960s, Ralph Erskine (1914–2005) co-ordinated one of the most sensitive participatory projects, Byker Housing Estate. His assistant, Vernon Gracie, set up an office in the neighborhood of a working-class commu-nity in the northern industrial town of Newcastle-upon-Tyne, England. The architects built a few dozen test units for the 10,000 inhabitants and analyzed the postoccupancy criti-cisms before producing their final scheme. This sympathy with the users led to a unique architectural outcome, the Byker Wall, an eight-story, undulating structure that on its north side appeared as closed as a fortified castle, with tiny windows overlooking the freeway. On its south side, how-ever, it opened into a riot of wooden balconies and colorful elevations, overlooking a tightly knit fabric of row houses on a series of pedestrian lanes. Most of the units in the wall were for assisted living and the elderly, with services particular to their needs. The wall protected the rest of the low-rise neighborhood from traffic while creating a distinc-tive identity derived from its own aesthetic initiative. Social housing had finally achieved the right mix of urban scale and program just as most governments began withdrawing support for it.

The Portuguese architect Alvaro Siza (b. 1933) proposed a viaduct as the formal solution for the Malagueira Project in Évora, a social housing estate of roughly the same scale as Byker. He began working on the scheme after the 1974 revolution and intended to continue construction over a twenty-year period as a natural process of growth. The resi-dents, stimulated by their new political freedom, pursued a communist ideology, demanding full participation in the process while declaring that the "architect is the tool of the people." Siza offered them a system similar to Habraken's method, executed according to strong formal criteria. In-spired by the sixteenth-century aqueduct nested in Évora's historic center, Siza proposed to channel the conduits for water, gas, electricity, and telephone service into an aerial viaduct raised on pylons. The dark gray concrete blocks of the viaduct stood a few meters above the level of the stark-white units' roofs. Neither the architect nor the resi-dents' association showed much concern for automobiles, giving more attention to parks and pedestrian networks. This resulted in narrow streets paved with cobblestones that posed the same problems for parking and through traffic seen in the historic center. Siza set the units back-to-back in *L*-shaped volumes. The uniform white walls and small win-dows evoked the traditions of the Mediterranean and North Africa, while the rational plan of each unit recalled the dem-ocratic rigor of fifth-century BCE Olynthus (see Section 4.2). High walls separated one from the next, while flat roofs and patios served as a site for luxuriant planting.

Herman Hertzberger (b. 1932) designed the most ac-claimed application of Habraken's "supports" theory, the Centraal Beheer in Apeldoorn, the Netherlands, in 1968 (Fig. 20.1-3). He organized the office complex for a large insurance company as terraces overlooking a canyon-like internal atrium, resulting in a nonhierarchical interior land-scape. The structure followed a tartan grid, leaving office modules to be completed in different configurations ac-cording to the occupants' desires, an approach that Hertz-berger dubbed "building the unfinished."

The mandate for a people's architecture came partly as a response to the 1964 exhibition "Architecture without Archi-tects," organized by the Austrian émigré Bernard Rudofsky (1905–1988) at the Museum of Modern Art in New York. In his survey of vernacular buildings Rudofsky demonstrated the compelling sense of materiality, charm, and meaning in "non-pedigreed" buildings. The return to the common sense of local vernaculars influenced the planning of Sea Ranch (1965) (Fig. 20.1-4), a vacation settlement on the windswept cliffs of the Mendocino coast of northern California. Lawrence Halprin (1916–2009) prepared the site plan, gathering the units into dense clusters near the thickets of trees to conserve as much of the natural conditions and beach lands as pos-sible. The principal architect, Charles Moore (1925–1993), and his colleagues at the firm of Moore, Turnbull, Lyndon & Whitaker borrowed from both Alvar Aalto's open courtyards and local vernacular sources to design Condominium One, ten units enclosing an irregularly shaped court of grassy plat-forms framed by timber treads. Bay windows pushed out of the sheer exterior elevations, providing special views, while the oblique placement of windows looking into the collec-tive courtyard guaranteed privacy. The contrasting profiles

▼ **1976**

Rogers and Piano's Centre Pompidou, the first mediathèque, opens in Paris

United States withdraws from Vietnam

▲ **1973**

Alexander and colleagues publish *A Pattern Language*

▲ **1977**

Figure 20.1-3 Apeldoorn, the Netherlands. Centraal Beheer office complex, Herman Hertzberger, 1968.

of the single-pitched roofs and the simple stave cladding derived from the large wood plank hay barns of the region.

The success of Sea Ranch influenced Christopher Alexander (b. 1936), a professor at the University of California at Berkeley who from a background in mathematics had previously supported a highly mechanistic "systems" theory, by which all possible variables could be analyzed in the formulation of a scientific solution to design. After 1968 he abandoned his positivist stance to embrace the charm and wisdom of vernacular buildings. His treatise *A Pattern Language: Towns, Buildings, Construction* (1977), written with several colleagues, proposed 253 patterns based on vernacular solutions from throughout the world that could be used by designers as sequences to create a cohesive environment. The scale ranged from the urban region to the window seat. In the few examples built by Alexander and his colleagues, such as the 1985 Eishin Campus on the outskirts of Tokyo (Fig. 20.1-5), the method resulted in a village-scale composition. The Japanese campus for a private high school offered traditional elements, from the small-paned windows to the stone paving. The new buildings resembled historic structures, substantiating Alexander's theory of a

Figure 20.1-4 Mendocino, California. Sea Ranch, Charles Moore/Moore, Turnbull, Lyndon & Whitaker, 1965.

1978

Bofill begins Antigone district of Montpellier, France

Graves's Portland Building and Johnson and Burgee's AT&T Building

1978–1982

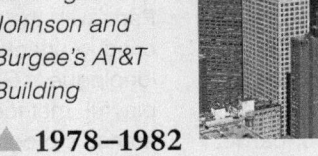

1982

Botta's Casa Rotonda built in Ticino, Switzerland

Figure 20.1-5 Tokyo. Eishen School, Christopher Alexander and Hajo Neis, 1985.

Figure 20.1-6 Mason's Bend, Alabama. Community Center, the Rural Studio, 2000.

samples. For the Mason's Bend Community Center (Fig. 20.1-6), completed in 2000, the architects constructed rammed-earth walls, used rafters fashioned from trees on the site, and glazed the north elevation with eighty recycled automobile windshields. The team kept costs, which were less than $20,000, at a fraction of market-rate building by using recycled materials and eliminating charges for design and construction. The users participated in the planning and construction processes, guaranteeing their satisfaction. While participatory design often left doubts of the viability of a work's value after the initial participants moved on, most projects that have included the user in the planning have resulted in buildings that enable rather than hinder life.

Radical Architecture: The Call to Nomadism

The politically charged atmosphere of the 1960s radicalized Western culture. Demonstrations, teach-ins, and occupations occurred as frequently as sports events, and students sought corresponding agitation in design. Both in Europe and in the United States the energy of political dissidents instigated the development of an architecture of liberation. For many innovators, the mythical freedom of the nomad became an ideal to be enhanced by advanced technology. In the background, the subversive nature of rock-and-roll music broke through cultural and social barriers, leading to mass festivals and new models of social organization. Electronically enhanced rock music arrived with both a primitive and a technological force, and radical architects responded by creating collectives with trendy names in emulation of rock bands.

The first signs of architecture's radicalization appeared in Paris with the Situationist International, whose Neo-Marxist critique attacked consumer society. The movement's chief ideologue, Guy Debord (1931–1994), developed the playful method of the *dérive* ("the drift") as the urban nomad's program for intentionally getting lost. He proposed

"timeless" way of building, whereby buildings should seem "as ancient in their form, as the trees and hills, and as our faces are."

One of the most extraordinary adventures in people's architecture occurred during the 1990s in Alabama, where Sam Mockbee (1944–2001) formed Rural Studio with his Auburn University students to design and build houses and public buildings in conjunction with the residents of poor rural communities. Unlike Alexander, who advocated "egoless" buildings and spurned originality, Mockbee produced work that bristled with innovative combinations of materials and ingenious structural solutions. The Rural Studio built one house with straw bales and another with stacks of carpet *psychogeography* as an alternative to the productivist logic of the capitalist city, which he illustrated by assembling a collage of disparate fragments of a map of Paris. His colleague, the Dutch artist Constant (b. Constant Nieuwenhuys, 1920–2005), designed a series of urban visions known collectively as New Babylon beginning in 1957 (Fig. 20.1-7). Constant imagined dense, multicolored volumes placed above ground level on pylons and spread randomly across vast territories without damaging the earth. Part megastructure and part patchwork, his New Babylon aspired to a highly nomadic condition.

The CIAM formally disbanded in 1958. In its wake, a group of young Japanese architects associated with Kenzo Tange (1913–2005) prepared the Metabolist Manifesto for the 1960 World Design Conference in Tokyo. The Japanese Metabolists, in particular Kisho Kurokawa (1934–2007), created futuristic proposals that incorporated constantly changing architectural elements. Tange designed a city for 10 million people that would stretch over Tokyo Bay on a net of floating infrastructures. His younger colleagues dreamed of ephemeral megastructures, culminating in Expo70, the World's Fair in Osaka, a completely futuristic landscape stocked with skeletal high-tech structures and inflatables. During the same year Kurokawa completed the emblematic Nagakin Capsule Towers (Fig. 20.1-8), two stacks of plug-in, prefabricated capsules bolted to hollow towers containing the elevators and services. The dimensions of the capsules, 2.3 × 3.8 × 2.1 m (7.5 × 12.5 × 7.9 ft), offered the bare ergonomic minimum for a single occupant, with a porthole window to look out on the Ginza district of Tokyo.

Figure 20.1-7 "View of Babylonian Sectors," from Constant, New Babylon, 1957–1970.

Figure 20.1-8 Tokyo. Nagakin Capsule Towers, Kisho Kurokawa, 1970.

colossal diagonal bracing served by mobile cranes that would constantly rearrange capsule components. *Walking City* (1964), by Ron Herron (1930–1994), proposed an octopod with retractable metal legs that would transport several thousand modern nomads from city to city for purposes of either leisure or work. *Archigram* picked up the Futurist idea of perpetual change and offered ephemeral solutions like the *Cushicle* (1967) by Mike Webb (b. 1937), an inflatable envelope for a single occupant, fit with all of one's needs and pleasures, that could be deflated and worn like a suit of clothes. *Archigram*'s nomadic projects, such as *Instant City* (1969) (Fig. 20.1-9a), intimated that future societies would no longer need buildings but would be composed of ingredients drawn from mass culture. The magazine folded in 1970, and very soon after Rogers and Piano won the competition to design the Centre Pompidou in Paris, a project that lived up to *Archigram*'s promise. Three decades later Cook finally realized a structure worthy of his youthful fantasies, the Kunsthaus (2003) in Graz, Austria. Its blob-shaped volume, studded with dozens of protruding nozzles, sat in the city center like a surgically extracted, shiny, black organ.

In Florence several radical groups appeared in the late 1960s. Archizoom, led by Andrea Branzi (b. 1938), produced an urban plan initially composed on a typewriter. The team's "No-Stop City" evoked an endless serial environment free of conflict (Fig. 20.1-9b). Superstudio, founded by Adolfo Natalini (b. 1941) and Cristiano Toraldo di Francia (b. 1941), created conceptual projects and furniture from 1966 to 1978. Their photocollages for the "Continuous Monument" project depicted a universal gridded space extending over cities and landscapes. Their fictional architecture spread with rational impunity over existing cities like Manhattan and across empty desert landscapes, pierced with gaps to allow either natural features or skyscrapers to pop through.

Youth culture entered architecture most visibly with the 1960 publication of *Archigram*, an architectural comic book edited by Peter Cook (b. 1936) with colleagues Warren Chalk, Dennis Crompton, Michael Webb, and David Greene. The continuing publication of issues of *Archigram* paralleled the career of the Beatles, and the song "Yellow Submarine" hinted at correspondences between the young architects and the rock group. Cook and his friends prepared such science fiction fantasies as *Plug-in City* (1964), a scaffold with

Figure 20.1-9 Radical urban visions of the 1960s. (a) *Archigram's Instant City*, an urban environment conceived of ephemeral elements of mass communication, Ron Herron, 1969. **(b)** "No-Stop City," Archizoom (Andrea Branzi), 1968–1972. **(c)** See next page.

Political issues motivated the youth culture of the early 1960s, but by the end of the decade the new ethos of "sex, drugs, and rock-and-roll" had taken hold. The anarchic hippie movement of dropouts from bourgeois society converged on San Francisco in 1967 for the Summer of Love, a mass experiment in collective living. For this "gathering of the tribes" the hippies organized free food, free clinics, free rock concerts, free drugs, and free love, relying on such technical support as electronic amplifiers, the chemical stimulation of hallucinogens, and birth control pills. The liquid light shows by artist Glenn McKay (b. 1936) enhanced the "trip" of the rock concerts that were staged at the Fillmore Auditorium, projecting colossal swirling patterns of oil-separated colors and collages of distorted images. It seemed for a brief moment that rock music, light shows, and hallucinogens could achieve the ephemeral ideals of a nomadic civilization without architecture. Many hippies moved to communes, like Drop City, founded by a group of four artists in 1965 near Trinidad, Colorado. In rural solitude they constructed modern versions of the nomadic yurt, using Buckminster Fuller's geodesic dome clad with recycled metal panels cut from abandoned automobiles. Drop City hosted a hippie festival in 1967, attracting hundreds of wanderers. The original owners later signed over their property to a nonprofit foundation, declaring it "forever free and open to all people," but the experiment in communal living lasted for less than a year.

In 1970 the Italian dreamer Paolo Soleri (1919–2013), who fantasized about grandiose megastructures combining architecture with ecology that he called "arcologies," established Arcosanti (Fig. 20.1-9c), which became a pilgrimage site for youth culture. During the next four decades he rallied successive waves of young volunteers to build his ideal city on a ravine in the middle of the desert, 110 km (70 miles) north of Phoenix, Arizona. Soleri's quest for a tangible alternative to the modern city resulted in grand vaulted concrete works embedded into the terrain, more like an outer space colony than a city.

In Denmark the collectivist urges of the 1960s generated the movement for *bofællesskab* ("living community"), or **co-housing**, which has continued as a viable alternative. Fresh out of college and motivated by the communitarian

Figure 20.1-9 (c) Phoenix, Arizona. Arcosanti, vaulted performance areas, Paolo Soleri, 1975–2000.

Centre Pompidou: The Spirit of 1968

Centre Pompidou in Paris, designed by Richard Rogers (b. 1933) and Renzo Piano (b. 1937), captured the spirit of 1960s radicalism. Their winning design in the 1971 competition against more than 600 rivals, with a jury that included Philip Johnson and Jean Prouvé, proposed an interactive scaffold, like *Plug-in City*, which could house flexible components and serve as an electronic billboard overlooking the sloping Place Beaubourg. They developed the design with engineer Peter Rice (1935–1992), from the London firm of Ove Arup, as a Lego-like assembly, exposing the structural and mechanical systems on the exterior in bright colors. Colossal curved exhaust pipes protruded from the lower levels like those on an ocean liner. The building's plexiglass-enclosed escalator snaked up the western facade like a carnival ride, giving dramatic views of the plaza and the rest of the city.

The program from the start was geared toward creating a cultural center that would be active day and night, with a library as well as a museum. It also included a bookstore, a *cinemathèque*, and a center for experimental music so that the institution could rightly claim to be the world's first *mediathèque*. The colossal steel "gerberettes," bone-shaped joints stacked like totems on each of the columns, cantilevered over the sides of the building. The radial joints for the diagonal braces were bolted to the tips of the gerberettes. The web trusses allowed each of the six levels column-free interiors. Attempting to appear as pragmatic and transitory as an oil rig, Centre Pompidou catered to the nomadic tastes of the 1960s, to the point of seeming a nonbuilding.

Paris. Centre Pompidou, Richard Rogers and Renzo Piano, 1971–1976.

spirit of the times, a group of fifty families, led by the Harvard-trained architect Jan Gudmand Høyer (b. 1936), settled in the first co-housing settlement of Saettedammen on the outskirts of Copenhagen in 1967. Høyer organized Saettedammen's densely clustered units around a common space for child care, collective meals, and socializing. Tegnestuen Vandkunsten perfected the co-housing type during the 1980s at Jystrup Savværket, an *L*-shaped composition. The twenty-one units were distributed to either side of a covered street, 5 m (16 ft) wide, lit with skylights, and paved with

Seaside, Florida: The Flagship of New Urbanism

The most significant aspect of Postmodernism was its critique of insensitive Modernist planning. Seaside was developed in 1979 as a summer resort along the beach of the Florida Panhandle and soon became the manifesto of "New Urbanism" through the master plan of Andrés Duany (b. 1949) and Elizabeth Plater-Zyberk (b. 1950). Its street pattern radiated from a central plaza, giving a semblance of the hierarchy and public space of historic cities, but because Seaside was not a municipality, the only real public building was the post office. On a site comparable to the subdivisions that served as a canvas for most American developers, the planners inserted pedestrian lanes in alternation with automobile streets. To ensure a feeling of coherence they set strict controls of typology and materials for the small houses, privileging porches, wooden board-and-batten siding, white picket fences, and pitched tin roofs. Despite this scenario of conformity, Seaside obtained considerable architectural variety through the participation of talented Postmodernist architects, including Leon Krier (b. 1946), the most outspoken exponent of New Urbanism.

Seaside, Florida. Summer resort, Andrés Duany and Elizabeth Plater-Zybeck, 1979.

wooden planks. The units were relatively small, ranging from 60 to 90 m² (645 to 969 ft²), but residents had use of the internal street and the common room as extensions of their personal space. They also had the option of using supplemental rooms planned as space for guests, cottage-offices, or semi-independent teenagers' apartments. The common room served as a clubhouse with billiards, a library, and a professional kitchen, where members took turns preparing meals for the community. While Drop City proved to be a brief anarchic flight from urban society, and Arcosanti a city without citizens, co-housing became a viable way of building communities and conserving resources.

Postmodernism: The Ironic Return to History

If Modernism seemed overly dogmatic in its goals, Postmodernism emerged with purposeful ambiguity. Architects, searching for alternatives, responded to linguistic theories of the late 1960s. With the debunking of positivism and the so-called modern project, modern architecture was often conceived as an agent of social control. Postmodern theorists turned to history for alternatives, often yielding ironic attacks on the functionalist premises of Modernism.

Italian architect Aldo Rossi (1931–1997) formulated a European response to Modernism in his 1966 essay *L'architettura della città* (*The Architecture of the City*). He interpreted the structure of the historic city and the conventional typologies of urban buildings as meaningful sources of form, similar to grammar and syntax. He condemned the "naive functionalism" of Modernist architects and their premise that "functions bring form together." For Rossi, most buildings in the historic city conformed to the rational repetition of a conventional type and responded to the dictates of their geographical context. Monuments performed as exceptional markers of *genius loci*, the divinity of the place. Rossi recuperated Enlightenment theories of architecture, relying on the definition of type by Quatremère de Quincy (1755–1845) as "a logical principle prior to form," which encouraged him to design pure forms drawn from a limited palette of urban precedents. The rationalism of the repeated type inspired him to design strict geometric projects analogous in their context, scale, and system to the structures of a historic city. His San Cataldo Cemetery in Modena (Fig. 20.1-10), begun in 1971, fulfilled many of his theories. The ossuary occupied a hollow red cube standing in the center of a grassy courtyard, its four walls punctured by a regular grid of small, square apertures. With stark arcades of triple-height pylons, it stood like a ghostly

presence, evoking thoughts of an abandoned prison removed from the world of the living.

Rossi's urban projects, such as the offices of the regional government in Perugia, built in 1988, were flawed by a disinterest in function, technique, and construction. Other exponents of the Neorationalist movement—known as *la tendenza* in Italy, Spain, and Switzerland—built with more attention to craft. Massimo Carmassi (b. 1943) designed San Michele in Borgo (Fig. 20.1-11) in 1983 for shops and housing in the historic center of Pisa with extraordinary attention to construction. Reviving the *muro a sacco* ("sack wall") technique of parallel brick walls with rubble and concrete infill, he structured the *U*-shaped compound using a stylized repetition of the local tower-house type. In new projects in suburban districts, such as the new university campus in Parma (2007), Carmassi continued to use tall brick pylons as an organizing device.

In Spain, Rafael Moneo (b. 1937) produced the most eloquent interpretations of Rossi's theories of typology. Although he was a master of several styles, Moneo frequently returned to the reduction to type. His Logroño City Hall (1981) set an *L*-shaped facade on a large triangular plaza. The slender three-story colonnades on the long side conveyed the rational, public nature of the institution. For the Murcia City Hall (Fig. 20.1-12), completed in 1998, Moneo engaged the rhythm of the historic buildings surrounding the plaza with a double-layered facade of smooth, golden sandstone verticals supported on white concrete transoms.

Figure 20.1-10 Modena, Italy. San Cataldo Cemetery, Aldo Rossi, 1971.

Figure 20.1-11 Pisa, Italy. San Michele in Borgo, Massimo Carmassi, 1983.

Figure 20.1-12 Murcia, Spain. City Hall, Rafael Moneo, 1998.

Figure 20.1-13 Lugano, Switzerland. Ransila I offices, Mario Botta, 1985.

A large double-height gap served as a balcony addressing the plaza.

In Ticino, the Italian canton of Switzerland, Mario Botta (b. 1943) used Rossi's method of the "urban analogue" for projects such as the Ransila I Building (1985) (Fig. 20.1-13). He evoked a medieval tower house by cutting into the volume on both sides of the corner. Inspired by Torre Guinigi in Lucca, he planted a tree on top, reinforcing the tower's verticality. Botta designed the 1982 Medici House, or Casa Rotonda (Fig. 20.1-14), in rural Stabio as a pure cylinder as monumental as a baptistery. He dramatically carved into the rounded walls, molding the solid stair shaft into a colossal column crowned with a primitive capital. One of the most prolific architects of the age, Botta continued to design pure, symmetrically composed volumes, usually clad with bricks or banded masonry.

In the United States Robert Venturi (b. 1925) launched his "gentle manifesto" against Modernism with *Complexity and Contradiction*, also published in 1966. Drawing upon an erudite collection of historic buildings, he recognized architectural figures of speech capable of ambiguity and irony. Venturi objected to orthodox Modernism's "puritanically moral language," quipping, "Less is a bore." His analysis of Mannerist and Baroque buildings celebrated "non-straightforwardness." Inspired by Pop Art, Venturi sought an architectural correspondence to the work of Andy Warhol (1928–1987) that would act as both a send-up and a celebration of popular culture. Warhol's silk-screened reproduction of the logo of the Campbell's tomato soup can, produced in 1968, prepared the way for Venturi's caricature of a colossal Ionic column, the "ironic order," set in the cut-out corner of his addition to the Oberlin Art Museum (1976) (Fig. 20.1-15).

In the house that Venturi designed for his mother, he created an elevation that looked like a child's drawing of a house with a pitched roof. Its complexity involved the interruption of the simple pitched roof with a 1 m (3.3 ft) wide gap, evoking a Mannerist broken pediment. In *Learning from Las Vegas*, written

Figure 20.1-14 Stabio, Switzerland. Casa Rotonda (Medici House), Botta, 1982.

Figure 20.1-15 Oberlin, Ohio.
Addition to Allen Memorial Art
Museum, Robert Venturi, 1976.

in 1972 with his wife, Denise Scott Brown (b. 1931), and Steven Izenour, Venturi elaborated the distinction between the "duck" and the "decorated shed." Most exponents of Modernism abhorred decoration, insisting that materials, structure, and articulated functions produced inherent beauty. Venturi categorized such work as "ducks," referring to a duck-shaped restaurant on Long Island, where the form became the signifier of meaning. He preferred the "decorated shed," the standard box of the commercial vernacular that specified its function by means of a sign. He chose to make the 1963 Guild House, an apartment building for the elderly in Philadelphia, "ugly and ordinary," responding to the Spartan taste of his Quaker clients and the brick tenements of the neighborhood. The block was clad in standard bricks and articulated by regular double-hung windows. A large billboard-like sign carried the institution's name over a polished granite column at the entry. On the roof of the top-floor recreation room, he pitched an oversized, gilded TV antenna, inspired by the sculptures of Claes Oldenburg (b. 1929), who in the early 1960s produced outsized versions in soft vinyl of such everyday objects as telephones and light switches. Venturi's nonfunctional TV antenna ironically referred to the chief activity of the elderly tenants. Like Pop artists, Venturi claimed that the "sources for modest buildings and images with social purpose will come, not from the industrial past, but from the everyday city around us, of modest buildings and modest spaces with symbolic appendages."

In 1977 the American critic Charles Jencks (b. 1939) appropriated Venturi's categories, such as "double functionality" and "super adjacency," to catalogue the changes in style that he classified under the rubric of "Postmodernism." Many of the works that broke with functionalist dogma offered ironic revivals of historic styles, such as Charles Moore's 1976 design for Piazza d'Italia in New Orleans (Fig. 20.1-16), a playful riff on the classical orders that arranged concave layers of colonnades around a fountain in the shape of the map of Italy. In the spirit of carnival the architect included a new "delicatessen order" made of sculpted sausages. Other Postmodernist projects ranged from Philip Johnson's AT&T Building in New York (now the Sony Building, but also known as the "Chippendale," 1978–1982) (Fig. 20.1-17), crowned with a Mannerist broken pediment, to the simulacrum of a Pompeian villa built in 1975 to house the Getty Museum in Malibu, designed with the advice of the archaeologist Norman Neuerburg.

Jencks's survey of Postmodernism anticipated some of the most significant examples of the style, such as the Portland Building (1982) by Michael Graves (1934–2015) for the municipal offices of Portland, Oregon; the Mississauga City Hall (1987) near Toronto by Ed Jones (b. 1938) and Michael Kirkland (b. 1943); and the Harold Washington Public Library (1991) by Thomas Beeby (b. 1941) in downtown Chicago. These three public buildings, large boxy volumes encrusted with overblown classical decorations, vaunted a sarcastic return to Greco-Roman iconography as an approach both accessible to the masses and amusing for professionals. Graves painted his building in contrasting pastel colors and decked it with superscaled classical pilasters and giant swags, clearly lampooning classicism. In 1991 he unveiled the Team Disney Building, the international headquarters of the world's largest entertainment corporation, in Burbank, California. Borrowing heavily from the classical porches and pavilions of Claude-Nicolas Ledoux, Graves created a temple front, setting six of the Seven Dwarfs, sculpted in polystyrene, as atlantids supporting a classical pediment. The seventh dwarf, Dopey, stood over them in the middle of the gable.

The grandest Postmodern projects in Europe appeared in the housing estates of the new towns outside Paris designed by Ricardo Bofill (b. 1939). Boasting that social housing could be treated as "Versailles for the people," he arranged prefabricated elements at Marne-la-Vallée in the form of Roman theaters. At Cergy-Pontoise he created a column-clad crescent. In Montpellier, between 1978 and 2000, he realized the consummate Postmodernist environment, the Antigone district, with its 1 km (0.6 mile) long array

Figure 20.1-16 New Orleans, Louisiana. Piazza d'Italia, Charles Moore et al., 1976.

Figure 20.1-17 New York. AT&T Building (now Sony Building), Philip Johnson, for Burgee and Johnson, 1978–1984.

Post-Functionalism

Peter Eisenman chose a different path in the attack against the functionalist premises of Modernism, reducing architecture to a game board of geometric rules that in many cases intentionally subverted the basic functions of architectural signifiers. In his most extreme realization, House VI in Cornwall, Connecticut (1975), commissioned by an architectural historian and her photographer husband, he began with two intersecting planes, around which he juxtaposed a green stair with a red one that led nowhere. He continued by interjecting a column into the middle of the dining table to align with the grid and culminated with a cut through the bedroom from the skylight to the floor that also divided the conjugal bed.

Cornwall, Connecticut. House VI, Peter Eisenman, 1975.

Figure 20.1-18 Montpellier, France. (a) Aerial view of Antigone district, Ricardo Bofill, 1980s. (b) See facing page.

Figure 20.1-18 Montpellier, France. (b) Central axis of the Antigone district.

of shaped urban sequences (Fig. 20.1-18a,b). The major square took the outline of Bramante's plan for St. Peter's, while adjacent to it stood a stadium-shaped plaza with the proportions of Piazza Navona.

In opposition to the dull urban settings of Modernism, Postmodernism attempted to generate a lively urban fabric. Kevin Lynch's *The Image of the City* (1960) defined a clear set of parameters for improving "urban cognition," or the ability to orient oneself in the city. He based his five principles of paths, boundaries, districts, nodes, and landmarks on an analysis of the urban fabric of Florence, Italy. A companion theory of "contextualism," by which architects attempted to respect the scale, typology, and materials of the traditional city, gained full sway in the replanning of Berlin for the Internationale Bauausstellung (1977–1984), which sponsored a series of projects to repair the patchy fabric of postwar West Berlin. Rob Krier (b. 1938) compiled an atlas of the urban spaces of historic cities and promoted the importance of the European block as the basic ingredient of the city. His Rauchstrasse block (1981–1985) gathered ten differently decorated cubic pavilions, each four stories high with four units per story, around a beautifully landscaped court. While the Postmodernists' playful iconography had a short-term impact, their attention to urban space and context would endure.

Further Reading

Jencks, Charles. *The Language of Postmodern Architecture*. New York: Rizzoli, 1977.

Nesbitt, Kate. *Theorizing A New Agenda for Architecture: An Anthology of Architectural Theory, 1965–1995*. New York: Princeton Architectural Press, 1996.

Rossi, Aldo. *The Architecture of the City*. Translated by Diane Ghirardo and Joan Ockman. Cambridge, MA: MIT Press, 1982.

Tzonis, Alexander, and Liane Lefaivre. *Architecture in Europe since 1968: Memory and Invention*. London: Thames & Hudson, 1992.

Tzonis, Alexander, Liane Lefaivre, and Richard Diamond. *Architecture in North America since 1960*. New York: Little, Brown, 1995.

Venturi, Robert. *Complexity and Contradiction in Architecture*. New York: Museum of Modern Art, 1966.

Venturi, Robert, Denise Scott-Brown, and Steven Izenour. *Learning from Las Vegas: The Forgotten Symbolism of Architectural Form*. Cambridge, MA: MIT Press, 1972.

20.2 MULTINATIONAL PRACTICE
Globalization, High-Tech, and Hypertecture

The increased flows of capital and technology, the speed of communications, and the ease of travel during the late twentieth century encouraged a new phenomenon: the multinational architect. By this time the largest American firms employed over 1,000 workers and maintained branch locations, often in different countries, that replicated the structure and operations of the multinational corporations they served. Individual architects who became famous for their theories or styles began to syndicate themselves for export, frequently working more outside their country of residence than in it. "Star" architects became a sort of luxury brand for ambitious patrons and institutions, tapping into the same promotional tactics and mobility seen in high fashion.

Until the oil embargo of 1973, the large corporate architecture firms tended to propose sealed office buildings that required extravagant energy use. Enormous hotels appeared in many American downtowns, providing ponderous air-conditioned atria as new social attractions. As the embargo enhanced the buying power of Southwest Asia, many corporate firms shifted their operations to oil-producing countries, following the new opportunities that emerged with the growth of East Asian economies and the full opening of the People's Republic of China to world trade in 1986.

The integration of economic networks and mass communications at the turn of the twenty-first century led to a general awareness of globalization. More than half of the world's population had moved to urban situations and were connected with others by cellphones and the Internet. Almost overnight megacities with more than 10 million inhabitants appeared in Asia, Africa, and Latin America, accompanied by the rapid production of Manhattan-inspired clusters of skyscrapers. Hypertecture, a term describing outscaled structures conceived as symbolic capital, became the built expression of this global trend.

Export Architecture in the Golden Age of Museums

After World War II, the commissioning of architects from abroad became a common practice. Such large American firms as Skidmore, Owings & Merrill (SOM) and Hellmuth, Obata & Kassabaum (HOK) became part of the global diffusion of multinational corporations. They offered complete design services, from town planning to landscaping, engineering, and interior work, designing hotels in Turkey, schools in Germany, airports in Saudi Arabia, and skyscrapers in London. Only museum commissions remained beyond their grasp. Museums during the late twentieth century assumed the symbolic status of cathedrals, capable of representing an entire city, and their design usually went to a select group of star architects who, through their mastery of forms and effects, could deliver an aura of distinction.

As cities sprawled upward and outward without aesthetic coordination, the museum became a kind of architectural ex-voto. Since 1975 nearly 10,000 have been produced in the United States alone, a record that will soon be surpassed by the People's Republic of China, which produces an average of 300 museums per year. The precedents for importing architects extend as far back as Bernini's design for the Louvre or Leo von Klenze's design for the Hermitage. The Postmodern call to famous outsiders began with the Neue Staatsgalerie in Stuttgart (Fig. 20.2-1) by the British architects James Stirling (1926–1992) and Michael Wilford (b. 1938) and the High Museum of Art in Atlanta by Richard Meier (b. 1934). Both museums opened in 1983 and generated tremendous publicity and tourism for their respective cities. Stirling, famous for technologically sophisticated details, surprised his peers with a witty variation on Karl Friedrich Schinkel's plan of the Altes Museum, cladding the circular court in alternating bands of sandstone similar to Renaissance structures. To this he added a ferrovitreous lobby like a parasitical growth, with a wavy glazed wall and transparent elevator, painting the exposed-steel members shocking tones of lime green and fuchsia.

The contextualism of Stirling's museum—which deferred to an existing Beaux-Arts wing set to one side and allowed visitors to walk over the new roof to an adjacent neighborhood—was completely absent from the High Museum (Fig. 20.2-2), which stood in isolation. Here Meier revived Le Corbusier's Purist style, producing an exoskeletal assembly derived from the unbuilt Palace of the Soviets. The cladding of bright

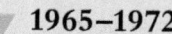

TIME LINE

▼ 1965–1972
Yamasaki's World Trade Center erected in New York City

Fuller builds U.S. pavilion at Montréal Expo, Québec, Canada

▲ 1967

▼ 1973
OPEC oil embargo, first petrol crisis

Koolhaas publishes *Delirious New York*

▲ 1978

Figure 20.2-1 Stuttgart, Germany. Addition to the Neue Staatsgalerie (New National Gallery), James Stirling and Michael Wilford, 1977–1983.

white enameled bakelite panels emphasized the museum's distinction as an exceptional presence in a part of town with many vacant lots. The High Museum focused on a four-story atrium skirted with spindly ramps that followed its curved perimeter of glazed walls. The design privileged circulation over display, allowing an abundance of daylight into the interlocking planes of the interior, which both charged the space with dynamic shadows while creating problems of overexposure for curating the galleries.

A raft of spectacular museums followed. Among the contextualists was Rafael Moneo, whose Museo de Arte Romano (1985) (Fig. 20.2-3) in Mérida offered a variation on the basilica type defined by a series of colossal brick arches between which were placed industrial monitor windows. He flanked the grand hall with an aisle on only one side, stacked three levels and cut to allow one to view from vertical positions the magnificent mosaics found in what had been Spain's most important Roman city. In Paris, Jean Nouvel at the Institut du Monde Arabe (1986) (Fig. 20.2-4) used the incongruous materials of sheer glass and stainless steel but retained the scale and volumes of the neighboring structures. The southern facade featured mechanical *mashrabiyya*, designed to open and close like the lenses of a camera. Nouvel returned to the

Figure 20.2-2 Atlanta, Georgia. High Museum, Richard Meier, 1979.

Figure 20.2-3 Mérida, Spain. Museo de Arte Romano, Moneo, 1985

massive piers to shelter low-rise structures for the exhibition spaces, arranged like a small village on canals.

The star system and the new demand for museums allowed architects whose work had been mostly theoretical to realize their potential. Aldo Rossi at the Bonnefantenmuseum in Maastricht (1994) finally achieved a well-constructed expression of his theory of typology by adding a coffee pot–like cupola to crown the end of the central wing of a severe *E*-shaped plan made of longitudinal galleries. Robert Venturi and Denise Scott Brown added the Sainsbury Wing (1991) to the National Gallery in London (Fig. 20.2-6), creating a synthesis of the duck with the decorated shed. The shape pragmatically followed the irregularity of the site, while the elevations carried ironically articulated classical pilasters, which appeared progressively farther apart and shallower as they moved away from the original neoclassical museum toward the shed.

concept of modern *mashrabiyya* for his greatest adventure and one of the key examples of hypertecture, the Louvre Abu Dhabi (2007–2017) (Fig. 20.2-5). There he unfurled a grand segmental dome, 180 m (590 ft) in diameter, using ten layers of fixed steel struts in star-shaped patterns forming a colossal mesh. The gigantic parasol is held up on four

Contemporary museums sponsored some of the most adventurous formal exercises of the times. Daniel Libeskind (b. 1946), after two decades of scribble-like designs, finally got his chance to build a complex structure at the Jewish Museum in Berlin (1993–1999), a zinc-clad zigzag scored with oblique window fissures. The avant-garde Austrian

2001

September 11 attack by al-Qaeda destroys World Trade Center in New York City

Toyo Ito's Sendai Mediathèque built in Japan

2001

2003

United States–led invasion of Iraq

Zaha Hadid awarded Pritzker Prize

2004

Figure 20.2-4 Paris. Institut du Monde Arabe, Jean Nouvel, 1986.

group Coop Himmel(b)lau created a swirling vortex for BMW Welt in Munich (2007). Likewise, Zaha Hadid (1950–2016), famous for her Neo-Constructivist graphic projects, designed several museums at the end of the 1990s, including the MAXXI in Rome (1998–2010) (Fig. 20.2-7), which, with its three-level atrium laced by multiple ramps and stairs, achieves a sublime Piranesian experience.

This dazzling parade of museums culminated at the end of the century with the scudded, titanium-clad Guggenheim Museum in Bilbao (1997) (Fig. 20.2-8) by Frank O. Gehry (b. 1929). During its first year of operation, it drew over a million visitors, a phenomenon soon known as the "Bilbao Effect." The crowds came to experience an indescribable figure composed of shrapnel-like forms that contradicted all previous notions of architectural geometry. Yet, aside from the atrium, with its three levels of glass and paneled surfaces that unfolded like the petals of a rose, the interior galleries conformed to typical orthogonal spaces independent of the outer shell. Like a bizarre sea creature beached on the riverbank at the edge of Bilbao's nineteenth-century grid, Gehry's Guggenheim transmitted the essence of "negative capability," in keeping with the avant-garde work it displayed.

Figure 20.2-5 Abu Dhabi. Louvre Abu Dhabi, Nouvel, 1986–2017.

▼ **2008**

Herzog & de Meuron and Ai Weiwei produce Olympic Stadium, Beijing

SOM completes Burj Khalifa, world's tallest structure, in Dubai, United Arab Emirates

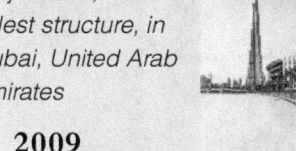

▲ **2009**

▼ **2010**

Hadid's MAXXI Museum built in Rome

Figure 20.2-6 London. Sainsbury Wing of the National Gallery, Robert Venturi and Denise Scott Brown, 1991.

Figure 20.2-7 Rome. MAXXI, Zaha Hadid, 1998–2010.

Figure 20.2-8 Bilbao, Spain. Guggenheim Museum, Frank O. Gehry, 1997.

In contrast to Gehry's wild scenography, Swiss architect Peter Zumthor (b. 1943) completed during the same year a paragon of understatement, the Kunsthaus, or KUB, in Bregenz (Fig. 20.2-9). He sheathed this enigmatic cube with an outer shell of etched-glass shingles set 1 m (3.3 ft) from the inner concrete walls. Delicate steel clamps held each panel so that it overlapped the next, leaving thin vertical **reveals** that allowed natural ventilation but shielded a direct view into the interior. Between each of the four floors a 2 m (7 ft) deep open mezzanine filtered natural light from the translucent exterior through the glass ceilings into the exhibition spaces. What appeared a simple box turned out to be as complex as a labyrinth. The difference of approach between Gehry and Zumthor reveals the extremes of contemporary museum design, which fluctuates between acrobatic spectacle and subtle revelation.

High-Tech: Buckminster Fuller's Progeny

High-Tech, a celebration of machine technology that was quite apparent in the aforementioned Centre Pompidou, emerged in the 1970s as one of the most attractive, if not expensive, postmodern attitudes available to multinational patrons. Inspired by the American engineer R. Buckminster Fuller (1895–1983), the movement sought to maximize the efficiency of building technologies. Fuller declared that humanity wastes 90% of its resources as a result of poor design, and his invocation to "make more with less," while quite similar to Mies's "less is more," came without the mystical connotations. In 1927 he presented the Dymaxion House (a combination of the words "dynamic," "maximum," and "ions"), a hexagonal volume suspended above ground from a

Figure 20.2-9 Bregenz, Austria. KUB Kunsthaus, Peter Zumthor, 1998.

Spaceship Earth

Fuller collaborated with the Japanese American architect Shoji Sadao (b. 1927) on a series of utopian megastructural projects, including a dome to enclose Midtown Manhattan, a colossal tetrahedron for 100,000 inhabitants that would float in San Francisco Bay, and "cloud spheres" for airborne cities. This last project inspired Fuller's metaphor of the planet as "spaceship earth." He advocated that construction around the globe achieve the same level of ergonomic and waste-free design used in the NASA space program.

a

b

(a) "Airborne cities," Fuller and Shoji Sadao, 1968. (b) St. Blazey, United Kingdom. Eden Project, an ecology exhibition of biomes based on Fuller's geodesic dome type, Nicholas Grimshaw, 2000. Each of the eight translucent domes is covered with polyhedron inflated pillows made of layered ETFE plastic to obtain optimal climates on the interior.

central service mast. Envisioning peaceful applications of military technology, he also proposed a ten-story Dymaxion apartment building that would be assembled in a factory and transported by zeppelin to a site where a bomb would clear the foundations before lowering the hexagonal tower into place. During World War II the U.S. Army commissioned Fuller to design transportable vaulted structures with prefabricated service components. After the war, he convinced an airplane factory to prepare the Wichita House (1946) (Fig. 20.2-10), a shiny aluminum dome set on a service mast, as a prototype for a mass-produced house. Conceived with the economic logic of an aircraft, the lightweight components could be assembled by six workers in a single day on virtually any site.

During his later career, Fuller pursued "tensegrity" as the key to structural efficiency. This desire to exploit tension for the reduction of the mass of structural materials led to his most important invention, the geodesic dome, conceived in 1949 at Black Mountain College in North Carolina. In the first prototype he covered a 4 m (13.5 ft) diameter with a network of polyhedrons made from metal rods, which reduced the bearing loads to a fraction of those seen in compression-based

Figure 20.2-10 Wichita, Kansas. Prototype prefabricated house, R. Buckminster Fuller, 1949 (model by Norman Foster Associates, 2010).

structures. Fuller went on to create the world's largest free span, stretching 115 m (377 ft), using his invention at the 1959 Union Tank Car Co. in Baton Rouge, Louisiana (demolished in 2007). During the next four decades, over 500,000 geodesic domes based on Fuller's patent were constructed, including the U.S. Pavilion at the Montréal Expo of 1967 designed with Shoji Sadao (Fig. 20.2-11).

Figure 20.2-11 Montréal. U.S. Pavilion for Expo '67, typical of Fuller's geodesic domes, 1967.

A Man's World No More

Two women emerged in the first decade of the twenty-first century as major protagonists in the globalized market of architecture, challenging what was previously an exclusively male realm. Both women received the Pritzker Prize, among many other awards. On one side, Zaha Hadid, born in Iraq but a naturalized British citizen, conceived extreme Neo-Expressionist projects, such as the zigzag Evelyn Grace Academy in Brixton, United Kingdom (2008), and the Galaxy Soho, a mounded, beehive-inspired shopping mall in Beijing. Since the 1980s she was assisted by the German master of parametrics, Patrik Schumacher. On the other side, the Japanese architect Kazuyo Sejima (b. 1956), who with her office of SANAA, co-directed by Ryue Nishizawa (b. 1966), has produced some of the most minimalist interventions of twenty-first-century architecture, which often defy structural logic, such as the immense perforated carpet of concrete at Lauzanne University's Rolex Learning Center (2010) or the brushed aluminum boxes for the Louvre-Lens Museum in Lens, France (2013), a 400 m (1,312 ft) long structure that seems to disappear in the clouds.

Lausanne, Switzerland. Rolex Learning Center, Kazuyo Sejima and Ryue Nishizawa, 2010.

The British architects Norman Foster (b. 1935) and Richard Rogers came to the United States to study with Fuller at Yale in 1961. Fuller's influence culminated in the two major expressions of High-Tech in the mid-1980s: Foster's Hong Kong and Shanghai Bank (HKSB) and Rogers's Lloyds of London (Fig. 20.2-12). Both towers used central columnar supports to suspend secondary structures and capped the whole with permanent cranes to continue servicing the buildings after construction. Foster squeezed the fifty-five-story HSKB into the dense core of Hong Kong using three vertical translucent slabs of differing heights. Every ten stories he inserted a series of double "coat-hanger" trusses to improve lateral support. The exoskeletal structural components permitted free-span interiors and generous atriums with ten-story hollows. Rogers's Lloyds building, a fourteen-story structure, was even more demonstrative of its structure and technology. He equipped three external towers with "plug-in" services, stainless-steel bathrooms, exposed ductwork, and transparent elevators. While the exterior appeared complex, the interior read as a simple rectangle, its full-height atrium capped by a glazed barrel-vault ceiling that reached 60 m (197 ft), taller than any of the great cathedrals. The two projects with their rooftop cranes flirted with the Futurist promise of the city as a "perpetual building site."

Foster also pursued less structurally expressive strategies in such projects as the Willis Faber & Dumas building (1975) (Fig. 20.2-13a) in Ipswich, England. Here, he wrapped the exterior with a uniform skin of highly reflective, brown-tinted glass. The glass wall followed the irregular contours of the site, while the interior remained open on a regular grid of columns interrupted by a central atrium for the escalators. The roof carried an extensive lawn, among the first green roofs on a modern office structure. Foster introduced metal plaques with four nubs to join the corners of four panes of the smoked glass facade in order to obtain the unprecedented smooth glass undulating curtain wall.

This inspired Peter Rice and his colleagues to invent the "Spiders," *X*-shaped metal clamps for the same function, first used in 1985 at La Cité des Sciences in Paris. The designers sealed the glass planes with Neoprene gaskets in a technology transfer from the automobile industry, first used by Eero Saarinen at the GM Tech Center in the early 1950s.

Most High-Tech projects suggest the logic of aircraft, and thus it should be no surprise that Foster, who pilots his own jet, has often been chosen as the architect of airports, including London Stansted (1991), where he spread a quilted rectangular roof over a forest of tree-like tetrapylons, and the Beijing International terminal (2008). His office also designed the stingray-shaped Spaceport America (2012) in the desert of New Mexico, planned as a launch pad for commercial space travel of the near future. Foster's Apple Headquarters in Cupertino, California (2017), commissioned by the digital wizard Steve Jobs, is usually described as a spaceship, comprising an immense four-story ring enclosing a woodsy landscape that has optimal thermal and lighting performance and uses only renewable

Figure 20.2-12 London. Lloyds of London, Richard Rogers, 1987.

energy to accommodate no fewer than 13,000 employees. With its uncompromised geometry and a site larger than most historic city centers, Apple presents the consummate horizontal expression of hypertecture, aspiring to embody the founder's conceit of the "infinite loop" (Fig. 20.2-13b).

The Spanish engineer Santiago Calatrava (b. 1951) diverged from High-Tech to develop a personal language of zoomorphic structures. He molded steel and concrete into sensual shapes inspired by bones and bird wings and then placed them in counteractive positions to exploit their tensile capacity. At the Alamillo Bridge in Seville (Fig. 20.2-14), built for the 1992 Expo, Calatrava poised a single pier tilted 15° away from the center and strung it with a series of steel cables like a colossal harp, exploiting the gravitational pull of the pier to counteract the draw on the cables. The dynamic equilibrium made the bridge seem like a bird's wing ready to spring into space, a metaphor emphasized by the beak-like tip at the top of the pylon. In numerous infrastructural projects executed during the mid-1990s, such as the Stadelhofen Station in Zurich, the Lyon Satolas Airport, and the City of Arts and Sciences in Valencia

(Fig. 20.2-15), Calatrava created exoskeletal structures that emulated the structural efficiency of animal anatomy.

The evolution of High-Tech toward an aesthetic of smooth amorphous "blobs" characterized the work of the London-based Future Systems of Jan Kaplický (1937–2009) and Amanda Levete (b. 1955). For the Selfridges building in Birmingham (2003) (Fig. 20.2-16) they produced a sinuous computer-generated profile for a free-form concrete envelope that looked like a molded rubber mound embossed with 15,000 aluminum hubcaps. Its impressive scenographic effect betrayed the functionalist ethos that technical solutions generate form. Despite Fuller's hopes to save the world through the increased efficiencies of well-made machines, High-Tech developed into a luxury style that proposed the beauty of custom-made technology, often resulting in significant deficits of embodied energy.

The architectural profession was one of the first to be affected by computer technologies. Computer-aided design was introduced through the aerospace industries in the early 1970s, and its software programs by the mid-1980s had

Figure 20.2-13 (a) Ipswich, England. Willis, Faber & Dumas building, Norman Foster, 1975. (b) Cupertino, California. Apple Headquarters, Norman Foster Associates, 2017.

Figure 20.2-14 Seville, Spain. Alamillo Bridge, Santiago Calatrava, 1992.

Figure 20.2-15 Valencia, Spain. City of Arts and Sciences, Calatrava, 2004.

become as important to design as word processors were to the preparation of texts, eliminating the tedious reproduction of drawings through graphic programs. Further programs for rendering and analysis made computer simulations, or *virtualism*, almost as important as real environments. Frank Gehry applied advanced computer techniques, using the CATIA program developed for French aeronautic companies, to produce the irrational forms of works such as the Disney Concert Hall in downtown Los Angeles (Fig. 20.2-17). The engineering, however, remained conventional and led to tolerances more than double the actual need.

The transition from High-Tech to computer-derived biomorphic designs influenced the development of Japanese architect Toyo Ito (b. 1941), a second-generation Metabolist who founded a studio initially called "Urban Robot" in emulation of the mechanomorphism of the 1970s. His cylindrical Yokohama Tower of the Winds and the blimp-shaped Egg of the Winds in Tokyo, in which he integrated perforated aluminum structures and multimedia, were ephemeral products of High-Tech. During the 1990s he was increasingly influenced by digital technologies. In the Sendai Mediathèque (2001) (Fig. 20.2-18a), Ito and avant-garde engineer Mutsuro Sasaki invented a biomimetic structural solution generated by computers, which they called "flux"

Figure 20.2-16 Birmingham, England. Selfridges, Future Systems, 2003.

structures, inspired by the swaying of underwater seaweed. The building rose as a glazed cube clad with a double layer of tinted shear glass walls that mediated the climate. Inside, thirteen mesh tubes, reminiscent of Vladimir Shukhov's hyperboloid shafts at the Moscow Tower, supported the seven levels while carrying the services, creating the effect of a bamboo forest. The tubes were structured on steel poles and compression rings like loosely woven baskets. Through computational analysis the architect and engineer eliminated as much weight and structure as possible, going

Figure 20.2-17 Los Angeles. Disney Concert Hall, Gehry, 1988–2005.

beyond mechanical metaphors to emulate the efficiency and fluidity of natural forms. The ultimate test came with the tsunami of 2011, which damaged the building's skin, but not its structure.

Computer technology in architecture evolved from a relatively passive role of saving labor to acquiring a nearly autonomous function known as **parametrics**, in which information is fed to programs that generate solutions, both practical and formal. The late work of Zaha Hadid, on which she was assisted by Patrik Schumacher (b. 1961), led to the undulating waves of the Heydar Aliyev cultural center in Baku, Azerbaijian (2010). The research of engineer Cecil Balmond resulted in the Arcelor Mittal Orbit Tower for the 2012 London Olympics, co-created with the artist Anish Kapoor. Like a vindication of the Tatlin Tower it stood as a paroxysm of complex geometry and aesthetically challenging forms that also challenged modes of construction (Fig. 20.2-18b).

The Architectural Consequences of Petroleum

Petroleum surpassed coal as the prime source of energy by the mid-twentieth century. Control of the oil supply became a major factor in both warfare and environmental degradation. Petrol literally fueled the sprouting of high-rise cities, suburban **sprawl**, and the rapid development of oil-rich nations. The relative ease of transporting and consuming oil encouraged an extreme level of energy waste, ranging from the construction of large enclosed structures with high-entropy heating and cooling systems to the development of an automobile-dependent way of life. The models that emerged in the United States spread to other countries desirous of attaining American levels of well-being.

Petroleum byproducts, including plastics and chemical fertilizers, became as pervasive as fuel. The immediate problem with fossil fuels became evident as brown clouds of smog, containing dangerous levels of carbon dioxide (CO_2) and fine particles, began to enshroud such cities as Los Angeles and Houston. Awareness grew during the 1980s of a greater problem: the cumulative effects of exhausts caused irreparable damage to the planet's biosphere, both decimating the protective ozone layer above the South Pole and throwing out of balance the planet's greenhouse gases. The hermetically sealed structures built at the point of petroleum import and the instant cities stocked with equally high-entropy structures at the points of export characterized the architecture of globalization.

Until 1973, the competitive world of multinational corporations spurred the race not only for the world's tallest building but also for the most energy-consuming structure. In Chicago, SOM produced the 100-story John Hancock Center (1969), a black-colored, steel-frame shaft that tapered like an obelisk and was crowned with twin horn-like radio antennae. The Bangladesh-born engineer Fazlur Khan (1929–1982) designed the tower's tubular structure of exposed diagonal cross-bracing, now called a **diagrid**, which eliminated the need for a grid of interior columns. The mixed-use project's open plan permitted new luxuries, including a "skylobby," where residents in the upper sixty stories had a small grocery store, and an indoor swimming pool. Four years later Khan and SOM completed the 110-story Sears Tower (now the Willis Tower, 1973), which reigned for a quarter of a century as the world's tallest building. Conceived as a bundle of tall, staggered boxes, it also relied on a tubular system, but with the cross-braces hidden behind the curtain wall.

RELIGION, PHILOSOPHY, FOLKLORE

Saddam Hussein's Monuments

After Saddam Hussein seized control of Iraq in 1979, he nationalized the oil companies, commissioned vast infrastructural improvements, restored archaeological sites such as Babylon and Ur, and completed a series of patriotic monuments to commemorate the war he launched against Iran (1980–1988). His projects ranged from the sublime al-Shaheed Martyrs Monument (1983), designed by the artist Ismael Fattah, to the ridiculous Hands of Victory. The 40 m (131 ft) high, ceramic-clad onion dome of the al-Shaheed was split in two, with half pushed to the side to reveal the concavity of the structure. Set in a park with surrounding reflecting pools, the two staggered shells were constructed on steel frames supporting resinous concrete walls covered with turquoise tiles.

The Hands of Victory monument (1987) came from a sketch made by Hussein. There a pair of colossal hands rose to either side of a parade street, each holding a 43 m (141 ft) long scimitar that crossed over the center of the street. The hands were modeled after the leader's own and the swords allegedly cast from the melted-down weapons of the enemy. The United States, which until 1989 had supported Hussein's regime, invaded Iraq first in 1991 and finally in 2003, searching for "weapons of mass destruction," only to find these relics of mass persuasion.

Baghdad, Iraq. Al-Shaheed Martyrs Monument, Ismael Fattah, 1983.

The Sears Tower inched out the 110-story Twin Towers of the World Trade Center (1965–1972) (Fig. 20.2-19) at the tip of Lower Manhattan for the distinction of the world's tallest structure. Designed by the Japanese American architect Minoru Yamasaki (1912–1986), these elongated parallelepipeds offered a dramatic formal contrast to the jagged skyline of the rest of the city. Like their Chicago rivals, they relied on a tubular structure. A service core for elevators and bathrooms occupied roughly one-quarter of each floor, while the outer frame used prefabricated stainless-steel columns placed at narrow 0.5 m (1.5 ft) intervals. At the bottom four levels every three columns merged into a single stem, creating the stylization of pointed Gothic arches. Venice's Piazza San Marco inspired the large plaza of the World

Figure 20.2-18 (a) Sendai, Japan. Mediathèque, Toyo Ito et al. (the interior of each floor was designed by a different architect), 2001. (b) London. Arcelor Mittal Orbit tower, designed for the 2012 Summer Olympics, Cecil Balmond and Anish Kapoor, 2012.

Figure 20.2-19 New York. World Trade Center, Minoru Yamasaki, 1965–1972.

Trade Center, set one level above the street and surrounded by low buildings and steel arcades. Unfortunately, the towers generated the Venturi effect, with a strong updraft, giving the space an unpleasant microclimate. Because of their imposing size and location, the Twin Towers became the symbol of the city, a major tourist attraction, and ultimately a target for the September 11, 2001, terrorist attack in which they were destroyed.

The possibilities of total climate control through cheap energy led to such hermetic architectural packages as Pennzoil Plaza (1972–1976) (Fig. 20.2-20) in Houston by Philip Johnson and John Burgee, two thirty-six-story trapezoidal towers linked at the base to a triple-height atrium with sloping roofs. The dark glazed obelisks rose like the pure volumes of minimalist sculpture, without any reference to human scale. Argentine-born Cesar Pelli (b. 1926) designed the similarly sculptural Pacific Design Center (1976) in Los Angeles. The opaque blue panels of its taut exterior earned the sobriquet "Blue Whale."

The works of architect-developer John Portman (b. 1924) best represented the high-entropy way of life as colossal, glazed volumes sheltering majestic voids. From the initial Hyatt Regency in Atlanta's Peachtree Place (1967), with its soaring twenty-story atrium animated by transparent elevators, he went on to create other spectacular hotels, including the mirror glass–clad cylinders of the Renaissance Center (1977) (Fig. 20.2-21) in downtown Detroit, Bonaventure Place in Los Angeles, and the San Francisco Hyatt Regency (1974). Portman's cavernous atria offered the feel of an amusement park in central city locations, completely cut off from the urban context and usually accessed through a parking garage. Such services as revolving rooftop restaurants and immense reception halls contributed to the energy extravagance.

All of these high-entropy projects were conceived before October 1973, when the Yom Kippur War in Israel led to the first energy crisis for the West. The predominantly Islamic membership of the Organization of Petroleum Exporting Countries (OPEC) imposed an oil embargo, which doubled the price of fuel, to contest Western support of Israel. The shah of Iran criticized the West: "You increased the price of wheat by 300%, and the same for sugar and cement. . . .

Figure 20.2-20 Houston, Texas. Pennzoil Plaza, Philip Johson and John Burgee, 1972–1976.

You buy our crude oil and sell it back to us, refined as pet-rochemicals, at a hundred times the price you've paid to us. . . . It's only fair that, from now on, you should pay more for oil. Let's say ten times more." The continued rise in energy costs during the 1970s led to stagnation in the U.S. building industry while boosting the research on energy-conscious design. Simultaneously the embargo fomented a building boom in the oil-producing countries. Because of the lack of professionals in these countries, most of the significant new buildings came from Western or Japanese offices.

Iraq, which was generally the most progressive of the OPEC countries, was home to only thirty native-born architects in 1950, most of them trained in England. The only country in Southwest Asia with a surplus of architects was Israel, owing to the immigration of many well-educated profession-als and the presence of a competent polytechnic university in Haifa. Tel Aviv, a city planned by Jewish settlers at the be-ginning of the twentieth century, had become known by the time of Israeli statehood in 1948 as the White City, a name due to its being almost completely composed of Modernist,

Figure 20.2-21 Detroit, Michigan. Renaissance Center, John Portman, 1977.

Bauhaus-style apartment buildings. Among the fine Modernist works built during the first years of statehood were the Maser Institute (1958) at the National University in Jerusalem and the Ramat Hadar housing blocks (1960–1964) by the Bauhaus-trained architect Munio Gitai Weinraub (1909–1970) and Al Mansfeld (1912–2004). But Israeli architects, despite their experience, were categorically excluded from working in OPEC countries for political reasons.

Many outsiders had worked in the region before the oil embargo. Le Corbusier designed a stadium in Iraq; Frank Lloyd Wright proposed an Opera House for Baghdad; Edward Durrell Stone (1902–1978) designed the 1962 Hotel Phoenicia in Beirut; and the Architect's Collaborative, an office founded by Walter Gropius in Boston, designed the extensive campus of Baghdad University from 1958 to 1970. A surprising difference in approach appeared after 1973, when some of the multinational offices became more considerate of environmental factors. Gordon Bunschaft (1909–1990) of SOM created a passive solar skyscraper, the National Commercial Bank (1983) (Fig. 20.2-22) in Jeddah, Saudi Arabia, which rose twenty-seven stories as a triangular prism with solid granite elevations pierced by two seven-story cutouts on the northeast side and a nine-story void on the south, protecting all of the glazing from direct exposure. The **section** reveals that the voids were connected to allow convection from the base to the top. The hollow spaces served as a site for hanging gardens.

The most poetic translation of the nomadic heritage of the region occurred at the King Abdulaziz Airport, known as the Hajj Airport (1987) (Fig. 20.2-23), near Jeddah, Saudi Arabia. Designed by SOM engineer Fazlur Khan as a series of tents, it could accommodate over 10 million pilgrims per year, most of them during the six-week *hajj* season in Mecca. The two parallel terminals were composed as hypostyles of steel poles from which white Teflon-coated tents, organized in three rows, stretched 45 m (148 ft) in each direction. An oculus at the apex of each tent

Figure 20.2-22 Jeddah, Saudi Arabia. National Commercial Bank, Gordon Bunschaft and SOM, 1983.

forced hot air out. Most of the terminal areas were completely exposed to the elements, relying on natural shading and ventilation to produce a comfortable temperature.

As globalization reached its zenith the vanity of owning the world's tallest tower passed to the source of petroleum. The skylines of the Persian Gulf cities of Kuwait, Doha, Abu Dhabi, and Dubai sprouted an improbable crop of glass and steel skyscrapers, most of them ignoring passive environmental controls and many of them with low occupancy rates. In 1999 the world's tallest hotel, the sixty-story Burj Al Arab, opened in Dubai (Fig. 20.2-24a) as a "seven-star" hotel that rose on its own island like a billowing sail with a central mast 333 m (1,093 ft) tall. Produced by the Atkins Company, the largest corporate office in Europe, it focused on a triangular atrium that surpassed Portman's vertiginous precedents. In the contest for the tallest structure, the state oil company of Malaysia financed the Petronas Towers (1998) (Fig. 20.2-24b) in Kuala Lumpur. The temples of Angkor inspired the stepped profiles of the twin towers, designed by Cesar Pelli, which were based on redented plans. Their 450 m (1,476 ft) spires have since been topped by the Burj Khalifa in Dubai (2010) (Fig. 20.2-24c), designed by Adrian Smith (b. 1944) of SOM, which rose 163 stories, or 828 m (2,717 ft), bringing distinction to Dubai as a trading network for the world's most coveted nonrenewable resource. Set on a triadic, crowfoot plan, it stepped up in bundles like a Gothic pinnacle, presenting a new Tower of Babel. The hubris of the builders of such proud towers will more than likely be punished not by divine wrath, but by the eventual absence of fuel.

The most important architectural theorist of the age of globalization, Rem Koolhaas (b. 1944), published *Delirious New York* in 1978 as a love song to the unconscious creative process of the skyscraper city of Manhattan. He defined the key to its magic as the "culture of congestion." In the meantime planners and developers throughout Asia and the oil-producing countries, and even in Koolhaas's own Rotterdam, tried their hand at Manhattanization but invariably fell short of yielding a metropolitan atmosphere. After two decades of practice with OMA (the Office of Metropolitan Architecture), Koolhaas published *S,M,X,XL* with the designer Bruce Mau, offering a confession that "Bigness," the power of banks, loan agents, developers, government officials, zoning authorities, subcontractors, and an endless lists of players, had guaranteed a sort of nearsightedness that only superscale projects could overcome. OMA's project in Beijing for CCTV (2012), the state television company, stood as a prime example of the resulting hypertecture, a building of immense scale, high iconic recognition, and no regard for the context (Fig. 20.2-25). Its uncanny composition, with two ground-level wings joined at a right angle and two towers that ascend obliquely from their opposite ends to meet two cantilevered horizontal wings that converge into a right angle, required the exceptional computing skill of Cecil Balmond. Occupying an entire block, the project rose like a lonely sphinx, its glass elevations scored by staggered diagonals exposing the complexities of an irregular diagrid structure, which at points of stress became denser. While bigness can be singled out as a means in architecture, here and elsewhere it seems to have become an end unto itself.

The Emergence of the Non-Western Architect

In 1979 Jay Pritzker (1922–1999), owner of the Hyatt Corporation and patron of several of John Portman's most audacious hotels, created the Pritzker Prize for architecture. That the first was awarded to Philip Johnson established a pattern of elitism, and over the course of four decades the prize has usually gone to Western star architects and a few from Japan, the tastemakers of globalization. In 1980 another

Figure 20.2-24 (a) Dubai, United Arab Emirates. Burj Al Arab hotel, Atkins Company, 1999. (b) Kuala Lumpur, Malaysia. Petronas Towers, Cesar Pelli, 1998. (c) See next page.

Figure 20.2-24 (c) Dubai. Burj Khalifa (Khalifa Tower), Adrian Smith/SOM, 2010.

architectural prize was founded by Aga Khan IV (b. 1936), the spiritual leader of the Ishmaili branch of the Shiite sect of Islam. The Aga Kahn Award for architecture, given every two or three years, acknowledges multiple projects, mostly in developing countries, many of which are mosques or concerned with heritage preservation districts. Some of the prize-winning projects have been designed by anonymous builders rather than architects. Hassan Fathy received the first Aga Khan Chairman's Award, and later prizes honored non-Western architects such as Sedad Eldem (1908–1988) of Turkey, who designed the Social Security Complex (1964) in Istanbul, and Rifat Chadirji (b. 1926), architect of the innovative Tobacco Monopoly Headquarters (1967) in Baghdad.

Geoffrey Bawa (1919–2003) of Sri Lanka received a career award for such projects as the Kandalama Hotel. The difference in the two awards programs underlines an obvious divergence in values: the Western prize has tended to promote celebrity careers, while the non-Western one tends to favor the quality of places and communities.

Contemporary architecture in Japan provides one of the few cases of resistance, revealing a modern, non-Western approach to design. Japan's long separation from the rest of the world as a result of the *sakoku* policy of the Edo government surely conditioned its cultural isolation. While the nation's building industry assimilated technologies from the West, Japanese architects pursued their own approach to

Figure 20.2-25 Beijing. CCTV state television offices, OMA (Rem Koolhaas and Ole Scheeren), 2012.

form. Kenzo Tange, one of the four Japanese architects to receive the Pritzker Prize, prevailed as the leader of an independent Japanese Modernism from the 1950s onward. Heavily influenced by Le Corbusier through his teacher Kunio Maekawa (1905–1986), who had worked for the French master in the 1930s, Tange came to the attention of the world with his Hiroshima Museum and Memorial Peace Park (1949–1955) (Fig. 20.2-26a), commemorating the city's survival of the first atomic bomb. The museum hovered in a long, thin box over a series of pylons, leaving the ground plane free. While conforming to many of Le Corbusier's criteria, the Hiroshima Museum also drew upon Japanese precedents such as the Ise shrine (see Section 7.2), a wooden structure raised on piles that is periodically dismantled and rebuilt. The atomic bomb killed as many as 100,000 and leveled the city, and Tange's museum responded as a flattened base for starting over.

Tange, who in his discussions of urban processes regularly used such biological analogies as "cells" and "metabolism," was selected by his students as the spokesperson for the Japanese Metabolist movement of the 1960s. His 1964 Yamanashi Center for Broadcasting in Kofu demonstrated the programmatic flux between structure and adaptation. The towering complex rose on a grid of masts, large cylinders used for services from which the variable parts of the building were hung. Tange's ability to coordinate complex

planning schemes, such as the 1964 Tokyo Olympics and the 1970 Osaka Expo, attracted many international clients, both in such Western cities as Bologna and San Francisco and in non-Western settings. His identity as a non-Western architect contributed to his attractiveness, especially in countries recently liberated from colonial status such as Algeria and Nigeria. Tange's project for the capital city of Abuja, Nigeria (1980s), aspired to the scale of Brasília but was not built as planned.

Tadao Ando (b. 1941), one of the few famous architects in Japan not connected to Tange, drew inspiration from the cosmic void found in Zen gardens. Working almost exclusively with planar concrete walls, Ando created spaces in which the daylight could filter through light traps. His Church of Light in Ibaraki (1989) (Fig. 20.2-26b) focused on the altar wall, a perfectly square plane inscribed with a cross that left a glaring crucifix of light. Ando shaped the structures of his houses and museums like blinders focusing on a particular view, similar to the function of windows in a Japanese teahouse. Without recourse to historic iconography, he captured the essence of Japanese identity in abstract modern forms.

A decade later in South Korea a similar development of an autonomous modern architecture took place. During the 1970s Kim Swoo Geun (1931–1986) promoted a cultural synthesis of arts and architecture after returning from his

Figure 20.2-26 (a) Hiroshima, Japan. Museum and Memorial Peace Park, Kenzo Tange, 1949–1955. (b) Ibaraki, Japan. Church of Light, Tadao Ando, 1989.

studies in Japan at Tange's University of Tokyo. His most accomplished collaborator, H-Sang Seung (b. 1952), continued to develop a new Asian alternative. In his works of the 1990s he created traditionally scaled courtyards using Corten surfaces and large panes of glass. His Dee Jeon Hospital in the new town of CheonAn took one of the most difficult **programs** in architecture, the modern hospital, and purposely attempted to avoid Western mechanistic environments by giving the "Oriental" hospital surprising elements of pleasure, such as small-scale windows, well-crafted

stone revetments, grassy rooftop courtyards lined with wood-panel elevations, and many structured views to gardens and landscapes. He eliminated the impersonal atmosphere of hospitals while establishing a fine grain for the rest of the new town's urban pattern.

Taiwan emerged during the 1980s in the same economic updraft that favored Korea. The office of C. Y. Lee (b. 1938), who had studied at Princeton during the period of Michael Graves's shift to Postmodernism, created the Hong Kuo Business Center (1990) (Fig. 20.2-27) in Taipei, a

Figure 20.2-27 Taipei, Taiwan. Hong Kuo Business Center, C. Y. Lee, 1990.

twenty-story structure similar to Graves's Portland Building. Instead of the inflated icons of Western classicism, Lee used overblown *duogong* brackets to create a Chinese equivalent of Postmodern historicism. Lee's Taipei 101 Tower (2004), a 101-story structure that rose pagoda-like from its base as a succession of eight eight-story stages with flaring eaves separating each stage, reigned for three years as the "world's tallest." The numbers 101 and 8 traditionally have been thought to bring good luck in Chinese culture.

Such literal use of Chinese iconography was extensively imitated for the crowning elements on the thousands of sky-scrapers built during the turn-of-the-century building boom in Beijing, Shanghai, and Shenzhen. After nearly a half-century of bureaucratic architecture under Communism, the

new mixed economy in the People's Republic of China liberalized the architectural profession. Western and Japanese architects arrived to create entire new cities, while a few small offices emerged as part of a new wave of local culture, attempting to establish a modern Chinese architecture that would comprehend the essence of traditional design without falling into the trap of iconographic kitsch. Yung-Ho Chang (b. 1956), after nearly two decades of training and teaching in the United States, opened the first private architectural studio in Beijing in 1993. He helped plan the Commune at the Great Wall, a group of twenty prototype vacation villas designed by different architects from East Asia. His own Split House (Fig. 20.2-28a), a variation on the traditional Chinese courtyard house, mixed exposed wooden beams,

Figure 20.2-28 Rural China. (a) Split House, Commune at the Great Wall, Yung-Ho Chang, 2000. (b) Ningbo Historic Museum, Wang Shu, 2009.

Figure 20.2-29 Beijing. Olympic Stadium, Herzog & de Meuron with Ai Weiwei, 2008.

metal tie-rods, rammed-earth walls, glass floors, and bamboo surfaces. Other architects have followed, such as Wang Lu (b. 1963) in Beijing, who designed the Museum at Tiantai (2003) using battered stone elevations and small courts. Ningbo Historic Museum (2009) (Fig. 20.2-28b) by Pritzker Prize winner Wang Shu (b. 1963) served as a moral response to the reckless destruction of Chinese historic patrimony, stacking twenty different types of brick, stone, and tile culled from demolished historic buildings into the elevations of a bastion-shaped volume.

Contrary to other architects' embrace of the insensitive scale and materials of the glass and steel high-rises of multinational firms, the new generation of independent Chinese architects has attempted to recuperate the subtle scale of the traditional Chinese environment without denying the arrival of modernity. The artist-architect Ai Weiwei (b. 1957) contributed the "bird's nest," woven with steel flanges, to cover the Olympic Stadium (2008) (Fig. 20.2-29) in Beijing, designed by Swiss architects Herzog & de Meuron as a new synthesis of traditional concepts, such as basket weaving, and modern structure.

In Africa after the fall of colonialism the new countries relied on Western technicians, and thus an Afro-centric modern architecture has been slow to emerge. Egyptian architect Hassan Fathy argued for a return to traditional building techniques as a means of resisting dependency on foreign materials and expertise. The Bank of West Africa commissioned several projects that drew on African traditions. Pierre Goudiaby Atepa (b. 1948) designed two of the bank's headquarters, one in Lomé, Togo, and the other in Dakar, Senegal, using monumental versions of rounded silos, with frieze decorations based on indigenous art. Wango Pierre Sauwadogo designed the same bank's headquarters in Ouagadougou, Burkina Faso (Fig. 20.2-30), using adobe as the infill of the three-story base.

Some of the more insightful works in Africa, inspired by the alarming rise of shantytown dwellers in cities like Lagos and Brazzaville, have come from Western aid. Laszlo Mester de Parajd (b. 1949), of Hungary and France, created modern works using mud walls at the Court of Justice in Agadez in Niger (1982). The Finnish architects Heikkenen and Kommonen designed the Kahere Eila School (1999) for poultry farming in Kindia, Guinea, as an example of a return to earth architecture, with a modern touch

Figure 20.2-30 Ouagadougou, Burkina Faso. Bank of West Africa, Wango Pierre Sauwadogo, 1990.

in the treatment of double roofs and crutch-like columns. Aside from the lessons of these self-built projects, African architecture has found its first hero in the success of David Adjaye (b. 1966), born of Ghanaian parents in Tanzania and educated in London, where he practices. After receiving acclaim for his Dirty House (2002) and the Idea Store library (2005) in Whitechapel, he emerged as an African star architect and served as principal designer of the National Museum of African American History in Washington, D.C. (2016) (Fig. 20.2-31), which stands with three levels of crown-like terraces in dark opposition to the whiteness of the Washington Monument. As in sports and music, earning distinction abroad has proved to have more influence in changing local attitudes than working exclusively in sub-Saharan Africa would have.

Most of the large cities in South America, like those in Africa and parts of Asia, are being pulled in all directions by informal shantytowns, where an estimated 1 billion human beings live in periurban squalor. During the 1970s John Turner proposed "sites and services" programs in the effort to secure infrastructure for water and sewage for the informal sector while leaving the dwellers "free to build."

Figure 20.2-31 Washington, D.C. National Museum of African American History, David Adjaye, 2016.

one of the most violent cities in the world. Since 2003, the city has been tamed by a new mayor, Sergio Fajardo, who initiated a widespread program of civic centers with libraries and public spaces, establishing a new sense of order and responsibility amid lawless urban sprawl. The Santo Domingo Library (Fig. 20.2-32) in the Parque España neighborhood, designed by Giancarlo Mazzanti (b. 1963), shows the creative response to the cultural program, raising mysterious polymorphic sheds on a hill. The library program included one of the last buildings by the Colombian Modernist master Rogelio Salmoná (1929–2007). Medellín's mixture of well-programmed modern public buildings, accessible public spaces, transparent police measures, and cultivation of human resources offers a creative model for taking back local control. While globalism may seem inevitable, strategies of local development often help to subvert its dehumanizing consequences.

Figure 20.2-32 Medellín, Colombia. Santo Domingo Library, Giancarlo Mazzanti, 2005.

Further Reading

Cohen, Jean-Louis. *The Future of Architecture Since 1889*. London: Phaedon, 2012.

Fernández Galiano, Luis. *Atlas: Global Architecture circa 2000*. Madrid: Fundación BBVA, 2007.

Frampton, Kenneth. *The Evolution of Twentieth Century Architecture: A Synoptic Account*. Vienna: Springer-Verlag, 2007.

Grimaldi, Roberto. *R. Buckminster Fuller, 1895–1983*. Rome: Officina, 1990.

Kayoko, Ota, ed. *Project Japan, Metabolism Talks . . .* Cologne, Germany: Taschen, 2011.

Koolhaas, Rem. *Delirious New York: A Retroactive Manifesto for Manhattan*. New York: Rizzoli, 1978.

Koolhaas, Rem, and Bruce Mau, *S,M,L,XL*, New York: Monacelli Press, 1995.

Kultermann, Udo. *Contemporary Architecture in the Arab States: Renaissance of a Region*. New York: McGraw-Hill, 1999.

Taylor, Brian Brace. *Miguel Angel Roca*. London: Mimar, 1992.

Tzonis, Alexander, and Liane Lefaivre. *Critical Regionalism: Architecture and Identity in a Globalized World*. Munich: Prestel, 2003.

Argentine architect Miguel Angel Roca (b. 1940) created a series of public buildings, cultural centers, and parks in his home city of Córdoba, Argentina, that attempted to recast development as a civic process. In La Paz, Bolivia, he continued a similar program of creating urban foci within shanty neighborhoods during the late 1980s by inserting a series of monumental public health centers. His brightly colored walls at the Florida Park pay homage to Luis Barragán, while at his San Antonio Health Center, an octagonal prism, a cube, and a sphere sitting under a single detached roof evoke the grand visions of his teacher, Louis I. Kahn.

During the 1990s Medellín, Colombia, was overrun by gangsters in the multinational narcotics trade, becoming

20.3 TOWARD AN ECOLOGICAL WORLDVIEW

Architecture and the Anthropocene

Since its origins architecture has provided humans with artificial climate. It is increasingly apparent, however, that modern architecture and urbanism have contributed substantially to the rapid alteration of the planet's climate. Public awareness of both the holes in the ozone stratum over Antarctica and the dramatic increase in greenhouses gases became a central political issue during the last two decades of the twentieth century and led to the popularization of the term *Anthropocene*, referring to the geological era dominated by human agency. During this time the polar ice caps lost 20% of their permafrost surface; the glaciers of Switzerland, Kenya, and Colorado melted; the rising levels of the oceans inundated coastal regions; and the frequency of freak storms and natural calamities increased exponentially. One response to the threat from the sky has been to design buildings as landscapes. Land architecture has become a symbolic effort to redeem humanity through integration with nature.

Since the 1992 United Nations–sponsored meeting in Rio de Janeiro and the Kyoto Accords of 1997, the demand for "**sustainable**" environments has infused architecture with a new functionalist imperative to reduce both the consumption of fossil fuels and the emission of CO_2 gases. The achievement of sustainability requires multiple strategies, beginning with the reorganization of transportation and urban densification. While new technologies, such as photovoltaics and sophisticated insulation, play an important role in this task, some of the best answers to the ecology question come from the common sense of traditional builders. In the age of global warming one's relation to the earth and the sky demands a new awareness of the wisdom of builders throughout time.

Land Architecture

Land architecture emerged as a symbolic response to the environmental crisis of the late twentieth century. Many architects treated their buildings as landscapes, returning to the land and local materials in an effort to compensate for the ecological damage caused by architecture and urbanism. How well land architecture performed in mitigating the impact of architectural scale and high entropy was less important than its intended message of appeasement of the earth.

The precursors of land architecture coincided with the first atomic bombs and their subsequent potential for nuclear overkill. The palpable fear that the biosphere was in mortal danger led to both activism and artistic acts of redemption. Frank Lloyd Wright, long an advocate of an architecture that connected to the land, designed the Second Jacobs House (1947) (Fig. 20.3-1a) in Middleton, Wisconsin, as a "solar hemi-cycle," lodging the structure into an earthen berm on

Figure 20.3-1 (a) Middleton, Wisconsin. Second Jacobs House, Frank Lloyd Wright, 1947. **(b)** Oakland, California. Oakland Museum, Kevin Roche, 1968.

Figure 20.3-2 Great Salt Lake, Utah. *Spiral Jetty*, Robert Smithson, 1970.

Smithson added material to the site, Heizer removed it. Both artists, in transforming uninhabited desert scenes, were performing ritual interventions with the land. The Bulgarian artist Christo offered less damaging methods of land art, performing ephemeral interventions with recyclable materials. His *Running Fence* (1976) stretched a continuous swath of white nylon sheets on metal poles over 40 km (25 miles) of northern California's chaparral hills. The work stood only for two weeks, an event that allowed viewers to appreciate in a new way the shape of the land.

the north while leaving it completely glazed on the south. Le Corbusier, who in the 1920s preached the value of the open ground plane and the rooftop garden, built several late projects with sod roofs. The vaulted, brick-walled Maisons Jaoul, in the suburbs of Paris (1956), carried a fully planted roof. Alvar Aalto created some of the most appealing precedents for land architecture, such as his 1953 Summer House at Muuratsalo, with its *U*-shaped courtyard spilling out into the woods. Kevin Roche (b. 1922) at the Oakland Museum (1968) (Fig. 20.3-1b) pursued an initial below-grade "bomb shelter"–type structure, covered with beautiful hanging gardens designed by Dan Kiley (1912–2004).

Later works that treated architecture as a landscape related more closely to the land art movement in the arts. During the late 1960s the sculptor Robert Smithson (1938–1973) proposed a geographic vision for works of art that he called Earthworks. Inspired by the movement of earth for infrastructure, he designed *Spiral Jetty* (1970) (Fig. 20.3-2) on the Great Salt Lake, using the same techniques as highway construction. His colleague Michael Heizer (b. 1944) made depressions in the desert, culminating in the ambitious excavation for *Double Negative* (1969), a deep trench cut through the rocky cliffs on either side of a desert canyon in Nevada. While

Land art crossed into architecture with the Vietnam Veterans Memorial by Maya Lin (b. 1959), completed in 1982 (Fig. 20.3-3). She proposed the reverse of the other monuments in Washington, D.C., designing a black wall sunk below grade and bent into an obliquely opened *V* shape. The two flanges of the wall carried the names of more than 58,000 Americans killed or missing in action, listed in the chronological order of their demise. One entered the memorial from either side on gently descending, paved ramps that transformed the site into an amphitheater-like enclosure. While searching for names on the wall, visitors saw themselves reflected in the polished black granite and behind them the glimmering monuments of the Washington Mall. This cut into the land generated small ritual acts, such as the rubbings visitors made by laying trace paper over the names.

Like land art, works of land architecture became inseparable from the landscape, through either addition or subtraction. The Dominus Winery (1997) (Fig. 20.3-4) in Napa Valley, California, by Jacques Herzog and Pierre de Meuron (b. 1950), added to the horizontal landscape of orderly

TIME LINE

 1962

Rachel Carson publishes
Silent Spring

EPA established, first Earth Day

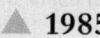 **1970**

 **1982**

Maya Lin's Vietnam Memorial opens in Washington, D.C.

Ozone hole over Antarctica officially recognized

▲ **1985**

Figure 20.3-3 Washington, D.C. Vietnam Veterans Memorial, Maya Lin, 1982.

Figure 20.3-4 Napa Valley, California. Dominus Winery, Jacques Herzog and Pierre de Meuron, 1997.

▼ **1986**

Nuclear disaster at Chernobyl, Ukraine, contaminates much of Europe

Zumthor's thermal baths constructed at Vals, Switzerland

▲ **1996**

▼ **1997**

Kyoto Accords, United Nations agreement (excluding United States) to significantly reduce greenhouse gases, signed

Figure 20.3-5 Barcelona. Igualada Cemetery, Enric Miralles and Carme Pinós, 1985–1994.

vineyards a long stone wall like that of an agricultural terrace. Built with steel gabion cages, similar to those found along highways to hold back landslides, the wall of unbound stones produced a long pile of rocks that appears similar to the works of sculptor Richard Long (b. 1945), who composes installations of stones and other natural materials in strict geometric patterns.

Many works connected to the renewal of Barcelona during the last two decades of the twentieth century fit the trend of land architecture. Enric Miralles (1955–2000) and Carme Pinós (b. 1954) designed the Igualada Cemetery (1985–1994) (Fig. 20.3-5) as a fissure in the hillside, partly sustained with gabion cages. Their archery range for the 1992 Barcelona Olympics (demolished in 2008) rolled in paraboloid humps from the edge of the ringroad incline, like the folding of land forms. Carlos Ferrater (b. 1944) and landscape architect Beth Figueras (1952–2010) conceived the Botanical Gardens of Montjuic (1996–2004) as a series of topographic pleats, articulated by V-shaped retaining walls made from sheets of Corten steel. The rusty color of the walls complemented the plant materials.

Farther afield, in Catalonia, RCR Arquitectes (led by Rafael Aranda, Carme Pigem, and Ramón Vilalta) emulated the bold steel forms of the sculptor Donald Judd. Their Bell-Lloc Winery (2007) (Fig. 20.3-6) in Palamós was entered through a series of Corten flanges that held back a mass of loosely stacked boulders. Where the path penetrated a shady vestibule, the offices

Figure 20.3-6 Palamós, Spain. Bell-Lloc Winery, RCR Arquitectes, 2007.

Piano's California Academy of Sciences built in San Francisco
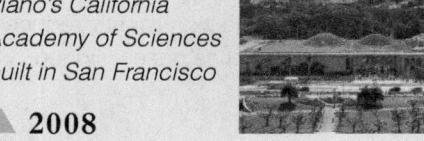
▲ 2008

▼ 2014
High Line Park in New York City completed

Chernobyl, New Safe Confinement vault completed
▲ 2017

Figure 20.3-7 Vals, Switzerland.
Thermal baths, Peter Zumthor, 1996.

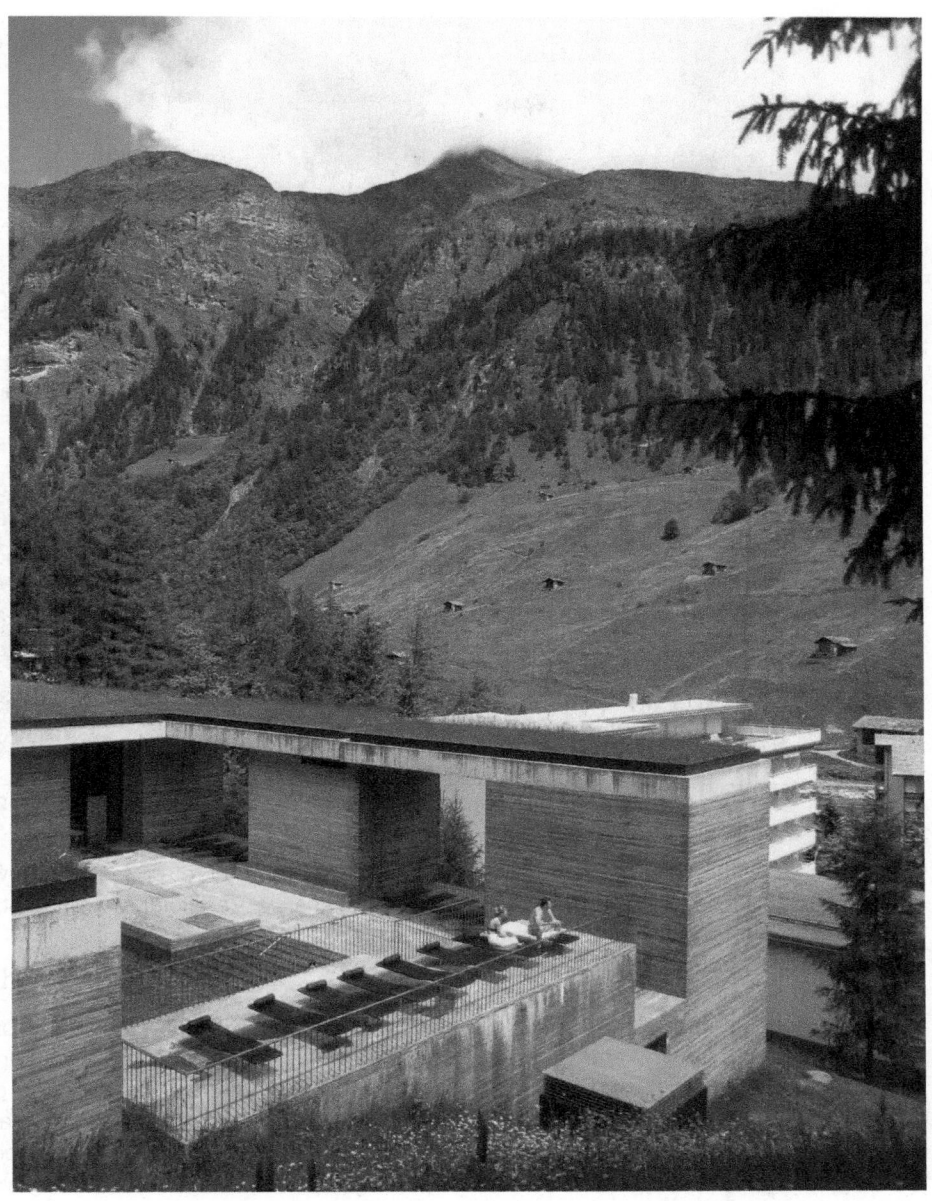

and services opened to glazed panels on the north side, while on the other side one found a subterranean labyrinth for the wine storage, completely structured in Corten panels. The folded steel roof plates supported 2 m (7 ft) of soil for growing rows of vines.

Peter Zumthor subtly integrated the thermal baths at Vals (1996) (Fig. 20.3-7) into the slopes of a spa town in the Swiss Alps, blending the planted roof effortlessly into the hill. One entered the spa through a tunnel to discover a subterranean, quarry-like chamber with ramps and mysterious pockets for a variety of thermal experiences tucked inside the stone-clad piers of the structure. Vals induced a ritual of discovery within its stone chasm, and after experimenting with the different interior spaces, one finally swam from the inside to an outer pool to discover a panoramic vision of the Alpine valley.

Peter Eisenman (b. 1932) progressed from an architect obsessed with geometric overlays to one fascinated by topographic patterns. In the late 1980s his work became more convoluted owing to the complex geometries made possible by computer modeling. Eisenman's largest project, the City of Culture in Santiago de Compostela, begun in 1999, covered a site as large as a traditional city, with undulating volumes that intermingled with folded landforms. In the Monument to the Murdered Jews of Europe (2004) (Fig. 20.3-8), a project that Eisenman planned for Berlin with sculptor Richard Serra (b. 1939), who subsequently withdrew from it, he erected 2,711 sarcophagus-size, squared-off slabs of differing heights across an entire block in the city center. The tallest of the dark gray chunks reached a little over twice human height. Moving toward midblock, the ground depressed on gentle rills, allowing the visitor to get lost in the site. Eisenman softened the rigidity of the project's organizing grid with the eccentric tilting of some of the slabs, which seemed to have been knocked askew by tectonic

Figure 20.3-8 Berlin. Monument to the Murdered Jews of Europe, Peter Eisenman, 2004.

plate shifts under the terrain. Like the ancient field of menhirs at Carnac (see Section 1.3), the monument carries no signs, no names, and no indication of its meaning but feels like a cemetery and could easily represent all of Europe's dead from the war as well as all the murdered Jews.

Renzo Piano, after his High-Tech exploit at Centre Pompidou, started his own firm and purposely toned down the exposed technology in his projects to devote more attention to landscapes. For the Schlumberger Headquarters (1983) in Paris, he renovated a series of old industrial buildings into offices, lining the court with a superb garden by Alexandre Chemetov and placing the three-level parking garage under a densely planted artificial hill. A concrete valley cut through the hill, carrying the sole residue of Piano's High-Tech moment: tensile structures supporting Teflon-coated tents, which provided a pleasant microclimate for the company's cafeteria and social spaces. His Jean Marie Tjibaou Cultural Center on the South Sea island of New Caledonia (1996) looked to local *kanak* traditions in the design of ten hut-like apses clad in double layers of wooden poles and set amid the trees on a small peninsula. The bowed wooden volumes peeked through the forest like gigantic crowns and produced Aeolian tones in the wind. At the California Academy of Sciences (2008) (Fig. 20.3-9) in San Francisco's Golden Gate Park, Piano placed a single, planted roof with seven bulging knolls on top of slender steel colonnades, wrapped with a rim of photovoltaic pergolas. Land architecture, either through digging into or rising out of the ground, keeps a building from being seen on its own. It interjects a symbolic gesture

of return to the land while promising a reconciliation of the artificial environment of architecture with nature.

Architects Respond to the Ecology Question

In 1962 Rachel Carson (1907–1964) published *Silent Spring*, interjecting the ecology question into politics. Her denunciation of the diffusion of DDT and other anthropogenic pollutants across the planet motivated the passage of the first restrictions on pesticides and other dangerous chemicals. In 1970 the U.S. government established the Environmental Protection Agency (EPA), and in the same year ecology activists set aside April 22 as the first Earth Day. Although architects were among the first to help plant trees, they did not generally recognize the connection of architecture and urbanism to the ecology question until the 1973 oil embargo. The ensuing energy crisis led to energy-conscious mandates and legislation spurring material changes, such as the production of more efficient insulation. U.S. president Jimmy Carter ordered a solar water heater installed on the roof of the White House. The governor of California, Jerry Brown, appointed one of the leading spokespeople for ecological architecture, Sim van der Ryn (b. 1934), as state architect, resulting in a series of energy-efficient office buildings. The 1977 Bateson Building in Sacramento (Fig. 20.3-10) demonstrated van der Ryn's effort to combine active and passive systems by creating natural climate control through enclosed courtyards assisted by mechanical devices.

As the research on ecological design advanced, the awareness of urbanism as the key to a sustainable future

Recycling Infrastructure: The High Line

The High Line in New York City (2009–2017) evolved as a privately funded community-organized project to convert the abandoned elevated rails of Lower Manhattan into a planted promenade. The landscape designer James Corner, working with Diller, Scofidio + Renfro, subtly retrofit the 2.3 km (1.4 mile) long viaduct with paving, planters, benches, lighting, and access points, occasionally preserving the rails as industrial archaeology. The Dutch landscaper Piet Oudolf introduced an atlas of wild grasses to line the route, while various artists have added many thought-provoking works of their own. An aerial work of land architecture, the High Line has become a major tourist attraction, drawing to its edges major projects such as Renzo Piano's new Whitney Museum of American Art, completed in 2015.

New York City. The High Line, James Corner with Diller, Sofidio + Renfro, 2009–2017.

began to take precedence. No matter how energy-efficient a building might be, if it requires its occupants to use automobile transportation, it contributes more to the problem than to the solution. Green urbanism involved rethinking infrastructure, replanning neighborhoods using the criteria of self-sufficiency and density, and revising the distribution of resources. Peter Calthorpe in the *Next American Metropolis* (1993) harked back to the ideas of Ebenezer Howard's Garden City in his proposals for reshaping the incoherent sprawl of American suburbs. Key to his "pedestrian pocket" concept was the creation of transportation nodes accessible to all residences in a ten-minute walk. In his 1990s regional plan for Portland, Oregon, Calthorpe began the process of creating a network of intermodal transportation centers with large areas for parking and public spaces for commercial amenities. Zaha Hadid's Hoenheimnord intermodal station (2001) on the outskirts of Strasbourg demonstrated that such a program for infrastructure could be approached as a pretext for art. The dynamic *S* shape of the station's roof extended through the graphics of the parking lot in a dramatic swath of white paving.

Curitiba, Brazil, became the first city to implement a program of comprehensive ecological urbanism. The impetus for planning came from the architect-mayor Jaime Lerner (b. 1937), who from 1971 on rearranged the city's infrastructure, channeling public transportation into a network of fast

Figure 20.3-9 San Francisco. California Academy of Sciences, Renzo Piano, 2008.

Figure 20.3-10 Sacramento, California. Bateson Building, Sim van der Ryn, 1977.

corridors for bus lanes with well-articulated transit nodes. More than 80% of Curitiba's 3 million inhabitants use public transportation, greatly reducing pollution. Most of the transit stops are combined with such cultural additions as neighborhood libraries and parks. Lerner turned environmental disadvantages, such as flood zones, into positive features such as parks, placing the cultural buildings in these areas on stilts. The city engaged the unemployed of Curitiba in a pilot program of recycling, initially exchanging bags of trash for transit tickets.

Freiburg in southwestern Germany became Europe's most progressive city in terms of "green" management. After the debacle of Chernobyl in 1986 the city rejected a state-funded nuclear power plant, devoting great effort to developing alternative energy sources and declaring itself a "solar region." Freiburg produces **photovoltaic panels** in two factories, and this technology now caps most public structures, including schools, garages, and stadia. The high-rise at the train station uses them as cladding. The Vauban district, built on the site of an abandoned military barracks, offers densely arranged apartments constructed with sophisticated insulation, natural materials, and a collective heating system using biomass fuel. Rolf Disch's Sunship and Solar Estate, with fifty townhouses and a long, ship-shaped five-story mixed-use building lining the main street, integrates photovoltaic elements as part of a sustainable aesthetic that has yielded "surplus energy" units.

Since sustainable cities can only be as good as their individual pieces, Bill Dunster (b. 1960) created BedZED (Beddington Zero Emissions Development) (Fig. 20.3-11) as a pilot project in the suburbs of west London to demonstrate an optimal model for an urban block. He built the project on a brownfield site as a renewal block of five compact rows for 100 units and forty work–live atelier spaces. Nearly self-sufficient in terms of energy, the densely set rows combine good insulation, solar orientation, triple-glazed windows, a biomass-fed furnace, wind pipes for ventilation, and planted roofs with recycled rainwater. Residents can enroll in car sharing to use a dozen electric cars that are charged by photovoltaic sources in the complex's garage. All of the materials used in the construction of BedZED came from local sources no farther than 35 km (21 miles) away, reducing the embodied energy of transportation.

Such alternatives as BedZED have become competitive with market-rate housing and have been shown to cut as much as 80% of an individual's energy use. For developing countries a different model was proposed at the Barefoot College, a village in the arid region of Rajasthan, India, founded by Bunker Roy in 1971. His community, which now serves more than 125,000 and has set up branches in other parts of India, revived Gandhi's principles of economic

Figure 20.3-11 London. BedZED (Beddington Zero Emissions Development), Bill Dunster, 2001.

Figure 20.3-12 London. 30 St. Mary Axe, Norman Foster, 2001–2003.

justice, nonhierarchical lifestyles, and self-sufficiency. Members are forced to conform to a $100 per month limit on income. The community produces intermediary technologies, such as solar cells and rainwater conservation tanks, for use in rural areas that lack power and water. In 1989 the Barefoot College added a new campus for its library, workshops, and residences, constructing over 150 geodesic domes to cover structures built of local materials. As in Drop City, the village blacksmiths covered the polyhedrons with panels taken from abandoned automobile hoods. The lesson of living well with less and producing enough energy to be self-sufficient can reduce a subalternate area's dependence on outside aid.

Some argue that if advanced technology caused global warming, it will also be part of the cure for it. The higher the technology, however, the more capital-intensive it is.

Norman Foster's optimally performing structures, such as the pickle-shaped high-rise 30 St. Mary Axe in London (2001–2003) (Fig. 20.3-12), rank among the most expensive buildings per square meter ever built. That the expense may someday be amortized by the energy savings is probable, but few can afford such an investment. Foster borrowed his concept of a "bioclimatic" high-rise from Malaysian architect Ken Yeang (b. 1948), who a decade earlier had built the Menara Mesinaga Tower as a spiraling series of voids that improved passive ventilation.

Most buildings could be made more sustainable simply through correct solar orientation and better insulation. Dutch architect Ton Alberts (1927–1999) pursued an integrated approach at the NMB Bank (now ING Bank, 1987) (Fig. 20.3-13) in the Bijlmermeer suburb of Amsterdam, the first large project in Europe to attract attention for its

Protection from Chernobyl, a Fearful Beauty

Apart from the intense alterations to the planet's biosphere that have been made by the exhausts of carbon fuels, there have been two major nuclear accidents that have substantiated the theory of the Anthropocene. While considered a "clean" source of energy, nuclear power has always offered the possibility of nuclear accidents through human error, such as that at Chernobyl, Ukraine, in 1986, or natural calamities, such as the 2011 tsunami at Fukushima, Japan. The fallout from Chernobyl put most of Europe at risk of contamination and led to more than 100,000 cancer-related deaths in the Ukraine. The concrete sarcophagus improvised to contain the reactor had a thirty-year life span, which prompted forty countries to contribute to the largest single building of the age, the great vault of the NSC (New Safe Confinement), a phenomenal structure produced by Novarka, a French engineering consortium. The 150 m (492 ft) long structure with a segmental vault that spans 240 m (787 ft) was assembled at a distance and rolled on rails into its permanent position. Its pure monolithic volume, the single most necessary building for human survival during the Anthropocene, stands as a sublime object in the midst of a forbidden territory, off-limits within a 30 km (98 ft) radius.

Pripyat, Ukraine. New Safe Confinement (NSC) for Chernobyl Nuclear Power Plant, Novarka, Vinci Construction, and Bouygues, 2017.

sustainable qualities. Inspired by Rudolph Steiner, the architect created an Expressionist composition of ten sloping midrise towers that rose with battered walls to pentagonal solar collectors crowning the roofs. Their star-shaped plans connected at the bottom two levels, forming a jagged *S* shape. Each tower contained a hollow circulation core that allowed air and daylight to penetrate the different levels. The designers strategically placed in the stairways gurgling fountains using recycled rainwater, as well as light sculptures that enhance the thermal and daylighting performance. The offices in the towers followed a narrow open plan, permitting all of the desks to be within 1 m (3.3 ft) of direct daylight. The energy savings proved to be the best of any large office complex of the time, but what surprised the evaluators after the first year's use was the reduction of attrition, from 5% absences per day to 0.3%. Alberts's building

Figure 20.3-13 Amsterdam, the Netherlands. NMB Bank (now ING Bank), Ton Alberts, 1987.

Figure 20.3-14 Phoenix, Arizona. Burton Barr Central Library, Will Bruder, 1995.

made workers feel comfortable at work and better adjusted as a community.

Will Bruder (b. 1946) designed one of the most energy-efficient buildings of the late twentieth century, the Burton Barr Phoenix Central Library (1995) (Fig. 20.3-14), like a colossal breadbox, integrating active and passive solar technologies. He draped the flanks with perforated copper "saddlebags," which carry the mechanicals, offices, bathrooms, and service stairs. A diaphanous membrane protects the inner concrete walls from direct exposure to the desert sun, allowing the structure to exhale the heat gain of the building's services. The completely glazed southern elevation is protected by computer-driven fins, like gigantic venetian blinds, that open and close during the day according to the intensity of sunlight. The north displays twenty-eight vertical ribbons of twisted white Teflon fabric,

fastened to steel pegs like tacking sails to protect the building from wind and glare. The internal concrete columns that support the five-level structure terminate in tapering cones that stop short of the vaulted ceiling of the reading room. They are capped with steel nozzles that hook into a Fuller-inspired space frame supporting the roof. An oculus above each of the columns poetically illuminates the structural novelty of these posts without beams. While most libraries are labyrinthine and sepulchral, with little relation to the outdoors, the Phoenix Library feels open, offering easy access to the stacks and exhilarating vistas to the horizon.

Several European architects have brought a new level of sophistication to sustainable design in large-scale projects. In Berlin the office of Sauerbruch Hutton has perfected insulation, solar orientation, and renewable energy using pixelated elevations with alternating bands of bright colors that attempt

Figure 20.3-15 Dessau, Germany. Federal Environmental Agency, Sauerbruch Hutton, 2005.

Figure 20.3-16 Bordeaux, France. Cité du Grand Parc, retrofit of social housing, Lacaton & Vassal, 2011–2015.

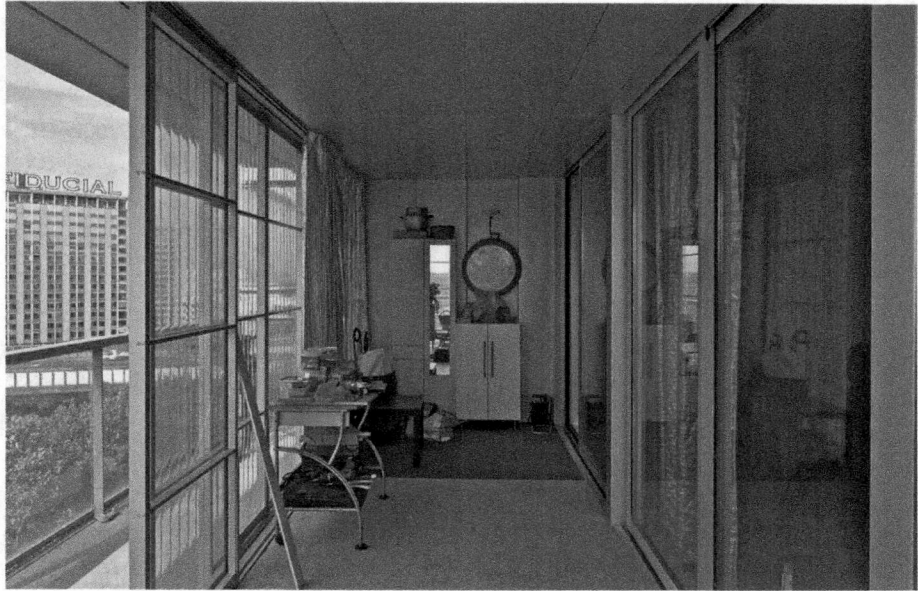

to mimic the colors of the context. Their addition of a slab tower and revision of an existing structure for GSW in Berlin in 1991 and their Federal Environmental Agency in Dessau proved that optimal sustainable buildings did not have to look primitive (Fig. 20.3-15). The French office of Lacaton & Vassal has proven that one of the most sustainable operations should be to revise existing buildings, especially large social housing projects, to improve thermal performance, aesthetics, and livability. Their retrofitting of the Tour Bois-le-Prêtre in Paris, and more recently the housing of Cité du Grand Parc in Bordeaux, transformed a typical concrete frame construction with poor insulation, wrapping the structures with 2 m (6.6 ft) wide greenhouse spaces that improved thermal comfort while offering expanded living space to residents at a cost that was a fraction of the expense of tearing down and rebuilding the structure from scratch (Fig. 20.3-16).

The call for "appropriate technology," a concept advanced in the 1970s by the economist E. F. Schumacher, referred to working within the limits that condition a project. The Australian architect Glenn Murcutt (b. 1936) has been particularly careful in his work to conserve resources and not use more technology than necessary to achieve a comfortable and sustainable environment. Like the Modernists Maxwell Fry and Jane Drew, he has frequently resorted to a double-roof solution to draw off excess heat. His Boyd Art Centre (1999) (Fig. 20.3-17) in Riversdale, on a rural site near Cambewarra, serves as a residence for seminars, with a large open hall, studios, and a dormitory structure. He anchored the project into the hill on a narrow concrete base, slipping each pair of wood-paneled bedrooms into the frame, like drawers in a dresser. The complex needs neither air-conditioning nor heating, maintaining optimal temperatures

Paper Architecture

While some architects during the 1960s willfully chose not to build, resulting in the development of "paper" architecture, the Japanese architect Shigeru Ban (b. 1957) literally used paper to construct both avant-garde luxury houses and experimental low-cost dwellings. For the "cardboard loghouses" (1995), emergency shelters produced after the earthquake in Kobe, he set cardboard tubes in foundations made from plastic beer crates, capped with an impermeable paper roof. The units were light, fireproof, moisture-proof, thermally efficient, and the price of cardboard.

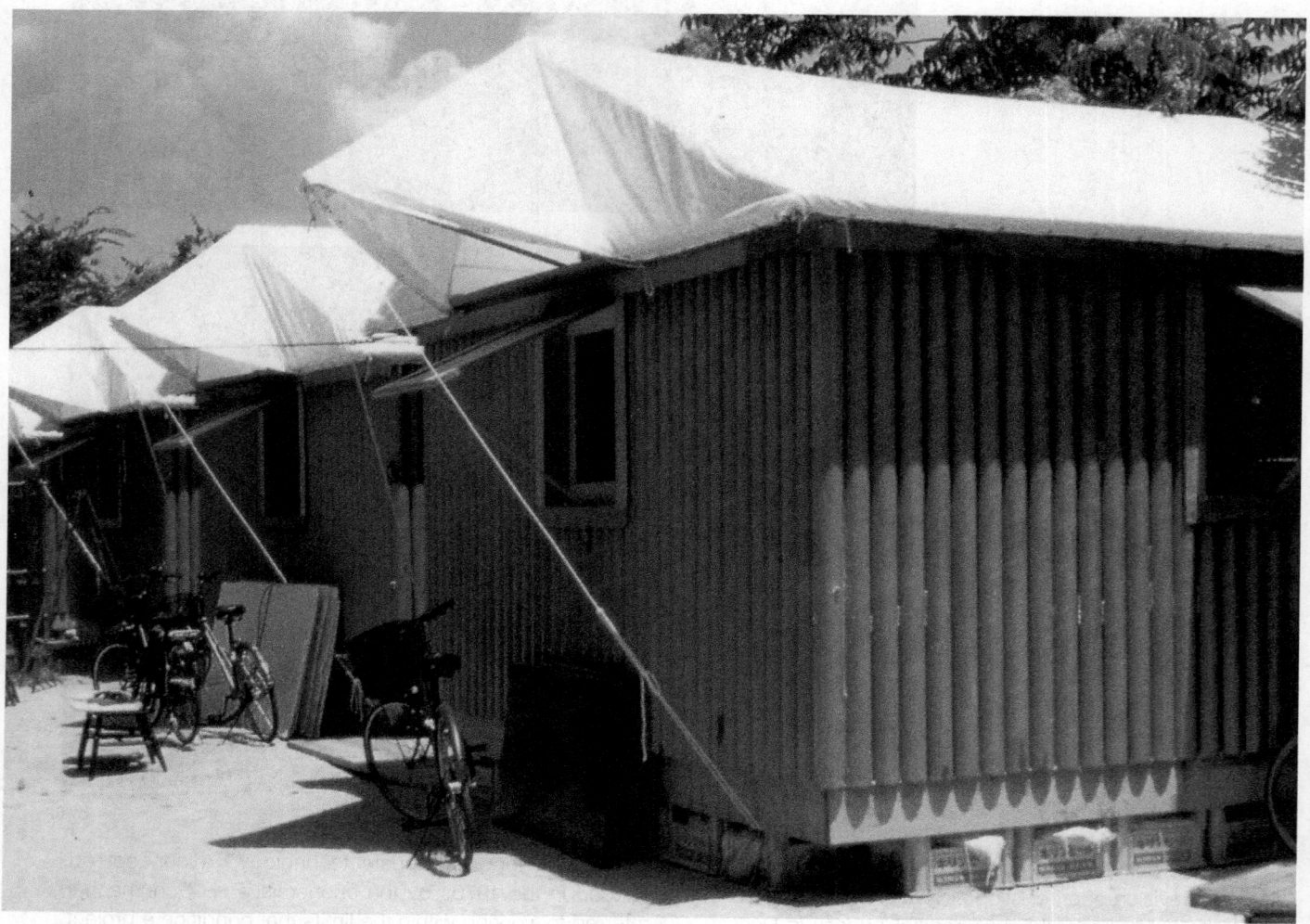

Kobe, Japan. Cardboard "loghouses," Shigeru Ban, 1995.

by adjusting the windows and shutters. Although Murcutt occasionally employs technically sophisticated features for the storage and heating of water, most of the sustainability in his work comes from common sense about orientation, construction, and patterns of dwelling.

The ecology question began with local concerns about the pollution of industrialized nations, but by now it has become a global discourse. The high-entropy patterns of development introduced by the West have created a negative legacy for developing countries. While many regions offer rays of hope for resource conservation and the respect of traditions, positive change at the global level can come only from collective and cumulative actions of the sort promoted by the Kyoto Accords and the Paris COP 21 agreement of 2015, ratified by 175 nations the following year. Models of sustainable environments need to come both from the most

Figure 20.3-17 Riversdale (near Cambewarra), Australia. Boyd Art Centre, Glenn Murcutt, 1999.

advanced economic zones and from developing situations, where people are still connected to local materials and traditional technologies. A fine alternative to the concrete boxes of globalization is the Primary School in Gando (2001) (Fig. 20.3-18a) by Diébédo Francis Kéré (b. 1965), a native of Burkina Faso who studied architecture and opened an office in Berlin before returning to his home village to build. The three rectangular volumes for the classrooms were built of mud bricks, with tall, narrow windows and adjustable louvers. A single detached roof spans the three volumes, set on a spindly space frame made from thin metal rebars that carry the curved tin hood from a small gap on the south to 2 m (7 ft) above the ceilings of the classrooms on the north. The roof induces air to pass naturally through the gap in response to the difference in temperatures between the upper tin layer and the lower brick ceiling. During the next decade Kéré continued to work with the villagers of Gando, who always participated in programming and construction, adding mud-brick structures with detached tin roofs for a second teaching volume, a secondary school, a teachers' residence, and an exquisite oval library capped with sawed-off ceramic pots inserted into the roof as skylights (Fig. 20.3-18b). Awarded the Aga Khan Prize in 2004, Kéré has spread his mixture of global technology and local materials to many other parts of West Africa.

A satisfactory answer to the ecology question can only be plural. Different places permit different possibilities. But in all cases the architectural imagination needs to assess the consequences of technology and return to origins to find new strategies for making forms and spaces that respond to the basic ecological principal of the circular economy. Architecture has always provided a second nature

Figure 20.3-18 Gando, Burkina Faso. (a) Primary School, Diébédo Francis Kéré, 2001. (b) Library, Kéré, 2012.

that has been both useful and beautiful. In the age of global warming, the utility and beauty of the built environment will depend on how well architects can replenish and enhance rather than waste what remains of nature.

Further Reading

Beatley, Timothy. *Green Urbanism: Learning from European Cities.* Washington, D.C.: Island Press, 2000.

Butti, Ken, and John Perlin. *A Golden Thread: 2500 Years of Solar Architecture and Technology.* Palo Alto, CA: Cheshire Books, 1980.

Calthorpe, Peter. *The Next American Metropolis: Ecology, Community, and the American Dream.* New York: Princeton Architectural Press, 1993.

Davis, Mike. *Planet of Slums.* London: Verso, 2006.

Fernandez Galiano, Luis. *Fire and Memory: On Architecture and Energy.* Cambridge, MA: MIT Press, 2000.

McDonough, William, and Michael Braungart. *Cradle to Cradle: Remaking the Way We Make Things.* New York: North Point Press, 2002.

↗ Visit the free website **www.oup.com/us/ingersoll** to view chapter outlines and study questions; Google Maps showing the location of key sites; links to UNESCO World Heritage Sites; and essays on topics that cross time and culture.

Glossary

abbey A Christian monastery or convent and its church. (8.3)

ablaq Arabic term for alternating bands of colored stones in Islamic masonry, derived from Byzantine *opus mixtum*. (7.1; 9.1)

acropolis (Akropolis) The upper town or elevated stronghold of an ancient Greek city, containing its chief temples. (4.2)

adobe Unbaked, sun-dried brick or building block made of a mixture of clay and straw. (1.2)

aedicule (1) A recess in a wall framed by columns supporting an entablature and pediment like a little temple front and intended as a shrine or shelter for a statue. (2) A door, window, or other opening framed by columns or pilasters and crowned with a pediment. (5.1; 6.3; 11.3)

agora The open meeting space or marketplace in an ancient Greek city. (4.2)

aisle A lateral division of a Christian church or an ancient Roman basilica running parallel to the central nave and separated from it by colonnades. (6.1)

all'antica Italian Renaissance expression signifying "in the style of the ancient Greeks and Romans." (10.1)

allée A broad avenue flanked by trees. (12.2)

altar A special table inside or in front of a temple or church for making sacrifices. (2.1)

ambulatory A processional passageway around a shrine or flanking the apse of a Christian church. (6.1)

amphitheater A round, semicircular, or oval outdoor arena surrounded by rising tiers of seats. (5.1)

andron The men's quarter in the ancient Greek house, used as the banqueting room. (4.2)

angled bastion A bastion, usually in the shape of an arrowhead, that slopes downward to resist cannon fire. (11.3)

annular vault A curving vault set in a ring-shaped pattern. (5.1)

apadana A columned audience hall in ancient Persian palaces. (4.1)

apotropaic A sculpted guardian figure placed at portals and thresholds. The neo-Assyrian figures were known as *shedus* and *lammasus*. (2.2; 3.1; 4.1)

apse A vaulted, semicircular, or semipolygonal space usually found at the sanctuary end of a Christian church. (6.1)

aqueduct An artificial channel for water, sometimes underground but often elevated on arches. (5.1)

arcade (1) A series of arches on columns or piers, either freestanding or attached to a wall. (13.2) (2) A covered walk lined with shops and offices, lit from a glazed ceiling. (16.1)

arch, true arch A curved structure, usually made of wedge-shaped stones (voussoirs), that spans an opening. (1.2; 5.1)

architecture parlante Literally, "speaking architecture," an eighteenth-century French phrase referring to works that narrate their function. (14.2)

architrave The beam that spans a pair of columns. (4.2)

ashlar masonry (1) Smooth blocks of rendered stone. (2.2) (2) Regularly placed, smooth-faced stones. (11.2)

atelier A studio for teaching art or architecture. (16.3)

atlantid Human figure used as a column-like support. (7.3)

atrium (1) The main inner court of a Roman house, with an open roof and a central basin to catch rainwater (see *impluvium*). (2) The colonnaded forecourt of a Christian church. (5.1)

attic The story above the main cornice in a classical facade. (5.1)

axis An imaginary straight line about which parts of a building or a group of buildings are arranged. (5.1)

axis mundi A monumental building marking the center of the world for Neolithic cultures. (2.1)

bailey An open court in a medieval fortification. (8.3)

baldacchino An ornamental canopy over a tomb, altar, or throne. (12.2)

balloon frame A system of light timber-frame construction in which vertical studs are nailed to horizontal supports. (16.1)

balustrade A decorative railing supported by a series of small posts or balusters. (11.3)

banco A wet-mud construction process, also called **cob**, in which balls of mud are stacked in spirals. (1.2; 9.3)

baptistery A central-plan structure, usually octagonal, for Christian baptism rites. (6.1)

barracks Modest longitudinal buildings for housing the military. (4.2; 6.1)

barrel vault A long, rounded vault. (5.1)

barrio Spanish term for a district or quarter of a town. (5.3; 13.3)

base The lowest supporting part of a column, pier, or wall. (4.2)

basilica (1) An ancient Roman meeting hall, oblong in plan, with a high central space lit by clerestory windows. (5.1) (2) The form of an early Christian church: oblong, with a high, clerestoried nave ending in an apse, flanked by two lower aisles and covered with a timber roof. (6.1)

bastide A new town in southwest France, preplanned and often laid out on an orthogonal grid. (9.2)

bastion A round, rectangular, or polygonal defensive projection of a fortress wall. (2.2)

battered wall A wall that slopes inward as it rises. (1.2)

battlement A low guarding wall or parapet with alternating depressed openings (embrasures or crenels) and solid parts (**merlons**). (8.3)

bay A regularly repeated spatial unit of a building or wall, defined by vaults, windows, orders, or other prominent vertical features. (1.2; 5.2)

bay window (or bow window) A window that projects outward from the wall. (16.2)

bazaar (**suq**) A covered market street in Islamic cities. (12.1)

belfry (**campanile**) The bell tower of a church or city hall. (9.1)

biforium A window or opening divided into two by a colonnette. (8.3)

blind window A window frame enclosing solid wall instead of glass, used to maintain the rhythm of fenestration. (8.1)

blockwork The assembly of notched logs into boxes. (1.2; 10.2)

bochka A pointed barrel-vault roof used in Russian churches. (10.2)

bosquet A cluster of trees in a formal French garden planted in quincunx patterns. (12.2)

bouleuterion An ancient Greek council hall. (4.2)

boulevard A broad city street, often with a planted strip of trees down its center or between its curb and sidewalks. (12.2)

brace frame A system of timber-frame construction using large, solid posts that extend the full height of the frame, into which horizontal members (girts) are fastened with interlocking joints (**mortise and tenon**). (1.2)

braces Horizontal or diagonal members in a timber-frame system of construction fastened with interlocking joints (**mortise and tenon**). (1.2)

bracket A projection from a vertical surface providing support under beams, cornices, balconies, and window frames. (10.1)

broken pediment A pediment with a gap at its apex. (13.3)

buttress An exterior mass, usually shaped like a thick rib or flange, that helps to support a wall. (2.1)

cairn Prehistoric mound containing passages lined with monoliths. (1.3)

caldarium The hot water room in an ancient Roman bath. (5.1)

camii A Turkish congregational mosque. (11.2)

campanile (or **belfry**) A bell tower, usually freestanding. (8.3)

cancha The typical Inca house with a large courtyard set behind a stone wall and sharing a party wall with the neighboring house. (10.3)

cantilever An overhang supported at only one end by a wall or a column. (1.2)

capital The upper element of a column or pilaster above the shaft. (4.2)

capstone A stone that fits into the top course of a masonry wall. (1.2)

caravansary An Islamic stopping place for caravans, also called a "khan." It was often a rectangular walled complex with a single large portal at one end opening onto a courtyard, with accommodations for travelers and animals along the sides of the complex and, at the end opposite the portal, a covered hall. (7.1)

cardo The principal north–south street in an ancient Roman city. (5.1)

caryatid (karyatid) A draped female figure used as a pillar. The name derives from rites performed for the goddess Artemis at the town of Karyai. (4.2)

casemate A room in a fortress wall with openings (embrasures) for the firing of weapons. (3.1)

castrum An ancient Roman walled military camp with a gridded rectangular layout. (5.1)

catacomb An underground system of passages used as a cemetery. (6.1)

Catalan vault A vault with a low pitch built with bricks set lengthwise rather than on their sides, making the vault's profile close to that of a segmental arch. (19.2)

catenary arch The paraboloid shape that a chain assumes when hung from two verticals that is then inverted for an upright arch or vault, much explored by Antoni Gaudí. (1.2)

cathedral A bishop's church, usually the principal church in a city. The word derives from *cathedra*, the bishop's throne. (6.1; 9.2)

causeway A raised road or path. (2.2)

cavea The tiered, semicircular seating area in an ancient Roman theater. (5.1)

cella The main room in a classical Greek or Roman temple, housing the cult statue. (4.2)

cenotaph Literally an "empty tomb," a monument to a person buried elsewhere. (14.2)

central plan A ground plan that is symmetrical in all directions. (6.1)

centuriation An ancient Roman grid system of land division. (15.1)

chacmol An altar made in the shape of a reclining person with the belly facing the sky, used by Aztecs and earlier Mesoamerican cultures for blood sacrifices. (10.3)

chaitya An Indian Buddhist cave temple or shrine carved out of a hillside, with a nave, side aisles, and a *stupa* in the apse. (6.3)

chamfer The groove or oblique surface made when an edge or corner is beveled or cut away, usually at a 45° angle, as in the chamfered corners of the Barcelona blocks. (16.1)

chancel The rear, usually eastern, section of a Christian church containing the choir and the principal altar. (13.1)

chapel (1) A small area within a Christian church containing an altar and used for private prayer. (6.1) (2) A room or building within a larger complex used for religious ceremonies. (3.1)

chapter house A place of assembly for the business meetings of a monastery. (8.3)

chevet A series of radiating chapels extending from the apse of a Gothic church. (8.3; 9.2)

chevron A succession of *V*-shaped decorative motifs. (1.3)

chhatri A decorative kiosk with a **dome** raised on slender columns, used mostly in northern India for sheltering statues. (12.1)

Chicago window A three-bay window used in early high-rise structures, with a broad central light flanked by two narrow, double-hung windows. (16.1)

choir The part of a church where the singers sit, either incorporated with the chancel or directly in front of it. (9.2)

church The principal Christian religious building, used in public worship, with a central apse for auditory functions, side aisles for processions, and an altar in an apse (usually located in the east). (6.1)

churrigueresque A highly ornamented Spanish or Spanish American style of the early eighteenth century, named after the architects José Benito, Joaquin, and Alberto Churriguera. (13.2)

circus (**hippodrome**) (1) An ancient Roman roofless enclosure, oblong in shape, with one straight end and tiers of seats along both sides and at the other end, which was curved. It was used for horse and chariot races and gladiatorial contests. (5.1) (2) An eighteenth-century circular or curved range of houses. (14.1)

citadel An elevated fort or stronghold. (2.3)

City Beautiful A late-nineteenth-century American city planning movement based on French academic principles of axiality, monumentality, and bilateral symmetry. (16.3)

cladding A protective layer of material added to an exterior wall. (2.1)

clapboard Overlapping horizontal boards used as a protective wall covering. (13.3)

classicism Ancient Greek and Roman architectural forms and principles or the revival of these forms in later periods. (4.2)

clerestory A window, usually in a series, disposed at an upper level, above head height. (2.2)

cloister (*claustrum*) A monastery courtyard, usually planted, enclosed by a covered ambulatory. (8.3)

cob technique Method of adobe construction, also called *banco*, in which mud balls are piled in a spiral pattern. (1.2)

coffer A square or polygonal decorative panel embossed into a ceiling or an arch. (6.1)

co-housing The voluntary collectivization of resources for a group of people sharing a residential complex. (20.1)

colonnade A row of columns supporting a beam or entablature. (3.1)

colossal order Columns or pilasters that rise more than a single story. (11.3)

colossus A statue that is much larger than life size. (4.2)

column A cylindrical, vertical support, usually tapering upward and made either in one piece (**monolithic**) or of shorter cylindrical sections, called **drums**. In classical architecture a column consists of a base, a shaft, and a capital. (1.2; 4.2)

common Public land belonging to the community at large. (13.3)

commune (1) A small administrative district, such as a city and its territory. (2) The inhabitants or government of such a district. (9.1)

compression The force within a structure that can crush or push together architectural members. (1.2)

concrete Artificial stone made of a mixture of cement, water, gravel, and sand. Reinforced concrete is embedded with steel rods, or rebars, to add tensile strength. (5.1)

corbelling Parallel masonry layers that extend in cantilever, each beyond the one below, usually to make an arch or a vault. (1.2)

Corinthian order The most attenuated and richly decorated of the three classical Greek orders. Acanthus leaves (*caucoli*) emerge from its capital and are topped by small volutes. (4.2)

cornice (1) A projecting ornamental molding along the top of a building or wall. (2) The top, projecting part of an entablature (see **order**). (10.1)

crenellation A pattern of repeated depressed openings (crenels) in a fortification wall (see **battlement**). (8.3)

crescent A concave, curving row of houses. (14.1)

crocket Bud-shaped decoration found on the roofs and pinnacles of Gothic churches. (9.2)

crossing The intersection of the nave and the transept in a Christian church. (6.1)

cross-vault The intersection of two barrel vaults. (3.1; 9.2)

crowfoot parapets Step-shaped battlements used throughout ancient Southwest Asia. (4.1)

cruck frame A wooden framing system made of matched pairs of large curved timbers (crucks) that are like slices of trees, forming a pointed arch where they meet at the top. (1.2)

crypt A room or story beneath the main floor of a church, sometimes lying underground, containing graves, relics, or chapels. (6.1)

cryptoporticus In Roman villas, a partly submerged service passageway lit with clerestories. (5.1)

cubit A unit of linear measurement, commonly eighteen inches, originally based on the length of the forearm from the elbow to the tip of the middle finger. (3.2)

cupola A small **dome**, particularly atop a roof or small tower. (6.2)

cyclopean masonry Walls made with large, irregularly shaped stones. (3.1)

diagrid The structural application of diagonal grids in tension, usually used in high-rise tubular structures. (20.2)

dike A wall or bank used to contain water. (2.1)

diwan (*divan*) (1) A Persian word indicating the executive council, which often referred to the space for assemblies, an open hypostyle hall in a Persian or Mughal palace. (12.1) (2) The Ottoman word for the council chamber, which was surrounded with low couches, leading to the name *divan* for the piece of furniture. (11.2)

dog-leg stair A stair that reaches one landing and makes a right angle turn (11.3)

dolmen A prehistoric tomb made of two upright megaliths, capped with a horizontal stone and buried under an earth mound. (1.3)

dome A curved roof usually spanning a circular or polygonal base and sometimes raised on a drum. (5.1).

domus An ancient Roman house for wealthy citizens, usually served by an atrium, or *impluvium* court, and an enclosed garden. (5.1)

donjon See **keep**. (8.3)

doorjamb The side of a door or window frame. (1.1)

Doric order The stoutest and least decorated of classical Greek columns, with a plain capital, a fluted shaft, and no base. The entablature is decorated with alternating squares filled with **triglyphs** and **metopes**. (4.2)

dormer A window that protrudes out of a pitched roof with its own pitched roof. (12.2)

double-ender A Carolingian church with apses at both east and west ends. (8.3)

dougong In Chinese architecture, a cantilevered bracket or cluster of brackets used to support a roof. (5.2; 7.2)

dromos A long, high-walled entrance to a Mycenaean tomb, or a space set aside for races in a Greek city. (3.1)

drum (1) A circular or polygonal enclosure supporting a **dome**. (9.1) (2) One of the cylindrical blocks of stone that forms a column. (4.1)

eave The overhang of a sloping roof projecting beyond a wall. (1.2; 5.2)

eclecticism The combination of elements from a variety of architectural styles, especially in late-nineteenth-century European and American architecture. (16.3)

elevation An exterior or interior vertical plane of a building, or a drawing of the same. (1.2; 3.1)

eminent domain The legal process of expropriating private property for public utility. (10.1)

enfilade The arrangement of rooms in a linear sequence, one opening to the next without a corridor. (10.1)

English garden The picturesque, irregular style of garden developed for English country houses in the seventeenth and eighteenth centuries. (14.1)

entablature The horizontal spanning element of a classical order divided into the architrave (bottom), frieze, and cornice (top). (4.2)

entasis The slight convex bulge given to a column to offset the optical illusion that it is thinner in the middle. (4.2)

esplanade A wide, open landscape foregrounding a monumental urban complex. (12.2)

estipite A pillar or pilaster carrying such extra decoration as secondary capitals, geometric panels, and scroll ornaments, used in seventeenth- and eighteenth-century Spanish and Latin American architecture. (13.2)

exedra A semicircular or rectangular recess, usually with seats or a bench and sometimes roofed. (5.1)

exoskeletal Referring to structures of support that stand outside of a building's volume. (9.2; 19.1)

ex-voto A work sponsored in thanks or anticipation of a benefice from heaven. (9.1)

falsework (or centering) Wooden scaffolds built to sustain arches and vaults during construction. (1.2; 10.1)

fastigium A window of appearances where the ruler assumes a divine semblance. (3.2; 6.1)

faubourg A suburb of a medieval French city, located outside the city's walls. (9.2)

feng shui A Chinese method of geomancy for the proper orientation of buildings. (5.2)

ferrovitreous A type of structure of the industrial age made with iron and glass for lightness and translucency. (15.3)

figure-ground A term taken from psychology and the fine arts signifying the balance of solid and void, which in maps relates to the relation of solid buildings to empty streets. (19.1)

finial An ornament that tops a pinnacle, spire, or vertical member, usually pointed and decorated with stylized foliage. (9.1)

fireproof construction A construction system with masonry load-bearing walls, interior iron columns and beams, and masonry arches to support floors used in nineteenth-century British industrial architecture. (14.3)

fluting (flutes) Shallow, vertical, concave grooves cut into a column shaft or pilaster. (4.1)

flying buttress An arch or half-arch that transfers the thrust of a vault or roof from an upper part of a wall to an external pylon. (9.2)

folly (folie) A structure, such as a tower or fake ruin, built in a garden or park to complement a view. (14.1)

fonduk A hospice for foreign traders in an Islamic city. (9.1)

forum A public civic and commercial square in ancient Roman cities, usually surrounded by colonnades and including a basilica, temple, and fountain. (5.1)

fresco A wall painting made on wet plaster with water-based colors. (3.1)

frieze (1) In a classical order, the middle horizontal division of an **entablature**, usually decorated with sculpture (4.2). (2) An elevated, horizontal decorative band on a wall. (3.1)

frigidarium A room with a cold pool in ancient Roman baths. (5.1)

functionalism A modern theory of design that promotes forms derived from use, structure, or function. (19.1)

gable The area where the wall meets the overhangs of a pitched or otherwise inclined roof. (4.2)

galerie (also **galleria, arcade, passage**) A covered walk lined with shops and offices that penetrates the interior of a city block and is lit by skylights. (15.3)

gallery (1) An upper story open on one side either to an interior space or to the exterior. In a church, the gallery runs above the side aisles and opens to the nave. (2) In secular architecture, a long room on an upper floor, often with windows along one side, used for recreation or the display of paintings. (9.1)

garbha griha The inner sanctum of a Hindu temple, usually capped with a pyramidal structure (*shikhara*). (6.3)

gargoyle A grotesque figure sculpted onto the downspouts of Gothic cathedrals. (9.2)

genius loci The god, or special spirit, of a place. (6.2)

glacis The bare, sloping embankment before a fortification. (3.1; 8.3)

glazing The surface of a structure covered in glass. (18.1)

gopura A monumental gateway into a Hindu temple. (6.3)

Greek cross A cross with four arms of equal length, often used in the plan of Byzantine churches. (6.2; 13.1)

groin vault The **cross-vault** spanning a bay of a Gothic structure. (9.2)

half-timbering A construction system in which a wooden frame is left exposed and filled in with brick or plaster. (5.1)

Hallenkirche (hall church) A church, typical of Germany, with side aisles as high, or nearly as high, as the central nave. (9.2)

hammam A Turkish or Islamic thermal bath. (11.2)

hasht bihisht In Persian architecture, the organization of a nine-square plan, literally "the eight paradises." (10.2; 12.1)

Hellenism The transmission of Greek culture at the time of Alexander the Great, resulting in very theatrical approaches to buildings and sculptures. (4.2)

henge A circle of upright stones or posts. (1.3)

herat A dead-end street in the typical Islamic city, usually reserved for kin groups or trades. (7.1)

hipped roof A pitched roof with sloping gable ends. (11.1)

hippodrome (1) An ancient Greek and Roman stadium for horse or chariot racing in the form of an oblong with one curved end. (6.1)

historiated column A freestanding monumental column, decorated with a spiral of friezes. (5.1)

historicism The use of forms from a variety of past styles, either separately or in combination, particularly during the nineteenth century. (16.3)

hospice A traveler's resort providing lodging and entertainment. (8.3)

hôtel particulier A French townhouse. (12.2)

hutong A neighborhood of courtyard houses in northern China. (11.1)

hypocaust An ancient Roman central heating system using hot air ducts in the floors of the building. (5.1)

hypostyle hall A room with a roof supported by many columns, usually in rows. (2.2; 3.1; 7.1)

I-beam A length of steel with an *I*-shaped section, used in modern steel-frame construction. (19.1)

imaret Literally "soup kitchen," a Turkish term that has come to mean the campus of a religious foundation that includes a **camii** (mosque), **madrasa** (school), **hammam** (bath), **turbe** (tomb), and charitable soup kitchen. (11.2)

impluvium A courtyard with roofs slanted toward the center so that the runoff spills into a small basin. (2.1; 5.1)

impost A horizontal projection from a wall or post on which an arch rests. (6.2)

insula An ancient Roman apartment block. (5.1)

intercolumnation The space between adjacent columns. (4.2)

interlacing arches An arcade or series of arches in which the arches intersect, creating a lattice, or basket-like, pattern. (8.2)

intrados The inner edge or circumference of an arch, as opposed to the outer edge, or extrados. (8.3)

Ionic order A Greek classical column, with a capital decorated with scrolls. (4.2)

iwan A large vaulted space open at one end used in Islamic palaces, **mosques**, and **madrasas**. (7.1; 12.1)

jalis The perforated stone screens used on the elevations of Mughal buildings. (12.1)

keep (donjon) The tower stronghold of a medieval castle, used as a residence in times of siege. (8.2)

keystone The central wedge-shaped stone (**voussoir**) in an arch, sometimes decorated. (5.1)

khanqah A Sufi convent similar to the *tekke* constructed for dervishes in Ottoman Turkey. (12.1)

kiva Male meeting hall used by the indigenous peoples of the American Southwest, usually round and below grade. (10.3)

kokoshnik A rounded gable, often with an ogive tip, similar in shape to a Russian woman's headdress. (10.2)

kufic script The rectangular, intertwined lettering used to decorate Islamic religious buildings. (7.1)

külliye (imaret) A Turkish building complex centered around a **mosque** and including educational, charitable, and medical facilities. (11.2)

kunda Sacred water tank adjacent to a Hindu temple, usually accessed by extravagant stairs. (8.1)

Lady chapel A round chapel dedicated to the Virgin Mary, usually set near the cloister of a convent. (8.3)

lantern A small, fenestrated tower on top of a roof or **dome**, admitting light to the space below. (10.1)

lingam A stout stone cylinder representing the Hindu god Shiva set in the inner cell (**garbha griha**) of a temple, usually interpreted as a phallic symbol. (6.3; 8.1)

lintel A horizontal spanning element between two uprights or posts. (1.3)

loggia A roofed porch or gallery with an open arcade or colonnade. (3.1; 10.1)

longhouse A long, rectangular structure raised on poles and usually covered with thatch that housed large extended families or communities and their animals, with the animals living in the side aisles. Found in Neolithic Europe, contemporary Southeast Asia, and pre-Contact America. (1.2)

lotus capital An Egyptian motif in which a column is capped with a closed lotus flower. (2.2) *lukovitsa* The bulbous, onion-shaped **dome** used as decoration atop Russian Orthodox churches. (10.2)

lunette A semicircular window or wall panel framed by an arch or vault. (15.3)

machicolation The arched cantilevers beneath the parapet of a defensive structure, with openings, or "murder holes," through which defenders could shoot or toss boiling oil on attackers. (9.1)

madrasa An Islamic theological or law school. (8.2)

maksura The screened-off area near the *mihrab* **niche** for the ruling elite in a royal **mosque**. (7.1)

malqaf A flue, or wind-catcher, in an Islamic residence that displaces hot air with cool air. (9.1)

Mamluk The slave-rulers of thirteenth- and fourteenth-century Cairo. (9.1)

mandala A magic diagram of the cosmos made from overlaid geometric patterns, used throughout India as the basis for the plan of monumental religious structures. (8.1)

manor A large country estate, usually with a grand patron's house and spaces for freehold tenants. (14.1)

mansard roof A roof with a steep lower slope and a flatter upper slope on all four sides. Also called a gambrel roof in Great Britain. (12.2)

martyrium A building (usually with a central plan) marking a holy site for Christians, such as places in the stories of Jesus and the apostles or where martyrs were sacrificed. (6.2)

mashrabiyya A perforated screen set over windows in traditional Islamic houses to protect the interior from harsh light and shield the women from public view. (9.1)

masjid (or *jami*) The congregational **mosque** in a Persian city. (12.1)

masonry Stonework or brickwork. (1.2)

mass The effect of bulk, density, and weight of matter in space. (2.2)

mastaba An Arabic word for "bench," signifying the ancient Egyptian flat-topped, rectangular tombs with sloping (battered) sides. (2.2)

mausoleum A monumental tomb deriving its name from the grand tomb of the tyrant Mausolus of Halicarnassus. (4.2)

maydan (*meydan*) A large open space used for public ceremonies in large Islamic cities. (7.1; 12.1)

megalith A huge, irregular stone. (1.3; 2.2)

megaron The principal hall of an Anatolian, Cretan, or Mycenaean palace or house, rectangular in plan, with a circular central hearth and a front porch formed by the prolongation of the side walls. A hairpin megaron is *U*-shaped, with the curved end walled off to make a back room. (3.1; 4.2)

megastructure A massive complex of buildings with a unitary style and a coordinated program of diverse functions, usually raised above grade on a plinth. (19.1)

menhir A prehistoric monument in the form of a large, upright stone. (1.3)

merlon A protruding part of a defensive parapet at the top of a fortified wall. (8.3)

metope The square space, often decorated with sculpture, between the **triglyphs** in a Doric frieze. (4.2)

mihrab A **niche** in the *qibla* wall of a Muslim religious building indicating the direction toward Mecca. (7.1)

minaret A tall, slender tower at a mosque, from which the faithful are called to prayer by the crier, or *muezzin*. (7.1; 11.2)

minbar The pulpit in a **mosque**. (7.1)

mithraeum An underground sanctuary used for the ceremonies of the mystery cult centered around the mythical Persian figure of Mithra. (6.1)

moat A wide protective ditch surrounding a medieval town or fortress, sometimes filled with water. (8.1)

module A unit of measurement to which parts of a building are related by simple ratios. In classical architecture, the module is usually the diameter of a column. (4.2)

monastery The enclosure for a religious order living apart from society. (8.3)

monolithic Made from a single stone. (1.3)

mortar A binding substance, such as cement or lime, used to hold rows of masonry together. (2.1)

mortise and tenon A wood-joining method in which a projecting tongue (tenon) of one member is fitted into a slot (mortise) of corresponding shape in another member. (1.2)

mosaic Surface decoration formed by small cubes of glass or stone (*tesserae*) set in mortar or plaster. (6.2)

mosque The Islamic prayer hall. (7.1)

motte A medieval fortification consisting of a conical earth mound surrounded by a ditch, topped with a wooden wall and tower, and set in an open court, or bailey. (8.3)

mudéjar The use of Islamic motifs in Spain after the Christian conquest of 1492. (8.2)

mullion An upright that divides windows or other openings. (3.2; 19.1)

muqarnas Honeycomb, or stalactite, decoration of a vault or overhang, usually made with plaster as a succession of small **niches**. (8.2)

narthex The transverse vestibule of an early Christian church. (6.1)

nave The taller central space in either an ancient Roman basilica or a Christian church lit by clerestories and flanked by aisles. (6.1)

necropolis Literally, a "city of the dead," a large, ancient burial ground. (7.2)

niche A scooped-out recess in a wall. (10.1)

obelisk A tall, square shaft, usually made of one piece of stone, that tapers upward and ends in a pyramidal tip. (2.2)

oculus A round window, usually at the apex of a **dome**. (1.2; 5.1)

ogive A pointed arch inflected at its apex with a darted shape. (9.1)

oikos An ancient Greek house, often divided into male and female areas. (4.2)

onion dome (*lukovitsa*) A bulbous-shaped dome found usually in either Islamic tombs or Russian Orthodox churches. (10.2)

orchestra In an ancient Greek or Roman theater, the circular or semicircular space between the auditorium and the stage building. (4.2)

order A classical column and entablature. The ancient Greeks developed the Doric, Ionic, and Corinthian orders, and the Romans, the Tuscan and Composite orders. (4.2)

oriole An extruded bay, usually on a street facade, serving as a site for a special window. (15.2)

orthostats Monolithic stone panels used to protect the interior walls in Neolithic monuments. (1.3; 3.1)

pagoda A multistoried Chinese or Japanese prayer tower with elaborately projecting roofs at each story. (7.2)

palace (1) The ruler's residence, deriving from the imperial residence on the Palatine Hill in Rome. (5.1) (2) A later term for the residence of the governor, the bishop, and finally the city hall. During the fourteenth century wealthy citizens appropriated the term for their residences in Italy. (9.1)

palaestra An ancient Greek or Roman building for athletic training. (5.1)

palatine chapel A chapel built into a palace, reserved for the royal court. (6.2)

palazzo The late medieval/Renaissance residence of a wealthy Italian family, built as a large block with an interior courtyard and sometimes an enclosed garden. (10.1)

palisade A series of wooden posts with pointed tops set in the ground vertically as a fence or fortification. (5.1)

Panopticon A cylindrical building with radiating outer cells that can be observed from a central point. (14.3)

parallax A change in the perception of a space or object due to different points of view. (4.2)

parallelepiped A rectangular box-shaped figure with parallel walls that meet at right angles. (2.1)

parametrics A design method based on algorithmic applications used to coordinate parameters and rules, sometimes leading to surprising self-generated formal results. (19.2)

parapet A low guarding wall at the top of a building. (3.3)

parti In the French Beaux-Arts system, the basic design layout for a building or group of buildings. (16.3)

party wall A shared wall on the dividing line between two properties or houses. (10.3)

parvis The open plaza serving a major church. (16.1)

passage tomb Prehistoric mounded tomb with an entry corridor made from megaliths. (1.3)

pastas A semienclosed space in front of the interior rooms of an ancient Greek house. (4.2)

patio Inner court of Spanish palaces, usually paved and surrounded by arcades. (5.3)

pedestal A support for a column, statue, or urn. (6.3; 10.1)

pediment (1) The triangular **gable** end of an ancient Greek or Roman temple. (4.2) (2) The crowning feature over a door or window that is sometimes curved, based on a segmental arch. (11.3)

pendentive A curving triangular surface or **spandrel** that makes the transition from the corners of a square or polygonal room to a circular **dome** or its **drum**. (6.2)

penthouse The top-story luxury apartment in a tall building. (18.2)

peripteral Surrounded on all sides by a single row of columns. (4.2)

peristyle A roofed, columned porch or colonnade surrounding a building or courtyard. (4.2)

per strigas An ancient Greek system of orthogonal city planning "by bands." The parallel east–west avenues created bands dissected by one or more north–south avenues. (4.2)

photovoltaic panel An energy-producing screen made of silicone cells that imitate the natural process of photosynthesis. (20.3)

piano nobile The main floor of an Italian palace, usually one story above the ground floor. (11.3)

piazza An Italian public square. (9.1)

picturesque An aesthetic theory seeking inspiration in nature and characterized by irregularity, the exotic, and the sublime. (14.1)

pier A solid masonry support, often rectangular or square in plan. (2.2)

pilaster A shallow, flattened rectangular column or pier attached to a wall and often modeled on an order. (10.1)

pilotis The French term, popularized by Le Corbusier, for the wooden piles of stilt houses raised over land or water, leaving the grade level open. (18.2)

pisé (or *terre pisé*) Rammed earth or clay used as a building material. (1.2)

pishtaq The entry facade to Persian monumental religious complexes framing an *iwan* with slender minarets. (12.1)

place A French public square. (12.2)

planar The quality of a flat surface. (2.2)

plasticity The molded quality of thick walls, using elements that protrude or recede to create deep shadows. (11.3)

Plattenbau Prefabricated, panel-constructed public housing produced in the Eastern Bloc countries. (19.1)

plaza Spanish word for an open public space in a city. (12.1)

poché French expression describing the filling of a wall. (1.3; 15.1)

podium A raised platform or base. (4.2)

point-loaded structure A frame construction in which bearing is concentrated on the columns. (5.2)

polis Greek word for a city and its territory. (4.2)

polychromy Architectural decoration using a variety of colors or varicolored materials. (2.1)

porch A covered entranceway to a building raised on slender columns. (3.1)

porphyry Purple igneous stone associated with royalty, often coming from Egypt. (5.1)

portal A monumental entranceway to a building or courtyard. (8.3)

portcullis A massive, movable defensive grating in a fortified gateway. (2.2)

portico (1) A covered entranceway or porch with columns on one or more sides. (10.1) (2) A continuous arcade. (11.2)

post and beam (or **post and lintel**) A construction system using vertical supports (posts) spanned by horizontal beams (also called lintels). (1.2)

prakaram A walled enclosure in a Hindu temple compound, like a *temenos*. (6.3; 8.1)

program A building's uses or activities. (2.2; 20.2)

propylaia A monumental entranceway to a sacred enclosure. (4.2)

propylon An ancient Egyptian freestanding monumental gateway before the pylon of a temple. (6.1)

prytaneion The public hall in an ancient Greek city that housed the sacred hearth and where official and public guests were entertained. (4.2)

pylon (1) The monumental truncated pyramidal towers flanking an entrance to an ancient Egyptian temple. (2) Sometimes refers to a substantial supporting pillar. (3.1)

pyramid A massive memorial or temple rising from a square or rectangular base to an elevated altar or a point, with either a succession of steps or a smooth incline. (2.2)

qibla The prescribed Muslim alignment to Mecca to which all **mosques** and tombs are oriented. (7.1)

quatrefoil A four-lobe motif often used in Gothic window decoration. (9.1)

quincunx (1) A pattern used by gardeners with five points arranged four on the edges of a square and one in the center. (2) The composition of a church where four domes are placed symmetrically around a larger central dome. (6.2)

quoin Rusticated stone placed on the corners of a building. (11.3)

radiating chapels (**chevet**) A series of chapels that extend from the curve of an ambulatory or apse. (9.2)

rampart A fortified wall. (2.2)

range The long arm of a building complex. (12.2)

ravelin A freestanding *V*-shaped bastion, placed as an advance guard between the principle and the moat. (12.2)

rayonnant Late Gothic style in which structures were made of increasingly thin, branching members (9.2)

redented A plan based on jogging lines like a sawtooth. (8.1)

refectory The eating hall in a religious or secular institution. (8.3)

refinements Distortions built into Greek temples to compensate for the curvatures of visual perception. (4.2)

reinforced concrete Concrete strengthened with a web of iron rebars. (17.1)

relief Carved or embossed decoration added to an architectural surface (4.2)

rendering The smoothing or elaboration of the surface of a wall, through either carving or plastering. (4.2)

retable A painted or carved altarpiece standing at the back of an altar. (13.2)

reveal The depth of a side of a doorway or window opening. (20.2)

reverse curve An *S*-shaped scroll motif. (10.1)

revetment A cladding, or **veneer**, of stone, **terra-cotta**, metal, wood, plaster, or other material. (1.3)

revival The use of older styles or forms in new architecture. (10.1; 15.2)

rhythmic trabeation The alternation of facade elements, such as pilasters and arches. (11.3)

riad A symmetrical patio surrounded by four *iwans*, found at the center of old Moroccan houses. (8.2)

rib A narrow, projecting band on a ceiling or vault, usually structural but sometimes merely decorative, enforcing the lines of structure. (9.2)

ribbed vault In Gothic cathedrals, the articulation of **groin vaults**. (9.2)

rondel (roundel) A round panel or hollow placed to relieve or decorate a spandrel between arches (9.1)

rood screen The screen, often elaborately carved, that separates the **nave** from the **chancel** in a Christian church. (15.2)

roofcomb A vertical addition that crowns a roof, making it appear higher; such features were very common in Mayan temples. (7.3)

rotunda A round hall or building, usually topped with a **dome**. (11.3)

roundel See **rondel**.

rustication The separation of regular masonry blocks by deeply cut, often wedge-shaped (**chamfered**) grooves. (10.1)

sack wall A wall made with rows of stones inside and outside filled with rubble in between. (1.2)

sacristy A room in a Christian church where altar vessels and robes are stored. (10.1)

sahn The open courtyard of an Islamic building. (7.1)

sanctuary A place of refuge from hostile forces. (1.1)

sash window A window, usually in two parts, that is opened by sliding one part in the vertical plane. (16.1)

saucer dome A low dome. (15.1)

scenae frons In an ancient Roman theater, the decorated backdrop of a stage, usually articulated with three doors and three stories of columned structures. (5.1)

section A drawing of a vertical slice through a building. (20.2)

segmental arch An arch based on a segment of a true arch, appearing flatter than such. (7.2; 10.1)

semidome A half-dome, such as the covering of an apse. (6.1)

serdab In ancient Egyptian tombs, the closed chamber for the statue of the deceased. (2.2)

serliana A central arch flanked by lower trabeated openings like a triumphal arch, sometimes called a palladian window. (11.3)

sgraffito Decoration made by scraping away one of two layers of differently colored plaster. (18.2)

shaft The main vertical part of a column, between the base and the **capital**. (4.2)

shakkei (borrowed landscape) Japanese design of gardens that incorporates natural features from outside the yard. (12.3)

sharawaggi William Temple's pseudo-Chinese term to describe planned irregularity in a garden or town design, referring to the irregularity of Chinese gardens. (14.1)

shear stress A force that occurs parallel to a plain, pulling it in several directions. (1.1)

shikhara A pyramidal tower built over the sanctuary (*garbha griha*) of a Hindu temple. (6.3; 8.1)

shoin The palace type built in Japan during the Edo period on an asymmetrical layout, like a flock of geese. (12.3)

shoji In Japanese traditional buildings, a sliding wall or screen made of translucent paper. (12.3)

siheyuan A Chinese dwelling with several individual pavilions set around an open court. (5.2)

silo A well-sealed structure, usually without windows, for storing grain. (9.3)

space frame A system of lightweight trusses used instead of beams to cover large interiors without the need for vertical supports. (19.2)

spandrel The area between two adjacent arches. (6.2)

spolia A fragment from another time or culture incorporated into a facade. (6.1)

sprawl The informal expansion of urban edges influenced by the capacity of automobiles to quickly move in all directions. (19.1; 20.2)

spur wall A short wall that projects at a right angle from a main wall. (2.1)

square (piazza, *place***, plaza)** An open area in a city, usually surrounded by buildings, and paved or landscaped. (12.1)

squinch A small arch or a series of gradually wider and increasingly projecting concentric arches across the interior corners of a square or polygonal room, forming a transition from the room shape to a circular **dome** or **drum** above. (8.2)

stela An upright stone slab marking a grave. (2.2)

stoa A long, roofed portico with columns along the front and a wall at the back, used for public life in ancient Greece. (4.2)

string course A projecting horizontal band across an exterior wall of a building. (11.3)

strut A sloping roof beam at right angles to a pitched-roof surface that joins a rafter to a collar beam. (6.3)

stucco An exterior plaster building finish. (2.2; 4.2)

stupa A Buddhist memorial mound that enshrines relics or marks a sacred site. (4.3)

stylobate The top step of a temple platform. (4.2)

suq (*bazaar*) A covered market street in Islamic cities. (8.2)

suspension bridge A bridge that uses two pylons, from the top of which are hung cables from which smaller vertical cables reach down to support the deck. (15.3)

sustainable design An approach to design, planning, and construction that eliminates waste both in the production and in the use of a building and lowers the dependence on carbon fuels. (20.3)

switchback stair A stair that ascends to a landing and turns 180° to meet the next level (4.1)

synagogue A Jewish hall for worship. (6.2; 10.2)

taberna An ancient Roman shop or booth. (5.1)

tablero In Meso-American architecture, a rectangular framed panel cantilevered over a sloping wall. (5.3)

tablinum The owner's office in an ancient Roman *domus*, which would have been oriented with one side looking toward the central atrium. (5.1)

tabula rasa An ancient term signifying the erasure of wax tablets, which when applied to cities indicates the wiping away of all previous constructions. (16.1)

talud-tablero An inclined plane supporting a cantilevered box used on the facades of ancient Mexican buildings. (5.3)

tatami A straw floor mat, usually 1 × 2 m (3.3 × 6.7 ft), that provides standard proportions in Japanese architecture. (12.3)

temenos A sacred enclosure built to separate the ancient temple from the rest of the city. (2.1)

temple front A building facade or porch, with columns and a pediment, that resembles an end of a classical temple. (15.1)

tenement A densely arranged apartment building, usually for lower-class tenants. (16.2)

tenshu A Japanese castle built in the sixteenth and seventeenth centuries. (12.3)

tension The force tending to bend, stretch, or pull apart an architectural member. (1.2)

tepidarium The moderately warm room in ancient Roman baths. (5.1)

terrace (1) A level embankment top, roof, or raised platform adjoining a building, often paved or landscaped for leisure use. (2.1) (2) A series of attached row houses with rear gardens set at a lower level than the street. (16.2)

terra-cotta Hard, molded, and fired clay used for ornamental wall covering or roof or floor tiles. (5.1)

thermae An ancient Roman bath complex. (5.1)

thermal window A rounded arch window with three divisions, used in ancient Roman baths to bring clerestory light into vault rooms. (11.3)

tholos (1) A round, corbel-vaulted Mycenaean tomb. (3.1) (2) Any round ancient Greek building. (4.2)

thrust Outward or lateral stress on a structure. (6.2)

tipi Nomadic structure used by Native Americans west of the Mississippi River, built with tall poles set leaning toward the center and covered with hides or canvas. (10.3)

tokonoma A raised, decorated alcove in the main hall of a Japanese palace. (12.3)

torana Decorated entrance gate to a Buddhist shrine. (4.3)

trabeation The horizontal span between two upright planes or columns. (1.3)

tracery A pattern of curvilinear, perforated ornament within the upper part of a medieval window or screen. (9.2)

transept The transverse arms of a cross-shaped church, crossing the main axis at a right angle. (6.1)

transom A horizontal ledge at the top of a door or a window. (1.3; 2.2)

travertine A type of pock-marked limestone. (5.1)

trefoil A three-lobed, cloverleaf pattern commonly used in Gothic windows. (9.1)

tribune (1) The apse of a church. (8.3) (2) The gallery in a church. (9.2)

triclinium Roman dining room lined on three sides with couches. (5.1)

triforium (1) A medieval window divided into three by two colonnettes. (2) In a medieval Christian church, a shallow arcaded passageway above the nave arcade and below the clerestory, each bay having three arches. (9.1)

triglyph In a Doric frieze, a panel with three vertical grooves set between the **metopes**. (4.2)

trilithon Two upright monoliths supporting a **lintel** stone, similar to a **dolmen**. (1.3)

triumphal arch A decorated Roman gateway, usually free-standing, with one or three arched openings celebrating the return of a victorious general. (5.1)

truss A horizontal spanning member made from a web of thin braces, usually arranged as triangles, achieving maximum strength while eliminating **mass**. (15.3)

tufa A porous, gray, volcanic building stone. (5.1)

tumulus An earth or stone mound over a grave. (1.3)

turbe An Ottoman tomb. (11.2)

typology (1) Building **type** that serves specific functions, such as a temple, school, hospital, or prison. (6.1) (2) **Type** of formal volumes, such as domes, cubes, parallelepipeds, or bars. (15.1)

vault An arched ceiling or roof. (1.2)

veneer An applied decorative surface. (3.1)

vestibule An anteroom to a larger hall. (2.1)

viaduct An aerial roadway or waterway carried on a series of arches. (8.3)

Vierendeel truss A spanning member made with square, rather than triangular, braces. (19.3)

vihara An Indian Buddhist monastery. (4.3)

villa A country house used as a getaway for urban elites and usually (but not always) the seat of a working farm. (5.1; 11.3)

volume The amount of space occupied by a three-dimensional object. (2.2)

volute A spiral or scroll. (4.2)

voussoir A wedge-shaped block that is one of the units in an arch or vault. (1.2)

wabi-sabi The taste for rustic simplicity applied to the design of Japanese teahouses. (12.3)

wattle and daub A construction system using woven branches and twigs plastered over with mud as filling between the larger members of a wooden frame. (1.2)

westwork (*westwerk*) The **narthex**, chapels, and twin towers set at the west entrance of Carolingian churches. (8.3)

wheel window (*roue*) The central round window on the west facade of a cathedral (often called the "rose" but usually depicting a wheel). (9.2)

wigwam Nomadic hut built by Native Americans in the central states region of the present-day United States, built with bent branches like a **dome**, and covered with hides and cloth. (1.2)

window A wall opening usually admitting light and air. (2.1)

yurt A nomadic dwelling used in the Central Asian steppes composed of a cylindrical base made from a trellis of intersecting poles, a roof of radiating poles attached to a tension ring, and a covering of felt cloth and hides. (1.2)

ziggurat A Mesopotamian temple-tower in the form of a staged pyramid. (2.1)

zoning The legal restrictions determining specific uses, such as commercial, industrial, or residential, for set zones of a city. (18.1)

Credits

All illustrations are by Nicola Jannucci, unless otherwise stated. All photos are by Richard J. Ingersoll, unless otherwise stated.

Chapter 1. **1.1-1**, © Stephen Harby; **1.1-2a**, Fabrizio Cigana; **1.1-4**, Sisse Brimberg/National Geographic Stock; **1.1-7b**, Teomancimit; Creative Commons Attribution-Share Alike 3.0 Unported license; **1.1-9a**, Thomas Sagory/www.du-ciel.com; **1.2-1**, © Luis Devin–www.pgymies.org; **1.2-2**, C. H. Grabill, Photo; Library of Congress, Prints and Photographs Division; **1.2-4a**, Qiong Mo; **1.2-5**, Stefano Bertocci; **1.2-7**, © SF photo/iStockphoto; **1.2-8b**, Wknight94; Creative Commons Attribution-Share Alike 3.0 Unported license; **1.2-9**, Gary Rollefson; **1.3-2**, Georg Gerster, Zumikon/Switzerland; **1.3-5a**, Fabrizio Nevola; **1.3-5b**, Fabrizio Nevola; **1.3-6a**, Fabrizio Nevola; **1.3-7**, Herschel Parnes; **1.3-9a**, Georg Gerster, Zumikon/Switzerland; **1.3-9b**, rnl/Shutterstock.com.

Chapter 2. **2.1-7**, Georg Gerster, Zumikon/Switzerland; **2.1-12**, World History Archive/Alamy Stock Photo; **2.2-3a**, © Stephen Harby; **2.2-4**, © Stephen Harby; **2.2-5a**, Yann Arthus-Bertrand/Getty Images; **2.2-6a**, © Stephen Harby; **2.3-1b**, Copyright J.M. Kenoyer/Harappa.com, Courtesy Dept. of Archaeology and Museums, Govt. of Pakistan; **2.3-2**, Copyright J.M. Kenoyer/Harappa.com, Courtesy Dept. of Archaeology and Museums, Govt. of Pakistan; **2.3-3**, Mike Goldwater/Alamy. **Text-box images:** "The Millennial Tell," p. 37, Georg Gerster; "A Map of Ancient Nippur's Territory," p. 48, Paul Fearn/Alamy Stock Photo; "The Sphinx," p. 61, © Stephen Harby.

Chapter 3. **3.1-4a**, Alick M. McLean; **3.1-4b**, Stefano Bertocchi; **3.1-5**, Scala/Art Resource, NY; **3.1-6**, Richard Ishida; **3.1-7**, Alick M. McLean; **3.1-8**, Stephanie Kaplan; **3.1-9**, Alick M. McLean; **3.1-11a**, Gerog Gerster, Zumikon/Switzerland; **3.1-11b**, Alick M. McLean; **3.1-12**, Sarah Dotson; **3.1-13a**, German Archaeological Institute, Bogazkoy-Hattusa Archive; **3.1-13b**, Sebastiano Brandolini; **3.1-14**, German Archaeological Institute, Bogazkoy-Hattusa Archive; **3.1-15**, German Archaeological Institute, Bogazkoy-Hattusa Archive; **3.1-17a**, Photo: Klaus-Peter Simon; Creative Commons Attribution 3.0 Unported license; **3.1-17b**, Creative Commons Attribution 3.0 Unported license; **3.2-3**, Dainel Toner Photos; **3.2-4**, Georg Gerster, Zumikon/Switzerland; **3.2-5**, bpk, Berlin/Aegyptisches Museum, Saatliche Museen, Berlin, Germany/Art Resource, NY; **3.2-6**, © Stephen Harby; **3.2-10**, Egyptian Museum of Berlin/Creative Commons Attribution-Share Alike 3.0 Unported license; **3.3-2b**, © Stephen Harby. **Text-box image:** "The Rock-Cut Temples at Abu Simbel," p. 99, © Stephen Harby.

Chapter 4. **4.1-6**, New Babylon. Model of the Entemanki tower, 570 BCE, inspired by Ur-Nammu's ziggurat at Ur. Pergamon Museum, Berlin; **4.1-7**, © red_moon_rise/iStockPhoto; **4.1-8**, Truth Seeker/Creative Commons Attribution-Share Alike 3.0 Unported license; **4.1-9**, Georg Gerster, Zumikon/Switzerland; **4.1-10**, Diego Delso, delso.photo, License CC-BY-SA; **4.1-11**, Carlo Pasquini; **4.2-6**, Wolfram Hoepfner; **4.2-10a**, Sebastiano Brandolini; **4.2-14b**, Georg Gerster, Zumikon/Switzerland; **4.2-15**, Peter Connolly; **4.2-18**, Peter Connolly; **4.2-23**, Lawrence Davis; **4.3-2a**, © Stephen Harby; **4.3-2b**, Borromeo/Art Resource, NY; **4.3-4**, © Stephen Harby; **4.3-5**, © Stephen Harby. **Text-box images:** "Rock-Cut Achaemenid Tombs and Monolithic Masonry," p. 117, Design Pics Inc/Alamy Stock Photo License; "The Greek Theater," p. 121, Alick M. McLean; "Pan-Hellenic Cult Sites of Olympia and Delphi," p. 127, (a), Alick M. McLean; "Buddhism and *Dharma*," p. 147, (a) and (b), © Stephen Harby.

Chapter 5. **5.1-13**, Massimo Carmassi; **5.1-14**, Massimo Carmassi; **5.1-20**, Capitol and Forum/Rome/Connoly/akg-images; **5.1-21**, Massimo Carmassi; **5.1-24**, Shutterstock/Mirek Hejnicki; **5.1-29b**, Massimo Carmassi; **5.1-30**, Massimo Carmassi; **5.1-31a**, Sergey Kelin/Shutterstock; **5.1-31b**, Art Collection 2/ Alamy Stock Photo; **5.2-1**, Ted Chang; **5.2-4a**, Ted Chang; **5.2-8**, Ted Chang; **5.3-2**, Maunus·X·/Creative Commons Attribution-Share Alike 3.0 Unported, 2.5 Generic, 2.0 Generic and 1.0 Generic license; **5.3-4a**, Georg Gerster, Zumikon/Switzerland; **5.3-4b**, Georg Gerster, Zumikon/Switzerland; **5.3-7**, Photo by Michele Pasquini; **5.3-8**, Photo by Michele Pasquini. **Text-box image:** "Vitruvius and Roman Architectural Theory," p. 154, © Vaara/iStockPhoto.

Chapter 6. **6.1-1**, Alick M. McLean; **6.1-2**, Massimo Carmassi; **6.1-8**, Alick M. McLean; **6.1-12**, Sebastiano Brandolini; **6.2-2**, Alick M. McLean; **6.2-7**, Sarah Dotson; **6.2-12**, Alick M. McLean; **6.3-1a**, Ted Chang; **6.3-2**, © Stephen Harby; **6.3-3**, © Stephen Harby; **6.3-4**, © Stephen Harby; **6.3-5**, © Stephen Harby; **6.3-6**, © Stephen Harby; **6.3-7a**, © Stephen Harby. **Text-box images:** "The Clandestine Church," p. 201, Vanni/Art Resource, NY; "Byzantine Capitals," p. 214, Alick M. McLean; "Byzantine Revisionism," p. 218, Alick M. McLean; "The Sex of the Hindu Temple," p. 224, (a), © Stephen Harby; "Buddha Leaves India," p. 229, robertharding/Alamy Stock Photo.

Chapter 7. **7.1-2**, Muhammad Mahdi Karim; edited by jjron; GNU Free Documentation License, Version 1.2; **7.1-4a**, Georg Gerster, Zumikon/Switzerland; **7.1-6**, Sebastiano Brandolini; **7.1-7**, Sebastiano Brandolini; **7.1-11a**, Georg Gerster, Zumikon/Switzerland; **7.1-11b**, Georg Gerster, Zumikon/Switzerland; **7.1-12**, Conrad Thake; **7.1-13**, © Stephen Harby; **7.2-1**, © View Stock/Alamy; **7.2-3**, Stefano Bertocci; **7.2-4**, Ted Chang; **7.2-5**, Ted Chang; **7.2-6**, Kenneth Dedeu/Shutterstock; **7.2-7**, Roberto d'Alessandria; **7.2-9**, Photo by Michele Pasquini; **7.3-3**, © Stephen Harby; **7.3-4**, Ted Chang; **7.3-5**, © Stephen Harby; **7.3-6a**, Stefano Bertocci; **7.3-6b**, Peter Andersen; **7.3-7**, Stefano Bertocci; **7.3-8**, tato grasso; **7.3-10a**, Daniel Toner Photos; **7.3-11**, Daniel Toner Photos; **7.3-12**, Daniel Toner Photos; **7.3-13**, Daniel Toner Photos. **Text-box images:** "The Islamic Horseshoe-Shaped Arch," p. 240, Sebastiano Brandolini; "*Dougong*: Tang Brackets," p. 245, Ted Chang; "The Shrines of Japanese Shintoism: Ise and Izumo," p. 249, (b), The Asahi Shimbun/Contributor.

Chapter 8. **8.1-2**, Georg Gerster, Zumikon/Switzerland; **8.1-3**, Ted Chang; **8.1-4**, Georg Gerster, Zumikon/Switzerland; **8.1-6a**, EC23T3; **8.1-7a**, Georg Gerster, Zumikon/Switzerland; **8.1-9a**, © Stephen Harby; **8.1-10**, Giacco Aurigi; **8.1-11**, © Stephen Harby; **8.1-12a**, © Stephen Harby; **8.1-12b**, Ted Chang; **8.2-2**, Toni Castillo/Getty; **8.2-7**, Dzarzycka/iStockphoto; **8.2-12**, Giacco Aurigi; **8.2-16**, Goerge Gerster; **8.3-2**, Alick M. McLean; **8.3-3**, Aeggy/ Creative Commons Attribution 3.0 Unported license; **8.3-4**, Alick M. McLean; **8.3-6**, CuboImages srl/ Alamy; **8.3-8**, Sebastiano Brandolini; **8.3-11**, Clark; **8.3-12**, Clark; **8.3-17**, Daniel Toner; **8.3-19**, Sebastiano Brandolini; **8.3-20**, Alick M. McLean; **8.3-21a**, Alick M. McLean.

Chapter 9. **9.1-7**, Alick M. McLean; **9.1-8a**, Alick M. McLean; **9.1-8b**, Alick M. McLean; **9.1-11**, Sebastiano Brandolini; **9.1-12**, Sebastiano Brandolini; **9.1-13**, Sebastiano Brandolini; **9.1-14a**, © Stephen Harby; **9.1-14b**, © Stephen Harby; **9.1-15**, Erich Lessing/Art Resource, NY; **9.1-21**, Alick M. McLean; **9.1-22**, Alick M. McLean; **9.1-24**, Jay Powell; **9.1-27**, Erich Lessing/Art Resource, NY; **9.2-10a**, Christophe Girot; **9.2-4**, © KIK-IRPA, Brussels; **9.2-7**, Ideal reconstruction of Castel San Giovanni, end of 14th century, Museo Delle Terre Nuove, San Giovanni Valdarno; **9.2-13a**, Didier B (Sam67fr); Creative Commons Attribution-Share Alike 2.5 Generic license; **9.2-14c**, © Stephen Harby; **9.2-15**, sborisov/123RF; **9.3-2**, Ted Chang; **9.3-3**, © Jason Gallier/Alamy; **9.3-4a**, Georg Gerster, Zumikon/Switzerland; **9.3-5**, Stefano Bertocci; **9.3-6**, Barnaby

Fitzgerald; **9.3-7**, upyernoz/Creative Commons Attribution 2.0 Generic license; **9.3-8**, Stefano Bertocci; **9.3-9**, Ted Chang. **Text-box images:** "The *Mashrabiyya* and the Women of the Cairene House," p. 332, (b), © Stephen Harby; "Pointed Arches, Ribbed Vaults, and Flying Buttresses," p. 353, © The Art Gallery Collection/Alamy; "The *Toguna*: A Male Meeting Hall," p. 370, Stefano Bertocci.

Chapter 10. 10.1-5, Alick M. McLean; **10.2-3**, Stefano Bertocci; **10.2-4a**, UserNo101/Creative Commons Attribution-Share Alike 3.0 Unported license; **10.2-5**, Ludvig14/Creative Commons Attribution-Share Alike 3.0 Unported license; **10.2-6b**, Anna Genina; **10.2-7**, Daniel Kruczynski/Creative Commons Uznanie autorstwa – Na tych samych warunkach 2.0; **10.2-8**, Gerard Janot; **10.2-9**, Gerard Janot; **10.2-10**, Smack; **10.2-11**, Ludvig14/Creative Commons Attribution-Share Alike 3.0 Unported license; **10.3-2**, Georg Gerster, Zumikon/Switzerland; **10.3-3**, William Iseminger; **10.3-4**, © Elementallmaging/iStockphotos; **10.3-7c**, Maunus/Public Domain; **10.3-8**, Georg Gerster, Zumikon/Switzerland; **10.3-9**, Alessio Battistella; **10.3-11b**, Alessio Battistella; **10.3-12**, © Stephen Harby. **Text-box images:** "Eastern European Blockwork," p. 402, (a), Stefano Bertocci; "The *Kiva*: A Sacred Space for the Male Retreat," p. 416, Georg Gerster, Zumikon/Switzerland; "The Sacred Stones of Machu Picchu," p. 426, (a), Avalon/Photoshot License/Alamy Stock Photo, and (b), Alessio Battistella; "Inca Masonry," p. 427, © Stephen Harby.

Chapter 11. 11.1-1, © Trustees of the British Museum; **11.1-6b**, View Stock/Getty; **11.2-6**, Sarah Dotson; **11.2-7a**, Leiden University Library, BPL 1758, sheet 13; **11.2-9**, Huseyin G. Citci; **11.2-12**, © Stephen Harby; **11.3-3**, Paul Fearn/Alamy Stock Photo; **11.3-7**, Scala/Art Resource, NY; **11.3-9**, Dailbor Jovanovic; **11.3-21**, © Stephen Harby; **11.3-23**, Alick M. McLean; **11.3-24**, Alick M. McLean; **11.3-26**, Erich Lessing/Art Resource, NY; **11.3-27**, © Stephen Harby. **Text-box images:** "The Counter-Reformation Church," p. 470, Tiziano Trevisiol; "Cardinals' Gardens and Papal Urbanism," p. 482, Étienne Dupérac.

Chapter 12. 12.1-1, Photo: David Stanley from Nanaimo, Canada/Creative Commons Attribution 2.0 Generic license; **12.1-2a**, imageBROKER/Alamy Stock Photo; **12.1-3**, Christophe Girot; **12.1-7**, Christophe Girot; **12.1-8**, Christophe Girot; **12.1-9a**, Christophe Girot; **12.1-9c**, Christophe Girot; **12.1-10**, Christophe Girot; **12.1-21**, Michael Hannemann; **12.1-22**, Michele Pasquini; **12.2-12**, Erich Lessing/Art Resource, NY; **12.2-13a**, Foto Marburg/Art Resource, NY; **12.2-21a**, © Stephen Harby; **12.2-22a**, © Stephen Harby; **12.3-1a**, Courtesy of the National Museum of Japanese History; **12.3-2a**, Michele Pasquini; **12.3-4a**, Don Choi; **12.3-6a**, Don Choi; **12.3-7**, Don Choi; **12.3-8a**, Don Choi; **12.3-8b**, Don Choi; **12.3-9**, Tibor Bognar/Alamy Stock Photo. **Text-box images:** "The French *Hôtel*," p. 512, (a), Ralf Treinen (license CC BY-SA 3.0); "Zen Buddhism in Japan," p. 532, Herschel Parnes.

Chapter 13. 13.1-1, © frans lemmens/Alamy; **13.1-2a**, British Library/HIP/Art Resource, NY; **13.1-3a**, Collection Rijksmuseum, Amsterdam; **13.1-5**, Collection Rijksmuseum, Amsterdam; **13.1-7**, Rainer Ebert; **13.1-9**, Joe Staines; **13.1-12**, Joe Staines; **13.1-13**, Don Choi; **13.1-14a**, Patrick Ducasse; **13.1-15**, Don Choi; **13.1-17a**, Patrick Ducasse; **13.1-17b**, Don Choi; **13.1-18**, Don Choi; **13.1-19**, © Stephen Harby; **13.1-20a**, © Stephen Harby; **13.1-20b**, © Stephen Harby; **13.2-1**, © Stephen Harby; **13.2-2**, © Stephen Harby; **13.2-5a**, © Stephen Harby; **13.2-8**, Photos by Hans Peter Schaefer; **13.2-10**, © Stephen Harby; **13.2-12a**, © Bildarchiv Monheim GmbH/Alamy; **13.2-14**, E-roxo; **13.3-4**, Brian Jannsen/Alamy Stock Photo; **13.3-5**, © Stephen Harby; **13.3-6a**, © BDphoto/iStockPhoto; **13.3-6b**, Library of Congress, Prints and Photographs Division; **13.3-7a**, Francis Nicholson, 1698, Library of Congress, Prints and Photographs Division; **13.3-7b**, Townsend Zeigler; **13.3-8**, LOC; **13.3-10**, Herschel Parnes; **13.3-11a**, Parlange Plantation Louisiana, circa 1750, Vincent de Ternant, Library of Congress, Prints and Photographs Division; **13.3-12**, Daderot/Creative Commons Attribution-Share Alike 3.0 Unported license; **13.3-15**, Redwood Library, P. Harrison, 1746, Library of Congress, Prints and Photographs Division; **13.3-16**, Redwood Library, P. Harrison, 1746, Library of Congress, Prints and Photographs Division. **Text-box images:** "The Dutch House and Feminine Order," p. 549, Collection Rijksmuseum, Amsterdam; "Of Bodies Bearing Buildings: Atlantids," p. 570, © Stephen Harby; "Portuguese *Azulejos* Cladding," p. 575, Tiziano Trevisiol; "The Plan of Savannah: The Brief Reign of Utopia," p. 586, Art Resource, NY; "The Puritan Meetinghouse," p. 588, Justin Sherma.

Chapter 14. 14.1-2, Joe Staines; **14.1-3**, 颐园新居; **14.1-4**, © Stephen Harby; **14.1-6a**, Joe Staines; **14.1-6b**, Joe Staines; **14.1-9b**, Matt Cardy/Stringer/Getty; **14.1-11**, Joe Staines; **14.2-3a**, akg-images/Bildarchiv Monheim; **14.2-9**, Don Choi; **14.2-11**, Don Choi; **14.2-20a**, Paris, BN/Design readingrm, Boullee 1785/akg-images; **14.2-20b**, Newton's Cenotaph/Drawing, Boullee 1784/akg-images; **14.2-21**, Federation Festival/1790/Monnet/akg-images; **14.2-23**, Don Choi; **14.3-1**, Jasonjsmith; **14.3-2**, © Blackbeck/iStockPhoto; **14.3-3**, © Brett Charlton/iStockPhoto; **14.3-9**, Elise Feiersinger; **14.3-12a**, Library of Congress, Prints and Photographs Division, HABS, Reproduction number HABS PA,51-PHILA,354—162 (CT); **14.3-12b**, LOC. **Text-box image:** "The Picturesque and Natural Law," p. 595, Don Choi.

Chapter 15. 15.1-4, Berlin-Britz, Hufeisensiedlung/akg-images; **15.1-5**, © Stephen Harby; **15.1-7a**, © Stephen Harby; **15.1-11a**, Glen Bowman/Creative Commons Attribution 2.0 Generic license; **15.1-13**, By Courtesy of the Trustees of Sir John Soane's Museum; **15.1-14a**, By Courtesy of the Trustees of Sir John Soane's Museum; **15.1-14b**, Joe Staines; **15.1-15**, Joe Staines; **15.1-17**, Boston, State House, C. Bulfinch, 1795, Library of Congress, Prints and Photographs Division; **15.1-18**, Philadelphia, Bank of Pennsylvania, B. Latrobe, 1800, Library of Congress, Prints and Photographs Division; **15.1-20**, Herschel Parnes; **15.1-21a**, Albert and Shirley Small Special Collection Library, University of Virginia; **15.1-21b**, University library, T. Jefferson, et al., begun 1822, Library of Congress, Prints and Photographs Division; **15.1-23a**, Jeff Howard; **15.1-23b**, Capital Mall and Washington Monument, R. Mills, 1833-84, Library of Congress, Prints and Photographs Division; **15.2-1**, Photos by Hans Peter Schaefer; **15.2-3**, © Stephen Harby; **15.2-4**, New York City, Trinity Church, etching from 1846. Library of Congress, Prints and Photographs Division; **15.2-5a**, Don Choi; **15.2-5b**, Don Choi; **15.2-8**, © Stephen Harby; **15.2-9**, Giacco Aurigi; **15.3-5**, Les Halles, Baltard, 1845-55, Library of Congress, Prints and Photographs Division; **15.3-6a**, Joe Staines; **15.3-9**, Photo 12/Alamy Stock Photo; **15.3-13**, Geof Sheppard. **Text-box images:** "Jefferson's Monticello: The Prototypical American House," p. 655, (a), Carol Highsmith/Library of Congress, and (b), Massachusetts Historical Society, Boston; "John Ruskin's *Seven Lamps of Architecture*," p. 665, © Fitzwilliam Museum, Cambridge/Art Resource, NY; "Emily Warren Roebling's Brooklyn Bridge," p. 685, Alfiero Zamponi.

Chapter 16. 16.1-6, Martin Feiersinger; **16.1-7a**, Martin Feiersinger; **16.1-7b**, Martin Feiersinger; **16.1-12a**, New York Public Library Digital Collections; **16.1-13**, New York City, Villard Houses, McKim, Mead & White, 1880s, Library of Congress, Prints and Photographs Division; **16.1-14b**, Ingfbruno/Creative Commons Attribution-Share Alike 3.0 Unported license; **16.1-15**, Riverside Historical Museum, Riverside, Illinois; **16.1-16a**, G. B. Post, 1890, Library of Congress, Prints and Photographs Division; **16.1-16b**, Tribune Building, R. M. Hunt, 1875-1903, Library of Congress, Prints and Photographs Division; **16.1-17**, Wotjek Palmowski; **16.1-18**, Wotjek Palmowski; **16.1-19**, Library of Congress, Prints and Photographs Division, HABS MO, 96-SALU, 49—1; **16.1-20**, Library of Congress, Prints & Photographs Division, HABS ILL, 16-CHIG,39—; **16.2-3**, Martin Feiersinger; **16.2-5**, H. J. Hardenbergh, 1880s, Library of Congress, Prints and Photographs Division; **16.2-6**, E. Flagg, 1898, Library of Congress, Prints and Photographs Division; **16.2-8**, Joe Staines; **16.2-9**, Snark/Art Resource, NY; **16.2-10**, Jon Farman/Public Domain; **16.2-11**, Don Choi; **16.2-13**, © Stephen Harby; **16.2-14**, McKim, Mead & White, 1887, Library of Congress, Prints and Photographs Division; **16.2-15b**, Fab5669; **16.3-2b**, © Directphoto.org/Alamy; **16.3-8**, R. M. Hunt, 1880s, Library of Congress, Prints and Photographs Division; **16.3-9**, Alfiero Zamponi; **16.3-10**, F. Furness, 1976, Library of Congress, Prints and Photographs Division; **16.3-12**, Docofoto; **16.3-13**, Justin Sherma; **16.3-14**, Library of Congress, Prints and Photographs Division, LC-USZ62-83107; **16.3-16**, The Art Institute of Chicago/Art Resource, NY. **Text-box images:** "American Mass-Produced Buildings," p. 705, James Bogardus, 1850s, Library of Congress, Prints and Photographs Division; "Chicago School Techniques for Tall Buildings," pp. 708–09, (a), Wotjek Palmowski, and (b), Library of Congress, Prints and Photographs Division; "The Model Tenement in New York," p. 713, LOC; "Thoreau's Cabin on Walden Pond," p. 723, Justin Sherma.

Chapter 17. 17.1-1, © Stephen Harby; **17.1-2**, Photo: Jonathan Billinger/Creative Commons Attribution-Share Alike 2.0 Generic License; **17.1-3**, © Stephen Harby; **17.1-4b**, Stephen Harby; **17.1-5**, © Stephen Harby; **17.1-7**, Jsvideos/Shutterstock; **17.1-8**, Joe Staines; **17.1-10**, Photo:

Index